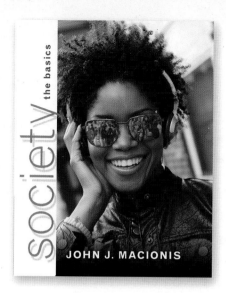

society the basics

JOHN J. MACIONIS

now features integration with MySocLab!

Each chapter now features three assignments from the lab that help students **Understand**, **Apply**, and **Do** Sociology.

D1304235

Understand
Core Concepts in Sociology Videos

Each chapter features a documentary-style video that explains core concepts in sociology. These videos are accompanied by multiple-choice review questions to help solidify students' understanding of important concepts.

Video: Individual Rights vs. the Common Good

While they're an essential element in any culture, shared values differ from one society to another. One of the most cherished American values, woven deep within the fabric of U.S. culture, is the importance of individual rights. Still, there is a long-standing tension between individual rights and the common good that can be traced to the very roots of American political culture.

Apply
MySocLibrary

With more than 200 primary source readings, **MySocLibrary** is a robust resource featuring the most popular classic and contemporary articles in sociology. Each chapter provides links to readings that are accompanied by a series of multiple-choice questions.

Do
Social Explorer Activity

Social Explorer activities in each chapter get students doing sociology and drawing their own conclusions about the social world. John Macionis leads students in an exploration of Census data through interactive maps, helping them connect concepts from the book with demographics in their local community and in counties across the United States.

PearsonChoices

With ever-increasing demands on time and resources, today's college instructors and students want greater value, innovation, and flexibility with their educational products. At Pearson, we've created a unique program that allows instructors and students to choose from a range of text and media formats to match personal teaching and learning styles.

Choose from the following:

- **Premium Print** and **Digital Resources** featuring **MySocLab**
- **Alternate Print Versions** including **Books à la Carte**
- **Custom Textbooks** and **Custom Media** that tailor content to specific course goals
- **Cost-Saving Digital eBooks** from CourseSmart eTextbooks Online that take advantage of the Internet as an alternative to the print textbook at half the price
- **Audio Books**, available through **MySocLab**, provide a great alternative for students who are auditory learners

With **PearsonChoices™**, you can empower your course with trusted content in a variety of formats to best meet your teaching goals and your students' learning goals.

society

the basics

eleventh edition

John J. Macionis

KENYON COLLEGE

Prentice Hall

Boston   Columbus   Indianapolis   New York   San Francisco   Upper Saddle River
Amsterdam   Cape Town   Dubai   London   Madrid   Milan   Munich   Paris   Montreal   Toronto
Delhi   Mexico City   Sao Paulo   Sydney   Hong Kong   Seoul   Singapore   Taipei   Tokyo

Planet Friendly Publishing
✔ Made in the United States
✔ Printed on Recycled Paper
Text: 10%   Cover: 10%
Learn more: www.greenedition.org

GREEN EDITION

At Pearson we're committed to producing books in an Earth-friendly manner and to helping our customers make greener choices. Manufacturing books in the United States ensures compliance with strict environmental laws and eliminates the need for international freight shipping, a major contributor to global air pollution.

And printing on recycled paper helps minimize our consumption of trees, water, and fossil fuels. The text of *Society: The Basics*, Eleventh Edition, was printed on paper made with 10% post-consumer waste, and the cover was printed on paper made with 10% post-consumer waste. According to Environmental Defense's Paper Calculator, by using this innovative paper instead of conventional papers, we achieved the following environmental benefits:

Trees Saved: 178 • Air Emissions Eliminated: 16,877 pounds
Water Saved: 81,256 gallons • Solid Waste Eliminated: 4,935 pounds

Editorial Director: *Craig Campanella*
Editor in Chief: *Dickson Musslewhite*
Senior Acquisitions Editor: *Brita Mess*
Editorial Assistant: *Seanna Breen*
Director of Marketing: *Brandy Dawson*
Executive Marketing Manager: *Kelly May*
Marketing Assistant: *Janell Bitor*
Managing Editor: *Maureen Richardson*
Production Editor: *Barbara Reilly*
Data Researcher: *Kimberlee Klesner*
Copy Editor: *Bruce Emmer*
Proofreaders: *Donna Mulder, Louise Rothman*
Manager, Text Rights and Permissions: *Charles Morris*
Text Permissions Research: *Margaret Gorenstein*
Manufacturing Manager: *Nick Sklitsis*

Operations Specialist: *Christina Amato*
AV Production Project Manager: *Maria Piper*
Senior Art Director: *Nancy Wells*
Art Director: *Anne Bonanno Nieglos*
Designer: *Ilze Lemesis*
Manager, Visual Research: *Beth Brenzel*
Photo Researcher: *Sheila Norman*
Manager, Cover Visual Research & Permissions: *Karen Sanatar*
Cover Art: © *Exactostock/Superstock*; © *Mark Richards/PhotoEdit*
Media Director: *Brian Hyland*
Media Editor: *Tom Scalzo*
Lead Media Project Manager: *Diane Lombardo*
Composition: *Nesbitt Graphics, Inc.*
Printer/Binder: *Courier Companies, Inc.*
Text Font: *10/12 Minion*

Credits and acknowledgments borrowed from other sources and reproduced, with permission, in this textbook appear on appropriate page within text (or on pages 696–98).

Microsoft® and Windows® are registered trademarks of the Microsoft Corporation in the U.S.A. and other countries. Screen shots and icons reprinted with permission from the Microsoft Corporation. This book is not sponsored or endorsed by or affiliated with the Microsoft Corporation.

Library of Congress Cataloging-in-Publication Data
Macionis, John J.
   Society : the basics / John J. Macionis.—11th ed.
      p. cm.
Includes bibliographical references and index.
ISBN 978-0-205-00378-5
   1. Sociology. I. Title.
   HM586.M1657 2010
   301—dc22

                                    2010027621

10 9 8 7 6 5 4 3 2

Prentice Hall
is an imprint of

PEARSON

www.pearsonhighered.com

Student edition ISBN 10:   0-205-00378-8
              ISBN 13: 978-0-205-00378-5
À la carte ISBN 10:   0-205-00513-6
              ISBN 13: 978-0-205-00513-0

Contents

3 Socialization: From Infancy to Old Age   66

4 Social Interaction in Everyday Life   92

5 Groups and Organizations   116

6 Sexuality and Society 142

7 Deviance 170

13 Family and Religion   366

14 Education, Health, and Medicine   404

15 Population, Urbanization, and Environment   444

Boxes

Seeing Sociology in Everyday Life

Thinking Globally

Thinking About Diversity: Race, Class, & Gender

Controversy & Debate

Seeing SOCIOLOGY in the NEWS

Maps

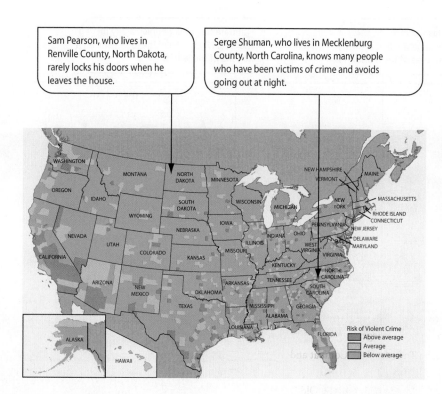

Sam Pearson, who lives in Renville County, North Dakota, rarely locks his doors when he leaves the house.

Serge Shuman, who lives in Mecklenburg County, North Carolina, knows many people who have been victims of crime and avoids going out at night.

Risk of Violent Crime
- Above average
- Average
- Below average

NATIONAL MAPS: Seeing Ourselves

Luz Alvarez Perez shops in fashionable boutiques in Santiago, Chile, a nation that is now among the high-income countries of the world.

Fatimata Ba earns pennies a day in Niamey, Niger, one of the low-income nations of the world.

Economic Development
- High-income countries
- Middle-income countries
- Low-income countries

GLOBAL MAPS: Window on the World

Preface

The world today challenges us like never before. We all know that the economy is uncertain, not only here at home but also around the globe. Technological disasters of our own making threaten the natural environment. There's a lot of anger about how our leaders in Washington are doing their jobs. Perhaps no one should be surprised to read polls that tell us most people are anxious about their economic future, unhappy with government, and worried about the state of the planet. Many of us simply feel overwhelmed, as if we were up against forces we can barely grasp.

That's where sociology comes in. For more than 150 years, sociologists have been working to better understand how society operates. We sociologists may not have all the answers, but we have learned quite a lot. A beginning course in sociology is your introduction to the fascinating and very useful study of the world around you. After all, we all have a stake in understanding our world and, as best we can, improving it.

Society: The Basics, Eleventh Edition, provides you with all the basics about how this world works. You will find this book to be informative and even entertaining. Before you have finished the first chapter, you will discover that sociology is more than useful—it is also fun. Sociology is a field of study that can change the way you see the world and open the door to many new opportunities. What could be more exciting than that?

A Word about Language

This text has a commitment to describe the social diversity of the United States and the world. This promise carries with it the responsibility to use language thoughtfully. In most cases, the book uses the terms "African American" and "person of color" rather than the word "black." Similarly, we use the terms "Latino," "Latina," and "Hispanic" to refer to people of Spanish descent. Most tables and figures refer to "Hispanics" because this is the term the Census Bureau uses when collecting statistical data about our population.

Students should realize, however, that many individuals do not describe themselves using these terms. Although the word "Hispanic" is commonly used in the eastern part of the United States and "Latino" and the feminine form "Latina" are widely heard in the West, across the United States people of Spanish descent identify with a particular ancestral nation, whether it be Argentina, Mexico, some other Latin American country, or Spain or Portugal in Europe.

The same holds for Asian Americans. Although this term is a useful shorthand in sociological analysis, most people of Asian descent think of themselves in terms of a specific country of origin, say, Japan, the Philippines, Taiwan, or Vietnam.

In this text, the term "Native American" refers to all the inhabitants of the Americas (including Alaska and the Hawaiian Islands) whose ancestors lived here prior to the arrival of Europeans. Here again, however, most people in this broad category identify with their historical society, such as Cherokee, Hopi, Seneca, or Zuni. The term "American Indian" refers to only those Native Americans who live in the continental United States, not including Native peoples living in Alaska or Hawaii.

On a global level, this text avoids the word "American"—which literally designates two continents—to refer to just the United States. For example, referring to this country, the term "the U.S. economy" is more precise than "the American economy." This convention may seem a small point, but it implies the significant recognition that we in this country represent only one society (albeit a very important one) in the Americas.

Supplements

Society: The Basics, Eleventh Edition, is the heart of an unprecedented multimedia learning package that includes a wide range of proven instructional aids as well as several new ones. I have personally written all the annotations for both students and instructors, the Test Item File, Instructor's Manual, and much of the material in MySocLab. I maintain a keen interest in all the supplements to ensure their quality and integration with the text.

For the Instructor

Annotated Instructor's Edition. (0-205-01011-3) The AIE is a complete student text with author annotations on every page. The annotations are especially useful to new instructors, but they are written to be helpful to even the most seasoned teachers. Margin notes include summaries of research findings, statistics from the United States and other nations, insightful quotations, information highlighting patterns of social diversity in the United States, and high-quality survey data from the General Social Survey conducted by the National Opinion Research Center (NORC) and from World Values Survey data from the Inter-University Consortium for Political and Social Research (ICPSR).

Instructor's Manual. (0-205-00550-0) This text offers an instructor's manual that will be of interest even to those who have never chosen to use one before. The manual provides the expected detailed chapter outlines and discussion questions and much more—summaries of important developments, recent articles from *Teaching Sociology* that are relevant to classroom discussions, suggestions for classroom activities, and supplemental lecture material for every chapter of the text.

Test Item File. (0-205-01010-5) This key author-created supplement reflects the material in the textbook—both in content and in language—far better than the testing file available with any other introductory sociology textbook. The file contains over 2,000 items—more than 100 per chapter—in multiple-choice, true-false, and essay formats. All of the questions are identified by level of difficulty.

MyTest. (0-205-01009-1) This online, computerized software allows instructors to create their own personalized exams, to edit any or all of the existing test questions, and to add new questions. Other special features of this program include random generation of test questions, creation of alternative versions of the same test, scrambling question sequence, and test preview before printing.

TestGen. (0-205-03271-0) The test item file is also available through TestGen EQ. This fully networkable test-generating software works with both Windows™ and Macintosh™ computers.

PowerPoint® Slides. (0-205-05846-9) These PowerPoint slides combine graphics and text in a colorful format to help you convey sociological principles in a visual and exciting way. Each chapter of the textbook has approximately fifteen to twenty-five slides that communicate the key concepts in that chapter. For easy access, they are available in the instructor portion of MySocLab for *Society: The Basics, Eleventh Edition.*

Media Supplements

PEARSON **mysoclab** is a learning and assessment tool that enables instructors to assess student performance and adapt course content—without investing additional time or resources. MySocLab is designed with instructor flexibility in mind—you decide the extent of integration into your course—from independent self-assessment to total course management. The lab is accompanied with an instructor's manual featuring easy-to-read media grids, activities, sample syllabi, and tips for integrating technology into your course.

For the Student

Study Guide. (0-205-01008-3) This complete guide helps students review and reflect on the material presented in *Society: The Basics, Eleventh Edition.* Each of the sixteen chapters in the Study Guide provides an overview of the corresponding chapter in the student text, summarizes its major topics and concepts, offers applied exercises, and features end-of-chapter tests with answers.

In Appreciation

The usual practice of crediting a book to a single author hides the efforts of dozens of women and men who have helped create *Society: The Basics, Eleventh Edition.* I offer my deep and sincere thanks to the Pearson editorial team, including Yolanda de Rooy, division president; Craig Campanella, editorial director; Dickson Musslewhite, editor-in-chief; and Brita Mess, senior acquisitions editor in sociology, for their steady enthusiasm in the pursuit of both innovation and excellence.

Day-to-day work on the book is shared by the author and the production team. Barbara Reilly, Pearson production editor, is a key member of the group who is responsible for the attractive page layout of the book; indeed, if anyone "sweats the details" as much as I do, it is Barbara! Kimberlee Klesner works with me to ensure that all the data in this revision are the very latest available. Kimberlee brings enthusiasm that matches her considerable abilities, and I thank her for both.

I also want to thank the members of the Pearson sales staff, the men and women who have given this text such remarkable support over the years. My hat goes off especially to Brandy Dawson and Kelly May, who share responsibility for our marketing campaign.

Thanks, too, to Ilze Lemesis for providing both the interior and cover design of the book, to Anne Nieglos for managing the design, and to Maria Piper for managing the line art program. Developmental and copy editing of the manuscript was skillfully done by Bruce Emmer.

It goes without saying that every colleague knows more about a number of topics covered in this book than the author does. For that reason, I am grateful to the hundreds of faculty and the many students who have written to me to offer comments and suggestions. More formally, I am grateful to the following people who have reviewed some or all of this manuscript:

Rebecca Riehm, Jefferson Community College
William Wood, California State University Fullerton
Rudy Harris, Des Moines Area Community College
Judi Kessler, Monmouth College
Dale Howard, NorthWest Arkansas Community College
Robert Atkins, North Seattle Community College
Richard Sweeney, Modesto Junior College
Dave Conz, Arizona State University
Robert Brainerd, Highland Community College

I also wish to thank the following colleagues for sharing their wisdom in ways that have improved this book:

Doug Adams (Ohio State University), Kip Armstrong (Bloomsburg University), Rose Arnault (Fort Hays State University), William Beaver (Robert Morris University), Scott Beck (Eastern Tennessee State University), Lois Benjamin (Hampton University), Philip Berg (University of Wisconsin, La Crosse), Kimberly H. Boyd (Germanna Community College), John R. Brouillette (Colorado State University), Cathryn Brubaker (DeKalb College), Brent Bruton (Iowa State University), Richard Bucher (Baltimore City Community College), Evandro Camara (Emporia State University), Bill Camp (Lucerne County Community College), Karen Campbell (Vanderbilt University), Francis N. Catano (Saint Anselm College), Harold Conway (Blinn College), Allison Cotton (Prairie View A&M University), Gerry Cox (Fort Hays State University), Lovberta Cross (Shelby State Community College), James A. Davis (Harvard University), Sumati Devadutt (Monroe Community College), Keith Doubt (Northeast Missouri State University), Thomas Dowdy (Oklahoma Baptist University), William Dowell (Heartland Community College), Doug Downey (Ohio State University), Denny Dubbs (Harrisburg Area Community College), Travis Eaton (Northeast Louisiana State University), Helen Rose Fuchs Ebaugh (University of Houston), John Ehle (Northern Virginia Community College), Roger Eich (Hawkeye Community College), Heather FitzGibbon (College of Wooster), Kevin Fitzpatrick (University of Alabama, Birmingham), Dona C. Fletcher (Sinclair Community College), Charles Frazier (University of Florida), Karen Lynch Frederick (Saint Anselm College), Patricia Gagné (University of Kentucky, Louisville), Pam Gaiter (Collin County Community College), Jarvis Gamble (Owens Technical College), Patricia L. Gibbs (Foothill College), Steven Goldberg (City College, City University of New York), Charlotte Gotwald (York College of Pennsylvania), Norma B. Gray (Bishop State Community College), Rhoda Greenstone (DeVry Institute), Jeffrey Hahn (Mount Union College), Harry Hale (Northeast Louisiana State University), Dean Haledjian (Northern Virginia Community College), Dick Haltin (Jefferson Community College), Marvin Hannah (Milwaukee Area Technical College), Chad Hanson (Casper College), Charles Harper (Creighton University), Michael Hart (Broward College), Gary Hodge (Collin County Community College), Elizabeth A. Hoisington (Heartland Community College), Kathleen Holmes (Darton College), Sara Horsfall (Stephen F. Austin State University), Peter Hruschka (Ohio Northern University), Glenna Huls (Camden County College), Jeanne Humble (Lexington Community College), Cynthia Imanaka (Seattle Central Community College), Craig Jenkins (Ohio State University), Sam Joseph (Lucerne County Community College), Ed Kain (Southwestern University), Audra Kallimanis (Mount Olive College), Paul Kamolnick (Eastern Tennessee State University), Irwin Kantor (Middlesex County College), Thomas Korllos (Kent State University), Rita Krasnow (Virginia Western Community College), Donald Kraybill (Elizabethtown College), Howard Kurtz (Oklahoma City University), Michael Lacy (Colorado State University), Carol Landry (Oakland Community College); George Lowe (Texas Tech University), Don Luidens (Hope College), Larry Lyon (Baylor University), Li-Chen Ma (Lamar University), Setma Maddox (Texas Wesleyan University), Errol Magidson (Richard J. Daley College), Kooros Mahmoudi (Northern Arizona University), Mehrdad Mashayekhi (Georgetown University), Allan Mazur (Syracuse University), Karen E. B. McCue (University of New Mexico, Albuquerque), Rodney A. McDanel (Benedictine University), Doug McDowell (Rider University), Ronald McGriff, (College of the Sequoias), Meredith McGuire (Trinity College), Karla McLucas (Bennett College), Lisa McMinn (Wheaton College), Jack Melhorn (Emporia State University), Will Melick (Kenyon College), Ken Miller (Drake University), Linda Miller (Queens University of Charlotte), Richard Miller (Navarro College), Joe Morolla (Virginia Commonwealth University), Peter B. Morrill (Bronx Community College), Craig Nauman (Madison Area Technical College), Dina B. Neal (Vernon College), Jody Nedley-Newcomb (Southwestern Community College), Therese Nemec (Fox Valley Technical College), Joong-Hwan Oh (Hunter College), Richard Perkins (Houghton College), Marla A. Perry (Iowa State University), Anne Peterson (Columbus State Community College), Marvin Pippert (Roanoke College), Lauren Pivnik (Monroe Community College), Scott Potter (Marion Technical College), Nevel Razak (Fort Hays State College), Lee Reineck (Stautzenberger College), George Reim (Cheltenham High School), Virginia Reynolds (Indiana University of Pennsylvania), Laurel Richardson (Ohio State University), Heather Rimes (Florida Southern College-Orlando), Keith Roberts (Hanover College), Ellen Rosengarten (Sinclair Community College), Frederick Roth (Marshall University), Mark Rubinfeld (Westminster College, Salt Lake City), Paulina Ruf (University of Tampa), Bill Ruth (Paris Junior College); Michael Ryan (Dodge City Community College), Marvin Scott (Butler University), Ray Scupin (Linderwood College), Steve Severin (Kellogg Community College), Tim Sexton (Chippewa Valley Technical College), Harry Sherer (Irvine Valley College), Walt Shirley (Sinclair Community College), Anson Shupe (Indiana University–Purdue University at Fort Wayne), Brenda Silverman (Onondaga Community College), Ree Simpkins (Missouri Southern State University), Scott Simpson (Arkansas Northeastern College), Glen Sims (Glendale Community College), Toni Sims (University of Louisiana, Lafayette), Sherry Smith (Georgia Perimeter College-Clarkston Campus), Sylvia Kenig Snyder (Coastal Carolina University), Thomas Soltis (Westmoreland Community College), Nancy Sonleitner (University of Oklahoma), Larry Stern (Collin County Community College), Randy Ston (Oakland Community College), Vickie H. Taylor (Danville Community College), Don Thomas (Ohio State University), Mark J. Thomas (Madison Area Technical College), Len Tompos (Lorain County Community College), Christopher Vanderpool (Michigan State University), Phyllis Watts (Tiffin University), Murray Webster (University of North Carolina, Charlotte), Debbie White (Collin County Community College), Marilyn Wilmeth (Iowa University), Stuart Wright (Lamar University), William Yoels (University of Alabama, Birmingham), Dan Yutze (Taylor University), Wayne Zapatek (Tarrant County Community College), Jin-kun Wei (Brevard Community College), Amy Wong (San Diego State University), and Frank Zulke (Harold Washington College).

Finally, I would like to dedicate this eleventh edition of the book to my wife, Amy. We have traveled a very long way together on our life journey. Amy, you bring me such deep joy simply by being the magnificent woman you are. Keep getting better!

With best wishes to my colleagues and love to all,

John J. Macionis

1 Sociology: Perspective, Theory, and Method

- What makes the sociological perspective a new and exciting way of seeing the world?

- Why is sociology an important tool for your future career?

- How do sociologists conduct research to learn about the social world?

Watch the *Core Concepts in Sociology* video "Sociologists at Work" on **mysoclab.com**

Chapter Overview

This chapter introduces the discipline of sociology. The most important skill to gain from this course is the ability to use what we call the *sociological perspective*. The chapter next introduces *sociological theory*, which helps us build understanding from what we see using the sociological perspective. The chapter continues by explaining how sociologists "do" sociology, describing three approaches to conducting research and four methods of data collection.

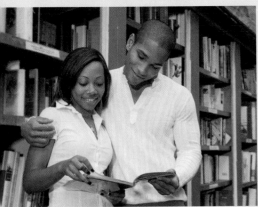

From the moment he first saw Tonya, as they both stepped off the subway train, Duane knew she was "the one." As the two walked up the stairs to the street and entered the building where they were both taking classes, Duane tried to get Tonya to stop and talk. At first, she ignored him. But after class, they met again, and she agreed to join him for coffee. That was three months ago. Today, they are engaged to be married.

If you were to ask people in the United States, "Why do couples like Tonya and Duane marry?" it is a safe bet that almost everyone would reply, "People marry because they fall in love." Most of us find it hard to imagine a marriage being happy without love; for the same reason, when people fall in love, we expect them to think about getting married.

But is the decision about whom to marry really just a matter of personal feelings? There is plenty of evidence that if love is the key to marriage, Cupid's arrow is carefully aimed by the society around us.

Society has many "rules" about whom we should and should not marry. In all states but Massachusetts, Vermont, New Hampshire, Connecticut, and Iowa, along with the District of Columbia, the law rules out half the population, banning people from marrying someone of the same sex, even if the couple is deeply in love. But there are other rules as well. Sociologists have found that people, especially when they are young, are very likely to marry someone close in age, and people of all ages typically marry someone of the same race, of similar social class background, of much the same level of education, and with the same degree of physical attractiveness (Schwartz & Mare, 2005; Schoen & Cheng, 2006; Feng Hou & Myles, 2008; Chapter 13, "Family and Religion," gives details). People end up making choices about whom to marry, but society narrows the field long before they do.

When it comes to love, our decisions do not simply result from what philosophers call "free will." Sociology teaches us that our social world guides our life choices in much the same way that the seasons influence our choice of clothing.

The Sociological Perspective

Sociology is *the systematic study of human society*. At the heart of this discipline is a distinctive point of view called the *sociological perspective*.

Seeing the General in the Particular

Years ago, Peter Berger (1963) described the **sociological perspective** as *seeing the general in the particular*. By this he meant that sociology helps us see *general* patterns in the behavior of *particular* people. Although every individual is unique, society shapes the lives of people in various *categories* (such as children and adults, women and men, the rich and the poor) very differently. We begin to see the world sociologically by realizing how the general categories into which we fall shape our particular life experiences.

This text explores the power of society to guide our actions, thoughts, and feelings. We may think that marriage results simply from the personal feeling of love. Yet the sociological perspective shows us that factors such as our sex, age, race, and social class guide our selection of a partner. It might be more accurate to think of love as a feeling we have for others who match up with what society teaches us to want in a mate.

Seeing the Strange in the Familiar

At first, using the sociological perspective may seem like *seeing the strange in the familiar*. Consider how you would react if someone were to say to you, "You fit all the right categories, which means you would make a wonderful spouse!" We are used to thinking that people fall in love and decide to marry based on personal feelings. But the sociological perspective reveals to us the initially strange idea that society shapes what we think and do.

Because we live in an individualistic society, learning to see how society affects us may take a bit of practice. Consider the decision by women to bear children. Like the selection of a mate, the choice

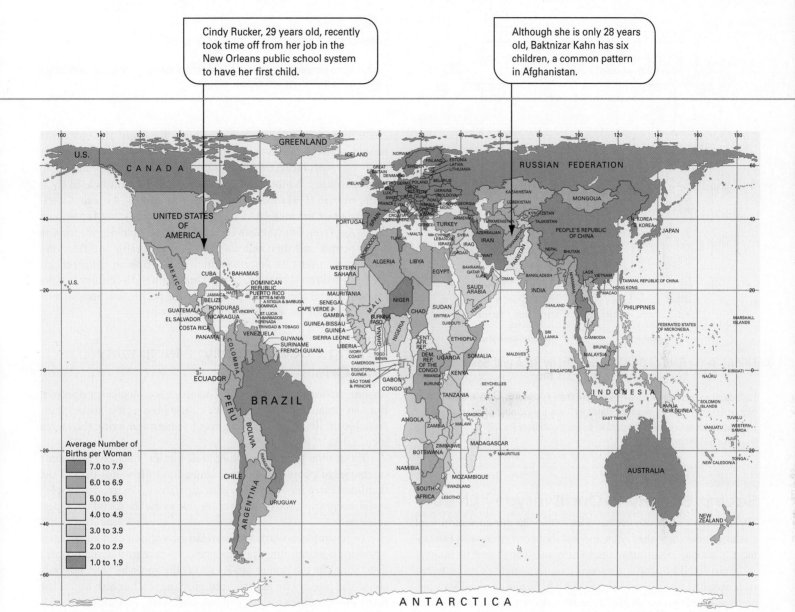

Cindy Rucker, 29 years old, recently took time off from her job in the New Orleans public school system to have her first child.

Although she is only 28 years old, Baktnizar Kahn has six children, a common pattern in Afghanistan.

Average Number of Births per Woman

- 7.0 to 7.9
- 6.0 to 6.9
- 5.0 to 5.9
- 4.0 to 4.9
- 3.0 to 3.9
- 2.0 to 2.9
- 1.0 to 1.9

Window on the World

GLOBAL MAP 1–1   Women's Childbearing in Global Perspective

Is childbearing simply a matter of personal choice? A look around the world shows that it is not. In general, women living in poor countries have many more children than women in rich nations. Can you point to some of the reasons for this global disparity? In simple terms, such differences mean that if you had been born into another society (whether you are female or male), your life might be quite different from what it is now.

Sources: Data from Hamilton, Martin, & Ventura (2009), Population Reference Bureau (2009), United Nations Development Programme (2009), and Central Intelligence Agency (2009). Map projection from *Peters Atlas of the World* (1990).

of having a child—or how many to have—would seem to be very personal. Yet there are social patterns here as well. As shown in Global Map 1–1, the average woman in the United States has about two children during her lifetime. In the Philippines, however, the "choice" is about three; in Guatemala, about four; in Ethiopia, about five; in Afghanistan, about six; and in Niger, about seven.

What accounts for these striking differences? Because poor countries provide women with less schooling and fewer economic opportunities, women's lives are centered in the home, and they are less likely to use contraception. The strange truth is that society has much to do with the familiar decisions that women and men make about childbearing.

sociology (p. 2) the systematic study of human society

sociological perspective (p. 2) the special point of view of sociology that sees general patterns of society in the lives of particular people

Diversity Snapshot

White men are more than 12 times more likely than black women to commit suicide.

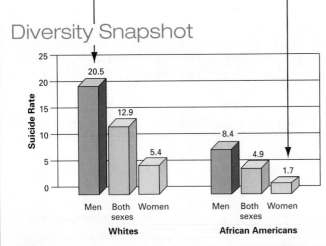

FIGURE 1–1 **Rate of Death by Suicide, by Race and Sex, for the United States**

Suicide rates are higher for white people than for black people and higher for men than for women. Rates indicate the number of deaths by suicide for every 100,000 people in each category for 2007.

Source: Xu et al. (2010).

Seeing Society in Our Everyday Lives

The society in which we live has a lot to do with our choices in food, clothing, music, schooling, jobs, and just about everything else. Even the most "personal" decisions we make turn out to be shaped by society.

What could be more personal than the lonely decision to end your own life? Emile Durkheim (1858–1917), one of sociology's pioneers, showed that social forces are at work even in such an intensely personal action as suicide. Examining official records in and around his native France, Durkheim (1966, orig. 1897) found that some categories of people were more likely than others to take their own lives. He found that men, Protestants, wealthy people, and the unmarried each had much higher suicide rates than women, Catholics and Jews, the poor, and married people. Durkheim explained these differences in terms of *social integration*: Categories of people with strong social ties had low suicide rates, and more individualistic people had high suicide rates.

In Durkheim's time, men had much more freedom than women. But despite its advantages, freedom weakens social ties and thus increases the rate of suicide. Likewise, more individualistic Protestants were more likely to commit suicide than more tradition-bound Catholics and Jews, whose rituals encourage stronger social ties. The wealthy have much more freedom than the poor—but once again, at the cost of a higher suicide rate.

A century later, Durkheim's analysis still holds true. Figure 1–1 shows suicide rates for four categories of the U.S. population. In

2007, there were 12.9 recorded suicides for every 100,000 white people, which is more than twice the rate for African Americans (4.9). For both races, suicide was more common among men than among women. White men (20.5) are almost four times as likely as white women (5.4) to take their own lives. Among African Americans, the rate for men (8.4) was almost five times that for women (1.7). Applying Durkheim's logic, the higher suicide rate among white people and men reflects their greater wealth and freedom, just as the lower rate among women and people of color reflects their limited social choices. Just as Durkheim did a century ago, we can see general sociological patterns in the personal actions of particular individuals. ● Go to **mysoclab.com**

Seeing Sociologically: Marginality and Crisis

Anyone can learn to see the world using the sociological perspective. But two situations help people see clearly how society shapes individual lives: living on the margins of society and living through a social crisis.

From time to time, everyone feels like an "outsider." For some categories of people, however, being an *outsider*—not part of the dominant category—is an everyday experience. The greater people's social marginality, the better they are able to use the sociological perspective.

For example, no African American grows up in the United States without understanding the importance of race in shaping people's lives. Songs by the rapper Jay-Z express the anger he feels, not only about the poverty he experienced growing up, but also about the many innocent lives he has seen lost to violence in a society of such wide racial disparities. His lyrics, and those of many similar artists, which are spread throughout the world by the mass media, show that some people of color—especially African Americans living in the inner city—feel like their hopes and dreams are crushed by society. But white people, as the dominant majority, think less often about race and the privileges it provides, believing that race affects only people of color and not themselves as well. People at the margins of social life, including women, gays and lesbians, people with disabilities, and the very old, are aware of social patterns that others rarely think about. To become better at using the sociological perspective, we must step back from our familiar routines and look at our lives with a new curiosity.

Periods of change or crisis make everyone feel a little off balance, encouraging us to use the sociological perspective. The sociologist C. Wright Mills (1959) illustrated this idea using the Great Depression of the 1930s. As the unemployment rate soared to 25 percent, people without jobs could not help but see general social forces at work in their particular lives. Rather than saying, "Something is wrong with

Go to the Multimedia Library at **mysoclab.com** to hear author John Macionis answer the question "How Do You Know Something Is True?"

global perspective the study of the larger world and our society's place in it

high-income countries	**middle-income countries**	**low-income countries**
the nations with the highest overall standards of living	nations with a standard of living about average for the world as a whole	nations with a low standard of living in which most people are poor

me; I can't find a job," they took a sociological approach and realized, "The economy has collapsed; there are no jobs to be found!" Mills believed that using what he called the "sociological imagination" in this way helps people understand their society and how it affects their own lives. The Seeing Sociology in Everyday Life box on page 6 takes a closer look.

The Importance of a Global Perspective

As new information technology draws even the farthest reaches of the planet closer together, many academic disciplines are taking a **global perspective,** *the study of the larger world and our society's place in it*. What is the importance of a global perspective for sociology?

First, global awareness is a logical extension of the sociological perspective. Sociology shows us that our place in society shapes our life experiences. It stands to reason, then, that the position of our society in the larger world system affects everyone in the United States.

The world's 194 nations can be divided into three broad categories according to their level of economic development (see Global Map 9–1 on page 247). **High-income countries** are *the nations with the highest overall standards of living*. The sixty-seven nations in this category include the United States and Canada, Argentina, the nations of Western Europe, Israel, Saudi Arabia, Japan, and Australia. Taken together, these nations generate most of the world's goods and services, and the people who live in them own most of the planet's wealth. Economically speaking, people in these countries are very well off, not because they are smarter or work harder than anyone else but because they were lucky enough to be born in a rich region of the world.

A second category is **middle-income countries,** *nations with a standard of living about average for the world as a whole*. People living in any of these seventy-one nations—many of the countries of Eastern Europe, South Africa and some other African nations, and almost all of Latin America and Asia—are as likely to live in rural villages

---

People with the greatest privileges tend to see individuals as responsible for their own lives. Those at the margins of society, by contrast, are quick to see how race, class, and gender can create disadvantages. The rap artist Jay-Z has given voice to the frustration felt by many African Americans living in this country's inner cities.

as in cities and to walk or ride tractors, scooters, bicycles, or animals as to drive automobiles. On average, they receive eight to ten years of schooling. Most middle-income countries also have considerable social inequality within their borders, meaning that some people are extremely rich (members of the business elite in nations across North Africa, for example) but many more lack safe housing and adequate nutrition (people living in the shanty settlements that surround Lima, Peru, or Mumbai, India).

The remaining fifty-six nations of the world are **low-income countries,** *nations with a low standard of living in which most people are poor*. Most of the poorest countries in the world are in Africa, and a few are in Asia. Here again, a few people are very rich, but the majority struggle to get by with poor housing, unsafe water, too little food, and perhaps most serious of all, little chance to improve their lives.

Chapter 9 ("Global Stratification") explains the causes and consequences of global wealth and poverty. But every chapter of this text makes comparisons between the United States and other nations for four reasons:

1. **Where we live shapes the lives we lead.** As you saw in Global Map 1–1 on page 5, women living in rich and poor nations have very different lives, as suggested by the number of children they have. To understand ourselves and appreciate how others live, we must understand something about how countries differ, which is easy to do by paying attention to the global maps found throughout this text.

2. **Societies throughout the world are increasingly interconnected.** Historically, people in the United States took only passing note of the countries beyond our own borders. In recent decades, however, the United States and the rest of the world have become linked as never before. Electronic technology now transmits pictures, sounds, and written documents around the globe in seconds.

   One effect of this new technology is that people all over the world now share many of the same tastes in food, clothing, movies, and music. Rich countries such as the United States influence other nations, whose people are ever more likely to gobble up our Big Macs and Whoppers, dance to the latest hip-hop music, and speak English.

   But the larger world also has an impact on us. We all know the contributions of famous immigrants such as Arnold Schwarzenegger (who came to the United States from Austria) and Gloria Estefan (who came from Cuba). More than 1.5 million immigrants enter the United States

◦ Making the Grade

Mills used the term "sociological imagination" to mean the same thing as the term "sociological perspective" used by Peter Berger and others.

◦ Making the Grade

The box below suggests that C. Wright Mills hoped the sociological imagination would spark social change toward a more equal society.

SEEING SOCIOLOGY IN EVERYDAY LIFE

The Sociological Imagination: Turning Personal Problems into Public Issues

As Mike opened the envelope, he felt the tightness in his chest. The letter he dreaded was in his hands—his job was finished at the end of the day. After eleven years! Years in which he had worked hard, sure that he would move up in the company. All those hopes and dreams were now suddenly gone. Mike felt like a failure. Anger at himself—for not having worked even harder, for having wasted so many years of his life in what had turned out to be a dead-end job—swelled up inside him.

But as he returned to his workstation to pack his things, Mike soon realized that he was not alone. Almost all his colleagues in the tech support group had received the same letter. Their jobs were moving to India, where the company was able to provide telephone tech support for less than half the cost of employing workers in California.

By the end of the weekend, Mike was sitting in the living room with a dozen other ex-employees. Comparing notes and sharing ideas, they now realized that they were simply a few of the victims of a massive outsourcing of jobs that is part of what analysts call the "globalization of the economy."

In good times and bad, the power of the sociological perspective lies in making sense of our individual lives. We see that many of our particular problems (and our successes as well) are not unique to us but are the result of larger social trends. Half a century ago, the sociologist C. Wright Mills pointed to the power of what he called the sociological imagination to help us understand everyday events. As he saw it, society—not people's personal failings—is the main cause of poverty and other social problems. By turning personal problems into public issues, the sociological imagination is also the key to bringing people together to create needed change. In this excerpt,* Mills (1959:3–5) explains the need for a sociological imagination:

> When society becomes industrialized, a peasant becomes a worker; a feudal lord is liquidated or becomes a businessman. When classes rise or fall, a man is employed or unemployed; when the rate of investment goes up or down, a man takes new heart or goes broke. When wars happen, an insurance salesman becomes a rocket launcher; a store clerk, a radar man; a wife lives alone; a child grows up without a father. Neither the life of an individual nor the history of a society can be understood without understanding both.
>
> Yet men do not usually define the troubles they endure in terms of historical change. . . . The well-being they enjoy, they do not usually impute to the big ups and downs of the society in which they live. Seldom aware of the intricate connection between the patterns of their own lives and the course of world history, ordinary men do not usually know what this connection means for the kind of men they are becoming and for the kinds of history-making in which they might take part. They do not possess the quality of mind essential to grasp the interplay of men and society, of biography and history, of self and world. . . .
>
> What they need . . . is a quality of mind that will help them [see] what is going on in the world and . . . what may be happening within themselves. It is this quality . . . [that] may be called the sociological imagination.

*In this excerpt, Mills uses "man" and male pronouns to apply to all people. As far as gender was concerned, even this outspoken critic of society reflected the conventional writing practices of his time.

WHAT DO YOU THINK?

1. As Mills sees it, how are personal troubles different from public issues? Explain this difference in terms of what happened to Mike.

2. Living in the United States, why do we often blame ourselves for the personal problems we face?

3. By using the sociological imagination, how do we gain the power to change the world?

each year, bringing their skills and talents along with their fashions and foods, greatly increasing the racial and cultural diversity of this country.

Trade across national boundaries has also created a global economy. Large corporations make and market goods worldwide. Stock traders in New York pay close attention to the financial markets in Tokyo and Hong Kong even as wheat farmers in Kansas watch the price of grain in the former Soviet republic of Georgia. Because most new U.S. jobs involve international trade, greater global understanding has never been more important.

3. **Many social problems that we face in the United States are far more serious elsewhere.** Poverty is a serious problem in this country, but as Chapter 9 ("Global Stratification") explains, poverty in Latin America, Africa, and Asia is both more common and more serious. In the same way, although women have lower social standing than men in the United States, gender inequality is much greater in the world's poor countries.

4. **Thinking globally helps us learn more about ourselves.** We cannot walk the streets of a distant city without thinking about what it means to live in the United States. Comparing life in various settings often leads to unexpected lessons. For instance, in

Making the Grade

Think of the global perspective as an extension of the sociological perspective. Here at home, where we are "placed" within society affects how we act, think, and feel. Expanding our vision shows that our nation's place in the world affects the lives of all who live in this country.

Seeing Sociology in Everyday Life

How would your life be different if you had been born into a family in a poor farming village in Asia? What might you be doing right now instead of reading this textbook?

We can easily see the power of society over the individual by imagining how different our lives would be had we been born in place of any of these children from, respectively, Bolivia, Ethiopia, Thailand, Mali, South Korea, and India.

Chapter 9, we visit a squatter settlement in Chennai, India. There, despite a desperate lack of basic material goods, people thrive in the love and support of family members. Why, then, are so many poor people in the United States angry and alone? Are material things—so central to our definition of a "rich" life—the best way to measure human well-being?

In sum, in an increasingly interconnected world, we can understand ourselves only to the extent that we understand others. Sociology is an invitation to learn a new way of looking at the world around us. Is this invitation worth accepting? What are the benefits of applying the sociological perspective?

Applying the Sociological Perspective

Applying the sociological perspective is useful in many ways. First, sociology is at work guiding many of the laws and policies that shape our lives. Second, on an individual level, making use of the sociological perspective leads to important personal growth and expanded awareness. Third, studying sociology is excellent preparation for the world of work.

Sociology and Public Policy

Sociologists have helped shape public policy—the laws and regulations that guide how people in communities live and work—in countless ways, from racial desegregation and school busing to laws regulating divorce. For example, in her study of how divorce affects people's income, the sociologist Lenore Weitzman (1985, 1996) discovered that women who leave marriages typically experience a dramatic loss of income. Recognizing this fact, many states passed laws that have increased women's claims to marital property and enforced fathers' obligations to provide support for women raising their children.

Sociology and Personal Growth

By applying the sociological perspective, we are likely to become more active and aware and to think more critically in our everyday lives. Using sociology pays off in four ways:

1. **The sociological perspective helps us assess the truth of "common sense."** We all take many things for granted, but that does not make them true. One good example is the idea that we are free individuals who are personally responsible for our lives. If

Seeing Sociology in Everyday Life

This discussion shows you that using the sociological perspective is valuable for changing society by shaping public policy, for your personal enrichment, and for advancing your career.

Go to the Multimedia Library at **mysoclab.com** to view the slideshow "The Functions of Sociologists"

we think we decide our own fate, we may be quick to praise successful people as superior and consider others with fewer achievements personally deficient. A sociological approach, by contrast, encourages us to ask whether common beliefs are really true and, to the extent that they are not, why they are so widely held.

2. **The sociological perspective helps us see the opportunities and constraints in our lives.** Sociological thinking leads us to see that in the game of life, we have a say in how to play our cards, but it is society that deals us the hand. The more we understand the game, the better players we will be. Sociology helps us learn more about the world around us so that we can pursue our goals more effectively.

3. **The sociological perspective empowers us to be active participants in our society.** The better we understand how society operates, the more effective citizens we become. As C. Wright Mills explained in the box on page 6, it is the sociological perspective that turns a private problem (such as being out of work) into a public issue (a lack of good jobs). As we come to see how society affects us, we may decide to support society as it is, or we may set out with others to change it.

4. **The sociological perspective helps us live in a diverse world.** North Americans represent just 5 percent of the world's population, and as the remaining chapters of this book explain, much of the other 95 percent lives very differently than we do.

Still, like people everywhere, we tend to view our own way of life as "right," "natural," and "better." The sociological perspective prompts us to think critically about the strengths and weaknesses of all ways of life, including our own.

Careers: The "Sociology Advantage"

Most students at colleges and universities today are very interested in getting a good job. A background in sociology is excellent preparation for the working world. Of course, completing a bachelor's degree in sociology is the right choice for people who decide they would like to go on to graduate work and eventually become a professor or researcher in this field. Throughout the United States, tens of thousands of men and women teach sociology in universities, colleges, and high schools. But just as many professional sociologists work as researchers for government agencies or private foundations and businesses, gathering important information on how people live, what they think, and how they spend their money. In today's cost-conscious world, agencies and companies want to be sure that the products, programs, and policies they create get the job done at the lowest cost. Sociologists, especially those with advanced research skills, are in high demand for this type of evaluation research (Deutscher, 1999).

In addition, a smaller but increasing number of people work as clinical sociologists. These women and men work, much as clinical psychologists do, with the goal of improving the lives of troubled clients. A basic difference is that sociologists focus on difficulties not in the personality but in the individual's web of social relationships. ● Go to **mysoclab.com**

But sociology is not just for people who want to be sociologists. People who work in criminal justice—including jobs in police departments, probation offices, and correction facilities—also gain the "sociology advantage" by learning what categories of people are most at risk of becoming criminals or victims, how effective various policing policies and programs are at preventing crime, and why people turn to crime in the first place. Similarly, people who work in the health care field—including physicians, nurses, and technicians—also gain a sociology advantage by learning about patterns of health and illness within the population, as well as how factors such as race, ethnicity, gender, and social class affect human health.

The American Sociological Association (2007) reports that sociology is also excellent preparation for jobs in dozens of fields, including advertising, banking, business, education, government, journalism, law, public relations, and social work. In almost any type of work, success depends on understanding how various categories of people differ in beliefs, family patterns, and other ways of life.

Just about every job in today's economy involves working with people. For this reason, studying sociology is good preparation for your future career. In what ways does having "people skills" help police officers perform their job?

Making the Grade

Looking back, we can see that sociology developed when and where social change was greatest.

positivism (p. 10) a scientific approach to knowledge based on "positive" facts as opposed to mere speculation

Unless you have a job that never involves dealing with people, you should consider the workplace benefits of taking courses in sociology.

The Origins of Sociology

Like the "choices" people make, major historical events rarely just "happen." Even sociology itself is the result of powerful social forces.

Social Change and Sociology

Striking changes in Europe during the eighteenth and nineteenth centuries made people think more about society and their place in it, spurring the development of sociology. Three kinds of changes were especially important in the development of sociology: the rise of a factory-based economy, the explosive growth of cities, and new ideas about democracy and political rights.

A New Industrial Economy

During the Middle Ages, most people in Europe plowed fields near their homes or engaged in small-scale *manufacturing* (a term derived from Latin words meaning "to make by hand"). By the end of the eighteenth century, inventors were using new sources of energy—the power of moving water and then steam—to operate large machines in mills and factories. As a result, instead of laboring at home or in tightly knit groups, workers became part of a large and anonymous labor force, under the control of strangers who owned the factories. This change in the system of production took people away from their homes, weakening the traditions that had guided community life for centuries.

The Growth of Cities

Across Europe, landowners took part in what historians call the *enclosure movement*—they fenced off more and more farmland to create grazing areas for sheep, the source of wool for the thriving textile mills. Without land, countless tenant farmers had little choice but to head to the cities in search of work in the new factories.

As cities grew larger, these urban migrants faced many social problems, including pollution, crime, and homelessness. Moving through streets crowded with strangers, they faced a new, impersonal social world.

Political Change

Economic development and the growth of cities also brought new ways of thinking. In the writings of Thomas Hobbes (1588–1679), John Locke (1632–1704), and Adam Smith (1723–1790), we see a shift in focus from people's moral duties to God and king to the pursuit of self-interest. Philosophers now spoke of *personal liberty* and *individual rights*. Echoing these sentiments, our own Declaration of Independence

What we see depends on our point of view. When gazing at the stars, lovers see romance, but scientists see thermal reactions. How does using the sociological perspective change what we see in the world around us?

clearly states that each citizen has "certain unalienable rights," including "life, liberty, and the pursuit of happiness."

The French Revolution, which began in 1789, was an even greater break with political and social tradition. As the French social analyst Alexis de Tocqueville (1805–1859) declared, the change in society in the wake of the French Revolution amounted to "nothing short of the regeneration of the whole human race" (1955:13, orig. 1856). As the new industrial economy, enormous cities, and fresh political ideas combined to draw attention to society, the new discipline known as sociology developed in France, Germany, and England, the countries where these changes were greatest.

Science and Sociology

Throughout history, the nature of society has fascinated people, including the brilliant philosophers K'ung Fu-tzu, or Confucius (551–479 B.C.E.), in China and Plato (427–347 B.C.E.) and Aristotle (384–322 B.C.E.) in Greece.[1] Later, the Roman emperor Marcus Aurelius (121–180), the medieval thinkers Saint Thomas Aquinas (c. 1225–1274) and Christine de Pizan (c. 1363–1431), and the great English playwright William Shakespeare (1564–1616) wrote about the workings of society.

---

[1]The abbreviation B.C.E. means "before the common era." We use this throughout the text instead of the traditional B.C. ("before Christ") to reflect the religious diversity of our society. Similarly, in place of the traditional A.D. (*anno Domini,* "in the year of our Lord"), we use the abbreviation C.E. ("common era").

Winston-Salem Journal

Back to School: In Poor Economy, Laid-off Workers Flocking to Community Colleges

By LISA O'DONNELL
February 10, 2009

Scores of laid-off workers are going back to the classroom, leading to an increase in enrollment in community colleges across North Carolina.

Historically, people have flocked to community colleges during recessions to learn new job skills. This time around, they are taking classes in such fields as health care and technical education, administrators said.

"At Forsyth Tech, and community colleges in general, we have an inverse relationship with the economy," said Gary Green, the president of Forsyth Technical Community College. "When you get a downturn, the job market tightens up and people look to community colleges to prop themselves up and get the skills they need to get back into the work force or to solidify their place in the work force. That's what we're seeing occur."

Mary Sue Antonucci of Pilot Mountain returned to the classroom last year because her job painting houses was not providing enough income. She is pursuing an associate's degree in art and hopes to open her own business.

"I realized, of course, that the job was not going to sustain me," said Antonucci, 50. "I knew I would not be able to take care of myself if I had no degree."

Although official full-time enrollment figures for degree-seeking students aren't yet available for the spring semester, administrators estimate that 12,500 new students enrolled in the state's fifty-eight community colleges this academic year, a 6.2 percent jump in enrollment from last year.

Typically, more students enroll in community colleges in the fall, but not this year, said Kennon Briggs, the executive vice president for the state's community-college system.

"Most companies gave their layoff notices in January and February rather than October or November," Briggs said. "We think for the first time in history that our spring-semester enrollment is going to be bigger than the fall's."

At Forsyth Tech, the number of students in fall 2008 increased 9.5 percent compared with fall 2007. For the spring semester, enrollment is up about 11.4 percent compared with last spring, Green said.

Colleges are being forced to serve more students with less money, Briggs said.

A few months ago, the governor's office asked the community-college system to trim 5 percent —$45 million—from its budget for the current fiscal year.

"What makes this a challenge is that we're growing at that rate at a time when we've been asked to return 5 percent of our current budget because state revenues have not materialized," Briggs said.

To compensate for the loss in funds, some colleges have increased class sizes and asked their faculty to teach more courses, Briggs said.

Forsyth Tech is dealing with the enrollment increase by offering some classes at 7 a.m. and adding part-time instructors, Green said.

Class sizes have not increased for the most part, Green said, because it would reduce the quality of instruction.

"We've had to work with the facilities we have and the personnel resources we have," he said.

Both Briggs and Green said they expect enrollment to continue to expand for at least another academic year based on the bleak economic forecast. . . .

WHAT DO YOU THINK?

1. This article describes the recent surge in community college enrollments in North Carolina, and a similar trend is occurring all across the country. How does this rise in community college enrollments reflect not just personal choices by individuals but also larger changes in society?

2. Can you point to other personal choices people have been making that may be linked to the weaker economy? What are they?

3. Did the weakening economy affect your life in terms of work? What about your decision to attend college? Explain.

Yet these thinkers were more interested in imagining the ideal society than they were in studying society as it really was. It was the French social thinker Auguste Comte (1798–1857) who coined the term *sociology* in 1838 to describe this new way of thinking. This makes sociology among the youngest of the academic disciplines— far newer than history, physics, or economics, for example.

Comte (1975, orig. 1851–54) saw sociology as the product of three stages of historical development. During the earliest *theological stage*, from the beginning of human history up to the end of the European Middle Ages about 1350 C.E., people took the religious view that society expressed God's will.

With the dawn of the Renaissance in the fifteenth century, Comte explained, the theological stage gave way to a *metaphysical stage* in which people came to see society as a natural rather than supernatural phenomenon. The English philosopher Thomas Hobbes (1588–1679), for example, suggested that society reflected not the perfection of God so much as the failings of selfish human nature.

What Comte called the *scientific stage* began with the work of early scientists such as the Polish astronomer Copernicus (1473–1543), the Italian astronomer and physicist Galileo (1564–1642), and the English physicist and mathematician Isaac Newton (1642–1727). Comte's contribution came in applying the scientific approach, originally used to analyze the physical world, to the study of society.[2]

Comte's approach is called **positivism,** *a scientific approach to knowledge based on "positive" facts as opposed to mere speculation.* Comte thought that knowledge based on tradition or metaphysics was really only speculation. A positivist approach to knowledge, however, is based on *science.* As a positivist, Comte believed that society operates according to certain laws, just as the physical world operates

---

[2]Illustrating Comte's stages, the ancient Greeks and Romans viewed the planets as gods; Renaissance metaphysical thinkers saw them as astral influences (giving rise to astrology); by the time of Galileo, scientists understood planets as natural objects moving according to natural laws.

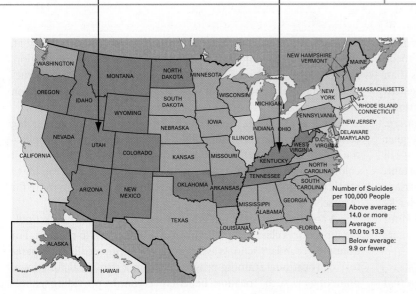

In the Plains and Mountain regions, and across the mountainous Appalachian region of the country, population density is very low, so people are more isolated. This isolation contributes to a higher rate of suicide.

Explore population density in your own state and across the United States on **mysoclab.com**. What conclusions can you draw about the relation between population density and suicide rate?

Seeing Ourselves

NATIONAL MAP 1–1
Suicide Rates across the United States

This map shows which states have high, average, and low suicide rates. Look for patterns. By and large, high suicide rates occur where people live far apart from one another. More densely populated states have low suicide rates. Do these data support or contradict Durkheim's theory of suicide? Why?

Explore on **mysoclab.com**

Source: Xu et al. (2010).

Number of Suicides per 100,000 People
- Above average: 14.0 or more
- Average: 10.0 to 13.9
- Below average: 9.9 or fewer

according to gravity and other laws of nature. Comte believed that by using science, people could come to understand the laws not only of the physical world but of society as well.

By the beginning of the twentieth century, sociology had taken hold in the United States and showed the influence of Comte's ideas. Today, most sociologists continue to consider science a crucial part of sociology, but we now realize that human behavior is far more complex than the movement of planets. We are creatures of imagination and spontaneity, so human behavior can never be explained by any rigid "laws of society." In addition, early sociologists such as Karl Marx (1818–1883) were troubled by the striking inequalities of the new industrial society. They hoped that the new discipline of sociology would not just help us understand society but also lead to change toward greater social justice.

Sociological Theory

The desire to translate observations into understanding brings us to the important part of sociology known as *theory*. A **theory** is *a statement of how and why specific facts are related*. The job of sociological theory is to explain social behavior in the real world. For example, recall Durkheim's theory that categories of people with low social integration (men, Protestants, the wealthy, and the unmarried) are at higher risk of suicide. Seeing Sociology in the News explains one consequence for young people of the recent economic recession.

Sociologists conduct research to test and refine their theories. National Map 1–1 shows the suicide rates for each of the fifty states and gives you a chance to do some theorizing of your own.

In building theory, sociologists face two basic questions: What issues should we study? And how should we connect the facts? In answering

these questions, sociologists look to one or more theoretical approaches as "road maps." Think of a **theoretical approach** as *a basic image of society that guides thinking and research*. Sociologists make use of three theoretical approaches: the *structural-functional approach*, the *social-conflict approach*, and the *symbolic-interaction approach*.

The Structural-Functional Approach

The **structural-functional approach** is *a framework for building theory that sees society as a complex system whose parts work together to promote solidarity and stability*. As its name suggests, this approach points to **social structure,** *any relatively stable pattern of social behavior*. Social structure gives our lives shape in families, the workplace, or the college classroom. This approach also looks for each structure's **social functions,** *the consequences of a social pattern for the operation of society as a whole*. All social patterns, from a simple handshake to complex religious rituals, function to tie people together and to keep society going, at least in its present form.

The structural-functional approach owes much to Auguste Comte, who pointed out the need to keep society unified when many traditions were breaking down. Emile Durkheim, who helped establish sociology in French universities, also based his work on this approach. A third structural-functional pioneer was the English sociologist Herbert Spencer (1820–1903). Spencer compared society to the human body: Just as the structural parts of the human body—the skeleton, muscles, and internal organs—function together to help the entire organism survive, social structures work together to preserve society. The structural-functional approach, then, leads sociologists to identify various structures of society and investigate their functions.

The U.S. sociologist Robert K. Merton (1910–2003) expanded our understanding of social function by pointing out that any social structure probably has many functions, some more obvious than others. He distinguished between **manifest functions,** *the recognized and intended consequences of any social pattern,* and **latent functions,** *the unrecognized and unintended consequences of any social pattern.* For example, the obvious function of this country's system of higher education is to give young people the information and skills they will need to hold jobs after graduation. Perhaps just as important, although less often acknowledged, is college's function as a "marriage broker," bringing together young people of similar social backgrounds. Another latent function of higher education is to limit unemployment by keeping millions of people out of the labor market, where many of them might not easily find jobs.

But Merton also recognized that not all the effects of social structure are good. Thus a **social dysfunction** is *any social pattern that may disrupt the operation of society.* Globalization of the economy, a rising flow of immigrants, and increasing inequality of income are all factors that—in the eyes of some people—disrupt existing social patterns. As these examples suggest, what is helpful and what is harmful for society is a matter about which people often disagree. In addition, what is functional for one category of people (say, a banking system that provides high profits for Wall Street executives) may well be dysfunctional for other categories of people (workers who lose pension funds invested in banks that fail or people who cannot pay their mortgages and end up losing their homes).

CRITICAL REVIEW The main idea of the structural-functional approach is its vision of society as stable and orderly. The main goal of sociologists who use this approach, then, is to figure out "what makes society tick."

In the mid-1900s, most sociologists favored the structural-functional approach. In recent decades, however, its influence has declined. By focusing attention on social stability and unity, critics point out, structural-functionalism ignores inequalities of social class, race, ethnicity, and gender, which cause tension and conflict. In general, its focus on stability at the expense of conflict makes this approach somewhat conservative. As a critical response, sociologists developed the social-conflict approach.

CHECK YOUR LEARNING How do manifest functions differ from latent functions? Give an example of a manifest function and a latent function of automobiles in the United States.

The Social-Conflict Approach

The **social-conflict approach** is *a framework for building theory that sees society as an arena of inequality that generates conflict and change.* Unlike the structural-functional emphasis on solidarity and stability, this approach highlights how factors such as class, race, ethnicity, gender, and age are linked to inequality in terms of money, power, education, and social prestige. A conflict analysis rejects the idea that social structure promotes the operation of society as a whole, focusing instead on how any social pattern benefits some people while hurting others.

Sociologists using the social-conflict approach look at ongoing conflict between dominant and disadvantaged categories of people—the rich in relation to the poor, white people in relation to people of color, and men in relation to women. Typically, people on top try to protect their privileges while the disadvantaged try to gain more for themselves.

A conflict analysis of our educational system shows how schooling reproduces class inequality from one generation to the next. For example, secondary schools assign students to either college preparatory or vocational training programs. From a structural-functional point of view, such "tracking" benefits everyone by providing schooling that fits students' abilities. But conflict analysis argues that tracking often has less to do with talent than with social background, meaning that well-to-do students are placed in higher tracks while poor children end up in lower tracks.

In this way, young people from privileged families get the best schooling, which leads them to college and later to high-income careers. The children of poor families, by contrast, are not prepared for college and, like their parents before them, typically get stuck in low-paying jobs. In both cases, the social standing of one generation is passed on to the next, with schools justifying the practice in terms of individual merit (Bowles & Gintis, 1976; Oakes, 1982, 1985).

Many sociologists use social-conflict analysis not just to understand society but also to reduce inequality. Karl Marx championed the cause of workers in what he saw as their battle against factory owners. In a well-known statement (inscribed on his monument in London's Highgate Cemetery), Marx declared, "The philosophers have only interpreted the world, in various ways; the point, however, is to change it."

Feminism and the Gender-Conflict Approach

One important type of conflict analysis is the **gender-conflict approach,** *a point of view that focuses on inequality and conflict between women and men.* The gender-conflict approach is closely linked to **feminism,** *support of social equality for women and men.*

The importance of the gender-conflict approach lies in making us aware of the many ways in which our society places men in positions of power over women, in the home (where men are usually considered the "head of the household"), in the workplace (where men earn more income and hold most positions of power), and in the mass media (how many hip-hop stars are women?).

Making the Grade

The feminist and gender-conflict approaches and the race-conflict approach are all examples of social-conflict theory.

Another contribution of the gender-conflict approach is making us aware of the importance of women to the development of sociology. Harriet Martineau (1802–1876) is regarded as the first woman sociologist. Born to a wealthy English family, Martineau made her mark in 1853 by translating the writings of Auguste Comte from French into English. She later documented the evils of slavery and argued for laws to protect factory workers, defending workers' right to unionize. She was particularly concerned about the position of women in society and fought for changes in education policy so that women could look forward to more in life than marriage and raising children.

In the United States, Jane Addams (1860–1935) was a sociological pioneer who in 1899 helped found Hull House, a Chicago settlement house that provided assistance to immigrant families. Although widely published—Addams wrote eleven books and hundreds of articles—she chose the life of a public activist over that of a university sociologist, speaking out on issues involving inequality, immigration, and the pursuit of peace. Though her pacifism during World War I was the subject of much controversy, she was awarded the Nobel Peace Prize in 1931.

All chapters of this book consider the importance of gender and gender inequality. For an in-depth look at feminism and the social standing of women and men, see Chapter 10 ("Gender Stratification").

The Race-Conflict Approach

Another important type of social-conflict analysis is the **race-conflict approach,** *a point of view that focuses on inequality and conflict between people of different racial and ethnic categories.* Just as men have power over women, white people have numerous social advantages over people of color, including, on average, higher incomes, more schooling, better health, and longer life expectancy.

The race-conflict approach also points out the contributions to the development of sociology made by people of color. Ida Wells Barnett (1862–1931) was born to slave parents but rose to become a teacher and then a journalist and newspaper publisher. She campaigned tirelessly for racial equality and, especially, to put an end to the lynching of black people. She wrote and lectured about racial inequality throughout her life (Lengerman & Niebrugge-Brantley, 1998).

An important contribution to understanding race in the United States was made by William Edward Burghardt Du Bois (1868–1963). Born to a poor Massachusetts family, Du Bois enrolled at Fisk University in Nashville, Tennessee, and then at Harvard University, where he earned the first doctorate awarded by that university to a person of color. Du Bois then founded the Atlanta Sociological Laboratory, which was an important center of sociological

We can use the sociological perspective to look at sociology itself. All of the most widely recognized pioneers of the discipline were men. This is because in the nineteenth century, it was all but unheard of for women to be college professors, and few women took a central role in public life. But Jane Addams was an early sociologist in the United States, who founded Hull House, a Chicago settlement house where she spent many hours helping young people.

research in the early decades of the last century. Like most people who follow the social-conflict approach (whether focusing on class, gender, or race), Du Bois believed that scholars should not simply learn about society's problems but also try to solve them. He therefore studied the black communities across the United States, pointing to numerous social problems ranging from educational inequality, a political system that denied people their right to vote, and the terrorist practice of lynching. Du Bois spoke out against racial inequality and participated in the founding of the National Association for the Advancement of Colored People (NAACP) (E. Wright, 2002a, 2002b). The Thinking About Diversity box on page 14 takes a closer look at the ideas of W. E. B. Du Bois.

CRITICAL REVIEW The various social-conflict approaches have gained a large following in recent decades, but like other approaches, they have met with criticism. Because any conflict analysis focuses on inequality, it largely ignores how shared values and interdependence can unify members of a society. In addition, say critics, to the extent that it pursues political goals, a social-conflict approach cannot claim scientific objectivity. Supporters of social-conflict analysis respond that *all* theoretical approaches have political consequences.

macro-level orientation a broad focus on social structures that shape society as a whole

    structural-functional approach (p. 11)
    social-conflict approach (p. 12)

micro-level orientation a close-up focus on social interaction in specific situations

    symbolic-interaction approach a framework for building theory that sees society as the product of the everyday interactions of individuals

THINKING ABOUT DIVERSITY: RACE, CLASS, & GENDER

W. E. B. Du Bois: A Pioneer in Sociology

One of sociology's pioneers in the United States, William Edward Burghardt Du Bois saw sociology as a key to solving society's problems, especially racial inequality. Du Bois earned a Ph.D. in sociology from Harvard University and established the Atlanta Sociological Laboratory, one of the first centers of sociological research in the United States. He helped his colleagues in sociology—and people everywhere—see the deep racial divisions in the United States. White people can simply be "Americans," Du Bois explained, but African Americans have a "double consciousness," reflecting their status as citizens who are never able to escape identification based on the color of their skin.

In his sociological classic *The Philadelphia Negro: A Social Study* (1899), Du Bois explored Philadelphia's African American community, identifying both the strengths and the weaknesses of people wrestling with overwhelming social problems on a day-to-day basis. He challenged the belief—widespread at that time—that blacks were inferior to whites, and he blamed white prejudice for the problems African Americans faced. He also criticized successful people of color for being so eager to win white acceptance

that they gave up all ties with the black community, which needed their help.

Despite notable achievements, Du Bois gradually grew impatient with academic study, which he felt was too detached from the everyday struggles of people of color. Du Bois wanted change. It was the hope of sparking public action against racial separation that led Du Bois, in 1909, to participate in the founding of the National Association for the Advancement of Colored People (NAACP), an organization that has been active in supporting racial equality for more than a century. As the editor of the organization's magazine, *Crisis*, Du Bois worked

tirelessly to challenge laws and social customs that deprived African Americans of the rights and opportunities enjoyed by the white majority.

Du Bois described race as the major problem facing the United States in the twentieth century. Early in his career, as a sociological researcher, he made enormous contributions to the study of racial inequality. Later, as an activist, he believed political reform might overcome deep racial divisions. But by the end of his life, he had grown bitter, believing that little had changed. At the age of ninety-three, Du Bois left the United States for the African nation of Ghana, where he died two years later.

WHAT DO YOU THINK?

1. If he were alive today, do you think that Du Bois would still consider race a major problem in the twenty-first century? Why or why not?

2. How much do you think African Americans today experience "double consciousness"?

3. In what ways can sociology help us understand and reduce racial conflict?

Sources: Based on Baltzell (1967), Du Bois (1967, orig. 1899), Wright (2002a, 2002b), and personal communication with Earl Wright II.

A final criticism of both the structural-functional and social-conflict approaches is that they paint society in broad strokes—in terms of "family," "social class," "race," and so on. A third theoretical approach views society less in general terms and more as the specific, everyday experiences of individual people.

  CHECK YOUR LEARNING Why do you think sociologists characterize the social-conflict approach as "activist"? What is it actively trying to achieve?

The Symbolic-Interaction Approach

The structural-functional and social-conflict approaches share a **macro-level orientation,** meaning *a broad focus on social structures that shape*

society as a whole. Macro-level sociology takes in the big picture, rather like observing a city from a helicopter and seeing how highways help people move from place to place or how housing differs from rich to poor neighborhoods. Sociology also uses a **micro-level orientation,** *a close-up focus on social interaction in specific situations.* Exploring city life in this way occurs at street level, where you might watch how children invent games on a school playground or observe how pedestrians respond to homeless people they pass on the street. The **symbolic-interaction approach,** then, is *a framework for building theory that sees society as the product of the everyday interactions of individuals.*

How does "society" result from the ongoing experiences of tens of millions of people? One answer, detailed in Chapter 4 ("Social Interaction in Everyday Life"), is that society is nothing more than the reality

Making the Grade

The Applying Theory table summarizes the three major theoretical approaches in sociology. Study the table to be sure you understand each one.

Seeing Sociology in Everyday Life

How would a structural-functional and a social-conflict analysis provide different answers to the question "What categories of people are you most likely to date and eventually marry?" How does a micro-level understanding of "romance" differ from a macro-level understanding?

APPLYING THEORY

Major Theoretical Approaches

	Structural-Functional Approach	Social-Conflict Approach	Symbolic-Interaction Approach
What is the level of analysis?	Macro-level	Macro-level	Micro-level
What image of society does the approach have?	Society is a system of interrelated parts that is relatively stable. Each part works to keep society operating in an orderly way. Members generally agree about what is morally right and morally wrong.	Society is a system of social inequalities based on class (Marx), gender (feminism and gender-conflict approach), and race (race-conflict approach). Society operates to benefit some categories of people and harm others. Social inequality causes conflict that leads to social change.	Society is an ongoing process. People interact in countless settings using symbolic communications. The reality people experience is variable and changing.
What core questions does the approach ask?	How is society held together? What are the major parts of society? How are these parts linked? What does each part do to help society work?	How does society divide a population? How do advantaged people protect their privileges? How do disadvantaged people challenge the system seeking change?	How do people experience society? How do people shape the reality they experience? How do behavior and meaning change from person to person and from one situation to another?

that people construct for themselves as they interact with one another. That is, we human beings live in a world of symbols, and we attach meaning to virtually everything, from the words on this page to the wink of an eye. We create "reality," therefore, as we define our surroundings, decide what we think of others, and shape our own identities.

The symbolic-interaction approach has roots in the thinking of Max Weber (1864–1920), a German sociologist who emphasized understanding a particular setting from the point of view of the people in it. Since Weber's time, sociologists have taken micro-level sociology in a number of directions. Chapter 3 ("Socialization: From Infancy to Old Age") discusses the ideas of George Herbert Mead (1863–1931), who explored how our personalities develop as a result of social experience. Chapter 4 ("Social Interaction in Everyday Life") presents the work of Erving Goffman (1922–1982), whose *dramaturgical analysis* describes how we resemble actors on a stage as we play out our various roles. Other contemporary sociologists, including George Homans and Peter Blau, have developed *social-exchange analysis*, the idea that interaction is guided by what each person stands to gain and lose from others. In the ritual of courtship, for example, people seek mates who can offer them at least as

much—in terms of physical attractiveness, intelligence, and social background—as they offer in return.

CRITICAL REVIEW Without denying the existence of macro-level social structures such as the family and social class, the symbolic-interaction approach reminds us that society basically amounts to *people interacting*. That is, micro-level sociology shows us how individuals construct and experience society. However, by emphasizing what is unique in each social scene, this approach risks overlooking the widespread influence of culture, as well as structural factors such as class, gender, and race.

CHECK YOUR LEARNING How does a micro-level analysis differ from a macro-level analysis? Provide an explanation of a social pattern at both levels.

The Applying Theory table summarizes the structural-functional, social-conflict, and symbolic-interaction approaches. Keep in mind that each is helpful in answering particular types of questions. As the Seeing Sociology in Everyday Life box on pages 16–17 shows, the fullest understanding of society comes from using all three approaches.

positivist sociology the study of society based on scientific observation of social behavior

empirical evidence information we can verify with our senses

science a logical system that develops knowledge from direct, systematic observation

● Seeing Sociology in Everyday Life

Think of three commonsense ideas that you were brought up to believe and that you later realized (perhaps thinking sociologically) were not entirely true.

SEEING SOCIOLOGY IN EVERYDAY LIFE

Sports: Playing the Theory Game

Who doesn't enjoy sports? Children and teens may play as many as two or three organized sports. For adults who don't participate themselves, weekend television is filled with sporting events, and whole sections of our newspapers are devoted to teams and players and scores. What can we learn by applying sociology's three theoretical approaches to this familiar element of life in the United States?

Structural-Functional Approach According to the structural-functional approach, the manifest functions of sports include recreation, getting in shape, and letting off steam in a relatively harmless way. Sports have important latent functions as well, from building social relationships to creating jobs. Perhaps the most important latent function of sports is to encourage competition, which is central to our society's way of life.

Of course, sports also have dysfunctional consequences. For example, colleges and universities that try to field winning teams sometimes recruit students for their athletic skill rather than their academic ability. This practice not only lowers a school's academic standards but also shortchanges athletes, who spend little time doing the academic work that will prepare them for future careers (Upthegrove, Roscigno, & Charles, 1999).

Social-Conflict Approach A social-conflict analysis points out how sports are linked to social inequality. Some sports—

tennis, swimming, golf, skiing—are expensive, so participation is largely limited to the well-to-do. Football, baseball, and basketball, however, are accessible to people at almost all income levels. Thus the games people play are not simply a matter of choice but also a reflection of their social standing.

Throughout history, men have dominated the world of sports. The first modern Olympic Games, held in 1896, excluded women from competition. Through most of the twentieth century, Little League teams barred girls based on the traditional ideas that girls lack the strength and the stamina to play sports and that they risk losing their femininity if they do. Both the

All Olympic games involve outstanding athletes. However, the sports that are central to the summer games, including track and field events, have a higher share of athletes of color. By contrast, the winter Olympics have fewer minorities and more well-to-do athletes. Can you explain why?

Olympics and the Little League are now open to females as well as males, but even today, women still take a back seat to men, particularly in sports with the greatest earnings and social prestige.

Although our society long excluded people of color from professional sports, opportunities have expanded in recent decades. In 1947, Jackie Robinson crossed the "color line" to become the first African American player in Major League Baseball. More than fifty years later, professional baseball retired the legendary Robinson's number 42 on *all* teams. In 2008, African Americans (12.8 percent of the U.S. population) accounted for 10.2 percent of Major League Baseball players, 67 percent of National Football League (NFL) players, and 77 percent of National Basketball Association (NBA) players (Lapchick, 2009).

But racial discrimination still exists in professional sports. For one thing, race is linked to the positions athletes play on the field, a pattern called "stacking." The figure shows the results of a 2009 study of race in Major League Baseball. Notice that white players are most concentrated in the central "thinking" positions of pitcher (66 percent white) and catcher (62 percent white). By contrast, African Americans represented only 5 percent of pitchers, and there were no black catchers. At the same time, 9 percent of infielders are African Americans, as are 32 percent of outfielders (positions characterized as requiring "speed and reactive ability") (Lapchick, 2009).

Three Ways to Do Sociology

All sociologists want to learn about the social world. But just as some may prefer one theoretical approach to another, many sociologists favor one research orientation. The following sections describe three ways to do sociological research: positivist, interpretive, and critical sociology.

Positivist Sociology

One popular way to do sociological research is **positivist sociology,** which is *the study of society based on scientific observation of social*

behavior. As explained earlier, positivist research discovers facts through the use of **science,** *a logical system that develops knowledge from direct, systematic observation.* Positivist sociology is sometimes called *empirical sociology* because it is based on **empirical evidence,** which is *information we can verify with our senses.*

Scientific research often challenges what we accept as "common sense." Here are three examples of widely held beliefs that are not supported by scientific evidence:

1. **"Differences in the behavior of females and males are just 'human nature.'"** Wrong. Much of what we call "human

---

Go to MySocLibrary at **mysoclab.com** to read "Names, Logos, Mascots, and Flags: The Contradictory Use of Sports Symbols" by Stanley D. Eitzen

○ Making the Grade

The pattern of "stacking," shown in the figure below, illustrates a social-conflict approach to understanding.

More broadly, African Americans have a large share of players in only five major sports: basketball, football, baseball, boxing, and track. And across all professional sports, the vast majority of managers, head coaches, and team owners are still white (Lapchick, 2009).

Who benefits most from professional sports? Although some players get sky-high salaries and millions of fans follow their teams, the vast profits sports generate are controlled by a small number of people—predominantly white men. In sum, sports in our country are bound up with inequalities based on gender, race, and wealth.

● Go to **mysoclab.com**

Symbolic-Interaction Approach At the micro-level, a sporting event is a complex, face-to-face interaction. In part, play is guided by the players' assigned positions and the rules of the game. But players are also spontaneous and unpredictable. Following the symbolic-interaction approach, we see sports less as a system and more as an ongoing process.

From this point of view, too, we would also expect each player to understand the game a little differently. Some players enjoy stiff competition; for others, love of the game may be greater than the need to win. In addition, the behavior of any single player is likely to change over time. A rookie in professional baseball, for example, may feel self-conscious during the

Diversity Snapshot

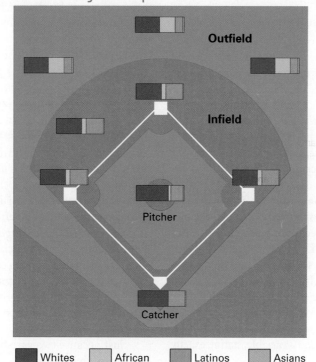

| ■ Whites | ☐ African Americans | ☐ Latinos | ☐ Asians |

"Stacking" in Professional Baseball

Does race play a part in professional sports? Looking at the various positions in professional baseball, we see that white players are more likely to play the central positions in the infield, while people of color are more likely to play in the outfield. What do you make of this pattern?

Source: Lapchick (2009).

first few games in the big leagues but go on to develop a comfortable sense of fitting in with the team. Coming to feel at home on the field was slow and painful for Jackie Robinson, who knew that many white players and millions of white fans resented his presence. In time, however, his outstanding ability and his confident, cooperative manner won him the respect of the entire nation.

The three theoretical approaches provide different insights into sports, and none is entirely correct. Applied to any issue, each approach provides part of a complex picture. To fully appreciate the power of the sociological perspective, you should become familiar with all three.

WHAT DO YOU THINK?

1. Describe how a macro-level approach to sports differs from a micro-level approach. Which theoretical approaches are macro-level, and which one is micro-level?

2. Make up three questions about sports that reflect the focus of each of the three theoretical approaches.

3. How might you apply the three approaches to other social patterns, such as the workplace or family life?

---

nature" is constructed by the society in which we live. We know this because researchers have found that definitions of "feminine" and "masculine" change over time and vary from one society to another (see Chapter 10, "Gender Stratification").

2. **"The United States is a middle-class society in which most people are more or less equal."** Not true. As Chapter 8 ("Social Stratification") explains, the richest 5 percent of U.S. families control more than 60 percent of the country's wealth, while almost half of all families have scarcely any wealth at all (Wolff, 2009).

3. **"People marry because they are in love."** Not exactly. In U.S. society, as already discussed, many social rules guide the selection of mates. Around the world, as Chapter 13 ("Family and Religion") explains, research indicates that marriages in most societies are arranged by parents and have little to do with love.

These examples confirm the old saying that "it's not what we *don't* know that gets us into trouble as much as the things we *do* know that *just aren't so*." The Seeing Sociology in Everyday Life box on page 19 explains why we also need to think critically about the "facts" we find in the popular media and on the Internet.

We have all been brought up hearing many widely accepted "truths," being bombarded by "expert" advice in the popular media, and feeling pressure to accept the opinions of those around us. As adults, we need to evaluate more critically what we see, read, and hear. Sociology can help us do that. Sociologists (and everyone else) can use science to assess many kinds of information.

Concepts, Variables, and Measurement

Let's take a closer look at how science works. A basic element of science is the **concept,** *a mental construct that represents some aspect of the world in a simplified form.* Sociologists use concepts to label aspects of social life, including "the family" and "the economy," and to categorize people in terms of their "gender" or "social class."

A **variable** is *a concept whose value changes from case to case.* The familiar variable "height," for example, has a value that varies from person to person. The concept "social class" can describe people's social standing using the values "upper-class," "middle-class," "working-class," and "lower-class."

The use of variables depends on **measurement,** *a procedure for determining the value of a variable in a specific case.* Some variables are easy to measure, as when a nurse checks our blood pressure. But measuring sociological variables can be far more difficult. For example, how would you measure a person's social class? You might start by looking at the clothing people wear, listening to how they speak, or noting where they live. Or trying to be more precise, you might ask about income, occupation, and education. Because there are many ways to measure a complex variable like social class, researchers must make decisions about how to *operationalize* a variable, stating exactly what they are measuring.

Statistics

Sociologists also face the problem of dealing with large numbers of people. For example, how do you report income for thousands or even millions of individuals? Listing streams of numbers would carry little meaning and tell us nothing about the people as a whole. To solve this problem, sociologists use *descriptive statistics* to state what is "average" for a large population. The most commonly used descriptive statistics are the *mean* (the arithmetic average of all measures, which you calculate by adding all the values and dividing by the number of cases), the *median* (the score at the halfway point in a listing of numbers from lowest to highest), and the *mode* (the score that occurs most often).

Reliability and Validity

For a measurement to be useful, it must be reliable and valid. **Reliability** refers to *consistency in measurement.* A measurement is reliable if repeated measurements give the same result time after time. But consistency does not guarantee **validity,** which is *actually measuring exactly what you intend to measure.* Valid measurement means more than hitting the same spot somewhere on a target again and again; it means hitting the exact target, the bull's-eye.

Say you want to know just how religious the students at your college are. You might ask students how often they attend religious services. But is going to a house of worship really the same thing as being religious? Maybe not, because people take part in religious rituals for many reasons, some of them having little to do with religion; in addition, some strong believers avoid organized religion altogether. Thus even when a measure yields consistent results (meaning that it is reliable), it can still miss the intended target (and therefore lack validity). Good sociological research depends on careful measurement, which is always a challenge to researchers.

Correlation and Cause

The real payoff in scientific research is determining how variables are related. **Correlation** means *a relationship in which two (or more) variables change together.* But sociologists want to know not just how variables change but which variable changes the other. The scientific ideal is to determine **cause and effect,** *a relationship in which change in one variable causes change in another.* As noted earlier, Emile Durkheim found that the degree of social integration (the cause) affected the suicide rate (the effect) among categories of people. Scientists refer to the cause as the *independent variable* and the effect as the *dependent variable.* Understanding cause and effect is valuable because it allows researchers to *predict* how one pattern of behavior will produce another.

Just because two variables change together does not necessarily mean that they have a cause-and-effect relationship. For instance, the marriage rate in the United States falls to its lowest point in January, which also happens to be the month when the national death rate is highest. Does this mean that people drop dead because they don't marry or that they don't marry because they die? Of course not. More likely, it is the cold and often stormy weather across much of the country in January (perhaps combined with the postholiday blues) that is responsible for both the low marriage rate and the high death rate.

When two variables change together but neither one causes the other, sociologists describe the relationship as a *spurious*, or false, correlation. A spurious correlation between two variables usually results from some third factor. For example, delinquency rates are high where young people live in crowded housing, but this is not because crowded housing causes youngsters to "turn bad." Both crowded housing and delinquency result from a third factor: poverty. To be sure of a real cause-and-effect relationship, we must show that (1) variables are correlated, (2) the independent (causal) variable occurs before the dependent variable, and (3) there is no evidence that a third variable has been overlooked, causing a spurious correlation.

Go to the Multimedia Library at **mysoclab.com** to view the *Core Concepts in Sociology* video "Objectivity: Fact or Fiction?"

● Seeing Sociology
in Everyday Life

Why do you think many doctors, teachers, and police officers avoid working professionally with their own children?

SEEING SOCIOLOGY IN EVERYDAY LIFE

Is What We Read in the Popular Press True? The Case of Extramarital Sex

Every day, we see stories in newspapers and magazines that tell us what people think and how they behave. But a lot of what you might read turns out to be misleading or worse.

Take the issue of extramarital sex, meaning married people having sex with someone other than their spouse. A look at the cover of many of the "women's magazines" you find in the checkout aisle at the supermarket or a quick reading of the advice column in your local newspaper might lead you to think that extramarital sex is a major issue facing married couples.

The "pop" media seem full of stories about how to keep your spouse from "cheating" or pointing out the clues that tip you off when your spouse is having an affair. Most of the studies reported in the popular press and on Internet Web sites suggest that more than half of married people—women as well as men—cheat on their spouse.

But is extramarital sex really that widespread? No. Researchers who conduct sound sociological investigation have found that in any given year, only 3 to 4 percent of married people have an extramarital relationship, and no more than 15 to 20 percent of married people have *ever* done so. Why, then, do surveys in the popular media report rates of extramarital sex that are so much higher? We can answer this question by taking a look at who fills out pop surveys.

First, it is people with a personal interest in some topic who are most likely to respond to an offer in the popular media or online to complete a survey. For this reason, people who have some personal experience with extramarital sex (either their own behavior or their partner's) are more likely to show up in these studies. In contrast, studies correctly done by skilled researchers carefully select subjects so that the results are representative of the entire population.

Second, because the readership of the magazines and online sources that conduct these surveys is, on average, young, their surveys end up attracting a high proportion of young respondents. And one thing we know about young people—married or unmarried—is that they are more likely to have sex. For example, the typical married person who is thirty years of age is more than twice as likely to have had an extramarital relationship than the typical married person over age sixty.

Third, women are much more likely than men to read the popular magazines that feature sex

TRIXIE August 2010
"How Much Cheating? New Survey Tells All!"
"10 Tips for a Sexy You"

surveys. Therefore, women are more likely to fill out the surveys. In recent decades, the share of women, especially younger women, who have had extramarital sex has gone up. Why are today's younger women more likely than women a generation or two earlier to have had extramarital sex? Probably because women today are working out of the home and many are traveling as part of their job. In general, today's women have a wider social network that brings them into contact with more men.

Chapter 8 ("Sexuality and Society") takes a close look at sexual patterns including extramarital relationships. For now, just remember that a lot of what you read in the popular media and online may not be as true as some people think.

WHAT DO YOU THINK?

1. Can you think of other issues on which pop media surveys may give misleading information? What are they?

2. Explain why we should have more trust in the results of sound research carried out by skilled sociologists than in the surveys conducted by the popular media.

3. Do you think companies are likely to sell more magazines or newspapers if they publish "research" results that distort the truth? Explain.

Sources: T. W. Smith (2006), Black (2007), Parker-Pope (2008).

The Ideal of Objectivity

A guiding principle of science is *objectivity*, or personal neutrality, in conducting research. Ideally, objective research allows the facts to speak for themselves and not be influenced by the personal values and biases of the researcher. In reality, of course, achieving total neutrality is impossible for anyone. But carefully observing the rules of scientific research will maximize objectivity. ● Go to **mysoclab.com**

The German sociologist Max Weber noted that people usually choose *value-relevant* research topics—topics they care about. But once their work is under way, he cautioned, researchers should try to be *value-free*. That is, we must be dedicated to finding truth as it *is* rather than as we think it *should be*. For Weber, this difference sets science apart from politics. Researchers (unlike politicians) must stay open-minded and be willing to accept whatever results come from their work, whether they personally agree with them or not.

Weber's argument still carries much weight in sociology, although most researchers realize that we can never be completely value-free or even aware of all our biases (Demerath, 1996). In addition, keep in mind that sociologists are not "average" people: Most are highly educated white men and women who are more politically

research orientations

positivist sociology (p. 16)
the study of society based on systematic observation of social behavior

interpretive sociology
the study of society that focuses on discovering the meanings people attach to their social world

critical sociology
the study of society that focuses on the need for social change

 Go to the Multimedia Library at **mysoclab.com** to view the *Core Concepts in Sociology* video "Qualitative vs. Quantitative Research"

liberal than the population as a whole. Sociologists need to remember that they, too, are influenced by their social backgrounds.

Interpretive Sociology

Not all sociologists agree that science is the only way—or even the best way—to study human society. This is because, unlike planets or other elements of the natural world, humans do not simply move around as objects that can be measured. On the contrary, people are active creatures who attach *meaning* to their actions, and meaning is not easy to observe directly. Therefore, sociologists have developed a second research orientation, known as **interpretive sociology,** *the study of society that focuses on discovering the meanings people attach to their social world*. Max Weber, the pioneer of this framework, argued that the proper focus of sociology is *interpretation*, or understanding the meanings people create in their everyday lives.

The Importance of Meaning

Interpretive sociology differs from positivist sociology in three ways. First, positivist sociology focuses on action—on what people do—because this is what we can observe directly. Interpretive sociology, focuses on people's understanding of their actions and their surroundings. Second, positivist sociology claims that objective reality exists "out there"; interpretive sociology counters that reality is subjective, constructed by people in the course of their everyday lives. Third, positivist sociology tends to favor *quantitative* data, numerical measurements of outward behavior; interpretive sociology favors *qualitative* data, researchers' perceptions of how people understand their world. In sum, the positivist orientation, close to science, is well suited for research in a laboratory, where investigators stand back and take careful measurements of what people do. The interpretive orientation, while not rejecting science outright, claims that we learn more by interacting with people, focusing on subjective meaning, and learning how people make sense of their everyday lives. This type of research is best carried out in a natural setting. ⬤ Go to **mysoclab.com**

Weber's Concept of *Verstehen*

Max Weber claimed that the key to interpretive sociology lies in *Verstehen* (pronounced "fair-SHTAY-en"), the German word for "understanding." It is the interpretive sociologist's job not just to observe *what* people do but also to share in their world of meaning, coming to appreciate *why* they act as they do. Subjective thoughts and feelings, which scientists tend to dismiss because they are difficult to measure, are the focus of the interpretive sociologist's attention.

Critical Sociology

Like the interpretive orientation, critical sociology developed in reaction to what many sociologists saw as the limitations of positivist

sociology. In this case, however, the problem involves the central principle of scientific research: objectivity. Positivist sociology holds that reality is "out there" and that the researcher's job is to study and document how society works. But Karl Marx, who founded the critical orientation, rejected the idea that society exists as a "natural" system. To assume that society is somehow "fixed," he claimed, is the same as saying that society cannot be changed. Positivist sociology, in his view, ends up supporting the status quo. **Critical sociology,** by contrast, is *the study of society that focuses on the need for social change*.

The Importance of Change

Rather than asking the positivist question "How does society work?" critical sociologists ask moral and political questions, especially "Should society exist in its present form?" Their answer, typically, is that it should not. Critical sociology does not reject science completely—Marx (like critical sociologists today) used scientific methods to learn about inequality. But critical sociology does reject the scientific neutrality that requires researchers to try to be "objective" and limit their work to studying the status quo.

One recent account of the critical orientation, echoing Marx, claims that the point of this type of sociology is "not just to research the social world but to change it in the direction of democracy and social justice" (Feagin & Hernán, 2001:1). In making value judgments about how society should be changed, critical sociology rejects Weber's goal that sociology be a value-free science and emphasizes instead that sociologists should be activists in pursuit of greater social equality.

Sociologists using the critical orientation seek to change not only society but also the character of research itself. They often identify personally with their research subjects and encourage them to help decide what to study and how to do the work. Often researchers and subjects use their findings to provide a voice for less powerful people and advance the political goal of a more equal society (Hess, 1999; Feagin & Hernán, 2001; Perrucci, 2001).

Sociology as Politics

Positivist sociologists object to taking sides in this way, claiming that critical sociology (whether feminist, Marxist, or of some other critical orientation) becomes political, lacks scientific objectivity, and cannot correct for its own biases. Critical sociologists respond that *all* research is political in that either it calls for change or it does not; sociologists thus have no choice about their work being political, but they can choose *which* positions to support.

Critical sociology is an activist approach that ties knowledge to action and seeks not just to understand the world as it exists but also to improve it. In general, positivist sociology tends to appeal to researchers who try to be nonpolitical or who have more conservative political views; critical sociology appeals to those whose politics ranges from liberal to radical left.

Imagine that you are a positivist sociologist. How might you criticize critical sociology? Now imagine that you are a critical sociologist. How might you criticize positivist sociology?

gender the personal traits and social positions that members of a society attach to being female or male

SUMMING UP

Three Research Orientations in Sociology

	Positivist Sociology	Interpretive Sociology	Critical Sociology
What is reality?	Society is an orderly system. There is an objective reality "out there."	Society is ongoing interaction. People construct reality as they attach meanings to their behavior.	Society is patterns of inequality. Reality is that some categories of people dominate others.
How do we conduct research?	Using a scientific orientation, the researcher carefully observes behavior, gathering empirical, ideally quantitative, data. Researcher tries to be a neutral observer.	Seeking to look "deeper" than outward behavior, the researcher focuses on subjective meaning. The researcher gathers qualitative data, discovering the subjective sense people make of their world. Researcher is a participant.	Seeking to go beyond positivism's focus on studying the world as it is, the researcher is guided by politics and uses research as a strategy to bring about desired social change. Researcher is an activist.
Corresponding theoretical approach	Structural-functional approach	Symbolic-interaction approach	Social-conflict approach

Research Orientations and Theory

Is there a link between research orientations and sociological theory? There is no precise connection, but each of the three ways to do sociology—positivist, interpretive, and critical—does stand closer to one of the theoretical approaches presented earlier in this chapter. The positivist orientation is linked to the structural-functional approach (because both are concerned with the scientific goal of understanding society as it is), the interpretive orientation to the symbolic-interaction approach (because both focus on the meanings people attach to their social world), and the critical orientation to the social-conflict approach (because both seek to reduce social inequality). The Summing Up table provides a quick review of the differences among the three ways to do sociology. Many sociologists favor one orientation over another; however, because each provides useful insights, it is a good idea to become familiar with all three.

Gender and Research

In recent years, sociologists have become aware that research is affected by **gender,** *the personal traits and social positions that members of a society attach to being female or male.* Gender can affect sociological research in five ways (Eichler, 1988; Giovannini, 1992):

1. **Androcentricity.** *Androcentricity* (literally, "focus on the male") means approaching an issue from a male perspective. Some-

times researchers act as if only men's activities are important, ignoring what women do. For years, sociologists studying occupations focused on the paid labor of men and overlooked the housework and child care traditionally performed by women. Research that tries to explain human behavior cannot ignore half of humanity.

   Gynocentricity—seeing the world from a female perspective—can also limit good sociological investigation. However, in our male-dominated society, this problem arises less often.

2. **Overgeneralizing.** This problem occurs when sociologists gather data only from men but then use that information to draw conclusions about all people. For example, a researcher might speak to a handful of male public officials and then form conclusions about an entire community.

3. **Gender blindness.** Failing to consider gender at all is called *gender blindness.* The lives of men and women differ in many ways. A study of growing old in the United States might suffer from gender blindness if it overlooked the fact that most elderly men live with spouses but elderly women generally live alone.

4. **Double standards.** Researchers must be careful not to judge men and women by different standards. For example, a family researcher who labels a couple "man and wife" may define the man as the "head of the household" and treat him as important while assuming that the woman simply engages in family "support work."

5. **Interference.** Another way gender can distort a study is if a subject reacts to the sex of the researcher, interfering with the

Seeing Sociology
in Everyday Life

Think of three research topics about U.S. society that might be
affected by the gender of the researcher. In each case, explain why.

Go to the Multimedia Library at **mysoclab.com**
to see Jeff Lucas discuss "Experiments"

If you ask only male subjects about their attitudes or actions, you may be
able to support conclusions about "men" but not more generally about
"people." What would a researcher have to do to ensure that research data
support conclusions about all of society?

research operation. While studying a small community in
Sicily, for instance, Maureen Giovannini (1992) found that
many men treated her as a *woman* rather than as a *researcher*.
Some thought it inappropriate for an unmarried woman to
speak privately with a man. Others denied Giovannini access
to places they considered off-limits to women.

There is nothing wrong with focusing research on people of one
sex or the other. But all sociologists, as well as people who read their
work, should be mindful of how gender can affect an investigation.

Research Ethics

Like all other scientific investigators, sociologists must be aware that
their work can harm as well as help subjects and communities. For this
reason, the American Sociological Association—the major profes-

sional organization of sociologists in North America—has established
formal guidelines for conducting research (1997).

Sociologists must try to be skillful and fair-minded in their work.
They must disclose all research findings without omitting significant data. They should make their results available to other sociologists who may want to conduct a similar study.

Sociologists must also make sure that subjects taking part in a
research project are not harmed, and they must stop work right away
if they suspect that any subject is at risk of harm. Researchers are also
required to protect the privacy of individuals involved in a research
project, even if they come under pressure from authorities, such as the
police or the courts, to release confidential information. Researchers
must also get the *informed consent* of participants, which means that
the subjects must fully understand their responsibilities and the risks
that the research involves and agree to take part before the work begins.

Another guideline concerns funding. Sociologists must include in
their published reports all sources of financial support. They must avoid
accepting money from a source if there is any question about a conflict
of interest. Researchers must never accept funding from any organization that seeks to influence the research results for its own purposes.

The federal government also plays a part in research ethics. Every
college and university that seeks federal funding for research involving human subjects must have an *institutional review board* (IRB)
that examines grant applications and ensures that research will not
violate ethical standards.

Finally, there are global dimensions to research ethics. Before beginning work in another country, an investigator must become familiar
enough with that society to understand what people *there* are likely to
regard as a violation of privacy or a source of personal danger. In a
diverse society such as our own, the same rule applies to studying people whose cultural background differs from that of the researcher. The
Thinking About Diversity box offers tips on the sensitivity outsiders
should apply when studying Hispanic communities.

Research Methods

A **research method** is *a systematic plan for doing research*. Four widely
used methods of sociological investigation are experiments, surveys,
participant observation, and the use of existing sources. None is better or worse than any other. Rather, just as a carpenter chooses a
particular tool for a particular job, researchers select a method according to whom they want to study and what they want to learn.

Testing a Hypothesis: The Experiment

The **experiment** is *a research method for investigating cause and effect
under highly controlled conditions*. Experiments closely follow the logic
of science, testing a specific *hypothesis*, a statement of how two (or

research method a systematic plan for doing research

experiment (p. 22)
a research method for investigating cause and effect under highly controlled conditions

survey (p. 24)
a research method in which subjects respond to a series of statements or questions on a questionnaire or in an interview

participant observation (p. 26)
a research method in which investigators systematically observe people while joining them in their routine activities

use of existing sources (p. 28)

THINKING ABOUT DIVERSITY: RACE, CLASS, & GENDER

Studying the Lives of Hispanics

JORGE: If you are going to include Latinos in your research, you need to learn a little about their culture.

MARK: I'm interviewing lots of different families. What's special about interviewing Latinos?

JORGE: Sit down and I'll tell you a few things you need to know. . . .

Because our society is socially diverse, sociologists often find themselves studying people who differ from themselves. Learning, in advance, the ways of life of any category of people can ease the research process and ensure that no hard feelings are caused along the way.

Gerardo Marín and Barbara Van Oss Marín (1991) have identified five areas of concern when conducting research with Hispanic people, currently the largest minority in the United States.

1. **Be careful with terms.** The Maríns point out that "Hispanic" is a label of convenience used by the U.S. Census Bureau. Few people from Spanish- and Portuguese-speaking cultures think of themselves as "Hispanic"; most identify with a particular country, such as Peru, Cuba, Argentina, or Spain.

2. **Be aware of cultural differences.** By and large, the U.S. population is individualistic and competitive. Many Hispanics, by contrast, place more value on cooperation and community. An outsider may judge the behavior of a Hispanic subject as

conformist or overly trusting when in fact the person is simply trying to be helpful. Researchers should also realize that Hispanic respondents might agree with a particular statement merely out of politeness.

3. **Anticipate family dynamics.** Hispanic cultures have strong family loyalties. Asking subjects to reveal information about another family member may make them uncomfortable or even angry. The Maríns add that a researcher's request to speak privately with a Hispanic woman in the home may provoke suspicion or outright disapproval from her husband or father.

4. **Take your time.** Spanish cultures, the Maríns explain, tend to place the quality of relationships above simply getting a job done. A non-Hispanic researcher who tries to hurry an interview with a Hispanic family out of a desire not to delay the family's dinner may be

considered rude for not proceeding at a more sociable and relaxed pace.

5. **Think about personal space.** Finally, Hispanics typically maintain closer physical contact than many non-Hispanics. Therefore, researchers who seat themselves across the room from their subjects may seem standoffish. Researchers might also wrongly label Hispanics "pushy" if they move closer than a non-Hispanic researcher finds comfortable.

Of course, Hispanics differ among themselves just as people in any category do, and these generalizations apply to some more than to others. But investigators should be aware of cultural dynamics when carrying out any research, especially in the United States, where hundreds of distinctive categories of people make up our multicultural society.

WHAT DO YOU THINK?

1. Give a specific example of damage to a study that might occur if researchers are not sensitive to the culture of their subjects.

2. What do researchers need to do to avoid the kinds of problems noted in this box?

3. Discuss the research process with classmates from various cultural backgrounds. In what ways are the concerns raised by people of different cultural backgrounds similar? In what ways do they differ?

---

more) variables are related. A hypothesis is really an educated guess about how variables are linked, usually expressed as an *if-then* statement: *If* this particular thing were to happen, *then* that particular thing will result. ● Go to **mysoclab.com**

An experimenter gathers the evidence needed to reject or not to reject the hypothesis in four steps: (1) State which variable is the *independent variable* (the "cause" of the change) and which is the *dependent variable* (the "effect," the thing that is changed). (2) Measure the initial value of the dependent variable. (3) Expose the

dependent variable to the independent variable (the "cause" or "treatment"). (4) Measure the dependent variable again to see what change, if any, took place. If the expected change took place, the experiment supports the hypothesis; if not, the hypothesis must be modified.

Successful experiments depend on careful control of all factors that might affect what the experiment is trying to measure. Control is easiest in a research laboratory. But experiments in an everyday location—"in the field," as sociologists say—have the advantage of letting researchers observe subjects in their natural settings.

Go to the Multimedia Library at **mysoclab.com** to view the video "The Stanford Prison Experiment"

Making the Grade

Sociologists use various research methods. Which one is chosen depends on the question being asked and also what resources are available for the study.

Illustration of an Experiment: The "Stanford County Prison"

Prisons can be violent settings, but is this due simply to the "bad" people who end up there? Or as Philip Zimbardo suspected, does prison itself somehow cause violent behavior? To answer this question, Zimbardo devised a fascinating experiment, which he called the "Stanford County Prison" (Zimbardo, 1972; Haney, Banks, & Zimbardo, 1973).

Zimbardo thought that once inside a prison, even emotionally healthy people are likely to engage in violence. So Zimbardo treated the *prison setting* as the independent variable capable of causing *violence*, the dependent variable.

To test this hypothesis, Zimbardo and his research team first constructed a realistic-looking "prison" in the basement of the psychology building on the campus of Stanford University. Then they placed an ad in a local newspaper, offering to pay young men to help with a two-week research project. To each of the seventy who responded they administered a series of physical and psychological tests and then selected the healthiest twenty-four.

The next step was to assign randomly half the men to be "prisoners" and half to be "guards." The plan called for the guards and prisoners to spend the next two weeks in the mock prison. The prisoners began their part of the experiment when real police officers "arrested" them at their homes. After searching and handcuffing the men, the police drove them to the local police station, where they were fingerprinted. Then police transported their captives to the Stanford prison, where the guards locked them up. Zimbardo started his video camera rolling and watched to see what would happen next. ● Go to **mysoclab.com**

The experiment turned into more than anyone had bargained for. Both guards and prisoners soon became embittered and hostile toward one another. Guards humiliated the prisoners by assigning them jobs such as cleaning toilets with their bare hands. The prisoners resisted and insulted the guards. Within four days, the researchers had removed five prisoners who displayed signs of "extreme emotional depression, crying, rage and acute anxiety" (Hanley, Banks, & Zimbardo, 1973:81). Before the end of the first week, the situation had become so bad that the researchers had to end the experiment.

The events that unfolded at the "Stanford County Prison" supported Zimbardo's hypothesis that prison violence is rooted in the social character of jails themselves, not in the personalities of individual guards and prisoners. This finding raised questions about our society's prisons, leading to some basic reforms. Zimbardo's experiment also shows the potential of research to threaten the physical and mental well-being of subjects. Such dangers are not always as obvious as they were in this case. Therefore, researchers must carefully consider the potential harm to subjects at all stages of their work and halt any study, as Zimbardo did, if subjects suffer harm of any kind.

○ **CRITICAL REVIEW** In carrying out the "Stanford County Prison" study, the researchers chose to do an experiment because they were interested in testing a hypothesis. In this case, Zimbardo and his colleagues wanted to find out if the prison setting itself (rather than the personalities of individual guards and prisoners) is the cause of prison violence. The fact that the "prison" erupted in violence—even using guards and prisoners with "healthy" profiles—supports their hypothesis.

○ **CHECK YOUR LEARNING** How might Zimbardo's findings help explain the abuse of Iraqi prisoners by U.S. soldiers after the 2003 invasion?

Asking Questions: Survey Research

A **survey** is *a research method in which subjects respond to a series of statements or questions on a questionnaire or in an interview.* The most widely used of all research methods, the survey is well suited to studying what cannot be observed directly, such as political attitudes or religious beliefs.

A survey targets some *population,* for example, unmarried mothers or adults living in rural counties in Wisconsin. Sometimes every adult in the country is the survey population, as in polls taken during national political campaigns. Of course, contacting a vast number of people is all but impossible, so researchers usually study a *sample,* a much smaller number of subjects selected to represent the entire population. Surveys using samples of as few as 1,500 people commonly give accurate estimates of public opinion for the entire country.

Beyond selecting subjects, the survey must have a specific plan for asking questions and recording answers. The most common way to do this is to give subjects a *questionnaire* with a series of written statements or questions. Often the researcher lets subjects choose possible responses to each item, as on a multiple-choice test. Sometimes, though, a researcher may want subjects to respond freely, to permit all opinions to be expressed. Of course, this free-form approach means that the researcher later has to make sense out of what can be a bewildering array of answers.

In an *interview,* a researcher personally asks subjects a series of questions, thereby solving one problem common to the questionnaire method: the failure of some subjects to return the questionnaire to the researcher. A further difference is that interviews give participants freedom to respond as they wish. Researchers often ask follow-up questions to clarify an answer or to probe a bit more deeply. In doing this, however, a researcher must avoid influencing the subject even in subtle ways, such as by raising an eyebrow as the subject offers an answer.

● Seeing Sociology
  in Everyday Life

Write three questions you might ask to measure people's social class. Why would you have to ask more than one question?

○ Making the Grade

In general, questionnaires allow a researcher to collect lots of easily reported information—age, sex, voter participation—from lots of people. Interviews allow researchers to explore in-depth attitudes on a particular topic from a few people.

Illustration of Survey Research: Studying the African American Elite

Do highly successful African Americans escape the sting of racism? The sociologist Lois Benjamin—herself a successful college professor and the first African American faculty member at the University of Tampa—thought the answer was no. To investigate the effects of racism on talented African American men and women, Benjamin set out to conduct survey research.

Benjamin (1991) chose to interview subjects rather than distribute a questionnaire because she wanted to enter into a conversation with her subjects, to ask follow-up questions, and to be able to pursue topics that might come up in conversation. A second reason Benjamin favored interviews over questionnaires is that racism is a sensitive topic. A supportive researcher can make it easier for subjects to answer painful questions more freely.

Because conducting interviews takes a great deal of time, Benjamin had to limit the number of people in her study. She settled for 100 men and women. Even this small number kept Benjamin busy for more than two years of scheduling, traveling, and meeting with respondents. She spent another two years transcribing the tapes of her interviews, sorting out what the hours of talk told her about racism, and writing up her results.

Benjamin began by interviewing people she knew and asking them to suggest others. This strategy is called *snowball sampling* because the number of individuals included grows rapidly over time. Snowball sampling is appealing because it is an easy way to do research: We begin with familiar people, who provide introductions to their friends and colleagues. The drawback, however, is that snowball sampling rarely produces a sample that is representative of the larger population. Benjamin's sample probably contained many like-minded individuals, and it was certainly biased toward people willing to talk openly about race. She understood these problems and tried to include in her sample people of both sexes, of different ages, and representing different regions of the country. The Thinking About Diversity box on pages 26–27 presents a statistical profile of Benjamin's respondents along with some tips on how to read tables.

Benjamin based all her interviews on a series of questions and allowed her subjects to answer however they wished. As usually happens, the interviews took place in a wide range of settings. She met subjects in offices (hers or theirs), in hotel rooms, and in cars. In each case, Benjamin tape-recorded the conversation, which lasted from two-and-one-half to three hours, so that she would not be distracted by taking notes.

As research ethics demand, Benjamin offered complete anonymity to participants. Even so, many of the women and men in her study—including notables such as Vernon E. Jordan Jr., the former president of the National Urban League, and Yvonne Walker-

Focus groups are a type of survey in which a small number of people representing a target population are asked for their opinions about some issue or product. Here a sociology professor asks students to evaluate textbooks for use in her introductory class.

Taylor, the first woman president of Wilberforce University—were accustomed to being in the public eye and permitted Benjamin to use their names.

What surprised Benjamin most about her research was how eagerly many subjects responded to her request for an interview. These normally busy men and women appeared to go out of their way to contribute to her project. Furthermore, once the interviews were under way, many of her subjects became very emotional. Benjamin reports that at some point in the conversation, about 40 of her 100 subjects cried. For them, apparently, the research provided an opportunity to release feelings and share experiences they had never revealed to anyone before. How did Benjamin respond to the expression of such sentiments? She reports that she cried along with her respondents.

Of the research orientations described earlier in this chapter, you will see that Benjamin's research fits best under interpretive sociology (she wanted to find out what race meant to her subjects) and critical sociology (she undertook the study partly to show that racial prejudice still exists). Many of her subjects reported fearing that race might someday undermine their success, and others spoke of a race-based "glass ceiling" preventing them from reaching the highest positions in U.S. society. Summarizing her findings, Benjamin concluded that despite the improving social standing of African Americans, black people in the United States still suffer the sting of racial hostility.

● Seeing Sociology
in Everyday Life

Suggest a research topic that might lead a researcher to use a
questionnaire. What about a topic that would call for interviews?

Go to the Multimedia Library at **mysoclab.com** to
view the slideshow "How to Read a Table"

THINKING ABOUT DIVERSITY: RACE, CLASS, & GENDER

Lois Benjamin's African American Elite: Using Tables in Research

Say you want to present a lot of information about a diverse population. How do you do it quickly and easily? The answer is by using a table. A table provides a lot of information in a small amount of space, so learning to read tables can increase your reading efficiency. When you spot a table, look first at the title to see what information it contains. The title of the table presented here provides a profile of the 100 subjects participating in Lois Benjamin's research. Across the top of the table, you will see eight variables that describe these men and women. Reading down each column, note the categories within each variable; the percentages in each column add up to 100.

Starting at the top left, we see that Benjamin's sample was mostly men (63 percent, versus 37 percent women). In terms of age, most of the respondents (68 percent) were in the middle stage of life, and most grew up in a predominantly black community in the South or in the North or Midwest region of the United States.

These individuals are indeed a professional elite. Notice that half have earned either a doctorate (32 percent) or a medical or law degree (17 percent). Given their extensive education (and Benjamin's own position as a professor), we should not be surprised that the largest share (35 percent) work in academic institutions. In terms of income, these are wealthy individuals, with most (64 percent) earning

more than $50,000 annually back in 1990 (a salary that only 39 percent of full-time workers make even today).

Finally, we see that these 100 individuals are generally left of center in their political views. In part, this reflects their extensive schooling (which encourages progressive thinking) and the tendency of academics to fall on the liberal side of the political spectrum.

● Go to **mysoclab.com**

WHAT DO YOU THINK?

1. Why are statistical data, such as those in this table, an efficient way to convey a lot of information?

2. Looking at the table, can you determine how long it took most people to become part of this elite? Explain your answer.

3. Do you see any ways in which this African American elite might differ from a comparable white elite? If so, what are they?

CRITICAL REVIEW Professor Benjamin chose the survey as her method because she wanted to ask a lot of questions and gather information from her subjects. Certainly, some of the information she collected could have been obtained using a questionnaire. But she decided to carry out interviews because she was dealing with a complex and sensitive topic. Interacting with her subjects one on one for several hours, Benjamin could put them at ease, discuss personal matters, and ask them follow-up questions.

CHECK YOUR LEARNING Could this research have been carried out by a white sociologist? Why or why not?

In the Field: Participant Observation

Participant observation is *a research method in which investigators systematically observe people while joining them in their routine activities.* This method lets researchers study everyday social life in any natural setting, from a nightclub to a religious seminary. Cultural anthropologists use participant observation to study other societies, calling this method *fieldwork.*

At the beginning of a field study, most researchers do not have a specific hypothesis in mind. In fact, they may not yet realize what the important questions will turn out to be. This makes most participant observation *exploratory* and *descriptive*, falling within interpretive sociology and producing mostly qualitative, rather than quantitative, data. Compared with experiments and surveys, participant observation has few hard-and-fast rules. But this flexibility allows investigators to explore the unfamiliar and adapt to the unexpected.

Participant observers try to gain entry into a setting without disturbing the routine behavior of others. Their role is twofold: To gain an insider's viewpoint, they must become participants in the setting, "hanging out" for months or even years, trying to act, think, and even feel the same way as the people they are observing; at the same time, they must remain observers, standing back from the action and applying the sociological perspective to social patterns that others take for granted.

Because the personal impressions of a single researcher play such a central role, critics claim that participant observation falls short of scientific standards. Yet its personal approach is also a strength: Where a high-profile team of sociologists administering a formal survey

┌─● Making the Grade

In her study of the African American elite, Lois Benjamin made great effort to explain who her subjects were. Always consider this question when reading anyone's research results.

┌─● Making the Grade

Another term for "participant observation" is "fieldwork" because this type of research is carried out in some natural setting.

The Talented 100: Lois Benjamin's African American Elite

Sex	Age	Childhood Racial Setting	Childhood Region	Highest Educational Degree	Job Sector	Income	Political Orientation
Male 63%	35 or younger 6%	Mostly black 71%	West 6%	Doctorate 32%	College or university 35%	More than $50,000 64%	Radical left 13%
Female 37%	36 to 54 68%	Mostly white 15%	North or Midwest 32%	Medical or law 17%	Private, for-profit 17%	$35,000 to $50,000 18%	Liberal 38%
	55 or older 26%	Racially mixed 14%	South 38%	Master's 27%	Private, nonprofit 9%	$20,000 to $34,999 12%	Moderate 28%
			Northeast 12%	Bachelor's 13%	Government 22%	Less than $20,000 6%	Conservative 5%
			Other 12%	Less 11%	Self-employed 14%		Depends on issue 14%
					Retired 3%		Unknown 2%
100%	100%	100%	100%	100%	100%	100%	100%

Source: Adapted from Lois Benjamin, *The Black Elite: Facing the Color Line in the Twilight of the Twentieth Century* (Chicago: Nelson-Hall, 1991), p. 276.

might disrupt a setting, a sensitive participant observer often can gain important insight into people's behavior.

Illustration of Participant Observation:
Street Corner Society

Did you ever wonder what everyday life was like in an unfamiliar neighborhood? In the late 1930s, a young graduate student at Harvard University named William Foote Whyte (1914–2000) set out to study social life in a rather rundown section of Boston. His curiosity led him to carry out four years of participant observation in this neighborhood, which he called "Cornerville."

At the time, Cornerville was home to first- and second-generation Italian immigrants. Most were poor, and many Bostonians considered Cornerville a place to avoid, a slum inhabited by criminals. Wanting to learn the truth, Whyte set out to discover for himself exactly what life was like inside this community. His celebrated book, *Street Corner Society* (1981, orig. 1943), describes Cornerville as a community with its own code of values, complex social patterns, and particular social conflicts.

To start, Whyte considered a range of research methods. He could have taken questionnaires to one of Cornerville's community centers and asked local people to fill them out. Or he could have invited members of the community to come to his Harvard office for interviews. But it is easy to see that such formal strategies would have gained little cooperation from the local people and produced few insights. Whyte decided, therefore, to ease into Cornerville life and slowly build a personal understanding of this rather mysterious place.

Soon enough, Whyte discovered the challenges of even getting started in field research. As an upper-middle-class WASP graduate student from Harvard, he stood out on the streets of Cornerville. Even a friendly overture from such an outsider could seem pushy and rude. Early on, Whyte dropped in at a local bar, hoping to buy a woman a drink and encourage her to talk about Cornerville. Looking around the room, he could find no woman alone. He thought he might have an opportunity when he saw a man sit down with two women. He walked over and asked, "Pardon me. Would you mind if I joined you?" Instantly, he realized his mistake:

> There was a moment of silence while the man stared at me. Then he offered to throw me down the stairs. I assured him that this would not be necessary, and demonstrated as much by walking right out of there without any assistance. (1981:289)

As the photo below suggests, conducting participant observation requires researchers to adapt to unfamiliar surroundings.

Read an account of participant observation research, "Hanging Tongues: A Social Encounter with the Assembly Line" by William E. Thompson, on **mysoclab.com**

Participant observation is a method of sociological research that allows a researcher to investigate people as they go about their everyday lives in some "natural" setting. At its best, participant observation makes you a star in your own reality show, but living in what may be a strange setting far from home for months at a time is always challenging.

As this incident suggests, gaining entry to a community is the vital—and sometimes hazardous—first step in field research. "Breaking in" requires patience, ingenuity, and a little luck. Whyte's big break came in the form of a young man named "Doc," whom he met in a local social service agency. Whyte complained to Doc about how hard it was to make friends in Cornerville. Doc responded by taking Whyte under his wing and introducing him to others in the community. With Doc's help, Whyte soon became a neighborhood regular.

Whyte's friendship with Doc illustrates the importance of a *key informant* in field research. Such people not only introduce a researcher to a community but often remain a source of information and help. But using a key informant also has its risks. Because any person has a particular circle of friends, a key informant's guidance is certain to "spin" the study in one way or another. Moreover, in the eyes of others, the reputation of the key informant, for better or worse, usually rubs off on the investigator. So although a key informant is helpful early on, a participant observer must seek a broader range of contacts.

Having entered the Cornerville world, Whyte quickly learned another lesson: A field researcher needs to know when to speak and when to shut up. One evening, he joined a group discussing neighborhood gambling. Wanting to get the facts straight, Whyte asked innocently, "I suppose the cops were all paid off?"

> The gambler's jaw dropped. He glared at me. Then he denied vehemently that any policeman had been paid off and immediately switched the conversation to another subject. For the rest of that evening I felt very uncomfortable.

The next day, Doc offered some sound advice:

> "Go easy on that 'who,' 'what,' 'why,' 'when,' 'where' stuff, Bill. You ask those questions and people will clam up on you. If people accept you, you can just hang around, and you'll learn the answers in the long run without even having to ask the questions." (1981:303)

In the months and years that followed, Whyte became familiar with everyday life in Cornerville and even married a local woman with whom he would spend the rest of his life. In the process, he learned that the common stereotypes were wrong. In Cornerville, most people worked hard, many were quite successful, and some even boasted of sending children to college. Even today, Whyte's book makes for fascinating reading about the deeds, dreams, and disappointments of immigrants and their children living in one ethnic community, and it contains the rich detail that can only come from years of participant observation.

CRITICAL REVIEW To study the community he called Cornerville, Professor Whyte chose participant observation—a good choice because he did not have a specific hypothesis to test, nor did he know at the outset exactly what the questions were. By moving into this community for several years, Whyte was able to come to know the place and to paint a complex picture of social life there. Read on **mysoclab.com**

CHECK YOUR LEARNING Give an example of a topic for sociological research that would be best studied using (1) an experiment, (2) a survey, and (3) participant observation.

Using Available Data: Existing Sources

Not all research requires that investigators collect new data. Sometimes sociologists make use of existing sources, data collected by others.

The data most widely used by researchers are gathered by government agencies such as the U.S. Census Bureau. Data about other nations in the world are found in various publications of the United Nations and the World Bank.

Using available information saves time and money. This method has special appeal to sociologists with low budgets. And in fact, government data are usually more extensive and more accurate than what researchers could obtain on their own.

But using available data has problems of its own. Data may not be available in the exact form that is needed. For example, you may be able to find the average salaries paid to professors at your school but not separate figures for the amounts paid to women and men. Further, there are always questions about how accurate the existing data are. In his nineteenth-century study of suicide, described earlier, Emile Durkheim used official records. But Durkheim had no way to know if a death classified as a suicide was really an accident or vice versa.

⊸◯ Making the Grade

Using existing sources—especially in clever and creative ways, as Baltzell did—is the key to conducting historical research in sociology.

⊸◯ Making the Grade

Can you describe a research project that might be carried out on your campus using existing sources? Explain your research question and what documents you would use.

Illustration of the Use of Existing Sources: A Tale of Two Cities

Why might one city have been home to many famous people and another have produced hardly any famous people at all? To those of us living in the present, historical data offer a key to unlocking secrets of the past. The award-winning study *Puritan Boston and Quaker Philadelphia*, by E. Digby Baltzell (1979), shows how a researcher can use available data to do historical research.

The story begins with Baltzell making a chance visit to Bowdoin College in Maine. As he walked into the college library, he saw on the wall three portraits—of the celebrated author Nathaniel Hawthorne, the famous poet Henry Wadsworth Longfellow, and Franklin Pierce, the fourteenth president of the United States. He soon learned that all three men were members of the same class at Bowdoin, graduating in 1825. How could it be, Baltzell wondered, that this small college had graduated more famous people in a single year than his own, much bigger University of Pennsylvania had graduated in its entire history? To answer this question, Baltzell was soon paging through historical documents to see whether the New England states had indeed produced more famous people than his native Pennsylvania.

What were Baltzell's data? He turned to the *Dictionary of American Biography*, twenty volumes profiling more than 13,000 outstanding men and women in fields such as politics, law, and the arts. The dictionary told Baltzell who was great, and he realized that the longer the biography, the more important the person is thought to be.

By the time Baltzell had identified the seventy-five individuals with the longest biographies, he saw a striking pattern. Massachusetts had the most by far, with twenty-one of the seventy-five top achievers. The New England states, combined, claimed thirty-one entries. By contrast, Pennsylvania could boast of only two, and all the states in the Middle Atlantic region had just twelve. Looking more closely, Baltzell discovered that most of New England's great achievers had grown up in and around the city of Boston. Again, in stark contrast, almost no one of comparable standing came from his own Philadelphia, a city with many more people than Boston.

What could explain this remarkable pattern? Baltzell drew inspiration from the German sociologist Max Weber (1958, orig. 1904–05), who argued that a region's record of achievement was influenced by its major religious beliefs (see Chapter 13, "Family and Religion"). In the religious differences between Boston and Philadelphia, Baltzell found the answer to his puzzle. Boston was a Puritan settlement, founded by people who highly valued the pursuit of excellence and public achievement. Philadelphia, by contrast, was settled by Quakers, who believed in equality and avoided public notice.

Both the Puritans and the Quakers had fled religious persecution in England, but once people settled in the new land, the two religious traditions produced quite different cultural patterns. Convinced of humanity's innate sinfulness, Boston Puritans built a rigid society in which family, church, and school regulated people's behavior. They celebrated hard work as a means of glorifying God and viewed public success as a reassuring sign of God's blessing. In short, Puritanism fostered a disciplined and ambitious life in which people both sought and respected achievement.

Philadelphia's Quakers, by contrast, built their way of life on the belief that all human beings are basically good. They saw little need for strong social institutions to "save" people from sinfulness. They believed in equality, so even those who became rich considered themselves no better than anyone else. Thus rich and poor alike lived modestly and discouraged one another from standing out by seeking fame or running for public office.

In Baltzell's sociological imagination, Boston and Philadelphia took the form of two social "test tubes": Puritanism was poured into one, Quakerism into the other. Centuries later, we can see that different "chemical reactions" occurred in each case. The two belief systems apparently led to different attitudes toward personal achievement, which in turn shaped the history of each region. Today, we can see that Boston's Kennedys (despite being Catholic) are only one of that city's many families that exemplify the Puritan pursuit of recognition and leadership. By contrast, there has never been even one family with such stature in the entire history of Philadelphia.

Baltzell's study uses scientific logic, but it also illustrates the interpretive approach by showing how people make sense of their world. His research reminds us that sociological investigation often involves mixing research orientations to fit a particular problem. The Summing Up table on page 30 provides a quick review of the four major methods of sociological investigation.

⊸◯ **CRITICAL REVIEW** The main reason Professor Baltzell chose to use existing sources is that this is a good way to learn about history. The *Dictionary of American Biography* offers a great deal of information about people who lived long ago and obviously are not available for an interview. At the same time, existing sources were not created with the purpose of answering a modern-day sociologist's questions. For this reason, using such documents requires a critical eye and a good deal of creative thinking.

⊸◯ **CHECK YOUR LEARNING** What other questions about life in the past might you wish to answer using existing sources?

Putting It All Together: Ten Steps in Sociological Research

The following ten questions will guide you through a research project in sociology:

1. **What is your topic?** Being curious and using the sociological perspective can generate ideas for social research at any time

○— Making the Grade

The ten steps listed below are a summary of what is needed to conduct good sociological research.

○— Making the Grade

Study the Summing Up table below to be sure that you understand the four major research methods.

SUMMING UP

Four Research Methods

	Experiment	Survey	Participant Observation	Existing Sources
Application	For explanatory research that specifies relationships between variables Generates quantitative data	For gathering information about issues that cannot be directly observed, such as attitudes and values Useful for descriptive and explanatory research Generates quantitative or qualitative data	For exploratory and descriptive study of people in a "natural" setting Generates qualitative data	For exploratory, descriptive, or explanatory research whenever suitable data are available
Advantages	Provides the greatest opportunity to specify cause-and-effect relationships Replication of research is relatively easy	Sampling, using questionnaires, allows surveys of large populations Interviews provide in-depth responses	Allows study of "natural" behavior Usually inexpensive	Saves time and expense of data collection Makes historical research possible
Limitations	Laboratory settings have an artificial quality Unless the research environment is carefully controlled, results may be biased	Questionnaires must be carefully prepared and may yield a low return rate Interviews are expensive and time-consuming	Time-consuming Replication of research is difficult Researcher must balance roles of participant and observer	Researcher has no control over possible biases in data Data may only partially fit current research needs

and in any place. Pick a topic you find interesting and that you think is important to study.

2. **What have others already learned?** You are probably not the first person with an interest in some issue. Visit the library and search the Internet to see what theories and methods other researchers have applied to your topic. In reviewing the existing research, note problems that have come up to avoid repeating past mistakes.

3. **What, exactly, are your questions?** Are you seeking to explore an unfamiliar setting? To describe some category of people? To investigate cause and effect between variables? Clearly state the goals of your research, and operationalize all variables.

4. **What will you need to carry out research?** How much time and money are available to you? What special equipment or skills does the research require? Can you do all the work yourself?

5. **Are there ethical concerns?** Might the research harm anyone? How can you minimize the chances for injury? Will you promise your subjects anonymity? If so, how will you ensure that anonymity will be maintained?

6. **What method will you use?** Consider all major research strategies and combinations of methods. The most suitable method will depend on the kinds of questions you are asking and the resources available to you.

7. **How will you record the data?** The research method you use guides your data collection. Be sure to record information accurately and in a way that will make sense to you later on (it may be months before you write up the results of your work). Watch out for any personal bias that may creep into your work.

8. **What do the data tell you?** Determine what the data say about your initial questions. If your study involves a specific hypothesis, you should be able to confirm, reject, or modify it on the basis of your findings. Keep in mind that there will be several ways to interpret your results, depending on the theoretical approach you apply, and you should consider them all.

9. **What are your conclusions?** Prepare a final report explaining what you have learned. Also, evaluate your own work. What problems arose during the research process? What questions were left unanswered?

stereotype a simplified description applied to every person in some category

CONTROVERSY & DEBATE

Is Sociology Nothing More Than Stereotypes?

JENA: (*raising her eyes from her notebook*) Today, in sociology class, we talked about stereotypes.

MARCIA: (*trying to focus on her science lab*) OK, here's one: Roommates don't like to be disturbed when they're studying.

JENA: Seriously, my studious friend, we all have stereotypes, even professors.

MARCIA: (*becoming faintly interested*) Like what?

JENA: Professor Chandler said today in class that Protestants are most likely to kill themselves. And later Yannina—this girl from, I think, Ecuador—said something like "You Americans are rich, but you don't take marriage seriously, and you love to divorce!"

MARCIA: My brother said to me last week that "everybody knows you have to be black to play professional basketball." Now there's a stereotype!

College students, like everyone else, are quick to make generalizations about people. As this chapter explains, sociologists, too, love to generalize by looking for social patterns in everyday life. However, beginning students of sociology may wonder if sociological generalizations aren't really the same thing as stereotypes. For example, are the statements reported by Jena and Marcia true generalizations or false stereotypes?

A **stereotype** is *a simplified description applied to every person in some category*. Each of the statements the students made is a stereotype that is false, for three reasons. First, rather than describing averages, each statement describes every person in some category in exactly the same way; second, even though many stereotypes often contain an element of truth, each of these three statements leaves out relevant

facts and distorts reality; and third, each statement is motivated by bias, spoken more as a put-down than as a fair-minded observation.

Good sociology makes generalizations, but they must meet three conditions. First, sociologists do not carelessly apply any generalization to everyone in a category. Second, sociologists make sure that a generalization squares with all available facts. And third, sociologists make generalizations fair-mindedly, in the interest of getting at the truth.

Jena recalled her professor saying that the suicide rate among Protestants is higher than the rate among Catholics or Jews. However, the statement "Protestants are most likely to kill themselves" is not a fair generalization because most Protestants take no such action. It would be just as wrong to jump to the conclusion that a particular friend, because he is a Protestant, is about to end his own life. (Imagine refusing to lend money to a roommate, who happens to be

A sociology classroom is a good place to get at the truth behind common stereotypes.

a Baptist, explaining, "Well, given your risk of suicide, I might never get paid back!")

Second, sociologists shape their generalizations to available facts. A more factual version of the statement Yannina made is that by world standards, the U.S. population has a very high standard of living, that almost everyone in our society does marry at some point with every intention of staying married, and that even though our divorce rate is among the world's highest, few people take pleasure in divorcing.

Third, sociologists try to be fair-minded and want to get at the truth. The statements made by Marcia's brother about African Americans and basketball is a stereotype and therefore not good sociology for two reasons. First, it is simply not true, and second, it seems motivated by racial bias rather than truth-seeking.

The bottom line, then, is that good sociological generalizations are *not* the same as stereotyping. But a college sociology course is an excellent setting for getting at the truths behind common stereotypes. The classroom encourages discussion and offers the factual information you need to decide whether a particular statement is a valid sociological generalization or a harmful or unfair stereotype.

WHAT DO YOU THINK?

1. Can you think of a common stereotype of sociologists? What is it? After reading this box, do you still think it is valid?

2. Do you think taking a sociology course can help correct people's stereotypes? Why or why not?

3. Can you think of a stereotype of your own that might be challenged by sociological analysis?

---

10. **How can you share what you have learned?** Consider making a presentation to a class or maybe even to a meeting of professional sociologists. The important point is to share what you have learned with others and to let them respond to your work.

The Controversy & Debate box discusses the use of the sociological perspective and reviews many of the ideas presented in this chapter. This box will help you apply what you have learned to the important question of how the generalizations made by sociologists differ from the common stereotypes we hear every day.

Seeing Sociology in Everyday Life

"Why do couples marry?"

We asked this question at the beginning of this chapter. The commonsense answer is that people marry because they are in love. But as this chapter has explained, society guides our everyday lives, affecting what we do, think, and feel. Look at the three photographs, each showing a couple who, we can assume, is "in love." In each case, can you provide some of the rest of the story? By looking at the categories that the people involved represent, explain how society is at work in bringing the two people together.

> **HINT**   Society is at work on many levels. Consider (1) rules about same-sex and other-sex marriage, (2) laws defining the number of people who may marry, (3) the importance of race and ethnicity, (4) the importance of social class, (5) the importance of age, and (6) the importance of social exchange (what each partner offers the other). All societies enforce various rules that state who should or should not marry whom.

Jada Pinkett met Will Smith in 1995 when she auditioned for a part on his hit show, *The Fresh Prince of Bel Air*. Two years later, they married. What social patterns do you see?

In 1997, during the fourth season of her hit TV show, *Ellen*, Ellen DeGeneres "came out" as a lesbian, which put her on the cover of *Time* magazine. Since then, she has been an activist on behalf of gay and lesbian issues. Following California's brief legalization of same-sex marriage in 2008, she married her longtime girlfriend, Australian actress Portia de Rossi.

In 2000, at the age of fifty-six, Michael Douglas ended a twenty-three-year marriage in order to marry actress Catherine Zeta-Jones, who was then thirty-one. How likely is it that a fifty-six-year-old woman would marry a thirty-one-year-old man?

Applying SOCIOLOGY in Everyday Life

1. Analyze the marriages of your parents, other family members, and friends in terms of class, race, age, and other factors. What evidence can you find that society guides the feeling we call "love"?

2. Figure 13–2 on page 380 shows the U.S. divorce rate over the past century. Using the sociological perspective, and with an eye to the timeline inside the back cover of this book, try to identify societal factors that caused the divorce rate to rise or fall.

3. Explore your local area, and draw a sociological map of the community. Include the types of buildings (for example, "big, single-family homes," "rundown business district," "new office buildings," "student apartments") found in various places, and guess at the categories of people who live or work there. What patterns do you see?

Making the Grade

👁️⊙–Watch on mysoclab.com

What Is the Sociological Perspective?

The **SOCIOLOGICAL PERSPECTIVE** reveals the power of society to shape individual lives.
- C. Wright Mills called this point of view the "sociological imagination," which transforms personal troubles into public issues.
- Being an outsider or experiencing social crisis can encourage the sociological perspective.

pp. 2–5

APPLYING THE SOCIOLOGICAL PERSPECTIVE has many benefits:
- helping us understand the barriers and opportunities in our lives
- giving us an advantage in our careers
- guiding public policy

pp. 7–9

✓ Global awareness is an important part of the sociological perspective because our society's place in the world affects us all (pp. 5–7).

sociology (p. 2) the systematic study of human society

sociological perspective (p. 2) the special point of view of sociology that sees general patterns of society in the lives of particular people

global perspective (p. 5) the study of the larger world and our society's place in it

high-income countries (p. 5) the nations with the highest overall standards of living

middle-income countries (p. 5) nations with a standard of living about average for the world as a whole

low-income countries (p. 5) nations with a low standard of living in which most people are poor

Origins of Sociology

RAPID SOCIAL CHANGE helped trigger the development of sociology:
- rise of an industrial economy
- explosive growth of cities
- new political ideas

p. 9

AUGUSTE COMTE named sociology in 1838.
- Early philosophers tried to describe the ideal society, but Comte wanted to understand society as it really is.
- Karl Marx and many later sociologists used sociology to try to make society better.

pp. 10–11

✓ The countries that experienced the most rapid social change were those in which sociology developed first (p. 9).

positivism (p. 10) a scientific approach to knowledge based on "positive" facts as opposed to mere speculation

theory (p. 11) a statement of how and why specific facts are related

theoretical approach (p. 11) a basic image of society that guides thinking and research

structural-functional approach (p. 11) a framework for building theory that sees society as a complex system whose parts work together to promote solidarity and stability

social structure (p. 11) any relatively stable pattern of social behavior

social functions (p. 11) the consequences of a social pattern for the operation of society as a whole

manifest functions (p. 12) the recognized and intended consequences of any social pattern

latent functions (p. 12) the unrecognized and unintended consequences of any social pattern

social dysfunction (p. 12) any social pattern that may disrupt the operation of society

social-conflict approach (p. 12) a framework for building theory that sees society as an arena of inequality that generates conflict and change

gender-conflict approach (p. 12) a point of view that focuses on inequality and conflict between women and men

feminism (p. 12) support of social equality for women and men

race-conflict approach (p. 13) a point of view that focuses on inequality and conflict between people of different racial and ethnic categories

macro-level orientation (p. 14) a broad focus on social structures that shape society as a whole

micro-level orientation (p. 14) a close-up focus on social interaction in specific situations

symbolic-interaction approach (p. 14) a framework for building theory that sees society as the product of the everyday interactions of individuals

Theory: Linking Facts to Create Meaning

 macro-level

The **STRUCTURAL-FUNCTIONAL APPROACH** explores how social structures work together to help society operate.
- Auguste Comte, Emile Durkheim, and Herbert Spencer helped develop the structural-functional approach.

pp. 11–12

The **SOCIAL-CONFLICT APPROACH** shows how inequality creates conflict and causes change.
- Two important types of conflict analysis are the **gender-conflict approach**, linked to **feminism**, and the **race-conflict approach**.
- Karl Marx helped develop the social-conflict approach.

pp. 12–14

✦–Explore on mysoclab.com

 micro-level

The **SYMBOLIC-INTERACTION APPROACH** studies how people, in everyday interaction, construct reality.
- Max Weber and George Herbert Mead helped develop the symbolic-interaction approach.

pp. 14–15

▭ See the Applying Theory table on page 15.

✓ To get the full benefit of the sociological perspective, apply all three approaches.

Research: Doing Sociology

POSITIVIST SOCIOLOGY uses the logic of science to understand how variables are related.

- tries to establish cause and effect
- demands that researchers try to be objective

`pp. 16–20`

INTERPRETIVE SOCIOLOGY focuses on the meanings that people attach to behavior.

- People construct reality in their everyday lives.
- Weber's *Verstehen* is learning how people understand their world.

`p. 20`

CRITICAL SOCIOLOGY uses research to bring about social change.

- focuses on inequality
- rejects the principle of objectivity, claiming that all research is political

`p. 20`

positivist sociology (p. 16) the study of society based on systematic observation of social behavior

science (p. 16) a logical system that develops knowledge from direct, systematic observation

empirical evidence (p. 16) information we can verify with our senses

concept (p. 18) a mental construct that represents some aspect of the world in a simplified form

variable (p. 18) a concept whose value changes from case to case

measurement (p. 18) a procedure for determining the value of a variable in a specific case

reliability (p. 18) consistency in measurement

validity (p. 18) actually measuring exactly what you intend to measure

correlation (p. 18) a relationship in which two (or more) variables change together

cause and effect (p. 18) a relationship in which change in one variable (the independent variable) causes change in another (the dependent variable)

interpretive sociology (p. 20) the study of society that focuses on discovering the meanings people attach to their social world

critical sociology (p. 20) the study of society that focuses on the need for social change

gender (p. 21) the personal traits and social positions that members of a society attach to being female or male

See the Summing Up table on page 21.

✓ Gender, involving both researcher and subjects, can affect all research (pp. 21–22).

✓ All researchers must follow professional ethical guidelines for conducting research (p. 22).

Methods: Strategies for Doing Research

The **EXPERIMENT** allows researchers to study cause and effect between two or more variables in a controlled setting.

- example of an experiment: Zimbardo's "Stanford County Prison"

`pp. 22–24`

SURVEY research uses questionnaires or interviews to gather subjects' responses to a series of questions.

- example of a survey: Benjamin's "Talented 100"

`pp. 24–26`

Through **PARTICIPANT OBSERVATION**, researchers join with people in a social setting for an extended period of time.

- example of participant observation: Whyte's *Street Corner Society*

`pp. 26–28`

Researchers use data collected by others from **EXISTING SOURCES** to save time and money.

- example of using existing sources: Baltzell's *Puritan Boston and Quaker Philadelphia*

`pp. 28–29`

research method (p. 22) a systematic plan for doing research

experiment (p. 22) a research method for investigating cause and effect under highly controlled conditions

survey (p. 24) a research method in which subjects respond to a series of statements or questions on a questionnaire or in an interview

participant observation (p. 26) a research method in which investigators systematically observe people while joining them in their routine activities

stereotype (p. 31) a simplified description applied to every person in some category

See the Summing Up table on page 30.

Read on mysoclab.com

✓ Which method the researcher uses depends on the question being asked.

✓ Researchers combine these methods, depending on the specific goals of their study.

2 Culture

- What is culture?

- Why is it so important to understand people's cultural differences?

- How does culture support social inequality?

Chapter Overview

This chapter focuses on the concept of "culture," which refers to a society's entire way of life. Notice that the root of the word "culture" is the same as that of the word "cultivate," suggesting that people living together actually "grow" their way of life over time.

It's late on a Tuesday night, but Fang Lin gazes intently at her computer screen. Dong Wang, who is married to Fang, walks up behind her chair.

"I'm trying to finish organizing our investments," Fang explains, speaking in Chinese.

"I didn't realize that we could do all this online in our own language," Dong says, reading the screen. "That's great. I like that a lot."

Fang and Dong are not alone in feeling this way. Back in 1990, executives of Charles Schwab & Co., a large investment brokerage corporation, gathered in a conference room at the company's headquarters in San Francisco to discuss ways to expand their business. They came up with the idea that the company would profit by giving greater attention to the increasing cultural diversity of the United States. Why? Pointing to data collected by researchers at the U.S. Census Bureau, they saw that the number of Asian Americans was rising rapidly, not just in San Francisco but all over the country. The data also showed company officials that Asian Americans, on average, are doing pretty well, with half of families earning more than $65,000 a year (in today's dollars).

Based on such data, Schwab launched a diversity initiative, assigning executives to work just on building awareness of the company among Asian Americans. Since then, the scope of the program has grown so that Schwab now employs more than 300 people who speak Chinese, Japanese, Korean, Vietnamese, or some other Asian language. Having account executives who speak languages other than English is important because research shows that most immigrants who come to the United States prefer to communicate in their first language, especially when dealing with important matters like investing their money. In addition, the company has launched Web sites using Korean, Chinese, and other Asian languages. Fang Lin and Dong Wang are just two of the millions of people who have opened accounts with companies that reach out to them in a familiar language other than English.

This initiative has been extremely successful for Schwab, which now manages a much larger share of investments made by Asian Americans. Asian Americans spent $250 billion in 2008, so any company would be smart to follow the lead Schwab has taken. Other racial and ethnic categories that represent even larger markets in the United States are Hispanic Americans and African Americans (each spending more than $500 billion in 2008) (Fattah, 2002; Karrfalt, 2003; U.S. Census Bureau, 2009; U.S. Bureau of Labor Statistics, 2009).

Businesses like Schwab have learned that the United States is the most *multicultural* of all the world's nations. This cultural diversity reflects our long history of receiving immigrants from all over the world. The ways of life found around the world differ not only in terms of languages and forms of dress but also in preferred foods, musical tastes, family patterns, and beliefs about right and wrong. Some of the world's people have many children, while others have few; some honor the elderly, while others seem to glorify youth. Some societies are peaceful and others warlike, and they embrace thousands of different religious beliefs and ideas about what is polite and rude, beautiful and ugly, pleasant and repulsive. This amazing human capacity for so many different ways of life is a matter of human culture. ● Go to **mysoclab.com**

What Is Culture?

Culture is *the ways of thinking, ways of acting, and material objects that together form a people's way of life.* When studying culture, sociologists consider both thoughts and things. *Nonmaterial culture* consists of the ideas created by members of a society, ranging from art

culture the ways of thinking, the ways of acting, and the material objects that together form a people's way of life

society (p. 40) people who interact in a defined territory and share a culture

culture shock (p. 40) personal disorientation when experiencing an unfamiliar way of life

 Go to the Multimedia Library at **mysoclab.com** to view the video "Sociologists and Culture"

Human beings around the globe create diverse ways of life. Such differences begin with outward appearance: Contrast the women shown here from Ethiopia, India, Kenya, Thailand, South Yemen, and the United States and the men from Taiwan (Republic of China), Ecuador, and Papua New Guinea. Less obvious but of even greater importance are internal differences, since culture also shapes our goals in life, our sense of justice, and even our innermost personal feelings.

● Go to the Multimedia Library at **mysoclab.com**
to explore the strange rituals of the Nacirema

● Seeing Sociology
in Everyday Life

Can you describe specific practices or patterns familiar to us in the
United States that would shock people living in some other part of
the world? Explain your response.

All societies contain cultural differences that can provoke a mild case of culture shock. This woman traveling on a British subway is not sure what to make of the woman sitting next to her, who is wearing the Muslim full-face veil known as the *niqab*.

to Zen; *material culture* refers to physical things, everything from armchairs to zippers.

The terms "culture" and "society" obviously go hand in hand, but their precise meanings differ. Culture is a shared way of life or social heritage; **society** refers to *people who interact in a defined territory and share a culture.* Neither society nor culture could exist without the other.

Culture shapes not only what we do but also what we think and how we feel—elements of what we commonly but wrongly describe as "human nature." The warlike Yanomamö of the Brazilian rain forest think aggression is natural, but halfway around the world, the Semai of Malaysia live quite peacefully. The cultures of the United States and Japan both stress achievement and hard work, but members of our society value individualism more than the Japanese, who value collective harmony. ● Go to **mysoclab.com**

Given the extent of cultural differences in the world and people's tendency to view their own way of life as "natural," it is no wonder that we often feel **culture shock,** *personal disorientation when experiencing an unfamiliar way of life.* People can experience culture shock right here in the United States when, say, African Americans shop in an Iranian neighborhood in Los Angeles, college students visit the Amish countryside in Ohio, or New Yorkers travel through small towns in the Deep South. But culture shock can be intense when we travel abroad. The Thinking Globally box tells the story of a U.S.

researcher making his first visit to the home of the Yanomamö people living in the Amazon region of South America.

> **January 2, high in the Andes Mountains of Peru.** In the rural highlands, people are poor and depend on one another. The culture is built on cooperation among families and neighbors who have lived nearby for many generations. Today, we spend an hour watching a new house being built. A young couple invited their families and friends, who arrived about 6:30 in the morning, and right away everyone began building. By midafternoon, most of the work had been done, and the couple then provided a large meal, drinks, and music that continued for the rest of the day.

No particular way of life is "natural" to humans, even though most people around the world view their own behavior that way. The cooperation that comes naturally in small communities high in the Andes Mountains of Peru is very different from the competitive lifestyle that is natural to so many people living in, say, Chicago or New York. Such variations come from the fact that we are creatures of culture who join together to create our own way of life. Every other animal, from ants to zebras, behaves very much the same all around the world because their behavior is determined by instincts, biological programming over which the species has no control. A few animals—notably chimpanzees and related primates—have some capacity for culture, as researchers have learned by observing them using tools and teaching simple skills to their offspring. But the creative power of humans is far greater than that of any other form of life. In short, *only humans rely on culture rather than instinct to ensure their survival* (Harris, 1987; Morell, 2008). To understand how human culture came to be, we need to look back at the history of our species.

Culture and Human Intelligence

Scientists tell us that our planet is 4.5 billion years old (see the timeline inside the back cover of this text). Life appeared about 1 billion years later. Fast-forward another 2 to 3 billion years, and we find dinosaurs ruling Earth. It was only after these giant creatures disappeared—some 65 million years ago—that our history took a crucial turn with the appearance of the animals we call primates.

The importance of primates is that they have the largest brains relative to body size of all living creatures. About 12 million years ago, primates began to evolve along two different lines, leading humans away from the great apes, our closest relatives. Some 3 million years ago, our distant human ancestors climbed down from the trees of Central Africa to move around in the tall grasses. There, walking upright, they learned the advantages of hunting in groups and made use of fire, tools, and weapons; built simple shelters; and fashioned basic clothing. These Stone Age achievements mark the

┌─● Making the Grade

Humans are not the only creatures who have culture, but we are the only creatures who *depend on* culture to survive.

┌─● Making the Grade

The United States is culturally diverse, reflecting our historically high level of immigration.

THINKING GLOBALLY

Confronting the Yąnomamö: The Experience of Culture Shock

A small aluminum motorboat chugged steadily along the muddy Orinoco River, deep within South America's vast tropical rain forest. The anthropologist Napoleon Chagnon was nearing the end of a three-day journey to the home territory of the Yąnomamö, one of the most technologically simple societies on Earth.

Some 12,000 Yąnomamö live in villages scattered along the border of Venezuela and Brazil. Their way of life could hardly be more different from our own. The Yąnomamö wear little clothing and live without electricity, cars, or other conveniences most people in the United States take for granted. They use bows and arrows for hunting and warfare, as they have for centuries. Many of the Yąnomamö have had little contact with the outside world, so Chagnon would be as strange to them as they would be to him.

By 2:00 in the afternoon, Chagnon had almost reached his destination. The hot sun and humid air were becoming unbearable. Chagnon's clothes were soaked with sweat, and his face and hands were swollen from the bites of gnats swarming around him. But he scarcely noticed, so focused was he on the fact that in just a few moments, he would be face to face with people unlike any he had ever known.

Chagnon's heart pounded as the boat slid onto the riverbank. He and his guide climbed from the boat and walked toward the Yąnomamö village, stooping as they pushed their way through the dense undergrowth. Chagnon describes what happened next:

> I looked up and gasped when I saw a dozen burly, naked, sweaty, hideous men staring at us down the shafts of their drawn arrows! Immense wads of green tobacco were stuck between their lower teeth and lips, making them look even more hideous, and strands of dark green slime dripped or hung from their nostrils—strands so long that they clung to their [chests] or drizzled down their chins.

My next discovery was that there were a dozen or so vicious, underfed dogs snapping at my legs, circling me as if I were to be their next meal. I just stood there holding my notebook, helpless and pathetic. Then the stench of the decaying vegetation and filth hit me and I almost got sick. I was horrified. What kind of welcome was this for the person who came here to live with you and learn your way of life, to become friends with you? (1992:11–12)

Fortunately for Chagnon, the Yąnomamö villagers recognized his guide and lowered their weapons. Reassured that he would survive the afternoon, Chagnon still was shaken by his inability to make any sense of these people. And this was to be his home for a year and a half! He wondered why he had given up physics to study human culture in the first place.

WHAT DO YOU THINK?

1. As they came to know Chagnon, might the Yąnomamö, too, have experienced culture shock? Why?

2. Can you think of an experience you had that is similar to the one described here?

3. How can studying sociology help reduce the experience of culture shock?

---

point at which our ancestors embarked on a distinct evolutionary course, making culture their primary strategy for survival. By about 250,000 years ago, our species, *Homo sapiens*—Latin for "intelligent person"—had emerged. Humans continued to evolve so that by about 40,000 years ago, people who looked more or less like us roamed the planet. With larger brains, these "modern" *Homo sapiens* developed culture rapidly, as the wide range of tools and cave art that have survived from this period suggests.

By 12,000 years ago, the founding of permanent settlements and the creation of specialized occupations in the Middle East (in portions of modern-day Iraq and Egypt) marked a turning point. About this time, the biological forces we call instincts had almost disappeared, replaced by a more efficient survival scheme: *fashioning the natural environment to our purposes.* Ever since, humans have made and remade their world in countless ways, resulting in today's fascinating cultural diversity.

How Many Cultures?

How many cultures are there in the United States? One indicator of culture is language; the Census Bureau lists more than 300 languages spoken in this country, most of which were brought by immigrants from nations around the world (U.S. Census Bureau, 2007).

symbol anything that carries a particular meaning recognized by people who share a culture

People throughout the world communicate not just with spoken words but also with bodily gestures. Because gestures vary from culture to culture, they can occasionally be the cause of misunderstandings. For instance, the commonplace "thumbs up" gesture we use to express "Good job!" can get a person from the United States into trouble in Greece, Iran, and a number of other countries, where people take it to mean "Up yours!"

Globally, experts document almost 7,000 languages, suggesting the existence of as many distinct cultures. Yet the number of languages spoken around the world is declining, and more than half are now spoken by fewer than 10,000 people (Lewis, 2009). Experts expect that the coming decades may see the disappearance of hundreds of these languages, including Gullah, Pennsylvania German, and Pawnee (all spoken in the United States), Han (northwestern Canada), Oro in the Amazon region (Brazil), Sardinian (Sardinia, Italy), Aramaic (the language of Jesus of Nazareth in the Middle East), Nu Shu (a language of southern China that is the only one known to be spoken exclusively by women), and Wakka Wakka and several other Aboriginal tongues spoken in Australia. What accounts for the decline? Likely reasons include high-technology communication, increasing international migration, and an expanding global economy, all of which are reducing global cultural diversity (UNESCO, 2001; Barovick, 2002; Hayden, 2003).

The Elements of Culture

Although cultures vary greatly, they all have common elements, including symbols, language, values, and norms. We begin our discussion with the one that is the basis for all the others: symbols.

Symbols

Like all creatures, human beings sense the surrounding world, but unlike others, we also give the world *meaning*. Humans transform the elements of the world into *symbols*. A **symbol** is *anything that carries a particular meaning recognized by people who share a culture*. A word, a whistle, a wall of graffiti, a flashing red light, a raised fist—all serve as symbols. The human capacity to create and manipulate symbols is almost limitless—think of the variety of meanings associated with the simple act of winking an eye, which can convey such messages as interest, understanding, or insult.

Societies create new symbols all the time. The Seeing Sociology in Everyday Life box describes some of the "cyber-symbols" that have developed along with our increasing use of computers for communication.

We are so dependent on our culture's symbols that we often take them for granted. We become keenly aware of the importance of a symbol, however, when it is used in an unconventional way, as when someone burns a U.S. flag during a political demonstration. Entering an unfamiliar culture also reminds us of the power of symbols; culture shock is really the inability to "read" meaning in unfamiliar surroundings. Not understanding the symbols of a culture leaves a person feeling lost and isolated, unsure of how to act, and sometimes frightened.

Culture shock is a two-way process. On one hand, the traveler *experiences* culture shock when meeting people whose way of life is dramatically different. For example, North Americans who consider dogs beloved household pets might be put off by the Masai of eastern Africa, who ignore dogs and never feed them. The same travelers might be horrified to find that in parts of Indonesia and in the northern regions of the People's Republic of China, people roast dogs for dinner.

On the other hand, a traveler can *inflict* culture shock on others by acting in ways that offend them. The North American who asks for a steak in an Indian restaurant is likely to offend Hindus working there because they consider cows sacred and never to be eaten. Global travel provides endless opportunities for misunderstanding.

Symbolic meanings also vary within a single society. In the debate about flying the Confederate flag over the South Carolina state house a few years ago, some people saw the flag as a symbol of regional pride or family heritage, while others saw it as a symbol of racial oppression.

Language

The heart of a symbolic system is **language,** *a system of symbols that allows people to communicate with one another*. Humans have created many alphabets to express the hundreds of languages we speak; several examples are shown in Figure 2–1 on page 44. Even rules for writing differ: Most people in Western societies write from left to right, people in northern Africa and western Asia write from right to left, and people in eastern Asia write from top to bottom. Global Map 2–1

Anything can serve as a symbol; what makes something a symbol is simply that humans attach meaning to it.

language a system of symbols that allows people to communicate with one another

cultural transmission the process by which one generation passes culture to the next

Sapir-Whorf thesis (p. 44) the idea that people see and understand the world through the cultural lens of language

---

SEEING SOCIOLOGY IN EVERYDAY LIFE

New Symbols in the World of Instant Messaging

MOLLY: gr8 2 c u!

GREG: u 2

MOLLY: jw about next time

GREG: idk, lotta work

MOLLY: no prb, xoxoxo

GREG: thanx, bcnu

The world of symbols changes all the time. One reason that people create new symbols is that we develop new ways to communicate. Today, more than 135 million people in the United States (most of them young and many of them students) use mobile text-messaging on a regular basis (Nielsen, 2008).

Here are some of the most common text-messaging symbols:

b   be
bc   because
b4   before
b4n   'bye for now
bbl   be back later
bcnu   be seeing you
brb   be right back
cu   see you
def   definitely
g2g   got to go
gal   get a life
gmta   great minds think alike
gr8   great
hagn   have a good night
h&k   hugs and kisses
idc   I don't care

idt   I don't think
idk   I don't know
imbl   it must be love
jk   just kidding
jw   just wondering
j4f   just for fun
kc   keep cool
l8r   later
lmao   laugh my ass off
ltnc   long time no see
myob   mind your own business
no prb   no problem
omg   oh my gosh
pcm   please call me
plz   please
prbly   probably

qpsa   *¿Que pasa?*
rt   right
thanx   thanks
u   you
ur   you are
w/   with
w/e   whatever
w/o   without
wan2   want to
wtf   what the freak
y   why
2l8   too late
?   question
2   to, too, two
4   for, four

WHAT DO YOU THINK?

1. What does the creation of symbols such as these suggest about culture?

2. Do you think that using such symbols is a good way to communicate? Does it lead to confusion or misunderstanding? Why or why not?

3. What other kinds of symbols can you think of that are new to your generation?

Sources: J. Rubin (2003), Berteau (2005), and Bacher (2009).

---

on page 45 shows where in the world we find the three most widely spoken languages, English, Chinese, and Spanish.

Language allows much more than communication; it is the key to **cultural transmission,** *the process by which one generation passes culture to the next.* Just as our bodies contain the genes of our ancestors, our cultural heritage contains countless symbols created by those who came before us. Language is the key that unlocks centuries of accumulated wisdom.

Language skills may link us to the past, but they also spark the human imagination to connect symbols in new ways, creating an almost limitless range of future possibilities. Language sets humans apart as the only creatures who are self-conscious, aware of our limitations and our ultimate mortality, yet are able to dream and hope for a future better than the present.

Does Language Shape Reality?

Does someone who speaks Cherokee, an American Indian language, experience the world differently from other North Americans who think in Spanish or English? Edward Sapir and Benjamin Whorf claimed that the answer is yes, because each language has its own

● Seeing Sociology
in Everyday Life

Think about the games you played when you were growing up, like Tag or Capture the Flag, or board games, like Monopoly or Chutes and Ladders. What cultural values do they teach? What about video games like Grand Theft Auto, God of War, or Rainbow Six Vegas?

FIGURE 2–1   Human Languages: A Variety of Symbols
Here the English word "read" is written in twelve of the hundreds of languages humans use to communicate with one another.

distinct symbols that serve as the building blocks of reality (Sapir, 1929, 1949; Whorf, 1956, orig. 1941). Further, they noted that each symbolic system has words or expressions not found in any other symbolic system. Finally, all languages connect symbols with distinctive emotions, so as multilingual people know, a single idea may "feel" different when it is expressed in Spanish rather than in English or Chinese.

Formally, the **Sapir-Whorf thesis** holds that *people see and understand the world through the cultural lens of language.* In the decades since Sapir and Whorf published their work, however, scholars have taken issue with this proposition. Current thinking is that although we do fashion reality out of our symbols, evidence does not support the notion that language *determines* reality in the way Sapir and Whorf claimed. For example, we know that children understand the idea of "family" long before they learn that word; similarly, adults can imagine new ideas or things before devising a name for them (Kay & Kempton, 1984; Pinker, 1994).

Values and Beliefs

What accounts for the popularity of movie characters such as James Bond, Neo, Erin Brockovich, Lara Croft, and Rocky Balboa? Each is ruggedly individualistic, going it alone and relying on personal skill and savvy to challenge "the system." In admiring such characters, we are supporting certain **values,** *culturally defined standards that people use to decide what is desirable, good, and beautiful and that serve as broad guidelines for social living.* Values are what people who share a culture use to make choices about how to live.

Values are broad principles that underlie **beliefs,** *specific ideas that people hold to be true.* In other words, values are abstract standards

of goodness, and beliefs are particular matters that people accept as true or false. For example, because most U.S. adults share the value of providing equal opportunity for all, they believe that a qualified woman could serve as president of the United States, as the 2008 presidential campaign of Hillary Rodham Clinton demonstrated (NORC, 2009:326).

Key Values of U.S. Culture

The sociologist Robin Williams Jr. (1970) identified ten values as central to our way of life:

1. **Equal opportunity.** People in the United States believe in not *equality of condition* but *equality of opportunity.* This means that society should provide everyone with the chance to get ahead according to individual talents and efforts.

2. **Individual achievement and personal success.** Our way of life encourages competition so that each person's rewards should reflect personal merit. A successful person is given the respect due a "winner."

3. **Material comfort.** Success in the United States generally means making money and enjoying what it will buy. Although people sometimes remark that "money won't buy happiness," most of us pursue wealth all the same.

4. **Activity and work.** Our heroes, from Olympic gold medalists to the winners of television's *American Idol,* are "doers" who get the job done. Our culture values action over reflection and taking control of events over passively accepting fate.

5. **Practicality and efficiency.** We value the practical over the theoretical, "doing" over "dreaming." "Major in something that will help you get a job!" parents tell their college-age children.

6. **Progress.** We are an optimistic people who, despite waves of nostalgia, believe that the present is better than the past. We celebrate progress, viewing the "very latest" as the "very best."

7. **Science.** We expect scientists to solve problems and to improve our lives. We believe that we are rational people, which probably explains our cultural tendency (especially among men) to devalue emotion and intuition as sources of knowledge.

8. **Democracy and free enterprise.** Members of our society recognize numerous individual rights that governments should not take away. We believe that a just political system is based on free elections in which adults select government leaders and on an economy that responds to the choices of individual consumers.

9. **Freedom.** We favor individual initiative over collective conformity. While we know that everyone has responsibilities to others, we believe that people should be free to pursue their personal goals.

Seeing Sociology in Everyday Life

How many languages are spoken by people on your campus? See if you can find out the extent of language diversity at your college.

Chinese

- Official language
- Widely spoken second language

English

- Official language
- Widely spoken second language

Spanish

- Official language
- Widely spoken second language

Window on the World

GLOBAL MAP 2–1

Language in Global Perspective

Chinese (including Mandarin, Cantonese, and dozens of other dialects) is the native tongue of nearly one-fifth of the world's people, almost all of whom live in Asia. Although all Chinese people read and write with the same characters, they use several dozen dialects. The "official" dialect, taught in schools throughout the People's Republic of China and the Republic of Taiwan, is Mandarin (the dialect of Beijing, China's capital). Cantonese, the language of Canton, is the second most common Chinese dialect; it differs in sound from Mandarin roughly the way French differs from Spanish.

English is the native tongue or official language in several world regions (spoken by 5 percent of humanity) and has become the preferred second language in most of the world.

The largest concentration of Spanish speakers is in Latin America and, of course, Spain. Spanish is also the second most widely spoken language in the United States.

Sources: *Peters Atlas of the World* (1990), Lewis (2009), and World Factbook (2009).

Seeing Sociology in Everyday Life

Would you say that physical fitness is an emerging cultural value? Why or why not?

norms rules and expectations by which a society guides the behavior of its members

mores norms that are widely observed and have great moral significance

folkways norms for routine or casual interaction

Every culture is a work in progress in that cultural values change over time. In the 2010 film *Avatar*, the "traditional" values of our own society are evident in the humans' efforts to exploit the resources of the planet Pandora, as well as their willingness to use force to accomplish this goal. At the same time, a competing set of values held by the native Pandora people—who live peacefully and simply by honoring the natural world—is now emerging among members of our society.

10. **Racism and group superiority.** Despite strong ideas about individualism and freedom, most people in the United States still judge others according to gender, race, ethnicity, and social class. In general, U.S. culture values males over females, whites over people of color, people with northwestern European backgrounds over those whose ancestors came from other parts of the world, and rich over poor. Although we describe ourselves as a nation of equals, there is little doubt that some of us are "more equal" than others.

Values: Often in Harmony, Sometimes in Conflict

In many ways, cultural values go together. Williams's list includes examples of *value clusters* in our way of life. For instance, we value activity and work because we expect effort to lead to achievement and success and result in material comfort.

Sometimes, however, one core cultural value contradicts another. Take the first and last items on Williams's list, for example: Members of our society say they believe in equality of opportunity, yet many also look down on others because of their sex or race. Value conflict causes strain and often leads to awkward balancing acts in our beliefs. Sometimes we decide that one value is more important

than another by, for example, supporting equal opportunity while opposing same-sex marriage. In these cases, we simply learn to live with the contradictions.

Emerging Values

Like all elements of culture, values change over time. People in the United States have always valued hard work. In recent decades, however, we have placed increasing importance on leisure—having time off from work to do things such as reading, travel, or community service that provide enjoyment and satisfaction. Similarly, although the importance of material comfort remains strong, more people are seeking personal growth through meditation and other spiritual activity.

Values: A Global Perspective

Values vary from culture to culture around the world. In general, the values that are important in higher-income countries differ somewhat from those in lower-income countries.

People in lower-income nations develop cultures that value survival. This means that people place a great deal of importance on physical safety and economic security. They worry about having enough to eat and a safe place to sleep at night. In addition, lower-income nations tend to be traditional, with values that celebrate the past and emphasize the importance of family and religious beliefs. These nations, in which men have most of the power, typically discourage or forbid practices such as divorce and abortion.

People in higher-income countries develop cultures that value individualism and self-expression. These countries are rich enough that most of the people take survival for granted, focusing their attention instead on which "lifestyle" they prefer and how to achieve the greatest personal happiness. In addition, these cultures tend to be secular and rational, placing less emphasis on family ties and religious beliefs and more on people thinking for themselves and being tolerant of others who differ from them. In higher-income nations, women have social standing more equal to men, and there is widespread support for practices such as divorce and abortion (World Values Survey, 2008). Figure 2–2 shows how selected countries of the world compare in terms of cultural values.

Norms

Most people in the United States are eager to gossip about "who's hot" and "who's not." Members of American Indian societies, however, typically condemn such behavior as rude and divisive. Both patterns illustrate the operation of **norms,** *rules and expectations by which a society guides the behavior of its members.* In everyday life, people respond to each other with *sanctions*, rewards or punishments that encourage conformity to cultural norms.

○─● Seeing Sociology
in Everyday Life

Give two examples of campus folkways and two examples of campus
mores. What are the likely consequences of violating each type of norm?

○─● Seeing Sociology
in Everyday Life

Figure 2–2 shows that as a rich nation, the United States ranks high in
terms of self-expression but is more traditional than many other high-
income nations, such as those in Europe. Can you point to specific beliefs
or practices that set us apart from Europeans as more traditional?

William Graham Sumner (1959, orig. 1906), an early U.S. sociologist, coined the term **mores** (pronounced "MORE-ayz") to refer to *norms that are widely observed and have great moral significance.* Certain mores include *taboos,* such as our society's insistence that adults not engage in sexual relations with children.

People pay less attention to **folkways,** *norms for routine or casual interaction.* Examples include ideas about appropriate greetings and proper dress. A man who does not wear a tie to a formal dinner party may raise an eyebrow for violating folkways or "etiquette." If he were to arrive at the dinner party wearing *only* a tie, however, he would violate cultural mores and invite a more serious response.

As we learn cultural norms, we gain the capacity to evaluate our own behavior. Doing wrong (say, downloading a term paper from the Internet) can cause both *shame*—the painful sense that others disapprove of our actions—and also *guilt*—a negative judgment we make of ourselves. Only cultural creatures can experience shame and guilt. This is what the writer Mark Twain had in mind when he remarked that people "are the only animals that blush—or need to."

Ideal and Real Culture

Values and norms do not describe actual behavior so much as they suggest how we *should* behave. We must remember that *ideal culture* always differs from *real culture,* which is what actually occurs in everyday life. For example, most women and men agree on the importance of sexual faithfulness in marriage. Even so, in one study, 17 percent of married people reported having been sexually unfaithful to their spouse at some point in the marriage (NORC, 2009:1955). But a culture's moral standards are important all the same, calling to mind the old saying "Do as I say, not as I do."

Technology and Culture

In addition to symbolic elements such as values and norms, every culture includes a wide range of physical human creations called *artifacts.* The Chinese eat with chopsticks rather than knives and forks, the Japanese place mats rather than rugs on the floor, and many men and women in India prefer flowing robes to the close-fitting clothing common in the United States. The material culture of a people can seem as strange to outsiders as their language, values, and norms.

A society's artifacts partly reflect underlying cultural values. The warlike Yąnomamö carefully craft their weapons and prize the

Global Snapshot

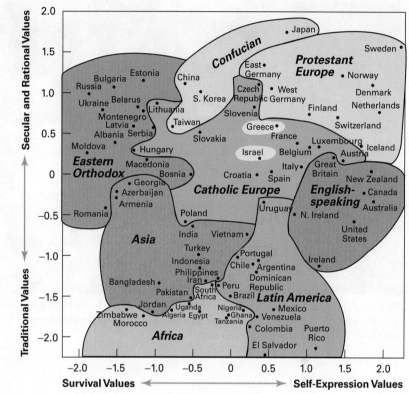

FIGURE 2–2   Cultural Values of Selected Countries

A general global pattern is that higher-income countries tend to be secular and rational and favor self-expression. By contrast, the cultures of lower-income countries tend to be more traditional and concerned with economic survival. Each region of the world, however, has distinctive cultural patterns, including religious traditions, that affect values. Looking at the figure, what patterns can you see?

Sources: Inglehart & Welzel (2005) and Inglehart (2009).

poison tips on their arrows. By contrast, our society's embrace of individuality and independence goes a long way toward explaining our high regard for the automobile: We own about 250 million motor vehicles—more than one for every licensed driver—and even in an age of high gasoline prices, many of these are the large sport utility vehicles that we might expect rugged, individualistic people to choose.

In addition to expressing values, material culture also reflects a society's level of **technology,** *knowledge that people use to make a way of life in their surroundings.* The more complex a society's technology, the easier it is for members of that society to shape the world for themselves.

● Seeing Sociology
in Everyday Life

Do some research in your own home: Look at the photographs that are displayed, and try to understand who is shown, what makes the event important, and what these photographs suggest about patterns of culture.

● Seeing Sociology
in Everyday Life

If archaeologists dig up our civilization 50,000 years from now, based on the artifacts they find, what kind of people will they think we were? Point to specific artifacts (such as SUVs, cell phones, and credit cards) and what they say about us.

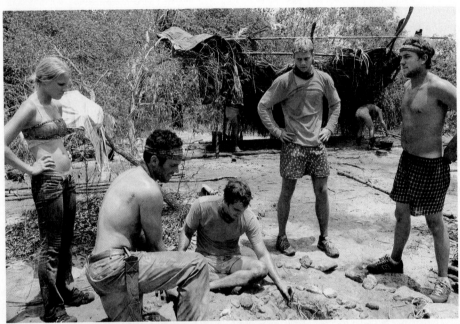

What would it be like to live in a society with simple technology? That's the premise of the television show *Survivor*. What advantages do societies with simple technology afford their members? What disadvantages do you see?

the primary food source for these peoples—while men do most of the hunting. Because the tasks they perform are of equal value, the two sexes are regarded as having about the same social importance (Leacock, 1978).

Hunters and gatherers do not have formal leaders. They may look to one person as a *shaman*, or priest, but holding such a position does not excuse the person from the daily work of finding food. Overall, hunting and gathering is a simple and egalitarian way of life.

Limited technology leaves hunters and gatherers vulnerable to the forces of nature. Storms and droughts can easily destroy their food supply, and they have few effective ways to respond to accidents or disease. Looking back at these societies, we see that many children died in childhood, and only half lived to the age of twenty.

As people with powerful technology steadily close in on them, hunting and gathering societies are vanishing. Fortunately, studying their way of life has provided us with valuable information about our sociocultural history and our fundamental ties to the natural environment.

Gerhard Lenski argued that a society's level of technology is crucial in determining what cultural ideas and artifacts emerge or are even possible (Nolan & Lenski, 2007). He pointed to the importance of *sociocultural evolution*—the historical changes in culture brought about by new technology—which unfolds in terms of four major levels of development: hunting and gathering, horticulture and pastoralism, agriculture, and industry.

Hunting and Gathering

The oldest and most basic way of living is **hunting and gathering,** *the use of simple tools to hunt animals and gather vegetation for food.* From the time of our earliest human ancestors 3 million years ago until about 1800, most people in the world lived as hunters and gatherers. Today, however, this technology supports only a few societies, including the Kaska Indians of northwestern Canada, the Pygmies of Central Africa, the Khoisan of southwestern Africa, the Aborigines of Australia, and the Semai of Malaysia. Typically, hunters and gatherers spend most of their time searching for game and edible plants. Their societies are small, generally with several dozen people living in a nomadic, familylike group, moving on as they use up an area's vegetation or follow migratory animals.

Everyone helps search for food, with the very young and the very old doing what they can. Women usually gather vegetation—

Horticulture and Pastoralism

Horticulture, *the use of hand tools to raise crops,* appeared around 10,000 years ago. The hoe and the digging stick (used to punch holes in the ground for planting seeds) first turned up in fertile regions of the Middle East and Southeast Asia, and by 6,000 years ago, these tools were in use from Western Europe to China. Central and South Americans also learned to cultivate plants, but rocky soil and mountainous land forced members of many societies to continue to hunt and gather even as they adopted this new technology (Fisher, 1979; Chagnon, 1992).

In especially dry regions, societies turned not to raising crops but to **pastoralism,** *the domestication of animals.* Throughout the Americas, Africa, the Middle East, and Asia, many societies combine horticulture and pastoralism.

Growing plants and raising animals allows societies to feed hundreds of members. Pastoral peoples remain nomadic, but horticulturalists make permanent settlements. In a horticultural society, a material surplus means that not everyone has to produce food; some people are free to make crafts, become traders, or serve as full-time priests. Compared with hunters and gatherers, pastoral and horticultural societies are more unequal, with some families operating as a ruling elite.

technology (p. 47) knowledge that people use to make a way of life in their surroundings

hunting and gathering
the use of simple tools to hunt animals and gather vegetation for food

→

horticulture
the use of hand tools to raise crops

pastoralism
the domestication of animals

→

agriculture
large-scale cultivation using plows harnessed to animals or more powerful energy sources

→

industry
the production of goods using advanced sources of energy to drive large machinery

→

postindustrialism the production of information using computer technology

Because hunters and gatherers have little control over nature, they generally believe that the world is inhabited by spirits. As they gain the power to raise plants and animals, however, people come to believe in one God as the creator of the world. The pastoral roots of Judaism and Christianity are evident in the term "pastor" and the common view of God as a "shepherd" who stands watch over all.

Agriculture

Around 5,000 years ago, technological advances led to **agriculture,** *large-scale cultivation using plows harnessed to animals or more powerful energy sources.* Agrarian technology first appeared in the Middle East and gradually spread throughout the world. The invention of the animal-drawn plow, the wheel, writing, numbers, and new metals changed societies so much that historians call this era the "dawn of civilization."

By turning the soil, plows allow land to be farmed for centuries, so agrarian people can live in permanent settlements. With large food surpluses that can be transported by animal-powered wagons, populations grow into the millions. As members of agrarian societies become more and more specialized in their work, money is used as a form of common exchange, replacing the earlier system of barter. Although the development of agrarian technology expands human choices and fuels urban growth, it also makes social life more individualistic and impersonal.

Agriculture also brings about a dramatic increase in social inequality. Most people live as serfs or slaves, but a few elites are freed from labor to cultivate a "refined" way of life based on the study of philosophy, art, and literature. At all levels, men gain pronounced power over women.

People with only simple technology live much the same the world over, with minor differences caused by regional variations in climate. But agrarian technology gives people enough control over the world that cultural diversity dramatically increases (Nolan & Lenski, 2007).

Industry

Industrialization occurred as societies replaced the muscles of animals and humans with new forms of power. Formally, **industry** is *the production of goods using advanced sources of energy to drive large machinery.* The introduction of steam power, starting in England about 1775, greatly boosted productivity and transformed culture in the process.

Agrarian people work in or near their homes, but most people in industrial societies work in large factories under the supervision of strangers. In this way, industrialization pushes aside the traditional cultural values that guided family-centered agrarian life for centuries.

Industry also made the world seem smaller. In the nineteenth century, railroads and steamships carried people across land and sea faster and farther than ever before. In the twentieth century, this process continued with the invention of the automobile, the airplane, radio, television, and computers.

Industrial technology also raises living standards and extends the human life span. Schooling becomes the rule because industrial jobs demand more and more skills. In addition, industrial societies reduce economic inequality and steadily extend political rights.

It is easy to see industrial societies as "more advanced" than those relying on simpler technology. After all, industry raises living standards and stretches life expectancy to the seventies and beyond—about twice that of the Yąnomamö. But as industry intensifies individualism and expands personal freedom, it weakens human community. Also, industry has led people to abuse the natural environment, which threatens us all. And although advanced technology gives us laborsaving machines and miraculous forms of medical treatment, it also contributes to unhealthy levels of stress and has created weapons capable of destroying in a flash everything that our species has achieved.

Postindustrial Information Technology

Going beyond the four categories discussed by Lenski, we see that many industrial societies, including the United States, have now entered a postindustrial era in which more and more economic production makes use of *new information technology.* **Postindustrialism** refers to *the production of information using computer technology.* Production in industrial societies centers on factories that make *things,* but postindustrial production centers on computers and other electronic devices that create, process, store, and apply *ideas and information.*

The emergence of an information economy changes the skills that define a way of life. No longer are mechanical abilities the only key to success. People find that they must learn to work with symbols by speaking, writing, computing, and creating images and sounds. One result of this change is that our society now has the capacity to create symbolic culture on an unprecedented scale as people work with computers to generate new words, music, and images.

Cultural Diversity

In the United States, we are aware of our cultural diversity when we hear several different languages being spoken while riding a subway in New York, Washington, D.C., or Los Angeles. Compared to a country such as Japan, whose historical isolation makes it the most *monocultural* of all high-income nations, centuries of heavy immigration have made the United States the most *multicultural* of all high-income countries.

high culture cultural patterns that distinguish a society's elite

popular culture cultural patterns that are widespread among a society's population

subculture cultural patterns that set apart some segment of a society's population

counterculture (p. 52) cultural patterns that strongly oppose those widely accepted within a society

■● Read "Gangstas, Thugs, and Hustlas: The Code of the Street in Rap Music" by Charis E. Kubrin on **mysoclab.com**

Sometimes the distinction between high culture and popular is not so clear. Bonham's Auction House in England recently featured spray-painted works by the graffiti artist Banksy. This particular one was expected to be sold for more than $250,000.

Between 1820 (when the government began keeping track of immigration) and 2009, more than 76 million people came to our shores. This cultural mix continues to increase as more than 1.5 million people arrive each year. A century ago, almost all immigrants came from Europe; today, the majority of newcomers arrive from Latin America and Asia. To understand the reality of life in the United States, we must move beyond shared cultural patterns to consider cultural diversity.

High Culture and Popular Culture

Cultural diversity can involve social class. In fact, in everyday talk, we usually use the term "culture" to mean art forms such as classical literature, music, dance, and painting. We describe people who attend the opera or the theater as "cultured," thinking that they appreciate the "finer things in life."

We speak less kindly of ordinary people, assuming that everyday culture is somehow less worthy. So we are tempted to judge the music of Haydn as "more cultured" than hip-hop, couscous as better than cornbread, and polo as more polished than Ping-Pong.

These differences arise because many cultural patterns are readily available to only some members of a society. Sociologists use the term **high culture** to refer to *cultural patterns that distinguish a*

society's elite and **popular culture** to describe *cultural patterns that are widespread among a society's population.*

Common sense may suggest that high culture is superior to popular culture, but sociologists are uneasy with such judgments, for two reasons. First, neither elites nor ordinary people share all the same tastes and interests; people in both categories differ in numerous ways. Second, do we praise high culture because it is really better than popular culture or simply because its supporters have more money, power, and prestige? For example, there is no difference between a violin and a fiddle; however, we name the instrument one way when it is used to produce a type of music typically enjoyed by a person of higher position and the other way when it produces music appreciated by people with lower social standing.

Subculture

The term **subculture** refers to *cultural patterns that set apart some segment of a society's population.* People who ride "chopper" motorcycles, traditional Korean Americans, New England "Yankees," Ohio State football fans, the southern California "beach crowd," Elvis impersonators, and wilderness campers all display subcultural patterns.

It is easy but often inaccurate to put people in subcultural categories because almost everyone participates in many subcultures without having much commitment to any one of them. In some cases, ethnicity and religion can be strong enough to set people apart from one another, with tragic results. Consider the former nation of Yugoslavia in southeastern Europe. The 1990s' civil war there was fueled by extreme cultural diversity. This *one* small country with a population about equal to the Los Angeles metropolitan area made use of *two* alphabets, embraced *three* major religions, spoke *four* major languages, was home to *five* major nationalities, was divided into *six* separate republics, and absorbed the cultural influences of *seven* surrounding countries. The cultural conflict that plunged this nation into civil war shows that subcultures are a source not only of pleasing variety but also of tension and even violence. ■● Read on **mysoclab.com**

Many people view the United States as a melting pot where many nationalities blend into a single "American" culture (Gardyn, 2002). But given so much cultural diversity, how accurate is the melting pot image? For one thing, subcultures involve not just *difference* but also *hierarchy.* Too often what we view as dominant or "mainstream" culture are the patterns favored by powerful segments of the population, and we view the lives of disadvantaged people as "subculture." But are the cultural patterns of rich skiers on the mountains of Aspen, Colorado, any less a subculture than the

multiculturalism a perspective recognizing the cultural diversity of the United States and promoting equal standing for all cultural traditions

Eurocentrism the dominance of European (especially English) cultural patterns

Afrocentrism emphasizing and promoting African cultural patterns

Making the Grade

State several arguments in favor of our society sharing a common culture; state several arguments in favor of our society recognizing cultural diversity.

A generation ago, most people regarded tattoos as a mark of low social status. Today, this cultural pattern is gaining popularity among people at all social class levels. Kat Von D is a tattoo artist on the nationwide television show *L.A. Ink*.

cultural patterns of skateboarders on the streets of Los Angeles? Some sociologists therefore prefer to level the playing field of society by emphasizing multiculturalism.

Multiculturalism

Multiculturalism is *a perspective recognizing the cultural diversity of the United States and promoting equal standing for all cultural traditions.* Multiculturalism represents a sharp change from the past, when U.S. society downplayed cultural diversity, defining itself in terms of its European and especially English immigrants. Today there is spirited debate about whether we should continue to focus on historical traditions or highlight contemporary diversity.

E pluribus unum, the Latin phrase that appears on each U.S. coin, means "out of many, one." This motto symbolizes not only our national political union but also the idea that the varied experiences of immigrants from around the world come together to form a new way of life.

But from the outset, the many cultures did not melt together as much as harden into a hierarchy. At the top were the English, who formed a majority and established English as the nation's dominant language. Further down, people of other backgrounds were advised to model themselves after "their betters" so that the "melting" was really a process of Anglicization—adoption of English ways. As multiculturalists see it, early in its history, U.S. society set up the English

way of life as an ideal that everyone else should imitate and by which everyone should be judged.

Since then, historians have reported events from the point of view of the English and others of European ancestry, paying little attention to the perspectives and accomplishments of Native Americans and people of African and Asian descent. Multiculturalists criticize this as **Eurocentrism,** *the dominance of European (especially English) cultural patterns.* Molefi Kete Asante, a supporter of multiculturalism, argues that like "the fifteenth-century Europeans who could not cease believing that the Earth was the center of the universe, many [people] today find it difficult to cease viewing European culture as the center of the social universe" (1988:7).

One controversial issue involves language. Some people believe that English should be the official language of the United States; by 2009, legislatures in thirty states had enacted laws making it the official language. But more than 55 million men and women—one in five—speak a language other than English at home. Spanish is the second most commonly spoken language in the United States, and several hundred other tongues are heard across the country, including Italian, German, French, Filipino, Japanese, Korean, Vietnamese, Russian, and a host of Native American languages. National Map 2–1 on page 52 shows where in the United States large numbers of people speak a language other than English at home.

Supporters of multiculturalism say it is a way of coming to terms with our country's increasing social diversity. With the Asian American and Hispanic American populations increasing rapidly, some analysts predict that today's children will live to see people of African, Asian, and Hispanic ancestry become the *majority* of this country's population.

Supporters also claim that multiculturalism is a good way to strengthen the academic achievement of African American children. To counter Eurocentrism, some multicultural educators are calling for **Afrocentrism,** *emphasizing and promoting African cultural patterns,* which they see as a strategy for correcting centuries of ignoring the cultural achievements of African societies and African Americans.

Although multiculturalism has found favor in recent years, it has drawn criticism as well. Opponents say it encourages divisiveness rather than unity because it urges people to identify with only their own category rather than with the nation as a whole. In addition, critics say, multiculturalism actually harms minorities themselves. Multicultural policies (from African American studies departments to all-black dorms) seem to support the same racial separation that our nation has struggled so long to overcome. Furthermore, in the early grades, an Afrocentric curriculum may deny children important knowledge and skills by forcing them to study only certain topics from a single point of view.

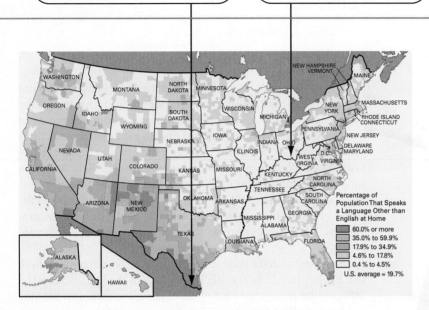

Elvira Martinez lives in Zapata County, Texas, where about three-quarters of the people in her community speak Spanish at home.

Jeffrey Steen lives in Adams County, Ohio, where almost none of his neighbors speaks a language other than English.

Explore the percentage of foreign-born people in your local community and in counties across the United States on mysoclab.com

Percentage of Population That Speaks a Language Other than English at Home

- 60.0% or more
- 35.0% to 59.9%
- 17.9% to 34.9%
- 4.6% to 17.8%
- 0.4 % to 4.5%

U.S. average = 19.7%

Seeing Ourselves

NATIONAL MAP 2–1
Language Diversity across the United States

Of more than 283 million people age five or older in the United States, the Census Bureau reports that nearly 56 million (20 percent) speak a language other than English at home. Of these, 62 percent speak Spanish and 15 percent use an Asian language (the Census Bureau lists thirty-nine languages and language categories, each of which is favored by more than 100,000 people). The map shows that non–English speakers are concentrated in certain regions of the country. Which ones? What do you think accounts for this pattern?

Explore on mysoclab.com

Sources: U.S. Census Bureau (2003, 2009).

Finally, the global war on terrorism has drawn the issue of multiculturalism into the spotlight. In 2005, British Prime Minister Tony Blair responded to a terrorist attack in London, stating, "It is important that the terrorists realize [that] our determination to defend our values and our way of life is greater than their determination to . . . impose their extremism on the world." He went on to warn that the British government would expel Muslim clerics who encouraged hatred and terrorism (Barone, 2005). In a world of cultural difference and conflict, we have much to learn about tolerance and peacemaking.

Counterculture

Cultural diversity also includes outright rejection of conventional ideas or behavior. **Counterculture** refers to *cultural patterns that strongly oppose those widely accepted within a society*.

During the 1960s, for example, a youth-oriented counterculture rejected mainstream culture as too competitive, self-centered, and materialistic. Instead, hippies and other counterculturalists favored a collective and cooperative lifestyle in which "being" was more important than "doing" and the capacity for personal growth—or "expanded consciousness"—was prized more highly than material possessions like fancy homes and cars. Such differences led some people to "drop out" of the larger society and join countercultural communities.

Countercultures are still flourishing. At the extreme, small militaristic communities (made up of people born and bred in this country) or bands of religious militants (from other countries) exist in the United States, some of them engaging in violence intended to threaten our way of life.

Cultural Change

Perhaps the most basic human truth is that "all things shall pass." Even the dinosaurs, which thrived on this planet for 160 million years, exist today only as fossils. Will humanity survive for millions of years to come? All we can say with certainty is that given our reliance on culture, the human record will show continuous change.

Figure 2–3 shows changes in student attitudes that have occurred between 1969 (the height of the 1960s' counterculture) and 2009. Some attitudes have changed only slightly: Today, as a generation ago, most men and women look forward to raising a family. But today's students are much less concerned than those of the 1960s with developing a philosophy of life and are much more interested in making money.

Change in one dimension of a cultural system usually sparks changes in others. For example, today's college women are far more interested in making money because women are much more likely to be in the labor force than their mothers or grandmothers were. Working for income may not change their interest in having a family, but it does increase their age at first marriage and the divorce rate. Such connections illustrate the principle of **cultural integration,** *the close relationships among various elements of a cultural system*.

Some parts of a cultural system change faster than others. William Ogburn (1964) observed that technology moves quickly, generating new elements of material culture (such as test-tube babies) faster than nonmaterial culture (such as ideas about parenthood) can keep up with them. Ogburn called this inconsistency **cultural lag,** *the fact that some cultural elements change more quickly than others, disrupting a cultural system*. In a world in which a woman can give birth to a child by using another woman's egg, which has

cultural integration the close relationships among various elements of a cultural system

cultural lag the fact that some cultural elements change more quickly than others, disrupting a cultural system

been fertilized in a laboratory with the sperm of a total stranger, how are we to apply traditional ideas about motherhood and fatherhood?

Cultural changes are set in motion in three ways. The first is *invention*, the process of creating new cultural elements, such as the telephone (1876), the airplane (1903), and the computer (late 1940s), each of which changed our way of life. The process of invention goes on all the time, as indicated by the thousands of applications submitted every year to the U.S. Patent Office. The timeline inside the back cover of this book shows other inventions that have helped change our culture.

Discovery, a second cause of change, involves recognizing and understanding more fully something already in existence, from a distant star to the foods of another culture to women's athletic ability. Many discoveries result from painstaking scientific research, and others happen by a stroke of luck, as in 1898 when Marie Curie unintentionally left a rock on a piece of photographic paper, noticed that emissions from the rock had exposed the paper, and thus discovered radium.

The third cause of cultural change is *diffusion*, the spread of objects or ideas from one society to another. Because new technology sends information around the globe in seconds, cultural diffusion has never been greater than it is today.

Our own way of life has contributed many significant cultural elements to the world, ranging from computers to jazz music. Of course, diffusion works the other way, too, so that much of what we assume is "American" actually comes from elsewhere. Most of the clothing we wear and the furniture we use, as well as the watch we carry and the money we spend, all had their origins in other cultures (Linton, 1937a).

It is certainly correct to talk about "American culture," especially when we are comparing our way of life to the culture of some other society. But this discussion of cultural change shows us that culture is always complex and always changing. The Thinking About Diversity box on pages 54–55 offers a good example of the diverse and dynamic character of culture with a brief look at the history of rock-and-roll music.

Ethnocentrism and Cultural Relativism

December 10, a small village in Morocco. Watching many of our fellow travelers browsing through a tiny ceramics factory, we have little doubt that North Americans are among the world's greatest shoppers. We delight in surveying hand-woven carpets in China or India, inspecting finely crafted metals in Turkey, or collecting the beautifully colored porcelain tiles we find here in Morocco. Of course, all these items are wonderful bargains. But one major reason for the low prices is unsettling to people living in rich countries: Many products from the world's low- and

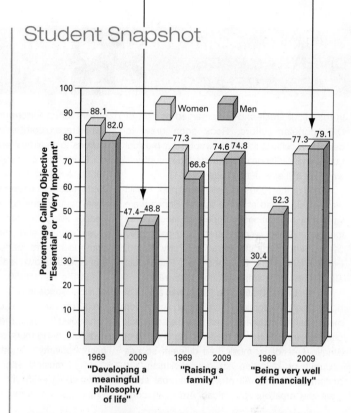

Compared to college students 40 years ago, today's students are less interested in developing a philosophy of life and more interested in making money.

Student Snapshot

FIGURE 2–3   Life Objectives of First-Year College Students, 1969 and 2009

Researchers have surveyed first-year college students every year since 1969. While attitudes about some things such as the importance of family have stayed about the same, attitudes about other life goals have changed dramatically.

Sources: Astin et al. (2002) and Pryor et al. (2009).

middle-income countries are made by children—some as young as five or six—who work long days for pennies per hour.

We think of childhood as a time of innocence and freedom from adult burdens such as work. In poor countries throughout the world, however, families depend on income earned by their children. So what people in one society think of as right and natural, people elsewhere find puzzling or even immoral. Perhaps the Chinese philosopher Confucius had it right when he noted that "all people are the same; it's only their habits that are different."

Just about every imaginable idea or behavior is commonplace somewhere in the world, and this cultural variation causes travelers both excitement and distress. Australians flip light switches down to

Making the Grade

Youth cultures tend to develop as societies industrialize because young people gain more independence from parents and have more money to spend on their own interests.

ethnocentrism the practice of judging another culture by the standards of one's own culture

cultural relativism the practice of judging a culture by its own standards

THINKING ABOUT DIVERSITY: RACE, CLASS, & GENDER

Early Rock-and-Roll: Race, Class, and Cultural Change

In the 1950s, rock-and-roll emerged as part of U.S. popular culture. Rock soon grew to become a cultural tide that swept away musical tastes and traditions and changed the country in ways we still experience today.

Early in the 1950s, mainstream "pop" music was largely aimed at white adults. Songs were written by professional composers, recorded by long-established record labels, and performed by well-known artists including Perry Como, Eddie Fisher, Doris Day, and Patti Page. Just about every big-name performer was white.

In the United States, the 1950s was a time of rigid racial segregation. This racial separation meant that the cultures of white people and black people were different. In the subcultural world of African Americans, music had different sounds and rhythms, reflecting jazz, gospel singing, and rhythm and blues. All of these musical styles were the creations of African American com-

posers and performers working with black-owned record companies and broadcast on radio stations to an almost entirely black audience.

Class, too, divided the musical world of the 1950s, even among whites. A second musical subculture was country and western, a musical style popular among poorer whites, especially people living in the South. Like rhythm and blues, country and western music had its own composers and performers, its own record labels, and its own radio stations.

In the early 1950s, there were a variety of musical worlds in U.S. society, separated by the walls of race and class. There was little "crossover" music, meaning that very rarely, if ever, did performers or songs from one world gain popularity in another.

This musical segregation began to break down about 1955 with the birth of rock-and-roll. Rock was a new mix of many existing musical

patterns, drawing on mainstream pop but including country and western and, especially, rhythm and blues.

The new rock-and-roll music drew together musical traditions, but it soon divided society in a new way—by age. Rock-and-roll was the first music clearly linked to the emergence of a youth culture—rock was all the rage among teenagers but was little appreciated or even understood by their parents. One reason for this age split was that in the prosperous 1950s, young people had more money to spend, and record companies realized that they could make a fortune selling music to the new "youth market."

Within a few years, the new youth culture presented young people with many new musical stars, and many definitely were not people who looked or acted like their parents. The rock-and-roll performers were men (and a few women) who looked young and took a rebellious stand

Elvis Presley (*center*) drew together the music of rhythm and blues singers, such as Big Mama Thornton (*left*), and country and western stars, including Carl Perkins (*right*). The development of rock-and-roll illustrates the ever-changing character of U.S. culture.

turn them on, but North Americans flip them up. The Japanese name city blocks; North Americans name city streets. Egyptians stand very close to others in conversation; North Americans are used to maintaining several feet of "personal space." Bathrooms lack toilet paper in much of rural Morocco, causing considerable discomfort for North Americans, who recoil at the thought of using the left hand for bathroom hygiene, as the locals do.

Given that a particular culture is the basis for everyday experiences, it is no wonder that people everywhere exhibit **ethnocentrism,** *the practice of judging another culture by the standards of one's own culture.* Some small degree of ethnocentrism is necessary for people to be emotionally attached to their way of life. But ethnocentrism can also generate misunderstanding and sometimes even leads to conflict.

○ Making the Grade

During the 1950s, rock-and-roll helped bring together black and white musical styles, but because this music was popular among the young, it also divided people by age.

● Seeing Sociology
in Everyday Life

Just for fun, go to http://www.TheSociologyPage.com, where you can hear one of the author's "cover" performances of oldies rock-and-roll.

against "adult" culture. The typical rocker was a young man who looked like what parents might have called a "juvenile delinquent" and who claimed to be "cool," an idea that most parents did not even understand.

The first band to make it big in rock-and-roll was Bill Haley and the Comets. These men (Haley lowered his stated age to gain greater acceptance) came out of the country and western tradition (his earlier bands included the Down Homers and the Saddlemen). Haley's first big hits in 1954—"Shake, Rattle, and Roll" and "Rock around the Clock"—were recordings of earlier rhythm and blues songs.

Very quickly, however, young people began to lose interest in older performers such as Bill Haley and turned their attention to younger performers who had a stronger juvenile delinquent image—musicians sporting sideburns, turned-up collars, and black leather jackets. By the end of 1955, the unquestioned star of rock-and-roll was a poor white southern boy from Tupelo, Mississippi, named Elvis Aron Presley. From his rural roots, Elvis knew country and western music, and after he moved to his adopted hometown of Memphis, Tennessee, he learned all about black gospel and rhythm and blues.

Before the 1950s ended, Presley had become the first superstar of rock-and-roll—not only because he had talent but also because he had great crossover power. With early hits including "Hound Dog" (a rhythm and blues song originally recorded by Big Mama Thornton) and "Blue Suede Shoes" (written by country and western star Carl Perkins), Presley broke down many of the walls of race and class in the music of the United States.

Elvis went on to a twenty-year career as "the King." But during that time, illustrating the expanding and changing character of culture, popular music developed in many new and different directions. By the end of the 1950s, popular musical styles included soft rock (Ricky Nelson, Pat Boone), rockabilly (Johnny Cash), and dozens of doo-wop groups, both black and white (often named for birds—the Falcons, the Penguins, and the Flamingos—or cars—the Imperials, the Impalas, the Fleetwoods).

During the 1960s, rock music grew even more popular and more diverse, including folk music (the Kingston Trio; Peter, Paul, and Mary; Bob Dylan), surf music (the Beach Boys, Jan and Dean), and the "British invasion" led by the Beatles.

At first, the Beatles were very close to the clean-cut, pop side of rock, but they soon shared the spotlight with another British band that was proud of its "delinquent" clothing and street fighter looks—the Rolling Stones. During the 1960s, the hard rock of the Beatles and Stones was joined by softer "folk rock" performed by the Byrds, Buffalo Springfield, the Mamas and the Papas, Simon and Garfunkel, and Crosby, Stills, and Nash. Mainstream rock continued with bands like the Who, and rhythm and blues gave birth to "Motown" (named after the "motor city," Detroit), as well as "soul" music, creating dozens of African American stars, including Aretha Franklin, James Brown, the Four Tops, the Temptations, and Diana Ross and the Supremes.

On the West Coast, San Francisco developed a different, more political rock music performed by Jefferson Airplane, the Grateful Dead, and Janis Joplin. West Coast spin-off musical styles included "acid rock," influenced by drug use, performed by the Doors and Jimi Hendrix. The jazz influence also returned to the world of rock, creating such "jazz rock" groups as Chicago and Blood, Sweat, and Tears.

This brief look at the early decades of rock-and-roll shows the power of race and class to divide and separate people, shaping different subcultural patterns. It also shows the power of music to bring people together. We also see that the production of culture—in terms of music as well as movies and music videos—has become a megabusiness. But most of all, it shows us that culture is not a rigid system that stands still but is better described as a living process, changing, adapting, and reinventing itself over time.

WHAT DO YOU THINK?

1. Many dimensions of our way of life shaped rock-and-roll. In what ways do you think the emergence of rock-and-roll changed U.S. culture?

2. Throughout this period of musical change, most musical performers were men. What does this tell us about our way of life? Is popular music still dominated by men today?

3. Can you carry on the story of musical change in the United States to the present? (Think of disco, heavy metal, punk rock, rap, and hip-hop.)

Source: Based on Stuessy & Lipscomb (2008).

Even language is culturally biased. Years ago, people in North America or Europe referred to China as the "Far East." But this term, unknown to the Chinese, is an ethnocentric term for a region that is far east *of us.* The Chinese name for their country translates as "Central Kingdom," suggesting that they, like us, see their society as the center of the world.

The alternative to ethnocentrism is **cultural relativism,** *the practice of judging a culture by its own standards.* Cultural relativism can be difficult for travelers to adopt: It requires not only openness to unfamiliar values and norms but also the ability to put aside cultural standards we have known all our lives. Even so, as people of the world increasingly come into contact with one another, the importance of understanding other cultures will become ever greater.

Widespread ethnocentrism in the world certainly contributes to armed conflict between nations. At the same time, today's military is

Associated Press

U.S. Troops Train for Both Combat and Conversation

BY DAN ELLIOTT
March 29, 2010

FORT CARSON, Colo.—Two young American soldiers in combat gear sit at a small table in a concrete block building, politely but insistently questioning a 66-year-old Afghan actor playing the role of a village elder.

Outside, in the thick red mud of a remote Fort Carson valley, other soldiers crouch in defensive positions, peering into their rifle sights in the cold morning. But inside, the soldiers are learning to negotiate, rather than shoot, trying to coax information from the Afghan elder about bomb-makers in a nearby village.

The soldiers are among about 4,000 members of Fort Carson's 1st Brigade Combat Team and supporting units who will deploy to Afghanistan this summer. They're practicing counterinsurgency tactics, cultivating trust and cooperation with the Afghan people at the same time they wage war on the insurgents.

The Army's top commanders and planners say that strategy is the key to success in Afghanistan.

"Understanding the culture, and the impact of your actions on the culture, is so essential to mission success that you won't succeed without it," Gen. George W. Casey, the Army chief of staff, said during a visit to Fort Carson this month.

The strategy, detailed in a 2006 Army manual, is a dramatic change in U.S. counterinsurgency doctrine, shifting the focus from the enemy to the population, said Conrad Crane, director of the Army Military History Institute at the Army War College at Carlisle Barracks, Pa.

"If you work with the people, the people are going to give you the intelligence you need for the next operation," said Crane, the lead author of the new doctrine. "It's a revolutionary type of intelligence."

The success of the approach will be measured by how much support and information the soldiers get, he said. "Are they telling you where the explosives are, are they telling you where the bad guys are?"

The strategy is getting its first major test in Afghanistan in Helmand province, where 10,000 U.S., NATO and Afghan troops pushed the Taliban out of the town of Marjah in February.

The allies are now trying to win over the townspeople with good governance, public services and aid.

Making it work in the long run will be tough, said Rick "Ozzie" Nelson, a counterterrorism expert at the Center for Strategic and International Studies.

The basic level of cultural knowledge and language skills the soldiers are getting might not be enough to navigate through Afghanistan's intricate web of ethnic and tribal groups, he said.

But any level of skills will help, Nelson said, noting, "There didn't used to be any cultural training."

At Fort Carson, several hundred soldiers from the 1st Brigade are being schooled in the details of Afghan religion, history, geography and tribal structure and taking lessons in Dari, one of Afghanistan's languages.

They'll learn between 600 and 1,500 Dari words, including basic greetings, requests for IDs

often called upon not only to fight but to win the hearts and minds of the local people in an unfamiliar setting. Seeing Sociology in the News explains how the U.S. Army is training combat soldiers to understand the culture of tribal people in rural Afghanistan.

As the opening to this chapter explained, businesses in the United States are learning the value of marketing to a culturally diverse population. Similarly, businesses now know that success in the global economy depends on awareness of cultural patterns around the world. IBM, for example, now provides technical support for its products on Web sites in more than thirty languages (IBM, 2009).

This embrace of difference is a change from the past, when many companies used marketing strategies that lacked sensitivity to cultural diversity. The translation of Coors beer's phrase "Turn It Loose" startled Spanish-speaking customers by proclaiming that the beer would cause diarrhea. Braniff Airlines translated its slo-

In the world's low-income countries, most children must work to provide their families with needed income. These young girls work long hours in a brick factory in the Kathmandu Valley, Nepal. Is it ethnocentric for people living in high-income nations to condemn the practice of child labor because we think youngsters belong in school? Why or why not?

gan "Fly in Leather" into Spanish so carelessly that it read "Fly Naked"; similarly, Eastern Airlines' slogan "We Earn Our Wings Every Day" became "We Fly Daily to Heaven," which is hardly comforting to air travelers. Even the poultry giant Frank Perdue fell victim to poor marketing when his pitch "It Takes a Tough Man to Make a Tender Chicken" was transformed into the Spanish phrase "A Sexually Excited Man Will Make a Chicken Affectionate" (Helin, 1992).

But cultural relativism creates problems of its own. If almost any behavior is the norm *somewhere* in the world, does that mean everything is equally right? Does the fact that some Indian and Moroccan families benefit from having their children work long hours justify child labor? Because we are all members of a single human species, surely there must be some universal standards of proper conduct. But what are they? And in trying to develop them, how can we avoid imposing our own standards on others? There are no simple answers to these questions. But when confronting an unfamiliar cultural practice, it is best to resist making judgments before grasping what members of that culture think of the issue. Remember also to think about your own and friendly questions like "How are you doing" and "How is your family," said Mowafiq Al-Anazi, an associate dean at the Defense Language Institute in Monterey, Calif.

"We see language and culture very inextricably intertwined," said Army Col. Sue Ann Sandusky, commandant at the institute. "You're learning a language in order to be able to communicate and understand communication, and to do that you have to be able to place the words and language in the cultural context."

The soldiers still train for combat, too. After meeting with the village elder in the Fort Carson exercise, the platoon was ambushed a few miles away by other soldiers playing the role of Taliban fighters. In a chaotic gun battle waged with blanks, the shouting and cursing platoon overcame the attackers and summoned a Black Hawk helicopter to evacuate a soldier with a make-believe wound. . . .

Veterans and relative newcomers in the 1st Brigade say both combat training and cultural training will help when they get to Afghanistan.

"If you get the people on your side, the enemy will go away," said Command Sgt. Maj. Martin Kelley, a 24-year Army veteran who has served three deployments to Iraq as well as previous stints in Bosnia and Kuwait.

Second Lt. Richard Groat, who negotiated with the village elder and then led the platoon as it fought off the mock Taliban attack, said it was his first patrol and felt like the real thing.

"This process provides experience for me that I don't have," he said.

Ahmad Shah Alam, who played the role of the village elder in the negotiation exercise, said the scenario was realistic, and that the brushy hills and snowy mountain backdrop of Fort Carson give the soldiers a good sense of what it's like to be in Afghanistan.

"I feel like I was home," said Alam, a professional actor who appeared in the 2007 movie "Kite Runner" in a role called "man in the park." . . .

He said he feels it's his duty to help the Americans fighting insurgents in Afghanistan.

"This is very tough," he said. "I do not wish to be an American soldier."

WHAT DO YOU THINK?

1. In what ways is cultural knowledge an important part of what today's military calls "counterinsurgency tactics"? Provide examples from the article.

2. One military officer claims, "If you get the people on your side, the enemy will go away." Do you think that combat soldiers in a foreign land can realistically expect to do that? Why or why not?

3. If the people of the world were able to greatly increase cultural understanding, do you think we might expect to put an end to war? Why or why not?

Adapted from "U. S. Troops Train for Both Combat and Conversation" by Dan Elliott. Associated Press Writer Brook Donald contributed to this report. Used with permission of The Associated Press. Copyright © 2010. All rights reserved.

way of life as others might see it. After all, what we gain most from studying others is better insight into ourselves.

A Global Culture?

Today more than ever, we can observe many of the same cultural patterns the world over. Walking the streets of Seoul, South Korea; Kuala Lumpur, Malaysia; Chennai, India; Cairo, Egypt; or Casablanca, Morocco, we see people wearing jeans, hear familiar music, and read ads for many of the same products we use at home.

Societies around the world now have more contact with one another than ever before, thanks to the flow of goods, information, and people:

1. **Global economy: The flow of goods.** International commerce is at an all-time high. The global economy has spread many consumer goods—from cars and TV shows to music and fashion—throughout the world.

2. **Global communications: The flow of information.** The Internet and satellite-assisted communications enable people to experience events taking place thousands of miles away, often as they happen. In addition, English has long been the dominant language of the Internet, helping spread the English language around the world. It was not until late in 2009 that a person could register a Web address in Korean, Chinese, Arabic, or another language that uses a non-Latin script. Recall from Global Map 2–1 that English is now the preferred second language in most parts of the world.

3. **Global migration: The flow of people.** Knowledge about the rest of the world motivates people to move where they imagine life will be better, and modern transportation technology, especially air travel, makes relocating easier than ever before. As a result, in most countries, significant numbers of people were born elsewhere (including some 38 million people in the United States, 12.5 percent of the population).

These global links help make the cultures of the world more similar. But there are three important limitations to the global culture thesis. First, the flow of information, goods, and people is uneven in different parts of the world. Generally speaking, urban areas (centers of commerce, communication, and people) have stronger ties to one another, and rural villages remain isolated. In addition, the greater economic and military power of North America and Western Europe means that nations in these regions influence the rest of the world more than the rest of the world influences them.

Second, the global culture thesis assumes that people everywhere are able to *afford* the new goods and services. As Chapter 9 ("Global Stratification") explains, desperate poverty in much of the world deprives people of even the basic necessities of a safe and secure life.

Third, although many cultural elements have spread throughout the world, people everywhere do not attach the same meanings to them. Do children in Tokyo draw the same lessons from reading the Harry Potter books as children in London or New York? Similarly, we

cultural universals traits that are part of every known culture

sociobiology a theoretical approach that explores ways in which human biology affects how we create culture

enjoy foods from around the world while knowing little about the lives of the people who created them. In short, people everywhere look at the world through their own cultural lenses.

Theoretical Analysis of Culture

Sociologists investigate how culture helps us make sense of ourselves and the surrounding world. Here we will examine several macro-level theoretical approaches to understanding culture. A micro-level approach to the personal experience of culture, which emphasizes how individuals not only conform to cultural patterns but also create new patterns in their everyday lives, is the focus of Chapter 4 ("Social Interaction in Everyday Life").

The Functions of Culture: Structural-Functional Analysis

The structural-functional approach explains culture as a complex strategy for meeting human needs. Drawing from the philosophical doctrine of *idealism*, this approach considers values to be the core of a culture (Parsons, 1966; R. M. Williams, 1970). In other words, cultural values direct our lives, give meaning to what we do, and bind people together. Countless other cultural traits have various functions that support the operation of society.

Thinking functionally helps us understand unfamiliar ways of life. Consider the Amish farmer in central Ohio plowing hundreds of acres with a team of horses. His methods may violate the U.S. cultural value of efficiency, but from the Amish point of view, hard work functions to develop the discipline necessary for a devoutly religious way of life. Long days of working together not only make the Amish self-sufficient but also strengthen family ties and unify local communities.

Of course, Amish practices have dysfunctions as well. The hard work and strict religious discipline are too demanding for some, who end up leaving the community. Also, strong religious beliefs sometimes prevent compromise, and as a result, slight differences in religious practices have caused the Amish to divide into different communities (Kraybill, 1989; Kraybill & Olshan, 1994).

If cultures are strategies for meeting human needs, we would expect to find many common patterns around the world. **Cultural universals** are *traits that are part of every known culture.* Comparing hundreds of cultures, George Murdock (1945) identified dozens of cultural universals. One common element is the family, which functions everywhere to control sexual reproduction and to oversee the care of children. Funeral rites, too, are found everywhere because all human communities cope with the reality of death. Jokes are another cultural universal, serving as a safe means of releasing social tensions.

○ **CRITICAL REVIEW** The strength of structural-functional analysis lies in showing how culture operates to meet human needs. Yet by emphasizing a society's dominant cultural patterns, this approach largely ignores cultural diversity. Also, because this approach emphasizes cultural stability, it downplays the importance of change. In short, cultural systems are neither as stable nor as universal as structural-functional analysis leads us to believe. The Applying Theory table summarizes this theoretical approach's main lessons about culture and places it alongside two other approaches that we consider next.

○ **CHECK YOUR LEARNING** In the United States, what are some of the functions of sports, July Fourth celebrations, and Black History Month?

Inequality and Culture: Social-Conflict Analysis

The social-conflict approach draws attention to the link between culture and inequality. From this point of view, any cultural trait benefits some members of society at the expense of others.

Why do certain values dominate a society in the first place? Many conflict theorists, especially Marxists, argue that culture is shaped by a society's system of economic production. Social-conflict theory, then, is rooted in the philosophical doctrine of *materialism*, which holds that a society's system of material production (such as our own capitalist economy) has a powerful effect on the rest of the culture. This materialist approach contrasts with the idealistic leanings of structural-functionalism.

Social-conflict analysis ties our society's cultural values of competitiveness and material success to our country's capitalist economy, which serves the interests of the nation's wealthy elite. The culture of capitalism teaches us to think that rich and powerful people work harder or longer than others and that they therefore deserve their wealth and privileges. It also encourages us to view capitalism as somehow "natural," discouraging us from trying to reduce economic inequality.

Eventually, however, the strains of inequality erupt into movements for social change. Two examples are the civil rights movement and the women's movement. Both sought greater equality, and both encountered opposition from defenders of the status quo.

○ **CRITICAL REVIEW** The social-conflict approach suggests that cultural systems do not address human needs equally, allowing some people to dominate others. This inequality in turn generates pressure toward change.

Yet by stressing the divisiveness of culture, this approach understates ways in which cultural patterns integrate members of a society. Thus we should consider both social-conflict and structural-functional insights for a fuller understanding of culture.

○ Making the Grade

The concept "cultural universal" is an older concept linked to the structural-functional approach. It is based on the idea that if some cultural trait is found everywhere, it must be very useful for society.

○ Making the Grade

Because multiculturalism supports greater social equality for people of various cultural backgrounds, this theory falls within sociology's social-conflict approach.

● APPLYING THEORY ●

Culture

	Structural-Functional Approach	Social-Conflict Approach	Sociobiology Approach
What is the level of analysis?	Macro-level	Macro-level	Macro-level
What is culture?	Culture is a system of behavior by which members of societies cooperate to meet their needs.	Culture is a system that benefits some people and disadvantages others.	Culture is a system of behavior that is partly shaped by human biology.
What is the foundation of culture?	Cultural patterns are rooted in a society's core values and beliefs.	Cultural patterns are rooted in a society's system of economic production.	Cultural patterns are rooted in humanity's biological evolution.
What core questions does the approach ask?	How does a cultural pattern help society operate? What cultural patterns are found in all societies?	How does a cultural pattern benefit some people and harm others? How does a cultural pattern support social inequality?	How does a cultural pattern help a species adapt to its environment?

└○ **CHECK YOUR LEARNING**　How might a social-conflict analysis of college fraternities and sororities differ from a structural-functional analysis?

Evolution and Culture: Sociobiology

We know that culture is a human creation, but does human biology influence how this process unfolds? A third way of thinking, standing with one leg in biology and the other in sociology, is **sociobiology,** *a theoretical approach that explores ways in which human biology affects how we create culture.*

Sociobiology rests on the theory of evolution proposed by Charles Darwin in his book *On the Origin of Species* (1859). Darwin asserted that living organisms change over long periods of time as a result of *natural selection*, a matter of four simple principles. First, all living things live to reproduce themselves. Second, the blueprint for reproduction is in the genes, the basic units of life that carry traits of one generation into the next. Third, some random variation in genes allows each species to "try out" new life patterns in a particular environment. This variation enables some organisms to survive better than others and to pass on their advantageous genes to their offspring. Fourth and finally, over thousands of generations, the genes that promote reproduction survive and become dominant. In this way, as biologists say, a species *adapts* to its environment, and dominant traits emerge as the "nature" of the organism.

Sociobiologists claim that the large number of cultural universals reflects the fact that all humans are members of a single biological species. It is our common biology that underlies, for example, the apparently universal "double standard" of sexual behavior. As the sex researcher Alfred Kinsey put it, "Among all people everywhere in the world, the male is more likely than the female to desire sex with a variety of partners" (quoted in Barash, 1981:49). But why?

We all know that children result from joining a woman's egg with a man's sperm. But the biological significance of a single sperm is very different from that of a single egg. For healthy men, sperm is a "renewable resource" produced by the testes throughout most of the life course. A man releases hundreds of millions of sperm in a single ejaculation (Barash, 1981:47). A newborn girl's ovaries, however, contain her entire lifetime supply of follicles, or immature eggs. A woman releases a single egg cell from the ovaries each month. So although men are biologically capable of fathering thousands of offspring, a woman is able to bear only a relatively small number of children.

Given this biological difference, men reproduce their genes most efficiently by being promiscuous—readily engaging in sex. But women look at reproduction differently. Each of a woman's pregnancies demands that she carry the child, give birth, and provide care for some time afterward. Efficient reproduction on the part of the woman therefore depends on selecting a man whose qualities (beginning with the likelihood that he will simply stay around) will contribute to her child's survival and, later, successful reproduction.

Making the Grade

Theories dealing with how biology affects human behavior do not have wide support in sociobiology. Sociobiology is a theory—supported by some sociologists, not by others—that has one foot in biology and the other in sociology.

Seeing Sociology in Everyday Life

What might be a sociobiological analysis of sibling rivalry? In other words, why do siblings often fight? Why do siblings often join forces when threatened by an "outsider"?

The double standard certainly involves more than biology and is tangled up with the historical domination of women by men. But sociobiology suggests that this cultural pattern, like many others, has an underlying "bio-logic." Simply put, the double standard exists around the world because women and men everywhere tend toward distinctive reproductive strategies.

CRITICAL REVIEW Sociobiology has generated intriguing insights into the biological roots of some cultural patterns. But this approach remains controversial for two reasons.

First, some critics fear that sociobiology may revive the biological arguments of a century ago that claimed the superiority of one race or sex. But defenders counter that sociobiology rejects the past pseudoscience of racial and gender superiority. In fact, they say, sociobiology unites all humanity because all people share a single evolutionary history. Sociobiology does assert that men and women differ biologically in some ways that culture cannot easily overcome. But far from claiming that males are somehow more important than females, sociobiology emphasizes that both sexes are vital to human reproduction and survival.

Second, say the critics, sociobiologists have little evidence to support their theories. Research to date suggests that biological forces do not *determine* human behavior in any rigid sense. Rather, humans *learn* behavior within a culture. The contribution of sociobiology, then, includes explaining why some cultural patterns are more common and seem easier to learn than others (Barash, 1981).

CHECK YOUR LEARNING Using the sociobiology approach, explain why some cultural patterns, such as sibling rivalry (the fact that children in the same family often compete and even fight with each other), are widespread.

Because any analysis of culture requires a broad focus on the workings of society, the three approaches discussed in this chapter are macro-level in scope. The symbolic-interaction approach, with its micro-level focus on people's behavior in specific situations, will be explored in Chapter 4 ("Social Interaction in Everyday Life").

Culture and Human Freedom

This entire chapter leads us to ask an important question: To what extent are human beings, as cultural creatures, free? Does culture bind us to each other and to the past? Or does it enhance our capacity for individual thought and independent choice?

As symbolic creatures, humans cannot live without culture. But the capacity for culture does have some drawbacks. We may be the only animals who name ourselves, but living in a symbolic world means that we are also the only creatures who experience alienation. In addition, culture is largely a matter of habit, which limits our choices and drives us to repeat troubling patterns, such as racial prejudice and gender discrimination, in each new generation.

Our society's emphasis on personal achievement urges us toward excellence, yet this same competitive behavior also isolates us from one another. Material things comfort us in some ways but divert us from the security and satisfaction that come from close relationships and spiritual strength.

For better and worse, human beings are cultural creatures, just as ants and bees are prisoners of their biology. But there is a crucial difference. Biological instincts create a ready-made world; culture forces us to choose as we make and remake a world for ourselves. No better evidence of this freedom exists than the cultural diversity of our own society and the even greater human diversity around the world.

Learning about this cultural diversity is one goal shared by sociologists. The Thinking Globally box offers some contrasts between the cultures of the United States and Canada. Wherever we may live, the better we understand the workings of the surrounding culture, the better prepared we will be to use the freedom it offers us.

Using an evolutionary perspective, sociobiologists explain that different reproductive strategies give rise to a double standard: Men treat women as sexual objects more than women treat men that way. While this may be so, many sociologists counter that behavior—such as that shown here—is more correctly understood as resulting from a culture of male domination.

THINKING GLOBALLY

The United States and Canada: Two National Cultures or One?

The United States and Canada are two of the largest high-income nations in the world, and they share a common border of about 4,000 miles. But do the United States and Canada share the same culture?

One important point to make right away is that both nations are *multicultural*. Not only do both countries have hundreds of Native American societies, but immigration has also brought people from all over the world to both the United States and Canada. In both countries, most early immigrants came from Europe, but in recent years, most immigrants have come from nations in Asia and Latin America. The Canadian city of Vancouver, for example, has a Chinese community about the same size as the Latino community in Los Angeles.

Canada differs from the United States in one important respect—historically, Canada has had *two* dominant cultures: French (about 16 percent of the population) and British (roughly 36 percent). Almost one-third of people in the provinces of Quebec (where French is the official language) and New Brunswick (which is officially bilingual) claim some French ancestry.

Are the dominant values of Canada much the same as those we have described for the United States? Seymour Martin Lipset (1985) finds that they differ to some degree. The United States declared its independence from Great Britain in 1776; Canada did not formally separate from Great Britain until 1982, and the British monarch is still Canada's official head of state. Thus, Lipset continues, the dominant culture of Canada lies between the culture of the United States and that of Great Britain.

The culture of the United States is more individualistic, and Canada's is more collective. In the United States, individualism is seen in the historical importance of the cowboy, a self-sufficient loner, and even outlaws such as Jesse James and Billy the Kid are regarded as heroes because they challenged authority. In Canada, it is the Mountie—Canada's well-known police officer on horseback—who is looked on with

great respect. Canada's greater emphasis on collective life is also evident in stronger unions: Canadian workers are almost three times as likely to be members of a union as workers in the United States (Steyn, 2008).

Politically, people in the United States tend to think that individuals ought to do things for themselves. In Canada, much as in Great Britain, there is a strong sense that government should look after the interests of everyone. The U.S. Constitution emphasizes the importance of "life, liberty, and the pursuit of happiness" (words that place importance on the individual), while Canadian society is based on "peace, order, and good government" (words that place importance on the government) (Steyn, 2008). One clear result of this difference today is that Canada has a much broader social welfare system (including universal health care) than the United States (the only high-income nation without such a program). It also helps explain the

fact that about one-third of all households in the United States own one or more guns, and the idea that individuals are entitled to own a gun, although controversial, is widespread. In Canada, by contrast, few households have a gun, and the government restricts gun ownership, as in Great Britain.

WHAT DO YOU THINK?

1. Why do you think some Canadians feel that their way of life is overshadowed by that of the United States?

2. Ask your friends to name the capital city of Canada (the correct answer is Ottawa, in the province of Ontario). Are you surprised by how few know the answer? Why or why not?

3. Why do many people in the United States not know very much about either Canada or Mexico, countries with which we share long borders?

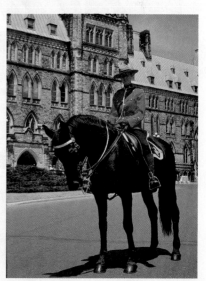

The individuals that a society celebrates as heroic are a good indication of that society's cultural values. In the United States, outlaws such as Jesse James (and later, Bonnie and Clyde) were regarded as heroes because they represented the individual standing strong against authority. In Canada, by contrast, people have always looked up to the Mountie, who symbolizes society's authority over the individual.

Seeing Sociology in Everyday Life

What clues do we have to a society's cultural values?

The values of any society—that is, what that society thinks is important—are reflected in various aspects of everyday life, including the things people have and the ways they behave. An interesting way to "read" our own culture's values is to look at the "superheroes" that we celebrate. Take a look at the characters in the three photos below, and in each case, describe what makes the character special and what each character represents in cultural terms.

Superman first appeared in an *Action Comic* book in 1938, as the United States struggled to climb out of economic depression and faced the rising danger of war. Since then, Superman has been featured in a television show as well as in a string of Hollywood films. One trait of most superheroes is that they have a secret identity; in this case, Superman's everyday identity is "mild-mannered news reporter" Clark Kent.

Buffy, the Vampire Slayer, a more recent star of television, film, comic books, and video games, is a rare example of a woman playing a superhero character.

HINT Superman (as well as Spider-Man and Buffy) defines our society as good; after all, Superman fights for "truth, justice, and the American way." Many superheroes have stories that draw on great people in our cultural history, including religious figures such as Moses and Jesus: They have mysterious origins (we never really know their true families), they are "tested" through great moral challenges, and they finally succeed in overcoming all obstacles. (Today's superheroes, however, are likely to win the day using force and often violence.) Having a "secret identity" means that superheroes can lead ordinary lives (and means we ordinary people can imagine being superheroes). But to keep their focus on fighting evil, superheroes must place their work ahead of any romantic interests ("Work comes first!"). Buffy also illustrates the special challenge to "do it all" faced by women in our society: Constantly called on to fight evil, she still must make time for her studies as well as her friends.

Another longtime superhero important to our culture is Spider-Man. In all three *Spider-Man* movies, Peter Parker (who transforms into Spider-Man when he confronts evil) is secretly in love with Mary Jane Watson, but—in true superhero style—he does not allow himself to follow his heart.

Applying SOCIOLOGY in Everyday Life

1. What traits define popular culture "heroes" such as Clint Eastwood's film character Dirty Harry, Sylvester Stallone's film characters Rocky and Rambo, and Arnold Schwarzenegger's character The Terminator?

2. Ask someone in the class who has lived in another country how the culture of that nation differs from the way of life here. Look for ways in which this person sees or understands U.S. culture differently from people who have lived here all their lives.

3. Watch a Disney film such as *Finding Nemo*, *The Lion King*, *The Little Mermaid*, *Aladdin*, or *Pocahontas*. One reason for the popularity of these films is that they all share culture themes that are important to our society. Using the list of key values of U.S. culture on pages 44–46, explain what makes any of these films "American."

Making the Grade

CHAPTER 2 Culture

What Is Culture?

👁 Watch on mysoclab.com

Culture is a **WAY OF LIFE**.
- Culture is shared by members of a society.
- Culture shapes how we act, think, and feel.

pp. 38–40

Culture is a **HUMAN TRAIT**.
- Although several species display a limited capacity for culture, only human beings rely on culture for survival.

p. 40

Culture is a **PRODUCT OF EVOLUTION**.
- As the human brain evolved, culture replaced biological instincts as our species' primary strategy for survival.

pp. 40–42

culture (p. 38) the ways of thinking, the ways of acting, and the material objects that together form a people's way of life

society (p. 40) people who interact in a defined territory and share a culture

culture shock (p. 40) personal disorientation when experiencing an unfamiliar way of life

- We experience **CULTURE SHOCK** when we enter an unfamiliar culture and are not able to "read" meaning in our new surroundings.
- We create culture shock for others when we act in ways they do not understand.

p. 40

✓ Approximately 200 different cultures exist in the United States. Worldwide, there are roughly 7,000 different cultures (pp. 41–42).

The Elements of Culture

Culture relies on **SYMBOLS** in the form of words, gestures, and actions to express meaning.

p. 42

LANGUAGE is the symbolic system by which one generation transmits culture to the next.

pp. 42–44

VALUES are abstract standards of what *ought to be* (for example, equality of opportunity).
BELIEFS are specific statements that people who share a culture hold to be true (for example, "A qualified woman could be elected president").

pp. 44–46

NORMS, which guide human behavior, are of two types:
- **mores** (for example, sexual taboos), which have great moral significance
- **folkways** (for example, greetings or dining etiquette), which are matters of everyday politeness

pp. 46–47

symbol (p. 42) anything that carries a particular meaning recognized by people who share a culture

language (p. 42) a system of symbols that allows people to communicate with one another

cultural transmission (p. 43) the process by which one generation passes culture to the next

Sapir-Whorf thesis (p. 44) the idea that people see and understand the world through the cultural lens of language

values (p. 44) culturally defined standards that people use to decide what is desirable, good, and beautiful and that serve as broad guidelines for social living

beliefs (p. 44) specific ideas that people hold to be true

norms (p. 46) rules and expectations by which a society guides the behavior of its members

mores (p. 47) norms that are widely observed and have great moral significance

folkways (p. 47) norms for routine or casual interaction

✓ Values and norms (standards for how we should behave) reflect **ideal culture**, which differs from **real culture** (what actually occurs in everyday life) (p. 47).

Technology and Culture

Culture is shaped by **TECHNOLOGY**. We understand technological development in terms of stages of **SOCIOCULTURAL EVOLUTION**:
- hunting and gathering
- horticulture and pastoralism
- agriculture
- industry
- postindustrial information technology

pp. 47–49

technology (p. 47) knowledge that people use to make a way of life in their surroundings

hunting and gathering (p. 48) the use of simple tools to hunt animals and gather vegetation for food

horticulture (p. 48) the use of hand tools to raise crops

pastoralism (p. 48) the domestication of animals

agriculture (p. 49) large-scale cultivation using plows harnessed to animals or more powerful energy sources

industry (p. 49) the production of goods using advanced sources of energy to drive large machinery

postindustrialism (p. 49) the production of information using computer technology

✓ Members of societies that possess sophisticated technology should be careful not to judge cultures with simpler technology as inferior (p. 49).

Cultural Diversity

We live in a **CULTURALLY DIVERSE SOCIETY**.
- This diversity is due to our history of immigration.
- Diversity reflects regional differences.
- Diversity reflects differences in social class that set off **high culture** (available only to elites) from **popular culture** (available to average people).

pp. 49–50

A number of values are central to our way of life. But **CULTURAL PATTERNS** are not the same throughout our society.
- **Subculture** is based on differences in interests as well as life experiences.
- **Multiculturalism** is an effort to enhance appreciation of cultural diversity.
- **Counterculture** is strongly at odds with conventional ways of life.

pp. 50–52

CULTURAL CHANGE results from
- **invention** (examples include the telephone and the computer)
- **discovery** (for example, the recognition that women are capable of political leadership)
- **diffusion** (for example, the growing popularity of various ethnic foods and musical styles)

CULTURAL LAG results when some parts of a cultural system change faster than others.

pp. 52–53

How do we understand cultural differences?
- **ETHNOCENTRISM** links people to their society but can cause misunderstanding and conflict between societies.
- **CULTURAL RELATIVISM** is increasingly important as people of the world come into more and more contact with each other.

pp. 53–56

Read on **mysoclab.com**

Explore on **mysoclab.com**

✓ Global cultural patterns result from the worldwide flow of goods, information, and people (pp. 56–57).

high culture (p. 50) cultural patterns that distinguish a society's elite

popular culture (p. 50) cultural patterns that are widespread among a society's population

subculture (p. 50) cultural patterns that set apart some segment of a society's population

multiculturalism (p. 51) a perspective recognizing the cultural diversity of the United States and promoting equal standing for all cultural traditions

Eurocentrism (p. 51) the dominance of European (especially English) cultural patterns

Afrocentrism (p. 51) emphasizing and promoting African cultural patterns

counterculture (p. 52) cultural patterns that strongly oppose those widely accepted within a society

cultural integration (p. 52) the close relationships among various elements of a cultural system

cultural lag (p. 52) the fact that some cultural elements change more quickly than others, disrupting a cultural system

ethnocentrism (p. 54) the practice of judging another culture by the standards of one's own culture

cultural relativism (p. 55) the practice of judging a culture by its own standards

Theoretical Analysis of Culture

The **STRUCTURAL-FUNCTIONAL APPROACH** views culture as a relatively stable system built on core values. All cultural patterns play some part in the ongoing operation of society.

p. 58

The **SOCIAL-CONFLICT APPROACH** sees culture as a dynamic arena of inequality and conflict. Cultural patterns benefit some categories of people more than others.

p. 58

SOCIOBIOLOGY explores how the long history of evolution has shaped patterns of culture in today's world.

pp. 59–60

cultural universals (p. 58) traits that are part of every known culture

sociobiology (p. 59) a theoretical approach that explores ways in which human biology affects how we create culture

See the Applying Theory table on page 59.

Culture and Human Freedom

- Culture can limit the choices we make.
- As cultural creatures, we have the capacity to shape and reshape our world to meet our needs and pursue our dreams.

p. 60

3 Socialization: From Infancy to Old Age

- Why is social experience the key to human personality?

- What familiar social settings have special importance to how we live and grow?

- How do our experiences change over the life course?

On a cold winter day in 1938, a social worker walked quickly to the door of a rural Pennsylvania farmhouse. Sent to investigate a case of possible child abuse, the social worker entered the house and soon discovered a five-year-old girl hidden in a second-floor storage room. The child, whose name was Anna, was wedged into an old chair with her arms tied securely above her head so that she couldn't move. She was wearing filthy clothes, and her arms and legs were as thin as matchsticks (K. Davis, 1940).

Anna's situation can only be described as tragic. She was born in 1932 to an unmarried and mentally impaired woman of twenty-six who lived with her strict father. Angry about his daughter's "illegitimate" motherhood, the grandfather did not even want the child in his house, so for the first six months of her life, Anna was passed among various welfare agencies. But her mother could not afford to pay for her care, and Anna returned to the hostile home of her grandfather.

To lessen the grandfather's anger, Anna's mother kept the child in the storage room and gave her just enough milk to keep her alive. There she stayed—day after day, month after month, with almost no human contact—for five long years.

Learning about Anna's rescue, the sociologist Kingsley Davis immediately went to see the child. He found her with local officials at a county home. Davis was stunned by the emaciated girl, who could not laugh, speak, or even smile. Anna was completely unresponsive, as if alone in an empty world.

Social Experience: The Key to Our Humanity

Socialization is so basic to human development that we sometimes overlook its importance. But in this terrible case of an isolated child, we can see what humans would be like without social contact. Although physically alive, Anna hardly seems human. We can see that without social experience, a child is not able to act or communicate in a meaningful way and seems to be as much an object as a person.

Sociologists use the term **socialization** to refer to *the lifelong social experience by which people develop their human potential and learn culture.* Unlike other species, whose behavior is biologically set, humans need social experience to learn their culture and to survive. Social experience is also the basis of **personality,** *a person's fairly consistent patterns of acting, thinking, and feeling.* We build a personality by internalizing—taking in—our surroundings. But without social experience, as Anna's case shows, personality hardly develops at all.

Human Development: Nature and Nurture

Anna's case makes clear the fact that humans depend on others to provide the care needed not only for physical growth but also for personality to develop. A century ago, however, people mistakenly believed that humans were born with instincts that determined their personality and behavior.

The Biological Sciences: The Role of Nature

Charles Darwin's groundbreaking study of evolution, described in Chapter 2 ("Culture"), led people to think incorrectly that human behavior was instinctive, simply our "nature." Such ideas led to claims that the U.S. economic system reflects "instinctive human competitiveness," that some people are "born criminals," or that women are "naturally" emotional and men are "naturally" more rational.

People trying to understand cultural diversity also misunderstood Darwin's thinking. Centuries of world exploration had taught Western Europeans that people around the world behaved quite differently from society to society. But Europeans linked these differences to

○ Making the Grade

Sociologists and others have long debated the relative importance of biology (nature) and social environment (nurture). Cases of isolated children show that nurture is crucial to human development. But the text ends up avoiding a "nature versus nurture" argument in favor of linking the two concepts: It is human nature to nurture.

biology rather than culture. It was an easy, although incorrect and very damaging, step to claim that members of technologically simple societies were biologically less evolved and therefore "less human." This ethnocentric view helped justify colonialism: Why not take advantage of others if they seem not to be as "fully human" as you are?

The Social Sciences: The Role of Nurture

In the twentieth century, biological explanations of human behavior came under fire. The psychologist John B. Watson (1878–1958) developed a theory called *behaviorism*, which held that behavior is not instinctive but learned. Thus people everywhere are equally human, differing only in their cultural patterns. In short, Watson rooted human behavior not in nature but in *nurture*.

Today, social scientists are cautious about describing *any* human behavior as instinctive. This does not mean that biology plays no part in human behavior. Human life, after all, depends on the functioning of the body. We also know that children often share biological traits (such as height and hair color) with their parents and that heredity plays a part in intelligence, musical and artistic talent, and personality (such as how you deal with frustration). However, whether you develop your inherited potential depends on how you are raised. For example, if children do not use their brain early in life, the brain fails to develop fully (Goldsmith, 1983; Begley, 1995).

Without denying the importance of nature, then, nurture matters more in shaping human behavior. More precisely, *nurture is our nature.*

Social Isolation

As the story of Anna shows, cutting people off from the social world is very harmful. For ethical reasons, researchers can never place human beings in total isolation to study what happens. But in the past, they have studied the effects of social isolation on nonhuman primates.

Research with Monkeys

In a classic study, the psychologists Harry and Margaret Harlow (1962) placed rhesus monkeys—whose behavior is in some ways surprisingly similar to human behavior—in various conditions of social isolation. They found that complete isolation (with adequate nutrition) for even six months seriously disturbed the monkeys' development. When returned to their group, these monkeys were passive, anxious, and fearful.

The Harlows then placed infant rhesus monkeys in cages with an artificial "mother" made of wire mesh with a wooden head and the nipple of a feeding tube where the breast would be. These monkeys

also survived but were unable to interact with others when placed in a group.

But monkeys in a third category, isolated with an artificial "mother" covered with soft terry cloth, did better. Each of these monkeys would cling to the "mother" closely. Because these monkeys showed less developmental damage than the earlier groups, the Harlows concluded that the monkeys benefited from this closeness. The experiment confirmed how important it is that adults cradle infants affectionately.

Finally, the Harlows discovered that infant monkeys could recover from as much as three months of isolation. But after about six months, isolation caused irreversible emotional and behavioral damage.

Studies of Isolated Children

The rest of Anna's story squares with the Harlows' findings. After her discovery, Anna received extensive social contact and soon showed improvement. When Kingsley Davis (1940) revisited her after ten days, he found her more alert and even smiling (perhaps for the first time in her life!). Over the next year, Anna made slow but steady progress, showing more interest in other people and gradually learning to walk. After a year and a half, she could feed herself and play with toys.

But as the Harlows might have predicted, Anna's five years of social isolation had caused permanent damage. At age eight, her mental development was still less than that of a two-year-old. Not until she was almost ten did she begin to use words. Because Anna's mother was mentally retarded, perhaps Anna was also. The riddle was never solved, however, because Anna died at age ten of a blood disorder, possibly related to the years of abuse she suffered (K. Davis, 1940, 1947).

A more recent case of childhood isolation involves a California girl abused by her parents (Curtiss, 1977; Rymer, 1994). From the time she was two, Genie was tied to a potty chair in a dark garage. In 1970, when she was rescued at age thirteen, Genie weighed only 59 pounds and had the mental development of a one-year-old. With intensive treatment, she became physically healthy, but her language ability remains that of a young child. Today, Genie lives in a home for developmentally disabled adults.

○ **CRITICAL REVIEW** All evidence points to the crucial role of social experience in forming personality. Human beings can sometimes recover from abuse and short-term isolation. But there is a point—exactly when is unclear from the small number of cases studied—at which isolation in infancy causes permanent developmental damage.

○ **CHECK YOUR LEARNING** What do studies of isolated children teach us about the importance of social experience?

Freud's Model of Personality

id Freud's term for the human being's basic drives → **ego** Freud's term for a person's conscious efforts to balance innate pleasure-seeking drives with the demands of society → **superego** Freud's term for the cultural values and norms internalized by an individual

Seeing Sociology in Everyday Life

Using Piaget's concepts, can you explain why young children will reach for a nickel rather than a dime?

Understanding Socialization

Socialization is a complex, lifelong process. The following sections highlight the work of six researchers—Sigmund Freud, Jean Piaget, Lawrence Kohlberg, Carol Gilligan, George Herbert Mead, and Erik H. Erikson—who made lasting contributions to our understanding of human development.

The personalities we develop depend largely on the environment in which we live. When a child's world is shredded by violence, the damage can be profound and lasting. This drawing was made by thirteen-year-old Rahid in the Darfur region of Sudan, where armed militia have killed more than 300,000 people since 2003. What are the likely effects of such experiences on a young person's self-confidence and capacity to form trusting ties with others?

Courtesy of Dr. Annie Sparrow, Human Rights Watch.

Sigmund Freud's Elements of Personality

Sigmund Freud (1856–1939) lived in Vienna at a time when most Europeans considered human behavior biologically fixed. Trained as a physician, Freud turned to the study of personality and eventually developed the celebrated theory of psychoanalysis.

Basic Human Needs

Freud claimed that biology plays a major part in human development, although not in terms of specific instincts, as is the case in other species. Rather, he theorized that humans have two basic needs or drives that are present at birth. First is a need for bonding, which he called the "life instinct," or *eros* (named after the Greek god of love). Second, we share an aggressive drive he called the "death instinct," or *thanatos* (the Greek word for "death"). These opposing forces, operating at an unconscious level, create deep inner tension.

Freud's Model of Personality

Freud combined basic human drives and the influence of society into a model of personality with three parts: id, ego, and superego. The **id** (Latin for "it") represents *the human being's basic drives*, which are unconscious and demand immediate satisfaction. Rooted in biology, the id is present at birth, making a newborn a bundle of demands for attention, touching, and food. But society opposes the self-centered id, which is why one of the first words a child usually learns is "no."

To avoid frustration, a child must learn to approach the world realistically. This is done through the **ego** (Latin for "I"), which is *a person's conscious efforts to balance innate pleasure-seeking drives with the demands of society*. The ego arises as we gain awareness of our distinct existence and face the fact that we cannot have everything we want.

In the human personality, **superego** (Latin for "above or beyond the ego") is *the cultural values and norms internalized by an individual*. The superego operates as our conscience, telling us *why* we cannot have everything we want. The superego begins to form as a child becomes aware of parental demands and matures as the child comes to understand that everyone's behavior should take account of cultural norms.

Personality Development

To the id-centered child, the world is a jumble of physical sensations that bring either pleasure or pain. As the superego develops, however, the child learns the moral concepts of right and wrong. Initially, in other words, children can feel good only in a physical way (as when being held and cuddled), but after three or four years, they feel good or bad according to how they judge their behavior against cultural norms (doing "the right thing").

Piaget's Stages of Development

sensorimotor stage
Piaget's term for the level of human development at which individuals experience the world only through their senses

→

preoperational stage
Piaget's term for the level of human development at which individuals first use language and other symbols

→

concrete operational stage
Piaget's term for the level of human development at which individuals first see causal connections in their surroundings

→

formal operational stage
Piaget's term for the level of human development at which individuals think abstractly and critically

The id and the superego remain in conflict, but in a well-adjusted person, the ego manages these opposing forces. If conflicts are not resolved during childhood, they may surface as personality disorders later on.

Culture, in the form of superego, *represses* selfish demands, forcing people to look beyond their own desires. Often the competing demands of self and society result in a compromise Freud called *sublimation*, which changes selfish drives into socially acceptable behavior. For example, marriage makes the satisfaction of sexual urges socially acceptable, and competitive sports are an outlet for aggression.

CRITICAL REVIEW In Freud's time, few people were ready to accept sex as a basic drive. More recent critics have charged that Freud's work presents humans in male terms and devalues women (Donovan & Littenberg, 1982). Freud's theories are also difficult to test scientifically. But Freud influenced everyone who later studied human personality. Of special importance to sociology are his ideas that we internalize social norms and that childhood experiences have a lasting impact on personality.

CHECK YOUR LEARNING What are the three elements in Freud's model of personality? What does each one mean?

Jean Piaget's Theory of Cognitive Development

The Swiss psychologist Jean Piaget (1896–1980) studied human *cognition*, how people think and understand. As Piaget watched his own three children grow, he wondered not just what they knew but how they made sense of the world. Piaget went on to identify four stages of cognitive development.

The Sensorimotor Stage

Stage one is the **sensorimotor stage,** *the level of human development at which individuals experience the world only through their senses.* For about the first two years of life, infants know the world only by touching, tasting, smelling, looking, and listening. "Knowing" to very young children amounts to what their senses tell them.

The Preoperational Stage

About age two, children enter the **preoperational stage,** *the level of human development at which individuals first use language and other symbols.* Now children begin to think about the world using their imagination. But "pre-op" children between about two and six attach meanings only to specific experiences and objects. They can identify a toy as their "favorite" but cannot describe what *types* of toys they like.

Lacking abstract concepts, a child cannot judge size, weight, or volume. In one of his best-known experiments, Piaget placed two

identical glasses containing equal amounts of water on a table. He asked several five- and six-year-olds whether the amount in each was the same. They nodded that it was. The children then watched Piaget take one of the glasses and pour its contents into a taller, narrower glass, raising the level of the water. He asked again whether each glass held the same amount. The typical five- or six-year-old now insisted that the taller glass held more water. By about age seven, children are able to think more abstractly and realize that the amount of water stays the same.

The Concrete Operational Stage

Next comes the **concrete operational stage,** *the level of human development at which individuals first see causal connections in their surroundings.* Between the ages of seven and eleven, children focus on how and why things happen. In addition, they attach more than one symbol to an event or object. If, for example, you say to a child of five, "Today is Wednesday," she might respond, "No, it's my birthday!" indicating that she can use just one symbol at a time. But an older child at the concrete operational stage would be able to respond, "Yes, and it's also my birthday."

The Formal Operational Stage

The last step in Piaget's model is the **formal operational stage,** *the level of human development at which individuals think abstractly and critically.* At about age twelve, young people begin to reason in the abstract rather than think only of concrete situations. For example, if you ask a child of seven, "What would you like to be when you grow up?" you will get a concrete response such as "a teacher." But most teenagers can consider the question more abstractly and might respond, "I would like a job that helps others." As they gain the capacity for abstract thought, young people also learn to understand metaphors. Hearing the phrase "A penny for your thoughts" might lead a child to ask for a coin, but a teenager will recognize a gentle invitation to intimacy.

CRITICAL REVIEW Freud saw human beings passively torn by opposing forces of biology and culture. Piaget saw the mind as active and creative. He saw the ability to engage the world unfolding in stages as the result of both biological maturation and social experience.

But do people in all societies pass through all four of Piaget's stages? Living in a traditional society that changes slowly probably limits the capacity for abstract and critical thought. Even in the United States, perhaps 30 percent of people never reach the formal operational stage (Kohlberg & Gilligan, 1971).

CHECK YOUR LEARNING What are Piaget's four stages of cognitive development? What does his theory teach us about socialization?

Making the Grade

Kohlberg's theory is similar to Piaget's theory, but Kohlberg focuses on one aspect of cognition—moral reasoning. Gilligan's theory is similar to Kohlberg's theory, but she focuses on the link between gender and moral reasoning.

self George Herbert Mead's term for the part of an individual's personality composed of self-awareness and self-image

looking-glass self Charles Horton Cooley's term for a self-image based on how we think others see us

Lawrence Kohlberg's Theory of Moral Development

Lawrence Kohlberg (1981) built on Piaget's work to study *moral reasoning,* how people come to judge situations as right or wrong. Here again, development occurs in stages.

Young children who experience the world in terms of pain and pleasure (Piaget's sensorimotor stage) are at the *preconventional* level of moral development. At first, "rightness" amounts to "what feels good to me." For example, a child may reach for something on a table that looks shiny, which is the reason parents of young children have to "childproof" their homes.

The *conventional* level, Kohlberg's second stage, appears by the teens (corresponding to Piaget's final, formal operational stage). At this point, young people lose some of their selfishness as they learn to define right and wrong in terms of what pleases parents and conforms to cultural norms. At this stage, individuals also become aware of not just action but also intention. They might realize, for example, that stealing food for hungry children is not the same as stealing an iPod to sell for pocket change.

In Kohlberg's final stage of moral development, the *postconventional* level, people move beyond their society's norms to consider abstract ethical principles. As they think about ideas such as liberty, freedom, or justice, they may argue that what is lawful still may not be right. When the African American civil rights activist Rosa Parks refused to give up her seat on a Montgomery, Alabama, bus back in 1955, she violated that city's segregation laws in order to call attention to the injustice of those laws.

CRITICAL REVIEW Like the work of Piaget, Kohlberg's model explains moral development in terms of distinct stages. But whether this model applies to people in all societies remains unclear. Further, many people in the United States apparently never reach the postconventional level of moral reasoning, although exactly why is still an open question.

Childhood is a time to learn principles of right and wrong. According to Carol Gilligan, however, boys and girls define what is "right" in different ways. After reading about Gilligan's theory, can you suggest what these two children might be arguing about?

Another problem with Kohlberg's research is that all his subjects were boys. He committed a common research error, described in Chapter 1 ("Sociology: Perspective, Theory, and Method"), by generalizing the results of male subjects to all people. This problem led a colleague, Carol Gilligan, to investigate how gender affects moral reasoning.

CHECK YOUR LEARNING What are Kohlberg's three stages of moral development? What does his theory teach us about socialization?

Carol Gilligan's Theory of Gender and Moral Development

Carol Gilligan (1982) set out to compare the moral development of girls and boys and concluded that the two sexes use different standards of rightness. Boys, she claims, have a *justice perspective,* relying on formal rules to define right and wrong. Girls, by contrast, have a *care and responsibility perspective,* judging a situation with an eye toward personal relationships and loyalties. For example, as boys see it, stealing is wrong because it breaks the law. Girls are more likely to wonder why someone would steal and to be sympathetic toward someone who steals, say, to feed her family.

Kohlberg treats rule-based male reasoning as morally superior to the person-based female perspective. Gilligan notes that impersonal rules have long governed men's lives in the workplace, but personal relationships are more relevant to women's lives as mothers and caregivers. Why, then, Gilligan asks, should we set up male standards as the norms by which to judge everyone?

CRITICAL REVIEW Gilligan's work sharpens our understanding of both human development and gender issues in research. Yet the question remains, does nature or nurture account for the differences between females and males? In Gilligan's view, cultural conditioning is at work, a view that finds support in other research. For example, Nancy Chodorow (1994) claims that children grow up in homes in which, typically, mothers do much more nurturing than fathers. As girls learn to identify with mothers, they become more concerned with care and responsibility to others. By contrast, boys become more like fathers, who are often

Go to the Multimedia Library at mysoclab.com to view the video "The Looking–Glass Self"

significant others people, such as parents, who have special importance for socialization

generalized other Mead's term for widespread cultural norms and values we use as a reference in evaluating ourselves

away from the home, and they may develop more detached personalities and a greater concern for abstract rules. Perhaps the moral reasoning of females and males will become more similar as more women organize their lives around the workplace.

CHECK YOUR LEARNING According to Gilligan, how do boys and girls differ in their approach to understanding right and wrong?

George Herbert Mead's Theory of the Social Self

George Herbert Mead (1863–1931) developed a theory of *social behaviorism* to explain how social experience develops an individual's personality (1962, orig. 1934).

The Self

Mead's central concept is the **self,** *the part of an individual's personality composed of self-awareness and self-image.* Mead's genius lay in seeing the self as the product of social experience.

First, said Mead, *the self develops only with social experience.* The self is not part of the body and does not exist at birth. Mead rejected the idea that personality is guided by biological drives (as Freud asserted) or even biological maturation (as Piaget claimed). For Mead, self develops only as the individual interacts with others. Without interaction, as we see from cases of isolated children, the body grows, but no self emerges.

Second, Mead explained, *social experience is the exchange of symbols.* Only people use words, a wave of the hand, or a smile to create meaning. We can train a dog using reward and punishment, but the dog attaches no meaning to its actions. By contrast, human beings find meaning in action by imagining people's underlying intentions. In short, a dog responds to *what you do*, but a human responds to *what you have in mind* as you do it. You can train a dog to go to the hallway and bring back an umbrella. But without understanding intention, if the dog cannot find the umbrella, it is incapable of the *human* response: to look for a raincoat instead.

Third, Mead continues, *understanding intention requires imagining a situation from the other's point of view.* Using symbols, we imagine ourselves in another person's shoes and see ourselves as that person does. This capacity lets us anticipate how others will respond to us even before we act. A simple toss of a ball, for example, requires stepping outside yourself to imagine how the other person will catch your throw. All symbolic interaction, then, involves seeing ourselves as others see us, a process Mead called *taking the role of the other.*

The Looking-Glass Self

In effect, others are a mirror (which people used to call a "looking glass") in which we see ourselves. What we think of ourselves, then, depends on how we think others see us. For example, if we think others see us as clever, we will think of ourselves in the same way. But if we feel they think of us as clumsy, then that is how we will see ourselves. Charles Horton Cooley (1864–1929) used the phrase **looking-glass self** to mean *a self-image based on how we think others see us* (1964, orig. 1902). Go to **mysoclab.com**

The I and the Me

Mead's fourth point is that *by taking the role of the other, we become self-aware.* Another way of saying this is that the self has two parts. One part of the self operates as subject, being active and spontaneous. Mead called the subjective side of the self the "I" (the subjective form of the personal pronoun). The other part of the self works as an object, the way we imagine others see us. Mead called the objective side of the self the "me" (the objective form of the personal pronoun). All social experience has both components: We initiate action (the I-phase, or subjective side, of the self), and we evaluate the action based on how others respond to us (the me-phase, or objective side, of the self).

Development of the Self

According to Mead, the key to developing the self is learning to take the role of the other. With limited social experience, infants can do this only through *imitation.* They mimic the behavior of other people without understanding the underlying intention, and so at this point, they have no self.

As children learn to use language and other symbols, the self emerges in the form of *play.* Play involves assuming roles modeled on **significant others,** *people, such as parents, who have special importance for socialization.* Playing "mommy" or "daddy" begins to teach children to imagine the world from a parent's point of view.

Gradually, children learn to take the roles of several others at once. This skill lets them move from simple play (say, playing catch) involving one other person to complex *games* (such as baseball) involving many others. By about age seven, most children have the social experience needed to engage in team sports.

Figure 3–1 on page 74 charts the progression from imitation to play to games. But there is a final stage in the development of the self. A game involves dealing with a limited number of other people in just one situation. Everyday life demands that we see ourselves in terms of cultural norms as *any* member of our society might. Mead used the term **generalized other** to refer to *widespread cultural norms and values we use as a reference in evaluating ourselves.*

As life goes on, the self continues to change along with our social experiences. But no matter how much the world shapes us, we always remain creative beings able to react to the world around us. Thus, Mead concluded, we play a key role in our own socialization.

○ Making the Grade

Be sure you understand how Mead's concepts—the I and the me—differ from the id and superego in Freud's theory. The Critical Review section below explains the difference.

○ Seeing Sociology
in Everyday Life

Have you ever seen young children put on their parents' shoes, literally putting themselves "in the shoes" of another person? How does this action help children learn to "take the role of the other"?

The self is able simultaneously to take the role of:	*no one* (no ability to take the role of the other)	*one* other in *one* situation	*many* others in *one* situation	*many* others in *many* situations
when:	engaging in imitation	engaging in play	engaging in games	recognizing the generalized other

FIGURE 3–1 Building on Social Experience

George Herbert Mead described the development of the self as a process of gaining social experience. That is, the self develops as we expand our capacity to take the role of the other.

○ **CRITICAL REVIEW** Mead's work explores the essence of social experience itself. In the symbolic interaction of human beings, he believed he had found the root of both self and society.

Mead's view is completely social, allowing no biological element at all. This is a problem for followers of Freud (who said our drives are rooted in the body) and Piaget (whose stages of development are tied to biological maturity).

Be careful not to confuse Mead's concepts of the I and the me with Freud's id and superego. For Freud, the id originates in our biology, but Mead rejected any biological element of self (although he never clearly spelled out the origin of the I). In addition, the id and the superego are locked in continual combat, but the I and the me work cooperatively together (Meltzer, 1978).

○ **CHECK YOUR LEARNING** Explain the meaning and importance of Mead's concepts of the I and the me. What did Mead mean by "taking the role of the other"? Why is this process so important to socialization?

Erik H. Erikson's Eight Stages of Development

Although some analysts discussed in this chapter (including Freud) point to childhood as the crucial time when personality takes shape, Erik H. Erikson (1902–1994) took a broader view of socialization. He explained that we face challenges throughout the life course (1963, orig. 1950).

Stage 1: Infancy—the challenge of trust (versus mistrust). Between birth and about eighteen months, infants face the first of life's challenges: to gain a sense of trust that their world is a safe place. Family members play a key role in how any infant meets this challenge.

Stage 2: Toddlerhood—the challenge of autonomy (versus doubt and shame). The next challenge, up to age three, is to learn skills to cope with the world in a confident way. Failure to gain self-control leads children to doubt their abilities.

Stage 3: Preschool—the challenge of initiative (versus guilt). Four- and five-year-olds must learn to engage their surroundings—including people outside the family—or experience guilt at having failed to meet the expectations of parents and others.

Stage 4: Preadolescence—the challenge of industriousness (versus inferiority). Between ages six and thirteen, children enter school, make friends, and strike out on their own more and more. They either feel proud of their accomplishments or fear that they do not measure up.

Stage 5: Adolescence—the challenge of gaining identity (versus confusion). During the teen years, young people struggle to establish their own identity. In part, teens identify with others, but they also want to be unique. Almost all teens experience some confusion as they struggle to establish an identity.

Stage 6: Young adulthood—the challenge of intimacy (versus isolation). The challenge for young adults is to form and keep intimate relationships with others. Making close friends (and especially falling in love) involves balancing the need to bond with the need to have a separate identity.

Stage 7: Middle adulthood—the challenge of making a difference (versus self-absorption). The challenge of middle age is to contribute to the lives of others in the family, at work, and in the larger world. Failing at this, people become self-centered, caught up in their own limited concerns.

Stage 8: Old age—the challenge of integrity (versus despair). Near the end of their lives, people hope to look back on what they have accomplished with a sense of integrity and satisfaction. For those who have been self-absorbed, old age brings only a sense of despair over missed opportunities.

○ **CRITICAL REVIEW** Erikson's theory views personality formation as a lifelong process, with success at one stage (say, an infant gaining trust) preparing us to meet the next challenge. However, not everyone faces these challenges in the exact order presented by Erikson. Nor is it clear that failure to meet a challenge at one stage of life means that a person is doomed to fail in life's later stages. A broader question, raised earlier in our discussion

┌─○ Making the Grade

Most theorists discussed in this chapter focus on childhood as the critical time when personality is formed. What sets Erik Erikson apart is the focus on socialization throughout the life course.

┌─○ Making the Grade

The family is considered first because it is widely considered to be the most important agent of socialization.

of Piaget's ideas, is whether people in other cultures and at other times in history would define a successful life in Erikson's terms.

In sum, Erikson's model points out how several factors, including the family and school, shape our personalities. In the next section, we take a closer look at these important agents of socialization.

─○ **CHECK YOUR LEARNING** In what ways does Erikson take a broader view of socialization than other thinkers presented in this chapter?

Agents of Socialization

Every social experience we have affects us in at least a small way. However, several familiar settings have special importance to the socialization process. Among them are the family, the school, the peer group, and the mass media.

The Family

The family affects socialization in many ways. For most people, the family may be the most important socializing agent of all.

Nurture in Early Childhood

Responsibility for the care of infants, who are totally dependent on others, typically falls on parents and other family members. For several years—at least until children begin school—the family has the job of teaching children skills, values, and beliefs. Overall, research suggests, nothing is more likely to produce a happy, well-adjusted child than a loving family (Gibbs, 2001).

Not all family learning results from intentional teaching by parents. Children also learn from the type of environment adults create. Whether children learn to see themselves as strong or weak, smart or stupid, loved or simply tolerated—and as Erik Erikson suggests, whether they see the world as trustworthy or dangerous—depends largely on the quality of the surroundings provided by parents and other caregivers.

Race and Class

The family also gives children a social identity. In part, social identity involves race. Racial identity is complex because, as Chapter 11 ("Race and Ethnicity") explains, societies define race in various ways. In addition, in the 2000 U.S. census, almost 7 million people (about 2.4 percent) said they consider themselves to be in two or more racial categories. This number is rising, and 4 percent of all births in the United States are now recorded as interracial. National Map 3–1 on page 76 shows where people who describe themselves as racially mixed live.

Social class, like race, plays a large part in shaping a child's personality. Whether born into families of high or low social position, children

gradually come to realize that their family's social standing affects how others see them and, in time, how they come to see themselves.

In addition, research shows that the class position of parents affects not just how much money parents have to spend on their children but also what parents expect of them (Ellison, Bartkowski, & Segal, 1996). When people in the United States were asked to pick from a list of traits they thought most desirable in a child, people at all social class levels chose hard work and helping others as the most important personal qualities. However, people with lower-class standing were nearly twice as likely as people in the upper classes to say that obedience and popularity are important personal traits.

Sociological research indicates that wealthy parents tend to encourage creativity in their children while poor parents tend to foster conformity. Although this general difference may be valid, parents at all class levels can and do provide loving support and guidance by simply involving themselves in their children's lives. Henry Ossawa Tanner's painting *The Banjo Lesson* stands as a lasting testament to this process.

Henry Ossawa Tanner, *The Banjo Lesson*, 1893. Oil on canvas. Hampton University Museum, Hampton, Virginia.

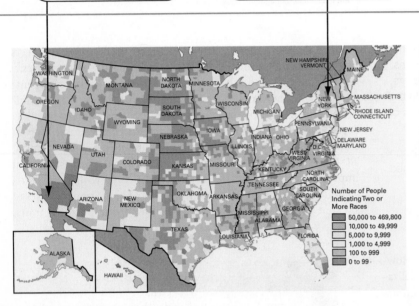

Alejo Gonzalez, a native of Los Angeles, considers himself white, African American, and Latino.

Emily Johnston attends school in Herkimer County in upstate New York, where almost all of her classmates are white.

Explore the percentage of racially mixed people in your local community and in counties across the United States on **mysoclab.com**

Seeing Ourselves

NATIONAL MAP 3–1

Racially Mixed People across the United States

This map shows the county-by-county distribution of people who described themselves as racially mixed in the 2000 census. How do you think growing up in an area with a high level of racially mixed people (such as Los Angeles or Miami) would be different from growing up in an area with few such people (for example, in upstate New York or the Plains States in the middle of the country)?

Explore on **mysoclab.com**

Source: U.S. Census Bureau (2001).

Number of People Indicating Two or More Races

- 50,000 to 469,800
- 10,000 to 49,999
- 5,000 to 9,999
- 1,000 to 4,999
- 100 to 999
- 0 to 99

Similarly, people of higher social class position are more likely to encourage imagination and creativity in their children (NORC, 2009).

What accounts for the difference? Melvin Kohn (1977) explains that people of lower social standing usually have only limited education and hold jobs that involve performing routine tasks under close supervision. Expecting that their children will grow up to take similar positions, they encourage obedience and may even use physical punishment such as spanking to get it. Because well-off parents generally have had more schooling, they usually have jobs that demand imagination and creativity, so they try to inspire the same qualities in their children. Consciously or not, all parents act in ways that encourage their children to follow in their footsteps.

Wealthier parents typically provide their children with an extensive program of leisure activities, including sports, vacation travel, and music lessons. These enrichment activities—far less available to children growing up in low-income families—build *cultural capital*, which advances learning and creates a sense of confidence in these children that they will be successful throughout their lives (Lareau, 2002).

Social class also affects how long the process of growing up takes, as the Seeing Sociology in Everyday Life box explains.

The School

Schooling enlarges children's social world to include people with backgrounds different from their own. It is only as they encounter people who differ from themselves that children come to understand the importance of factors such as race and social position. As they do, they are likely to cluster together in play groups made up of their own class, race, and gender.

Gender

Schools join with families in socializing children into gender roles. Studies show that at school, boys engage in more physical activities and spend more time outdoors and girls are more likely to help teachers with various housekeeping chores. Boys also engage in more aggressive behavior in the classroom, where girls are typically quieter and better behaved (Best, 1983; Jordan & Cowan, 1995).

What Children Learn

Schooling is not the same for children living in rich and poor communities. As Chapter 14 ("Education, Health, and Medicine") explains, children from well-off families typically have a far richer experience in school than children whose families are poor.

What children learn in school goes beyond the formally planned lessons. Schools informally teach many things, which together might be called the *hidden curriculum*. Activities such as spelling bees, for example, teach children not only how to spell and to think on their feet but also that society divides the population into "winners" and "losers." Sports help students develop their strength and skills and also teach children important lessons in cooperation and competition.

For most children, school is also their first experience with bureaucracy. The school day is based on impersonal rules and a strict time schedule. Not surprisingly, these are also the traits of the large organizations that will employ them later in life.

The Peer Group

By the time they enter school, children have also discovered the **peer group,** *a social group whose members have interests, social position, and age in common.* Unlike the family and the school, the peer group

SEEING SOCIOLOGY IN EVERYDAY LIFE

Are We Grown Up Yet? Defining Adulthood

SOLLY: (*seeing several friends walking down the dorm hallway, just returned from dinner*) Yo, guys! Jeremy's twenty-one today. We're going down to the Box Car to celebrate.

MATT: (*shaking his head*) Dunno, dude. I got a lab to finish up. It's just another birthday.

SOLLY: Not just any birthday, my friend. He's twenty-one—an *adult!*

MATT: (*sarcastically*) If turning twenty-one would make me an adult, I wouldn't still be clueless about what I want to do with my life!

Are you an adult or still an adolescent? Does turning twenty-one make you a "grown-up"? According to the sociologist Tom Smith (2003), in our society, no one factor announces the onset of adulthood. In fact, the results of his survey—using a representative sample of 1,398 people over the age of eighteen—suggest that many factors play a

part in our decision to consider a young person as "grown up."

According to the survey, the single most important transition in claiming adult standing in the United States today is the completion of schooling. But other factors are also important: Smith's respondents linked adult standing to taking on a full-time job, gaining the ability to support a family financially, no longer living with parents, and finally, marrying and becoming a parent. In other words, almost everyone in the United States thinks a person who has done *all* of these things is fully "grown up."

At what age are these transitions likely to be completed? On average, about age twenty-six. But such an average masks an important difference based on social class. People who do not attend college (more common among people growing up in lower-income families) typically finish school before age twenty, and a full-time job,

independent living, marriage, and parenthood may follow in a year or two. Those from more privileged backgrounds are likely to attend college and may even go on to graduate or professional school, delaying the process of becoming an adult for as long as ten years, past the age of thirty.

WHAT DO YOU THINK?

1. Do you consider yourself an adult? At what age did your adulthood begin?

2. Consider a woman whose children are grown, who has had a recent divorce, and is now going to college getting a degree so that she can find a job. Is she likely to feel that she is suddenly not quite "grown up" now that she's back in school? Why or why not?

3. How does the research described in this box show that adulthood is a socially defined concept rather than a biological stage of life?

---

allows children to escape the direct supervision of adults. Among their peers, children learn how to form relationships on their own. Peer groups also offer the chance to discuss interests that adults may not share (such as clothes and popular music) or permit (such as drugs and sex).

It is not surprising, then, that parents express concern about who their children's friends are. In a rapidly changing society, peer groups have great influence, and the attitudes of young and old may be different enough to form a "generation gap." The importance of peer groups typically peaks during adolescence, when young people begin to break away from their families and think of themselves as adults.

Even during adolescence, however, parental influence on children remains strong. Peers may affect short-term interests such as music or television shows, but parents have greater influence on long-term goals such as going to college (Davies & Kandel, 1981).

Finally, any neighborhood or school is made up of many peer groups. As Chapter 5 ("Groups and Organizations") explains, individuals tend to view their own group in positive terms and put down other groups. In addition, people are influenced by peer groups they would like to join, a process sociologists call **anticipatory socialization,** *learning that helps a person achieve a desired position.* In school,

for example, young people may copy the styles and slang of a group they hope will accept them. Later in life, a young lawyer who hopes to move up may conform to the attitudes and behavior of the firm's partners in order to be accepted.

The Mass Media

August 30, Isle of Coll, off the west coast of Scotland. The last time we visited this remote island, there was no electricity and most people spoke the ancient Gaelic language. Now that a power cable comes from the mainland, homes have lights, appliances, television, and the Internet! Almost with the flip of a switch, this tiny place has been thrust into the modern world. It is no surprise that traditions are fast disappearing and a rising share of the population is now mainlanders who ferry over with their cars to spend time in their vacation homes. And everyone now speaks English.

The **mass media** are *the means for delivering impersonal communications to a vast audience.* The term *media* (plural of *medium*) comes from the Latin word for "middle," suggesting that the media

In high-income countries such as the United States, television is an important part of socialization.

In low-income countries such as Nigeria, the mass media play a smaller role in socialization.

Global Snapshot

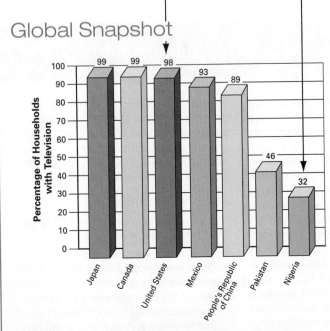

FIGURE 3–2 Television Ownership in Global Perspective

Television is popular in high- and middle-income countries, where almost every household owns at least one TV set.

Sources: U.S. Census Bureau (2008) and International Telecommunication Union (2008).

typically spend even more time—about 6½ hours a day—in front of video screens. Younger children favor watching television and playing video games; as children get older, music videos, social networking, and Web surfing become a bigger part of the mix (Roberts, Foehr, & Rideout, 2006; Nielsen Media Research, 2009; U.S. Bureau of Labor Statistics, 2009).

Years before children learn to read, television watching is a part of their daily routine. As they grow, children spend as many hours in front of a television as they do in school or interacting with their parents. This continues to be so despite research that suggests that television makes children more passive, less physically fit, and less likely to use their imagination (American Psychological Association, 1993; Fellman, 1995).

Television and Politics

The comedian Fred Allen once quipped that we call television a "medium" because it is "rarely well done." For a variety of reasons, television (as well as other mass media) provokes plenty of criticism. Some liberal critics argue that for most of television's history, racial and ethnic minorities have been invisible or have been shown only in stereotypical roles (such as African Americans playing butlers, Asian Americans playing gardeners, or Hispanics playing new immigrants). In recent years, however, minorities have moved closer to center stage on television. There are now far more Hispanic actors on prime-time television than there were a generation ago, and they play a far wider range of characters (Lichter & Amundson, 1997; Fetto, 2003b).

On the other side of the fence, conservative critics charge that the television and film industries are dominated by a liberal "cultural elite." In recent years, they claim, "politically correct" media have advanced liberal causes including feminism and gay rights (Rothman, Powers, & Rothman, 1993; B. Goldberg, 2002). But not everyone agrees, and some counter that the popularity of the Fox Network, home to Sean Hannity, Bill O'Reilly, Glenn Beck, and other conservative commentators, suggests that television programming offers "spin" from both sides of the political spectrum.

Television and Violence

In 1996, the American Medical Association (AMA) issued the startling statement that violence in television and films had reached such a high level that it posed a hazard to our health. More recently, a study found a strong link between aggressive behavior and the amount of time elementary school children spend watching television and using video games (Robinson et al., 2001). The public is concerned about this issue: Three-fourths of U.S. adults have either walked out of a movie or turned off television because of too much violence. About two-thirds of parents say that they are "very concerned" that their children are exposed to too much media violence. There may be reason

connect people. *Mass* media resulted as communications technology (first newspapers and then radio, television, films, and the Internet) spread information on a massive scale. The mass media are important not only because they are so powerful but also because their influence is likely to differ from that of the family, the local school, and the peer group. In short, the mass media introduce people to ideas and images that are new and different.

In the United States, television, introduced in the 1930s, quickly became the dominant medium after World War II. Today, 98 percent of U.S. households have at least one TV set, and 54 percent have three or more. As Figure 3–2 indicates, the United States has one of the highest rates of television ownership in the world.

The Extent of Television Viewing

Just how "glued to the tube" are we? Some categories of people watch television more than others, of course. Generally, minorities, older people, and people with lower incomes spend the most time watching TV. National surveys show that people in this country spend half their free time watching television, about 4½ hours a day. A study by the Kaiser Family Foundation found that school-age youngsters

Making the Grade

The chapter now turns to stages of the life course. Although we think of these stages as biological (children are children because they are young and immature), comparing our society past and present and comparing various societies today show that culture shapes all stages of the life course.

Go to the Multimedia Library at **mysoclab.com** to view the video "Child Labor in Africa"

for this concern: Almost two-thirds of television programs contain violence, and in most such scenes, violent characters show no remorse and are not punished (Rideout, 2007).

In 1997, the television industry adopted a rating system for programs. But we are left to wonder whether watching sexual or violent programming harms people as much as critics say. More important, why do the mass media contain so much sex and violence in the first place?

Television and other mass media have enriched our lives with entertaining and educational programming. The media also increase our exposure to other cultures and provoke discussion of current issues. At the same time, the power of the media—especially television—to shape how we think remains controversial.

Of course, the effects of mass media on how we grow up and how we understand the world around us also include new computer technology. Evidence suggests that the rate of technological change is increasing, with new forms of computer-based communication introduced all the time. Seeing Sociology in the News on pages 80–81 takes a look at how iPhones and text messaging are shaping the kind of people we become.

CRITICAL REVIEW This section shows that socialization is complex, with many factors shaping our personalities as we grow. In addition, these factors do not always work together, with children learning things from peer groups and the mass media that may conflict with what they learn at home.

Beyond family, school, peer group, and the media, other spheres of life also play a part in social learning. For most people in the United States, these include religious organizations, the workplace, the military, and social clubs. In the end, socialization is not a simple learning process but a complex balancing act as we absorb information from a variety of sources. In the process of sorting and weighing all the information we receive, we form our own distinctive personalities.

CHECK YOUR LEARNING Identify all the major agents of socialization discussed in this section. What are some of the unique ways that each helps us develop our individual personalities?

Socialization and the Life Course

Although childhood has special importance in the socialization process, learning continues throughout our lives. An overview of the life course reveals how society organizes human experience according to age—namely, the stages of life we know as childhood, adolescence, adulthood, and old age.

Concern with violence and the mass media involves not just television and films, but also the video games that are so popular among children, especially boys. Many games involve graphic violence; almost all games encourage players to be aggressive towards opponents. Do you think such video games are harmful to young people? Do you think the current rating code is sufficient to guide parents and children who buy the games, or would you support greater restrictions on game content?

Childhood

The next time you go shopping for athletic shoes, check where the shoes on display are made. Most are manufactured in countries such as Taiwan and Indonesia where wages are far lower than they are in the United States. What is not stated anywhere on the shoes is that many are made by children who spend their days working in factories instead of going to school. More than 160 million of the world's children work, half of them full time, and almost half of these boys and girls do work that is dangerous to their physical and mental health. For their efforts, they earn very little—typically, about 50 cents an hour (International Labour Organization, 2006; U.S. Bureau of International Labor Affairs, 2008). Global Map 3–1 on page 82 shows that child labor is most common in the nations of Africa and Asia. ● Go to **mysoclab.com**

The idea of children working long days in factories bothers people who live in high-income nations because we think of *childhood*— roughly the first twelve years of life—as a carefree time of learning and play. In fact, as the historian Philippe Ariès (1965) explains, the whole idea of "childhood" is fairly new. In the Middle Ages, children of four or five were treated like adults and expected to fend for themselves.

We support our view of childhood by pointing out that youngsters are biologically immature. But a look back in time and around the world shows that the concept of childhood is grounded not in

The New York Times

The Children of Cyberspace: Old Fogies by Their Twenties

BY BRAD STONE
January 9, 2010

My two-year-old daughter surprised me recently with two words: "Daddy's book." She was holding my Kindle electronic reader.

Here is a child only beginning to talk, revealing that the seeds of the next generation gap have already been planted. She has identified the Kindle as a substitute for words printed on physical pages. I own the device and am still not completely sold on the idea.

My daughter's worldview and life will be shaped in very deliberate ways by technologies like the Kindle and the new magical high-tech gadgets coming out this year. . . . She'll know nothing other than a world with digital books, Skype video chats with faraway relatives, and toddler-friendly video games on the iPhone. She'll see the world a lot differently from her parents.

But these are also technology tools that children even ten years older did not grow up with, and I've begun to think that my daughter's generation will also be utterly unlike those that preceded it.

Researchers are exploring this notion too. They theorize that the ever-accelerating pace of technological change may be minting a series of mini-generation gaps, with each group of children uniquely influenced by the tech tools available in their formative stages of development.

"People two, three or four years apart are having completely different experiences with technology," said Lee Rainie, director of the Pew Research Center's Internet and American Life Project. "College students scratch their heads at what their high school siblings are doing, and they scratch their heads at their younger siblings. It has sped up generational differences.". . .

These mini-generation gaps are most visible in the communication and entertainment choices made by different age groups. According to a survey last year by Pew, teenagers are more likely to send instant messages than slightly older twenty-somethings (68 percent versus 59 percent)

and to play online games (78 percent versus 50 percent).

Larry Rosen, a professor of psychology at California State University, Dominguez Hills, and the author of the coming "Rewired: Understanding the iGeneration and the Way They Learn," has also drawn this distinction between what he calls the Net Generation, born in the 1980s, and the iGeneration, born in the '90s and this decade.

Now in their twenties, those in the Net Generation, according to Dr. Rosen, spend two hours a day talking on the phone and still use e-mail frequently. The iGeneration—conceivably their younger siblings—spends considerably more time texting than talking on the phone, pays less attention to television than the older group and tends to communicate more over instant messenger networks.

Dr. Rosen said that the newest generations, unlike their older peers, will expect an instant response from everyone they communicate with, and won't have the patience for anything less.

---

biology but in culture (LaRossa & Reitzes, 2001). In rich countries today, not everyone has to work, so childhood is extended to allow time for young people to learn the skills they will need in a high-technology workplace.

Because childhood in the United States lasts such a long time, some people worry when children seem to be growing up too fast. In part, this "hurried child" syndrome results from changes in the family—including high divorce rates and both parents in the labor

Many of us experienced adolescence as a difficult stage of life. The popular television show *The Secret Life of the American Teenager* is centered on the character Amy Juergens, played by Shailene Woodley (in the center of the photo), a high school student who becomes pregnant while attending a summer band camp. As Amy deals with her situation, she discovers that just about all her teenage friends have "secret lives" in which they are facing similar challenges.

force—that leave children with less supervision. In addition, "adult" programming on television, in films, and on the Internet carries grown-up concerns such as sex, drugs, and violence into young people's lives. Today's ten- to twelve-year-olds, says one executive of a children's television channel, have about the same interests and experiences typical of twelve- to fourteen-year-olds a generation ago (K. S. Hymowitz, 1998). Perhaps this is why today's children, compared to kids fifty years ago, have higher levels of stress and anxiety (Gorman, 2000).

Adolescence

At the same time that industrialization created childhood as a distinct stage of life, adolescence emerged as a buffer between childhood and adulthood. We generally link *adolescence*, or the teenage years, with emotional and social turmoil as young people develop their own identities.

"They'll want their teachers and professors to respond to them immediately, and they will expect instantaneous access to everyone, because after all, that is the experience they have growing up," he said. "They should be just like their older brothers and sisters, but they are not."

The boom of kid-focused virtual worlds and online games like Club Penguin and Moshi Monsters especially intrigues Mizuko Ito, a cultural anthropologist and associate researcher at the University of California Humanities Research Institute.

Dr. Ito said that children who play these games would see less of a distinction between their online friends and real friends; virtually socializing might be just as fulfilling as a Friday night party. And they would be more likely to participate actively in their own entertainment, clicking at the keyboard instead of leaning back on the couch. . . .

Another bubbling intra-generational gap, as any modern parent knows, is that younger children tend to be ever more artful multitaskers. Studies performed by Dr. Rosen at Cal State show that 16- to 18-year-olds perform seven tasks, on average, in their free time—like texting on the phone, sending instant messages and checking Facebook while sitting in front of the television.

People in their early twenties can handle only six, Dr. Rosen found, and those in their thirties perform about five and a half.

That versatility is great when they're killing time, but will a younger generation be as focused at school and work as their forebears? . . .

It's not yet clear whether these disparities between adjacent groups of children and teenagers will simply fade away, as the older groups come to embrace the new technology tools, or whether they will deepen into more serious rifts between various generations.

But the children, teenagers and young adults who are passing through this cauldron of technological change will also have a lot in common. They'll think nothing of sharing the minutiae of their lives online, staying connected to their friends at all times, buying virtual goods, and owning one über-device that does it all.

They will believe the Kindle is the same as a book. And they will all think their parents are hopelessly out of touch.

WHAT DO YOU THINK?

1. What technological changes shaped the lives of the baby-boomers (today aged fifty to sixty-five) in ways different from the lives of their parents?

2. Do you think that the pace of technological change has been accelerating? Do you experience this change as good or bad? Why?

3. How might people in generations brought up to communicate with handwritten letters, the telephone, or instant messaging develop different expectations about interaction with others, such as how quickly people respond to them?

Again, we are tempted to attribute teenage rebelliousness and confusion to the biological changes of puberty. But it really comes from cultural inconsistency. For example, the mass media glorify sex and schools hand out condoms, even as parents urge restraint. Consider, too, that an eighteen-year-old may face the adult duty of going to war but lacks the adult right to drink a beer. In short, adolescence is a time of social contradictions, when people are no longer children but not yet adults.

Like all stages of life, adolescence varies according to social background. Most young people from working-class families move right from high school to the adult world of work and parenting. Such men and women are typically considered adults by the time they reach age twenty. Wealthier teens, however, have the resources to attend college and perhaps graduate school, thereby stretching adolescence to the late twenties and even the thirties (T. W. Smith, 2003). The Thinking About Diversity box on page 83 provides an example of how race and ethnicity can shape the academic performance of high school students.

Adulthood

If stages of the life course were based on biological changes, it would be easy to define *adulthood*. Regardless of exactly when it begins, adulthood is the time of life when most accomplishments take place, including pursuing a career and raising a family. Personalities are largely formed by then, although dramatic change in a person's environment—such as unemployment, divorce, or serious illness—can cause significant changes to the self.

During early adulthood—until about age forty—young adults learn to manage day-to-day affairs for themselves, often juggling conflicting priorities: parents, partner, children, schooling, work, and leisure activities. Women are especially likely to try to "do it all" because our culture gives them major responsibility for child rearing and household chores even if they have demanding jobs outside the home.

In middle adulthood—roughly between ages forty and sixty-five—people sense that their life circumstances are pretty well set. They also become more aware of the fragility of health, which the young typically take for granted. Women who have devoted many years to raising a family can find middle adulthood emotionally trying. Children grow up and require less attention, and husbands become absorbed in their careers, leaving some women with spaces in their lives that are difficult to fill. Many women who divorce during middle adulthood also face serious financial problems (Weitzman, 1985, 1996). For all these reasons, an increasing number of women in middle adulthood decide to return to school and seek new careers.

For everyone, growing older means facing physical decline, a prospect our culture makes especially painful for women. Because good looks are considered more important for women, the

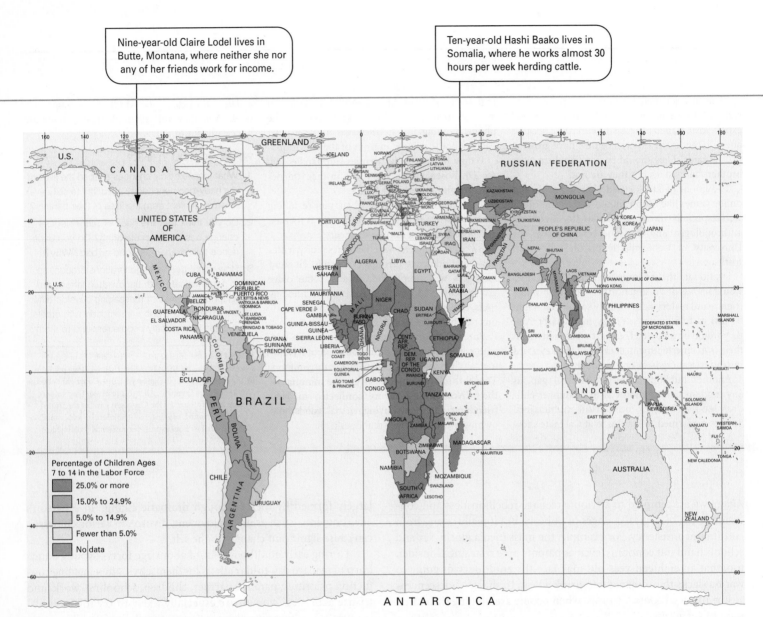

Nine-year-old Claire Lodel lives in Butte, Montana, where neither she nor any of her friends work for income.

Ten-year-old Hashi Baako lives in Somalia, where he works almost 30 hours per week herding cattle.

Percentage of Children Ages 7 to 14 in the Labor Force

- 25.0% or more
- 15.0% to 24.9%
- 5.0% to 14.9%
- Fewer than 5.0%
- No data

Window on the World

GLOBAL MAP 3–1
Child Labor in Global Perspective

Industrialization extends childhood and discourages children from work and other activities considered suitable only for adults. This is why child labor is uncommon in the United States and other high-income countries. In less economically developed nations of the world, however, children are a vital economic asset, and they typically begin working as soon as they are able. How would childhood in, say, the African nations of Chad or Somalia differ from that in the United States or Canada?

Sources: Global March against Child Labor (2008), World Bank (2008), and UNICEF (2009).

appearance of wrinkles and graying hair can be traumatic. Men have their own particular difficulties as they grow older. Some must admit that they are never going to reach earlier career goals. Others realize that the price of career success has been neglect of family or personal health.

Old Age

Old age—the later years of adulthood and the final stage of life—begins around the mid-sixties. With people living longer, the elderly population is growing nearly as fast as the U.S. population as a whole. As Figure 3–3 on page 84 shows, about one person in

THINKING ABOUT DIVERSITY: RACE, CLASS, & GENDER

The Development of Self among High School Students

Adolescence is a time when people ask questions like "Who am I?" and "What do I want to become?" In the end, we all have to answer these questions for ourselves. But race and ethnicity are likely to have an effect on what our answers turn out to be.

Grace Kao (2000) investigated the identity and goals of students enrolled in Johnstown High School, a large (3,000-student) school in a Chicago suburb. Johnstown High is considered a good school, with above-average test scores. It is also racially and ethnically diverse: 47 percent of the students are white, 43 percent are African American, 7 percent are Hispanic, and 3 percent are of Asian descent.

Kao interviewed sixty-three Johnstown students, female and male, both individually and in small groups with others of the same race and ethnicity. Talking with them, she learned how important racial and ethnic stereotypes are in young people's developing sense of self.

What are these stereotypes? White students are seen as hardworking, studious, and concerned about getting high grades. African American students are thought to study less, either because they are not as smart or because they just don't try as hard. In any case, students see African Americans as at high risk of failure in school. Because the stereotype says that Hispanics are

headed for manual occupations—as gardeners or laborers—they are seen as not caring very much about doing well in school. Finally, Asian American students are seen as hardworking high achievers, either because they are smarter or because they focus on academics rather than, say, sports.

From her interviews, Kao learned that most students think these stereotypes are true and take them personally. They expect people, including themselves, to perform in school more or less the way the stereotype predicts. In addition, young people—whether white, black, Hispanic, or Asian—mostly hang out with others

like themselves, which gives them little chance to find out that their assumptions are wrong.

Students of all racial and ethnic categories say they *want* to do well in school. But not getting to know those who differ from themselves means that they measure success *only in relation to their own category*. To African American students, in other words, "success" means doing as well as other black students and not flunking out. To Hispanics, "success" means avoiding manual labor and ending up with any job in an office. Whites and Asians define "success" as earning high grades and living up to the high-achievement stereotype. For all these young people, then, "self" develops to reflect how our society defines race and ethnicity.

WHAT DO YOU THINK?

1. Were you aware of racial and ethnic stereotypes similar to those described here in your high school? What about your college?

2. Do you think gender stereotypes affect the performance of women and men in school as much as racial and ethnic stereotypes? Explain your answer.

3. What can be done to reduce the damaging effects of racial and ethnic stereotypes?

---

eight is over age sixty-five, and the elderly now outnumber teenagers. By 2030, the number of seniors will double to 72 million, and the "average" person in the United States will be almost forty (U.S. Census Bureau, 2009).

We can only begin to imagine the full consequences of the "graying of the United States." As more and more people retire from the labor force, the share of nonworking adults—already ten times greater than in 1900—will go up, increasing demand for health care and other social products and services. But perhaps most important, elderly people will be more visible in everyday life. As the twenty-first century goes on, the young and the old will interact more and more.

The aging of the U.S. population is the focus of **gerontology** (*geron* in Greek means "old person"), *the study of aging and the elderly.* Gerontologists study both the physical and the social dimensions of growing old.

Aging and Biology

For most of our population, gray hair, wrinkles, and declining energy begin in middle age. After about age fifty, bones become more brittle, injuries take longer to heal, and the risks of chronic illnesses (such as arthritis and diabetes) and life-threatening conditions (such as heart disease and cancer) rise steadily. Sensory abilities—taste, sight,

gerontology (p. 83) the study of aging and the elderly

gerontocracy a form of social organization in which the elderly have the most wealth, power, and prestige

ageism prejudice and discrimination against older people

○ Making the Grade

Looking at the figure below, notice that projections show the median age of our society leveling off at about 39 years by mid-century. If this is correct, about half the population will be below this age and half will be above it.

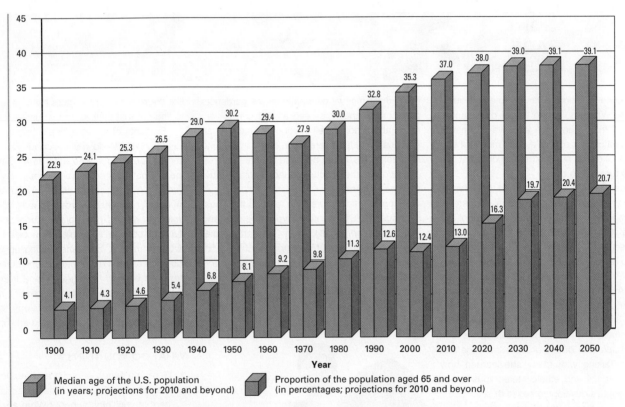

Median age of the U.S. population (in years; projections for 2010 and beyond)

Proportion of the population aged 65 and over (in percentages; projections for 2010 and beyond)

FIGURE 3–3   The Graying of U.S. Society

The proportion of the U.S. population over the age of sixty-five tripled during the last century. The median age of the U.S. population has now passed thirty-five years and will continue to rise.

Source: U.S. Census Bureau (2009).

touch, smell, and especially hearing—become less sharp with age (Treas, 1995; Metz & Miner, 1998).

Even so, most older people are neither disabled nor discouraged by their physical condition. In 2007, only 16 percent of seniors said that they could not walk a quarter mile by themselves, and fewer than one in twenty needs care in a hospital or nursing home. Overall, only 28 percent of people over age seventy-five characterize their health as "fair" or "poor"; 72 percent consider their overall condition "good" to "excellent." On average, the health of U.S. seniors is steadily improving (Pleis, Lucas, & Ward, 2009; National Center for Health Statistics, 2010).

Aging and Culture

Culture shapes how we understand growing old. In low-income countries, old age gives people great influence and respect because elders control the most land and have wisdom gained over the course of a lifetime. For these reasons, a preindustrial society usually takes the

form of a **gerontocracy,** *a form of social organization in which the elderly have the most wealth, power, and prestige.*

Industrialization lessens the social standing of the elderly, giving more wealth, power, and prestige to younger people. This trend seems to be continuing: The average age of today's corporate executives, which was fifty-nine back in 1980, was just fifty-four in 2008 (Spencer Stuart, 2008). In an industrial society, older people typically live apart from their grown children, and rapid social change makes much of what seniors know obsolete, at least from the point of view of younger people. A problem common to industrial societies, then, is **ageism,** *prejudice and discrimination against older people.*

November 1, approaching Kandy, Sri Lanka. Our little van struggles up the steep mountain incline. Breaks in the lush vegetation offer spectacular views that interrupt our conversation about growing old.

Read "Men and Women: Together and Apart in Later Years" by Katherine Newman on **mysoclab.com**

● Seeing Sociology
in Everyday Life

The text claims that, in our society, death typically occurs in old age. How do you think class, and perhaps race, affect this pattern?

Mick Jagger and Keith Richard's of the Rolling Stones, Paul McCartney of the Beatles, and Judy Collins and Joan Baez of the folk music scene all became celebrities in the 1960s when they were teenagers. Fifty years later, they are all approaching old age. Yet they remain active in their careers and continue to attract new fans. What do these facts suggest about our changing view of old age?

> "Then there are no old-age homes in your country?" I ask. "In Colombo and other cities, I am sure," our driver responds, "but not many. We are not like you Americans." "And how is that?" I ask, stiffening a bit. His eyes remain fixed on the road: "We would not leave our fathers and mothers to live alone."

Not surprisingly, growing old in the United States is challenging. When we're young, becoming older means taking on new roles and responsibilities. In old age, the opposite happens as people leave behind roles that have given them identity, pleasure, and prestige. When people retire from familiar work routines, some find restful recreation or new activities, but others lose their sense of self-worth and suffer outright boredom. **Read** on **mysoclab.com**

Aging and Income

Reaching old age means living with less income. But today, the U.S. elderly population is doing better than ever. In 1960, some 35 percent of the elderly were poor; by 2008, this figure had fallen to 9.7 percent—less than the poverty rate of 13.2 percent for the population as a whole (U.S. Census Bureau, 2009). A generation ago, old age carried the highest risk of poverty; today, that is true of young people ages eighteen to twenty-four.

What changed? An increasing share of older couples earned double incomes during their working years, which helped them save more. In addition, better health allows older people to continue to work for income. Government programs have become more generous, so that almost half of all government spending now goes to programs that assist the elderly even as spending on children has remained more or less flat. But the recent economic downturn has canceled out many of these advantages as people have lost some of the pension income they were counting on, and more of today's workers are not receiving pension benefits at all.

If many seniors are struggling, they are doing better than many younger people. Since 1980, on average, seniors have posted a 36 percent increase in income (in constant dollars), which is five times the increase for people under thirty-five (U.S. Census Bureau, 2009). Today's average senior has a net worth of about $200,000. A reasonable question, then, is whether we should continue to favor the oldest members of our society and risk slighting younger members, who now suffer most from poverty.

Death and Dying

Throughout most of human history, low living standards and limited medical technology meant that death, caused most often by disease or accident, could come at any stage of life. Today, however, 84 percent of people in the United States die after age fifty-five (Heron et al., 2009).

◯ Making the Grade

Each stage of life has its own joys and challenges, but in our society, early stages of life typically involve *adding* roles and responsibilities; old age differs in that it typically involves *losing* roles and responsibilities.

cohort a category of people with something in common, usually their age

total institution a setting in which people are isolated from the rest of society and controlled by an administrative staff

resocialization radically changing an inmate's personality by carefully controlling the environment

In the 2007 film *The Bucket List*, two terminally ill men, played by Jack Nicholson (shown above) and Morgan Freeman, set out to experience many grand adventures before they "kick the bucket." Approaching the end of life—if we see it coming—can provide opportunities to resolve many issues that we have carried with us for decades.

differently or not at all. Second, in any society, the stages of the life course present certain problems and transitions that involve learning something new and, in many cases, unlearning familiar routines.

Societies organize the life course according to age, but other forces such as class, race, ethnicity, and gender also shape people's lives. Thus the general patterns described in this chapter apply somewhat differently to various categories of people.

People's life experiences also vary, depending on when, in the history of a society, they are born. A **cohort** is *a category of people with something in common, usually their age*. Because members of a particular age cohort are generally influenced by the same economic and cultural trends, they tend to develop similar attitudes and values. Women and men born in the late 1940s and 1950s grew up during a period of economic expansion that gave them a sense of optimism. Today's college students, who have grown up in an age of economic uncertainty, are less confident about the future.

After observing many dying people, the psychologist Elisabeth Kübler-Ross (1969) described death as an orderly transition involving five distinct stages. Typically, a person first reacts to the prospect of dying with *denial*, perhaps to be expected in a culture that doesn't like to talk about death. The second phase is *anger* as the person facing death sees it as a gross injustice. Third, anger gives way to *negotiation* as the person imagines it might be possible to avoid death by striking a bargain with God. The fourth stage, *resignation*, is often accompanied by psychological depression. Finally, a complete adjustment to death requires *acceptance*. At this point, no longer paralyzed by fear and anxiety, the person whose life is ending sets out to make the most of whatever time remains.

As older people become a larger share of the U.S. population, we can expect our culture to become more comfortable with the idea of death. In recent years, for example, people in the United States and in other high-income nations have been discussing death more openly, and the trend is toward viewing dying as preferable to prolonged suffering. More married couples are taking steps to prepare for death with legal and financial planning; this openness may help ease the pain of the surviving spouse, a consideration for women who, more often than not, outlive their husbands.

The Life Course: Patterns and Variations

This brief examination of the life course points to two major conclusions. First, although each stage of life reflects the biological process of aging, the life course is largely a social construction. For this reason, people in different societies may experience a stage of life quite

Resocialization: Total Institutions

A final type of socialization, experienced by more than 2 million people in the United States at any one time, involves being confined—often against their will—in prisons or mental hospitals. This is the special world of the **total institution,** *a setting in which people are isolated from the rest of society and controlled by an administrative staff*.

According to Erving Goffman (1961), total institutions have three important characteristics. First, staff members supervise all aspects of daily life, including where residents (often called "inmates") eat, sleep, and work. Second, life in a total institution is controlled and standardized, with the same food, uniforms, and activities for everyone. Third, formal rules dictate when, where, and how inmates perform their daily routines.

The purpose of such rigid routines is **resocialization,** *radically changing an inmate's personality by carefully controlling the environment*. Prisons and mental hospitals physically isolate inmates behind fences, barred windows, and locked doors and control their access to the telephone, computers, mail, and visitors. The institution becomes their entire world, making it easier for the staff to bring about personality change—or at least obedience—in the inmate.

Resocialization is a two-part process. First, the staff breaks down a new inmate's existing identity. For example, an inmate must surrender personal possessions, including clothing and grooming articles used to maintain a distinctive appearance. Instead, the staff

◦ Making the Grade

Of the theories of human development we have considered in this chapter, Freud's probably points to the least human freedom, because we are all caught between two powerful forces—biology (id) and culture (superego).

◦ Making the Grade

Mead's theory of human development points to the most human freedom, because he saw no biological drives as Freud did and saw humans as spontaneous and creative.

CONTROVERSY & DEBATE

Are We Free within Society?

MIKE: Sociology is a good course. Since my professor started telling us to look at our lives with a sociological eye, I'm realizing that a lot of who, what, and where I am is because of society.

KIM: (*teasingly*) Oh, so society is responsible for making you so smart and witty and handsome?

MIKE: No, that's all me. But I'm seeing that being at college and playing football is maybe not all me.

What do you think? How free are we, really? This chapter stresses one key theme: Society shapes how we think, feel, and act. If this is so, then in what sense are we free? To answer this important question, consider the Muppets, puppet stars of television and film. Watching the antics of Kermit the Frog, Miss Piggy, and the rest of the troupe, we almost believe they are real rather than objects controlled from offstage. As the sociological perspective points out, human beings are like puppets in that we, too, respond to offstage forces. Society gives us a culture and shapes our lives according to class, race, and gender. If this is so, can we really claim to be free?

Sociologists answer this question with many voices. The politically liberal response is that individuals are *not* free of society—in fact, as social creatures, we never could be. But if we are condemned to live in a society with power over us, it is important to do what we can to make our world as just as possible, by working to lessen class differences and other

barriers to opportunity for minorities, including women. Conservatives agree that society shapes our lives but also point out that we *are* free because society can never dictate our dreams or stand in our way if we are determined to succeed. Our history as a nation, right from the revolutionary act that led to its found-

Does understanding more about how society shapes our lives give us greater power to "cut the strings" and choose for ourselves how to live?

ing, is one story after another of individuals pursuing their personal goals despite great odds.

Both attitudes are found in George Herbert Mead's analysis of socialization. Mead recognized that society makes demands on us, sometimes limiting our options. But he also reminded us that human beings are spontaneous and creative, capable of acting on society and bringing about change. Mead noted the power of society while still affirming the human capacity to evaluate, criticize, and ultimately choose and change.

In the end, we may seem like puppets, but only on the surface. A crucial difference is that we can stop, look up at the "strings" that make us move, and even yank on them defiantly (Berger, 1963:176). If our pull is strong enough, we may accomplish more than we might think. As Margaret Mead is said to have remarked, "Never doubt that a small group of thoughtful, committed citizens can change the world. Indeed, it is the only thing that ever has."

WHAT DO YOU THINK?

1. Do you think that our society gives more freedom to males than to females? Why or why not?

2. Do you think that most people in our society feel that they have some control over their lives or not? Why?

3. Has learning about socialization increased or decreased your feeling of freedom? Why?

provides standard-issue clothes so that everyone looks alike. The staff subjects new inmates to "mortifications of self," which can include searches, medical examinations, head shaving, fingerprinting, and assignment of a serial number. Once inside the walls, individuals also give up their privacy as guards routinely inspect their living quarters.

In the second part of the resocialization process, the staff tries to build a new self in the inmate through a system of rewards and punishments. Having a book to read, watching television, or making a telephone call may seem like minor pleasures to the outsider, but in the rigid environment of the total institution, the opportunity to

gain such simple privileges as these can be a powerful motivation to conform. The length of confinement typically depends on how well the inmate cooperates with the staff.

Total institutions affect people in different ways. Some inmates may end up "rehabilitated" or "recovered," but others may change little, and still others may become hostile or bitter. Over a long period of time, living in a rigidly controlled environment can leave some *institutionalized*, without the capacity for independent living.

But what about the rest of us? Does socialization crush our individuality or empower us to reach our creative potential? The Controversy & Debate box takes a closer look at this vital question.

Seeing Sociology in Everyday Life

When do we grow up and become adults?

As this chapter explains, many factors come into play in the process of moving from one stage of the life course to another. In global perspective, what makes our society unusual is that there is no one event that clearly tells everyone (and us, too) that the milestone of adulthood has been reached. We have important events that say, for example, when someone completes high school (graduation ceremony) or gets married (wedding ceremony). Look at the photos below. In each case, what do we learn about how the society defines the transition from one stage of life to another?

> **HINT** Societies differ in how they structure the life course, including which stages of life are defined as important, what years of life various stages correspond to, and how clearly movement from one stage to another is marked. Given our cultural emphasis on individual choice and freedom, many people tend to say "You're only as old as you feel" and let people decide these things for themselves. When it comes to reaching adulthood, our society is not very clear—the Seeing Sociology in Everyday Life box on page 77 points out many factors that figure into becoming an adult. So there is no widespread "adult ritual" as we see in the photos. Keep in mind that for us, class matters a lot in this process, with young people of higher social standing staying in school and delaying full adulthood until well into their twenties or even their thirties. Finally, in these tough economic times, the share of young people in their twenties living with parents goes way up, which can delay adulthood for an entire cohort.

Among the Hamer people in the Omo Valley of Ethiopia, young boys must undergo a test to mark their transition to manhood. Usually the event is triggered by the boy's expressing a desire to marry. In this ritual, witnessed by everyone in his society, the boy must jump over a line of bulls selected by the girl's family. If he succeeds in doing this three times, he is declared a man and the wedding can take place (marking the girl's transition to womanhood). Does our society have any ceremony or event similar to this to mark the transition to adulthood?

On the San Carlos Reservation in Arizona, young Apache girls perform the Sunrise Dance to mark their transition to adulthood. Carefully painted by an elder according to Apache tradition, each girl holds a special staff, which symbolizes her hope for a long and healthy life and spiritual happiness. Many of the world's societies time these coming-of-age rituals to correspond to a girl's first menstrual cycle. Why do you think this is so?

These young men and women in Seoul, South Korea, are participating in a Confucian ceremony to mark their becoming adults. This ritual, which takes place on the twentieth birthday, defines young people as full members of the community and also reminds them of all the responsibilities they are now expected to fulfill. If we had such a ritual in the United States, at what age would it take place? Would a person's social class affect the timing of this ritual?

Applying SOCIOLOGY in Everyday Life

1. Across the United States, many families plan elaborate parties to celebrate a daughter's or son's graduation from high school. In what respects is this a ritual that marks reaching adulthood? How does social class affect whether or not people define this event as the beginning of adulthood?

2. In the United States, when does the stage of life we call "old age" begin? Is there an event that marks the transition to old age? Does social class play a part in this process? If so, how?

3. Watch several hours of prime-time programming on network or cable television. Keep track of every time any element of violence is shown, and calculate the number of violent scenes per hour. On the basis of observing a small and unrepresentative sample of programs, what are your conclusions?

Making the Grade

CHAPTER 3 Socialization: From Infancy to Old Age

What Is Socialization?

Watch on mysoclab.com

Socialization is a **LIFELONG PROCESS**.
- Socialization develops our humanity as well as our particular personalities.
- The importance of socialization is seen in the fact that extended periods of social isolation result in permanent damage (cases of Anna and Genie).

pp. 68–69

Socialization is a matter of **NURTURE** rather than **NATURE**.
- A century ago, most people thought human behavior resulted from biological instinct.
- For us as human beings, it is our nature to nurture.

pp. 68–69

socialization (p. 68) the lifelong social experience by which people develop their human potential and learn culture

personality (p. 68) a person's fairly consistent patterns of acting, thinking, and feeling

Important Contributions to Our Understanding of Socialization

SIGMUND FREUD'S model of the human personality has three parts:
- **id**: innate, pleasure-seeking human drives
- **superego**: the demands of society in the form of internalized values and norms
- **ego**: our efforts to balance innate, pleasure-seeking drives and the demands of society

pp. 70–71

LAWRENCE KOHLBERG applied Piaget's approach to stages of moral development:
- We first judge rightness in **preconventional** terms, according to our individual needs.
- Next, **conventional** moral reasoning takes account of parental attitudes and cultural norms.
- Finally, **postconventional** reasoning allows us to criticize society itself.

p. 72

To **GEORGE HERBERT MEAD**:
- The self is part of our personality and includes self-awareness and self-image.
- The self develops only as a result of social experience.
- Social experience involves the exchange of symbols.
- Social interaction depends on understanding the intention of another, which requires taking the role of the other.
- Human action is partly spontaneous (the I) and partly in response to others (the me).
- We gain social experience through imitation, play, games, and understanding the **generalized other**.

pp. 73–74

JEAN PIAGET believed that human development involves both biological maturation and gaining social experience. He identified four stages of cognitive development:
- The **sensorimotor stage** involves knowing the world only through the senses.
- The **preoperational stage** involves starting to use language and other symbols.
- The **concrete operational stage** allows individuals to understand causal connections.
- The **formal operational stage** involves abstract and critical thought.

p. 71

CAROL GILLIGAN found that gender plays an important part in moral development, with males relying more on abstract standards of rightness and females relying more on the effects of actions on relationships.

pp. 72–73

CHARLES HORTON COOLEY used the term **looking-glass self** to explain that we see ourselves as we imagine others see us.

p. 73

ERIK H. ERIKSON identified challenges that individuals face at each stage of life from infancy to old age.

pp. 74–75

id (p. 70) Freud's term for the human being's basic drives

ego (p. 70) Freud's term for a person's conscious efforts to balance innate pleasure-seeking drives with the demands of society

superego (p. 70) Freud's term for the cultural values and norms internalized by an individual

sensorimotor stage (p. 71) Piaget's term for the level of human development at which individuals experience the world only through their senses

preoperational stage (p. 71) Piaget's term for the level of human development at which individuals first use language and other symbols

concrete operational stage (p. 71) Piaget's term for the level of human development at which individuals first see causal connections in their surroundings

formal operational stage (p. 71) Piaget's term for the level of human development at which individuals think abstractly and critically

self (p. 73) George Herbert Mead's term for the part of an individual's personality composed of self-awareness and self-image

looking-glass self (p. 73) Charles Horton Cooley's term for a self-image based on how we think others see us

significant others (p. 73) people, such as parents, who have special importance for socialization

generalized other (p. 73) Mead's term for widespread cultural norms and values we use as a reference in evaluating ourselves

Agents of Socialization

The **FAMILY** is usually the first setting of socialization.

- Family has the greatest impact on attitudes and behavior.
- A family's social position, including race and social class, shapes a child's personality.
- Ideas about gender are learned first in the family.

pp. 75–76

Explore on mysoclab.com

The **PEER GROUP** helps shape attitudes and behavior.

- The peer group takes on great importance during adolescence.
- The peer group frees young people from adult supervision.

pp. 76–77

SCHOOLS give most children their first experience with bureaucracy and impersonal evaluation.

- Schools teach knowledge and skills needed for later life.
- Schools expose children to greater social diversity.
- Schools reinforce ideas about gender.

p. 76

The **MASS MEDIA** have a huge impact on socialization in modern, high-income societies.

- The average U.S. child spends about 6½ hours a day watching television and playing video games—as much time as attending school and interacting with parents.
- The mass media often reinforce stereotypes about gender and race.
- The mass media expose people to a great deal of violence.

pp. 77–79

peer group (p. 76) a social group whose members have interests, social position, and age in common

anticipatory socialization (p. 77) learning that helps a person achieve a desired position

mass media (p. 77) the means for delivering impersonal communications to a vast audience

Socialization and the Life Course

The concept of **CHILDHOOD** is grounded not in biology but in culture. In high-income countries, childhood is extended.

pp. 79–80

ADULTHOOD is the stage of life when most accomplishments take place. Although personality is now formed, it continues to change with new life experiences.

pp. 81–82

Acceptance of **DEATH AND DYING** is part of socialization for the elderly. This process typically involves five stages: denial, anger, negotiation, resignation, and acceptance.

pp. 85–86

The emotional and social turmoil of **ADOLESCENCE** results from cultural inconsistency in defining people who are not children but not yet adults. Adolescence varies by social class.

pp. 80–81

OLD AGE is defined as much by culture as biology.

- In high-income countries, old age is a time of disengagement and loss of social importance.
- The "graying of the United States" means that our country's average age is going up.

pp. 82–85

Read on mysoclab.com

gerontology (p. 83) the study of aging and the elderly

gerontocracy (p. 84) a form of social organization in which the elderly have the most wealth, power, and prestige

ageism (p. 84) prejudice and discrimination against older people

cohort (p. 86) a category of people with something in common, usually their age

✓ Every stage of life is socially constructed in ways that vary from society to society (p. 86).

Total Institutions

TOTAL INSTITUTIONS include prisons, mental hospitals, and monasteries.

- Staff members supervise all aspects of life.
- Life is standardized, with all inmates following set rules and routines.

pp. 86–87

RESOCIALIZATION is a two-part process:

- breaking down inmates' existing identity
- building a new self through a system of rewards and punishments

pp. 86–87

total institution (p. 86) a setting in which people are isolated from the rest of society and controlled by an administrative staff

resocialization (p. 86) radically changing an inmate's personality by carefully controlling the environment

4 Social Interaction in Everyday Life

- How do we create reality in our face-to-face interactions?

- Why do employers try to control their workers' feelings on the job as well as their behavior?

- What makes something funny?

 Watch the *Core Concepts in Sociology* video "Social Interaction and Social Roles" on **mysoclab.com**

Chapter Overview

This chapter takes a micro-level look at society, examining patterns of everyday social interaction. First, the chapter identifies important social structures, including status and role. Then it explains how we construct reality in social interaction. Finally, it applies the lessons learned to three everyday experiences: emotion, gender, and humor.

Harold and Sybil are on their way to another couple's home in an unfamiliar area near Fort Lauderdale, Florida. For the last twenty minutes, as Sybil sees it, they have been driving in circles, searching in vain for Coconut Palm Road.

"Look, Harold," says Sybil. "There are some people up ahead. Let's ask for directions."

Harold, gripping the wheel ever more tightly, begins muttering under his breath. "I know where I am. I don't want to waste time talking to strangers. Just let me get us there."

"I'm sure you know where you are, Harold," Sybil responds, looking straight ahead. "But I don't think you know where you're going."

Harold and Sybil are lost in more ways than one: Not only can't they find where their friends live, but they also cannot understand why they are growing angrier with each other with each passing minute.

What's going on? Like most men, Harold cannot stand getting lost. The longer he drives around, the more incompetent he feels. Sybil can't understand why Harold doesn't pull over to ask someone the way to Coconut Palm Road. If she were driving, she thinks to herself, they would already be comfortably settled in with their friends.

Why don't men like to ask for directions? Because men value their independence, they are uncomfortable asking for any type of help and are reluctant to accept it. To ask another person for assistance is the same as saying, "You know something I don't know." If it takes Harold a few more minutes to find Coconut Palm Road on his own—and to keep his sense of being in control—he thinks that's the way to go.

Women are more in tune with others and strive for connectedness. From Sybil's point of view, asking for help is right because sharing information builds social bonds and at the same time gets the job done. Asking for directions seems as natural to her as searching on his own is to Harold. Obviously, getting lost is sure to create conflict for Harold and Sybil as long as neither one of them understands the other's point of view.

Such everyday social patterns are the focus of this chapter. The central concept is **social interaction,** *the process by which people act and react in relation to others.* We begin by presenting the rules and building blocks of everyday experience and then explore the almost magical way in which face-to-face interaction creates the reality in which we live.

Social Structure: A Guide to Everyday Living

October 21, Ho Chi Minh City, Vietnam. This morning we leave the ship and make our way along the docks toward the center of Ho Chi Minh City, known to an earlier generation as Saigon. Government security officers wave us through the heavy iron gates. Pressed against the fence are dozens of men who operate cyclos (bicycles with small carriages attached to the front), the Vietnamese version of taxicabs. We spend the next twenty minutes shaking our heads at several persistent drivers who pedal alongside us, pleading for our business. The pressure is uncomfortable. We decide to cross the street but realize suddenly that there are no stop signs or signal lights—and the street is an unbroken stream of bicycles, cyclos, motorbikes, and small trucks. The locals don't bat an eye; they just walk at a steady pace across the street, parting waves of vehicles that immediately close in again behind them. Walk right into traffic? With our small children on our backs? Yup, we did it; that's the way it works in Vietnam.

Members of every society rely on social structure to make sense out of daily situations. As our family's introduction to the streets of

social interaction the process by which people act and react in relation to others

status a social position that a person holds

ascribed status a social position a person receives at birth or takes on involuntarily later in life

achieved status a social position a person takes on voluntarily that reflects personal ability and effort

status set all the statuses a person holds at a given time

master status a status that has special importance for social identity, often shaping a person's entire life

Vietnam suggests, the world can be disorienting, even frightening, when society's rules are unclear. Let's take a closer look at the ways in which society organizes everyday life.

Status

In every society, people build their lives using the idea of **status,** *a social position that a person holds.* In everyday use, the word "status" generally refers to prestige, as when a college president is said to have more "status" than a newly hired assistant professor. But sociologically speaking, both "president" and "professor" are statuses, or positions, within the collegiate organization.

Status is part of our social identity and defines our relationships to others. As Georg Simmel (1950:307, orig. 1902), one of the founders of sociology, pointed out, before we can deal with anyone, we need to know who the person is.

Each of us holds many statuses at once. The term **status set** refers to *all the statuses a person holds at a given time,* A teenage girl may be a daughter to her parents, a sister to her brother, a student at her school, and a goalie on her soccer team.

Status sets change over the life course. A child grows up to become a parent, a student graduates to become a lawyer, and a single person marries to become a husband or a wife, sometimes becoming single again as a result of death or divorce. Joining an organization or finding a job enlarges our status set; retirement or withdrawing from activities makes it smaller. Over a lifetime, people gain and lose dozens of statuses.

Ascribed and Achieved Status

Sociologists classify statuses in terms of how people attain them. An **ascribed status** is *a social position a person receives at birth or takes on involuntarily later in life.* Exam-

Members of our society celebrate the achievement of Olympic athletes such as Apolo Ohno not only because he has won eight medals in speed skating (not to mention winning in the reality television show *Dancing with the Stars*), but because he was able to do all this even after a challenging childhood during which his parents divorced, he lost contact with his mother, and his father had to spend long hours working.

ples of ascribed statuses are being a daughter, a Cuban, a teenager, or a widower. Ascribed statuses are matters about which we have little or no choice.

By contrast, an **achieved status** refers to *a social position a person takes on voluntarily that reflects personal ability and effort.* Achieved statuses in the United States include honors student, Olympic athlete, software writer, and thief.

In the real world, of course, most statuses involve a combination of ascription and achievement. That is, people's ascribed statuses influence the statuses they achieve. People who achieve the status of lawyer, for example, are likely to share the ascribed benefit of being born into relatively well-off families. By the same token, many less desirable statuses, such as convicted criminal, drug addict, or unemployed worker, are more easily achieved by people who were born into poverty.

Master Status

Some statuses matter more than others. A **master status** is *a status that has special importance for social identity, often shaping a person's entire life.* For most people, a job is a master status because it reveals a great deal about social background, education, and income. In a few cases, a person's name is a master status; being in the Bush or Kennedy family attracts attention and creates opportunities.

A master status can be negative as well as positive. Consider serious illness. Sometimes people, even lifelong friends, avoid cancer patients or people with AIDS because of their illnesses. As another example, the fact that all societies limit opportunities for women makes gender a master status.

Sometimes a physical disability can serve as a master status to the point that we dehumanize people by seeing them only in terms of their disability. The Thinking About Diversity box on page 96 shows how.

Role

A second important social structure is **role,** *behavior expected of someone who holds a particular status.* A person *holds* a status and *performs* a role (Linton, 1937b). For example, holding the status of student leads you to perform the role of attending classes and completing assignments.

Make a list of ten important statuses in your own life. Indicate whether each one is ascribed or achieved. Is this sometimes difficult to do? Why?

Go to the Multimedia Library at **mysoclab.com** to listen to an NPR report, "Housework: Hope for Men, No Thanks for Women"

THINKING ABOUT DIVERSITY: RACE, CLASS, & GENDER

Physical Disability as a Master Status

Physical disability works in much the same way as class, gender, or race in defining people in the eyes of others. In the following interviews, two women explain how a physical disability can become a master status—a trait that overshadows everything else about them. The first voice is of twenty-nine-year-old Donna Finch, who lives with her husband and son in Muskogee, Oklahoma, and holds a master's degree in social work. She is also blind.

Most people don't expect handicapped people to grow up; they are always supposed to be children. . . . You aren't supposed to date; you aren't supposed to have a job; somehow you're just supposed to disappear. I'm not saying this is true of anyone else, but in my own case I think I was more intellectually mature than most children, and more emotionally immature. I'd say that not until the last four or five years have I felt really whole.

Rose Helman is an elderly woman who has retired and lives near New York City. She suffers from spinal meningitis and is also blind.

You ask me if people are really different today than in the '20s and '30s. Not too

much. They are still fearful of the handicapped. I don't know if fearful is the right word, but uncomfortable at least. But I can

Modern technology means that most soldiers who lose limbs in war now survive. How do you think the loss of an arm or a leg affects a person's social identity and sense of self?

understand it somewhat; it happened to me. I once asked a man to tell me which staircase to use to get from the subway out to the street. He started giving me directions that were confusing, and I said, "Do you mind taking me?" He said, "Not at all." He grabbed me on the side with my dog on it, so I asked him to take my other arm. And he said, "I'm sorry, I have no other arm." And I said, "That's all right, I'll hold onto the jacket." It felt funny hanging onto the sleeve without the arm in it.

WHAT DO YOU THINK?

1. Have you ever had a disease or disability that became a master status? If so, how did others react?

2. How might such a master status affect someone's personality?

3. Can being very fat or very thin serve as a master status? Why or why not?

Source: Based on Orlansky & Heward (1981).

Both statuses and roles vary by culture. In the United States, the status "uncle" refers to a brother of either mother or father; in Vietnam, however, the word for "uncle" is different when referring to the mother's or father's side of the family, and the two men have different responsibilities. In every society, actual role performance varies according to a person's unique personality, although some societies permit more individual expression of a role than others.

Because we hold many statuses at once in our status set, everyday life is a mix of many roles. Robert Merton (1968) introduced the term **role set** to identify *a number of roles attached to a single status.*

Figure 4–1 shows four statuses of one person, each linked to a different role set. First, as a professor, this woman interacts with students (the teacher role) and other academics (the colleague role). Second, as a researcher, she gathers and analyzes data (the field-work role) that she uses in her publications (the author role). Third,

the same woman holds the status of "wife," with a marital role (such as confidante and sexual partner) toward her spouse, with whom she shares a domestic role toward the household. Fourth, she holds the status of "mother," with routine responsibilities for her children (the maternal role) as well as involvement in their school and other organizations (the civic role).

A global perspective shows us that the roles people use to define their lives differ from society to society. In low-income countries, people spend fewer years as students, and family roles are typically very important to social identity. In high-income nations, people spend more years as students, and family roles may or may not be very important to social identity. Another dimension of difference involves housework. As Global Map 4–1 on page 98 shows, especially in poor nations of the world, doing housework is an important role that falls heavily on women. ● Go to **mysoclab.com**

○ Making the Grade

Remember that *status* refers to a social position and *role* refers to behavior. We *hold* a status and *perform* a role.

role (p. 95) behavior expected of someone who holds a particular status

role set a number of roles attached to a single status

role conflict conflict among the roles connected to two or more statuses

role strain tension among the roles connected to a single status

Role Conflict and Role Strain

People in modern, high-income countries juggle many responsibilities demanded by their various statuses and roles. As most mothers can testify, being a parent and working outside the home both involve physically and emotionally draining roles. Sociologists thus recognize **role conflict** as *conflict among the roles connected to two or more statuses.*

We experience role conflict when we find ourselves pulled in various directions as we try to respond to the many statuses we hold. One response to role conflict is deciding that "something has to go." More than one politician, for example, has decided not to run for office because of the conflicting demands of a hectic campaign schedule and family life. In other cases, people put off having children in order to stay on the "fast track" for career success.

Even roles linked to a single status can make competing demands on us. **Role strain** is *tension among the roles connected to a single status.* A college professor may enjoy being friendly with students. At the same time, however, the professor must maintain the personal distance needed to evaluate students objectively and fairly. In short, performing the roles of even a single status can be something of a balancing act.

One strategy for minimizing role conflict is separating parts of our lives so that we perform roles for one status at one time and place and carry out roles for another status in a completely different setting. A familiar example of this pattern is deciding to "leave the job at work" before heading home to the family.

Role Exit

After she left the life of a Catholic nun to become a university sociologist, Helen Rose Fuchs Ebaugh began to study her own experience of *role exit,* the process by which people disengage from important social roles. In studying a range of "exes," including ex-nuns, ex-doctors, ex-husbands, and ex-alcoholics, Ebaugh saw a pattern in the process of becoming an "ex."

According to Ebaugh (1988), the process begins as people come to doubt their ability to continue in a certain role. As they imagine alternative roles, they ultimately reach a tipping point when they decide to pursue a new life. Even at this point, however, a past role can continue to influence their lives. Exes carry with them a self-image shaped by an earlier role, which can interfere with building a new sense of self. For example, an ex-nun may hesitate to wear stylish clothing and makeup.

Exes must also rebuild relationships with people who knew them in their earlier life. Learning new social skills is another challenge. For example, Ebaugh reports, ex-nuns who enter the dating scene after decades in the church are often surprised to learn that today's sexual norms are very different from those they knew when they were teenagers.

FIGURE 4–1   **Status Set and Role Sets**

A status set includes all the statuses a person holds at a given time. The status set defines *who we are* in society. The many roles linked to each status define *what we do.*

The Social Construction of Reality

In 1917, the Italian playwright Luigi Pirandello wrote a play titled *The Pleasure of Honesty,* about a character named Angelo Baldovino, a brilliant man with a checkered past. Baldovino enters the fashionable home of the Renni family and introduces himself in a peculiar way:

> Inevitably we construct ourselves. Let me explain. I enter this house and immediately I become what I have to become, what I can become: I construct myself. That is, I present myself to you in a form suitable to the relationship I wish to achieve with you. And, of course, you do the same with me. (act 1, scene 1)

Baldovino suggests that although behavior is guided by status and role, we have considerable ability to shape what happens from moment to moment. In other words, "reality" is not as fixed as we may think.

The **social construction of reality** is *the process by which people creatively shape reality through social interaction.* This idea is the foundation of the symbolic-interaction approach, described in Chapter 1 ("Sociology: Perspective, Theory, and Method"). As

Lucila Herrerade Nuñez is a 28-year-old mother of two in Lima, Peru, who works full time and also does all the housework.

Donna Murray, also 28, shares a Boston apartment with her fiancé. Although they agreed to share housework, she still does most of it.

Percentage of Household Work Done by Women
- 90.0% and over
- 80.0% to 89.9%
- 70.0% to 79.9%
- 60.0% to 69.9%

Window on the World

GLOBAL MAP 4–1   **Housework in Global Perspective**

Throughout the world, housework is a major part of women's routines and identities. This is especially true in poor nations of Latin America, Africa, and Asia, where the social position of women is far below that of men. But our society also defines housework and child care as "feminine" activities, even though women and men have the same legal rights and most women work outside the home.

Source: *Peters Atlas of the World* (1990); updated by the author.

Baldovino's remark suggests, quite a bit of "reality" remains unclear in everyone's mind, especially in unfamiliar situations. So we present ourselves in terms that suit the setting and our purposes, and as others do the same, reality takes shape.

Social interaction, then, is a complex negotiation that builds reality. Most everyday situations involve at least some agreement about what's going on. But how people see events depends on their different backgrounds, interests, and intentions. One example of changing patterns in everyday interaction involves greeting another person. Seeing Sociology in the News on pages 100–101 takes a look at how young people have embraced hugging as a form of greeting, replacing the handshakes that are common among their parents.

social construction of reality (p. 97) the process by which people creatively shape reality through social interaction

Thomas theorem W. I. Thomas's claim that situations defined as real are real in their consequences

ethnomethodology Harold Garfinkel's term for the study of the way people make sense of their everyday surroundings

Explore how education shapes reality construction on **www.mysoclab.com**

"Street Smarts"

What people commonly call "street smarts" is actually a form of constructing reality. In his autobiography, *Down These Mean Streets,* Piri Thomas recalls moving to a new apartment in Spanish Harlem. Returning home one evening, young Piri found himself cut off by Waneko, the leader of the local street gang, who was flanked by a dozen others.

> "Whatta ya say, Mr. Johnny Gringo," drawled Waneko.
>
> *Think man,* I told myself, *think your way out of a stomping. Make it good.* "I hear you 104th Street coolies are supposed to have heart," I said. "I don't know this for sure. You know there's a lot of streets where a whole 'click' is made out of punks who can't fight one guy unless they all jump him for the stomp." I hoped this would push Waneko into giving me a fair one. His expression didn't change.
>
> "Maybe we don't look at it that way."
>
> *Crazy, man,* I cheer inwardly, *the* cabron *is falling into my setup.* . . . "I wasn't talking to you," I said. "Where I come from, the pres is president 'cause he got heart when it comes to dealing."
>
> Waneko was starting to look uneasy. He had bit on my worm and felt like a sucker fish. His boys were now light on me. They were no longer so much interested in stomping me as seeing the outcome between Waneko and me. "Yeah," was his reply. . . .
>
> I knew I'd won. Sure, I'd have to fight; but one guy, not ten or fifteen. If I lost, I might still get stomped, and if I won I might get stomped. I took care of this with my next sentence. "I don't know you or your boys," I said, "but they look cool to me. They don't feature as punks."
>
> I had left him out purposely when I said "they." Now his boys were in a separate class. I had cut him off. He would have to fight me on his own, to prove his heart to himself, to his boys, and most important, to his turf. He got away from the stoop and asked, "Fair one, Gringo?" (1967:56–57)

This situation reveals the drama—sometimes subtle, sometimes savage—by which human beings creatively build everyday reality. Of course, not everyone enters a situation with equal power. Should a police officer on patrol have come upon the fight that took place between Piri and Waneko, both young men might have ended up in jail.

Explore on **mysoclab.com**

Flirting is an everyday experience in reality construction. Each person offers information to the other and hints at romantic interest. Yet the interaction proceeds with a tentative and often humorous air so that either individual can withdraw at any time without further obligation.

The Thomas Theorem

By using his wits and fighting with Waneko until they both tired, Piri Thomas won acceptance by the gang. What took place that evening in Spanish Harlem is an example of the **Thomas theorem,** named after W. I. Thomas and Dorothy Thomas (1928; Thomas, 1966:301, orig. 1931): *Situations that are defined as real are real in their consequences.*

Applied to social interaction, the Thomas theorem means that although reality is "soft" as it is being shaped, it can become "hard" in its effects. In the situation just described, local gang members saw Piri Thomas act in a worthy way, so in their eyes, he *became* worthy.

Ethnomethodology

Most of the time, we take social reality for granted. To become more aware of the social world we help create, Harold Garfinkel (1967) came up with **ethnomethodology,** *the study of the way people make sense of their everyday surroundings.* This approach begins by pointing out that everyday behavior rests on a number of assumptions. For instance, when you ask someone the simple question "How are you?" you usually want to know how someone is doing in general, but you might be wondering how a person is dealing with a specific physical, mental, spiritual, or financial challenge. However, the person being asked probably assumes that you are not really interested in the details about any of these things and that you are just "being polite."

One good way to investigate the assumptions we make about everyday reality is to break the rules. For example, the next time someone asks, "How are you?" offer details from your last physical examination or explain all the good and bad things that have happened since you woke up that morning and see how the person reacts.

The results are predictable, because we all have some idea of what the "rules" of everyday interaction are. The person will most likely become confused or irritated by your unexpected behavior—a reaction that helps us see not only what the rules are but how important they are to everyday reality.

The New York Times

For Teenagers, Hello Means "How About a Hug?"

BY SARAH KERSHAW
May 28, 2009

There is so much hugging at Pascack Hills High School in Montvale, New Jersey, that students have broken down the hugs by type:

There is the basic friend hug, probably the most popular, and the bear hug, of course. But now there is also the bear claw, when a boy embraces a girl awkwardly with his elbows poking out.

There is the hug that starts with a high-five, then moves into a fist bump, followed by a slap on the back and an embrace.

There's the shake and lean; the hug from behind; and, the newest addition, the triple—any combination of three girls and boys hugging at once.

"We're not afraid, we just get in and hug," said Danny Schneider, a junior at the school, where hallway hugging began shortly after 7 a.m. on a recent morning as students arrived. "The guy friends, we don't care. You just get right in there and jump in."

There are romantic hugs, too, but that is not what these teenagers are talking about.

Girls embracing girls, girls embracing boys, boys embracing each other—the hug has become the favorite social greeting when teenagers meet or part these days. Teachers joke about "one hour" and "six hour" hugs, saying that students hug one another all day as if they were separated for the entire summer.

A measure of how rapidly the ritual is spreading is that some students complain of peer pressure to hug to fit in. And schools from Hillsdale, New Jersey, to Bend, Oregon, wary in a litigious era about sexual harassment or improper touching—or citing hallway clogging and late arrivals to class—have banned hugging or imposed a three-second rule.

Parents, who grew up in a generation more likely to use the handshake, the low-five or the high-five, are often baffled by the close physical contact. "It's a wordless custom, from what I've observed," wrote Beth J. Harpaz, the mother of two boys, 11 and 16, and a parenting columnist

for The Associated Press, in a new book, *13 Is the New 18.*

"And there doesn't seem to be any other overt way in which they acknowledge knowing each other," she continued, describing the scene at her older son's school in Manhattan. "No hi, no smile, no wave, no high-five—just the hug. Witnessing this interaction always makes me feel like I am a tourist in a country where I do not know the customs and cannot speak the language."

For teenagers, though, hugging is hip. And not hugging?

"If somebody were to not hug someone, to never hug anybody, people might be just a little wary of them and think they are weird or peculiar," said Gabrielle Brown, a freshman at Fiorello H. LaGuardia High School in Manhattan.

Comforting as the hug may be, principals across the country have clamped down. "Touching and physical contact is very dangerous territory," said Noreen Hajinlian, the principal of George G. White School, a junior high school in Hillsdale, New Jersey, who banned hugging two years ago. . . .

Reality Building: Class and Culture

People do not build everyday experience out of thin air. In part, how we act or what we see in our surroundings depends on our interests. Gazing at the sky on a starry night, for example, lovers discover romance and scientists see hydrogen atoms fusing into helium. Social background also affects what we see, which is why the residents of Spanish Harlem experience a different world than people living on Manhattan's pricey Upper East Side.

In global perspective, reality construction varies even more. Consider these everyday situations: People waiting for a bus in London typically "queue up" in a straight line; people in New York City are rarely so orderly. The law in Saudi Arabia forbids women to drive cars, a ban unthinkable in the United States. In this country, a "short walk" means a few blocks or a few minutes; in the Andes Mountains of Peru, this same phrase means a few miles.

The point is that people build reality from the surrounding culture. Chapter 2 ("Culture") explains how people the world over find different meanings in specific gestures, so inexperienced travelers can find themselves building an unexpected and unwelcome reality. Similarly, in a study of popular culture, JoEllen Shively (1992) screened films set in the American West to men of European descent and to Native American men. The men in both categories claimed to enjoy the films, but for different reasons. White

People build reality from their surrounding culture. Yet because cultural systems are marked by diversity and even outright conflict, reality construction always involves tensions and choices. Turkey is a nation with a mostly Muslim population, but it has also embraced Western culture. Here, women confront starkly different definitions of what is "feminine."

Staton R. Winter, *The New York Times.*

But pro-hugging students say it is not a romantic or sexual gesture, simply the "hello" of their generation. "We like to get cozy," said Katie Dea, an eighth grader at Claire Lilienthal Alternative School in San Francisco. "The high-five is, like, boring."

Some sociologists said that teenagers who grew up in an era of organized play dates and close parental supervision are more cooperative with one another than previous generations—less cynical and individualistic and more loyal to the group.

But Amy L. Best, a sociologist at George Mason University, said the teenage embrace is more a reflection of the overall evolution of the American greeting, which has become less formal since the 1970s. "Without question, the boundaries of touch have changed in American culture," she said. "We display bodies more readily, there are fewer rules governing body touch and a lot more permissible access to other people's bodies."

Hugging appears to be a grass-roots phenomenon and not an imitation of a character or custom on TV or in movies. The prevalence of boys' nonromantic hugging (especially of other boys) is most striking to adults. Experts say that over the last generation, boys have become more comfortable expressing emotion, as embodied by the MTV show "Bromance," which is now a widely used term for affection between straight male friends.

But some sociologists pointed out that African American boys and men have been hugging as part of their greeting for decades, using the word "dap" to describe a ritual involving handshakes, slaps on the shoulders and, more recently, a hug, also sometimes called the gangsta hug among urban youth. . . .

There are, too, some young critics of hugging.

Amy Heaton, a freshman at Bethesda-Chevy Chase High School in Bethesda, Maryland, said casual social hugging seemed disingenuous to her. . . . "It's like air-kissing. It's really superficial."

But Carrie Osbourne, a sixth-grade teacher at Claire Lilienthal Alternative School, said hugging was a powerful and positive sign that children are inclined to nurture one another, breaking down barriers. "And it gets to that core that every person wants to feel cared for, regardless of your age or how cool you are or how cool you think you are," she said.

WHAT DO YOU THINK?

1. The handshake of the adult world has been replaced by the hug of the teenage world. Can you think of other everyday life gestures that differ from one generation to another? Explain.

2. Have you ever felt "not hip" for not hugging someone? If so, explain what happened.

3. Why do you think many older people consider hugging (or other physical touching) "dangerous territory," while younger people seem more casual about this?

men interpreted the films as praising rugged people striking out for the frontier and conquering the forces of nature. Native American men saw in the same films a celebration of land and nature. Given their different cultures, it is as if people in the two categories saw two different films.

Films also have an effect on the reality we all experience. The 2009 film *Adam,* for example, about a young man with Asperger syndrome, is one of a series of recent films that have changed people's awareness of the struggle of coping with mental disorders.

Dramaturgical Analysis: The "Presentation of Self"

Erving Goffman (1922–1982) was another sociologist who analyzed social interaction, explaining how people live their lives much like actors performing on a stage. If we imagine ourselves as directors observing what goes on in the theater of everyday life, we are doing what Goffman called **dramaturgical analysis,** *the study of social interaction in terms of theatrical performance.*

Dramaturgical analysis offers a fresh look at the concepts of status and role. A status is like a part in a play, and a role is a script, supplying dialogue and action for the characters. Goffman described each person's performance as the **presentation of self,** *a person's efforts to create specific impressions in the minds of others.* This process, sometimes called *impression management,* begins with the idea of personal performance (Goffman, 1959, 1967).

Performances

As we present ourselves in everyday situations, we reveal information to others both consciously and unconsciously. Our performances include the way we dress (in theatrical terms, our costume), the objects we carry (props), and our tone of voice and the way we carry ourselves (our demeanor). In addition, we vary our performances according to where we happen to be (the set). We may joke loudly in a restaurant or at a sporting event, for example, but we lower our voices when entering a house of worship. People design settings, such as homes or offices, to bring about desired reactions in others.

An Application: The Doctor's Office

Consider how the operation of a physician's office conveys important information to an audience of patients. The fact that medical doctors enjoy high prestige and power in the United States is clear upon entering a doctor's office. First, the doctor is nowhere to be seen. Instead, in what Goffman describes as the "front region" of the setting, the patient encounters a receptionist, who works as a gatekeeper, deciding whether and when the patient can meet the doctor. A simple

Read "The Presentation of Self in Everyday Life" by Erving Goffman on **mysoclab.com**

Seeing Sociology in Everyday Life

Members of every culture have rules about how close people should stand while talking. To see what the rules are in your social world, during a conversation, slowly move closer and closer to the other person and see what happens.

I didn't ask you to undress so I could examine you. I asked you to undress because it's essential to the doctor-patient relationship that I be fully clothed and you be sitting there in your underwear.

SIPRESS

glance around the doctor's waiting room, with patients (often impatiently) waiting to be invited into the inner sanctum, leaves little doubt that the doctor and staff are in charge.

The "back region" is composed of the examination rooms as well as the doctor's private office. Once inside the office, the patient can see a wide range of props, such as medical books and framed degrees, that give the impression that the doctor has the specialized knowledge necessary to call the shots. The doctor is usually seated behind a desk—the larger and grander the desk, the greater the statement of power—and the patient is given only a chair.

The doctor's appearance and manner offer still more information. The usual white lab coat (costume) may have the practical function of keeping clothes from becoming dirty, but its social function is to let others know the physician's status at a glance. A stethoscope around the neck and a black medical bag in hand (more props) have the same purpose. The doctor uses highly technical language that is often mystifying to the patient, again emphasizing that the doctor is in charge. Finally, patients use the title "doctor," but they, in turn, are often addressed only by their first names, which further shows the doctor's dominant position. The overall message of a doctor's performance is clear: "I will help you, but you must allow me to take charge." **Read on mysoclab.com**

Nonverbal Communication

The novelist William Sansom describes the performance of a character named Mr. Preedy, an English vacationer on a beach in Spain:

> He took care to avoid catching anyone's eye. First, he had to make it clear to those potential companions of his holiday that they were of no concern to him whatsoever. He stared through them, round them, over them—eyes lost in space. The beach might have been empty. If by chance a ball was thrown his way, he looked surprised; then let a smile of amusement light his face (Kindly Preedy), looked around dazed to see that there were people on the beach, tossed it back with a smile to himself and not a smile *at* the people. . . .
>
> [He] then gathered together his beach-wrap and bag into a neat sand-resistant pile (Methodical and Sensible Preedy), rose slowly to stretch his huge frame (Big-Cat Preedy), and tossed aside his sandals (Carefree Preedy, after all). (1956:230–31)

Without saying a single word, Mr. Preedy offers a great deal of information about himself to anyone watching him. This is the process of **nonverbal communication,** *communication using body movements, gestures, and facial expressions rather than speech.*

Many parts of the body can be used to generate *body language,* that is, to convey information to others. Facial expressions are the most significant form of body language. Smiling, for example, shows pleasure, although we distinguish among the deliberate smile of Kindly Preedy on the beach, a spontaneous smile of joy at seeing a friend, a pained smile of embarrassment, and the full, unrestrained smile of self-satisfaction we often associate with winning some important contest.

Eye contact is another crucial element of nonverbal communication. Generally, we use eye contact to invite social interaction. Someone across the room "catches our eye," sparking a conversation. Avoiding another's eyes, by contrast, discourages communication. Hands also speak for us. Common hand gestures within our culture convey, among other things, an insult, a request for a ride, an invitation for someone to join us, or a demand that others stop in their tracks. Gestures also add meaning to spoken words. For example, pointing in a threatening way gives greater emphasis to a word of warning, shrugging the shoulders adds an air of indifference to the phrase "I don't know," and rapidly waving the arms lends urgency to the single word "Hurry!"

Body Language and Deception

As any actor knows, it is very difficult to pull off a perfect performance in front of others. In everyday life, unintended body language can contradict our planned meaning: A teenage boy explains why he is getting home so late, for example, but his mother doubts his words because he avoids looking her in the eye; the movie star on a television talk show claims that her recent flop at the box office is "no big deal," but the nervous swing of her leg suggests otherwise. Because

dramaturgical analysis (p. 101) Erving Goffman's term for the study of social interaction in terms of theatrical performance

presentation of self (p. 101) Erving Goffman's term for a person's efforts to create specific impressions in the minds of others

nonverbal communication communication using body movements, gestures, and facial expressions rather than speech

personal space the surrounding area over which a person makes some claim to privacy

Seeing Sociology in Everyday Life

After reading the analysis of doctors' offices (pp. 101–2), try doing a similar analysis of the offices of several faculty members on your campus. What differences do you notice? How can you explain the patterns?

nonverbal communication is hard to control, it provides clues to deception, in much the same way that changes in breathing, pulse rate, perspiration, and blood pressure recorded on a lie detector suggest that a person is lying.

Recognizing dishonest performances is difficult because no single bodily gesture tells us for sure that someone is lying. But because any performance involves so many bits of body language, few people can keep up a lie without some slip-up, raising the suspicions of a careful observer. Therefore, the key to detecting lies is to view the whole performance with an eye for inconsistencies.

Gender and Performances

Because women are socialized to respond to others, they tend to be more sensitive than men to nonverbal communication. In fact, gender is a central element in personal performances.

Demeanor

Demeanor—the way we act and carry ourselves—is a clue to social power. Simply put, powerful people enjoy more personal freedom in how they act. Off-color remarks, swearing, or putting one's feet on the desk may be acceptable for the boss but rarely for employees. Similarly, powerful people can interrupt others, but less powerful people are expected to show respect through silence (Smith-Lovin & Brody, 1989; Henley, Hamilton, & Thorne, 1992; C. Johnson, 1994).

Because women generally occupy positions of less power, demeanor is a gender issue as well. As Chapter 10 ("Gender Stratification") explains, 40 percent of all working women in the United States hold secretarial or service jobs under the control of supervisors who are usually men. Women, then, learn to craft their personal performances more carefully than men and defer to men more often in everyday interaction.

Use of Space

How much space does a personal performance require? Power plays a key role here; the more power you have, the more space you use. Men typically command more space than women, whether pacing back and forth before an audience or casually stretching out on a bench. Why? Our culture has traditionally measured femininity by how *little* space women occupy—the standard of "daintiness"—and masculinity by how *much* territory a man controls—the standard of "turf" (Henley, Hamilton, & Thorne, 1992).

For both sexes, **personal space** is *the surrounding area over which a person makes some claim to privacy.* In the United States, people generally stay several feet apart when speaking; throughout the Middle East, by contrast, people stand much closer. But just about every-

When we observe the performances of other people, we are often aware that what we see is not completely "real." In the 2009 film *Surrogates,* people of the future are able to buy robots that look just like themselves—only without any human flaws—and allow these "surrogates" to live for them while they remain electronically linked to the action in the safety of their homes. Why do you think this film was so popular with audiences?

where, men (with their greater social power) often intrude into women's personal space. If a woman moves into a man's personal space, however, he is likely to take it as a sign of sexual interest.

Staring, Smiling, and Touching

Eye contact encourages interaction. In conversations, women hold eye contact more than men. But men have their own brand of eye contact: staring. When men stare at women, they are claiming social dominance and defining women as sexual objects.

Although it often shows pleasure, smiling can also be a sign of trying to please someone or of submission. In a male-dominated world, it is not surprising that women smile more than men (Henley, Hamilton, & Thorne, 1992).

Finally, mutual touching suggests intimacy and caring. Apart from close relationships, however, touching is generally something men do to women (but rarely, in our culture, to other men). A male doctor touches the shoulder of his female nurse as they examine a report, a young man touches the back of his woman friend as he guides her across the street, or a male instructor touches the arms of young women as he teaches them to ski. In such examples, the intent of the touching may be harmless and may bring little response, but it

○— Seeing Sociology
in Everyday Life

Watch female-male couples holding hands. Which person has the
hand to the front and which has the hand to the rear? Can you see
a pattern and offer an explanation?

○— Seeing Sociology
in Everyday Life

Using Goffman's approach, offer examples of performances,
nonverbal communication, idealization, and tact in your own life.

Hand gestures vary widely from one culture to another. Yet people everywhere chuckle, grin, or
smirk to indicate that they don't take another person's performance seriously. Therefore, the world
over, people who cannot restrain their mirth tactfully cover their faces.

amounts to a subtle ritual by which men claim dominance over
women.

Idealization

People behave the way they do for many, often complex reasons. Even
so, Goffman suggests, we construct performances to *idealize* our
intentions. That is, we try to convince others (and perhaps ourselves)
that our actions reflect ideal cultural standards rather than selfish
motives.

Idealization is easily illustrated by returning to the world of doctors and patients. In a hospital, doctors engage in a performance
known as "making rounds." Upon entering a patient's room, the doctor often stops at the foot of the bed and silently examines the
patient's chart. Afterward, doctor and patient talk briefly. In ideal
terms, this routine represents a personal visit to check on a patient's
condition.

In reality, the picture is not so perfect. A doctor may see dozens
of patients a day and remember little about many of them. Reading
the chart is a chance to recall the patient's name and medical problems, but revealing the impersonality of the patient's care would
undermine the cultural ideal of the doctor as deeply concerned about
the welfare of others.

Doctors, college professors, and other professionals typically
idealize their motives for entering their chosen careers. They are
quick to describe their work as "making a contribution to science,"
"serving the community," or even "answering a call from God."
Rarely do people admit the more common, less honorable motives:
the income, power, prestige, and leisure time that these occupations
provide.

We all use idealization to some degree. When was the last time
you smiled and made polite remarks to someone you did not like?
Such little lies ease our way through social interactions. Even when
we suspect that others are putting on an act, we are unlikely to challenge their performance, for reasons that we shall examine next.

Embarrassment and Tact

The famous speaker giving a campus lecture keeps mispronouncing
the college's name; the visiting ambassador rises from the table to
speak, unaware of the napkin that still hangs from his neck; the president becomes ill at a state dinner. As carefully as people may craft
their performances, slip-ups of all kinds happen. The result is
embarrassment, or discomfort after a spoiled performance. Goffman
describes embarrassment as "losing face."

Embarrassment is an ever-present danger because idealized performances typically contain some deception. In addition, most performances involve juggling so many elements that one thoughtless
moment can shatter the intended impression.

A curious fact is that an audience often overlooks flaws in a
performance, allowing the actor to avoid embarrassment. If we do
point out a misstep ("Excuse me, but your fly is open"), we do it
quietly and only to help someone avoid even greater loss of face. In
Hans Christian Andersen's classic fable "The Emperor's New
Clothes," the child who blurts out the truth, that the emperor is
parading about naked, is scolded for being rude.

Often members of an audience actually help the performer
recover from a flawed performance. *Tact* is helping someone "save
face." After hearing a supposed expert make an embarrassingly inaccurate remark, for example, we might ignore the comment, as if it

◦ Making the Grade

In terms of this discussion, embarrassment amounts to a ruined performance that causes an actor to "lose face." Tact is efforts to help others maintain a successful performance, or to "save face" after some interactional slip-up.

◦ Making the Grade

Emotions are complex and reflect both biological and cultural forces. Sociologists are interested in how culture affects our emotional life.

To most people in the United States, these expressions convey anger, fear, disgust, happiness, surprise, and sadness. But do people elsewhere in the world define them in the same way? Research suggests that all human beings experience the same basic emotions and display them to others in the same basic ways. But culture plays a part by specifying the situations that trigger one emotion or another.

had never been spoken. Or with mild laughter we could treat what was said as a joke. Or we could simply respond, "I'm sure you didn't mean that," hearing the statement but not allowing it to destroy the performance. With these options in mind, it is easier to understand Abraham Lincoln's observation that "tact is the ability to describe others the way they see themselves."

Why is tact so common? Embarrassment creates discomfort not only for the actor but also for everyone else. Just as the entire audience feels uneasy when an actor forgets a line, people who observe the awkward behavior of others are reminded of how fragile their own performances often are. Socially constructed reality thus functions like a dam holding back a sea of chaos. Should one person's performance spring a leak, others tactfully help make repairs. After all, everyone lends a hand in building reality, and no one wants it suddenly swept away.

In sum, Goffman's research shows that although behavior is spontaneous in some respects, it is more patterned than we like to think. Almost 400 years ago, William Shakespeare captured this idea in lines that still ring true:

> All the world's a stage,
> And all the men and women merely players:
> They have their exits and their entrances;
> And one man in his time plays many parts.

> (*As You Like It*, act 2, scene 7)

Interaction in Everyday Life: Three Applications

The final sections of this chapter illustrate the major elements of social interaction by focusing on three important dimensions of everyday life: emotions, language, and humor.

Emotions: The Social Construction of Feeling

Emotions, more commonly called *feelings,* are an important dimension of everyday life. Indeed, what we *do* often matters less than how we *feel* about it. Emotions seem very personal because they are "inside." Even so, just as society guides our behavior, it guides our emotional life.

The Biological Side of Emotions

Studying the social interaction of men and women all over the world, Paul Ekman (1980a, 1980b) reported that people everywhere express six basic emotions: happiness, sadness, anger, fear, disgust, and surprise. In addition, Ekman found that people in every society use much the same facial expressions to show these emotions. To help us understand this universal problem, Ekman explains that some emotional responses seem to be "wired" into human beings; that is, they are biologically programmed in our facial features, muscles, and central nervous system.

Why? Over centuries of evolution, emotions developed in the human species because they serve a social purpose: supporting group life. Emotions are powerful forces that allow us to overcome our individualism and build connections with others. Thus the capacity for emotion arose in our ancestors along with the capacity for culture (Turner, 2000).

The Cultural Side of Emotions

But culture does play an important role in guiding human emotions. First, Ekman explains, culture defines *what triggers* an emotion. Whether people define the departure of an old friend as joyous (causing happiness), insulting (arousing anger), a loss (creating sadness), or mystical (causing surprise and awe) has a lot to do with the culture.

Seeing Sociology in Everyday Life

What emotions are (or are not) expected of a college professor in front of a class?

Seeing Sociology in Everyday Life

What are the "emotional scripts" that students might apply to college graduation? That is, why might people see this event in positive or negative terms?

CONTROVERSY & DEBATE

Managing Feelings: Women's Abortion Experiences

Liz: I just *can't* be pregnant! There's no way I can deal with a baby at this point in my life! I'm going to see my doctor tomorrow about an abortion.

Jen: I can't believe you'd do that, Liz! How are you going to feel in a couple of years when you think of what that *child* would be doing if you'd let it live?

Few issues today generate as much emotion as abortion. In a study of women's abortion experiences, the sociologist Jennifer Keys (2002) discovered emotional scripts or "feeling rules" that guide how women feel about ending a pregnancy.

Keys explains that different emotional scripts arise from the political controversy surrounding abortion. The antiabortion movement defines abortion as a personal tragedy, the "killing of an unborn child." Given this definition, which we see in Jen's comment above, women who end a preg-

nancy through abortion are doing something very wrong and can expect to feel grief, guilt,

The words that doctors and nurses use guide whether a woman having an abortion defines the experience in positive or negative terms.

and regret. So intense are these feelings, according to supporters of this position, that such women often suffer from "postabortion syndrome."

Those who take the pro-choice position have an opposing view of abortion. From this point of view, illustrated by Liz's comment, the woman's problem is the *unwanted pregnancy*; abortion is an acceptable medical solution. Therefore, the emotion to be expected in a woman who ends a pregnancy is not guilt but relief.

In her research, Keys conducted in-depth interviews with forty women who had recently had abortions and found that all of them used such scripts to "frame" their situation in an antiabortion or pro-choice manner. In part, this construction of reality reflects the woman's own attitude about abortion. In addition, however, women's partners and friends typically encouraged specific feelings

---

Second, culture provides rules for the *display* of emotions. For example, most people in the United States express emotions more freely with family members than with others in the workplace. Similarly, we expect children to express emotions to parents, although parents tend to hide their emotions from their children. Third, culture guides how we *value* emotions. Some societies encourage the expression of emotion, while others expect members to control their feelings and maintain a "stiff upper lip." Gender also plays a part; traditionally at least, many cultures expect women to show emotions while condemning emotional expression by men as a sign of weakness. In some cultures, of course, this pattern is less pronounced or even reversed.

Emotions on the Job

In the United States, most people are freer to express their feelings at home than on the job. This is because, as Arlie Russell Hochschild (1979, 1983) explains, the typical corporation or other place of busi-

ness does indeed try to control not only the behavior of its employees but also their emotions. Take the case of an airline flight attendant who offers passengers a drink, a snack, and a smile. Do you think that this smile might convey real pleasure at serving the customer? It may. But Hochschild's study of flight attendants points to a different conclusion: The smile is an emotional script demanded by the airline as the right way to do the job. Therefore, from Hochschild's research we see an added dimension of the "presentation of self" described by Erving Goffman. Not only do our everyday life presentations to others involve surface acting but they also involve the "deep acting" of emotions.

With these patterns in mind, it is easy to see that we socially construct our emotions as part of our everyday reality, a process sociologists call *emotion management*. The Controversy & Debate box relates the very different emotions displayed by women who decide to have an abortion, depending on their personal view of terminating a pregnancy.

Seeing Sociology in Everyday Life

List words that people use to describe a very sexually active female. How many such terms are there? Are they positive or negative in meaning? Repeat this exercise for a very sexually active male. What differences do you notice?

Making the Grade

The language we use has the effect of reflecting and reinforcing patterns of male dominance.

about the event. Ivy, one young woman in the study, had a close friend who was also pregnant. "Congratulations!" she exclaimed when she learned of Ivy's condition. "We're going to be having babies together!" Such a statement established one "feeling rule"—having a baby is *good*—which sent the message to Ivy that her planned abortion should trigger guilt. Working in the other direction, Jo's partner was horrified at the news that she was pregnant. Doubting his own ability to be a father, he blurted out, "I would rather put a gun to my head than have this baby!" His panic not only defined having the child as a mistake but alarmed Jo as well. Clearly, her partner's reaction made the decision to end the pregnancy a matter of relief from a terrible problem.

Medical personnel also play a part in the process of reality construction by using specific terms. Nurses and doctors who talk about "the baby" encourage the antiabortion framing of abortion and provoke grief and guilt. On the

other hand, those who use language such as "pregnancy tissue," "fetus," or "the contents of the uterus" encourage the pro-choice framing of abortion as a simple medical procedure leading to relief. Olivia began using the phrase "products of conception," which she picked up from her doctor. Denise spoke of her procedure as "taking the extra cells out of my body. Yeah, I did feel some guilt when I thought that this was the beginning of life, but my body is full of life—you have lots of cells in you."

After the procedure, most women reported actively trying to manage their feelings. Explained Ivy, "I never used the word 'baby.' I kept saying to myself that it was not formed yet. There was nothing there yet. I kept that in my mind." On the other hand, Keys found that all of the women in her study who had undergone abortions but nevertheless leaned toward the antiabortion position did use the term "baby." When interviewed, Gina explained, "I do think of it as a baby. The truth is that I ended my

baby's life and I should not have done that. Thinking that makes me feel guilty. But—considering what I did—maybe I *should* feel guilty." Believing that what she had done was wrong, in other words, Gina actively called out the feeling of guilt—in part, Keys concluded, to punish herself.

WHAT DO YOU THINK?

1. In your own words, explain "emotional scripts" or "feeling rules."

2. Can you apply the idea of "scripting feelings" to the experience of getting married?

3. In light of this discussion, to what extent is it correct to say that our feelings are not as personal as we may think they are?

Language: The Social Construction of Gender

As Chapter 2 ("Culture") explains, language is the thread that weaves members of a society in the symbolic web we call culture. Language conveys not only a surface message but also deeper levels of meaning. One important level involves gender. Language defines men and women differently in terms of both power and value (Henley, Hamilton, & Thorne, 1992; Thorne, Kramarae, & Henley, 1983).

Language and Power

A young man proudly rides his new motorcycle up his friend's driveway and asks, "Isn't she a beauty?" On the surface, the question has little to do with gender. Yet why does he use the pronoun *she* rather than *he* or *it* to refer to his prized possession?

The answer is that language helps men establish control over their surroundings. That is, a man attaches a female pronoun to a motorcycle (or car, boat, or other object) because doing so reflects

ownership. Perhaps this is also why, in the United States and elsewhere, traditionally a woman who marries takes the last name of her husband. But some women today (currently about 18 percent) are asserting their independence by keeping their own name or combining the two family names.

Language and Value

Typically, the English language treats as masculine whatever has greater value, force, or significance. For instance, the adjective *virtuous,* meaning "morally worthy" or "excellent," is derived from the Latin word *vir,* meaning "man." On the other hand, the adjective *hysterical,* meaning "emotionally out of control" comes from the Greek word *hyster,* meaning "uterus."

In many familiar ways, language also confers a different value on the two sexes. Traditional masculine terms such as *king* or *lord* have a positive meaning, while comparable terms, such as *queen, madam,* or *dame,* can have negative meanings. Similarly, the use of the suffixes *-ess* and *-ette* to indicate femininity usually devalues the words

● Seeing Sociology
in Everyday Life

Can you describe other examples of types of work that not only
demand particular behavior but also require people to display
particular emotions? Explain.

┌● Making the Grade

The foundation of humor follows from the earlier discussion of the
social construction of reality—building and contrasting two different
definitions of reality.

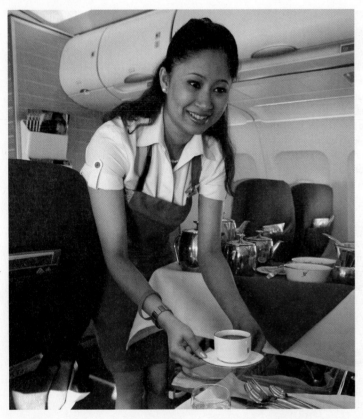

Many of us think emotions are simply part of our biological makeup. While
there is a biological foundation to human emotion, sociologists have demonstrated that what triggers an emotion—as well as when, where, and to whom
the emotion is displayed—is shaped by culture. For example, many
occupations not only regulate a worker's on-the-job behavior but also
expect workers to display a particular emotion, as in the case of the
always-smiling airline flight attendant. Can you think of other jobs that
regulate emotions in this way?

to which they are added. For example, a *major* has higher standing
than a *majorette*, as does a *host* in relation to a *hostess* or a *master* to a
mistress. Thus language both mirrors social attitudes and helps perpetuate them.

Given the importance of gender to social interaction in everyday life, perhaps we should not be surprised that women and men
sometimes have trouble communicating with each other. In the
Thinking About Diversity box, Harold and Sybil, whose misadven-
tures finding their friends' home were described in the opening to this
chapter, return to illustrate how the two sexes often seem to be speaking different languages.

Reality Play: The Social Construction of Humor

Humor plays an important part in everyday life. Everyone laughs at
a joke, but few people think about what makes something funny. We
can apply many of the ideas developed in this chapter to explain how,
by using humor, we "play with reality" (Macionis, 1987).

The Foundation of Humor

Humor is produced by the social construction of reality; specifically,
it arises as people create and contrast two different realities. Generally, one reality is *conventional,* that is, what people in a specific situation expect. The other reality is *unconventional,* an unexpected
violation of cultural patterns. In short, humor arises from the contradictions, ambiguities, and double meanings found in differing definitions of the same situation.

There are countless ways to mix realities and thereby generate
humor. Contrasting realities emerge from statements that contradict themselves, such as "Nostalgia is not what it used to be"; statements that repeat themselves, such as Yogi Berra's line "It's *déjà vu* all
over again"; or statements that mix up words, such as Oscar Wilde's
line, "Work is the curse of the drinking class." Even switching around
syllables does the trick, as in the case of the country song "I'd Rather
Have a Bottle in Front of Me than a Frontal Lobotomy."

You can also build a joke the other way around, leading the audience to expect an unconventional answer and then delivering a very
ordinary one. When a reporter asked the famous criminal Willy Sutton why he robbed banks, for example, he replied dryly, "Because
that's where the money is." Regardless of how a joke is constructed,
the greater the opposition or difference between the two definitions
of reality, the greater the humor.

When telling jokes, the comedian uses various strategies to
strengthen this opposition and make the joke funnier. One common
technique is to present the first, conventional remark in conversation with another actor but then turn toward the audience or the
camera to deliver the second, unexpected line. In a Marx Brothers
movie, Groucho remarks, "Outside of a dog, a book is a man's best
friend." Then, raising his voice and turning to the camera, he adds,
"And *inside* of a dog, it's too dark to read!" Such "changing channels" emphasizes the difference between the conventional and unconventional realities. Following the same logic, many stand-up
comedians also "reset" the audience to conventional expectations by
adding "But seriously, folks, . . ." between jokes. Monty Python comedian John Cleese did this with his trademark line, "And now for
something completely different."

Comedians pay careful attention to their performances—the
precise words they use and the timing with which they deliver their

THINKING ABOUT DIVERSITY: RACE, CLASS, & GENDER

Gender and Language: "You Just Don't Understand!"

In the story that opened this chapter, Harold and Sybil faced a situation that rings all too true to many people: When they are lost, men grumble to themselves and perhaps blame their partners but avoid asking for directions. For their part, women can't understand why men refuse help when they need it.

Deborah Tannen (1990) explains that men typically define most everyday encounters as competitive. Therefore, getting lost is bad enough without asking for help, which lets someone else get "one up." By contrast, because women have traditionally had a subordinate position, they find it easy to ask for help. Sometimes, Tannen points out, women ask for assistance even when they don't need it.

A similar gender-linked pattern involves what women consider "trying to be helpful" and men call "nagging." Consider the following exchange (adapted from Adler, 1990):

SYBIL: What's wrong, honey?

HAROLD: Nothing.

SYBIL: Something is bothering you. I can tell.

HAROLD: I told you nothing is bothering me. Leave me alone.

SYBIL: But I can see that something is wrong.

HAROLD: OK. Just why do you think something is bothering me?

SYBIL: Well, for one thing, you're bleeding all over your shirt.

HAROLD: (*now irritated*) Yeah, well, it doesn't bother me.

SYBIL: (*losing her temper*) WELL, IT SURE IS BOTHERING ME!

HAROLD: (*walking away*) Fine. I'll go change my shirt.

The problem couples face in communicating is that what one partner *intends* by a comment is not always what the other *hears* in the words. To Sybil, her opening question is an effort at cooperative problem solving. She can see that

something is wrong with Harold (who has cut himself while doing yard work), and she wants to help him. But Harold interprets her pointing out his problem as belittling him and tries to close off the discussion. Sybil, confident that Harold would be more positive toward her if he just understood that she only wants to be helpful, repeats her question. This sets in motion a vicious circle in which Harold, thinking his wife is trying to make him feel incapable of looking after himself, responds by digging in his heels. This, in turn, makes his wife all the more sure that she needs to do something. And around it goes until somebody gets really angry.

In the end, Harold agrees to change his shirt but still refuses to discuss the original problem. Defining his wife's concern as "nagging," Harold just wants Sybil to leave him alone. For her part, Sybil fails to understand her husband's view of the situation and walks away convinced that he is a stubborn grouch.

WHAT DO YOU THINK?

1. Based on this box, how would you describe the basic difference between the way men and women talk?

2. What are the reasons for any gender differences in language?

3. Do you think that understanding Tannen's conclusions would help female-male couples communicate better? Why or why not?

---

lines. A joke is well told if the comic times the lines to create the sharpest possible opposition between the realities; in a careless performance, the joke falls flat. Because the key to humor lies in the collision of realities, we can see why the climax of a joke is termed the "*punch* line."

The Dynamics of Humor: "Getting It"

After hearing a joke, did you ever say, "I don't get it"? To "get" humor, members of an audience must understand the two realities involved well enough to appreciate their difference. A comedian may make getting the joke harder by leaving out some important information. In such cases, the audience must pay attention to the stated elements of the joke and fill in the missing pieces. As a simple example, consider the comment of movie producer Hal Roach upon reaching his hundredth birthday: "If I had known I would live to be one hundred, I would have taken better care of myself!" Here, getting the joke depends on realizing the unstated fact that Roach must have taken pretty good care of himself because he did make it to one hundred.

Seeing Sociology in Everyday Life

Here is a joke about sociologists: How many sociologists does it take to change a light bulb? Answer: None. There is nothing wrong with the light bulb; it's *the system* that needs to be changed! What makes this joke funny? What sort of people are likely to get it? What kind of people probably won't? Why?

Seeing Sociology in Everyday Life

Can you remember some of the first jokes you ever heard as a child? Can you explain why very young people's humor focuses on certain topics?

Humor provides an opportunity to express sentiments that are potentially dangerous or disruptive. For this reason, people in every society use humor when they talk about those in power. With this thought in mind, can you explain why just about every president has been the target of jokes? Here, Dwayne "The Rock" Johnson impersonates President Obama on *Saturday Night Live*.

Or take one of W. C. Fields's lines: "Some weasel took the cork out of my lunch!" "What a lunch!" we think to ourselves to "finish" the joke.

Here is an even more complex joke: What do you get if you cross an insomniac, a dyslexic, and an agnostic? Answer: A person who stays up all night wondering if there is a dog. To get this one, you must know that insomnia is an inability to sleep, that dyslexia causes a person to reverse letters in words, and that an agnostic doubts the existence of God.

Why would a comedian require the audience to make this sort of effort to understand a joke? Our enjoyment of a joke is increased by the pleasure of figuring out all the pieces needed to "get it." In addition, "getting" the joke makes you an "insider" compared to

those who don't get it. We have all experienced the frustration of not getting a joke: fear of being judged stupid, coupled with a sense of being excluded from a pleasure shared by others. Sometimes someone may tactfully explain a joke so the other person doesn't feel left out. But as the old saying goes, if a joke has to be explained, it isn't very funny.

The Topics of Humor

All over the world, people smile and laugh, making humor a universal element of human culture. But because the world's people live in different cultures, humor rarely travels well.

> **October 1, Kobe, Japan.** Can you share a joke with people who live halfway around the world? At dinner, I ask two Japanese college women to tell me a joke. "You know 'crayon'?" Asako asks. I nod. "How do you ask for a crayon in Japanese?" I respond that I have no idea. She laughs out loud as she says what sounds like "crayon crayon." Her companion Mayumi laughs too. My wife and I sit awkwardly, straight-faced. Asako relieves some of our embarrassment by explaining that the Japanese word for "give me" is kureyo, which sounds like "crayon." I force a smile.

What is humorous to the Japanese, then, may be lost on the Chinese, Brazilians, or people in the United States. Even the social diversity of this country means that people will find humor in different situations. New Englanders, southerners, and westerners have their own brands of humor, as do Latinos and Anglos, fifteen- and fifty-year-olds, Wall Street bankers and rodeo riders.

But for everyone, topics that lend themselves to double meanings or controversy generate humor. For example, in the United States, the first jokes many of us learned as children concerned bodily functions kids are not supposed to talk about. The mere mention of "unmentionable acts" or certain parts of the body can dissolve young faces in laughter.

Are there jokes that can break through the cultural barrier? Yes, but they must touch on universal human experiences such as, say, turning on a friend:

> I think of a number of jokes, but none seems likely to work. Understanding jokes about the United States is difficult for people who know little about our culture. Is there something more universal? Inspiration: "Two men are walking in the woods

● Seeing Sociology
in Everyday Life

Humor is most common among people with roughly the same social
standing. Why is it risky to joke with people who have more power
than you do? What about joking with people who have less power?

● Making the Grade

Why would comedians doing "blue-collar humor" have to look
and sound like "Larry the cable guy"?

and come upon a huge bear. One guy leans over and tightens up the laces on his running shoes. 'Jake,' says the other, 'what are you doing? You can't outrun that bear!' 'I don't have to outrun the bear,' responds Jake. 'I just have to outrun you!'" Smiles all around.

The controversy found in humor often walks a fine line between what is funny and what is "sick." During the Middle Ages, people used the word "humors" (derived from the Latin *humidus,* meaning "moist") to mean a balance of bodily fluids that regulated a person's health. Researchers today document the power of humor to reduce stress and improve health. One recent study of cancer patients, for example, found that the greater a patient's sense of humor, the greater the odds of surviving the disease. Such findings confirm the old saying "Laughter is the best medicine" (Bakalar, 2005; Sven Svebak, cited in M. Elias, 2007). At the extreme, however, people who always take conventional reality lightly risk being defined as deviant or even mentally ill (a common stereotype shows insane people laughing uncontrollably, and for a long time mental hospitals were known as "funny farms").

Then, too, every social group considers certain topics too sensitive for humorous treatment. If you joke about such things, you risk criticism for telling a "sick" joke (and being labeled "sick" yourself). People's religious beliefs, tragic accidents, or appalling crimes are some of the subjects of "sick" jokes or no jokes at all. Even years later, there have been no jokes about the victims of the September 11, 2001, terrorist attacks.

The Functions of Humor

Humor is found everywhere because it works as a safety valve for potentially disruptive statements and ideas. Put another way, humor provides an acceptable way to discuss a sensitive topic without appearing to be serious or being offensive. Having said something controversial, people often use humor to defuse the situation by simply stating, "I didn't mean anything by what I said—it was just a joke!"

People also use humor to relieve tension in uncomfortable situations. One study of medical examinations found that most patients try to joke with doctors to ease their own nervousness (Baker et al., 1997).

Humor and Conflict

Humor holds the potential to liberate those who laugh, but it can also be used to put down other people. Men who tell jokes about women, for example, are typically expressing some measure of hostility toward them. Similarly, jokes about gay people reveal tensions about sexual orientation. Real conflict can be masked by humor when people choose not to bring the conflict out into the open (Primeggia & Varacalli, 1990).

"Put-down" jokes make one category of people feel good at the expense of another. After collecting and analyzing jokes from many societies, Christie Davies (1990) confirmed that ethnic conflict is a driving force behind humor in most of the world. The typical ethnic joke makes fun of some disadvantaged category of people, at the same time making the joke teller feel superior. Given the Anglo-Saxon traditions of U.S. society, Poles and other ethnic and racial minorities have long been the butt of jokes, as have Newfoundlanders in eastern Canada, Scots in England, Irish in Scotland, Sikhs in India, Turks in Germany, Hausas in Nigeria, Tasmanians in Australia, and Kurds in Iraq.

Disadvantaged people also make fun of the powerful, although usually with some care. Women in the United States joke about men, just as African Americans find humor in white people's ways and poor people poke fun at the rich. Throughout the world, people target their leaders with humor, and officials in some countries take such jokes seriously enough to arrest those who do not show proper respect (Speier, 1998).

In sum, humor is much more important than we may think. It is a means of mental escape from a conventional world that is not entirely to our liking (Flaherty, 1984, 1990; Yoels & Clair, 1995). This fact helps explain why so many of our nation's comedians come from the ranks of historically marginalized peoples, including Jews and African Americans. As long as we maintain a sense of humor, we assert our freedom and are never prisoners of reality. By putting a smile on our faces, we change ourselves and the world just a little and for the better.

Chris Rock is an African American comedian who likes to make jokes involving race, sometimes at the expense of black people. No doubt, many whites have commented, "If I made a joke like that, wow . . ." All people make fun of themselves. But when people of one racial category (especially those who have historically been dominant) make fun of people of another race, their humor can easily seem like a racially insensitive "put down."

Seeing Sociology in Everyday Life

How do we all construct the reality we experience?

This chapter suggests that Shakespeare might have had it right when he said "All the world's a stage." And if so, then the Internet may be the latest and greatest stage so far. When we use Web sites such as Facebook, as Goffman explains, we present ourselves as we want others to see us. Everything we write about ourselves as well as how we arrange our page creates an impression in the mind of anyone interested in "checking us out." Take a look at the Facebook page below, paying careful attention to all the details. What is the young man explicitly saying about himself? What can you read "between the lines"? That is, what information can you identify that he may be trying to conceal or at least purposely not be mentioning? How honest do you think his "presentation of self" is? Why? Do a similar analysis of the young woman's Facebook profile shown on the next page.

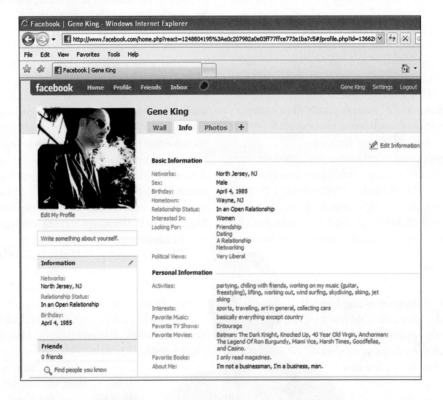

> **HINT**   Just about every element of a presentation conveys information about us to others, so all the information found on a Web site like this one is significant. Some information is intentional—for example, what people write about themselves and the photos they choose to post. Other information may be unintentional but is nevertheless picked up by the careful viewer, who may be noting the following things:
>
> - The length and tone of the person's profile (Is it a long-winded list of talents and accomplishments or humorous and modest?)
> - The language used (Poor grammar may be a clue to educational level.)
> - What hour of the day or night the person wrote the material (A person creating his profile at 11 o'clock on a Saturday night may not be quite the party person he describes himself to be.).

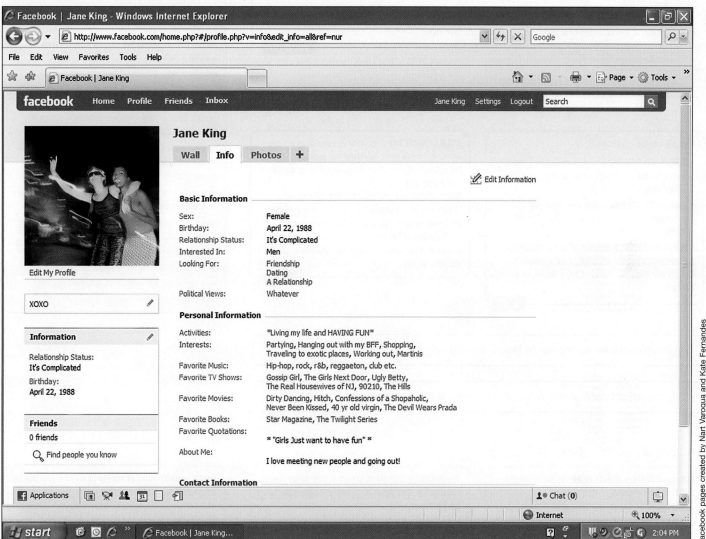

Applying SOCIOLOGY in Everyday Life

1. Identify five important ways in which you present yourself to others, including, for example, the way you decorate your dorm room, apartment, or house; the way you dress; and the way you behave in the classroom. In each case, think about what you are trying to say about yourself. Have your presentations changed in recent years? If so, how, and why?

2. During one full day, every time somebody asks, "How are you?" or "How's it goin'?" stop and actually give a com-plete, truthful answer. What happens when you respond to a polite question in an honest way? Listen to how people respond, and also watch their body language. What can you conclude?

3. Stroll around downtown or at a local mall. Pay attention to how many women and men you find at each location. From your observations, are there stores that are "gendered" so that there are "female spaces" and "male spaces"? How and why are spaces "gendered"?

Making the Grade

CHAPTER 4 Social Interaction in Everyday Life

What Is Social Structure?

Watch on mysoclab.com

SOCIAL STRUCTURE refers to social patterns that guide our behavior in everyday life. The building blocks of social structure are

- **STATUS**—a social position that is part of our social identity and that defines our relationships to others
- **ROLE**—the action expected of a person who holds a particular status

pp. 94–97

✓ A person holds a status and performs a role.

A status can be either an

- **ASCRIBED STATUS**, which is involuntary (for example, being a teenager, an orphan, or a Mexican American), or an
- **ACHIEVED STATUS**, which is earned (for example, being an honors student, a pilot, or a thief).

A **MASTER STATUS**, which can be either ascribed or achieved, has special importance for a person's identity (for example, being blind, a doctor, or a Kennedy).

p. 95

ROLE CONFLICT results from tension among roles linked to two or more statuses (for example, a woman who juggles her responsibilities as a mother and a corporate CEO).

ROLE STRAIN results from tension among roles linked to a single status (for example, the college professor who enjoys personal interaction with students but at the same time knows that social distance is necessary in order to evaluate students fairly).

p. 97

social interaction (p. 94) the process by which people act and react in relation to others

status (p. 95) a social position that a person holds

status set (p. 95) all the statuses a person holds at a given time

ascribed status (p. 95) a social position a person receives at birth or takes on involuntarily later in life

achieved status (p. 95) a social position a person takes on voluntarily that reflects personal ability and effort

master status (p. 95) a status that has special importance for social identity, often shaping a person's entire life

role (p. 95) behavior expected of someone who holds a particular status

role set (p. 96) a number of roles attached to a single status

role conflict (p. 97) conflict among the roles connected to two or more statuses

role strain (p. 97) tension among the roles connected to a single status

✓ A person's status set changes over the life course (p. 95).

✓ The role sets attached to a single status vary from society to society around the world (pp. 96–97).

The Social Construction of Reality

Through **SOCIAL INTERACTION**, we construct the reality we experience.

- For example, two people interacting both try to shape the reality of their situation.

pp. 97–98

Explore on mysoclab.com

ETHNOMETHODOLOGY is a strategy to reveal the assumptions people have about their social world.

- We can expose these assumptions by intentionally breaking the "rules" of social interaction and observing the reactions of other people.

p. 99

The **THOMAS THEOREM** says that the reality people construct in their interaction has real consequences for the future.

- For example, a teacher who believes a certain student to be intellectually gifted may well encourage exceptional academic performance.

p. 99

Both **CULTURE** and **SOCIAL CLASS** shape the reality people construct.

- For example, a "short walk" for a New Yorker is a few city blocks, but for a peasant in Latin America, it could be a few miles.

pp. 100–101

social construction of reality (p. 97) the process by which people creatively shape reality through social interaction

Thomas theorem (p. 99) W. I. Thomas's claim that situations defined as real are real in their consequences

ethnomethodology (p. 99) Harold Garfinkel's term for the study of the way people make sense of their everyday surroundings

✓ Through the social construction of reality, people creatively shape their social world.

Dramaturgical Analysis: The "Presentation of Self"

DRAMATURGICAL ANALYSIS explores social interaction in terms of theatrical performance: A status operates as a part in a play and a role is a script.
PERFORMANCES are the way we present ourselves to others.

- Performances are both conscious (intentional action) and unconscious (nonverbal communication).
- Performances include costume (the way we dress), props (objects we carry), and demeanor (tone of voice and the way we carry ourselves).

pp. 101–103

Read on mysoclab.com

GENDER affects performances because men typically have greater social power than women. Gender differences involve *demeanor, use of space*, and *staring, smiling, and touching*.

- **DEMEANOR**—With greater social power, men have more freedom in how they act.
- **USE OF SPACE**—Men typically command more space than women.
- **STARING** and **TOUCHING** are generally done by men to women.
- **SMILING**, as a way to please another, is more commonly done by women.

pp. 103–104

IDEALIZATION of performances means we try to convince others that our actions reflect ideal culture rather than selfish motives.

p. 104

EMBARRASSMENT is the "loss of face" in a performance. People use **TACT** to help others "save face."

pp. 104–105

dramaturgical analysis (p. 101) Erving Goffman's term for the study of social interaction in terms of theatrical performance

presentation of self (p. 101) Erving Goffman's term for a person's efforts to create specific impressions in the minds of others

nonverbal communication (p. 102) communication using body movements, gestures, and facial expressions rather than speech

personal space (p. 103) the surrounding area over which a person makes some claim to privacy

Interaction in Everyday Life: Three Applications

EMOTIONS: The Social Construction of **FEELING**

The same basic emotions are biologically programmed into all human beings, but culture guides what triggers emotions, how people display emotions, and how people value emotions. In everyday life, the presentation of self involves managing emotions as well as behavior.

pp. 105–106

LANGUAGE: The Social Construction of **GENDER**

Gender is an important element of everyday interaction. Language defines women and men as different types of people, reflecting the fact that society attaches greater power and value to what is viewed as masculine.

pp. 107–108

REALITY PLAY: The Social Construction of **HUMOR**

Humor results from the difference between conventional and unconventional definitions of a situation. Because humor is a part of culture, people around the world find different situations funny.

pp. 108–111

5 Groups and Organizations

- How do groups affect how we behave?

- Why can "who you know" be as important as "what you know"?

- In what ways have large business organizations changed in recent decades?

Chapter Overview

This chapter analyzes social groups, both small and large, highlighting the differences between them. Then the focus shifts to formal organizations that carry out various tasks in our modern society and provide most of us with jobs.

With the workday over, Juan and Jorge pushed through the doors of the local McDonald's restaurant. "Man, am I hungry," announced Juan, heading right into line. "Look at all the meat I'm gonna eat." But Jorge, a recent immigrant from a small village in Guatemala, is surveying the room with a sociological eye. "There is much more than food to see here. This place is all about America!"

And so it is, as we shall see. But back in 1948, when the story of McDonald's began, people in Pasadena, California, paid little attention to the opening of a new restaurant by brothers Maurice and Richard McDonald. The McDonald brothers' basic concept, which was soon called "fast food," was to serve meals quickly and cheaply to large numbers of people. The brothers trained employees to do highly specialized jobs: One person grilled hamburgers while others "dressed" them, made French fries, whipped up milkshakes, and handed the food to the customers in assembly-line fashion.

As the years went by, the McDonald brothers prospered, and they opened several more restaurants, including one in San Bernardino. It was there, in 1954, that Ray Kroc, a traveling blender and mixer salesman, paid them a visit.

Kroc was fascinated by the efficiency of the McDonald brothers' system and saw the potential for expanding into a nationwide chain of fast-food restaurants. The three launched the plan as partners. Soon Kroc bought out the McDonalds (who returned to running their original restaurant) and went on to become one of the greatest success stories of all time. Today, McDonald's is one of the mostly widely known brand names in the world, with 32,000 restaurants serving 58 million people daily throughout the United States and in 117 other countries.

The success of McDonald's points to more than just the popularity of hamburgers and French fries. The organizational principles that guide this company are coming to dominate social life in the United States and elsewhere. As Jorge correctly observed, this one small business not only transformed the restaurant industry but also changed our way of life.

We begin this chapter by looking at *social groups,* the clusters of people with whom we interact in our daily lives. As you will learn, the scope of group life expanded greatly during the twentieth century. From a world of families, local neighborhoods, and small businesses, our society now relies on the operation of huge corporations and other bureaucracies that sociologists describe as *formal organizations.* Understanding this expansion of social life and appreciating what it means for us as individuals are the main objectives of this chapter.

Social Groups

Almost everyone wants a sense of belonging, which is the essence of group life. A **social group** is *two or more people who identify with and interact with one another.* Human beings come together as couples, families, circles of friends, churches, clubs, businesses, neighborhoods, and large organizations. Whatever the form, groups contain people with shared experiences, loyalties, and interests. While keeping their individuality, members of social groups also think of themselves as a special "we."

Not every collection of individuals forms a group. People with a status in common, such as women, African Americans, homeowners, soldiers, millionaires, college graduates, and Roman Catholics, are not a group but a *category.* Though they know that others hold the same status, most are strangers to one another. Similarly, students sitting in a large stadium interact to a very limited extent. Such a loosely formed collection of people in one place is a *crowd* rather than a group.

However, the right circumstances can quickly turn a crowd into a group. Events from power failures to terrorist attacks can make people bond quickly with strangers.

Primary and Secondary Groups

People often greet one another with a smile and a simple "Hi! How are you?" The response is usually "Fine, thanks. How about you?" This

Seeing Sociology in Everyday Life

List all the groups in your life that you think of as "we." Is each a primary or secondary group?

answer is often more scripted than sincere. Explaining how you are *really* doing might make people feel so awkward that they would beat a hasty retreat.

Social groups are of two types, based on their members' degree of genuine personal concern for one another. According to Charles Horton Cooley, a **primary group** is *a small social group whose members share personal and lasting relationships.* Joined by *primary relationships,* people spend a great deal of time together, engage in a wide range of activities, and feel that they know one another pretty well. In short, they show real concern for one another. The family is every society's most important primary group.

Cooley called personal and tightly integrated groups "primary" because they are among the first groups we experience in life. In addition, family and friends have primary importance in the socialization process, shaping our attitudes, behavior, and social identity.

Members of primary groups help one another in many ways, but they generally think of their group as an end in itself rather than as a means to other ends. In other words, we tend to think that family and friendship link people who "belong together." Members of a primary group also tend to view each other as unique and irreplaceable. Especially in the family, we are bound to others by emotion and loyalty. Brothers and sisters may not always get along, but they always remain "family."

In contrast to the primary group, the **secondary group** is *a large and impersonal social group whose members pursue a specific goal or activity.* In most respects, secondary groups have characteristics opposite those of primary groups. *Secondary relationships* involve weak emotional ties and little personal knowledge of one another. Many secondary groups exist for only a short time, beginning and ending without particular significance. Students enrolled in the same course at a large university—people who may or may not see one another after the semester ends—are one example of a secondary group.

Secondary groups include many more people than primary groups. For example, dozens or even hundreds of people may work in the same company, yet most of them pay only passing attention to one another. Sometimes the passage of time transforms a group from secondary to primary, as with co-workers who share an office for many years and develop closer relationships. But generally, members of a secondary group do not think of themselves as "we." Secondary ties need not be hostile or cold, of course. Interactions among students, co-workers, and business associates are often quite pleasant even if they are impersonal.

Unlike members of primary groups, who display a *personal orientation,* people in secondary groups have a *goal orientation.* Primary group members define each other according to *who* they are in

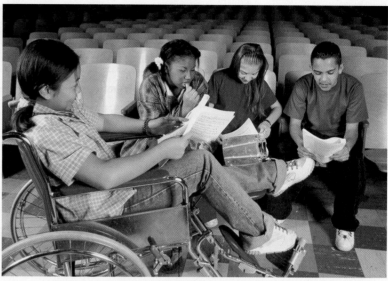

As human beings, we live our lives as members of groups. Such groups may be large or small, temporary or long-lasting, and can be based on kinship, cultural heritage, or some shared interest.

terms of family ties or personal qualities, but people in secondary groups look to one another for *what* they are, that is, what they can do for each other. In secondary groups, we tend to "keep score," aware of what we give others and what we receive in return. This goal orientation means that secondary group members usually remain formal and polite. It is in a secondary relationship, therefore, that we ask the question "How are you?" without expecting a truthful answer.

The Summing Up table on page 120 reviews the characteristics of primary and secondary groups. Keep in mind that these traits define two types of groups in ideal terms; most real groups contain elements of both. For example, a women's group on a university campus may be quite large (and therefore secondary), but its members may identify strongly with one another and provide lots of mutual support (making it seem primary).

Many people think that small towns and rural areas emphasize primary relationships and that large cities are characterized by secondary ties. This generalization is partly true, but some urban neighborhoods—especially those populated by people of a single ethnic or religious category—can be very tightly knit.

Group Leadership

How do groups operate? One important element of group dynamics is leadership. Although a small circle of friends may have no leader at all, most large secondary groups place leaders in a formal chain of command.

Making the Grade

Look closely at the Summing Up table below to be sure you understand how primary and secondary groups differ. The arrows at the top indicate that these two concepts form a continuum—that is, any particular group is primary and secondary to some degree.

instrumental leadership group leadership that focuses on the completion of tasks

expressive leadership group leadership that focuses on the group's well-being

SUMMING UP

Primary Groups and Secondary Groups

	Primary Group ←———————→ Secondary Group	
Quality of relationships	Personal orientation	Goal orientation
Duration of relationships	Usually long-term	Variable; often short-term
Breadth of relationships	Broad; usually involving many activities	Narrow; usually involving few activities
Perception of relationships	Ends in themselves	Means to an end
Examples	Families, circles of friends	Co-workers, political organizations

Two Leadership Roles

Groups typically benefit from two kinds of leadership. **Instrumental leadership** refers to *group leadership that focuses on the completion of tasks.* Members look to instrumental leaders to make plans, give orders, and get things done. **Expressive leadership,** by contrast, is *group leadership that focuses on the group's well-being.* Expressive leaders take less of an interest in achieving goals and focus on promoting the well-being of members and minimizing tension and conflict among members.

Because they concentrate on performance, instrumental leaders usually have formal, secondary relationships with other members. These leaders give orders and reward or punish people according to how much they contribute to the group's efforts. Expressive leaders build more personal, primary ties. They offer sympathy to members going through tough times, keep the group united, and lighten serious moments with humor. Typically, successful instrumental leaders enjoy more *respect* from members and expressive leaders generally receive more personal *affection.*

Three Leadership Styles

Sociologists also describe leadership in terms of its decision-making style. *Authoritarian leadership* focuses on instrumental concerns, takes personal charge of decision making, and demands that group members obey orders. Although this leadership style may win little affection from the group, a fast-acting authoritarian leader is appreciated in a crisis.

Democratic leadership is more expressive, making a point of including everyone in the decision-making process. Although less successful in a crisis situation, when there is little time for discussion, democratic leaders generally draw on the ideas of all members to develop creative solutions to problems.

Laissez-faire leadership allows the group to function more or less on its own (*laissez-faire* in French means "leave it alone"). This style is typically the least effective in promoting group goals (White & Lippitt, 1953; Ridgeway, 1983).

Group Conformity

Groups influence the behavior of their members, often promoting conformity. "Fitting in" provides a secure feeling of belonging, but at the extreme, group pressure can be unpleasant and even dangerous. Interestingly, as experiments by Solomon Asch and Stanley Milgram showed, even strangers can encourage group conformity.

Asch's Research

Solomon Asch (1952) recruited students for what he told them was a study of visual perception. Before the experiment began, he explained to all but one member of a small group that their real purpose was to put pressure on the remaining person. Placing six to eight students around a table, Asch showed them a "standard" line, as drawn on Card 1 in Figure 5–1, and asked them to match it to one of the three lines on Card 2.

Anyone with normal vision can see that the line marked "A" on Card 2 is the correct choice. Initially, as planned, everyone made the matches correctly. But then Asch's secret accomplices began answering incorrectly, leaving the uninformed student (seated at the table so as to answer next to last) bewildered and uncomfortable.

What happened? Asch found that one-third of all subjects chose to conform by answering incorrectly. Apparently, many of us are willing to compromise our own judgment to avoid the discomfort of being different, even from people we do not know.

Go to the Multimedia Library at **mysoclab.com** to view the video "Milgram Obedience Study Today"

groupthink the tendency of group members to conform, resulting in a narrow view of some issue

Milgram's Research

Stanley Milgram, a former student of Solomon Asch's, conducted conformity experiments of his own. In Milgram's controversial study (1963, 1965; A. G. Miller, 1986), a researcher explained to male recruits that they would be taking part in a study of how punishment affects learning. One by one, he assigned them to the role of teacher and placed another person—actually an accomplice of Milgram's—in a connecting room to pose as a learner.

The teacher watched as the learner sat down in what looked like an electric chair. The researcher applied electrode paste to one of the learner's wrists, explaining that this would "prevent blisters and burns." The researcher then attached an electrode to the wrist and secured the leather straps, explaining that they would "prevent excessive movement while the learner was being shocked." Although the shocks would be painful, the researcher reassured the teacher, they would cause "no permanent tissue damage."

The researcher then led the teacher back into the adjoining room, pointing out that the "electric chair" was connected to a "shock generator," actually a phony but realistic-looking piece of equipment with a label that read "Shock Generator, Type ZLB, Dyson Instrument Company, Waltham, Mass." On the front was a dial that supposedly regulated electric current from 15 volts (labeled "Slight Shock") to 300 volts ("Intense Shock") to 450 volts ("Danger: Severe Shock"). ● Go to **mysoclab.com**

Seated in front of the "shock generator," the teacher was told to read aloud pairs of words. Then the teacher was to repeat the first word of each pair and wait for the learner to recall the second word. Whenever the learner failed to answer correctly, the teacher was told to apply an electric shock.

The researcher directed the teacher to begin at the lowest level (15 volts) and to increase the shock by 15 volts every time the learner made a mistake. And so the teacher did. At 75, 90, and 105 volts, the teacher heard moans from the learner; at 120 volts, shouts of pain; by 270 volts, screams; at 315 volts, pounding on the wall; after that, dead silence. Only a few of the forty subjects assigned to the role of teacher during the initial research even questioned the procedure before reaching the dangerous level of 300 volts, and twenty-six of the subjects—almost two-thirds—went all the way to the potentially lethal 450 volts. Even Milgram was surprised at how readily people obeyed authority figures.

Milgram (1964) then modified his research to see whether ordinary people—not authority figures—could pressure strangers to administer electrical shocks, in the same way that Asch's groups had pressured individuals to match lines incorrectly.

This time, Milgram formed a group of three teachers, two of whom were his accomplices. Each of the teachers was to suggest a shock level when the learner made an error; the rule was that the group would then administer the *lowest* of the three suggested

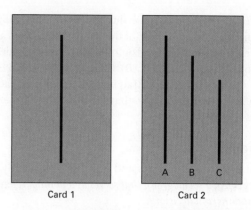

FIGURE 5–1 **Cards Used in Asch's Experiment in Group Conformity**

In Asch's experiment, subjects were asked to match the line on Card 1 to one of the lines on Card 2. Many subjects agreed with the wrong answers given by others in their group.

Source: Asch (1952).

levels. This arrangement gave the person who was not in on the experiment the power to deliver a lesser shock regardless of what the others said.

The accomplices suggested increasing the shock level with each error the learner made, putting pressure on the third person to do the same. The subjects in these groups applied voltages three to four times higher than those applied by subjects acting alone. Thus Milgram's research suggests that people are likely to follow the directions not only of legitimate authority figures but also of groups of ordinary individuals, even if doing so means harming another person.

Janis's "Groupthink"

Experts also cave in to group pressure, says Irving Janis (1972, 1989). Janis argues that a number of U.S. foreign policy blunders, including the failure to foresee the Japanese attack on Pearl Harbor during World War II and our ill-fated involvement in the Vietnam War, resulted from group conformity among our highest-ranking political leaders.

Common sense tells us that group discussion improves decision making. Janis counters that group members often seek agreement that closes off other points of view. Janis called this process **groupthink,** *the tendency of group members to conform, resulting in a narrow view of some issue.*

A classic example of groupthink resulted in the disastrous U.S. invasion of the Bay of Pigs in Cuba in 1961. Looking back, Arthur Schlesinger Jr., an adviser to President Kennedy at the time, confessed

Seeing Sociology
in Everyday Life

In terms of in-groups and out-groups, explain what happens when people who may not like each other discover that they have a common enemy.

feeling guilty "for having kept so quiet during those crucial discussions in the Cabinet Room," adding that the group discouraged anyone from challenging what, in hindsight, Schlesinger considered "nonsense" (quoted in Janis, 1972:30, 40). Groupthink may also have been a factor in the U.S. invasion of Iraq in 2003, when U.S. leaders were led to believe—erroneously—that Iraq had stockpiles of weapons of mass destruction.

Reference Groups

How do we assess our own attitudes and behavior? Frequently, we use a **reference group,** *a social group that serves as a point of reference in making evaluations and decisions.*

A young man who imagines his family's response to a woman he is dating is using his family as a reference group. A supervisor who tries to predict her employees' reaction to a new vacation policy is using them in the same way. As these examples suggest, reference groups can be primary or secondary. In either case, our need to conform shows how others' attitudes affect us.

We also use groups we do *not* belong to for reference. Being well prepared for a job interview means showing up dressed the way people in that company dress for work. Conforming to groups we do not belong to is a strategy to win acceptance and illustrates the process of *anticipatory socialization,* described in Chapter 3 ("Socialization: From Infancy to Old Age").

Stouffer's Research

Samuel Stouffer and his colleagues (1949) conducted a classic study of reference groups during World War II. Researchers asked soldiers to rate their own, or any competent soldier's, chances of promotion in their army unit. You might guess that soldiers serving in outfits with high promotion rates would be optimistic about advancement. Yet Stouffer's research pointed to the opposite conclusion: Soldiers in army units with low promotion rates were actually more positive about their chances to move ahead.

The key to understanding Stouffer's results lies in the groups against which soldiers measured themselves. Those assigned to units with lower promotion rates looked around them and saw people making no more headway than they were. Although they had not been promoted, neither had many others, so they did not feel deprived. However, soldiers in units with higher promotion rates could think of many people who had been promoted sooner or more often than they had. With such people in mind, even soldiers who had been promoted themselves were likely to feel shortchanged.

The point is that we do not make judgments about ourselves in isolation, nor do we compare ourselves with just anyone. Regardless of our situation in *absolute* terms, we form a subjective sense of our well-being by looking at ourselves *relative* to specific reference groups (Merton, 1968; Mirowsky, 1987).

In-Groups and Out-Groups

Each of us favors some groups over others, whether because of political outlook, social prestige, or just manner of dress. On some college campuses, for example, left-leaning student activists may look down on fraternity members, whom they view as conservative; fraternity members, in turn, may snub the "nerds" who work too hard. People in just about every social setting make similar positive and negative evaluations of members of other groups.

Such judgments illustrate another key element of group dynamics: the opposition of in-groups and out-groups. An **in-group** is *a social group toward which a member feels respect and loyalty.* An **out-group,** by contrast, is *a social group toward which a person feels a sense of competition or opposition.* In-groups and out-groups are based on the idea that "we" have valued traits that "they" lack.

Tensions between groups sharpen the groups' boundaries and give people a clearer social identity. However, members of in-groups generally hold overly positive views of themselves and unfairly negative views of various out-groups.

Power also plays a part in intergroup relations. A powerful in-group can define others as a lower-status out-group. Historically, in countless U.S. cities and towns, many white people viewed people of color as an out-group and subordinated them socially, politically, and economically. Internalizing these negative attitudes, minorities often struggled to overcome negative self-images. In this way, in-groups and out-groups foster loyalty but also generate conflict (Tajfel, 1982; Bobo & Hutchings, 1996).

Group Size

The next time you go to a party, try to arrive first. If you do, you will be able to observe some fascinating group dynamics. Until about six people enter the room, every person who arrives usually joins in a single conversation. As more people arrive, the group divides into two or more clusters, and it divides again and again as the party grows. This process shows that group size plays a crucial role in how group members interact.

To understand why, note the mathematical number of relationships possible among two to seven people. As shown in Figure 5–2, two people form a single relationship; adding a third person results in three relationships; a fourth person yields six. Increasing the number of people further boosts the number of relationships much more rapidly because every new individual can interact with everyone already there. Thus by the time seven people join one conversation, twenty-one "channels" connect them. With so many open channels, at this point the group usually divides into smaller conversation groups.

The Dyad

The German sociologist Georg Simmel (1858–1918) explored the dynamics in the smallest social groups. Simmel (1950, orig. 1902) used the term **dyad** (Greek for "pair") to designate *a social group with two members.* Simmel explained that social interaction in a dyad is typically more intense than in larger groups because neither member must share the other's attention with anyone else. In the United States, love affairs, marriages, and the closest friendships are dyadic.

But like a stool with only two legs, dyads are unstable. Both members of a dyad must work to keep the relationship going; if either withdraws, the group collapses. To make marriage more stable, society supports the marital dyad with legal, economic, and often religious ties.

The Triad

Simmel also studied the **triad,** *a social group with three members.* A triad contains three relationships, each of which unites two of the three people. A triad is more stable than a dyad because one member can act as a mediator if relations between the other two become strained. This analysis of group dynamics helps explain why members of a dyad (say, spouses having conflict) often seek out a third person (such as a marriage counselor) to discuss tensions between them.

On the other hand, two of the three can pair up to press their views on the third, or two may intensify their relationship, leaving the other feeling left out. For example, when two of the three members of a triad develop a romantic interest in each other, they will come to understand the meaning of the old saying, "Two's company, three's a crowd."

As groups grow beyond three people, they become more stable and capable of withstanding the loss of one or more members. At the same time, increases in group size reduce the intense interaction possible in only the smallest groups. This is why larger groups are based less on personal attachments and more on formal rules and regulations.

Social Diversity: Race, Class, and Gender

Race, ethnicity, class, and gender each play a part in group dynamics. Peter Blau (1977; Blau, Blum, & Schwartz, 1982; South & Messner, 1986) points out three ways in which social diversity influences intergroup contact:

1. **Large groups turn inward.** Blau explains that the larger a group is, the more likely its members are to concentrate relationships among themselves. Say a college is trying to enhance social diversity by increasing the number of international students. These students may add a dimension of difference, but as their numbers rise, they become more likely to form their own social group. Thus efforts to promote social diversity may have the unintended effect of promoting separatism.

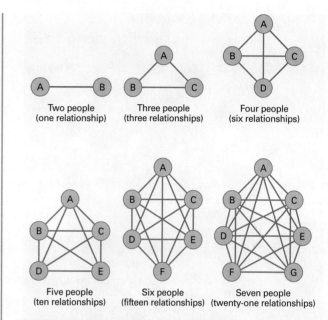

FIGURE 5–2 **Group Size and Relationships**

As the number of people in a group increases, the number of relationships that link them increases much faster. By the time six or seven people share a conversation, the group usually divides into two. Why are relationships in smaller groups typically more intense?

2. **Heterogeneous groups turn outward.** The more socially diverse a group is, the more likely its members are to interact with outsiders. Campus groups that recruit people of both sexes and various social backgrounds typically have more intergroup contact than those with members of one social category.

3. **Physical boundaries create social boundaries.** To the extent that a social group is physically segregated from others (by having its own dorm or dining area, for example), its members are less likely to interact with other people.

Networks

A **network** is *a web of weak social ties.* Think of a network as a "fuzzy" group containing people who come into occasional contact but lack a sense of boundaries and belonging. If you think of a *group* as a "circle of friends," think of a *network* as a "social web" expanding outward, often reaching great distances and including large numbers of people.

The largest network of all is the World Wide Web of the Internet. But the Internet has expanded much more in some global regions than in others. Global Map 5–1 on page 125 shows that Internet use is high in rich countries and far less common in poor nations.

Go to the Multimedia Library at **mysoclab.com** to listen to the NPR report "Scientists Debate Six Degrees of Separation"

formal organizations large secondary groups organized to achieve their goals efficiently

The triad, illustrated by Jonathan Green's painting *Friends,* includes three people. A triad is more stable than a dyad because conflict between any two persons can be mediated by the third member. Even so, should the relationship between any two become more intense in a positive sense, those two are likely to exclude the third.

Jonathan Green, *Friends,* 1992. Oil on masonite, 14 in. × 11 in. © Jonathan Green.
http://www.jonathangreenstudios.com

Some networks come close to being groups, as in the case of college friends who stay in touch years after graduation by e-mail and telephone. More commonly, however, a network includes people we know of or who know of us but with whom we interact rarely, if at all. As one woman known as a community organizer puts it, "I get calls at home, [and] someone says, 'Are you Roseann Navarro? Somebody told me to call you. I have this problem . . .'" (Kaminer, 1984:94).

Network ties often give us the sense that we live in a "small world." In a classic experiment, Stanley Milgram (1967; Watts, 1999) gave letters to subjects in Kansas and Nebraska intended for specific people in Boston who were unknown to the original subjects. No addresses were given, and the subjects in the study were told to send the letters to others they knew personally who might know the target people. Milgram found that the target people received the letters

with, on average, six people passing them on. This result led Milgram to claim that everyone is connected to everyone else by "six degrees of separation." Later research, however, has cast doubt on Milgram's claim. Examining Milgram's original data, Judith Kleinfeld noted that most of Milgram's letters (240 out of 300) never arrived at all (Wildavsky, 2002). Most of those that did reach their destination had been given to people who were wealthy, a fact that led Kleinfeld to conclude that rich people are better connected across the country than ordinary men and women. ● Go to **mysoclab.com**

Network ties may be weak, but they can be a powerful resource. For immigrants trying to become established in a new community, businesspeople seeking to expand their operations, or new college graduates looking for a job, *whom* you know often is just as important as *what* you know (Hagan, 1998; Petersen, Saporta, & Seidel, 2000).

Networks are based on people's colleges, clubs, neighborhoods, political parties, religious organizations, and personal interests. Obviously, some networks are made up of people with more wealth, power, and prestige than others; that explains the importance of being "well connected." The networks of more privileged categories of people—such as the members of a country club—are a valuable form of "social capital," which is more likely to lead people in these categories to higher-paying jobs (Green, Tigges, & Diaz, 1999; Lin, Cook, & Burt, 2001).

Some people also have denser networks than others; that is, they are connected to more people. Typically, the largest social networks include people who are young, well educated, and living in large cities (Fernandez & Weinberg, 1997; Podolny & Baron, 1997).

Gender also shapes networks. Although the networks of men and women are typically of the same size, women include more relatives (and more women) in their networks, and men include more co-workers (and more men). Women's ties, therefore, may not be quite as powerful as typical "old boy" networks. But research suggests that as gender equality increases in the United States, the networks of men and women are becoming more alike (Reskin & McBrier, 2000; Torres & Huffman, 2002).

Formal Organizations

As noted earlier, a century ago, most people lived in small groups of family, friends, and neighbors. Today, our lives revolve more and more around **formal organizations,** *large secondary groups organized to achieve their goals efficiently.* Formal organizations such as corporations and government agencies differ from small primary groups in their impersonality and their formally planned atmosphere.

When you think about it, organizing more than 300 million members of U.S. society is truly remarkable, whether it involves paving roads, collecting taxes, schooling children, or delivering the mail. To carry out most of these tasks, we rely on large formal organizations.

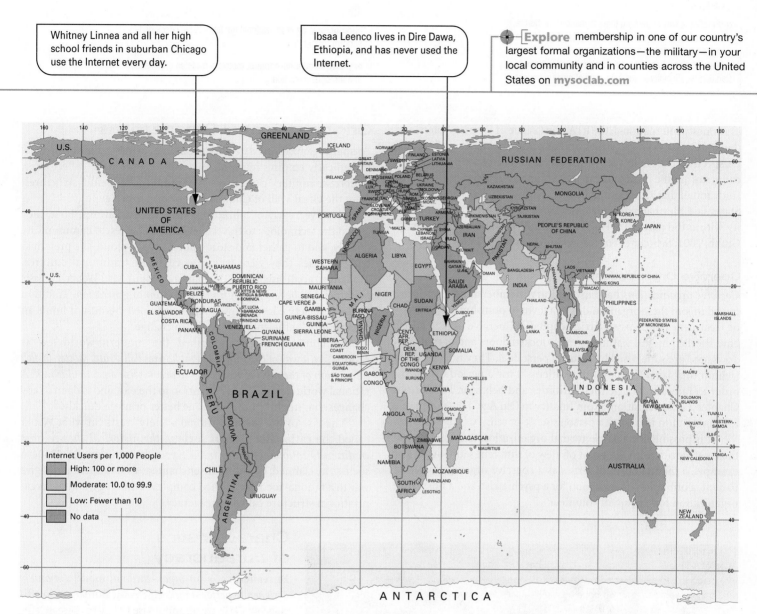

Whitney Linnea and all her high school friends in suburban Chicago use the Internet every day.

Ibsaa Leenco lives in Dire Dawa, Ethiopia, and has never used the Internet.

Explore membership in one of our country's largest formal organizations—the military—in your local community and in counties across the United States on **mysoclab.com**

Internet Users per 1,000 People
- High: 100 or more
- Moderate: 10.0 to 99.9
- Low: Fewer than 10
- No data

Window on the World

GLOBAL MAP 5–1   Internet Users in Global Perspective

This map shows how the Information Revolution has affected countries around the world. In most high-income nations, at least one-third of the population uses the Internet. By contrast, only a small share of people in low-income nations does so. What effect does this pattern have on people's access to information? What does this mean for the future in terms of global inequality?

Source: International Telecommunication Union (2009).

Types of Formal Organizations

Amitai Etzioni (1975) identified three types of formal organizations, distinguished by the reasons people participate in them: utilitarian organizations, normative organizations, and coercive organizations.

Utilitarian Organizations

Just about everyone who works for income belongs to a *utilitarian organization,* one that pays people for their efforts. Becoming part of

a utilitarian organization—a business, government agency, or school system, for example—is usually a matter of individual choice, although most people must join one or another such organization to make a living. **Explore on mysoclab.com**

Normative Organizations

People join *normative organizations* not for income but to pursue some goal they think is morally worthwhile. Sometimes called *voluntary associations,* these include community service groups (such

Groups and Organizations   CHAPTER 5   **125**

as Amnesty International, the PTA, the League of Women Voters, and the Red Cross), political parties, and religious organizations. In global perspective, people in the United States and in other high-income countries are the most likely to join voluntary associations. A recent study found that 72 percent of first-year college students in the United States said they had participated in some organized volunteer activity within the past year (Pryor et al., 2009; see also Curtis, Baer, & Grabb, 2001; Schofer & Fourcade-Gourinchas, 2001).

Coercive Organizations

Coercive organizations have involuntary memberships. People are forced to join these organizations as a form of punishment (prisons) or treatment (some psychiatric hospitals). Coercive organizations have special physical features, such as locked doors and barred windows, and are supervised by security personnel. They isolate people (whom they label "inmates" or "patients") for a period of time in order to radically change their attitudes and behavior. Recall from Chapter 3 ("Socialization: From Infancy to Old Age") the power of a total institution to change a person's sense of self.

It is possible for a single formal organization to fall into *all* of these categories from the point of view of different individuals. For example, a mental hospital serves as a coercive organization for a patient, a utilitarian organization for a psychiatrist, and a normative organization for a hospital volunteer.

Origins of Formal Organizations

Formal organizations date back thousands of years. Elites who controlled early empires relied on government officials to collect taxes, undertake military campaigns, and build monumental structures, from the Great Wall of China to the pyramids of Egypt.

However, early organizations had two limitations. First, they lacked the technology to travel over large distances, to communicate quickly, and to gather and store information. Second, the preindustrial societies they were trying to rule had traditional cultures. **Tradition,** according to the German sociologist Max Weber, consists of *values and beliefs passed from generation to generation.* Tradition makes a society conservative, Weber explained, because it limits an organization's efficiency and ability to change.

By contrast, Weber described the modern worldview as **rationality,** *a way of thinking that emphasizes deliberate, matter-of-fact calculation of the most efficient way to accomplish a particular task.* A rational worldview pays little attention to the past and is open to any changes that might get the job done better or more quickly.

The rise of the "organizational society" rests on what Weber called the **rationalization of society,** *the historical change from tradition to rationality as the main type of human thought.* Modern society, he claimed, becomes "disenchanted" as sentimental ties give way to a rational focus on science, complex technology, and the organizational structure called bureaucracy.

Characteristics of Bureaucracy

Bureaucracy is *an organizational model rationally designed to perform tasks efficiently.* Bureaucratic officials regularly create and revise policy to increase efficiency. To appreciate the power and scope of bureaucratic organization, consider that any one of almost 400 million phones in the United States can connect you within seconds to any other phone in a home, a business, an automobile, or even a hiker's backpack on a remote trail in the Rocky Mountains. Such instant communication is beyond the imagination of people who lived in the ancient world.

Our telephone system depends on technology such as electricity, fiber optics, and computers. But the system could not exist without the organizational capacity to keep track of every telephone call—recording which phone called which other phone, when, and for how long—and presenting all this information to more than 200 million telephone users in the form of a monthly bill (Federal Communications Commission, 2008; CTIA, 2009).

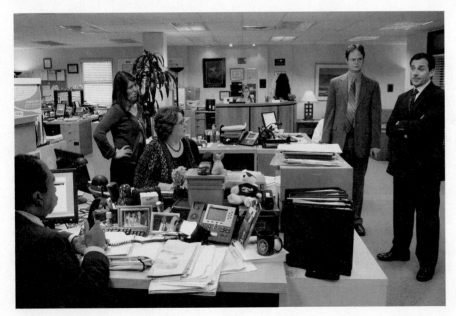

Weber described the operation of the ideal bureaucracy as rational and highly efficient. In real life, actual large organizations often operate very differently from Weber's model, as can be seen on the television show *The Office.*

Seeing Sociology in Everyday Life

Give an example of each of the factors listed here in the operation of your college or university bureaucracy.

Making the Grade

The six traits listed here defined, for Weber, the *ideal* bureaucracy. This means that in its pure form, bureaucracy has all these traits. Actual organizations, of course, may differ in some way from the ideal.

SUMMING UP

Small Groups and Formal Organizations

	Small Groups	Formal Organizations
Activities	Much the same for all members	Distinct and highly specialized
Hierarchy	Often informal or nonexistent	Clearly defined according to position
Norms	General norms, informally applied	Clearly defined rules and regulations
Membership criteria	Variable; often based on personal affection or kinship	Technical competence to carry out assigned tasks
Relationships	Variable and typically primary	Typically secondary, with selective primary ties
Communications	Typically casual and face to face	Typically formal and in writing
Focus	Person-oriented	Task-oriented

What specific traits promote organizational efficiency? Max Weber (1978, orig. 1921) identified six key elements of the ideal bureaucratic organization:

1. **Specialization.** Our ancestors spent most of their time looking for food and finding shelter. Bureaucracy, by contrast, assigns individuals highly specialized jobs.

2. **Hierarchy of offices.** Bureaucracies arrange workers in a vertical ranking. Each person is thus supervised by someone "higher up" in the organization while in turn supervising others in lower positions. Usually, with few people at the top and many at the bottom, bureaucratic organizations take the form of a pyramid.

3. **Rules and regulations.** Rationally enacted rules and regulations guide a bureaucracy's operation. Ideally, a bureaucracy seeks to operate in a completely predictable way.

4. **Technical competence.** Bureaucratic officials have the technical competence to carry out their duties. Bureaucracies typically hire new members according to set standards and then monitor their performance. Such impersonal evaluation contrasts with the ancient custom of favoring relatives, whatever their talents, over strangers.

5. **Impersonality.** Bureaucracy puts rules ahead of personal whim so that both clients and workers are all treated in the same way. From this impersonal approach comes the commonplace image of the "faceless bureaucrat."

6. **Formal, written communications.** It is often said that the heart of bureaucracy is not people but paperwork. Rather than casual, face-to-face talk, bureaucracy depends on formal, written memos and reports, which accumulate in vast files.

Bureaucratic organization promotes efficiency by carefully hiring workers and limiting the unpredictable effects of personal taste and opinion. The Summing Up table reviews the differences between small social groups and large formal organizations.

Organizational Environment

All organizations exist in the larger world. How well any organization performs depends not only on its own goals and policies but also on the **organizational environment,** *factors outside an organization that affect its operation.* These factors include technology, economic and political trends, current events, the available workforce, and other organizations.

Modern organizations are shaped by *technology,* including copiers, telephones, and computer equipment. Computers give employees access to more information and people than ever before. At the same time, computer technology allows managers to closely monitor the activities of workers (Markoff, 1991).

Economic and political trends affect organizations. All organizations are helped or hurt by periodic economic growth or recession. Most industries also face competition from abroad as well as changes in laws—such as new environmental standards—at home.

Making the Grade

Just because an organization is efficient doesn't mean that people enjoy being part of it or that it is actually good for people. Weber feared the opposite: The more rational and bureaucratic society became, the less it would advance human well-being.

Seeing Sociology in Everyday Life

Do you think FEMA or other large government organizations are inherently inefficient, or do you think their leaders sometimes make bad decisions? Explain your answer.

Current events can have significant effects even on organizations that are far away. Events such as the rise in energy prices that followed the 2005 hurricanes that devastated the Gulf states, the 2006 elections that transferred leadership in Congress from Republicans to Democrats, and the 2008 elections that handed control of both the White House and Congress to the Democrats affected the operation of both government and business organizations.

Population patterns also affect organizations. The average age, typical level of education, social diversity, and size of a local community determine the available workforce and sometimes the market for an organization's products or services.

Other organizations also contribute to the organizational environment. To be competitive, a hospital must be responsive to the insurance industry and to organizations representing doctors, nurses, and other health care workers. It must also be aware of the medical equipment, health care procedures, and prices available at nearby facilities.

The Informal Side of Bureaucracy

Weber's ideal bureaucracy deliberately regulates every activity. In real-life organizations, however, human beings are creative (and stubborn) enough to resist bureaucratic regulation. Informality may amount to cutting corners on the job at times, but it can also provide the flexibility needed for an organization to adapt and be successful.

In part, informality comes from the personalities of organizational leaders. Studies of U.S. corporations document that the qualities and quirks of individuals—including personal charisma, interpersonal skills, and the ability to recognize problems—can have a great effect on organizational performance (Halberstam, 1986; Baron, Hannan, & Burton, 1999).

Authoritarian, democratic, and laissez-faire types of leadership (described earlier in this chapter) reflect individual personality as much as any organizational plan. Then, too, in the "real world" of organizations, leaders sometimes seek to benefit personally through abuse of organizational power. Many of the corporate leaders of banks and insurance companies that collapsed during the financial meltdown of 2008 walked off with multimillion-dollar "golden parachutes." More commonly, leaders take credit for the efforts of the people who work for them. For example, the responsibilities—and authority—of many secretaries are far greater than their official job titles and salaries suggest.

Communication offers another example of organizational informality. Memos and other written documents are the formal way to spread information through the organization. Typically, however, people create informal networks, or "grapevines," that spread information quickly, if not always accurately. Grapevines, using word of mouth and e-mail, are particularly important to rank-and-file workers because higher-ups often try to keep important information from them.

The spread of e-mail has "flattened" organizations somewhat, allowing even the lowest-ranking employee to bypass immediate superiors to communicate directly with the organization's leader or all fellow employees at once. Some organizations consider such "open channel" communication unwelcome and limit the use of e-mail. Leaders may also seek to protect themselves from a flood of messages each day. Microsoft Corporation (whose founder, Bill Gates, has an "unlisted" address that helps him limit his e-mail to hundreds of messages each day) has developed screens that filter out all messages except those from approved people (Gwynne & Dickerson, 1997).

Using new information technology together with age-old human ingenuity, members of formal organizations often find ways to personalize their work and surroundings. Such efforts suggest that we should take a closer look at some of the problems of bureaucracy.

Problems of Bureaucracy

We rely on bureaucracy to manage everyday life efficiently, but many people are uneasy about large organizations gaining too much influence. Bureaucracy can dehumanize and manipulate us, and some say it poses a threat to political democracy. These dangers are discussed in the following sections.

Bureaucratic Alienation

Max Weber held up bureaucracy as a model of productivity. Yet Weber was keenly aware of bureaucracy's potential to *dehumanize* the people it is supposed to serve. The impersonality that fosters efficiency also keeps officials and clients from responding to each other's unique personal needs. Typically, officials treat each client impersonally as a standard "case." Sometimes the tendency toward dehumanization goes too far, as in 2008 when the U.S. Army accidentally sent letters to family members of soldiers killed in Iraq and Afghanistan, addressing the recipients as "John Doe" ("Army Apologizes," 2009).

Formal organizations create *alienation,* according to Weber, by reducing the human being to "a small cog in a ceaselessly moving mechanism" (1978:988, orig. 1921). Although formal organizations are designed to benefit humanity, Weber feared that people might well end up serving formal organizations.

Bureaucratic Inefficiency and Ritualism

On Labor Day 2005, as people in New Orleans and other coastal areas were battling to survive in the wake of Hurricane Katrina, 600 firefighters from around the country assembled in a hotel meeting room in Atlanta awaiting deployment. Officials of the Federal Emergency Management Agency (FEMA) explained to the crowd that they were first going to be given a lecture on "equal opportunity, sexual harassment, and customer service." Then, the official continued, they would each be given a stack of FEMA pamphlets with the agency's phone number to distribute to people in the devastated areas. A firefighter stood up and shouted, "This is ridiculous. Our fire departments and mayors sent us down here to save lives, and you've got us doing *this?*" The FEMA official thundered back, "You are now employees of FEMA, and you will follow orders and do what you are told" ("Places," 2005:39).

Finally, new technology has greatly expanded networking in today's world, especially among younger people who typically make use of Facebook and other social networking Web sites. Once in cyberspace, however, information we post may end up being read by almost anyone, which can cause some serious problems. The Seeing Sociology in the News article on pages 130–31 takes a closer look.

People sometimes describe inefficiency by saying that an organization has too much "red tape," meaning that important work does not get done. The term "red tape" is derived from the ribbon used by slow-working eighteenth-century English administrators to wrap official parcels and records (Shipley, 1985).

To Robert Merton (1968), red tape amounts to a new twist on the familiar concept of group conformity. He coined the term **bureaucratic ritualism** to describe *focusing on rules and regulations to the point of undermining an organization's goals.* In short, rules and regulations should be a means to an end, not an end in themselves that takes the focus away from the organization's stated goals. After the terrorist attacks of September 11, 2001, the U.S. Postal Service continued to help deliver mail addressed to Osama bin Laden to a post office in Afghanistan, despite the objections of the FBI. It took an act of Congress to change the policy (Bedard, 2002).

Bureaucratic Inertia

If bureaucrats sometimes have little reason to work very hard, they have every reason to protect their jobs. Thus officials typically work to keep their organization going even when its goal has been realized. As Max Weber put it, "Once fully established, bureaucracy is among the social structures which are hardest to destroy" (1978:987, orig. 1921).

Bureaucratic inertia refers to *the tendency of bureaucratic organizations to perpetuate themselves.* Formal organizations tend to take on a life of their own beyond their formal objectives. For example, the U.S. Department of Agriculture still has offices in nearly every county in all fifty states, even though only about one county in seven has any working farms. Usually, an organization manages to stay in business by redefining its goals; for example, the Agriculture Department now performs a broad range of work not directly related to farming, including nutritional and environmental research.

George Tooker's painting *Government Bureau* is a powerful statement about the human costs of bureaucracy. The artist paints members of the public in a drab sameness—reduced from human beings to mere "cases" to be disposed of as quickly as possible. Set apart from others by their positions, officials are "faceless bureaucrats" concerned more with numbers than with providing genuine assistance (notice that the artist places the fingers of the officials on calculators).

George Tooker, *Government Bureau*, 1956. Egg tempera on gesso panel, 19⅝ × 29⅝ inches. The Metropolitan Museum of Art, George A. Hearn Fund, 1956 (56.78). Photograph © 1984 The Metropolitan Museum of Art.

Oligarchy

Early in the twentieth century, Robert Michels (1876–1936) pointed out the link between bureaucracy and political **oligarchy,** *the rule of the many by the few* (1949, orig. 1911). According to what Michels called the "iron law of oligarchy," the pyramid shape of bureaucracy places a few leaders in charge of the resources of the entire organization.

Weber believed that a strict hierarchy of responsibility resulted in high organizational efficiency. But Michels countered that hierarchy also weakens democracy because officials can and often do use their access to information, resources, and the media to promote their own personal interests.

Furthermore, bureaucracy helps distance officials from the public, as in the case of the corporate president or public official who is "unavailable for comment" to the local press or the national president who withholds documents from Congress claiming "executive privilege." Oligarchy, then, thrives in the hierarchical structure of bureaucracy and reduces the accountability of leaders to the people (Tolson, 1995).

Political competition, term limits, a system of checks and balances, and the law prevent the U.S. government from becoming an out-and-out oligarchy. Even so, in U.S. political races, candidates who have the

ABC News

Professor Suspended After Joke About Killing Students on Facebook

BY DALIA FAHMY
March 3, 2010

The list of Facebook faux-pas just grew longer.

Gloria Gadsden, a sociology professor at East Stroudsburg University in Pennsylvania, says she was suspended last week after updating her Facebook status with complaints about work that alluded to violence.

In January, she wrote: "Does anyone know where I can find a very discreet hitman? Yes, it's been that kind of day." Then in February: "had a good day today. DIDN'T want to kill even one student.:-). Now Friday was a different story."

Gadsden says she posted the comments in jest, on a profile she thought could only be seen by friends and family. She says officials were notified of the posts by a student—even though she says she had no students in her "friend" list.

"I was just having a bad day, and I was venting to family and friends," says Gadsden, who says she didn't realize her comments could be read by the

public after Facebook relaxed its privacy standards in December. "My friends and family knew I was being facetious. They knew I wasn't targeting anyone."

Nevertheless, university officials were unhappy about the allusions to violence in the posts, she says, and in a meeting with her even mentioned the recent shooting spree by a disgruntled biologist at the University Alabama-Huntsville.

"Given the climate of security concerns in academia, the university has an obligation to take all threats seriously and act accordingly," Marilyn Wells, ESU's interim provost and vice president for academic affairs, told *The Chronicle of Higher Education* last week. Wells and other university officials did not return calls from ABC News seeking comment.

Workers have been getting in trouble often over their online vents. Not only do employers want to control their online image as closely as they can, but they are also vulnerable, like anybody else, to hurt pride.

"When you badmouth your boss and the boss is hearing, whether you're doing it online or at the coffee maker, the boss isn't going to be happy," says Jonathan Ezor, assistant professor of law and technology at Touro Law Center in Huntington, New York. "The fact that it's online makes it more easily findable and have a broader potential impact."

The comments that provoke employers into action usually contain obscenities or exaggerations that could hurt relations with customers.

Last year, for example, Dan Leone, a stadium worker for the Philadelphia Eagles, was fired after he reacted with an online obscenity to news that one of the Eagles' star players was leaving to join the Denver Broncos.

"Dan is [deleted] devastated about Dawkins signing with Denver. Dam Eagles R Retarted," was the comment that cost Leone his job.

Although he later apologized and tried to get his job back, his employer wouldn't budge. . . .

In the U.K., Virgin Atlantic Airlines fired thirteen cabin crew members after they made fun of

visibility, power, and money that come with already being in office enjoy a significant advantage. In recent congressional elections, as few as 6 percent of congressional officeholders running for reelection were defeated by their challengers (Center for Responsive Politics, 2009).

The Evolution of Formal Organizations

The problems of bureaucracy—especially the alienation it produces and its tendency toward oligarchy—stem from two organizational traits: hierarchy and rigidity. To Weber, bureaucracy is a top-down system: Rules and regulations made at the top guide every part of people's work down the chain of command. A century ago in the United States, Weber's ideas took hold in an organizational model called *scientific management*. We take a look at this model and then examine three challenges over the course of the twentieth century that gradually have led to a new model: the *flexible organization.*

Scientific Management

Frederick Winslow Taylor (1911) had a simple message: Most businesses in the United States were sadly inefficient. Managers had little idea of how to increase their business's output, and workers relied on the same tired skills of earlier generations. To increase efficiency, Taylor explained, business should apply the principles of modern

science. **Scientific management,** then, is *the application of scientific principles to the operation of a business or other large organization.*

Scientific management involves three steps. First, managers carefully observe the job performed by each worker, identifying all the operations involved and measuring the time needed for each. Second, managers analyze their data, trying to discover ways for workers to perform each job more efficiently. For example, managers might decide to give workers different tools or to reposition various work operations within the factory. Third, management provides guidance and incentives for workers to do their jobs more efficiently. If a factory worker moves 20 tons of pig iron in one day, for example, management would show the worker how to do the job more efficiently and then provide higher wages as the worker's productivity rises. Taylor concluded that if scientific principles were applied to all the steps of the production process, companies would become more profitable, workers would earn higher wages, and consumers would pay lower prices.

A century ago, the auto pioneer Henry Ford put it this way: "Save ten steps a day for each of 12,000 employees, and you will have saved fifty miles of wasted motion and misspent energy" (Allen & Hyman, 1999:209). In the early 1900s, the Ford Motor Company and many other businesses followed Taylor's lead and experienced dramatic improvements in efficiency.

The successful application of scientific management suggested that decision-making power in the workplace should rest with the owners and executives, who paid little attention to the ideas of their workers. As the decades passed, however, formal organizations faced passengers in their postings and quipped about defective engines.

The discount airline, owned by Sir Richard Branson, told *The Guardian* at the time that the postings were "totally inappropriate" and "brought the company into disrepute."

Social media mavens can even get in trouble before they've been hired. Remember the case of the Cisco fatty that went viral last year?

One Twitter user posted an update last year saying "Cisco just offered me a job! Now I have to weigh the utility of a fatty paycheck against the daily commute to San Jose and hating the work."

A Cisco employee responded, "Who is the hiring manager? I'm sure they would love to know that you will hate the work. We here at Cisco are versed in the Web."

Needless to say, the applicant did not end up working at Cisco.

Several Web sites, such as JobVent.com, have sprung up in recent years to make it easier for employees to vent their job frustrations online.

There's even a website called IhateDell.net that allows employees (and customers) to air their complaints about the computer maker.

In some cases, online postings by disgruntled employees can seriously damage a company's bottom line. Just ask Domino's Pizza.

Domino's sales dropped last year after an employee posed for five YouTube videos. In one, he stuffed cheese up his nose and put it into a sandwich. In another, he sneezed into a cheese steak sandwich.

Once the poser and the photographer—also a Domino's employee—were identified, they were fired and sued by Dominos.

In this case, the transgression seemed very clear. But employees often complain that their online posts are only used as excuses to fire them.

Gadsden, the professor from East Stroudsburg, says that university officials have been discriminating against her ever since she wrote an essay in *The Chronicle of Higher Education* saying universities don't do enough to retain minority faculty. . . .

"Their reaction (to the posts) was exaggerated," says Gadsden, noting that she was not given a warning or a chance to correct her actions before she was suspended.

WHAT DO YOU THINK?

1. Do you have a Facebook page? If so, whom do you allow to view it? Could something like what happened to Professor Gadsden or others mentioned in this article happen to you?

2. Is "badmouthing" your boss online more serious than verbal gossip among coworkers? Why or why not?

3. Do you think the university was justified in suspending Professor Gadsden? What would you have done to resolve this case?

"Professor Suspended After Joke About Killing Students on Facebook" by Dalia Fahmy. Copyright © 2010 ABC News Internet Ventures. Source: http://abcnews.go.com/Business/PersonalFinance/facebook-firings-employees-online-vents-twitter-postings-cost/story?id=9986796

important challenges involving race and gender, rising competition from abroad, and the changing nature of work itself. We now take a brief look at each of these challenges and how they prompted organizations to change.

The First Challenge: Race and Gender

In the 1960s, critics claimed that big businesses and other organizations engaged in unfair hiring practices. Rather than hiring on the basis of competence as Weber had proposed, they routinely excluded women and other minorities, especially from positions of power. Hiring on the basis of competence is partly a matter of fairness; it is also a matter of enlarging an organization's talent pool to promote efficiency.

Patterns of Privilege and Exclusion

In the early twenty-first century, as shown in Figure 5–3 on page 132, non-Hispanic white men in the United States—33 percent of the working-age population—still held 63 percent of senior-level management jobs. Non-Hispanic white women also made up 33 percent of the population, but they held just 24 percent of executive positions (U.S. Equal Employment Opportunity Commission, 2009). The members of other minorities lagged further behind.

Rosabeth Moss Kanter (1977; Kanter & Stein, 1979) points out that excluding women and minorities from the workplace ignores the talents of more than half the population. Furthermore, underrepresented people in an organization often feel like socially isolated out-groups: uncomfortably visible, taken less seriously, and with fewer chances for promotion. Sometimes what passes for "merit" or good work in an organization is simply being of the right social category (Castilla, 2008).

Opening up an organization so that change and advancement happen more often, Kanter claims, improves everyone's on-the-job performance by motivating employees to become "fast-trackers" who work harder and are more committed to the company. By contrast, an organization with many dead-end jobs turns workers into less productive "zombies" who are never asked for their opinion on anything. An open organization also encourages leaders to seek out the ideas of all employees, which usually improves decision making.

The "Female Advantage"

Some organizational researchers argue that women bring special management skills that strengthen an organization. According to Deborah Tannen (1994), women have a greater "information focus" and more readily ask questions in order to understand an issue. Men, by contrast, have an "image focus" that makes them wonder how asking questions in a particular situation will affect their reputation.

In another study of women executives, Sally Helgesen (1990) found three other gender-linked patterns. First, women place greater value on communication skills and share information more than men do. Second, women are more flexible leaders who typically give their employees greater freedom. Third, compared to men, women tend to emphasize the interconnectedness of all organizational

Think of the jobs people in your family do—are they industrial
jobs (making things) or postindustrial jobs (processing
information)?

Diversity Snapshot

Compared to their percentage of the total population, white men are overrepresented in senior management positions.

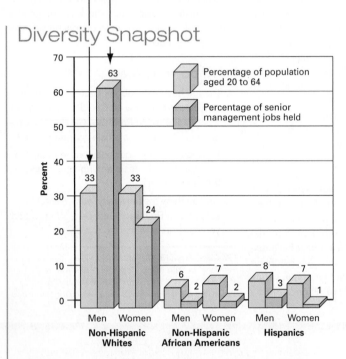

FIGURE 5–3   U.S. Managers in Private Industry by Race, Sex, and Ethnicity, 2007

White men are more likely than their population size suggests to be senior managers in private industry. The opposite is true for white women and other minorities. What factors do you think may account for this pattern?

Sources: U.S. Census Bureau (2009) and U.S. Equal Employment Opportunity Commission (2009).

operations. These patterns, which Helgesen dubbed the *female advantage,* help make companies more flexible and democratic.

In sum, one challenge to conventional bureaucracy is to become more open and flexible in order to take advantage of the experience, ideas, and creativity of everybody, regardless of race or gender. The result goes right to the bottom line: greater profits.

The Second Challenge: The Japanese Work Organization

In 1980, the corporate world in the United States was shaken to discover that the most popular automobile model sold in this country was not a Chevrolet, Ford, or Plymouth but the Honda Accord, made in Japan. And the trend continued: In 2008, the Japanese corporation Toyota passed General Motors to become the largest carmaker in the world (Fowler, 2008). Ironically, as late as the 1950s, the label "Made in Japan" generally indicated that a product was cheap and poorly made. But times have changed. The success of the Japanese auto

industry, as well as companies making electronics, cameras, and many other products, has drawn attention to the "Japanese work organization." How has so small a country been able to challenge the world's economic powerhouse?

Japanese organizations reflect that nation's strong collective spirit. In contrast to the U.S. emphasis on rugged individualism, the Japanese value cooperation. In effect, formal organizations in Japan are more like large primary groups. A generation ago, William Ouchi (1981) highlighted differences between formal organizations in Japan and in the United States. First, Japanese companies hired new workers in groups, giving everyone the same salary and responsibilities. Second, many Japanese companies hired workers for life, fostering a strong sense of loyalty. Third, with the idea that employees would spend their entire careers there, many Japanese organizations trained workers in all phases of their operations. Fourth, although Japanese corporate leaders took ultimate responsibility for their organizations' performance, they involved workers in "quality circles" to discuss decisions that affected them. Fifth, Japanese companies played a large role in the lives of workers, providing home mortgages, sponsoring recreational activities, and scheduling social events. Together, such policies encouraged much more loyalty among members of Japanese organizations than was the case in their U.S. counterparts.

Not everything has worked out well for Japanese corporations. Around 1990, the Japanese economy entered a downward trend that has persisted for two decades. During this downturn, many Japanese companies changed their policies, no longer offering workers jobs for life or many of the other benefits noted by Ouchi. Japanese society is also aging—with a large share of the population over age sixty-five and not working—and this pattern is likely to slow economic growth in the future.

For the widely admired Toyota corporation, 2010 turned out to be a year of trouble. Having expanded its operations to become the world's largest auto company, Toyota was forced to announce recalls of millions of its vehicles due to mechanical problems, suggesting that one consequence of its rapid growth was the loss of some of the company's focus on what had been the key to its success all along—quality (Saporito, 2010).

The Third Challenge: The Changing Nature of Work

Beyond rising global competition and the need to provide equal opportunity for all, pressure to modify conventional work organizations is also coming from changes in the nature of work itself. Over the past few decades, the economy of the United States has moved from industrial to postindustrial production. Rather than working in factories using heavy machinery to make *things,* more people today are using computers and other electronic technology to create or

┌─● Seeing Sociology
  in Everyday Life

Have you ever had a "dead-end" job? A job that demanded
creativity? Which would you prefer and why?

┌─● Making the Grade

As you read the discussion that follows, be sure you understand and
remember the four principles of McDonaldization.

process *information.* A postindustrial society, then, is characterized by information-based organizations.

Frederick Taylor developed his concept of scientific management at a time when most jobs involved tasks that, though often backbreaking, were routine. Workers shoveled coal, poured liquid iron into molds, welded body panels to automobiles on an assembly line, or shot hot rivets into steel girders to build skyscrapers. In addition, a large part of the U.S. labor force in Taylor's day was made up of immigrants, most of whom had little schooling and many of whom knew little English. The routine nature of industrial jobs, coupled with the limited skills of the labor force, led Taylor to treat work as a series of fixed tasks set down by management and followed by employees.

Many of today's information age jobs are very different: The work of designers, artists, consultants, writers, editors, composers, programmers, business owners, and others now demands creativity and imagination. What does this mean for formal organizations? Here are several ways in which today's organizations differ from those of a century ago:

1. **Creative freedom.** As one Hewlett-Packard executive put it, "From their first day of work here, people are given important responsibilities and are encouraged to grow" (Brooks, 2000:128). Today's organizations treat employees with information age skills as a vital resource. Executives can set production goals but cannot dictate how to accomplish tasks that require imagination and discovery. This gives highly skilled workers *creative freedom,* which means they are subject to less day-to-day supervision as long as they generate good results in the long run.

2. **Competitive work teams.** Many organizations allow several groups of employees to work on a problem and offer the greatest rewards to the group that comes up with the best solution. Competitive work teams—a strategy first used by Japanese organizations—draw out the creative contributions of everyone and at the same time reduce the alienation often found in conventional organizations (Maddox, 1994; Yeatts, 1994).

3. **A flatter organization.** By spreading responsibility for creative problem solving throughout the workforce, organizations take on a flatter shape. That is, the pyramid shape of conventional bureaucracy is replaced by an organizational form with fewer levels in the chain of command, as shown in Figure 5–4 on page 134.

4. **Greater flexibility.** The typical industrial age organization was a rigid structure guided from the top. Such organizations may accomplish a good deal of work, but they are not especially creative or able to respond quickly to changes in their larger environment. The ideal model in the information age is a *more open* and *flexible* organization that both generates new ideas and adapts quickly to the rapidly changing global marketplace.

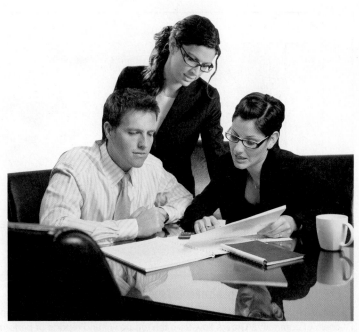

During the last fifty years in the United States, women have moved into management positions throughout the corporate world. While some men initially opposed women's presence in the executive office, it is now clear that women bring particular strengths to the job, including leadership flexibility and communication skills. Thus, some analysts speak of women offering a "female advantage."

What does this all mean for organizations? As David Brooks puts it, "The machine is no longer held up as the standard that healthy organizations should emulate. Now, it's the ecosystem" (2000:128). Today's "smart" companies seek out intelligent, creative people (AOL calls its main buildings "Creative Centers") and nurture the growth of their talents.

Keep in mind, however, that many of today's jobs do not involve creative work at all. More correctly, the postindustrial economy has created two very different types of work: high-skill creative work and low-skill service work. Work in the fast-food industry, for example, is routine and highly supervised and thus has much more in common with factory work of a century ago than with the creative teamwork typical of today's information organizations. Therefore, at the same time that some organizations have taken on a flatter, more flexible form, others continue to use a rigid chain of command.

The "McDonaldization" of Society

As noted in the opening to this chapter, McDonald's has enjoyed enormous success, now operating more than 32,000 restaurants in the United States and around the world. Japan has more than 3,700

Is your college or university a top-down bureaucracy or a flatter, more flexible organization? How might you find out?

[●]—Read "The McDonaldization of Society" by George Ritzer on **mysoclab.com**

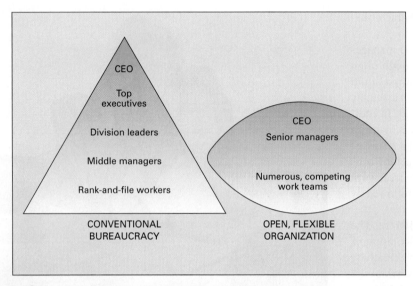

FIGURE 5–4   Two Organizational Models

The conventional model of bureaucratic organizations has a pyramid shape, with a clear chain of command. Orders flow from the top down, and reports of performance flow from the bottom up. Such organizations have extensive rules and regulations, and their workers have highly specialized jobs. More open and flexible organizations have a flatter shape, more like a football. With fewer levels in the hierarchy, responsibility for generating ideas and making decisions is shared throughout the organization. Many workers do their jobs in teams and have a broad knowledge of the entire organization's operation.

Golden Arches, and the world's largest McDonald's is found in China's capital, Beijing. [●]—Read on **mysoclab.com**

McDonald's is far more than a restaurant chain; it is a symbol of U.S. culture. Not only do people around the world associate McDonald's with the United States, but here at home, one poll found that 98 percent of schoolchildren could identify Ronald McDonald, making him as well known as Santa Claus.

Even more important, the organizational principles that underlie McDonald's are coming to dominate our entire society. Our culture is becoming "McDonaldized,"[1] a clever way of saying that we model many aspects of life on the approach taken by the restaurant chain: Parents buy toys at worldwide chain stores all carrying identical merchandise; we drop in at a convenient shop for a ten-minute drive-through oil change; face-to-face communication is being replaced more and more with electronic methods such as voice mail,

e-mail, and instant messaging; more vacations take the form of resorts and tour packages; television packages the news in the form of ten-second sound bites; college admissions officers size up applicants they have never met by glancing at their GPAs and SAT scores; and professors assign ghostwritten textbooks[2] and evaluate students using tests mass-produced for them by publishing companies.

Can you tell what all these developments have in common?

Four Principles

According to George Ritzer (1993), the McDonaldization of society involves four basic organizational principles:

1. **Efficiency.** Ray Kroc, the marketing genius behind the expansion of McDonald's, set out to serve a hamburger, French fries, and a milkshake to a customer in fifty seconds. Today, one of the company's most popular items is the Egg McMuffin, an entire breakfast packaged into a single sandwich. In the restaurant, customers pick up their meals at a counter, dispose of their own trash, and stack their own trays as they walk out the door or, better still, drive away from the pickup window taking whatever mess they make with them. Such efficiency is now central to our way of life. We tend to think that anything done quickly is, for that reason alone, good.

2. **Predictability.** An efficient organization wants to make everything it does as predictable as possible. McDonald's prepares all food using set formulas. Company policies guide the performance of every job.

3. **Uniformity.** The first McDonald's operating manual declared the weight of a regular raw hamburger to be 1.6 ounces, its size to be 3.875 inches across, and its fat content to be 19 percent. A slice of cheese weighs exactly half an ounce, and French fries are cut precisely 9/32 inch thick.

   Think about how many of the objects we see every day around the home, the workplace, and the campus are designed and mass-produced uniformly according to a standard plan. Not just our environment but our everyday life experiences—

---

[1]The term "McDonaldization" was coined by Jim Hightower (1975); much of this discussion is based on the work of George Ritzer (1993, 1998, 2000) and Eric Schlosser (2002).

[2]A number of popular sociology textbooks were not written by the person whose name appears on the cover. This book is not one of them. Even the test bank that accompanies this text was written by the author.

Seeing Sociology in Everyday Life

Can you point to examples of McDonaldization beyond those noted below? What are they?

Go to the Multimedia Library at **mysoclab.com** to hear George Ritzer explain "The McDonaldization of Society"

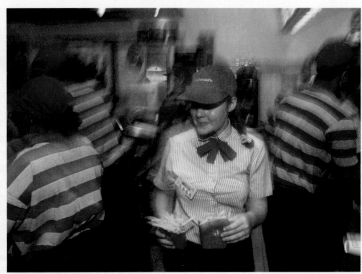

The best of today's information age jobs—including working at Google, the popular search engine Web site—allow people lots of personal freedom as long as they produce good ideas. At the same time, many other jobs, such as working the counter at McDonald's, involve the same routines and strict supervision found in factories a century ago.

from traveling the nation's interstate highways to sitting at home viewing national TV shows—are more standardized than ever before.

Almost anywhere in the world, a person can walk into a McDonald's restaurant and buy the same sandwiches, drinks, and desserts prepared in the same way.[3] Uniformity results from a highly rational system that specifies every action and leaves nothing to chance.

4. **Control.** The most unreliable element in the McDonald's system is human beings. After all, people have their good and bad days, and they sometimes let their minds wander or decide to do something a different way. To minimize the unpredictable human element, McDonald's has automated its equipment to cook food at a fixed temperature for a set length of time. Even the cash registers at McDonald's are keyed to pictures of the

menu items so that ringing up a customer's order is as simple as possible.

Similarly, automatic teller machines are replacing banks, highly automated bakeries produce bread while people stand back and watch, and chickens and eggs (or is it eggs and chickens?) emerge from automated hatcheries. In supermarkets, laser scanners at self-checkouts are phasing out human checkers. Much of our shopping now occurs in malls, where everything from temperature and humidity to the kinds of stores and products sold are subject to continuous control and supervision (Ide & Cordell, 1994). ● Go to **mysoclab.com**

Can Rationality Be Irrational?

There is no doubt about the popularity or efficiency of McDonald's. But there is another side to the story.

Max Weber was alarmed at the increasing rationalization of the world, fearing that formal organizations would cage our imaginations and crush the human spirit. As he saw it, rational systems are efficient but dehumanizing. McDonaldization bears him out. Each of the principles we have just discussed limits human creativity, choice, and freedom. Echoing Weber, Ritzer reaches the conclusion that "the ultimate irrationality of McDonaldization is that people could lose control over the system and it would come to control us" (1993:145). Perhaps even McDonald's understands the limits of

---

[3]As McDonald's has "gone global," a few products have been added or changed according to local tastes. For example, in Uruguay, customers enjoy the McHuevo (a hamburger with a poached egg on top); Norwegians can buy McLaks (grilled salmon sandwiches); the Dutch favor the Groenteburger (vegetable burger); in Thailand, McDonald's serves Samurai pork burgers; the Japanese can purchase a Chicken Tatsuta Sandwich (chicken seasoned with soy and ginger); Filipinos eat McSpaghetti (spaghetti with tomato sauce and bits of hot dog); and in India, where Hindus eat no beef, McDonald's sells a vegetarian Maharaja Mac (B. Sullivan, 1995).

⌐● Making the Grade

The McDonaldization thesis is that rational organization is coming to define our way of life and this trend is in important ways harmful to our well-being.

⌐● Making the Grade

The opposing trends are (1) expansion of flatter, more flexible organizations that value creativity and (2) the large number of routine service jobs that reflect the "McDonaldization of society."

CONTROVERSY & DEBATE

Computer Technology, Large Organizations, and the Assault on Privacy

JAKE: I'm doing MySpace. It's really cool.

DUNCAN: Why do you want to put your whole life out there for everyone to see?

JAKE: I'm famous, man!

DUNCAN: Famous? Ha! You're throwing away whatever privacy you have left.

Jake completes a page on MySpace.com, which includes his name and college, e-mail, photo, biography, and current personal interests. It can be accessed by billions of people around the world.

Late for a meeting with a new client, Sarah drives her car through a yellow light as it turns red at a main intersection. A computer linked to a pair of cameras notes the violation and takes one picture of her license plate and another of her sitting in the driver's seat. Seven days later, she receives a summons to appear in traffic court.

Julio looks through his mail and finds a letter from a Washington, D.C., data services company telling him that he is one of about 145,000

people whose name, address, Social Security number, and credit file have recently been sold to criminals in California posing as businesspeople. With this information, these crooks can obtain credit cards or take out loans in his name.

These are all cases showing that today's organizations—which know more about us than ever before and more than most of us even realize—pose a growing threat to personal privacy. Large organizations are necessary for today's society

to operate. In some cases, organizations using information about us may actually be helpful. But cases of identity theft are on the rise, and personal privacy is on the decline.

In the past, small-town life gave people little privacy. But at least if people knew something about you, you were just as likely to know something about them. Today, unknown people "out there" can access information about each of us all the time without our learning about it.

In part, the loss of privacy is a result of more and more complex computer technology. Are you aware that every e-mail you send and every Web site you visit leaves a record in one or more computers? Most of these records can be retrieved by people you don't know, as well as by employers and other public officials.

Another part of today's loss of privacy reflects the number and size of formal organizations. As explained in this chapter, large organizations tend to treat people impersonally, and they have a huge appetite for information. Mix large organizations with ever more complex computer technology, and it is no wonder that

---

rationalization—the company has now expanded its offerings of more upscale foods, such as premium roasted coffee and salad selections that are more sophisticated, fresh, and healthful (Philadelphia, 2002).

The Future of Organizations: Opposing Trends

Early in the twentieth century, ever-larger organizations arose in the United States, most taking on the bureaucratic form described by Max Weber. In many respects, these organizations were like armies led by powerful generals who issued orders to their captains and lieu-

tenants. Ordinary soldiers, working in the factories, did what they were told.

With the emergence of the postindustrial economy after 1950, as well as rising competition from abroad, many organizations evolved toward the flatter, more flexible model that encourages communication and creativity. Such "intelligent organizations" (Pinchot & Pinchot, 1993; Brooks, 2000) have become more productive than ever. Just as important, for highly skilled people who enjoy creative freedom, these organizations create less of the alienation that so worried Weber.

But this is only half the story. Although the postindustrial economy created many highly skilled jobs, it created even more routine

● Seeing Sociology
in Everyday Life

Have large organizations reduced your privacy in ways you don't like?
Explain.

● Seeing Sociology
in Everyday Life

Are we giving away our own privacy by posting so much information
about ourselves on social networking sites such as Facebook?
Explain.

most people in the United States are concerned about who knows what about them and what people are doing with this information.

For decades, the level of personal privacy in the United States has been declining. Early in the twentieth century, when state agencies began issuing driver's licenses, for example, they generated files for every licensed driver. Today, officials can send this information at the touch of a button not only to the police but also to all sorts of other organizations. The Internal Revenue Service and the Social Security Administration, as well as government agencies that benefit veterans, students, the unemployed, and the poor, all collect mountains of personal information.

Business organizations now do much the same thing, and many of the choices we make end up in a company's database. Most of us use credit—the U.S. population now has more than 1 billion credit cards, an average of five per adult—but the companies that do "credit checks" collect and distribute information about us to almost anyone who asks, including criminals planning to steal our identity.

Then there are the small cameras found not only at traffic intersections but also in stores, public buildings, and parking garages and across college campuses. The number of surveillance cameras that monitor our movements is rapidly increasing with each passing year. So-called security cameras may increase public safety in some ways—say, by discouraging a mugger or even a terrorist—at the cost of the little privacy we have left.

After the September 11, 2001, terrorist attacks, the federal government took steps (including the USA PATRIOT Act) to strengthen national security. Today, government officials more closely monitor not just who enters the country but the activities of all of us. Increased national security and privacy do not mix.

Some legal protections remain. Each of the fifty states has laws that give citizens the right to examine some records about themselves kept by employers, banks, and credit bureaus. The federal Privacy Act of 1974 also limits the exchange of personal information among government agencies and permits citizens to examine and correct most government files. In response to rising levels of identity theft, Congress is likely to pass more laws to regulate the sale of credit information. But so many organizations, private as well as public, now have information about us—experts estimate that 90 percent of U.S. households are profiled in databases somewhere—that current laws simply cannot effectively address the privacy problem.

WHAT DO YOU THINK?

1. Do you believe that our concern about national security is destroying privacy? How can the loss of privacy threaten our security?

2. Do you use Internet sites such as http://www.myspace.com? Why do you think so many young people are eager to spread personal information in this way?

3. Have you checked your credit history recently? Do you know how to reduce the chances of having your identity stolen? (If not, one place to start is http://www.stopidentitytheft.org).

Sources: Robert Wright (1998), "Online Privacy" (2000), J. Rosen (2000), A. Hamilton (2001), Heymann (2002), O'Harrow (2005), and Bruxelles (2009).

service jobs, such as those offered by McDonald's. Fast-food companies now represent the largest pool of low-wage labor, aside from migrant workers, in the United States (Schlosser, 2002). Work of this kind, which Ritzer terms "McJobs," offers few of the benefits that today's highly skilled workers enjoy. On the contrary, the automated routines that define work in the fast-food industry, telemarketing, and similar fields are not very different from those that Frederick Taylor described a century ago.

Today, the organizational flexibility that gives better-off workers more freedom carries, for rank-and-file employees, the ever-present threat of "downsizing" (Sennett, 1998). Organizations facing global competition are eager to attract creative employees, but they are just as eager to cut costs by eliminating as many routine jobs as possible. The net result is that some people are better off than ever while others worry about holding their jobs and struggle to make ends meet—a trend that we will explore in detail in Chapter 8 ("Social Stratification").

U.S. organizations remain the envy of the world for their productive efficiency. Indeed, there are few places on Earth where the mail arrives as quickly and dependably as it does in this country. But we should remember that the future is far brighter for some people than for others. In addition, as the Controversy & Debate box explains, formal organizations pose a mounting threat to our privacy, something to keep in mind as we envision our organizational future.

Seeing Sociology in Everyday Life

To what extent is the concept of McDonaldization a part of our everyday lives?

This chapter explains that since the opening of the first McDonald's restaurant in 1948, the principles that underlie the fast-food industry—efficiency, predictability, uniformity, and control—have spread to many aspects of our everyday lives. Here is a chance to identify aspects of McDonaldization in several familiar routines. In each of the two photos on the facing page, can you identify specific elements of McDonaldization? That is, in what ways does the organizational pattern or the technology involved increase efficiency, predictability, uniformity, and control? In the photo below, what elements do you see that are clearly not McDonaldization? Why?

> **HINT** This process, which is described as the "McDonaldization of society," has made our lives easier in some ways, but it has also made our society ever more impersonal, gradually diminishing our range of human contact. Also, although this organizational pattern is intended to serve human needs, it may end up doing the opposite by forcing people to live according to the demands of machines. Max Weber feared that our future would be an overly rational world in which we all might lose much of our humanity.

Small, privately owned stores like this one were once the rule in the United States. But the number of "mom and pop" businesses is declining as "big box" discount stores expand. Why are small stores disappearing? What social qualities of these stores are we losing in the process?

Automated teller machines (ATMs) became common in the United States in the early 1970s. A customer with an electronic identification card can complete certain banking operations (such as withdrawing cash) without having to deal with a human bank teller. What makes the ATM one example of McDonaldization? Do you enjoy using ATMs? Why or why not?

At checkout counters in many supermarkets and large discount stores, the customer lifts each product through a laser scanner linked to a computer in order to identify what the product is and what it costs. The customer then inserts a credit or debit card to pay for the purchase and proceeds to bag the items.

Applying SOCIOLOGY in Everyday Life

1. Have colleges and universities been affected by the process called McDonaldization? Do large, anonymous lecture courses qualify as an example? Why? What other examples of McDonaldization can you identify on the college campus?

2. Visit any large public building with an elevator. Observe groups of people as they approach the elevator, and enter the elevator with them. Watch their behavior: What happens to conversations as the elevator doors close? Where do people fix their eyes? Can you explain these patterns?

3. Using campus publications or your school's Web page (and some assistance from an instructor), try to draw an organizational pyramid for your college or university. Show the key offices and how they supervise and report to one another.

Making the Grade

What Are Social Groups?

Watch on mysoclab.com

SOCIAL GROUPS are two or more people who identify with and interact with one another.
p. 118

A **PRIMARY GROUP** is small, personal, and lasting (examples include family and close friends).
pp. 118–19

A **SECONDARY GROUP** is large, impersonal, goal-oriented, and often of shorter duration (examples include a college class or a corporation).
p. 119

See the Summing Up table on page 120.

Elements of Group Dynamics

GROUP LEADERSHIP
- *Instrumental leadership* focuses on completing tasks.
- *Expressive leadership* focuses on a group's well-being.
- *Authoritarian leadership* is a "take charge" style that demands obedience; *democratic leadership* includes everyone in decision making; *laissez-faire leadership* lets the group function mostly on its own.
pp. 119–20

GROUP CONFORMITY
- The Asch, Milgram, and Janis research shows that group members often seek agreement and may pressure one another toward conformity.
- Individuals use *reference groups*—including both *in-groups* and *out-groups*—to form attitudes and make evaluations.
pp. 120–22

GROUP SIZE and DIVERSITY
- Georg Simmel described the *dyad* as intense but unstable; the *triad*, he said, is more stable but can dissolve into a dyad by excluding one member.
- Peter Blau claimed that larger groups turn inward, socially diverse groups turn outward, and physically segregated groups turn inward.
pp. 122–23

NETWORKS are relational webs that link people with little common identity and limited interaction. Being "well connected" in networks is a valuable type of social capital.
pp. 123–24

social group (p.118) two or more people who identify with and interact with one another

primary group (p. 119) a small social group whose members share personal and lasting relationships

secondary group (p. 119) a large and impersonal social group whose members pursue a specific goal or activity

instrumental leadership (p. 120) group leadership that focuses on the completion of tasks

expressive leadership (p. 120) group leadership that focuses on the group's well-being

groupthink (p. 121) the tendency of group members to conform, resulting in a narrow view of some issue

reference group (p. 122) a social group that serves as a point of reference in making evaluations and decisions

in-group (p. 122) a social group toward which a member feels respect and loyalty

out-group (p. 122) a social group toward which a person feels a sense of competition or opposition

dyad (p. 123) a social group with two members

triad (p. 123) a social group with three members

network (p. 123) a web of weak social ties

What Formal Organizations?

FORMAL ORGANIZATIONS are large secondary groups organized to achieve their goals efficiently.
p. 124

UTILITARIAN ORGANIZATIONS pay people for their efforts (examples include businesses and government agencies).
p. 125

NORMATIVE ORGANIZATIONS have goals people consider worthwhile (examples include voluntary associations such as the PTA).
pp. 125–26

COERCIVE ORGANIZATIONS are organizations people are forced to join (examples include prisons and mental hospitals).
p. 126

Explore on mysoclab.com

formal organization (p. 124) a large secondary group organized to achieve its goals efficiently

tradition (p. 126) values and beliefs passed from generation to generation

rationality (p. 126) a way of thinking that emphasizes deliberate, matter-of-fact calculation of the most efficient way to accomplish a particular task

rationalization of society (p. 126) Weber's term for the historical change from tradition to rationality as the main type of human thought

What Are Formal Organizations? *(continued)*

All formal organizations operate in an **ORGANIZATIONAL ENVIRONMENT** that is influenced by
- technology
- political and economic trends
- current events
- population patterns
- other organizations

pp. 127–28

See the Summing Up table on page 127.

bureaucracy (p. 126) an organizational model rationally designed to perform tasks efficiently

organizational environment (p. 127) factors outside an organization that affect its operation

bureaucratic ritualism (p. 129) a focus on rules and regulations to the point of undermining an organization's goals

bureaucratic inertia (p. 129) the tendency of bureaucratic organizations to perpetuate themselves

oligarchy (p. 129) the rule of the many by the few

scientific management (p. 130) Frederick Taylor's term for the application of scientific principles to the operation of a business or other large organization

Modern Formal Organizations: Bureaucracy

BUREAUCRACY, which Max Weber saw as the dominant type of organization in modern societies, is based on
- specialization
- hierarchy of offices
- rules and regulations
- technical competence
- impersonality
- formal, written communication

pp. 126–27

PROBLEMS OF BUREAUCRACY include
- bureaucratic alienation
- bureaucratic inefficiency and ritualism
- bureaucratic inertia
- oligarchy

pp. 128–30

The Evolution of Formal Organizations

CONVENTIONAL BUREAUCRACY

In the early 1900s, Frederick Taylor's **SCIENTIFIC MANAGEMENT** applied scientific principles to increase productivity.

pp. 130–31

⌐ **MORE OPEN, FLEXIBLE ORGANIZATIONS** ¬

In the 1960s, Rosabeth Moss Kanter proposed that opening up organizations for all employees, especially women and other minorities, increased organizational efficiency.

p. 131

In the 1980s, global competition drew attention to the Japanese work organization's collective orientation.

p. 132

The Changing Nature of Work

Recently, the rise of a postindustrial economy has created two very different types of work:
- highly skilled and creative work (examples include designers, consultants, programmers, and executives)
- low-skilled service work associated with the "McDonaldization" of society, based on efficiency, uniformity, and control (examples include jobs in fast-food restaurants and telemarketing)

pp. 132–36

📖⊕ Read on **mysoclab.com**

6 Sexuality and Society

- What was the sexual revolution, and how did it change U.S. society?

- Why do societies try to control people's sexual behavior?

- How does sexuality play a part in social inequality?

 Watch the *Core Concepts in Sociology* video "Alternative Sexual Orientation" on **mysoclab.com**

Chapter Overview

This chapter explains how society shapes human sexuality and also how sexuality figures into our everyday lives. Although sexuality is biological, society (including culture and patterns of inequality) shapes how we experience sexuality.

Pam Goodman walks along the hallway with her friends Jennifer Delosier and Cindy Thomas. The three young women are sophomores at Jefferson High School, in Jefferson City, a small town in the Midwest.

"What's happening after school?" Pam asks.

"Dunno," replies Jennifer. "Maybe Todd is coming over."

"Got the picture," adds Cindy. "We're so gone."

"Shut up!" Pam stammers, smiling. "I hardly know Todd." The three girls break into laughter.

It is no surprise that young people spend a lot of time thinking and talking about sex. But as the sociologist Peter Bearman discovered, sex involves more than just talk. Bearman and two colleagues (Bearman, Moody, & Stovel, 2004) conducted confidential interviews with 832 students at the high school in a Midwestern town they called Jefferson City, learning that 573 (69 percent of the students) had had at least one "sexual and romantic relationship" during the previous eighteen months. So most, but not all, of these students were sexually active.

Bearman wanted to learn about sexual activity in order to understand the problem of sexually transmitted diseases (STDs) among young people. Why are the rates of STDs so high? And why can there be sudden "outbreaks" of disease that involve dozens of young people in a community?

To find the answers to these questions, Bearman and colleagues asked the students to identify their sexual partners (promising, of course, not to reveal any confidential information). This information allowed them to trace connections between individual students in terms of sexual activity and produced a surprising pattern: Sexually active students were linked to each other through common partners much more than anyone might have expected. In all, common partners linked half of the sexually active students, as shown in the diagram.

Other relationships
(If a pattern was observed more than once, numeral indicates frequency.)

Source: Bearman, Moody, & Stovel (2004).

Awareness of the connections among people can help us understand how STDs spread from one infected person to another in a short period of time. Bearman's study also shows that research can teach us a great deal about human sexuality, which is an important dimension of social life. You will also see that sexual attitudes and behavior have changed dramatically over the past century in the United States.

Understanding Sexuality

How much of your thoughts and actions every day have something to do with sexuality? If you are like most people, the answer is "quite a lot," because sexuality is about much more than just having sex. Sexuality is a theme found almost everywhere—in sports, on campus, in

We claim that beauty is in the eye of the beholder, which suggests the importance of culture in setting standards of attractiveness. All of the people pictured here—from Kenya, Arizona, New Zealand, Thailand, South Africa, and Ecuador—are considered beautiful by members of their own society. At the same time, sociobiologists point out that in every society on Earth, people are attracted to youthfulness. The reason, as sociobiologists see it, is that attractiveness underlies our choices about reproduction, which is most readily accomplished in early adulthood.

the workplace, and especially in the mass media. There is also a sex industry that includes pornography and prostitution, both of which are multibillion-dollar businesses in this country. The bottom line is that sexuality is an important part of how we think about ourselves as well as how others think about us. For this reason, there are few areas of social life in which sexuality does not play some part.

Nevertheless, U.S. culture has long treated sex as taboo; even today, many people avoid talking about it. As a result, although sex can produce much pleasure, it also causes confusion, anxiety, and sometimes outright fear. Even scientists long considered sex off limits as a topic to study. It was not until the middle of the twentieth century that researchers turned their attention to this vital dimension of social life. Since then, as this chapter explains, we have discovered a great deal about human sexuality. ● Go to **mysoclab.com**

Sex: A Biological Issue

Sex refers to *the biological distinction between females and males.* From a biological point of view, sex is the way humans reproduce. A female ovum and a male sperm, each containing twenty-three chromosomes (biological codes that guide physical development), combine to form an embryo. To one of these pairs of chromosomes, which determines the child's sex, the mother contributes an X chromosome and the father contributes either an X or a Y. An X from the father produces a female (XX) embryo; a Y from the father produces a male (XY) embryo. A child's sex is thus determined biologically at the moment of conception.

The sex of an embryo guides its development. If the embryo is male, the growth of testicular tissue starts to produce large amounts

primary sex characteristics the genitals, organs used for reproduction

secondary sex characteristics bodily development, apart from the genitals, that distinguishes biologically mature females and males

intersexual people people whose bodies (including genitals) have both female and male characteristics

transsexuals people who feel they are one sex even though biologically they are the other

Chaz Bono, on the right, is the only child of entertainers Sonny and Cher Bono. Born Chastity Bono, she "came out" as a lesbian in the 1990s and became a gay-rights advocate. In 2010, Chaz legally changed his name after completing a female-to-male gender transition.

of testosterone, a hormone that triggers the development of male genitals (sex organs). If little testosterone is present, the embryo develops female genitals.

Sex and the Body

Some differences in the body set males and females apart. Right from birth, the two sexes have different **primary sex characteristics,** namely, *the genitals, organs used for reproduction.* At puberty, as people reach sexual maturity, additional sex differentiation takes place. At this point, people develop **secondary sex characteristics,** *bodily development, apart from the genitals, that distinguishes biologically mature females and males.* Sexually mature females have wider hips for giving birth, milk-producing breasts for nurturing infants, and soft, fatty tissue that provides a reserve supply of nutrition during pregnancy and breast feeding. Sexually mature males typically develop more muscle in the upper body, more extensive body hair, and deeper voices. Of course, these are general differences; some males are smaller and have less body hair and higher voices than some females.

Keep in mind that sex is not the same thing as gender. *Gender* is an element of culture and refers to the personal traits and patterns of behavior (including responsibilities, opportunities, and privileges) that a culture attaches to being female or male. Chapter 10 ("Gender Stratification") explains that gender is an important dimension of social inequality.

Intersexual People

Sex is not always as clear-cut as has been just described. The term **intersexual people** refers to *people whose bodies (including genitals) have both female and male characteristics.* Intersexuality is both natural and very rare, involving well below 1 percent of a society's population. An older term for intersexual people is *hermaphrodite* (a word derived from Hermaphroditus, the child of the mythological Greek gods Hermes and Aphrodite, who embodied both sexes). A true hermaphrodite has both a female ovary and a male testis.

However, our culture demands that sex be clear-cut, a fact evident in the requirement that parents record the sex of their child at birth as either female or male. In the United States, some people respond to intersexual people with confusion or even disgust. But attitudes in other cultures are quite different: The Pokot of eastern Africa, for example, pay little attention to what they consider a simple biological error, and the Navajo look on intersexual people with awe, seeing in them the full potential of both the female and the male (Geertz, 1975).

Transsexuals

Transsexuals are *people who feel they are one sex even though biologically they are the other.* Estimates suggest that one or two of every 1,000 people who are born have experienced the feeling of being trapped in a body of the wrong sex and a desire to be the other sex. Sometimes called transgender people, many begin to disregard conventional ideas about how females and males should look and behave. Some also go one step further and undergo *gender reassignment,* surgical alteration of their genitals, which is usually accompanied by hormone treatments. This medical process is complex and takes months or even years, but it helps many people gain a joyful sense of finally becoming on the outside who they feel they are on the inside (Gagné, Tewksbury, & McGaughey, 1997; Olyslager & Conway, 2007).

Sex: A Cultural Issue

Sexuality has a biological foundation. But like all other elements of human behavior, sexuality is also very much a cultural issue. Biology may explain some animals' mating rituals, but humans have no similar biological program. Although there is a biological "sex drive" in the sense that people find sex pleasurable and may seek to engage in sexual activity, our biology does not dictate any specific ways of being

In Montana, marriage between first cousins is against the law.

In Indiana, first cousins Shawn and Delia Dawson were able to marry only because they are both 70 years old.

incest taboo a norm forbidding sexual relations or marriage between certain relatives

Seeing Ourselves

NATIONAL MAP 6–1

First-Cousin Marriage Laws across the United States

There is no single view on first-cousin marriages in the United States: Twenty-four states forbid such unions, twenty allow them, and six allow them with restrictions.* In general, states that permit first-cousin marriages are found in New England, the Southeast, and the Southwest.

*Of the six states that allow first-cousin marriages with restrictions, five permit them only when couples are past childbearing age.

Source: National Conference of State Legislatures (2009).

First-Cousin Marriages
- Allowed
- Allowed with restrictions
- Not allowed

sexual any more than our desire to eat dictates any particular foods or table manners.

Cultural Variation

Almost every sexual practice shows considerable variation from one society to another. In his pioneering study of sexuality in the United States, Alfred Kinsey and his colleagues (1948) found that most couples reported having intercourse in a single position: face to face, with the woman on the bottom and the man on top. Halfway around the world, in the South Seas, most couples *never* have sex in this way. In fact, when the people of the South Seas learned of this practice from Western missionaries, they poked fun at it as the strange "missionary position."

Even the simple practice of displaying affection varies from society to society. Most people in the United States kiss in public, but the Chinese kiss only in private. The French kiss publicly, often twice (once on each cheek), and Belgians kiss three times (starting on either cheek). The Maori of New Zealand rub noses, and most people in Nigeria don't kiss at all.

Modesty, too, is culturally variable. If a woman stepping into a bath is disturbed, what body parts does she cover? Helen Colton (1983) reports that an Islamic woman covers her face, a Laotian woman covers her breasts, a Samoan woman covers her navel, a Sumatran woman covers her knees, and a European woman covers her breasts with one hand and her genital area with the other.

Around the world, some societies restrict sexuality, and others are more permissive. In China, for example, societal norms so closely regulate sexuality that few people have sexual intercourse before they marry. In the United States, at least in recent decades, intercourse prior to marriage has become the norm, and some people choose to have sex even without strong commitment.

The Incest Taboo

When it comes to sex, do all societies agree on anything? The answer is yes. One cultural universal—an element found in every society the world over—is the **incest taboo,** *a norm forbidding sexual relations or marriage between certain relatives.* In the United States, the law, reflecting cultural mores, prohibits close relatives (including brothers and sisters, parents and children) from having sex or marrying. But in another example of cultural variation, exactly which family members are included in our society's incest taboo varies from state to state. National Map 6–1 shows that about half the states outlaw marriage between first cousins and about half do not; a few permit this practice but with restrictions (National Conference of State Legislatures, 2009).

Some societies (such as the North American Navajo) apply incest taboos only to the mother and others on her side of the family. There are also societies on record (including ancient Peru and Egypt) that have approved brother-sister marriages among the nobility as a strategy to keep power within a single family (Murdock, 1965, orig. 1949).

Why does some form of incest taboo exist everywhere? Part of the reason is biology: Reproduction between close relatives of any species increases the odds of producing offspring with mental or physical problems. But why, of all living species, do only humans observe an incest taboo? This fact suggests that controlling sexuality between close relatives is a necessary element of *social* organization. For one thing, the incest taboo limits sexual competition in families by restricting sex to spouses (ruling out, for example, sex between parent and child). Second, because family ties define people's rights and obligations toward one another, reproduction between close relatives would hopelessly confuse kinship; if a mother and son had a daughter, would the child consider the male a father or a brother?

⊙ Making the Grade

Be sure you understand why the incest taboo is more about society than biology.

⊙ Making the Grade

Be sure you understand the differences between the "sexual revolution" and the "sexual counterrevolution."

Over the course of the past century, social attitudes in the United States have become more accepting of most aspects of human sexuality. What do you see as some of the benefits of this greater openness? What are some of the negative consequences?

Third, by requiring people to marry outside their immediate families, the incest taboo integrates the larger society as people look beyond their close kin when seeking to form new families.

The incest taboo has long been a sexual norm in the United States and throughout the world. But in this country, many other sexual norms have changed over time. In the twentieth century, as the next section explains, our society experienced both a sexual revolution and a sexual counterrevolution.

Sexual Attitudes in the United States

What do people in the United States think about sex? Our culture's attitudes toward sexuality have always been somewhat contradictory. The early Puritan settlers of New England demanded strict conformity in attitudes and behavior, and they imposed severe punishment for any sexual misconduct, even if it took place in the privacy of the home. Later on, most European immigrants arrived with rigid ideas about "correct" sexuality, typically limiting sex to reproduction within marriage. Some regulation of sexual activity has continued ever since. As late as the 1960s, for example, some states legally prohibited the sale of condoms in stores. Until 2003, when the Supreme Court struck them down, thirteen states had laws banning sexual acts between partners of the same sex. Even today, "fornication"

laws, which forbid intercourse by unmarried couples, are still on the books in eight states.

But this is just one side of the story. As Chapter 2 ("Culture") explains, because U.S. culture is individualistic, many of us believe that people should be free to do pretty much as they wish, as long as they cause no direct harm to others. The idea that what people do in the privacy of their own homes is no one else's business makes sex a matter of individual freedom and personal choice.

When it comes to sexuality, is the United States restrictive or permissive? The answer is both. On one hand, many people in the United States still view sexual conduct as an important indicator of personal morality. On the other hand, sex has become more and more a part of popular culture carried by the mass media—one recent report concluded that the number of scenes in television shows with sexual content doubled in a mere ten years (Kunkel et al., 2005). Within this complex framework, we turn now to changes in sexual attitudes and behavior that have occurred over the course of the past century.

The Sexual Revolution

Over the past century, the United States witnessed profound changes in sexual attitudes and practices. The first indications of this change came in the 1920s as millions of people migrated from farms and small towns to rapidly growing cities. There, living apart from their families and meeting new people in the workplace, young men and

● Seeing Sociology
  in Everyday Life

Can you point to elements of everyday life that are linked to the
sexual revolution or the sexual counterrevolution?

women enjoyed considerable sexual freedom, one reason that decade
became known as the "Roaring Twenties."

In the 1930s and 1940s, the Great Depression and World War II
slowed the rate of change. But in the postwar period, after 1945,
Alfred Kinsey set the stage for what later came to be known as the
sexual revolution. In 1948, Kinsey and his colleagues published their
first study of sexuality in the United States, and it raised eyebrows
everywhere. The national uproar resulted mostly from the fact that
scientists were actually studying sex, a topic many people were uneasy
talking about even in the privacy of their homes.

Kinsey also had some interesting things to say. His two books
(Kinsey, Pomeroy, & Martin, 1948; Kinsey et al., 1953) became best-
sellers because they revealed that people in the United States, on average, were far less conventional in sexual matters than most had
thought. These books encouraged a new openness toward sexuality,
which helped set the sexual revolution in motion.

In the late 1960s, the sexual revolution truly came of age. Youth culture dominated public life, and expressions such as "sex, drugs, and rock-
and-roll" and "if it feels good, do it!" summed up the new, freer attitude
toward sex. The baby boom generation, born between 1946 and 1964,
became the first cohort in U.S. history to grow up with the idea that sex
was part of people's lives, whether they were married or not.

New technology also played a part in the sexual revolution. The
birth control pill, introduced in 1960, not only prevented pregnancy
but also made having sex more convenient. Unlike a condom or a
diaphragm, which has to be applied at the time of intercourse, the pill
could be taken like a daily vitamin supplement. Now women as well
as men could engage in sex without any special preparation.

Because women were historically subject to greater sexual regulation than men, the sexual revolution had special significance for
them. Society's traditional "double standard" allows (and even encourages) men to be sexually active but expects women to be virgins until
marriage and faithful to their husbands afterward. The survey data in
Figure 6–1 show the narrowing of the double standard as a result of
the sexual revolution. Among people born between 1933 and 1942
(that is, people who are in their late sixties and seventies today),
56 percent of men but just 16 percent of women report having had
two or more sexual partners by age twenty. Compare this wide gap
with the pattern among those born between 1953 and 1962 (people
now in their late forties and fifties), who came of age after the sexual
revolution. In this category, 62 percent of men and 48 percent of women
say they had two or more sexual partners by age twenty (Laumann
et al., 1994:198). The sexual revolution increased sexual activity overall, and it changed women's behavior even more than men's.

Greater openness about sexuality develops as societies become
richer and the opportunities for women increase. With these facts
in mind, look for a pattern in the global use of birth control shown
in Global Map 6–1 on page 150.

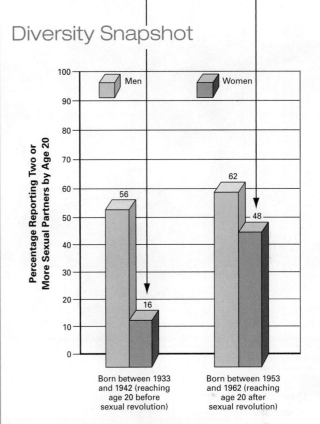

Nancy Houck, now 73 years old, has lived most of her life in a social world where men have had much more sexual freedom than women.

Sarah Roholt, 47, is a baby boomer who feels that she and her women friends have pretty much the same sexual freedom as men.

Diversity Snapshot

FIGURE 6–1   **The Sexual Revolution:
Closing the Double Standard**

A larger share of men than women report having had two or more sexual partners by age twenty. But the sexual revolution greatly reduced
this gender difference.

Source: Laumann et al. (1994:198).

The Sexual Counterrevolution

The sexual revolution made sex a topic of everyday discussion and
sexual activity more a matter of individual choice. However, by 1980,
the climate of sexual freedom that had marked the late 1960s and
1970s was criticized by some people as evidence of our country's
moral decline, and the *sexual counterrevolution* began.

Politically speaking, the sexual counterrevolution was a conservative call for a return to "family values" and a change from sexual
freedom back toward what critics saw as the sexual responsibility valued by earlier generations. Critics of the sexual revolution objected not
just to the idea of "free love" but to trends such as cohabitation (living together without being married) and unmarried couples having
children.

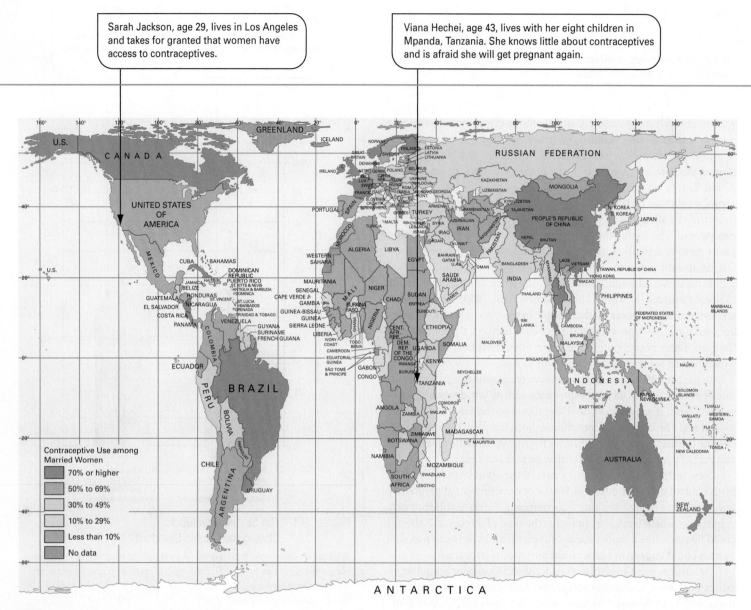

Sarah Jackson, age 29, lives in Los Angeles and takes for granted that women have access to contraceptives.

Viana Hechei, age 43, lives with her eight children in Mpanda, Tanzania. She knows little about contraceptives and is afraid she will get pregnant again.

Contraceptive Use among Married Women

- 70% or higher
- 50% to 69%
- 30% to 49%
- 10% to 29%
- Less than 10%
- No data

Window on the World

GLOBAL MAP 6–1   Contraceptive Use in Global Perspective

The map shows the percentage of married women using modern contraception methods (such as barrier methods, contraceptive pill, implants, injectables, intrauterine devices, or sterilization). In general, how do high-income nations differ from low-income nations? Can you explain this difference?

Sources: Data from United Nations (2008) and Population Reference Bureau (2009).

Looking back, the sexual counterrevolution did not greatly change the idea that people should decide for themselves when and with whom to have a sexual relationship. But whether for moral reasons or concerns about sexually transmitted diseases, more people began choosing to limit their number of sexual partners or not to have sex at all.

Is the sexual revolution over? It is true that people are making more careful decisions about sexuality. But as the rest of this chapter explains, the ongoing sexual revolution is evident in the fact that there is now greater acceptance of premarital sex as well as increasing tolerance for various sexual orientations.

Premarital Sex

In light of the sexual revolution and the sexual counterrevolution, how much has sexual behavior in the United States really changed?

Seeing Sociology
in Everyday Life

Go to the Multimedia Library at **mysoclab.com**
to listen to the NPR report "Adultery"

Why do you think U.S. society has become more accepting of
premarital sex but not of extramarital sex?

One interesting trend involves premarital sex—sexual intercourse before marriage—among young people.

Consider first what U.S. adults *say* about premarital intercourse. Table 6–1 shows that 30 percent characterize sexual relations before marriage as "always wrong" or "almost always wrong." Another 16 percent consider premarital sex "wrong only sometimes," and about 52 percent say premarital sex is "not wrong at all." Public opinion is far more accepting of premarital sex today than was the case a generation ago, but our society clearly remains divided on this issue (NORC, 2009).

Now let's look at what young people *do*. For women, there has been marked change over time. The Kinsey studies reported that for people born in the early 1900s, about 50 percent of men but just 6 percent of women had premarital sexual intercourse before age nineteen. Studies of baby boomers, born after World War II, show a slight increase in premarital sex among men but a large increase—to about one-third—among women. The most recent studies show that by the time they are seniors in high school, slightly more than half of young men and women have had premarital sexual intercourse. In addition, sexual experience among high school students who are sexually active is limited—only 15 percent of students report four or more sexual partners. These statistics have remained much the same for the past twenty years (Laumann et al., 1994:323–24, Centers for Disease Control and Prevention, 2008; Yabroff, 2008).

A common belief is that an even larger share of young people engage in oral sex. This choice reflects the fact that this practice avoids the risk of pregnancy; in addition, many young people see oral sex as something less than "going all the way." Recent research suggests that the share of young people who have had oral sex is greater than the share having had intercourse, but only by about 10 percent. Therefore, mass-media claims of an "oral sex epidemic" among young people in the United States are almost certainly exaggerated.

Finally, a significant minority of young people choose abstinence (not having sexual intercourse). Many also choose not to have oral sex, which, like intercourse, can transmit disease. Even so, research confirms the fact that premarital sex is widely accepted among young people today.

Sex between Adults

Judging from the mass media, people in the United States are very active sexually. But do popular images reflect reality? The Laumann study (1994), the largest study of sexuality since Kinsey's groundbreaking research, found that frequency of sexual activity varies widely in the U.S. population. One-third of adults report having sex with a partner a few times a year or not at all, another one-third have sex once or several times a month, and the remaining one-third have sex with a partner two or more times a week. In short, no single stereotype accurately describes sexual activity in the United States.

Table 6–1 How We View Premarital and Extramarital Sex

Survey Question: "There's been a lot of discussion about the way morals and attitudes about sex are changing in this country. If a man and a woman have sexual relations before marriage, do you think it is always wrong, almost always wrong, wrong only sometimes, or not wrong at all? What about a married person having sexual relations with someone other than the marriage partner?"

	Premarital Sex	Extramarital Sex
"Always wrong"	22.9%	80.5%
"Almost always wrong"	6.8	10.7
"Wrong only sometimes"	15.5	5.6
"Not wrong at all"	52.1	1.5
"Don't know"/No answer	2.7	1.8

Source: *General Social Surveys, 1972–2008: Cumulative Codebook* (Chicago: National Opinion Research Center, 2009), p. 339.

Despite the widespread image of "swinging singles" promoted on television shows such as *Sex and the City*, it is married people who have sex with partners the most. In addition, married people report the highest level of satisfaction—both physical and emotional—with their partners (Laumann et al., 1994).

Extramarital Sex

What about married people having sex outside of marriage? This practice, commonly called "adultery" (sociologists prefer the more neutral term *extramarital sex*), is widely condemned in the United States. Table 6–1 shows that more than 90 percent of U.S. adults consider a married person's having sex with someone other than the marital partner to be "always wrong" or "almost always wrong." The norm of sexual fidelity within marriage has been and remains a strong element of U.S. culture.

But actual behavior falls short of the cultural ideal. The Laumann study reports that about 25 percent of married men and 10 percent of married women have had at least one extramarital sexual experience. Stating this the other way around, it means that 75 percent of men and 90 percent of women have remained sexually faithful to their partners (Laumann et al., 1994:214; T. W. Smith, 2006; NORC, 2009:339). ● Go to **mysoclab.com**

Sex over the Life Course

Patterns of sexual activity change with age. In the United States, most young men become sexually active by the time they reach sixteen and women by the age of seventeen. By the time they reach their mid-twenties, about 90 percent of both women and men reported being sexually active with a partner at least once during the past year.

The picture begins to change by about age fifty, after which advancing age is linked to a decline in the share of people who are

Diversity Snapshot

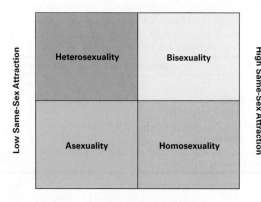

High Opposite-Sex Attraction

Heterosexuality	Bisexuality
Asexuality	Homosexuality

Low Same-Sex Attraction / High Same-Sex Attraction

Low Opposite-Sex Attraction

FIGURE 6–2   Four Sexual Orientations

A person's levels of same-sex attraction and opposite-sex attraction are two distinct dimensions that combine in various ways to produce four major sexual orientations.

Source: Adapted from Storms (1980).

sexually active. By age sixty, just 85 percent of men and 60 percent of women say they have been sexually active with a partner in the past year. By age seventy, only half of women claim to be sexually active; by age eighty, half of men say the same (Laumann et al., 1994, T.W. Smith, 2006). Sexual activity does decline with advancing age. Contrary to popular stereotypes, however, these data show that sexual activity is a normal part of life for most older adults.

Sexual Orientation

In recent decades, public opinion about sexual orientation has shown a remarkable change. **Sexual orientation** is *a person's romantic and emotional attraction to another person*. The norm in all human societies is **heterosexuality** (*hetero* is Greek for "the other of two"), meaning *sexual attraction to someone of the other sex*. Yet in every society, a certain share of people experience **homosexuality** (*homo* is Greek for "the same"), *sexual attraction to someone of the same sex*. Keep in mind that people do not necessarily fall into just one of these categories; they may have varying degrees of attraction to both sexes.

The idea that sexual orientation is often not clear-cut points to the existence of a third category: **bisexuality,** *sexual attraction to*

people of both sexes. Some bisexual people are attracted equally to males and females; many others are attracted more strongly to one sex than the other. Finally, **asexuality** is *a lack of sexual attraction to people of either sex.* Figure 6–2 places each of these sexual orientations in relation to the others.

It is important to remember that sexual *attraction* is not the same thing as sexual *behavior.* Many people have experienced some attraction to someone of the same sex, but far fewer ever actually engage in same-sex behavior. This is in large part because our culture discourages such actions.

In the United States and around the world, heterosexuality is the norm because, biologically speaking, heterosexual relations permit human reproduction. Even so, most societies tolerate homosexuality. Among the ancient Greeks, upper-class men considered homosexuality the highest form of relationship, partly because they looked down on women as intellectually inferior. As men saw it, heterosexuality was necessary only so they could have children, and "real" men preferred homosexual relations (Kluckhohn, 1948; Ford & Beach, 1951; Greenberg, 1988).

What Gives Us a Sexual Orientation?

The question of how people come to have a particular sexual orientation is strongly debated. The arguments cluster into two general positions: sexual orientation as a product of society and sexual orientation as a product of biology.

Sexual Orientation: A Product of Society

This approach argues that people in any society attach meanings to sexual activity, and these meanings differ from place to place and over time. As Michel Foucault (1990, orig. 1978) points out, for example, there was no distinct category of people called "homosexuals" until a century ago, when scientists and eventually the public as a whole began defining people that way. Throughout history, many people no doubt had what we would call "homosexual experiences." But neither they nor others saw in this behavior the basis for any special identity.

Anthropological studies show that patterns of homosexuality differ greatly from one society to another. In Siberia, for example, the Chukchee Eskimo perform a ritual during which one man dresses as a woman and does a woman's work. The Sambia, who dwell in the Eastern Highlands of New Guinea, have a ritual in which young boys perform oral sex on older men in the belief that eating semen will make them more masculine. In southeastern Mexico, a region in which religions recognize gods who are both female and male, the local culture defines people not only as female and male but also as *muxes* ("MOO-shayss"), a third sexual category. *Muxes* are men who dress and act as women, some only on ritual occasions, some all the

● Seeing Sociology
in Everyday Life

What evidence of transgender people do you see in the mass media?

○ Making the Grade

Sexual orientation results from both social and biological influences; evidence suggests that biology plays the more important part in this process.

THINKING ABOUT DIVERSITY: RACE, CLASS, & GENDER

A Third Gender: The *Muxes* of Mexico

Alejandro Taledo, sixteen years old, stands on a street corner in Juchitán, a small town in the state of Oaxaca, in southeastern Mexico. Called Alex by her friends, she has finished a day of selling flowers with her mother and now waits for a bus to ride home for dinner.

As you may know, Alejandro is commonly a boy's name. In fact, this young Mexican was born a boy. But several years ago, Alex decided that whatever her sex, she felt she was a girl, and she decided to live according to her own feelings.

In this community, she is not alone. Juchitán and the surrounding region is well known not only for beautiful black pottery and delicious food but also for the large number of gays, lesbians, and transgender people who live there. At first glance, this fact may surprise people who think of Mexico as a traditional country, especially when it comes to gender and sexuality. In Mexico, the stereotype goes, men control the lives of women, especially their sexuality. But like all stereotypes, this one misses some important facts. Nationally, Mexico has become more tolerant of diverse sexual expression. In 2009, Mexico City, the nation's capital, began recognizing same-sex marriages. And nowhere is tolerance for sexual orientation greater than it is in the region around Juchitán.

There, transgender people are called *muxes* (pronounced "MOO-shayss"), which is based on the Spanish word *mujer,* meaning "woman." *Muxes* are considered neither male nor female but of a third gender. Some *muxes* wear women's clothing and act almost entirely in a feminine way. Others adopt a feminine look and behavior only on special occasions. One of the most popular events is the region's grand celebration, which is held every November and is attended by more than 2,000 *muxes* and their families. A highlight of this event is a competition for the title of "transvestite of the year."

The acceptance of transgender people in central Mexico has its roots in the culture that existed before the Spanish arrived. At that time, anyone with ambiguous gender was viewed as especially wise and talented. The region's history includes accounts of Aztec priests and Mayan gods who cross-dressed or were considered to be both male and female. In the sixteenth century, the coming of the Spanish colonists and the influence of the Catholic church reduced much of this gender tolerance. But acceptance of mixed sexual identity continues today in this region, where many people hold so tightly to their traditions that they speak only their ancient Zapotec language rather than Spanish.

And so it is in Juchitán that *muxes* are respected, accepted, and even celebrated. *Muxes* are successful in business and take leadership roles in the church and in politics. Most important, they are commonly accepted by friends and family alike. Alejandro lives with her parents and five siblings and helps her mother both selling flowers on the streets and also at home. Her father, Victor Martinez Jimenez, is a local construction worker who speaks only Zapotec. He still refers to Alex as "him" but says "it was God who sent him, and why would I reject him? He helps his mother very much. Why would I get mad?" Alex's mother, Rosa Taledo Vicente, adds, "Every family considers it a blessing to have one gay son. While daughters marry and leave home, a *muxe* cares for his parents in their old age."

WHAT DO YOU THINK?

1. Do you think that U.S. society is tolerant of people wishing to combine masculine and feminine dress and behavior? Why or why not?

2. *Muxes* are people who were born biologically male. How do you think the local people in this story would feel about women who wanted to dress and act like men? Would you expect equal tolerance for such people? Why or why not?

3. How do you personally feel about the existence of a third category of sexual identity? Explain your views.

Sources: Gave (2005), Lacey (2008), and Rosenberg (2008).

time. The Thinking About Diversity box takes a closer look. Such diversity of sexual expression around the world shows that sexual expression is socially constructed (Blackwood & Wieringa, 1999; Gave, 2005; Lacey, 2008; Rosenberg, 2008).

Sexual Orientation: A Product of Biology

A growing body of research suggests that sexual orientation is innate, or rooted in human biology, in much the same way that people are born right-handed or left-handed. Arguing this position, Simon LeVay

homophobia discomfort over close personal interaction with people thought to be gay, lesbian, or bisexual

pornography (p. 156) sexually explicit material intended to cause sexual arousal.

prostitution (p. 157) the selling of sexual services

Seeing Sociology in Everyday Life

What changes in laws regarding gay marriage do you expect over the next ten years? Why?

(1993) links sexual orientation to the structure of a person's brain. LeVay studied the brains of both homosexual and heterosexual men and found a small but important difference in the size of the hypothalamus, a part of the brain that regulates hormones. Such an anatomical difference, he claims, plays a part in shaping sexual orientation.

Genetics may also influence sexual orientation. One study of forty-four pairs of brothers, all homosexual, found that thirty-three pairs had a distinctive genetic pattern involving the X chromosome. Moreover, the gay brothers had an unusually high number of gay male relatives—but only on their mother's side. Such evidence leads some researchers to think there may be a "gay gene" located on the X chromosome (Hamer & Copeland, 1994).

CRITICAL REVIEW Mounting evidence supports the conclusion that sexual orientation is rooted in biology, although the best guess at present is that both nature and nurture play a part. Remember that sexual orientation is not a matter of neat categories. Most people who think of themselves as homosexual have had one or more heterosexual experiences, just as many people who think of themselves as heterosexual have had one or more homosexual experiences. Explaining sexual orientation, then, is not easy.

There is also a political issue here with great importance for gay men and lesbians. To the extent that sexual orientation is based in biology, homosexuals have no more choice about their sexual orientation than they do about their skin color. If this is so, shouldn't gay men and lesbians expect the same legal protection from discrimination as African Americans?

CHECK YOUR LEARNING What evidence supports the position that sexual behavior is constructed by society? That sexual orientation is rooted in biology?

How Many Gay People Are There?

What share of our population is gay? This is a hard question to answer because, as noted earlier, sexual orientation is not a matter of neat categories. In addition, people are not always willing to discuss their sexuality with strangers or even family members. Alfred Kinsey estimated that about 4 percent of males and 2 percent of females have an exclusively same-sex orientation, although he pointed out that most people experience same-sex attraction at some point in their lives.

Some social scientists put the gay share of the population at 10 percent. But research surveys show that how homosexuality is defined makes a big difference in the results (Mosher, Chandra, & Jones, 2005). As Figure 6–3 shows, just 6 percent of men and 11 percent of women between the ages of fifteen and forty-four reported engaging in homosexual activity *at some time in their lives*. At the same time, just 2.3 percent of men and 1.3 percent of women defined themselves as "partly" or "entirely" homosexual.

In recent surveys, about 1.8 percent of men and 2.8 percent of women described themselves as bisexual. But bisexual experiences appear to be more common among younger people, especially while they live on college and university campuses (Laumann et al., 1994; Mosher, Chandra, & Jones, 2005). Many bisexuals do not think of themselves as either gay or straight, and their behavior reflects elements of both gay and straight living.

The Gay Rights Movement

The public's attitude toward homosexuality has been moving toward greater acceptance. Back in 1973, about three-fourths of U.S. adults claimed that homosexual relations were "always wrong" or "almost always wrong." Although that percentage changed little in the 1970s and 1980s, by 2008 it had dropped to 52 percent (NORC, 2009:340). Among college students, who are generally more tolerant of homosexual relationships than the population as a whole, we see a similar trend. In 1980, about half of college students supported laws prohibiting homosexual relationships; by 2008, as Figure 6–4 shows, roughly one-quarter felt the same way (Astin et al., 2002; Pryor et al., 2010).

One of the most difficult challenges for many gay and lesbian people is winning the acceptance and support of family members. In the popular television show *Grey's Anatomy*, Callie introduces her partner to a disapproving father. Would your parents respond in the same way? Would you?

Go to the Multimedia Library at mysoclab.com to view the ABC News *Nightline* video "One Town's Struggle with God, Gays, and Bigotry"

In large measure, this change was brought about by the gay rights movement, which arose in the middle of the twentieth century. Up to that time, most people in this country did not discuss homosexuality, and it was common for companies (including the federal government and the armed forces) to fire anyone who was accused of being gay. Mental health professionals also took a hard line, describing homosexuals as "sick" and sometimes placing them in mental hospitals, where it was hoped they might be "cured." It is no surprise that most lesbians and gay men remained "in the closet," closely guarding the secret of their sexual orientation. But the gay rights movement gained strength during the 1960s. One early milestone for the movement occurred in 1973 when the American Psychiatric Association declared that homosexuality was not an illness but simply "a form of sexual behavior."

The gay rights movement also began using the term **homophobia** to describe *discomfort over close personal interaction with people thought to be gay, lesbian, or bisexual* (Weinberg, 1973). The concept

Diversity Snapshot

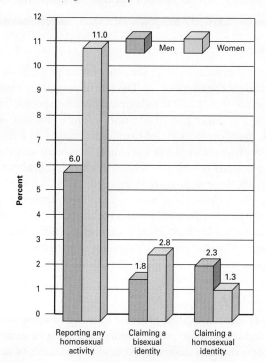

FIGURE 6–3 Share of the Population That Is Bisexual or Homosexual

Although more women than men report having had a homosexual experience, more men than women claim to have a homosexual identity.

Source: Adapted from Mosher, Chandra, & Jones (2005).

Student Snapshot

Since 1980, college students' opposition to homosexual relationships has declined sharply.

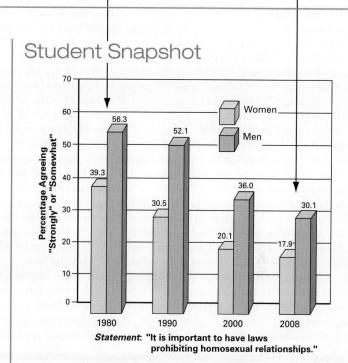

Statement: "It is important to have laws prohibiting homosexual relationships."

FIGURE 6–4 Opposition to Homosexual Relationships: Attitudes of First-Year College Students, 1980–2008

The historical trend among college students is toward greater tolerance of homosexual relationships, a view held by a large majority.

Sources: Astin et al. (2002) and Pryor et al. (2009).

of homophobia turns the tables on society: Instead of asking "What's wrong with gay people?" the question becomes "What's wrong with people who can't accept a different sexual orientation?"

In 2004, a number of cities and towns began to allow gay couples to marry, although these unions were later invalidated. But gay marriage is now legal in Massachusetts (2004), Connecticut (2008), Vermont (2009), Iowa (2009), New Hampshire (2009), and the District of Columbia (2010). A number of other states, including California (which briefly legalized gay marriage in 2008), Washington, and New Jersey, recognize either "domestic partnerships" or "civil unions" that provide most or all of the benefits of marriage. At the same time, a majority of the states have enacted laws that forbid gay marriage and prohibit recognizing such marriages performed elsewhere. ● Go to **mysoclab.com**

The law regulating marriage is not the only public issue involving same-sex relationships. In recent years, an increasing number of high schools have had requests from gay and lesbian students to bring a same-sex date to the senior prom. In many cases, this request sparks a controversy, as Seeing Sociology in the News on pages 156–57 explains.

The New York Times

Making a Prom Date Changes His Fate

BY MARK DAVIS
March 28, 2010

COCHRAN, Ga.—Derrick Martin had a question he couldn't answer, so he did what any eighteen-year-old would. Fingers tapping, he logged on to his computer last December and Googled the following words, which changed his life:

"I'm gay. Can I go to the prom?"

He can, and will. But those eight little words have done more than ensure the high school senior can take a same-sex date to Bleckley High School's prom next month.

Seeking that answer has thrust him to the forefront of a national discussion. It's touched off heated discussions in beauty salons and restaurants here and elsewhere, and made this small middle Georgia town a focal point in the debate over gay rights. Some applaud him for bravery. Others say his soul's in peril.

All he really wanted, he says, was a night to remember.

"I didn't anticipate this," Derrick said earlier this week, a few days after news got out that he would bring his boyfriend, a young man from Tift County, to his prom. "I thought this might run on the second page of the paper."

Instead, he's Derrick Martin, sudden celebrity. As he sat on a bench underneath a bare oak tree outside a Bleckley school building, a Ford pickup, kids hanging out of its cab, zipped by. Derrick! Derrick! young voices yelled. . . .

Derrick sighed. "If I could have just brought him without asking, I would have done that." ...

As he searched Web sites, Derrick came across the legal defense site for the national gay-rights organization Lambda. A representative of the group told him that if a school system didn't have rules forbidding same-sex dates, then Derrick likely could bring his boyfriend.

"They did warn me that the school system could cancel the prom," he said.

That wasn't just conjecture. School officials in Itawamba County, Mississippi, canceled a prom recently after eighteen-year-old Constance McMillen said she wanted to bring a girl to her school's April 2 dance. The American Civil Liberties Union, claiming the school board violated her right to free expression, has demanded that McMillen be allowed to attend.

Nothing like that occurred in January, when Derrick requested a meeting with Bleckley High Principal Michelle Masters. Because his date isn't a Bleckley student, school rules required Derrick to fill out a form identifying him. He decided to check with Masters first. . . .

Masters took the request to the Bleckley County Board of Education. . . . In early March, the board announced that Derrick could bring his boyfriend to the prom. . . .

Bleckley High School, home of the Royals, would hold its prom April 17, as originally planned. The junior class would plan it, as well as decorate the school gym. This is a BHS tradition.

But tradition, people soon learned, was about to get a test.

Cochran, about two hours south of Atlanta, is a confluence of U.S. and state roads that come together for a few blocks before fanning out again

Sexual Issues and Controversies

Sexuality lies at the heart of a number of controversies in the United States today. Here we take a look at four key issues: teen pregnancy, pornography, prostitution, and sexual violence.

Teen Pregnancy

Because of the risk of pregnancy, engaging in sexual activities—especially having intercourse—demands a high level of responsibility. Teenagers may be biologically mature enough to conceive, but many are not emotionally secure enough to appreciate the consequences of their actions. Surveys show that there are almost 750,000 teen pregnancies in the United States each year, most of them unplanned (Alan Guttmacher Institute, 2006; Ventura et al., 2009). This country's rate of births to teenage women is higher than that of all other high-income countries and is twice the rate in Canada (Darroch et al., 2001; Population Reference Bureau, 2010).

For young women of all racial and ethnic categories, weak families and low income sharply increase the likelihood of becoming sexually active and having an unplanned child. To make matters worse, having unplanned children raises the risk that young women (as well as young fathers-to-be) will not complete a high school education and will end up living in poverty (Alan Guttmacher Institute, 2002).

Did the sexual revolution raise the rate of teenage pregnancy? Perhaps surprisingly, the answer is no. The rate of pregnancy among teens in 1950 was higher than it is today, partly because people back then married at a younger age. In addition, because abortion was against the law, many pregnancies led to quick marriages. As a result, there were many pregnant teenagers, but almost 90 percent were married. Today, the number of pregnant teens has fallen, but in about 80 percent of all cases, these women are unmarried. In a slight majority (57 percent) of such cases, these women keep their babies; in the remainder, they have abortions (27 percent) or miscarriages (16 percent) (Alan Guttmacher Institute, 2006; Ventura et al., 2009). National Map 6–2 on page 158 shows pregnancy rates for women between the ages of fifteen and nineteen throughout the United States.

Pornography

Pornography is *sexually explicit material intended to cause sexual arousal.* But what is and is not pornographic has long been a matter of debate. Recognizing that different people view portrayals of sexuality differently, the U.S. Supreme Court gives local communities the power to decide for themselves what type of material violates "community standards" of decency and lacks "redeeming social value."

Definitions aside, pornography is very popular in the United States: X-rated videos, telephone "sex lines," sexually explicit movies and magazines, and thousands of Internet Web sites make up a thriving industry that takes in more than $10 billion each year, which is across rolling land that yields peanuts and cotton. A museum near the police department is dedicated to those agricultural staples.

About 5,200 people live here. Wednesdays at noon, much of downtown adheres to a practice that has just about gone the way of the mule. Stores close. People head to the municipal golf course, visit Macon to shop, or catch up on the latest events.

A lot of catching up these days focuses on Derrick's decision, and how it reflects change—not just in Cochran, either.

Barbara Anderson's shears snipped quickly, as if they were as indignant as she.

"I think they [the school board] ought to do like that other state and cancel the prom," said Anderson, who owns a styling salon here. "They won't allow us to have God in school, but they'll allow this?"

Across the street, waitress Victoria Cagle took a break after the lunch rush. She is a 2009 Bleckley grad who hopes to attend nearby Middle Georgia College and teach high school biology.

"I think what they [the board] did was the right thing," said Cagle, 19. "I think what he's doing is awesome."

Merchant Jason Ledbetter isn't so sure.

"It bothers me," said Ledbetter, 47, part-owner of a downtown music store. "By him doing that, it shows we accept it." ...

The boys may face a divine reckoning, said resident Faye Ortiz. "What they do is up to them," said Ortiz, 45. . . . "They've got to answer to God."

Opinions aside, Derrick's action has come at a cost. He's no longer living at home. Staying there, he said, became intolerable as news spread that he was taking his boyfriend to the prom. For now he's staying with a friend, the girl he escorted to last year's prom.

"She's my best friend," he said.

He also has friends who are gay, Derrick said. He expected some of them to stand with him when he took his request to school officials.

"I thought I would have had a little bit of backup," he said, disappointment creeping in his voice. "But it's just me."

His boyfriend, who's also eighteen and a school senior, has not made any public comments.

Derrick's parents are remaining silent, too. . . .

"I only wanted to be honest," [Derrick] said. Now, he feels an obligation. If he has to be the face of gay rights, OK.

A big lesson to learn from eight little words.

WHAT DO YOU THINK?

1. Has your high school ever experienced controversy about bringing same-sex dates to the prom or other events? Explain.

2. Do you think Derrick Martin wanted to become a symbol of gay rights or did he simply want to go to his school's prom? Explain.

3. What about you? Would you take a public stand in a case like this? Explain.

---

more than the revenues of ABC, CBS, and NBC combined. The vast majority of consumers of pornography are men.

Traditionally, people have criticized pornography on *moral* grounds. National surveys confirm the concern of 60 percent of U.S. adults that "sexual materials lead to a breakdown of morals" (NORC, 2009:341). Today, however, pornography is also seen as a *political* issue because most of it degrades women, portraying them as the sexual playthings of men.

Some critics also claim that pornography is a cause of violence against women. Although it is difficult to prove a scientific cause-and-effect relationship between what people view and how they act, the public shares a concern about pornography and violence, with almost half of adults holding the opinion that pornography encourages people to commit rape (NORC, 2009:341).

Although people everywhere object to sexual material they find offensive, many also value the principle of free speech and the protection of artistic expression. Nevertheless, pressure to restrict pornography is building from an unlikely coalition of conservatives, who oppose pornography on moral grounds, and liberals as well as feminists who condemn it for political reasons.

Prostitution

Prostitution is *the selling of sexual services.* Often called the "world's oldest profession," prostitution has existed throughout recorded history. In the United States today, about one in six adult men reports having paid for sex at some time (NORC, 2009). Because most people think that sex should be an expression of intimacy, they find the idea of sex for money disturbing. As a result, prostitution is against the law everywhere in the United States except for parts of rural Nevada.

Around the world, prostitution is greatest in poor countries where patriarchy is strong and traditional cultural norms limit women's ability to earn a living. Global Map 6–2 on page 159 shows where prostitution is most widespread.

Types of Prostitution

Most prostitutes (many prefer the morally neutral term "sex workers") are women, but they fall into different categories. *Call girls* are elite prostitutes, typically young, attractive, and well-educated women who arrange their own "dates" with clients by telephone. The classified pages of any large city newspaper contain numerous ads for "escort services," by which women and men offer both companionship and sex for a fee.

In the middle category are prostitutes who are employed in "massage parlors" or brothels under the control of managers. These sex workers typically have less choice about their clients, receive less money for their services, and get to keep no more than half of what they make.

At the bottom of the sex worker hierarchy are *streetwalkers,* women and men who "work the streets" of large cities. Some female

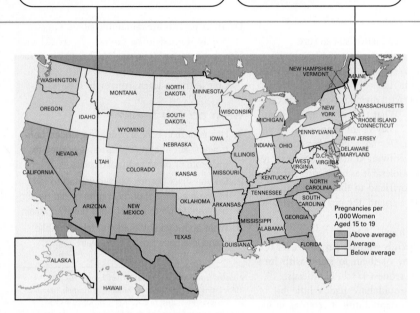

In Tucson, Arizona, 18-year-old Ramona Ramirez was just given a baby shower by her high school classmates, many of whom are already married and have children.

In Bangor, Maine, Sandy Johnson, also 18, reports that only "one or two" girls in her high school have become pregnant.

Explore the percentage of 15- to 17-year-olds who are married in your local community and in counties across the United States on **mysoclab.com**

Seeing Ourselves

NATIONAL MAP 6–2
Teenage Pregnancy Rates across the United States

The map shows pregnancy rates for women aged fifteen to nineteen. In what regions of the country are rates high? Where are they low? What explanation can you offer for these patterns?

Explore on **mysoclab.com**

Source: Alan Guttmacher Institute (2006).

Pregnancies per 1,000 Women Aged 15 to 19
- Above average
- Average
- Below average

streetwalkers are under the control of male pimps who take most of their earnings. Many others are addicted to drugs and sell sex to buy the drugs they need. Both types of people are at high risk of becoming the victims of violence (Davidson, 1998; Estes, 2001).

Most prostitutes offer heterosexual services. However, gay prostitutes also trade sex for money. Researchers report that many gay prostitutes end up selling sex after having suffered rejection by family and friends because of their sexual orientation (Weisberg, 1985; Boyer, 1989; Kruks, 1991).

A Victimless Crime?

Prostitution is against the law almost everywhere in the United States, but many people consider it a victimless crime (defined in Chapter 7, "Deviance," as a crime in which there is no obvious victim). Consequently, instead of enforcing prostitution laws consistently, police stage only occasional crackdowns. This policy reflects a desire to control prostitution while recognizing that it is impossible to eliminate it entirely.

Many people take a "live and let live" attitude about prostitution and say that adults ought to be free to do as they please as long as no one is forced to do anything. But is prostitution really victimless? The sex trade subjects many women to abuse and outright violence and also plays a part in spreading sexually transmitted diseases, including AIDS. In addition, many poor women, especially in low-income nations, become trapped in a life of selling sex. Thailand, in Southeast Asia, has 2 million prostitutes, representing about 10 percent of all women in the labor force. Many of these women begin working before they are teenagers, are often subjected to physical abuse, and run a high risk of contracting HIV (Wonders & Michalowski, 2001).

In the past, the focus of law enforcement has been on the women who earn money as sex workers. But prostitution would not exist without demand on the part of men. For this reason, police officers are now more likely to target "Johns" when they attempt to buy sex.

Sexual Violence: Rape and Date Rape

Ideally, sexual activity occurs within a loving relationship between consenting adults. In reality, however, sex can sometimes be twisted by hatred and violence. Here we consider two types of sexual violence: rape and date rape.

Rape

Although some people think rape is motivated only by a desire for sex, it is actually an expression of power, a violent act that uses sex to hurt, humiliate, or control another person. According to the Federal Bureau of Investigation (2009), almost 90,000 women each year report to the police that they have been raped. The actual number of rapes is likely several times higher.

The official government definition of rape is "the carnal knowledge of a female forcibly and against her will." Thus official rape statistics include only victims who are women. But men, too, are raped—in perhaps 10 percent of all cases. Most men who rape men are not homosexual; they are heterosexuals who are motivated by a desire not for sex but to dominate another person.

Date Rape

A common myth is that rape involves strangers. In reality, however, only about one-third of all rapes fit this pattern. Two of every three rapes involve people who know each other—more often than not, pretty well—and these crimes usually take place in familiar surroundings, such

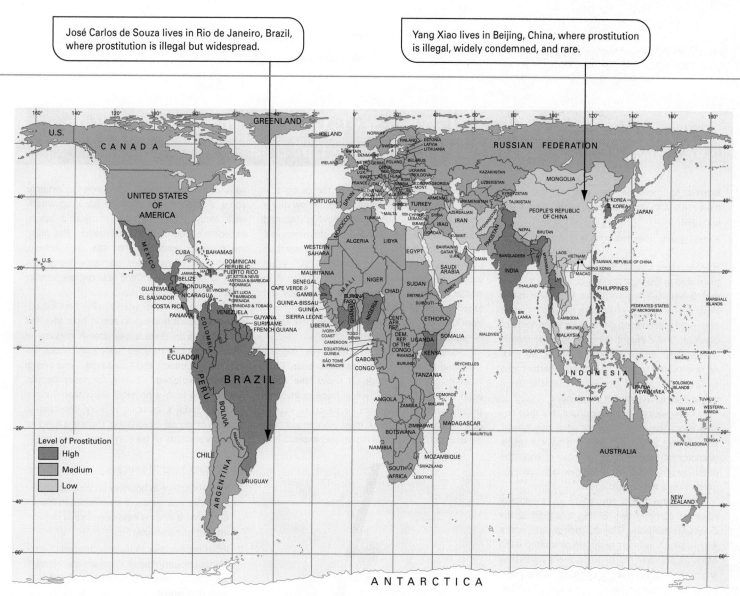

José Carlos de Souza lives in Rio de Janeiro, Brazil, where prostitution is illegal but widespread.

Yang Xiao lives in Beijing, China, where prostitution is illegal, widely condemned, and rare.

Level of Prostitution
- High
- Medium
- Low

Window on the World

GLOBAL MAP 6–2 Prostitution in Global Perspective

Generally speaking, prostitution is widespread in societies where women have low standing. Officially, at least, the People's Republic of China boasts of gender equality, including the elimination of "vice" such as prostitution, which oppresses women. By contrast, in much of Latin America, where patriarchy is strong, prostitution is common. In many Islamic societies, patriarchy is also strong, but religion is a counterbalance, so prostitution is limited. Western, high-income nations have a moderate amount of prostitution.

Sources: *Peters Atlas of the World* (1990) and Mackay (2000).

as the home or a college campus. The term "date rape" or "acquaintance rape" refers to forcible sexual violence against women by men they know (Laumann et al., 1994; U.S. Bureau of Justice Statistics, 2009).

A second myth, often linked specifically to date rape, is the idea that a woman who has been raped must have done something to encourage the man and make him think she wanted to have sex. Perhaps the victim agreed to go out with the offender. Maybe she even

invited him to her room. But of course, such actions no more justify rape than they would any other kind of physical assault.

Although rape is a physical attack, it also leaves emotional and psychological scars. Beyond the brutality of being physically violated, rape by an acquaintance also affects a victim's ability to trust others. Psychological scars are especially serious among the two-thirds of sexual assault victims who are under eighteen and even

● Seeing Sociology
in Everyday Life

Is there much discussion of "hooking up" on your campus? Why or why not?

📖● Read "Human Rights, Sex Trafficking, and Prostitution" by
Alice Leuchtag on **mysoclab.com**

**SEEING SOCIOLOGY
IN EVERYDAY LIFE**

When Sex Is Only Sex: The Campus Culture of "Hooking Up"

BRYNNE: My mom told me once that she didn't have sex with my dad until after they were engaged.

KATY: I guess times really have changed!

Have you ever been in a sexual situation and not been sure of the right thing to do? Most colleges and universities highlight two important rules. First, sexual activity must take place only when both participants have given clear statements of consent. The consent principle is what makes "having sex" different from date rape. Second, no one should knowingly expose a partner to a sexually transmitted disease, especially when the partner is unaware of the danger.

These rules are very important, but they say little about the larger issue of what sex *means*. For example, when is it "right" to have a sexual relationship? How well do you have to know the other person? If you do have sex, are you obligated to see the person again?

Two generations ago, there were informal rules for campus sex. Dating was part of the courtship process. That is, "going out" was a way in which women and men evaluated each other as possible marriage partners while they sharpened their own sense of what they wanted in a mate. Because, on average, marriage took place when people were in their early twenties, many college students became engaged and married while they were still in school. In this cultural climate, sex became part of a relationship along with commitment— a serious interest in the other person as a possible marriage partner.

Today, the sexual culture of the campus is very different. Partly because people now marry much later, the culture of courtship has declined dramatically. About three-fourths of women in a recent national survey point to a new campus pattern, the culture of "hooking up." What exactly is "hooking up"? Most describe it in words like these: "When a girl and a guy get together for a physical encounter—anything from kissing to having sex—and don't necessarily expect anything further."

Student responses to the survey suggest that "hookups" have three characteristics. First, most couples who hook up know little about each other. Second, a typical hookup involves people who have been drinking alcohol, usually at a campus party. Third, most women are critical of the culture of hooking up and express little

satisfaction with these encounters. Certainly, some women (and men) who hook up simply walk away, happy to have enjoyed a sexual experience free of further obligation. But given the powerful emotions that sex can unleash, hooking up often leaves someone wondering what to expect next. "Will you call me tomorrow?" "Will I see you again?"

The survey asked women who had experienced a recent hookup to report how they felt about the experience a day later. A majority of respondents said they felt "awkward," about half felt "disappointed" and "confused," and one in four felt "exploited." Clearly, for many people, sex is more than a physical encounter. Further, because today's campus is very sensitive to charges of sexual exploitation, there is a need for clearer standards of fair play.

WHAT DO YOU THINK?

1. How extensive is hooking up on your campus? Are you aware of differences in these encounters among heterosexuals and among homosexuals?

2. What do you see as the advantages of sex without commitment? What are the disadvantages of this kind of relationship? Are men and women likely to answer these questions differently? Explain.

3. Do you think college students need more guidance about sexual issues? If so, who should provide this guidance?

Source: Based in part on Marquardt & Glenn (2001).

more so among the one-third who are under the age of twelve. The home is no refuge from rape: One-third of all victims under the age of eighteen are attacked by their own fathers or stepfathers (Snyder, 2000).

How common is date rape? Recent surveys have found that about 10 percent of all teens and 20 percent of high school girls in the United States reported having been victims of sexual or

physical violence inflicted by the boys they were dating (Centers for Disease Control and Prevention, 2008; Teenage Research Unlimited, 2008).

Nowhere has the issue of date rape been more widely discussed than on college campuses, where the danger of date rape is high. The collegiate environment promotes easy friendships and encourages trust. At the same time, many young students have much to learn

○ Making the Grade

Use the Applying Theory table below to review the theoretical approaches to sexuality.

● Seeing Sociology
in Everyday Life

How free do you think you are (or were) in choosing a life partner?
In what ways does society guide this selection process?

● APPLYING THEORY ●

Sexuality

	Structural-Functional Approach	Symbolic-Interaction Approach	Social-Conflict/Feminist Approach
What is the level of analysis?	Macro-level	Micro-level	Macro-level
What is the importance of sexuality for society?	Society depends on sexuality for reproduction. Society uses the incest taboo and other norms to control sexuality in order to maintain social order.	Sexual practices vary among the many cultures of the world. Some societies allow individuals more freedom than others in matters of sexual behavior.	Sexuality is linked to social inequality. U.S. society regulates women's sexuality more than men's, which is part of the larger pattern of men dominating women.
Has sexuality changed over time? How?	Yes. As advances in birth control technology separate sex from reproduction, societies relax some controls on sexuality.	Yes. The meanings people attach to virginity and other sexual matters are all socially constructed and subject to change.	Yes and no. Some sexual standards have relaxed over time, but society still defines women in sexual terms, just as homosexual people are harmed by society's heterosexual bias.

about relationships and about themselves. As the Seeing Sociology in Everyday Life box explains, although college life encourages communication, it provides few social norms to help guide young people's sexual experiences. To counter the problem, many schools now actively address myths about rape. In addition, greater attention is now focused on the use of alcohol, which increases the likelihood of sexual violence. 📖●⌐Read on mysoclab.com

Theoretical Analysis of Sexuality

Applying sociology's various theoretical approaches gives us a better understanding of human sexuality. The following sections discuss the three major approaches. The Applying Theory table highlights the key insights of each approach.

Structural-Functional Analysis

The structural-functional approach explains the contribution of any social pattern to the overall operation of society. Because sexuality

can have such important consequences, society regulates this type of behavior.

The Need to Regulate Sexuality

From a biological point of view, sex allows our species to reproduce. But culture and social institutions regulate *with whom* and *when* people reproduce. For example, most societies condemn married people who have sex with someone other than a spouse. To allow the forces of sexual passion to go unchecked would threaten family life, especially the raising of children.

The fact that the incest taboo exists everywhere shows clearly that no society permits a completely free choice of sexual partners. Reproduction by family members other than married partners would break down the kinship system and hopelessly confuse human relationships.

Historically, the social control of sexuality was strong, mostly because sex often led to childbirth. We see these controls at work in the old-fashioned distinction between "legitimate" reproduction (within marriage) and "illegitimate" reproduction (outside marriage). But once a society develops the technology to control births, its sexual norms become more permissive. This occurred in the

● Seeing Sociology
in Everyday Life

Chastity belts may not be used today, but can you point to other
ways in which society controls women's sexuality?

● Seeing Sociology
in Everyday Life

Do you and your parents differ in your understanding of the
importance of virginity at first marriage or other issues involving
sexuality? Explain.

The control of women's sexuality is a common theme throughout human history. During the Middle Ages, Europeans devised the "chastity belt"—a metal device locked about a woman's groin that prevented sexual intercourse (and probably interfered with other bodily functions as well). While such devices are all but unknown today, the social control of sexuality continues. Can you point to examples?

United States, where over the course of the twentieth century, sex moved beyond its basic reproductive function and became mainly a form of intimacy and even recreation (Giddens, 1992).

Latent Functions: The Case of Prostitution

It is easy to see that prostitution is harmful because it spreads disease and exploits women. But does it have latent functions that help explain why prostitution is so widespread? According to Kingsley Davis (1971), prostitution is one way to meet the sexual needs of a large number of people who do not have ready access to sex, including soldiers, travelers, and people who are not physically attractive enough or are too poor to attract a marriage partner. Some people favor prostitution because they want sex without the "trouble" of a relationship. As one team of analysts put it, "Men don't pay for sex; they pay so they can leave" (Miracle, Miracle, & Baumeister, 2003:421).

○ **CRITICAL REVIEW**   The structural-functional approach helps us appreciate the important role sexuality plays in the organization of society. The incest taboo and other cultural norms suggest that society has always paid attention to who has sex with whom and, especially, who reproduces with whom.

Functional analysis sometimes ignores gender; when Kingsley Davis wrote of the benefits of prostitution for society, he was really talking about the benefits to *men.* In addition, the fact that sexual patterns change over time, just as they differ around the world, is ignored by this perspective. To appreciate the varied and changeable nature of sexuality, we now turn to the symbolic-interaction approach.

○ **CHECK YOUR LEARNING**   Compared to traditional societies, why do modern societies give people more choice about matters involving sexuality?

Symbolic-Interaction Analysis

The symbolic-interaction approach highlights how as people interact, they construct everyday reality. As explained in Chapter 4 ("Social Interaction in Everyday Life"), different people construct different realities, so the views of one group or society may well differ from those of another. In the same way, our understanding of sexuality can and does change over time, just as it differs from one society to another.

The Social Construction of Sexuality

Almost all social patterns involving sexuality saw a lot of change over the course of the past century. One good illustration is the changing importance of virginity. A century ago, our society's norm—for women, at least—was virginity before marriage. This norm was strong because there was no effective means of birth control available, and virginity was the only assurance a man had that his bride-to-be was not carrying another man's child.

Today, because we have gone a long way toward separating sex from reproduction, the virginity norm has weakened considerably. In the United States, among people born between 1963 and 1974, just 16.3 percent of men and 20.1 percent of women report being virgins at first marriage (Laumann et al., 1994:503).

Another example of our society's construction of sexuality involves young people. A century ago, childhood was a time of innocence in sexual matters. In recent decades, however, thinking has changed. Although few people encourage sexual activity between children, most people believe that children should be educated about sex so that they can make intelligent choices about their behavior as they grow older.

Global Comparisons

Around the world, different societies attach different meanings to sexuality. For example, Ruth Benedict (1938), an anthropologist who spent years learning the ways of life of the Melanesian people of southeastern New Guinea, reported that adults paid little attention when young children engaged in sexual experimentation with one another. Parents in Melanesia shrugged off such activity because before puberty, sex cannot lead to reproduction. Is it likely that most parents in the United States would respond the same way?

Sexual practices also vary from culture to culture. Circumcision of infant boys (the practice of removing all or part of the foreskin

● Seeing Sociology
in Everyday Life

Can you point to other sexual patterns that vary around the world?
Explain.

┌─● Making the Grade

Social-conflict analysis suggests that, by defining people in
tems of their sexuality, we ignore their full range of talents and
abilities, thus diminishing them.

of the penis) is common in the United States but rare in most other parts of the world. A practice sometimes referred to as female circumcision (removal of the clitoris) is rare in the United States but common in parts of Africa and the Middle East (Crosette, 1995; Huffman, 2000). (For more about this practice, more accurately called "female genital mutilation," see the Thinking About Diversity box on page 286).

● **CRITICAL REVIEW** The strength of the symbolic-interaction approach lies in revealing the socially constructed character of familiar social patterns. Understanding that people "construct" sexuality, we can better appreciate the variety of sexual attitudes and practices found over the course of history and around the world.

One limitation of this approach is that not all sexual practices are so variable. Men everywhere have always been more likely to see women in sexual terms than the other way around. Some broader social structure must be at work in a pattern that is this widespread, as we shall see in the following section on the social-conflict approach.

● **CHECK YOUR LEARNING** What evidence can you provide showing that human sexuality is socially constructed?

Social-Conflict and Feminist Analysis

As you have seen in earlier chapters, the social-conflict approach highlights dimensions of inequality. This approach reveals how sexuality both reflects patterns of social inequality and helps perpetuate them. Feminism, a social-conflict approach focusing on gender inequality, links sexuality to the domination of women by men.

Sexuality: Reflecting Social Inequality

Recall our discussion of prostitution, a practice outlawed almost everywhere

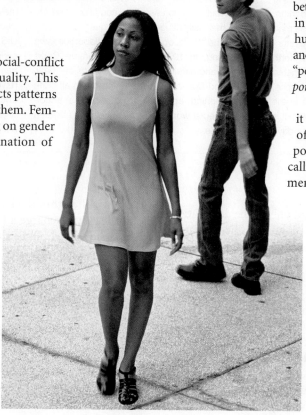

From a social-conflict point of view, sexuality is not so much a "natural" part of our humanity as it is a socially constructed pattern of behavior. Sexuality plays an important part in social inequality: By defining women in sexual terms, men devalue them as objects. Would you consider the behavior shown here to be "natural" or socially directed? Why?

in our society. Enforcement of prostitution laws is uneven at best, especially when it comes to who is and is not likely to be arrested. Gender bias is evident here: Although two people are involved, the record shows that police are far more likely to arrest (less powerful) female prostitutes than (more powerful) male clients. Class inequality, too, is involved: It is streetwalkers—women with the least income and most likely to be minorities—who face the highest risk of arrest (Saint James & Alexander, 2004). A feminist approach also leads us to ask whether so many women would be involved in prostitution in the first place if they had economic opportunities equal to those of men.

More generally, which categories of people in U.S. society are most likely to be defined in terms of their sexuality? The answer, once again, is those with less power: women compared to men, people of color compared to whites, and gays and lesbians compared to heterosexuals. In this way, sexuality, a natural part of human life, is used by society to define some people as less worthy.

Sexuality: Creating Social Inequality

Social-conflict theorists, especially feminists, point to sexuality as the root of inequality between women and men. Defining women in sexual terms devalues them from full human beings to objects of men's interest and attention. Is it any wonder that the word "pornography" comes from the Greek word *porne*, meaning "harlot" or "prostitute"?

If men define women in sexual terms, it is easy to see pornography—almost all of which is consumed by males—as a power issue. Because pornography typically shows women focused on pleasing men, it supports the idea that men have power over women.

Some radical critics doubt that this element of power can ever be removed from heterosexual relations (A. Dworkin, 1987). Most social-conflict theorists do not reject heterosexuality, but they do agree that sexuality can and does degrade women. Our culture often describes sexuality in terms of sport (men "scoring" with women) and violence ("slamming," "banging," and "hitting on," for example, are verbs used for both fighting and sex).

queer theory a body of research findings that challenges the heterosexual bias in U.S. society

heterosexism a view that labels anyone who is not heterosexual as "queer"

● Seeing Sociology
in Everyday Life

Can you think of three social patterns that are examples of heterosexism?

CONTROVERSY & DEBATE

The Abortion Controversy

FRANK: The abortion people are marching again across campus.

MARVIN: For or against?

FRANK: Both. I'm not sure which came first, but somebody said there have already been some fights. . . .

A black van pulls up in front of the storefront in a busy section of the city. Two women get out of the front seat and cautiously look up and down the street. After a moment, one nods to the other, and they open the rear door to let a third woman out of the van. Standing to the right and left of the woman, the two quickly escort her inside the building.

This scene might describe two federal marshals taking a convict to a police station, but it is actually an account of two clinic workers helping a woman who has decided to have an abortion. Why are they so cautious? Anyone who has read the papers in recent years knows about the angry confrontations at abortion clinics across North America. Some opponents have even targeted and killed doctors who carried out abortions, some 1.2 million of which are performed in the United States each year (Ventura et al., 2009). It is one of the most hotly debated issues of our day.

Abortion has not always been so controversial. In colonial times, midwives and other healers performed abortions with little community opposition and with full approval of the law. But controversy arose about 1850, when early medical doctors wanted to eliminate the competition they faced from midwives and other traditional health providers, whose income came largely from ending pregnancies. By 1900, medical doctors had succeeded in getting every state to pass a law banning abortion.

Such laws greatly reduced the number of abortions. Those that did occur were performed "underground," as secretly as possible. Many women who wanted abortions—especially those who were poor—had little choice but to seek help from unlicensed "back alley" abortionists, sometimes with tragic results due to unsanitary conditions and the use of medically dangerous techniques.

By the 1960s, opposition to antiabortion laws was rising. In 1973, the U.S. Supreme Court made a landmark decision (in the cases of *Roe* v. *Wade* and *Doe* v. *Bolton*), striking down all state laws banning abortion. In effect, this action established a woman's legal access to abortion nationwide.

Even so, the abortion controversy continues. On one side of the issue are people who describe themselves as "pro-choice," supporting a woman's right to choose abortion. On the other side are those who call themselves "pro-life," opposing abortion as morally wrong; these people would like to see the Supreme Court reverse its 1973 decision.

How strong is the support for each side of the abortion controversy? A recent national survey asked a sample of adults the question "Should it be possible for a pregnant woman to obtain a legal abortion if the woman wants it for any reason?" In response, 41 percent said yes (placing them in the pro-choice camp) and 55 percent said no (expressing the pro-life position); the remaining 4 percent offered no opinion (NORC, 2009:331).

A closer look shows that circumstances make a big difference in how people see this issue. The figure shows that large majorities of U.S. adults favor legal abortion if a pregnancy seriously threatens a woman's health, if the pregnancy is a result of rape, or if a fetus is likely to have a serious defect. The bottom line is that about 41 percent support access to abortion under *any* circumstances, but 85 percent support access to abortion under *some* circumstances.

Queer Theory

Social-conflict theory has taken aim not only at the domination of women by men but also at heterosexuals dominating homosexuals. In recent years, as many lesbians and gay men have sought public acceptance, a gay voice has risen in sociology. The term **queer theory** refers to *a body of research findings that challenges the heterosexual bias in U.S. society.*

Queer theory begins with the claim that our society is characterized by **heterosexism,** *a view that labels anyone who is not heterosexual as "queer."* Our heterosexual culture victimizes a wide range of people, including gay men, lesbians, bisexuals, transsexuals, and even asexual people. Furthermore, although most people agree that bias against women (sexism) and people of color (racism) is wrong, heterosexism is widely tolerated and some-

times well within the law. For example, U.S. military forces cannot legally discharge a female soldier for "acting like a woman" because that would be a clear case of gender discrimination. But, as long as its "Don't ask, don't tell" policy remains in effect, the military forces can discharge her for homosexuality if she is a sexually active lesbian.

Heterosexism is also part of everyday culture (Kitzinger, 2005). When we describe something as "sexy," for example, don't we really mean attractive to *heterosexuals*?

○ **CRITICAL REVIEW** The social-conflict approach shows how sexuality is both a cause and an effect of inequality. In particular, it helps us understand men's power over

abortion the deliberate termination of a pregnancy

Many of those who take the pro-life position feel strongly that abortion amounts to killing unborn children—more than 45 million since *Roe* v. *Wade* was passed. To them, people never have the right to end innocent life in this way. But pro-choice advocates are no less committed to the position that women must have control over their own bodies. If pregnancy decides the course of women's lives, women will never be able to compete with men on equal terms, whether it is on campus or in the workplace. Therefore, access to legal, safe abortion is a necessary condition to women's full participation in society.

Survey Question: "It should be possible for a pregnant woman to obtain a *legal abortion* . . ."

Percentage Answering Yes						
84.8	72.6	70.4	42.8	41.1	40.7	39.6
"... if the woman's own health is seriously endangered by the pregnancy."	"... if she became pregnant as a result of rape."	"... if there is a strong chance of serious defect in the baby."	"... if she is married and does not want any more children."	"... if the family has a very low income and cannot afford any more children."	"... if the woman wants it for any reason."	"... if she is not married and does not want to marry the man."

When Should the Law Allow a Woman to Choose Abortion?
The extent of public support for legal abortion depends on how the issue is presented.
Source: NORC (2009:229–31).

WHAT DO YOU THINK?

1. The more conservative, pro-life position sees abortion as a moral issue, and the more liberal, pro-choice position views abortion as a power issue. Compare these positions to how conservatives and liberals view the issue of pornography.

2. Surveys show that men and women have almost the same opinions on the subject of abortion. Does this surprise you? Why or why not?

3. Why do you think the abortion controversy is often so bitter? Do you think it is possible for our nation to find a middle ground on this issue?

women and heterosexual people's domination of homosexual people.

At the same time, this approach overlooks the fact that many people do not see sexuality as a power issue. On the contrary, many couples enjoy a vital sexual relationship that deepens their commitment to one another. In addition, the social-conflict approach pays little attention to steps our society has made toward reducing inequality. Today's men are less likely to describe women as sex objects than they were a few decades ago. One of the most important issues in the workplace today is ensuring that all employees remain free from sexual harassment. Rising public concern (see Chapter 10, "Gender Stratification") has reduced sex abuse in the work-

place. There is also ample evidence that the gay rights movement has won greater opportunities and social acceptance for gay people.

CHECK YOUR LEARNING How does sexuality play a part in creating social inequality?

This chapter closes with a look at what is perhaps the most divisive sexuality-related issue of all: **abortion,** *the deliberate termination of a pregnancy*. There seems to be no middle ground in the debate over this controversial issue. The Controversy & Debate box helps explain why.

How do the mass media play into our society's views of human sexuality?

Far from it being a "natural" or simply "biological" concept, cultures around the world attach all sorts of meanings to human sexuality. The photos below show how the mass media—in this case, popular magazines—reflect our own culture's ideas about sexuality. In each case, can you "decode" the magazine cover and explain its messages? To what extent do you think the messages are true?

Magazines like this one are found at the checkout lines of just about every supermarket and discount store in the United States. Looking just at the cover, what can you conclude about women's sexuality in our society?

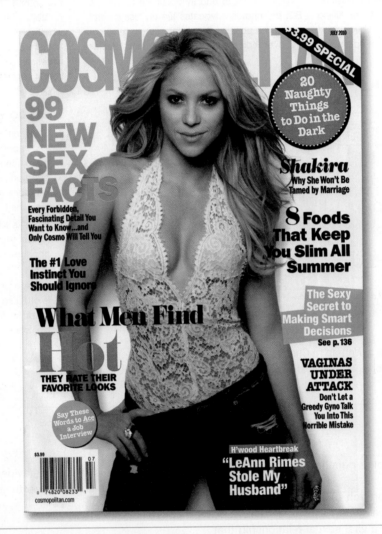

HINT The messages we get from mass media sources like these not only tell us about sexuality but also tell us what sort of people we ought to be. There is a lot of importance attached to sexuality for women, placing pressure on women to look good to men and to define life success in terms of attracting men with their sexuality. Similarly, being masculine means being successful, sophisticated, in charge, and, of course, able to attract desirable women. When the mass media endorse sexuality, it is almost always according to the norm of heterosexuality.

Messages about sexuality are directed to men as well as to women. Here is a recent issue of *GQ*. What messages about masculinity can you find? Do you see any evidence of heterosexual bias?

Applying SOCIOLOGY in Everyday Life

1. Looking at the *Cosmopolitan* cover, what evidence of heterosexual bias do you see? Explain.
2. Contact your school's student services office, and ask for information about the extent of sexual violence on your campus. Do people typically report such crimes? What policies and procedures does your school have to respond to sexual violence?
3. Use the campus library and Internet sources to learn more about the experiences of women and men involved in prostitution. As you learn more, decide whether you think prostitution should be considered a "victimless crime."

Making the Grade

CHAPTER 6 Sexuality and Society

👁 Watch on mysoclab.com

What Is Sexuality?

SEX is biological, referring to bodily differences between females and males.

p. 145

GENDER is cultural, referring to behavior, power, and privileges a society attaches to being female or male.

p. 146

---

sex (p. 145) the biological distinction between females and males

primary sex characteristics (p. 146) the genitals, organs used for reproduction

secondary sex characteristics (p. 146) bodily development, apart from the genitals, that distinguishes biologically mature females and males

intersexual people (p. 146) people whose bodies (including genitals) have both female and male characteristics

transsexuals (p. 146) people who feel they are one sex even though biologically they are the other

incest taboo (p. 147) a norm forbidding sexual relations or marriage between certain relatives

---

Sexuality is a **BIOLOGICAL ISSUE**.

- Sex is determined at conception as a male sperm joins a female ovum.
- Males and females have different genitals (*primary sex characteristics*) and bodily development (secondary sex characteristics).
- *Intersexual people* (*hermaphrodites*) have some combination of male and female genitalia.
- *Transsexual people* feel they are one sex although biologically they are the other.

pp. 145–46

Sexuality is a **CULTURAL ISSUE**.

- For humans, sex is a matter of cultural meaning and personal choice rather than biological programming.
- Sexual practices vary considerably from one society to another (examples include kissing, ideas about modesty, and standards of beauty).
- The *incest taboo* exists in all societies because regulating sexuality, especially reproduction, is a necessary element of social organization. Specific taboos vary from one society to another.

pp. 146–48

✓ Sexuality is a theme found throughout most areas of social life in the United States (pp. 144–45).

Sexual Attitudes in the United States

The **SEXUAL REVOLUTION**, which peaked in the 1960s and 1970s, drew sexuality out into the open. Baby boomers were the first generation to grow up with the idea that sex was a normal part of social life.

pp. 148–49

The **SEXUAL COUNTERREVOLUTION**, which was evident by 1980, aimed criticism at "permissiveness" and urged a return to more traditional "family values."

pp. 149–50

Beginning with the work of Alfred Kinsey, researchers have studied sexual behavior in the United States and reached many interesting conclusions:

- Premarital sexual intercourse became more common during the twentieth century.
- More than half of young men and two-thirds of young women have intercourse by their senior year in high school.
- Among all U.S. adults, sexual activity varies: One-third report having sex with a partner a few times a year or not at all; another one-third have sex once to several times a month; the remaining one-third have sex two or more times a week.
- Extramarital sex is widely condemned, and just 25 percent of married men and 10 percent of married women report being sexually unfaithful to their spouses at some time.

pp. 150–52

Sexual Orientation

SEXUAL ORIENTATION is a person's romantic or emotional attraction to another person. Four sexual orientations are
- heterosexuality
- homosexuality
- bisexuality
- asexuality

p. 152

- About 6% of adult men and 11% of adult women report engaging in some homosexual activity; 2.3% of men and 1.3% of women consider themselves homosexual
- About 1.8% of men and 2.8% of women claim a bisexual identity.

p. 154

Most research supports the claim that sexual orientation is rooted in biology in much the same way as being right-handed or left-handed.

p. 153

Sexual orientation is not a matter of neat categories because many people who think of themselves as heterosexual have homosexual experiences; the reverse is also true.

p. 154

The gay rights movement helped change public attitudes toward greater acceptance of homosexuality. Still, 52 percent of U.S. adults say homosexuality is wrong.

pp. 154–55

sexual orientation (p. 152) a person's romantic and emotional attraction to another person

heterosexuality (p. 152) sexual attraction to someone of the other sex

homosexuality (p. 152) sexual attraction to someone of the same sex

bisexuality (p. 152) sexual attraction to people of both sexes

asexuality (p. 152) a lack of sexual attraction to people of either sex

homophobia (p. 155) discomfort over close personal interaction with people thought to be gay, lesbian, or bisexual

Sexual Issues and Controversies

TEEN PREGNANCY About 750,000 U.S. teenagers become pregnant each year. The rate of teenage pregnancy has dropped since 1950, when many teens married and had children. Today, most pregnant teens are not married and are at high risk of dropping out of school and being poor.

p. 156

⊕ Explore on mysoclab.com

PROSTITUTION The selling of sexual services is illegal almost everywhere in the United States. Many people view prostitution as a victimless crime, but it victimizes women and spreads sexually transmitted diseases.

pp. 157–58

📖 Read on mysoclab.com

PORNOGRAPHY The law allows local communities to set standards of decency. Conservatives condemn pornography on moral grounds; liberals view pornography as a power issue, condemning it as demeaning to women.

pp. 156–57

SEXUAL VIOLENCE Some 90,000 rapes are reported each year in the United States, but the actual number is probably several times higher. Rapes are violent crimes in which victims and offenders typically know one another.

pp. 158–61

pornography (p. 156) sexually explicit material intended to cause sexual arousal

prostitution (p. 157 the selling of sexual services

ABORTION Laws banned abortion in all states by 1900. Opposition to these laws rose during the 1960s, and in 1973, the U.S. Supreme Court declared these laws unconstitutional. Today, some 1.2 million abortions are performed each year. People who describe themselves as "pro-choice" support a woman's right to choose abortion; people who call themselves "pro-life" oppose abortion on moral grounds.

pp. 164–65

Theoretical Analysis of Sexuality

The **STRUCTURAL-FUNCTIONAL APPROACH** highlights society's need to regulate sexual activity and especially reproduction. One universal norm is the incest taboo, which keeps family relations clear.

pp. 161–62

The **SYMBOLIC-INTERACTION APPROACH** emphasizes the various meanings people attach to sexuality. The social construction of sexuality can be seen in sexual differences between societies and in changing sexual patterns over time.

pp. 162–63

The **SOCIAL-CONFLICT/FEMINIST APPROACH** links sexuality to social inequality. *Feminist theory* claims that men dominate women by devaluing them to the level of sexual objects. *Queer theory* claims our society has a heterosexual bias, defining anything different as "queer."

pp. 163–65

queer theory (p. 164 a body of research findings that challenges the heterosexual bias in U.S. society

heterosexism (p. 164) a view that labels anyone who is not heterosexual as "queer"

abortion (p. 165) the deliberate termination of a pregnancy

7 Deviance

- Why does every society have deviance?

- How does *who* and *what* are defined as deviant reflect social inequality?

- What effect has punishment had in reducing crime in the United States?

● **Watch** the *Core Concepts in Sociology* video "Infidelity" on **mysoclab.com**

Chapter Overview

This chapter investigates how society encourages both conformity and deviance, and it also provides an introduction to crime and the criminal justice system.

"I was like the guy lost in another dimension, a stranger in town, not knowing which way to go." With these words, Bruce Glover recalls the day he returned to his hometown of Detroit, Michigan, after being away for twenty-six years—a long stretch in a state prison. Now fifty-six years of age, Glover was a young man of thirty when he was arrested for running a call girl ring. Found guilty at trial, he was given a stiff jail sentence.

"My mother passed while I was gone," Glover continues, shaking his head. "I lost everything." On the day he walked out of prison, he realized just how true that statement was. He had nowhere to go and no way to get there. He had no valid identification, which he would need to find a place to live and a job. He had no money to buy the clothes he needed to go out and start looking. He turned to a prison official and asked for help. Only with the assistance of a state agency was he finally able to get some money and temporary housing (C. Jones, 2007).

This chapter explores issues involving crime and criminals, asking not only how our criminal justice system handles offenders but also why societies develop standards of right and wrong in the first place. As you will see, the law is simply one part of a complex system of social control: Society teaches us all to conform, at least most of the time, to countless rules. We begin our investigation by defining several basic concepts.

What Is Deviance?

Deviance is *the recognized violation of cultural norms.* Norms guide virtually all human activities, so the concept of deviance is quite broad. One category of deviance is **crime,** *the violation of a society's formally enacted criminal law.* Even criminal deviance spans a wide range, from minor traffic violations to prostitution, sexual assault, and murder.

Most familiar examples of nonconformity are negative instances of rule breaking, such as stealing from a campus bookstore, assaulting a fellow student, or driving while intoxicated. But we also define especially righteous people—students who speak up too much in class or people who are overly enthusiastic about the latest electronic gadgets—as deviant, even if we give them a measure of respect. What all deviant actions or attitudes, whether negative or positive, have in common is some element of *difference* that causes us to think of another person as an "outsider" (H. S. Becker, 1966).

Not all deviance involves action or even choice. The very *existence* of some categories of people can be troublesome to others.

To the young, elderly people may seem hopelessly "out of touch," and to some whites, the mere presence of people of color may cause discomfort. Able-bodied people often view people with disabilities as an out-group, just as rich people may shun the poor for falling short of their high-class standards.

Social Control

All of us are subject to **social control,** *attempts by society to regulate people's thoughts and behavior.* Often this process is informal, as when parents praise or scold their children or when friends make fun of a classmate's choice of music. Cases of serious deviance, however, may bring action by the **criminal justice system,** *the organizations—police, courts, and prison officials—that respond to alleged violations of the law.*

How a society defines deviance, *who* is branded as deviant, and *what* people decide to do about deviance all have to do with the way a society is organized. Only gradually, however, have people come to understand that the roots of deviance are deep in society, as the chapter now explains.

The Biological Context

Chapter 3 ("Socialization: From Infancy to Old Age") explained that a century ago, most people understood—or more correctly, misunderstood—human behavior to be the result of biological instincts. Early interest in criminality therefore focused on biological

deviance the recognized violation of cultural norms

crime the violation of a society's formally enacted criminal law

social control attempts by society to regulate people's thoughts and behavior

criminal justice system the organizations—police, courts, and prison officials—that respond to alleged violations of the law

causes. In 1876, Cesare Lombroso (1835–1909), an Italian physician who worked in prisons, theorized that criminals stand out physically, with low foreheads, prominent jaws and cheekbones, protruding ears, hairy bodies, and unusually long arms. All in all, Lombroso claimed that criminals look like our apelike ancestors.

Had Lombroso looked more carefully, he would have found the physical features he linked to criminality throughout the entire population. We now know that no physical traits distinguish criminals from noncriminals.

In the middle of the twentieth century, William Sheldon took a different approach, suggesting that body structure might predict criminality (Sheldon, Hartl, & McDermott, 1949). He cross-checked hundreds of young men for body type and criminal history and concluded that delinquency was most common among boys with muscular, athletic builds. Sheldon Glueck and Eleanor Glueck (1950) confirmed that conclusion but cautioned that a powerful build does not necessarily *cause* or even *predict* criminality. Parents, they suggested, tend to be somewhat distant from powerfully built sons, who in turn grow up to show less sensitivity toward others. In a self-fulfilling prophecy, people who expect muscular boys to be bullies may act in ways that bring about the aggressive behavior they expect.

Today, genetics research seeks possible links between biology and crime. In 2003, scientists at the University of Wisconsin reported results of a twenty-five-year study of crime among 400 boys. The researchers collected DNA samples from each boy and noted any history of trouble with the law. The researchers concluded that genetic factors (especially defective genes that, say, make too much of an enzyme) together with environmental factors (especially abuse early in life) were strong predictors of adult crime and violence. They noted, too, that these factors together were a better predictor of crime than either one alone (Lemonick, 2003; Pinker, 2003).

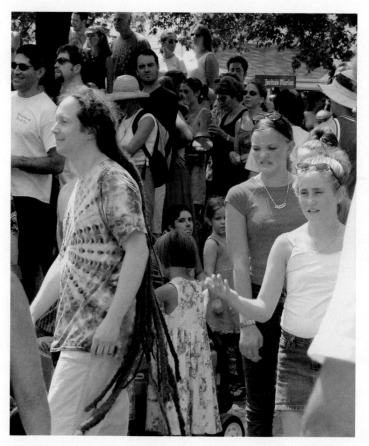

Deviance is always a matter of difference. Deviance emerges in everyday life as we encounter people whose appearance or behavior differs from what we consider "normal." Who is the "deviant" in this photograph? From whose point of view?

CRITICAL REVIEW Biological theories offer a limited explanation of crime. The best guess at present is that biological traits in combination with environmental factors explain some serious crime. Most of the actions we define as deviant are carried out by people who are physically quite normal.

In addition, because a biological approach looks at the individual, it offers no insight into how some kinds of behaviors come to be defined as deviant in the first place. Therefore, although there is much to learn about how human biology may affect behavior, research currently puts far greater emphasis on social influences.

CHECK YOUR LEARNING What does biological research add to our understanding of crime? What are the limitations of this approach?

Personality Factors

Like biological theories, psychological explanations of deviance focus on individual abnormality. Some personality traits are inherited, but most psychologists think personality is shaped primarily by social experience. Deviance, then, is viewed as the result of "unsuccessful" socialization.

Classic research by Walter Reckless and Simon Dinitz (1967) illustrates the psychological approach. Reckless and Dinitz began by asking teachers to categorize twelve-year-old male students as either likely or unlikely to get into trouble with the law. They then interviewed both the boys and their mothers to assess each boy's self-concept and how he related to others. Analyzing their results, the researchers found that the "good boys" displayed a strong conscience (what Freud called superego), could handle frustration, and identified

┌─○ Making the Grade

Deviance, the violation of norms, is a broad concept. Crime,
the violation of formally enacted law, is one type of deviance.

┌─○ Making the Grade

The three arguments below explain why we cannot fully understand
deviance only by looking at the deviant person. We need a broader,
sociological perspective to examine society.

with cultural norms and values. The "bad boys," by contrast, had a
weaker conscience, displayed little tolerance for frustration, and felt
out of step with conventional culture.

As we might expect, the "good boys" went on to have fewer run-
ins with the police than the "bad boys." Because all the boys lived in
areas where delinquency was widespread, the investigators attributed staying out of trouble to a personality that controlled deviant
impulses. Based on this conclusion, Reckless and Dinitz called their
analysis *containment theory*.

┌─○ **CRITICAL REVIEW**   Psychologists have shown that personality patterns have some connection to deviance. Some serious criminals are psychopaths who do not feel guilt or shame,
have no fear of punishment, and have little sympathy for the people they harm (Herpertz & Sass, 2000). However, as noted in the
case of biological factors, most serious crimes are committed by
people whose psychological profiles are normal.

Both biological and psychological research views deviance
as a trait of individuals. The reason these approaches have limited value in explaining deviance is that wrongdoing has more to
do with the organization of society. We now turn to a sociological approach, which explores where ideas of right and wrong
come from, why people define some rule breakers but not others as deviant, and what role power plays in this process.

└─○ **CHECK YOUR LEARNING**   Why do biological and psychological analyses not explain deviance very well?

Why is it that street-corner gambling like this is usually against the law but playing the
same games in a fancy casino is not?

The Social Foundations of Deviance

Although we tend to view deviance as the free choice or personal failings of individuals, all behavior—deviance as well as conformity—is
shaped by society. Three social foundations of deviance identified
here will be detailed later in this chapter:

1. **Deviance varies according to cultural norms.** No thought or
   action is inherently deviant; it becomes deviant only in relation to particular norms. State law permits prostitution in rural
   areas of Nevada, although the practice is outlawed in the rest of
   the United States. Twelve states have gambling casinos, twenty-
   nine have casinos on Indian reservations, and four other states
   have casinos at racetracks. In all other states, casino gambling
   is illegal. Text-messaging while driving is legal in thirty-three
   states but against the law in seventeen others (six other states
   forbid the practice for young drivers). Until 2008, when a
   court struck down the law, only Florida legally banned gay men
   and lesbians from adopting a child (Ruggieri, 2008; American
   Gaming Association, 2009; National Conference of State Legislatures, 2010).

   Further, most cities and towns have at least one unique
   law. For example, Mobile, Alabama, outlaws the wearing of
   stiletto-heeled shoes; Pine Lawn, Missouri, bans saggy, "low-
   rider" pants; South Padre Island, Texas, bans the wearing of
   neckties; Mount Prospect, Illinois, has a law against keeping
   pigeons or bees; Topeka, Kansas, bans snowball fights; Hoover,
   South Dakota, does not allow fishing with a kerosene lantern;
   and Beverly Hills, California, regulates the number of
   tennis balls allowed on the court at one time (R. Steele,
   2000; Wittenauer, 2007).

   Around the world, deviance is even more diverse.
   Albania outlaws any public display of religious faith,
   such as "crossing" oneself; Cuba bans citizens from
   owning personal computers; Vietnam can prosecute
   citizens for meeting with foreigners; Malaysia does not
   allow tight-fitting jeans for women; Saudi Arabia bans
   the sale of red flowers on Valentine's Day; Iran does
   not allow women to wear makeup and forbids the
   playing of rap music (Chopra, 2008).

2. **People become deviant as others define them that way.**
   Everyone violates cultural norms at one time or
   another. For example, have you ever walked around
   talking to yourself or "borrowed" a pen from your
   workplace? Whether such behavior defines us as mentally ill or criminal depends on how others perceive,
   define, and respond to it.

3. **Both norms and the way people define rule breaking
   involve social power.** The law, claimed Karl Marx, is

○ Making the Grade

Notice that Durkheim considered deviance to be a natural and necessary part of all social organization.

● Seeing Sociology
in Everyday Life

Keeping in mind Durkheim's claim that society creates deviance to mark moral boundaries, can you suggest why we often define people only in terms of their deviance, for example, by calling someone an "addict" or a "thief"?

the means by which powerful people protect their interests. A homeless person who stands on a street corner speaking out against the government risks arrest for disturbing the peace; a mayoral candidate during an election campaign doing exactly the same thing gets police protection. In short, norms and how we apply them reflect social inequality.

The Functions of Deviance: Structural-Functional Analysis

The key insight of the structural-functional approach is that deviance is a necessary element of social organization. This point was made a century ago by Emile Durkheim.

Durkheim's Basic Insight

In his pioneering study of deviance, Emile Durkheim (1964a, orig. 1893; 1964b, orig. 1895) made the surprising statement that there is nothing abnormal about deviance. In fact, it performs four essential functions:

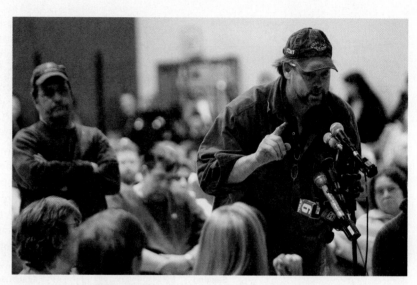

Durkheim claimed that deviance is a necessary element of social organization, serving several important functions. After a man convicted of killing a child settled in their New Hampshire town, residents came together to affirm their community ties as well as their understanding of right and wrong. Has any event on your campus caused a similar reaction?

1. **Deviance affirms cultural values and norms.** As moral creatures, people must prefer some attitudes and behaviors to others. But any definition of virtue rests on an opposing idea of vice: There can be no good without evil and no justice without crime. Deviance is needed to define and support morality.

2. **Responding to deviance clarifies moral boundaries.** By defining some individuals as deviant, people draw a boundary between right and wrong. For example, a college marks the line between academic honesty and deviance by disciplining students who cheat on exams.

3. **Responding to deviance brings people together.** People typically react to serious deviance with shared outrage. In doing so, Durkheim explained, they reaffirm the moral ties that bind them. For example, after the September 11, 2001, terrorist attacks, people across the United States were joined by a common desire to protect the country and bring the perpetrators to justice.

4. **Deviance encourages social change.** Deviant people push a society's moral boundaries, suggesting alternatives to the status quo and encouraging change. Today's deviance, declared Durkheim, can become tomorrow's morality (1964b:71, orig. 1895). For example, rock-and-roll, condemned as immoral in the 1950s, became a mainstream, multibillion-dollar industry just a few years later (see the Thinking About Diversity box on

pages 54–55). In recent decades, hip-hop music has followed the same path toward respectability.

An Illustration: The Puritans of Massachusetts Bay

Kai Erikson's classic study of the Puritans of Massachusetts Bay brings Durkheim's theory to life. Erikson (2005b, orig. 1966) shows that even the Puritans, a disciplined and highly religious group, created deviance to clarify their moral boundaries. In fact, Durkheim might well have had the Puritans in mind when he wrote:

> Imagine a society of saints, a perfect cloister of exemplary individuals. Crimes, properly so called, will there be unknown; but faults which appear [insignificant] to the layman will create there the same scandal that the ordinary offense does in ordinary consciousness. . . . For the same reason, the perfect and upright man judges his smallest failings with a severity that the majority reserve for acts more truly in the nature of an offense. (1964b:68–69, orig. 1895)

Deviance is thus not a matter of a few "bad apples" but a necessary condition of "good" social living.

Deviance may be found in every society, but the *kind* of deviance people generate depends on the moral issues they seek to clarify. The Puritans, for example, experienced a number of "crime waves," including the well-known outbreak of witchcraft in 1692. With each response, the Puritans answered questions about the range of proper beliefs by celebrating some of their members and condemning others as deviant.

⌐● Making the Grade

Merton's strain theory shows how people's opportunities (or lack of opportunities) to achieve cultural goals can encourage both deviance and conformity. In addition, what sociologists call people's "structure of opportunities" helps explain the type of deviance they engage in.

⌐● Making the Grade

Study the definition of labeling theory, which is the key idea of the symbolic-interaction approach. Be sure you understand this statement: Deviance results not so much from what people do as from how others respond to what they do.

FIGURE 7–1   Merton's Strain Theory of Deviance

Combining a person's view of cultural goals and the conventional means to obtain them allowed Robert Merton to identify various types of deviance.

Source: Merton (1968).

strain between our culture's emphasis on wealth and the lack of opportunities to get rich may encourage some people, especially the poor, to engage in stealing, drug dealing, and other forms of street crime. Merton called this type of deviance *innovation*—using unconventional means (street crime) rather than conventional means (hard work at a "straight" job) to achieve a culturally approved goal (wealth).

The inability to reach a cultural goal may also prompt another type of deviance that Merton calls *ritualism*. For example, people who believe they cannot achieve the cultural goal of becoming rich may stick rigidly to the rules (the conventional means) in order at least to feel respectable.

A third response to the inability to succeed is *retreatism:* rejecting both cultural goals and means so that one in effect "drops out." Some alcoholics, drug addicts, and street people are retreatists. The deviance of retreatists lies in their unconventional lifestyles and, perhaps more seriously, in what seems to be their willingness to live this way.

The fourth response to failure is *rebellion*. Like retreatists, rebels such as radical "survivalists" reject both the cultural definition of success and the conventional means of achieving it but go one step further by forming a counterculture supporting alternatives to the existing social order.

Deviant Subcultures

Richard Cloward and Lloyd Ohlin (1966) extended Merton's theory, proposing that crime results not simply from limited legitimate (legal) opportunity but also from readily accessible illegitimate (illegal) opportunity. In short, deviance or conformity depends on the *relative opportunity structure* that frames a person's life.

The life of Al Capone, a notorious gangster, illustrates Cloward and Ohlin's theory. As a son of poor immigrants, Capone faced barriers of poverty and ethnic prejudice, which lowered his odds of achieving success in conventional terms. Yet as a young man during the Prohibition era (the years between 1920 and 1933, when alcoholic beverages were banned in the United States), Capone found in his neighborhood people who could teach him how to sell alcohol illegally—a source of illegitimate opportunity. Where the structure of opportunity favors criminal activity, Cloward and Ohlin predict the development of *criminal subcultures,* such as Capone's criminal organization or today's inner-city street gangs.

But what happens when people are unable to find *any* opportunities, legal or illegal? Then deviance may take one of two forms. One is *conflict subcultures,* such as armed street gangs that regularly engage in violence, ignited by frustration and a desire for respect. Another possible outcome is the development of *retreatist subcultures,* in which deviants drop out and abuse alcohol or other drugs.

Albert Cohen (1971, orig. 1955) suggests that criminality is most common among lower-class youths because they have the least

Erikson discovered that although the offenses changed, the proportion of the population the Puritans defined as deviant remained steady over time. This stability, he concluded, confirms Durkheim's claim that society creates deviants to mark its changing moral boundaries. In other words, by constantly defining a small number of people as deviant, the Puritans maintained the moral shape of their society.

Merton's Strain Theory

Some deviance may be necessary for a society to function, but Robert Merton (1938, 1968) argued that too much deviance results from particular social arrangements. Specifically, the extent and kind of deviance depend on whether a society provides the *means* (such as schooling and job opportunities) to achieve cultural *goals* (such as financial success). Merton's strain theory of deviance is illustrated in Figure 7–1.

Conformity lies in pursuing cultural goals through approved means. Thus the U.S. "success story" is someone who gains wealth and prestige through talent, schooling, and hard work. But not everyone who wants conventional success has the opportunity to attain it. For example, people living in poverty may see little hope of becoming successful if they play by the rules. According to Merton, the

Seeing Sociology in Everyday Life

An old saying goes, "Sticks and stones can break my bones, but names can never hurt me." What might labeling theory have to say about this claim?

labeling theory (p. 178) the idea that deviance and conformity result not so much from what people do as from how others respond to those actions

stigma (p. 178) a powerfully negative label that greatly changes a person's self-concept and social identity

medicalization of deviance (p. 179) the transformation of moral and legal deviance into a medical condition

opportunity to achieve success by conventional means. Neglected by society, they seek self-respect by creating a deviant subculture that defines as worthy the traits these youths do have. Being feared on the street may win few points with society as a whole, but it may satisfy a youth's desire to "be somebody" in a local neighborhood.

Walter Miller (1970, orig. 1958) adds that deviant subcultures are characterized by (1) *trouble,* arising from frequent conflict with teachers and police; (2) *toughness,* the value placed on physical size, strength, and agility, especially among males; (3) *smartness,* the ability to succeed on the streets, to outsmart or "con" others; (4) *a need for excitement,* the search for thrills, risk, or danger; (5) *a belief in fate,* a sense that people lack control over their own lives; and (6) *a desire for freedom,* often expressed as anger toward authority figures.

Finally, Elijah Anderson (1994, 2002; Kubrin, 2005) explains that in poor urban neighborhoods, most people manage to conform to conventional ("decent") values. Yet faced every day with neighborhood crime and violence, indifference or even hostility from police, and sometimes even neglect from their own parents, some young men decide to live by the "street code." To show that he can survive on the street, a young man displays "nerve," a willingness to stand up to any threat. Following this street code, the young man believes that even a violent death is better than being "dissed" (disrespected) by others. Some manage to escape the dangers, but the risk of ending up in jail—or worse—is very high for these young men, who have been pushed to the margins of our society.

CRITICAL REVIEW Durkheim made an important contribution by pointing out the functions of deviance. However, there is evidence that a community does not always come together in reaction to crime; sometimes fear of crime drives people to withdraw from public life (Liska & Warner, 1991; Warr & Ellison, 2000).

Merton's strain theory also has been criticized for explaining some kinds of deviance (stealing, for example) better than others (crimes of passion or mental illness). Furthermore, not everyone seeks success in conventional terms of wealth, as strain theory suggests.

The general argument of Cloward and Ohlin, Cohen, and Miller—that deviance reflects the opportunity structure of society—has been confirmed by later research (Allan & Steffensmeier, 1989; Uggen, 1999). However, these theories fall short by assuming that everyone shares the same cultural standards for judging right and wrong. If we define crime as including not just burglary and auto theft but also fraud and other crimes carried out by corporate executives and Wall Street tycoons, many more high-income people will be counted among criminals. There is evidence that people of all social backgrounds

Young people cut off from legitimate opportunity often form subcultures that many people view as deviant. Gang subcultures are one way young people gain the sense of belonging and respect denied to them by the larger culture.

have become more casual about breaking the rules, as the Seeing Sociology in Everyday Life box on page 180 explains.

Finally, all structural-functional theories suggest that everyone who breaks the rules will be labeled deviant. However, becoming deviant is actually a highly complex process, as the next section explains.

CHECK YOUR LEARNING Why do you think many of the theories just discussed seem to say that crime is more common among people with lower social standing?

Deviant subcultures affect specific segments of the population. At the same time, as the economy rises and falls, the level of criminal activity typically goes up and down. Hard times, in short, tend to encourage widespread anxiety and a belief that we have to look out for ourselves any way we can. Seeing Sociology in the News on pages 178–79 offers a recent chapter in this very old story.

Labeling Deviance: Symbolic-Interaction Analysis

The symbolic-interaction approach explains how people come to see deviance in everyday situations. From this point of view, definitions of deviance and conformity are surprisingly flexible.

San Francisco Chronicle

Ex-Employees Turn to Cyber Crime after Layoffs

BY ALEJANDRO MARTINEZ-CABRERA
April 8, 2010

SAN FRANCISCO—When a slumping economy and historically high unemployment rates dropped the ax on the country's workforce and left the survivors wondering if—or when—they'd be next, law enforcers and security experts braced themselves for what they considered would be an almost inevitable rise in data breaches and high-tech crimes. And they were right.

National unemployment rates peaked in October at 10.1 percent and remained at 9.7 percent during the first two months of the year. Local law enforcers say the inability to find gainful employment has been a recurrent motivation behind new cases of identity theft and software piracy that drop on their desks almost daily.

"We're constantly coming across people who typically we wouldn't see and wouldn't engage in this criminal behavior if the economy was better. They see it as a way out," said Detective Sgt. Ken Taylor of California's Silicon Valley high-tech crimes task force Rapid Enforcement Allied Computer Team.

In one recent case under investigation, Taylor said, an unemployed San Mateo, California, woman in her twenties was detained with a large number of re-encoded credit cards in her possession. She said she was using them to buy food.

And a Fremont, California, man who had been recently laid off was arrested in February for selling pirated copies of a $2,500 Adobe design program for $150 on Craigslist. Task force members could look at cases of workers-turned-software-pirates all day every day, Taylor said.

According to cyber-security researchers, corporations across all industries have been dealing with a steadily growing number of internal data breaches since the financial meltdown.

A Verizon data-loss report noted that individuals with insider knowledge of organizations accounted for 20 percent of all breaches last year, and that number has been increasing as economic malaises drag on, said Chris Novak, managing principal of Verizon Business's Global Investigative Response Team.

Even though external attacks made up the bulk of the breaches, the report found that each internal incident compromised on average 100,000 individual pieces of sensitive information—at least 60,000 pieces more than external hacks.

Researchers say that anyone from top-level executives and IT personnel to low-level support employees can have access to data that can be sold illegally. A 2009 survey of almost 1,000 laid-off individuals found that 59 percent admitted keeping company data after leaving the business, according to the Ponemon Institute, a privacy research center in Traverse City, Michigan.

Labeling Theory

The central contribution of symbolic-interaction analysis is **labeling theory,** *the idea that deviance and conformity result not so much from what people do as from how others respond to those actions.* Labeling theory stresses the relativity of deviance, meaning that people may define the same behavior in any number of ways.

Consider these situations: A college student takes a sweater off the back of a roommate's chair and packs it for a weekend trip, a married woman at a convention in a distant city has sex with an old boyfriend, and a mayor gives a big city contract to a major campaign contributor. We might define the first situation as carelessness, borrowing, or theft. The consequences of the second situation depend largely on whether the woman's behavior becomes known back home. In the third situation, is the mayor choosing the best contractor or paying off a political debt? The social construction of reality is a highly variable process of detection, definition, and response.

Primary and Secondary Deviance

Edwin Lemert (1951, 1972) observed that some norm violations—say, skipping school or underage drinking—may provoke some reaction from others, but this process has little effect on a person's self-concept. Lemert calls such passing episodes *primary deviance.*

But what happens if people take notice of someone's deviance and really make something of it? After an audience has defined some action as primary deviance, the individual may begin to change, taking on a deviant identity by talking, acting, or dressing in a different way, rejecting the people who are critical, and repeatedly breaking the rules. Lemert (1951:77) calls this change of self-concept *secondary deviance.* He explains that "when a person begins to employ . . . deviant behavior as a means of defense, attack, or adjustment to the . . . problems created by societal reaction . . . , deviance [becomes] secondary." For example, say that people have begun describing a young man as an "alcohol abuser," which establishes primary deviance. These people may then exclude him from their friendship network. His response may be to become bitter toward them, start drinking even more, and seek the company of others who approve of his drinking. These actions mark the beginning of secondary deviance, a deeper deviant identity.

Stigma

Secondary deviance marks the start of what Erving Goffman (1963) called a *deviant career.* As people develop a deeper commitment to their deviant behavior, they typically acquire a **stigma,** *a powerfully negative label that greatly changes a person's self-concept and social identity.*

A stigma operates as a master status (see Chapter 4, "Social Interaction in Everyday Life"), overpowering other dimensions of identity so that a person is discredited in the minds of others and consequently becomes socially isolated. Often a person gains a stigma informally as others begin to see the individual in deviant terms. Sometimes, however, an entire community stigmatizes a person in a public way through what Harold Garfinkel (1956) calls a *degradation ceremony.* A criminal prosecution is one example, operating much like a high school graduation ceremony in reverse: A person stands before the community to be labeled in negative rather than positive terms.

In fact, data breach originators are "moving from being just the administrators and super-type users to your everyday users," Novak said.

"When data breaches are caused by administrators or super users, it's a big deal and the organization loses a great deal of information," he said. "When they come from average users, they're smaller pinpricks but can drag on longer and cost the company more in the long run."

Stolen data can range from employees' health care records or clients' credit card numbers to merger and acquisition plans, confidential agreements or valuable source code, said Rick Kam, president and co-founder of data breach prevention firm ID Experts.

Thieves can easily sell the information to cyber-criminal rings or use it as a bargaining chip to get a job with their former employer's competitors. According to the Ponemon Institute study, 67 percent of respondents said they would use "their former company's confidential, sensitive or proprietary information to leverage a new job."

"The issue of identity theft is all about opportunity," Kam said. "And our first instinct is to protect ourselves."

In one case handled by Kam's company six months ago, a disgruntled man went as far as trying to extort his former employer, a large health care provider, by threatening to release thousands of sensitive patient records that would have triggered an avalanche of lawsuits.

Those who remain employed but fear being the next to go can also grow alienated or resentful toward their companies and may be tempted to steal corporate data, said Kevin Rowney, director of breach response at Symantec.

"It's a common trend in economic history. Rising stress creates the circumstances that motivate people to go into financial fraud," Rowney said. "Employees in this economy feel it's every man for himself."

Retrospective and Projective Labeling

Once people stigmatize a person as deviant, they may engage in *retrospective labeling,* a reinterpretation of the person's past in light of some present deviance (Scheff, 1984). For example, after discovering that a priest has sexually molested a child, others rethink his past, perhaps offering comments such as "He always did want to be around young children." Retrospective labeling, which distorts a person's biography by being highly selective, typically deepens a deviant identity.

Similarly, people may engage in *projective labeling* of a stigmatized person, using a deviant identity to predict the person's future actions. Regarding the priest, people might say, "He's going to keep at it until he's caught." The more people in someone's social world think such things and act accordingly, the more these definitions affect the individual's self-concept, and the greater the chance that the predictions will come true.

Labeling Difference as Deviance

Is a homeless man who refuses to allow police to take him to a city shelter on a cold night simply trying to live independently, or is he "crazy"? People have a tendency to treat behavior that irritates or threatens them not simply as "different" but as deviance or even mental illness.

The psychiatrist Thomas Szasz (1961, 1970, 2003, 2004) claims that people are too quick to apply the label of mental illness to conditions that simply amount to differences we don't like. The only way to avoid this troubling practice, Szasz concludes, is to stop using the idea of mental illness entirely. The world is full of people whose differences in thought or action may irritate us, but such differences are not grounds for defining someone as mentally ill. Such labeling, Szasz says, simply enforces conformity to the standards of people powerful enough to impose their will on others.

Most mental health professionals reject the idea that mental illness does not exist. But they agree that it is important to think carefully about how we define "difference." First, people who are mentally ill are no more to blame for their condition than people who suffer from cancer or some other physical problem. Therefore, having a mental or physical illness is no grounds for a person being labeled "deviant." Second, people (especially those without the medical knowledge to diagnose mental illness) should avoid applying such labels just to make others conform to their own standards of behavior.

The Medicalization of Deviance

Labeling theory, particularly the ideas of Szasz and Goffman, helps explain an important shift in the way our society understands deviance. Over the past fifty years, the growing influence of psychiatry and medicine has led to the **medicalization of deviance,** *the transformation of moral and legal deviance into a medical condition.*

Medicalization amounts to swapping one set of labels for another. In moral terms, we judge people or their behavior as either "bad" or "good." However, the scientific objectivity of medicine passes no moral judgment, instead using clinical diagnoses such as "sick" or "well."

Making the Grade

The development of secondary deviance is one application of the Thomas theorem (see Chapter 6, "Social Interaction in Everyday Life"), which states that situations people define as real become real in their consequences.

Seeing Sociology in Everyday Life

Explain in your own words sociologist Howard Becker's (1966) statement that deviance is nothing more than behavior that people define as deviant.

SEEING SOCIOLOGY IN EVERYDAY LIFE

Deviant Subculture: Has It Become OK to Break the Rules?

ASTRID: Simon! You're downloading that music illegally. You'll get us both into trouble!

SIMON: Look, everyone cheats. Rich CEOs cheat in business. Ordinary people cheat on their taxes. Politicians lie. What else is new?

ASTRID: So it's OK to steal? Is that what you really believe?

SIMON: I'm not saying it's OK. I'm just saying everyone does it. . . .

It's been a couple of bad years for the idea of playing by the rules. First we learn that the executives of not just one but many U.S. corporations are guilty of fraud and outright stealing on a scale that most of us cannot even imagine. More recently, we realize that the Wall Street leaders running the U.S. economy not only did a pretty bad job of it but paid themselves tens of millions of dollars for doing so. And of course, even the Catholic church, which we hold up as a model of moral behavior, is still trying to recover from the charges that hundreds of priests have sexually abused parishioners (most of them under the age of consent) for decades while church officials covered up the crimes.

There have been plenty of theories offered about what is causing this widespread wrongdoing. Some suggest that the pressure to win—by whatever means necessary—in the highly competitive world of business and politics can be overwhelming. As one analyst put it, "You can get away with your embezzlements and your lies, but you can never get away with *failing*."

Such thinking helps explain the wrongdoing among many CEOs in the corporate world and the conviction of several members of Congress for ethics violations, but it offers little insight into the problem of abusive priests. In some ways at least, wrongdoing seems to have

Do you consider cheating in school wrong? Would you turn in someone you saw cheating? Why or why not?

become a way of life for just about everybody. For example, the Internal Revenue Service reports that Simon is right—millions of U.S. taxpayers cheat on their taxes, failing to pay an estimated $345 billion each year. The music industry claims that it has lost billions of dollars to illegal piracy of recordings, a practice especially common among young people. Perhaps most disturbing of all, surveys of students in high school, college, and also graduate school show that about half say that they cheated on a test at least once during the past year (Gallup, 2004; Morin, 2006).

Emile Durkheim viewed society as a moral system, built on a set of rules about what people should and should not do. Years earlier, another French thinker named Blaise Pascal made the opposite claim that "cheating is the foundation of society." Today, which of the two statements is closer to the truth?

WHAT DO YOU THINK?

1. In your opinion, how widespread is wrongdoing in U.S. society today?

2. Do you think the people who break the rules usually think that their actions are wrong? Why or why not?

3. What do you think are the reasons for the apparent increase in dishonesty?

Sources: Based on "Our Cheating Hearts" (2002) and Bono (2006).

To illustrate this idea, until the mid-twentieth century, most people viewed alcoholics as morally weak people easily tempted by the pleasure of drink. Gradually, however, medical specialists redefined alcoholism so that most people now consider it a disease, leading us to define alcoholics as "sick" rather than "bad." In the same way, obesity, drug addiction, child abuse, sexual promiscuity, and other behaviors that used to be strictly moral matters are widely defined today as illnesses for which people need help rather than punishment.

The Difference Labels Make

Whether we define deviance as a moral or a medical issue has three consequences. First, it affects *who responds* to deviance. An offense against common morality typically brings a reaction from members of the community or the police. A medical label, however, places the situation under the control of clinical specialists, including counselors, psychiatrists, and physicians.

A second issue is *how people respond* to deviance. A moral approach defines deviants as offenders subject to punishment. Medically, however,

○ Making the Grade

Deviance can be defined as either a moral or a medical issue. Be sure you understand the three key differences between defining deviance one way or the other.

● Seeing Sociology in Everyday Life

Context guides how we define someone's action. For example, Amy Bishop shot and killed her brother in 1986; back then, her action was ruled accidental. In light of this recent shooting, authorities reopened the earlier case and indicted Bishop.

they are patients who need treatment. Punishment is designed to fit the crime, but treatment programs are tailored to the patient and may involve any therapy that a specialist thinks might prevent future illness.

Third, and most important, the two labels differ on the issue of *the competence of the deviant person.* From a moral standpoint, whether we are right or wrong, at least we are responsible for our own behavior. Once we are defined as sick, however, we are seen as unable to control (or if "mentally ill," even to understand) our actions. People who are labeled incompetent are subject to treatment, often against their will. For this reason alone, defining deviance in medical terms should be done with extreme caution.

Sutherland's Differential Association Theory

Learning any social pattern, whether conventional or deviant, is a process that takes place in groups. According to Edwin Sutherland (1940), a person's tendency toward conformity or deviance depends on the amount of contact with others who encourage or reject conventional behavior. This is Sutherland's theory of *differential association.*

A number of studies confirm the idea that young people are more likely to engage in delinquent behavior if they believe that members of their peer group encourage such activity (Akers et al., 1979; Miller & Matthews, 2001). One recent investigation focused on sexual activity among eighth-grade students. Two strong predictors of such behavior in young girls were having a boyfriend who encouraged sexual relations and having girlfriends they believed would approve of such activity. Similarly, boys were encouraged to become sexually active by friends who rewarded them with high status in the peer group (Little & Rankin, 2001).

Hirschi's Control Theory

The sociologist Travis Hirschi (1969; Gottfredson & Hirschi, 1995) developed *control theory,* which states that social control depends on people's anticipating the consequences of their behavior. Hirschi assumes that everyone finds at least some deviance tempting. But the thought of a ruined career keeps most people from breaking the rules; for some, just imagining the reactions of family and friends is enough. On the other hand, people who think that they have little to lose from deviance are likely to become rule breakers.

Specifically, Hirschi links conformity to four different types of social control:

1. **Attachment.** Strong social attachments encourage conformity. Weak family, peer, and school relationships leave people freer to engage in deviance.

2. **Opportunity.** The greater a person's access to legitimate opportunity, the greater the advantages of conformity. By contrast,

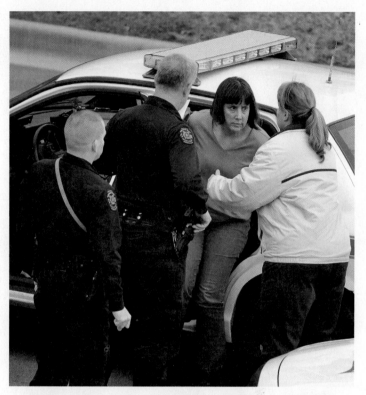

In 2010, Amy Bishop, a biology professor with a Harvard Ph.D., was denied tenure by her colleagues at the University of Alabama Huntsville. Soon after that, she took a gun to a campus faculty meeting and killed three colleagues, wounding three others. What effect does the social standing of the offender have in our assessment of her as "crazy" or "sick" as opposed to simply "evil"?

someone with little confidence in future success is more likely to drift toward deviance.

3. **Involvement.** Extensive involvement in legitimate activities—such as holding a job, going to school, or playing sports—inhibits deviance (Langbein & Bess, 2002). By contrast, people who simply "hang out" waiting for something to happen have the time and energy to engage in deviant activity.

4. **Belief.** Strong beliefs in conventional morality and respect for authority figures restrain tendencies toward deviance. By contrast, people with a weak conscience (and who are left unsupervised) are more open to temptation (Stack, Wasserman, & Kern, 2004).

Hirschi's analysis calls to mind our earlier discussions of the causes of deviant behavior. Here again, a person's relative social privilege and family and community environment affect the risk of deviant behavior (Hope, Grasmick, & Pointon, 2003).

Seeing Sociology in Everyday Life

Why do you think that politicians and other well-known people who get into trouble with the law often claim they have a problem with alcohol or other drugs and check into "rehab"?

Making the Grade

Students often have difficulty clearly defining secondary deviance and distinguishing it from primary deviance. Carefully review these concepts.

All social groups teach their members skills and attitudes that encourage certain behavior. In recent years, discussion on college campuses has focused on the dangers of binge drinking, which results in several dozen deaths each year among young people in the United States. How much of a problem is binge drinking on your campus?

○ **CRITICAL REVIEW** The various symbolic-interaction theories all see deviance as a process. Labeling theory links deviance not to action but to the *reaction* of others. Thus some people are defined as deviant but others who think or behave in the same way are not. The concepts of secondary deviance, deviant career, and stigma show how being labeled deviant can become a lasting self-concept.

Yet labeling theory has several limitations. First, because it takes a highly relative view of deviance, labeling theory ignores the fact that some kinds of behavior—such as murder—are condemned just about everywhere. Therefore, labeling theory is most usefully applied to less serious issues, such as sexual promiscuity or mental illness. Second, research on the consequences of deviant labeling does not clearly show whether deviant labeling produces further deviance or discourages it (Smith & Gartin,

1989; Sherman & Smith, 1992). Third, not everyone resists being labeled as deviant; some people actively seek it (Vold & Bernard, 1986). For example, people engage in civil disobedience and willingly subject themselves to arrest in order to call attention to social injustice.

Sociologists consider Sutherland's differential association theory and Hirschi's control theory important contributions to our understanding of deviance. But why do society's norms and laws define certain kinds of activities as deviant in the first place? This important question is addressed by social-conflict analysis, the focus of the next section.

○ **CHECK YOUR LEARNING** Clearly define primary deviance, secondary deviance, deviant career, and stigma.

Deviance and Inequality: Social-Conflict Analysis

The social-conflict approach links deviance to social inequality. That is, who or what is labeled "deviant" depends on which categories of people hold power in a society.

Deviance and Power

Alexander Liazos (1972) points out that the people we tend to define as deviants—the ones we dismiss as "nuts" and "sluts"—are typically not those who are bad or harmful as much as they are *powerless*. Bag ladies and unemployed men on street corners, not corporate polluters or international arms dealers, carry the stigma of deviance.

Social-conflict theory explains this pattern in three ways. First, all norms—especially the laws of any society—generally reflect the interests of the rich and powerful. People who threaten the wealthy are likely to be labeled deviant, whether it's by taking people's property ("common thieves") or advocating a more egalitarian society ("political radicals"). Karl Marx, a major architect of the social-conflict approach, argued that the law and all social institutions support the interests of the rich. Or as Richard Quinney puts it, "Capitalist justice is by the capitalist class, for the capitalist class, and against the working class" (1977:3).

Second, even if their behavior is called into question, the powerful have the resources to resist deviant labels. The majority of the corporate executives who were involved in the corporate scandals of recent years were not arrested, and only a small number ever went to jail.

Third, the widespread belief that norms and laws are "just" and "good" masks their political character. For this reason, although we may condemn the unequal application of the law, most of us give little thought to whether the laws themselves are really fair or not.

Seeing Sociology
in Everyday Life

How would a Marxist analysis explain the fact that hundreds of miners have died in coal mines in West Virginia and other states in recent decades without anyone being charged with any crime?

white-collar crime crime committed by people of high social position in the course of their occupations

corporate crime (p. 184) the illegal actions of a corporation or people acting on its behalf

organized crime (p. 184) a business supplying illegal goods or services

Deviance and Capitalism

In the Marxist tradition, Steven Spitzer (1980) argues that deviant labels are applied to people who interfere with the operation of capitalism. First, because capitalism is based on private control of property, people who threaten the property of others—especially the poor who steal from the rich—are prime candidates for being labeled deviant. Conversely, the rich who take advantage of the poor are less likely to be labeled deviant. For example, landlords who charge poor tenants high rents and evict those who cannot pay are not considered criminals; they are simply "doing business."

Second, because capitalism depends on productive labor, people who cannot or will not work risk being labeled deviant. Many members of our society think people who are out of work, even through no fault of their own, are somehow deviant.

Third, because the operation of the capitalist system depends on respect for authority figures, people who resist authority are likely to be labeled deviant. Examples are children who skip school or talk back to parents or teachers and adults who do not cooperate with employers or police.

Fourth, anyone who directly challenges the capitalist status quo is likely to be defined as deviant. Such has been the case with labor organizers, radical environmentalists, civil rights and antiwar activists, and feminists.

On the other side of the coin, society positively labels whatever supports the operation of capitalism. For example, winning athletes enjoy celebrity status because they make money and express the values of individual achievement and competition, both vital to capitalism. Also, Spitzer notes, we condemn using drugs of escape (marijuana, psychedelics, heroin, and crack) as deviant but promote drugs (such as alcohol and caffeine) that encourage adjustment to the status quo.

The capitalist system also tries to control people who don't fit into the system. The elderly, people with mental or physical disabilities, and Robert Merton's "retreatists" (people addicted to alcohol or other drugs) represent a "costly yet relatively harmless burden" to society. Such people, claims Spitzer, are subject to control by social welfare agencies. But people who openly challenge the capitalist system, including the inner-city "underclass" and revolutionaries—Merton's "innovators" and "rebels"—are controlled by the criminal justice system and, if necessary, military forces such as police SWAT teams and the National Guard.

Note that both the social welfare and criminal justice systems blame individuals, not the system, for social problems. Welfare recipients are considered unworthy freeloaders, poor people who rage at their plight are labeled rioters, anyone who actively challenges the government is branded a radical or a communist, and those who attempt to gain illegally what they will never get legally are rounded up as common criminals.

White-Collar Crime

In a sign of things to come, a Wall Street stockbroker named Michael Milken made headlines in 1987 when he was jailed for business fraud. Milken attracted attention because not since the days of Al Capone had anyone made so much money in one year: $550 million—about $1.5 million a day (Swartz, 1989).

Milken engaged in **white-collar crime,** defined by Edwin Sutherland in 1940 as *crime committed by people of high social position in the course of their occupations.* White-collar crime does not involve violence and rarely brings police with guns drawn to the scene. Rather, white-collar criminals use their powerful offices illegally to enrich themselves or others, often causing significant public harm in the process. For this reason, sociologists sometimes call white-collar offenses "crime in the suites" as opposed to "crime in the streets."

The most common white-collar crimes are bank embezzlement, business fraud, bribery, and violating antitrust laws that

Perhaps no one better symbolized the greed that drove the Wall Street meltdown of 2008 than Bernard Madoff, who swindled thousands of people and organizations out of some $50 billion. In 2009, after pleading guilty to eleven felony counts, Madoff was sentenced to 150 years in prison. Do you think white-collar offenders are treated fairly by our criminal justice system? Why or why not?

● Seeing Sociology
in Everyday Life

Imagine police holding a street gang, but not its individual
members, responsible for an outbreak of violence. This is what
happens in the case of corporate crime. What does this fact suggest
about the link between crime and power?

○ Making the Grade

White-collar crime and corporate crime are similar concepts, and
there is not always a clear line separating the two. White-collar
criminals are *individuals* of high social position who commit crimes
while doing their jobs. Corporate crime occurs when a *company*
acts in violation of the law.

require businesses to be competitive. Sutherland (1940) explains that such white-collar offenses typically end up in a civil hearing rather than a criminal courtroom. *Civil law* regulates business dealings between private parties; *criminal law* defines a person's moral responsibilities to society. In practice, someone who loses a civil case pays for damage or injury but is not labeled a criminal. Furthermore, corporate officials are protected by the fact that most charges of white-collar crime target the organization rather than individuals.

In the rare cases that white-collar criminals are charged and convicted, they usually escape punishment. A government study found that those convicted of fraud and punished with a fine ended up paying less than 10 percent of what they owed; most managed to hide or transfer their assets to avoid paying up. Among white-collar criminals convicted of embezzlement, only about half ever served a day in jail. One accounting found that just 57 percent of the embezzlers convicted in the U.S. federal courts served prison sentences; the rest were put on probation or issued a fine (U.S. Bureau of Justice Statistics, 2010). As some analysts see it, until courts impose more prison terms, we should expect white-collar crime to remain widespread (Shover & Hochstetler, 2006).

Corporate Crime

Sometimes whole companies, not just individuals, break the law. **Corporate crime** consists of *the illegal actions of a corporation or people acting on its behalf.*

Corporate crime ranges from knowingly selling faulty or dangerous products to deliberately polluting the environment (Derber, 2004). The collapse of a number of corporations in recent years, linked to criminal conduct on the part of company officials, has cost tens of thousands of people their jobs and their pensions.

In addition, companies often violate safety regulations, resulting in injury or death. Between 2006 and 2010, more than 125 people died in underground coal mines in the United States, in many cases amid allegations of safety violations. We might also wonder whether any "safe" mines really exist in light of the fact that hundreds more people died from "black lung" disease resulting from years of inhaling coal dust. The death toll for all job-related hazards in the United States runs into the thousands, and more than 1 million people are injured on the job seriously enough to require time away from work (Jafari, 2008; U.S. Census Bureau, 2009; Mine Safety and Health Administration, 2009).

Organized Crime

Organized crime is *a business supplying illegal goods or services.* Sometimes crime organizations force people to do business with them, as when a gang extorts money from shopkeepers for "protection."

In most cases, however, organized crime involves selling illegal goods and services—often sex, drugs, or gambling—to willing buyers.

Organized crime has flourished in the United States for more than a century. The scope of its operations expanded among immigrants who found that this society was not willing to share its opportunities with them. Thus some ambitious minorities (such as Al Capone, mentioned earlier) made their own success, especially during Prohibition, when the government banned the production and sale of alcohol.

The Italian Mafia is a well-known example of organized crime. But other criminal organizations involve African Americans, Chinese, Colombians, Cubans, Haitians, Nigerians, and Russians, as well as others of almost every racial and ethnic category. Organized crime today involves a wide range of activities, from selling illegal drugs to prostitution to credit card fraud and selling false identification papers to illegal immigrants (Valdez, 1997; Federal Bureau of Investigation, 2008).

○ **CRITICAL REVIEW** According to social-conflict theory, a capitalist society's inequality in wealth and power shapes its laws and how they are applied. The criminal justice and social welfare systems thus act as political agents, controlling categories of people who are a threat to the capitalist system.

Like other approaches to deviance, social-conflict theory has its critics. First, this approach implies that laws and other cultural norms are created directly by the rich and powerful. At the very least, this is an oversimplification because the law also protects workers, consumers, and the environment, sometimes opposing the interests of corporations and the rich.

Second, social-conflict analysis argues that criminality springs up only to the extent that a society treats its members unequally. However, as Durkheim noted, deviance exists in all societies, whatever the economic system and their degree of inequality.

The various sociological explanations for crime and other types of deviance are summarized in the Applying Theory table.

○ **CHECK YOUR LEARNING** Define white-collar crime, corporate crime, and organized crime.

Deviance, Race, and Gender

What people consider deviant reflects the relative power and privilege of different categories of people. The following sections offer two examples: how racial and ethnic hostility motivates hate crimes and how gender is linked to deviance.

● APPLYING THEORY ●

Deviance

	Structural-Functional Approach	Symbolic-Interaction Approach	Social-Conflict Approach
What is the level of analysis?	Macro-level	Micro-level	Macro-level
What is deviance? What part does it play in society?	Deviance is a basic part of social organization. By defining deviance, society sets its moral boundaries.	Deviance is part of socially constructed reality that emerges in interaction. Deviance comes into being as individuals label something deviant.	Deviance results from social inequality. Norms, including laws, reflect the interests of powerful members of society.
What is important about deviance?	Deviance is universal: It exists in all societies.	Deviance is variable: Any act or person may or may not be labeled deviant.	Deviance is political: People with little power are at high risk of being labeled deviant.

Hate Crimes

A **hate crime** is *a criminal act against a person or a person's property by an offender motivated by racial or other bias.* A hate crime may express hostility toward someone based on race, religion, ancestry, sexual orientation, or physical disability. The federal government recorded 7,783 hate crimes in 2008 (U.S. Department of Justice, 2009).

In 1998, people across the country were stunned by the brutal killing of Matthew Shepard, a gay student at the University of Wyoming, by two men filled with hatred toward homosexuals. But such crimes are far from isolated cases. The National Coalition of Anti-Violence Programs reports that 40 percent of lesbians and gay men in the United States say that they have been the victims of hate violence in their adult lifetimes, and about 90 percent of such people report experiencing verbal abuse. People who contend with multiple stigmas, such as gay men of color, are especially likely to be victimized (Dang & Vianney, 2007; National Coalition of Anti-Violence Programs, 2010). Yet hate crimes can happen to anyone: In 2008, more than one of every six hate crimes based on race targeted white people (Federal Bureau of Investigation, 2009).

By 2009, forty-five states and the federal government had enacted legislation that raises penalties for crimes motivated by hatred. Supporters are gratified, but opponents charge that such laws, which increase the penalty for a crime based on the attitudes of the offender, amount to punishing "politically incorrect" thoughts. The Thinking About Diversity box on page 186 takes a closer look at the issue of hate crime laws.

The Feminist Perspective: Deviance and Gender

Virtually every society in the world tries to control the behavior of women more than men. Historically, our own society has centered women's lives around the home. In the United States even today, women's opportunities in the workplace, in politics, in athletics, and in the military are more limited than men's. In some other parts of the world, the constraints on women are greater still. In Saudi Arabia, women cannot vote or legally operate motor vehicles; in Iran, women who expose their hair or wear makeup in public can be whipped; and not long ago, a Nigerian court convicted a divorced woman of bearing a child out of wedlock and sentenced her to death by stoning; her life was later spared out of concern for her child (Eboh, 2002).

Gender also figures into the theories about deviance noted earlier. For example, Robert Merton's strain theory defines cultural goals in terms of financial success. Traditionally at least, this goal has had more to do with the lives of men, because women have been socialized to define success in terms of relationships, particularly marriage and motherhood (E. B. Leonard, 1982). A more woman-focused theory might recognize the "strain" that results from the cultural ideal of equality clashing with the reality of gender-based inequality.

According to labeling theory, gender influences how we define deviance because people commonly use different standards to judge the behavior of females and males. Further, because society puts men

● Seeing Sociology
in Everyday Life

Why do you think that women are much less likely than men
to be arrested for a serious crime?

crimes against the person (violent crimes) crimes that direct violence or the
threat of violence against others

crimes against property (property crimes) crimes that involve theft of money
or property belonging to others

victimless crimes violations of law in which there are no obvious victims

THINKING ABOUT DIVERSITY: RACE, CLASS, & GENDER

Hate Crime Laws: Do They Punish Actions or Attitudes?

On a cool October evening, Todd Mitchell, an African American teenager, was standing with some friends in front of their apartment complex in Kenosha, Wisconsin. They had just seen the film *Mississippi Burning* and were fuming over a scene that showed a white man beating a young black boy as he knelt in prayer.

"Do you feel hyped up to move on some white people?" asked Mitchell. Minutes later, they saw a young white boy walking toward them on the other side of the street. Mitchell commanded, "There goes a white boy. Go get him!" The group swarmed around the youngster, beating him bloody and leaving him on the ground in a coma. The attackers took the boy's tennis shoes as a trophy.

Police soon arrested the boys and charged them with the beating. Todd Mitchell went to trial as the ringleader, and the jury found him guilty of aggravated battery *motivated by racial hatred*. Instead of receiving the usual two-year prison sentence, Mitchell was sent to jail for four years.

As this case illustrates, hate crime laws punish a crime more severely if the offender is motivated by bias against some category of people. Supporters make three arguments in favor of hate crime legislation. First, the offender's intentions are always important in weighing criminal responsibility, so considering hatred as an intention is nothing new. Second, victims of hate crimes typically suffer more serious injuries than victims of crimes with other motives. Third, a crime motivated by racial or other bias is more harmful because it can inflame an entire community more than a crime carried out, say, for money.

Critics counter that while some hate crime cases involve hard-core racism, most are impul-

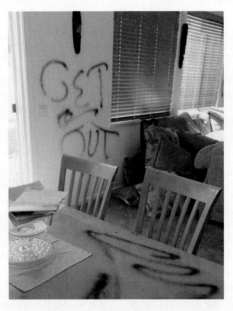

Do you think this example of vandalism should be prosecuted as a hate crime? In other words, should the punishment be more severe than if the spray painting were just "normal" graffiti? Why or why not?

sive acts by young people. Even more important, critics maintain, hate crime laws are a threat to First Amendment guarantees of free speech. Hate crime laws allow courts to sentence offenders not just for their actions but also for their attitudes. As the Harvard University law professor Alan Dershowitz cautions, "As much as I hate bigotry, I fear much more the Court attempting to control the minds of citizens." In short, according to critics, hate crime laws open the door to punishing beliefs rather than behavior.

In 1993, the U.S. Supreme Court upheld the sentence handed down to Todd Mitchell. In a unanimous decision, the justices reaffirmed that the government should not punish an individual's beliefs. But, they reasoned, a belief is no longer protected when it becomes the motive for a crime.

WHAT DO YOU THINK?

1. Do you think crimes motivated by hate are more harmful than those motivated by, say, greed? Why or why not?

2. Do you think minorities such as African Americans should be subject to the same hate crime laws as white people? Why or why not?

3. On balance, do you favor or oppose hate crime laws? Why?

Sources: Terry (1993), A. Sullivan (2002), and Hartocollis (2007).

in positions of power over women, men often escape direct responsibility for actions that victimize women. In the past, at least, men who sexually harassed or assaulted women were labeled only mildly deviant and sometimes escaped punishment entirely.

By contrast, women who are victimized may have to convince others—even members of a jury—that they are not to blame for their own sexual harassment or assault. Research confirms an important truth: Whether people define a situation as deviant—and, if they do, who in the situation is defined as deviant—depends on the sex of both the audience and the actors (King & Clayson, 1988).

Finally, despite its focus on inequality, much social-conflict analysis does not address the issue of gender. If economic disadvantage is a primary cause of crime, as conflict theory suggests, why do women (whose economic position is much worse than men's) commit far *fewer* crimes than men?

Crime

Crime is the violation of criminal laws enacted by a locality, a state, or the federal government. All crimes are composed of two distinct

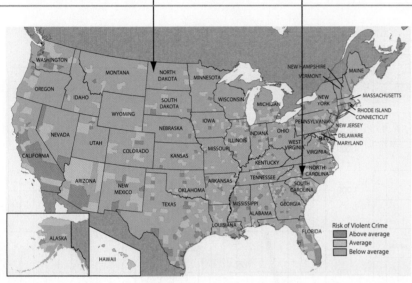

Sam Pearson, who lives in Renville County, North Dakota, rarely locks his doors when he leaves the house.

Serge Shuman, who lives in Mecklenburg County, North Carolina, knows many people who have been victims of crime and avoids going out at night.

Explore the share of the population in prison in your local community and in counties across the United States on mysoclab.com

Seeing Ourselves

NATIONAL MAP 7–1

The Risk of Violent Crime across the United States

This map shows the risk of becoming a victim of violent crime. In general, the risk is highest in low-income, rural counties that have a large population of men between the ages of fifteen and twenty-four. After reading this section of the text, see whether you can explain this pattern.

Explore on mysoclab.com

Source: CAP Index (2009).

Risk of Violent Crime
- Above average
- Average
- Below average

elements: the *act* itself (or in some cases, a failure to do what the law requires) and *criminal intent* (in legal terminology, *mens rea*, or "guilty mind"). Intent is a matter of degree, ranging from willful conduct to negligence. Someone who is negligent does not set out deliberately to hurt anyone but acts (or fails to act) in a way that results in harm. Prosecutors weigh the degree of intent in determining whether, for example, to charge someone with first-degree murder, second-degree murder, or negligent manslaughter. Alternatively, they may consider a killing justifiable, as in self-defense.

Types of Crime

In the United States, the Federal Bureau of Investigation (FBI) gathers information on criminal offenses and regularly reports the results in a publication called *Crime in the United States.* Two major types of crime make up the FBI "crime index."

Crimes against the person, also referred to as *violent crimes,* are *crimes that direct violence or the threat of violence against others.* Violent crimes include murder and manslaughter (legally defined as "the willful killing of one human being by another"), aggravated assault ("an unlawful attack by one person on another for the purpose of inflicting severe or aggravated bodily injury"), forcible rape ("the carnal knowledge of a female forcibly and against her will"), and robbery ("taking or attempting to take anything of value from the care, custody, or control of a person or persons, by force or threat of force or violence and/or putting the victim in fear"). National Map 7–1 shows the risk of violent crime for all the counties in the United States.

Crimes against property, also referred to as *property crimes,* are *crimes that involve theft of money or property belonging to others.* Property crimes include burglary ("the unlawful entry of a structure to commit a [serious crime] or a theft"), larceny-theft ("the unlawful

taking, carrying, leading, or riding away of property from the possession of another"), motor vehicle theft ("the theft or attempted theft of a motor vehicle"), and arson ("any willful or malicious burning or attempt to burn the personal property of another").

A third category of offenses, not included in major crime indexes, is **victimless crimes,** *violations of law in which there are no obvious victims.* Also called *crimes without complaint,* they include illegal drug use, prostitution, and gambling. The term "victimless crime" is misleading, however. How victimless is a crime when young drug users embark on a life of crime to support their drug habit? What about a pregnant woman who, by smoking crack, permanently harms her baby? Or a gambler who loses the money needed to support himself and his family? Perhaps it is more correct to say that people who commit such crimes are both offenders and victims.

Because public views of victimless crime vary greatly, laws differ from place to place. Although gambling and prostitution are legal in only limited areas, both activities are common across the country.

Criminal Statistics

Statistics gathered by the FBI show crime rates rising from 1960 to 1990 and then declining after that. Even so, police count more than 11 million serious crimes each year. Figure 7–2 on page 188 shows the trends for various serious crimes over the past four decades.

Always read crime statistics with caution, however, because they include only crimes known to the police. Almost all murders are reported, but other assaults—especially between people who know one another—often are not. Police records include an even smaller proportion of property crimes, especially when the losses are small.

Researchers check official crime statistics by conducting *victimization surveys,* in which they ask a representative sample of

● Seeing Sociology
  in Everyday Life

Do you think a student who downloads music in violation of
the law is guilty of theft? Why or why not?

○ Making the Grade

The profile of the street criminal is based on arrest data and
not on convictions in a court of law. This is because the data
made available by the FBI are based on arrests.

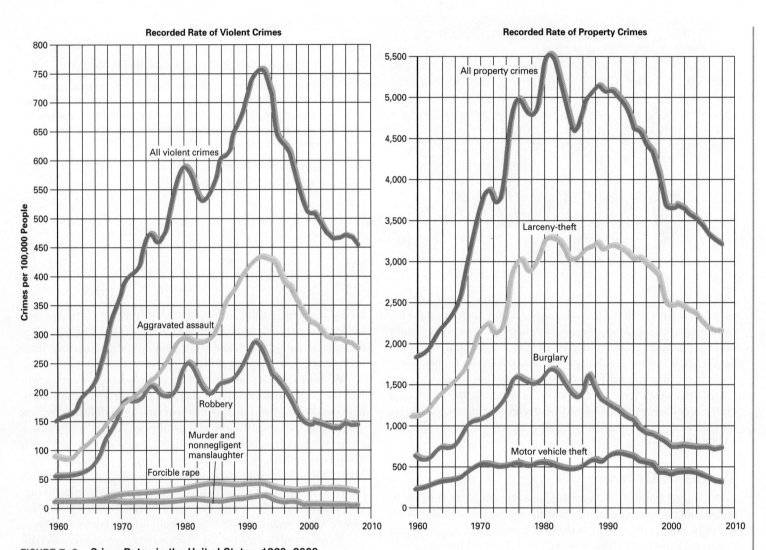

FIGURE 7–2   Crime Rates in the United States, 1960–2008

The graphs show the rates for various violent crimes and property crimes during recent decades. Since about 1990,
the trend has been downward.

Source: Federal Bureau of Investigation (2009).

people about their experiences with crime. Victimization surveys
carried out in 2008 showed that the actual number of serious crimes
was more than twice as high as police reports indicate (Rand, 2009).

The Street Criminal: A Profile

Using various government crime reports, we can draw a general
description of the categories of people most likely to be arrested for
crimes.

Gender

Although each sex makes up roughly half the population, police col-
lared males in 65.2 percent of all property crime arrests in 2008; the
other 34.8 percent of arrests involved women. In other words, men are
arrested almost twice as often as women for property crimes. In the
case of violent crimes, the difference is even greater, with 81.7 percent
of arrests involving males and just 18.3 percent females (more than
a four-to-one ratio).

Go to the Multimedia Library at **mysoclab.com** to watch the ABC *20/20* video "Justice and Privilege"

Read "Race and Class in the Criminal Justice System" by David Cole on **mysoclab.com**

It may be that law enforcement officials are reluctant to define women as criminals. In global perspective, the greatest gender difference in crime rates occurs in societies that most severely limit the opportunities of women. In the United States, the difference in arrest rates for women and men has been narrowing, which probably indicates increasing gender equality in our society. Between 1999 and 2008, there was a 11.6 percent *increase* in arrests of women and a 3.1 percent *drop* in arrests of men (Federal Bureau of Investigation, 2009).

Age

Official crime rates rise sharply during adolescence, peak in the late teens, and fall as people get older. People between the ages of fifteen and twenty-four represent just 14 percent of the U.S. population, but in 2008, they accounted for 41.5 percent of all arrests for violent crimes and 48.3 percent of arrests for property crimes.

Social Class

The FBI does not assess the social class of arrested persons, so no statistical data of the kind given for age and gender are available. But research has long indicated that street crime is more widespread among people of lower social position (Thornberry & Farnsworth, 1982; Wolfgang, Thornberry, & Figlio, 1987).

Yet the connection between class and crime is more complicated than it appears on the surface. For one thing, many people see the poor as less worthy than the rich, whose wealth and power confer "respectability" (Tittle, Villemez, & Smith, 1978; Elias, 1986). And although crime—especially violent crime—is a serious problem in the poorest inner-city communities of the United States, most of these crimes are committed by a few hard-core offenders. The majority of people in inner-city neighborhoods have no criminal record at all (Wolfgang, Figlio, & Sellin, 1972; Elliott & Ageton, 1980; Harries, 1990).

The connection between social standing and criminality also depends on the type of crime. If we expand our definition of crime beyond street offenses to include white-collar crime, the "common criminal" suddenly looks much more affluent and may live in a $100 million home. ● Go to **mysoclab.com**

Race and Ethnicity

Both race and ethnicity are strongly linked to crime rates, although the reasons are many and complex. Official statistics indicate that 69.2 percent of arrests for index crimes in 2008 involved white people. However, arrests of African Americans are higher in proportion to their share of the general population. African Americans make up 12.8 percent of the population of the United States but account for 30.1 percent of the arrests for property crimes (versus 67.4 percent for whites) and 39.4 percent of arrests for violent crimes (versus 58.3 percent for whites) (Federal Bureau of Investigation, 2009).

"You look like this sketch of someone who's thinking about committing a crime."

There are several reasons for the disproportionate number of arrests among African Americans. First, in the United States, race is closely linked to social standing, which, as already explained, affects the likelihood of engaging in street crimes. Many poor people living in the midst of wealth come to see society as unjust and therefore are more likely to turn to crime to get their share (Blau & Blau, 1982; E. Anderson, 1994; Martinez, 1996).

Second, black and white family patterns differ: Seventy-two percent of non-Hispanic black children (compared with 28 percent of non-Hispanic white children) are born to single mothers. There are two risks associated with single parenting: Children get less supervision, and they are at greater risk of living in poverty. With more than one-third of African American children growing up in poor families (compared with one in nine white children), no one should be surprised at proportionately higher crime rates for African Americans (Courtwright, 1996; Jacobs & Helms, 1996; Hamilton, Martin, and Ventura, 2009; U.S. Census Bureau, 2009).

Third, prejudice prompts white police to arrest black people more readily and leads citizens to report African Americans more willingly, so people of color are overly criminalized (Chiricos, McEntire, & Gertz, 2001; Quillian & Pager, 2001; Demuth & Steffensmeier, 2004). Read on **mysoclab.com**

Fourth, remember that the official crime index does not include arrests for offenses ranging from drunk driving to white-collar violations. This omission contributes to the view of the typical criminal

⊙ Making the Grade

Remember that the profile of a criminal depends on the type of crime. Street crime involves a larger share of lower-income people; corporate crime involves mostly high-income people. With regard to race, most street crime is committed by whites.

⊙ Seeing Sociology in Everyday Life

Do you think stricter gun control laws would lower the level of deadly violence in the United States? Why or why not?

as a person of color. If we broaden our definition of crime to include drunk driving, business fraud, embezzlement, stock swindles, and cheating on income tax returns, the proportion of white criminals rises dramatically.

Keep in mind, too, that categories of people with high arrest rates are also at higher risk of being victims of crime. In the United States, for example, African Americans are six times as likely to die as a result of homicide as white people (Rogers et al., 2001; Heron et al., 2009).

Finally, some categories of the population have unusually low rates of arrest. People of Asian descent, who account for 4.5 percent of the population, figure in only 1.1 percent of all arrests. As Chapter 11 ("Race and Ethnicity") explains, Asian Americans enjoy higher than average educational achievement and income. Also, Asian American culture emphasizes family solidarity and discipline, both of which keep criminality down.

Crime in Global Perspective

By world standards, the U.S. crime rate is high. Although recent crime trends are downward, there were 16,272 murders in this country in 2008, which amounts to one every half hour around the clock. In large cities such as New York, never does a week go by without someone being killed.

The rate of violent crime (but not property crime) in the United States is several times higher than in Europe. The contrast is even greater between our country and the nations of Asia, including India and Japan, where violent and property crime rates are among the lowest in the world.

Elliott Currie (1985) suggests that crime arises from our culture's emphasis on individual economic success, often at the expense of strong families and neighborhoods. The United States also has extraordinary cultural diversity—a result of centuries of immigration—that can lead to conflict. In addition, economic inequality is higher in this country than in most other high-income nations. Our society's relatively weak social fabric, combined with considerable frustration among the poor, increases the level of criminal behavior.

Another factor contributing to violence in the United States is extensive private ownership of guns. About two-thirds of murder victims in the United States die from shootings. The U.S. rate of handgun homicides is about five times higher than in Canada, a country that strictly limits handgun ownership (Federal Bureau of Investigation, 2009; Statistics Canada, 2009).

Surveys show that about one-third of U.S. households have at least one gun. In fact, there are more guns (about 283 million) than adults in this country, and 40 percent of these weapons are handguns, which are commonly used in violent crimes. In large part, gun ownership reflects people's fear of crime, yet easy availability of guns in this country makes crime more deadly (Brady Campaign, 2008; NORC, 2009).

Supporters of gun control claim that restricting gun ownership would reduce the number of murders in the United States. For example, the number of murders each year in Canada, where the law prevents most people from owning guns, is about the same as the number of murders in just the cities of New York and Newark in this country. But as critics of gun control point out, laws regulating gun ownership do not keep guns out of the hands of criminals, who almost always obtain guns illegally. They also claim that gun control is no magic bullet in the war on crime: The number of people in the United States killed each year by knives alone is three times the number of Canadians killed by weapons of all kinds (J. D. Wright, 1995; Munroe, 2007; Federal Bureau of Investigation, 2009; Statistics Canada, 2009).

By the end of 2008, gun sales to private citizens were up sharply, reflecting the fears on the part of many gun owners that the Obama administration would act to curtail gun ownership. Changes in the law may or may not occur in the next few years, but debate over the consequences of widespread gun ownership will continue (Potter, 2008).

December 24–25, traveling through Peru. In Lima, Peru's capital city, the concern with crime is obvious. Almost every house is fortified with gates, barbed wire, or broken glass embedded in cement at the top of a wall. Private security forces are everywhere in the rich areas along the coast, where we find the embassies, expensive hotels, and the international airport.

The picture is very different as we pass through small villages high in the Andes to the east. The same families have lived in these communities for generations, and people know one another. No gates or fences here. And we've seen only one police car all afternoon.

Crime rates are high in some of the largest cities of the world, such as Manila, Philippines, and São Paulo, Brazil, which have rapid population growth and millions of desperately poor people. Outside of big cities, however, the traditional character of low-income societies and their strong family structure allow local communities to control crime informally.

Some types of crime have always been multinational, such as terrorism, espionage, and arms dealing. But today, the globalization we are experiencing on many fronts also extends to crime. A case in point is the illegal drug trade. In part, the problem of illegal drugs in the United States is a *demand* issue. That is, the demand for cocaine and other drugs in this country is high, with high rates of addiction and many young people who are willing to risk arrest or even violent death for a chance to get rich in the drug trade. But the *supply* side of the issue is just as important. In the South American nation of Colombia, at least 20 percent of the people depend on cocaine production

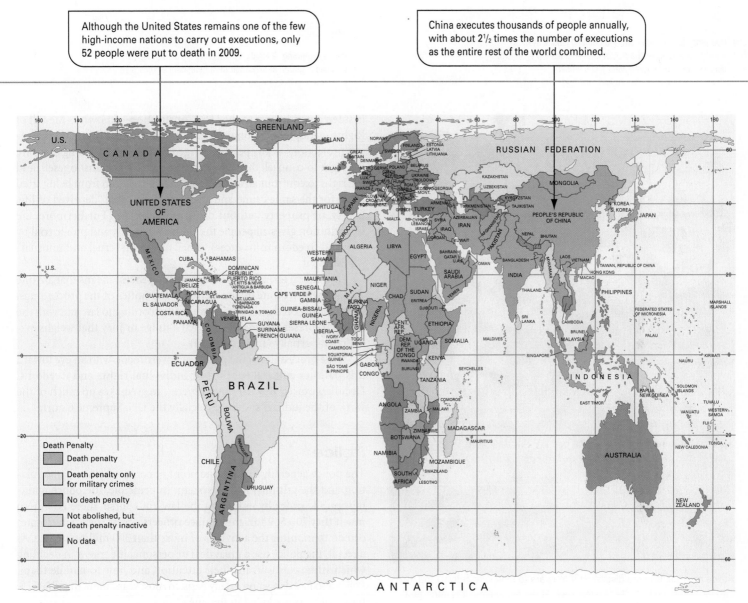

Although the United States remains one of the few high-income nations to carry out executions, only 52 people were put to death in 2009.

China executes thousands of people annually, with about 2½ times the number of executions as the entire rest of the world combined.

Death Penalty

Death penalty

Death penalty only for military crimes

No death penalty

Not abolished, but death penalty inactive

No data

Window on the World

GLOBAL MAP 7–1 **Capital Punishment in Global Perspective**

The map identifies fifty-eight countries in which the law allows the death penalty for ordinary crimes; in nine more, the death penalty is reserved for exceptional crimes under military law or during times of war. The death penalty does not exist in ninety-five countries; in thirty-five more, although the death penalty remains in law, no execution has taken place in more than ten years. Compare rich and poor nations: What general pattern do you see? In what way are the United States and Japan exceptions to this pattern?

Source: Amnesty International (2010a).

for their livelihood. Not only is cocaine Colombia's most profitable export, but it outsells all other exports combined, including coffee. Clearly, then, drug dealing and many other crimes are closely related to social conditions both in this country and elsewhere.

Different countries have different strategies for dealing with crime. The use of capital punishment (the death penalty) is one

example. According to Amnesty International (2010b), five nations account for 93 percent of the world's executions carried out by governments. Global Map 7–1 shows which countries currently use capital punishment. The global trend is toward abolishing the death penalty: Amnesty International (2010a) reports that since 1985, more than sixty nations have ended this practice.

Due process—the idea that the criminal justice system should operate under the rule of law—guides the actions of police, court officials, and corrections officers.

plea bargaining a legal negotiation in which a prosecutor reduces a charge in exchange for a defendant's guilty plea

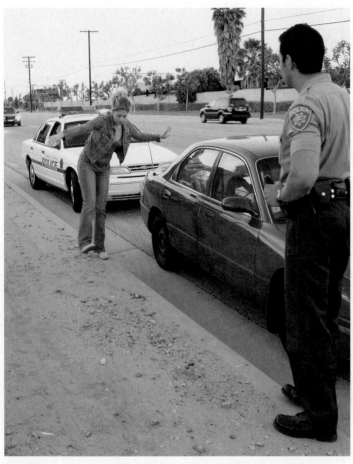

Police must be allowed discretion if they are to handle effectively the many different situations they face every day. At the same time, it is important that the police treat people fairly. Here we see a police officer deciding whether or not to charge a young woman with driving while intoxicated. What factors do you think enter into this decision?

The U.S. Criminal Justice System

The criminal justice system is a society's formal response to crime. We shall briefly examine the key elements of the U.S. criminal justice system: police, the courts, and the system of punishment and corrections. First, however, we must understand an important principle that underlies the entire system, the idea of due process.

Due Process

Due process is a simple but very important idea: The criminal justice system must operate according to law. Criminal law is grounded in the first ten amendments to the U.S. Constitution—known as the Bill of Rights—adopted by Congress in 1791. The Constitution offers various protections to any person charged with a crime. Among these are the right to counsel, the right to refuse to testify against oneself, and the right to confront all accusers, as well as freedom from being tried twice for the same crime and freedom from being "deprived of life, liberty, or property without due process of law." Furthermore, the Constitution gives all people the right to a speedy and public trial by jury and freedom from excessive bail and from "cruel and unusual" punishment.

In general terms, the concept of due process means that anyone charged with a crime must receive (1) fair notice of the proceedings, (2) a hearing on the charges conducted according to law and with the ability to present a defense, and (3) a judge or jury that weighs evidence impartially (Inciardi, 2000).

Due process limits the power of government, with an eye toward this nation's cultural support of individual rights and freedoms. Deciding exactly how far government can go makes up much of the work of the judicial system, especially the U.S. Supreme Court.

Police

The police generally serve as the point of contact between a population and the criminal justice system. In principle, the police maintain public order by enforcing the law. Of course, there is only so much that 708,569 full-time police officers across the United States can do to monitor the activities of more than 300 million people. As a result, the police use a great deal of personal judgment in deciding which situations warrant their attention and how to handle them. Police also face danger on a daily basis. In most years, more than 100 U.S. police officers are killed in the line of duty.

Given these facts, how do police officers carry out their duties? In a study of police behavior in five cities, Douglas Smith and Christy Visher (1981; D. A. Smith, 1987) concluded that because they must act swiftly, police quickly size up situations in terms of six factors. First, the more serious they think the situation is, the more likely they are to make an arrest. Second, police take account of the victim's wishes in deciding whether or not to make an arrest. Third, the odds of arrest go up the more uncooperative a suspect is. Fourth, police are more likely to take into custody someone they have arrested before, presumably because this suggests guilt. Fifth, the presence of bystanders increases the chances of arrest. According to Smith and Visher, the presence of observers prompts police to take stronger control of a situation, if only to move the encounter from the street (the suspect's turf) to the police department (where law officers have the edge). Sixth, all else being equal, police are more likely to arrest people of color than to arrest whites, perceiving people of African or Latino descent as either more dangerous or more likely to be guilty.

Four Justifications for Punishment

retribution an act of moral vengeance by which society makes the offender suffer as much as the suffering caused by the crime

deterrence the attempt to discourage criminality through the use of punishment

rehabilitation (p. 194) a program for reforming the offender to prevent later offenses

societal protection (p. 194) rendering an offender incapable of further offenses temporarily through imprisonment or permanently by execution

Courts

After arrest, a court determines a suspect's guilt or innocence. In principle, U.S. courts rely on an adversarial process involving attorneys—one representing the defendant and another the state—in the presence of a judge who monitors legal procedures.

In practice, however, about 90 percent of criminal cases are resolved before court appearance through **plea bargaining,** *a legal negotiation in which a prosecutor reduces a charge in exchange for a defendant's guilty plea.* For example, the state may offer a defendant charged with burglary a lesser charge, perhaps possession of burglary tools, in exchange for a guilty plea.

Plea bargaining is widespread because it spares the system the time and expense of trials. A trial is usually unnecessary if there is little disagreement as to the facts of the case. Moreover, because of the high number of cases entering the system, prosecutors could not possibly bring every case to trial even if they wanted to. By quickly resolving most of their work, then, the courts can devote their resources to the most important cases.

But plea bargaining pressures defendants (who are presumed innocent) to plead guilty. A person can exercise the right to a trial, but only at the risk of receiving a more severe sentence if found guilty. Furthermore, low-income defendants must often rely on a public defender—typically an overworked and underpaid attorney who may devote little time to even the most serious cases (Novak, 1999). Plea bargaining may be efficient, but it undercuts both the adversarial process and the rights of defendants.

Punishment

In 2009, a man with a long criminal record who was out on bail on charges of raping a child walked into a coffee shop in Parkland, Washington, and shot and killed four uniformed police officers as they were doing "paperwork" on their laptops. Two days later, a massive manhunt ended when the man was killed in a confrontation with another police officer (MSNBC, 2009).

Such cases force us to wonder about the reasons that drive some people to deadly violence and also to ask how a society should respond to such acts. In the case of the Parkland shootings, the crime was resolved through gunfire. But typically, of course, a suspect is apprehended and put on trial. If found guilty, the next step is punishment.

What does a society gain through the punishment of wrongdoers? Scholars answer with four basic reasons, which are described in the following sections: retribution, deterrence, rehabilitation, and societal protection.

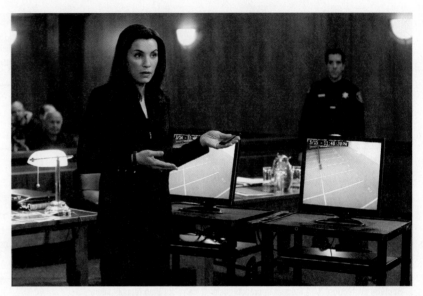

Many of our most popular television shows, including *The Good Wife*, show dedicated and skillful people moving our judicial system forward. We like to think that the court system carefully weighs the guilt and innocence of every person accused of a crime. As explained below, however, only 10 percent of criminal cases are actually resolved through a formal trial.

Retribution

The oldest justification for punishment is to satisfy a society's need for **retribution,** *an act of moral vengeance by which society makes the offender suffer as much as the suffering caused by the crime.* Retribution rests on the view that society exists in a moral balance. When criminality upsets this balance, punishment in equal measure restores the moral order, as suggested in the ancient code calling for "an eye for an eye, a tooth for a tooth."

In the Middle Ages, most people viewed crime as sin—an offense against God as well as society—that required a harsh response. Although critics point out that retribution does little to reform the offender, many people today still consider vengeance reason enough for punishment.

Deterrence

A second justification for punishment is **deterrence,** *the attempt to discourage criminality through the use of punishment.* Deterrence is based on the eighteenth-century Enlightenment idea that as calculating and rational creatures, humans will not break the law if they think that the pain of the punishment will outweigh the pleasure of the crime.

Deterrence emerged as a reform measure in response to harsh punishments based on retribution. Why put someone to death for stealing if theft can be discouraged by a prison sentence? As the concept of deterrence gained acceptance in industrial societies, execution

○ Making the Grade

Carefully review the Summing Up table below to ensure that you understand the four justifications for punishment.

Go to the Multimedia Library at **mysoclab.com** to watch the ABC *Primetime* video "Juvenile Corrections"

SUMMING UP

Four Justifications for Punishment

Retribution	The oldest justification for punishment. Punishment is society's revenge for a moral wrong. In principle, punishment should be equal in severity to the crime itself.
Deterrence	An early modern approach. Crime is considered social disruption, which society acts to control. People are viewed as rational and self-interested; deterrence works because the pain of punishment outweighs the pleasure of crime.
Rehabilitation	A modern strategy linked to the development of social sciences. Crime and other deviance are viewed as the result of social problems (such as poverty) or personal problems (such as mental illness). Social conditions are improved; treatment is tailored to the offender's condition.
Societal protection	A modern approach easier to carry out than rehabilitation. Even if society is unable or unwilling to rehabilitate offenders or reform social conditions, people are protected by the imprisonment or execution of the offender.

and physical mutilation of criminals were replaced by milder forms of punishment such as imprisonment.

Punishment may deter crime in two ways. *Specific deterrence* convinces an individual offender that crime does not pay. Through *general deterrence,* punishing one person serves as an example to others.

Rehabilitation

The third justification for punishment, **rehabilitation,** is *a program for reforming the offender to prevent later offenses.* Rehabilitation arose along with the social sciences in the nineteenth century. Since then, sociologists have claimed that crime and other deviance spring from a social environment marked by poverty or lack of parental supervision. Logically, then, if offenders learn to be deviant, they can also learn to obey the rules; the key is controlling the environment. *Reformatories* or *houses of correction* provided a controlled setting where people could learn proper behavior (recall the description of total institutions in Chapter 3, "Socialization: From Infancy to Old Age").

Like deterrence, rehabilitation motivates the offender to conform. In contrast to deterrence and retribution, which simply make the offender suffer, rehabilitation encourages constructive improvement. Unlike retribution, which demands that the punishment fit the crime, rehabilitation tailors treatment to each offender. Thus identical crimes would prompt similar acts of retribution but different rehabilitation programs. ● Go to **mysoclab.com**

Societal Protection

A final justification for punishment is **societal protection,** *rendering an offender incapable of further offenses temporarily through imprisonment or permanently by execution.* Like deterrence, societal protection is a rational approach to punishment intended to protect society from crime.

In 2010, some 2.4 million people were in prison in the United States. Although the crime rate has gone down since 1980, the number of offenders locked up has increased nearly fivefold. This rise in the prison population reflects both tougher public attitudes toward crime and an increasing number of arrests for drug-related crimes. As a result, the United States now imprisons a larger share of its population than any other country in the world (Pew Center on the States, 2008; Sentencing Project, 2008; U.S. Bureau of Justice Statistics, 2010).

○ **CRITICAL REVIEW** The Summing Up table reviews the four justifications for punishment. However, an accurate assessment of the consequences of punishment is no simple task.

The value of retribution lies in Durkheim's claim that punishing the deviant person increases society's moral awareness. For this reason, punishment was traditionally a public event. Although the last public execution in this country took place in Kentucky more than seventy years ago, today's mass media ensure public awareness of executions carried out inside prison walls (Kittrie, 1971).

● Seeing Sociology
in Everyday Life

Although there has been little change in public support for the death penalty as recorded in surveys, the long-term trend is toward fewer executions. Can you suggest reasons for this pattern?

Does punishment deter crime? Despite our extensive use of punishment, our society has a high rate of **criminal recidivism**, *later offenses by people previously convicted of crimes.* A government study reported that two-thirds of state prison inmates released from jail in 1994 were rearrested for a serious crime within three years. Other research tells us that about three-fourths of state prisoners have been incarcerated before (DeFina & Arvanites, 2002; Langan & Levin, 2002). So does punishment really deter crime? Fewer than one-half of all crimes are known to police, and of these, only about one in five results in an arrest. Most crimes, therefore, go unpunished, leading us to conclude, perhaps, that the old saying "crime doesn't pay" may not be entirely true.

Prisons provide short-term societal protection by keeping offenders off the streets, but they do little to reshape attitudes or behavior in the long term (Carlson, 1976; R. A. Wright, 1994). Perhaps rehabilitation is an unrealistic expectation, because according to Sutherland's theory of differential association, locking up criminals together for years probably strengthens criminal attitudes and skills. Imprisonment also breaks whatever social ties inmates may have in the outside world, which, following Hirschi's control theory, makes inmates likely to commit more crimes upon release.

─● **CHECK YOUR LEARNING** What are society's four justifications for punishment? Does sending offenders to prison accomplish each of them? How?

The Death Penalty

Perhaps the most controversial issue involving punishment is the death penalty. From 1993 through 2009, more than 3,500 people were sentenced to death in U.S. courts; 1,000 executions were carried out. In thirty-six states, the law allows the state to execute offenders convicted of very serious crimes such as first-degree murder. But while a majority of states do permit capital punishment, only a few states are likely to carry out executions. Across the United States, half of the 3,207 people on death row at the end of 2008 were in just four states: California, Texas, Florida, and Pennsylvania (U.S. Bureau of Justice Statistics, 2010).

Opponents of capital punishment point to research suggesting that the death penalty has limited value as a crime deterrent. Countries such as Canada, where the death penalty has been abolished, have not seen a rise in the number of murders. Critics also point out that the United States is the only Western, high-income nation that routinely executes offenders. As public concern about the death penalty has increased, the use of capital punishment declined from as many as ninety-eight executions in 1999 to thirty-seven in 2008 but rising again in 2009 to fifty-two.

To increase the power of punishment to deter crime, capital punishment was long carried out in public. Here is a photograph from the last public execution in the United States, with twenty-two-year-old Rainey Bethea standing on the scaffold moments from death in Owensboro, Kentucky, on August 16, 1937. Children as well as adults were in the crowd. Now that the mass media report the story of executions across the country, states carry out capital punishment behind closed doors.

Public opinion surveys reveal that the share of U.S. adults who claim to support the death penalty as a punishment for murder remains high (62 percent) and has been fairly stable over time (NORC, 2009:214). College students hold about the same attitudes as everyone else, with about two-thirds of first-year students expressing support for the death penalty (Pryor et al., 2008).

But judges, criminal prosecutors, and members of trial juries are less and less likely to call for the death penalty. One reason is that because the crime rate has come down in recent years, the public now has less fear of crime and is less interested in applying the most severe punishment.

A second reason is public concern that the death penalty may be applied unjustly. The analysis of DNA evidence—a recent advance—from old crime scenes has shown that many people were wrongly convicted of a crime. Across the country, between 1975 and 2010, at least 137 people who had been sentenced to death were released from death row after new DNA evidence demonstrated their innocence. Such findings were one reason that in 2000, the governor of Illinois stated that he could no longer support the death penalty, leading him to commute the death sentences of every person on that state's death row (S. Levine, 2003; Death Penalty Information Center, 2010).

○ Making the Grade

"Community-based corrections" refers to ways of dealing with offenders without sending them to prison.

A third reason for the decline in the use of the death penalty is that more states now permit judges and juries to sentence serious offenders to life in prison without the possibility of parole. Such punishment offers to protect society from dangerous criminals who can be "put away" forever without requiring an execution.

Fourth and finally, many states now shy away from capital punishment because of the high cost of prosecuting capital cases. Death penalty cases require more legal work and demand superior defense lawyers, often at public expense. In addition, such cases commonly include testimony by various paid "experts," including physicians and psychiatrists, which also runs up the costs of trial. Then there is the cost of many appeals that almost always follow a conviction leading to the sentence of death. When all these factors are put together, the cost of a death penalty case typically exceeds the cost of sending an offender to prison for life. So it is easy to see why states often choose not to seek the death penalty. One accounting, for example, reveals that the state of New Jersey has been spending more than $10 million a year prosecuting death penalty cases that have yet to result in a single execution (Thomas & Brant, 2007).

Organizations opposed to the death penalty are challenging this punishment in court. In 2008, for example, the U.S. Supreme Court upheld the use of lethal injection against the charge that this procedure amounts to cruel and unusual punishment, which would be unconstitutional. There is no indication at present that the United States will end the use of the death penalty. But the trend is away from this type of punishment.

Community-Based Corrections

Prison is at the center of our system of corrections. Prisons keep convicted criminals off the streets. The thought of prison probably deters many people from committing serious crime. But the evidence suggests that locking people up does little to rehabilitate most offenders. Further, prisons are expensive, costing more than $25,000 per year to support each inmate, in addition to the high cost of building the facilities.

A recent alternative to prison that has been adopted by many cities and states across the country is **community-based corrections,** *correctional programs operating within society at large rather than behind prison walls.* Community-based corrections have three main advantages: They reduce costs, they reduce overcrowding in prisons, and they allow for supervision of convicts while eliminating the hardships of prison life and the stigma that accompanies going to jail. In general, the idea of community-based corrections is not so much to punish as to reform; such programs are therefore usually offered to individuals who have committed less serious offenses and who appear to be good prospects for avoiding future criminal violations (Inciardi, 2000).

Probation

One form of community-based corrections is *probation,* a policy of permitting a convicted offender to remain in the community under conditions imposed by a court, including regular supervision. Courts may require that a probationer receive counseling, attend a drug treatment program, hold a job, avoid associating with "known criminals," or anything else a judge thinks is appropriate. Typically, a probationer must check in with an officer of the court (the probation officer) on a regular schedule to make sure the guidelines are being followed. Should the probationer fail to live up to the conditions set by the court or commit a new offense, the court may revoke probation and send the offender to jail.

Shock Probation

A related strategy is *shock probation,* a policy by which a judge orders a convicted offender to prison for a short time and then suspends the remainder of the sentence in favor of probation. Shock probation is thus a mix of prison and probation that is intended to impress on the offender the seriousness of the situation while still withholding full-scale imprisonment. In some cases, shock probation takes place in a special "boot camp" facility where offenders might spend up to three months in a military-style setting intended to teach discipline and respect for authority (Cole & Smith, 2002).

Parole

Parole is a policy of releasing inmates from prison to serve the remainder of their sentences in the local community under the supervision of a parole officer. Although courts may sometimes sentence an offender to prison without the possibility of parole, most other inmates become eligible for parole after serving a certain portion of their sentence. At this time, a parole board evaluates the risks and benefits of an inmate's early release from prison. If parole is granted, the parole board then monitors the offender's conduct until the sentence is completed. Should the offender not comply with the conditions of parole or be arrested for another crime, the board can revoke parole, returning the offender to prison to complete the original sentence.

○ **CRITICAL REVIEW** Evaluations of probation and parole have been mixed. There is little question that community-based programs are much less expensive than conventional imprisonment; they also free up room in prisons for people who commit more serious crimes. Yet research suggests that although probation and shock probation do seem to work for some people, they do not significantly reduce criminal recidivism. Similarly, parole is useful to prison officials as a means to encourage good behavior among prison inmates who hope for early release. Yet levels of crime among those released on parole are so high that

CONTROVERSY & DEBATE

Violent Crime Is Down—but Why?

DUANE: I'm a criminal justice major, and I want to be a police officer. Crime is a huge problem in America, and police are what keeps the crime rate low.

SANDY: I'm a sociology major. As for combating crime, I'm not sure it's quite that simple....

During the 1980s, crime rates shot upward. Just about everyone lived in fear of violent crime, and in many larger cities, the numbers of people killed and wounded made whole neighborhoods seem like war zones. There seemed to be no solution to the problem.

Yet in the 1990s, serious crime rates began to fall so that in recent years they have returned to levels not seen in more than a generation. Why? Researchers point to several reasons:

1. **A reduction in the youth population.** It was noted earlier that young people (particularly males) are responsible for much violent crime. Between 1990 and 2000, the share of the population aged fifteen to twenty-four dropped by about 5 percent (in part because of the legalization of abortion in 1973).

2. **Changes in policing.** Much of the drop in crime (like the earlier rise in crime) has taken place in large cities. In New York City, the number of murders fell from 2,245 in 1990 to 475 in 2009, the lowest figure since the city started keeping reliable records in 1963. Part of the reason for the decline is that the city adopted a policy of *community policing,* which means that police are concerned not just with making arrests but with preventing crime. Officers get to know the areas they patrol and frequently stop

young men for jaywalking or other minor infractions so they can check them for concealed weapons (the word is out that you can be arrested for carrying a gun). In addition, there are more police at work in large cities. For example, Los Angeles added more than 2,000 police in the 1990s, and it, too, saw its violent crime rate fall during that period.

3. **More prisoners.** Between 1985 and 2009, the number of inmates in U.S. prisons soared from 750,000 to 2.4 million. The main reason for this increase is tough new laws that demand prison time for many crimes, especially drug offenses. As one analyst put it, "When you lock up an extra million people, it's got to have some effect on the crime rate" (Franklin Zimring, quoted in Witkin, 1998:31).

4. **A better economy.** The U.S. economy boomed during the 1990s. With unemployment down, more people were working, reducing the likelihood that some would turn to

One reason that crime has gone down is that there are more than 2 million people incarcerated in this country. This has caused severe overcrowding of facilities such as this Maricopa County, Arizona, prison.

crime out of economic desperation. The logic here is simple: More jobs, fewer crimes. By the same token, the recent economic downturn has slowed the downward crime trend.

5. **The declining drug trade.** Many analysts think that the most important factor in reducing rates of violent crime is the decline of crack cocaine. Crack came on the scene around 1985, and violence spread, especially in the inner cities, as young people—facing few legitimate job opportunities and increasingly armed with guns—became part of a booming drug trade.

By the early 1990s, however, the popularity of crack had begun to fall as people saw the damage the drug was causing to entire communities. This realization, coupled with steady economic improvement and stiffer sentences for drug offenses, helped bring about the turnaround in violent crime.

The current picture looks better relative to what it was a decade or two ago. But one researcher cautions, "It looks better, but only because the early 1990s were so bad. So let's not fool ourselves into thinking everything is resolved. It's not."

WHAT DO YOU THINK?

1. Do you support the policy of community policing? Why or why not?

2. What do you see as the pros and cons of building more prisons?

3. Of all the factors mentioned here, which do you think is the most important in crime control? Which is least important? Why?

Sources: Winship & Berrien (1999), Donahue & Levitt (2000), Rosenfeld (2002), Liptak (2008), and C. Mitchell (2008).

a number of states have ended their parole programs entirely (Inciardi, 2000).

Such evaluations point to a sobering truth: By itself, the criminal justice system cannot eliminate crime. As the Controversy & Debate box explains, although police, courts, and pris-

ons do affect crime rates, crime and other deviance are not just the acts of "bad people" but reflect the operation of society itself.

CHECK YOUR LEARNING What are three types of community-based corrections? What are their advantages?

Seeing Sociology in Everyday Life

Why do most of us—at least most of the time—obey the rules?

As this chapter explains, every society is a system of social control that encourages conformity to certain norms and discourages deviance or norm breaking. One way society does this is through the construction of heroes and villains. Heroes, of course, are people we are supposed to look up to and use as role models. Villains are people whom we look down on and reject their example. Organizations of all types create heroes that serve as guides to everyday behavior. In each case below, who is being made into a hero? Why? What are the values or behaviors that we are encouraged to copy in our own lives?

> **HINT** A society without heroes and villains would be one in which no one cared how people think or act. Societies create heroes as role models that are supposed to inspire us to be more like them. Societies create heroes by emphasizing one aspect of someone's life and ignoring lots of other things. For example, Babe Ruth was a great ball player, but his private life was sometimes less than inspiring. Perhaps this is why the Catholic church never considers anyone a candidate for sainthood until after—usually long after—the person has died.

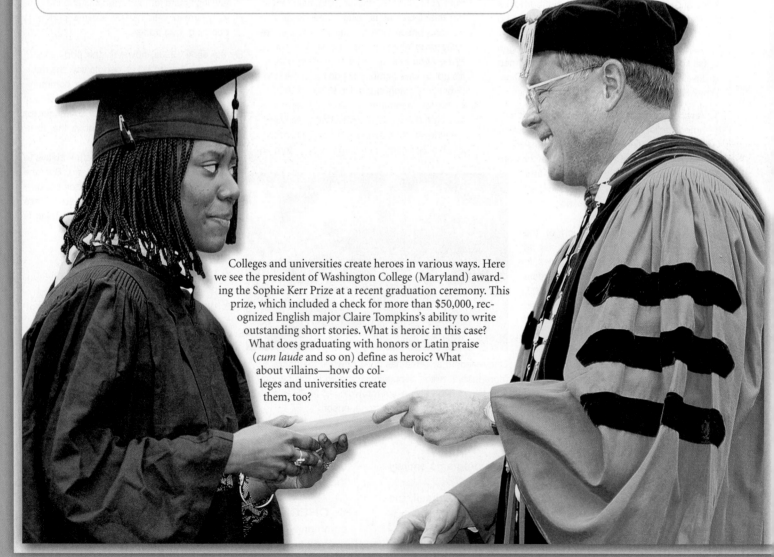

Colleges and universities create heroes in various ways. Here we see the president of Washington College (Maryland) awarding the Sophie Kerr Prize at a recent graduation ceremony. This prize, which included a check for more than $50,000, recognized English major Claire Tompkins's ability to write outstanding short stories. What is heroic in this case? What does graduating with honors or Latin praise (*cum laude* and so on) define as heroic? What about villains—how do colleges and universities create them, too?

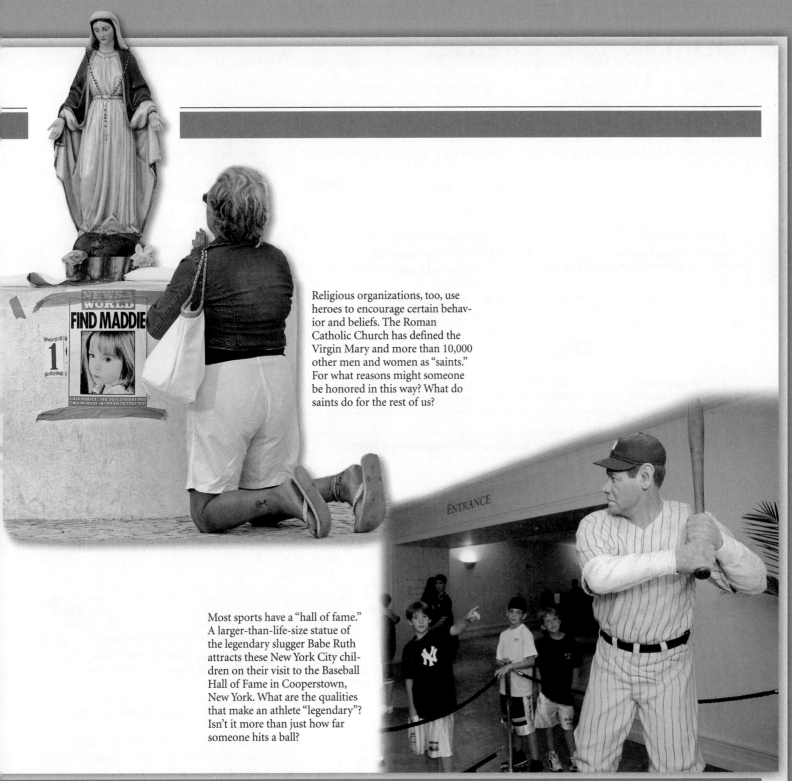

Religious organizations, too, use heroes to encourage certain behavior and beliefs. The Roman Catholic Church has defined the Virgin Mary and more than 10,000 other men and women as "saints." For what reasons might someone be honored in this way? What do saints do for the rest of us?

Most sports have a "hall of fame." A larger-than-life-size statue of the legendary slugger Babe Ruth attracts these New York City children on their visit to the Baseball Hall of Fame in Cooperstown, New York. What are the qualities that make an athlete "legendary"? Isn't it more than just how far someone hits a ball?

Applying SOCIOLOGY in Everyday Life

1. Do athletic teams, fraternities and sororities, and even people in a college classroom create heroes and villains? Explain how and why.

2. Identity theft is a new type of crime that victimizes as many as 10 million people each year in the United States. Research this phenomenon, and explain how this offense differs from property crime that takes place "on the street." (Consider differences in the crime, the offenders, and the victims.)

3. Watch an episode of a real-action police show such as *Cops*. Based on what you see, how would you profile the people who commit crimes?

Making the Grade

⊙ Watch on mysoclab.com

What Is Deviance?

DEVIANCE refers to norm violations ranging from minor infractions, such as bad manners, to major infractions, such as serious violence.

p. 172

deviance (p. 172) the recognized violation of cultural norms

crime (p. 172) the violation of a society's formally enacted criminal law

social control (p. 172) attempts by society to regulate people's thoughts and behavior

criminal justice system (p. 172) the organizations—police, courts, and prison officials—that respond to alleged violations of the law

Theories of Deviance

BIOLOGICAL THEORIES

- focus on individual abnormality
- explain human behavior as the result of biological instincts

Lombroso claimed criminals have apelike physical traits; later research links criminal behavior to certain body types and genetics.

pp. 172–73

PSYCHOLOGICAL THEORIES

- focus on individual abnormality
- see deviance as the result of "unsuccessful socialization"

Reckless and Dinitz's *containment theory* links delinquency to weak conscience.

pp. 173–74

✓ *Biological and psychological theories provide a limited understanding of crime and other deviance because most violations are carried out by people who are normal (pp. 173, 174).*

SOCIOLOGICAL THEORIES view all behavior—deviant as well as conforming—as products of society. Sociologists point out that

- what is deviant varies from place to place according to cultural norms
- behavior and individuals become deviant as others define them that way
- what and who a society defines as deviant reflect who has social power and who does not

pp. 174–75

Theoretical Analysis of Deviance

The Functions of Deviance: Structural-Functional Analysis

Durkheim claimed that deviance is a normal element of society that

- affirms cultural norms and values
- clarifies moral boundaries
- brings people together
- encourages social change

pp. 175–76

Merton's **strain theory** explains deviance in terms of a society's cultural goals and the means available to achieve them.

Deviant subcultures are discussed by Cloward and Ohlin, Cohen, Miller, and Anderson.

pp. 176–77

labeling theory (p. 178) the idea that deviance and conformity result not so much from what people do as from how others respond to those actions

stigma (p. 178) a powerfully negative label that greatly changes a person's self-concept and social identity

medicalization of deviance (p. 179) the transformation of moral and legal deviance into a medical condition

white-collar crime (p. 183) crime committed by people of high social position in the course of their occupations

corporate crime (p. 184) the illegal actions of a corporation or people acting on its behalf

organized crime (p. 184) a business supplying illegal goods or services

hate crime (p. 185) a criminal act against a person or a person's property by an offender motivated by racial or other bias

Labeling Theory: Symbolic-Interaction Analysis

Labeling theory claims that deviance depends less on what someone does than on how others react to that behavior. If people respond to primary deviance by stigmatizing a person, secondary deviance and a deviant career may result.

pp. 178–79

The **medicalization of deviance** is the transformation of moral and legal deviance into a medical condition. In practice, this means a change in labels, replacing "good" and "bad" with "sick" and "well."

pp. 179–81

Sutherland's **differential association theory** links deviance to how much others encourage or discourage such behavior.

p. 181

Hirschi's **control theory** states that imagining the possible consequences of deviance often discourages such behavior. People who are well integrated into society are less likely to engage in deviant behavior.

pp. 181–82

▤ *See the Applying Theory table on page 185.*

Deviance and Inequality: Social-Conflict Analysis

Based on Karl Marx's ideas, social-conflict theory holds that laws and other norms operate to protect the interests of powerful members of any society.

- **White-collar offenses** are committed by people of high social position as part of their jobs. Sutherland claimed such offenses are rarely prosecuted and are most likely to end up in civil rather than criminal court.
- **Corporate crime** refers to illegal actions by a corporation or people acting on its behalf. Although corporate crimes cause considerable public harm, most cases of corporate crime go unpunished.
- **Organized crime** has a long history in the United States, especially among categories of people with few legitimate opportunities.

pp. 182–84

Deviance, Race, and Gender

- What people consider deviant reflects the relative power and privilege of different categories of people.
- **Hate crimes** are crimes motivated by racial or other bias; they target people with disadvantages based on race, gender, or sexual orientation.
- In the United States and elsewhere, societies control the behavior of women more closely than that of men.

pp. 184–86

What Is Crime?

CRIME is the violation of criminal laws enacted by local, state, or federal governments. There are two major categories of serious crime:

- crimes against the person (violent crime), including murder, aggravated assault, forcible rape, and robbery
- crimes against property (property crime), including burglary, larceny-theft, auto theft, and arson

pp. 186–87

 Explore on mysoclab.com

PATTERNS OF CRIME IN THE UNITED STATES

- Official statistics show that arrest rates peak in late adolescence and drop steadily with advancing age.
- About 65% of people arrested for property crimes and 82% of people arrested for violent crimes are male.
- Street crime is more common among people of lower social position. Including white-collar and corporate crime makes class differences in criminality smaller.
- More whites than African Americans are arrested for street crimes. However, more African Americans are arrested than whites in relation to their population size. Asian Americans have a lower-than-average rate of arrest.
- By world standards, the U.S. crime rate is high.

pp. 187–91

crimes against the person (p. 187) crimes that direct violence or the threat of violence against others; also known as *violent crimes*

crimes against property (p. 187) crimes that involve theft of money or property belonging to others; also known as *property crimes*

victimless crimes (p. 187) violations of law in which there are no obvious victims

Read on mysoclab.com

The U.S. Criminal Justice System

Police

The police maintain public order by enforcing the law.

- Police use personal discretion in deciding whether and how to handle a situation.
- Research suggests that police are more likely to make an arrest if the offense is serious, if bystanders are present, or if the suspect is African American or Latino.

p. 192

Courts

Courts rely on an adversarial process in which attorneys—one representing the defendant and one representing the state—present their cases in the presence of a judge who monitors legal procedures.

- In practice, U.S. courts resolve most cases through plea bargaining. Though efficient, this method puts less powerful people at a disadvantage.

p. 193

Punishment

There are four justifications for punishment:

- retribution
- deterrence
- rehabilitation
- societal protection

pp. 193–95

See the Summing Up table on page 194.

The **death penalty** remains controversial in the United States, the only high-income Western nation that routinely executes serious offenders. The long-term trend is toward fewer executions.

p. 195

Community-based corrections include probation and parole. These programs lower the cost of supervising people convicted of crimes and reduce prison overcrowding but have not been shown to reduce recidivism.

pp. 196–97

plea bargaining (p. 193) a legal negotiation in which a prosecutor reduces a charge in exchange for a defendant's guilty plea

retribution (p. 193) an act of moral vengeance by which society makes the offender suffer as much as the suffering caused by the crime

deterrence (p. 193) the attempt to discourage criminality through the use of punishment

rehabilitation (p. 194) a program for reforming the offender to prevent later offenses

societal protection (p. 194) rendering an offender incapable of further offenses temporarily through imprisonment or permanently by execution

criminal recidivism (p. 195) later offenses by people previously convicted of crimes

community-based corrections (p. 196) correctional programs operating within society at large rather than behind prison walls

8 Social Stratification

- What is social stratification?

- Why does social inequality exist?

- How do social classes in the United States differ from one another?

Watch the *Core Concepts in Sociology* video "Social Class in the United States: Fact or Fiction?" on **mysoclab.com**

Chapter Overview

This chapter introduces the central concept of social stratification, which is important because our social standing affects almost everything about our lives. While making comparisons to other societies, the chapter surveys social stratification in the United States, identifying important measures of inequality and describing the U.S. class system.

On April 10, 1912, the ocean liner *Titanic* slipped away from the docks of Southampton, England, on its first voyage across the North Atlantic to New York. A proud symbol of the new industrial age, the towering ship carried 2,300 men, women, and children, some of them enjoying more luxury than most travelers today could imagine. Many poor immigrants crowded the lower decks, journeying to what they hoped would be a better life in the United States.

Two days out, the crew received reports of icebergs in the area but paid little notice. Then, near midnight, as the ship steamed swiftly westward, a stunned lookout reported a massive shape rising out of the dark ocean directly ahead. Moments later, the *Titanic* collided with a huge iceberg, as tall as the ship itself, that split open its side as if the grand vessel were a giant tin can.

Seawater flooded into the vessel's lower levels, pulling the ship down by the bow. Within twenty-five minutes of impact, people were rushing for the lifeboats. By 2:00 A.M., the bow was completely submerged, and the stern rose high above the water. Clinging to the deck, quietly observed by those in lifeboats, hundreds of helpless passengers and crew solemnly passed their final minutes before the ship disappeared into the frigid Atlantic (W. Lord, 1976).

The tragic loss of more than 1,600 lives made news around the world. Looking back on this terrible event with a sociological eye, we see that some categories of passengers had much better odds of survival than others. In keeping with that era's traditional ideas about gender, women and children boarded the lifeboats first, with the result that 80 percent of those who died were men. Class was also a factor in who survived and who did not. More than 60 percent of the passengers traveling on first-class tickets were saved because they were on the upper decks, where warnings were sounded first and lifeboats were accessible. Only 36 percent of the second-class passengers survived, and of the third-class passengers on the lower decks, only 24 percent escaped drowning. On board the *Titanic,* class meant more than the quality of accommodations; it was a matter of life or death.

The fate of the passengers on the *Titanic* dramatically illustrates how social inequality affects the way people live—and sometimes whether they live at all. This chapter explores the important concept of social stratification and examines social inequality in the United States.

What Is Social Stratification?

Every society is marked by inequality, with some people having more money, schooling, health, and power than others. **Social stratification,** defined as *a system by which a society ranks categories of people in a hierarchy,* is based on four important principles:

1. **Social stratification is a trait of society, not simply a reflection of individual differences.** Many of us think of social standing in terms of personal talent and effort, and as a result, we often exaggerate the extent to which we control our own fate. Did a higher percentage of the first-class passengers on the *Titanic* survive because they were better swimmers than second- and third-class passengers? No. They did better because of their privileged position on the ship. Similarly, children born into wealthy families are more likely than children born into poverty to enjoy good health, do well in school, succeed in a career, and live a long life. Neither the rich nor the poor are responsible for creating social stratification, yet this system shapes the lives of us all.

2. **Social stratification carries over from generation to generation.** We have only to look at how parents pass their social position on to their children to understand that stratification is a trait of societies rather than individuals. Some individuals, especially in industrial societies, do experience **social mobility,** *a change in position within the social hierarchy.* Social mobility may be upward or downward. We celebrate the achievements of rare individuals such as Christina Aguilera and Michael Jordan, who rose from modest beginnings to fame and fortune. Some people also move downward in the social hierarchy because of business setbacks, unemployment, or illness. More often people move *horizontally;* they switch one job for another

social stratification a system by which a society ranks categories of people in a hierarchy

social mobility a change in position within the social hierarchy

Seeing Sociology in Everyday Life

Are there elements of caste in U.S. society? To what extent do parents pass on their social position to children? What about the idea that there are "women's jobs" and "men's jobs"?

at about the same social level. The social standing of most people remains much the same over their lifetime.

3. **Social stratification is universal but variable.** Social stratification is found everywhere. Yet *what* is unequal and *how* unequal it is vary from one society to another. In some societies, inequality is mostly a matter of prestige; in others, wealth or power is the key element of difference. In addition, some societies contain more inequality than others.

4. **Social stratification involves not just inequality but beliefs as well.** Any system of inequality not only gives some people more than others but also defines these arrangements as fair. Like the *what* of social inequality, the explanations of *why* people should be unequal differ from society to society.

Caste and Class Systems

In rural India, the traditional caste system still shapes people's lives. This girl is a member of the "untouchables," a category below the four basic castes. She and her family are clothes washers, people who clean material "polluted" by blood or human waste. Such work is defined as unclean for people of higher caste position.

When comparing societies in terms of inequality, sociologists distinguish between *closed systems,* which allow little change in social position, and *open systems,* which permit much more social mobility. Closed systems are called *caste systems,* and more open systems are called *class systems.*

The Caste System

A **caste system** is *social stratification based on ascription, or birth.* A pure caste system is closed because birth alone determines a person's entire future, with little or no social mobility based on individual effort. People live out their lives in the rigid categories into which they were born, without the possibility for change for the better or worse.

An Illustration: India

Many of the world's agrarian societies are caste systems. Although India's economy is growing rapidly, much of the population still lives in traditional villages, where the caste system is part of everyday life. The traditional Indian system includes four major castes (or *varnas,* from a Sanskrit word that means "color"): Brahmin, Kshatriya, Vaishya, and Sudra. On the local level, however, each of these is composed of hundreds of subcaste groups (*jatis*).

From birth, caste position determines the direction of a person's life. First, with the exception of farming, which is open to everyone, families in each caste perform one type of work, as priests, soldiers, barbers, leather workers, sweepers, and so on.

Second, a caste system demands that people marry others of the same ranking. If people were to have "mixed" marriages with members of other castes, what rank would their children hold? Sociologists call this pattern of marrying within a social category *endogamous* marriage (*endo-* stems from the Greek word for "within"). According to tradition—this practice is now rare and found only in remote rural areas—Indian parents select their children's marriage partners, often before the children reach their teens.

Third, caste guides everyday life by keeping people in the company of "their own kind." Norms reinforce this practice by teaching, for instance, that a "purer" person of a higher caste position is "polluted" by contact with someone of lower standing.

Fourth, caste systems rest on powerful cultural beliefs. Indian culture is built on the Hindu tradition that doing the caste's life work and accepting an arranged marriage are moral duties.

Caste and Agrarian Life

Caste systems are typical of agrarian societies because agriculture demands a lifelong routine of hard work. By teaching a sense of moral duty, a caste system ensures that people are disciplined for a lifetime of work and are willing to perform the same jobs as their parents.

caste system (p. 205) social stratification based on ascription, or birth

class system social stratification based on both birth and individual achievement

meritocracy social stratification based on personal merit

Thus the caste system has hung on in rural India more than seventy years after being formally outlawed. People living in the industrial cities of India have many more choices about work and marriage partners than people in rural areas.

Another country dominated by caste is South Africa, although the racial system of *apartheid* is no longer legal and now in decline. The Thinking Globally box takes a closer look.

The Class System

Because a modern economy must attract people to work in many occupations other than farming, it depends on developing people's talents in diverse fields. This process of schooling and specialization gives rise to a **class system,** *social stratification based on both birth and individual achievement.*

Class systems are more open than caste systems, so people who gain schooling and skills may experience social mobility. As a result, class distinctions become blurred, and even blood relatives may have different social standings. Categorizing people according to their color, sex, or social background comes to be seen as wrong in modern societies as all people gain political rights and, in principle, equal standing before the law. In addition, work is no longer fixed at birth but involves some personal choice. Greater individuality also translates into more personal freedom in the process of selecting a marital partner.

Meritocracy

The concept of **meritocracy** refers to *social stratification based on personal merit.* Because industrial societies need to develop a broad range of abilities beyond farming, stratification is based not just on the accident of birth but also on *merit* (from a Latin word meaning "earned"), which includes a person's knowledge, abilities, and effort. A rough measure of merit is the importance of a person's job and how well it is done. To increase meritocracy, industrial societies expand equality of opportunity and teach people to expect unequal rewards based on individual performance.

In a pure meritocracy, which has never existed, social position would depend entirely on a person's ability and effort. Such a system would have ongoing social mobility, blurring social categories as individuals continuously move up or down in the system, depending on their latest performance.

Caste societies define merit in different terms, emphasizing loyalty to the system—that is, dutifully performing whatever job comes with the social position a person has at birth. Because they assign jobs before anyone can know anything about a person's talents or interests, caste systems waste human potential. On the other hand, because caste systems clearly assign everyone a "place" in society and a specific type of work, they are very orderly. A need for some amount of order is the reason that even industrial and postindustrial societies keep some elements of caste—such as letting wealth pass from

generation to generation—rather than becoming complete meritocracies. A pure meritocracy, with individuals moving up and down the social ranking all the time, would pull apart families and other social groupings. After all, economic performance is not everything: Would we want to evaluate our family members solely on how successful they are in their jobs outside of the home? Probably not. Class systems in industrial societies move toward meritocracy to promote productivity and efficiency; but at the same time, they keep caste elements, such as family, to maintain order and social unity.

Status Consistency

Status consistency is *the degree of uniformity in a person's social standing across various dimensions of social inequality.* A caste system has little social mobility and high status consistency, so the typical person has the same relative standing with regard to wealth, power, and prestige as everyone else in the same caste. However, the greater mobility of class systems produces less status consistency. In the United States, most college professors with advanced degrees enjoy high social prestige but earn only modest incomes. Low status consistency means that it is much harder to define people's social position. Therefore, *classes* are much harder to define than *castes.*

Caste and Class: The United Kingdom

The mix of meritocracy and caste in class systems is well illustrated by the United Kingdom (Great Britain—composed of England, Wales, and Scotland—and Northern Ireland), an industrial nation with a long agrarian history.

Aristocratic England

In the Middle Ages, England had a system of aristocracy that resembled a caste. The aristocracy included the leading members of the church, who were thought to speak with the authority of God. Some clergy were local priests, who were not members of the aristocracy and who lived simple lives. But the highest church officials lived in palaces and presided over an organization that owned much land, which was the major source of wealth. Church leaders, who were typically referred to as the *first estate* in France and other European countries, also had a great deal of power to shape the political events of the day.

The rest of the aristocracy, which in France and other European countries was called the *second estate,* was a hereditary nobility that made up barely 5 percent of the population. The royal family—the king and queen at the top of the power structure—as well as lesser nobles (including several hundred families headed by men titled as dukes, earls, and barons) together owned most of the nation's land. Most of the men and women within the aristocracy were wealthy due to their land, and they had many servants for their homes as well as ordinary farmers to work their fields. With all their work done for

How much of your social position is due to merit (personal ability and effort), and how much is due to caste (passed on from your parents)?

status consistency the degree of uniformity in a person's social standing across various dimensions of social inequality

---

THINKING GLOBALLY

Race as Caste: A Report from South Africa

JEROME: I've been reading about racial caste in South Africa. I'm glad that's over.

REGGIE: But racial inequality is far from over. . . .

At the southern tip of the African continent lies South Africa, a country about the size of Alaska with a population of about 50 million. For 300 years, the native Africans who lived there were ruled by white people, first by the Dutch traders and farmers who settled there in the mid-seventeenth century and then by the British, who colonized the area early in the nineteenth century. By the early 1900s, the British had taken over the entire country, naming it the Union of South Africa.

In 1961, the nation declared its independence from Britain, calling itself the Republic of South Africa, but freedom for the black majority was still decades away. To ensure their political control over the black population, whites instituted the policy of *apartheid,* or racial separation. Apartheid, written into law in 1948, denied blacks national citizenship, ownership of land, and any voice in the nation's government. As a lower caste, blacks received little schooling and performed menial, low-paying jobs. White people with even average wealth had at least one black household servant.

The members of the white minority claimed that apartheid protected their cultural traditions from the influence of people they considered inferior. When blacks resisted apartheid, whites used brutal military repression to maintain their power. Even so, steady resistance—especially from younger blacks, who demanded a political voice and economic opportunity—gradually forced the country to change. Criticism from other industrial nations added to the pressure. By the mid-1980s, the tide began to turn as the South African government granted limited political rights to people of mixed race and Asian ancestry. Next came the right of all people to form labor unions, to enter occupations once limited to whites, and to own property. Officials also repealed apartheid laws that separated the races in public places.

The pace of change increased in 1990 with the release from prison of Nelson Mandela, who led the fight against apartheid. In 1994, the first national election open to all races made Mandela president, ending centuries of white minority rule.

Despite this dramatic political change, social stratification in South Africa is still based on race. Even with the right to own property, one-fourth of black South Africans have no work, and half the population lives below the poverty line. The worst off are some 7 million *ukuhleleleka,* which means "marginal people" in the Xhosa language. Soweto-by-the-Sea may sound like a summer getaway, but it is a shantytown, home to hundreds of thousands of people crammed into shacks made of packing cases, corrugated metal, cardboard, and other discarded materials. Recent years have seen some signs of prosperity. But for most families, there is no electricity for lights or refrigeration. Without plumbing, the majority of people use buckets to haul sewage. The community's women line up to take a turn at various water taps that each serves more than 1,000 people. Jobs are hard to come by, and those who do find work are lucky to earn $250 a month.

South Africa's current president, Jacob Zuma, who was elected in 2009, leads a nation still crippled by its history of racial caste. Tourism is up and holds the promise of an economic boom in years to come, but the country can break from the past only by providing real opportunity to all its people.

WHAT DO YOU THINK?

1. How has race been a form of caste in South Africa?

2. Although apartheid is no longer law, why does racial inequality continue to shape South African society?

3. Does race operate as an element of caste in the United States? Explain your answer.

Sources: Mabry & Masland (1999), Murphy (2002), and Perry (2009).

---

them by others, members of the aristocracy had no occupation and thought that engaging in any work for income was beneath them. They used their time to develop skills in horseback riding and warfare and to cultivate refined tastes in art, music, and literature.

To prevent their vast landholdings from being divided by heirs when they died, aristocrats devised the law of *primogeniture* (from the Latin meaning "firstborn"), which required that all property pass to the oldest son or other male relation. Younger sons had to find other means of support. Some of these men became leaders in the church, where they would live as well as they were used to, and helped tie together the church and the state by having members of the same families running both. Other younger sons within the aristocracy became military officers or judges or took up other professions considered honorable for gentlemen. In an age when no woman

● Seeing Sociology
in Everyday Life

Are there any aristocratic elements of U.S. society? What are they?

● Seeing Sociology
in Everyday Life

What do the distinctive accents in the speech of people in
poor rural areas or poor inner cities in the United States say
about their social history?

One of the major events of the twentieth century was the socialist revolution in Russia,
which led to the creation of the Soviet Union. Following the ideas of Karl Marx, the
popular uprising overthrew a feudal aristocracy, as depicted in the 1920 painting
Bolshevik by Boris Mikhailovich Kustodiev.

could inherit her father's property and few women had the opportunity to earn a living on their own, a noble daughter depended for
her security on marrying well.

Below the high clergy and the rest of the aristocracy, the vast
majority of men and women were called *commoners* or, in France and
other European countries, the *third estate.* Most commoners were serfs
working land owned by nobles or the church. Unlike members of the
aristocracy, most commoners had little schooling and were illiterate.

As the Industrial Revolution expanded England's economy, some
commoners living in cities made enough money to challenge the
nobility. More emphasis on meritocracy, the growing importance of
money, and the expansion of schooling and legal rights eventually
blurred the differences between aristocrats and commoners and gave
rise to a class system.

Perhaps it is a sign of the times that these days, traditional titles
are put up for sale by aristocrats who need money. In 1996, for example, Earl Spencer—the brother of Princess Diana—sold one of his
titles, Lord of Wimbledon, to raise the $300,000 he needed to redo
the plumbing in one of his large homes (McKee, 1996).

The United Kingdom Today

The United Kingdom has a class system today, but caste elements
of the past are still evident. A small number of British families still

hold considerable inherited wealth and enjoy high prestige,
schooling at excellent universities, and substantial political
influence. A traditional monarch, Queen Elizabeth II, is the
United Kingdom's head of state, and Parliament's House of
Lords is composed of "peers," about half of whom are of
noble birth. However, control of government has passed to
the House of Commons, where the prime minister and other
ministers typically reach their positions by achievement—
winning an election—rather than by birth.

Lower in the class hierarchy, roughly one-fourth of the
British people fall into the middle class. Some earn comfortable incomes from professions and businesses and are
likely to have investments in the form of stocks and bonds.
Below the middle class, perhaps half of all Britons consider
themselves "working-class," earning modest incomes
through manual labor. The remaining one-fourth of the
British people make up the lower class, the poor who lack
steady work or who work full time but are paid too little to
live comfortably. Most lower-class Britons live in the
nation's northern and western regions, which have been
plagued by closings of mines and factories.

The British mix of caste elements and meritocracy has
produced a highly stratified society with some opportunity to move upward or downward, much the same as exists
in the United States (Long & Ferrie, 2007). Historically,
British society has been somewhat more castelike than is the case in
the United States, a fact reflected in the importance attached to lin-
guistic accent. Distinctive patterns of speech develop when people
are set off from one another over several generations. People in the
United States treat accent as a clue to where a person lives or grew
up (we can easily identify a midwestern "twang" or a southern
"drawl"). In the United Kingdom, however, accent is more a mark
of social class (upper-class people speak "the King's English," but
most people speak "like commoners"). So different are these two
accents that the British seem to be, as the saying goes, "a single people divided by a common language."

Classless Societies? The Former Soviet Union

Nowhere in the world do we find a society without some degree of
social inequality. Yet some nations have claimed to be classless.

The Russian Revolution

The Union of Soviet Socialist Republics (USSR), which rivaled the
United States as a military superpower in the mid- to late twentieth
century, was born out of a revolution in Russia in 1917. The Russian
Revolution ended the feudal estate system ruled by a hereditary

structural social mobility a shift in the social position of large numbers of people due more to changes in society itself than to individual efforts

nobility and transferred most farms, factories, and other productive property from private ownership to state control. Following the lead of Karl Marx, who believed that private ownership of property was the source of social stratification, Soviet leaders boasted of becoming a classless society.

Critics, however, pointed out that based on their jobs, the Soviet people were actually stratified into four unequal categories. At the top were high government officials, known as *apparatchiks*. Next came the Soviet intelligentsia, including lower government officials, college professors, scientists, physicians, and engineers. Below them were manual workers and, at the lowest level, the rural peasantry.

In reality, the Soviet Union was not classless at all, and political power was concentrated in only a small percentage of the population. But putting factories, farms, colleges, and hospitals under state control did create greater economic equality (although with sharp differences in power) than in capitalist societies such as the United States.

The Modern Russian Federation

In 1985, Mikhail Gorbachev came to power with a new economic program known as *perestroika* ("restructuring"). Gorbachev saw that although the Soviet system had significantly reduced economic inequality, overall living standards lagged far behind those of other industrial nations. Gorbachev tried to generate economic growth by reducing the centralized control of the economy, which had proved to be inefficient.

Gorbachev's economic reforms turned into one of the most dramatic social movements in history. People throughout Eastern Europe blamed their poverty and lack of basic freedoms on the repressive ruling class of Communist party officials. Beginning in 1989, people throughout Eastern Europe toppled their socialist governments, and in 1991, the Soviet Union itself collapsed, with its largest republic remaking itself as the Russian Federation.

The Soviet Union's story shows that social inequality involves more than economic resources. Soviet society may not have had the extremes of wealth and poverty found in the United Kingdom and the United States. But an elite class existed all the same, based on political power rather than wealth.

What about social mobility in so-called classless societies? In the twentieth century, there was as much upward social mobility in the Soviet Union as in the United Kingdom or the United States. Rapidly expanding industry and government drew many poor rural peasants into factories and offices. This trend illustrates what sociologists call **structural social mobility,** *a shift in the social position of large numbers of people due more to changes in society itself than to individual efforts.*

November 24, Odessa, Ukraine. The first snow of our voyage flies over the decks as our ship docks at Odessa, the former Soviet Union's southern port on the Black Sea. Not far from the dock, we gaze up at the Potemkin Steps, the steep stairway up to the city, where the first shots of the Russian Revolution rang out. It has been six years since our last visit, and much has changed; indeed, the Soviet Union itself has collapsed. Has life improved? For some people, certainly. There are now chic boutiques in which well-dressed shoppers buy fine wines, designer clothes, and imported perfumes. Outside, shiny new Volvos, Mercedeses, and even a few Cadillacs stand out against the small Ladas from the "old days." But for most people, life seems much worse. Flea markets line the curbs as families sell their home furnishings. When meat sells for $4 a pound and the average person earns about $30 a month, people become desperate. Even the city has to save money by turning off streetlights after 8:00 P.M. The spirits of most people seem as dim as Odessa's streets.

During the 1990s, structural social mobility in the Russian Federation turned downward as that country experienced something similar to the Great Depression of the 1930s in the United States. One indicator is that the average life span for men dropped by eight years and for women by two years. Many factors contributed to this decline, including Russia's poor health care system, but the Russian people clearly have suffered in the turbulent period of economic change that began in 1991 (Bohlen, 1998; Gerber & Hout, 1998; Mason, 2004).

The hope was that in the long run, closing inefficient state industries would improve the nation's economic performance. The economy has expanded, but living standards have fallen and millions of Russians face hard times. The few people who made huge fortunes have seen much of their new wealth vanish in the recent recession. This fact, along with more government control over the Russian economy, has caused economic inequality to decline. At the same time, however, many people wonder what a return to a more socialist society will mean for their living standards and political freedoms (Zuckerman, 2006; Wendle, 2009).

China: Emerging Social Classes

Sweeping political and economic change has affected not just the Russian Federation but also the People's Republic of China. After the Communist revolution in 1949, the state took control of all farms, factories, and other productive property. Communist party leader Mao Zedong declared all work to be equally important, so officially, social classes no longer existed.

Seeing Sociology in Everyday Life

A statement like "People get what they deserve" is an example of ideology that supports our market-based economy. Can you think of other common examples of ideology?

ideology cultural beliefs that justify particular social arrangements, including patterns of inequality

Davis-Moore thesis the functional analysis claiming that social stratification has beneficial consequences for the operation of society

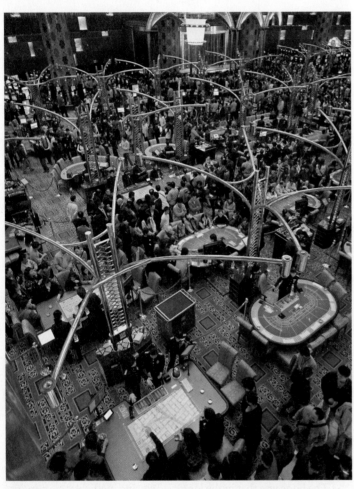

By allowing a market economy to expand, especially in the coastal regions, China has experienced remarkable economic growth. The gambling industry in Macao now rivals that of Las Vegas.

The new program greatly reduced economic inequality. But as in the Soviet Union, social differences remained. The country was ruled by a political elite with enormous power and considerable privilege; below them were managers of large factories and skilled professionals; next came industrial workers; at the bottom were rural peasants, who were not even allowed to leave their villages to migrate to cities.

Further economic change came in 1978, when Mao died and Deng Xiaoping became China's leader. The state gradually loosened its hold on the economy, allowing a new class of business owners to emerge. Communist party leaders remain in control of the country, and some have prospered as they have joined the ranks of the small but wealthy elite who control new, privately run industries. China's

economy has experienced rapid growth, and the nation has now moved into the middle-income category. Much of this new prosperity has been concentrated in coastal areas where living standards have soared far above those in China's rural interior.

Since the late 1990s, the booming cities along China's coast have become home to many thousands of people made rich by the expanding economy. In addition, these cities have attracted more than 100 million young migrants from rural areas in search of better jobs and a better life. Many more have wanted to move to the booming cities, but the government still restricts movement, which has the effect of slowing upward social mobility. For those who have been able to move, the jobs that are available are generally better than the work that people knew before. But many of these new jobs are dangerous, and most pay wages that barely meet the higher costs of living in the city, so the majority of the migrants remain poor. To make matters worse, the weakening global economy has caused many Chinese factories to lay off workers or even to shut down. As a result, beginning in 2008, some people began to migrate from cities back to the countryside—a case of downward social mobility (Atlas, 2007; Wu & Treiman, 2007; Chang, 2008; Powell, 2008).

A new category in China's social hierarchy consists of the *hai gui*, a term derived from words meaning "returned from overseas" or "sea turtles." The ranks of the "sea turtles" are increasing by tens of thousands each year as young men and women return from educations in other countries, in many cases from college and university campuses in the United States. These young people, most of whom were from privileged families to begin with, typically return to China to find many opportunities and soon become very influential (Liu & Hewitt, 2008).

In China, a new class system is emerging, a mix of the old political hierarchy and a new business hierarchy. Economic inequality in China has increased as members of the new business elite have become millionaires and even billionaires; as Figure 8–1 shows, it is now as great as in the United States. With so much change in China, patterns of social stratification are likely to remain in flux for some time to come (Bian, 2002; Kuhn, 2007).

Ideology: The Power behind Stratification

How do societies persist without sharing their resources more equally? The highly stratified British aristocracy lasted for centuries, and for 2,000 years people in India accepted the idea that they should be privileged or poor based on the accident of birth.

A major reason that social hierarchies endure is **ideology,** *cultural beliefs that justify particular social arrangements, including patterns of inequality.* A belief—for example, the idea that the rich are smart and the poor are lazy—is ideological to the extent that it supports inequality by defining it as fair.

○ Making the Grade

The Davis-Moore thesis does not endorse any level or type of social stratification. It simply states that societies devise some system of unequal rewards to enhance efficient productivity.

Plato and Marx on Ideology

According to the ancient Greek philosopher Plato (427–347 B.C.E.), every culture considers some type of inequality fair. Although Karl Marx understood this, he was far more critical of inequality than Plato. Marx criticized capitalist societies for defending wealth and power in the hands of a few as a "law of the marketplace." Capitalist law, he continued, defines the right to own property, which encourages money to remain within the same families from one generation to the next. In short, Marx concluded, culture and institutions combine to support a society's elite, which is why established hierarchies last such a long time.

Historical Patterns of Ideology

Ideology changes along with a society's economy and technology. Because agrarian societies depend on most of their people performing a lifetime of labor, they develop caste systems that make carrying out the duties of a person's social position or "station" a moral responsibility. With the rise of industrial capitalism, an ideology of meritocracy arises, defining wealth and power as prizes to be won by the individuals who perform the best. This change means that the poor—often given charity under feudalism—are looked down on as personally undeserving. This harsh view is linked to the ideas of Herbert Spencer, as explained in the Thinking About Diversity box on page 212.

History shows how difficult it is to change social stratification. However, challenges to the status quo always arise. Traditional ideas about "a woman's place," for example, have given way to economic opportunity for women in societies today. The continuing progress toward racial equality in South Africa is another case of widespread rejection of the ideology of apartheid.

The Functions of Social Stratification

Why does social stratification exist at all? According to the structural-functional approach, social stratification plays a vital part in the operation of society. This argument was presented many years ago by Kingsley Davis and Wilbert Moore (1945).

The Davis-Moore Thesis

The **Davis-Moore thesis** states that *social stratification has beneficial consequences for the operation of a society.* How else, ask Davis and Moore, can we explain the fact that some form of social stratification has been found in every society?

Davis and Moore note that modern societies have hundreds of occupational positions of varying importance. Certain jobs—say, washing cars or answering a telephone—are fairly easy and can be

Driving to work in São Paulo, Brazil, Fabio Campos passes both gated mansions of the very rich and rundown shacks of the very poor.

On her way to work in Stockholm, Sweden, Sylvia Arnbjörg passes through mostly middle-class neighborhoods.

Global Snapshot

FIGURE 8–1 **Economic Inequality in Selected Countries, 2008**

Many low- and middle-income countries have greater economic inequality than the United States. But this country has more economic inequality than most high-income nations.

These data are the most recent available, representing income share for various years between 1998 and 2008.

Sources: U.S. Census Bureau (2009) and World Bank (2010).

performed by almost anyone. Other jobs—such as designing a new generation of computers or transplanting human organs—are very difficult and demand the scarce talents of people with extensive and expensive training.

Therefore, Davis and Moore explain, the greater the functional importance of a position, the more rewards a society attaches to it. This strategy promotes productivity and efficiency because rewarding important work with income, prestige, power, or leisure encourages people to do these things and to work better, longer, and harder. In short, unequal rewards (which is what social stratification is) benefit society as a whole.

Davis and Moore claim that any society could be egalitarian, but only to the extent that people are willing to let *anyone* perform *any* job. Equality also demands that someone who performs a job poorly be rewarded just as much as someone who performs the job well. Such a system clearly offers little incentive for people to try their best, reducing the society's productive efficiency.

The Davis-Moore thesis suggests the reason stratification exists; it does not state precisely what rewards a society should give to any

● Making the Grade

Stratification systems produce ideas and beliefs that define their operation as just. In short, stratification involves not just who has what but also beliefs about justice—why people should have what they have.

● Seeing Sociology in Everyday Life

Following Davis and Moore's thinking, why do professors give grades from A to F? What would happen if they gave every student the same grade? Explain.

THINKING ABOUT DIVERSITY: RACE, CLASS, & GENDER

The Meaning of Class: Is Getting Rich "the Survival of the Fittest"?

JAKE: "My dad is amazing. He's really smart!"
FRANK: "You mean he's rich. He owns I don't know how many businesses."
JAKE: "Do you think people get rich without being smart?"

It's a question we all wonder about. How much is our social position a matter of intelligence? What about hard work? Being born to the "right family"? Even "dumb luck"?

More than in most societies, in the United States we link social standing to personal abilities including intelligence. This idea goes back a long time. We have all heard the words "the survival of the fittest," which describes our society as a competitive jungle in which the "best" survive and the rest fall behind. The phrase was coined by one of sociology's pioneers, Herbert Spencer (1820–1903), whose ideas about social inequality are still widespread today.

Spencer, who lived in England, eagerly followed the work of the natural scientist Charles Darwin (1809–1882). Darwin's theory of biological evolution held that a species changes phys-

ically over many generations as it adapts to the natural environment. Spencer incorrectly applied Darwin's theory to the operation of society, which does not operate according to biological principles. In Spencer's distorted view, society became the "jungle," with the "fittest" people rising to wealth and the "failures" sinking into miserable poverty.

As wrong as they were, it is no surprise that Spencer's views were popular among the rising U.S. industrialists of the day. John D. Rockefeller (1839–1937), who made a vast fortune building the oil industry, recited Spencer's "social gospel" to young children in Sunday school. As Rockefeller saw it, the growth of giant corporations—and the astounding wealth of their owners—was merely the result of the survival of the fittest, a basic fact of nature. Neither Spencer nor Rockefeller had much sympathy for the poor, seeing poverty as evidence of individuals' failing to measure up in a competitive world. Spencer opposed social welfare programs because he thought they penalized society's "best" people (through taxes) and

rewarded its "worst" members (through welfare benefits). By incorrectly using Darwin's theory, the rich could turn their backs on everyone else, assuming that inequality was inevitable and somehow "natural."

Today, sociologists point out that our society is far from a meritocracy, as Spencer claimed. And it is not the case that companies or individuals who generate lots of money necessarily benefit society. The people who made hundreds of millions of dollars selling subprime mortgages in recent years certainly ended up hurting just about everyone. But Spencer's view that the "fittest" rise to the top remains widespread in our very unequal and individualistic culture.

WHAT DO YOU THINK?

1. How much do you think inequality in our society can correctly be described as "the survival of the fittest"? Why?

2. Why do you think Spencer's ideas are still popular in the United States today?

3. Is how much you earn a good measure of your importance to society? Why or why not?

occupational position or how unequal rewards should be. It merely points out that positions a society considers crucial must offer enough rewards to draw talented people away from less important work.

○ **CRITICAL REVIEW** Although the Davis-Moore thesis is an important contribution to understanding social stratification, it has provoked criticism. Melvin Tumin (1953) wondered, first of all, how we assess the importance of a particular occupation. Perhaps the high rewards our society gives to physicians result partly from deliberate efforts by medical schools to limit the supply of physicians and thereby increase the demand for their services.

Furthermore, do rewards actually reflect the contribution someone makes to society? With income of about $275 million per year, Oprah Winfrey earns more in one day than the president of the United States earns all year. Would anyone argue that hosting a talk show is more important than leading a country? And what about members of the U.S. military serving in Iraq or Afghanistan? Although they face the daily risk of combat, a new

private first class in the United States Army earned a base salary of $20,500 in 2010 (Defense Finance and Accounting Service, 2010). And what about the heads of the big Wall Street financial firms that collapsed in 2008? It seems reasonable to conclude that these corporate leaders made some bad decisions, yet their salaries were astronomical. Even after finishing its worst year ever, with losses of $27 billion, Merrill Lynch paid bonuses of more than $1 million to each of more than 700 employees (Fox, 2009). The top people in the financial industry made out even better. In 2007, James Dimon, head of JPMorganChase, had earnings of more than $55 million; the same year, Lloyd Blankfein, head of Goldman Sachs, made more than $70 million—an amount it would take a typical U.S. Army private more than 3,000 years to earn. Do corporate executives deserve such megasalaries for their contributions to society?

Second, Tumin claimed that Davis and Moore ignore how the caste elements of social stratification can *prevent* the development of individual talent. Born to privilege, rich children have

○ Seeing Sociology
in Everyday Life

Have you ever had a job that caused you to experience the alienation that concerned Karl Marx? Explain.

opportunities to develop their abilities, which is something many gifted poor children never have.

Third, living in a society that places so much importance on money, we tend to overestimate the importance of high-paying work; how do stockbrokers or people who trade international currencies really contribute to society? For the same reason, it is difficult for us to see the importance of work not oriented toward making money, such as parenting, creative writing, playing in a symphony, or just being a good friend to someone in need (Packard, 2002).

Finally, by suggesting that social stratification benefits all of society, the Davis-Moore thesis ignores how social inequality promotes conflict and can even provoke revolution. This criticism leads to the social-conflict approach, which provides a very different explanation for social inequality.

○ **CHECK YOUR LEARNING** State the Davis-Moore thesis in your own words. What are Tumin's criticisms of this thesis?

Stratification and Conflict

Social-conflict analysis argues that rather than benefiting society as a whole, social stratification benefits some people and disadvantages others. This analysis draws heavily on the ideas of Karl Marx, with contributions from Max Weber.

Karl Marx: Class Conflict

As Marx saw it, the Industrial Revolution promised humanity a society free from want. Yet during Marx's lifetime, the capitalist economy had done little to improve the lives of most people. Marx set out to explain a glaring contradiction: how, in a society so rich, so many could be so poor.

In Marx's view, social stratification is rooted in people's relationship to the means of production. People either own productive property (such as factories and businesses) or sell their labor to others. In feudal Europe, the aristocracy and the church owned the productive land; the peasants toiled as farmers. Under industrial capitalism, the aristocracy was replaced by **capitalists** (sometimes called the *bourgeoisie,* a French word meaning "town dwellers"), *people who own and*

Oprah Winfrey consistently earns more than $200 million a year and enjoys fame to match her fortune. Guided by the Davis-Moore thesis, why would societies reward some people so much more than others? How would Karl Marx answer this question differently?

operate factories and other businesses in pursuit of profits. Peasants became the **proletarians,** *people who sell their labor for wages.* Capitalists and proletarians have opposing interests and are separated by a vast gulf of wealth and power, making class conflict inevitable.

Marx lived during the nineteenth century, a time when a small number of industrialists in the United States were amassing great fortunes. Andrew Carnegie, J. P. Morgan, and John Jacob Astor (one of the few rich passengers to drown on the *Titanic*) lived in fabulous mansions that were filled with priceless works of art and staffed by dozens of servants. Even by today's standards, their incomes were staggering. For example, Carnegie earned more than $20 million in 1900 (roughly $530 million in today's dollars), when the average worker earned roughly $500 a year (Baltzell, 1964; Williamson, 2010).

In time, Marx believed, the working majority would overthrow the capitalists once and for all. Capitalism would bring about its own downfall, Marx reasoned, because it makes workers poorer and poorer and gives them little control over what they make or how they make it. Under capitalism, work produces only **alienation,** *the experience of isolation and misery resulting from powerlessness.*

To replace capitalism, Marx imagined a *socialist* system that would meet the needs of all rather than just the needs of the elite few: "The proletarians have nothing to lose but their chains. They have a world to win" (Marx & Engels, 1972:362, orig. 1848).

○ **CRITICAL REVIEW** Marx has had enormous influence on sociological thinking. But his revolutionary ideas, calling for the overthrow of capitalist society, also make his work highly controversial.

One of the strongest criticisms of the Marxist approach is that it ignores a central idea of the Davis-Moore thesis: that a system of unequal rewards is needed to place people in the right jobs and to motivate people to work hard. Marx separated reward from performance; his egalitarian ideal was based on the principle "from each according to ability, to each according to need" (Marx & Engels, 1972:388, orig. 1848). However, failure to reward individual performance may be precisely what caused the low productivity of the former Soviet Union and other socialist economies around the world. Defenders respond to such criticism by asking why we assume that humanity is inherently selfish rather than social; individual rewards are not the only way to motivate people to perform their social roles (M. S. Clark, 1991).

A second problem is that the revolutionary change Marx predicted has failed to happen, at least in advanced capitalist societies. The next section explains why.

blue-collar occupations lower-prestige jobs that involve mostly manual labor

white-collar occupations higher-prestige jobs that involve mostly mental activity

● Seeing Sociology
in Everyday Life

Using what you have learned so far about social inequality in the United States, how correct do you think Marx was about capitalism? Explain your answer.

○ **CHECK YOUR LEARNING**   How does Marx's view of social stratification differ from the Davis-Moore thesis?

Why No Marxist Revolution?

Despite Marx's prediction, capitalism is still thriving. Why have industrial workers not overthrown capitalism? Ralf Dahrendorf (1959) suggested four reasons:

1. **Fragmentation of the capitalist class.**   Today, tens of millions of stockholders, rather than single families, own most large companies. Day-to-day corporate operations are in the hands of a large class of managers, who may or may not be major stockholders. With stock so widely held—about 50 percent of U.S. households own stocks—more and more people have a direct stake in the capitalist system (U.S. Census Bureau, 2010).

2. **A higher standard of living.**   As Chapter 12 ("Economics and Politics") explains, a century ago, most U.S. workers were in factories or on farms in **blue-collar occupations**, *lower-prestige jobs that involve mostly manual labor.* Today, most workers are in **white-collar occupations**, *higher-prestige jobs that involve mostly mental activity.* These jobs are in sales, customer support, management, and other service fields. Most of today's white-collar workers do not think of themselves as an "industrial proletariat." Just as important, the average income in the United States rose almost tenfold over the course of the twentieth century, even allowing for inflation, and the number of hours in the workweek decreased. Most workers today are far better off than workers were a century ago, an example of structural social mobility. One result of this rising standard of living is that more people support the status quo.

3. **More worker organizations.**   Workers today have the right to form labor unions that make demands of management, backed by threats of work slowdowns and strikes. As a result, labor disputes are settled without threatening the capitalist system.

4. **Greater legal protections.**   Over the past century, new laws made the workplace safer, and unemployment insurance, disability protection, and Social Security now provide workers with greater financial security.

A Counterpoint

These developments suggest that our society has smoothed many of capitalism's rough edges. Yet many observers claim that Marx's analysis of capitalism is still largely valid (Domhoff, 1983; Stephens, 1986; Boswell & Dixon, 1993; Hout, Brooks, & Manza, 1993). First, wealth remains highly concentrated, with 35 percent of all privately owned property in the hands of 1 percent of the U.S. population (Keister, 2000; Wolff, 2009). Second, many of today's white-collar jobs offer no more income, security, or satisfaction than factory work did a century ago. Third, many benefits enjoyed by today's workers came about through the class conflict Marx described; workers still struggle to hold on to what they have; and in recent years, many workers have actually lost pensions and other benefits. Fourth, although workers have gained legal protections, ordinary people still face disadvantages that the law cannot overcome. Therefore, social-conflict theorists conclude, even without a socialist revolution in the United States, Marx was still mostly right about capitalism.

Max Weber: Class, Status, and Power

Max Weber agreed with Karl Marx that social stratification causes social conflict, but he viewed Marx's two-class model as too simple. Instead, he viewed social stratification as involving three distinct dimensions of inequality.

The first dimension, economic inequality—the issue so important to Marx—Weber called *class* position.

Back in the Great Depression of the 1930's, "tent cities" that were home to desperately poor people could be found in much of the United States. The depression came to an end, but poverty persisted. The recent recession sparked a resurgence of tent cities, including this one in Fresno, California. How would structural-functional analysis explain such poverty? What about the social-conflict approach?

○ Making the Grade

Marx viewed social stratification in terms of classes. Weber viewed inequality in terms of a socioeconomic status hierarchy with multiple dimensions. Individuals stand higher on some dimensions and lower on others, so there are no clear-cut classes.

● APPLYING THEORY ●

Social Stratification

	Structural-Functional Approach	Social-Conflict Approach	Symbolic-Interaction Approach
What is the level of analysis?	Macro-level	Macro-level	Micro-level
What is social stratification?	Stratification is a system of unequal rewards that benefits society as a whole.	Stratification is a division of a society's resources that benefits some people and harms others.	Stratification is a factor that guides people's interactions in everyday life.
What is the reason for our social position?	Social position reflects personal talents and abilities in a competitive economy.	Social position reflects the way society divides resources.	The products we consume all say something about social position.
Are unequal rewards fair?	Yes. Unequal rewards boost economic production by encouraging people to work harder and try new ideas. Linking greater rewards to more important work is widely accepted.	No. Unequal rewards only serve to divide society, creating "haves" and "have-nots." There is widespread opposition to social inequality.	Maybe. People may or may not define inequality as fair. People may view their social position as a measure of self-worth, justifying inequality in terms of personal differences.

Weber did not think of classes as well-defined categories but as a continuum ranging from high to low. Weber's second dimension is *status,* or social prestige, and the third is *power.*

Weber's Socioeconomic Status Hierarchy

Marx viewed prestige and power as simple reflections of economic position and did not treat them as distinct dimensions of inequality. But Weber noted that status consistency in modern societies is often quite low: A local government official might exercise great power yet have little wealth or social prestige.

Weber, then, characterizes stratification in industrial societies as a multidimensional ranking rather than a hierarchy of clearly defined classes. In line with Weber's thinking, sociologists use the term **socioeconomic status (SES)** to refer to *a composite ranking based on various dimensions of social inequality.*

Inequality in History

Weber observed that each of his three dimensions of social inequality stands out at a different time in the history of human societies. Status or social prestige is the main dimension of difference in agrarian societies, taking the form of honor. Members of these societies gain prestige by conforming to cultural norms that apply to their particular rank.

Industrialization and the development of capitalism eliminate traditional rankings based on birth but create striking financial inequality. Thus in an industrial society, the crucial difference between people is the economic dimension of class.

Over time, industrial societies witness the growth of a bureaucratic state. Bigger government and the spread of all types of other organizations make power more important in the stratification system. Especially in socialist societies, where government regulates many aspects of life, high-ranking officials become the new ruling elite.

This historical analysis points to a final difference between Weber and Marx. Marx thought societies could eliminate social stratification by abolishing private ownership of productive property. Weber doubted that overthrowing capitalism would significantly lessen social stratification. It might reduce economic differences, he reasoned, but socialism would increase inequality by expanding government and concentrating power in the hands of a political elite. The popular uprisings against socialist bureaucracies in Eastern Europe and the former Soviet Union show that discontent can be generated by socialist political elites and thus support Weber's position.

Making the Grade

Be sure you understand Weber's claim about the changing basis of stratification in agrarian (prestige), industrial-capitalist (money), and socialist (power) societies.

conspicuous consumption buying and using products because of the "statement" they make about social position

SEEING SOCIOLOGY IN EVERYDAY LIFE

When Class Gets Personal: Picking (with) Your Friends

The sound of banjo music drifted across the field late one summer afternoon. I laid my brush down, climbed over the fence I had been painting, and walked toward the sound of the music to see what was going on. That's how I met my neighbor Max, a retired factory worker who lived just up the road. Max was a pretty good "picker," and within an hour, I was back on his porch with my guitar. I called Howard, a friend who teaches at the college, and he showed up a little while later, six-string in hand. The three of us jammed for a couple of hours, smiling all the while.

The next morning, I was mowing the grass in front of the house when Max came walking down the road. I turned off the lawnmower as he came down the driveway. "Hi, Max," I said. "Thanks for having us over last night. I really had fun."

"Don't mention it," Max responded. Then he shook his head a little and added, "Ya know, I

was thinkin' after you guys left. I mean, it was really somethin' how you guys looked like you

were having a great time. With somebody like me!"

"Well, yeah," I replied, not sure what he meant. "You sure played better than we did."

Max looked down at the ground, embarrassed by the compliment. Then he added, "What I mean is that you guys were having a good time with somebody like *me.* You're both professors, right? *Doctors,* even . . ."

WHAT DO YOU THINK?

1. Why do you think Max felt that two college teachers would not enjoy spending time with him?

2. How does his reaction suggest that people take social position personally?

3. Can you think of a similar experience you have had with someone of a different social position?

CRITICAL REVIEW Weber's multidimensional view of social stratification greatly influenced sociologists and made the concept of socioeconomic status hierarchy popular. But critics (particularly those who favor Marx's ideas) argue that although social class boundaries may have blurred, industrial and postindustrial nations still show striking patterns of social inequality.

As will be explained shortly, economic inequality has increased recently in the United States. Although some people favor Weber's multidimensional hierarchy, others think, in light of this trend, that Marx's view of the rich versus the poor is closer to the truth.

CHECK YOUR LEARNING What are Weber's three dimensions of social inequality? According to Weber, which of them would you expect to be most important in the United States? Why?

Stratification and Interaction

Because social stratification has to do with the way an entire society is organized, sociologists (Marx and Weber included) typically treat it as a macro-level issue. But a micro-level analysis of social stratification is also important because people's social standing affects their everyday

interactions. The Applying Theory table on page 215 summarizes the contributions of three theoretical approaches to social stratification.

In most communities, people interact primarily with others of about the same social standing. This pattern begins with the fact that due to social stratification, people tend to live with others like themselves. In larger public spaces, such as a large shopping mall, we often see couples or groups made up of individuals whose appearance and shopping habits are similar. At the same time, people with very different social standing commonly keep their distance from one another. Well-dressed people walking down the street on their way to an expensive restaurant, for example, might move across the sidewalk or even cross the street to avoid getting close to others they think are homeless people. The Seeing Sociology in Everyday Life box gives another example of how differences in social class position can affect interaction.

Finally, just about everyone realizes that the way we dress, the car we drive (or the bus we ride), and even the food and drink we order at the campus snack bar say something about our budget and personal tastes. Sociologists use the term **conspicuous consumption** to refer to *buying and using products because of the "statement" they make about social position.* Ignoring the water fountain in favor of paying for bottled water tells people that you have extra money to spend. And

● Seeing Sociology
in Everyday Life

Have you recently had an everyday life experience that brought
home the importance of social stratification in our society?
Explain.

● Seeing Sociology
in Everyday Life

Can you identify aspects of everyday life that seem to suggest
that economic inequality is increasing? Explain.

no one needs a $100,000 automobile to get around, of course, but driving up in such a vehicle says "I have arrived" in more ways than one.

○ **CRITICAL REVIEW** A micro-level analysis of social stratification helps us see patterns of social inequality in our everyday lives. At the same time, the limitation of this approach is that it has little to say about how and why broad patterns of social inequality exist, which was the focus of the structural-functional and social-conflict approaches.

○ **CHECK YOUR LEARNING** Point to several ways in which social stratification shapes the way people of different social positions behave in the course of a typical day.

Stratification and Technology: A Global Perspective

We can weave together a number of observations made in this chapter by considering the relationship between a society's technology and its type of social stratification. This analysis draws on Gerhard Lenski's model of sociocultural evolution discussed in Chapter 2 ("Culture").

Hunting and Gathering Societies

With simple technology, hunters and gatherers produce only what is necessary for day-to-day living. Some people may produce more than others, but the group's survival depends on all sharing what they have. Thus no categories of people are better off than others.

Horticultural, Pastoral, and Agrarian Societies

As technological advances create a surplus, social inequality increases. In horticultural and pastoral societies, a small elite controls most of the surplus. Larger-scale agriculture is more productive still, and striking inequality—as great as at any time in history—places the nobility in an almost godlike position over the masses.

Industrial Societies

Industrialization pushes inequality downward. Prompted by the need to develop people's talents, meritocracy takes hold and weakens the power of traditional elites. Industrial productivity also raises the living standards of the historically poor majority. Specialized work demands schooling for all, sharply reducing illiteracy. A literate population demands a greater voice in political decision making, reducing social inequality and lessening men's domination of women.

Over time, even wealth becomes somewhat less concentrated (contradicting Marx's prediction). In the 1920s, the richest 1 percent of U.S. families owned about 40 percent of all wealth, a figure that fell

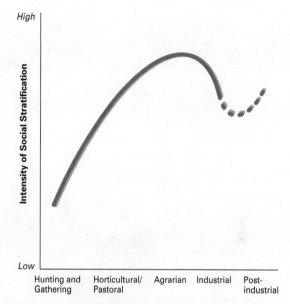

FIGURE 8–2 **Social Stratification and Technological Development: The Kuznets Curve**

The Kuznets curve shows that greater technological sophistication generally is accompanied by more pronounced social stratification. The trend reverses itself as industrial societies relax rigid, castelike distinctions in favor of greater opportunity and equality under the law. Political rights are more widely extended, and there is even some leveling of economic differences. However, the emergence of postindustrial society has brought an upturn in economic inequality, as indicated by the broken line added by the author.

Sources: Drawn by the author based on Kuznets (1955) and Lenski (1966).

to 30 percent by the 1980s as taxes—with higher tax rates for people with higher incomes—paid for new government programs benefiting the poor (Williamson & Lindert, 1980; Beeghley, 1989; U.S. House of Representatives, 1991). Such trends help explain why Marxist revolutions occurred in *agrarian* societies, such as Russia (1917), Cuba (1959), and Nicaragua (1979), where social inequality is most pronounced, rather than in *industrial* societies as Marx predicted. However, wealth inequality turned upward again after 1990 and is once again about the same as it was in the 1920s (Keister, 2000; Wolff, 2009). With the goal of reducing this trend, the Obama administration has expressed its intention to raise federal income tax rates on high-income individuals.

The Kuznets Curve

In human history, then, technological advances first increase but then moderate the intensity of social stratification. Greater inequality is functional for agrarian societies, but industrial societies benefit from

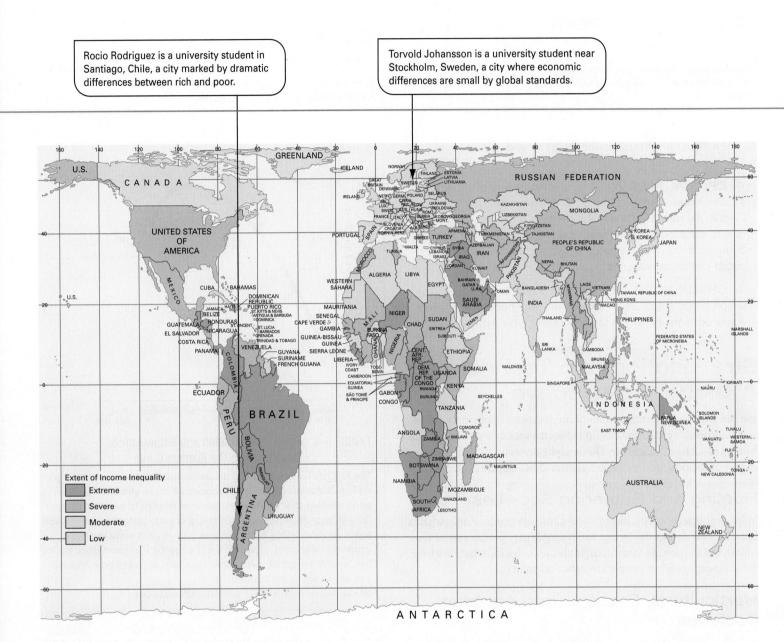

Rocio Rodriguez is a university student in Santiago, Chile, a city marked by dramatic differences between rich and poor.

Torvold Johansson is a university student near Stockholm, Sweden, a city where economic differences are small by global standards.

Window on the World

GLOBAL MAP 8–1   Income Inequality in Global Perspective

Societies throughout the world differ in the rigidity and extent of their social stratification and their overall standard of living. This map highlights income inequality. Generally speaking, the United States stands out among high-income nations, such as Great Britain, Sweden, Japan, and Australia, as having greater income inequality. The less economically developed countries of Latin America and Africa, including Colombia, Brazil, and the Central African Republic, as well as much of the Arab world, exhibit the most pronounced inequality of income. Is this pattern consistent with the Kuznets curve?

Source: Based on Gini coefficients obtained from World Bank (2008) and Central Intelligence Agency (2009).

a more equal system. This historical trend, recognized by the Nobel Prize–winning economist Simon Kuznets (1955, 1966), is illustrated by the Kuznets curve, shown in Figure 8–2 on page 217.

Social inequality around the world generally supports the Kuznets curve. Global Map 8–1 shows that high-income nations that have passed through the industrial era (including the United States,

Canada, and the nations of Western Europe) have somewhat less income inequality than nations in which a larger share of the labor force remains in farming (as is common in Latin America and Africa). At the same time, it is important to remember that income inequality reflects not just technological development but also a society's political and economic priorities. Income inequality in the

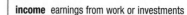

Making the Grade

Notice in the two pie-charts below that wealth is
more unequally distributed than income.

income earnings from work or investments

wealth (p. 220) the total value of money and other assets, minus
outstanding debts

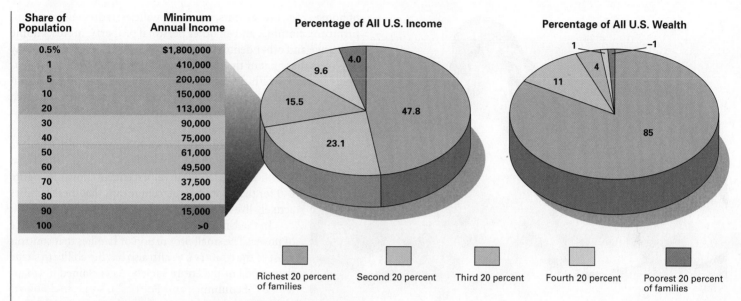

Share of Population	Minimum Annual Income
0.5%	$1,800,000
1	410,000
5	200,000
10	150,000
20	113,000
30	90,000
40	75,000
50	61,000
60	49,500
70	37,500
80	28,000
90	15,000
100	>0

Percentage of All U.S. Income

4.0 | 9.6 | 15.5 | 47.8 | 23.1

Percentage of All U.S. Wealth

1 | −1 | 4 | 11 | 85

■ Richest 20 percent of families ■ Second 20 percent ■ Third 20 percent ■ Fourth 20 percent ■ Poorest 20 percent of families

FIGURE 8–3 **Distribution of Income and Wealth in the United States**

Income, and especially wealth, is divided unequally in U.S. society.

Sources: Income data from U.S. Census Bureau (2009); wealth data based on Bucks et al. (2009), Wolff (2009), and author estimates.

United States may have declined during much of the last century, but this country still has more economic inequality than Canada, countries throughout Europe, and Japan.

Another criticism of the Kuznets curve is that it was developed by comparing societies at different levels of economic development (using what sociologists call "cross-sectional data"). Such data do not tell us about the future of any one society. In the United States, recent trends showing increases in economic inequality suggest that the Kuznets curve may require serious revision—represented by the broken line in Figure 8–2. The fact that U.S. society is now experiencing greater economic inequality suggests that the long-term trend may differ from what Kuznets projected half a century ago.

Inequality in the United States

The United States differs from most European nations and Japan in never having had a titled nobility. With the significant exception of our racial history, we have never known a caste system that rigidly ranks categories of people.

Even so, U.S. society is highly stratified. Not only do the rich have most of the money, but they also receive the most schooling, enjoy the best health, and consume the most goods and services. Such privilege contrasts sharply with the poverty of millions of women and men who worry about paying next month's rent or a

doctor's bill when a child becomes ill. Many people think of the United States as a "middle-class society" in which people are more or less alike. But is this really the case?

Income, Wealth, and Power

One important dimension of economic inequality is **income,** *earnings from work or investments.* The Census Bureau reports that the median U.S. family income in 2008 was $61,521. The pie chart in the middle of Figure 8–3 shows the distribution of income among all U.S. families.[1] The richest 20 percent of families (earning at least $113,000 annually, with a mean of about $190,000) received 47.8 percent of all income, and the bottom 20 percent (earning less than $28,000, with a mean of about $16,000) received only 4.0 percent.

The table at the left in Figure 8–3 takes a closer look at income distribution. In 2008, the highest-paid 5 percent of U.S. families

[1]The Census Bureau reports both mean and median incomes for families ("two or more persons related by blood, marriage, or adoption") and households ("two or more persons sharing a living unit"). In 2008, mean family income was $79,634, higher than median family income ($61,521) because high-income families pull up the mean but not the median. For households, these figures are somewhat lower—a mean of $68,424 and a median of $50,303—because families average 3.15 people and households average 2.57.

● Seeing Sociology
in Everyday Life

Why do you think so many people view the United States as a
middle-class society in which most people have more or less
equal social standing?

● Seeing Sociology
in Everyday Life

People of all social classes have the same right to vote. But
can you think of ways in which the rich have more power to
shape U.S. society than the rest of us?

Members of our society tend to think of social class in terms of income and wealth, as if
to say "I am what I own." For this reason, conspicuous consumption—buying and
displaying various goods partly with an eye toward gaining social standing in the eyes of
others—is a common pattern. How have you engaged in conspicuous consumption?

of homes, cars, investments, insurance policies, retirement pensions, furniture, clothing, and all other personal property, minus a home mortgage and other debts. The wealth of average people is not only less than that of the rich but also different in kind. Most people's wealth centers on a home and a car—property that generates no income—but the greater wealth of the rich is mostly in the form of stocks and other income-producing investments.

When financial assets are balanced against debts, the lowest-ranking 40 percent of families have virtually no wealth at all. The negative percentage shown in Figure 8–3 for the poorest 20 percent means that these families actually live in debt.

In the United States, wealth is an important source of power. The small proportion of families that controls most of the country's wealth also has the ability to shape the agenda of the entire society. As explained in Chapter 12 ("Economics and Politics"), some sociologists argue that such concentrated wealth weakens democracy because the political system primarily serves the interests of the super-rich.

Occupational Prestige

In addition to generating income, work is also an important source of prestige. We commonly evaluate each other according to the kind of work we do, giving greater respect to those who do what we consider to be more important work and less to others with more modest jobs.

Sociologists measure the relative social prestige of various occupations (NORC, 2009). Table 8–1 shows that people give high prestige to occupations, such as medicine, law, and engineering, that require extensive training and generate high income. By contrast, less prestigious work—as a waitress or janitor, for example—not only pays less but requires less ability and schooling. Occupational prestige rankings are much the same in all high-income nations (Lin & Xie, 1988).

In any society, high-prestige occupations go to privileged categories of people. In Table 8–1, for example, the highest-ranking occupations are dominated by men. We have to go more than a dozen jobs down the list to find "registered nurse" and "secondary school teacher," careers chosen mostly by women. Similarly, many of the lowest-prestige jobs are commonly performed by people of color.

Schooling

Industrial societies have expanded opportunities for schooling, but some people still receive much more than others. In 2009, although almost 87 percent of women and men aged twenty-five and older had

earned at least $200,000 (averaging almost $327,000), or 20.5 percent of all income, more than the total earnings of the lowest-paid 40 percent. At the very top of the pyramid, the richest 0.5 percent earned at least $1.8 million. In short, while a small number of people earn very high incomes, the majority make do with far less.

Income is only one part of a person's or family's **wealth,** *the total value of money and other assets, minus outstanding debts.* Wealth—including stocks, bonds, and real estate—is distributed even more unequally than income.

The pie chart at the right in Figure 8–3 shows the approximate distribution of wealth in the United States. The richest 20 percent of U.S. families own roughly 85 percent of the country's entire wealth. High up in this privileged category are the top 5 percent of families, the "very rich," who own 62 percent of all private property. Richer still, with wealth into the tens of millions of dollars, are the 1 percent of families that qualify as "super-rich" and possess about 35 percent of the nation's privately held resources (Keister, 2000; Keister & Moller, 2000; Bucks et al., 2009; Wolff, 2009). At the top of the wealth pyramid, the ten richest individuals in our society have a combined net worth of more than $225 billion (Miller & Greenberg, 2009). This amount equals the total property of nearly 2 million average families, enough people to fill the cities of Chicago, Houston, and San Francisco.

The wealth of the average U.S. family is currently about $120,300 (Bucks et al., 2009). Family wealth reflects the total value

● Seeing Sociology
in Everyday Life

Identify the jobs in Table 8–1 that have traditionally been
performed by people of color. What pattern do you discover?

● Seeing Sociology
in Everyday Life

Reading down from the top of Table 8–1, how far do you
have to go before you see a job in which most workers would
be women?

Table 8–1   The Relative Social Prestige of Selected Occupations in the United States

White-Collar Occupations	Prestige Score	Blue-Collar Occupations	White-Collar Occupations	Prestige Score	Blue-Collar Occupations
Physician	86		Funeral director	49	
Lawyer	75		Real estate agent	49	
College/university professor	74		Bookkeeper	47	
Architect	73			47	Machinist
Chemist	73			47	Mail carrier
Physicist/astronomer	73		Musician/composer	47	
Aerospace engineer	72			46	Secretary
Dentist	72		Photographer	45	
Member of the clergy	69		Bank teller	43	
Psychologist	69			42	Tailor
Pharmacist	68			42	Welder
Optometrist	67			40	Farmer
Registered nurse	66			40	Telephone operator
Secondary school teacher	66			39	Carpenter
Accountant	65			36	Bricklayer/stonemason
Athlete	65			36	Child care worker
Electrical engineer	64		File clerk	36	
Elementary school teacher	64			36	Hairdresser
Economist	63			35	Baker
Veterinarian	62			34	Bulldozer operator
Airplane pilot	61			31	Auto body repairer
Computer programmer	61		Retail apparel salesperson	30	
Sociologist	61			30	Truck driver
Editor/reporter	60		Cashier	29	
	60	Police officer		28	Elevator operator
Actor	58			28	Garbage collector
Radio/TV announcer	55			28	Taxi driver
Librarian	54			28	Waiter/waitress
	53	Aircraft mechanic		27	Bellhop
	53	Firefighter		25	Bartender
Dental hygienist	52			23	Farm laborer
Painter/sculptor	52			23	Household laborer
Social worker	52			22	Door-to-door salesperson
	51	Electrician		22	Janitor
Computer operator	50			09	Shoe shiner

Source: Adapted from *General Social Surveys, 1972–2008: Cumulative Codebook* (Chicago: National Opinion Research Center, 2009), pp. 2310–2317.

○ Making the Grade

Notice in the section below how ancestry, race and ethnicity, and gender can operate as caste elements.

○ Seeing Sociology in Everyday Life

To what extent is gender still an element of caste? That is, as you look around you, do women seem to have the same opportunities and privileges as men?

completed high school, just 29 percent of women and 30 percent of men were college graduates (U.S. Census Bureau, 2010).

Schooling affects both occupation and income because most (but not all) of the better-paying, white-collar jobs listed in Table 8–1 require a college degree or other advanced study. Most blue-collar jobs, which bring lower income and less prestige, require less schooling.

Ancestry, Race, and Gender

A class system rewards individual talent and effort. But nothing affects social standing as much as birth into a particular family, which has a strong bearing on future schooling, occupation, and income. Research suggests that more than one-third of our country's richest people—those with hundreds of millions of dollars in wealth—derived their fortunes mostly from inheritance (Miller & Newcomb, 2005; Harford, 2007). Inherited poverty shapes the future of tens of millions of others.

Also closely linked to social position in the United States is race. White people have a higher overall occupational standing than African Americans and also receive more schooling. The median African American family income was $39,879 in 2008, just 57 percent of the $70,070 earned by non-Hispanic white families. This difference in income makes a real difference in people's lives. For example, non-Hispanic white families are more likely to own their homes (75 percent do) than black families (47 percent) (U.S. Census Bureau, 2009).

Some of the racial difference in income results from the larger proportion of single-parent families among African Americans. Comparing only families that include a married couple, African American families earned 80 percent as much as non-Hispanic white families.

Over time, this income difference builds into a huge wealth gap (Altonji, Doraszelski, & Segal, 2000). A survey of families by the government's Federal Reserve found that median wealth for minority families, including African Americans, Hispanics, and Asian Americans ($27,800), is just 16 percent of the median ($170,400) for non-Hispanic white families (Bucks et al., 2009).

Social ranking involves ethnicity as well. Historically, people of English ancestry have enjoyed the most wealth and wielded the greatest power in U.S. society. The Latino population—the largest U.S. racial or ethnic minority—has long been disadvantaged. In 2008, the median income among Hispanic families was $40,500, which is 58 percent of the median income for non-Hispanic white families. A detailed examination of how race and ethnicity affect social standing is presented in Chapter 11 ("Race and Ethnicity").

Of course, both men and women are found in families at every social level. Yet on average, women have less income, wealth, and occupational prestige than men. Among single-parent families, those headed by a woman are more than twice as likely to be poor as those headed by a man. Chapter 10 ("Gender Stratification") examines the link between gender and social stratification.

Social Classes in the United States

As noted earlier, rankings in a caste system are rigid and obvious to all. Defining the social categories in a more fluid class system, however, is not so easy. Followers of Karl Marx see two major social classes: capitalists and proletarians. Other sociologists find as many as six classes (Warner & Lunt, 1941) or even seven (Coleman & Rainwater, 1978). Still others side with Max Weber, believing that people form not clear-cut classes but a multidimensional status hierarchy.

Defining classes in the United States is difficult because of the relatively low level of status consistency. Especially toward the middle of the hierarchy, people's social position on one dimension may not be the same as their standing on another. For example, a government official may have the power to administer a multimillion-dollar budget yet earn only a modest personal income. Similarly, many members of the clergy enjoy ample prestige but only moderate power and low pay. Or consider the casino poker player who wins little respect but makes a lot of money.

Finally, the social mobility characteristic of class systems—again, most pronounced near the middle—means that social position may change during a person's lifetime, further blurring class boundaries. With these issues in mind, we can examine four general rankings: the upper class, the middle class, the working class, and the lower class.

The Upper Class

Families in the upper class—the top 5 percent of the U.S. population—earn at least $200,000, and some earn ten times that much or more. As a general rule, the more a family's income comes from inherited wealth in the form of stocks and bonds, real estate, and other investments, the stronger a family's claim to being upper-class.

In 2009, *Forbes* magazine profiled the richest 400 people in the United States who were worth at least $950 million (and as much as $50 billion) (Miller & Greenberg, 2009). These people form the core of the upper class or Karl Marx's "capitalists"—the owners of the means of production and thus of most of the nation's private wealth. Many of these people spend much of their time managing their own wealth. Many upper-class people with smaller fortunes are business owners, top executives in large corporations, or senior government officials. Historically, the upper class has been composed of white Anglo-Saxon Protestants, but this is less true today (Pyle & Koch, 2001).

Making the Grade

Pay attention to a key difference between the small number of "upper-uppers," who are almost always born (or occasionally marry) into "old money," and the much larger number of "lower-uppers," who move upward socially as they earn lots of "new money."

Seeing Sociology in Everyday Life

When you think about the "American dream," you imagine rising to which part of the upper class? Explain your answer.

People often distinguish between the "new rich" and families with "old money." Men and women who suddenly begin to earn high incomes tend to spend their money on status symbols because they enjoy the new thrill of high-roller living and they want others to know of their success. Those who grow up surrounded by wealth, by contrast, are used to a privileged way of life and are more quiet about it. Thus the conspicuous consumption of the lower-upper class (*left*) can differ dramatically from the more private pursuits and understatement of the upper-upper class (*right*).

Upper-Uppers

The *upper-upper class*, sometimes called "blue bloods" or simply "society," includes less than 1 percent of the U.S. population (Baltzell, 1995). Membership is almost always the result of birth, as suggested by the old remark that the easiest way to become an upper-upper is to be born one. Most of these families possess enormous wealth that is primarily inherited. For this reason, members of the upper-upper class are said to have "old money."

Set apart by their wealth, upper-uppers live in exclusive neighborhoods such as Beacon Hill in Boston, the Rittenhouse Square section of Philadelphia, the Gold Coast of Chicago, and Nob Hill in San Francisco. Their children typically attend private schools with others of similar background and complete their formal education at high-prestige colleges and universities. In the historical pattern of European aristocrats, they study liberal arts rather than vocational skills.

Women of the upper-upper class often do volunteer work for charitable organizations. Such activities serve a dual purpose: They help the larger community, and they build networks that broaden this elite's power (Ostrander, 1980, 1984).

Lower-Uppers

Most upper-class people actually fall into the *lower-upper class*. And lower-uppers include some of the richest people in the world. The

queen of England is in the upper-upper class based not only on her fortune of $450 million but on her family tree. J. K. Rowling, author of the Harry Potter books, is easily worth twice as much—more than $1 billion—but this self-made woman (who was once on welfare) stands at the top of the lower-upper class. The major difference, in other words, is that members of the lower-upper class are the "working rich" who get their money mostly by earning it rather than inheritance. These "new rich" families—who make up 3 to 4 percent of the U.S. population—generally live in large homes in expensive neighborhoods, own vacation homes near the water or in the mountains, and send their children to private schools and good colleges. Yet most do not gain entry into the clubs and associations of "old money" families.

The Middle Class

Made up of 40 to 45 percent of the U.S. population, the large middle class has a tremendous influence on our culture. Television and movies usually show middle-class people, and most commercial advertising is directed at these average consumers. The middle class contains far more ethnic and racial diversity than the upper class.

Upper-Middles

People near the top of this category are called the *upper-middle class,* based on their above-average income in the range of $113,000 to

● Seeing Sociology
in Everyday Life

What low-wage jobs have you held? Assess those
experiences in light of the box below.

Go to the Multimedia Library at **mysoclab.com**
to view the ABC *20/20* video "Poverty in
Camden, New Jersey"

SEEING SOCIOLOGY IN EVERYDAY LIFE

Nickel and Dimed: On (Not) Getting By in America

All of us know people who work at low-wage jobs as waitresses at diners, clerks at drive-throughs, or sales associates at discount stores such as Walmart. We see such people just about every day. Many of us actually *are* such people. In the United States, "common sense" tells us that the jobs people have and the amount of money they make reflect their personal abilities as well as their willingness to work hard.

Barbara Ehrenreich (2001) had her doubts. To find out what the world of low-wage work is really like, the successful journalist and author decided to leave her comfortable upper-middle-class life to live and work in the world of low-wage jobs. She began in Key West, Florida, taking a job as a waitress for $2.43 an hour plus tips. Right away, she found out she had to work much harder than she ever imagined. By the end of a shift, she was exhausted, but after sharing tips with the kitchen staff, she averaged less than $6.00 an hour. This was barely above the national minimum wage at the time and provided just enough income to pay the rent on her tiny apartment, buy food, and cover other basic expenses. She had to hope that she didn't get sick, because the job did not provide health insurance and

she couldn't afford to pay for a visit to a doctor's office.

After working for more than a year at a number of other low-wage jobs, including cleaning motels in Maine and working on the floor of a Walmart in Minnesota, she had rejected quite a bit of "common sense." First, she now knew that tens of millions of people with low-wage jobs work very hard every day. If you don't think so, Ehrenreich says, take on one of these jobs for yourself. Second, these jobs require not only hard work (imagine thoroughly cleaning three motel rooms every hour all day long) but also special skills and real intelligence (try waiting on ten tables in a restaurant at the same time and keeping everybody happy). She found that the people she worked with were, on aver-

age, just as smart, clever, and funny as others she knew who wrote books for a living or taught at a college.

Why, then, do we think of low-wage workers as lazy or as having less ability? It surprised Ehrenreich to learn that many low-wage workers felt this way about themselves. In a society that teaches us to believe that personal ability is everything, we learn to size people up by their job. Ehrenreich discovered that many low-wage workers, subject to constant supervision, random drug tests, and other rigid rules that usually come with such jobs, end up feeling unworthy, even to the point of not trying for anything better. Such beliefs, she concludes, help support a society of extreme inequality in which some people live very well because of the low wages paid to the rest.

WHAT DO YOU THINK?

1. Have you ever held a low-wage job? If so, would you say you worked hard? What was your pay? Were there any benefits?

2. Ehrenreich claims that most well-off people in the United States are dependent on low-wage workers. What does she mean by this?

3. How much of a chance do most people with jobs at Wendy's or Walmart have to enroll in college and to work toward a different career? Explain.

$200,000 a year. Such income allows upper-middle-class families to live in a comfortable house in a fairly expensive area, own several nice automobiles, and build investments. Two-thirds of upper-middle-class children graduate from college, and postgraduate degrees are common. Many go on to high-prestige occupations as physicians, engineers, lawyers, accountants, and business executives. Lacking the power of the richest people to influence national or international events, upper-middles often play an important role in local political affairs.

Average-Middles

The rest of the middle class falls close to the center of the U.S. class structure. *Average-middles* typically work at less prestigious white-collar occupations as bank branch managers or high school teachers

or in highly skilled blue-collar jobs such as electrical work and carpentry. Family income falls between $49,000 and $113,000 a year, which is roughly the national average.[2]

Middle-class people generally build up a small amount of wealth over the course of their working lives, mostly in the form of a house and a retirement account. Most average-middle-class men and women are likely to be high school graduates, but the odds are just fifty-fifty that they will complete a college degree, usually at a less expensive, state-supported school.

---

[2]In some parts of the United States where the cost of living is very high (say, San Francisco), a family might need as much as $150,000 in annual income to reach the middle class.

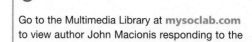
Go to the Multimedia Library at **mysoclab.com** to view author John Macionis responding to the question "What Difference Does Class Make?"

The Working Class

About one-third of the population falls within the working class (sometimes called the *lower-middle class*). In Marxist terms, the working class forms the core of the industrial proletariat. The blue-collar jobs held by members of the working class yield a family income of between $28,000 and $49,000 a year, somewhat below the national average. Working-class families have little or no wealth and are vulnerable to financial problems caused by unemployment or illness.

Many working-class jobs provide little personal satisfaction—requiring discipline but rarely imagination—and subject workers to continual supervision. These jobs also offer fewer benefits, such as medical insurance and pension plans. About two-thirds of working-class families own their homes, usually in lower-cost neighborhoods. College becomes a reality for only about one-third of working-class children.

The Lower Class

The remaining 20 percent of the population make up the lower class. Low income makes their lives insecure and difficult. In 2008, the federal government classified 40 million people (13.2 percent of the population) as poor. Millions more—called the "working poor"—are slightly better off, holding low-prestige jobs that provide little satisfaction and minimal income. Barely half manage to complete high school, and only one in four ever reaches college. In the Seeing Sociology in Everyday Life box, one sociologist describes the experience of trying to survive day-to-day doing low-wage work.

Society segregates the lower class, especially when the poor are racial or ethnic minorities. About 45 percent of lower-class families own their own home, typically in the least desirable neighborhoods. Although poor neighborhoods are often found in inner cities, lower-class families also live in rural areas, especially across the South.
● Go to **mysoclab.com**

The Difference Class Makes

Social stratification affects nearly every dimension of our lives. In the following sections, we will briefly examine some of the ways social standing is linked to our health, values, politics, and family life.
● Go to **mysoclab.com**

Health

Health is closely related to social standing. Children born into poor families are three times more likely to die from disease, neglect, accidents, or violence during their first year of life than children born into privileged families. Among adults, people with above-average incomes are almost twice as likely as low-income people to describe their health as excellent. In addition, on average, richer people live five years longer because they eat more nutritious food, live in safer and less stressful environments, and receive better medical care (Congressional Budget Office, 2008; Pleis & Lucas, 2009).

Values and Attitudes

Some values and attitudes vary from class to class. The "old rich" have an unusually strong sense of family history because their position is based on wealth passed down from generation to generation. Secure in their birthright privileges, upper-uppers also favor understated manners and tastes; many "new rich" people engage in conspicuous consumption, using homes, cars, and even airplanes as status symbols to make a statement about their social position.

Affluent people with greater education and financial security are also more tolerant of controversial behavior such as homosexuality. Working-class people, who grow up in an atmosphere of greater supervision and discipline and are less likely to attend college, tend to be less tolerant (Lareau, 2002; NORC, 2007).

Compared to high-income people, low-income people are half as likely to report good health and, on average, live about five fewer years. The toll of low income—played out in inadequate nutrition, little medical care, and high stress—is easy to see on the faces of the poor, who look old before their time.

Making the Grade

Be sure you understand how social class position involves not only money but also "cultural capital."

Seeing Sociology in Everyday Life

After reading the box below, think about times when you have felt out of place in some setting based on your social class position. Why did you feel this way? How do such feelings show that we often understand class differences in terms of personal worthiness?

THINKING ABOUT DIVERSITY: RACE, CLASS, & GENDER

The Power of Class: A Low-Income Student Asks, "Am I as Good as You?"

Marcella grew up without the privileges that most other students on the campus of this private, liberal arts college take for granted. During her senior year, she and I talked at length about her college experiences and why social class presented a huge challenge to her. Marcella is not her real name; she wishes to remain anonymous. I have summarized what she has said about her college life in the story that follows.

When I came here, I entered a new world. I found myself in a strange and dangerous place. All around me were people with habits and ideas I did not understand. A thousand times, I thought to myself, I hope all of you will realize that there are other worlds out there and that I am from one of them. Will you accept me?

I am a child of poverty, a young woman raised in a world of want and violence. I am now on the campus of an elite college. I may have a new identity as a college student. But my old life

is still going on in my head. I have not been able to change how I think of myself.

Do you want to find out more about me? Learn more about the power of social class to shape how we feel about ourselves? Here is what I want to say to you.

When I was growing up, I envied most of you. You lived in a middle-class bubble, a world that held you, protected you, and com-

forted you. Not me. While your parents were discussing current events, planning family trips, and looking out for you, my father and mother were screaming at each other. I will never be able to forget summer nights when I lay in my bed, sticky with sweat, biting my fingernails as a telephone crashed against the wall that separated my room from theirs. My father was drunk and out of control; my mother ducked just in time.

Your fathers and mothers work in office buildings. They have good jobs, as doctors, lawyers, and architects; they are corporate managers; they run small businesses. Your mothers and fathers are people who matter. My mom takes the bus to a hospital where she works for $10 an hour cleaning up after people. She spends her shift doing what she is told. My dad? Who knows. He was a deadbeat, a drunk, a drug addict. I don't know if he still is or not. I haven't heard from him in eight years.

You grew up in a neighborhood and probably lived for many years in one

---

Social class has a great deal to do with an individual's self-concept. People with higher social standing experience more confidence in everyday interaction for the simple reason that others tend to view them as having greater importance. The Thinking About Diversity box describes the challenges faced by one young woman from a poor family attending a college where most students are from elite families.

Politics

Do political attitudes follow class lines? The answer is yes, but the pattern is complex. A desire to protect wealth prompts well-off people to take a more conservative approach to *economic* issues, favoring, for example, lower taxes. But on *social* matters such as abortion and gay rights, highly educated, more affluent people are more liberal. People of lower social standing, by contrast, tend to be economic liberals, favoring government social programs that benefit

them, but typically hold more conservative views on social issues (NORC, 2007).

A clearer pattern emerges when it comes to political involvement. Higher-income people, who are better served by the system, are more likely to vote and to join political organizations than people with low incomes. In presidential elections, more than three-fourths of adults with family incomes of at least $75,000 vote, compared to about half of adults with family incomes below $30,000 (Samuelson, 2003; U.S. Census Bureau, 2009).

Family and Gender

Social class also shapes family life. Generally, lower-class families are somewhat larger than middle-class families because of earlier marriage and less use of birth control. Another family pattern is that working-class parents encourage children to conform to conventional norms and respect authority figures. Parents of higher social standing

● Seeing Sociology
in Everyday Life

An interesting mini-project is to ask your parents
(and also ask yourself) about changes in your family's
social position over the last several generations. What
factors are linked to these changes?

● Making the Grade

Remember that social mobility has many forms—
including upward and downward—and also takes
place over one generation (intragenerational mobility)
or several generations (intergenerational mobility).

house. My family lived in low-cost rental housing. We moved a lot. When there was no money for rent, we packed up our stuff and moved to a new place. It seemed like we were always running away from something.

You grew up with books, with trips to the library, with parents who read to you. You learned how to speak well and have an impressive vocabulary. I never heard a bedtime story, and I had maybe one inspiring teacher. Most of what I know I had to learn on my own. Maybe that's why I always feel like I am trying to catch up to you.

You know how to use forks, knives, and spoons the right way. You know how to eat Chinese food and what to order at a Thai restaurant. You have favorite Italian dishes. You know how to order wine. You know about German beers, Danish cheeses, and French sauces. Me? I grew up having Thanksgiving dinner on paper plates, eating turkey served by social service volunteers. When you ask me to go with you to some special restaurant, I make some excuse and stay home. I can't afford it. I am afraid you will find out how little I know about things you take for granted.

How did I ever get to this college? I remember one of my teachers telling me that I "have promise." The college admission office accepted me. But I am not sure why. I was given a scholarship that covers most of my tuition. That solved one big problem, and now I am here. But sometimes I am not sure I will stay. I have to study more than many of you to learn things you already know. I have to work two part-time jobs to make the money I needed to buy a used computer, clothes, and the occasional pizza at the corner place where many of you spend so much time.

It's amazing to me that I am here. I realize how lucky I am. But now that I am here, I realize that the road is so much longer than I thought it would be. Getting to this college was only part of the journey. The scholarship was only part of the answer. The biggest challenge for me is what goes on every day—the thousands of ways in which you live a life that I still don't really understand, the thousands of things that I won't know or that I will do wrong that will blow my cover, and show me up for the fraud I am.

WHAT DO YOU THINK?

1. How does this story show that social class involves much more than how much money a person has?

2. Why does Marcella worry that other people will think she is a "fraud"? If you could speak to her about this fear, what would you say?

3. Have you ever had similar feelings about being less important than—or better than—someone else based on social class position? Explain.

pass on a different "cultural capital" to their children, teaching them to express their individuality and imagination more freely (Kohn, 1977; McLeod, 1995; Lareau, 2002).

The more money a family has, the more opportunities parents have to develop their children's talents and abilities. An affluent family earning more than $98,470 a year will spend $483,750 raising a child born in 2008 to the age of eighteen. Middle-class people, with an average income of about $75,000 a year, will spend $291,570, and a lower-class family earning less than $56,870 will spend $210,340 (Lino & Carlson, 2009). Privilege leads to privilege as family life reproduces the class structure in each generation.

Class also shapes our world of relationships. In a classic study of married life, Elizabeth Bott (1971, orig. 1957) found that most working-class couples divide their responsibilities according to traditional gender roles; middle-class couples, by contrast, are more egalitarian, sharing more activities and expressing greater intimacy. More recently, Karen Walker (1995) discovered that working-class friendships typically serve as sources of material assistance; middle-class friendships are likely to involve shared interests and leisure pursuits.

Social Mobility

Ours is a dynamic society marked by quite a bit of social movement. Earning a college degree, landing a higher-paying job, or marrying someone who has a good income contributes to *upward social mobility;* dropping out of school, losing a job, or becoming divorced (especially for women) may result in *downward social mobility.*

Over the long term, though, social mobility is not so much a matter of individual changes as changes in society itself. In the first half of the twentieth century, for example, industrialization expanded the U.S. economy, pushing up living standards. Even people who were not good swimmers rode the rising tide of prosperity. More

○ Making the Grade

The changes in median family income shown below in Figure 8–4 are examples of structural social mobility.

FIGURE 8–4   **Median Annual Income, U.S. Families, 1950–2008**

Average U.S. family income grew rapidly between 1950 and 1970. Since then, however, the increase has been smaller.

Source: U.S. Census Bureau (2009).

recently, the "outsourcing" of jobs and the closing of U.S. factories and other business operations has brought downward structural social mobility, dealing economic setbacks to many people. The economic downturn that hit hard in 2008 and 2009 reduced the income and economic opportunities of millions of people.

Sociologists distinguish between shorter- and longer-term changes in social position. **Intragenerational social mobility** is *a change in social position occurring during a person's lifetime* (*intra* is Latin for "within"). **Intergenerational social mobility,** *upward or downward social mobility of children in relation to their parents,* is important because it reveals long-term changes in society that affect everyone (*inter* is Latin for "between").

Myth versus Reality

In few societies do people think about "getting ahead" as much as in the United States. Moving up, after all, is the American dream. But is there as much social mobility in our country as we like to think?

One recent study of intergenerational mobility shows that about 32 percent of U.S. men had the same type of work as their fathers, 37 percent were upwardly mobile (for example, a son born to a father with a blue-collar job ends up doing white-collar work), and 32 percent were downwardly mobile (for example, the father has a white-collar job and the son does blue-collar work). Among women, 46 percent were upwardly mobile, 28 percent were downwardly mobile, and 27 percent showed no change compared to their fathers (Beller & Hout, 2006).

Horizontal social mobility—changing jobs at the same class level—is even more common. Overall, about 80 percent of children show some type of social mobility in relation to their parents (Hout, 1998; Beller & Hout, 2006).

Research points to four general conclusions about social mobility in the United States:

1. **Social mobility over the course of the past century has been fairly high.** A high level of mobility is what we would expect in an industrial class system.

2. **Within a single generation, social mobility is usually small.**
   Most young families increase their income over time as they
   gain education and skills. A typical family headed by a thirty-
   year-old earned about $59,000 in 2008; a typical family headed
   by a fifty-year-old earned $77,000 (U.S. Census Bureau, 2009).
   Yet only a few people move from "rags to riches" (the way J. K.
   Rowling did) or lose a lot of money (a number of rock stars
   who made it big had little money left a few years later). Most
   social mobility involves small movement within one class level
   rather than large movement between classes.

3. **The long-term trend in social mobility has been upward.**
   Industrialization, which greatly expanded the U.S. economy,
   and the growth of white-collar work over the course of the
   twentieth century have raised living standards.

4. **Social mobility since the 1970s has been uneven.** Real
   income (adjusted for inflation) rose during the twentieth century until the 1970s. Since then, as shown in Figure 8–4, real
   income has risen and fallen, with overall smaller gains than was
   the case before 1970. Most recently, the economic recession that
   began in 2007 resulted in downward social mobility for many
   U.S. families. But general historical trends do not show the
   experiences of different categories of people, as the next section explains.

Mobility by Income Level

Figure 8–5 shows how U.S. families at different income levels made
out between 1980 and 2008. Well-to-do families (the highest 20 percent, but not all the same families over the entire period) saw their
incomes jump 55 percent, from an average $122,519 in 1980 to
$190,400 in 2008. People in the middle of the population also had
gains, but more modest ones. The lowest-income 20 percent actually
lost ground, making an average of $43 less in 2008 than in 1980
(adjusted for inflation).

For families at the top of the income scale (the highest 5 percent), recent decades have brought a windfall. These families, with
average income of almost $175,000 in 1980, were making $326,928
in 2008—nearly twice as much as they had made in 1980 (U.S. Census Bureau, 2009).

Mobility: Race, Ethnicity, and Gender

White people in the United States have always been in a more privileged position than people of African or Hispanic descent. Through
the economic expansion of the 1980s and 1990s, more African Americans entered the ranks of the wealthy. But overall, the real income
of African Americans has changed little in three decades. African
American family income as a percentage of white family income has

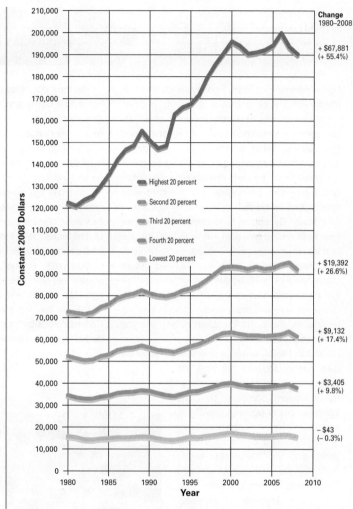

FIGURE 8–5 **Mean Annual Income, U.S. Families, 1980–2008
(in 2008 dollars, adjusted for inflation)**

The gap between high-income and low-income families is wider today
than it was in 1980.

Source: U.S. Census Bureau (2009).

fallen slightly to 57 percent in 2008 from 61 percent in 1975. Compared with white families, Latino families lost ground between 1975
(when their average income was 66 percent of that of white families) and 2008 (when it had slipped to 58 percent) (Pomer, 1986; U.S.
Census Bureau, 2009).

Feminists point out that historically, women have had less chance
for upward mobility than men because most working women hold
clerical jobs (such as secretary) and service positions (such as food
server) that offer few opportunities for advancement.

SEEING SOCIOLOGY IN EVERYDAY LIFE

As CEOs Get Richer, the Great Mansions Return

I grew up in Elkins Park, Pennsylvania, an older Philadelphia suburb that is a mostly middle-class community, although like most of suburbia, some neighborhoods boast bigger houses than others. What made Elkins Park special was that a century ago, a handful of great mansions were built by early Philadelphia industrialists. Back then, all there was to the town was these great "estates," separated by fields and meadows. By about 1940, however, most of this land had been split off into lots for the homes of newer middle-class suburbanites. The great mansions suddenly seemed out of place, with heirs disagreeing over who should live there and how to pay the rising property taxes. As a result, many of the great mansions were sold, the buildings taken down, and the land subdivided.

In the 1960s, when I was a teenager, a short bike ride could take me past the Breyer estate (built by the founder of the ice-cream company, now the township police building), the Curtis estate (built by a magazine publisher and transformed into a community park), and the Wanamaker estate (built by the founder of a large Philadelphia department store, now the site of high-rise apartments). Probably the grandest of them all was the Wiedner estate, modeled after a French chateau, complete with doorknobs and window pulls covered in gold; it now stands empty.

In their day, these structures were not just home to a family and many servants; they were also monuments to a time when the rich were, well, *really* rich. By contrast, the community that emerged on the grounds once owned by these rich families is middle-class, with modest homes on small lots.

But did the so-called Gilded Age of great wealth disappear forever? No. By the 1980s, a new wave of great mansions was being built in the United States. Take the architect Thierry Despont, who designs huge houses for the super-rich. One of Despont's "smaller" homes might be 20,000 square feet (about ten times the size of the average U.S. house), and they go all the way up to 60,000 square feet (as big as any of the Elkins Park mansions built a century ago and almost the size of the White House). These megahomes have

kitchens as large as college classrooms, exercise rooms, indoor swimming pools, and even indoor tennis courts (Krugman, 2002).

Megahouses are being built by newly rich chief executive officers (CEOs) of large corporations. Although CEOs have always made more money than most people, recent years have seen executive compensation soar. Between 1970 and 2008, the average U.S. family saw only a modest increase in income (about 26 percent after inflation is taken into account). During the same period, the average compensation for the 100 highest-paid CEOs skyrocketed from $1.3 million (about 40 times the earnings of an average worker at that time) to $29.7 million (equal to 494 times the compensation of today's average worker). Richer still, the twenty highest-earning investment fund managers in 2008 (a terrible year for the stock market) had, on average, $465 million *each* in income, earning more in ten minutes than an average worker made all year (Story, 2009; Corporate Library, 2010; U.S. Census Bureau, 2010).

WHAT DO YOU THINK?

1. Do you consider increasing economic inequality a problem? Why or why not?

2. How many times more than an average worker should a CEO earn? Explain your answer.

3. Does very high CEO pay help or hurt stockholders? What about the general public? Explain your reasoning.

Over time, however, the earnings gap between women and men has been narrowing. Women working full time in 1980 earned 60 percent as much as men working full time; by 2008, women were earning 77 percent as much (U.S. Census Bureau, 2009).

Mobility and Marriage

Research points to the conclusion that marriage has an important effect on social standing. In a study of women and men in their for-

ties, Jay Zagorsky (2006) found that people who marry and stay married accumulate about twice as much wealth as people who remain single or who divorce. Reasons for this difference include the fact that couples who live together typically enjoy double incomes and also pay only half the bills they would have if they were single and living in separate households.

It is also likely that compared to single people, married men and women work harder in their jobs and save more money. Why? Primarily because they are working not just for themselves but to

Seeing Sociology in Everyday Life

In your opinion, how significantly has the recent economic downturn affected people's optimism about their ability to realize the "American dream"?

relative poverty (p. 232) the lack of resources of some people in relation to those who have more

absolute poverty (p. 232) a lack of resources that is life-threatening

feminization of poverty (p. 233) the trend of women making up an increasing proportion of the poor

support children and spouses who are counting on them (Popenoe, 2006).

Just as marriage pushes social standing upward, divorce usually makes social position go down. Couples who divorce take on the costs of supporting two households, which leaves them with less money for savings or other investment. After divorce, women are hurt more than men because typically the man earns more. Many women who divorce lose not only most of their income but also benefits such as health care and insurance coverage (Weitzman, 1996).

The American Dream: Still a Reality?

The expectation of upward social mobility is deeply rooted in U.S. culture. Through much of our history, the economy has grown steadily, raising living standards. Today, at least for some people, the American dream is alive and well. In 2008, fully 26 percent of U.S. families earned $100,000 or more, compared with just 7 percent back in 1967 (in dollars controlled for inflation). There are now at least 7 million millionaires in the United States, five times the number a decade ago (Rank & Hirschl, 2001; L. Eisenberg, 2007; U.S. Census Bureau, 2009; Wolff, 2009).

Yet not all indicators are so positive. Note these disturbing trends:

1. **For many workers, earnings have stalled.** The annual income of a fifty-year-old man working full time climbed by 65 percent between 1958 and 1974 (from $29,345 to $48,367 in constant 2008 dollars). Between 1974 and 2008, however, this worker's income fell by 6 percent to $45,540, even as the number of hours worked increased and the cost of necessities such as housing, education, gasoline, and medical care went way up (Russell, 1995a; U.S. Census Bureau, 2009).

2. **More jobs offer little income.** The expanding global economy has moved many industrial jobs overseas, reducing the availability of high-paying factory work here in the United States. At the same time, the expansion of our service economy means more of today's jobs—in fast-food restaurants or large discount stores—offer relatively low wages.

3. **Young people are remaining at home.** Currently, more than half of young people aged eighteen to twenty-four, unable to support a household, are still living with their parents. Since 1975, the average age at first marriage has moved upward four years (to 25.9 years for women and 28.1 years for men).

Over the past generation, more people have become rich, and the rich have become richer; as the Seeing Sociology in Everyday Life box explains, the highest-paid corporate executives have enjoyed a runaway rise in their earnings. But at the same time, the increasing share of low-paying jobs has brought downward mobility for millions of families, feeding the fear that the chance to enjoy a middle-class lifestyle is slipping away. As a glance back at Figure 8–4 on page 228 shows, although median family income doubled between 1950 and 1973, it has grown by only 18 percent since then (U.S. Census Bureau, 2009).

For years, the mass media have presented the American Dream as alive and well in "reality" shows such as *American Idol*, which is based on the idea that talent and effort can make anyone rich and famous. More recently, as Seeing Sociology in the News on pages 232–33 explains, television shows are presenting a more pessimistic view of people's chances to get ahead.

The Global Economy and the U.S. Class Structure

Underlying the shifts in U.S. class structure over recent decades is global economic change. Much of the industrial production that gave U.S. workers high-paying jobs a generation ago has been moved overseas, where wages are cheaper. With less industry at home, the United States now serves as a vast consumer market for industrial goods such as cars, stereos, cameras, and computers made in China, Japan, South Korea, and elsewhere.

High-paying jobs in manufacturing, held by 28 percent of U.S. workers in 1960, support fewer than 10 percent of workers today. In their place, the economy offers service work, which pays far less. Traditionally high-paying corporations such as USX (formerly United States Steel) now employ fewer people than the expanding McDonald's chain, and fast-food clerks make only a fraction of what steelworkers earn.

The global reorganization of work has not been bad news for everyone. The global economy is driving upward social mobility for educated people who specialize in law, finance, marketing, and computer technology. Even allowing for the downturn in 2008 and 2009, the global economic expansion also helped push up the stock market more than tenfold between 1980 and 2010, reaping profits for families with money to invest.

But the same trend has hurt many average workers, who have lost their factory jobs and now perform low-wage service work. In addition, many companies (General Motors and Ford are recent examples) have downsized—cutting the ranks of their workforce—in an attempt to stay competitive in world markets. As a result, although more than 50 percent of all married-couple families today contain two or more people in the labor force—more than twice the share in 1950—many families are working harder than ever before simply to hold on to what they have (A. L. Nelson, 1998; Sennett, 1998; U.S. Census Bureau, 2009).

The New York Times

Waking Up from American Dreams

By ANAND GIRIDHARADAS
February 13, 2010

The recent Super Bowl triumph of the New Orleans Saints fits the traditional narrative of limitless American possibility: a long-shot victory by a written-off team from a fate-battered city. But for the 38.6 million Americans who kept their televisions on after the game to watch the new reality show *Undercover Boss*, a different narrative was on offer, with a darker portrait of the extant American Dream.

American Idol–style contests have dominated reality television in the United States in recent years, with the Horatio Alger–style story line that anyone with talent and pluck can rise. *Undercover Boss* was built very differently, for a nation that is day by day growing more skeptical of that story line and more susceptible to other, less hopeful narratives.

Each week, the show dispatches a top executive at a leading American company to labor anonymously among his rank-and-file workers. It plays not on the traditional American fantasy that you, too, can begin in the mailroom and become C.E.O. Instead, as the viewer comments online suggest, the show taps into a feeling that many Americans once considered un-American: pleasure in seeing the high and mighty humbled.

In the first episode, Larry O'Donnell, the president of Waste Management . . . is stunned to discover working-class realities. He is shocked that workers must punch in after lunch and lose two minutes of pay for every minute they are late. He encounters a worker with chronic kidney problems who must keep working. . . .

This being American television, there is, of course, a narrative twist. Mr. O'Donnell returns to his real life, shaken by his excursion among people.

He summons his new working-class friends to headquarters one by one to disclose his identity. But it is revealing of present American realities that he makes no effort to change the system overall. . . . Rather, he throws them scraps—changing the lunch-tardiness policy, switching a working mother he met from an hourly to a salaried position. . . .

The Horatio Alger narrative maintains its hold in the United States. A Gallup/*USA Today* poll last year found that three-quarters of Americans still believe that if you work hard and follow the rules, you can achieve the American Dream.

But a large number of people also tell pollsters that it is becoming harder to get ahead, that tension is rising between rich and poor, that the rich are rich because of connections and fortunate birth. And for this writer, who recently returned to America after six years in India, it is hard to ignore a quiet turning in the culture . . . toward ideas more familiar in feudal places: that class is a fate, not a situation; that the contest is rigged against the underdog.

In India, a suffix enforces such stratification. It is "-wallah," and can be added to a service to denote the kind of person who provides it, generation after generation. A dhobiwallah is an inevitable launderer, a chaiwallah an inevitable server of tea. At times, it feels as if America, too, is becoming a Wallah Society.

Two sociologists, Greggor Mattson and Claude Fischer . . . recently concluded in the *Annual*

Poverty in the United States

Social stratification creates both "haves" and "have-nots." All systems of social inequality create poverty, or at least **relative poverty,** *the lack of resources of some people in relation to those who have more.* A more serious but preventable problem is **absolute poverty,** *a lack of resources that is life-threatening.*

As Chapter 9 ("Global Stratification") explains, about 1.4 billion human beings around the world—one person in five—are at risk of absolute poverty. Even in the affluent United States, families go hungry, sleep in parked cars or on the streets, and suffer from poor health simply because they are poor.

The Extent of Poverty

In 2008, the government classified 39.8 million men, women, and children—13.2 percent of the U.S. population—as poor. This count of relative poverty refers to families with income below an official poverty line, which, for a family of four, was set that year at $22,025. The poverty line is about three times what the government estimates a family will spend for food. But the income of the average poor family was just 59 percent of this amount. This means that the typical poor family had to get by on less than $13,000 in 2008 (U.S. Census Bureau, 2009).

Who Are the Poor?

Although no single description fits all poor people, poverty is greater among certain categories of our population. Where these categories overlap, the problem is especially serious.

Age

A generation ago, the elderly were the category of the population at greatest risk for poverty. But thanks to better retirement programs offered today by private employers and the government, the poverty rate for people over age sixty-five fell from 30 percent in 1967 to 9.7 percent—well below the national average—in 2008. Looking at it from another angle, about 9.2 percent (3.7 million) of the poor are elderly.

Today the burden of poverty falls most heavily on children and young adults. In 2008, some 19 percent of people under age eighteen (14.1 million children) and 18.4 percent of people ages eighteen to twenty-four (5.3 million young adults) were poor. Put another way, 49 percent of the U.S. poor are young people under the age of twenty-five.

Race and Ethnicity

Seventy percent of all poor people are white (including some who also describe themselves as Hispanic); 24 percent are African

Review of Sociology that class, among the least-discussed fault lines, has become the most salient—even more salient than race.... Increasingly, they write, rich and poor Americans live in separate, impermeable worlds: one of relatively plentiful salaried jobs [and] vibrant neighborhoods ... and another that sees those things, and the larger dream, receding.

The shift can be sensed in American restaurants. What once distinguished them from restaurants elsewhere was an idea of classlessness: that the person with the grease-stained notepad and aching feet could, with luck and effort, become the person at the table; that there was no essential difference between them.

But the archetypal American waiter today is no longer the eager-eyed college student, paying his way through school, hatching big plans. Waiting tables is increasingly a profession, as in France, with older, brusquer servers whose vision of the world is tinged with resentment.

There is a quiet but unmistakable defensiveness in their voices, which ask in every interaction, "What, you think you're better than me?"...

Humor can be more revealing than seriousness, and fiction more revealing than truth. So a good place to watch this turning in American ideas is *30 Rock*, the hit television show....

Jack Donaghy, played by Alec Baldwin, is a suave, arrogant, heavily bonused television executive who lives in a world of private jets, secret restaurants, and [custom-made] suits. If earlier New York comedies like *Seinfeld* and *Friends* airbrushed class, giving everyone nice apartments regardless of occupation, *30 Rock* depicts a Goldman Sachsed America where the rich and not-rich spin in different orbits.

Alexis de Toqueville once marveled at an America where servants were "equals of their masters." ... Yet in Jack Donaghy's America the classes have so diverged as to be physically distinct. When Mr. Donaghy crashes a younger colleague's high-school reunion and blends right in, he explains it thus: "Rich 50 is middle-class 38."

In another episode, in an echo of recent economic history, Mr. Donaghy convinces Kenneth ... to surrender his life savings of $4,000 to be invested on his behalf....

"Next stop: homeownership," Mr. Donaghy mocks. "I'm just kidding. The middle class is dying. You'll be renting forever."

Moments later, Kenneth learns that the stock has collapsed. All his money is lost.

WHAT DO YOU THINK?

1. Do you think reality shows like *American Idol* realistically portray people's ability to rise in the class system based on talent and hard work?

2. How realistic is the portrayal of our class system in *30 Rock*, which presents the rich and poor as living in different and disconnected worlds?

3. Do you feel that, if you work hard and follow the rules, you can achieve the American Dream? Explain your personal views on this question.

Adapted from the original article, "Waking Up from American Dreams," by Anand Giridharadas published in *The New York Times* on February 13, 2010. Copyright © by The New York Times Company. All rights reserved. Used by permission and protected by the Copyright Laws of the United States. The printing, copying, redistribution, or retransmission of the Material without express permission is prohibited.

American (also including some who say they are also Hispanic). But in relation to their overall numbers, African Americans are about three times as likely as whites to be poor. In 2008, some 24.7 percent of African Americans (9.4 million people) lived in poverty, compared with 23.2 percent of Hispanics (11 million), 11.8 percent of Asian Americans (1.6 million), and 8.6 percent of non-Hispanic whites (17 million). The poverty gap between whites and minorities has changed little since 1975.

People of color have especially high rates of child poverty. Among African American children, 34.7 percent are poor; the comparable figures are 30.6 percent among Hispanic children and 10.6 percent among non-Hispanic white children (U.S. Census Bureau, 2009).

Gender and Family Patterns

Of all poor people age eighteen or older, 59 percent are women and 41 percent are men. This difference reflects the fact that women who head households are at high risk of poverty. Of all poor families, 48 percent are headed by women with no husband present, and just 8 percent are headed by single men.

The United States has experienced a **feminization of poverty,** which is defined as *the trend of women making up an increasing proportion of the poor.* In 1960, only 25 percent of all poor households were headed by women; the majority of poor families had both wives and husbands in the home. By 2008, however, the proportion of poor families headed by single women had nearly doubled to 48 percent.

The feminization of poverty is one result of a larger trend: the rapidly increasing number of households at all class levels headed by single women. This trend, coupled with the fact that households headed by women are at high risk of poverty, helps explain why women and their children now make up an increasing share of the U.S. poor.

Urban and Rural Poverty

In the United States, the greatest concentration of poverty is found in central cities, where the 2008 poverty rate stood at 17.7 percent. The poverty rate in suburbs is 9.8 percent. Thus the poverty rate for urban areas as a whole is 12.9 percent, lower than the 15.1 percent found in rural areas. National Map 8–1 on page 234 shows that most of the counties with the highest poverty rate in the United States are rural.

Explaining Poverty

The richest nation on Earth contains tens of millions of poor people, a fact that raises serious questions. It is true, as some analysts remind us, that most poor people in the United States are far better off than

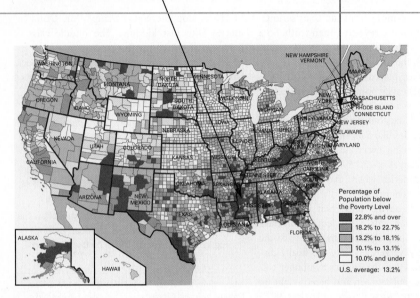

Anna Mae Peters lives in Nitta Yuma, Mississippi. Almost everyone she knows lives below the government's poverty line.

Julie Garland lives in Greenwich, Connecticut, where people have very high income and there is little evidence of poverty.

Explore the percentage of people living in poverty in your local community and in counties across the United States on mysoclab.com

Seeing Ourselves

NATIONAL MAP 8–1

Poverty across the United States

This map shows that the poorest counties in the United States—where the poverty rate is more than twice the national average—are in Appalachia, spread across the Deep South, along the border with Mexico, near the Four Corners region of the Southwest, and in the Dakotas. Can you suggest some reasons for this pattern?

Explore on mysoclab.com

Source: U.S. Census Bureau (2009).

Percentage of Population below the Poverty Level

- 22.8% and over
- 18.2% to 22.7%
- 13.2% to 18.1%
- 10.1% to 13.1%
- 10.0% and under

U.S. average: 13.2%

the poor in other countries: 34 percent of U.S. poor families own a home, 70 percent own a car, and only about 19 percent say they often go without food (U.S. Census Bureau, 2009). But there is little doubt that poverty harms the overall well-being of millions of people in this country.

Why is there poverty in the first place? We will examine two opposing explanations that lead to a lively and important political debate.

One View: Blame the Poor

One view holds that *the poor are primarily responsible for their own poverty.* Throughout the nation's history, people have placed a high cultural value on self-reliance, convinced that a person's social standing is mostly a matter of individual talent and effort. According to this view, society offers plenty of opportunities to anyone who is able and willing to take advantage of them, and the poor are people who cannot or will not work due to a lack of skills, schooling, or motivation.

In his study of Latin American cities, the anthropologist Oscar Lewis (1961) concluded that the poor become trapped in a *culture of poverty,* a lower-class subculture that can destroy people's ambition to improve their lives. Socialized in poor families, children become resigned to their situation, producing a self-perpetuating cycle of poverty.

In 1996, hoping to free people from what some saw as a culture of poverty in the United States, Congress changed the welfare system, which had provided a federal guarantee of financial assistance to poor people since 1935. The federal government continues to send money to the states to distribute to needy people, but benefits now carry strict limits—in most cases, no more than two years at a stretch

and a total of five years altogether if a person moves in and out of the welfare system. The stated purpose of this reform was to force people to be self-supporting and move them away from dependency on government.

Another View: Blame Society

A different position, argued by the sociologist William Julius Wilson (1996a, 1996b; see also Mouw, 2000), holds that *society is primarily responsible for poverty.* Wilson points to the loss of jobs in our inner cities as the primary cause of poverty, claiming that there is simply not enough work to support families. Wilson sees any apparent lack of trying on the part of the poor as a result of little opportunity rather than as a cause of poverty. From Wilson's point of view, Lewis's analysis amounts to *blaming the victim,* that is, saying that victims are responsible for their own suffering (W. Ryan, 1976). To combat poverty and reduce the need for welfare, Wilson argues, the government should fund jobs and provide affordable child care for low-income mothers and fathers.

CRITICAL REVIEW The U.S. public is evenly divided over whether government or people themselves should take responsibility for reducing poverty (NORC, 2009:403). Government statistics show that 53 percent of the heads of poor families did not work at all during 2008, and an additional 31 percent worked only part time (U.S. Census Bureau, 2009). Such facts seem to support the "blame the poor" position because a major cause of poverty is not holding a job.

But the reasons that people do not work are more in step with the "blame society" position. Middle-class women may be able to combine working and child rearing, but this is much harder for poor

234   CHAPTER 8   Social Stratification

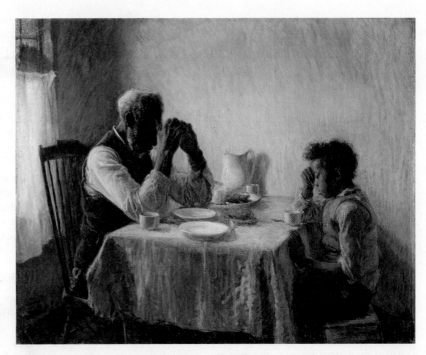

Read "The Compassion Gap in American Poverty Policy" by Fred Block et al. on **mysoclab.com**

Seeing Sociology in Everyday Life

Our society has been more generous with the "worthy" poor (such as elderly people) than with the "unworthy" poor (such as able-bodied people who, we assume, should take care of themselves). Why do you think we have not done more to reduce poverty among children, who surely fall into the "worthy" category?

women who cannot afford child care, and few employers provide child care programs. As William Julius Wilson explains, many people are jobless not because they are avoiding work but because there are not enough jobs to go around. In short, the most effective way to reduce poverty is to ensure a greater supply of jobs as well as child care for parents who work (W. J. Wilson, 1996a; Pease & Martin, 1997; Duncan, 1999; Bainbridge, Meyers, & Waldfogel, 2003). **Read** on **mysoclab.com**

CHECK YOUR LEARNING Explain the view that the poor should take responsibility for poverty and the view that society is responsible for poverty. Which is closer to your own view?

The Working Poor

Not all poor people are jobless, and the *working poor* command the sympathy and support of people on both sides of the poverty debate. In 2008, some 16 percent of heads of poor families (1.3 million women and men) worked at least fifty weeks of the year and yet could not escape poverty. Another 31 percent of these heads of families (2.5 million people) remained poor despite having part-time employment. Put differently, 3.2 percent of heads of families who work full time earn so little that they remain poor (U.S. Census Bureau, 2009). Since July 2009, the the federal minimum wage has been $7.25 per hour. But at this level, working is no guarantee of escaping poverty—even earning $8.00 per hour, a full-time worker cannot lift an urban family of four above the poverty line.

Individual ability and personal initiative do play a part in shaping social position. However, the weight of sociological evidence points toward society, not individual character traits, as the primary source of poverty, because more and more available jobs offer only low wages. In addition, the poor are *categories* of people—female heads of families, people of color, people in inner-city neighborhoods isolated from the larger society—who face special barriers and limited opportunities.

The Controversy & Debate box on pages 236–37 takes a closer look at the current welfare debate. Understanding this important social issue can help us decide how our society should respond to the problem of poverty, as well as the problem of homelessness discussed next.

Homelessness

Each year, the government's Department of Housing and Urban Development conducts a national survey of cities and towns to find

The African American artist Henry Ossawa Tanner captured the humility and humanity of impoverished people in his painting *The Thankful Poor*. This insight is important in a society that tends to define poor people as morally unworthy and deserving of their bitter plight.

Henry Ossawa Tanner (1859–1937), *The Thankful Poor*. Private collection. Art Resource, New York.

out how many people in the United States are homeless. The 2008 survey found about 664,414 people living in shelters, in transitional housing, and on the street on a single night in January. But, the government estimates, a much larger number—approximately 1.6 million people—are homeless for at least some time during the course of the year (U.S. Department of Housing and Urban Development, 2009). As with earlier estimates of the homeless population, critics claimed that the HUD estimate undercounted the homeless, who may well have numbered several million people. Some estimates suggest that as many as 3 million people are homeless for at least one night in a given year. In addition, they add, evidence suggests that the number of homeless people in the United States is increasing (L. Kaufman, 2004; National Coalition for the Homeless, 2009).

The familiar stereotypes of homeless people—men sleeping in doorways and women pushing rickety shopping carts containing everything they own—have been replaced by the "new homeless": people thrown out of work because of plant closings, women who take their children and leave home to escape domestic violence, women and men forced out of apartments by rent increases, and

Go to the Multimedia Library at **mysoclab.com** to listen to the NPR report "A Few Small Steps to Homelessness"

Seeing Sociology in Everyday Life

Do you think people in the United States consider homelessness to be a serious problem? Why or why not?

CONTROVERSY & DEBATE

The Welfare Dilemma

MARCO: *(rushing in through the door)* Sorry I'm late. I stopped at the store and got stuck behind some welfare mother in the checkout lane.

SERGEI: *(looking back with a confused grin)* Exactly what does a person on welfare look like?

What is *your* image of a welfare recipient? If you are like many people in the United States, you might think of a middle-aged African American woman. But you would be wrong. In truth, the typical person receiving welfare in this country is a child who is white.

There is a lot of confusion about welfare. There is also disagreement about whether this type of assistance is a good or bad idea. In 1996, Congress debated the issue and enacted a new law that ended the federal government's role in providing income assistance to poor households. In place of this federal program, new state-run programs now offer limited help to the poor, but they require people who receive aid to get job training or find work—or have their benefits cut off.

To understand how we got to where we are, let's begin by explaining what, exactly, welfare is. The term "welfare" refers to an assortment of policies and

programs designed to improve the well-being of some low-income people. Until the welfare reform of 1996, most people used the term to refer to just one part of the overall system: Aid for Families with Dependent Children (AFDC), a federal program of monthly financial support for parents (mostly single women) to care for themselves and their children. In 1996, about 5 million households in the United States received AFDC for at least some part of the year.

Is society responsible for poverty or are individuals themselves to blame? When it comes to homeless families, most people think society should do more.

Conservatives opposed AFDC, claiming that rather than reducing child poverty, AFDC made the problem worse, in two ways. First, they claimed that AFDC weakened families, because for years after the program began, it paid benefits to poor mothers only if no husband lived in the home. As a result, the government was actually providing an economic incentive to women to have children outside of marriage, and they blame it for the rapid rise of out-of-wedlock births among poor people. To conservatives, marriage is one key to reducing poverty: Only about one in twenty married-couple families are poor; more than nine in ten AFDC families were headed by an unmarried woman.

Second, conservatives believe that welfare encourages poor people to become dependent on government handouts, the main reason that eight out of ten poor heads of households did not have full-time jobs. Furthermore, only 5 percent of single mothers receiving AFDC worked full time, compared to more than half of nonpoor single mothers. Conservatives say that welfare gradually moved well beyond its original purpose of short-term help to non-working women with children (say, after

others unable to meet mortgage or rent payments because of low wages or no work at all. Today, no stereotype paints a complete picture of the homeless.

The large majority of homeless people report that they do not work, although about 20 percent have at least a part-time job (U.S. Conference of Mayors, 2007). Working or not, all homeless people have one thing in common: poverty. For that reason, the explanations of poverty just presented also apply to homelessness. Some people blame the *personal traits* of the homeless. More than one-third of homeless people are substance abusers, and one-fourth are mentally ill. More broadly, a fraction of 1 percent of our population, for one reason or another, seems unable to cope with our complex and highly

competitive society (U.S. Department of Housing and Urban Development, 2009). ● Go to **mysoclab.com**

Others see homelessness resulting from *societal factors,* including low wages and a lack of affordable housing (Kozol, 1988; Bohannan, 1991; L. Kaufman, 2004). Supporters of this position point out that about one-third of the homeless consist of families, and children are the fastest-growing category of the homeless.

No one disputes that a large proportion of homeless people are personally impaired to some degree, but cause and effect are difficult to untangle. Long-term structural changes in the U.S. economy, cutbacks in social service budgets, and the recent economic downturn have all contributed to the problem of homelessness.

● Seeing Sociology
in Everyday Life

Do you see evidence of homelessness in your community?
Has the problem become worse during the recent economic
recession?

● Seeing Sociology
in Everyday Life

What are the arguments typically made by Democratic and
Republican politicians on the issue of poverty?

divorce or death of a husband) and gradually became a way of life. Once trapped in dependency, poor women would raise children who were themselves likely to be poor as adults.

Liberals have a different view. Why, they ask, do people object to government money going to poor mothers and children when most "welfare" actually goes to richer people? The cost of AFDC was as high as $25 billion annually—no small sum, to be sure, but much less than the $516 billion in annual Social Security benefits Uncle Sam provides to more than 40 million of our senior citizens, most of whom are not poor. And it is just a small fraction of the more than $1 trillion "bailout money" Congress voted in 2008 and 2009 to assist the struggling financial industry.

Liberals insist that most poor families who turn to public assistance are truly needy. Most of the people who are helped in this way are children. And they don't get very much. The typical household receives only about $500 per month in assistance, hardly enough to attract people to a life of welfare dependency. Even adding some additional money in the form of food stamps, households assisted by welfare still struggle well below the poverty line everywhere in the country. Therefore, liberals see

public assistance as a "Band-Aid approach" to the serious social problems of too few jobs and too much income inequality in the United States. As for the charge that public assistance weakens families, liberals agree that the share of families with one parent has gone up, but they see single parenting as a broad trend found at all class levels in many countries.

Back in 1996, the conservative arguments carried the day, ending the AFDC program. Our society's individualistic culture has always encouraged us to blame people themselves (rather than society) for poverty, which becomes a sign not of need but of laziness and personal failure (Inglehart et al., 2000). This view of the poor is probably the biggest reason that led Congress to replace the federal AFDC program with state-run programs called Temporary Assistance for Needy Families (TANF), requiring poor adults to get job training and limiting income assistance to two consecutive years with a lifetime limit of five years.

By 2008, the new TANF policy had cut the number of households receiving income assistance by more than half. This means that many single parents who were once on welfare have taken jobs or are receiving job training. With this mind, conservatives who

supported welfare reform see the new program as a huge success. The welfare rolls have been cut, and more people have moved from receiving a check to working to support themselves. But liberals claim that the reform is far from successful. They point out that many of the people who are now working earn so little pay that they are hardly better off than before. In other words, the reform has greatly reduced the number of people receiving welfare, but it has done little to reduce the extent of poverty.

WHAT DO YOU THINK?

1. How does our cultural emphasis on self-reliance help explain the controversy surrounding public assistance? Why do people not criticize benefits (such as home mortgage deductions) for people who are better off?

2. Do you approve of the time limits on benefits built into the TANF program? Why or why not?

3. Why do you think the welfare reforms have done little to reduce poverty?

Sources: Lichter & Crowley (2002), Lichter & Jayakody (2002), Von Drehle (2008), and U.S. Census Bureau (2009).

Class, Welfare, Politics, and Values

We have reviewed many facts about social inequality. In the end, however, our opinions about wealth and poverty depend not just on facts but also on our politics and values. As we might expect, the idea that social standing reflects personal merit is popular among well-off people; the opposing idea, that government should spread wealth more equally, finds favor among those who are less well off (NORC, 2009).

In the United States, our cultural emphasis on individual responsibility encourages us to see successful people as personally worthy and to view poor people as personally falling short. Such attitudes go a long way toward explaining why our society spends much more than other high-income nations on education (to promote opportu-

nity) but much less on public assistance programs (which directly support the poor).

Most members of our society are willing to accept a high level of income inequality, and many hold a harsh view of the poor. To the extent that we define poor people as undeserving, we look on public assistance programs as at best a waste of money and at worst a substitute for personal initiative.

Finally, the drama of social stratification extends far beyond the borders of the United States. The most striking social inequality is found not by looking inside one country but by comparing living standards in various parts of the world. In Chapter 9, we broaden our focus by investigating global stratification.

Seeing Sociology in Everyday Life

How do we understand inequality in our society?

This chapter sketches the class structure of the United States and also explains how factors such as race are linked to social standing. You already know, for example, that the rate of poverty is three times higher for African Americans than for whites, and you have also learned that the typical black family earns just 57 percent as much as the typical (non-Hispanic) white family. But rich people—here, we'll define "rich" as a family earning more than $75,000 a year—come in all colors. Here's a chance to test your sociological thinking by answering several questions about how race affects being rich. Look at each of the statements below: Does the statement reflect reality or is it a myth?

Q

1. In the United States, all rich people are white. *Reality or myth?*

2. Rich white families are actually richer than rich African American families. *Reality or myth?*

3. People in rich black families don't work as hard as members of rich white families. *Reality or myth?*

4. When you are rich, color doesn't matter. *Reality or myth?*

1. *Of course, this is a myth.* But when it comes to being rich, race does matter: About 23 percent of African American families are affluent (for Hispanic families, 22 percent), compared to about 46 percent of non-Hispanic white families.

2. *Reality.* Rich white, non-Hispanic families have a mean (average) income more than $200,000 per year. Rich African American families average about $130,000 per year.

3. *Myth.* On average, rich black families are more likely to rely on multiple incomes (that is, they have more people working) than their white counterparts. In addition, rich white families receive more unearned income—income from investments—than rich African American families.

4. *Myth.* Rich African Americans still face social barriers based on their race, just as rich whites benefit from the privileges linked to their color.

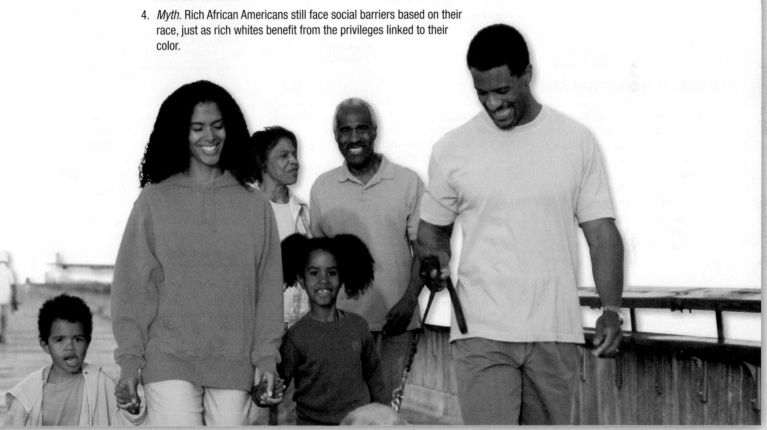

Applying SOCIOLOGY in Everyday Life

1. Identify three ways in which social stratification is evident in the everyday lives of students on your campus. In each case, explain exactly what is unequal and what difference it makes. Do you think individual talent or family background is more important in creating these social differences?

2. Sit down with parents, grandparents, or other relatives, and assess the social position of your family over the last three generations. Has social mobility taken place? How much? Why?

3. During an evening of television viewing, assess the social class level of the characters you see on various shows. In each case, explain why you assign someone a particular social position. Do you find many clearly upper-class people? Middle-class people? Working-class people? Poor people? Describe the patterns you find.

Making the Grade

VISUAL SUMMARY

What Is Social Stratification?

SOCIAL STRATIFICATION is a system by which a society ranks categories of people in a hierarchy, so that some people have more money, power, and prestige than others.
Social stratification

- is a trait of society, not simply a reflection of individual differences
- carries over from one generation to the next
- is supported by a system of cultural beliefs that defines certain kinds of inequality as just
- takes two general forms: caste systems and class systems

pp. 204–6

CASTE SYSTEMS

- are based on birth (ascription)
- permit little or no social mobility
- shape a person's entire life, including occupation and marriage
- are common in traditional, agrarian societies

pp. 205–6

CLASS SYSTEMS

- are based on both birth (ascription) and **meritocracy** (individual achievement)
- permit some social mobility
- are common in modern industrial and postindustrial societies

pp. 206–11

social stratification (p. 204) a system by which a society ranks categories of people in a hierarchy

social mobility (p. 204) a change in position within the social hierarchy

caste system (p. 205) social stratification based on ascription, or birth

class system (p. 206) social stratification based on both birth and individual achievement

meritocracy (p. 206) social stratification based on personal merit

status consistency (p. 206) the degree of uniformity in a person's social standing across various dimensions of social inequality

structural social mobility (p. 209) a shift in the social position of large numbers of people due more to changes in society itself than to individual efforts

ideology (p. 210) cultural beliefs that justify particular social arrangements, including patterns of inequality

Theoretical Analysis of Social Stratification

The **STRUCTURAL-FUNCTIONAL APPROACH** points to ways social stratification helps society operate.

- The **Davis-Moore thesis** states that social stratification is universal because of its functional consequences.
- In caste systems, people are rewarded for performing the duties of their position at birth.
- In class systems, unequal rewards attract the ablest people to the most important jobs and encourage effort.

pp. 211–13

The **SOCIAL-CONFLICT APPROACH** claims that stratification divides societies into classes, benefiting some categories of people at the expense of others and causing social conflict.

- Karl Marx claimed that capitalism places economic production under the ownership of capitalists, who exploit the proletarians who sell their labor for wages.
- Max Weber identified three distinct dimensions of social stratification: economic class, social status or prestige, and power. Conflict exists between people at various positions on a multidimensional hierarchy of **socioeconomic status (SES)**.

pp. 213–16

Davis-Moore thesis (p. 211) the functional analysis claiming that social stratification has beneficial consequences for the operation of society

capitalists (p. 213) people who own and operate factories and other businesses in pursuit of profits

proletarians (p. 213) people who sell their labor for wages

alienation (p. 213) the experience of isolation and misery resulting from powerlessness

blue-collar occupations (p. 214) lower-prestige jobs that involve mostly manual labor

white-collar occupations (p. 214) higher-prestige jobs that involve mostly mental activity

socioeconomic status (SES) (p. 215) a composite ranking based on various dimensions of social inequality

conspicuous consumption (p. 216) buying and using products because of the "statement" they make about social position

The **SYMBOLIC-INTERACTION APPROACH**, a micro-level analysis, explains that we size people up by looking for clues to their social standing. **Conspicuous consumption** refers to buying and displaying products that make a "statement" about one's position in the social class system. Most people tend to socialize with others whose social standing is similar to their own.

pp. 216–17

See the Applying Theory table on page 215.

Social Stratification and Technology: A Global Perspective

Hunting and Gathering → Horticultural and Pastoral → Agrarian ——————→ Industrial ——————————————→ Postindustrial

- Gerhard Lenski explains that advancing technology initially increases social stratification, which is most intense in agrarian societies.

p. 217

- Industrialization reverses the trend, reducing social stratification.

p. 217

- In postindustrial societies, social stratification again increases.

p. 218–19

See the Kuznets curve (Figure 8–2 on page 217).

Inequality in the United States

SOCIAL STRATIFICATION involves many dimensions:

- *Income*: Earnings from work and investments are unequal, with the richest 20% of families earning twelve times as much as the poorest 20% of families.
- *Wealth*: The total value of all assets minus debts, wealth is distributed more unequally than income, with the richest 20% of families holding 85% of all wealth.
- *Power*: Income and wealth are important sources of power.
- *Prestige*: Work generates not only income but also prestige. White-collar jobs generally offer more income and prestige than blue-collar jobs. Many lower-prestige jobs are performed by women and people of color.
- *Family ancestry, race and ethnicity*, and *gender* all affect social standing.

pp. 219–22

income (p. 219) earnings from work or investments

wealth (p. 220) the total value of money and other assets, minus outstanding debts

Social Classes in the United States

$200,000
$200,000
$61,000
$61,000
$28,000
$28,000

UPPER CLASS—5% of the population. Most members of the upper-upper class, or "old rich," inherited their wealth; the lower-upper class, or "new rich," work at high-paying jobs.

MIDDLE CLASS—40 to 45% of the population. People in the upper-middle class have significant wealth; average-middles have less prestige and do white-collar work, and most attend college.

WORKING CLASS—30 to 35% of the population. People in the lower-middle class do blue-collar work; only about one-third of children attend college.

LOWER CLASS—20% of the population. Most people in the lower class lack financial security due to low income; many live below the poverty line; half do not complete high school.

pp. 222–25

intragenerational social mobility (p. 228) a change in social position occurring during a person's lifetime

intergenerational social mobility (p. 228) upward or downward social mobility of children in relation to their parents

- People with higher social standing generally have better health, hold certain values and political attitudes, and pass on advantages in the form of "cultural capital" to their children.
- Social mobility is common in the United States, as it is in other high-income countries, but typically only small changes occur from one generation to the next.
- Due to the expansion of the global economy, the richest families now earn more than ever; families near the bottom of the class system have seen only small increases.

pp. 225–31

Poverty in the United States

POVERTY PROFILE

- The government classifies 40 million people—13.2% of the population—as poor.
- About 49% of the poor are young people under age 24.
- About 70% of the poor are white, but in relation to their population, African Americans and Hispanics are more likely to be poor.
- The "feminization of poverty" means that more poor families are headed by women.
- About 47% of the heads of poor families are among the "working poor" who work at least part time but do not earn enough to lift a family of four above the poverty line.
- Estimates place the number of people who are homeless at some time over the course of a year at between 1.6 and 3 million.

pp. 232–33, 235–37

EXPLANATIONS OF POVERTY

- Blame individuals: The culture of poverty thesis states that poverty is caused by shortcomings in the poor themselves (Oscar Lewis).
- Blame society: Poverty is caused by society's unequal distribution of wealth and lack of good jobs (William Julius Wilson).

pp. 233–35

📖┤Read on mysoclab.com

⊕┤Explore on mysoclab.com

relative poverty (p. 232) the lack of resources of some people in relation to those who have more

absolute poverty (p. 232) a lack of resources that is life-threatening

feminization of poverty (p. 233) the trend of women making up an increasing proportion of the poor

9 Global Stratification

- What share of the world's people live in absolute poverty?

- Why are some of the world's countries so rich and others so poor?

- Are rich nations making global poverty better or worse? How?

 Watch the *Core Concepts in Sociology* video "Globalization" on **mysoclab.com**

More than a thousand workers were busily sewing together polo shirts on the fourth floor of the garment factory in Narsingdi, a small town about 30 miles northeast of Bangladesh's capital city of Dhaka. The thumping of hundreds of sewing machines produced a steady roar throughout the long working day.

But in an instant everything changed when an electric gun used to shoot spot remover onto stained fabric gave off a spark, which ignited the flammable liquid. Suddenly, a worktable burst into flames. People rushed to smother the fire with shirts, but there was no stopping the blaze: In a room filled with combustible materials, the flames spread quickly.

The workers scrambled toward the narrow staircase that led to the street. At the bottom, however, the human wave pouring down the steep steps collided with a folding metal gate across the doorway that was kept locked to prevent workers from leaving during working hours. Panicked, the people turned, only to be pushed back by the hundreds behind them. In a single terrifying minute of screaming voices, thrusting legs, and pounding hearts, dozens were crushed and trampled. By the time the gates were opened and the fire was put out, fifty-two garment workers lay dead.

Garment factories like this one are big business in Bangladesh, where clothing accounts for 75 percent of the country's total economic exports. Half of these garments end up in stores in the United States. The reason so much of the clothing we buy is made in poor countries like Bangladesh is simple economics—Bangladeshi garment workers labor for as many as twelve hours a day, often seven days a week, and most earn the minimum wage of only $25 a month—as little as 12 cents an hour, which is just a few percent of what a garment worker makes in the United States.

Tanveer Chowdhury manages this garment factory, which his family owns. Speaking to reporters, he complained bitterly about the tragedy. "This fire has cost me $586,373, and that does not include $70,000 for machinery and $20,000 for furniture. I made commitments to meet deadlines, and I still have the deadlines. I am now paying for air freight at $10 a dozen when I should be shipping by sea at 87 cents a dozen."

There was one other cost Chowdhury did not mention. To compensate families for the loss of their loved ones in the fire, the factory eventually agreed to pay $1,952 per person. In Bangladesh, life—like labor—is cheap (based on Bearak, 2001, and Lynch, 2006).

Garment workers in Bangladesh are part of the roughly 1.4 billion of the world's people who work hard every day and yet remain poor. As this chapter explains, although poverty is a reality in the United States and other nations, the greatest social inequality is not *within* nations but *between* them (Goesling, 2001; Chen & Ravallion, 2008). We can understand the full dimensions of poverty only by exploring **global stratification,** *patterns of social inequality in the world as a whole.*

Global Stratification: An Overview

Chapter 8 ("Social Stratification") described inequality in the United States. In global perspective, however, social stratification is far greater. The left pie chart in Figure 9–1 divides the world's total income by quintiles (fifths) of the population. Recall from Chapter 8 that the richest 20 percent of the U.S. population earns about 48 percent of the national income (see Figure 8–3 on page 219). The richest 20 percent of the global population, however, receives about 77 percent of world income. At the other extreme, the poorest 20 percent of the U.S. population earns 4 percent of our national income; the poorest fifth of the world's people, by contrast, struggles to survive on just 2 percent of global income (Milanovic, 2009).

In terms of wealth, as the chart at the right in Figure 9–1 shows, global inequality is even greater. A rough estimate is that the richest 20 percent of the world's adults own more than 90 percent of the planet's wealth. About half of all wealth is owned by just 2 percent of the world's adult population; about 40 percent, by the richest 1 percent. On the other hand, the poorest half of the world's adults own barely 1 percent of all global wealth. In terms of dollars, about half the world's families have less than $2,500 in total wealth, far less than the $120,300 in wealth for the typical family in the United States (Davies et al., 2008; Bucks et al., 2009).

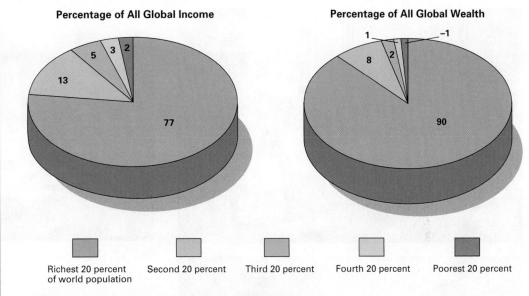

Percentage of All Global Income

Percentage of All Global Wealth

Richest 20 percent of world population   Second 20 percent   Third 20 percent   Fourth 20 percent   Poorest 20 percent

FIGURE 9–1   Distribution of Global Income and Wealth

Global income is very unequal, with the richest 20 percent of the world's people earning almost forty times as much as the poorest 20 percent. Global wealth is even more unequally divided, with the richest 20 percent owning 90 percent of private wealth and the poorest half of the world's people having barely anything at all.

Source: Author calculations based on Davies et al. (2006, 2008) and Milanovic (2009).

Because some countries are so much richer than others, even people in the United States with income below the government's poverty line live far better than the majority of people on the planet. The average person in a rich nation such as the United States is extremely well off by world standards. Any one of the world's richest people (in 2009, the world's three richest people—Bill Gates and Warren Buffett in the United States and Carlos Slim Helu in Mexico—were *each* worth more than $35 billion) has more personal wealth than the total economic output of the world's thirty-four poorest *countries* (United Nations Development Programme, 2008; Kroll, Miller, & Serafin, 2009). ● Go to **mysoclab.com**

A Word about Terminology

Classifying the 194 nations on Earth into categories ignores many striking differences. These nations have rich and varied histories, speak different languages, and take pride in their distinctive cultures. However, various models have been developed that classify countries in order to study global stratification (U.S. Department of State, 2008).

One global model, developed after World War II, labeled the rich, industrial countries the "First World"; the less industrialized, socialist countries the "Second World"; and the nonindustrialized, poor countries the "Third World." But the "three worlds" model is less useful today. For one thing, it was a product of Cold War politics, when the capitalist West (the First World) faced off against the socialist East (the Second World) while other nations (the Third World) remained more or less on the sidelines. But the sweeping changes in Eastern Europe and the collapse of the Soviet Union in the early 1990s mean that a distinctive Second World no longer exists.

Another problem is that the "three worlds" model lumped together more than 100 countries as the Third World. In reality, some better-off nations of the Third World (such as Chile in South America) have thirteen times the per-person productivity seen in the poorest countries of the world (such as Ethiopia in East Africa).

These facts call for a modestly revised system of classification. The sixty-seven **high-income countries** are defined as *the nations with the highest overall standards of living*. These nations have a per capita gross domestic product (GDP) greater than $12,000. The world's seventy-one **middle-income countries** are not as rich; they are *nations with a standard of living about average for the world as a*

○ Making the Grade

Low-income nations have per-capita GDP under $2,500; middle-income nations have per capita GDP above $2,500 but below $12,000; high-income nations have per-capita GDP above $12,000.

○ Seeing Sociology
in Everyday Life

There are communities within the United States that resemble the three photos below. Are you familiar with "low-income America"? What about "middle-income America" and "high-income America"?

Japan (*above, left*) is among the world's high-income countries, in which industrial technology and economic expansion have produced material prosperity. The presence of market forces is evident in this view of downtown Tokyo. India (*above, right*) has recently become one of the world's middle-income countries. An increasing number of motor vehicles fill city streets. Ethiopia (*left*) is among the world's low-income countries. As the photograph suggests, these nations have limited economic development and rapidly increasing populations. The result is widespread poverty.

whole. Their per capita GDP is less than $12,000 but greater than $2,500. The remaining fifty-six **low-income countries** are *nations with a low standard of living in which most people are poor.* In these nations, per capita GDP is less than $2,500.

This model has two advantages over the "three worlds" system. First, it focuses on economic development rather than political system (capitalist or socialist). Second, it gives a better picture of the relative economic development of various countries because it does not lump together all lower-income nations into a single "Third World."

When ranking countries, keep in mind that there is social stratification within every nation. In Bangladesh, for example, members of the Chowdhury family, who own the garment factory described in the chapter-opening story, earn as much as $1 million per year, which is several thousand times more than one of their workers earns. The full extent of global inequality is even greater, because the wealthiest

people in rich countries such as the United States live worlds apart from the poorest people in low-income countries such as Bangladesh, Haiti, and Sudan.

High-Income Countries

In nations where the Industrial Revolution first took place more than two centuries ago, productivity increased more than 100-fold. To understand the power of industrial and computer technology, consider that any one of the rich nations of Europe (such as the United Kingdom, France, Germany, or Italy) is more productive than the whole continent of Africa south of the Sahara, where industrialization and Internet connections are limited.

Global Map 9–1 shows that the high-income nations of the world include the United States, Canada, and Mexico, Argentina and

Luz Alvarez Perez shops in fashionable boutiques in Santiago, Chile, a nation that is now among the high-income countries of the world.

Fatimata Ba earns pennies a day in Niamey, Niger, one of the low-income nations of the world.

Economic Development
- High-income countries
- Middle-income countries
- Low-income countries

Window on the World

GLOBAL MAP 9–1 Economic Development in Global Perspective

In high-income countries—including the United States, Canada, Mexico, Chile, Argentina, the nations of Western Europe, Israel, Saudi Arabia, Malaysia, Australia, the Russian Federation, and Japan—a highly productive economy provides people, on average, with material plenty. Middle-income countries—including most of Latin America and Asia—are less economically productive, with a standard of living about average for the world as a whole but far below that of the United States. These nations also have a significant share of poor people who are barely able to feed and house themselves. In the low-income countries of the world, poverty is severe and widespread. Although small numbers of elites live very well in the poorest nations, most people struggle to survive on a small fraction of the income common in the United States.

Note: Data for this map are provided by the United Nations. Each country's economic productivity is measured in terms of its gross domestic product (GDP), which is the total value of all the goods and services produced by a country's economy within its borders in a given year. Dividing each country's GDP by the country's population gives us the per capita (per-person) GDP and allows us to compare the economic performance of countries of different population sizes. High-income countries have a per capita GDP of more than $12,000. Many are far richer than this, however; the figure for the United States exceeds $45,000. Middle-income countries have a per capita GDP ranging from $2,500 to $12,000. Low-income countries have a per capita GDP of less than $2,500. Figures used here reflect the United Nations' "purchasing power parities" system, which is an estimate of what people can buy using their income in the local economy.

Source: Data from United Nations Development Programme (2009).

THINKING ABOUT DIVERSITY: RACE, CLASS, & GENDER

Las Colonias: "America's Third World"

"We wanted to have something for ourselves," explains Olga Ruiz, who has lived in the border community of College Park, Texas, for two decades. There is no college in College Park, nor does this dusty stretch of rural land have sewer lines or even running water. Yet this town is one of some 1,800 settlements that have sprouted up in southern Texas along the 1,200-mile border with Mexico that runs from El Paso to Brownsville. Together, they are home to an estimated 1 million people.

Many people speak of *las colonias* (Spanish for "the colonies") as "America's Third World" because these desperately poor communities look much like their counterparts in Mexico or many other middle- or low-income nations. But almost all of the people living in the *colonias* are Latino, 85 percent of them are legal residents, and more than half are U.S. citizens.

Anastacia Ledsema, seventy-two years old, moved to a *colonia* called Sparks more than forty years ago. Born in Mexico, Ledsema married a Texas man, and together they paid $200 for a quarter-acre lot in a new border community. For months, they camped out on their land. Step by step, however, they

invested their labor and their money to build a modest house. Not until 1995 did their small community get running water—a service promised by developers years before. After the water line came, things changed more than they expected. "When we got water," recalls Ledsema, "that's when so many people came in." The population of Sparks quickly doubled to about 3,000, overwhelming the water supply so that sometimes the faucet does not run at all.

The residents of all the *colonias* know that they are poor. Indeed, the Census Bureau

declared the county surrounding one border community the poorest in the United States. Concerned over the lack of basic services in so many of these communities, Texas officials have banned any new settlements. But most of the people who move here—even those who start off sleeping in their cars or trucks—see these communities as the first step on the path to the American dream. Oscar Solis, a neighborhood leader in Panorama Village, with a population of about 150, is proud to show visitors around the small but growing town. "All of this work we have done ourselves," he says with a smile, "to make our dream come true."

WHAT DO YOU THINK?

1. Are you surprised that such poverty exists in a rich country like the United States? Why or why not?

2. Why do you think such communities get little attention from the U.S. mass media?

3. To what extent do you think the people living in these communities will have their "dreams come true"? Explain your answer.

Source: Based on Schaffer (2002).

Chile, the nations of Western Europe, Israel, Saudi Arabia, Singapore, Hong Kong (part of the People's Republic of China), Japan, South Korea, the Russian Federation, Malaysia, Australia, and New Zealand.

These countries cover roughly 47 percent of Earth's land area, including parts of five continents, and lie mostly in the Northern Hemisphere. In 2009, the population of these nations was about 1.6 billion, or about 23 percent of the world's people. About three-fourths of the people in high-income countries live in or near cities (World Bank, 2009; Population Reference Bureau, 2010).

Significant cultural differences exist among high-income countries; for example, the nations of Europe recognize more than thirty official languages. But these societies all produce enough economic

goods and services to enable their people to lead comfortable material lives. Per capita annual income (that is, average income per person per year) ranges from about $12,000 annually (in Venezuela and Turkey) to more than $45,000 annually (in the United States and Norway). In fact, people in high-income countries enjoy 80 percent of the world's total income.

Keep in mind that high-income countries have many low-income people. The Thinking About Diversity box profiles the striking poverty that exists in *las colonias* along the southern border of the United States.

Production in rich nations is capital-intensive. This means that it is based on the use of factories, big machinery, and advanced

┌─○ Making the Grade

The photos below show that even natural disasters reflect
patterns of global stratification, with greater loss of life in
lower-income nations. In so many ways, poverty leaves
people vulnerable.

┌─○ Making the Grade

The full exent of global stratification reflects both differences
among countries and internal stratification.

When natural disasters strike high-income nations, property damage may be great, but the loss of life
is relatively low. For example, the 2010 earthquake in Chile (*left*) forced people from damaged homes
but the death toll for the entire nation was about 400. By contrast, when another earthquake hit Haiti
in 2010 (*right*), less well-built structures came tumbling down, resulting in more than 100,000 deaths.

technology. Most of the largest corporations that design and market computers, as well as most computer users, are located in high-income countries. In addition, high-income countries also control the world's financial markets, so daily events on the stock exchanges of New York, London, and Tokyo affect people throughout the world. In short, rich nations are very productive because of their advanced technology and also because they control the global economy.

Middle-Income Countries

Middle-income countries have per capita annual incomes ranging from $2,500 to $12,000, roughly the median for the world's nations. Typically, 55 to 60 percent of the people in middle-income countries live in or near cities, and industrial jobs are common. The remaining 40 to 45 percent of the people live in rural areas, where most are poor and lack access to schools, medical care, adequate housing, and even safe drinking water.

Looking at Global Map 9–1, we see that seventy-one of the world's nations fall in the middle-income category. At the high end are Panama (Latin America), Bulgaria (Europe), and Iran (Asia), where annual income is about $11,000. At the low end are Nicaragua (Latin America), Congo (Africa), and Vietnam (Asia), with roughly $3,000 annually in per capita income.

One cluster of middle-income nations used to be part of the Second World. These countries, found in Eastern Europe and Western Asia, had mostly socialist economies until popular revolts between 1989 and 1991 swept their governments aside. Since then, these nations have introduced more free-market economies. These middle-income countries include Belarus and Ukraine, as well as Kazakhstan, Georgia, and Turkmenistan.

Other middle-income countries include Peru and Brazil in South America and Namibia and Angola in Africa. Both India and the People's Republic of China have entered the middle-income category, which now includes most of Asia.

Taken together, middle-income countries span roughly 35 percent of the world's land area and are home to about 3.9 billion people, or about 57 percent of humanity. Some very large countries (such as China) are far less crowded than others (such as El Salvador), but compared to high-income countries, these societies are densely populated (World Bank, 2009; Population Reference Bureau, 2010).

Low-Income Countries

Low-income countries, where most people are very poor, are mostly agrarian societies with some industry. Fifty-six nations, identified on Global Map 9–1, are spread across Central and East Africa and Asia. Low-income countries cover 18 percent of the planet's land area and are home to 20 percent of its people. Population density is generally high, although it is greater in Asian countries (such as Bangladesh and Pakistan) than in Central African nations (such as Chad and the Democratic Republic of the Congo).

Have you ever visited or lived in a middle- or low-income nation? If so, make a list of some of the most striking differences between life there and here in the United States.

Have you traveled to a low-income country? If so, can you recall an experience similar to the one described in the author's journal entry below?

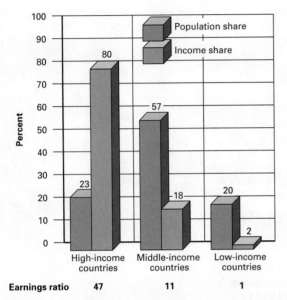

FIGURE 9–2   The Relative Share of Income and Population by Level of Economic Development

For every dollar earned by people in low-income countries, people in high-income countries earn $47.

Sources: United Nations Development Programme (2009) and Population Reference Bureau (2010).

In poor countries, about one-third of the people live in cities; most inhabit villages and farms as their ancestors have done for centuries. In fact, half the world's people are farmers, most of whom follow cultural traditions. With limited industrial technology, they cannot be very productive—one reason that many endure severe poverty. Hunger, disease, and unsafe housing shape the lives of the world's poorest people.

Those of us who live in rich nations such as the United States find it hard to understand the scope of human need in much of the world. From time to time, televised pictures of famine in very poor countries such as Ethiopia and Bangladesh give us shocking glimpses into the poverty that makes every day a life-and-death struggle for many in low-income nations. Behind these images lie cultural, historical, and economic forces that we shall explore in the remainder of this chapter.

Global Wealth and Poverty

October 14, Manila, Philippines. What caught my eye was how clean she was—a girl no more than seven or eight years old, wearing a freshly laundered dress and with her hair carefully combed. She followed us with her

eyes: Camera-toting Americans stand out here, in one of the poorest neighborhoods in the entire world.

Fed by methane from the decomposing garbage, the fires never go out on Smokey Mountain, the vast garbage dump on the north side of Manila. Smoke covers the hills of refuse like a thick fog. But Smokey Mountain is more than a dump; it is a neighborhood that is home to thousands of people. It is hard to imagine a setting more hostile to human life. Amid the smoke and the squalor, men and women do what they can to survive. They pick plastic bags from the garbage and wash them in the river, and they collect cardboard boxes or anything else they can sell. What chance do their children have, coming from families that earn only a few hundred dollars a year, with hardly any opportunity for schooling, year after year, breathing this foul air? Against this backdrop of human tragedy, one lovely little girl has put on a fresh dress and gone out to play.

Now our taxi driver threads his way through heavy traffic as we head for the other side of Manila. The change is amazing: The smoke and smell of the dump give way to neighborhoods that could be in Miami or Los Angeles. A cluster of yachts floats on the bay in the distance. No more rutted streets; now we glide quietly along wide boulevards lined with trees and filled with expensive Japanese cars. We pass shopping plazas, upscale hotels, and high-rise office buildings. Every block or so we see the gated entrance to an exclusive residential community with security guards standing watch. Here, in large, air-conditioned homes, the rich of Manila live—and many of the poor work.

Low-income nations are home to some rich and many poor people. The fact that most people live with incomes of a few hundred dollars a year means the burden of poverty is far greater than among the poor of the United States. This is not to suggest that U.S. poverty is a minor problem. In so rich a country, too little food, substandard housing, and no medical care for tens of millions of people—almost half of them children—amount to a national tragedy.

The Severity of Poverty

Poverty in poor countries is more severe than it is in rich countries. A key reason that quality of life differs so much around the world is that economic productivity is lowest in precisely the regions where population growth is highest. Figure 9–2 shows the proportion of world population and global income for countries at each level of economic development. High-income countries are by far the most advantaged, with 80 percent of global income supporting just 23 percent of humanity. In middle-income nations, 57 percent of the

○ Making the Grade

As you look at Table 9–1, remember that GDP depends on both level of economic development and the country's population size; per capita GDP is a good measure of average living standards; the UN quality of life index reflects not only income levels but also a society's health and levels of inequality.

Read "The Global Economy and the Privileged Class" by Robert Perrucci and Earl Wysong on **mysoclab.com**

world's people earn 18 percent of global income. This leaves 20 percent of the planet's population with just 2 percent of global income (World Bank, 2009; Population Reference Bureau, 2010). For every dollar received by an individual in a low-income country, someone in a high-income nation takes home $47.

Table 9–1 shows the extent of wealth and well-being in specific countries around the world. The first column of figures gives the gross domestic product (GDP) for a number of high-, middle-, and low-income countries. The United States, a large industrial nation, had a 2008 GDP of more than $14 trillion; Japan's GDP that same year was approaching $5 trillion. A comparison of GDP figures shows that the world's richest nations are thousands of times more productive than the poorest countries. Read on **mysoclab.com**

The second column of figures in Table 9–1 divides GDP by the entire population size to give an estimate of what people can buy using their income in the local economy. The per capita GDP for the richest high-income countries, including the United States, Sweden, and Canada, is very high, exceeding $35,000. For middle-income countries, such as India, Uruguay, and Bulgaria, the figures range from less than $3,000 in India to more than $10,000 in Uruguay and Bulgaria. In the world's low-income countries, per capita GDP is just a few hundred dollars. In Niger or Ethiopia, a typical person labors all year to make what the average worker in the United States earns in a week.

The last column of Table 9–1 is a measure of quality of life in the various nations. This index, calculated by the United Nations, combines income, education (extent of adult literacy and average years of schooling), and longevity (how long people typically live). Index values are decimals that fall between extremes of 1 (highest) and 0 (lowest). By this calculation, Norwegians enjoy the highest quality of life (.971), with residents of the United States close behind (.956). At the other extreme, people in the African nation of Niger have the lowest quality of life (.340).

Relative versus Absolute Poverty

The distinction between relative and absolute poverty, made in Chapter 8 ("Social Stratification"), has an important application to global inequality. People living in rich countries generally focus on *relative poverty,* meaning that some people lack resources that are taken for granted by others. By definition, relative poverty exists in every society, rich or poor.

More important in global perspective, however, is *absolute poverty,* a lack of resources that is life-threatening. Human beings in absolute poverty lack the nutrition necessary for health and long-term survival. To be sure, some absolute poverty exists in the United States. But such immediately life-threatening poverty strikes only a small proportion of the U.S. population; in low-income countries, by contrast, one-third or even half of the people are in desperate need.

Table 9–1 Wealth and Well-Being in Global Perspective, 2008

Country	Gross Domestic Product (US$ billions)	GDP per Capita (PPP US$)*	Quality of Life Index
High-Income			
Norway	450	53,433	.971
Australia	1,015	34,923	.970
Canada	1,400	35,812	.966
Sweden	480	36,712	.963
Japan	4,909	33,632	.960
United States	14,204	45,592	.956
United Kingdom	2,646	35,130	.947
South Korea	929	24,801	.937
Middle-Income			
Eastern Europe			
Bulgaria	50	11,222	.840
Albania	12	7,041	.818
Ukraine	180	6,914	.796
Latin America			
Uruguay	32	11,216	.865
Brazil	1,613	9,567	.813
Ecuador	53	7,449	.806
Asia			
Thailand	261	8,135	.783
People's Republic of China	4,326	5,383	.772
India	1,218	2,753	.612
Middle East			
Iran	385	10,955	.782
Syria	55	4,511	.742
Africa			
Algeria	174	7,740	.754
Namibia	9	5,155	.686
Low-Income			
Latin America			
Haiti	7	1,155	.532
Asia			
Laos	5	2,165	.619
Pakistan	168	2,496	.572
Bangladesh	79	1,241	.543
Africa			
Guinea	4	1,140	.435
Ethiopia	27	779	.414
Niger	5	627	.340

*These data are the United Nations' purchasing power parity (PPP) calculations, which avoid currency rate distortion by showing the local purchasing power of each domestic currency.

Source: United Nations Development Programme, 2009; World Bank, 2009).

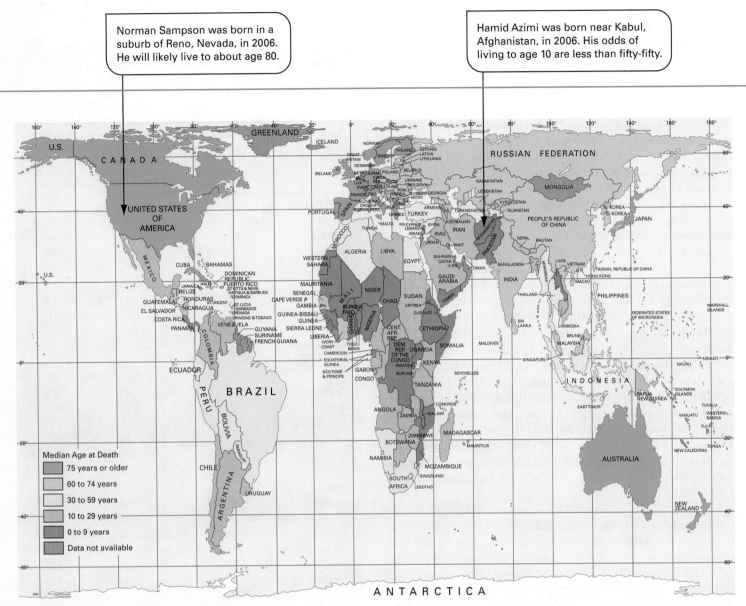

Window on the World

GLOBAL MAP 9–2   Median Age at Death in Global Perspective

This map identifies the age below which half of all deaths occur in any year. In the high-income countries of the world, including the United States, it is mostly the elderly who face death, that is, people aged seventy or older. In middle-income countries, including most of Latin America, most people die years or even decades earlier. In low-income countries, especially in Africa and parts of Asia, it is children who die, more than one-third of them never reaching their fourteenth birthday.

Sources: World Bank (1993) and World Health Organization, 2008.

Because absolute poverty is deadly, one global indicator of this problem is the median age at death. Global Map 9–2 identifies the age by which half of all people born in a nation die. In rich countries, more than two-thirds of all people die after the age of seventy, but in poor countries, over a third of all deaths occur among children under the age of fourteen. In the world's poorest nations, half of all children never live to the age of ten (World Health Organization, 2008).

The Extent of Poverty

Poverty in poor countries is more widespread than it is in rich nations such as the United States. Chapter 8 ("Social Stratification") noted that the U.S. government officially classifies 13.2 percent of the population as poor. In low-income countries, however, most people live no better than the poor in the United States, and many are far worse off. As Global Map 9–2 shows, the high death rates among children in Africa indicate that absolute poverty is greatest there, where 30 percent of the

Go to the Multimedia Library at **mysoclab.com**
to listen to the NPR report "Haiti's Dark Secret
(Child Slavery)"

○ Making the Grade

As explained below, gender inequality is greater in
low-income countries than in high-income countries.

population is malnourished. In the world as a whole, at any given time, 13 percent of the people—more than 1 billion—suffer from chronic hunger, which leaves them less able to work and puts them at high risk of disease (Chen & Ravallion, 2008; United Nations Food and Agriculture Organization, 2010).

The typical adult in a rich nation such as the United States consumes about 3,500 calories a day, which is actually too much and leads to obesity and related health problems. The typical adult in a low-income country not only does more physical labor but consumes just 2,500 calories a day. The result is undernourishment: too little food or not enough of the right kinds of food.

In the ten minutes it takes to read this section of the chapter, about 100 people in the world who are sick and weakened from hunger will die. This amounts to about 25,000 people a day, or 9 million people each year. Clearly, easing world hunger is one of the most serious challenges facing humanity today.

Poverty and Children

Death comes early in poor societies, where families lack adequate food, safe drinking water, secure housing, and access to medical care. In the world's low- and middle-income nations, one-third of all children do not receive enough nutrition to be healthy (Levinson & Bassett, 2007). ● Go to **mysoclab.com**

Poor children live in poor families, and many share in the struggle to get through each day. Organizations fighting child poverty estimate that at least 100 million city children in poor countries beg, steal, sell sex, or work for drug gangs to provide income for their families. Such a life almost always means dropping out of school and puts children at high risk of disease and violence. Many girls, with little or no access to medical assistance, become pregnant, a case of children who cannot support themselves having children of their own.

Analysts also estimate that millions of children in poor countries leave their families altogether, sleeping and living on the streets as best they can or perhaps trying to migrate to the United States. Roughly half of all street children are found in Latin American cities such as Mexico City and Rio de Janeiro, where half of all children grow up in poverty. Many people in the United States know these cities as exotic travel destinations, but they are also home to thousands of children living in makeshift huts, under bridges, or in alleyways (United Nations Development Programme, 2000; Collymore, 2002; Leopold, 2007).

In cities around the world, officials engage in "urban cleansing," rounding up street children in an effort to make the city more attractive to visitors. As Seeing Sociology in the News on pages 254–55 explains, these efforts are especially common when cities host major events such as the World Cup in soccer.

Millions of children fend for themselves every day on the streets of poor cities where many fall victim to disease, drug abuse, and violence. What do you think must be done to put an end to scenes like this one in Kolkata, India?

Poverty and Women

In rich societies, a lot of the work women do is undervalued, underpaid, or overlooked entirely. In poor societies, women face even greater disadvantages. Most of the people who work under poor or even dangerous conditions in sweatshops like the one described in the opening to this chapter are women.

To make matters worse, in many low-income nations, tradition keeps women out of many jobs. In Bangladesh, for example, women work in garment factories because that nation's conservative Muslim religious norms bar them from most other paid work and limit their opportunities for advanced schooling (Bearak, 2001). Traditional norms also give women primary responsibility for child rearing and maintaining the household. As a result, many of the world's women are overworked and underpaid. One United Nations (2004) study concluded that worldwide, women perform 66 percent of all the work and produce 50 percent of all the food but earn just 10 percent of all the income and own only 1 percent of all the wealth. It is no surprise, then, that about 70 percent of the world's 1.4 billion people living near absolute poverty are women (UNICEF, 2004; Moghadam, 2005).

Finally, most women in poor countries receive little or no reproductive health care. Limited access to birth control keeps women at home with their children, keeps the birth rate high, and limits the economic production of the country. In addition, the world's poorest

The Sun

The Child Catchers

By SHARON HENRY
March 27, 2010

DURBAN, South Africa—It has just gone 10 A.M. and the searing South African sun is beating down, forcing city dwellers to seek shade under newly planted palm trees.

Only the many teams of workmen preparing Durban for the gaze of World Cup visitors must continue their heavy toil in temperatures exceeding 30°C [86° Fahrenheit].

With seventy-six days to go before the eyes of the world fall upon this city, time is running out.

Above the whirr of drills and heavy-duty diggers, a different and more harrowing sound begins to emerge from behind the wire mesh covering the windows of a parked police van.

On closer inspection, tiny fingers can be seen reaching out desperately through the holes, as the voices inside beg for help.

"Please, please come. We will die in this heat," a small voice pleads before collapsing into pitiful sobs.

Shockingly, the van contains eight street children aged nine to fifteen.

In the build-up to the biggest football show on earth, these helpless youngsters are being rounded up each day by police and dumped miles outside Durban in a bid to keep the city looking pristine.

To an extent it is a pointless exercise, as the children simply embark on the 24-hour trek back to Durban as soon as they are dumped.

To the outside world, they appear in desperate need of rehabilitation. But to Durban Municipal Police they are unsightly vermin in need of urgent removal.

The Sun witnessed the police's heavy-handed tactics firsthand, less than a day after arriving in Durban last week.

Sun photographer Marc Giddings was detained and interrogated by police for more than two hours after taking pictures of children locked in the back of a van without food or water.

Inside the city's Metropolitan police station, he was shocked to discover a poster on display entitled "Operation Beach Clean-Up."

It blatantly revealed police tactics in the build-up to the World Cup. Street children were listed alongside vagrants and debris on a register of rubbish to be removed from the city centre. . . .

Later we traced one of the girls who had been detained in the police truck.

Her harrowing story reveals a different side to the sun-and-surf South Africa that its government officials would like World Cup fans to buy into.

It is more in tune with official figures that show one in four South Africans are jobless and live daily on less than 84p [U.S. $1.30].

Nobuhle Sishi is still only fifteen but she has lived on the streets of Durban for two years. . . .

She said, "Life was always very difficult for us because we are very poor and Mum and Dad's drinking meant we all had to fend for ourselves and raise each other. And there was a lot of violence that we all witnessed daily.

---

women typically give birth without help from trained health care personnel. Figure 9–3 on page 256 draws a stark contrast between low- and high-income countries in this regard.

Slavery

Poor societies have many problems in addition to hunger, including illiteracy, warfare, and slavery. The British Empire banned slavery in 1833, followed by the United States in 1865. But slavery is a reality for at least 12 million men, women, and children, and as many as 200 million people (about 3 percent of humanity) live today in conditions that come close to slavery (Anti-Slavery International, 2008; U.S. Department of Labor, 2009).

Anti-Slavery International (ASI) describes four types of slavery. First is *chattel slavery,* in which one person owns another. In spite of the fact that this practice is against the law almost everywhere, about 27 million people fall into this category. The buying and selling of slaves still takes place in many countries in Asia, the Middle East, and especially Africa. The Thinking Globally box on page 257 describes the reality of one slave's life in the African nation of Mauritania.

A second, more common form of bondage is *child slavery,* in which desperately poor families let their children take to the streets to do what they can to survive. The International Labour Organization estimates that more than 200 million children are at work, at least 8 million of whom are in forced and hazardous forms of labor. In 2009, the U.S. Department of Labor identified more than 100 goods—including cotton, sugarcane, tobacco, and coffee—produced in more than fifty nations with forced labor, mostly by children.

Third, *debt bondage* is the practice by which employers hold workers captive by paying them too little to meet their debts. In this case, workers receive a wage, but it is too small to cover the food and housing provided by the employer; for practical purposes, they are enslaved. Many sweatshop workers in low-income nations fall into this category.

Fourth, *servile forms of marriage* may also amount to slavery. In India, Thailand, and some African nations, families marry off women against their will. Many end up as slaves to their husband's family; some are forced into prostitution.

One additional form of slavery is *human trafficking,* the movement of men, women, and children from one place to another for the purpose of performing forced labor. In many cases, women or men are brought to a new country on the promise of a job and then find themselves held captive, forced to become prostitutes or farm laborers. In other cases, "parents" adopt children from another country and then force them to work in sweatshops. Such activity is big business: Next to trading in guns and drugs, trading in people brings the greatest profits to organized crime around the world (Orhant, 2002).

In 1948, the United Nations issued the Universal Declaration of Human Rights, which states, "No one shall be held in slavery or

"But the hardest thing for me was when I was raped by someone in our village when I was just thirteen. After that I just felt I had to get away—anywhere was better than being at home."

Nobuhle sprinted away barefoot from her family home—a corrugated iron shack—and hitched twenty miles into Durban, where other street children told her to make her home in the Emagghumeri area.

She said, "At first I thought it would be a better life but I soon realised the truth. At night, I had just a small blanket to sleep under and I was regularly beaten up and abused by men."

Shockingly, Nobuhle has been raped a further five times on the streets. It is estimated that 500,000 rapes are committed annually in South Africa and 52 people are murdered every day.

Nobuhle added, "Who would seriously choose a life on the streets? The only way to survive it is by sniffing pots of glue that dull every feeling. But I have seen the terrible effects it has had on my friends, crippling their joints so they can no longer walk."

Recalling the round-up witnessed by *The Sun*, Nobuhle said, "The police pulled up in a van and dragged us into it from across the street.

"Then they beat us with sticks and sprayed pepper in our faces until our chests felt like they were on fire. On this occasion we were driven to the police station and kept with adult criminals in the back of the van while the sun was beating down on us.

"At other times, the police drive us round the city all day before taking us out to townships far away and dumping us.

"Sometimes it takes us a whole night and day to walk back to the city, and then the whole round-up process begins again the next day. It has been getting more and more frequent in recent weeks."

As a temporary measure, the street charity Umthombo has rescued Nobuhle and taken her back to her family home, where social workers are monitoring her progress.

They say she will be safer there during the period of intense pre–World Cup police activity.

But Nobuhle said, "I don't know how long I will be able to stay. . . . All I wish for is a space . . . where I can go to school. I would like to learn computers and become a teacher so I can help other children to avoid a life of misery." . . .

WHAT DO YOU THINK?

1. Does it surprise you that, in cities around the world, officials "clean up" evidence of poverty, especially when events attract the eyes of the world? Can you point to other examples of this pattern?

2. How would you respond to the existence of street children in cities such as Durban?

3. Do you think street children are the problem or are they a symptom of larger problems in a society? Explain.

"The Child Catchers" by Sharon Henry from *The Sun*, March 27, 2010, copyright © 2010 The Sun, is reprinted by permission of NI Syndication/nisyndication.com.

---

servitude; slavery and the slave trade shall be prohibited in all their forms." Unfortunately, more than six decades later, this social evil still exists.

Explanations of Global Poverty

What accounts for severe and widespread poverty in much of the world? The rest of this chapter provides answers to this question using the following facts about poor societies:

1. **Technology.** About one-quarter of people in low-income countries farm the land using human muscles or animal power. With such limited energy sources, agricultural production is modest.

2. **Population growth.** As Chapter 15 ("Population, Urbanization, and Environment") explains, the poorest countries have the world's highest birth rates. Despite the death toll from poverty, the populations of poor countries in Africa double their numbers every twenty-five years. In sub-Saharan Africa, 43 percent of the people are under the age of fifteen. With such a large share of the population just entering the childbearing years, the wave of population growth will continue to roll into the future. For example, in recent years, the population of Uganda has swelled by more than 3 percent annually, so even with economic development, living standards have fallen (Population Reference Bureau, 2009).

3. **Cultural patterns.** Poor societies are usually traditional. People who hold to long-established ways of life resist change—even change that promises a richer material life.

4. **Social stratification.** Low-income nations distribute their wealth very unequally. Chapter 8 ("Social Stratification") explained that social inequality is greater in agrarian societies than in industrial societies. In Brazil, for example, 75 percent of all farmland is owned by just 4 percent of the people (Bergamo & Camarotti, 1996; Galano, 1998).

5. **Gender inequality.** Extreme gender inequality in poor societies keeps women from holding jobs, which typically means they have many children. An expanding population, in turn, slows economic development. Many analysts conclude that raising living standards in much of the world depends on improving the social standing of women.

6. **Global power relationships.** A final cause of global poverty lies in the relationships between the nations of the world. Historically, wealth flowed from poor societies to rich nations through **colonialism**, *the process by which some nations enrich themselves through political and economic control of other nations.* The countries of Western Europe colonized much of Latin America beginning roughly 500 years ago. Such global exploitation allowed some nations to develop economically at the expense of other nations.

○ Making the Grade

The list on page 255 identifies six factors that play a part in explaining global poverty. As you read on, you will see that the first three are closer to modernization theory and the next three are closer to dependency theory.

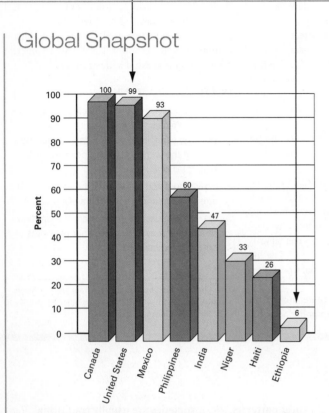

> Compared to a woman in the United States, an Ethiopian woman is far less likely to give birth with the help of medical professionals and is much more likely to die in childbirth.

Global Snapshot

FIGURE 9–3 **Percentage of Births Attended by Skilled Health Staff**

In the United States, most women give birth with the help of medical professionals, but this is usually not the case in low-income nations.

Source: World Bank (2009).

Although 130 former colonies gained their independence during the twentieth century, exploitation continues through **neocolonialism,** *a new form of global power relationships that involves not direct political control but economic exploitation by multinational corporations.* A **multinational corporation** is *a large business that operates in many countries.* Corporate leaders can impose their will on countries in which they do business to create favorable economic conditions, just as colonizers did in the past (Bonanno, Constance, & Lorenz, 2000).

Global Stratification: Theoretical Analysis

There are two major explanations for the unequal distribution of the world's wealth and power: *modernization theory* and *dependency theory.* Each theory suggests a different solution to the suffering of hungry people in much of the world.

Modernization Theory

Modernization theory is *a model of economic and social development that explains global inequality in terms of technological and cultural differences between nations.* Modernization theory, which follows the structural-functional approach, emerged in the 1950s, a time when U.S. society was fascinated with new developments in technology. To showcase the power of protective technology and also to counter the growing influence of the Soviet Union and socialism in much of the world, U.S. policymakers drafted a market-based foreign policy that has been with us ever since (Rostow, 1960, 1978; Bauer, 1981; Berger, 1986; Firebaugh, 1996; Firebaugh & Sandu, 1998).

Historical Perspective

Until a few centuries ago, the entire world was poor. Because poverty has been the norm throughout human history, modernization theory proposes that it is *affluence* that demands an explanation.

Affluence came within reach of a growing share of people in Western Europe during the late Middle Ages as world exploration and trade expanded. Soon the Industrial Revolution was under way, transforming first Western Europe and then North America. Industrial technology, together with the spirit of capitalism, created new wealth as never before. At first, this new wealth benefited only a few individuals. But industrial technology was so productive that gradually the living standards of even the poorest people began to improve. Absolute poverty, which had plagued humanity throughout history, was finally in decline.

In high-income countries where the Industrial Revolution began, the standard of living jumped at least fourfold during the twentieth century. As middle-income nations in Asia and Latin America have industrialized, they too have become richer. But with limited industrial technology, low-income countries have changed much less.

The Importance of Culture

Why didn't the Industrial Revolution sweep away poverty the world over? Modernization theory points out that not every society wants to adopt new technology. Doing so takes a cultural environment that emphasizes the benefits of innovation as well as material wealth.

Modernization theory identifies *tradition* as the greatest barrier to economic development. A reverence for the past may discourage people from adopting new technologies that would raise their living standards. Even today, many people—from the Amish in North America to traditional Islamic people in the Middle East to the Semai of Malaysia—oppose new technology because they see it as a threat to their family relationships, customs, and religious beliefs.

Max Weber (1958, orig. 1904–05) found that at the end of the Middle Ages, Western Europe's cultural environment favored change. As Chapter 13 ("Family and Religion") explains, the Protestant

colonialism (p. 255) the process by which some nations enrich themselves through political and economic control of other nations

neocolonialism a new form of global power relationships that involves not direct political control but economic exploitation by multinational corporations

multinational corporation a large business that operates in many countries

modernization theory a model of economic and social development that explains global inequality in terms of technological and cultural differences between nations

THINKING GLOBALLY

"God Made Me to Be a Slave"

Fatma Mint Mamadou is a young woman living in North Africa's Islamic Republic of Mauritania. Asked her age, she pauses, smiles, and shakes her head. She has no idea when she was born. Nor can she read or write. What she knows is tending camels, herding sheep, hauling bags of water, sweeping, and serving tea to her owners. This young woman is one of perhaps 90,000 slaves in Mauritania.

In the central region of this nation, having very dark skin almost always means being a slave to an Arab owner. Fatma accepts her situation; she has known nothing else. She explains in a matter-of-fact voice that she is a slave, like her mother before her and her grandmother before that. "Just as God created a camel to be a camel," she shrugs, "he created me to be a slave."

Fatma, her mother, and her brothers and sisters live together in a squatter settlement on the edge of Nouakchott, Mauritania's capital city. Their home is a 9-by-12-foot hut they built from wood scraps and other materials taken from construction sites. The roof is nothing more than a piece of cloth; there is no plumbing or furniture. The nearest water comes from a well a mile down the road.

In this region, slavery began more than 500 years ago, about the time Columbus sailed west toward the Americas. As Arab and Berber tribes moved across the African continent spreading Islam, they raided local villages and made slaves of the people, a practice that was continued for dozens of generations. In 1905, the French colonial rulers of Mauritania banned slavery. After the nation gained independence in 1961, the new government reaffirmed the ban.

Human slavery continues to exist in the twenty-first century.

However, slavery was not officially abolished until 1981, and even then, it was not made a crime. In 2007, the nation passed legislation making the practice of slavery punishable by up to ten years in prison, and the government now provides monetary compensation to victims of slavery. But the new laws have done little to change strong traditions. The sad truth is that people like Fatma still have no idea of the concept of "freedom to choose."

The next question is more personal: "Are you and other girls ever raped?" Again, Fatma hesitates. With no hint of emotion, she responds, "Of course, in the night the men come to breed us. Is that what you mean by rape?"

WHAT DO YOU THINK?

1. How does tradition play a part in keeping people in slavery?

2. What might explain the fact that the world still tolerates slavery?

3. Explain the connection between slavery and poverty.

Source: Based on Burkett (1997).

Reformation reshaped traditional Catholic beliefs to generate a progress-oriented way of life. Wealth—looked on with suspicion by the Roman Catholic Church—became a sign of personal virtue, and the growing importance of individualism steadily replaced the traditional emphasis on family and community. These new cultural patterns laid the groundwork for the Industrial Revolution.

Rostow's Stages of Modernization

Modernization theory holds that the door to affluence is open to all. As technological advances spread around the world, all societies should gradually industrialize. According to Walt Rostow (1960, 1978), modernization occurs in four stages:

1. **Traditional stage.** Socialized to honor the past, people in traditional societies cannot easily imagine that life can or should be

any different. They therefore build their lives around families and local communities, following well-worn paths that allow little individual freedom or change. Life is often spiritually rich but lacking in material goods.

A century ago, much of the world was in this initial stage of economic development. Nations such as Bangladesh, Niger, and Somalia are still at the traditional stage and remain poor. Even in countries such as India that have recently joined the ranks of middle-income nations, certain elements of the population have remained highly traditional. The Seeing Sociology in Everyday Life box on page 258 takes a look at traditional life in India.

2. **Take-off stage.** As a society shakes off the grip of tradition, people start to use their talents and imagination, sparking economic growth. A market emerges as people produce goods not

Rostow's stages of economic development describe an airplane, first on the ground, then moving fast down the runway, then climbing to cruising altitude, and then flying high. In the 1950s, when Rostow was writing, U.S. society was fascinated with jet planes, scientific achievement, and progress.

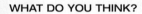 **Explore** which areas of the United States have attracted large numbers of immigrants seeking the high standard of living available in a country at this stage of modernization on **mysoclab.com**

SEEING SOCIOLOGY IN EVERYDAY LIFE

"Happy Poverty" in India: Making Sense of a Strange Idea

Although India has become a middle-income nation, its per capita GDP is only $2,753, less than one-tenth that in the United States. For this reason, India is home to more than one-quarter of the world's hungry people.

But most North Americans do not easily understand the reality of poverty in India. Many of the country's 1.2 billion people live in conditions far worse than those our society labels "poor." A traveler's first experience of Indian life can be shocking. Chennai (formerly known as Madras), for example, one of India's largest cities with 7 million inhabitants, seems chaotic to the outsider, with streets choked by motorbikes, trucks, carts pulled by oxen, and waves of people. Along the roadway, vendors sit on burlap cloths selling fruits, vegetables, and cooked food while people a few yards away work, talk, bathe, and sleep.

Although some people live well, Chennai is dotted by more than 1,000 shanty settlements, home to half a million people from rural villages who have come in search of a better life. Shantytowns are clusters of huts built with branches, leaves, and pieces of discarded cardboard and tin. These dwellings offer little privacy and lack refrigeration, running water, and bathrooms. A visitor from the United States may feel uneasy in such an area, knowing that the poorest sections of our

own inner cities seethe with frustration and sometimes explode with violence.

But India's people understand poverty differently than we do. No restless young men hang out at the corner, no drug dealers work the streets, and there is little danger of violence. In the United States, poverty often means anger and isolation; in India, even shantytowns are organized around strong families—children, parents, and often grandparents—who offer a smile of welcome to a stranger.

For traditional people in India, life is shaped by *dharma,* the Hindu concept of duty and destiny that teaches people to accept their fate, whatever it may be. Mother Teresa, a Catholic nun who worked among the poorest of India's

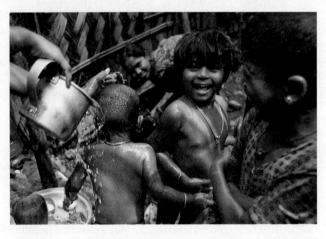

people, went to the heart of the cultural differences: "Americans have angry poverty," she explained. "In India, there is worse poverty, but it is a happy poverty."

Perhaps we should not describe anyone who clings to the edge of survival as happy. But poverty in India is eased by the strength and support of families and communities, a sense that life has a purpose, and a worldview that encourages each person to accept whatever life offers. As a result, a visitor may come away from a first encounter with Indian poverty rather confused: "How can people be so poor and yet seem content, active, and *joyful?*"

WHAT DO YOU THINK?

1. What did Mother Teresa mean when she said that in India there is "happy poverty"?

2. How might a visit to an Indian shantytown change the way you think of being "rich"?

3. Do you know of any poor people in the United States who have attitudes toward poverty similar to these people in India? What would make people seem to accept their poverty?

---

just for their own use but to trade with others for profit. Greater individualism, a willingness to take risks, and a desire for material goods also take hold, often at the expense of family ties and time-honored norms and values.

Great Britain reached take-off by about 1800, the United States by 1820. Thailand, a middle-income country in eastern Asia, is now in this stage. Such development is typically speeded by progressive influences from rich nations, including foreign aid, the availability of advanced technology and investment capital, and opportunities for schooling abroad.

3. **Drive to technological maturity.** As this stage begins, "growth" is a widely accepted idea that fuels a society's pursuit of higher living standards. A diversified economy drives a population eager to enjoy the benefits of industrial technology. At the same time, people begin to realize (and sometimes regret) that industrialization is weakening traditional family and local community life. Great Britain entered this stage by about 1840, the United States by 1860. Today, Mexico, the U.S. territory of Puerto Rico, and South Korea are among the nations driving to technological maturity.

○ Making the Grade

The photos below show us how stages of life—in this case, childhood—are constructed by society, as discussed in Chapter 3.

○ Seeing Sociology in Everyday Life

How would our society define work performed by children as young as those shown below?

In rich nations such as the United States, most parents expect their children to enjoy years of childhood, largely free from the responsibilities of adult life. This is not the case in poor nations across Latin America, Africa, and Asia. Poor families depend on whatever income their children can earn, and many children as young as six or seven work full days weaving or performing other kinds of manual labor. Child labor lies behind the low prices of many products imported for sale in this country.

At this stage of development, absolute poverty is greatly reduced. Cities swell with people who have left rural villages in search of economic opportunity. Specialization gives rise to the wide range of jobs that we find in our economy today. An increasing focus on work makes relationships less personal. Growing individualism generates social movements demanding greater political rights. Societies approaching technological maturity also provide basic schooling for all their people and advanced training for some. The newly educated consider tradition "backward" and push for further change. The social position of women steadily approaches that of men.

4. **High mass consumption.** Economic development steadily raises living standards as mass production stimulates mass consumption. Simply put, people soon learn to "need" the expanding selection of goods that their society produces. The United States, Japan, Australia, and the nations of Western Europe entered this stage of development by 1900. Reaching this level of economic prosperity today are two former British colonies in eastern Asia: Hong Kong (now part of the People's Republic of China) and Singapore (independent since 1965). ✦─ Explore on mysoclab.com

The Role of Rich Nations

Modernization theory claims that high-income countries play four important roles in global economic development:

1. **Controlling population.** Because population growth is greatest in the poorest societies, rising population can overtake eco-

nomic advances. Rich nations can help limit population growth by exporting birth control technology and promoting its use. Once economic development is under way, birth rates should decline, as they have in industrialized nations, because children are no longer an economic asset and now cost a great deal of money to raise.

2. **Increasing food production.** Rich nations can export high-tech farming methods to poor nations to help increase their agricultural yields. Such techniques, collectively referred to as the Green Revolution, include new hybrid seeds, modern irrigation methods, chemical fertilizers, and pesticides for insect control.

3. **Introducing industrial technology.** Rich nations can encourage economic growth in poor societies by introducing machinery and information technology, which raise productivity. Industrialization also shifts the labor force from farming to skilled industrial and service jobs.

4. **Providing foreign aid.** Investment capital from rich nations can boost the prospects of poor societies striving to reach Rostow's take-off stage. Foreign aid can raise farm output by making it possible for poor countries to buy more fertilizer and build irrigation projects. In addition, financial and technical assistance to build power plants and factories improves industrial output. Each year, the United States provides about $29 billion in foreign aid to developing countries (U.S. Census Bureau, 2010).

○ Making the Grade

Modernization theory is linked to structural-functional analysis; dependency theory is linked to social-conflict analysis.

dependency theory a model of economic and social development that explains global inequality in terms of the historical exploitation of poor nations by rich ones

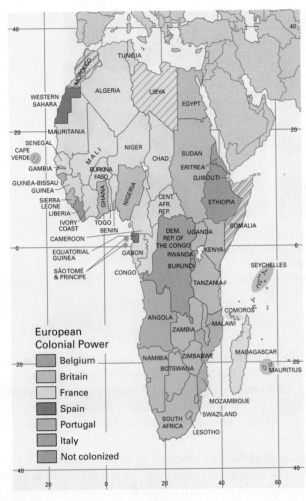

FIGURE 9–4   Africa's Colonial History

For more than a century, most of Africa was colonized by European nations, with France dominating in the northwestern region of the continent and Great Britain dominating in the east and south.

○ **CRITICAL REVIEW**   Modernization theory has many influential supporters among social scientists (Parsons, 1966; Moore, 1977, 1979; Berger, 1986; Firebaugh, 1996; Firebaugh & Sandu, 1998). For decades, it has shaped the foreign policy of the United States and other rich nations. Supporters point to rapid economic development in Asia—especially in South Korea, Taiwan, Singapore, and Hong Kong—as proof that the affluence created in Western Europe and North America is within the reach of all countries.

But modernization theory faces criticism from socialist countries (and left-leaning analysts in the West) as little more than a defense of capitalism. Its most serious flaw, according to critics, is

that modernization has simply not occurred in many poor countries. The United Nations reported that living standards in a number of nations, including Haiti and Nicaragua in Latin America and Sudan, Ghana, and Rwanda in Africa, are actually lower today than they were in 1960 (United Nations Development Programme, 2009).

A second criticism of modernization theory is that it fails to recognize how rich nations, which benefit from the status quo, often block the path to development for poor countries. Centuries ago, rich countries industrialized from a position of global strength. Can we expect poor countries today to do so from a position of global weakness?

Third, modernization theory treats rich and poor societies as separate worlds, ignoring the fact that the global economy affects all nations. Many countries in Latin America and Asia are still struggling to overcome the harm caused by colonization, which boosted the fortunes of Europe.

Fourth, modernization theory holds up the world's most developed countries as the standard for judging the rest of humanity, revealing an ethnocentric bias. We need to remember that our Western idea of "progress" has caused us to rush headlong into a competitive, materialistic way of life, which uses up the world's scarce resources and damages the natural environment.

Fifth and finally, modernization theory suggests that the causes of global poverty lie almost entirely within the poor societies themselves. Critics see this analysis as little more than blaming the victims for their own problems. Instead, they argue, an analysis of global inequality should focus just as much on the behavior of rich nations as it does on the behavior of poor ones and also on the global economic system.

Concerns such as these reflect a second major approach to understanding global inequality, dependency theory.

○ **CHECK YOUR LEARNING**   State the main ideas of modernization theory, including Rostow's four stages of economic development. Point to strengths and weaknesses of this theory.

Dependency Theory

Dependency theory is *a model of economic and social development that explains global inequality in terms of the historical exploitation of poor nations by rich ones.* This analysis, which follows the social-conflict approach, puts primary responsibility for global poverty on rich nations, which for centuries have systematically impoverished low-income countries and made them dependent on the rich ones. This destructive process continues today.

Historical Perspective

Everyone agrees that before the Industrial Revolution, there was little affluence in the world. However, dependency theory asserts that people

⌐○ Making the Grade

Be sure you understand the differences between colonialism
and neocolonialism.

⌐○ Making the Grade

What we learn about in school as the "great explorers"
discovering the new world is characterized by dependency
theory as "colonialism" and the exploitation of native
peoples.

living in poor countries were actually better off economically in the past than their descendants are now. André
Gunder Frank (1975), a noted supporter of this theory,
argues that the colonial process that helped develop rich
nations also *underdeveloped* poor societies.

Dependency theory is based on the idea that the economic positions of the rich and poor nations of the world
are linked and cannot be understood apart from one
another. Poor nations are not simply lagging behind rich
ones on the "path of progress"; rather, the prosperity of
the most developed countries came largely at the expense
of less developed ones. In short, some nations became
rich only because others became poor. Both are the result
of the global economic system that began to take shape
five centuries ago.

The Importance of Colonialism

Late in the fifteenth century, Europeans began surveying
the Americas to the west, Africa to the south, and Asia to
the east in order to establish colonies. They were so successful that a century ago, Great Britain controlled about
one-fourth of the world's land, boasting that "the sun
never sets on the British Empire." The United States, itself
originally a patchwork of small British colonies on the
eastern seaboard of North America, soon pushed across
the continent, purchased Alaska, and gained control of
Haiti, Puerto Rico, Guam, the Philippines, the Hawaiian
Islands, and Guantanamo Bay in Cuba.

As colonialism spread, there emerged a brutal form of human
exploitation—the international slave trade—from about 1500 until
1850. Even as the world was turning away from slavery, Europeans
took control of most of the African continent, as Figure 9–4 shows,
and dominated most of the continent until the early 1960s.

Formal colonialism has almost disappeared from the world.
However, according to dependency theory, political liberation has
not translated into economic independence. Far from it—the economic relationship between poor and rich nations continues the
colonial pattern of domination. This *neocolonialism* is the heart of the
capitalist world economy.

Wallerstein's Capitalist World Economy

Immanuel Wallerstein (1974, 1979, 1983, 1984) explains global stratification using a model of the "capitalist world economy." Wallerstein's
term "world economy" suggests that the prosperity of some nations
and the poverty and dependency of other countries result from a
global economic system. He traces the roots of the global economy to
the beginning of colonization more than 500 years ago, when Europeans began gathering wealth from the rest of the world. Because the

Modernization theory claims that corporations that build factories in low-income nations
help people by providing them with jobs and higher wages than they had before;
dependency theory views these factories as "sweatshops" that exploit workers. In
response to the Olympic Games selling sports clothing produced by sweatshops, these
women staged a protest in Athens, Greece; they are wearing white masks to symbolize
the "faceless" workers who make much of what we wear. Is any of the clothing you
wear made in sweatshop factories?

global economy is based in high-income countries, it is capitalist in
character.[1]

Wallerstein calls the rich nations the *core* of the world economy.
Colonialism enriched this core by funneling raw materials from
around the world to Western Europe, where they fueled the Industrial Revolution. Today, multinational corporations operate prof-
itably worldwide, channeling wealth to North America, Western
Europe, Australia, and Japan.

Low-income countries are the *periphery* of the global economy.
Drawn into the world economy by colonial exploitation, poor nations
continue to support rich ones by providing inexpensive labor and a
vast market for industrial products. The remaining countries are the
semiperiphery of the world economy. They include middle-income
countries such as India and Brazil that have closer ties to the global
economic core.

According to Wallerstein, the world economy benefits rich societies (by generating profits for them) and harms the rest of the world

---

[1]This discussion also draws on A. G. Frank (1980, 1981), Delacroix & Ragin (1981),
Bergesen (1983), Dixon & Boswell (1996), and Kentor (1998).

Making the Grade

Modernization theory assumes that all of the world was poor before the Industrial Revolution and that some nations were able to become rich. Dependency theory assumes that today's poor countries were actually better off before colonialism drained them of their wealth.

Go to the Multimedia Library at **mysoclab.com** to listen to the NPR report "Experts Fear Financial Crisis Will Hurt World's Poor"

How does modernization theory view investment by global corporations such as Coca-Cola in low-income nations like Mozambique? How does the view of dependency theory differ?

(by causing poverty). The world economy thus makes poor nations dependent on rich ones. This dependency involves three factors:

1. **Narrow, export-oriented economies.** Poor nations produce only a few crops for export to rich countries. Examples include coffee and fruits from Latin American nations, oil from Nigeria, hardwoods from the Philippines, and palm oil from Malaysia. Today's multinational corporations buy raw materials cheaply in poor societies and transport them to core nations, where factories process them for profitable sale. Thus poor nations develop few industries of their own.

2. **Lack of industrial capacity.** Without an industrial base, poor societies face a double bind: They count on rich nations to buy their inexpensive raw materials, and they must then try to buy from the rich nations whatever expensive manufactured goods they can afford. In a classic example of this dependency, British colonialists encouraged the people of India to raise cotton but prevented them from weaving their own cloth. Instead, the British shipped Indian cotton to English textile mills in Birmingham and Manchester, manufactured the cloth, and shipped finished goods back to India, where the very people who harvested the cotton bought the garments.

   Dependency theorists claim that the Green Revolution—widely praised by modernization theorists—works the same way. Poor countries sell cheap raw materials to rich nations and then try to buy expensive fertilizers, pesticides, and machinery in return. Typically, rich countries profit from this exchange more than poor nations.

3. **Foreign debt.** Unequal trade patterns have plunged poor countries into debt. Collectively, the poor nations of the world owe rich countries some $3 trillion; hundreds of billions of dollars are owed to the United States alone. Such staggering debt paralyzes a country, causing high unemployment and rampant inflation (World Bank, 2010). ◉ Go to **mysoclab.com**

The Role of Rich Nations

Modernization theory and dependency theory assign very different roles to rich nations. Modernization theory holds that rich societies *produce wealth* through capital investment and new technology. Dependency theory views global inequality in terms of how countries *distribute wealth,* arguing that rich nations have *overdeveloped* themselves as they have *underdeveloped* the rest of the world.

Dependency theorists dismiss the idea that programs developed by rich countries to control population and boost agricultural and industrial output raise living standards in poor countries. Instead, they claim, such programs actually benefit rich nations and the ruling elites, not the poor majority, in low-income countries (Kentor, 2001).

Frances Moore Lappé and Joseph Collins (1986) maintain that the capitalist culture of the United States encourages people to think of poverty as somehow inevitable. In this line of reasoning, they explain, poverty results from "natural" processes, including people having too many children, and from natural disasters such as droughts. But global poverty is far from inevitable; in their view, it results from deliberate government policies. Lappé and Collins point out that the world already produces enough food to allow every person on the planet to become quite fat. In fact, most of Africa actually exports food, even though many people in African nations go hungry.

According to Lappé and Collins, the contradiction of poverty amid plenty stems from the rich-nation policy of producing food for profit, not people. That is, corporations in rich nations cooperate with elites in poor countries to grow and export profitable crops such as coffee, which means using land that could otherwise produce basics such as beans and corn for local families. Governments of poor countries support the practice of growing for export because they need food profits to repay foreign debt. According to Lappé and Collins, the capitalist corporate structure of the global economy is at the core of this vicious circle.

● Seeing Sociology
in Everyday Life

When we see images of life in "exotic" countries in the mass
media, do we confront the extensive poverty that is found
there? Explain.

●Making the Grade

One key difference between modernization theory and
dependency theory is their view of rich nations. The first
approach sees rich nations as a solution to the problem of
poverty; the second sees them as a cause of the problem.

CRITICAL REVIEW The main idea of dependency theory is that no nation becomes rich or poor in isolation because a single global economy shapes the future of all nations. Pointing to continuing poverty in Latin America, Africa, and Asia, dependency theorists claim that development simply cannot proceed under the constraints now imposed by rich countries. Rather, they call for radical reform of the entire world economy so that it operates in the interests of the majority of people.

Critics charge that dependency wrongly treats wealth as if no one gets richer without someone else getting poorer. Farmers, small business owners, and corporations can and do create new wealth through hard work and imaginative use of new technology. After all, they point out, the entire world's wealth has increased six-fold since 1950.

Second, dependency theory is wrong in blaming rich nations for global poverty because many of the world's poorest countries (such as Ethiopia) have had little contact with rich nations. On the contrary, a long history of trade with rich countries has dramatically improved the

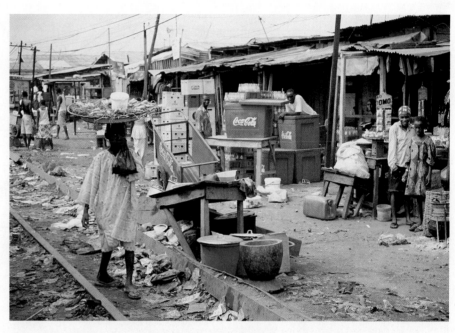

Although the world continues to grow richer, billions of people are being left behind. This shantytown in Lagos, Nigeria, is typical of many cities in low-income countries. What can you say about the quality of life in such a place?

economies of nations including Sri Lanka, Singapore, and Hong Kong (all former British colonies), as well as South Korea and Japan. In short, say the critics, most evidence shows that foreign investment by rich nations encourages economic growth, as modernization theory claims, and not economic decline, as dependency theory holds (E. F. Vogel, 1991; Firebaugh, 1992).

Third, critics call dependency theory simplistic for pointing the finger at a single factor—the capitalist market system—as the cause of global inequality (Worsley, 1990). Dependency theory views poor societies as passive victims and ignores factors inside these countries that contribute to their economic problems. Sociologists have long recognized the vital role of culture in shaping people's willingness to embrace or resist change. Under the rule of the ultratraditional Muslim Taliban, for example, Afghanistan became economically isolated, and its living standards sank to among the lowest in the world. Is it reasonable to blame high-income, capitalist societies for that country's stagnation?

Nor can rich societies be held responsible for the reckless behavior of foreign leaders whose corruption and militarism impoverish their countries. Examples include the regimes of Ferdinand Marcos in the Philippines, François Duvalier in Haiti, Manuel Noriega in Panama, Mobutu Sese Seko in Zaire (today's

Democratic Republic of the Congo), and Saddam Hussein in Iraq. Some leaders even use food supplies as a weapon in internal political struggles, leaving the masses starving, as in the African nations of Ethiopia, Sudan, and Somalia. Likewise, many countries throughout the world have done little to improve the status of women or control population growth.

Fourth, critics say dependency theory is wrong to claim that global trade always makes rich nations richer and poor nations poorer. For example, in 2008, the United States had a trade deficit of $821 billion, meaning that this nation imports that much more goods than it sells abroad. Our country's single greatest debt was to China, whose profitable trade has now pushed that country into the ranks of the world's middle-income nations (U.S. Census Bureau, 2009).

Fifth, critics fault dependency theory for offering only vague solutions to global poverty. Most dependency theorists urge poor nations to end all contact with rich countries, and some call for nationalizing foreign-owned industries. In other words, dependency theory is really an argument for some sort of world socialism. In light of the difficulties socialist countries (even better-off socialist countries such as Russia) have had in meeting the needs of their own people, critics ask, should we really expect such a system to rescue the entire world from poverty?

● Seeing Sociology
in Everyday Life

An increasingly popular idea is "fair trade," paying people in
poor nations a fair price for their products. Would you pay more
for a cup of coffee made using beans for which a farmer in a
low-income country was paid a higher price? Why or why not?

○ Making the Grade

Carefully review the Applying Theory table below to be sure you
understand the two theories of poverty.

● APPLYING THEORY ●

Global Poverty

	Modernization Theory	Dependency Theory
Which theoretical approach is applied?	Structural-functional approach	Social-conflict approach
How did global poverty come about?	The whole world was poor until some countries developed industrial technology, which allowed mass production and created affluence.	Colonialism moved wealth from some countries to others, making some nations poor as it made other nations rich.
What are the main causes of global poverty today?	Traditional culture and a lack of productive technology.	Neocolonialism—the operation of multinational corporations in the global, capitalist economy.
Are rich countries part of the problem or part of the solution?	Rich countries are part of the solution, contributing new technology, advanced schooling, and foreign aid.	Rich countries are part of the problem, making poor countries economically dependent and in debt.

The Applying Theory table summarizes the main arguments
of modernization theory and dependency theory.

○ **CHECK YOUR LEARNING**   State the main ideas of
dependency theory. What are several strengths and weaknesses
of this theory?

Global Stratification: Looking Ahead

Among the most important trends of recent decades is the development of a global economy. In the United States, rising production and
sales abroad bring profits to many corporations and their stockholders, especially those who already have substantial wealth. At the same
time, the global economy has moved manufacturing jobs abroad, closing factories in this country and hurting many average workers. The
net result: greater economic inequality in the United States.

People who support the global economy claim that the expansion of trade results in benefits for all countries involved. For this
reason, they endorse policies such as the North American Free Trade
Agreement (NAFTA) signed by the United States, Canada, and
Mexico, which took effect in 1994. Critics of expanding globalization make other claims: Manufacturing jobs are being lost in the

United States, and more manufacturing now takes place abroad in
factories where workers are paid little and few laws ensure workplace
safety. In addition, other critics of expanding globalization point to
the ever-greater stresses that our economy places on the natural
environment.

But perhaps the greatest concern is the vast economic inequality that exists between the world's countries. The concentration of
wealth in high-income countries, coupled with grinding poverty in
low-income nations, may well be the biggest problem facing humanity in the twenty-first century.

Both modernization theory and dependency theory offer some
understanding of this urgent problem. In evaluating these theories,
we must consider empirical evidence. Over the course of the twentieth century, living standards rose in most of the world. Even the
economic output of the poorest 25 percent of the world's people
increased fourfold during those 100 years. As a result, the number of
people living on less than $1.25 per day fell from about 1.9 billion in
1981 to about 1.4 billion in 2005 (Chen & Ravallion, 2008). In short,
most people around the world are better off than ever before in
absolute terms.

The greatest reduction in poverty has taken place in Asia, a
region generally regarded as an economic success story. In 1981,
almost 80 percent of global $1.25-per-day poverty was in East Asia;

● Seeing Sociology
in Everyday Life

Based on what you have read here and elsewhere, do you
think that, fifty years from now, the problem of global hunger
will be more or less serious? Explain your answer.

● Making the Grade

The figure below shows that both the richest and the
poorest people in the world are getting richer. At the same
time, the gap between rich and poor is getting larger.

by 2005, that figure had fallen to 17 percent. Since then, two very
large Asian countries—India and China—have joined the ranks of
the middle-income nations. The economic growth in India and
China has been so great that in the last two decades, global economic
inequality has actually decreased as economic prosperity has spread
from Europe and North America to Asia (Sala-i-Martin, 2002; Bussollo
et al., 2007; Chen & Ravallion, 2008; Davies et al., 2008).

Latin America represents a mixed case. In the 1970s, this world
region enjoyed significant economic growth; during the 1980s and
1990s, however, there was little overall improvement. The share of
the global $1.25-per-day poverty was slightly higher in 2005 (3 percent)
than it was in 1981 (2 percent) (Chen & Ravallion, 2008).

In Africa, about half of the nations are showing economic
growth greater than in the past. In many countries, however, especially those south of the Sahara, the extent of extreme poverty has
become worse. In 1981, sub-Saharan Africa accounted for 11 percent of $1.25-per-day poverty; by 2005, this share had risen to 28
percent (Sala-i-Martin, 2002; Chen & Ravallion, 2008).

Overall, then, most people are doing better than in the past.
However, richer people in the world are moving ahead much faster
than poor people, so that the world's *relative* poverty has been
increasing (United Nations Development Programme, 2009). In
2007, the gap between the rich and the poor in the world was almost
three times as big as it was back in 1900. Figure 9–5 shows that the
poorest of the world's people are being left behind.

Recent trends suggest the need to look critically at both modernization theory and dependency theory. The fact that governments
have played a large role in the economic growth that has occurred in
Asia and elsewhere challenges modernization theory and its free-
market approach to development. On the other hand, since the
upheavals in the former Soviet Union and Eastern Europe, a global
reevaluation of socialism has also been taking place. Because socialist nations have a record of poor economic performance and political repression, many low-income nations are unwilling to follow the
advice of dependency theory and place economic development
entirely under government control.

Although the world's future is uncertain, we have learned a great
deal about global stratification. One major insight, offered by modernization theory, is that poverty is partly a *problem of technology*. A
higher standard of living for a growing world population depends on
the ability of poor nations to raise their agricultural and industrial
productivity. A second insight, derived from dependency theory, is
that global inequality is also a *political issue*. Even with higher productivity, the human community must address crucial questions
concerning the distribution of resources, both within societies and
around the globe.

Although economic development raises living standards, it also
places greater strains on the natural environment. As nations such as

Global Snapshot

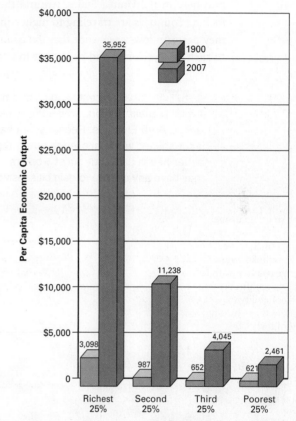

FIGURE 9–5 **The World's Increasing Economic Inequality**
The gap between the richest and poorest people in the world is nearly
three times as big as it was a century ago.
Source: United Nations Development Programme (2009).

India and China—with a combined population of 2.5 billion—
become more affluent, their people will consume more energy and
other natural resources (China has recently passed Japan to become
the second-largest consumer of oil, behind the United States, which
is one reason that oil prices have been rising). Richer nations, in
which people consume more, also produce more solid waste and create more pollution.

Finally, the vast gulf that separates the world's richest and poorest people puts everyone at greater risk of war and terrorism as the
poorest people challenge the social arrangements that threaten their
existence (Lindauer & Weerapana, 2002). In the long run, it is probably true that we can achieve peace on this planet only by ensuring
that all the world's people enjoy a significant measure of dignity and
security.

Seeing Sociology in Everyday Life

How much social inequality can we find if we look around the world?

This chapter explains that a global perspective reveals even more social stratification than we find here in the United States. Around the world, an increasing number of people in lower-income countries are traveling to higher-income nations in search of jobs. As "guest workers," they perform low-wage work that the country's own more well-off citizens do not wish to do. In such cases, the rich and poor truly live "worlds apart."

> **HINT** Dubai's recent building boom has been accomplished using the labor of about 1 million guest workers, who actually make up about 85 percent of the population of the United Arab Emirates. Recent years have seen a rising level of social unrest, including labor strikes, which has led to some improvements in working and living conditions and better health care. But guest workers have no legal rights to form labor unions, nor do they have any chance to gain citizenship.

With so little income, many guest workers sleep six to a small room. How do you think living in a strange country, with few legal rights, affects these workers' ability to improve their working conditions?

Oil wealth has made some of the people of Dubai, in the United Arab Emirates, among the richest in the world. Dubai's wealthiest people can afford to ski on snow—in one of the hottest regions of the world—on enormous indoor ski slopes like this one. Is there anything about this picture that makes you uncomfortable? Explain your reaction.

Many guest workers come to Dubai from India to take jobs building this country's new high-rise hotels and business towers. Workers labor about twelve hours a day but earn only between $50 and $175 a month—typically, twice what people can earn at home. Do you think the chance to take a job like this in a foreign country is an opportunity or a form of exploitation?

Applying SOCIOLOGY in Everyday Life

1. What comparisons can you make between the pattern of guest workers coming to places like Dubai in the Middle East and workers coming to the United States from Mexico and other countries in Latin America?

2. Page through several issues of any current newsmagazine or travel magazine to find any stories or advertising mentioning lower-income countries (selling, say, coffee from Colombia or exotic vacations to India). What picture of life in low-income countries does the advertising present? In light of what you have learned in this chapter, how accurate does this image seem to you?

3. Millions of students from abroad study on U.S. campuses. Find a woman and a man on your campus who were raised in a low-income country. After explaining that you have been studying global inequality, ask if they are willing to share information about what life is like back home. If they are, ask about stratification in general, as well as their own social position, in their home country.

Making the Grade

VISUAL SUMMARY

Global Stratification: An Overview

HIGH-INCOME COUNTRIES

- contain 23% of the world's people
- receive 80% of global income
- have a high standard of living based on advanced technology
- produce enough economic goods to enable their people to lead comfortable lives
- include 67 nations, among them the United States, Canada, Mexico, Argentina, Chile, the nations of Western Europe, Israel, Saudi Arabia, the Russian Federation, Japan, South Korea, Malaysia, and Australia

pp. 245–49

MIDDLE-INCOME COUNTRIES

- contain 57% of the world's people
- receive 19% of global income
- have a standard of living about average for the world as a whole
- include 71 nations, among them the nations of Eastern Europe, Peru, Brazil, Namibia, Egypt, Indonesia, India, and the People's Republic of China

p. 249

LOW-INCOME COUNTRIES

- contain 20% of the world's people
- receive 2% of global income
- have a low standard of living due to limited industrial technology
- include 56 nations, generally in Central and East Africa and Asia, among them Chad, the Democratic Republic of the Congo, Ethiopia, Bangladesh, and Pakistan

pp. 249–50

See Global Map 9–1 on page 247.

✓ Although poverty is a reality in the United States and other nations, the greatest social inequality is not within nations but between them.

global stratification (p. 244) patterns of social inequality in the world as a whole

high-income countries (p. 245) the nations with the highest overall standards of living

middle-income countries (p. 245) nations with a standard of living about average for the world as a whole

low-income countries (p. 246) nations with a low standard of living in which most people are poor

Global Wealth and Poverty

All societies contain **RELATIVE POVERTY**, but low-income nations face widespread **ABSOLUTE POVERTY** that is life-threatening.

- Worldwide, about 1 billion people are at risk due to poor nutrition.
- About 9 million people, most of them children, die each year from diseases caused by poverty.
- Throughout the world, women are more likely than men to be poor. Gender bias is strongest in poor societies.
- As many as 200 million men, women, and children (about 3% of humanity) live in conditions that can be described as slavery.

pp. 250–55

FACTORS CAUSING POVERTY

- Lack of technology limits production.
- High birth rates produce rapid population increase.
- Traditional cultural patterns make people resist change.
- Extreme social inequality distributes wealth very unequally.
- Extreme gender inequality limits the opportunities of women.
- Colonialism allowed some nations to exploit other nations; neocolonialism continues today.

pp. 255–56

colonialism (p. 255) the process by which some nations enrich themselves through political and economic control of other nations

neocolonialism (p. 256) a new form of global power relationships that involves not direct political control but economic exploitation by multinational corporations

multinational corporation (p. 256) a large business that operates in many countries

▢⊙—Read on mysoclab.com

Global Stratification: Theoretical Analysis

MODERNIZATION THEORY maintains that nations achieve affluence by developing advanced technology. This process depends on a culture that encourages innovation and change toward higher living standards. Walt Rostow identified four stages of development:

- *Traditional stage*—People's lives are built around families and local communities. (Example: Bangladesh)

- *Take-off stage*—A market emerges as people produce goods not just for their own use but to trade with others for profit. (Example: Thailand)

- *Drive to technological maturity*—The ideas of economic growth and higher living standards gain widespread support; schooling is widely available; the social standing of women improves. (Example: Mexico)

- *High mass consumption*—Advanced technology fuels mass production and mass consumption as people now "need" countless goods. (Example: the United States)

pp. 256–59

modernization theory (p. 256) a model of economic and social development that explains global inequality in terms of technological and cultural differences between nations

dependency theory (p. 260) a model of economic and social development that explains global inequality in terms of the historical exploitation of poor nations by rich ones

⊕⌐**Explore** on **mysoclab.com**

MODERNIZATION THEORY CLAIMS

- Rich nations can help poor nations by providing technology to control population size, increase food production, and expand industrial and information economy output and by providing foreign aid to pay for new economic development.

- Rapid economic development in Asia shows that affluence is within reach of other nations of the world.

p. 259

CRITICS CLAIM

- Rich nations do little to help poor countries and benefit from the status quo. Low living standards in much of Africa and South America result from the policies of rich nations.

- Because rich nations, including the United States, control the global economy, many poor nations struggle to support their people and cannot follow the path to development taken by rich countries centuries ago.

p. 260

DEPENDENCY THEORY maintains that global wealth and poverty were created by the colonial process beginning 500 years ago that overdeveloped rich nations and underdeveloped poor nations. This capitalist process continues today in the form of neocolonialism—economic exploitation of poor nations by multinational corporations. Immanuel Wallerstein's model of the capitalist world economy identified three categories of nations:

- *Core*—the world's high-income countries, which are home to multinational corporations

- *Semiperiphery*—the world's middle-income countries, with ties to core nations

- *Periphery*—the world's low-income countries, which provide low-cost labor and a vast market for industrial products

pp. 260–62

DEPENDENCY THEORY CLAIMS

- Three key factors—export-oriented economies, a lack of industrial capacity, and foreign debt—make poor countries dependent on rich nations and prevent their economic development.

- Radical reform of the entire world economy is needed so that it operates in the interests of the majority of people.

p. 262

CRITICS CLAIM

- Dependency theory overlooks the sixfold increase in global wealth since 1950 and the fact that the world's poorest countries have had weak, not strong, ties to rich countries.

- Rich nations are not responsible for cultural patterns or political corruption that block economic development in many poor nations.

pp. 263–64

See the Applying Theory table on page 264.

Gender Stratification

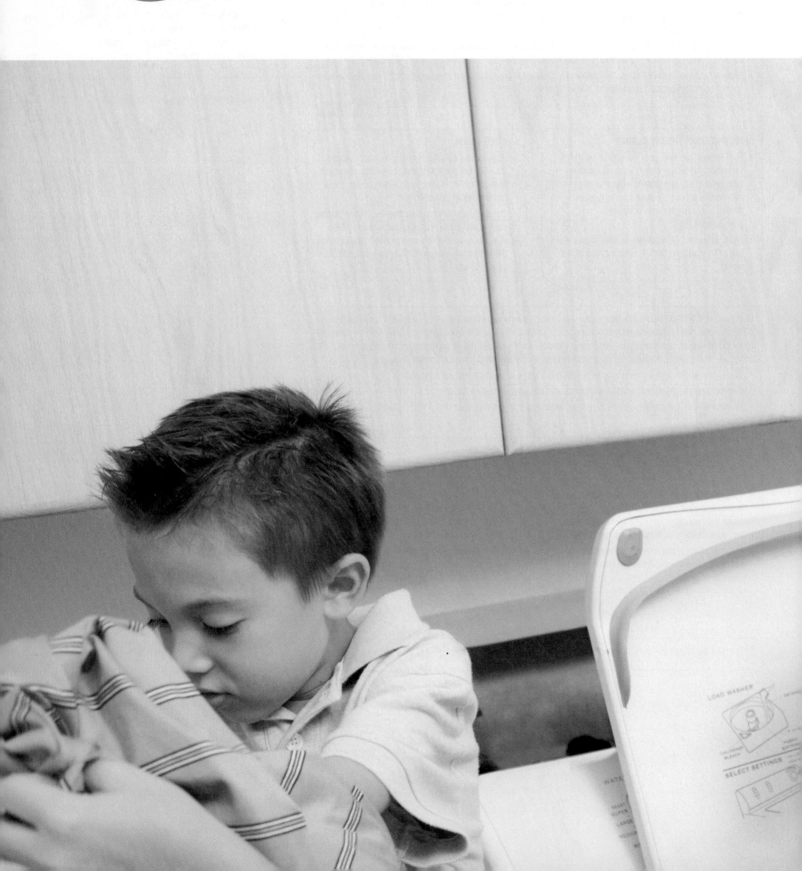

- How is gender a creation of society?

- What differences does gender make in people's lives?

- Why is gender an important dimension of social stratification?

Watch the *Core Concepts in Sociology* video "Similarities and Differences between Men and Women" on **mysoclab.com**

At first we traveled quite alone . . . but before we had gone many miles, we came on other wagon-loads of women, bound in the same direction. As we reached different cross-roads, we saw wagons coming from every part of the country and, long before we reached Seneca Falls, we were a procession.

So wrote Charlotte Woodward in her journal as she made her way in a horse-drawn wagon along the rutted dirt roads leading to Seneca Falls, a small town in upstate New York. The year was 1848, a time when slavery was legal in much of the United States and the social standing of all women, regardless of color, was far below that of men. Back then, in much of the country, women could not own property, keep their own wages if they were married, draft a will, file lawsuits in a court (including lawsuits seeking custody of their own children), or attend college, and husbands were widely viewed as having unquestioned authority over their wives and children.

Some 300 women gathered at Wesleyan Chapel in Seneca Falls to challenge this second-class citizenship. They listened as their leader, Elizabeth Cady Stanton, called for expanding women's rights and opportunities, including the right to vote. At that time, most people considered such a proposal absurd and outrageous. Even many of those attending the conference were shocked by the idea: Stanton's husband, Henry, rode out of town in protest (Gurnett, 1998).

Much has changed since the Seneca Falls convention, and many of Stanton's proposals are now accepted as matters of basic fairness. But as this chapter explains, women and men still lead different lives in the United States and elsewhere in the world; in most respects, men are still in charge. This chapter explores the importance of gender and explains that gender, like class position, is a major dimension of social stratification.

Gender and Inequality

Chapter 6 ("Sexuality and Society") explained that biological differences divide the human population into categories of female and male. **Gender** refers to *the personal traits and social positions that members of a society attach to being female or male.* Gender, then, is a dimension of social organization, shaping how we interact with others and even how we think about ourselves. More important, gender also involves *hierarchy,* placing men and women in different positions in terms of power, wealth, and other resources. This is why sociologists speak of **gender stratification,** *the unequal distribution of wealth, power, and privilege between men and women.* In short, gender affects the opportunities and constraints we face throughout our lives.

Male-Female Differences

Many people think there is something "natural" about gender distinctions because biology does make one sex different from the other. But we must be careful not to think of social differences in biological terms. In 1848, for example, women were denied the vote because many people assumed that women did not have enough intelligence or interest in politics. Such attitudes had nothing to do with biology; they reflected the *cultural patterns* of that time and place.

Another example is athletic performance. In 1925, most people—both women and men—believed that the best women runners could never compete with men in a marathon. Today, as Figure 10–1 shows, the gender gap has greatly narrowed, and the best women runners routinely post better times than the fastest men of decades past. Here again, most of the differences between men and women turn out to be socially created.

Differences in physical ability between the sexes do exist. On average, males are 10 percent taller than women, 20 percent heavier, and 30 percent stronger, especially in the upper body (Ehrenreich, 1999). On the other hand, women outperform men in the ultimate

gender the personal traits and social positions that members of a society attach to being female or male

gender stratification the unequal distribution of wealth, power, and privilege between men and women

game of life itself: Life expectancy for men is 75.1 years, and women can expect to live 80.2 years (Heron et al., 2009).

In adolescence, males do a bit better on the mathematics and reading portions of the SAT, while females show stronger writing skills, differences that reflect both biology and socialization (Lewin, 2008; College Board, 2009). However, research does not point to any overall differences in intelligence between males and females.

Biologically, then, men and women differ in limited ways, with neither one naturally superior. But culture can define the two sexes differently, as the global study of gender described in the next section shows.

Gender in Global Perspective

The best way to see how gender is based in culture is by comparing one society to another. Three important studies highlight just how different "masculine" and "feminine" can be.

The Israeli Kibbutz

In Israel, collective Jewish settlements are called *kibbutzim*. The *kibbutz* (the singular form of the word) has been an important setting for gender research because gender equality is one of its stated goals; men and women share in both work and decision making.

In recent decades, kibbutzim have become less collective and thus less distinctive organizations. But for much of their history, both sexes shared most everyday jobs. Many men joined women in taking care of children, and women joined men in repairing buildings and providing armed security. Both sexes made everyday decisions for the group. Girls and boys were raised in the same way; in many cases, young children were raised together in dormitories away from parents. Women and men in the kibbutzim achieved remarkable (although not complete) social equality, evidence that culture defines what is feminine and what is masculine.

Margaret Mead's Research

The anthropologist Margaret Mead carried out groundbreaking research on gender. If gender is based in the biological differences between men and women, she reasoned, people everywhere should define "feminine" and "masculine" in the same way; if gender is cultural, these concepts should vary.

Mead (1963, orig. 1935) studied three societies in New Guinea. In the mountainous home of the Arapesh, Mead observed men and women with remarkably similar attitudes and behavior. Both sexes, she reported, were cooperative and sensitive to others—in short, what our culture would label "feminine."

Moving south, Mead studied the Mundugumor, whose headhunting and cannibalism stood in striking contrast to the gentle ways of the Arapesh. In this culture, both sexes were typically selfish and aggressive, traits we define as "masculine."

> The women's movement of the 1960s encouraged women to show their true abilities.

Diversity Snapshot

FIGURE 10–1   Men's and Women's Athletic Performance

Do men naturally outperform women in athletic competition? The answer is not obvious. Early in the twentieth century, men outpaced women by more than an hour in marathon races. But as opportunities for women in athletics have increased, women have been closing the performance gap. Only eleven minutes separate the current world marathon records for women (set in 2003) and for men (set in 2008).

Source: Marathonguide.com (2010).

Finally, traveling west to the Tchambuli, Mead discovered a culture that, like our own, defined females and males differently. But, Mead reported, the Tchambuli *reversed* many of our ideas of gender: Females were dominant and rational, and males were submissive, emotional, and nurturing toward children. Based on her observations, Mead concluded that culture is the key to gender distinctions because what one society defines as masculine another may see as feminine.

Some critics view Mead's findings as "too neat," as if she saw in these societies just the patterns she was looking for. Deborah Gewertz (1981) challenged what she called Mead's "reversal hypothesis," pointing out that Tchambuli males are really the more aggressive sex. Gewertz explains that Mead visited the Tchambuli (who themselves spell their name Chambri) during the 1930s, after they had lost much of their property in tribal wars, and observed men rebuilding their homes, a temporary role for Chambri men.

Seeing Sociology
in Everyday Life

Do you think female and male athletes should compete on the
same teams? Why or why not? Do you think men and women
see this issue differently?

matriarchy a form of social organization in which females dominate males

patriarchy a form of social organization in which males dominate females

sexism the belief that one sex is innately superior to the other

George Murdock's Research

In a broader study of more than 200 preindustrial societies, George
Murdock (1937) found some global agreement on which tasks are
feminine and which masculine. Hunting and warfare, Murdock
observed, generally fall to men, and home-centered tasks such as cooking and child care tend to be women's work. With their simple technology, preindustrial societies apparently assign roles reflecting men's
and women's physical characteristics. With their greater size and
strength, men hunt game and protect the group; because women bear
children, they do most of the work in the home.

Beyond this general pattern, Murdock found much variety. Consider agriculture: Women did the farming in about the same number of societies as men; in most societies, the two sexes divided this
work. When it came to many other tasks, from building shelters to
tattooing the body, Murdock found that preindustrial societies were
as likely to turn to one sex as the other.

CRITICAL REVIEW Global comparisons show that
overall, societies do not consistently define tasks as feminine or
masculine. With industrialization, the importance of muscle power
declines, further reducing gender differences (Nolan & Lenski,

2007). In sum, gender is too variable to be a simple expression
of biology; what it means to be female and male is mostly a creation of society.

CHECK YOUR LEARNING By comparing many cul-
tures, what do we learn about the origin of gender differences?

Patriarchy and Sexism

Conceptions of gender vary, and there is evidence of societies in which
women have greater power than men. One example is the Musuo, a
very small society in southwestern China's Yunnan province, in which
women control most property, select their sexual partners, and make
most decisions about everyday life. The Musuo appear to be a case of
matriarchy ("rule by mothers"), *a form of social organization in which
females dominate males,* which has only rarely been documented in
human history.

The pattern found almost everywhere in the world is **patriarchy**
("rule by fathers"), *a form of social organization in which males dominate females.* Global Map 10–1 shows the great variation in the relative power and privilege of women that exists from country to
country. According to the United Nations' gender development index,
Australia, Iceland, and Norway give women the highest social
standing; by contrast, women in the Central African Republic,
Sierra Leone, Mali, Afghanistan, and Niger have the lowest social
standing compared with men. Of the world's 194 nations, the
United States was ranked nineteenth in terms of gender equality (United Nations Development Programme, 2009).

The justification for patriarchy is **sexism,** *the belief that
one sex is innately superior to the other.* Sexism is not just a matter of individual attitudes; it is built into the institutions of
our society. *Institutional sexism* is found throughout the economy, with women highly concentrated in low-paying jobs. Similarly, the legal system has long excused violence against
women, especially on the part of boyfriends, husbands, and
fathers.

The Costs of Sexism

Sexism limits the talents and the ambitions of the half of the
human population who are women. Although men benefit in
some respects from sexism, their privilege comes at a high price.
Masculinity in our culture encourages men to engage in many
high-risk behaviors: using tobacco and alcohol, playing dangerous sports, and even driving recklessly. As Marilyn French
(1985) argues, patriarchy drives men to relentlessly seek control, not only of women but also of themselves and their world.
Thus masculinity is linked not only to accidents but also to
suicide, violence, and stress-related diseases. The *Type A personality*—marked by chronic impatience, driving ambition, com-

In every society, people assume that certain jobs, patterns of behavior, and ways of
dressing are "naturally" feminine while others are just as obviously masculine. But in
global perspective, we see remarkable variety in such social definitions. These men,
Wodaabe pastoral nomads who live in the African nation of Niger, are proud to
engage in a display of beauty most people in our society would consider feminine.

Astrid Brügger, age 19, lives in Norway; like most girls growing up in high-income nations, she enjoys most of the rights and opportunities available to men.

Jendayi Gattuso, age 20, lives in Mozambique, a low-income nation that limits the rights and opportunities of women.

Women's Social Standing
High
Above average
Average
Below average
Low
No data

Window on the World

GLOBAL MAP 10–1 Women's Power in Global Perspective

Women's social standing in relation to men's varies around the world. In general, women live better in rich countries than in poor countries. Even so, some nations stand out: In Australia, Iceland, and Norway women come closest to social equality with men.

Source: United Nations Development Programme (2009).

petitiveness, and free-floating hostility—is one cause of heart disease and an almost perfect match with the behavior our culture considers masculine (Ehrenreich, 1983).

Finally, as men seek control over others, they lose opportunities for intimacy and trust. As one analyst put it, competition is supposed to "separate the men from the boys." In practice, however, it separates men from men and everyone else (Raphael, 1988).

Must Patriarchy Go On?

In preindustrial societies, women have little control over pregnancy and childbirth, which limits the scope of their lives. In those same societies, men's greater height and physical strength are valued resources that give them power. But industrialization, including birth control technology, increases people's choices about how to live. In societies like our own, biological differences offer little justification for patriarchy.

● Seeing Sociology
in Everyday Life

Did you grow up in a home in which females and males had
different jobs and responsibilities? How did this experience
affect your view of gender?

gender roles (also known as **sex roles**) attitudes and activities
that a society links to each sex

But males are dominant in the United States and elsewhere.
Does this mean that patriarchy is inevitable? Some researchers claim
that biological factors such as differences in hormones and slight
differences in brain structure "wire" the sexes with different moti-
vations and behaviors—especially aggressiveness in males—making patriarchy difficult or perhaps even impossible to change (S.
Goldberg, 1974; Rossi, 1985; Popenoe, 1993b; Udry, 2000). However, most sociologists believe that gender is socially constructed
and *can* be changed. The fact that no society has completely eliminated patriarchy does not mean that we must remain prisoners of
the past.

To understand why patriarchy continues today, we next examine how gender is rooted and reproduced in society, a process that
begins in childhood and continues throughout our lives.

Gender and Socialization

From birth until death, gender shapes human feelings, thoughts, and
actions. Children quickly learn that their society considers females
and males different kinds of people; by about age three, they begin to
think of themselves in these terms.

In the past, many people in the United States traditionally
described women using terms such as "emotional," "passive," and
"cooperative." By contrast, men were described as "rational," "active,"
and "competitive." It is curious that we were taught for so long to
think of gender in terms of one sex being opposite to the other,
especially because women and men have so much in common and
also because research suggests that most people develop personalities that are a mix of feminine and masculine traits (Bem,
1993).

Just as gender affects how we think of ourselves, so it teaches
us how to behave. **Gender roles** (also known as **sex roles**) are
attitudes and activities that a society links to each sex. A culture that
defines males as ambitious and competitive encourages them
to seek out positions of leadership and play team sports. To
the extent that females are defined as deferential and emotional, they are expected to be supportive helpers and
quick to show their feelings.

Sex is a biological distinction that develops prior to
birth. Gender is the meaning that a society attaches to
being female or male. Gender differences are a matter of
power, because what is defined as masculine typically
has more importance than what is defined as feminine.
Infants begin to learn the importance of gender by the
way parents treat them. Do you think this child is a girl
or a boy? Why?

Gender and the Family

The first question people usually ask about a newborn—"Is it a boy or
a girl?"—has great importance because the answer involves not just
sex but the likely direction of the child's life. In fact, gender is at work
even before a child is born, because especially in lower-income nations,
parents hope their firstborn will be a boy rather than a girl.

Soon after birth, family members welcome infants into the "pink
world" of girls or the "blue world" of boys (Bernard, 1981). People
even send gender messages in the way they handle infants. One
researcher at an English university presented an infant dressed as
either a boy or a girl to a number of women; her subjects handled the
"female" child tenderly, with frequent hugs and caresses, while treating the "male" child more aggressively, often lifting him up high in
the air or bouncing him on a knee (Bonner, 1984; Tavris & Wade,
2001). The lesson is clear: The female world revolves around cooperation and emotion, and the male world puts a premium on independence and action.

Gender and the Peer Group

About the time they enter school, children begin to move outside the
family and make friends with others of the same age. Considerable
research points to the fact that young children tend to form single-sex
play groups (Martin & Fabes, 2001).

Peer groups teach additional lessons about gender.
After spending a year watching children at play, Janet Lever
(1978) concluded that boys favor team sports with complex rules and clear objectives such as scoring runs or
making touchdowns. Such games nearly always have
winners and losers, reinforcing masculine traits of
aggression and control.

Girls, too, play team sports. But, Lever explains,
girls also play hopscotch, jump rope, or simply
talk, sing, or dance. These activities have few
rules, and rarely is victory the ultimate goal.
Instead of teaching girls to be competitive, Lever
explains, female peer groups promote the interpersonal skills of communication and
cooperation, presumably the basis for
girls' future roles as wives and mothers.

The games we play offer important
lessons for our later lives. Lever's observations recall Carol Gilligan's gender-
based theory of moral reasoning,
discussed in Chapter 3 ("Socialization:
From Infancy to Old Age"). Boys, Gilligan
(1982) claims, reason according to abstract
principles. For them, "rightness" amounts to

● Seeing Sociology
in Everyday Life

Consider the statements "He fathered the child" and "She mothered the child." How do you think gender shapes the meaning of parenting?

● Seeing Sociology
in Everyday Life

What is your declared or likely major? Based on the classes you have taken, what share of students in this major are female and what share are male? Does this pattern agree with those described here?

In our society, the mass media have enormous influence on our attitudes and behavior, and what we see shapes our views of gender. In the 2009 film *Twilight,* we see a strong, "take charge" male playing against a more passive female. Do you think the mass media create these gender patterns? Or it is more correct to say that they reproduce them? Is there another option?

"playing by the rules." By contrast, girls consider morality a matter of responsibility to others.

Gender and Schooling

Gender shapes our interests and beliefs about our own abilities, guiding areas of study and, eventually, career choices (Correll, 2001). In high school, more girls than boys learn secretarial skills and take vocational classes such as cosmetology and food services. Classes in woodworking and auto mechanics attract mostly young men.

Women have now become a majority (57 percent) of the students on college campuses across the United States. As their numbers have increased, women have become well represented in many fields of study that once excluded them, including mathematics, chemistry, and biology. But men still predominate in many fields, including engineering, physics, and philosophy, and women cluster in the fine arts (including music, dance, and drama) as well as the social sciences (including anthropology and sociology). Newer areas of study are also gender-typed: More men than women take computer science, and courses in gender studies enroll mostly women.

Gender and the Mass Media

Since television captured the public imagination in the early 1950s, white males have held center stage; racial and ethnic minorities were all but absent from television until the early 1970s. And when both sexes appeared on camera, men generally played the brilliant detectives, fearless explorers, and skilled surgeons. Women played the less capable characters, often unnecessary except for the sexual interest they added to the story.

Historically, advertisements have shown women in the home, cheerfully using cleaning products, serving food, trying out appliances, and modeling clothes. Men predominate in ads for cars, travel, banking services, industrial companies, and alcoholic beverages. The authoritative voiceover—the voice that describes a product on television and radio—is almost always male (D. M. Davis, 1993).

A careful study of gender in advertising reveals that men usually appear taller than women, implying male superiority. Women, by contrast, are more frequently presented lying down (on sofas and beds) or, like children, seated on the floor. Men's facial expressions and behavior give off an air of competence and imply dominance; women often appear childlike, submissive, and sexual. Men focus on the products being advertised, and women often focus on the men (Goffman, 1979; Cortese, 1999).

Finally, advertising perpetuates what Naomi Wolf (1990) calls the "beauty myth." The Seeing Sociology in Everyday Life box on page 278 takes a closer look at how this myth affects both women and men.

Gender and Social Stratification

Gender involves more than how people think and act. It is also about how society is organized, how our lives are affected by social hierarchy. The reality of gender stratification can be seen in just about every aspect of our everyday lives. We look, first, to the world of working women and men.

Working Women and Men

In 1900, just one-fifth of women were in the U.S. labor force. Today, this figure has tripled, to 60 percent, and 75 percent of these working women work full time. The once common view that earning income is a man's role no longer holds true.

Factors that have contributed to change in the U.S. labor force include the decline of farming, the growth of cities, shrinking family size, and a rising divorce rate. The United States, along with most other nations of the world, considers women working for income the rule rather than the exception. Women make up almost half the U.S. paid labor force, and more than half of U.S. married couples depend on two incomes.

In the past, many younger women in the labor force were childless. But today, 60 percent of married women with children under age six are in the labor force, as are 74 percent of married women with children between six and seventeen years of age. For widowed, divorced, or separated women with children, the comparable figures are 64 percent of women with younger children and 76 percent of women with older children (U.S. Department of Labor, 2009).

Read "Maid to Order: The Politics of Other Women's Work" by Barbara Ehrenreich on **mysoclab.com**

Seeing Sociology in Everyday Life

Do you think women on your campus are overly concerned with looking thin? Explain.

SEEING SOCIOLOGY IN EVERYDAY LIFE

The Beauty Myth

BETH: "I can't eat lunch. I need to be sure I can get into that black dress for tonight."

SARAH: "Maybe eating is more important than looking good for Tom."

BETH: "That's easy for you to say. You're a size 2 and Jake adores you!"

The Duchess of Windsor once remarked, "A woman can never be too rich or too thin." The first half of her observation might apply to men as well, but certainly not the second. After all, the vast majority of ads placed by the $10-billion-a-year U.S. cosmetics industry and the $35-billion diet industry target women.

According to Naomi Wolf (1990), certain cultural patterns create a "beauty myth" that is damaging to women. The beauty myth arises, first, because society teaches women to measure their worth in terms of physical appearance. Yet the standards of beauty embodied by the *Playboy* centerfold or the 100-pound New York fashion model are out of reach for most women.

The way society teaches women to prize relationships with men, whom they presumably attract with their beauty, also contributes to the beauty myth. Striving for beauty not only drives women to be extremely disciplined but also forces them to be highly attentive and responsive to men. In short, beauty-minded women try to please men and avoid challenging male power.

Belief in the beauty myth is one reason so many young women are focused on body image,

One way our culture supports the beauty myth is through beauty pageants for women; over the years, contestants have become thinner and thinner.

particularly being as thin as possible, often to the point of endangering their health. During the past several decades, the share of young women who develop an eating disorder such as anorexia nervosa (dieting to the point of starvation) or bulimia (binge eating followed by vomiting) has risen dramatically.

The beauty myth affects males as well: Men are told repeatedly that they should want to possess beautiful women. Such ideas about beauty reduce women to objects and motivate men to think of women as if they were dolls rather than human beings.

There can be little doubt that the idea of beauty is important in everyday life. According to Wolf, the question is whether beauty is about how we look or how we act.

WHAT DO YOU THINK?

1. Is there a "money myth" that states that people's income is a reflection of their worth? Does it apply more to one sex than to the other?

2. Can you see a connection between the beauty myth and the rise of eating disorders among young women in the United States?

3. Among people with physical disabilities, do you think that issues of "looking different" are more serious for women or for men? Why?

Gender and Occupations

Although women are closing the gap with men as far as working for income is concerned, the work done by the two sexes remains very different. The U.S. Department of Labor (2009) reports a high concentration of women in two types of jobs. Administrative support work draws 24 percent of working women, most of whom are secretaries or other office workers. These are called "pink-collar jobs" because 75 percent are filled by women. Another 16 percent of employed women perform service work. Most of these jobs are in the food service industries, child care, and health care. Read on **mysoclab.com**

Table 10–1 shows the ten occupations with the highest concentrations of women. These jobs tend to be at the low end of the pay

scale, with limited opportunities for advancement and with men as supervisors (U.S. Department of Labor, 2009).

Men dominate most other job categories, including the building trades, where 99 percent of brickmasons, stonemasons, and heavy-equipment mechanics are men. Likewise, men make up 87 percent of architects and engineers, 85 percent of police officers, 70 percent of physicians and surgeons, 66 percent of lawyers, and 57 percent of corporate managers. According to a recent survey, just 15 of the *Fortune* 500 companies in the United States have a woman as their chief executive officer, and just 15 percent of the seats on corporate boards of directors are held by women. In 2009, the highest-paid woman CEO in the United States had the same total compensation

Seeing Sociology
in Everyday Life

As you look at Table 10–1, think about which jobs have a
high concentration of men (some are noted in the text). How
do they differ from the "feminine" jobs in Table 10–1?

Go to the Multimedia Library at **mysoclab.com**
to listen to the NPR report "Women's Pay
Disparity a Growing Campaign Issue"

as the ninth-highest-paid male CEO. Increasing the leadership role
of women in the business world is not just a matter of fairness;
research into the earnings of this country's 500 largest corporations
showed that the companies with more women on the board also are
the most profitable (Dickler, 2007; Graybow, 2007; Loomis, 2007;
U.S. Department of Labor, 2009; Catalyst, 2010; *Fortune*, 2010).

Gender stratification in everyday life is easy to see: Female nurses
assist male physicians, female secretaries serve male executives, and
female flight attendants are under the command of male airline
pilots. In any field, the greater a job's income and prestige, the
more likely it is to be held by a man. For example, women represent
98 percent of kindergarten teachers, 81 percent of elementary and
middle school teachers, 56 percent of secondary school educators,
46 percent of professors in colleges and universities, and 23 percent
of college and university presidents (Chronicle of Higher Education,
2007; U.S. Department of Labor, 2009).

How are women kept out of certain jobs? By defining some kinds
of work as "men's work," society defines women as less competent
than men. In a study of coal mining in southern West Virginia,
Suzanne Tallichet (2000) found that most men considered it "unnat-
ural" for women to work in the mines. Women who did so were
defined as deviant and subject to labeling as "sexually loose" or as
lesbians. Such labeling made these women outcasts, presented a challenge to holding the job, and made advancement all but impossible.

In the corporate world, too, the higher in the company we look,
the fewer women we find. You hardly ever hear anyone say out loud
that women don't belong at the top levels of a company. But many
people seem to feel this way, which can prevent women from being
promoted. Sociologists describe this barrier as a *glass ceiling* that is
not easy to see but blocks women's careers all the same (Benokraitis
& Feagin, 1995).

One challenge to male domination in the workplace comes from
women who are entrepreneurs. In 2008, there were more than 10 million
woman-owned businesses in the United States, double the number of a
decade ago; they employed more than 13 million people and generated
$2 trillion in sales. By starting their own businesses, women have shown
that they can make opportunities for themselves apart from large, male-
dominated companies (Center for Women's Business Research, 2009).

Of course, gender stratification shapes the workforce not only in
the United States but in other nations as well. Seeing Sociology in
the News on page 280 provides a close look at Japan, a nation where,
traditionally, patriarchy has been very strong, but where evidence of
change is now beginning to appear.

Gender, Income, and Wealth

In 2008, the median earnings for women working full time were
$35,903, and men working full time earned $46,566. This means that

Table 10–1 Jobs with the Highest Concentrations of Women, 2008	Number of Women Employed	Percentage in Occupation Who Are Women
Occupation		
1. Speech-language pathologist	133,000	98.1
2. Dental hygienist	143,000	97.7
3. Preschool or kindergarten teacher	685,000	97.6
4. Dental assistant	263,000	96.3
5. Secretary or administrative assistant	3,296,000	96.1
6. Occupational therapist	87,000	95.9
7. Child care worker	1,314,000	95.6
8. Medical records and health information technician	98,000	95.0
9. Receptionist or information clerk	1,413,000	93.6
10. Licensed practical nurse	566,000	93.3

Source: U.S. Department of Labor (2009).

for every dollar earned by men, women earned about 77 cents. These
earnings differences are greatest among older workers because older
working women typically have less education and less seniority than
older working men. Earnings differences are smaller among younger
workers because younger men and women tend to have similar
schooling and work experience.

Among full-time workers of all ages, 26 percent of women
earned less than $25,000 in 2008, compared with 16 percent of com-
parable men. At the upper end of the income scale, men were more
than twice as likely as women (22.2 percent versus 10.1 percent) to
earn more than $75,000 (U.S. Census Bureau, 2009).

The main reason women earn less is the *type* of work they do:
largely clerical and service jobs. In effect, jobs and gender interact.
People still perceive jobs with less clout as "women's work," just as
people devalue certain work simply because it is performed by
women (England, Hermsen, & Cotter, 2000; Cohen & Huffman,
2003).

In recent decades, supporters of gender equality have proposed
a policy of "comparable worth," paying people not according to the
historical double standard but according to the level of skill and
responsibility involved in the work. Several nations, including Great
Britain and Australia, have adopted comparable worth policies, but
these policies have found limited acceptance in the United States. As
a result, women in this country lose as much as $1 billion in income
annually. ● Go to **mysoclab.com**

A second cause of gender-based income inequality has to do
with society's view of the family. Both men and women have children, of course, but our culture gives more of the responsibility of
parenting to women. Pregnancy and raising small children keep
many younger women out of the labor force at a time when their

CNN.com

Women on Board: Breaking the "Bamboo Ceiling"

By KYUNG LAH
April 22, 2010

TOKYO—Change a few circumstances in her life and Sakie Fukushima says she would have been a housewife. She was raised to be a good Japanese wife and homemaker, after all. That's what was expected of women of her generation—to sit behind their men, make their bentos, iron their shirts and watch them rise to lead Japan's economy.

Life did not go as Fukushima expected.

Sixty-year-old Fukushima is one of Japan's most powerful executives, sitting on the board of both U.S. and Japanese-based multinational companies. The fact that she is a female in one of the most male-dominated business cultures is a stunning backstory in one woman's remarkable ascent through the so-called "bamboo ceiling." Bamboo bends, and unlike glass, never breaks. But Fukushima managed to crack through, by working for a U.S. company.

"I was lucky to be in a place where the hard work was appreciated," said Fukushima, of her corporate beginnings at Korn-Ferry International. The American company saw her sales output, the highest in the Asia-Pacific region, as the reason for promotion.

An American mentor and her supportive husband urged Fukushima to push beyond her Japanese cultural expectations.

"If I was to work for a Japanese company, a large Japanese company, I don't think I would have come this far."

The World Economic Forum's Global Gender Gap Index ranks Japan 101 out of 134 countries. Part of the reason for the low ranking is that just 1.4 percent of Japanese executives are women.

What that has meant for women in the workplace is they are pushed to traditionally female roles: secretary and store clerk. It is a dismal reality for the world's second-largest economy, said Beth Brooke, Ernst and Young's Global vice chairwoman and a *Forbes* Magazine 100 most powerful woman.

"Japan is a very homogeneous society. So on the spectrum of diversity, not just gender, it is more difficult to embrace diversity because it's not a terribly diverse culture to begin with."

Ironically, Brooke believes the global economic slowdown and Japan's aging population is a chance to rediscover the people underutilized in the workforce.

"I think we have an opportunity to change the conversation here. Whether you're a country or a company, you need growth. Japan has an enormous opportunity, frankly, to see the opportunity to spark innovation through a gender lens of diversity. I think gender diversity is a big part of the solution."

Fukushima agreed, as she celebrates her recent appointment to the Bridgestone Corporation board. She is the first female to be elected to the Japanese company's boardroom.

"Experimenting is the best way to say it," said Fukushima, describing Japan's corporate senti-

ment toward women. "They know they have to have diversity but they don't know how to do it and how to use it effectively. As a result of increasing competition outside of Japan from China and Korea, the Japanese business community has realized it has to change. They can't rely on the past successful model of the 1970s and '80s. They will have to increase diversity, change the way of doing business in order to compete."

Fukushima's new colleague, Bridgestone Americas, Inc. CEO and President Gary Garfield, said he is encouraged that his company in Japan is catching up to other global companies.

He calls having a female on the board a no-brainer. His advice to Japanese companies: "Just branch out and do it. They'll be stronger for it. I think they'll be better companies for it."

WHAT DO YOU THINK?

1. What does the article say about why Japan has such strong gender stratification?

2. Are there reasons to think that Japan's future will be different from its past? What are they?

3. Does the "glass ceiling" in the United States differ from the "bamboo ceiling" in Japan? If so, how?

"Women on Board: Breaking the 'Bamboo Ceiling'" by Kyung Lah is reprinted by permission. Source: CNN.com, April 22, 2010.

---

male peers are making significant career advancements. When women workers return to the labor force, they have less job experience and seniority than their male counterparts (Stier, 1996; Waldfogel, 1997).

In addition, women who choose to have children may be unable or unwilling to take on fast-paced jobs that tie up their evenings and weekends. To avoid role strain, they may take jobs that offer shorter commuting distances, more flexible hours, and employer-provided child care services. Women pursuing both a career and a family are torn between their dual responsibilities in ways that men are not. One study found that almost half of women in competitive jobs took time off to have children, compared to about 12 percent of men (Hewlett & Luce, 2005). Role conflict is also experienced by women on campus, where one study concluded that young female professors with at least one child were at least 20 percent less likely to have tenure than comparable men in the same field (Shea, 2002).

The two factors noted so far—type of work and family responsibilities—account for about two-thirds of the earnings difference between women and men. A third factor—discrimination against women—accounts for most of the remainder (Fuller & Schoenberger, 1991). Because overt discrimination is illegal, it is practiced in subtle ways. Women on their way up the corporate ladder often run into the glass ceiling described earlier; company officials may deny its existence, but it effectively prevents many women from rising above middle management.

For all these reasons, women earn less than men in all major occupational categories. Even so, many people think that women own most of the country's wealth, perhaps because women typically outlive men. Government statistics tell a different story: Fifty-seven percent of people with $1.5 million or more in assets are men, although widows are highly represented in this elite club (Johnson & Raub, 2006; Internal Revenue Service, 2008). Just 10 percent of the people

● Seeing Sociology
in Everyday Life

How is gender related to doing housework in your current
home or in the home in which you grew up?

identified by *Forbes* magazine as the richest people in the United States in 2009 were women (Miller & Greenberg, 2009).

Housework: Women's "Second Shift"

In the United States, housework has always presented a cultural contradiction: We claim that it is essential for family life, but people get little reward for doing it (Bernard, 1981). Here, as around the world, taking care of the home and children has been considered "women's work" (see Global Map 4–1 on page 98). As women have entered the labor force, the amount of housework women do has gone down, but the *share* done by women has stayed the same. Figure 10–2 shows that overall, women average 15.2 hours of housework per week, compared with 9.0 hours for men. As the figure shows, women in all categories do significantly more housework than men (Bureau of Labor Statistics, 2010).

Men do support the idea of women entering the paid labor force, and most count on the money women earn. But many men resist taking on an equal share of household duties (Heath & Bourne, 1995; Harpster & Monk-Turner, 1998; Stratton, 2001).

Gender and Education

In the past, our society considered schooling more necessary for men, who worked outside the home. But times have changed. By 1980, women earned a majority of all associate and bachelor's degrees; in 2008, their share was 59 percent (National Center for Education Statistics, 2010).

College doors have opened wider to women in recent decades, and differences in men's and women's majors are becoming smaller. In 1970, for example, women accounted for just 17 percent of bachelor's degrees in the natural sciences, computer science, and engineering; by 2008, the proportion had doubled to 34 percent.

In 1992, for the first time, women earned a majority of postgraduate degrees, which are often a springboard to high-prestige jobs. In all areas of study in 2008, women earned 61 percent of all master's degrees and 50 percent of all doctorates (including 61 percent of all Ph.D. degrees in sociology). Women have also broken into many graduate fields that used to be almost all male. For example, in 1970, only a few hundred women received a master's of business administration (M.B.A.) degree, compared to more than 69,000 in 2008 (45 percent of all such degrees) (National Center for Education Statistics, 2010).

Despite this progress, men still predominate in some professional fields. In 2008, men received 53 percent of law degrees (LL.B. and J.D.), 51 percent of medical degrees (M.D.), and 56 percent of dental degrees (D.D.S. and D.M.D.) (National Center for Education Statistics, 2010). Our society still defines high-paying professions (and the drive and competitiveness needed to succeed in them) as masculine. But the share of women in all these profes-

Diversity Snapshot

> On average, women spend considerably more time doing housework than men.

FIGURE 10–2 **Housework: Who Does How Much?**

Regardless of employment or family status, women do more housework than men. What effect do you think the added burden of housework has on women's ability to advance in the workplace?

Source: Bureau of Labor Statistics (2010).

sions has risen and is now close to half. When will parity be reached? Probably not in the next few years. For example, the American Bar Association (2010) reports that in 2009, men still accounted for 53 percent of law school students across the United States.

Gender and Politics

A century ago, almost no women held elected office in the United States. In fact, women were legally barred from voting in national elections until the passage of the Nineteenth Amendment to the Constitution in 1920. However, a few women were candidates for political office even before they could vote. The Equal Rights party supported Victoria Woodhull for the U.S. presidency in 1872; perhaps it was a sign of the times that she spent election day in a New York City jail. Table 10–2 on page 282 identifies milestones in women's gradual movement into U.S. political life.

Today, thousands of women serve as mayors of cities and towns across the United States, and tens of thousands more hold responsi-

minority any category of people distinguished by physical or cultural difference that a society sets apart and subordinates

intersection theory analysis of the interplay of race, class, and gender, often resulting in multiple dimensions of disadvantage

Table 10–2 Significant Firsts for Women in U.S. Politics

1869	Law allows women to vote in Wyoming Territory.
1872	First woman to run for the presidency (Victoria Woodhull) represents the Equal Rights party.
1917	First woman elected to the House of Representatives (Jeannette Rankin of Montana).
1924	First women elected state governors (Nellie Taylor Ross of Wyoming and Miriam "Ma" Ferguson of Texas); both followed their husbands into office. First woman to have her name placed in nomination for the vice presidency at the convention of a major political party (Lena Jones Springs, a Democrat).
1931	First woman to serve in the Senate (Hattie Caraway of Arkansas); completed the term of her husband upon his death and won reelection in 1932.
1932	First woman appointed to the presidential cabinet (Frances Perkins, secretary of labor in the cabinet of President Franklin D. Roosevelt).
1964	First woman to have her name placed in nomination for the presidency at the convention of a major political party (Margaret Chase Smith, a Republican).
1972	First African American woman to have her name placed in nomination for the presidency at the convention of a major political party (Shirley Chisholm, a Democrat).
1981	First woman appointed to the U.S. Supreme Court (Sandra Day O'Connor).
1984	First woman to be successfully nominated for the vice presidency (Geraldine Ferraro, a Democrat).
1988	First woman chief executive to be elected to a consecutive third term (Madeleine Kunin, governor of Vermont).
1992	Political "Year of the Woman" yields record number of women in the Senate (six) and the House (forty-eight), as well as first African American woman to win election to U.S. Senate (Carol Moseley-Braun of Illinois), first state (California) to be served by two women senators (Barbara Boxer and Dianne Feinstein), and first woman of Puerto Rican descent elected to the House (Nydia Velazquez of New York).
1996	First woman appointed secretary of state (Madeleine Albright).
2000	First former First Lady to win elected political office (Hillary Rodham Clinton, senator from New York).
2001	First woman to serve as national security adviser (Condoleezza Rice); first Asian American woman to serve in a presidential cabinet (Elaine Chao).
2005	First African American woman appointed secretary of state (Condoleezza Rice).
2007	First woman elected as Speaker of the House (Nancy Pelosi). Record number of women in the Senate (sixteen) and the House (seventy).
2008	For the first time, women make up a majority of a state legislature (New Hampshire).
2009	Record number of women in the Senate (seventeen) and the House (seventy-three).

ble administrative jobs in the federal government. At the state level, 24 percent of state legislators in 2009 were women (up from just 5 percent in 1971). National Map 10–1 shows where in the United States women have made the greatest political gains.

Change is coming more slowly at the highest levels of power, although a majority of U.S. adults claim they would support a qual-

ified woman for any office, including the presidency. In 2008, Hillary Clinton came close to gaining the presidential nomination of the Democratic party, losing out to Barack Obama, who became the nation's first African American president. In 2009, 6 of the 50 state governors were women (12 percent), and in Congress, women held 73 of the 435 seats in the House of Representatives (17 percent) and 17 of the 100 seats in the Senate (17 percent) (Center for American Women and Politics, 2009a).

Women make up half of Earth's population, but they hold just 19 percent of seats in the world's 187 parliamentary governments. Although this represents a rise from the 3 percent of seats they held fifty years ago, only in sixteen countries, among them Sweden and Norway, do women represent more than one-third of the members of parliament (Paxton, Hughes, & Green, 2006; Inter-Parliamentary Union, 2009).

Gender and the Military

Since colonial times, women have served in the U.S. armed forces. Yet in 1940, at the outset of World War II, just 2 percent of armed forces personnel were women. In the fall of 2009, women represented 14 percent of all deployed U.S. troops as well as people serving in all capacities in the armed forces.

Clearly, women make up a growing share of the U.S. military, and almost all military assignments are now open to both women and men. But law prevents women from engaging in offensive warfare. Even so, the line between troop support and outright combat is easily crossed, as women serving in Iraq have learned. In fact, between May 2003 and January 2010, the war in Iraq claimed the lives of 103 female soldiers.

The debate on women's role in the military has been going on for centuries. Some people object to opening doors in this way, claiming that women lack the physical strength of men. Others reply that military women are better educated and score higher on intelligence tests than military men. But the heart of the issue is our society's deeply held view of women as *nurturers*—people who give life and help others—which clashes with the image of women trained to kill.

Whatever our views of women and men, the reality is that military women are in harm's way. In part, this fact reflects the strains of a military short of personnel. In addition, the type of insurgency that surrounds our troops in Iraq and Afghanistan can bring violent combat to any soldier at any time. Finally, our modern warfare technology blurs the distinction between combat and noncombat personnel. A combat pilot can fire missiles at a target miles away; by contrast, nonfighting medical evacuation teams must travel directly into the line of fire (Segal & Hansen, 1992; Wilcox, 1992; Kaminer, 1997; McGirk, 2006).

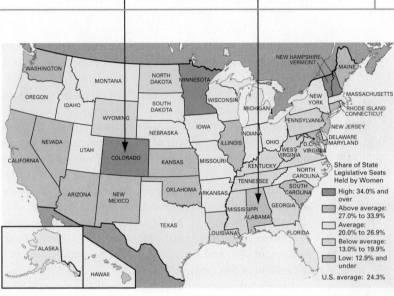

In general, the western states have a higher percentage of legislators who are women than the southern states.

Explore the percentage of women in management, business, and finance in your local community and in counties across the United States on **mysoclab.com**

Seeing Ourselves

NATIONAL MAP 10–1
Women in State Government across the United States

Although women make up half of U.S. adults, just 24 percent of the seats in state legislatures are held by women. Look at the state-by-state variations in the map. In which regions of the country have women gained the greatest political power? What do you think accounts for this pattern?

Explore on **mysoclab.com**

Source: Center for American Women and Politics (2009b).

Share of State Legislative Seats Held by Women

High: 34.0% and over

Above average: 27.0% to 33.9%

Average: 20.0% to 26.9%

Below average: 13.0% to 19.9%

Low: 12.9% and under

U.S. average: 24.3%

Are Women a Minority?

A **minority** is *any category of people distinguished by physical or cultural difference that a society sets apart and subordinates.* Given the clear economic disadvantage of being a woman in our society, it seems reasonable to say that women are a minority in the United States even though they outnumber men.[1]

Even so, most white women do not think of themselves in this way (Lengermann & Wallace, 1985). This is partly because, unlike racial minorities (including African Americans) and ethnic minorities (say, Hispanics), white women are well represented at all levels of the class structure, including the very top.

Bear in mind, however, that at every class level, women typically have less income, wealth, education, and power than men. Patriarchy makes women depend on men—first their fathers and later their husbands—for their social standing (Bernard, 1981).

Minority Women: Intersection Theory

If women are defined as a minority, what about minority women? Are they doubly handicapped? This question lies at the heart of **intersection theory,** *analysis of the interplay of race, class, and gender, which often results in multiple dimensions of disadvantage.* Research shows that disadvantages linked to race and gender often combine to produce especially low social standing for some people (Ovadia, 2001).

Income data confirm this theory. Looking first at race and ethnicity, the median income in 2008 for African American women working full time was $31,525, which is 84 percent as much as the $37,610 earned by non-Hispanic white women; Hispanic women earned $26,997—just 72 percent as much as their white counterparts. Looking at gender, African American women earned 84 percent as much as African American men, and Hispanic women earned 87 percent as much as Hispanic men.

Combining these disadvantages, African American women earned 61 percent as much as non-Hispanic white men, and Hispanic women earned 53 percent as much (U.S. Census Bureau, 2009). These differences reflect minority women's lower positions in the occupational and educational hierarchies. These data confirm that although gender has a powerful effect on our lives, it does not operate alone. Class position, race and ethnicity, gender, and sexual orientation form a multilayered system that provides disadvantages for some and privileges for others (Saint Jean & Feagin, 1998).

Violence against Women

In the nineteenth century, men claimed the right to rule their households, even to the point of using physical discipline against their wives, and a great deal of "manly" violence is still directed against women. A government report estimates that 364,000 aggravated assaults against women occur annually. To this number can be added 164,000 rapes or sexual assaults and perhaps 1.5 million simple assaults (U.S. Bureau of Justice Statistics, 2009).

Gender violence is also an issue on college and university campuses. According to research carried out by the U.S. Department

---

[1]Sociologists use the term "minority" instead of "minority group" because, as explained in Chapter 5 ("Groups and Organizations"), women make up a *category,* not a group. People in a category share a status or identity but generally do not know one another or interact.

Feminists argue that rape is not about sex but about power. It is this claim that makes sexual violence against women not just a crime but a matter of gender stratification.

sexual harassment comments, gestures, or physical contacts of a sexual nature that are deliberate, repeated, and unwelcome

that face a great deal of stress; low-income women also have fewer options to get out of a dangerous home (Smolowe, 1994; Frias & Angel, 2007).

Violence toward women also occurs in casual relationships. As noted in Chapter 7 ("Deviance"), most rapes involve men known, and often trusted, by their victims. Dianne Herman (2001) argues that the extent of sexual abuse shows that the tendency toward sexual violence is built into our way of life. All forms of violence against women—from the catcalls that intimidate women on city streets to a pinch in a crowded subway to physical assaults that occur at home—express what she calls a "rape culture" of men trying to dominate women. Feminists explain that sexual violence is fundamentally about *power,* not sex, and therefore should be understood as a dimension of gender stratification.

In global perspective, violence against women is built into other cultures in many different ways. One case in point is the practice of female genital mutilation, a painful and often dangerous surgical procedure that is performed in more than two dozen countries and is also known to occur in the United States, as shown in Global Map 10–2. The Thinking About Diversity box on page 286 describes an instance of female genital mutilation that took place in California and asks whether this practice, which some people defend as promoting "morality," amounts to a case of violence against women.

The basic insight of intersection theory is that various dimensions of social stratification—including race and gender—can add up to great disadvantages for some categories of people. Just as African Americans earn less than whites, women earn less than men. Thus African American women confront a "double disadvantage," earning just 61 cents for every dollar earned by non-Hispanic white men. How would you explain the fact that some categories of people are much more likely to end up in low-paying jobs like this one?

of Justice, in a given academic year, about 3 percent of female college students become victims of rape (either attempted or completed). Projecting these figures over a typical five-year college career, about 20 percent of college women experience rape. In 90 percent of all campus cases, the victim knew the offender, and most of the assaults took place in the woman's living quarters (Karjane, Fisher, & Cullen, 2005).

Off campus as well, most gender-linked violence occurs where men and women interact most: in the home. Richard Gelles (cited in Roesch, 1984) argues that with the exception of the police and the military, the family is the most violent organization in the United States, and it is women who suffer most of the injuries. The risk of violence is especially great for low-income women living in families

Violence against Men

If our way of life encourages violence against women, it may encourage even more violence against men. As noted in Chapter 7 ("Deviance"), in more than 80 percent of cases in which a police officer makes an arrest for a violent crime, including murder, robbery, and assault, the offender is a male. In addition, 54 percent of all victims of violent crime are also men (Federal Bureau of Investigation, 2009; U.S. Bureau of Justice Statistics, 2009).

Our culture tends to define masculinity in terms of aggression and violence. "Real men" work and play hard, speed on the highways, and let nothing stand in their way. A higher crime rate is one result. But even when no laws are broken, men's lives involve more stress and isolation than women's lives, which is one reason that the suicide rate for men is four times higher than for women (Heron et al., 2009). In addition, as noted earlier, men live, on average, about five fewer years than women.

Violence is not simply a matter of choices made by individuals. It is built into our very way of life, with resulting harm to both men and women. In short, the way any culture constructs gender plays an important part in how violent or peaceful that society will be.

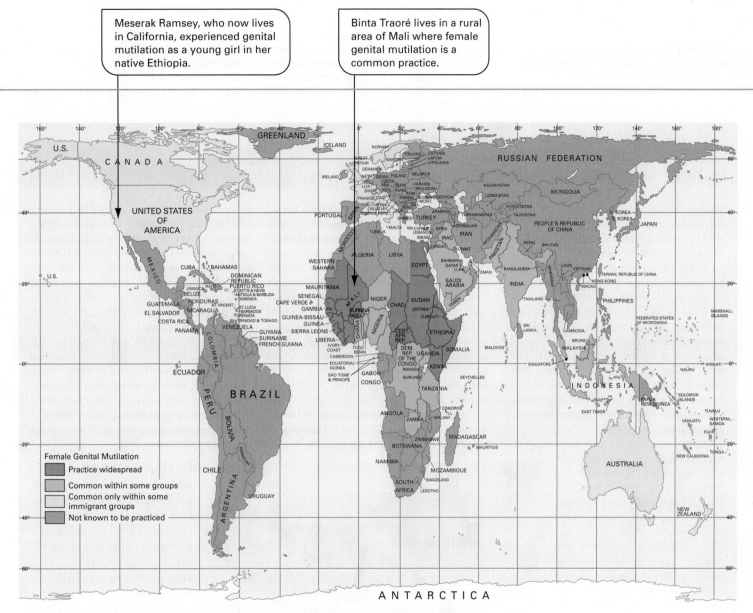

Meserak Ramsey, who now lives in California, experienced genital mutilation as a young girl in her native Ethiopia.

Binta Traoré lives in a rural area of Mali where female genital mutilation is a common practice.

Female Genital Mutilation

- Practice widespread
- Common within some groups
- Common only within some immigrant groups
- Not known to be practiced

Window on the World

GLOBAL MAP 10–2   Female Genital Mutilation in Global Perspective

Female genital mutilation is known to be performed in at least twenty-eight countries around the world. Across Africa, the practice is common and affects a majority of girls in the eastern African nations of Sudan, Ethiopia, and Somalia. In several Asian nations, including India, the practice is limited to a few ethnic minorities. In the United States, Canada, several European nations, and Australia, there are reports of the practice among some immigrants.

Sources: Seager (2003), World Health Organization (2006), and UNICEF (2009).

Sexual Harassment

Sexual harassment refers to *comments, gestures, or physical contacts of a sexual nature that are deliberate, repeated, and unwelcome.* During the 1990s, sexual harassment became an issue of national importance that rewrote the rules for workplace interaction between women and men.

Most (but not all) victims of sexual harassment are women. The reason is that, first, our culture encourages men to be sexually assertive and to see women in sexual terms. As a result, social interaction between men and women in the workplace, on campus, and elsewhere can easily take on sexual overtones. Second, most people in positions of power—including business executives, doctors, bureau chiefs, assembly line supervisors, professors, and military

THINKING ABOUT DIVERSITY: RACE, CLASS, & GENDER

Female Genital Mutilation: Violence in the Name of Morality

Meserak Ramsey, a woman born in Ethiopia and now working as a nurse in California, paid a visit to an old friend's home. Soon after arriving, she noticed her friend's eighteen-month-old daughter huddled in the corner of a room in obvious distress. "What's wrong with her?" she asked.

Ramsey was shocked when the woman said her daughter had recently had a clitoridectomy, the surgical removal of the clitoris. This type of female genital mutilation—performed by a midwife, a tribal practitioner, or a doctor and typically without anesthesia—is common in Nigeria, Sierra Leone, Senegal, Sudan, Ethiopia, Somalia, and Egypt and is known to be practiced in certain cultural groups in other nations around the world. It is illegal in the United States.

Among members of highly patriarchal societies, husbands demand that their wives be virgins at marriage and remain sexually faithful thereafter. The point of female genital mutilation is to eliminate sexual feeling, which, people assume, makes the girl less likely to violate sexual norms and thus be more desirable to men. In about one-fifth of all cases, an even more severe procedure, called infibulation, is performed, in which the entire external genital area is removed and the surfaces are stitched together, leaving only a small hole for urination and menstruation. Before marriage, a husband has the right to open the wound and ensure himself of his bride's virginity.

How many women have undergone female genital mutilation? Worldwide, estimates place the number at more than 100 million (World Health Organization, 2010). In the United States, hundreds or even thousands of such procedures are performed every year. In most cases, immigrant mothers and grandmothers who have themselves been mutilated insist that young girls in their family follow their example. Indeed, many immigrant women demand the procedure *because* their daughters now live in the United States, where sexual mores are more lax. "I don't have to worry about her now," the girl's mother explained to Meserak Ramsey. "She'll be a good girl."

Medically, the consequences of female genital mutilation include more than loss of sexual pleasure. Pain is intense and can last for

These young women have just undergone female genital mutilation. What do you think should be done about this practice?

years. There is also the danger of infection, infertility, and even death. Ramsey knows the anguish all too well: She herself underwent genital mutilation as a young girl. She is one of the lucky ones who has had few medical problems since. But the extent of her suffering is suggested by this story: She invited a young U.S. couple to stay at her home. Late at night, she heard the woman's cries and burst into their room to investigate, only to learn that the couple was making love and the woman had just had an orgasm. "I didn't understand," Ramsey recalls. "I thought that there must be something wrong with American girls. But now I know that there is something wrong with me." Or with a system that inflicts such injury in the name of traditional morality.

WHAT DO YOU THINK?

1. Is female genital mutilation a medical procedure or a means of social control? Explain your answer.

2. Can you think of other examples of physical mutilation imposed on women? What are they?

3. What do you think should be done about the practice of female genital mutilation in places where it is widespread? Do you think respect for human rights should override respect for cultural differences in this case?

Sources: Crossette (1995) and Boyle, Songora, & Foss (2001).

officers—are men who oversee the work of women. Surveys carried out in widely different work settings show that about 5 percent of women claim that they have been harassed on the job in the last year and about half of women say they receive unwanted sexual attention (NORC, 2009).

Sexual harassment is sometimes obvious and direct: A supervisor may ask for sexual favors from an employee and make threats if the advances are refused. Courts have declared that such *quid pro quo* sexual harassment (the Latin phrase means "one thing in return for another") is a violation of civil rights.

More often, however, the problem of unwelcome sexual attention is a matter of subtle behavior—sexual teasing, off-color jokes, comments about someone's looks—that may or may not be intended to harass anyone. But based on the *effect* standard, which

○ Seeing Sociology
in Everyday Life

The Internet has made pornography more accessible; do
you think it has become more socially acceptable as well?
Why or why not?

○ Making the Grade

Functional analysis essentially claims that gender
differences were functional in the past but, due to
changes in technology, these differences are much less
functional now.

is favored by many feminists, such actions add up to creating a *hostile environment* for women in the workplace. Incidents of this kind are far more complex because they involve different perceptions of the same behavior. For example, a man may think that repeatedly complimenting a co-worker on her appearance is simply being friendly. The co-worker, on the other hand, may believe the man is thinking of her in sexual terms and is not taking her work seriously, an attitude that could harm her job performance and prospects for advancement.

Pornography

Chapter 6 ("Sexuality and Society") defined *pornography* as sexually explicit material that causes sexual arousal. However, people take different views of exactly what is or is not pornographic; the law gives local communities the power to define whether sexually explicit material violates "community standards of decency" and lacks "any redeeming social value."

Traditionally, people have raised concerns about pornography as a *moral* issue. But pornography also plays a part in gender stratification. From this point of view, pornography is really a *power* issue because most pornography dehumanizes women, treating them as the playthings of men.

In addition, there is widespread concern that pornography encourages violence against women by portraying them as weak and undeserving of respect. Men show contempt for women defined in this way by striking out against them. Surveys show that about half of U.S. adults think that pornography encourages people to commit rape (NORC, 2009:341).

Like sexual harassment, pornography raises complex and sometimes conflicting concerns. Despite the fact that some material may offend just about everyone, many people defend the rights of free speech and artistic expression. Nevertheless, pressure to restrict pornography has increased in recent decades, reflecting both the long-standing concern that pornography weakens morality and the more recent concern that it is demeaning and threatening to women.

Theoretical Analysis of Gender

Why does gender exist in all known societies? Sociology's macro-level approaches—the structural-functional and social-conflict approaches—address the central place of gender in social organization. In addition, the symbolic-interaction approach helps us see the importance of gender in everyday life. The Applying Theory table on page 288 summarizes the important insights offered by each of these approaches.

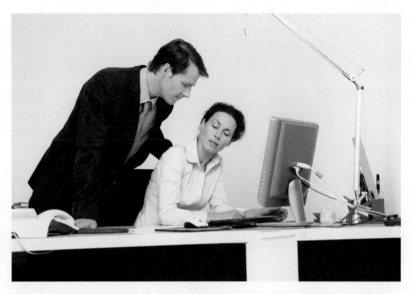

In recent decades, our society has recognized sexual harassment as an important problem. As a result, at least officially, unwelcome sexual attention is no longer tolerated in the workplace. To what extent do you think sexual comments, off-color jokes, and unnecessary touching still take place on the job?

Structural-Functional Analysis

The structural-functional approach views society as a complex system of many separate but integrated parts. From this point of view, gender serves as a means to organize social life.

As Chapter 2 ("Culture") explained, the earliest hunting and gathering societies had little power over biology. Lacking effective birth control, women could do little to prevent pregnancy, and the responsibilities of child care kept them close to home. At the same time, men's greater strength made them better suited for warfare and hunting. Over the centuries, this sex-based division of labor became institutionalized and largely taken for granted (Lengermann & Wallace, 1985; Freedman, 2002).

Industrial technology opens up a much greater range of cultural possibilities. With human muscle power no longer the main energy source, the physical strength of men becomes less important. In addition, the ability to control reproduction gives women greater choices about how to live. Modern societies relax traditional gender roles as the societies become more meritocratic because rigid roles waste an enormous amount of human talent. Yet change comes slowly because gender is deeply rooted in culture.

Talcott Parsons: Gender and Complementarity

As Talcott Parsons (1942, 1951, 1954) observed, gender helps integrate society, at least in its traditional form. Gender forms a

●━ Making the Grade

Carefully review the Applying Theory table below
to be sure that you understand the three theoretical
approaches to gender.

●━ Seeing Sociology
in Everyday Life

Based on your observations, do you think women
make more eye contact than men do? What other
gender-related patterns have you noticed?

● APPLYING THEORY ●

Gender

	Structural-Functional Approach	Symbolic-Interaction Approach	Social-Conflict Approach
What is the level of analysis?	Macro-level	Micro-level	Macro-level
What does gender mean?	Parsons described gender in terms of two complementary patterns of behavior: masculine and feminine.	Numerous sociologists have shown that gender is part of the reality that guides social interaction in everyday situations.	Engels described gender in terms of the power of one sex over the other.
Is gender helpful or harmful?	Helpful. Gender gives men and women distinctive roles and responsibilities that help society operate smoothly. Gender builds social unity as men and women come together to form families.	Hard to say; gender is both helpful and harmful. In everyday life, gender is one of the factors that helps us relate to one another. At the same time, gender shapes human behavior, placing men in control of social situations. Men tend to initiate most interactions, while women typically act in a more deferential manner.	Harmful. Gender limits people's personal development. Gender divides society by giving power to men to control the lives of women. Capitalism makes patriarchy stronger.

complementary set of roles that links women and men into family units and gives each sex responsibility for carrying out important tasks. Women take the lead in managing the day-to-day life of the household and raising children. Men connect the family to the larger world as they participate in the labor force.

Thus gender plays an important part in socialization. Society teaches boys—presumably destined for the labor force—to be rational, self-assured, and competitive. Parsons called this complex of traits *instrumental* qualities. To prepare girls for child rearing, socialization stresses *expressive* qualities, such as emotional responsiveness and sensitivity to others.

Society encourages gender conformity by instilling in men and women a fear that straying too far from accepted standards of masculinity or femininity will cause rejection by the opposite sex. In simple terms, women learn to reject nonmasculine men as sexually unattractive, and men learn to reject unfeminine women. In sum, gender integrates society both structurally (in terms of what we do) and morally (in terms of what we believe).

●━ **CRITICAL REVIEW** Influential in the 1950s, this approach has lost much of its standing today. First, structural-functionalism assumes a singular vision of society that is not shared by everyone. For example, historically, many women have worked outside the home because of economic necessity, a fact

not reflected in Parsons's conventional, middle-class view of social life. Second, Parsons's analysis ignores the personal strains and social costs of rigid gender roles. Third, in the eyes of those seeking sexual equality, Parsons's gender "complementarity" amounts to little more than women submitting to male domination.

●━ **CHECK YOUR LEARNING** In Parsons's analysis, what functions does gender perform for society?

Symbolic-Interaction Analysis

The symbolic-interaction approach takes a micro-level view of society, focusing on face-to-face interaction in everyday life. As suggested in Chapter 4 ("Social Interaction in Everyday Life"), gender affects everyday interaction in a number of ways.

Gender and Everyday Life

If you watch women and men interacting, you will probably notice that women typically engage in more eye contact than men do. Why? Holding eye contact is a way of encouraging the conversation to continue; in addition, looking directly at someone clearly shows the other person that you are paying attention.

This pattern is an example of sex roles, defined earlier as the way a society defines how women and men should think and behave. To understand such patterns, consider the fact that people with more power tend to take charge of social encounters. When men and women engage one another, as they do in families and in the workplace, it is men who typically initiate the interaction. That is, men speak first, set the topics of discussion, and control the outcomes. With less power, women are expected to be more *deferential,* meaning that they show respect for others of higher social position. In many cases, this means that women (just like children or others with less power) spend more time being silent and also encouraging men (or others with more power) not just with eye contact but by smiling or nodding in agreement. As a technique to control a conversation, men often interrupt others, just as they typically feel less need to ask the opinions of other people, especially those with less power (Tannen, 1990, 1994; Henley, Hamilton, & Thorne, 1992; Ridgeway & Smith-Lovin, 1999).

○ **CRITICAL REVIEW** The strength of the symbolic-interaction approach is helping us see how gender plays a part in shaping almost all our everyday experiences. Because our society defines men (and everything that is defined as masculine) as having more value than women (and what is defined as feminine), just about every familiar social encounter is "gendered," so that men and women interact in distinctive and unequal ways.

The symbolic-interaction approach suggests that individuals socially construct the reality they experience as they interact every day, using gender as one element of their personal "performances." Gender can be a useful guide to how we behave. Yet gender, as a structural dimension of society, is beyond the immediate control of any of us as individuals and also gives some people power over others. Therefore, patterns of everyday social interaction reflect our society's gender stratification. Everyday interaction also helps reinforce this inequality. For example, to the extent that fathers take the lead in family discussions, the entire family learns to expect men to "display leadership" and "show their wisdom"; to the extent that mothers let them take the lead, the family learns to expect women to be deferential to men.

A limitation of the symbolic-interaction approach is that by focusing on situational social experience, it says little about the broad patterns of inequality that set the rules for our everyday lives. To understand the roots of gender stratification, we have to "look up" to see more closely how society makes men and women unequal. We will do this using the social-conflict approach.

○ **CHECK YOUR LEARNING** Point to several ways that gender shapes the everyday face-to-face interactions of individuals.

In the 1950s, Talcott Parsons proposed that sociologists interpret gender as a matter of *differences.* As he saw it, masculine men and feminine women formed strong families and made for an orderly society. In recent decades, however, social-conflict theory has reinterpreted gender as a matter of *inequality.* From this point of view, U.S. society places men in a position of dominance over women.

Social-Conflict Analysis

From a social-conflict point of view, gender involves differences not just in behavior but in power as well. Consider the striking similarity between the way traditional ideas about gender benefit men and the way oppression of racial and ethnic minorities benefits white people. Conventional ideas about gender do not make society operate smoothly; on the contrary, they create division and tension, with men seeking to protect their privileges as women challenge the status quo.

As earlier chapters noted, the social-conflict approach draws heavily on the ideas of Karl Marx. Yet as far as gender is concerned, Marx was a product of his times, and his writings focused almost entirely on men. However, his friend and collaborator Friedrich Engels did develop a theory of gender stratification.

Friedrich Engels: Gender and Class

Looking back through history, Engels saw that in hunting and gathering societies, the activities of women and men, though different, had equal importance. A successful hunt brought men great prestige, but the vegetation gathered by women provided most of a group's food supply. As technological advances led to a productive surplus,

feminism support of social equality for women and men, in opposition to patriarchy and sexism

social equality and communal sharing gave way to private property and ultimately a class hierarchy. At this point, men gained significant power over women. With surplus wealth to pass on to heirs, upper-class men needed to be sure that their sons were their own, which led them to control the sexuality of women. The desire to control property brought about monogamous marriage and the family. Women were taught to remain virgins until marriage, to remain faithful to their husbands thereafter, and to build their lives around bearing and raising one man's children.

According to Engels (1902, orig. 1884), capitalism makes male domination even stronger. First, capitalism creates more wealth, which gives greater power to men as income earners and owners of property. Second, an expanding capitalist economy depends on turning people, especially women, into consumers who seek personal fulfillment by buying and using products. Third, society assigns women the task of maintaining the home to free men to work in factories. The double exploitation of capitalism, as Engels saw it, lies in paying low wages for male labor and paying women no wages at all.

○ **CRITICAL REVIEW**   Social-conflict analysis is strongly critical of conventional ideas about gender, claiming that society would be better off if we minimized or even did away with this dimension of social structure. That is, this approach regards conventional families, which traditionalists claim are personally and socially positive, as a social evil. A problem with social-conflict analysis, then, is that it minimizes the extent to which women and men live together cooperatively and often happily in families. A second problem lies in the assertion that capitalism is the basis of gender stratification. In fact, agrarian societies are typically more patriarchal than industrial-capitalist societies. Although socialist nations, including the People's Republic of China and the former Soviet Union, did move women into the labor force, by and large they provided

women with very low pay in sex-segregated jobs (Rosendahl, 1997; Haney, 2002).

○ **CHECK YOUR LEARNING**   According to Engels, how does gender support social inequality in a capitalist class system?

Feminism

Feminism is *support of social equality for women and men, in opposition to patriarchy and sexism.* The first wave of feminism in the United States began in the 1840s as women opposed to slavery, including Elizabeth Cady Stanton and Lucretia Mott, drew parallels between the oppression of African Americans and the oppression of women. Their main objective was obtaining the right to vote, which was finally achieved in 1920. But other disadvantages persisted, causing a second wave of feminism to arise in the 1960s that continues today.

Basic Feminist Ideas

Feminism views the everyday lives of women and men through the lens of gender. How we think of ourselves (gender identity), how we act (gender roles), and our social standing as women or men (gender stratification) are all rooted in the operation of society.

Although feminists disagree about many things, most support five general principles:

1. **Working to increase equality.** Feminist thinking is political; it relates ideas to action. Feminism is critical of the status quo, pushing for change toward social equality for women and men.

2. **Expanding human choice.** Feminists argue that cultural ideas about gender divide the full range of human qualities into two opposing and limiting spheres: the female world of emotion and cooperation and the male world of rationality and competition. As an alternative, feminists propose a "reintegration of humanity" by which all individuals develop all human traits (French, 1985).

3. **Eliminating gender stratification.** Feminism opposes laws and cultural norms that limit the education, income, and job opportunities of women. For this reason, feminists have long supported passage of the Equal Rights Amendment

NASCAR racing has always been a masculine world. But Danica Patrick has made a name for herself as an outstanding driver. At the same time, she has made much of her income from trading on her good looks, including the 2009 *Sports Illustrated* swimsuit edition. Are men as likely to do the same? Why or why not?

● Seeing Sociology
in Everyday Life

On your campus, do men's organizations (such as fraternities
and athletic teams) enjoy any special privileges? What about
women's organizations?

(ERA) to the U.S. Constitution, which states, in its entirety, "Equality of rights under the law shall not be denied or abridged by the United States or any State on account of sex." The ERA was first proposed in Congress in 1923. Although it has widespread support, it has yet to become law.

4. **Ending sexual violence.** Today's women's movement seeks to eliminate sexual violence. Feminists argue that patriarchy distorts relationships between women and men, encouraging violence against women in the form of rape, domestic abuse, sexual harassment, and pornography (A. Dworkin, 1987; Freedman, 2002).

5. **Promoting sexual freedom.** Finally, feminism advocates women's control over their sexuality and reproduction. Feminists support the free availability of birth control information. As Figure 10–3 shows, about two-thirds of married U.S. women of childbearing age use contraception; the use of contraceptives is far less common in many lower-income nations. Most feminists also support a woman's right to choose whether to have children or to end a pregnancy, rather than allowing men—husbands, physicians, and legislators—to control their reproduction. Many feminists also support gay people's efforts to end prejudice and discrimination in a largely heterosexual culture (Ferree & Hess, 1995; Armstrong, 2002).

Types of Feminism

Although feminists agree on the importance of gender equality, they disagree on how to achieve it: through liberal feminism, socialist feminism, or radical feminism (Stacey, 1983; L. Vogel, 1983; Ferree & Hess, 1995; Armstrong, 2002; Freedman, 2002). The Applying Theory table on page 292 highlights key arguments made by each type of feminist thinking.

Liberal Feminism

Liberal feminism is rooted in classic liberal thinking that individuals should be free to develop their own talents and pursue their own interests. Liberal feminists accept the basic organization of our society but seek to expand the rights and opportunities of women; they look to passage of the Equal Rights Amendment as an important step to achieving this goal. Liberal feminists also support reproductive freedom for all women. They respect the family as a social institution but seek changes in society, including more widely available maternity and paternity leave and child care for parents who work.

Given their beliefs in the rights of individuals, liberal feminists think that women should advance according to their individual efforts and merit, rather than by working collectively for change. Both women and men, through personal achievement, are capable of improving their lives, as long as society removes legal and cultural barriers.

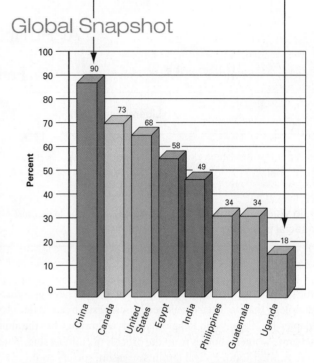

Global Snapshot

> Achen Eke, age 24 and mother of three, lives in Uganda, where most women do not have access to contraception.

> Chen-chi Bai, age 31 and the mother of one boy, lives in China, where contraception is encouraged and widely practiced.

FIGURE 10–3 **Use of Contraception by Married Women of Childbearing Age**

In the United States, most married women of childbearing age use contraception. In many lower-income countries, however, most women do not have the opportunity to make this choice.

Source: Population Reference Bureau (2009).

Socialist Feminism

Socialist feminism evolved from the ideas of Karl Marx and Friedrich Engels. From this point of view, capitalism increases patriarchy by concentrating wealth and power in the hands of a small number of men. Socialist feminists do not think the reforms supported by liberal feminists go far enough. They believe that the family form fostered by capitalism must change in order to replace "domestic slavery" with some collective means of carrying out housework and child care. Replacing the traditional family can come about only through a socialist revolution that creates a state-centered economy to meet the needs of all.

Radical Feminism

Like socialist feminism, *radical feminism* finds liberal feminism inadequate. Radical feminists believe that patriarchy is so firmly entrenched that even a socialist revolution would not end it. Instead, reaching the goal of gender equality means that society must eliminate gender itself.

◦ Making the Grade

Feminism is one type of social-conflict approach to understanding gender.

◦ Making the Grade

The three types of feminism all agree on the importance of gender and the need to make women and men more socially equal. They disagree on the way to do that, with liberal feminism involving the least societal change and radical feminism involving the most.

● APPLYING THEORY ●

Feminism

	Liberal Feminism	Socialist Feminism	Radical Feminism
Does it accept the basic order of society?	Yes. Liberal feminism seeks change only to ensure equality of opportunity.	No. Socialist feminism supports an end to social classes and to family gender roles that encourage "domestic slavery."	No. Radical feminism supports an end to the family system.
How do women improve their social standing?	Individually, according to personal ability and effort.	Collectively, through socialist revolution.	Collectively, by working to eliminate gender itself.

One possible way to achieve this goal is to use the new reproductive technology that has been developed by scientists in recent decades (see Chapter 13, "Family and Religion"). This technology has the ability to separate women's bodies from the process of childbearing. With an end to motherhood, radical feminists reason, society could leave behind the entire family system, liberating women, men, and children from the oppression of family, gender, and sex itself (A. Dworkin, 1987). Radical feminism seeks an egalitarian and gender-free society, a revolution much more sweeping than that sought by Marx.

Opposition to Feminism

Because feminism calls for significant change, it has always been controversial. But today, just 20 percent of U.S. adults say they oppose feminism, a share that has declined over time (NORC, 2009). Figure 10–4 shows a similar downward trend in opposition to feminism among college students after 1970. Note, however, that little change has occurred in recent years and that more men than women express antifeminist attitudes.

Feminism provokes criticism and resistance from both men and women who hold conventional ideas about gender. Some men oppose sexual equality for the same reasons that many white people have historically opposed social equality for people of color: They do not want to give up their privileges. Other men and women, including those who are neither rich nor powerful, distrust a social movement (especially its radical expressions) that attacks the traditional family and rejects patterns that have guided male-female relations for centuries.

Men who have been socialized to value strength and dominance may feel uneasy about feminist ideals of men as gentle and warm (Doyle, 1983). Similarly, some women whose lives center on their husbands and children may think that feminism does not value the social roles that give meaning to their lives. In general, opposition to feminism is greatest among women who have the least education and those who do not work outside the home (Marshall, 1985; Ferree & Hess, 1995).

Race and ethnicity play some part in shaping people's attitudes toward feminism. In general, African Americans (especially African American women) express the greatest support of feminist goals, followed by whites, with Hispanic Americans holding somewhat more traditional attitudes when it comes to gender (Kane, 2000).

Resistance to feminism is also found within academic circles. Some sociologists charge that feminism ignores a growing body of evidence that men and women do think and act in somewhat different ways, which may make complete gender equality impossible. Furthermore, say critics, with its drive to increase women's presence in the workplace, feminism undervalues the crucial and unique contribution women make to the development of children, especially in

● Seeing Sociology
in Everyday Life

Do you think women should get ahead primarily through
individual effort or by collective action? Explain.

● Seeing Sociology
in Everyday Life

Looking at the figure below, why do you think that,
over the years, more male students than female
students have opposed feminism?

the first years of life (Baydar & Brooks-Gunn, 1991; Popenoe,
1993b; Gibbs, 2001).

Finally, there is the question of *how* women should go
about improving their social standing. A large majority of
adults in the United States think that women should have
equal rights, but 70 percent also say that women should
advance individually, according to their training and abilities; only 10 percent favor women's rights groups or collective action (NORC, 2007:430).

For these reasons, most opposition to feminism is
directed toward its socialist and radical forms, while support for liberal feminism is widespread. In addition, we are
seeing an unmistakable trend toward gender equality. In
1977, 65 percent of all adults endorsed the statement "It is
much better for everyone involved if the man is the achiever
outside the home and the woman takes care of the home
and family." By 2008, the share supporting this statement
had dropped to 36 percent (NORC, 2009:360).

Gender: Looking Ahead

Predictions about the future are no more than educated
guesses. Just as economists disagree about the likely inflation
rate a year from now, sociologists can offer only general observations about the likely future of gender and society.

Change so far has been remarkable. A century ago,
women were second-class citizens, without access to many
jobs, barred from public office, and with no right to vote.
Although women remain socially disadvantaged, the movement toward equality has surged ahead. Two-thirds of people entering the workforce in the 1990s were women, and in
2000, for the first time, a majority of families had both husband and
wife in the paid labor force. Today's economy depends a great deal on
the earnings of women. In addition, as recent research shows, 22 percent of married men in the United States have wives who earn more
than they do (Fry & Cohn, 2010).

Many factors have contributed to this transformation. Perhaps most
important, industrialization and advances in computer technology have
shifted the nature of work from physically demanding tasks that favored
male strength to jobs that require thought and imagination. This change

Student Snapshot

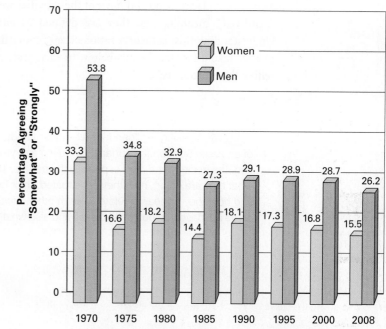

**Statement: "The activities of married women are best
confined to the home and family."**

FIGURE 10–4   Opposition to Feminism among First-Year College Students,
1970–2008

The share of college students expressing antifeminist views declined after 1970.
Men are still more likely than women to hold such attitudes.

Sources: Astin et al. (2002) and Pryor et al. (2009).

puts women and men on an even footing. Also, because birth control
technology has given us greater control over reproduction, women's
lives are less constrained by unwanted pregnancies.

Many women and men have deliberately pursued social equality. For example, sexual harassment complaints in the workplace are
taken much more seriously today than they were a generation ago.
As more women assume positions of power in the corporate and
political worlds, social changes in the twenty-first century may be as
great as those that have already taken place.

Seeing Sociology in Everyday Life

Can you spot "gender messages" in the world around you?

As this chapter makes clear, gender is one of the basic organizing principles of everyday life. Most of the places we go and most of the activities we engage in as part of our daily routines are "gendered," meaning that they are defined as either more masculine or more feminine. Understanding this fact, corporations keep gender in mind when they market products to the public. Take a look at the ads below. In each case, can you explain how gender is at work in selling these products?

> **HINT** Looking for "gender messages" in ads is a process that involves several levels of analysis. Start on the surface, by noting everything obvious in the ad, including the setting, the background, and especially the people. Then notice how the people are shown— what they are doing, how they are situated, their facial expressions, how they are dressed, and how they appear to relate to each other. Finally, state what you think is the message of the ad, based on both the ad itself and also what you know about the surrounding society.

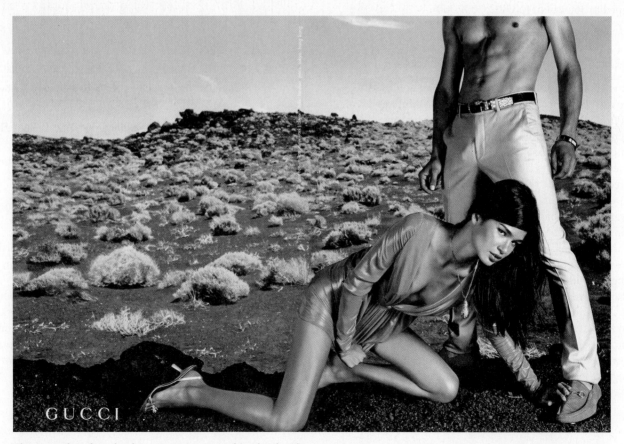

There are a lot of gender dynamics going on in this ad. What do you see?

Generally, our society defines cosmetics as feminine because most cosmetics are marketed toward women. How and why is this ad different?

What gender messages do you see in this ad?

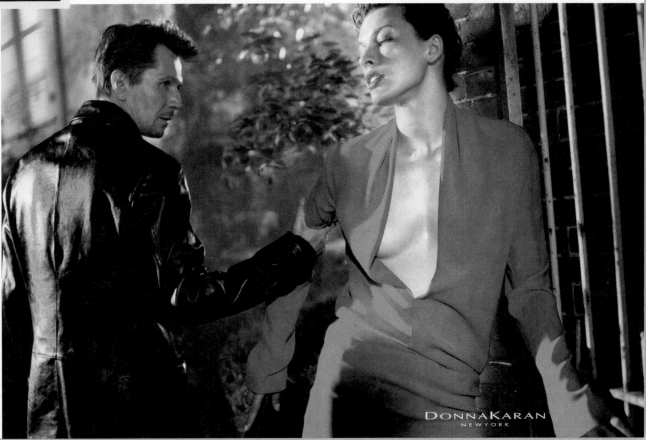

DONNA KARAN
NEW YORK

Applying SOCIOLOGY in Everyday Life

1. Look through some recent magazines, and select three advertisements that involve gender. In each case, provide analysis of how gender is used in the ad.

2. Watch several hours of children's television programming on a Saturday morning. Notice the advertising, which mostly sells toys and breakfast cereal. Keep track of what share of toys are "gendered," that is, aimed at one sex or the other. What traits do you associate with toys intended for boys and those intended for girls?

3. Do some research on the history of women's issues in your state. When was the first woman sent to Congress? What laws once existed that restricted the work women could do? Do any such laws exist today? Did your state support the passage of the Equal Rights Amendment or not? What share of political officials today are women?

Making the Grade

Gender Stratification 👁—Watch on mysoclab.com

Gender and Inequality

GENDER refers to the meaning a culture attaches to being female or male.
- Evidence that gender is rooted in culture includes global comparisons by Margaret Mead and others showing how societies define what is feminine and masculine in various ways.
- Gender is not only about difference: Because societies give more power and other resources to men than to women, gender is an important dimension of social stratification. **Sexism** is built into the operation of social institutions.
- Although some degree of **patriarchy** is found almost everywhere, it varies throughout history and from society to society.

pp. 272–76

gender (p. 272) the personal traits and social positions that members of a society attach to being female or male

gender stratification (p. 272) the unequal distribution of wealth, power, and privilege between men and women

matriarchy (p. 274) a form of social organization in which females dominate males

patriarchy (p. 274) a form of social organization in which males dominate females

sexism (p. 274) the belief that one sex is innately superior to the other

Gender and Socialization

Through the socialization process, gender becomes part of our personalities (**gender identity**) and our actions (**gender roles**). All the major agents of socialization—family, peer groups, schools, and the mass media—reinforce cultural definitions of what is feminine and masculine.

pp. 276–77

gender roles (sex roles) (p. 276) attitudes and activities that a society links to each sex

Gender and Social Stratification

Gender stratification shapes **THE WORKPLACE**:
- A majority of women are now in the paid labor force, but 40% hold clerical or service jobs.
- Comparing full-time U.S. workers, women earn 77% as much as men.
- This gender difference in earnings results from differences in jobs, differences in family responsibilities, and discrimination.

pp. 277–81

Gender stratification shapes **FAMILY LIFE**:
- Most unpaid housework is performed by women, whether or not they hold jobs outside the home.
- Pregnancy and raising small children keep many women out of the labor force at a time when their male peers are making important carrer gains.

p. 281

Gender stratification shapes **EDUCATION**:
- Women now earn 59% of all associate's and bachelor's degrees.
- Women make up 47% of law school students and are an increasing share of graduates in professions traditionally dominated by men, including medicine and business administration.

p. 281

📖—Read on mysoclab.com

minority (p. 283) any category of people distinguished by physical or cultural difference that a society sets apart and subordinates

intersection theory (p. 283) analysis of the interplay of race, class, and gender, often resulting in multiple dimensions of disadvantage

sexual harassment (p. 285) comments, gestures, or physical contacts of a sexual nature that are deliberate, repeated, and unwelcome

Gender stratification shapes **POLITICS**:
- Until a century ago, almost no women held elected office in the United States.
- In recent decades, the number of women in politics has increased significantly.
- Even so, the vast majority of elected officials, especially at the national level, are men.
- Women make up only about 14% of U.S. military personnel.

pp. 281–82

INTERSECTION THEORY investigates the intersection of race, class, and gender, factors that combine to cause special disadvantages to some categories of people.
- Women of color encounter greater social disadvantages than white women and earn much less than white men.
- Because all women have a distinctive social identity and are disadvantaged, they are a minority, although most white women do not think of themselves this way.

p. 283

VIOLENCE AGAINST WOMEN AND MEN is a widespread problem that is linked to how a society defines gender. Related issues include
- **sexual harassment**, which mostly victimizes women because our culture encourages men to be assertive and to see women in sexual terms.
- **pornography**, which portrays women as sexual objects. Many see pornography as a moral issue; because pornography dehumanizes women, it is also a power issue.

pp. 283–87

⊕—Explore on mysoclab.com

VISUAL SUMMARY

Theoretical Analysis of Gender

The **STRUCTURAL-FUNCTIONAL APPROACH** suggests that

- in preindustrial societies, distinctive roles for males and females reflect biological differences between the sexes.
- in industrial societies, marked gender inequality becomes dysfunctional and gradually decreases.

Talcott Parsons described gender differences in terms of complementary roles that promote the social integration of families and society as a whole.

pp. 287–88

The **SYMBOLIC-INTERACTION APPROACH** suggests that

- individuals use gender as one element of their personal performances as they socially construct reality through everyday interactions.
- gender plays a part in shaping almost all our everyday experiences.

Because our society defines men as having more value than women, the sex roles that define how women and men should behave place men in control of social situations; women play a more deferential role.

pp. 288–89

The **SOCIAL-CONFLICT APPROACH** suggests that

- gender is an important dimension of social inequality and social conflict.
- gender inequality benefits men and disadvantages women.

Friedrich Engels tied gender stratification to the rise of private property and a class hierarchy. Marriage and the family are strategies by which men control their property through control of the sexuality of women. Capitalism exploits everyone by paying men low wages and assigning women the task of maintaining the home.

pp. 289–90

See the Applying Theory table on page 288.

Feminism

FEMINISM

- endorses the social equality of women and men and opposes patriarchy and sexism.
- seeks to eliminate violence against women.
- advocates giving women control over their reproduction.

There are three types of feminism:

- Liberal feminism seeks equal opportunity for both sexes within the existing society.
- Socialist feminism claims that gender equality will come about by replacing capitalism with socialism.
- Radical feminism seeks to eliminate the concept of gender itself and to create an egalitarian and gender-free society.

Today, only 20% of U.S. adults say they oppose feminism. Most opposition is directed toward socialist and radical feminism. Support for liberal feminism is widespread.

pp. 290–93

feminism (p. 290) support of social equality for women and men, in opposition to patriarchy and sexism

See the Applying Theory table on page 292.

- What are race and ethnicity, and how are they created by society?

- Why does the United States have so much racial and ethnic diversity?

- How are race and ethnicity important dimensions of social inequality today?

Watch the *Core Concepts in Sociology* video "Racial Stereotypes and Discrimination" on **mysoclab.com**

This chapter explains how race and ethnicity are created by society. Both race and ethnicity are not only matters of difference but also dimensions of social inequality.

On a cool November morning in New York City, an instructor in a sociology class at Bronx Community College is leading a small-group discussion of race and ethnicity. He explains that the meaning of both concepts is far less clear than most people think. Then he asks, "How do you describe yourself?"

Eva Rodriguez leans forward in her chair and is quick to respond. "Who am I? Or should I say *what* am I? This is hard for me to answer. Most people think of race as black and white. But it's not. I have both black and white ancestry in me, but you know what? I don't think of myself in that way. I don't think of myself in terms of race at all. It would be better to call me Puerto Rican or Hispanic. Personally, I prefer the term 'Latina.' Calling myself Latina says I have mixed racial heritage, and that's what I am. I wish more people understood that race is not clear-cut."

This chapter examines the meaning of race and ethnicity. There are now millions of people in the United States who, like Eva Rodriguez, do not think of themselves in terms of a single category but as having a mix of ancestry.

The Social Meaning of Race and Ethnicity

As the story that opened this chapter suggests, people often confuse "race" and "ethnicity." For this reason, we begin with some basic definitions.

Race

A **race** is *a socially constructed category of people who share biologically transmitted traits that members of a society consider important.* People may classify one another racially on the basis of physical characteristics such as skin color, facial features, hair texture, and body shape.

Racial diversity appeared among our human ancestors as the result of living in different geographic regions of the world. In regions of intense heat, people developed darker skin (from the natural pigment melanin), which offers protection from the sun; in moderate climates, people developed lighter skin. Such traits are literally only skin deep because human beings the world over are members of a single biological species.

The striking variety of racial traits found today is also the product of migration; genetic characteristics once common to a single place are now found in many lands. Especially pronounced is the racial mix in the Middle East (that is, western Asia), historically a crossroads of migration. Greater racial uniformity characterizes more isolated peoples such as the island-dwelling Japanese. But every population has some genetic mixture, and increasing contact ensures even more racial blending of physical characteristics in the future.

Although we often think of race in terms of biological elements, race is a socially constructed concept. It is true that human beings differ in any number of ways involving physical traits, but a "race" comes into being only when the members of a society decide that some particular physical trait (such as skin color or eye shape) actually *matters*.

Because race is a matter of social definitions, it is a highly variable concept. For example, the members of U.S. society consider racial differences more important than people of many other countries. We also tend to "see" three racial categories—typically, black, white, and Asian—while other societies identify many more categories. People in Brazil, for instance, distinguish between *branca* (white), *parda* (brown), *morena* (brunette), *mulata* (mulatto), *preta* (black), and *amarela* (yellow) (Inciardi, Surratt, & Telles, 2000).

In addition, race may be defined differently by various categories of people within a society. In the United States, for example, research shows that white people "see" black people as having darker skin color than black people do (Hill, 2002).

The meaning and importance of race not only differ from place to place but also change over time. Back in 1900, for example, it was common in the United States to consider people of Irish, Italian, or Jewish ancestry as "nonwhite." By 1950, however, this was no longer the case, and such people today are considered part of the "white" category (Loveman, 1999; Brodkin, 2007).

race a socially constructed category of people who share biologically transmitted traits that members of a society consider important

ethnicity (p. 302) a shared cultural heritage

Seeing Sociology in Everyday Life

Researchers have found that biracial and multiracial people choose different racial identities in different settings, depending on whom they are with (Harris & Sim, 2002). Have you ever experienced such a "racial shift"? Explain.

The range of biological variation in human beings is far greater than any system of racial classification allows. This fact is made obvious by trying to place all of the people pictured here into simple racial categories.

Today, the Census Bureau allows people to describe themselves using more than one racial category (offering six single-race options and fifty-seven multiracial options). Our society officially recognizes a wide range of multiracial people (U.S. Census Bureau, 2008).

Racial Types

Scientists invented the concept of race more than a century ago as they tried to organize the world's physical diversity into three racial types. They called people with relatively light skin and fine hair *Caucasoid,* people with darker skin and coarse hair *Negroid,* and people with yellow or brown skin and distinctive folds on the eyelids *Mongoloid.*

Sociologists consider such terms misleading at best and harmful at worst. For one thing, no society contains biologically "pure" people. The skin color of people we might call "Caucasoid" (or "Indo-European," "Caucasian," or more commonly, "white") ranges from very light (typical in Scandinavia) to very dark (in southern India). The same variation exists among so-called "Negroids" ("Africans" or, more commonly, "black" people) and "Mongoloids" ("Asians"). In fact, many "white" people (say, in southern India) actually have darker skin than many "black" people (the Aborigines of Australia).

Overall, the three racial categories differ in just 6 percent of their genes, and there is actually more genetic variation *within* each category than *between* categories. This means that two people in the European nation of Sweden, randomly selected, are likely to have at least as much genetic difference as a Swede and a person in the African nation of Senegal (Harris & Sim, 2002; American Sociological Association, 2003; California Newsreel, 2003).

So just how important is race? From a biological point of view, knowing people's racial category allows us to predict almost nothing about them. Why, then, do societies make so much of race? Such categories allow societies to rank people in a hierarchy, giving some people more money, power, and prestige than others and allowing some people to feel that they are inherently "better" than others.

Because race may matter so much, societies sometimes construct racial categories in extreme ways. Throughout much of the twentieth century, for example, many southern states labeled as "colored" anyone with as little as one thirty-second African ancestry (that is, one African American great-great-great-grandparent). Today, the law allows parents to declare the race of a child (or not) as they wish. Even so, most members of our society are still very sensitive to people's racial backgrounds.

minority any category of people distinguished by physical or cultural
difference that a society sets apart and subordinates

Table 11–1 Racial and Ethnic Categories
in the United States, 2008

Racial or Ethnic Classification*	Approximate U.S. Population	Share of Total Population
Hispanic descent	**46,943,613**	**15.4%**
Mexican	30,783,559	10.1
Puerto Rican	4,216,533	1.4
Cuban	1,617,010	0.5
Other Hispanic	10,371,511	3.4
African descent	**39,058,834**	**12.8**
Nigerian	266,204	0.1
Ethiopian	165,747	0.1
Somalian	82,716	<
Other African	38,544,167	12.6
Native American descent	**2,443,422**	**0.8**
American Indian	1,993,316	0.7
Alaska Native	101,365	<
Other Native American	348,741	0.1
Asian or Pacific Island descent	**14,111,185**	**4.6**
Chinese	3,077,783	1.0
Asian Indian	2,495,998	0.8
Filipino	2,425,697	0.8
Vietnamese	1,431,980	0.5
Korean	1,344,267	0.4
Japanese	710,063	0.2
Cambodian	186,068	0.1
Other Asian or Pacific Islander	2,439,329	0.8
West Indian descent	**2,560,348**	**0.8**
Arab descent	**1,573,530**	**0.5**
Non-Hispanic European descent	**199,491,458**	**65.6**
German	50,272,200	16.5
Irish	36,278,332	11.9
English	27,517,339	9.0
Italian	17,749,037	5.8
Polish	9,887,099	3.3
French	9,446,927	3.1
Scottish	5,827,046	1.9
Dutch	4,928,917	1.6
Norwegian	4,643,339	1.5
Other Non-Hispanic European	32,941,222	10.8
Two or more races	**7,013,872**	**2.3**

*People of Hispanic descent may be of any race. Many people also identify with more than
one ethnic category. Therefore, figures total more than 100 percent.*
< indicates less than 0.1 percent.

Source: U.S. Census Bureau (2009).

A Trend toward Mixture

Over many generations and throughout the Americas, genetic traits from around the world have become mixed. Many "black" people have a significant Caucasoid ancestry, just as many "white" people have some Negroid genes. Whatever people may think, race is not a black-and-white issue.

Today, people are more willing to define themselves as multiracial. On the U.S. Census Bureau's American Community Survey (2009), more than 7 million people described themselves by checking two or more racial categories. The number of interracial births in the United States has been increasing. In 2008, some 4 percent of children under the age of five were multiracial, compared to less than 1 percent of people age sixty-five and older.

Ethnicity

Ethnicity is *a shared cultural heritage.* People define themselves—or others—as members of an *ethnic category* based on common ancestors, language, and religion that give them a distinctive social identity. The United States is a multiethnic society that favors the English language; even so, almost 56 million people (20 percent of the U.S. population over the age of five) speak Spanish, Italian, German, French, Chinese dialects, or some other language in their homes. In California, more than 40 percent of the population does so (U.S. Census Bureau, 2009).

With regard to religion, the United States is a predominantly Protestant nation, but most people of Spanish, Italian, and Polish ancestry are Roman Catholic, and many others of Greek, Ukrainian, and Russian descent belong to the Eastern Orthodox Church. More than 6 million Jewish Americans have ancestral ties to various nations around the world. The population of Muslim men and women is increasing and is variously estimated at between 2 and 3 million (Pew Research Center, 2007b).

Like the reality of race, the meaning of ethnicity is socially constructed, becoming important only because society defines it that way. For example, U.S. society defines people of Spanish descent as "Latin," even though Italy probably has a more "Latin" culture than Spain. People of Italian descent are viewed not as Latin but as "European" and thus less "different" (Camara, 2000; Brodkin, 2007). Like racial differences, the importance of ethnic differences can change over time. A century ago, Catholics and Jews were considered "different" in the predominantly Protestant United States. This is much less true today.

Keep in mind that race is constructed from *biological* traits and ethnicity is constructed from *cultural* traits. Of course, the two may go hand in hand. For example, Japanese Americans have distinctive physical traits and, for those who maintain a traditional way of life, a distinctive culture as well. Table 11–1 provides the most recent data on the racial and ethnic diversity of the United States.

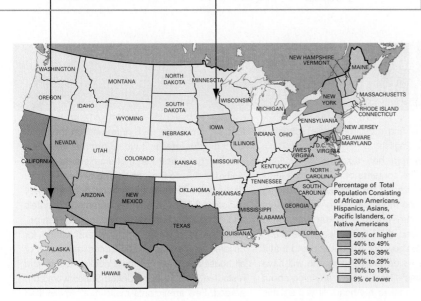

Marcos Chapa attends college in San Diego and lives in a community where most people are in some minority category.

Marianne Blumquist attends a community college in a small town an hour west of Minneapolis, where there are few racial or ethnic minorities.

Explore the percentage of foreign-born people in your local community and in counties across the United States on mysoclab.com

Seeing Ourselves

NATIONAL MAP 11–1

Where the Minority Majority Already Exists

In 2008, minorities were a majority in four states—Hawaii, California, New Mexico, and Texas—as well as the District of Columbia. At the other extreme, Vermont and Maine have the lowest share of racial and ethnic minorities (about 5 percent each). Why are states with high minority populations located in the South and Southwest?

Explore on mysoclab.com

Source: U.S. Census Bureau (2009).

Percentage of Total Population Consisting of African Americans, Hispanics, Asians, Pacific Islanders, or Native Americans

- 50% or higher
- 40% to 49%
- 30% to 39%
- 20% to 29%
- 10% to 19%
- 9% or lower

On an individual level, people either play up or play down their ethnicity, depending on whether they want to fit in or stand apart from the surrounding society: Immigrants may drop their cultural traditions over time or, like many people of Native American descent in recent years, try to revive their heritage. For most people, ethnicity is a more complex issue than race because they identify with several ethnic backgrounds. The golf star Tiger Woods, for example, describes himself as one-eighth American Indian, one-fourth Thai, one-fourth Chinese, one-eighth white, and one-fourth black (J. E. White, 1997).

Minorities

> **March 3, Dallas, Texas.** Spending a day or two in just about any hotel in a major U.S. city presents a lesson in contrasts: The majority of the guests checking in and out are white; the majority of the employees who carry the luggage, serve the food, and clean the rooms are racial or ethnic minorities.

As defined in Chapter 10 ("Gender Stratification"), a **minority** is *any category of people distinguished by physical or cultural difference that a society sets apart and subordinates.* Minority standing can be based on race, ethnicity, or both. As shown in Table 11–1, white people of non-Hispanic background (65.6 percent of the total) are still a majority of the U.S. population. But the share of minorities is increasing. Today, minorities are a majority in four states (California, New Mexico, Texas, and Hawaii) and in half of the country's 100 largest cities. By about 2042, minorities are likely to form a majority of the U.S. population (Mather & Pollard, 2008). National Map 11–1 shows where a minority majority already exists.

Minorities have two important characteristics. First, society imposes on them a *distinct identity,* which may be based on physical or cultural traits. Second, minorities experience *subordination.* As this chapter shows, U.S. minorities typically have lower income, lower occupational prestige, and limited schooling. Class, race, and ethnicity, as well as gender, are overlapping and reinforcing dimensions of social stratification. The Thinking About Diversity box on page 304 describes the struggles of recent Latin American immigrants to the United States.

Of course, not all members of a particular minority category are disadvantaged. For example, some Latinos are quite wealthy, certain Chinese Americans are celebrated business leaders, and African Americans are among our nation's political leaders. But even job success rarely allows individuals to escape their minority standing. As described in Chapter 4 ("Social Interaction in Everyday Life"), race or ethnicity often serves as a *master status* that overshadows personal accomplishments.

Minorities usually make up a small proportion of a society's population, but that is not always the case. Black South Africans are disadvantaged even though they are a numerical majority in their country. In the United States, women make up slightly more than half the population but are still struggling for the opportunities and privileges enjoyed by men.

Prejudice and Stereotypes

> **November 19, Jerusalem, Israel.** We are driving along the edge of this historical city, a holy place to Jews, Christians, and Muslims, when Razi, our taxi driver, spots a small group of Falasha—Ethiopian Jews—on a street corner. "Those people over there," he begins, "they are different.

● Seeing Sociology
in Everyday Life

Do you see stereotypes in common phrases such as "French kiss," "Dutch treat," "Indian giver," or being "gypped" (a reference to Gypsies)? Explain.

prejudice a rigid and unfair generalization about an entire category of people

stereotype a simplified description applied to every person in some category

racism the belief that one racial category is innately superior or inferior to another

---

THINKING ABOUT DIVERSITY: RACE, CLASS, & GENDER

Hard Work: The Immigrant Life in the United States

Early in the morning, it is already hot in Houston as a line of pickup trucks snakes slowly into a dusty yard, where 200 laborers have been gathered since dawn, hoping for a day's work. The driver of the first truck opens his window and tells the foreman that he is looking for a crew to spread boiling tar on a roof. Abdonel Cespedes, the foreman, turns to the crowd, and after a few minutes, three workers step forward and climb into the back of the truck. The next driver is looking for two experienced housepainters. The scene is repeated over and over as men and a few women leave to dig ditches, spread cement, hang drywall, open clogged septic tanks, or crawl under houses to poison rats.

As each driver pulls into the yard, the foreman asks, "How much?" Most of the people in the trucks offer $5 an hour. Cespedes automatically responds, "$7.25; the going rate is $7.25 for an hour's hard work." Sometimes he convinces people to pay that much, but usually not. The workers, who come from Mexico, El Salvador, and Guatemala, know that dozens of them will end up with no work at all this day. Most accept $5 or $6 an hour because they know that when the day is over, $50 is better than nothing.

Labor markets like this one are common in large cities, especially across the southwestern United States. The surge in immigration in recent years has brought millions of people to this country in

search of work, and most have little schooling and speak little English.

Manuel Barrera has taken a day's work moving the entire contents of a store to a storage site. He arrives at the boarded-up building and gazes at the mountains of heavy furniture that he must carry out to a moving van, drive across town, and then carry again. He sighs when he realizes how hot it is outside and that it is even hotter inside the building. He will have no break for lunch. No one says anything about toilets. Barrera shakes his head. "I will do this

These immigrants gather on a New York City street corner every morning hoping to be hired for construction work that pays about $60 a day with no benefits.

kind of work because it puts food on the table. But I did not foresee it would turn out like this."

The hard truth is that immigrants to the United States do the jobs that no one else wants. At the bottom level of the national economy, they perform low-skill jobs in restaurants and hotels and on construction crews, and they work in private homes cooking, cleaning, and caring for children. Across the United States, about half of all housekeepers, household cooks, tailors, and restaurant waiters in the United States were born abroad. Few immigrants make much more than the minimum wage ($7.25 in 2009), and rarely do immigrant workers receive any health or pension benefits. Many well-off families take the labor of immigrants as much for granted as they do their air-conditioned cars and comfortable homes.

WHAT DO YOU THINK?

1. In what ways do you or members of your family depend on the low-paid labor of immigrants?

2. Do you favor allowing the 12 million immigrants who entered this country illegally to earn citizenship? What should be done?

3. Should the U.S. government act to reduce the number of immigrants entering the country in the future? Why or why not?

Sources: Based on Booth (1998), Tumulty (2006), and U.S. Department of Labor (2008).

They don't drive cars. They don't want to improve themselves. Even when our country offers them schooling, they don't take it." He shakes his head at the Ethiopians and drives on.

Prejudice is *a rigid and unfair generalization about an entire category of people.* Prejudice is unfair because *all* people in some category are described as the same, based on little or no direct evidence. Prejudice may target people of a particular social class, sex, sexual orientation, age, political affiliation, race, or ethnicity.

Prejudices are *prejudgments* that can be either positive or negative. Our positive prejudices exaggerate the virtues of people like ourselves, and our negative prejudices condemn those who are different from us. Negative prejudice can be expressed as anything from mild dislike to outright hostility. Because such attitudes are rooted in culture, everyone has at least some prejudice.

Prejudice often takes the form of a **stereotype** (*stereo* is derived from a Greek word meaning "solid"), which is *a simplified description applied to every person in some category.* Many white people hold

● Seeing Sociology in Everyday Life

Do you think students on your campus have become more accepting of social diversity? Explain why or why not.

stereotypical views of minorities. Stereotyping is especially harmful to minorities in the workplace. If company officials see minority workers only in terms of a stereotype, they will make assumptions about their abilities, steer them toward certain jobs, and limit their access to better opportunities (R. L. Kaufman, 2002).

Minorities, too, stereotype whites and also other minorities (T. W. Smith, 1996; Cummings & Lambert, 1997). Surveys show, for example, that more African Americans than whites express the belief that Asians engage in unfair business practices and that more Asians than whites criticize Hispanics for having too many children (Perlmutter, 2002).

Measuring Prejudice: The Social Distance Scale

One measure of prejudice is *social distance,* how closely people are willing to interact with members of some category. In the 1920s, Emory Bogardus developed the *social distance scale* shown in Figure 11–1 on page 306. Bogardus (1925) asked students at colleges and universities in the United States how closely they were willing to interact with people in thirty racial and ethnic categories. People express the greatest social distance (most negative prejudice) by declaring that some category of people should be barred from the country entirely (point 7 in the figure); at the other extreme, people express the least social distance (most social acceptance) by saying they would accept a member of some category into their family through marriage (point 1).

Bogardus (1925, 1967; Owen, Elsner, & McFaul, 1977) found that people felt much more social distance from some categories than from others. In general, students in his surveys expressed the most social distance from Hispanics, African Americans, Asians, and Turks by indicating that they would accept such people as co-workers but not as neighbors, close friends, or family members. People expressed the least social distance from those from northern and western Europe, including English and Scottish people, and also Canadians, indicating that they were willing to include them in their families by marriage. ● Go to **mysoclab.com**

Recent research measuring student attitudes confirms the trend of declining prejudice toward all racial and ethnic categories. On your campus, does race or ethnicity guide people's choice in romantic attachments? Do some racial and ethnic categories mix more often than others? Explain your answer.

What patterns of social distance do we find among college students today? A recent study using the same social distance scale[1] reported three major findings (Parrillo & Donoghue, 2005):

1. **Student opinion shows a trend toward greater social acceptance.** Today's students express less social distance from all minorities than students did decades ago. Figure 11–1 shows that the mean (average) score on the social distance scale declined from 2.14 in 1925 to 1.93 in 1977 and to 1.44 in 2001. Respondents (81 percent of whom were white) showed notably greater acceptance of African Americans, a category of people that moved up from near the bottom in 1925 to the top one-third in 2001.

2. **People see less difference between various minorities.** The earliest studies found the difference between the highest- and lowest-ranked minorities (the range of averages) equal to almost three points on the scale. As the figure shows, the most recent research produced a range of averages of less than one point, indicating that today's students tend to see fewer differences between various categories of people.

3. **The terrorist attacks of September 11, 2001, may have reduced social acceptance of Arabs and Muslims.** The most recent study was conducted just a few weeks after September 11, 2001. Perhaps the fact that the nineteen men who attacked the World Trade Center and the Pentagon were Arabs and Muslims is part of the reason that students ranked these categories last on the social distance scale. However, not a single student gave Arabs or Muslims a 7, indicating that they should be barred from the country. On the contrary, the 2001 mean scores (1.94 for Arabs and 1.88 for Muslims) show higher social acceptance than students in 1977 expressed toward eighteen of the thirty categories of people studied.

Racism

A powerful and harmful form of prejudice, **racism** is *the belief that one racial category is innately superior or inferior to another.* Racism has existed throughout world

[1] Parrillo and Donoghue dropped seven of the categories used by Bogardus (Armenians, Czechs, Finns, Norwegians, Scots, Swedes, and Turks), claiming that they were no longer visible minorities. He added nine new categories (Africans, Arabs, Cubans, Dominicans, Haitians, Jamaicans, Muslims, Puerto Ricans, and Vietnamese), claiming that these are visible minorities today. This change probably encouraged higher social distance scores, making the trend toward decreasing social distance all the more significant.

○ Making the Grade

On the social distance scale, the higher the number, the greater the social distance, meaning more negative prejudice.

○ Making the Grade

The text presents four theories of prejudice. Check your understanding of each by completing this sentence: "This theory explains that prejudice is caused by . . ."

Student Snapshot

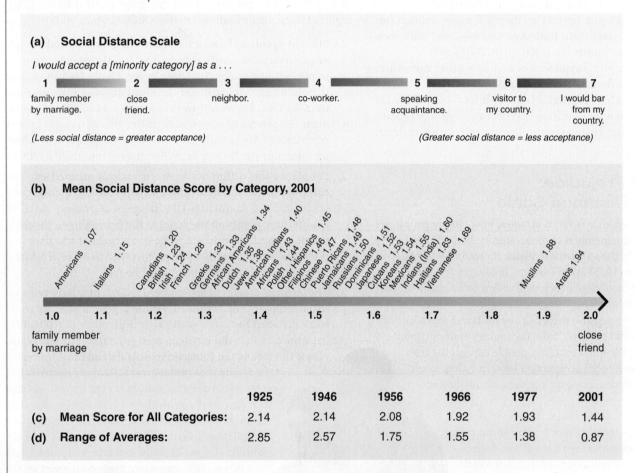

(a) **Social Distance Scale**

I would accept a [minority category] as a . . .

| 1 | 2 | 3 | 4 | 5 | 6 | 7 |

family member by marriage.   close friend.   neighbor.   co-worker.   speaking acquaintance.   visitor to my country.   I would bar from my country.

(Less social distance = greater acceptance)   *(Greater social distance = less acceptance)*

(b) **Mean Social Distance Score by Category, 2001**

Americans 1.07 · Italians 1.15 · Canadians 1.20 · British 1.23 · Irish 1.24 · French 1.28 · Greeks 1.32 · Germans 1.33 · African Americans 1.34 · Dutch 1.35 · Jews 1.38 · American Indians 1.40 · Africans 1.43 · Polish 1.44 · Other Hispanics 1.45 · Filipinos 1.46 · Chinese 1.47 · Puerto Ricans 1.48 · Jamaicans 1.49 · Russians 1.50 · Dominicans 1.51 · Japanese 1.52 · Cubans 1.53 · Koreans 1.54 · Mexicans 1.55 · Indians (India) 1.60 · Haitians 1.63 · Vietnamese 1.69 · Muslims 1.88 · Arabs 1.94

| 1.0 | 1.1 | 1.2 | 1.3 | 1.4 | 1.5 | 1.6 | 1.7 | 1.8 | 1.9 | 2.0 |

family member by marriage   close friend

		1925	1946	1956	1966	1977	2001
(c)	**Mean Score for All Categories:**	2.14	2.14	2.08	1.92	1.93	1.44
(d)	**Range of Averages:**	2.85	2.57	1.75	1.55	1.38	0.87

FIGURE 11–1 **Bogardus Social Distance Research**

The social distance scale is a good way to measure prejudice. Part (a) illustrates the complete social distance scale, from least social distance at the far left to greatest social distance at the far right. Part (b) shows the mean (average) social distance score received by each category of people in 2001. Part (c) presents the overall mean score (the average of the scores received by all racial and ethnic categories) in specific years. These scores have fallen from 2.14 in 1925 to 1.44 in 2001, showing that students express less social distance from minorities today than they did in the past. Part (d) shows the range of averages, the difference between the highest and lowest scores in given years (in 2001, for instance, it was 0.87, the difference between the high score of 1.94 for Arabs and the low score of 1.07 for Americans). This figure has also become smaller since 1925, indicating that today's students tend to see fewer differences between various categories of people.

Source: Parrillo & Donoghue (2005).

history. Despite their many achievements, the ancient Greeks, the peoples of India, and the Chinese all considered people unlike themselves inferior.

Racism has also been widespread throughout the history of the United States, where ideas about racial inferiority supported slavery.

Today, overt racism in this country has decreased because more people believe in evaluating others, in the words of Martin Luther King Jr., "not by the color of their skin but by the content of their character."

Even so, racism remains a serious social problem, as some people still argue that certain racial and ethnic categories are smarter than

Go to the Multimedia Library at **mysoclab.com**
to listen to the NPR report "Race and Intelligence:
Politicizing the Findings"

scapegoat (p. 308) a person or category of people, typically with little
power, whom people unfairly blame for their own troubles

SEEING SOCIOLOGY IN EVERYDAY LIFE

Does Race Affect Intelligence?

As we go through an average day, we encounter people of various racial and ethnic categories. We also deal with people who are very intelligent as well as those whose abilities are more modest. But is there a connection between race or ethnicity and intelligence?

Common stereotypes say that Asian Americans are smarter than white people and that the typical white person is more intelligent than the average African American. Throughout the history of the United States, many people have assumed that some categories of people are smarter than others. Just as important, people have used this thinking to justify the privileges of the allegedly superior category and even to bar supposedly inferior people from entering this country.

So what do we know about intelligence? Scientists know that people, as individuals, differ in mental abilities. The distribution of human intelligence forms a "bell curve". A person's *intelligence quotient* (IQ) is calculated as the person's mental age in years, as measured by a test, divided by the person's actual age in years, with the result multiplied by 100. An eight-year-old who performs like a ten-year-old has an IQ of 10 ÷ 8 = 1.25 × 100 = 125. Average performance is defined as an IQ of 100.

In a controversial study of intelligence and social inequality, Richard Herrnstein and Charles Murray (1994) claim that race is related to measures of intelligence. More specifically, they say that the average IQ for people of European ancestry is 100, for people of East Asian ancestry is 103, and for people of African ancestry is 90.

Such assertions go against our democratic and egalitarian beliefs that no racial type is naturally better than another. Because these findings can increase prejudice, critics argue that intelligence tests are not valid and even that the concept of intelligence has little real meaning.

Most social scientists believe that IQ tests do measure something important that we think of as intelligence, and they agree that *individuals* vary in intellectual aptitude. But they reject the idea that any *category* of people, on average, is naturally smarter than any other. So how do we explain the overall differences in IQ scores by race?

Thomas Sowell (1994, 1995) explains that most of this difference results not from biology but from environment. In some skillful sociological detective work, Sowell traced IQ scores for various racial and ethnic categories throughout the twentieth century. He found that on average, early-twentieth-century immigrants from European nations such as Poland, Lithuania, Italy, and Greece, as well as from Asian countries including China and Japan, scored 10 to 15 points below the U.S. average. But by the end of the twentieth century, people in these same categories had IQ scores that were average or above average. Among Italian Americans, for example, average IQ jumped almost 10 points; among Polish and Chinese Americans, the increase was almost 20 points.

Because genetic changes occur over thousands of years and most people in these categories marry others like themselves, biological factors cannot explain such a rapid rise in IQ scores. The only reasonable explanation is

changing cultural patterns. The descendants of early immigrants improved their intellectual performance as their standard of living rose and their opportunity for schooling increased.

Sowell found that much the same was true of African Americans. Historically, the average IQ score of African Americans living in the North has been about 10 points higher than the average score of those living in the South. Among the descendants of African Americans who migrated from the South to the North after 1940, IQ scores went up, just as they did for descendants of European and Asian immigrants. Thus environmental factors appear to be critical in explaining differences in IQ among various categories of people.

According to Sowell, these test score differences tell us that *cultural patterns matter.* Asians who score high on tests are no smarter than other people, but they have been raised to value learning and pursue excellence. For their part, African Americans are no less intelligent than anyone else, but they carry a legacy of disadvantage that can undermine self-confidence and discourage achievement. ● Go to **mysoclab.com**

WHAT DO YOU THINK?

1. If IQ scores reflect people's environment, are they valid measures of intelligence? Could they be harmful?

2. According to Thomas Sowell, why do some racial and ethnic categories show dramatic short-term gains in average IQ scores?

3. Do you think parents and schools influence a child's IQ score? If so, how?

others. The Seeing Sociology in Everyday Life box explains that these commonsense stereotypes fail to recognize that racial differences in mental abilities result from environment rather than from biology.

Theories of Prejudice

Where does prejudice come from? Social scientists provide several answers to this vexing question, focusing on frustration, personality, culture, and social conflict.

Scapegoat Theory

Scapegoat theory holds that prejudice springs from frustration among people who are themselves disadvantaged (Dollard et al., 1939). Take the case of a white woman who is frustrated by her low-paying job in a textile factory. Directing her hostility at the powerful factory owners carries the obvious risk of being fired; therefore, she may blame her low pay on the presence of minority co-workers. Her prejudice does not improve her situation, but it is a relatively safe way to express

The New York Times

In Job Hunt, College Degree Can't Close Racial Gap

By MICHAEL LUO
December 1, 2009

Johnny R. Williams, 30, would appear to be an unlikely person to have to fret about the impact of race on his job search, with companies like JPMorgan Chase and an M.B.A. from the University of Chicago on his résumé.

But after graduating from business school last year and not having much success garnering interviews, he decided to retool his résumé, scrubbing it of any details that might tip off his skin color. His membership, for instance, in the African American business students association? Deleted.

"If they're going to X me," Mr. Williams said, "I'd like to at least get in the door first."

Similarly, Barry Jabbar Sykes, 37, who has a degree in mathematics from Morehouse College, a historically black college in Atlanta, now uses Barry J. Sykes in his continuing search for an information technology position, even though he has gone by Jabbar his whole life.

"Barry sounds like I could be from Ireland," he said.

That race remains a serious obstacle in the job market for African Americans, even those with degrees from respected colleges, may seem to some people a jarring contrast to decades of progress by blacks, culminating in President Obama's election.

But there is ample evidence that racial inequities remain when it comes to employment. Black joblessness has long far outstripped that of whites. And strikingly, the disparity . . . has been even more pronounced for those with college degrees, compared with those without. Education, it seems, does not level the playing field—in fact, it appears to have made it more uneven. . . .

The unemployment rate for black male college graduates 25 and older in 2009 has been nearly twice that of white male college graduates—8.4 percent compared with 4.4 percent.

Various academic studies have confirmed that black job seekers have a harder time than whites. A study published several years ago in *The American Economic Review* titled "Are Emily and Greg More Employable than Lakisha and Jamal?" found that applicants with black-sounding names received 50 percent fewer callbacks than those with white-sounding names.

A more recent study, published this year in *The Journal of Labor Economics* found white, Asian, and Hispanic managers tended to hire more whites and fewer blacks than black managers did.

The discrimination is rarely overt, according to interviews with more than two dozen college-educated black job seekers around the country. . . . Instead, those interviewed told subtler stories, referring to surprised looks and offhand comments, interviews that fell apart almost as soon as they began, and the sudden loss of interest from companies after meetings. . . .

Mr. Williams recently applied to a Dallas money management firm that had posted a position with top business schools. The hiring manager had seemed ecstatic to hear from him, telling him they had trouble getting people from prestigious business schools to move to the area. . . . .

But when Mr. Williams later met two men from the firm for lunch, he said they appeared stunned when he strolled up to introduce himself.

anger, and it may give her the comforting feeling that at least she is superior to someone.

A **scapegoat,** then, is *a person or category of people, typically with little power, whom other people unfairly blame for their own troubles.* Because they have little power and thus are usually "safe targets," minorities often are used as scapegoats.

Authoritarian Personality Theory

Theodor Adorno and his colleagues (1950) considered extreme prejudice a personality trait of certain individuals. This conclusion is supported by research indicating that people who show strong prejudice toward one minority are usually intolerant of all minorities. These *authoritarian personalities* rigidly conform to conventional cultural values and see moral issues as clear-cut matters of right and wrong. According to Adorno, people who grow up developing authoritarian personalities also view society as naturally competitive, with "better" people (like themselves) dominating those who are weaker (all minorities).

Adorno and colleagues also found the opposite pattern to be true: People who express tolerance toward one minority are likely to be accepting of all. Such people tend to be more flexible in their moral judgments and treat all people as equals.

Adorno thought that people with little education and those raised by cold and demanding parents tend to develop authoritarian personalities. Filled with anger and anxiety as children, they grow into hostile and aggressive adults who seek out scapegoats.

Culture Theory

A third theory claims that although extreme prejudice is found in certain people, some prejudice is found in everyone. Why? Because prejudice is part of the culture in which we all live and learn. The Bogardus social distance studies help prove the point. Bogardus found that students across the country had mostly the same attitudes toward specific racial and ethnic categories, feeling closer to some and more distant from others.

More evidence that prejudice is rooted in culture is the fact that minorities express the same attitudes as white people toward categories other than their own. Such patterns suggest that individuals hold prejudices because we live in a "culture of prejudice" that has taught us to view certain categories of people as "better" or "worse" than others.

Do we live a "culture of prejudice"? Seeing Sociology in the News explains that minority job-seekers, especially those with good training, have reason to think that the answer may be yes.

Conflict Theory

A fourth explanation proposes that prejudice is used as a tool by powerful people not only to justify privilege for themselves but also to

"Their eyes kind of hit the ceiling a bit," he said. "It was kind of quiet for about 45 seconds."

The company's interest in him quickly cooled, setting off the inevitable questions in his mind.

Discrimination in many cases may not even be intentional, some job seekers pointed out, but simply a matter of people gravitating toward similar people, casting about for the right "cultural fit," a buzzword often heard in corporate circles.

There is also the matter of how many jobs, especially higher-level ones, are never even posted and depend on word-of-mouth and informal networks, in many cases leaving blacks at a disadvantage. A recent study published in the academic journal *Social Problems* found that white males receive substantially more job leads for high-level supervisory positions than women and members of minorities.

Many interviewed, however, wrestled with "pulling the race card," groping between their cynicism and desire to avoid the stigma that blacks are too quick to claim victimhood. After all, many had gone to good schools and had accomplished résumés. Some had grown up in well-to-do settings, with parents who had raised them never to doubt how high they could climb. Moreover, there is President Obama, perhaps the ultimate embodiment of that belief.

Certainly, they conceded, there are times when their race can be beneficial, particularly with companies that have diversity programs. But many said they sensed that such opportunities had been cut back over the years . . . Others speculated there was now more of a tendency to deem diversity unnecessary after Mr. Obama's triumph.

In fact, whether Mr. Obama's election has been good or bad for their job prospects is hotly debated. Several interviewed went so far as to say that they believed there was only so much progress that many in the country could take, and that there was now a backlash against blacks. . . .

It is difficult to overstate the degree that they say race permeates nearly every aspect of their job searches, from how early they show up to interviews to the kinds of anecdotes they try to come up with. . . .

Nearly all said they agonized over job applications that asked them whether they would like to identify their race. Most said they usually did not.

oppress others. Anglos who look down on Latino immigrants in the Southwest, for example, can get away with paying the immigrants low wages for hard work. Similarly, all elites benefit when prejudice divides workers along racial and ethnic lines and discourages them from working together to advance their common interests (Geschwender, 1978; Olzak, 1989; Rothenberg, 2008).

According to another conflict-based argument, made by Shelby Steele (1990), minorities themselves encourage *race consciousness* (which is sometimes called "identity politics") in order to win greater power and privileges. Because of their historical disadvantage, minorities claim that they are victims entitled to special consideration based on their race. Although this strategy may bring short-term gains, Steele cautions that such thinking often sparks a backlash from whites or others who oppose "special treatment" on the basis of race or ethnicity.

Discrimination

Closely related to prejudice is **discrimination,** *unequal treatment of various categories of people.* Prejudice refers to *attitudes;* discrimination is a matter of *action.* Like prejudice, discrimination can be either positive (providing special advantages) or negative (creating obstacles) and ranges from subtle to extreme.

Institutional Prejudice and Discrimination

We typically think of prejudice and discrimination as the hateful ideas or actions of specific people. But Stokely Carmichael and Charles Hamilton (1967) point out that far greater harm results from **institutional prejudice and discrimination,** *bias built into the operation of society's institutions,* including schools, hospitals, law enforcement, and the workplace. For example, researchers have shown that banks reject home mortgage applications from minorities at a higher rate—or charge higher rates for the same mortgage—compared to white applicants, even when income and quality of neighborhood are held constant (Gotham, 1998; Blanton, 2007).

According to Carmichael and Hamilton, people are slow to condemn or even recognize institutional prejudice and discrimination because it often involves respected public officials and long-established traditions. A case in point is *Brown* v. *Board of Education of Topeka,* the 1954 Supreme Court decision that ended the legal segregation of U.S. schools. The principle of "separate but equal" schooling had been the law of the land, supporting racial inequality by allowing school segregation. Despite this change in the law, more than half a century later, most U.S. students still attend schools in which one race overwhelmingly predominates (KewalRamani et al., 2007). In 1991, the courts pointed out that neighborhood

Read "Use of Black English and Racial Discrimination in Urban Housing Markets" by Douglas S. Massey and Garvey Lundy on mysoclab.com

prejudice (p. 304) a rigid and unfair generalization about an entire category of people

discrimination (p. 309) unequal treatment of various categories of people

institutional prejudice and discrimination (p. 309) bias built into the operation of society's institutions

miscegenation biological reproduction by partners of different racial categories

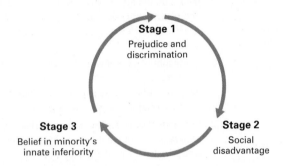

Stage 1: Prejudice and discrimination begin, often as an expression of ethnocentrism or an attempt to justify economic exploitation.

Stage 2: As a result of prejudice and discrimination, a minority is socially disadvantaged, occupying a low position in the system of social stratification.

Stage 3: This social disadvantage is then interpreted not as the result of earlier prejudice and discrimination but as evidence that the minority is innately inferior, unleashing renewed prejudice and discrimination by which the cycle repeats itself.

FIGURE 11–2   **Prejudice and Discrimination: The Vicious Circle**

Prejudice and discrimination can form a vicious circle, perpetuating themselves.

schools will never provide equal education as long as our population is racially segregated, with most African Americans living in central cities and most white people and Asian Americans living in suburbs. Read on mysoclab.com

Prejudice and Discrimination: The Vicious Circle

Prejudice and discrimination reinforce each other. The Thomas theorem, discussed in Chapter 4 ("Social Interaction in Everyday Life"), offers a simple explanation of this fact: *Situations that are defined as real become real in their consequences* (Thomas & Thomas, 1928; Thomas, 1966:301, orig. 1931).

As Thomas recognized, stereotypes become real to people who believe them and sometimes even to those victimized by them. Prejudice on the part of white people toward people of color does not produce *innate* inferiority, but it can produce *social* inferiority, pushing minorities into low-paying jobs, inferior schools, and racially segregated housing. Then, as white people interpret that social disadvantage as evidence that minorities do not measure up, they unleash a new round of prejudice and discrimination, giving rise to a vicious circle in which each perpetuates the other, as shown in Figure 11–2.

Majority and Minority: Patterns of Interaction

Social scientists describe interaction between majority and minority members of a society in terms of four models: pluralism, assimilation, segregation, and genocide.

Pluralism

Pluralism is *a state in which people of all races and ethnicities are distinct but have equal social standing.* In other words, people who differ in appearance or social heritage all share resources roughly equally.

The United States is pluralistic to the extent that almost all categories of people (convicted felons are one exception; see page 352) have equal standing under the law. In addition, large cities contain countless "ethnic villages" where people proudly display the traditions of their immigrant ancestors. These include New York's Spanish Harlem, Little Italy, and Chinatown; Philadelphia's Italian "South Philly"; Chicago's "Little Saigon"; and Latino East Los Angeles. New York City alone supports hundreds of magazines, newspapers, and radio stations in more than ninety languages (Paul, 2001; Logan, Alba, & Zhang, 2002; New York Community Media Alliance, 2008).

But the United States is not truly pluralistic, for three reasons. First, although most people value their cultural heritage, few want to live exclusively with others exactly like themselves (NORC, 2009). Second, our tolerance for social diversity goes only so far. One reaction to the growing proportion of minorities in the United States is a social movement to make English the nation's official language. Third, as you will see later in this chapter, people of various colors and cultures do *not* have equal social standing.

Assimilation

Many people think of the United States as a "melting pot" in which different nationalities blend together. But rather than everyone "melting" into some new cultural pattern, most minorities have adopted the dominant culture established by the earliest settlers. Why? Because doing so is both the avenue to upward social mobility and a way to escape the prejudice and discrimination directed against more visible foreigners. Sociologists use the term **assimilation** to describe *the process by which minorities gradually adopt patterns of the dominant culture.* Assimilation involves changing styles of dress, values, religion, language, and friends.

The amount of assimilation varies by category. For example, in the United States, Canadians have "melted" more than Cubans, the Dutch more than Dominicans, Germans more than the Japanese. Multiculturalists oppose making assimilation a goal because it suggests that minorities are "the problem" and the ones who need to do all the changing.

Note that assimilation involves changes in ethnicity but not in race. For example, many descendants of Japanese immigrants have discarded their ethnic traditions but retain their racial identity. For racial traits to diminish over generations, **miscegenation,** or *biological reproduction by partners of different racial categories,* must occur. Although interracial marriage is becoming more common, it still amounts to only 7 percent of all U.S. marriages (U.S. Census Bureau, 2010).

Segregation

Segregation is *the physical and social separation of categories of people.* Sometimes minorities, especially religious orders such as the Amish, voluntarily segregate themselves. Usually, however, majorities segregate minorities by excluding them. Neighborhoods, schools, occupations, hospitals, and even cemeteries may be segregated. Pluralism encourages cultural distinctiveness without disadvantage; segregation enforces separation that harms a minority.

Racial segregation has a long history in the United States, beginning with slavery and evolving into racially separate housing, schooling, buses, and trains. Decisions such as the 1954 *Brown* case have reduced *de jure* (Latin, "by law") discrimination in the United States. However, *de facto* ("in fact") segregation continues in the form of countless neighborhoods that are home to people of a single race.

Despite some recent decline, segregation continues in the United States. For example, Livonia, Michigan, is 92 percent white, and neighboring Detroit is 83 percent African American. Kurt Metzger (2001) explains, "Livonia was pretty much created by white flight [from Detroit]." Research shows that across the country, whites (especially those with young children) continue to avoid neighborhoods where African Americans live (Emerson, Yancey, & Chai, 2001; Krysan, 2002). At the extreme, Douglas Massey and Nancy Denton (1989) documented the *hypersegregation* of poor African Americans in some inner cities. Hypersegregation means having little contact of any kind with people beyond the local community. Hypersegregation is the daily experience of about 20 percent of poor African Americans

and is a pattern found in about twenty-five large U.S. cities (Wilkes & Iceland, 2004).

Genocide

Genocide is *the systematic killing of one category of people by another.* This deadly form of racism and ethnocentrism violates nearly every recognized moral standard, yet it has occurred time and again in human history.

Genocide was common in the history of contact between Europeans and the original inhabitants of the Americas. From the sixteenth century on, the Spanish, Portuguese, English, French, and Dutch forcibly colonized vast empires. Although most native people died from diseases brought by Europeans, against which they had no natural defenses, many who opposed the colonizers were killed deliberately (Matthiessen, 1984; Sale, 1990).

Genocide also occurred in the twentieth century. Beginning in 1915, more than 1 million Armenians were killed by the Ottoman Empire. Likewise, unimaginable horror befell European Jews during Adolf Hitler's reign of terror. During the Holocaust that lasted from about 1935 to 1945, the Nazis murdered more than 6 million Jewish men, women, and children, along with gay people, Gypsies, and people with handicaps. The Soviet dictator Josef Stalin murdered on an even greater scale, killing some 30 million real and imagined enemies during decades of violent rule. Between 1975 and 1980, Pol Pot's Communist regime in Cambodia butchered all "capitalists," which included anyone able to speak a Western language. In all, some 2 million people (one-fourth of the population) perished in the Cambodian "killing fields."

Tragically, genocide continues in the modern world. Recent examples include Hutus killing Tutsis in the African nation of Rwanda, Serbs killing Bosnians in the Balkans of Eastern Europe, and the killing of hundreds of thousands of people in the Darfur region of Sudan.

These four patterns of minority-majority contact have all been played out in the United States. Although many people proudly point to patterns of pluralism and assimilation, it is also important to recognize the degree to which U.S. society has been built on segregation (of African Americans) and genocide (of Native Americans). The remainder of this chapter examines how these four patterns have shaped the past and present social standing of major racial and ethnic categories in the United States.

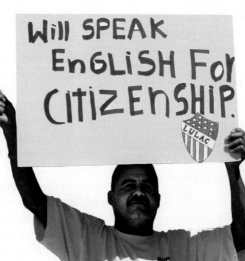

Should we expect people who come to the United States to change their language and other cultural patterns in order to "fit in," or should we expect them to hold onto their own traditions? Why?

Seeing Sociology
in Everyday Life

In your city or town, are there minority neighborhoods? Which categories of people live there? To what degree is your community racially or ethnically segregated?

Making the Grade

As the maps on the facing page show, Native peoples were the original inhabitants of the Americas, and new immigrants pushed them farther west as the United States took form.

In an effort to force assimilation, the U.S. Bureau of Indian Affairs took American Indian children from their families and placed them in boarding schools like this one, Oklahoma's Riverside Indian School. There they were taught to speak English by non-Indian teachers with the goal of making them into "Americans."

Race and Ethnicity in the United States

> Give me your tired, your poor,
> Your huddled masses yearning to breathe free,
> The wretched refuse of your teeming shore,
> Send these, the homeless, tempest-tossed to me:
> I lift my lamp beside the golden door.

These words by Emma Lazarus, inscribed on the base of the Statue of Liberty, express cultural ideals of human dignity, personal freedom, and economic opportunity. Indeed, the United States has provided more of the "good life" to more immigrants than any other nation. More than 1.5 million immigrants come to this country every year, and their ways of life create a social mosaic that is especially evident in large cities.

However, as a survey of racial and ethnic minorities in the United States will show, our country's golden door has opened more widely for some than for others. We turn to the history and current social standing of the major categories of the U.S. population.

Native Americans

The term "Native Americans" refers to the hundreds of societies—including Aleuts, Cherokee, Zuni, Sioux, Mohawk, Aztec, and Inca—who first settled the Western Hemisphere. Some 30,000 years before

Christopher Columbus landed in the Americas, migrating peoples crossed a land bridge from Asia to North America where the Bering Strait (off the coast of Alaska) lies today. Gradually, they spread throughout North and South America.

When the first Europeans arrived late in the fifteenth century, Native Americans numbered in the millions. But by 1900, after centuries of conflict and acts of genocide, the "vanishing Americans" numbered just 250,000 (Dobyns, 1966; Tyler, 1973). The land they controlled also shrank dramatically, as National Map 11–2 shows.

Columbus first referred to the Native Americans that he encountered as "Indians" because he mistakenly thought he had reached the coast of India. Columbus found the native people passive and peaceful, in stark contrast to the materialistic and competitive Europeans (Matthiessen, 1984; Sale, 1990). Yet Europeans justified the seizure of Native Americans' lands by calling them thieves and murderers (Josephy, 1982; Matthiessen, 1984; Sale, 1990).

After the Revolutionary War, the new U.S. government adopted a pluralistic approach to Native American societies and tried to gain more land through treaties. Payment for land was far from fair, however, and when Native Americans resisted surrendering their homelands, the U.S. government simply used its superior military power to evict them. By the early 1800s, few Native Americans remained east of the Mississippi River.

In 1871, the United States declared Native Americans wards of the government and adopted a strategy of forced assimilation. Relocated to specific territories designated as "reservations," Native Americans continued to lose their land and were on their way to losing their culture as well. Reservation life encouraged dependency on outsiders, replacing ancestral languages with English and traditional religion with Christianity. Officials took many children from their parents and handed them over to boarding schools, where they were resocialized as "Americans." Authorities gave local control of reservations to the few Native Americans who supported government policies, and they distributed reservation land, traditionally held collectively, as private property to individual families (Tyler, 1973).

Not until 1924 were Native Americans entitled to U.S. citizenship. After that, many migrated from the reservations, adopting mainstream cultural patterns and marrying non–Native Americans. Today, one-half of Native Americans consider themselves biracial or multiracial (U.S. Census Bureau, 2009), and many large cities now contain sizable Native American populations. However, as Table 11–2 shows, the income of Native Americans is far below the U.S. average, and relatively few Native Americans earn a college degree.[2]

From in-depth interviews with Native Americans in a western city, Joan Albon (1971) concluded that their low social standing was a result of cultural factors, including their noncompetitive view of life

○ Making the Grade

People tend to think about race and ethnicity when they deal with categories of people whom they think of as "other." WASPs have race and ethnicity, too, of course, but U.S. society does not construct these into a minority identity.

● Seeing Sociology in Everyday Life

In what ways does being a WASP (or simply being white) confer privilege on people?

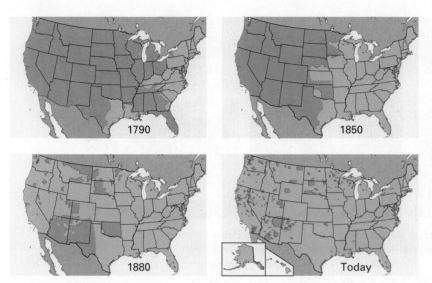

1790   1850   1880   Today

Seeing Ourselves

NATIONAL MAP 11–2

Land Controlled by Native Americans, 1790 to Today

In 1790, Native Americans controlled three-fourths of the land (blue-shaded areas) that eventually became the United States. Today, Native Americans control 304 reservations, scattered across the United States, that account for just 2 percent of the country's land area. How would you characterize these locations?

Source: Published in *The New York Times* on March 18, 1998. Copyright © 1998 by The New York Times Company. All rights reserved. Used by permission and protected by the Copyright Laws of the United States. The printing, copying, redistribution, or retransmission of the Material without express written permission is prohibited.

and reluctance to pursue higher education. In addition, she noted, many Native Americans have dark skin, which makes them targets of prejudice and discrimination.

Members of the more than 200 American Indian nations in the United States today are reclaiming pride in their cultural heritage. Traditional cultural organizations report a surge in new membership applications, and many children can now speak native languages better than their parents. The legal right of Native Americans to govern their reservations has enabled some tribes to build profitable gaming casinos. But the wealth produced from gambling has enriched relatively few Native peoples, and most profits go to non-Indian investors (Bartlett & Steele, 2002). While some prosper, most Native Americans remain severely disadvantaged, with a profound sense of the injustice they have suffered at the hands of white people.

White Anglo-Saxon Protestants

White Anglo-Saxon Protestants (WASPs) were not the first people to inhabit the United States, but they soon dominated the nation after European settlement began. Most WASPs are of English ancestry, but this category also includes people from Scotland and Wales. With some 35 million people claiming English, Scottish, or Welsh ancestry, 12 percent of our society has some WASP background, and WASPs are found at all class levels (U.S. Census Bureau, 2009).

Many people associate WASPs with elite communities along the East and West Coasts. But the highest concentrations of WASPs are in Utah (because of migrations of Mormons with English ancestry), Appalachia, and northern New England (also due to historical patterns of immigration).

Looking back in time, WASP immigrants were highly skilled and motivated to achieve by what we now call the Protestant work ethic. Because of their numbers and power, WASPs were not subject to the prejudice and discrimination experienced by other categories of immigrants. In fact, the historical dominance of WASPs has led others to want to become more like them (K. W. Jones, 2001).

WASPs were never one single group; especially during colonial times, hostility separated English Anglicans from Scottish Presbyterians (Parrillo, 1994). But in the nineteenth century, most WASPs joined together to oppose the arrival of "undesirables" such as the Germans in the 1840s and Italians in the 1880s. Those who could afford it sheltered themselves in exclusive suburbs and restrictive clubs. Thus the 1880s—the decade when the Statue of Liberty first welcomed immigrants to the United States—also saw the

[2]In making comparisons of education and income, keep in mind that various categories of the U.S. population have different median ages. In 2008, the median age for all U.S. people was 36.8 years; for Native Americans, the figure was 31.2 years. Because people's schooling and income increase over time, this age difference accounts for some of the disparities shown in Table 11–2.

Table 11–2   The Social Standing of Native Americans, 2008

	Native Americans	Entire U.S. Population
Median family income	$43,190	$61,521
Percentage in poverty	24.2%	13.2%
Completion of four or more years of college (age 25 and over)	12.7%	29.5%

Source: U.S. Census Bureau (2009).

Seeing Sociology in Everyday Life

Do you think that Marian Anderson, who broke a "color line" in 1936 by being invited to the White House, would have imagined our nation having an African American president?

Seeing Sociology in Everyday Life

In your opinion, how much change has there been in racial prejudice and discrimination against African Americans during your lifetime? Explain your position.

The efforts of these four women greatly advanced the social standing of African Americans in the United States. Pictured from left to right: Sojourner Truth (1797–1883), born a slave, became an influential preacher and outspoken abolitionist who was honored by President Lincoln at the White House. Harriet Tubman (1820–1913), after escaping from slavery herself, masterminded the flight from bondage of hundreds of African American men and women via the "Underground Railroad." Ida Wells-Barnett (1862–1931), born to slave parents, became a partner in a Memphis newspaper and served as a tireless crusader against the terror of lynching. Marian Anderson (1897–1993), an exceptional singer whose early career was restrained by racial prejudice, broke symbolic "color lines" by singing in the White House in 1936 and on the steps of the Lincoln Memorial to a crowd of almost 100,000 people in 1939.

founding of the first country club with exclusively WASP members (Baltzell, 1964).

By about 1950, however, WASP wealth and power had peaked, as indicated by the 1960 election of John Fitzgerald Kennedy, the first Irish Catholic president. Yet the WASP cultural legacy remains. English is this country's dominant language and Protestantism the majority religion. Our legal system also reflects its English origins. But the historical dominance of WASPs is most evident in the widespread use of the terms "race" and "ethnicity" to describe everyone but them.

African Americans

Africans accompanied European explorers to the New World in the fifteenth century. But most accounts trace the beginning of black history in the United States to 1619, when a Dutch trading ship brought twenty Africans to Jamestown, Virginia. Many more ships filled with African laborers followed. Whether these people arrived as slaves or as indentured servants (who paid for their passage by agreeing to work for a period of time), being of African descent on these shores soon became virtually synonymous with being a slave. In 1661, Virginia enacted the first law in the new colonies recognizing slavery (Sowell, 1981).

Slavery was the foundation of the southern colonies' plantation system. White people ran plantations using slave labor, and until 1808, some were also slave traders. Traders—including North Americans, Africans, and Europeans—forcibly transported some 10 mil-

lion Africans to various countries in the Americas, including 400,000 to the United States. On small sailing ships, hundreds of slaves were chained for the several weeks it took to cross the Atlantic Ocean. Filth and disease killed many and drove others to suicide. Overall, perhaps half died en route (Franklin, 1967; Sowell, 1981).

The reward for surviving the miserable journey was a lifetime of servitude. Although some slaves worked in cities at various trades, most labored in the fields, often from daybreak until sunset and even longer during the harvest. The law allowed owners to use whatever disciplinary measures they deemed necessary to ensure that slaves were obedient and hardworking. Even killing a slave rarely prompted legal action. Owners also divided slave families at public auctions, where human beings were bought and sold as property. Unschooled and dependent on their owners for all their basic needs, slaves had little control over their lives (Franklin, 1967; Sowell, 1981).

Some free people of color lived in both the North and the South, laboring as small-scale farmers, skilled workers, and small business owners. But the lives of most African Americans stood in glaring contradiction to the principles of freedom on which the United States was founded. The Declaration of Independence states, "We hold these Truths to be self-evident, that all Men are created equal, that they are endowed by their Creator with certain unalienable Rights, that among these are Life, Liberty, and the Pursuit of Happiness." However, most white people did not apply these ideals to African Americans. In the *Dred Scott* case in 1857, the U.S. Supreme Court addressed the

Go to the Multimedia Library at **mysoclab.com** to watch the Reverend Martin Luther King Jr. deliver his famous "I Have a Dream" speech

Making the Grade

Jim Crow laws are a clear example of institutional discrimination.

question "Are slaves citizens?" by writing, "We think they are not, and that they are not included, and were not intended to be included, under the word 'citizens' in the Constitution, and can therefore claim none of the rights and privileges which that instrument provides for and secures for citizens of the United States" (quoted in Blaustein & Zangrando, 1968:160). Thus arose what the Swedish sociologist Gunnar Myrdal (1944) called the "American dilemma": a democratic society's denial of basic rights and freedoms to one category of people. People would speak of equality, in other words, but then fail to extend the same rights and freedoms to all categories of people. Many white people resolved this dilemma by defining black people as naturally inferior and therefore undeserving of equality (Leach, 2002).

In 1865, the Thirteenth Amendment to the Constitution outlawed slavery. Three years later, the Fourteenth Amendment reversed the *Dred Scott* ruling, granting citizenship to all people born in the United States. The Fifteenth Amendment, ratified in 1870, stated that neither race nor previous condition of servitude should deprive any (male) citizen of the right to vote. However, so-called *Jim Crow laws*—classic cases of institutionalized discrimination—segregated U.S. society into two racial castes. Especially in the South, white people beat and lynched black people (and some white people) who challenged the racial hierarchy.

The twentieth century brought dramatic changes for African Americans. After World War I, tens of thousands of women and men fled the rural South for jobs in northern factories. Although most did find economic opportunities, few escaped racial prejudice and discrimination, which placed them lower in the social hierarchy than white immigrants arriving from Europe.

In the 1950s, a national civil rights movement set the climate for a landmark judicial decision that outlawed segregated schools, and in the 1960s, legislation outlawed overt discrimination in employment and public accommodations. The Black Power movement in the 1960s and 1970s gave African Americans a renewed sense of pride and purpose. ● Go to **mysoclab.com**

Despite these gains, people of African descent continue to occupy a lower social position in the United States, as shown in Table 11–3. The median income of African American families in 2008 ($39,879) was only 57 percent of non-Hispanic white family income ($70,070), a ratio that has changed little in thirty years.[3] Black families remain three times as likely as white families to be poor.

The number of African American families securely in the middle class rose by more than half between 1980 and 2008; 41 percent

Table 11–3 The Social Standing of African Americans, 2008		
	African Americans	**Entire U.S. Population**
Median family income	$39,879	$61,521
Percentage in poverty	24.7%	13.2%
Completion of four or more years of college (age 25 and over)	19.3%	29.5%
Source: U.S. Census Bureau (2009).		

earn $50,000 or more each year. This means that the African American community is now economically diverse. Even so, a majority of African Americans are still working-class or poor. In recent years, many have seen earnings slip as urban factory jobs, vital to residents of central cities, have been lost to other countries where labor costs are lower. This is one reason that black unemployment is almost twice as high as white unemployment; among African American teenagers in many cities, the unemployment figure exceeds 40 percent (R. A. Smith, 2002; U.S. Department of Labor, 2010).

Since 1980, African Americans have made remarkable educational progress. The share of adults completing high school rose from half to 84 percent in 2008, nearly closing the gap between blacks and whites. Between 1980 and 2008, the share of African American adults with at least a college degree rose from 8 percent to more than 19 percent. But as Table 11–3 shows, African Americans are still well below the national average when it comes to completing four years of college.

The political clout of African Americans has greatly increased. As a result of both black migration to the cities and white flight to the suburbs, African Americans have gained greater political power in urban places, and many of this country's largest cities have had African American mayors. At the national level, the election of Barack Obama as this country's forty-fourth president—the first African American to hold this office—is a historic and hugely important event. It demonstrates that our society has moved beyond the assumption that race is a barrier to the highest office in the land (West, 2008). Yet in early 2010, African Americans accounted for just 39 members of the House of Representatives (9 percent of 435), one member (out of 100) in the Senate, and two state governors (National Governors Association, 2010; U.S. House of Representatives, 2010; U.S. Senate, 2010).

In sum, for nearly 400 years, people of African ancestry in the United States have struggled for social equality. As a nation, the United States has come far in this pursuit. Overt discrimination is now illegal, and research documents a long-term decline in prejudice against African Americans (Firebaugh & Davis, 1988; J. Q. Wilson, 1992; NORC, 2009).

Fifty years after the abolition of slavery, W. E. B. Du Bois (1913) pointed to the extent of black achievement but cautioned that racial

[3]Here again, a median age difference (non-Hispanic whites, 41.1; blacks, 33.3) accounts for some of the income and educational disparities. More important is a higher proportion of one-parent families among blacks than whites. If we compare only married-couple families, African Americans (median income $61,509 in 2008) earned 80 percent as much as non-Hispanic whites ($77,356).

Table 11–4 The Social Standing of Asian Americans, 2008

	All Asian Americans	Chinese Americans	Japanese Americans	Asian Indian Americans	Filipino Americans	Korean Americans	Entire U.S. Population
Median family income	$73,578	$81,823	$83,762	$99,783	$87,069	$66,055	$61,521
Percentage in poverty	11.8%	11.9%	8.9%	7.8%	5.4%	13.4%	13.2%
Completion of four or more years of college (age 25 and over)	52.3%	52.1%	46.3%	70.1%	48.0%	49.8%	29.5%

Source: U.S. Census Bureau (2009).

caste remained strong in the United States. Almost a century later, this racial hierarchy persists.

Asian Americans

Although Asian Americans share some racial traits, enormous cultural diversity marks this category of people. In 2008, the total number of Asian Americans exceeded 13.5 million, or about 4.5 percent of the U.S. population. The largest category of Asian Americans is people of Chinese ancestry (3.1 million), followed by those of Asian Indian (2.5 million), Filipino (2.4 million), Vietnamese (1.5 million), Korean (1.3 million), and Japanese (710,000) descent. More than one-third of Asian Americans live in California.

Many young Asian Americans have commanded attention and respect as academic high achievers and are disproportionately represented at our country's best colleges and universities. Many of their elders have also made economic and social gains; most Asian Americans now live in middle-class suburbs. Yet despite (and sometimes because of) their achievements, Asian Americans are sometimes avoided or treated with hostility (Chua-Eoan, 2000; Lee & Marlay, 2007).

The achievement of some Asian Americans has given rise to a "model minority" stereotype that is misleading because it hides the differences in class standing found among their ranks. We will focus on the history and current standing of Chinese Americans and Japanese Americans—the longest-established Asian American minorities—and conclude with a brief look at the most recent arrivals.

Chinese Americans

Chinese immigration to the United States began in 1849 with the economic boom of California's Gold Rush. New towns and businesses sprang up overnight, and the demand for cheap labor attracted some 100,000 Chinese immigrants. Most Chinese workers were young, hard-working men willing to take low-status jobs that whites did not want. But the economy soured in the 1870s, and desperate whites began to compete with the Chinese for whatever work could be found. Suddenly, the hardworking Chinese were seen as a threat. Economic hard times led to prejudice and discrimination (Ling, 1971; Boswell, 1986).

Soon laws were passed barring Chinese people from many occupations, and public opinion turned strongly against the "Yellow Peril."

In 1882, the U.S. government passed the first of several laws limiting Chinese immigration. This action caused domestic hardship because in the United States, Chinese men outnumbered Chinese women by twenty to one. This sex imbalance drove the Chinese population down to only 60,000 by 1920. Because Chinese women already in the United States were in high demand, they soon lost much of their traditional submissiveness to men (Hsu, 1971; Lai, 1980; Sowell, 1981).

Responding to racial hostility, some Chinese moved east; many more sought the relative safety of urban Chinatowns. There Chinese traditions flourished, and kinship networks, called *clans,* offered financial assistance to individuals and represented the interests of all. At the same time, however, living in an all-Chinese community discouraged people from learning English, which limited their job opportunities (Wong, 1971).

A renewed need for labor during World War II prompted President Franklin Roosevelt to end the ban on Chinese immigration in 1943 and to extend the rights of citizenship to Chinese Americans born abroad. Many responded by moving out of Chinatowns and seeking cultural assimilation. In turn-of-the-century Honolulu, for example, 70 percent of the Chinese people lived in Chinatown; today, the figure is below 20 percent.

By 1950, many Chinese Americans had experienced upward social mobility. Today, people of Chinese ancestry are no longer limited to self-employment in laundries and restaurants; many hold high-prestige positions, especially in fields related to science and technology.

As shown in Table 11–4, the median family income of Chinese Americans in 2008 was $81,823, higher than the national average of $61,521. However, the higher income of all Asian Americans reflects a larger number of family members in the labor force.[4]

---

[4]Median age for all Asian Americans in 2008 was 35.8 years, somewhat below the national median of 36.8 and the non-Hispanic white median of 41.1. But specific categories vary widely in median age: Japanese, 45.4; Filipino, 38.9; Chinese, 38.3; Korean, 37.1; Asian Indian, 32.6; Cambodian, 30.9; Hmong, 20.6 (U.S. Census Bureau, 2009).

Seeing Sociology
in Everyday Life

On your campus, do students of any one race or ethnic category
tend to hang out together? Explain the patterns you see.

Seeing Sociology
in Everyday Life

Recent research on social distance (see pages 305–6)
indicates that most of today's college students say they are
more accepting of African Americans than Asian Americans.
Does this square with your experiences? What about people
in the country as a whole—are they more accepting of
Asian Americans or African Americans? Why?

Chinese Americans also have an enviable record of educational achievement, standing significantly above the national average in college graduation.

Despite their success, many Chinese Americans still deal with subtle (and sometimes blatant) prejudice and discrimination. Such hostility is one reason that poverty among Chinese Americans stands near the national average. The problem of poverty is most common among those who remain in the socially isolated Chinatowns working in restaurants or other low-paying jobs, raising the question of whether racial and ethnic enclaves help their residents or exploit them (Portes & Jensen, 1989; Kinkead, 1992; Gilbertson & Gurak, 1993).

Japanese Americans

Japanese immigration to the United States began slowly in the 1860s, reaching only 3,000 by 1890. Most of these immigrants came to the Hawaiian Islands (annexed by the United States in 1898 and made a state in 1959) to take low-paying jobs. After 1900, as the number of Japanese immigrants to California increased (reaching 140,000 by 1915), white hostility increased (Takaki, 1998). In 1907, the United States signed an agreement with Japan limiting the entry of men—the chief economic threat—while allowing Japanese women to immigrate to ease the sex ratio imbalance. In the 1920s, state laws in California and dozens of other states mandated segregation and banned interracial marriage, virtually ending further Japanese immigration. Not until 1952 did the United States extend citizenship to foreign-born Japanese.

Japanese and Chinese immigrants differed in three important ways. First, there were fewer Japanese immigrants, so they escaped some of the hostility directed at the more numerous Chinese. Second, the Japanese knew much more about the United States than the Chinese did, which helped them assimilate (Sowell, 1981). Third, Japanese immigrants preferred rural farming to clustering in cities, which made them less visible. But many white people objected to Japanese ownership of farmland, so in 1913, California barred further purchases. Many foreign-born Japanese (called the *Issei*) responded by placing farmland in

On average, Asian Americans have income above the national median. At the same time, however, the poverty rate in many Asian American communities—including San Francisco's Chinatown—is well above average.

the names of their U.S.-born children (*Nisei*), who were constitutionally entitled to citizenship.

Japanese Americans faced their greatest crisis after Japan bombed the U.S. naval fleet at Pearl Harbor, Hawaii, on December 7, 1941. Rage was directed at the Japanese living in the United States. Some people feared that the Japanese here would spy for Japan or commit acts of sabotage. Within a year, President Franklin Roosevelt signed Executive Order 9066, an unprecedented action designed to ensure national security by detaining people of Japanese descent in military camps. Authorities soon relocated 120,000 people of Japanese descent (90 percent of all U.S. Japanese) to remote inland reservations (Sun, 1998; Ewers, 2008).

Concern about national security always rises in times of war, but Japanese internment was sharply criticized. First, it targeted an entire category of people, not one of whom was ever known to have committed a disloyal act. Second, roughly two-thirds of those imprisoned were *Nisei*, U.S. citizens by birth. Third, the United States was also at war with Germany and Italy, but no comparable action was taken against people of German or Italian ancestry.

Relocation meant selling homes, furnishings, and businesses on short notice for pennies on the dollar. As a result, almost the entire Japanese American population was economically devastated. Herded into military prisons, surrounded by barbed wire, and guarded by armed soldiers, families crowded into single rooms, often in buildings that had previously sheltered livestock. The internment ended in 1944 when the Supreme Court declared it unconstitutional, although the last camp did not close until March 1946 (after the war had ended). In 1988, Congress awarded $20,000 to each of the victims as token compensation for the hardships they endured.

After World War II, Japanese Americans staged a dramatic recovery. Having lost their traditional businesses, many entered new occupations, and driven by cultural values stressing the importance of education and hard work, Japanese Americans have enjoyed remarkable success. In 2008, the median income of Japanese American households was more than 35 percent above the national average, and the rate of poverty among Japanese Americans was well below the national figure.

○ Making the Grade

Compare the data in the various tables in this section
of the chapter to assure that you have learned the
social standing of each racial and ethnic category.

● Seeing Sociology
in Everyday Life

Do you think Latinos are fairly represented in today's
television shows and films? Explain your position.

Table 11–5   The Social Standing of Hispanic Americans, 2008

	All Hispanics	Mexican Americans	Puerto Ricans	Cuban Americans	Entire U.S. Population
Median family income	$40,466	$41,538	$43,944	$51,290	$61,521
Percentage in poverty	23.2%	22.9%	24.0%	14.2%	13.2%
Completion of four or more years of college (age 25 and over)	13.2%	9.0%	15.8%	25.4%	29.5%

Source: U.S. Census Bureau (2009).

Upward social mobility has encouraged cultural assimilation and intermarriage. Younger Japanese Americans rarely live in residential enclaves, as many Chinese Americans still do, and most marry non-Japanese partners. In the process, many have abandoned their traditions, including the Japanese language. A large share of Japanese Americans, however, belong to ethnic associations as a way of maintaining their ethnic identity. Still, some appear to be caught between two worlds, no longer culturally Japanese yet, because of racial differences, not completely accepted in the larger society.

Recent Asian Immigrants

More recent immigrants from Asia include Filipinos, Indians, Koreans, Vietnamese, Guamanians, and Samoans. Overall, the Asian American population increased by 86 percent between 1990 and 2008 and currently accounts for more than one-third of all immigration to the United States (U.S. Department of Homeland Security, 2009).

The entrepreneurial spirit is strong among Asian immigrants. In part this reflects cultural patterns that stress achievement and self-reliance, but having one's own small business is also a strategy for dealing with societal prejudice and discrimination. Small business success is one reason that Asian American family income is above the national average, but it is also true that in many of these businesses, a number of family members work long hours.

Another factor that raises the family income of Asian Americans is a high level of schooling. As shown in Table 11–4, for all categories of Asian Americans, the share of adults with a four-year college degree is well above the national average. Among Asian Indian Americans, who have the highest educational achievement of all Asian Americans, more than two-thirds of all men and women over the age of twenty-five have completed college, a proportion that is more than twice the national average. This remarkable educational achievement is one reason that Asian Indian Americans had a median family income of almost $100,000 in 2008, about 62 percent higher than the national average.

In sum, a survey of Asian Americans presents a complex picture. The Japanese come closest to having achieved social acceptance. But some surveys reveal greater prejudice against Asian Americans than against African Americans (Parrillo & Donoghue,

2005). Median income data suggest that many Asian Americans have prospered. But these numbers reflect the fact that many Asian Americans live in Hawaii, California, or New York, where incomes are high but so are living costs (Takaki, 1998). Then, too, many Asian Americans remain poor. One thing is clear—their high immigration rate means that people of Asian ancestry will play a central role in U.S. society in the decades to come.

Hispanic Americans/Latinos

In 2008, the number of Hispanics in the United States topped 46 million (15.4 percent of the U.S. population), surpassing the number of Asian Americans (13.6 million, or 4.5 percent of the U.S. population) and even African Americans (39 million, or 12.8 percent) and making Hispanics the largest racial or ethnic minority. However, keep in mind that few who fall in this category describe themselves as "Hispanic" or "Latino." Like Asian Americans, Hispanics are really a cluster of distinct populations, each of which identifies with a particular ancestral nation (Marín & Marín, 1991). About two out of three Hispanics (some 31 million) are Mexican Americans. Puerto Ricans are next in number (4.2 million), followed by Cuban Americans (1.6 million). Many other nations of Latin America are represented by smaller numbers.

Although the Hispanic population is increasing all over the country, most Hispanic Americans live in the Southwest. One of three Californians is Latino (in greater Los Angeles, almost half the people are Latino). National Map 11–3 on page 320 shows the distribution of the Hispanic, African American, Asian American, and Arab American populations across the United States.

Median family income for all Hispanics—$40,466 in 2008—stands well below the national average.[5] As the following sections explain, however, some categories of Hispanics have fared better than others.

Mexican Americans

Some Mexican Americans are descendants of people who lived in a part of Mexico annexed by the United States after the Mexican

---

[5]The 2008 median age of the U.S. Hispanic population was 27.7 years, far below the non-Hispanic white median of 41.1 years. This difference accounts for some of the disparity in income and education.

American War (1846–48). However, most Mexican Americans are recent immigrants. Today, more immigrants come to the United States from Mexico than from any other country.

Like many other immigrants, many Mexican Americans have worked as low-wage laborers, on farms or elsewhere. Table 11–5 shows that the 2008 median family income for Mexican Americans was $41,538, about two-thirds the national average. Almost one-fourth of Mexican American families are poor—nearly twice the national average. Finally, despite gains since 1980, Mexican Americans still have a high dropout rate and receive much less schooling, on average, than the U.S. population as a whole.

Puerto Ricans

The island of Puerto Rico, like the Philippines, became a U.S. possession when Spain was defeated at the end of the Spanish-American War in 1898. In 1917, Congress passed the Jones Act, which made Puerto Ricans (but not Filipinos) U.S. citizens and made Puerto Rico a territory of the United States.

New York City is home to more than 750,000 Puerto Ricans. About one-third of this community is severely disadvantaged. Adjusting to cultural patterns on the U.S. mainland—including, for many, learning English—is one major challenge; also, Puerto Ricans with darker skin encounter prejudice and discrimination. As a result, more people now return to Puerto Rico each year than arrive: Between 1990 and 2008, the Puerto Rican population of New York actually fell by more than 100,000 (Navarro, 2000; U.S. Census Bureau, 2009).

This "revolving door" pattern limits assimilation. Two out of three Puerto Rican families in the United States speak Spanish at home. Speaking only Spanish maintains a strong ethnic identity but limits economic opportunity. Puerto Ricans also have a much higher rate of woman-headed households than other Hispanics, a pattern that puts families at greater risk of poverty (U.S. Census Bureau, 2009).

Table 11–5 shows that the 2008 median family income for Puerto Ricans was $43,944, or about 71 percent of the national average. Although long-term mainland residents have made economic gains, more recent immigrants from Puerto Rico struggle to find work. Overall, Puerto Ricans remain the most socially disadvantaged Hispanic minority.

Cuban Americans

In little more than a decade after the 1959 Marxist revolution led by Fidel Castro, 400,000 Cubans had fled to the United States. Most settled with other Cuban Americans in Miami. Many immigrants were highly educated business and professional people who wasted little time becoming as successful in the United States as they had been in their homeland.

Table 11–5 shows that the median family income for Cuban Americans in 2008 was $51,290, above that of other Hispanics but still well below the national average. The 1.6 million Cuban Americans living in the United States today have managed a delicate balancing act, achieving in the larger society while holding on to much of their traditional culture. Of all Hispanics, Cubans are the most likely to speak Spanish in their homes: more than eight out of ten families do so. However, cultural distinctiveness and living in highly visible communities such as Miami's Little Havana provoke hostility from some people.

Arab Americans

Arab Americans are another U.S. minority whose numbers are increasing. Like Hispanic Americans, these are people whose ancestors lived in a variety of countries. What is sometimes called "the Arab world" includes twenty-two nations and stretches across northern Africa, from Mauritania and Morocco on Africa's west coast to Egypt and Sudan on Africa's east coast, and extends into the Middle East (western Asia), including Iraq and Saudi Arabia. Not all the people who live in these nations are Arabs, however; for example, the Berber people in Morocco and the Kurds of Iraq are not Arabs.

In 2010, claiming the federal government is not securing our borders, Arizona officials enacted a new law making law enforcement officials more proactive in determining the immigrant status of people they have a lawful reason to engage. While popular in Arizona, the new law drew the fire of critics who saw the law as an attack on people of Hispanic descent.

● Seeing Sociology
in Everyday Life

Look closely at the maps. Can you explain why various categories of people tend to be concentrated in certain regions of the United States?

● Making the Grade

Remember that Hispanic Americans are the largest racial/ethnic minority in the United States, representing more than 15 percent of the nation's population.

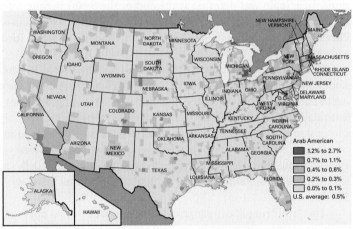

Seeing Ourselves

NATIONAL MAP 11–3

The Concentration of Hispanics or Latinos, African Americans, Asian Americans, and Arab Americans, by County

In 2008, people of Hispanic or Latino descent represented 15.4 percent of the U.S. population; 12.8 percent were African Americans, 4.6 percent Asian Americans, and 0.5 percent Arab Americans. These maps show the geographic distribution of these categories of people in 2000. Comparing them, we see that the southern half of the United States is home to far more minorities than the northern half. But do they all concentrate in the same areas? What patterns do the maps reveal?

Sources: U.S. Census Bureau (2001, 2009).

Arab cultures differ from society to society, but they share widespread use of the Arabic alphabet and language and have Islam as their dominant religion. But keep in mind that "Arab" (an ethnic category) is not the same as "Muslim" (a follower of Islam). A majority of the people living in most Arab countries are Muslims, but some Arabs are Christians or followers of other religions. In addition, most of the world's Muslims do not live in Africa or the Middle East and are not Arabs.

Because many of the world's nations have large Arab populations, immigration to the United States has created a culturally diverse population of Arab Americans. Some Arab Americans are Muslims and some are not; some speak Arabic and some do not; some maintain the traditions of their homeland and some do not. As is the case with Hispanic Americans and Asian Americans, some are recent immigrants and some have lived in this country for decades or even for generations.

Seeing Sociology in Everyday Life

Do you know of any highly educated immigrants who worked as professionals in their birth nations and who are now performing working-class jobs here in the United States? Why might immigrants have to do this?

Seeing Sociology in Everyday Life

Do any members of your family consider themselves to be "white ethnics"? Do you? Explain.

As noted back in Table 11–1, the government gives the official number of Arab Americans as 1.6 million, but because people may not declare their ethnic background, it is likely that the actual number is at least twice as high.[6] The largest populations of Arab Americans have ancestral ties to Lebanon (32 percent of all Arab Americans), Egypt (12 percent), and Syria (10 percent). Most Arab Americans (69 percent) report ancestral ties to one nation, but 30 percent report ancestors in more than one nation, which may include both Arab and non-Arab countries (U.S. Census Bureau, 2009). National Map 11–3 shows that the Arab American population is distributed throughout the United States.

Included in the Arab American population are people of all social classes. Some are highly educated professionals who work as physicians, engineers, and educators; others are working-class people who perform various skilled jobs in factories or on construction sites; still others do service work in restaurants, hospitals, or other settings or work in small family businesses. As shown in Table 11–6, median family income for Arab Americans is above the national average ($70,073 compared to the national median of $61,521 in 2008), but Arab Americans have a higher than average poverty rate (16.1 percent, versus 13.2 percent for the population as a whole). Arab Americans are highly educated; 46 percent have a college degree, compared to 30 percent of the adult population as a whole (U.S. Census Bureau, 2009).

There are large, visible Arab American communities in a number of U.S. cities, including New York, Chicago, Los Angeles, Houston, and Dearborn (Michigan). Even so, Arab Americans may choose to downplay their ethnicity as a way to avoid prejudice and discrimination. The fact that many of the recent terrorist attacks against the United States and other nations have been carried out by Arabs has fueled a stereotype that links being Arab (or Muslim) with being a terrorist. This stereotype, like all stereotypes, is unfair because it blames an entire category of people for the actions of a few individuals. But it is probably the reason that the social distance research discussed earlier in this chapter shows students expressing more negative attitudes toward Arabs than toward any other racial or ethnic category. It also helps explain why Arab Americans have been targets of an increasing number of hate crimes and why many Arab Americans feel that they are subject to "ethnic profiling" by police officers and security personnel that threatens their privacy and civil liberties (Ali & Juarez, 2003; Ali, Lipper, & Mack, 2004; Hagopian, 2004).

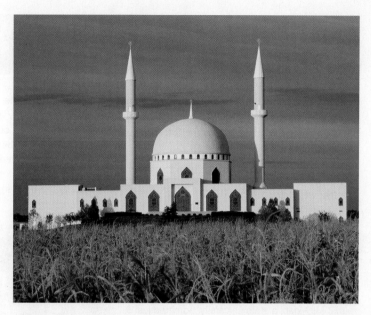

Arab American communities can be found in many large cities on the East and West Coasts of the United States, but the heaviest concentrations are found across the upper Midwest. This mosque rises above the cornfields in a rural area near Toledo, Ohio.

White Ethnic Americans

The term "white ethnics" recognizes the ethnic heritage and social disadvantages of many white people. White ethnics are non-WASPs whose ancestors lived in Ireland, Poland, Germany, Italy, or other European countries. More than half of the U.S. population falls into one or more white ethnic categories.

High rates of emigration from Europe in the nineteenth century first brought Germans and Irish and then Italians and Jews to this country. Despite cultural differences, all shared the hope that the United States would offer greater political freedom and economic opportunity than their homelands. Most did live better in this country, but the belief that "the streets of America were paved with gold" turned out to be a far cry from reality. Many immigrants found only hard labor for low wages.

White ethnics also endured their share of prejudice and discrimination. Many employers shut their doors to new immigrants, posting signs such as "None need apply but Americans" (Handlin, 1941:67). In 1921, Congress enacted a quota system that greatly limited immigration, especially by southern and eastern Europeans, who

Table 11–6 The Social Standing of Arab Americans, 2008

	Arab Americans	Entire U.S. Population
Median family income	$70,073	$61,521
Percentage in poverty	16.1%	13.2%
Completion of four or more years of college (age 25 and over)	45.5%	29.5%

Source: U.S. Census Bureau (2009).

---

[6]The 2008 median age for Arab Americans was 30.6 years, below the national median of 36.8 years.

● Seeing Sociology
in Everyday Life

Do you know your school's policy on affirmative action?

● Seeing Sociology
in Everyday Life

Do you support affirmative action in college admission for some or all minorities? Explain your point of view.

CONTROVERSY & DEBATE

Affirmative Action: Solution or Problem?

STEPHANIE: I think Barbara Gruttner got, well, a raw deal. She should have been admitted.

GINA: Perhaps. But diversity is important. I believe in affirmative action.

MARCO: Maybe some people do get into college more easily. But that includes guys like me whose father went here.

Barbara Gruttner, who is white, claimed that she was the victim of racial discrimination and that the University of Michigan Law School unfairly denied her application for admission while admitting many less qualified African American applicants. The basis of her claim was the fact that Michigan, a state university, admitted just 9 percent of white students with her grade point average and law school aptitude test scores while admitting 100 percent of African American applicants with comparable scores.

In 2003, the U.S. Supreme Court heard Gruttner's complaint in a review of the admissions policies of both the law school and the undergraduate program at the University of Michigan. In a six-to-three decision, the Court ruled against Gruttner, claiming that the University of Michigan Law School could use a policy of affirmative action that takes account of the race of applicants in the interest of creating a socially diverse student body. At the same time, however, the

Court struck down the university's undergraduate admissions policy, which awarded points not only for grades and college board scores but also for being a member of an underrepresented minority. A point system of this kind, the Court ruled, is too close to the rigid quota systems rejected by the Court in the past.

With this ruling, the Supreme Court continued to oppose quotalike systems while at the same time reaffirming the importance of racial diversity on campus. Thus colleges and universities can take account of race in order to increase the number of traditionally underrepresented students as long as race is treated as just one variable in a process that evaluates each applicant as an individual (Stout, 2003).

How did the controversial policy of affirmative action begin? The answer takes us back to the end of World War II, when the U.S. government funded higher education for veterans of all races. The so-called G.I. Bill held special promise for African Americans, most of whom needed financial assistance to enroll in college. By 1960, government funding helped 350,000 black men and women attend college.

There was just one problem: Even with advanced schooling, these individuals were not finding the kinds of jobs for which they were qualified. So the Kennedy administration devised a program of "affirmative action" to provide broader opportunities to qualified minorities. Businesses and universities were instructed to monitor hiring, promotion, and admissions policies to eliminate discrimination against minorities, even if unintended.

were likely to have darker skin and different cultural backgrounds than the dominant WASPs. This quota system continued until 1968.

In response to prejudice and discrimination, many white ethnics formed supportive residential enclaves. Some also gained footholds in businesses and trades: Italian Americans entered the construction industry, Irish Americans worked in construction and civil service jobs, Jews predominated in the garment industry, and many Greeks (like the Chinese) worked in the retail food business (W. M. Newman, 1973).

Many white ethnics still live in traditional working-class neighborhoods, although those who prospered have gradually assimilated. Most descendants of immigrants who labored in sweatshops and lived in crowded tenements now make enough money to lead comfortable lives. As a result, their ethnic heritage has become a source of pride.

Race and Ethnicity: Looking Ahead

The United States has been, and will remain, a land of immigrants. Immigration has brought striking cultural diversity and tales of hope, struggle, and success told in hundreds of languages.

Most immigrants arrived in a great wave that peaked about 1910. The next two generations brought economic gains and at least some assimilation. The government also extended citizenship to Native Americans (1924), foreign-born Filipinos (1942), Chinese Americans (1943), and Japanese Americans (1952).

Another wave of immigration began after World War II and swelled as the government relaxed immigration laws in the 1960s.

● Seeing Sociology in Everyday Life

Can you provide examples of xenophobia in our society today?

● Making the Grade

Reading the box below, be sure you see that the policy of affirmative action has changed over time, largely as the result of court decisions.

Defenders of affirmative action see it, first, as a sensible response to our nation's racial and ethnic history, especially for African Americans, who suffered through two centuries of slavery and a century of segregation under Jim Crow laws. Throughout our history, they claim, being white gave people a big advantage. They see minority preference today as a step toward fair compensation for unfair majority preference in the past.

Second, given our racial history, many analysts doubt that the United States will ever become a color-blind society. They claim that because prejudice and discrimination are rooted deep in U.S. culture, simply claiming that we are color-blind does not mean that everyone will be treated fairly.

Third, supporters maintain that affirmative action has worked. Where would minorities be today if the government had not enacted this policy in the 1960s? Major employers, such as fire and police departments in large cities, began hiring minorities and women for the first time only because of affirmative action. This program has helped expand the African American middle class and increased racial diversity on college campuses and in the workplace.

Only about 10 percent of white people say they support racial preferences for African Americans. Even among African Americans themselves, just 46 percent support this policy

(NORC, 2009). Critics point out, first of all, that affirmative action was intended as a temporary remedy to ensure fair competition but soon became a system of "group preferences" and quotas—in short, a form of "reverse discrimination," favoring people not because of talent and effort but because of race, ethnicity, or sex.

Second, critics say, if racial preferences were wrong in the past, they are wrong now. Why should whites today, many of whom are far from privileged, be penalized for past discrimination that was in no way their fault? Our society has undone most of the institutional prejudice and discrimination of earlier times—doesn't the election of an African American president suggest that? Giving entire categories of people special treatment compromises standards of excellence and calls into question the real accomplishments of minorities.

A third argument against affirmative action is that it benefits those who need it least. Favoring minority-owned corporations or holding places in law school helps already privileged people. Affirmative action has done little for the African American underclass that needs the most help.

There are good arguments for and against affirmative action, and people who want our society to have more racial and ethnic equality fall on both sides of the debate. Voters in a num-

ber of states, including California, Washington, Michigan, and Nebraska, have passed ballot initiatives banning the use of affirmative action based on gender or race. In 2008, however, voters in Colorado voted down such a proposal. So the country remains divided on this issue. The disagreement is not whether people of all backgrounds should have equal opportunity but whether the current policy of affirmative action is part of the solution or part of the problem.

WHAT DO YOU THINK?

1. In view of the fact that society has historically favored males over females and whites over people of color, would you agree that white males have received more "affirmative action" than anyone? Why or why not?

2. Should affirmative action include only disadvantaged categories of minorities (say, African Americans and Native Americans) and exclude more affluent categories (such as Japanese Americans)? Why or why not?

3. Do you think the election of Barack Obama as the nation's first African American president suggests that affirmative action is no longer needed? Why or why not?

Sources: Bowen & Bok (1999), Kantrowitz & Wingert (2003), Flynn (2008), Leff (2008), and NORC (2009).

Today, about 1.5 million people come to the United States each year—about 1.1 million legally and another 400,000 illegally. This is almost twice the number that arrived during the "Great Immigration" a century ago (although newcomers now enter a country that has five times as many people). Most of today's immigrants come not from Europe but from Latin America and Asia, with Mexicans, Chinese, Indians, and Filipinos arriving in the largest numbers.

Many new arrivals face much the same prejudice and discrimination experienced by those who came before them. In 1994, California voters passed Proposition 187, which stated that illegal immigrants should be denied health care, social services, and public education; it was later overturned in federal court. More recently, voters there mandated that all children learn English in school. Some landowners in the

Southwest have taken up arms to discourage illegal immigrants crossing the border from Mexico. Even so, we continue to debate how to best deal with the more than 12 million illegal immigrants already here.

Even minorities who have been in the United States for generations feel the sting of prejudice and discrimination. Affirmative action, a policy meant to provide opportunities for racial and ethnic minorities, is also hotly debated, as the Controversy & Debate box describes.

Like those of earlier generations, today's immigrants hope to blend into U.S. society without completely giving up their traditional culture. Some still build racial and ethnic enclaves, so the Little Havanas and Koreatowns of today stand alongside the Little Italys and Chinatowns of the past. In addition, new arrivals carry the hope that racial and ethnic diversity can be a source of pride rather than a badge of inferiority.

Seeing Sociology in Everyday Life

Is our society becoming more accepting of racially and ethnically mixed couples and friendship groups?

As the social distance research presented in this chapter shows, today's college students express greater acceptance of social diversity. Look at the two corporate advertisements shown here. What evidence of greater acceptance do you see? In your opinion, does this evidence mean that our society has really changed? Why or why not?

Here's an ad from 1957, when the civil rights movement was just getting under way. Based on what you have read in this chapter, how does this reflect what U.S. society was like fifty years ago in terms of racial segregation?

> **HINT** On the face of it, today's ads suggest far greater racial and ethnic tolerance than was true in the 1950s, when we rarely saw images of people of different categories interacting with one another. The social distance research noted in this chapter also supports the idea that tolerance is increasing. Being more racially inclusive is also a smart business policy, in light of of the increasing economic resources of various minority categories of the U.S. population.

Especially in the case of advertising aimed at young people, racial and ethnic mixing has become the rule. How accurately does this image reflect everyday life? Do you think young people differ from older people in their degree of social tolerance? Explain.

Applying SOCIOLOGY in Everyday Life

1. Thinking about your own campus, can you point to ways in which race does not matter in students' lives? In what ways does race still matter? On balance, how important is race today?

2. Does your college or university take account of race and ethnicity in its admissions policies? Ask to speak with an admissions officer to see what you can learn about your school's use of race and ethnicity in admissions. Ask whether there is a "legacy" policy that favors children of parents who attended the school.

3. Give several of your friends or family members a quick quiz, asking them what share of the U.S. population is white, Hispanic, African American, and Asian (see Table 11–1 on page 302). You will probably find that most white people exaggerate the size of the African American population (C. A. Gallagher, 2003). Why do you think this is so?

Making the Grade

CHAPTER 11 Race and Ethnicity   ◉ Watch on mysoclab.com

The Social Meaning of Race and Ethnicity

RACE refers to socially constructed categories based on biological traits a society defines as important.

- The meaning and importance of race vary from place to place and over time.
- Societies use racial categories to rank people in a hierarchy, giving some people more money, power, and prestige than others.
- In the past, scientists created three broad categories—Caucasoids, Mongoloids,and Negroids—but there are no biologically pure races.

pp. 300–2

ETHNICITY refers to socially constructed categories based on cultural traits a society defines as important.

- Ethnicity reflects common ancestors, language, and religion.
- The importance of ethnicity varies from place to place and over time.
- People choose to play up or play down their ethnicity.
- Societies may or may not set categories of people apart based on differences in ethnicity.

pp. 302–3

race (p. 300) a socially constructed category of people who share biologically transmitted traits that members of a society consider important

ethnicity (p. 302) a shared cultural heritage

minority (p. 303) any category of people distinguished by physical or cultural difference that a society sets apart and subordinates

Minorities are people of various racial and ethnic categories who are visually distinctive and disadvantaged by a society (p. 303).

◈ Explore on mysoclab.com

Prejudice and Stereotypes

PREJUDICE is a rigid and unfair generalization about a category of people.

- The social distance scale is one measure of prejudice.
- One type of prejudice is the **STEREOTYPE,** a simplified description applied to every person in some category.
- **RACISM,** a very destructive type of prejudice, asserts that one race is innately superior or inferior to another.

pp. 303–7

There are four **THEORIES OF PREJUDICE:**

- **Scapegoat theory** claims that prejudice results from frustration among people who are disadvantaged.
- **Authoritarian personality theory** (Adorno) claims that prejudice is a personality trait of certain individuals, especially those with little education and those raised by cold and demanding parents.
- **Culture theory** (Bogardus) claims that prejudice is rooted in culture; we learn to feel greater social distance from some categories of people.
- **Conflict theory** claims that prejudice is a tool used by powerful people to divide and control the population.

pp. 307–9

prejudice (p. 304) a rigid and unfair generalization about an entire category of people

stereotype (p. 304) a simplified description applied to every person in some category

racism (p. 305) the belief that one racial category is innately superior or inferior to another

scapegoat (p. 308) a person or category of people, typically with little power, whom other people unfairly blame for their own troubles

Discrimination

DISCRIMINATION is treating various categories of people unequally.

- Prejudice refers to *attitudes*; discrimination involves *actions*.
- Institutional prejudice and discrimination is bias built into the operation of society's institutions, including schools, hospitals, the police, and the workplace.
- Prejudice and discrimination perpetuate themselves in a vicious circle, resulting in social disadvantage that fuels additional prejudice and discrimination.

pp. 309–10

discrimination (p. 309) unequal treatment of various categories of people

institutional prejudice and discrimination (p. 309) bias built into the operation of society's institutions

 Read on mysoclab.com

Majority and Minority: Patterns of Interaction

PLURALISM requires that racial and ethnic categories, although distinct, have roughly equal social standing.

- U.S. society is pluralistic in that all people in the United States, regardless of race or ethnicity, have equal standing under the law.
- U.S. society is not pluralistic in that all racial and ethnic categories do not have equal social standing.

p. 310

ASSIMILATION is the process by which minorities gradually adopt the patterns of the dominant culture.

- Assimilation involves changes in dress, language, religion, values, and friends.
- Assimilation is a strategy to escape prejudice and discrimination and to achieve upward social mobility.
- Some categories of people have assimilated more than others.

pp. 310–11

pluralism (p. 310) a state in which people of all races and ethnicities are distinct but have equal social standing

assimilation (p. 310) the process by which minorities gradually adopt patterns of the dominant culture

miscegenation (p. 311) biological reproduction by partners of different racial categories

segregation (p. 311) the physical and social separation of categories of people

genocide (p. 311) the systematic killing of one category of people by another

SEGREGATION is the physical and social separation of categories of people.

- Although some segregation is voluntary (for example, the Amish), majorities usually segregate minorities by excluding them from neighborhoods, schools, and occupations.
- *De jure* segregation is segregation by law; *de facto* segregation describes settings that contain only people of one category.
- Hypersegregation means having little social contact with people beyond the local community.

p. 311

GENOCIDE is the systematic killing of one category of people by another.

- Historical examples of genocide include the extermination of Jews by the Nazis and the killing of Western-leaning people in Cambodia by Pol Pot.
- Recent examples of genocide include Hutus killing Tutsis in the African nation of Rwanda, Serbs killing Bosnians in the Balkans of Eastern Europe, and the systematic killing in the Darfur region of Sudan.

p. 311

Race and Ethnicity in the United States

NATIVE AMERICANS, the earliest human inhabitants of the Americas, have endured genocide, segregation, and forced assimilation. Today, the social standing of Native Americans is well below the national average.

pp. 312–13

WHITE ANGLO-SAXON PROTESTANTS (WASPs) were most of the original European settlers of the United States, and many continue to enjoy high social position today.

pp. 313–14

AFRICAN AMERICANS experienced two centuries of slavery. Emancipation in 1865 gave way to segregation by law (the so-called Jim Crow laws). In the 1950s and 1960s, a national civil rights movement resulted in legislation that outlawed segregated schools and overt discrimination in employment and public accommodations. Today, despite legal equality, African Americans are still disadvantaged.

pp. 314–16

ASIAN AMERICANS have suffered both racial and ethnic hostility. Although some prejudice and discrimination continue, both Chinese and Japanese Americans now have above-average income and schooling. Asian immigrants—especially Chinese, Indians, and Filipinos—now account for more than one-third of all immigration to the United States.

pp. 316–18

HISPANIC AMERICANS OR LATINOS, the largest U.S. minority, include manyethnicities sharing a Spanish heritage. Mexican Americans, the largest Hispanicminority, are concentrated in the Southwest and are the poorest Hispanic category. Cubans, concentrated in Miami, are the most affluent Hispanic category.

pp. 318–19

ARAB AMERICANS are a growing U.S. minority. Because they come to the United States from so many different nations, Arab Americans are a culturally diverse population, and they are represented in all social classes. They have been a target of prejudice and hate crimes in recent years as a result of a stereotype that links all Arab Americans with terrorism.

pp. 319–21

WHITE ETHNIC AMERICANS are non-WASPs whose ancestors emigrated from Europe in the nineteenth and twentieth centuries. In response to prejudice and discrimination, many white ethnics formed supportive residential enclaves.

pp. 321–22

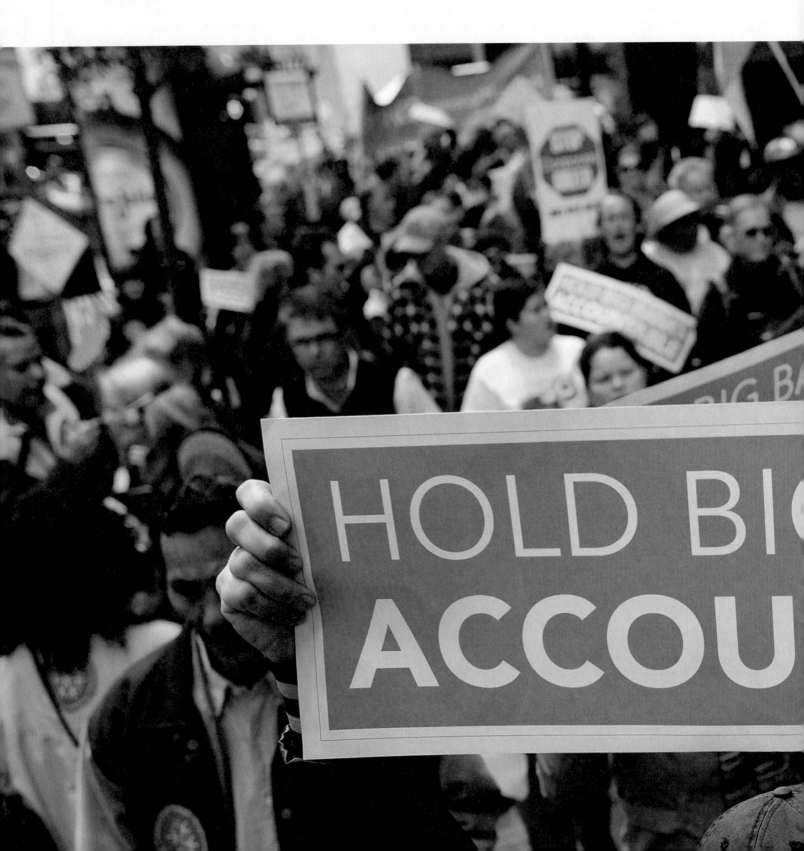

12 Economics and Politics

- What is a social institution?

- How does change in the economy reshape society?

- Why do some critics say the United States is not really a democracy?

Watch the Core Concepts in Sociology video "Money and Politics" on mysoclab.com

This chapter explores the operation of the economy, a major social institution, and explains how changes in economic production have reshaped society. The chapter then examines politics, a second major social institution, with attention to the character and causes of war and terrorism.

Here's a quick quiz about the U.S. economy. (Hint: All six questions have the same right answer.)

- Which business do 137 million people in the United States visit each week?
- Which business sells the products of more than 61,000 companies?
- Which U.S. company, on average, opens a new or remodeled store every day?
- Which U.S. company buys more than $18 billion worth of goods each year from China, which, if the company were a country, would be China's seventh largest trading partner?
- Which U.S. company created 33,000 new jobs domestically (and another 30,000 in other countries) in 2008?
- Which single company actually grew in size during the recent economic downturn?

The answer, of course, is Walmart, the global discount store chain founded by Sam Walton, who opened his first store in Arkansas in 1962. In 2009, Walmart announced revenues of $401 billion in annual sales through more than 4,000 stores in the United States and 3,615 stores in other countries from Brazil to China, making it the second-largest corporation in the nation.

But not everyone is pleased with the expansion of Walmart. Across the United States, many people have joined a social movement to keep Walmart out of their local communities, fearing the loss of local businesses and, in some cases, local culture. Critics claim that the merchandising giant pays low wages, keeps out unions, and sells many products made in sweatshops abroad. In 2010, a federal court ruled that a Walmart would go to trial to defend against claims by women of sex discrimination (Saporito, 2003; Walsh, 2007; A. Clark, 2010; Walmart, 2010).

This chapter explores the economy and the closely related institution of politics. A number of very large corporations, including Walmart, are at the center of the U.S. economy, raising questions about just how the economy operates, whose interests it ought to serve, and to what extent big business shapes the political life of the United States.

Economics and politics are **social institutions,** *major spheres of social life or societal subsystems organized to meet human needs.* The two chapters that follow consider other social institutions: Chapter 13 focuses on family and religion, and Chapter 14 highlights education, health, and medicine. These discussions explain how social institutions have changed over the course of history, describe how they operate today, and point out controversies that are likely to shape them tomorrow.

The Economy: Historical Overview

The **economy** is *the social institution that organizes a society's production, distribution, and consumption of goods and services.* The economy operates, for better or worse, in a generally predictable manner. *Goods* are commodities ranging from necessities (such as food, clothing, and shelter) to luxury items (such as cars, swimming pools, and yachts). *Services* are activities that benefit people (including the work

of priests, physicians, teachers, and computer software specialists). Three times in the past, technological revolutions reorganized the economy and, in the process, transformed social life.

The Agricultural Revolution

As Chapter 2 ("Culture") explained, the earliest societies were made up of hunters and gatherers living off the land. In these technologically simple societies, there was no distinct economy; producing and consuming were part of family life.

Harnessing animals to plows around 5,000 years ago permitted the development of agriculture, which was fifty times more productive than hunting and gathering. The resulting surpluses meant that not everyone had to produce food, so many people took on other specialized work: making tools, raising animals, and building dwellings. Soon towns sprang up, linked by networks of traders dealing in food, animals, and other goods. These four factors—agricultural technology, specialized work, permanent settlements, and trade—made the economy a distinct social institution.

The Industrial Revolution

By the mid-eighteenth century, a second technological revolution was under way, starting in England and spreading to the United States

Seeing Sociology in Everyday Life

Can you list several jobs in today's economy that represent industrial work and postindustrial work?

social institution a major sphere of social life or societal subsystem, organized to meet human needs

economy the social institution that organizes a society's production, distribution, and consumption of goods and services

postindustrial economy a productive system based on service work and high technology

and elsewhere. Industrialization changed the economy in five fundamental ways:

1. **New sources of energy.** Throughout history, "energy" had meant the muscle power of people or animals. Then, in 1765, the English inventor James Watt introduced the steam engine. A hundred times more powerful than animal muscles, early steam engines soon drove heavy machinery.

2. **Centralization of work in factories.** Steam-powered machinery moved work from homes to factories, centralized workplaces that housed the machines.

3. **Manufacturing and mass production.** Before the Industrial Revolution, most people grew or gathered raw materials such as grain, wood, or wool. In an industrial economy, the focus shifts so that most people turn raw materials into a wide range of finished products such as furniture and clothing.

4. **Specialization.** Centuries ago, people worked at home making products from start to finish. In the factory, a laborer repeats a single task over and over, making only a small contribution to the finished product.

5. **Wage labor.** Instead of working for themselves, factory workers became wage laborers working for strangers, who often cared less for them than for the machines they operated.

The Industrial Revolution gradually raised the standard of living as countless new products fueled an expanding marketplace. Yet the benefits of industrial technology were shared very unequally, especially at the beginning. Some factory owners made huge fortunes, while the majority of industrial workers lived close to poverty. Children, too, worked in factories or in coal mines for pennies a day. As time went on, workers formed labor unions to represent their interests collectively to factory owners. In the twentieth century, new laws banned child labor, set minimum wage levels, improved workplace safety, and extended schooling and political rights to a larger segment of the population.

The Information Revolution and Postindustrial Society

By about 1950, the nature of production was changing once again. The United States was creating a **postindustrial economy,** *a productive system based on service work and high technology.* Automated machinery (and later, robotics) reduced the role of human labor in factory production and expanded the ranks of clerical workers and managers. The postindustrial era is marked by a shift from industrial work to service work.

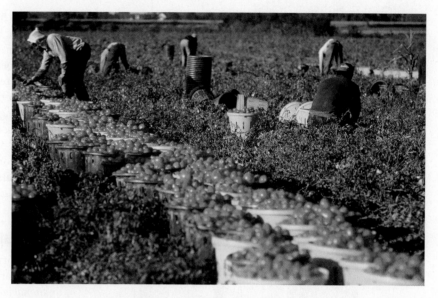

As societies industrialize, a smaller share of the labor force works in agriculture. In the United States, much of the agricultural work that remains is performed by immigrants from lower-income nations. These farm workers from Mexico travel throughout Florida during the tomato harvest.

Driving this economic change is a third technological breakthrough: the computer. Just as the Industrial Revolution did two-and-a-half centuries ago, the Information Revolution has introduced new kinds of products and new forms of communication and has changed the character of work. There have been three significant changes:

1. **From tangible products to ideas.** The industrial era was defined by the production of goods; in the postindustrial era, people work with symbols. Computer programmers, writers, financial analysts, advertising executives, architects, editors, and various types of consultants make up more of the labor force in the information age.

2. **From mechanical skills to literacy skills.** The Industrial Revolution required mechanical skills, but the Information Revolution requires literacy skills: speaking and writing well and, of course, knowing how to use a computer. People able to communicate effectively are likely to do well; people without these skills face fewer opportunities.

3. **From factories to almost anywhere.** Industrial technology drew workers to factories located near power sources, but computer technology allows people to work almost anywhere. Laptop and wireless computers and cell phones now turn the home, car, or even an airplane into a "virtual office." What this means for everyday life is that new information technology blurs the line between our lives at work and at home.

Global Snapshot

In high-income nations such as the United States, almost three out of four jobs are in the tertiary or service sector of the economy.

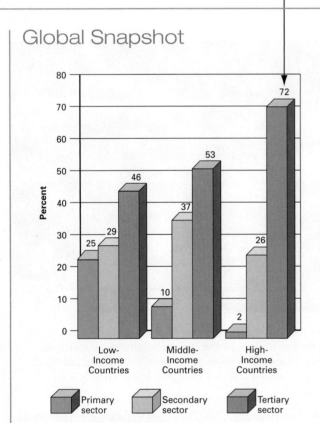

FIGURE 12–1 **The Size of Economic Sectors, by National Income Level**

As countries become richer, the primary sector becomes a smaller part of the economy and the tertiary or service sector becomes larger.

Source: Estimates based on World Bank (2009).

Sectors of the Economy

The three revolutions just described reflect a shifting balance among the three sectors of a society's economy. The **primary sector** is *the part of the economy that draws raw materials from the natural environment.* The primary sector—agriculture, raising animals, fishing, forestry, and mining—is largest in low-income nations. Figure 12–1 shows that 25 percent of the economic output of low-income countries is in the primary sector, compared with 10 percent of economic activity among middle-income nations and just 2 percent in high-income countries like the United States.

The **secondary sector** is *the part of the economy that transforms raw materials into manufactured goods.* This sector expands quickly as societies industrialize. It includes operations such as refining petroleum into gasoline and turning metals into tools and automobiles. The globalization of industry means that just about all the world's

countries have a significant share of workers employed in the secondary sector. Figure 12–1 shows that the secondary sector now accounts for a greater share of economic output in middle-income nations than it does in high-income countries.

The **tertiary sector** is *the part of the economy that involves services rather than goods.* The tertiary sector grows with industrialization, accounting for 46 percent of economic output in low-income countries, 53 percent in middle-income countries, and 72 percent in high-income countries. About 80 percent of the U.S. labor force is in service work, including secretarial and clerical jobs and work in food service, sales, law, health care, advertising, and teaching (U.S. Department of Labor, 2009).

The Global Economy

New information technology is drawing people around the world together and creating a **global economy,** *economic activity that crosses national borders.* The development of a global economy has five major consequences.

First, we see a global division of labor: Different regions of the world specialize in one sector of economic activity. As Global Map 12–1 shows, agriculture represents about half the total economic output of the world's poorest countries. Global Map 12–2 shows that most of the economic output of high-income countries, including the United States, is in the service sector. In short, the world's poorest nations specialize in producing raw materials, and the richest nations specialize in the production of services.

Second, an increasing number of products pass through more than one nation. Look no further than your morning coffee: The beans may have been grown in Colombia and transported to New Orleans on a freighter that was registered in Liberia, made in a shipyard in Japan using steel from Korea, and fueled by oil from Venezuela.

Third, national governments no longer control the economic activity that takes place within their borders. In fact, governments cannot even accurately regulate the value of their national currencies because dollars, euros, pounds sterling, and yen are traded around the clock in the financial markets of New York, London, and Tokyo.

A fourth consequence of the global economy is that a small number of businesses operating internationally now control a vast share of the world's economic activity. Using the latest available data, the 1,500 largest multinational companies account for half the world's economic output (DeCarlo, 2009; World Bank, 2010).

Fifth and finally, the globalization of the economy raises concerns about the rights and opportunities of workers. Critics of this trend claim that the United States is losing jobs—especially factory

Window on the World

GLOBAL MAP 12–1

Agricultural Employment in Global Perspective

The primary sector of the economy is largest in the nations that are least developed. In the poor countries of Africa and Asia, up to half of all workers are farmers. This picture is altogether different in the world's most economically developed countries—including the United States, Canada, Great Britain, and Australia—which have a mere 2 percent of their labor force in agriculture.

Source: Data from International Labour Organization (2010).

GLOBAL MAP 12–2

Service-Sector Employment in Global Perspective

The tertiary sector of the economy becomes larger as a nation's income level rises. In the United States, Canada, the countries of Western Europe, much of South America, Australia, and Japan, about two-thirds of the labor force performs service work.

Source: Data from International Labour Organization (2010).

jobs—to low-income nations. This means that workers here face lower wages and higher unemployment. At the same time, many workers abroad are paid extremely low wages. As a result, say critics, the global expansion of capitalism threatens the well-being of workers throughout the world.

The world is still divided into 194 politically distinct nations. But the rising level of international economic activity makes nationhood less significant than it was even a decade ago.

Economic Systems: Paths to Justice

October 20, Saigon, Vietnam. Sailing up the narrow Saigon River is an unsettling experience for anyone who came of age in the 1960s. People like me need to remember that Vietnam is a country, not a war, and that nearly forty years have passed since the last U.S. helicopter lifted off the rooftop of the U.S. embassy, ending our country's presence there.

Saigon is now a boomtown. Neon signs bathe the city's waterfront in color; hotels, bankrolled by Western corporations, push skyward from a dozen construction sites; taxi meters record fares in U.S. dollars, not Vietnamese dong; and Visa and American Express stickers decorate the doors of trendy restaurants and fashionable shops that cater to tourists from Japan, France, and the United States.

There is heavy irony here: After decades of fighting, millions of lives lost on both sides, and the victory of Communist forces, the Vietnamese are doing an about-face and turning toward capitalism. What we see today is what might well have happened had the U.S. forces won the war.

Every society's economic system makes a statement about justice by determining who is entitled to what. Two general economic models are capitalism and socialism. However, no nation anywhere in the world has an economy that is completely one or the other; rather, capitalism and socialism are two ends of a continuum along which all real-world economies can be located. We will look at each of these models in turn.

Capitalism

Capitalism is *an economic system in which natural resources and the means of producing goods and services are privately owned.* An ideal capitalist economy has three distinctive features:

1. **Private ownership of property.** In a capitalist economy, individuals can own almost anything. The more capitalist an economy is, the more private ownership there is of wealth-producing property such as factories, real estate, and natural resources.

2. **Pursuit of personal profit.** A capitalist society seeks to create profit and wealth. The profit motive is the reason people take new jobs, open new businesses, or try to improve products. Making money is considered the natural way of economic life. Just as important, the Scottish philosopher Adam Smith (1723–1790) claimed that as individuals pursue their self-interest, the entire society prospers (1937, orig. 1776).

3. **Competition and consumer choice.** A purely capitalist economy is a free-market system with no government interference (sometimes called a *laissez-faire economy,* from the French words meaning "leave it alone"). Adam Smith stated that a freely competitive economy regulates itself by the "invisible hand" of the law of supply and demand.

Consumers guide a market economy, Smith explained, by selecting the goods and services offering the greatest value. As producers compete for the customer's business, they provide the highest-quality goods at the lowest possible prices. In Smith's time-honored phrase, from narrow self-interest comes "the greatest good for the greatest number of people." Government control of an economy, on the other hand, distorts market forces by reducing the quantity and quality of goods, shortchanging consumers in the process.

Justice in a capitalist system amounts to freedom of the marketplace, where anyone can produce, invest, buy, and sell according to individual self-interest. The increasing popularity of Walmart, described in the opening to this chapter, reflects the fact that the company's customers think they get a lot for their money when shopping there.

The United States is considered a capitalist nation because most businesses are privately owned. However, it is not completely capitalist because the government plays a large role in the economy. The government owns and operates a number of businesses, including almost all of this country's schools, roads, parks, museums, the U.S. Postal Service, the Amtrak railroad system, and the entire U.S. military. The U.S. government also had a major hand in building the Internet. In addition, governments use taxation and other forms of regulation to influence what companies produce, to control the quality and cost of merchandise, and to motivate consumers to conserve natural resources.

The U.S. government also sets minimum wage levels, enforces workplace safety standards, regulates corporate mergers, provides farm price supports, taxes everyone on what they earn, and also supplements the income of a majority of its people in the form of Social Security, public assistance, student loans, and veterans' benefits. Local, state, and federal governments combined are the nation's biggest employer, with 17 percent of the nonfarm labor force on their payrolls (U.S. Bureau of Labor Statistics, 2010).

Socialism

Socialism is *an economic system in which natural resources and the means of producing goods and services are collectively owned.* In its ideal form, a socialist economy rejects each of the three characteristics of capitalism just described in favor of three opposite features:

1. **Collective ownership of property.** A socialist economy limits rights to private property, especially property used to generate income. Government controls such property and makes housing and other goods available to all, not just to the people with the most money.

2. **Pursuit of collective goals.** The individualistic pursuit of profit goes against the collective orientation of socialism. What

○ Making the Grade

What do you see as advantages and disadvantages of capitalism and socialism?

Capitalism still thrives in Hong Kong (*left*), evident in streets choked with advertising and shoppers. Socialism is more the rule in China's capital, Beijing (*right*), a city dominated by government buildings rather than a downtown business district.

capitalism celebrates as the "entrepreneurial spirit," socialism condemns as greed; individuals are urged to work for the common good of all.

3. **Government control of the economy.** Socialism rejects capitalism's laissez-faire approach in favor of a *centrally controlled* or *command economy* operated by the government. Commercial advertising thus plays little role in socialist economies.

Justice in a socialist context means not competing to gain wealth but meeting everyone's basic needs in a roughly equal manner. From a socialist point of view, the common capitalist practice of giving workers as little in wages and benefits as possible to boost company earnings is unjust because it puts profits before people.

North Korea and more than two dozen other nations in Asia, Africa, and Latin America model their economies on socialism, placing almost all wealth-generating property under state control (Miller, Holmes, & Kim, 2010). The extent of world socialism declined during the 1990s as countries in Eastern Europe and the former Soviet Union geared their economies toward a market system. More recently, however, voters in Bolivia, Venezuela, Ecuador, and other nations in South America have elected leaders who are moving the national economies in a socialist direction.

Welfare Capitalism and State Capitalism

Most of the nations in Western Europe—especially Sweden, Denmark, and Italy—have market-based economies but also offer broad social welfare programs. Analysts call this third type of economic

system **welfare capitalism,** *an economic and political system that combines a mostly market-based economy with extensive social welfare programs.*

Under welfare capitalism, a nation's government owns some of the largest industries and services, such as transportation, the mass media, and health care. In Sweden and Italy, about 12 percent of economic production is *nationalized,* under state control. Most industry is left in private hands, but all economic activity is subject to extensive government regulation. High taxation (aimed especially at the rich) funds a wide range of social welfare programs, including universal health care and child care, that benefit the entire population (Olsen, 1996; CQ Press, 2009).

Another alternative is **state capitalism,** *an economic and political system in which companies are privately owned but cooperate closely with the government.* State capitalism is the rule in the nations along the Pacific Rim. Japan, South Korea, and Singapore are all capitalist countries, but their governments work in partnership with large companies, supplying financial assistance and controlling foreign imports to help their businesses compete in world markets (Gerlach, 1992).

Relative Advantages of Capitalism and Socialism

Which economic system works best? Comparing economic models is difficult because all nations mix capitalism and socialism to varying degrees. In addition, nations differ in cultural attitudes toward work, access to natural resources, levels of technological development, and

Making the Grade

Both capitalism and socialism have advantages and disadvantages. One general point on which most experts agree is that capitalism is more productive and socialism generates more social equality.

Seeing Sociology
in Everyday Life

Do you think the United States is moving toward capitalism or socialism at the moment? Explain.

Directly comparing the economic performance of capitalism and socialism is difficult because nations differ in many ways. But a satellite image of socialist North Korea and capitalist South Korea at night shows the dramatically different electrical output of the two nations, one indication of economic activity.

patterns of trade. Despite such complicating factors, some crude comparisons are revealing.

Economic Productivity

One key dimension of economic performance is productivity. A commonly used measure of economic output is *gross domestic product* (GDP), the total value of all goods and services produced within the nation's borders each year. Per capita (per-person) GDP allows us to compare the economic performance of nations of different population sizes.

The output of mostly capitalist countries in the late 1980s—before the end of socialist economies in the Soviet Union and Eastern Europe—varied somewhat but averaged about $13,500 per person. The comparable figure for the mostly socialist former Soviet Union and nations of Eastern Europe was about $5,000. This means that the capitalist countries outproduced the socialist nations by a ratio of 2.7 to 1 (United Nations Development Programme, 1990).

A recent comparison of socialist North Korea (per capita GDP of $1,800) and capitalist South Korea ($24,801) provides an even sharper contrast (United Nations Development Programme, 2009; Central Intelligence Agency, 2010).

Economic Equality

The distribution of resources within the population is another important measure of how well an economic system works. A comparative study of Europe in the mid-1970s, when that region was split between mostly capitalist and mostly socialist countries, compared the earnings of the richest 5 percent of the population and the poorest 5 percent (Wiles, 1977). Societies with mostly capitalist economies had an income ratio of about 10 to 1; the figure for socialist countries was 5 to 1. In other words, capitalist economies support a higher overall standard of living but with greater income inequality. Said another way, socialist economies create more economic equality but provide a lower overall living standard.

Personal Freedom

One additional consideration in evaluating capitalism and socialism is the personal freedom each system gives its people. Capitalism emphasizes the *freedom to pursue self-interest* and depends on the ability of producers and consumers to interact with little interference by the state. Socialism, by contrast, emphasizes *freedom from basic want*. The goal of equality requires the state to regulate the economy, which in turn limits personal choices and opportunities for citizens.

Can a single society offer both political freedom and economic equality? In the capitalist United States, our political system offers many personal freedoms, but the economy generates a lot of inequality, and freedom is not worth as much to a poor person as to a rich one. By contrast, North Korea or Cuba has considerable economic equality, but people cannot speak out or travel freely within or outside of the country. Perhaps the closest any countries have come to "having it all" is Denmark—the Thinking Globally box takes a closer look.

Changes in Socialist and Capitalist Countries

In 1989 and 1990, the nations of Eastern Europe, which had been seized by the former Soviet Union at the end of World War II, overthrew their socialist regimes. These nations—including the former German Democratic Republic (East Germany), the Czech Republic, Slovakia, Hungary, Romania, and Bulgaria—are all moving toward capitalist market systems after decades of state-controlled economies. At the end of 1991, the Soviet Union itself formally dissolved, and many of its former republics introduced some free-market principles into their economies. Within a decade, three-fourths of former Soviet

THINKING GLOBALLY

Want Equality and Freedom? Try Denmark

Denmark is a small nation in northwestern Europe with about 5.5 million people. This country is a good example of the economic and political system called welfare capitalism, in which a market economy is mixed with broad government programs that provide for the welfare of all Danish people.

Most Danes consider life in their country to be very good. There is a high standard of living—Denmark's per-person GDP is $36,130, which lags a bit behind the figure of $45,592 for the United States. But Denmark has only 60 percent as much income inequality as we have in this country. Its unemployment rate for 2009 was 6.4 percent, lower than the 9.3 percent in the United States.

Low inequality and low unemployment are largely the result of government regulation of the economy. Taxes in Denmark are the highest in the world, with most people paying about 40 percent of their income in taxes and those earning over about $70,000 paying more than 50 percent. That's in addition to a sales tax of 25 percent on everything people buy. These high taxes increase economic equality (by taking more taxes from the rich and giving more benefits to the poor), and they also allow the government to fund the social welfare programs that provide benefits to everyone. For example, every Danish citizen is

To enable men and women to work for income, the government of Denmark grants paid child-care leave to both fathers and mothers.

entitled to government-funded schooling and government-funded health care, and each worker receives at least five weeks of paid vacation leave each year. People who lose their jobs receive about 90 percent of their prior income from the government for up to four years.

Many people—especially the Danes themselves—feel that Denmark offers an ideal mix of political freedom (Danes have extensive political rights and elect their leaders) and economic security (all citizens benefit from extensive government services and programs).

WHAT DO YOU THINK?

1. What evidence of less income inequality might you expect to see in Denmark if you were to visit that country?

2. Would you be willing to pay most of your income in taxes if the government provided you with benefits such as schooling and health care? Why or why not?

3. Do you think most people in the United States would like to have our society become more like Denmark? Why or why not?

government enterprises were partly or entirely in private hands (Montaigne, 2001).

There were many reasons for these sweeping changes. First, the capitalist economies far outproduced their socialist counterparts. The socialist economies were successful in achieving economic equality, but living standards were low compared with those of Western Europe. Second, Soviet socialism was heavy-handed, rigidly controlling the media and restricting individual freedoms. In other words, socialism did away with *economic* elites, as Karl Marx predicted, but as Max Weber foresaw, socialism increased the power of *political* elites.

So far, the market reforms in Eastern Europe are proceeding unevenly. Some nations (Czech Republic, Slovakia, Poland, and the Baltic states of Latvia, Estonia, and Lithuania) are doing relatively well. But other countries (Romania, Bulgaria, and the Russian Federation) have been buffeted by price increases and falling living standards. Officials hope that expanding production will gradually bring

a turnaround. However, the introduction of a market economy has brought with it an increase in economic inequality (Ignatius, 2008; World Bank, 2008).

A number of countries, primarily in South America, have recently been heading in a more socialist direction. In 2005, the people of Bolivia elected Evo Morales, a former farmer, union leader, and activist, as their new president, over a wealthy business leader who was educated in the United States. This election placed Bolivia in a group of South American nations—including Ecuador, Venezuela, Brazil, Chile, and Uruguay—that are moving toward more socialist economies. The reasons for the shift toward socialism vary from country to country, but the common element is economic inequality. In Bolivia, for example, the economy has grown in recent decades, but most of the benefits have gone to a wealthy business elite. By contrast, more than half the country's people remain very poor (Howden, 2005).

Seeing Sociology in Everyday Life

Have you or someone in your family ever been a member of a labor union? What advantages or disadvantages did union membership provide?

Go to the Multimedia Library at **mysoclab.com** to see author John Macionis describe the changing nature of work

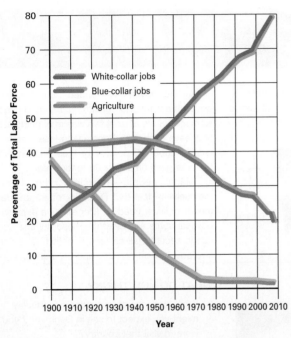

FIGURE 12–2 The Changing Pattern of Work in the United States, 1900–2009

Compared to a century ago, when the economy involved a larger share of factory and farm work, making a living in the United States now involves mostly white-collar service jobs.

Source: Estimates based on U.S. Department of Labor (2010).

Work in the Postindustrial U.S. Economy

Economic change is occurring not just in the socialist world but also in the United States. In 2009, a total of 138 million people in this country—58 percent of those aged sixteen and over—were working for income. A larger share of men (63 percent) than women (54 percent) had jobs, a gap that is holding steady over time. Among men, 57.3 percent of African Americans were employed, compared with 67.2 percent of whites, and 71.9 percent of Hispanics. Among women, 54.5 percent of African Americans were employed, compared with 55.9 percent of whites and 53.2 percent of Hispanics; 60.2 percent of Asian men and women were employed (U.S. Department of Labor, 2010).

The Changing Workplace

In 1900, roughly 40 percent of U.S. workers were farmers. In 2009, 1.6 percent were in agriculture. The family farm of yesterday has been replaced by *corporate agribusinesses.* Land is now more productive, but this change has caused painful adjustments across the country as a way of life is lost (Dudley, 2000). Figure 12–2 illustrates the shrinking role of the primary sector in the U.S. economy.

A century ago, industrialization swelled the ranks of blue-collar workers. By 1950, however, a white-collar revolution had moved most workers from factories into service occupations. By 2009, some 80 percent of the labor force worked in the service sector, and almost all new jobs were being created in this sector (U.S. Department of Labor, 2009).

As Chapter 8 ("Social Stratification") explained, much service work—including sales, clerical positions, and work in hospitals and restaurants—pays much less than older factory jobs. This means that many jobs in the postindustrial era provide only a modest standard of living. Women and other minorities, as well as many young people just starting their working careers, are the most likely to have jobs doing low-paying service work (Kalleberg, Reskin, & Hudson, 2000; Greenhouse, 2006). ● Go to **mysoclab.com**

Labor Unions

The changing U.S. economy has seen a decline in *labor unions,* organizations that seek to improve wages and working conditions. During the Great Depression of the 1930s, union membership increased rapidly until it reached more than one-third of nonfarm workers by 1950. Union rolls peaked around 1970 at almost 25 million. Since then, membership has declined to about 12.3 percent of nonfarm workers, or some 15.3 million men and women. Looking more closely, 37.4 percent of government workers are members of unions, compared with just 7.2 percent of private (nongovernment) workers (Clawson & Clawson, 1999; U.S. Department of Labor, 2010).

The pattern of union decline holds in most other high-income countries, yet unions claim a far smaller share of workers in the United States than elsewhere. Union membership is around 18 percent in Japan, between 20 and 40 percent in much of Europe, and 29 percent in Canada, and it reaches a high of 71 percent in Sweden (Visser, 2006; OECD, 2010).

The widespread decline in union membership in the United States reflects the shrinking industrial sector of the economy. Newer service jobs—such as sales jobs at retailers like Walmart, described in the opening to this chapter—are unlikely to be unionized. Citing low wages and worker complaints, unions are trying to organize Walmart employees, so far without winning over a single store. The weak economy of the past few years has given unions a short-term boost. The Obama administration is supporting new laws that may make it easier for workers to form unions. But long-term gains probably depend on the ability of unions to adapt to the new global economy. Union members in the United States, used to seeing foreign workers as "the enemy," will have to build new international alliances (Rousseau, 2002; Dalmia, 2008; M. Allen, 2009).

Professions

All kinds of jobs today are called *professional;* there are professional tennis players, professional housecleaners, and even professional exterminators. As distinct from an *amateur* (from the Latin for "lover," meaning one who acts out of love for the activity itself), a professional performs some task to earn a living. But what exactly is a profession?

A **profession** is *a prestigious white-collar occupation that requires extensive formal education.* People performing this kind of work make a *profession,* or public declaration, of their willingness to work according to certain principles. Professions include the ministry, medicine, law, academia, and fields such as architecture, accountancy, and social work. An occupation is considered a profession to the extent that it demonstrates four basic characteristics (W. J. Goode, 1960; Ritzer & Walczak, 1990):

1. **Theoretical knowledge.** Professionals have a theoretical understanding of their field rather than mere technical training. Anyone can master first-aid skills, for example, but doctors have a theoretical understanding of human health. This means that although playing tennis, cleaning houses, and exterminating insects may be important, they do not really qualify as professions.

2. **Self-regulating practice.** The typical professional is self-employed, "in private practice" rather than working for a company. Professionals oversee their own work and observe a code of ethics.

3. **Authority over clients.** Because of their expertise, professionals are sought out by clients, who value their advice and follow their directions.

4. **Community orientation rather than self-interest.** The traditional professing of duty states an intention to serve the community rather than merely to seek income.

In almost all cases, professional work requires not just a college degree but a graduate degree. Not surprisingly, professions are well represented among the jobs beginning college students say they hope to get after graduation, as shown in Figure 12–3.

Many occupations that do not qualify as true professions nonetheless seek to *professionalize* their services. Claiming professional standing usually begins by renaming the work to suggest special, theoretical knowledge, moving the field away from its original, lesser reputation. Stockroom workers become "inventory supply managers," and exterminators are reborn as "insect control specialists."

Interested parties may also form a professional association that certifies their skills. The organization then licenses its members,

> In a society such as ours, with so many different types of work, no one career attracts the interest of more than a small share of today's students.

Student Snapshot

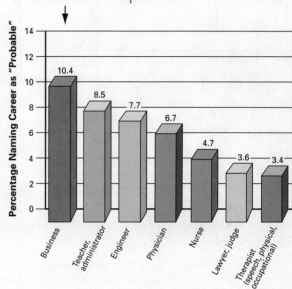

FIGURE 12–3 **The Careers Most Commonly Named as Probable by First-Year College Students, 2009**

Today's college students expect to enter careers that pay well and carry high prestige.

Source: Pryor et al. (2009).

writes a code of ethics, and emphasizes the work's importance in the community. To win public acceptance, a professional association may also establish schools or other training facilities and perhaps start a professional journal. Not all occupations try to claim professional status. Some *paraprofessionals,* including paralegals and medical technicians, have specialized skills but lack the extensive theoretical education required of full professionals.

Self-Employment

Self-employment—earning a living without being on the payroll of a large organization—was once common in the United States. About 80 percent of the labor force was self-employed in 1800, compared with just 7 percent of workers today (8.4 percent of men and 5.0 percent of women) (U.S. Department of Labor, 2010).

Lawyers, physicians, architects, and other professionals are well represented among the ranks of the self-employed in the United States. But most self-employed workers are small business owners, plumbers, farmers, carpenters, freelance writers and editors, artists, and long-distance truck drivers. In all, the self-employed are more likely to have blue-collar than white-collar jobs.

Seeing Sociology
in Everyday Life

Has the current recession affected you or members of your
family? Explain.

Go to the Multimedia Library at **mysoclab.com**
to view the video "Consequences of Poverty"

In the film *Up in the Air,* George Clooney plays the character Ryan Bingham, a corporate "downsizer." In this role, Bingham travels around the country presiding over layoffs and is paid by company executives who are too cowardly to fire people themselves. In your opinion, what do companies owe their employees—just pay for work performed, or is everyone entitled to broader job security?

Women own 28 percent of this nation's small businesses, and the share is rising. The 6.5 million firms owned by U.S. women employ almost 7 percent of the labor force and generate close to $1 trillion in annual sales (U.S. Small Business Administration, 2006).

Unemployment and Underemployment

Every society has some level of unemployment. For one thing, few young people entering the labor force find a job right away; workers may leave their jobs to seek new work or to stay at home raising children; others may be on strike or suffer from long-term illnesses; and still others lack the skills to perform useful work.

But unemployment is not just an individual problem; it is also caused by the economy. Jobs disappear as occupations become obsolete and companies change the way they operate. Since 1980, the 500 largest U.S. businesses eliminated more than 5 million jobs while creating even more new ones.

Generally, companies downsize to become more competitive or close down entirely in the face of foreign competition or economic recession. During the recession that began in 2008 in the United States, several million jobs were lost, with unemployment rising in just about every part of the economy. Jobs have been lost not only by blue-collar workers but also by white-collar workers who had typically weathered downturns in the past (U.S. Department of Labor, 2010).

In 2008, just as the country was falling into recession, 7 million people over the age of sixteen were unemployed, about 4.6 percent of the civilian labor force (U.S. Department of Labor, 2008b). But by the end of 2009, more than 15 million were unemployed, pushing the unemployment rate to 10 percent. In some regions of the country, especially rural areas, unemployment rates are usually far worse—about double the national average.

Figure 12–4 shows that unemployment among African Americans (14.8 percent) is nearly twice the rate among white people (8.5 percent). Among all categories of people, unemployment is lower among whites than among African Americans, although the gap between white and black teenagers is especially large. For all categories of people, a good way to reduce the risk of unemployment is to earn a college degree: As the figure shows, the unemployment rate for college graduates is around 4.5 percent—less than half the national average.

Underemployment is also a problem for millions of workers. In an era of corporate bankruptcy, the failure of large banks, and downsizing by companies throughout the U.S. economy, millions of workers—the lucky ones who still have their jobs—have been left with lower salaries, fewer benefits such as health insurance, and disappearing pensions. Rising global competition, weaker worker organizations, and economic recession have combined to allow many people to keep their jobs only by agreeing to cutbacks in pay or to the loss of other benefits (K. Clark, 2002; Gutierrez, 2007; McGeehan, 2009).

In addition, the government reports that more than 28 million people work part time, defined as less than thirty-five hours a week. Although most say they are satisfied with this arrangement, at least one-third claim that they want more work but cannot find it (U.S. Department of Labor, 2010). In all, as the country struggles to climb out of the recent recession, it is likely that one in five workers is working less than what is desired, is out of work and looking for a job, or is a "discouraged worker" who has given up entirely. ● Go to **mysoclab.com**

Workplace Diversity: Race and Gender

In the past, white men were the mainstay of the U.S. labor force. However, the nation's proportion of minorities is rising rapidly. The African American population is increasing faster than the population of non-Hispanic white people. The rate of increase in the Asian American and Hispanic populations is even greater.

Such dramatic changes are likely to affect U.S. society in countless ways. Not only will more and more workers be women and

Can you think of advantages and disadvantages of being able to work almost anywhere? Do the benefits of the "anywhere office" outweigh the downsides?

> The best strategy to reduce your risk of being without a job is to complete a college education.

minorities, but the workplace will have to develop programs and policies that meet the needs of a socially diverse workforce and also encourage everyone to work together effectively and respectfully. The Thinking About Diversity box on page 342 takes a closer look at some of the issues involved in our changing workplace.

New Information Technology and Work

> **July 2, Ticonderoga, New York.** The manager of the local hardware store scans the bar codes of a bagful of items. "The computer doesn't just total the costs," she explains. "It also keeps track of inventory, places orders with the warehouse, and decides which products to continue to sell and which to drop." "Sounds like what you used to do, Maureen," I respond with a smile. "Yep," she nods, with no smile at all.

Another workplace issue is the increasing role of computers and other new information technology. The Information Revolution is changing what people do in a number of ways (Rule & Brantley, 1992; Vallas & Beck, 1996):

1. **Computers are deskilling labor.** Just as industrial machines replaced the master craftsworkers of an earlier era, computers now threaten the skills of managers. More business operations are based not on executive decisions but on computer modeling. In other words, a machine decides whether to place an order, stock a dress in a certain size and color, or approve a loan application.

2. **Computers are making work more abstract.** Most industrial workers have a hands-on relationship with their product. Postindustrial workers use symbols to perform abstract tasks, such as making a company more profitable or making software more user-friendly.

3. **Computers limit workplace interaction.** Spending time at computer terminals, workers become isolated from one another.

4. **Computers increase employers' control of workers.** Computers allow supervisors to check employees' output continuously, whether they work at keyboard terminals or on assembly lines.

5. **Computers allow companies to relocate work.** Because computer technology allows information to flow almost anywhere instantly, the symbolic work in today's economy may not take place where we might think. We have all had the experience of calling a business (for instance, a hotel or bookstore) located in our own town only to find out that we are talking to a person at a computer workstation thousands of miles away. Computer

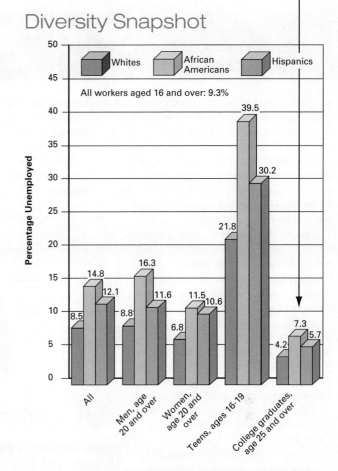

Diversity Snapshot

FIGURE 12–4 Official U.S. Unemployment Rates for Various Categories of Adults, 2009

Although college graduates have a low risk of unemployment, race is related to unemployment for all categories of people.

Source: U.S. Department of Labor (2010).

technology provides the means to outsource many jobs—especially service work—to other places where wages may be lower.

Perhaps in the wake of widespread failures on Wall Street, there will be a trend away from allowing computers to manage risk, putting responsibility for business decisions back in the hands of people (Kivant, 2008). Or perhaps both computers and people have flaws that will always prevent us from living in a perfect world. But the rapidly increasing reliance on computers in business reminds us that new technology is never socially neutral. It changes the relationships between people in the workplace, shapes the way we work, and often

corporation an organization with a legal existence, including rights and liabilities, separate from that of its members

Corporation are one example of the formal organizations discussed in Chapter 5, "Groups and Organizations."

THINKING ABOUT DIVERSITY: RACE, CLASS, & GENDER

Twenty-First-Century Diversity: Changes in the Workplace

An upward trend in the U.S. minority population is changing the workplace. As the figure shows, the number of non-Hispanic white men in the U.S. labor force will rise by less than 1 percent between 2010 and 2018, but the number of African American men will increase by 9 percent, the number of Hispanic men will increase by 25 percent, and the number of Asian men will increase by 22 percent.

Among non-Hispanic white women, the projected rise is less than 1 percent; among African American women, 10 percent; and among Asian women, 24 percent. Hispanic women will show the greatest gains, estimated at 30 percent.

Within a decade, non-Hispanic white men will represent 34 percent of all workers, and that figure will continue to drop. As a result, companies that welcome social diversity will tap the largest pool of talent and enjoy a competitive advantage leading to higher profits (Graybow, 2007; Toossi, 2007; Harford, 2008; U.S. Department of Labor, 2009).

Welcoming social diversity means, first, recruiting talented workers of both sexes and all racial and cultural backgrounds. But developing the potential of all employees requires meeting the needs of women and

other minorities, which may not be the same as those of white men. For example, child care at the workplace is a big issue for working mothers with small children.

Second, businesses must develop effective ways to deal with tension that arises from social differences. They will have to work harder to

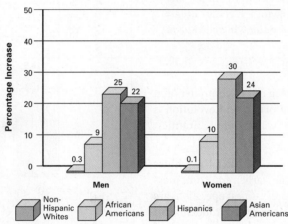

Projected Increase in the Number of People in the U.S. Labor Force, 2010–2018

Looking ahead, the share of minorities in the U.S. labor force will increase much faster than the share of white men and women.

Source: U.S. Department of Labor (2009).

ensure that workers are treated equally and respectfully, which means having zero tolerance for racial or sexual harassment.

Third, companies will have to rethink current promotion practices. At present, 72 percent of the directors of *Fortune* 100 companies are white men; 28 percent are women or other minorities (Executive Leadership Council, 2008). In a survey of U.S. companies, the U.S. Equal Employment Opportunity Commission (2009) confirmed that non-Hispanic white men, who make up 33 percent of adults aged twenty-five to sixty-four, hold 53 percent of management jobs; the comparable figures are 34 and 29 percent, respectively, for non-Hispanic white women, 12 and 7 percent for non-Hispanic African Americans, and 14 and 6 percent for Hispanics.

WHAT DO YOU THINK?

1. What underlying factors are increasing the social diversity of the U.S. workplace?

2. In what specific ways do you think businesses should support minority workers?

3. In what other settings (such as schools) is social diversity becoming

---

alters the balance of power between employers and employees. Understandably, then, people welcome some aspects of the Information Revolution and oppose others.

Corporations

At the core of today's capitalist economy is the **corporation,** *an organization with a legal existence, including rights and liabilities, separate from that of its members.* Incorporating makes an organization a legal entity, able to enter into contracts and own property. Of the more than 30 million businesses in the United States, 6 million are incorporated (U.S. Census Bureau, 2009). Incorporating protects the wealth

of owners from lawsuits that result from business debts or harm to consumers; it can also mean a lower tax rate on the company's profits.

Economic Concentration

Most U.S. corporations are small, with assets of less than $500,000, so it is the largest corporations that dominate our nation's economy. In 2006, the government listed 2,568 corporations with assets exceeding $2.5 billion, representing 80 percent of all corporate assets (Internal Revenue Service, 2009).

The largest U.S. corporation, measured in terms of sales, is Exxon Mobil, with 2009 revenue of more than $440 billion. This is more money than the combined tax revenues collected by forty-three states.

monopoly the domination of a market by a single producer

oligopoly the domination of a market by a few producers

Seeing Sociology in Everyday Life

Have you ever had a job like that shown in the photo below? What were the advantages and disadvantages of such work?

Second in line is Walmart, with annual sales of more than $400 billion.

Conglomerates and Corporate Linkages

Economic concentration creates *conglomerates,* giant corporations composed of many smaller corporations. Conglomerates form as corporations enter new markets, spin off new companies, or merge with other companies. For example, PepsiCo is a conglomerate that includes Pepsi-Cola, Frito-Lay, Gatorade, Tropicana, and Quaker.

Many conglomerates are linked because they own each other's stock, the result being worldwide corporate alliances of staggering size. Until 2009, General Motors, for example, owned Opel (Germany), Vauxhall (Great Britain), Saab (Sweden), and a share of Daewoo (South Korea) and had partnerships with Suzuki and Toyota (Japan). Similarly, Ford owned Volvo (Sweden) and still maintains a small interest in Aston Martin (Great Britain) and Mazda (Japan).

Corporations are also linked through *interlocking directorates,* networks of people who serve as directors of many corporations (Weidenbaum, 1995; Kono et al., 1998). These boardroom connections provide access to valuable information about other companies' products and marketing strategies. While perfectly legal, such linkages encourage illegal activity, such as price fixing, as companies share information about their pricing policies.

Corporations: Are They Competitive?

According to the capitalist model, businesses operate independently in a competitive market. But in light of the extensive linkages that exist between them, it is obvious that large corporations do not operate independently. Also, a few large corporations dominate many markets, so they are not truly competitive.

Federal law forbids any company from establishing a **monopoly,** *domination of a market by a single producer,* because with no competition, such a company could simply charge whatever is wanted for its products. But **oligopoly,** *domination of a market by a few producers,* is both legal and common. Oligopoly arises because the huge investment needed to enter a major market, such as the auto industry, is beyond the reach of all but the biggest companies. In addition, true competition involves risk, which big business tries to avoid.

The federal government seeks to regulate corporations in order to protect the public interest. Yet as corporate scandals have shown—most recently, involving the housing mortgage business and the collapse of so many banks—regulation is often too little too late, resulting in harm to millions of people. The U.S. government is also the

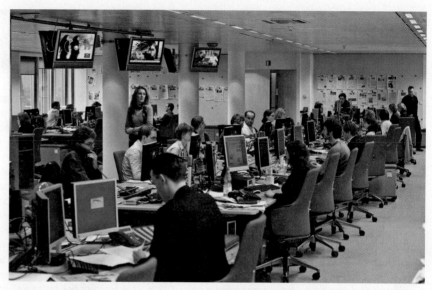

In today's corporate world, computers are changing the nature of work just as factories did more than a century ago. In what ways is computer-based work different from factory work? In what ways do you think it is very much the same?

corporate world's single biggest customer, and in 2008 and 2009, it stepped in to support many struggling corporations with multibillion-dollar bailout programs. Especially during tough economic times, the public tends to support a greater role for the government in the economy (Sachs, 2009).

Corporations and the Global Economy

Corporations have grown so large that they now account for most of the world's economic output. The biggest corporations are based in the United States, Japan, and Western Europe, but their marketplace is the entire world. Many large companies such as McDonald's and the chipmaker Intel earn most of their money outside the United States.

Global corporations know that poor countries contain most of the world's people and resources. In addition, labor costs there are attractively low: A manufacturing worker in Mexico, who earns about $2.88 an hour, labors for more than a week to earn about what a worker in Japan (who averages about $19.68 an hour) or the United States ($24.03 an hour) earns in a single day (U.S. Department of Labor, 2009).

As Chapter 9 ("Global Stratification") explained, the impact of multinational corporations on low-income countries is controversial. Modernization theorists claim that multinational corporations, by unleashing the great productivity of capitalism, raise living standards in poor nations, offering tax revenues, capital investment, new jobs, and advanced technology that together accelerate economic growth (Berger, 1986; Firebaugh & Beck, 1994; Firebaugh & Sandu, 1998).

○ Making the Grade

Supporters of a market economy point to the productive efficiency of the market; critics point to the market's effects in generating economic inequality.

○ Seeing Sociology in Everyday Life

Compare National Map 12–1 with National Map 15–1 on page 448. The regions losing jobs (such as the Great Plains) are also losing population (especially young people), which is why the average person there is older.

CONTROVERSY & DEBATE

The Market: Does the "Invisible Hand" Look Out for Us or Pick Our Pockets?

The market or government planning? Governments rely on one or the other to determine the products and services companies will produce and what people will consume. So important is this question that the answer has much to do with how nations define themselves, choose their allies, and identify their enemies.

Historically, U.S. society has relied on the "invisible hand" of the market to make economic decisions. Market dynamics move prices up or down according to the supply of products and buyer demand. The market thus links the efforts of countless people, each of whom—to restate Adam Smith's insight—is motivated only by self-interest. Defenders of the market system—including the economists Milton Friedman and Rose Friedman (1980)—claim that a more or less freely operating market system is the key to this country's high standard of living.

But others point to the contributions government makes to the U.S. economy. First, government must step in to carry out tasks that no private company could do as well, such as defending the country against enemies abroad or terrorists at home. Government (in partnership with private companies) also plays a key role in building and maintaining public projects such as roads, utilities, schools, libraries, and museums.

The Friedmans counter that whatever the task, government usually ends up being very inefficient. They claim that for most people, the least satisfying goods and services available today—public schools, the postal service, and passenger railroad service—are government-operated. The products we enjoy most—household appliances, computers and other electronics, fashionable clothes—are products of the market. The Friedmans and other supporters of free markets believe that minimal state regulation serves the public interest best.

But supporters of government intervention in the economy make other arguments. First, they claim that the market has incentives to produce only what is profitable. Few private companies set out to meet the needs of poor people because by definition, poor people have little money to spend.

Second, the market has certain self-destructive tendencies that only the government can curb. In 1890, for example, the government passed the Sherman Antitrust Act to break up the monopolies that controlled the nation's oil and steel production. In the decades since then—and especially after President Franklin Roosevelt's New Deal of the 1930s—government has taken a strong regulatory role to control inflation (by setting interest rates), enhance the well-being of workers (by imposing workplace safety standards), and benefit consumers (by setting standards for product quality). Especially after the failure of the market to prevent a serious economic downturn in 2008, the public voiced support

To what extent do you think government regulation of the economy is necessary?

for a larger government presence in the national economy.

Third, because the market magnifies social inequality, the government must step in on the side of social justice. Since capitalist economies concentrate income and wealth in the hands of a few, it is necessary for government to tax the rich at a higher rate to ensure that wealth reaches more of the population.

Does the market's "invisible hand" look out for us or pick our pockets? Although most people in the United States favor a free market, they also support government intervention that benefits the public. In recent years, public confidence in corporations has fallen, and confidence in the federal government has gone up. Government's job is not only to ensure national security but also to maintain economic stability. The Obama administration claims that the government needs to expand its efforts to put people to work by, for example, repairing the nation's roads and bridges as well as developing new sources of energy.

During the 1980s, support for the free market was strong; today, we see a swing back to support for a larger government role in the economy. In the decades to come, we should expect to see people in the United States, and also around the world, continuing to debate the best balance of market forces and government decision making.

WHAT DO YOU THINK?

1. Do you agree or disagree with the statement that "the government is best that governs least"? Why?

2. Do you think people support less government control of the economy in good times and more government control in bad times? Why or why not?

3. In what ways has the Obama administration expanded the role of government in the U.S. economy? What about the auto industry? The regulation of Wall Street?

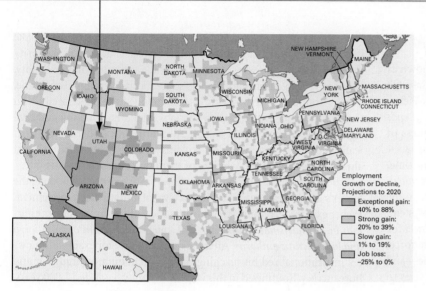

Leon Acosta, age 23 and just out of college, has relocated to Park City, Utah, where he has found a good job and lots of friends his own age.

⊕ Explore dominant industries in your local community and in counties across the United States on mysoclab.com

Employment Growth or Decline, Projections to 2020

■ Exceptional gain: 40% to 88%

□ Strong gain: 20% to 39%

□ Slow gain: 1% to 19%

■ Job loss: −25% to 0%

Seeing Ourselves

NATIONAL MAP 12–1
Where the Jobs Will Be: Projections to 2020

The economic prospects for people living in counties across the United States are not the same. Gains in jobs are projected to be strong for most areas in the Western states as well as for Florida; some areas in the East and the Midwest are also expected to gain jobs. But job growth will be slow at best in the midsection of the country, with a number of counties even projected to lose jobs in the years to come.

⊕ Explore on mysoclab.com

Source: Woods & Poole Economics, Washington, D.C. Copyright © 2007.

Dependency theorists respond that multinationals in fact make global inequality worse by blocking the development of local industries and by pushing poor countries to produce goods for export rather than food and other products for local people. From this standpoint, multinationals make poor nations increasingly dependent on rich nations (Wallerstein, 1979; Dixon & Boswell, 1996; Kentor, 1998).

In short, modernization theory praises the market as the key to progress and affluence for all the world's people. Dependency theory takes a different position, calling for replacing markets with government-based economic policies. The Controversy & Debate box takes a closer look at the issue of market versus government economies.

The Economy: Looking Ahead

Social institutions are a society's ways of meeting people's needs. But as we have seen, the U.S. economy only partly succeeds in this mission. As the years go by, our economy experiences alternating periods of expansion and recession. And in both good times and bad, our economy provides for some people much better than for others.

One important trend that underlies change in the economy is the Information Revolution. First, the share of the U.S. labor force engaged in manufacturing is less than half of what it was in 1960; service work, especially computer-related jobs, makes up the difference. For industrial workers, the postindustrial economy has brought unemployment and declining wages. Our society must face up to the challenge of providing millions of men and women with the language and computer skills they need to succeed in the modern economy. Yet in recent years, millions of people in "good" service jobs have found themselves out of work. In addition, there are regional differences in the economic outlook: National Map 12–1 shows

which regions are projected to gain jobs and which are expected to lose them by the year 2020.

A second transformation of recent years is the expansion of the global economy. Two centuries ago, the ups and downs people experienced reflected events and trends in their own town. One century ago, communities were economically linked so that one town's prosperity depended on producing goods demanded by people elsewhere in the country. Today, we have to look beyond the national economy because, for example, the historical rise in the cost of gasoline at our local gas station has as much to do with increasing demand for oil around the world, especially in India and China. As both producers and consumers, we are now subject to factors and forces that are both distant and unseen.

Finally, analysts around the world are rethinking conventional economic models. The global economy shows that socialism is less productive than capitalism, one important reason behind the collapse of socialist regimes in Eastern Europe and the Soviet Union. But capitalism has its own problems, including high levels of inequality and a steady stream of corporate scandal—two important reasons that the economy now operates with significant government regulation.

What will be the long-term effects of all these changes? Two conclusions seem certain. First, the economic future of the United States and other nations will be played out in a global arena. The new postindustrial economy in the United States has emerged as more industrial production has moved to other nations. Second, it is imperative that we address the urgent challenges of global inequality and population increase. Whether the world reduces or enlarges the gap between rich and poor societies may well steer our planet toward peace or war.

politics the social institution that distributes power, sets a society's goals, and makes decisions

government a formal organization that directs the political life of a society

power the ability to achieve desired ends despite resistance from others

authority power that people perceive as legitimate rather than coercive

routinization of charisma the transformation of charismatic authority into some combination of traditional and bureaucratic authority

Seeing Sociology in Everyday Life

Why do you think there are no monarchies in North and South America?

Politics: Historical Overview

There is a close link between economics and **politics** (also known as the "polity"), *the social institution that distributes power, sets a society's goals, and makes decisions.* Early in the twentieth century, Max Weber (1978, orig. 1921) defined **power** as *the ability to achieve desired ends despite resistance from others.* The use of power is the business of **government,** *a formal organization that directs the political life of a society.* Governments typically claim to help people, but at the same time, governments demand that people obey the rules. Yet, as Weber noted, most governments do not openly threaten their people. Most of the time, people respect (or at least accept) their society's political system.

No government, Weber explained, is likely to keep its power for very long if compliance comes only from the threat of brute force, because there could never be enough police to watch everyone—and who would watch the police? Every government therefore tries to make itself seem legitimate in the eyes of the public.

This brings us to the concept of **authority,** *power that people perceive as legitimate rather than coercive.* A society's source of authority depends on its economy. According to Weber, preindustrial societies rely on *traditional authority,* power legitimized by respect for long-established cultural patterns. Woven into a society's collective memory, traditional authority may seem almost sacred. Chinese emperors in centuries past were legitimized by tradition, as were the nobles in medieval Europe.

Traditional authority declines as societies industrialize. For example, royal families still exist in ten European nations, but the democratic cultures of countries such as the United Kingdom, Sweden, and Denmark have shifted power to commoners elected to office. Weber explained that the expansion of rational bureaucracy is the modern foundation of authority. *Rational-legal authority* (sometimes called *bureaucratic authority*) is power legitimized by rationally enacted law.

Traditional authority is tied to family; rational-legal authority flows from offices in governments. A traditional monarch passes power on to heirs; a modern president takes office and gives up power according to law.

Weber described one additional type of authority that has surfaced throughout history. *Charismatic authority* is power legitimized by

Monarchy is linked to both religion and family. In 2004, the coronation ceremony of Cambodia's first new king in fifty years, Norodom Sihamoni, included a religious ritual performed by his father.

the extraordinary personal qualities—the *charisma*—of a leader. Unlike its traditional and rational-legal counterparts, charismatic authority depends less on a person's ancestry or office and more on personality. Followers see in charismatic leaders some special, perhaps even divine, power. Examples of charismatic leaders include Jesus of Nazareth; Nazi Germany's Adolf Hitler; India's liberator, Mahatma Gandhi; and civil rights leader Martin Luther King Jr. All charismatic leaders aim to radically transform society, which explains why charismatics are almost always controversial and why few of them die of old age.

Because charismatic authority flows from a single individual, the leader's death creates a crisis. The survival of a charismatic movement, Weber explained, requires the **routinization of charisma:** *the transformation of charismatic authority into some combination of traditional and bureaucratic authority.* After the death of Jesus, for example, followers institutionalized his teachings in a church, built on tradition and bureaucracy. Routinized in this way, Christianity has lasted 2,000 years.

Politics in Global Perspective

The world's political systems differ in countless ways. Generally, however, they fall into four categories: monarchy, democracy, authoritarianism, and totalitarianism.

Monarchy

Monarchy (with Latin and Greek roots meaning "one ruler") is *a political system in which a single family rules from generation to generation.* Monarchy is commonly found in agrarian societies; for example, the Bible tells of great kings such as David and Solomon. In the world today, twenty-seven nations have royal families; most trace their ancestry back centuries. In Weber's analysis, then, monarchy is legitimized by tradition.

During the Middle Ages, *absolute monarchs* in much of the world claimed a monopoly of power based on divine right (or God's will). In some nations—including Oman, Saudi Arabia, and Swaziland—monarchs (not necessarily with divine support) still exercise virtually absolute control over their people.

With industrialization, however, monarchs gradually pass from the scene in favor of elected officials. All the European societies with royal families today are *constitutional monarchies,* meaning that their monarchs are little more than

Go to the Multimedia Library at **mysoclab.com** to view the ABC/*Nightline* video "Old-Fashioned Democracy"

monarchy a political system in which a single family rules from generation to generation

democracy a political system that gives power to the people as a whole

authoritarianism a political system that denies the people participation in government

totalitarianism (p. 348) a highly centralized political system that extensively regulates people's lives

symbolic heads of state; actual governing is the responsibility of elected officials, led by a prime minister and guided by a constitution. In these countries, nobility *reigns*, but elected officials actually *rule*.

Democracy

The historical trend throughout most of the world has been toward **democracy,** *a political system that gives power to the people as a whole.* Because it is unrealistic to expect all citizens to be involved in governing, our system is in fact a *representative democracy*, which puts authority in the hands of leaders who from time to time compete for office in elections.

Most high-income countries of the world, including those that still have royal families, claim to be democratic. Industrialization and democracy go together because both require a literate populace. Also, with industrialization, the traditional legitimization of power in a monarchy gives way to rational-legal authority. Thus democracy and rational-legal authority are linked just like monarchy and traditional authority.

But high-income countries such as the United States are not truly democratic, for two reasons. First, there is the problem of bureaucracy. The U.S. federal government has 2.7 million regular employees and several million more paid for by special funding. Add to this the 1.45 million uniformed service personnel and 64,000 legislative and judicial branch personnel—more than 4 million workers in all. Another 19.7 million people work in 89,500 local governments across the country. Most of the officials who run the government are never elected by anyone and do not have to answer directly to the people.

The second problem involves economic inequality: Rich people have far more political power than poor people. Most of our political leaders have been wealthy men and women, and in politics, "money talks." Given the even greater resources of billion-dollar corporations, how well does our "democratic" system listen to the voices of "average people"? ● Go to **mysoclab.com**

Still, democratic nations do provide many rights and freedoms. Global Map 12–3 on page 348 shows one assessment of political freedom around the world. According to Freedom House, an organization that tracks political trends, eighty-nine of the world's nations (with 46 percent of the global population) were "free," respecting many civil liberties, in 2009. This represents a gain for democracy: Just eighty-five nations were free a decade earlier (Freedom House, 2010).

Authoritarianism

Some governments prevent their people from having any voice in politics. **Authoritarianism** is *a political system that denies the people participation in government.* An authoritarian government is indifferent to people's needs and offers them no voice in selecting leaders. The absolute monarchies in Saudi Arabia and Oman are authoritarian, as is the military junta in Ethiopia.

Totalitarianism

October 30, Beijing, China. Several U.S. students are sitting around a computer in the lounge of a Chinese university dormitory. They are taking turns running Internet searches on keywords such as "democracy" and "Amnesty International." They soon realize that China's government filters the results of Internet searches, permitting only officially approved sites to appear. One Chinese student who

In early 2010, Google users placed flowers and candles outside the company's headquarters in Beijing after government leaders demanded that the Web giant accept state censorship. Rather than comply with government demands, Google chose to close down its operations within China, although they continued to operate in Hong Kong. If you were a company leader, would you support this principled action or would you agree to state censorship in order to gain access to the vast Chinese market?

Rosa Canellas Perez lives in Madrid, the capital of Spain, a high-income nation with extensive political freedom.

Nguyen Hung Anh lives near Hanoi, Vietnam, a middle-income nation that restricts political freedom and closely monitors the movements, actions, and speech of its people.

2009
- Free
- Partly free
- Not free

Window on the World

GLOBAL MAP 12–3   Political Freedom in Global Perspective

In 2009, a total of 89 of the world's 194 nations at that time, containing 46 percent of all people, were politically "free"; that is, they offered their citizens extensive political rights and civil liberties. Another 58 countries, which included 20 percent of the world's people, were "partly free," with more limited rights and liberties. The remaining 47 nations, home to 34 percent of humanity, fall into the category of "not free." In these countries, government sharply restricts individual initiative. While there have been some setbacks in recent years, between 1989 and 2009, democracy made significant gains, largely in Latin America and Eastern Europe. In Asia, India (containing 1.1 billion people) returned to the "free" category in 1999. In 2000, Mexico joined the ranks of nations considered "free" for the first time.

Source: Freedom House (2010).

is watching points out that things could be worse—in North Korea, she explains, most students have no access to computers at all.

The most intensely controlled political form is **totalitarianism,** *a highly centralized political system that extensively regulates people's lives.* Totalitarianism emerged in the twentieth century as governments gained the ability to rigidly control their populations.

The Vietnamese government closely monitors the activities of all its citizens. Similarly, the government of North Korea uses surveillance equipment and powerful computers to control its people by collecting and storing information about them.

Although some totalitarian governments claim to represent the will of the people, most seek to bend people to the will of the government.

Seeing Sociology in Everyday Life

In your opinion, what is the most important way in which people can be "free"? Are civil liberties or economic security more important? Explain your answer.

As the term "totalitarian" implies, such governments have a *total* concentration of power, allowing no organized opposition. Denying the people the right to assemble and controlling access to information, these governments create an atmosphere of isolation and fear. In the former Soviet Union, for example, most citizens had no access to telephone directories, copiers, fax machines, or accurate city maps.

Socialization in totalitarian societies is highly political, seeking obedience and commitment to the system. In North Korea, one of the world's strictest totalitarian states, pictures of leaders and political messages are everywhere, reminding citizens that they owe total allegiance to the state. Government-controlled schools and mass media present only official versions of events.

Totalitarian governments span the political spectrum from fascist (including Nazi Germany) to communist (such as North Korea). In all cases, however, one party claims total control of the society and permits no opposition.

A Global Political System?

Is globalization changing politics in the same way that it is changing the economy? On one level, the answer is no. Although most of today's economic activity is international, the world remains divided into nation-states just as it has been for centuries. The United Nations (founded in 1945) was a small step toward global government, but its political role in world affairs has been limited.

On another level, however, politics has become a global process. For some analysts, multinational corporations represent a new political order because of their enormous power to shape events throughout the world. In other words, politics is dissolving into business as corporations grow larger than governments.

Also, the Information Revolution has moved national politics onto the world stage. With e-mail, text messaging, and cell phones everywhere, few countries can conduct their political affairs in complete privacy.

Finally, several thousand *nongovernmental organizations* (NGOs) seek to advance global issues, such as human rights (Amnesty International) and environmental protection (Greenpeace). NGOs will continue to play a key role in expanding the global political culture.

In sum, just as individual nations are losing control of their own economies, governments cannot fully manage the political events occurring within their borders.

Politics in the United States

After fighting a war against Great Britain to gain political independence, the United States replaced the British monarchy with a representative democracy. Our nation's political development reflects its cultural history as well as its capitalist economy.

U.S. Culture and the Rise of the Welfare State

The political culture of the United States can be summed up in one word: individualism. This emphasis is found in the Bill of Rights, which guarantees freedom from undue government interference. It was this individualism that the nineteenth-century poet and philosopher Ralph Waldo Emerson had in mind when he said, "The government that governs best is the government that governs least."

But most people stop short of Emerson's position, believing that government is necessary to defend the country, operate highway systems and schools, maintain law and order, and help people in need. To accomplish these things, the United States has developed a complex **welfare state,** *a system of government agencies and programs that provides benefits to the population.* Government benefits begin even before birth (through prenatal nutrition programs) and continue into old age (through Social Security and Medicare). Some programs are especially important to the poor, who are not well served by our capitalist economic system; but students, farmers, homeowners, small business operators, veterans, performing artists, and even executives of giant corporations get various subsidies and supports. In fact, a majority of U.S. adults looks to government for at least part of their income.

Today's welfare state is the result of a gradual increase in the size and scope of government. In 1789, when the presence of the federal government amounted to little more than a flag in most communities, the entire federal budget was a mere $4.5 million ($1.50 for every person in the nation). Since then, it has steadily risen, reaching $3.6 trillion in 2010 ($11,697 for every person in the country).

Similarly, when our nation was founded, one government employee served every 1,800 citizens. Today, about one in six people in the United States is a government employee—more than are engaged in manufacturing (U.S. Census Bureau, 2009; U.S. Bureau of Labor Statistics, 2010).

Despite this growth, the U.S. welfare state is still smaller than those of many other high-income nations. Figure 12–5 on page 350 shows that government is larger in most of Europe, especially in Scandinavian countries such as Denmark and Sweden.

The Political Spectrum

Who supports a bigger welfare state? Who wants to cut it back? Answers to such questions reveal attitudes that form the *political spectrum,* which ranges from the extremely liberal on the left to the extremely conservative on the right. In the United States, about one-fourth of adults fall on the liberal or "left" side, and one-third say they are conservative, placing themselves on the political "right." The remaining 40 percent claim to be moderates, in the political "middle" (NORC, 2009:189).

Where do you fall on the political spectrum? On social issues,
are you more liberal or more conservative? What about on
economic issues?

Global Snapshot

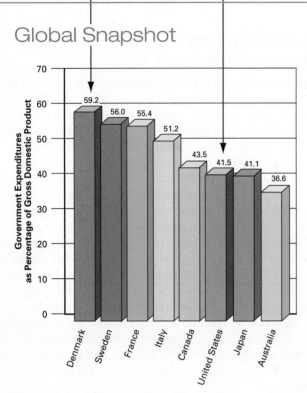

FIGURE 12–5   The Size of Government, 2010

Government activity accounts for a smaller share of economic output in
the United States than in other high-income countries.

Source: OECD (2010).

In Denmark, people look to government for a much greater share of goods and services than they do in the United States.

The political spectrum helps us understand the ways people think about the economy. *Economic issues* focus on economic inequality. On economic issues, liberals support extensive government regulation of the economy and a larger welfare state in order to reduce income inequality. Economic conservatives want to limit the hand of government in the economy and allow market forces more freedom.

The political spectrum can also be applied to *social issues,* which are moral questions about how people ought to live. Social issues include abortion, the death penalty, gay rights, and the treatment of minorities. Social liberals support equal rights and opportunities for all categories of people, view abortion as a matter of individual choice, and oppose the death penalty because it has been unfairly applied to minorities. The "family values" agenda of social conservatives supports traditional gender roles and opposes gay marriage, affirmative action, and other "special programs" for minorities. Social conservatives condemn abortion as morally wrong and support the death penalty as a just response to the most serious crimes.

Of the two major political parties in the United States, the Republican party is more conservative on both economic and social issues and the Democratic party is more liberal. But both parties favor big government when it advances their particular aims. During the 2008 presidential campaign, for example, Republican John McCain supported bigger government in the form of a stronger military; Democrat Barack Obama also favored enlarging government to expand the social "safety net" that would provide, for example, health care coverage for all.

Most people mix conservative and liberal attitudes. With wealth to protect, many higher-income people hold conservative views on economic issues. Yet their extensive schooling and secure social standing lead most to be social liberals. Lower-income people show the opposite pattern, with most being liberal on economic issues but supporting a socially conservative agenda (NORC, 2007; Ohlemacher, 2008). African Americans, both rich and poor, tend to be liberal (especially on economic issues) and for half a century have voted Democratic (95 percent cast ballots for the Democratic candidate, Barack Obama, in 2008). Historically, Latinos, Asian Americans, and Jews have also supported the Democratic party (Kohut, 2008).

Women tend to be somewhat more liberal than men. Among U.S. adults, more women lean toward the Democratic party, while more men vote for Republican candidates. In 2008, for example, 56 percent of women but just 49 percent of men voted for Barack Obama. Figure 12–6 on page 352 shows how this pattern has changed over time among college students. Although there have been shifts in student attitudes—to the right in the 1970s and to the left beginning in the mid-1990s—college women have remained consistently more liberal than college men (Astin et al., 2002; Sax et al., 2003; NORC, 2007; Pryor et al., 2007).

Party Identification

Because many people hold mixed political attitudes, with liberal views on some issues and conservative stands on others, party identification in this country is weak. Surveys show that about 49 percent favor the Democratic party and about 33 percent the Republican party, yet just 19 percent claim to be "strong Democrats" and 10 percent to be "strong Republicans." About 16 percent say they are "independent" (NORC, 2009:179). This lack of strong party identification is one reason each of the two major parties gains or loses power from election to election. Democrats held the White House in 1996 and gained ground in Congress in 1996, 1998, and 2000. In 2002 and 2004, the tide turned as Republicans made gains in Congress and kept control of the White House. In 2006, the tide turned again, with Democrats gaining control of Congress and winning the White House in 2008. In special elections in 2009 and 2010, Republicans were picking up seats again.

Go to the Multimedia Library at
mysoclab.com to view the video
"Lobbying and Special Interest Groups"

Read "Is Congress Really for Sale?"
by Paul Burstein on mysoclab.com

Lower-income people have more pressing financial needs, and so they tend to focus on economic issues, such as job wages and benefits. Higher-income people, by conrast, provide support for many social issues, such as animal rights.

There is also a rural-urban divide in U.S. politics. People in urban areas typically vote Democratic, and those in rural areas vote Republican. National Map 12–2 on page 353 shows the county-by-county results for the 2008 presidential election.

Special-Interest Groups

For years, a debate has raged across the United States about the private ownership of firearms. Organizations such as the Brady Campaign to Prevent Gun Violence support stricter gun-control laws; other organizations, including the National Rifle Association, strongly oppose such measures. Each is an example of a *special-interest group*, people organized to address some economic or social issue. Special-interest groups, which include associations of older adults, farmers, fireworks producers, and environmentalists, are strong in nations where political parties tend to be weak. Many special-interest groups employ *lobbyists* to support their political goals. Washington, D.C., is home to about 14,000 lobbyists (Center for Responsive Politics, 2010). Go to mysoclab.com

Political action committees (PACs) are formed by special-interest groups to raise and spend money in support of political aims. PACs channel most of their funds directly to candidates likely to support their interests. Since they were created in the 1970s, the number of PACs has grown rapidly to more than 5,200 (Federal Election Commission, 2009).

Because of the rising costs of campaigns, most candidates eagerly accept financial support from PACs. In the 2008 congressional elections, 27 percent of all campaign funding came from PACs, and senators who were seeking reelection received, on average, $2 million each in PAC contributions. Supporters maintain that PACs represent the interests of a vast assortment of businesses, unions, and church groups, thereby increasing political participation. Critics counter that organizations supplying cash to politicians expect to be treated favorably in return, so that in effect PACs try to buy political influence ("Abramoff Effect," 2006; Federal Election Commission, 2009). Read on mysoclab.com

In 2008, the candidates for the U.S. presidency spent more than $1 billion on their campaigns, and another $1.4 billion was spent by congressional candidates and people running for all other political offices. Does having the most money matter? The answer is yes: In 94 percent of the congressional races, the candidate with the most money ended up winning the election. Concerns about the power of money led to much discussion of campaign financing. In 2002, Congress passed a modest reform, limiting the amount of unregulated money that candidates can collect. Despite this change, both presidential races since then set new records for campaign spending (Center for Responsive Politics, 2009). And in 2010, the Supreme Court rejected limits on the election spending of corporations, unions, and other large organizations (Liptak, 2010).

As Figure 12–6 suggests, college students have always been more liberal than the population as a whole.

Why do you think that almost half of today's young people do not vote? Have you registered to vote?

Go to the Multimedia Library at **mysoclab.com** to view the video "Democracy: Those Who Don't Participate"

Student Snapshot

FIGURE 12–6 **Left-Right Political Identification of College Students, 1970–2006**

Student attitudes moved to the right after 1970 and shifted left in the late 1990s. College women tend to be more liberal than college men.

Sources: Astin et al. (2002), Sax et al. (2003), and Pryor et al. (2007).

Voter Apathy

A disturbing fact of U.S. political life is that many people in this country do not vote. In fact, U.S. citizens are less likely to vote today than they were a century ago. In the 2000 presidential election, which was decided by a few hundred votes, only half the registered voters went to the polls. In 2008, participation rose to 63 percent, which was the highest turnout since 1960. But this turnout is still lower than in almost all other high-income countries (Center for the Study of the American Electorate, 2009).

Who is and who is not likely to vote? Research shows that women are slightly more likely than men to cast a ballot. People over sixty-five are much more likely to vote than college-age adults (almost half of whom have not even registered). Non-Hispanic whites are more likely to vote (66 percent voted in 2008) than African Americans (65 percent in 2008, up from 56 percent in 2004) and Hispanics (50 percent). Generally speaking, people with a bigger stake in society—homeowners, parents with children at home, people with extensive schooling and good jobs—are more likely to vote. Income matters, too: People earning more than $75,000 a year are much more likely

to vote (79 percent in 2008) than people earning less than $10,000 (49 percent) (U.S. Census Bureau, 2009).

Of course, we should expect some nonvoting because at any given time, millions of people are sick or disabled; millions more are away from home at college or elsewhere or have moved to a new neighborhood and have forgotten to reregister. In addition, registering and voting depend on the ability to read and write, which discourages the tens of millions of U.S. adults who have limited literacy skills. Finally, people with physical disabilities that limit mobility have a lower turnout than the general population (Schur & Kruse, 2000; Brians & Grofman, 2001).

Conservatives suggest that apathy amounts to *indifference* to politics because most people are content with their lives. Liberals and especially political radicals on the far left of the political spectrum counter that apathy reflects *alienation* from politics among people who are so deeply dissatisfied with society that they doubt that elections will make any real difference. The fact that candidates such as Barack Obama have drawn so many new voters into the political process and the fact that the disadvantaged and powerless are least likely to vote suggest that the liberal explanation for voter apathy is probably closer to the truth. ● Go to **mysoclab.com**

Should Convicted Criminals Vote?

Although the right to vote is at the very foundation of our country's claim to being democratic, all states except Vermont and Maine have laws that bar people in jail from voting. More than half the states bar people convicted of serious crimes from voting while they are on probation or on parole. Eleven states ban voting even after people have completed their sentences, subject to various appeals to restore voting rights. Overall, 5.3 million people (including 1.4 million African American men) in the United States do not have the right to vote (Sentencing Project, 2009).

Should government take away people's political rights as a punishment for criminal acts? The legislatures in most of our fifty states have said yes. But critics point out that this practice may be politically motivated, because preventing convicted criminals from voting makes a difference in the way elections in this country turn out. Convicted felons (who tend to be lower-income people) show better than a two-to-one preference for Democratic over Republican candidates. Even allowing for expected voter apathy, one study concluded that if these laws had not been in force, Democrats would have won more congressional races and in 2000 Al Gore would have defeated George W. Bush for the presidency (Uggen & Manza, 2002). In 2009, such political considerations led Congress to debate the Democracy Restoration Act, which would establish a process to restore voting rights for convicted criminals who have completed their sentences.

pluralist model an analysis of politics that sees power as spread among many competing interest groups

power-elite model an analysis of politics that sees power as concentrated among the rich

Marxist political-economy model an analysis that explains politics in terms of the operation of a society's economic system

Go to the Multimedia Library at **mysoclab.com** to view 2004 presidential election results in your local community. What similarities and differences in voting patterns across the country do you see between 2004 and 2008?

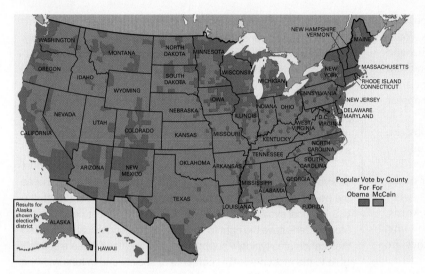

Seeing Ourselves

NATIONAL MAP 12–2

The Presidential Election, 2008: Popular Vote by County

Barack Obama won the 2008 presidential election with 53 percent of the total popular vote, but he received a majority of the vote in only about one-fourth of the nation's counties. Obama and other Democrats did well in more densely populated urban areas, while John McCain and other Republicans did well in less populated rural areas. Can you explain why rural areas are mostly Republican and urban areas mostly Democratic? What other social differences do you think distinguish the areas that voted Republican and Democratic? ● Go to **mysoclab.com**

Theoretical Analysis of Power in Society

Sociologists have long debated how power is spread throughout the U.S. population. Power is a very difficult topic to study because decision making is complex and often takes place behind closed doors. Despite this difficulty, researchers have developed three competing models of power in the United States.

The Pluralist Model: The People Rule

The **pluralist model,** closely linked to structural-functional theory, is *an analysis of politics that sees power as spread among many competing interest groups.* Pluralists claim, first, that politics is an arena of negotiation. No single organization can expect to achieve all of its goals. Organizations therefore operate as *veto groups,* realizing some goals but mostly keeping opponents from achieving all of theirs. The political process relies heavily on creating alliances and compromises among numerous interest groups so that policies gain wide support. In short, pluralists see power as spread widely throughout society, with all people having at least some voice in the political system (Dahl, 1961, 1982; Rothman & Black, 1998).

The Power-Elite Model: A Few People Rule

The **power-elite model,** based on social-conflict theory, is *an analysis of politics that sees power as concentrated among the rich.* The term "power elite" was coined by C. Wright Mills (1956), a social-conflict theorist who argued that the upper class holds most of society's wealth, prestige, and power.

Mills claimed that members of the power elite are in charge of the three major sectors of society: the economy, government, and the military. The power elite is made up of the "super-rich" (corporate executives and major stockholders); top officials in Washington, D.C. and state capitals; and the highest-ranking officers in the U.S. military.

Further, Mills explained that these elites move from one sector to another, building power as they go. Former Vice President Dick Cheney, for example, moved back and forth between powerful positions in the corporate world and the federal government. General Colin Powell moved from a top position in the U.S. military to become secretary of state. More broadly, when presidents fill cabinet posts, most of these powerful public officials are millionaires. This was true in the Bush administration and is probably the case for about half of those in the Obama administration.

Power-elite theorists say that the United States is not a democracy because our economic and political systems give a few people so much power that the average person's voice cannot be heard. They reject the pluralist idea that various centers of power serve as checks and balances on one another; according to the power-elite model, those at the top are powerful enough that they face no real opposition (Bartlett & Steele, 2000; Moore et al., 2002).

The Marxist Model: The System Is Biased

A third approach to understanding U.S. politics is the **Marxist political-economy model,** *an analysis that explains politics in terms of the operation of a society's economic system.* Like the power-elite model, the

Making the Grade

Generally, the pluralist model is close to sociology's structural-functional approach; the power-elite model is based on social-conflict theory, as is the Marxist political-economy model, which is more radical because it implies that changes in basic social institutions are needed to make the country truly democratic.

political revolution the overthrow of one political system in order to establish another

Marxist approach rejects the idea that the United States is a political democracy. But the power-elite model focuses on the enormous wealth and power of certain individuals; the Marxist model goes further and sees bias rooted in the nation's institutions, especially its economy. Karl Marx believed that a society's economic system (capitalist or socialist) shapes its political system. Therefore, power elites do not simply appear out of nowhere; they are creations of the capitalist economy.

From this point of view, reforming the political system—by, say, limiting the amount of money that rich people can contribute to political candidates—is unlikely to bring about true democracy. The problem does not lie in the people who exercise great power or the people who don't vote; the problem is the system itself—what Marxists call the "political economy of capitalism." In other words, as long as the United States has a predominantly capitalist economy, the majority of people will be shut out of politics, just as they are exploited in the workplace.

CRITICAL REVIEW The Applying Theory table summarizes the three models of the U.S. political system. Which model is most accurate? Over the years, research has shown support for each one. In the end, of course, how you think our political system ought to work is as much a matter of political values as it is of scientific fact.

Classic research by Nelson Polsby (1959) supports the pluralist model. Polsby studied the politics of New Haven, Connecticut, where he found that key decisions involving urban renewal, choosing political candidates, and running the city's schools were made by different groups. Polsby concluded that in New Haven, no one group—not even the upper class—ruled all the others.

Robert Lynd and Helen Lynd (1937) studied Muncie, Indiana (which they called "Middletown," to suggest that it was a typical city), and documented the fortune amassed by a single family, the Balls, from its business producing glass jars. Their findings support the power-elite position. The Lynds showed how the Ball family dominated the city's life, pointing to that family's name on a local bank,

One of the most significant political forces to develop in recent years is the "tea party" movement. Supporters claim that government has grown too big, too expensive, and now threatens the freedom of ordinary people. Do you see government as a "problem" the way many people on the right side of the political spectrum do? Or do you see it as the "solution" the way many people on the left side of the political spectrum do? Why?

university, hospital, and department store. In Muncie, according to the Lynds, the power elite boiled down to more or less a single family.

From the Marxist perspective, the point is not which individuals make decisions. Rather, as Alexander Liazos (1982:13) explains, "The basic tenets of capitalist society shape everyone's life: the inequalities of social classes and the importance of profits over people." As long as the basic institutions of society are organized to meet the needs of the few rather than the many, Liazos concludes, a democratic society is impossible.

Clearly, the political system in the United States gives almost everyone the right to participate in politics through elections. But as the power-elite and Marxist models point out, at the very least, the U.S. political system is far less democratic than most people think. Most citizens have the right to vote, but the major political parties and their candidates typically support only the positions that are acceptable to the most powerful segments of society and in tune with the operation of our capitalist economy.

Whatever the reasons, many people in the United States appear to be losing confidence in their leaders. Only about 60 percent of U.S. adults report having "some" or "a great deal" of confidence that members of Congress and other government officials will do what is best for the country (NORC, 2009:282–84).

CHECK YOUR LEARNING What is the main argument of the pluralist model of power? What about the power-elite model? The Marxist political-economy model?

Power beyond the Rules

Politics is always a matter of disagreement over a society's goals and the means to achieve them. A political system tries to settle controversy within a system of rules. But political activity sometimes breaks the rules or even tries to do away with the entire system.

Revolution

Political revolution is *the overthrow of one political system in order to establish another.* Revolution goes beyond *reform*, or change within a system, and even beyond a *coup d'état* (in French, literally, "blow to

○ Making the Grade

Use the Applying Theory table to review the three political models.

○ Making the Grade

Revolution, in which one political system is replaced by another, involves far greater change than reform, which implies change within the present system.

● APPLYING THEORY ●

Politics

	Pluralist Model	Power-Elite Model	Marxist Political-Economy Model
Which theoretical approach is applied?	Structural-functional approach	Social-conflict approach	Social-conflict approach
How is power spread throughout society?	Power is spread widely so that all groups have some voice.	Power is concentrated in the hands of top business, political, and military leaders.	Power is directed by the operation of the capitalist economy.
Is the United States a democracy?	Yes. Power is spread widely enough to make the country a democracy.	No. Power is too concentrated for the country to be a democracy.	No. The capitalist economy sets political decision making, so the country is not a democracy.

the state"), as when one leader topples another. Revolution involves change in the type of system itself.

No political system is immune to revolution, nor does revolution produce any one type of government. Our own Revolutionary War (1775–76) replaced colonial rule by the British monarchy with a representative democracy. French revolutionaries in 1789 also overthrew a monarch, only to set the stage for the return of monarchy in the person of Napoleon. In 1917, the Russian Revolution replaced a monarchy with a socialist government built on the ideas of Karl Marx. In 1991, a second Russian revolution dismantled the socialist Soviet Union, and the nation was reborn as fifteen independent republics, the largest of which—known as the Russian Federation—has moved closer to a market system with a somewhat greater political voice for its people.

Despite their striking variety, revolutions share a number of traits (Tocqueville, 1955, orig. 1856; Skocpol, 1979; Tilly, 1986):

1. **Rising expectations.** Common sense suggests that revolution is more likely when people are severely deprived, but history shows that most revolutions occur when people's lives are improving. Rising expectations, rather than bitterness and despair, make revolution more likely.

2. **Unresponsive government.** Revolution becomes more likely when a government is unwilling to reform itself, especially when demands for change being made by powerful segments of society are ignored.

3. **Radical leadership by intellectuals.** The English philosopher Thomas Hobbes (1588–1679) claimed that intellectuals provide

the justification for revolution and universities are often at the center of political change. Students played a key role in China's prodemocracy movement and in the uprisings in Eastern Europe.

4. **Establishing a new legitimacy.** Overthrowing a political system is not easy, but ensuring a revolution's long-term success is harder still. Some revolutionary movements are held together merely by hatred of the past regime and fall apart once new leaders are installed. Revolutionaries must also guard against counterrevolutionary drives led by overthrown leaders. This explains the speed and ruthlessness with which victorious revolutionaries typically dispose of former leaders.

Scientific research cannot declare that a revolution is good or bad. That judgment depends on the personal values of the citizenry, and the full consequences of such an upheaval become evident only after many years.

Terrorism

The terrorist attacks on the United States on September 11, 2001, involving four commercial airliners, killed nearly 3,000 innocent people (from sixty-eight nations), injured many thousands more, destroyed the twin towers of the World Trade Center in New York City, and seriously damaged the Pentagon in Washington, D.C. Not since the attack on Pearl Harbor at the outbreak of World War II had the United States suffered such a blow. This event was the most serious terrorist act ever recorded.

terrorism refers to acts of violence or the threat of violence used as a political strategy by an individual or a group

war organized, armed conflict among the people of two or more nations, directed by their governments

military-industrial complex (p. 358) the close association of the federal government, the military, and defense industries

Making the Grade

Explain why one person's "terrorist" is another person's "freedom fighter."

Kiefer Sutherland is special agent Jack Bauer in the popular television drama, *24*. In the show, Bauer works for the Los Angeles Counter Terrorism unit, and typically supports taking "any means necessary" to prevent terror attacks. Should the same standards that guide police work in criminal cases always apply to potential terrorist situations? Why or why not?

Terrorism refers to *acts of violence or the threat of violence used as a political strategy by an individual or a group*. Like revolution, terrorism is a political act beyond the rules of established political systems. According to Paul Johnson (1981), terrorism has four distinguishing characteristics.

First, terrorists try to paint violence as a legitimate political tactic, despite the fact that such acts are condemned by virtually every nation. Terrorists also bypass (or are excluded from) established channels of political negotiation. Therefore, terrorism is a weak organization's strategy against a stronger enemy. In recent decades, terrorism has become commonplace in international politics. In 2008, there were 11,770 acts of terrorism worldwide, which claimed 15,765 lives (including the deaths of 33 U.S. citizens) and injured more than 34,000 people. Most of those killed were in Iraq, but major terrorist attacks took place in many nations, including Afghanistan, India, and Somalia (National Center for Counterterrorism, 2009).

Second, terrorism is used not just by groups but also by governments against their own people. *State terrorism* is the use of violence, generally without support of law, by government officials. State terrorism is lawful in some authoritarian and totalitarian states, which survive by creating widespread fear and intimidation. Saddam Hussein, for example, relied on secret police and state terror to protect his power in Iraq.

Third, democratic societies reject terrorism in principle, but they are especially vulnerable to terrorists because they give broad civil liberties to their people and have less extensive police networks. In contrast, totalitarian regimes make widespread use of state terrorism, but their vast police power gives individuals few opportunities for acts of terror against the government.

Fourth and finally, terrorism is always a matter of definition. Governments claim the right to maintain order, even by force, and may label opposition groups who use violence as "terrorists." Political differences may explain why one person's "terrorist" is another's "freedom fighter" (Jenkins, 2003).

Although hostage taking and outright killing provoke popular anger, taking action against terrorists is difficult. Most terrorist groups have no formal connection to any established state, so identifying the parties responsible may be all but impossible. In addition, a military response may risk confrontation with other governments. Yet as the terrorism expert Brian Jenkins warns, a failure to respond "encourages other terrorist groups, who begin to realize that this can be a pretty cheap way to wage war" (quoted in Whitaker, 1985:29).

War and Peace

Perhaps the most critical political issue is **war**, *organized, armed conflict among the people of two or more nations, directed by their governments*. War is as old as humanity, but understanding it is crucial today because we now have weapons that can destroy the entire planet.

At almost any moment during the twentieth century, nations somewhere in the world were engaged in violent conflict. In its short history, the United States has participated in eleven major wars. From the Revolutionary War to our current engagement in Iraq and Afghanistan, more than 1.3 million U.S. men and women have been killed in armed conflicts, as shown in Figure 12–7, and many times that number have been injured. Thousands more have died in undeclared wars and limited military actions around the world.

The Causes of War

Wars occur so often that we might think that there is something natural about armed conflict. But there is no evidence that human beings must wage war under any particular circumstances. On the contrary, governments around the world usually have to force their people to go to war.

Like other forms of social behavior, warfare is a product of society that is more common in some places than in others. The Semai

● Seeing Sociology
in Everyday Life

Do you think you will live to see a world free from terrorism? What
will have to happen to create such a world?

● Seeing Sociology
in Everyday Life

Does it seem fair or unfair that the defense of this country falls
heavily on working-class people? Explain your position.

of Malaysia, among the most peace-loving of the world's peoples,
rarely resort to violence. In contrast, the Yąnomamö (see the box on
page 41) are quick to wage war.

If society holds the key to war or peace, under what circumstances do humans go to war? Quincy Wright (1987) cites five factors that promote war:

1. **Perceived threats.** Nations mobilize in response to a perceived
   threat to their people, territory, or culture. Leaders justified
   the U.S.-led military campaign against Iraq, for example, by
   stressing the threat that Saddam Hussein posed to neighboring
   countries and also to the United States.

2. **Social problems.** When internal problems cause widespread
   frustration at home, a nation's leaders may try to divert public attention by attacking an external "enemy" as a form of
   scapegoating. Although U.S. leaders defended the 2003 invasion of Iraq as a matter of national security, the start of the
   war effectively shifted the nation's attention away from the
   struggling national economy and boosted the popularity of
   then-President George W. Bush.

3. **Political objectives.** Poor nations, such as Vietnam, have used
   wars to end foreign domination. Powerful countries such as
   the United States may benefit from periodic shows of force to
   increase global political standing.

4. **Moral objectives.** Nations rarely claim that they are going to war
   to gain wealth and power. Instead, their leaders infuse military
   campaigns with moral urgency. By calling the 2003 invasion of
   Iraq "Operation Iraqi Freedom," U.S. leaders portrayed the mission as a morally justified war of liberation from an evil tyrant.

5. **The absence of alternatives.** A fifth factor promoting war is
   the lack of alternatives. Although the goal of the United
   Nations is to maintain international peace by finding alternatives to war, the organization has had limited success in preventing conflict between nations.

Social Class, Gender, and the Military

In World War II, three out of every four men in the United States in
their late teens and twenties served in the military, either voluntarily
or by being *drafted*—called to service. Only those who were ruled
ineligible due to some physical or mental problem performed no military service. Today, by contrast, there is no draft, and fighting is done
by a volunteer military. But not every member of our society is equally
likely to volunteer.

One recent study concluded that the military has few young people who are rich and few who are very poor. Rather, working-class people look to the military for a job, to become eligible for money to go to
college, or simply to get out of the small town where they grew up. In

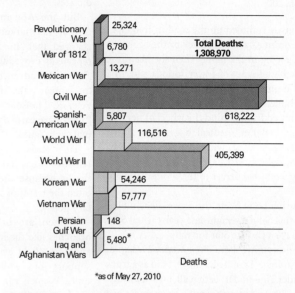

FIGURE 12–7 Deaths of Americans in Eleven U.S. Wars

Almost half of all U.S. deaths in war occurred during the Civil
War (1861–65).

Sources: Compiled from various sources by Maris A. Vinovskis (1989) and the author.

addition, the largest number of volunteers comes from the South, where
regional culture is more supportive of the military and where most military bases are located. As two analysts put it, "America's military seems
to resemble the makeup of a two-year commuter or trade school outside Birmingham or Biloxi far more than that of a ghetto or barrio or
four-year university in Boston" (Halbfinger & Holmes, 2003:1).

Throughout our nation's history, women have been a part of the
U.S. military. In recent decades, however, women have taken on
greater importance in the armed forces. For one thing, the share of
women is on the rise, now standing at 15 percent of all military personnel. Just as important, although regulations continue to keep
many military women out of harm's way, more women are now
engaging in combat. Seeing Sociology in the News on pages 358–59
takes a closer look at the changes under way.

Is Terrorism a New Kind of War?

People speak of terrorism as a new kind of war. War has historically
followed certain patterns: It is played out according to basic rules, the
warring parties are known to each other, and the objectives of the
warring parties—which generally involve control of territory—are
clearly stated.

Terrorism breaks from these patterns. The identity of terrorist
individuals and organizations may not be known, those involved

The New York Times

G.I. Jane Breaks the Combat Barrier

BY LIZETTE ALVAREZ
August 16, 2009

As the convoy rumbled up the road in Iraq, Specialist Veronica Alfaro was struck by the beauty of fireflies dancing in the night. Then she heard the unmistakable pinging of tracer rounds and, in a Baghdad moment, realized the insects were illuminated bullets.

She jumped from behind the wheel of her gun truck, grabbed her medical bag and sprinted fifty yards to a stalled civilian truck. On the way, bullets kicked up dust near her feet. She pulled the badly wounded driver to the ground and got to work.

Despite her best efforts, the driver died, but her heroism that January night last year earned Specialist Alfaro a Bronze Star for valor. . . .

"I did everything there," Ms. Alfaro, 25, said of her time in Iraq. "I gunned. I drove. I ran as a truck commander. And underneath it all, I was a medic."

Before 2001, America's military women had rarely seen ground combat. Their jobs kept them mostly away from enemy lines, as military policy dictates.

But the Afghanistan and Iraq wars, often fought in marketplaces and alleyways, have changed that. In both countries, women have repeatedly proved their mettle in combat. . . .

"Iraq has advanced the cause of full integration for women in the Army by leaps and bounds," said Peter R. Mansoor, a retired Army colonel. . . . "They have earned the confidence and respect of male colleagues."

Their success, widely known in the military, remains largely hidden from public view. In part, this is because their most challenging work is often the result of a quiet circumvention of military policy.

Women are barred from joining combat branches like the infantry, armor, Special Forces and most field artillery units and from doing support jobs while living with those smaller units. Women can lead some male troops into combat as officers, but they cannot serve with them in battle.

Yet, over and over, in Iraq and Afghanistan, Army commanders have resorted to bureaucratic trickery when they needed more soldiers for crucial jobs, like bomb disposal and intelligence. On paper, for instance, women have been "attached" to a combat unit rather than "assigned."

This quiet change has not come seamlessly—and it has altered military culture on the battlefield in ways large and small. Women need separate bunks and bathrooms. They face sexual discrimination and rape, and counselors and rape kits are now common in war zones. Commanders also confront a new reality: that soldiers have sex, and some will be evacuated because they are pregnant.

Nonetheless, as soldiers in the Iraq and Afghanistan wars, women have done nearly as much in battle as their male counterparts: patrolled streets with machine guns, served as gunners on vehicles, disposed of explosives, and driven trucks down bomb-ridden roads. They have proved indispensable in their ability to interact with and search Iraqi and Afghan women for

may deny their responsibility, and their goals may be unclear. The 2001 terrorist attacks against the United States were not attempts to defeat the nation militarily or to secure territory. They were carried out by people representing not a country but a cause, one not well understood in the United States. In short, they were expressions of anger and hate intended to create widespread fear.

Conventional warfare is symmetrical, with two nations sending armies into battle. By contrast, terrorism is a new kind of war: an asymmetrical conflict in which a small number of attackers use terror and their own willingness to die as a means to level the playing field against a much more powerful enemy. Although the terrorists may be ruthless, the nation under attack must use caution in its response to terrorism because little may be known about the identity and location of the parties responsible.

The Costs and Causes of Militarism

The cost of armed conflict extends far beyond battlefield casualties. Together, the world's nations spend more than $1.4 trillion annually for military-related purposes. Spending this much diverts resources from the desperate struggle for survival by hundreds of millions of poor people.

Defense is the U.S. government's second biggest expenditure (after Social Security), accounting for about 20 percent of all federal spending, which amounted to more than $700 billion in 2010. The United States has emerged as the world's single military superpower, accounting for about 42 percent of the world's military spending. Put another way, the United States spends nearly as much on the military as the rest of the world's nations combined (Stockholm International Peace Research Institute, 2009; U.S. Office of Management and Budget, 2010).

For decades, military spending went up because of the *arms race* between the United States and the former Soviet Union, which dropped out of the race after its collapse in 1991. But some analysts (who support power-elite theory) link high military spending to the domination of U.S. society by a **military-industrial complex,** *the close association of the federal government, the military, and defense industries.* The roots of militarism, then, lie not just in external threats but also in institutional structures here at home (Marullo, 1987; Barnes, 2002b).

A final reason for continuing militarism is regional conflict. In the 1990s, localized wars broke out in Bosnia, Chechnya, and Zambia and long-standing conflict continues between Israel and the Palestinians. Even limited wars have the potential to grow and involve other countries, including the United States. India and Pakistan—both nuclear powers—moved to the brink of war in 2002 and then pulled back. In 2003, the announcement by North Korea that it, too, had nuclear weapons raised tensions in Asia. Iran continues to pursue nuclear technology, raising fears that this nation may soon have an atomic bomb.

weapons, a job men cannot do for cultural reasons. The Marine Corps has created revolving units—"lionesses"—dedicated to just this task....

[In some] cases, the rules were bent to get women into combat positions.

In 2004 and 2005, Michael A. Baumann, now a retired lieutenant colonel, commanded thirty enlisted women and six female officers as part of a unit patrolling in the Rashid district of Baghdad, an extremely dangerous area at the time.

On paper, he followed military policy. The women were technically assigned to a separate chemical company of the division. In reality, they were core members of his field artillery battalion. Mr. Baumann said the women trained and fought alongside his male soldiers. Everyone from Mr. Baumann's commanders to the commanding general knew their true function, he said....

Brought up as an old-school Army warrior, Mr. Baumann said he had seriously doubted that women could physically handle infantry duties, citing the weight of the armor and the gear, the heat of Baghdad and the harshness of combat.

"I found out differently," said Mr. Baumann.... "Not only could they handle it, but in the same way as males.... I had full trust and confidence in their abilities."...

War is different today, they say. Technology has changed the way some of these jobs are done, making them more mechanized and less strength-dependent. Warfare in Iraq involves a lot more driving than walking.

What is more, not all combat jobs are the same. Handling field artillery or working in Bradleys [the Army's armored fighting vehicle], for example, are jobs more suited to some women than light infantry duties, which can require carrying heavy packs for miles....

Any change to the policy would require Congressional approval, which lawmakers say is unlikely in the middle of two wars. But women in the military and their allies want their performance in combat to count for something....

In Mr. Baumann's view, the reality on the ground long ago outpaced the debate.

"We have crossed that line in Iraq," he said. "Debate it all you want folks, but the military is going to do what the military needs to do. And they are needing to put women in combat."

WHAT DO YOU THINK?

1. Do you consider the work being done by Veronica Alfaro to be a step forward for women? Why or why not?

2. Looking at the wars in Iraq and Afghanistan, what factors have moved more U.S. women into combat?

3. Would you support a policy that allowed women to take all military assignments, including combat branches? Why or why not?

Nuclear Weapons

Despite the easing of superpower tensions, the world still contains more than 8,000 operational nuclear warheads, representing a destructive power of several tons of TNT for every person on the planet. If even a small fraction of this stockpile is used in war, life as we know it would end. Albert Einstein, whose genius contributed to the development of nuclear weapons, reflected, "The unleashed power of the atom has changed everything save our modes of thinking and we thus drift toward unparalleled catastrophe" ("Atomic Education," 1946). In short, nuclear weapons make full-scale war unthinkable in a world not yet capable of peace.

The United States, the Russian Federation, Great Britain, France, the People's Republic of China, Israel, India, Pakistan, and probably North Korea all have nuclear weapons. A few nations stopped the development of nuclear weapons—Argentina and Brazil halted work in 1990, and South Africa dismantled its arsenal in 1991. But by 2015, there could be ten new nations in the "nuclear club," and as many as fifty countries by 2025 (Grier, 2006). Such a trend makes any regional conflict very dangerous to the entire planet.

Mass Media and War

The 2003 U.S.-led invasion of Iraq was the first war in which television crews traveled with U.S. troops, reporting as the campaign unfolded. The mass media provided ongoing and detailed reports of events; cable television made available live coverage of the war twenty-four hours a day, seven days a week.

Media outlets "frame" the news according to their own politics. Those media outlets that were critical of the war—especially the Arab news channel Al-Jazeera—tended to report the slow pace of the conflict, the casualties to the U.S. and allied forces, and the deaths and injuries suffered by Iraqi civilians, all of which was information that would increase pressure to end the war. Media outlets that were supportive of the war—including most news organizations in the United States—tended to report the rapid pace of the war and the casualties to Iraqi forces and to downplay any harm to Iraqi civilians as minimal and unintended. In short, the power of the mass media to provide selective information to a worldwide audience means that television and other media may be almost as important to the outcome of a conflict as the military forces who are doing the actual fighting.

Pursuing Peace

How can the world reduce the dangers of war? Here are the most recent approaches to peace:

1. **Deterrence.** The logic of the arms race holds that security comes from a "balance of terror" between the superpowers. The principle of *mutual assured destruction* (MAD) means that a nation launching a first strike against another will face greater

● Seeing Sociology
in Everyday Life

Do you think the world is getting better at avoiding war? Explain.

⌐● Making the Grade

Identify and explain the four approaches to peace discussed below.

One reason to pursue peace is the rising toll of death and mutilation caused by millions of land mines placed in the ground during wartime and left there afterward. Civilians—many of them children—maimed by land mines receive treatment in this Kabul, Afghanistan, clinic.

But disarmament has limitations. No nation wants to be weakened by eliminating its defenses. Successful diplomacy depends on everyone involved sharing responsibility for a common problem (Fisher & Ury, 1988). Although the United States and the Russian Federation continue to negotiate arms reduction agreements, the world now faces threats from other nations such as North Korea and Iran.

4. **Resolving underlying conflict.** In the end, reducing the dangers of war may depend on resolving underlying conflicts by promoting a more just world. Poverty, hunger, and illiteracy are all root causes of war. Perhaps the world needs to reconsider the wisdom of spending thousands of times as much money on militarism as we do on efforts to find peaceful solutions (Sivard, 1988; Kaplan & Schaffer, 2001).

retaliation. This deterrence policy kept the peace for almost fifty years during the Cold War. Yet it encouraged an enormous arms race and cannot control nuclear proliferation, which represents a growing threat to peace. Deterrence also does little to stop terrorism or to prevent wars that are started by a stronger nation (such as the United States) against a weaker foe (such as the Taliban government in Afghanistan or Saddam Hussein's Iraq).

2. **High-technology defense.** If technology created the weapons, perhaps it can also protect us from them; such is the claim of the *strategic defense initiative* (SDI). Under SDI, satellites and ground installations would destroy enemy missiles soon after they were launched. In a survey shortly after the 2001 terrorist attacks, two-thirds of U.S. adults supported SDI (Thompson & Waller, 2001; "Female Opinion," 2002). However, critics claim that the system, which they refer to as "Star Wars," would be, at best, a leaky umbrella. Others worry that building such a system will spark another massive arms race. In 2009, the Obama administration stated that as part of its Ballistic Missile Defense System, the United States was expanding land- and sea-based missile defense systems in the Persian Gulf but not in Eastern Europe.

3. **Diplomacy and disarmament.** Some analysts believe that the best road to peace is diplomacy rather than technology (Dedrick & Yinger, 1990). Teams of diplomats working together can increase security by reducing, rather than building, weapons stockpiles.

Politics: Looking Ahead

Just as economies are changing, so are political systems. Several problems and trends are likely to be important in the decades to come.

One troublesome problem in the United States is inconsistency between our democratic ideals and our low turnout at the polls. Perhaps, as conservative pluralist theorists say, many people do not bother to vote because they are content with their lives. On the other hand, the liberal power-elite theorists may be right when they say that people withdraw from a system that concentrates so much wealth and power in the hands of a few people. Or perhaps, as radical Marxist critics claim, people find that our political system offers little real choice, limiting options and policies to those that support our capitalist economy. In any case, the current high level of apathy and distrust in our nation's government reflect a widespread desire for political change.

A second issue is the global rethinking of political models. The Cold War between the United States and the Soviet Union encouraged people to think of politics in terms of two opposing models, capitalism and socialism. Today, however, people are more likely to consider a broader range of political systems that link government to the economy in various ways. Welfare capitalism, as found in Sweden and Denmark, or state capitalism, as found in South Korea and Japan, are just two possibilities. The Thinking Globally box takes a look at the debate over the chances for the emergence of democratic governments in the world's Islamic countries.

Third, we still face the danger of war in many parts of the world. Even as the United States and the Russian Federation dismantle

THINKING GLOBALLY

Islam and Freedom: A "Democracy Gap"?

One of the reasons given by the U.S. government for sending troops to Iraq was to encourage the spread of democracy in the Middle East, especially in countries with Islamic populations.

But does the Middle East really need democracy? Is democracy a goal that is sought—and equated with freedom—everywhere? The answer is not entirely clear because nations have unique political histories and "freedom" means different things in different cultural settings.

Political freedom is a basic element of all democracies. Freedom House, an organization that monitors political freedom around the world, tracks people's right to vote, to express ideas freely, and to move about without undue interference from government. It reports that the region of the world with the least political freedom stretches from Africa through the Middle East to Asia (look back at Global Map 12–3 on page 22).

Many of the nations that Freedom House characterizes as "not free" have populations that are largely Islamic. According to the Pew Forum on Religion and Public Life in 2008, 50 of the world's 194 nations had an Islamic majority population. Just 9 of these countries had democratic governments (18 percent). Of the 144 nations without a majority Islamic population, 109 (76 percent) had democratic governments. In other words, countries without Islamic majorities are four times more likely to have democratic governments than countries with Islamic majorities. Freedom House concludes that countries with Islamic majority populations display a "democracy gap."

This relative lack of political democracy was found in all world regions that have Islamic-majority nations—in Africa, central Europe, the Middle East, and Asia. The pattern is especially strong among the sixteen Islamic-majority states in the Middle East and North Africa that are ethnically Arabic: Not one is an electoral democracy.

What explains this "democracy gap"? Freedom House points to four factors. First, Islamic-majority countries are typically less developed economically, with widespread poverty and limited schooling for their people. Second, these countries have cultural traditions that provide women with few economic, educational, or political opportunities. Third, while most countries limit the power of religious elites in government, and some (including the United States) even require a "separation of church and state," Islamic-majority nations support giving Islamic leaders political power. In two recent cases—Iran and Afghanistan under the Taliban—Islamic leaders have had formal control of government; in many more countries, religious leaders exert considerable influence on political outcomes.

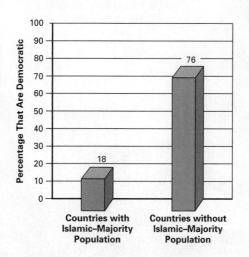

Democracy and Islam

Today, democratic government is much less common in countries with Islamic-majority populations. Fifty years ago, the same was true of countries with Catholic-majority populations.

Fourth and finally, the enormous wealth that comes from Middle Eastern oil plays a part in preventing democratic government. In Iraq, Saudi Arabia, Kuwait, Qatar, the United Arab Emirates, and other nations, this resource has provided astounding riches to a small number of families, money they can use to shore up their political control. In addition, oil wealth permits elites to build airports and other modern facilities without encouraging broader economic development that would raise the living standards of the majority.

For all these reasons, Freedom House concludes that the road to democracy for Islamic-majority nations is likely to be long. But today's patterns may not predict those of tomorrow. In 1950, very few Catholic-majority countries (mostly in Europe and Latin America) had democratic governments. Today, however, most of these nations are democratic. Note too that 40 percent of the world's Muslims—who live in Nigeria, Turkey, Bangladesh, India, Indonesia, and the United States—already live under democratic governments. But perhaps the best indicator that change is already under way is that by the end of 2009, Freedom House had added two more countries with Islamic majorities (Indonesia and Mali) to the list of "free" nations of the world.

WHAT DO YOU THINK?

1. Is the United States right or wrong in trying to bring about a democratic political system in Iraq? Explain your answer.

2. Do you expect to see greater democracy in Islamic-majority countries fifty years from now? Why or why not?

3. Can you point to several reasons that Muslims might object to the kind of political system we call "democracy"? Explain.

Sources: Karatnycky (2002), Pew Forum on Religion and Public Life (2008), and Freedom House (2010).

some warheads, vast stockpiles of nuclear weapons remain, and nuclear technology continues to spread around the world. In addition, new superpowers are likely to arise (the People's Republic of China and India are likely candidates), just as regional conflicts and terrorism are likely to continue. We can only hope (and vote!) for leaders who will work toward finding nonviolent solutions to the age-old problems that provoke war, thereby putting us on the road to world peace.

Seeing Sociology in Everyday Life

How important are you to the political process?

Historically, as this chapter explains, young people have been less likely than older people to take part in politics. But, as a study of the 2008 election suggests, that trend may be changing as evidence builds that young people intend to have their voices heard.

> **HINT**   In the 2008 presidential campaign, thousands of young people served as volunteers for both major political candidates, telephoning voters or walking door to door in an effort to increase public interest, raise money, and get people to the polls on Election Day. Many celebrities—including musicians and members of the Hollywood entertainment scene—also spoke out in favor of a candidate, most of them favoring the Democratic Party. But most important of all is voting, and your vote counts as much as that of any celebrity. Are you registered to vote? Will you turn out next Election Day?

Thousands of young people volunteered to assist the 2008 presidential candidates in their campaigns. In what ways do you think young people helped their candidates simply by using the telephone?

You don't need to be a campaign worker to make a difference. What is the easiest—and in the end, the most important—way to be a part of the political process?

Tom Morello, guitarist for "Rage Against the Machine" and other bands, has made political activism a central part of his career as a musician, speaking for various left-of-center causes. Can you identify other celebrities who have tried to shape public opinion?

Applying SOCIOLOGY in Everyday Life

1. The following Web site provides data on how people voted in the 2008 presidential election by gender, age, race, income, religion, and other variables: http://www.cnn.com/ELECTION/2008. Visit this site, and develop a profile of the typical Democratic voter and the typical Republican voter. Which variables best predict differences in voting preference?

2. Freedom House, an organization that studies civil rights and political liberty around the world, publishes an annual report,

"Freedom in the World." Find a copy in the library, or examine global trends and the political profile of any country on the Web at http://www.freedomhouse.org.

3. Visit a discount store such as Walmart or Kmart and do a little "fieldwork" in an area of the store that interests you. Pick ten products and see where they are made. Do the results support the existence of a global economy?

Making the Grade

CHAPTER 12 Economics and Politics 👁 Watch on mysoclab.com

The Economy: Historical Overview

The **ECONOMY** is the major social institution through which a society produces, distributes, and consumes goods and services.

- In technologically simple societies, economic activity is simply part of family life.
- The Agricultural Revolution (5,000 years ago) made the economy a distinct social institution based on agricultural technology, specialized work, permanent settlements, and trade.
- The Industrial Revolution (beginning around 1750) expanded the economy based on new sources of energy and specialized work in factories that turned raw materials into finished products.
- The postindustrial economy is based on a shift to service work and computer technology.

pp. 330–31

✓ *Today's expanding global economy produces and consumes products and services with little regard for national borders. The world's 1,500 largest corporations account for half of the world's economic output (p. 332).*

PRIMARY SECTOR
- draws raw materials from the natural environment
- is of greatest importance (25% of the economy) in low-income nations

p. 332

SECONDARY SECTOR
- transforms raw materials into manufactured goods
- is a significant share (26–37%) of the economy in low-, middle-, and high-income nations

p. 332

TERTIARY SECTOR
- produces services rather than goods
- is the largest sector (46–72%) in low-, middle-, and high-income countries

p. 332

social institution (p. 330) a major sphere of social life, or societal subsystem, organized to meet human needs

economy (p. 330) the social institution that organizes a society's production, distribution, and consumption of goods and services

postindustrial economy (p. 331) a productive system based on service work and computer technology

primary sector (p. 332) the part of the economy that draws raw materials from the natural environment

secondary sector (p. 332) the part of the economy that transforms raw materials into manufactured goods

tertiary sector (p. 332) the part of the economy that involves services rather than goods

global economy (p. 332) economic activity that crosses national borders

Economic Systems: Paths to Justice

CAPITALISM is based on private ownership of property and the pursuit of profit in a competitive marketplace. Capitalism results in

- greater productivity ⟷
- higher overall standard of living ⟷
- greater income inequality ⟷
- freedom to act according to self-interest ⟷

SOCIALISM is grounded in collective ownership of productive property through government control of the economy. Socialism results in

- less productivity
- lower overall standard of living
- less income inequality
- freedom from basic want

pp. 333–37

capitalism (p. 334) an economic system in which natural resources and the means of producing goods and services are privately owned

socialism (p. 334) an economic system in which natural resources and the means of producing goods and services are collectively owned

welfare capitalism (p. 335) an economic and political system that combines a mostly market-based economy with extensive social welfare programs

state capitalism (p. 335) an economic and political system in which companies are privately owned but cooperate closely with the government

Work in the Postindustrial U.S. Economy

JOBS
- Agricultural work represents about 1.5% of jobs.
- Blue-collar, industrial work has declined to 18.5% of jobs.
- White-collar, service work has increased to 80% of jobs.

p. 338

SELF-EMPLOYMENT
- 7.7% of U.S. workers are self-employed.
- Many professionals fall into this category, but most self-employed people have blue-collar jobs.

p. 339

UNEMPLOYMENT
- Unemployment has many causes, including the operation of the economy itself.
- In 2009, 10% of the country's labor force was unemployed.
- At highest risk for unemployment are young people and African Americans.

p. 340

profession (p. 339) a prestigious white-collar occupation that requires extensive formal education

Explore on mysoclab

corporation (p. 342) an organization with a legal existence, including rights and liabilities, separate from that of its members

monopoly (p. 343) the domination of a market by a single producer

oligopoly (p. 343) the domination of a market by a few producers

Corporations

CORPORATIONS form the core of the U.S. economy.
- The largest corporations, which are conglomerates, account for most corporate assets and profits.
- Many large corporations operate as multinationals, producing and distributing products in nations around the world.

pp. 342–43

Politics: Historical Overview

POLITICS is the major social institution by which a society distributes power and organizes decision making. Max Weber claimed that raw power is transformed into *legitimate authority* in three ways:

- Preindustrial societies rely on tradition to transform power into authority. Traditional authority is closely linked to kinship.
- As societies industrialize, tradition gives way to rationality. *Rational-legal authority* underlies the operation of bureaucratic offices as well as the law.
- At any time, however, some individuals transform power into authority through charisma. *Charismatic authority* is linked to extraordinary personal qualities (as found in Jesus of Nazareth, Adolf Hitler, and Mahatma Gandhi).

`p. 346`

politics (p. 346) the social institution that distributes power, sets a society's goals, and makes decisions

power (p. 346) the ability to achieve desired ends despite resistance from others

government (p. 346) a formal organization that directs the political life of a society

authority (p. 346) power that people perceive as legitimate rather than coercive

routinization of charisma (p. 346) the transformation of charismatic authority into some combination of traditional and bureaucratic authority

Politics in Global Perspective

MONARCHY is common in agrarian societies; leadership is based on kinship.
`p. 346`

DEMOCRACY is common in modern societies; leadership is linked to elective office.
`p. 347`

AUTHORITARIANISM is any political system that denies the people participation in government.
`p. 347`

TOTALITARIANISM concentrates all political power in one centralized leadership.
`pp. 347–49`

✓ *The world is divided into 194 politically independent nation-states. A political trend, however, is the growing wealth and power of multinational corporations. In an age of computers and other new information technology, governments can no longer control the flow of information across their borders (p. 349).*

monarchy (p. 346) a political system in which a single family rules from generation to generation

democracy (p. 347) a political system that gives power to the people as a whole

authoritarianism (p. 347) a political system that denies the people participation in government

totalitarianism (p. 348) a highly centralized political system that extensively regulates people's lives

welfare state (p. 349) a system of government agencies and programs that provides benefits to the population

Politics in the United States

U.S. government has expanded over the past two centuries, although the *welfare state* in the United States is smaller than in most other high-income nations.
`p. 349`

The *political spectrum*, from the liberal left to the conservative right, involves attitudes on both economic issues and social issues.
`pp. 349–50`

Special-interest groups advance the political aims of specific segments of the population.
`p. 351`

Voter apathy runs high in the United States: Only 63% of eligible voters went to the polls in the 2008 presidential election.
`p. 352`

Read on mysoclab.com

Theoretical Analysis of Power

The **PLURALIST MODEL** claims that political power is spread widely in the United States.
`p. 353`

The **POWER-ELITE MODEL** claims that power is concentrated in a small, wealthy segment of the population.
`p. 353`

The **MARXIST POLITICAL-ECONOMY MODEL** claims that our political agenda is determined by a capitalist economy, so true democracy is impossible.
`pp. 353–54`

pluralist model (p. 353) an analysis of politics that sees power as spread among many competing interest groups

power-elite model (p. 353) an analysis of politics that sees power as concentrated among the rich

Marxist political-economy model (p. 353) an analysis that explains politics in terms of the operation of a society's economic system

 See the Applying Theory table on page 355.

Power beyond the Rules

- **REVOLUTION** radically transforms a political system.
- **TERRORISM** employs violence in the pursuit of political goals and is used by a group against a much more powerful enemy.

`pp. 354–56`

War and Peace

- The development and spread of nuclear weapons have increased the threat of global catastrophe.
- World peace ultimately depends on resolving the tensions and conflicts that fuel militarism.

`pp. 356–60`

political revolution (p. 354) the overthrow of one political system in order to establish another

terrorism (p. 356) acts of violence or the threat of violence used as a political strategy by an individual or a group

war (p. 356) organized, armed conflict among the people of two or more nations, directed by their governments

military-industrial complex (p. 358) the close association of the federal government, the military, and defense industries

13 Family and Religion

- What is a family?

- How is religion linked to social inequality?

- Why are both family and religion changing in today's world?

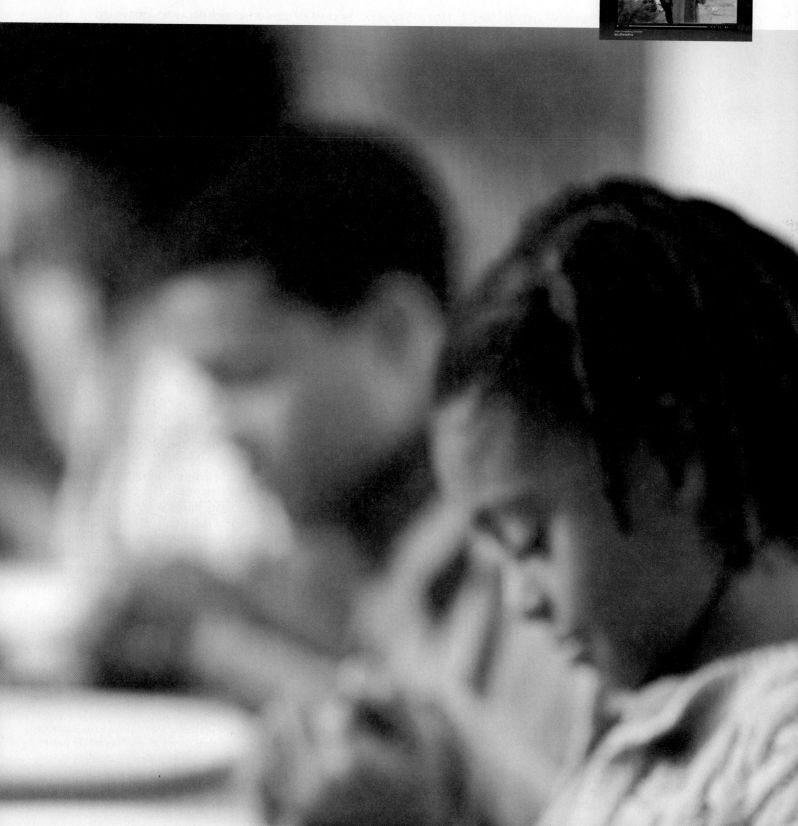

Chapter Overview

This chapter explores the importance of the family for society and also analyzes the meaning and importance of religion, another major social institution, which is based on the concept of the sacred.

Rosa Yniguez is one of seven children who grew up in Jalisco, Mexico, in a world in which families worked hard, went to church regularly, and were proud of having many children. Rosa remembers friends of her parents who had a clock in their living room with a picture of each of their twelve children where the numbers on the clock face would be.

Now thirty-five years old, Rosa is living in San Francisco, attends a local Catholic church, and works as a cashier in a department store. In some respects, she has carried on her parents' traditions—but not in every way. Recalling her childhood, she says, "In Mexico, many of the families I knew had six, eight, ten children. Sometimes more. But I came to this country to get ahead. That is simply impossible with too many kids." As a result of her desire to keep her job and make a better life for her family, Rosa has decided to have no more than the three children she has now.

A tradition of having large families has helped make Hispanics the largest racial or ethnic minority in the United States. But today, more and more Latinas are making the same decision as Rosa Yniguez and opting to have fewer children. Studies show that the birth rate for all immigrant women has been dropping for at least the past ten years (Navarro, 2004; U.S. Census Bureau, 2008).

Families have been with us for a very long time. But as this story indicates, U.S. families are changing in response to a number of factors, including the desire of women to have more career options and to provide better lives for their children. In fact, the family is changing faster than any other social institution (Bianchi & Spain, 1996).

Religion is changing too as membership in long-established denominations is declining and new religious organizations are flourishing. This chapter examines family and religion, which are closely linked as society's *symbolic institutions*. Both the family and religion help set standards of morality, maintain traditions, and join people together. Focusing on the United States and making comparisons to other countries, we will examine why many people consider family and religion the foundations of society while others predict—and may even encourage—the decline of both institutions.

Family: Basic Concepts

The **family** is *a social institution found in all societies that unites people in cooperative groups to care for one another, including any children.* Family ties also reflect **kinship,** *a social bond based on common ancestry, marriage, or adoption.* All societies contain families, but exactly who people call their kin has varied through history and varies today from one culture to another. Here and in other countries, families form around **marriage,** *a legal relationship, usually involving economic cooperation, sexual activity, and childbearing.*

Today, some people object to defining only married couples or parents and children as families because it endorses a narrow standard of how to live. Because some business and government programs still use this conventional definition, many unmarried but committed partners of the same or opposite sex are excluded from family health care and other benefits. However, organizations are gradually coming to recognize as families people with or without legal or blood ties who feel they belong together and define themselves as a family.

Because the U.S. Census Bureau uses the conventional definition of family,[1] sociologists who use Census Bureau data describing "families" must accept it. But the national trend is toward a broader definition.

---

[1] According to the Census Bureau, there were 117.2 million U.S. households in 2009. Of these, 78.9 million (67 percent) meet the bureau's definition of "family." The remaining living units contained single people or unrelated people living together. In 1950, 90 percent of all households were families.

Family: Global Variations

In preindustrial societies, people take a broad view of family ties, recognizing the **extended family,** *a family composed of parents and children as well as other kin.* This group is also called the *consanguine family* because it includes everyone with "shared blood." With industrialization, however, increasing social mobility and geographic migration give rise to the **nuclear family,** *a family composed of one or two parents and their children.* The nuclear family is also called the *conjugal family*, meaning "based on marriage." Although many people in our society live in extended families, far more live in nuclear families.

Marriage Patterns

Cultural norms—and often laws—identify people as suitable or unsuitable marriage partners. Some norms promote **endogamy,** *marriage between people of the same social category.* Endogamy limits marriage prospects to others of the same age, village, race, ethnicity, religion, or social class. By contrast, **exogamy** is *marriage between people of different social categories.* In rural India, for example, a person is expected to marry someone from the same caste (endogamy) but from a different village (exogamy). The reason for endogamy is that people of similar position pass along their standing to their children, maintaining the traditional social hierarchy. Exogamy, on the other hand, links distant communities and encourages the spread of culture.

In higher-income nations, laws permit only **monogamy** (from the Greek, meaning "one union"), *marriage that unites two partners.* Global Map 13–1 on page 370 shows that monogamy is the rule throughout the Americas and Europe. But many lower-income countries, especially in Africa and southern Asia, permit **polygamy** (Greek, "many unions"), *marriage that unites a person with two or more spouses.* Polygamy has two forms. By far the more common is *polygyny* (Greek, "many women"), a form of marriage that unites one man and two or more women. For example, Islamic nations in the Middle East and Africa permit men up to four wives. Even so, most Islamic families are monogamous because few men can afford to support several wives and even more children. *Polyandry* (Greek, "many men") unites one woman and two or more men. This extremely rare pattern exists in Tibet, a mountainous land where agriculture is difficult. There, polyandry discourages the division of land into parcels too small to support a family and divides the work of farming among many men.

Most of the world's societies at some time have permitted more than one marital pattern. Even so, most marriages have been monogamous (Murdock, 1965, orig. 1949). The historical preference

What does the modern family look like? If we look to the mass media, this is a difficult question to answer. In the television series *Modern Family*, Jay Pritchett's family includes his much younger new wife, his stepson Manny, his daughter Claire (who is married with three children) and his son Mitchell (who, with his gay partner, has an adopted Vietnamese daughter). How would you define "the family"?

for monogamy reflects two facts of life: Supporting several spouses is very expensive, and the number of men and women in most societies is roughly equal.

Residential Patterns

Just as societies regulate mate selection, they also designate where a couple may live. In preindustrial societies, most newlyweds live with one set of parents who offer protection and assistance. Most often married couples live with or near the husband's family, an arrangement called *patrilocality* (Greek, "place of the father"). But some societies, including the North American Iroquois, favor *matrilocality* ("place of the mother"), in which couples live with or near the wife's family.

Industrial societies show yet another pattern. Finances permitting, they favor *neolocality* (Greek, "new place"), in which a married couple lives apart from both sets of parents.

Patterns of Descent

Descent refers to *the system by which members of a society trace kinship over generations.* Most preindustrial societies trace kinship through

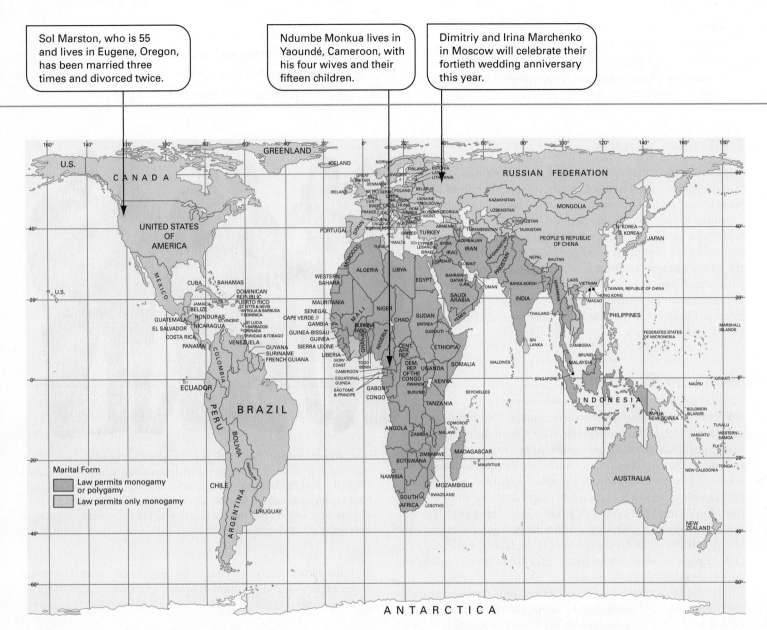

Sol Marston, who is 55 and lives in Eugene, Oregon, has been married three times and divorced twice.

Ndumbe Monkua lives in Yaoundé, Cameroon, with his four wives and their fifteen children.

Dimitriy and Irina Marchenko in Moscow will celebrate their fortieth wedding anniversary this year.

Window on the World

GLOBAL MAP 13–1   Marital Form in Global Perspective

Monogamy is the only legal form of marriage throughout the Western Hemisphere and in much of the rest of the world. In most African nations and in southern Asia, however, polygamy is permitted by law. In many cases, this practice reflects the influence of Islam, a religion that allows a man to have up to four wives. Even so, most marriages in these countries are monogamous, primarily for financial reasons.

Source: *Peters Atlas of the World* (1990), updated by the author.

either the father's side or the mother's side of the family. *Patrilineal descent,* the more common pattern, traces kinship through males, so that fathers pass property on to their sons. Patrilineal descent characterizes most pastoral and agrarian societies, in which men produce the most valued resources. *Matrilineal descent,* by which people define only the mother's side as kin and property passes from mothers to daughters, is found in horticultural societies where women are the main food producers.

Industrial societies with greater gender equality recognize *bilateral descent* ("two-sided descent"), a system tracing descent through both men and women. In this pattern, children include people on both the father's side and the mother's side among their relatives.

● Seeing Sociology
in Everyday Life

In terms of patterns of descent, how would you describe the
common practice in the United States of a woman adopting
her husband's last name after marriage?

descent   (p. 369) the system by which members of a society trace
kinship over generations

incest taboo   a norm forbidding sexual relations or marriage between
certain relatives

Patterns of Authority

Worldwide, the family patterns discussed so far—polygyny, patrilocality, and patrilineal descent—are dominant and reflect the global
pattern of patriarchy. In industrial societies such as the United States,
men are still typically heads of households, and most U.S. parents
give children their father's last name. However, more egalitarian families are evolving, especially as the share of women in the labor force
goes up.

Theoretical Analysis
of Families

As in earlier chapters, the various theoretical approaches offer a range
of insights about families.

Functions of Family:
Structural-Functional Analysis

According to the structural-functional approach, the family performs
many vital tasks. For this reason, the family is sometimes called the
"backbone of society."

1. **Socialization.** As noted in Chapter 3 ("Socialization: From
   Infancy to Old Age"), the family is the first and most important setting for child rearing. Ideally, parents help children develop into well-integrated and contributing
   members of society. Of course, family socialization
   continues throughout the life cycle. Adults change
   within marriage, and as any parent knows, mothers
   and fathers learn as much from their children as their
   children learn from them.

2. **Regulation of sexual activity.** Every culture regulates
   sexual activity in the interest of maintaining kinship
   organization and property rights. As discussed in Chapter 6 ("Sexuality and Society"), the **incest taboo** is *a
   norm forbidding sexual relations or marriage between certain relatives.* Although the incest taboo exists in every
   society, exactly which relatives cannot marry varies from
   one culture to another (Murdock, 1965, orig. 1949).

   Reproduction between close relatives of any
   species can result in mental and physical damage to
   offspring. Yet only humans observe an incest taboo,
   suggesting that the key reason for controlling incest
   is social. Why? First, the incest taboo limits sexual
   competition in families by restricting sex to spouses.
   Second, because kinship defines people's rights and
   obligations toward one another, reproduction between

close relatives would hopelessly confuse kinship ties and
threaten the social order. Third, forcing people to marry
beyond their immediate families ties together the larger society.

3. **Social placement.** Families are not needed for people to reproduce biologically, but they do help maintain social organization. Parents pass on their own social identity—in terms of
   race, ethnicity, religion, and social class—to their children at
   birth.

4. **Material and emotional security.** Many people view the family as a "haven in a heartless world," offering physical protection, emotional support, and financial assistance. Perhaps this
   is why people living in families tend to be happier, healthier,
   and wealthier than people living alone (Goldstein & Kenney,
   2001; U.S. Census Bureau, 2009).

○ **CRITICAL REVIEW**   Structural-functional analysis explains
why society, at least as we know it, is built on families. But this
approach glosses over the diversity of U.S. family life and ignores
how other social institutions (such as government) could meet
at least some of the same human needs. Finally, structural-functionalism overlooks the negative aspects of family life, including
patriarchy and family violence.

○ **CHECK YOUR LEARNING**   What four important functions does the family provide for society?

Often, we experience modern society as cold and impersonal. In this context, the
family can be a haven in a heartless world. Not every family lives up to this promise,
of course, but people in families do live happier and longer than those who live alone.

● Seeing Sociology in Everyday Life

Thinking about the "marriage marketplace," why do you think women have traditionally been less willing than men to reveal their age?

Inequality and Family: Social-Conflict and Feminist Analysis

Like the structural-functional approach, the social-conflict approach, which includes feminist analysis, considers the family central to our way of life. But instead of focusing on ways that kinship benefits society, this approach points out how family perpetuates social inequality. ☐●☐Read on **mysoclab.com**

1. **Property and inheritance.** Friedrich Engels (1902, orig. 1884) traced the origin of the family to men's need (especially in the higher classes) to identify heirs so that they could hand down property to their sons. Families thus concentrate wealth and reproduce the class structure in each new generation.

2. **Patriarchy.** Feminists link the family to patriarchy. To know who their heirs are, men must control the sexuality of women. Families therefore transform women into the sexual and economic property of men. A century ago in the United States,

most wives' earnings belonged to their husbands. Today, women still bear most of the responsibility for child rearing and housework (Stapinski, 1998; England, 2001).

3. **Race and ethnicity.** Racial and ethnic categories persist over generations only to the degree that people marry others like themselves. Endogamous marriage supports racial and ethnic inequality.

CRITICAL REVIEW Social-conflict and feminist analysis shows another side of family life: its role in social stratification. Friedrich Engels criticized the family as part and parcel of capitalism. But noncapitalist societies also have families (and family problems). The family may be linked to social inequality, as Engels argued, but it carries out societal functions not easily accomplished by other means.

CHECK YOUR LEARNING Point to three ways in which families support social inequality.

Constructing Family Life: Micro-Level Analysis

Both the structural-functional and social-conflict approaches view the family as a structural system. By contrast, micro-level analysis explores how individuals shape and experience family life.

The Symbolic-Interaction Approach

Ideally, family living offers an opportunity for *intimacy*, a word with Latin roots that mean "sharing fear." As family members share many activities and establish trust, they build emotional bonds. Of course, the fact that parents act as authority figures often limits their closeness with younger children. Only as young people approach adulthood do kinship ties open up to include sharing confidences with greater intimacy (Macionis, 1978).

The Social-Exchange Approach

Social-exchange analysis, another micro-level approach, describes courtship and marriage as forms of negotiation (Blau, 1964). Dating allows each person to assess the advantages and disadvantages of a potential spouse. In essence, exchange analysts suggest, people "shop around" to make the best "deal" they can.

In patriarchal societies, gender roles dictate the elements of exchange: Men bring wealth and power to the marriage marketplace, and women bring beauty. The importance of beauty explains women's traditional concern with their appearance and sensitivity about revealing their age. But as women have joined the labor force, they have become less dependent on men to support them, and so the terms of exchange are converging for men and women.

According to social exchange theory, people form relationships based on what each offers to the other. Generally partners see the exchange as fair or "about even." What do you think is the exchange involved in this marriage?

Recall from Chapter 8 ("Social Stratification") that arranged marriage is a pattern associated with caste systems. In class systems, we see a greater emphasis on love and personal choice in mate selection.

Go to the Multimedia Library at **mysoclab.com** to listen to the NPR report "Arranged Marriages"

● APPLYING THEORY ●

Family

	Structural-Functional Approach	Social-Conflict and Feminist Approaches	Symbolic-Interaction and Social-Exchange Approaches
What is the level of analysis?	Macro-level	Macro-level	Micro-level
What is the importance of family for society?	The family performs vital tasks, including socializing the young and providing emotional and financial support for members.	The family perpetuates social inequality by handing down wealth from one generation to the next.	The symbolic-interaction approach explains that the reality of family life is constructed by members in their interaction.
	The family helps regulate sexual activity.	The family supports patriarchy as well as racial and ethnic inequality.	The social-exchange approach shows that courtship typically brings together people who offer the same level of advantages.

CRITICAL REVIEW Micro-level analysis balances structural-functional and social-conflict visions of the family as an institutional system. Both the symbolic-interaction and social-exchange approaches focus on the individual experience of family life. However, micro-level analysis misses the bigger picture: The experience of family life is similar for people in the same social and economic categories. The Applying Theory table summarizes what we learn from the three theoretical approaches to family life.

CHECK YOUR LEARNING How does a micro-level approach to understanding family differ from a macro-level approach?

Stages of Family Life

Members of our society recognize several distinct stages of family life across the life course.

Courtship and Romantic Love

November 2, Kandy, Sri Lanka. Winding through the rain forest of this beautiful island, our van driver, Harry, recounts how he met his wife. Actually, it was more of an arrangement: The two families were Buddhist and of the same caste. "We got along well, right from the start," recalls Harry. "We had the same background. I suppose either she or I could have said no. But love marriages happen in the city, not in the village where I grew up."

In rural Sri Lanka, as in rural areas of low- and middle-income countries throughout the world, most people consider courtship too important to be left to the young. *Arranged marriages* are alliances between two extended families of similar social standing and usually involve an exchange not just of children but also of wealth and favors. Romantic love has little to do with marriage, and parents may make such arrangements when their children are very young. A century ago in Sri Lanka and India, half of all girls married before age fifteen (Mayo, 1927; Mace & Mace, 1960). As the Thinking Globally box on page 374 explains, child marriage still occurs in some parts of the world today. ● Go to **mysoclab.com**

Industrialization both erodes the importance of extended families and weakens traditions. As young people begin the process of choosing their own mate, dating sharpens courtship skills and allows sexual experimentation. Marriage is delayed until young people complete their education and gain the experience needed to select a suitable partner.

Our culture celebrates *romantic love*—affection and sexual passion toward another person—as the basis for marriage. We find it hard to imagine marriage without love, and popular culture, from fairy tales such as "Cinderella" to today's television sitcoms and dramas, portrays love as the key to a successful marriage.

Our society's emphasis on romantic love motivates young people to "leave the nest" to form families of their own; physical passion may also help a new couple through difficult adjustments in living together (W. J. Goode, 1959). On the other hand, because feelings change over time, romantic love is a less stable foundation for marriage

Go to the Multimedia Library at **mysoclab.com** to watch sociologist Pepper Schwartz discuss "Internet Dating"

Seeing Sociology in Everyday Life

How similar are your parents (or you and your spouse) in terms of age, social class, race, ethnicity, and education?

THINKING GLOBALLY

Early to Wed: A Report from Rural India

Sumitra Jogi cries as her wedding is about to begin. Are they tears of joy? Not exactly. This "bride" is an eighteen-month-old squirming in the arms of her mother. The groom? A boy of seven.

In a remote village in India's western state of Rajasthan, the two families gather at midnight to celebrate a traditional wedding ritual. It is May 2, in Hindu tradition an especially good day to marry. Sumitra's father smiles as the ceremony begins; her mother cradles the infant, who has fallen asleep. The groom, wearing a special costume and a red and gold turban on his head, gently reaches up and grasps the baby's hand. Then, as the ceremony ends, the young boy leads the child and mother around the wedding fire 3½ times while the audience beams at the couple's first steps together as husband and wife.

Child weddings are illegal in India, but traditions are strong in rural regions, and laws against child marriage are hard to enforce. As a result, thousands of children marry each year. "In rural Rajasthan,"

explains one social worker, "all the girls are married by age fourteen. These are poor, illiterate families, and they don't want to keep girls past their first menstrual cycle."

The eighteen-month-old girl on the left is breastfeeding during her wedding ceremony in a small village in the state of Rajasthan, India; her new husband is seven years old. Although outlawed, such arranged marriages involving children are still known to take place in traditional, remote areas of India.

For now, Sumitra Jogi will remain with her parents. But in eight or ten years, a second ceremony will send her to live with her husband's family, and her married life will begin.

If the reality of marriage is years in the future, why do families push their children to marry at such an early age? Parents of girls know that the younger the bride, the smaller the dowry they must offer to the groom's family. Also, when girls marry this young, there is no question about their virginity, which raises their value on the marriage market. No one in these situations thinks about love or the fact that the children are too young to understand what is taking place (J. W. Anderson, 1995).

WHAT DO YOU THINK?

1. Why are arranged marriages common in very traditional communities?

2. List several advantages and disadvantages of arranged marriages from the point of view of the families involved.

3. Can you point to ways in which mate selection in the United States is "arranged" by society?

than social and economic considerations, one reason that the divorce rate is much higher in the United States than in nations where societal traditions are a stronger guide in the choice of a partner. Responding to concern about the possibility of eventual separation, an increasing share of couples in the United States now includes creating a prenuptial agreement as part of their wedding preparations. Seeing Sociology in the News on pages 376–77 provides details.

But even in our country, sociologists point out, society aims Cupid's arrow more than we like to think. Most people fall in love with others of the same race who are close in age and of similar social class. Our society "arranges" marriages by encouraging **homogamy** (literally, "like marrying like"), *marriage between people with the same social characteristics.* ● Go to **mysoclab.com**

The extent of homogamy is greater for some categories of our population (such as younger people and immigrants from traditional

societies) than for others (older people and those who do not live according to strict traditions).

Settling In: Ideal and Real Marriage

Our culture gives young people an idealized, "happily ever after" picture of marriage. Such optimism can lead to disappointment, especially for women, who are taught that marriage is the key to personal happiness. Also, romantic love involves a lot of fantasy: We fall in love with others not always as they are but as we want them to be.

Sexuality, too, can be a source of disappointment. In the romantic haze of falling in love, people may see marriage as an endless sexual honeymoon, only to face the sobering realization that sex eventually becomes a less-than-all-consuming passion. Although the frequency of marital sex does decline over time, about two in three married people report that they are satisfied with the sexual dimension of their relationship. In general, couples with the best sexual relationships experience the most satisfaction in their marriages. Sex may not be the key to marital happiness, but more often than not, good sex and good relationships go together (Laumann et al., 1994; T.W. Smith, 2006).

Infidelity—sexual activity outside marriage—is another area where the reality of marriage does not match our cultural ideal. In a recent survey, 91 percent of U.S. adults said sex outside of marriage is "always wrong" or "almost always wrong." Even so, 22 percent of men and 10 percent of women indicated (in a private, written questionnaire) that they had been sexually unfaithful to their partners at least once (NORC, 2009:339, 1955).

Child Rearing

Despite the demands children make on us, U.S. adults overwhelmingly identify raising children as one of life's great joys (NORC, 2009:1714). Today, about half of U.S. adults say that two children is the ideal number, and few people want more than three (NORC, 2009:335). This is a change from two centuries ago, when *eight* children was the U.S. average.

Big families pay off in preindustrial societies because children supply needed labor. People therefore regard having children as a wife's duty, and in the absence of effective birth control, childbearing is a regular event. Of course, a high death rate in preindustrial societies prevents many children from reaching adulthood; as late as 1900, one-third of children in the United States died by age ten.

Economically speaking, industrialization transforms children from an asset to a liability. It now costs middle-class parents almost $300,000 to raise one child, including college tuition (Lino & Carlson, 2010). No wonder the U.S. average steadily dropped during the twentieth century to one child per family![2]

The trend toward smaller families is most pronounced in high-income nations. The picture differs in low-income regions in Latin America, Asia, and especially Africa, where many women have few alternatives to bearing children. In many African nations, as a glance back at Global Map 1–1 on page 3 shows, between four and six children is still the norm.

Parenting is a very expensive, lifelong commitment. As our society has given people greater choice about family life, more U.S. adults have decided to delay childbirth or to remain childless. In 1960, almost 90 percent of women between the ages of twenty-five

"Son, you're all grown up now. You owe me two hundred and fourteen thousand dollars."

and twenty-nine who had ever married had at least one child; today, this proportion is just 69 percent (U.S. Census Bureau, 2008).

About half of parents in the United States claim they would like to devote more of their time to child rearing (Cohn, 2007). But unless we accept a lower standard of living, the need for income demands that most parents pursue careers outside the home, even if that means giving less attention to their families. For many families, including Rosa Yniguez's family described in the opening to this chapter, having fewer children is an important step toward resolving the tension between work and parenting (Gilbert, 2005).

Children of working parents spend most of the day at school. But after school, about 5.6 million youngsters (14 percent of five- to fourteen-year-olds) are *latchkey kids* who must fend for themselves (U.S. Census Bureau, 2008). Traditionalists in the "family values" debate charge that many mothers work at the expense of their children, who receive less parenting. Progressives reply that such criticism unfairly blames women for wanting the same opportunities men have long enjoyed.

---

[2]According to the U.S. Census Bureau, the mean number of related children per family was 0.93 in 2008. Among all families, the medians were 0.78 for non-Hispanic whites, 1.19 for African Americans, and 1.43 for Hispanics.

USA Today

Prenuptial Agreements: Unromantic, but Important

BY LAURA PETRECCA
March 7, 2010

Let's face it: The afterglow of that Valentine's Day proposal often begins to dim as discussions of wedding details get started.

The happy couples face potential buzz killers that are financial (how to keep reception costs down), logistical (where to seat relatives not on speaking terms) and, in recent years, even more controversial (So, honey, I love you, but how about that prenuptial agreement . . .).

The prenup seems so utterly unromantic—or just plain wrong—but it's also become so right for so many these days: those keenly aware that a marriage may end up in a legal separation, divorce or death. Most prenups tackle financial issues such as real estate, division of bank accounts, and potential spousal support in the case of divorce or separation.

"More and more of these agreements are being drafted," says American Academy of Matrimonial Lawyers President Marlene Eskind Moses. "It's not just something for the rich and famous any longer. It's for people that have assets and/or income that they want to protect."

Nearly one-third of single adults say they would ask a significant other to sign a prenup, according to a February survey of 2,323 adults by Harris Interactive. . . .

LeAnna Kruckeberg, 24, of Iowa City, says that she has already told her boyfriend of about one year that she would like him to sign a prenup if they get married.

"Family money stays in the family and should be passed down from generation to generation," she says. "Why should those businesses that my grandparents and my parents built on good old-fashioned hard work be given to someone who marries into a family?

"Any inheritance or trust funds should go to my kids and completely bypass my husband."

Her boyfriend knows the stories of her relatives' struggles as they built businesses, so "he understands and respects" her prenup thinking, she says. . . .

A number of factors are fueling the prenup bump. At a broad level, they have gained more acceptance as a financial-planning tool. . . .

In a recession, people want to hang onto the assets they have, so they increasingly look to these pacts as an option, says Robert Nachshin, co-author of the prenup guide *I Do, You Do . . . But Just Sign Here.*

Also, as marital trends change, so do attitudes. Many couples are tying the knot at an older age, so those folks—as well as those entering a second or third marriage—are bringing more assets into the relationship than, say, a 23-year-old would have.

And of course, prenups are an extremely popular topic on the Internet (particularly on wedding, news and celebrity sites). The gritty details of actor Dennis Hopper's and golf aces Tiger Woods's and Greg Norman's prenups have all been hot topics. . . .

Among married Americans, the median duration of their wedded life in 2008 was 18 years, according to Pew Research Center's analysis of government data.

Congress took a small step toward easing the conflict between family and job responsibilities by passing the Family and Medical Leave Act in 1993. This law allows up to ninety days' unpaid leave from work for either parent to care for a new child or deal with a serious family emergency. Still, most adults in this country have to juggle parental and job responsibilities. When mothers work, who cares for the kids? Half of children under age five receive care from a parent (23 percent) or a relative (27 percent). Of the remaining 50 percent of young children, 25 percent attend day care or preschool, 9 percent are cared for in a nonrelative's home, 8 percent are cared for in their own home by a nanny or babysitter, and 8 percent have no regular arrangement (U.S. Census Bureau, 2008).

The Family in Later Life

Increasing life expectancy in the United States means that couples who stay married do so for a longer time. By age sixty, most have completed the task of raising children. At this point, marriage brings a return to living with only a spouse.

Like the birth of children, their departure—creating an "empty nest"—requires adjustments, although a marriage often becomes closer and more satisfying. Years of living together may lessen a couple's sexual passion, but understanding and commitment often increase.

Personal contact with children usually continues because most older adults live near at least one of their grown children. One-third of all U.S. adults (about 60 million) are grandparents, many of whom help with child care and other responsibilities. Among African Americans (who have a high rate of single parenting), grandmothers have an especially important position in family life (U.S. Census Bureau, 2006; AARP Foundation, 2007).

The other side of the coin is that adults in midlife now provide more care for aging parents. The "empty nest" may not be filled by a parent coming to live in the home, but many adults find that caring for parents living to eighty, ninety, and beyond can be as taxing as raising young children. The oldest of the "baby boomers"—now past sixty—are called the "sandwich generation" because many of them, especially women, will spend as many years caring for their aging parents as they did caring for their children (Lund, 1993).

The final and surely the most difficult transition in married life comes with the death of a spouse. Wives typically outlive husbands because of their greater life expectancy and the fact that women usually marry men several years older than themselves. Wives can thus expect to spend some years as widows. The challenge of living alone after the death of a spouse is especially great for men, who usually have fewer friends than widows and may lack housekeeping skills.

Given those odds, "Hope is not a financial plan," says [personal-finance expert Suze] Orman, who urges that every couple get a prenup. "The time to plan for a divorce is not when you're in a state of hate," she says. . . .

Financial, legal and marriage experts do agree on one front: Before getting hitched, couples should sort through issues such as credit card debt, discrepancies in each person's wealth and the possibility of future inheritances. [Divorce mediator Marietta] Shipley advises the marriage-bound to not only share lifelong dreams but to also review each other's credit reports. . . .

Some prenups touch upon more sentimental topics, such as who keeps the heirloom silverware received as a wedding present.

Prenups can even outline what is expected of a spouse's behavior.

"I had a client who was willing to pay his wife a special amount each year provided she didn't do cocaine," says prenup guide author Nachshin. "The agreement was to pay her $25,000 a year. He had the right to drug test her, and if she was clean, she was able to get $25,000." . . .

Some prenups address issues such as adultery, frequency of intimacy, limitations of weight gain, the scheduling of housekeeping and provisions for pets, says attorney Eskind Moses.

Those clauses may seem unnecessary to some folks, but nailing down what is important to each individual—be it the ownership of a ski house, retaining the rights to an antique tea set or determining who keeps Fido—is vital to do before the marriage laws kick in, say pro-prenup lawyers and financial advisers.

Madison, Wisconsin–based entrepreneur Penelope Trunk agrees that it's important to outline expectations when it comes to asset division, but she says these agreements are about emotional security as much as monetary security: You can't fully insulate yourself against marital heartbreak, but at least you can protect your assets.

"It's about everyone feeling secure in a relationship," she says. "You can't have a contract for your heart, but you can have a contract for the rest of this stuff."

WHAT DO YOU THINK?

1. What are some of the reasons that more people are including a prenuptial agreement in their wedding plans?

2. To what extent can partners set terms for their marriage that regulate things other than money, such as personal behavior? What examples of behavioral issues are mentioned in the article?

3. If you were getting married in the near future, would you wish to have both partners sign a prenuptial agreement? Why or why not?

Adapted from "Prenuptial Agreements: Unromantic, but Important" by Laura Petrecca. Source: USA Today, a division of Gannett Co., Inc., March 7, 2010. Reprinted by permission.

U.S. Families: Class, Race, and Gender

Dimensions of inequality—social class, ethnicity, race, and gender—are powerful forces that shape marriage and family life. This discussion addresses each of these factors in turn, but bear in mind that they overlap in our lives.

Social Class

Social class determines both a family's financial security and its range of opportunities. Interviewing working-class women, Lillian Rubin (1976) found that wives thought a good husband was a man who held a steady job, did not drink too much, and was not violent. Rubin's middle-class respondents, by contrast, never mentioned such things; these women simply *assumed* that a husband would provide a safe and secure home. Their ideal husband was a man with whom they could talk easily, sharing feelings and experiences.

Clearly, what women (and men) hope for in marriage—and what they end up with—is linked to their social class. Much the same holds for children: Boys and girls lucky enough to be born into more affluent families enjoy better mental and physical health, develop more self-confidence, and go on to greater achievement than children born to poor parents (McLeod & Shanahan, 1993; Duncan et al., 1998).

Ethnicity and Race

Although ethnicity and race also shape families, American Indian, Latino, and African American families (like all families) do not fit any single generalization or stereotype (Allen, 1995).

American Indian Families

American Indians display a wide variety of family types. Some patterns emerge, however, among people who migrate from tribal reservations to cities. Women and men who arrive in cities often seek out others—especially kin and members of the same tribe—for help in getting settled. One study tells the story of two women migrants to the San Francisco area who met at a meeting of an Indian organization and realized they were of the same tribe. The women and their children decided to share an apartment, and soon after, the children began to refer to one another as brothers, sisters, and cousins. As the months passed, the two mothers came to think of themselves as sisters (Lobo, 2002).

Migration also creates "fluid households" with changing membership. In another case from this same study, a woman, her aunt, and their children rented a large apartment in San Francisco. Over the course of several months, they welcomed into their home more than thirty other urban migrants, each of whom stayed for a short time while looking for housing of their own. Such patterns of mutual assistance, involving real or fictional kinship, are common among low-income people.

┌─● Making the Grade

Remember that family patterns for American Indians, Latinos, or any other racial or ethnic category vary by social class and that the experiences of family life may also differ for women and men.

┌─● Seeing Sociology in Everyday Life

Surveys report that most U.S. teens now claim they have dated someone of another race. Do you think the proportion of mixed-race marriages will rise in the next twenty years? Why or why not?

Diversity Snapshot

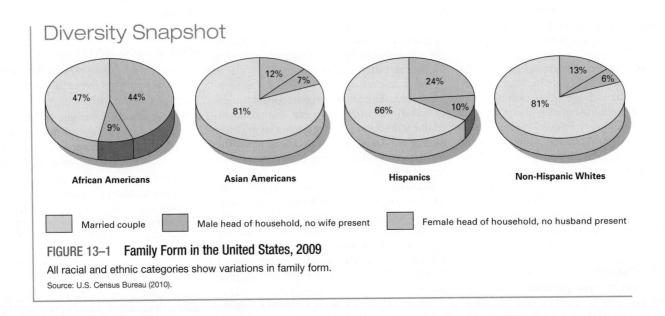

African Americans: 47%, 44%, 9%
Asian Americans: 81%, 12%, 7%
Hispanics: 66%, 24%, 10%
Non-Hispanic Whites: 81%, 13%, 6%

☐ Married couple   ☐ Male head of household, no wife present   ☐ Female head of household, no husband present

FIGURE 13–1 Family Form in the United States, 2009

All racial and ethnic categories show variations in family form.

Source: U.S. Census Bureau (2010).

American Indians who leave tribal reservations for the cities are typically better off than those who stay behind. Because people in reservations have a hard time finding work, they cannot easily form stable marriages, and problems such as alcoholism and drug abuse shatter the ties between parent and child.

Latino Families

Many Latinos enjoy the loyalty and support of extended families. Traditionally, Hispanic parents exercise greater control over children's courtship, considering marriage an alliance of families and not just a union based on romantic love. Some Hispanic families also follow conventional gender roles, prizing *machismo*—strength, daring, and sexual conquest—among men and treating women with respect but also close supervision.

However, assimilation into the larger society is changing these traditional patterns. As the story opening this chapter explained, many women who come to California from Mexico favor smaller families. Similarly, many Puerto Ricans who migrate to New York do not maintain the strong extended families they knew in Puerto Rico. In recent decades, the traditional authority of men over women has also lessened, especially among wealthy Latino families, whose number has more than tripled in the past twenty-five years (Navarro, 2004; Raley, Durden, & Wildsmith, 2004; U.S. Census Bureau, 2009).

Overall, however, the typical Hispanic family had an income of just $40,466 in 2008, or 68 percent of the national average (U.S. Census Bureau, 2009). Many Hispanic families suffer the stress of unemployment and other poverty-related problems.

African American Families

The U.S. Census Bureau reports that the typical African American family earned $39,879 in 2008, which was 65 percent of the national average. People of African ancestry are three times as likely as non-Hispanic whites to be poor, and poverty means that parents and children are likely to experience unemployment, substandard housing, and poor health.

Under these circumstances, maintaining stable family ties is difficult. Consider that 31 percent of African American women in their forties have never married, compared with about 9 percent of non-Hispanic white women of the same age. This means that African American women—often with children—are more likely to be single heads of households. Figure 13–1 shows that women headed 44 percent of African American families in 2009, compared with 24 percent of Hispanic families, 13 percent of non-Hispanic white families, and 12 percent of Asian and Pacific Islander families (U.S. Census Bureau, 2009).

Regardless of race, single-mother families are always at high risk of poverty. Twenty-one percent of U.S. families headed by non-Hispanic white women are poor. The higher poverty rate among families headed by African American women (37 percent) and Hispanic women (39 percent) is strong evidence of how the intersection of class, race, and gender can put women at a disadvantage. African American families with both wife and husband in the home, which represent 47 percent of the total, are much stronger economically, earning 80 percent as much as comparable non-Hispanic white families. But 70 percent of African American children are born to single

Go to the Multimedia Library at
mysoclab.com to view the *Core Concepts in Sociology* video "Changing Gender Roles at Home"

● Seeing Sociology
in Everyday Life

Given the high level of divorce in the United States, do you think it would be more accurate to call our marriage system "serial monogamy" (one partner after another)? Explain.

women, and 35 percent of African American boys and girls are growing up poor today, meaning that these families carry much of the burden of child poverty in the United States (Martin et al., 2009; U.S. Census Bureau, 2009).

Ethnically and Racially Mixed Marriages

Most spouses have similar social backgrounds with regard to class and race. But over the course of the twentieth century, ethnicity came to matter less and less. A woman of German or French ancestry might readily marry a man of Irish or English background without inviting disapproval from their families or from society in general.

Race has been a more powerful barrier. Before a 1967 Supreme Court decision (*Loving* v. *Virginia*), interracial marriage was actually illegal in sixteen states. Today, African, Asian, and Native Americans make up 18 percent of the U.S. population; if people ignored race in choosing spouses, we would expect about the same share of marriages to be mixed. The actual proportion of mixed marriages is 4 percent, showing that race still matters in social relations. But most people claim that race and ethnicity should not matter in choosing a partner. In addition, the age at first marriage has been rising to an average of 28.1 for men and 25.9 for women. Young people who marry a little later in life are more likely to make choices about partners with less input from parents.

One consequence of this increasing freedom of choice is that the share of ethnically and racially mixed marriages is increasing (Rosenfeld & Kim, 2005; U.S. Census Bureau, 2009). The most common type of interracial married couple is a white husband and an Asian wife, which accounts for about 21 percent of all interracial married couples. When ethnicity is considered, the most common type of "mixed" couple includes one partner who is Hispanic and one who is not. In nearly half of all "mixed" marriages, one partner claims a multiracial or multiethnic identity. Interracial married couples are most likely to live in the West; in five states—Hawaii, Alaska, California, Nevada, and Oklahoma—more than 10 percent of all married couples are interracial (Lee & Edmonston, 2005).

For most of our nation's history, interracial marriage was illegal. The last of these laws was struck down forty years ago. Although race and ethnicity continue to guide the process of courtship and marriage, interracial relationships are becoming more and more common.

Gender

The sociologist Jessie Bernard (1982) says that every marriage is actually two different relationships: the woman's marriage and the man's marriage. The reason is that few marriages have two equal partners. Although patriarchy has diminished, many people still expect husbands to be older and taller than their wives and to have more important, better-paid jobs. ● Go to **mysoclab.com**

Why, then, do many people think that marriage benefits women more than men? The positive stereotype of the carefree bachelor contrasts sharply with the negative image of the lonely spinster, suggesting that women are fulfilled only through being wives and mothers.

However, Bernard points out, married women actually have poorer mental health, less happiness, and more passive attitudes toward life than single women do. Married men, on the other hand, generally live longer, are mentally better off, and report being happier than single men. These differences suggest why, after divorce, men are more eager than women to find a new partner.

Bernard concludes that there is no better assurance of long life, health, and happiness for a man than having a woman devote her life to taking care of him and providing the security of a well-ordered home. She is quick to add that marriage *could* be healthful for women if husbands did not dominate wives and expect them to do almost all the housework. Survey responses confirm that couples rank "sharing household chores" as one of the most important factors that contribute to a successful marriage (Pew Research Center, 2007a).

Transitions and Problems in Family Life

The newspaper columnist Ann Landers once remarked that one marriage in twenty is wonderful, five in twenty are good, ten in twenty are tolerable, and the remaining four are "pure hell." Families can be a source of joy, but the reality of family life can also fall short of the ideal.

Divorce

Our society strongly supports marriage, and about nine out of ten people in the United States at some point "tie the knot." But many of today's marriages unravel. Figure 13–2 on page 380 shows that the U.S. divorce rate has more than tripled over the past century. Today, almost four in ten marriages eventually end in divorce (for African Americans, the rate is about six in

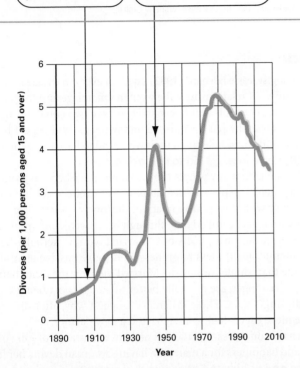

Go to the Multimedia Library at **mysoclab.com**
to listen to the NPR report "Marital Stress"

A century ago, many people regarded divorce as a mark of personal failure.

The divorce rate rose during World War II, when many couples were separated for long periods of time.

FIGURE 13–2 Divorce Rate for the United States, 1890–2008

Over the long term, the U.S. divorce rate has gone up. Since about 1980, however, the trend has been downward.

Sources: Tejada-Vera & Sutton (2009) and U.S. Census Bureau (2009).

dependency on their husbands. Thus women find it easier to leave unhappy marriages.

4. **Many of today's marriages are stressful.** With both partners working outside the home in most cases, people have less time and energy for family life. This makes raising children harder than ever. Children do stabilize some marriages, but divorce is most common during the early years of marriage when many couples have young children. ● Go to **mysoclab.com**

5. **Divorce has become socially acceptable.** Divorce no longer carries the powerful stigma it did just a few generations ago. Family and friends are now less likely to discourage couples in conflict from divorcing.

6. **Legally, a divorce is easier to get.** In the past, courts required divorcing couples to demonstrate that one or both were guilty of behavior such as adultery or physical abuse. Today, all states allow divorce if a couple simply states that the marriage has failed. Concern about easy divorce, shared by about half of U.S. adults, has led some states to consider rewriting their marriage laws (Phillips, 2001; NORC, 2009).

Who Divorces?

At greatest risk of divorce are young couples—especially those who marry after a brief courtship—who tend to lack money and emotional maturity. The chance of divorce also rises if a couple marries after an unexpected pregnancy or if one or both partners have substance abuse problems. People who are not religious are more likely to divorce than those who have strong religious beliefs. Finally, people whose parents divorced also have a higher divorce rate themselves. Research suggests that a role-modeling effect is at work: Children who see parents go through divorce are more likely to consider divorce themselves (Amato, 2001; Pew Research Center, 2008).

Divorce is also more common when both partners have successful careers, perhaps because of the strains of a two-career marriage but also because financially secure people may not feel that they have to remain in an unhappy home. In addition, men and women who divorce once are more likely to divorce again, probably because high-risk factors follow them from one marriage to another.

Divorce and Children

Because mothers usually gain custody of children but fathers typically earn more income, the well-being of many children depends on fathers' making court-ordered child support payments. Courts award child support in 57 percent of all divorces involving children. Yet in any given year, half of children legally entitled to support receive partial payments or no payments at all. Some 3.2 million "deadbeat dads" fail to support their youngsters. In response, federal legislation now requires employers to withhold money from the earnings of fathers or mothers

ten). From another angle, of all people over the age of fifteen, 21 percent of men and 23 percent of women have been divorced at some point. Ours is the highest divorce rate in the world; it is about 1½ times as high as in Canada and Japan and four times higher than in Italy and Ireland (European Union, 2010; OECD, 2010).

Causes of Divorce

The high U.S. divorce rate has many causes (Furstenberg & Cherlin, 1991; Etzioni, 1993; Popenoe, 1999; Greenspan, 2001):

1. **Individualism is on the rise.** Today's family members spend less time together. We have become more individualistic, more concerned with our own personal happiness and earning income than about the happiness and well-being of our partners and children.

2. **Romantic love fades.** Because our culture bases marriage on romantic love, relationships may fail as sexual passion fades. Many people end a marriage in favor of a new relationship that promises renewed excitement and romance.

3. **Women are less dependent on men.** Women's increasing participation in the labor force has reduced wives' financial

● Seeing Sociology
in Everyday Life

A girl who has been an only child becomes part of a "blended family" and suddenly has two older brothers. What adjustments might she have to make?

who fail to pay up; it is a serious crime to refuse to make child support payments or to move to another state to avoid making them (U.S. Census Bureau, 2009).

Remarriage and Blended Families

Three out of four people who divorce remarry, most within four years. Nationwide, more than one-third of all marriages are now remarriages for at least one partner. Men, who benefit more from wedlock, are more likely than women to remarry.

Remarriage often creates *blended families,* composed of children and some combination of biological parents and stepparents. With brothers, sisters, half-siblings, a stepparent—not to mention a biological parent who may live elsewhere and be married to someone else with other children—young people in blended families face the challenge of defining many new relationships and deciding just who is part of the nuclear family. Parents often have trouble defining responsibility for household work among people unsure of their relationships to each other. When the custody of children is an issue, ex-spouses can be an unwelcome presence for people in a new marriage. Although blended families require a great deal of new adjustment, they also offer both young and old the chance to relax rigid family roles (Furstenberg & Cherlin, 2001; McLanahan, 2002).

Family Violence

The ideal family is a source of pleasure and support. However, the disturbing reality of many homes is **family violence,** *emotional, physical, or sexual abuse of one family member by another.* The sociologist Richard J. Gelles calls the family "the most violent group in society with the exception of the police and the military" (quoted in Roesch, 1984:75).

Violence against Women

Family brutality often goes unreported to police. Even so, the U.S. Bureau of Justice Statistics (2009) estimates that about 550,000 people are victims of domestic violence each year. Family violence harms both sexes, but not equally—women are three times more likely than men to be a victim. In cases of deadly violence, the gender disparity is very large—fully 35 percent of women who are victims of homicide, but just 2 percent of men, are killed by spouses, partners, or ex-partners. Nationwide, the death toll from family violence is about 1,100 women each year. Overall, women are more likely to be injured by a family member than to be mugged or raped by a stranger or hurt in an automobile accident (Shupe, Stacey, & Hazlewood, 1987; Blankenhorn, 1995; U.S. Bureau of Justice Statistics, 2009).

Historically, the law defined wives as the property of their husbands, so no man could be charged with raping his wife. Today, however, all fifty states have *marital rape laws.* The law no longer regards

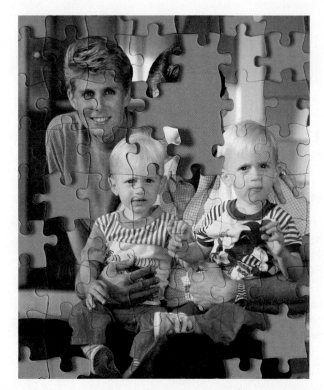

Divorce may be a solution for a couple in an unhappy marriage, but it can be a problem for children who experience the withdrawal of a parent from their social world. In what ways can divorce be harmful to children? Is there a positive side to divorce? How might separating parents better prepare their children for the transition of parental divorce?

domestic violence as a private family matter; it gives victims more options. Now, even without separation or divorce, a woman can obtain court protection from an abusive spouse, and all states have stalking laws that prohibit one ex-partner from following or otherwise threatening the other. Communities across North America have established shelters to provide counseling and temporary housing for women and children driven from their homes by domestic violence. Finally, the harm caused by domestic violence goes beyond the physical injuries. Victims often lose their ability to trust others. One study found that women who had been physically or sexually abused were much less likely than nonvictims to form stable relationships later on (Cherlin et al., 2004).

Violence against Children

Family violence also victimizes children. Each year, there are roughly 3.5 million reports of alleged child abuse or neglect. In 2007, 1,760 of the cases involved a child's death. Child abuse involves more than

● Seeing Sociology
in Everyday Life

In what ways do children benefit from growing up in a
household with both biological parents?

For a discussion of stereotyping of single parents,
go to the Multimedia Library at **mysoclab.com**
to view the *Core Concepts in Sociology* video
"Racial Stereotypes and Discrimination"

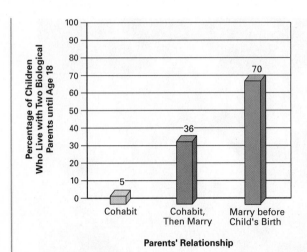

FIGURE 13–3 **Parental Involvement in Children's Lives:
Cohabiting and Married Parents**

Marriage increases the odds that children will remain in the same
household with both biological parents as they grow up.

Source: Phillips (2001).

physical injury; abusive adults can also misuse power and trust to
damage a child's emotional well-being. Child abuse and neglect are
most common among the youngest and most vulnerable children
(Besharov & Laumann, 1996; U.S. Department of Health and Human
Services, 2009).

Although child abusers conform to no simple stereotype, they
are more likely to be women (57 percent) than men (43 percent). But
almost all abusers share one trait: having been abused themselves as
children. Researchers have found that violent behavior in close relationships is learned; in families, violence begets violence (S. Levine,
2001; U.S. Department of Health and Human Services, 2009).

Alternative Family Forms

Most families in the United States are composed of a married couple
who raise children. But in recent decades, our society has displayed
increasing diversity in family life.

One-Parent Families

Thirty percent of U.S. families with children under eighteen have only
one parent in the household, a proportion that more than doubled
since 1970. Put another way, 26 percent of U.S. children now live with
only one parent, and about half will do so before reaching eighteen.

One-parent families, 85 percent of which are headed by a single
mother, result from divorce, death, or an unmarried woman's decision
to have a child.

Single parenthood increases a woman's risk of poverty because
it limits her ability to work and to further her education. The opposite is also true: Poverty raises the odds that a woman will become
a single mother. But single parenthood goes well beyond the poor:
One-third of women in the United States become pregnant as
teenagers, and many decide to raise their children whether they
marry or not. Even more important, the number of unmarried
women in their twenties, thirties, and forties who decide to have a
child is increasing (Pew Research Center, 2007a; Martin et al., 2009).
Looking back at Figure 13–1 on page 378, note that 53 percent of
African American families are headed by a single parent. Single
parenthood is less common among Hispanics (34 percent), Asian
Americans (19 percent), and non-Hispanic whites (19 percent). In
many single-parent families, mothers turn to their own mothers
for support. In the United States, then, the rise in single parenting
is tied to a declining role for fathers and the growing importance
of grandmothers. ● Go to **mysoclab.com**

Research shows that growing up in a one-parent family usually
puts children at a disadvantage. Some studies claim that because a
father and a mother each make a distinctive contribution to a child's
social development, one parent has a hard time doing as good a job
alone. But the most serious problem for one-parent families,
especially if that parent is a woman, is poverty. On average, children
growing up in a single-parent family start out poorer, get less schooling, and end up with lower incomes as adults. Such children are also
more likely to become single parents themselves (Popenoe, 1993a;
Blankenhorn, 1995; Kantrowitz & Wingert, 2001; McLanahan, 2002;
U.S. Census Bureau, 2010).

Cohabitation

Cohabitation is *the sharing of a household by an unmarried couple.*
In global perspective, cohabitation as a long-term form of family life,
with or without children, is especially common in Sweden and other
Scandinavian countries and is gaining in popularity in other European
nations. In the United States, the number of cohabiting couples has
increased from about 500,000 in 1970 to about 6.2 million today
(5.6 million heterosexual couples and 565,000 homosexual couples),
or about 5 percent of all households. Almost half of people between
twenty-five and forty-four years of age have cohabited at some point
(U.S. Census Bureau, 2009).

Cohabiting tends to appeal more to independent-minded people and those who favor gender equality (Brines & Joyner, 1999).
Most couples cohabit for no more than a few years; at that point,
about half decide to marry and half split up. Mounting evidence

cohabitation the sharing of a household by an unmarried couple

● Seeing Sociology
in Everyday Life

Have you ever lived with a partner informally? How does cohabitation differ from marriage?

suggests that living together may actually discourage marriage because partners (especially men) become used to low-commitment relationships. For this reason, cohabiting couples who have children—currently representing one-eighth of all births—are not always long-term parents. Figure 13–3 shows that just 5 percent of children born to cohabiting couples will live until age eighteen with both biological parents if the parents remain unmarried. The share rises to 36 percent among children whose parents marry at some point, but this is still half of the 70 percent figure for children whose parents married before they were born. When cohabiting couples with children separate, the involvement of both parents, especially with respect to financial support, is highly uncertain (Popenoe & Whitehead, 1999; Booth & Crouter, 2002; Scommegna, 2002).

Gay and Lesbian Couples

In 1989, Denmark became the first country to permit registered partnerships with the benefits of marriage for same-sex couples. Since then, more than fifteen countries, including Norway (1993), Sweden (1994), Iceland (1996), Finland (2001), the United Kingdom (2004), and Australia (2008) have followed suit. However, only seven countries have extended marriage—in name as well as in practice—to same-sex couples: the Netherlands (2001), Belgium (2003), Canada (2005), Spain (2005), South Africa (2006), Norway (2008), and Sweden (2009).

In the United States, Massachusetts became the first state to legalize same-sex marriage in 2004. As of 2010, Iowa, Vermont, Connecticut, New Hampshire, and the District of Columbia have also changed their laws to allow same-sex marriage. New Jersey, California, Oregon, and Nevada permit same-sex civil unions or domestic partnerships with nearly all the rights of marriage.

Back in 1996, Congress passed a law defining marriage as joining one man and one woman. Since then, a total of thirty states have amended their constitutions to permit marriage only between one man and one woman. Nonetheless, the trend in public opinion is toward greater acceptance of same-sex marriage. Currently, more than one-third of U.S. adults support gay marriage, and over half support civil unions providing the rights enjoyed by married couples (Newport, 2005; NORC, 2009:1712; Pew Research Center, 2009).

Most gay couples with children in the United States are raising the offspring of previous heterosexual unions; others have adopted children. But many gay parents are quiet about their sexual orientation, not wanting to draw unwelcome attention to their children or to themselves. In several widely publicized cases, courts have removed children from the custody of homosexual couples, citing the "best interests" of the children.

In 2009, Iowa joined the growing number of states that allow same-sex couples to marry. Some people oppose any same-sex relationships; others support civil unions; still others believe that same-sex marriage should be lawful throughout the United States. Where do you stand on this issue? Why?

Gay parenting challenges many traditional ideas. But it also shows that many gay couples value family life as highly as heterosexuals do.

Singlehood

Because nine out of ten people in the United States marry, we tend to see singlehood as a temporary stage of life. However, increasing numbers of people of all ages are living alone, often by choice. In 1950, only one household in ten contained a single person. By 2009, this share had risen to 27 percent, a total of 31 million single adult households (U.S. Census Bureau, 2010).

Most striking is the rising number of single young women. In 1960, some 28 percent of women aged twenty to twenty-four were single; by 2009, the proportion had soared to 77 percent. Underlying this trend is women's greater participation in the labor force. Women who are economically secure view a husband as a matter of choice rather than a financial necessity and marry later or, in some cases, not at all (Edwards, 2000).

By midlife, many unmarried women sense a lack of available men. Because our society expects women to "marry up," the older a woman is, the more education she has, and the better her job, the more difficulty she has finding a suitable husband.

○ Seeing Sociology
in Everyday Life

Do you think developments in genetic manipulation
that permit parents to have "designer children" are,
on balance, helpful or harmful? Why?

○ Making the Grade

Whatever your view of traditional families, be sure you can
point to ways U.S. families have changed since 1960.

CONTROVERSY & DEBATE

Should We Save the Traditional Family?

AARON: My parents were really goin' at each other last night. Man, I don't know whether they're going to stay together.

ABDUL: I hope they do, my friend. Families are what ties society together.

TAWNEESHA: Listen to you guys! The important thing is for each person to be happy. If being married does it for you, great. But there's lots of different ways for people to find happiness.

What are "traditional families"? Are they vital to our way of life or a barrier to progress? People use the term *traditional family* to mean a married couple who at some point in their lives raise children. Statistically speaking, traditional families are less common than they used to be. In 1950, as the figure shows, 90 percent of U.S. households were families—using the Census Bureau's definition of two or more persons related by blood, marriage, or adoption. By 2009, just 67 percent of households were families, due to rising levels of divorce, cohabitation, and singlehood.

"Traditional family" is more than just a handy expression; it is also a moral statement. Belief in the traditional family implies giving high value to becoming and staying married, putting children ahead of careers, and favoring two-parent families over various alternatives.

"Traditional Families Are the Solution"

On one side of the debate, David Popenoe (1993a) warns that there has been a serious erosion of the traditional family since 1960. At that time, married couples with young children accounted for almost half of all households; today, the figure is 21 percent. Singlehood is up, from 10 percent of households in 1960 to

Share of U.S. Households That the Census Bureau Classifies as Families, 1950 and 2009

Families made up a smaller share of all U.S. households in 2009 than they did in 1950.

27 percent today. And the divorce rate has risen by 59 percent since 1960, so that nearly four in ten of today's marriages end in permanent separation. Because of both divorce and the increasing number of children born to single women, the share of youngsters who live with just one parent has almost tripled since 1960 to 26 percent (Tejada-Vera & Sutton, 2009; U.S. Census Bureau, 2010). In other words, just one in four of today's children will grow up with two parents and go on to maintain a stable marriage as an adult.

In light of such data, Popenoe concludes, it may not be an exaggeration to say that the family is falling apart. He sees a fundamental shift from a "culture of marriage" to a "culture of divorce," where traditional vows of marital commitment—"till death do us part"—now amount to little more than "as long as I am happy."

The negative consequences of the cultural trend toward weaker families, Popenoe continues, are obvious and can be found everywhere: As we pay less and less attention to children, the crime rate among young people goes up, along with a host of other problem behaviors including underage smoking and drinking, premarital sex, and teen suicide.

As Popenoe sees it, we must work hard and act quickly to reverse current trends. Government cannot be the solution and may even be

New Reproductive Technologies and Family

Medical advances involving new reproductive technologies are also changing families. In 1978, England's Louise Brown became the world's first "test-tube baby"; since then, tens of thousands of children have been conceived outside the womb.

Test-tube babies are the product of *in vitro fertilization*, in which doctors unite a woman's egg and a man's sperm "in glass" (usually not a test tube but a shallow dish) rather than in a woman's body. Doctors then either implant the resulting embryo in the womb of the woman who is to bear the child or freeze it for implantation at a later time.

Modern reproductive technologies allow some couples who cannot conceive normally to have children. These techniques may also eventually help reduce the incidence of birth defects. Genetic screening of sperm and eggs would allow medical specialists to increase the odds for the birth of a healthy baby. But new reproductive technologies also raise difficult and troubling questions: When one woman carries an embryo developed from the egg of another, who is the mother? When a couple divorces, which spouse is entitled to use, or destroy, their frozen embryos? Should parents use genetic screening to select the traits of their child? Such questions remind us that technology changes faster than our ability to understand the consequences of its use.

● Seeing Sociology
in Everyday Life

How important do you think strong families are to the health
of our society? What makes a family "strong"?

● Seeing Sociology
in Everyday Life

Make a list of three or four changes you expect to see in
U.S. families fifty years from now. Are these changes for the
better or not? Why?

part of the problem: Since 1960, as families have weakened, government spending on social programs has soared fivefold. To save the traditional family, says Popenoe, we need a cultural turnaround similar to what happened with regard to cigarette smoking. In this case, we must replace our "me first" attitudes with commitment to our spouse and children and publicly endorse the two-parent family as best for the well-being of children.

"Traditional Families Are the Problem"
Judith Stacey (1993) provides a feminist viewpoint, saying "good riddance" to the traditional family. In her view, the traditional family is more problem than solution: "The family is not here to stay. Nor should we wish it were. On the contrary, I believe that all democratic people, whatever their kinship preferences, should work to hasten its demise" (Stacey, 1990:269).

The main reason for rejecting the traditional family, Stacey explains, is that it perpetuates social inequality. Families play a key role in maintaining the class hierarchy by transferring wealth as well as "cultural capital" from one generation to another. Feminists criticize the traditional family's patriarchal form, which subjects women to their husbands' authority and gives them most of the

responsibility for housework and child care. From a gay rights perspective, she adds, a society that values traditional families also denies homosexual men and women equal participation in social life.

Stacey thus applauds the breakdown of the family as social progress. She does not view the family as a necessary social institution but as a political construction that elevates one category of people—affluent white males—above others, including women, homosexuals, and poor people.

Stacey also claims that the concept of the "traditional family" is increasingly irrelevant in a diverse society in which both men and women work for income. What our society needs, Stacey concludes, is not a return to some golden age of the family but political and economic change, including income parity for women, universal health care and child care, programs to reduce unemployment, and expanded sex education in the schools. Such measures not only help families but also ensure that people in diverse family forms receive the respect and dignity they deserve.

Whether the traditional family is a positive force in U.S. society or a negative one depends on your point of view.

WHAT DO YOU THINK?

1. To strengthen families, David Popenoe suggests that parents put children ahead of their own careers by limiting their joint workweek to sixty hours. Do you agree? Why or why not?

2. Judith Stacey thinks that marriage is weaker today because women are rejecting patriarchal relationships. What do you think about this argument?

3. Do we need to change family patterns for the well-being of our children? As you see it, what specific changes are called for?

Families: Looking Ahead

Family life in the United States will continue to change in years to come, and with change comes controversy. Advocates of "traditional family values" line up against those who support greater personal choice; the Controversy & Debate box outlines some of the issues. Sociologists cannot predict the outcome of this debate, but based on ongoing research on family patterns, we can suggest five likely future trends.

First, the divorce rate is likely to remain high, even in the face of evidence that marital breakups put children at higher risk of poverty. Today's marriages are about as durable as they were a century ago, when many were cut short by death. The difference is that now more

couples *choose* to end marriages that fail to meet their expectations. Although the divorce rate has declined since 1980, it is unlikely that we will ever return to the low rates that marked the early decades of the twentieth century.

Second, family life in the future will be more diverse. Cohabiting couples, one-parent families, gay and lesbian families, and blended families are all on the rise. Most families are still based on marriage, and most married couples still have children. But the diversity of family forms implies a trend toward more personal choice.

Third, men will play a limited role in child rearing. In the 1950s, a decade many people consider the "golden age" of families, men began to withdraw from active parenting (Snell, 1990; Stacey, 1990).

profane included as an ordinary element of everyday life

sacred set apart as extraordinary, inspiring awe and reverence

religion a social institution involving beliefs and practices based on recognizing the sacred

faith belief based on conviction rather than on scientific evidence

totem an object in the natural world collectively defined as sacred

Seeing Sociology in Everyday Life

Can you recall instances of people turning to sacred symbols after a tragic event? Explain what happened.

In recent years, a countertrend has become evident, with some older, highly educated fathers making the choice to stay at home with young children, many using computer technology to continue their work. But we should not overestimate the importance of this trend because the stay-at-home dad represents only about 1 percent of all fathers of young children (U.S. Census Bureau, 2010). The bigger picture is that the high divorce rate in the United States and the increase in single motherhood are weakening children's ties to fathers and increasing children's risk of poverty.

Fourth, families will continue to feel the effects of economic changes. In many homes, both household partners work, increasing income but reducing marriage and family to the interaction of weary men and women trying to fit a little "quality time" with their children into an already full schedule. The long-term effects of the two-career couple on families as we have known them are likely to be mixed.

Fifth and finally, the importance of new reproductive technologies will increase. Ethical concerns about whether what *can* be done *should* be done will surely slow these developments, but new reproductive technologies will continue to alter the traditional experience of parenthood.

Despite the changes and controversies that have shaken the family in the United States, most people in our society still report being happy in their roles as partners and parents. Marriage and family life will likely remain a foundation of our society for generations to come.

Religion: Basic Concepts

Like family, religion plays an important part in human society. Families have long used religious rituals to celebrate birth, recognize adulthood, and mourn the dead.

The French sociologist Emile Durkheim stated that religion involves "things that surpass the limits of our knowledge" (1965:62, orig. 1915). As human beings, we regard most objects, events, and experiences as **profane** (from Latin, meaning "outside the temple"), *included as an ordinary part of everyday life.* But we also consider some things **sacred,** *set apart as extraordinary, inspiring awe and reverence.* Setting the sacred apart from the profane is the essence of all religious belief. **Religion,** then, is *a social institution involving beliefs and practices based on recognizing the sacred.*

There is great diversity in matters of faith, and nothing is sacred to everyone on Earth. Although people regard most books as profane, Jews believe that the Torah (containing the first five books of the Hebrew Bible, also known as the Old Testament) is sacred, in the same way that Christians revere the Old and New Testaments of the Bible and Muslims exalt the Qur'an (Koran).

But no matter how a community of believers draws religious lines, Durkheim (1965:62, orig. 1915) explained, people understand profane things in terms of their everyday usefulness: We log on to the Internet with our computer or turn a key to start our car. What is sacred we reverently set apart from daily life, giving it a "forbidden" or "holy" aura. For example, Muslims remove their shoes before entering a mosque to avoid defiling a sacred place with soles that have touched the profane ground outside.

The sacred is embodied in *ritual,* or formal ceremonial behavior. Holy Communion is the central ritual of Christianity; to the Christian faithful, the wafer and wine consumed during Communion are treated not in a profane way as food but as the sacred symbols of the body and blood of Jesus Christ.

Because religion deals with ideas that transcend everyday experience, neither common sense nor sociology can prove or disprove religious doctrine. Religion is a matter of **faith,** *belief based on conviction rather than on scientific evidence.* The New Testament of the Bible defines faith as "the conviction of things not seen" (Hebrews 11:1) and urges Christians to "walk by faith, not by sight" (2 Corinthians 5:7).

Some people with strong religious beliefs may be disturbed by the thought of sociologists turning a scientific eye on what they hold sacred. However, sociological study is no threat to anyone's faith. Sociologists study religion just as they study family, to understand religious experiences around the world and how religion is tied to other social institutions. They make no judgments about whether a specific religion is "right" or "wrong." Sociological analysis takes a more worldly approach, seeking to understand what religions have in common and how they differ as well as how religious activity affects society as a whole.

Although it began as a cult, Christianity's 2 billion followers make it now the most widespread of the world's religions.

Go to the Multimedia Library at **mysoclab.com** to view the *Core Concepts in Sociology* video "History of Religion in America"

Seeing Sociology in Everyday Life

Sports culture has a semireligious character. What is the function for local communities of supporting teams, such as the Ohio State Buckeyes, the Iowa State Cyclones, or the San Francisco 49ers?

Theoretical Analysis of Religion

Sociologists apply the major theoretical approaches to the study of religion just as they do to any other topic. Each provides distinctive insights about the ways religion shapes social life.

Functions of Religion: Structural-Functional Analysis

According to Emile Durkheim (1965, orig. 1915), society has a life and power of its own beyond the life of any individual. In a sense, society itself is godlike, shaping the lives of its members and living on beyond them. Practicing religion, people everywhere celebrate the awesome power of their society.

No wonder people around the world transform everyday objects into sacred symbols of their collective life. Members of technologically simple societies do this with a **totem,** *an object in the natural world collectively defined as sacred.* The totem—perhaps an animal or an elaborate work of art—becomes the centerpiece of ritual and symbolizes the power of collective life over the individual. In our society, the flag is a quasi-religious totem that is not to be used in a profane way (say, as clothing) or allowed to touch the ground.

Durkheim identified three major functions of religion that contribute to the operation of society:

1. **Social cohesion.** Religion unites people through shared symbolism, values, and norms. Religious thought and ritual establish rules of fair play, organizing our social life.

2. **Social control.** Society uses religious ideas to promote conformity. By defining God as a "judge," many religions encourage people to obey cultural norms. Religion can also be used to back up political systems. In medieval Europe, for example, monarchs claimed to rule by "divine right." Even today, our leaders publicly ask for God's blessing, implying that their efforts are right and just.

3. **Providing meaning and purpose.** Religious belief offers the comforting sense that our lives serve some greater purpose. Strengthened by such beliefs, people are less likely to despair in the face of change or even tragedy. For this reason, we mark major life transitions—including birth, marriage, and death—with religious observances.

 Go to **mysoclab.com**

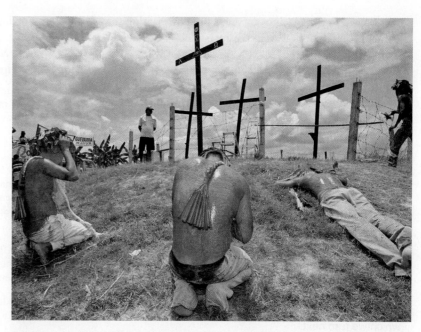

Religion is founded on the concept of the sacred—aspects of our existence that are set apart as extraordinary and demand our submission. Bowing, kneeling, or prostrating oneself are all ways of symbolically surrendering to a higher power. These Filipino Christians seek atonement for their sins in an annual Lenten ritual.

CRITICAL REVIEW In Durkheim's structural-functional analysis, religion represents the collective life that helps hold society together. The major weakness of this approach is that it downplays religion's dysfunctions, especially the fact that strongly held beliefs can generate social conflict. Terrorists have claimed that God supports their actions, and nations march to war under the banner of their God. Looking around the world, few people would deny that religious beliefs have provoked more violence in the world than differences of social class.

CHECK YOUR LEARNING What are Durkheim's three functions of religion for society?

Constructing the Sacred: Symbolic-Interaction Analysis

From a symbolic-interaction point of view, religion (like all of society) is socially constructed (although perhaps with divine inspiration). Through various rituals—from daily prayer to annual events such as Easter, Passover, or Ramadan—people sharpen the distinction between the sacred and the profane. Furthermore, says Peter

● Seeing Sociology
in Everyday Life

Can you point to rituals other than marriage that
involve religious leaders and sacred meanings?
Explain.

● Seeing Sociology
in Everyday Life

Can you think of an example of one society using the idea of
"converting heathens" to justify controlling another society?
Explain.

Berger (1967:35–36), placing our small, brief lives within some "cosmic frame of reference" gives us the appearance of "ultimate security and permanence."

Marriage is a good example. If two people look on marriage as a simple contract, they can walk away whenever they want. Their bond makes much stronger claims on them when it is defined as holy matrimony, which is surely one reason for the lower divorce rate among people with strong religious beliefs. More generally, whenever humans face uncertainty or life-threatening situations—such as illness, natural disaster, terrorist attack, or war—we find comfort in our sacred symbols.

○ **CRITICAL REVIEW** Using the symbolic-interaction approach, religion gives everyday life sacred meaning. Berger adds that the sacred's ability to give meaning and stability to society depends on ignoring the fact that it is socially constructed. After all, how much strength could we gain from sacred beliefs if we saw them merely as strategies for coping with tragedy? Also, this micro-level view ignores religion's link to social inequality, to which we turn next.

○ **CHECK YOUR LEARNING** Following Berger's thinking, why would religious people have a low divorce rate?

Inequality and Religion: Social-Conflict Analysis

The social-conflict approach highlights religion's support of social inequality. Religion, proclaimed Karl Marx, serves elites by legitimizing the status quo and diverting people's attention from social inequities.

Today, the British monarch is the formal head of the Church of England, illustrating the close ties between religious and political elites. In practical terms, working for political change may mean opposing the church and, by implication, opposing God. Religion also encourages people to accept the social problems of this world while they look hopefully to a "better world to come." In a well-known statement, Marx dismissed religion as "the sigh of the oppressed creature, the sentiment of a heartless world, and the soul of soulless conditions. It is the opium of the people" (1964:27, orig. 1848).

Religion and social inequality are also linked through gender because virtually all the world's major religions are patriarchal. For example, the Qur'an, the sacred text of Islam, gives men social dominance over women by defining gender roles: "Men are in charge of women. . . . Hence good women are obedient. . . . As for those whose rebelliousness you fear, admonish them, banish them from your bed, and scourge [punish] them" (Qur'an 4:34, quoted in W. Kaufman, 1976:163).

Christianity, the major religion in the Western Hemisphere, has also supported patriarchy throughout history. Although Christians revere Mary, the mother of Jesus, the New Testament contains the following passages:

A man . . . is the image and glory of God; but woman is the glory of man. For man was not made from woman, but woman from man. Neither was man created for woman, but woman for man. (1 Corinthians 11:7–9)

As in all the churches of the saints, the women should keep silence in the churches. For they are not permitted to speak, but should be subordinate, as even the law says. If there is anything they desire to know, let them ask their husbands at home. For it is shameful for a woman to speak in church. (1 Corinthians 14:33–35)

Wives, be subject to your husbands, as to the Lord. For the husband is the head of the wife as Christ is the head of the church. . . . As the church is subject to Christ, so let wives also be subject in everything to their husbands. (Ephesians 5:22–24)

Judaism has also traditionally supported patriarchy. Male Orthodox Jews recite the following prayer each day:

Blessed art thou, O Lord our God, King of the Universe, that I was not born a gentile.
　　Blessed art thou, O Lord our God, King of the Universe, that I was not born a slave.
　　Blessed art thou, O Lord our God, King of the Universe, that I was not born a woman.

Despite patriarchal traditions, most religions now have women in leadership roles, and many are introducing more gender-neutral language in hymnals and prayer books. Such changes involve not just organizational patterns but also conceptions of God. The theologian Mary Daly puts the matter bluntly: "If God is male, then male is God" (cited in Woodward, 1989:58).

○ **CRITICAL REVIEW** Social-conflict analysis emphasizes the power of religion to support social inequality. Yet religion also promotes change toward equality. For example, nineteenth-century religious groups in the United States played an important role in the movement to abolish slavery. In the 1950s and 1960s, religious organizations and their leaders were at the core of the civil rights movement. In the 1960s and 1970s, many clergy actively opposed the Vietnam War, and today many support any number of progressive causes such as feminism and gay rights.

The Applying Theory table summarizes the three theoretical approaches to understanding religion.

○ **CHECK YOUR LEARNING** How does religion help maintain class inequality and gender stratification?

○ Making the Grade

Carefully review the Applying Theory table below to ensure that you understand the three theoretical approaches to religion.

liberation theology the combining of Christian principles with political activism, often Marxist in character

● APPLYING THEORY ●

Religion

	Structural-Functional Approach	Symbolic-Interaction Approach	Social-Conflict Approach
What is the level of analysis?	Macro-level	Micro-level	Macro-level
What is the importance of religion for society?	Religion performs vital tasks, including uniting people and controlling behavior.	Religion strengthens marriage by giving it (and family life) sacred meaning.	Religion supports social inequality by claiming that the social order is just.
	Religion gives life meaning and purpose.	People often turn to sacred symbols for comfort when facing danger and uncertainty.	Religion turns attention from problems in this world to a "better world to come."

Religion and Social Change

Religion can be the conservative force portrayed by Karl Marx. But at some points in history, as Max Weber (1958, orig. 1904–05) explained, religion has promoted dramatic social change.

Max Weber: Protestantism and Capitalism

Weber believed that particular religious ideas set into motion a wave of change that brought about the industrialization of Western Europe. The rise of industrial capitalism was encouraged by Calvinism, a movement within the Protestant Reformation.

Central to the religious thought of John Calvin (1509–1564) is the doctrine of *predestination:* An all-knowing, all-powerful God has selected some people for salvation while condemning most to eternal damnation. Each person's fate, sealed before birth and known only to God, is either eternal glory or endless hellfire.

Driven by anxiety over their fate, Calvinists understandably looked for signs of God's favor in this world and came to see prosperity as a sign of divine blessing. Religious conviction and a rigid devotion to duty thus led Calvinists to work hard, and many amassed great wealth. But money was not for selfish spending or even for sharing with the poor, whose plight they saw as a mark of God's rejection. As agents for God's work on Earth, Calvinists believed that they could best fulfill their "calling" by reinvesting profits and achieving ever-greater success in the process.

All the while, the Calvinists lived thrifty lives and embraced technological advances, thereby laying the groundwork for the rise of industrial capitalism. In time, the religious fervor that motivated early Calvinists weakened, resulting in a profane "Protestant work ethic." To Max Weber, industrial capitalism itself was a "disenchanted" religion, further showing the power of religion to change the shape of society.

Liberation Theology

Historically, Christianity has reached out to suffering and oppressed people, urging all to strengthen their faith in a better life to come. In recent decades, however, some church leaders and theologians have taken a decidedly political approach and endorsed **liberation theology,** *the combining of Christian principles with political activism, often Marxist in character.*

This social movement started in the late 1960s in Latin America's Roman Catholic Church. Today, Christian activists continue to help people in poor nations liberate themselves from abysmal poverty. Their message is simple: Social oppression runs counter to Christian morality, so as a matter of faith and justice, Christians must promote greater social equality.

Pope Benedict XVI, like Pope John Paul II before him, condemns liberation theology for distorting church doctrine with left-wing politics. Nevertheless, the liberation theology movement has gained strength in the poorest countries of Latin America, where many people's Christian faith drives them to improve conditions for the world's poor (Neuhouser, 1989; J. E. Williams, 2002).

Types of Religious Organizations

Sociologists categorize the hundreds of different religious organizations in the United States along a continuum with *churches* at one end and *sects* at the other. We can describe any religious organization in relation to these two ideal types by placing it on the church-sect continuum.

Church

Drawing on the ideas of his teacher Max Weber, Ernst Troeltsch (1931) defined a **church** as *a religious organization that is well integrated into the larger society*. Churchlike organizations typically persist for centuries and include generations of the same families. Churches have

In global perspective, the range of religious activity is truly astonishing. Members of this Southeast Asian cult show their devotion to God by suspending themselves in the air using ropes and sharp hooks that pierce their skin. What religious practices that are common in the United States might seem astonishing to people living in other countries?

well-established rules and regulations and expect leaders to be formally trained and ordained.

Though concerned with the sacred, a church accepts the ways of the profane world. Church members conceive of God in intellectual terms (say, as a force for good) and favor abstract moral standards ("Do unto others as you would have them do unto you"). By teaching morality in safely abstract terms, church leaders avoid social controversy. For example, many churches celebrate the unity of all peoples but say little about their own lack of social diversity. By downplaying this type of conflict, a church makes peace with the status quo (Troeltsch, 1931).

A church may operate with or apart from the state. A **state church** is *a church formally linked to the state*. For centuries, Roman Catholicism was the official religion of the Roman Empire, and Confucianism was the official religion in China until the early twentieth century. Today, the Anglican church is the official church of England, and Islam is the official religion of Pakistan and Iran. State churches count everyone in a society as a member, which sharply limits tolerance of religious differences.

A **denomination** is *a church, independent of the state, that recognizes religious pluralism*. Denominations exist in nations, including the United States, that formally separate church and state. This nation has dozens of Christian denominations, including Catholics, Baptists, Episcopalians, Methodists, and Lutherans, as well as various branches of Judaism, Islam, and other traditions. Although members of a denomination hold to their own beliefs, they recognize the right of others to have different beliefs.

Sect

Unlike a church, which tries to fit into the larger society, a **sect** is *a religious organization that stands apart from the larger society*. Sect members have rigid religious convictions and deny the beliefs of others. In extreme cases, members of a sect may withdraw completely from society to practice their faith without interference. The Amish community is one example of a North American sect that isolates itself. Because U.S. culture generally considers religious tolerance a virtue, members of sects are sometimes accused of being narrow-minded in insisting that they alone follow the true religion (Kraybill, 1994; P. W. Williams, 2002).

In organizational terms, sects are less formal than churches. Sect members may be highly spontaneous and emotional in worship, compared to members of churches, who tend to listen passively to their leaders. Sects also reject the intellectualized religion of churches, stressing instead the personal experience of divine power. Rodney Stark (1985:314) contrasts a church's vision of a distant God ("Our Father, who art in Heaven") with a sect's more immediate God ("Lord, bless this poor sinner kneeling before you now").

Churches and sects also have different patterns of leadership. The more churchlike an organization, the more likely that its leaders

Seeing Sociology in Everyday Life

Think about the process by which a religious organization that begins as a cult ends up becoming a church. What has to change?

Making the Grade

In general, the importance of charisma is greatest in cults, less so in sects, and least important in churches.

are formally trained and ordained. Sectlike organizations, which celebrate the personal presence of God, expect their leaders to show divine inspiration in the form of **charisma** (from Greek, meaning "divine favor"), *extraordinary personal qualities that can infuse people with emotion and turn them into followers.*

Sects generally form as breakaway groups from established religious organizations (Stark & Bainbridge, 1979). Their psychic intensity and informal structure make them less stable than churches, and many sects form only to disappear soon after. The sects that do endure typically become more like churches, with declining emphasis on charismatic leadership as they become more bureaucratic.

To sustain their membership, many sects actively recruit (*proselytize*) new members. Sects value highly the experience of *conversion,* or religious rebirth. For example, Jehovah's Witnesses go door to door to share their faith with others in the hope of attracting new members.

Finally, churches and sects differ in their social composition. Because they are more closely tied to the world, well-established churches tend to include people of high social standing. Sects attract more disadvantaged people. A sect's openness to new members and promise of salvation and personal fulfillment appeal to people who feel they are social outsiders.

Cult

A **cult** is *a religious organization that is largely outside a society's cultural traditions.* Most sects spin off from a conventional religious organization. However, a cult typically forms around a highly charismatic leader who offers a compelling message of a new and very different way of life. Researchers have counted as many as 5,000 cults in the United States (Marquand & Wood, 1997).

Because some cult principles or practices are unconventional, many people view cults as deviant or even evil. The suicides of thirty-nine members of California's Heaven's Gate cult in 1997—people who claimed that dying was the doorway to a higher existence, perhaps in the company of aliens from outer space—confirmed the negative image the public holds of many cults. In short, say some scholars, calling a religious community a "cult" amounts to dismissing its members as crazy (Shupe, 1995; Gleick, 1997).

This charge is unfair because there is nothing basically wrong with this kind of religious organization. Many religions—Christianity, Islam, and Judaism included—began as cults. Of course, few cults exist for very long. One reason is that they are even more at odds with the larger society than sects. Many cults demand that members not only accept their teaching but also adopt a radically new lifestyle. This is why people sometimes accuse cults of brainwashing their members, although research suggests that most people who join cults suffer no psychological harm (Kilbourne, 1983; P. W. Williams, 2002).

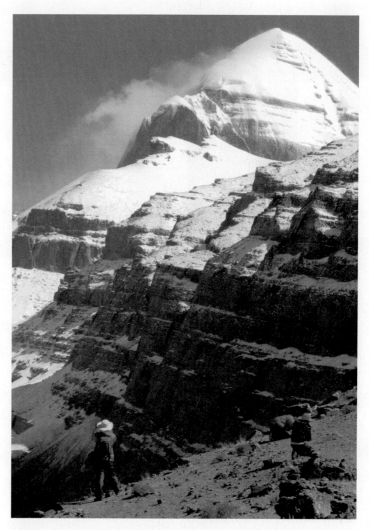

Animism is widespread in traditional societies, whose members live respectfully within the natural world on which they depend for their survival. Animists see a divine presence not just in themselves but in everything around them. Their example has inspired "New Age" spirituality, described on pages 396–97.

Religion in History

Like family, religion is a part of every known society. Also like family, religion shows marked variation over time and from place to place.

Early hunters and gatherers embraced **animism** (from the Latin, meaning "breath of life"), *the belief that elements of the natural world are conscious life forms that affect humanity.* Animists view forests, oceans, mountains, and the wind as spiritual forces. Many Native

Global Snapshot

In general, people in higher-income countries are less religious than those in lower-income nations. The U.S. population is an important exception to this pattern.

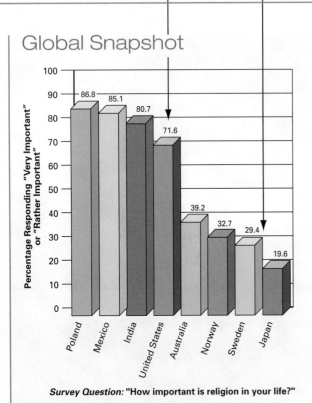

Survey Question: **"How important is religion in your life?"**

FIGURE 13–4   Religiosity in Global Perspective

Religion is stronger in the United States than in many other nations.

Source: Inglehart & Welzel (2010).

American societies are animistic, which accounts for their reverence for the natural environment.

Belief in a single divine power responsible for creating the world arose with pastoral and horticultural societies, which first appeared 10,000 to 12,000 years ago. The conception of God as a "shepherd" arose because Judaism, Christianity, and Islam all had their beginnings among pastoral peoples.

Religion becomes more important in agrarian societies. The central role of religion in social life is seen in the huge cathedrals that dominated the towns of medieval Europe.

The Industrial Revolution introduced the growing importance of science to everyday life. More and more, people looked to physicians and scientists for the knowledge and comfort they used to get from priests. However, religion persists in industrial societies because science is powerless to address issues of ultimate meaning in human life. In other words, *how* this world works is a matter for scientists, but *why* we and the rest of the universe exist is a question of faith.

Religion in the United States

Compared to almost every other high-income nation in the world, as Figure 13–4 suggests, the United States is a religious country (Inglehart & Welzel, 2010). But measuring the strength of religion in our society turns out to be difficult, as the following section explains.

Religious Commitment

Not only do about seven in ten people in our society claim that religion is important in their lives, but about 84 percent of adults in the United States identify with a specific religious tradition (NORC, 2009:202). More than half of U.S. adults consider themselves Protestants, one-fourth are Catholics, and 2 percent are Jews. Significant numbers of people also hold to dozens of other religions, from animism to Zen Buddhism, making our society not only religious but also religiously diverse (Eck, 2001). The remarkable religious diversity of the United States stems from a constitutional ban on a government-sponsored religion and from our historically high numbers of immigrants from all over the world. National Map 13–1 shows the share of people across the United States who claim to belong to a religious organization.

National Map 13–2 goes a step further, showing that the religion most people identify with varies by region. New England and the Southwest are predominantly Catholic, the South is overwhelmingly Baptist, and Lutherans predominate in the northern Plains states. In and around Utah, there is a heavy concentration of members of the Church of Jesus Christ of Latter-Day Saints (Mormons).

Religiosity is *the importance of religion in a person's life.* However, exactly how religious we are depends on precisely how we operationalize this concept. For example, 92 percent of adults in the United States claim to believe in a divine power, although just 61 percent claim that they "know that God exists and have no doubts about it" (NORC, 2009:474). Fifty-eight percent of adults say they pray at least once a day, but just 31 percent report attending religious services on a weekly or almost weekly basis (NORC, 2009:230, 223).

Clearly, the question "How religious are we?" has no easy answer, and it is likely that many people claim to be more religious than they really are. Overall, although most people in the United States claim to be at least somewhat religious, probably no more than one-third actually are. Religiosity also varies among denominations. Members of sects are the most religious of all, followed by Catholics and then "mainstream" Protestant denominations such as Episcopalians, Methodists, and Presbyterians (Sherkat & Ellison, 1999; Miller & Stark, 2002).

What difference does being more religious make? Researchers have linked a number of social patterns to holding strong religious beliefs, including low rates of delinquency among young people and

The United States is religiously diverse, but because certain religions predominate in particular regions of the country, most people do not experience the full range of this diversity in their everyday lives.

◆ Explore patterns of religious membership in your local community and in counties across the United States on mysoclab.com

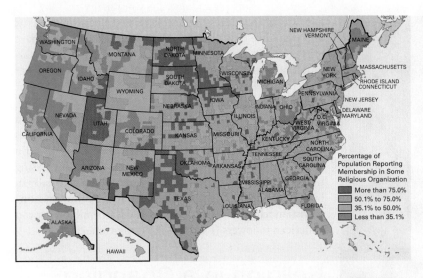

Seeing Ourselves

NATIONAL MAP 13–1

Religious Membership across the United States

In general, people in the United States are more religious than people in other high-income nations. Yet membership in a religious organization is more common in some parts of the country than in others. What pattern do you see in the map? Can you explain the pattern?

◆ Explore on mysoclab.com

Source: Glenmary Research Center (2002).

Percentage of Population Reporting Membership in Some Religious Organization
- More than 75.0%
- 50.1% to 75.0%
- 35.1% to 50.0%
- Less than 35.1%

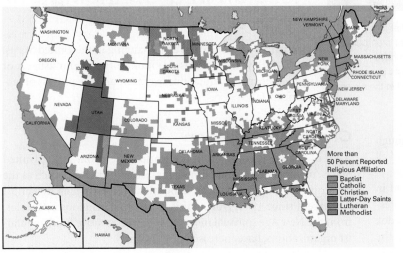

NATIONAL MAP 13–2

Religious Diversity across the United States

In most counties, at least 25 percent of people who report having an affiliation are members of the same religious organization. So although the United States is religiously diverse at the national level, most people live in communities where one denomination predominates. What historical facts might account for this pattern?

*When two or more churches have 25 to 49 percent of the membership in a county, the largest is shown. When no church has 25 percent of the membership, that county is left blank.

Source: Glenmary Research Center (2002).

More than 50 Percent Reported Religious Affiliation
- Baptist
- Catholic
- Christian
- Latter-Day Saints
- Lutheran
- Methodist

low rates of divorce among adults. According to one study, religiosity helps unite children, parents, and local communities in ways that benefit young people, enhancing their educational achievement (Muller & Ellison, 2001).

Religion: Class, Ethnicity, and Race

Religious affiliation is related to a number of other factors, including social class, ethnicity, and race.

Social Class

A study of *Who's Who in America*, which profiles U.S. high achievers, showed that 33 percent of the people who gave a religious affiliation were Episcopalians, Presbyterians, and United Church of Christ members, denominations that together account for less than 10 percent of

the population. Jews also enjoy high social position, with this 2 percent of the population accounting for 12 percent of listings in *Who's Who*.

Research shows that on average, members of other denominations, including Methodists and Catholics, have moderate social standing. Lower social standing is typical of Baptists, Lutherans, and members of sects. Of course, there is considerable variation within all denominations (Waters, Heath, & Watson, 1995; Keister, 2003; Pyle, 2006).

Ethnicity

Throughout the world, religion is tied to ethnicity, largely because one religion stands out in a single nation or geographic region. Islam predominates in the Arab societies of the Middle East, Hinduism is fused with the culture of India, and Confucianism runs deep in Chinese

● Seeing Sociology
  in Everyday Life

Do you think our society would be better off if more people
were religious? Or would it be worse off? Explain your
answer.

○ Making the Grade

The development of sociology itself as a rational view of the
world may be one expression of historical secularization.

Religious affiliation in the United States is surprisingly dynamic. In the last fifty years, traditional, "mainstream" religious organizations have lost about half their membership; during the same period, fundamentalist and new spiritualist movements have increased their numbers. As a result, recent research shows that about 44 percent of U.S. adults report having changed their religious affiliation at some point in their lives.

a major role in addressing problems of dislocation, poverty, and prejudice (Pattillo-McCoy, 1998). Black churches have also provided an important avenue of achievement for talented men and women. Ralph Abernathy, Martin Luther King Jr., and Jesse Jackson all achieved world recognition for their work as religious leaders.

Today, with 87 percent of African Americans claiming a religious affiliation, this category is somewhat more religious than the population as a whole. The vast majority favor a Protestant denomination. However, there is an increasing number of non-Christian African Americans, especially in large U.S. cities. Among them, the most common non-Christian religion is Islam, with as many as 1 million African American followers (Paris, 2000; Pew Forum, 2009).

Religion in a Changing Society

Like family life, religion is also changing in the United States. In the following sections, we look at two major aspects of change: changing affiliations over time and the process of secularization.

society. Christianity and Judaism do not follow this pattern; although these religions are mostly Western, Christians and Jews are found all over the world.

Religion and national identity are joined to a certain extent in the United States as well. For example, we have Anglo-Saxon Protestants, Irish Catholics, Russian Jews, and people of Greek Orthodox heritage. This linking of nation and religious belief results from the arrival of immigrants from nations with a distinctive major religion. Still, nearly every ethnic category displays some religious diversity. For example, people of English ancestry may be Protestants, Roman Catholics, Jews, Hindus, Muslims, or followers of other religions.

Race

Scholars claim that the church is both the oldest and the most important social institution in the African American community. Transported to the Western Hemisphere in slave ships, most Africans became Christians, the dominant religion in the Americas, but they blended Christian beliefs with elements of African religions they brought with them. Guided by this religious mix, African American Christians have developed rituals that seem, by European standards, far more spontaneous and emotional (Frazier, 1965; Roberts, 1980; Paris, 2000).

When African Americans migrated from the rural South to the industrial cities of the North starting around 1940, the church played

Changing Affiliation

A lot of change is going on in the world of religion. In the United States, membership in established, mainstream churches such as the Episcopalian and Presbyterian denominations has fallen by almost 50 percent since 1960. During this time, other religious categories, from the New Age spiritual movement to conservative fundamentalist organizations, have increased in popularity.

Many people are moving from one religious organization to another. A survey by the Pew Forum on Religion and Public Life (2008) reveals that 44 percent of U.S. adults report having switched religious affiliation at some point in their lives. The pattern of being born and raised with a religious affiliation one keeps throughout one's life is no longer the case for almost half of the U.S. population.

Such personal changes mean that religious organizations experience a pattern of people coming and going. For some time, for example, Catholics have represented almost one-fourth of the U.S. adult population. But this fairly stable statistic hides the fact that about one-third of all people raised Catholic have left the church. At the same time, about the same number of people—including many immigrants—have joined this church. A more extreme example is the Jehovah's Witnesses: Two-thirds of the people raised in this church have left, but their numbers have been more than replaced by converts recruited by members who travel from door to door spreading their message.

This pattern of religious "churn" has created an active and competitive marketplace of religious organization in the United States. Perhaps one result of this competition for members is that U.S. society remains among the most religious in the world. But it also reflects a loosening of people's ties to the religious organizations they are born into so that men and women now have more choice about their religious beliefs and affiliation.

Secularization

If people are less connected to the religious organization of their childhood, should we conclude that religion is getting weaker? Investigating this question brings us to the concept of **secularization,** *the historical decline in the importance of the supernatural and the sacred.* Secularization (from a Latin word for "worldly," meaning literally "of the present age") is commonly associated with modern, technologically advanced societies in which science is the major way of understanding.

Today, we are more likely to experience the transitions of birth, illness, and death in the presence of physicians (people with scientific knowledge) than church leaders (whose knowledge is based on faith). This shift alone suggests that religion's importance for our everyday lives has declined. Harvey Cox (1971:3) explains:

> The world looks less and less to religious rules and rituals for its morality or its meanings. For some [people] religion provides a hobby, for others a mark of national or ethnic identification, for still others an aesthetic delight. For fewer and fewer does it provide an inclusive and commanding system of personal and cosmic values and explanations.

If Cox is right, should we expect religion to disappear someday? Most sociologists say no. Although significant secularization does appear to have taken place in Europe, the vast majority of people in the United States still profess a belief in God, and nearly as many people claim to pray each day as vote in national elections. In addition, religious affiliation today in this country is higher than it was in 1850. In short, although people may be switching their affiliation from one religious organization to another, they remain religious all the same (Van Biema, 2008).

Our society does not seem to be on the road to secularization. Some dimensions of religiosity (such as belief in life after death) have declined, but others (such as religious affiliation) have increased. People move from one religious organization to another. From another perspective, some religious organizations have lost members, but for others membership is increasing. Among college students, as Figure 13–5 shows, the share of first-year students saying they have no religious preference has gone up, more than

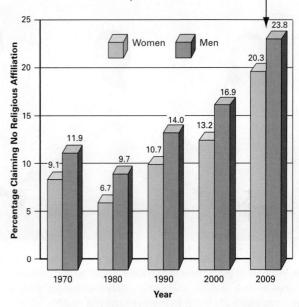

Although the share has been increasing, fewer than one-quarter of women and men on U.S. campuses claim no religious affiliation.

Student Snapshot

FIGURE 13–5   Religious Nonaffiliation among First-Year College Students, 1970–2009

The share of students claiming no religious affiliation has risen in recent decades.

Sources: Astin et al. (2002) and Pryor et al. (2009).

doubling between 1980 and 2009 (a trend mirrored in the larger adult population). But this share is still just a minority. Putting it all together, the claim that religion is declining in this country may be off the mark (Gorski, 2000; Stark & Finke, 2000; Hout & Fischer, 2002; Pryor et al., 2009).

As we look at religious change, people disagree whether it is good or bad. Conservatives see any weakening of religion as a mark of moral decline. Progressives view secularization as liberation from the dictatorial beliefs of the past, giving people greater choice about what to believe. Secularization has also brought many traditional religious practices, such as ordaining only men, into line with modern social attitudes that support greater gender equality.

According to the secularization thesis, religion should weaken in high-income nations as people enjoy higher living standards and greater security. A global perspective shows that this thesis holds for the nations of Western Europe, where most measures of religiosity have declined and are now low. But the United States, the richest country of all, is an exception; religion remains quite strong in our country.

civil religion a quasi-religious loyalty linking individuals in a basically secular society

New Age "seekers" are people in pursuit of spiritual growth, often using the age-old technique of meditation. The goal of this activity is to quiet the mind so that by moving away from everyday concerns, one can hear an inner, divine voice. Countless people attest to the spiritual value of meditation; it has also been linked to improved physical health.

> small stone building and reverently places offerings—corn and beans, sugar, plants of all colors, and even bits of gold and silver—in front of him as gifts to Mother Earth as he prays for harmony, joy, and the will to do good for one another. His words and the magic of the setting make the ceremony a very powerful experience.

In recent decades, an increasing number of people have sought spiritual development outside of established religious organizations. This trend has led some analysts to conclude that the United States is becoming a *postdenominational society.* In simple terms, more people seem to be spiritual seekers, believing in a vital spiritual dimension to human existence that they pursue more or less separately from any formal denomination.

What exactly is the difference between this "New Age" focus on spirituality and a traditional concern with religion? As one analysis puts it, spirituality is

> the search for . . . a religion of the heart, not the head. It . . . downplays doctrine and dogma, and revels in direct experience of the divine—whether it's called the "holy spirit" or "divine consciousness" or "true self." It's practical and personal, more about stress reduction than salvation, more therapeutic than theological. It's about feeling good rather than being good. It's as much about the body as the soul. (Cimino & Lattin, 1999:62)

Millions of people across in the United States today take part in New Age spirituality. Hank Wesselman (2001:39–42), an anthropologist and spiritual teacher, identifies five core values that define this approach:

1. **Seekers believe in a higher power.** There exists a higher power, a vital force that is within all things and all people. Each of us, then, is partly divine, just as the divine spirit exists in the world around us.

2. **Seekers believe we're all connected.** Everything and everyone is interconnected as part the universal divine pattern that seekers call spirit.

3. **Seekers believe in a spirit world.** The physical world is not all there is; a more important spiritual reality (or "spirit world") also exists.

4. **Seekers want to experience the spirit world.** Spiritual development means gaining the ability to experience the spirit world.

Civil Religion

One dimension of secularization is what Robert Bellah (1975) calls **civil religion,** *a quasi-religious loyalty binding individuals in a basically secular society.* In other words, formal religion may lose power, but citizenship has its own religious qualities. Most people in the United States consider our way of life a force for moral good in the world. Many people also find religious qualities in political movements, whether liberal or conservative (Williams & Demerath, 1991).

Civil religion involves a range of rituals, from standing to sing the national anthem at sporting events to waving the flag at public parades. At all such events, the U.S. flag serves as a sacred symbol of our national identity, and we expect people to treat it with respect.

"New Age" Seekers: Spirituality without Formal Religion

> **December 29, Machu Picchu, Peru.** We are ending the first day exploring this magnificent city built by the Inca people at the top of the Andes Mountains. Lucas, a local shaman, or religious leader, is leading a group of twelve members of our tour group in a ceremony of thanks. He kneels on the dirt floor of the

fundamentalism a conservative religious doctrine that opposes intellectualism and worldly accommodation in favor of restoring traditional, otherworldly religion

Seeing Sociology in Everyday Life

Do you think the rise of fundamentalist Islam in some parts of the world challenges the secularization thesis? Why or why not?

Many seekers come to understand that helpers and teachers who dwell in the spirit world can and do touch their lives.

5. **Seekers pursue transcendence.** Various techniques (such as yoga, meditation, and prayer) give people an increasing ability to rise above the immediate physical world (the experience of "transcendence"), which seekers believe to be the larger purpose of life.

From a traditional point of view, this New Age concern with spirituality may seem more like psychology than religion. Perhaps it would be fair to say that New Age spirituality combines elements of rationality (an emphasis on individualism as well as tolerance and pluralism) with a spiritual focus (search for meaning beyond our everyday concerns). It is this combination that makes New Age seeking particularly popular in the modern world (Tucker, 2002; Besecke, 2003, 2005).

Religious Revival: "Good Old-Time Religion"

At the same time as New Age spirituality is flourishing, a great deal of change has been going on in the world of organized religion. As noted earlier, membership in established, mainstream churches has fallen in recent decades. Since then, not only has interest in New Age spirituality increased, but affiliation with other formal religious organizations, including the Mormons, Seventh-Day Adventists, and especially Christian sects, has risen dramatically.

These opposing trends suggest that secularization itself may be self-limiting: As churchlike organizations become more worldly, many people leave them in favor of sectlike communities offering a more intense religious experience (Roof & McKinney, 1987; Jacquet & Jones, 1991; Warner, 1993; Iannaccone, 1994; Hout, Greeley, & Wilde, 2001).

One striking religious trend today is the growth of **fundamentalism,** *a conservative religious doctrine that opposes intellectualism and worldly accommodation in favor of restoring traditional, otherworldly religion.* In the United States, fundamentalism has made the greatest gains among Protestants. Southern Baptists, for example, are the largest Protestant religious community in the United States. But fundamentalist groups have also grown among Roman Catholics, Jews, and Muslims.

In response to what they see as the growing influence of science and the weakening of the conventional family, religious fundamentalists defend what they call "traditional values." As they see it, liberal churches are simply too open to compromise and change. Religious fundamentalism is distinctive in five ways (Hunter, 1983, 1985, 1987):

1. **Fundamentalists take the words of sacred texts literally.** Fundamentalists insist on a literal reading of sacred texts such as the Bible to counter what they see as excessive intellectualism among more liberal religious organizations. For example, fundamentalist Christians believe that God created the world in seven days precisely as described in the biblical book of Genesis.

2. **Fundamentalists reject religious pluralism.** Fundamentalists believe that tolerance and relativism water down personal faith. Therefore, they maintain that their religious beliefs are true and other beliefs are not.

3. **Fundamentalists pursue the personal experience of God's presence.** In contrast to the worldliness and intellectualism of other religious organizations, fundamentalists encourage a return to "good old-time religion" and spiritual revival. Among fundamentalist Christians, being "born again" and having a personal relationship with Jesus Christ should be evident in a person's everyday life.

In this outstanding example of U.S. folk art, Anna Bell Lee Washington's *Baptism 3* (1924) depicts the life-changing experience by which many people enter the Christian faith.

Go to the Multimedia Library at **mysoclab.com** to view the *Core Concepts in Sociology* video "Religion and Polarization"

○ Making the Grade

Can you define and distinguish between fundamentalism and secular humanism?

CONTROVERSY & DEBATE

Does Science Threaten Religion?

CIHAN: I think someday science will prove religion to be false.

RASHEED: I don't think science and religion are talking about the same thing at all.

About 400 years ago, the Italian physicist and astronomer Galileo (1564–1642) helped launch the Scientific Revolution with a series of startling discoveries. Dropping objects from the Leaning Tower of Pisa, he discovered some of the laws of gravity; making his own telescope, he observed the solar system and found that Earth orbited the sun, not the other way around.

For his trouble, Galileo was challenged by the Roman Catholic Church, which had preached for centuries that Earth stood motionless at the center of the universe. Galileo only made matters worse by responding that religious leaders had no business talking about matters of science.

Before long, he found his work banned and himself under house arrest.

As Galileo's treatment shows, right from the start, science has had an uneasy relationship with religion. In the nineteenth century, the two clashed again over the issue of creation. Charles Darwin's masterwork, *On the Origin of Species,* states that humanity evolved from lower forms of life over the course of a billion years—a theory that seems to fly in the face of the biblical account of creation found in Genesis, which

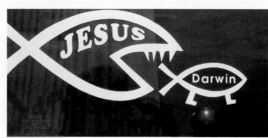

states that "God created the heavens and the earth," introducing living things on the third day and, on the fifth and sixth days, animals, including human beings fashioned in God's own image.

Galileo would have been an eager observer of the famous "Scopes monkey trial." In 1925, the state of Tennessee put a small-town science teacher named John Thomas Scopes on trial for teaching Darwinian evolution in the local high school. State law forbade teaching "any theory that denies the story of the Divine Creation of man as taught in the Bible" and especially the idea that "man descended from a lower order of animals." Scopes was found guilty and fined $100. His conviction was reversed on appeal, so the case never reached the U.S. Supreme Court, and the Tennessee law stayed on the books until 1967. A year later, the Supreme Court, in *Epperson* v. *Arkansas,* struck down all such laws as unconstitutional government support of religion.

---

4. **Fundamentalists oppose "secular humanism."** Fundamentalists think accommodation to the changing world weakens religious faith. They reject "secular humanism," our society's tendency to look to scientific experts rather than God for guidance about how to live. There is nothing new in this tension between science and religion, as the Controversy & Debate box explains.
   ● Go to **mysoclab.com**

5. **Many fundamentalists endorse conservative political goals.** Although fundamentalism tends to back away from worldly concerns, some fundamentalist leaders (including the Christian fundamentalists Jerry Fallwell, Pat Robertson, and Gary Bauer) have entered politics to oppose the "liberal agenda," which includes feminism and gay rights. Fundamentalists oppose abortion, same-sex marriage, and liberal bias in the media; they support the traditional two-parent family, seek a return of prayer in schools, and criticize the mass media for approaching stories from a liberal

viewpoint (Manza & Brooks, 1997; Thomma, 1997; Rozell, Wilcox, & Green, 1998).

Some people regard fundamentalism as judgmental, rigid, and self-righteous. But many believers find in fundamentalism, with its greater religious certainty and emphasis on experiencing God's presence, an appealing alternative to the more intellectual, tolerant, and worldly "mainstream" denominations (Marquand, 1997).

Which religious organizations are fundamentalist? In recent years, the world has become aware of an extreme form of fundamentalist Islam that supports violence directed against Western culture. In the United States, the term is most commonly applied to conservative Christian organizations in the evangelical tradition, including Pentecostals, Southern Baptists, Seventh-Day Adventists, and the Assemblies of God. Several national religious movements, including Promise Keepers (a men's organization) and

Seeing Sociology in Everyday Life

Go to the Multimedia Library at **mysoclab.com** to watch the ABC News *Nightline* video "A Battle between Faith and Science"

Were you raised in a particular religious tradition? If yes, would you describe it as "fundamentalist," "moderate," or "liberal"? What beliefs do you hold now?

Today—almost four centuries after Galileo was silenced—many people still debate the apparently conflicting claims of science and religion. Almost one-third of U.S. adults believe that the Bible is the literal word of God, and many of them reject any scientific findings that run counter to it (NORC, 2009:250). In 2005, all eight members of the school board in Dover, Pennsylvania, were voted out of office after they took a stand that many townspeople saw as weakening the teaching of evolution; at the same time, the Kansas state school board ordered the teaching of evolution to include its weaknesses and limitations from a religious point of view ("Much Ado about Evolution," 2005).

But a middle ground is emerging: Nearly half of U.S. adults (and also many church leaders) say the Bible is a book of truths *inspired* by God without being correct in a literal, scientific sense. That is, science and religion are two different ways of understanding that answer different questions. Both Galileo and Darwin devoted their lives to investigating *how* the natural world works. Yet only religion can address *why* we and the natural world exist in the first place.

This basic difference between science and religion helps explain why our nation is both the most scientific and the most religious in the world. As one scientist noted, the mathematical odds that a cosmic "big bang" 12 billion years ago created the universe and led to the formation of life as we know it are even smaller than the chance of winning a state lottery twenty weeks in a row. Doesn't such a scientific fact suggest an intelligent and purposeful power in our creation? Can't a person be a religious believer and at the same time a scientific investigator?

In 1992, a Vatican commission concluded that the church's silencing of Galileo was wrong. Today, most scientific and religious leaders agree that science and religion represent important but different truths. Many also believe that in today's rush to scientific discovery, our world has never been more in need of the moral guidance provided by religion.

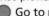 Go to **mysoclab.com**

WHAT DO YOU THINK?

1. Why do you think some scientific people reject religious accounts of human creation? Why do some religious people reject scientific accounts?

2. Does the sociological study of religion challenge anyone's faith? Why or why not?

3. About half of U.S. adults think science is changing our way of life too fast. Do you agree? Why or why not?

Sources: Gould (1981), Huchingson (1994), Applebome (1996), and Greely (2008).

Chosen Women, have a fundamentalist orientation. In national surveys, 31 percent of U.S. adults describe their religious upbringing as "fundamentalist," 41 percent claim a "moderate" religious upbringing, and 24 percent cite a "liberal" background (NORC, 2009:243).

In contrast to local congregations of years past, some religious organizations, especially fundamentalist ones, have become *electronic churches* dominated by "prime-time preachers" (Hadden & Swain, 1981). Electronic religion is found only in the United States. It has made James Dobson, Joel Osteen, Billy and Franklin Graham, Robert Schuller, and others "televangelists" more famous than all but a few clergy in the past. Perhaps 5 percent of the national television audience (about 10 million people) are regular viewers of religious television, and 20 percent (about 40 million) watch some religious programming every week (NORC, 2009:474).

Religion: Looking Ahead

The popularity of media ministries, the growth of religious fundamentalism, new forms of spirituality, and the connection of millions of people to mainstream churches show that religion will remain a major part of modern society for decades to come. High levels of immigration from Latin America and elsewhere should intensify as well as diversify the religious character of U.S. society in the twenty-first century (Yang & Ebaugh, 2001).

The world is becoming more complex, and social change seems to move at a faster pace than our capacity to make sense of it all. But rather than weakening religion, this process fires the religious imagination. As new technology gives us the power to alter, sustain, and even create life, we face increasingly difficult moral questions. Against this backdrop of uncertainty, it is little wonder that many people look to their faith for guidance and hope.

Seeing Sociology in Everyday Life

Chapter 13   Family and Religion

How religious is our society?

Compared to most other high-income nations, the United States has a relatively high level of religious belief and activity. We consider ourselves to be a modern, secular society, yet as this chapter explains, most people claim to be religious and at least one-third of the population is. Civil religion is also evident in many aspects of our everyday lives. Look at the photos below: Can you point to elements of civil religion in each of these familiar situations?

> **HINT**   As this chapter explains, civil religion is a quasi-religious loyalty linking members of a mostly secular society. Important events that qualify as civil religion are not formally religious but are typically defined as holidays (a word derived from "holy days"); involve gatherings of family, neighbors, and friends; and include ritual activities and the sharing of specific foods and beverages.

On Thanksgiving Day, most families across the United States gather to share a special dinner and give thanks for their good fortune. What religious or quasi-religious elements are part of a typical Thanksgiving celebration?

What about the Fourth of July? How is this special day an example of civil religion?

In recent decades, football's Super Bowl has emerged as an important annual event. What elements of civil religion can you find in Super Bowl Sunday?

Applying SOCIOLOGY in Everyday Life

1. Make a list of other events, activities, and pastimes that might be considered examples of civil religion. (Start off with Election Day; what about baseball?) Are there any local college events or rituals that might be included? In each case, explain the religious element that you see and the way the event or activity affects members of a community.

2. Is religion in the United States getting weaker? To evaluate the claim that our society is undergoing secularization, go to the library or local newspaper office and obtain an issue of your local newspaper published fifty years ago and, if possi-

ble, one published 100 years ago. Compare the amount of attention given to religious issues then and now. What pattern do you see?

3. Parents and grandparents can be a wonderful source of information about changes in marriage and family. Ask them at what ages they married, what their married lives have been like, and what changes in family life today stand out to them. Compare the answers of people of different generations—how are they different?

Making the Grade

Family: Basic Concepts

All societies are built on kinship. The **FAMILY** varies across cultures and over time:
- In industrialized societies such as the United States, *marriage* is monogamous.
- Many preindustrial societies permit *polygamy*, of which there are two types: *polygyny* and *polyandry*.
- In global perspective, *patrilocality* is most common, but industrial societies favor *neolocality* and a few societies have *matrilocal* residence.
- Industrial societies use bilateral *descent*; preindustrial societies are either patrilineal or matrilineal.

pp. 368–71

Theoretical Analysis of Family

The **STRUCTURAL-FUNCTIONAL APPROACH** identifies major family functions: socialization of the young, regulation of sexual activity, social placement, and providing material and emotional support.

p. 371

The **SOCIAL-CONFLICT** and **FEMINIST APPROACHES** explore how the family perpetuates social inequality by transmitting divisions based on class, ethnicity, race, and gender.

p. 372

The **SYMBOLIC-INTERACTION** and **SOCIAL-EXCHANGE APPROACHES** highlight the variety of family life as experienced by various family members.

pp. 372–73

📖 Read on mysoclab.com

▭ *See the Applying Theory table on page 373.*

Stages of Family Life

COURTSHIP AND ROMANTIC LOVE
- Courtship based on romantic love is central to mate selection in the United States.
- Arranged marriages are common in preindustrial societies.

pp. 373–75

CHILD REARING
- Family size has decreased over time as industrialization increases the costs of raising children.
- Fewer children are born as more women go to school and join the labor force.

pp. 375–76

THE FAMILY IN LATER LIFE
- Many middle-aged couples care for aging parents, and many older couples are active grandparents.
- The final transition in marriage begins with the death of a spouse.

p. 376

✓ *Most spouses have similar social background with regard to class and race, but over the last century, ethnicity has mattered less and less (p. 379).*

Transitions and Problems in Family Life

- Four in ten of today's marriages will end in **DIVORCE**. Remarriage creates blended families that include children from previous marriages.
- **FAMILY VIOLENCE** is a widespread problem. Most adults who abuse family members were themselves abused as children.

pp. 379–82

Alternative Family Forms

Family life is becoming more varied:
- One-parent families, cohabitation, gay and lesbian couples, and singlehood have become more common in recent years.

- Although only five states and the District of Columbia have lawful same-sex marriage, many gay men and lesbians form long-lasting relationships and, increasingly, are becoming parents.

pp. 382–84

family (p. 368) a social institution found in all societies that unites people in cooperative groups to care for one another, including any children

kinship (p. 368) a social bond based on common ancestry, marriage, or adoption

marriage (p. 368) a legal relationship, usually involving economic cooperation, sexual activity, and childbearing

extended family (p. 369) a family composed of parents and children as well as other kin; also known as a *consanguine family*

nuclear family (p. 369) a family composed of one or two parents and their children; also known as a *conjugal family*

endogamy (p. 369) marriage between people of the same social category

exogamy (p. 369) marriage between people of different social categories

monogamy (p. 369) marriage that unites two partners

polygamy (p. 369) marriage that unites a person with two or more spouses

descent (p. 369) the system by which members of a society trace kinship over generations

incest taboo (p. 371) a norm forbidding sexual relations or marriage between certain relatives

homogamy (p. 374) marriage between people with the same social characteristics

family violence (p. 381) emotional, physical, or sexual abuse of one family member by another

cohabitation (p. 382) the sharing of a household by an unmarried couple

New Reproductive Technologies

- Although ethically controversial, new reproductive technologies are changing conventional ideas of parenthood.

pp. 384–86

Religion: Basic Concepts

- **RELIGION** is a major social institution based on setting the *sacred* apart from the *profane*.
- Religion is grounded in *faith* rather than scientific evidence, and people express their religious beliefs through various rituals.

pp. 386–87

Theoretical Analysis of Religion

- The **STRUCTURAL-FUNCTIONAL APPROACH** suggests that religion unites people, promotes cohesion, and gives meaning and purpose to life; through religion, we celebrate the power of our society (Emile Durkheim).
- The **SYMBOLIC-INTERACTION APPROACH** explains that we socially construct religious beliefs; we are especially likely to seek religious meaning when faced with life's uncertainties and disruptions (Peter Berger).
- The **SOCIAL-CONFLICT APPROACH** claims that religion justifies the status quo. In this way, religion supports inequality and discourages change toward a more just and equal society (Karl Marx).

pp. 387–89

See the Applying Theory table on page 389.

Religion and Social Change

- Max Weber argued, in opposition to Marx, that religion can encourage social change. He showed how Calvinist beliefs promoted the rise of industrial capitalism.
- **LIBERATION THEOLOGY**, a fusion of Christian principles and political activism, tries to encourage social change.

pp. 389–90

Types of Religious Organizations

- **CHURCHES** are religious organizations well integrated into their society. Churches fall into two categories: state churches and denominations.
- **SECTS** are the result of religious division and are marked by charismatic leadership and members' suspicion of the larger society.
- **CULTS** are religious organizations based on new and unconventional beliefs and practices.

pp. 390–91

Religion in the United States

The United States is one of the most religious and religiously diverse nations. How researchers operationalize "religiosity" affects how "religious" our people seem to be:
- 84% of adults identify with a religion.
- 61% profess a firm belief in God.
- Just 31% say they attend religious services weekly.

pp. 392–93

Explore on **mysoclab.com**

Religion in a Changing Society

- In the United States, while some indicators of religiosity (like membership in mainstream churches) have declined, others (such as membership in sects) have increased.
- Almost half of U.S. adults have changed religious affiliation at some point in their lives.
- **SECULARIZATION** is a decline in the importance of the supernatural and the sacred.
- Today, **CIVIL RELIGION** takes the form of a quasi-religious patriotism that ties people to their society.
- *Spiritual seekers* are part of the "New Age" movement, which pursues spiritual development outside conventional religious organizations.
- **FUNDAMENTALISM** opposes religious accommodation to the world, interprets religious texts literally, and rejects religious diversity.

pp. 394–99

---

profane (p. 386) included as an ordinary part of everyday life

sacred (p. 386) set apart as extraordinary, inspiring awe and reverence

religion (p. 386) a social institution involving beliefs and practices based on recognizing the sacred

faith (p. 386) belief based on conviction rather than on scientific evidence

totem (p. 387) an object in the natural world collectively defined as sacred

liberation theology (p. 389) the combining of Christian principles with political activism, often Marxist in character

church (p. 390) a religious organization that is well integrated into the larger society

state church (p. 390) a church formally linked to the state

denomination (p. 390) a church, independent of the state, that recognizes religious pluralism

sect (p. 390) a religious organization that stands apart from the larger society

charisma (p. 391) extraordinary personal qualities that can infuse people with emotion and turn them into followers

cult (p. 391) a religious organization that is largely outside a society's cultural traditions

animism (p. 391) the belief that elements of the natural world are conscious life forms that affect humanity

religiosity (p. 392) the importance of religion in a person's life

Religious affiliation is tied to social class, ethnicity, and race:
- On average, Episcopalians, Presbyterians, and Jews enjoy high standing; lower social standing is typical of Baptists, Lutherans, and members of sects.
- Religion is often linked to ethnic background because people came to the United States from countries that have a major religion (e.g., most Irish Americans are Catholic).
- Transported to this country in slave ships, most Africans became Christians, but they blended Christian beliefs with elements of African religions they brought with them.

pp. 393–94

secularization (p. 395) the historical decline in the importance of the supernatural and the sacred

civil religion (p. 396) a quasi-religious loyalty binding individuals in a basically secular society

fundamentalism (p. 397) a conservative religious doctrine that opposes intellectualism and worldly accommodation in favor of restoring traditional, otherworldly religion

14 Education, Health, and Medicine

- How are schooling and health linked to social inequality in the United States?

- What changes in schooling and health have taken place in the United States in recent generations?

- Why do people in poor nations have little access to schooling and medical care?

Watch the *Core Concepts in Sociology* video "Inequities in Education" on **mysoclab.com**

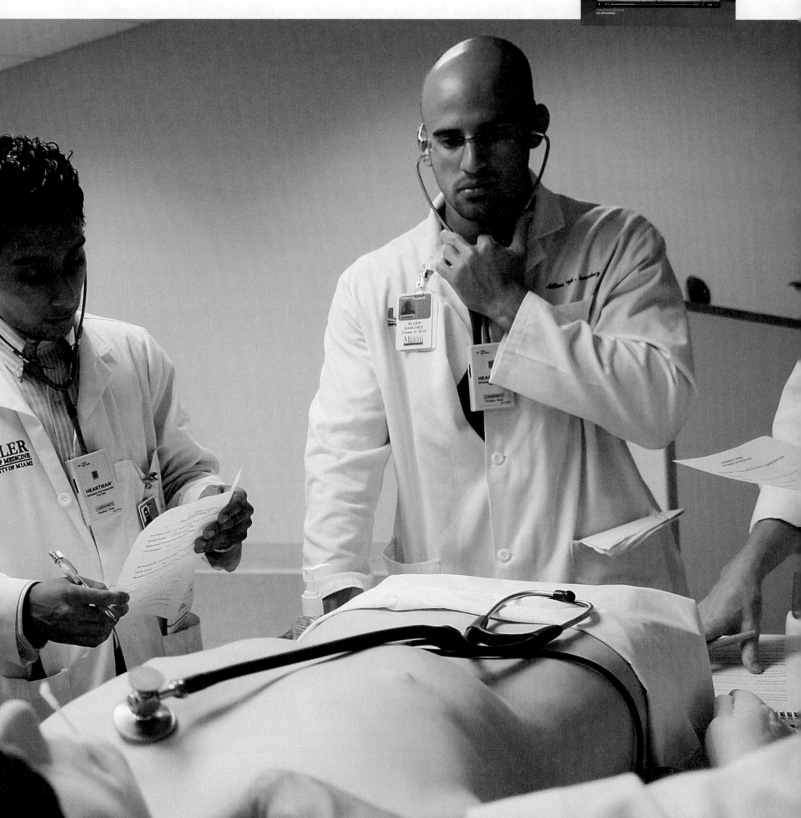

This chapter explains the operation of education and health care, two major social institutions that emerge in modern societies. The discussion offers both a global perspective and a focus on the United States.

When Lisa Addison was growing up in Baltimore, she always smiled when her teachers said she was smart and should go to college. "I liked hearing that," she recalls. "But I didn't know what to do about it. No one in my family had ever gone to college. I didn't know what courses to take in high school. I had no idea of how to apply to a college. How would I pay for it? What would it be like if I got there?"

Uncertain about her future, Addison found herself "kind of goofing off in school." After finishing high school, she took a job as a waitress and as a kitchen helper in a catering company. One day she realized that fifteen years had gone by and her dream of going to college seemed further away than ever.

But at the age of thirty-eight, Addison made the decision to go back to school. It was hard to give up the steady paycheck. But she was looking for more: "I don't want to do this kind of work for the rest of my life. I *am* smart. I can do better. At this point, I am ready for college."

Addison took a giant step through the door of the Community College of Baltimore County and, with the help of career counselors, set her sights on an associate's degree in business. She is now almost finished with this two-year program, and she plans to transfer to a four-year university to complete a bachelor's degree. Then she hopes to go back into the food service industry—but this time as a manager at higher pay (Toppo & DeBarros, 2005).

Education is a social institution that has particular importance to people looking to advance their careers. This chapter explains *why* schooling is more important than ever for success in the United States today and also describes *who* benefits most from schooling. The second half of the chapter examines *health* and the social institution of *medicine*. Good health, like good schooling, is distributed unequally throughout our society's population. In addition, like education, the practice of medicine reveals striking differences from society to society.

Education: A Global Survey

Education is *the social institution through which society provides its members with important knowledge, including basic facts, job skills, and cultural norms and values.* Education takes many forms, from informal family discussions around the dinner table to lectures and labs at large universities. In high-income nations, education depends largely on **schooling**, *formal instruction under the direction of specially trained teachers.*

Schooling and Economic Development

The extent of schooling in any society is tied to its level of economic development. In low- and middle-income countries, which are home to most of the world's people, families and local communities teach young people important knowledge and skills. Formal schooling, especially learning that is not directly connected to survival, is available mainly to wealthy people who can afford to pursue personal enrichment. The word *school* is from a Greek root that means "leisure." In ancient Greece, famous teachers such as Plato, Socrates, and Aristotle taught aristocratic, upper-class men who had plenty of spare time. The same was true in ancient China, where the famous philosopher K'ung Fu-tzu (Confucius) shared his wisdom with just a privileged few.

December 30, the Cuzco region, Peru. High in the Andes Mountains of Peru, families send their children to the local school. But "local" can mean 3 miles away or more, and there are no buses, so these children, almost all from poor families, walk an hour or more each way. Schooling is required by law, but in the rural highlands, some parents prefer to keep their children at home where they can help with the farming and livestock.

Today, schooling in low-income countries reflects the national culture. In Iran, for example, schooling is closely tied to Islam. Similarly, schooling in Bangladesh (Asia), Zimbabwe (Africa), and Nicaragua (Latin America) has been shaped by the distinctive cultural traditions of these nations.

Rate of Illiteracy

50.0% and greater

20.0% to 49.9%

5.0% to 19.9%

Less than 5.0%

Window on the World

GLOBAL MAP 14–1   Illiteracy in Global Perspective

Reading and writing skills are widespread in high-income countries, where illiteracy rates generally are below 5 percent. In much of Latin America, however, illiteracy is more common, one consequence of limited economic development. In fourteen nations—most of them in Africa—illiteracy is the rule rather than the exception; there people rely on the oral tradition of face-to-face communication rather than the written word.

Source: UNESCO (2010).

All low-income countries have one trait in common when it comes to schooling: There is not very much of it. In the poorest nations (including several in Central Africa), more than one-fourth of all children never get to school (World Bank, 2010); worldwide, one-third of all children never make it as far as the secondary grades. As a result, about one-sixth of the world's people cannot read or write. Global Map 14–1 shows the extent of illiteracy around the world, and the national comparisons in the text illustrate the link between schooling and economic development.

Schooling in India

India has recently become a middle-income country, but people there still earn only about 6 percent of the average U.S. income, and most

Table 14–1 Educational Achievement in the United States, 1910–2009

Year	High School Graduates	College Graduates	Median Years of Schooling
1910	13.5%	2.7%	8.1
1920	16.4	3.3	8.2
1930	19.1	3.9	8.4
1940	24.1	4.6	8.6
1950	33.4	6.0	9.3
1960	41.1	7.7	10.5
1970	55.2	11.0	12.2
1980	68.7	17.0	12.5
1990	77.6	21.3	12.4
2000	84.1	25.6	12.7
2009	86.7	29.5	13.0*

Notes: Figures are for people twenty-five years of age and over. Percentage of high school graduates includes those who go on to college. Percentage of high school dropouts can be calculated by subtracting the percentage of high school graduates from 100 percent.
*Author's estimate.

Source: U.S. Census Bureau (2010).

poor families depend on the earnings of children. Even though India has outlawed child labor, many children continue to work in factories—weaving rugs or making handicrafts—up to sixty hours a week, which greatly limits their opportunities for schooling.

Today, 90 percent of children in India complete primary school, typically in crowded schoolrooms where one teacher may face as many as sixty children, twice as many as in the average U.S. public school classroom. Almost 60 percent go on to secondary education, and very few enter college. As a result, 34 percent of India's people are unable to read and write (UNESCO, 2009).

Patriarchy also shapes Indian education. Indian parents are joyful at the birth of a boy because he and his future wife will both contribute income to the family. But there are economic costs to raising a girl: Parents must provide a dowry (a gift of wealth to the groom's family), and after her marriage, a daughter's work benefits her husband's family. Therefore, many Indians see less reason to invest in the schooling of girls, which is why only 52 percent of girls (compared with 61 percent of boys) reach the secondary grades. So what do the girls do while the boys are in school? Most of the children working in Indian factories are girls—a family's way of benefiting from their daughters while they can (UNESCO, 2009).

Schooling in Japan

Schooling has not always been part of the Japanese way of life. Before industrialization brought mandatory education in 1872, only a privileged few attended school. Today, Japan's educational system is widely praised for training some of the world's highest achievers.

The early grades concentrate on transmitting Japanese traditions, especially a sense of obligation to family. Starting in their early teens, students take a series of rigorous and highly competitive examinations. These written tests, which are like the Scholastic Assessment Tests (SATs) in the United States, decide the future of all Japanese students.

More men and women graduate from high school in Japan (97 percent) than in the United States (87 percent). But competitive examinations allow for just 47 percent of high school graduates to enter college—compared to 69 percent in the United States. Understandably, Japanese students take entrance examinations very seriously, and about half attend special "cram schools" to prepare for them.

Japanese schooling produces impressive results. In a number of fields, notably mathematics and science, young Japanese students outperform students in most other high-income nations, including the United States.

Schooling in the United States

The United States was among the first countries to set a goal of mass education. By 1850, about half the young people between the ages of five and nineteen were enrolled in school. By 1918, all states had passed *mandatory education laws* requiring children to attend school until the age of sixteen or completion of the eighth grade. Table 14–1 shows that this country reached a milestone in the mid-1960s, when for the first time a majority of U.S. adults had high school diplomas. In 2009, 86.7 percent of adults have high school educations, and 29.5 percent have a four-year college degree.

The U.S. educational system is shaped by both our high standard of living (which means that most young people do not have to work) and our democratic principles (the idea that schooling should be available to everyone). Thomas Jefferson thought the new nation could become democratic only if people learned to read. Today, the United States has an outstanding record of higher education for its people: The United States is ranked behind only Norway in terms of the share of adults who have earned a university degree (OECD, 2009).

Schooling in the United States also tries to promote *equal opportunity*. National surveys show that most people think schooling is crucial to personal success, and a majority believe that everyone has the chance to get an education consistent with personal ability and talent (NORC, 2009). However, this opinion expresses cultural ideals rather than reality. A century ago, for example, women were all but excluded from higher education; even today, most people who attend college come from families with above-average incomes.

In the United States, the educational system stresses the value of *practical* learning, knowledge that prepares people for their future

● Seeing Sociology
  in Everyday Life

What is your career goal? Are the courses you are taking
geared to helping you realize this goal?

┌● Making the Grade

In the United States, women represent a majority of college
students. In lower-income nations, men make up a large
majority of those attending college.

jobs. This is in line with what the education philosopher John
Dewey (1859–1952) called *progressive education,* having the
schools make learning relevant to people's lives. Students seek
out subjects of study that they believe will give them an advantage when they are ready to compete in the job market. For
example, as concerns about international terrorism have risen
in recent years, so have the numbers of students choosing to
study geography, international conflict, and Middle Eastern
history and culture (M. Lord, 2001).

The Functions of Schooling

Structural-functional analysis focuses on ways in which schooling supports the operation and stability of society:

1. **Socialization.** Technologically simple societies look to
   families to transmit a way of life from one generation to the
   next. As societies gain complex technology, they turn to
   trained teachers to pass on specialized knowledge that
   adults will need for their future jobs.

2. **Cultural innovation.** Faculty at colleges and universities
   invent culture as well as pass it along to students. Especially at centers of higher education, scholars conduct
   research that leads to discoveries and changes our way of life.

3. **Social integration.** Schools mold a diverse population into
   one society sharing norms and values. This is one reason that
   states enacted mandatory education laws a century ago when
   immigration became very high. In light of the ethnic diversity
   of many urban areas today, schooling continues to serve this
   purpose.

4. **Social placement.** Schools identify talent and match instruction to ability. Schooling increases meritocracy by rewarding
   talent and hard work regardless of social background and provides a path to upward social mobility.

5. **Latent functions.** Schooling serves several less widely recognized functions. It provides child care for the growing number
   of parents who work outside the home. In addition, it occupies
   thousands of young people in their twenties who would otherwise be competing for limited opportunities in the job market. High schools, colleges, and universities also bring together
   people of marriageable age. Finally, school networks can be a
   valuable career resource throughout life.

└● **CRITICAL REVIEW**   Structural-functional analysis
stresses ways in which formal education supports the operation
of a modern society. However, this approach overlooks the fact
that the classroom behavior of teachers and students can vary

In many low-income nations, children are as likely to work as they are to attend
school, and girls receive less schooling than boys. But the doors to schooling are
now opening to more girls and women. These young women are studying nursing
at Somalia University in downtown Mogadishu.

from one setting to another, a focus of the symbolic-interaction
approach discussed next. In addition, structural-functional analysis says little about many problems of our educational system
and how schooling helps reproduce the class structure in each
generation, which is the focus of the social-conflict approach,
covered in the final theoretical section on schooling.

└● **CHECK YOUR LEARNING**   Identify five functions of
schooling for the operation of society.

Schooling and Social Interaction

The basic idea of the symbolic-interaction approach is that people
create the reality they experience in their day-to-day interactions. We
use this approach to explain how stereotypes can shape what goes on
in the classroom.

The Self-Fulfilling Prophecy

Chapter 4 ("Social Interaction in Everyday Life") presented the
Thomas theorem, which states that situations people define as real
become real in their consequences. Put another way, people who
expect others to act in certain ways often encourage that very behavior. In doing so, people set up a *self-fulfilling prophecy.*

○ Seeing Sociology
in Everyday Life

"In school, as in life, you will only do as well as you think you can."
How true do you think this statement is? Explain.

○ Making the Grade

This discussion of the symbolic-interaction approach to
education echoes the labeling approach to deviance in
Chapter 9 ("Deviance"). Review pages 177–81.

girl named Carol had changed from a "brilliant, carefree, excited little girl to a frightened, timid, uncertain, almost-person." Not surprisingly, in the hours that followed, the brown-eyed students came to life, speaking up more and performing better than they had before. The prophecy had been fulfilled: Because the brown-eyed children thought they were superior, they became superior in their classroom performance; they also became "arrogant, ugly, and domineering" toward the blue-eyed children. For their part, the blue-eyed children began underperforming, becoming the inferior people they believed themselves to be.

At the end of the day, Elliott explained to the students what they had experienced. She applied the lesson to race, pointing out that if white children thought they were superior to black children, they would expect to do better in school, just as many children of color who live in the shadow of the same stereotypes would underperform in school. The children also realized that the society that teaches these stereotypes, as well as the hate that often accompanies them, encourages the kind of violence that ended the life of Martin Luther King Jr. (Kral, 2000).

○ **CRITICAL REVIEW** The symbolic-interaction approach explains how we all build reality in our everyday interactions with others. When school officials define some students as "gifted," for example, we can expect teachers to treat them differently and expect the students themselves to behave differently as a result of having been labeled in this way. If students and teachers come to believe that one race is academically superior to another, the behavior that follows may be a self-fulfilling prophecy.

One limitation of this approach is that people do not just make up such beliefs about superiority and inferiority. Rather, these beliefs are built into a society's system of social inequality, which brings us to the social-conflict approach.

○ **CHECK YOUR LEARNING** How can the labels that schools place on some students affect the students' actual performance and the reactions of others?

Schooling and Social Inequality

Social-conflict analysis challenges the structural-functional idea that schooling develops everyone's talents and abilities. Instead, this approach emphasizes three ways in which schooling causes and perpetuates social inequality:

1. **Social control.** As Samuel Bowles and Herbert Gintis (1976) see it, the demand for public education in the late nineteenth century was based on capitalist factory owners' need for an obedient and

How good are you as a student? The answer is that you are as good as you and your teachers think you are. The television show *Glee* demonstrates how with the help of an inspiring teacher, students can accomplish more than they expect.

Jane Elliott, an elementary school teacher in the all-white community of Riceville, Iowa, carried out a simple experiment that showed how a self-fulfilling prophecy can take place in the classroom. In 1968, Elliott was teaching a fourth-grade class when Martin Luther King Jr. was murdered. Her students were puzzled and asked why a national hero had been brutally shot. Elliott responded by asking her white students what they thought about people of color and was stunned to learn that they held many powerful negative stereotypes.

To show the class the harmful effects of such stereotypes, Elliott performed a classroom experiment. She found that almost all of the children in her class had either blue eyes or brown eyes. She told the class that children with brown eyes were smarter and worked harder than children with blue eyes. To be sure everyone could easily tell which category a child fell into, a piece of brown or blue cloth was pinned to each student's collar.

Elliott recalls the effect of this "lesson" on the way students behaved: "It was just horrifying how quickly they became what I told them they were." Within half an hour, Elliott continued, a blue-eyed

● Seeing Sociology
in Everyday Life

Assess the quality of your own schooling. Did your family's social
standing affect the quality of schools you attended? Explain.

tracking assigning students to different types of educational programs

Sociological research has documented the fact that young children living in low-income communities typically learn in classrooms like the one on the left, with large class sizes and low budgets that do not provide for high technology and other instructional materials. Children from high-income communities typically enjoy classroom experiences such as the one shown on the right, with small classes and the latest learning technology.

disciplined workforce. Once in school, immigrants learned not only the English language but also the importance of following orders.

2. **Standardized testing.** Critics claim that the assessment tests widely used by schools reflect our society's dominant culture, placing minority students at a disadvantage. By defining majority students as smarter, standardized tests unfairly transform privilege into personal merit (Crouse & Trusheim, 1988; Putka, 1990).

3. **Tracking.** Despite controversy over standardized tests, most U.S. schools use them for **tracking,** *assigning students to different types of educational programs,* such as college preparatory classes, general education, and vocational and technical training. Tracking supposedly helps teachers meet each student's individual abilities and interests. However, the education critic Jonathan Kozol (1992) considers tracking one of the "savage inequalities" in our school system. Most students from privileged backgrounds get into higher tracks, where they receive the best the school can offer. Students from disadvantaged backgrounds end up in lower tracks, where teachers stress memorization and put little focus on creativity (Bowles & Gintis, 1976; Oakes, 1985; Kilgore, 1991; Gamoran, 1992).

Public and Private Education

Across the United States, about 90 percent of 62 million primary and secondary school children attend state-funded public schools. The rest go to private schools.

About 40 percent of private school students attend one of the more than 7,500 *parochial* ("of the parish") schools operated by the Roman Catholic Church. The Catholic school system grew rapidly a century ago as cities swelled with immigrants. Today, after decades of flight from the inner city by white people, many parochial schools enroll non-Catholics, including a growing number of African Americans whose families seek an alternative to the neighborhood public school.

Protestants also have private schools, often known as Christian academies. These schools are favored by parents who want religious instruction for their children, as well as parents of all backgrounds who seek higher academic and disciplinary standards. Another 40 percent of private school students attend one of these 15,000 religious schools.

The remaining 20 percent of private school students attend one of the 10,800 nonreligious private schools that enroll mostly young people from well-to-do families. These are typically prestigious and expensive preparatory ("prep") schools, modeled on British boarding schools, that not only provide strong academic programs but also teach the way of life of the upper class. Many "preppies" maintain lifelong school-based networks of personal contacts that provide numerous social advantages.

Are private schools better than public schools? Research shows that holding social background constant, students in private schools do outperform those in public schools. The advantages of private schools include smaller classes, more demanding coursework, and greater discipline (Coleman, Hoffer, & Kilgore, 1981; Coleman & Hoffer, 1987; Peterson & Llaudet, 2006).

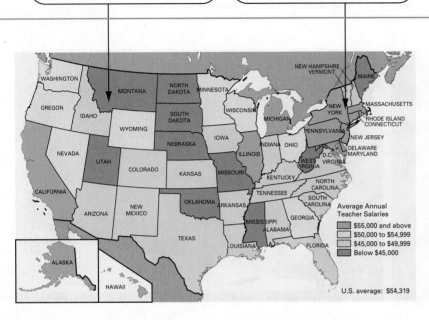

Now in his tenth year of middle school teaching, Tom Samuels lives near Butte, Montana, and earns $42,400 a year.

Fresh out of college, J. P. Saunders just landed a teaching job in Albany, New York, with a starting salary of $42,000 a year.

Average Annual Teacher Salaries

$55,000 and above
$50,000 to $54,999
$45,000 to $49,999
Below $45,000

U.S. average: $54,319

Explore the percentage of people without a high school education in your local community and in counties across the United States on mysoclab.com

Seeing Ourselves

NATIONAL MAP 14–1
Teachers' Salaries across the United States

In 2009, the average public school teacher in the United States earned $54,319. The map shows the average teacher salary for all the states; they range from a low of $35,070 in South Dakota to a high of $69,118 in New York. Looking at the map, what pattern do you see? What do high-salary (and low-salary) states have in common?

Explore on mysoclab.com

Source: National Education Association, *Rankings and Estimates: Rankings of the States, 2009, and Estimates of School Statistics, 2010.* Washington, D.C.: National Education Association, 2009, p. 19.

But even public schools are not all the same. Differences in funding between rich and poor communities result in unequal resources; this means that children in more affluent areas receive a better education than children in low-income communities. National Map 14–1 shows one key dimension of difference: Average teacher salaries vary by as much as $34,000 in state-by-state comparisons.

At the local level, differences in school funding can be dramatic. Winnetka, Illinois, one of the richest suburbs in the United States, spends more than $13,000 each year on each of its students, compared to a poor district such as Alpine, Utah, that spends only $5,000 each year. In recent years, these differences have increased (Edwards, 1998; Winter, 2004). The Thinking About Diversity box shows the effects of funding differences in the everyday lives of students.

Because school funding is most often based on the collection of local property taxes, schools in more affluent areas will offer better schooling than schools in poor communities. This difference also benefits whites over minorities, which is why some districts started a policy of *busing,* transporting students to achieve racial balance and equal opportunity in schools. Beginning in the 1970s, about 5 percent of U.S. students were bused to schools outside their neighborhoods, and this policy was very controversial. Supporters claimed that given the reality of racial segregation, the only way governments would adequately fund schools in poor, minority neighborhoods was if white children from richer areas attended. Critics responded that busing was expensive and undermines the concept of neighborhood schools. But almost everyone agreed on one thing: Given the racial imbalance of most urban areas, an effective busing policy would have to join inner cities and suburbs—a plan that has never been politically possible. Although racial segregation in U.S. public schools showed a modest decline between 1970 and 1990, there has been little change since then (Logan, Oakley, & Stowell, 2008).

But other policies to address unequal schools have emerged. One policy is to provide money equally across a state. This is the approach taken by Vermont, which passed Act 60, a law that distributes per-student tax money equally to all communities.

Not everyone thinks money is the key to good schooling. A classic report by a research team headed by James Coleman (1966) confirmed that schools in low-income communities and with mostly minority populations suffer problems ranging from large class size to insufficient libraries and too few science labs. But the Coleman report cautioned that more money by itself will not magically improve schooling. More important are the cooperative efforts of teachers, parents, and the students themselves. In other words, even if school funding were exactly the same everywhere (as in Vermont), students who benefit from more *cultural capital*—that is, those whose families value schooling, read to their children, and encourage the development of imagination—would still perform better. In short, we should not expect schools alone to overcome marked social inequality in the United States (Schneider et al., 1998; Israel, Beaulieu, & Hartless, 2001).

Further research confirms the difference the home environment makes in a student's school performance. A research team studied the rate at which school-age children gain skills in reading and mathematics (Downey, von Hippel, & Broh, 2004). Because U.S. children go to school six to seven hours a day, five days a week, and do not attend school during summer months, the researchers calculate that children spend only about 13 percent of their waking hours in school. During the school year, high-income children learn somewhat more quickly than low-income children, but the learning gap is far greater during the summer season when children are not in school. The researchers conclude that when it comes to student performance, schools matter, but the home and local environment matter more. Put another way,

THINKING ABOUT DIVERSITY: RACE, CLASS, & GENDER

Schooling in the United States: Savage Inequality

"Public School 261? Head down Jerome Avenue and look for the mortician's office." Off for a day studying the New York City schools, Jonathan Kozol parks his car and walks toward PS 261. Finding PS 261 is not easy because the school has no sign. In fact, the building is a former roller rink and doesn't look much like a school at all.

The principal explains that this is in a minority area of the North Bronx, so the population of PS 261 is 90 percent African American and Hispanic. Officially, the school should serve 900 students, but it actually enrolls 1,300. The rules say class size should not exceed thirty-two, but Kozol observes that it sometimes approaches forty. Because the school has just one small cafeteria, the children must eat in three shifts. After lunch, with no place to play, students squirm in their seats until they are told to return to their classrooms. Only one classroom in the entire school has a window to the world outside.

Toward the end of the day, Kozol remarks to a teacher about the overcrowding and the poor condition of the building. She sums up her thoughts: "I had an awful room last year. In the winter, it was 56 degrees. In the summer, it was up to 90." "Do the children ever comment on the building?" Kozol asks. "They don't say," she responds, "but they know. All these kids see TV. They know what suburban schools are like.

Then they look around them at their school. They don't comment on it, but you see it in their eyes. They understand."

Several months later, Kozol visits PS 24, in the affluent Riverdale section of New York City. This school is set back from the road, beyond a lawn planted with magnolia and dogwood trees, which are now in full bloom. On one side of the building is a playground for the youngest children; behind the school are playing fields for the older kids. Many people pay the high price of a house in Riverdale because the local schools have such an excellent reputation. There are 825 children here; most are white and a few are Asian, Hispanic, or African American. The building is in good repair. It has a large library and even a planetarium. All the classrooms have windows with bright curtains.

Entering one of the many classes for gifted students, Kozol asks the children what they are doing today. A young girl answers confidently, "My name is Laurie, and we're doing problem solving." A tall, good-natured boy continues, "I'm David. One thing that we do is logical thinking. Some problems, we find, have more than one good answer." Kozol asks if such reasoning is innate or if it is something a child learns. Susan, whose smile reveals her braces, responds, "You know some things to start with when you enter school. But we learn some things that other children don't. We learn certain things that other children don't know because we're *taught* them."

WHAT DO YOU THINK?

1. Are there differences between schools in your city or town? Explain.
2. Why is there so little public concern about schooling inequality?
3. What changes would our society have to make to eliminate schooling inequality? Would you support such changes? Why or why not?

Source: Adapted from Kozol (1992:85–88, 92–96).

schools close some of the learning gap that is created by differences in family resources, but they do not "level the playing field" between rich and poor children the way we like to think they do.

Access to Higher Education

For most people, advanced schooling is the key to a good job. But only 69 percent of U.S. high school graduates enroll in college immediately after graduation. Among young people aged eighteen to twenty-four years, about 40 percent are enrolled in college (National Center for Education Statistics, 2010).

A crucial factor affecting access to higher education is income. College is expensive: Even at state-supported colleges and universities, annual tuition and fees are about $7,000, and admission to the most expensive private colleges and universities exceeds $50,000 a year. As a result, two-thirds of the children in families with incomes above $75,000 per year (roughly the richest 30 percent, who fall within the upper-middle or upper class) attend college, but only 25 percent of children from families earning less than $20,000 a year go on to higher education (U.S. Census Bureau, 2006).

Seeing Sociology in Everyday Life

Are there specific things parents can do to improve their children's learning? How did your parents affect your learning?

Go to the Multimedia Library at **mysoclab.com** to view the video "Education and Financial Success"

Diversity Snapshot

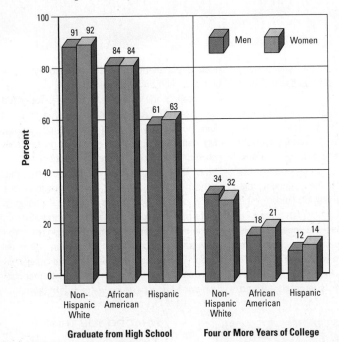

FIGURE 14–1 Educational Achievement for Various Categories of People, Aged 25 Years and Over, 2009

U.S. society still provides less education to minorities.

Source: U.S. Census Bureau (2010).

These economic differences are one reason that the educational gap between whites and minorities widens at the college level. As Figure 14–1 shows, African Americans are not quite as likely as non-Hispanic whites to graduate from high school and are much less likely to complete four or more years of college. Schooling is an important path to social mobility in our society, but the promise of schooling has not overcome the racial inequality that exists in the United States.

Completing college brings many rewards, including higher earnings. In the past forty years, as our economy has shifted to work that requires processing information, the gap in average income between people who complete only high school and those who earn a four-year college degree has more than doubled. In fact, today, a college degree can add as much as $1 million to a person's lifetime income. Table 14–2 gives details. In 2008, men who were high school graduates averaged $39,009, and college graduates averaged $65,800. The ratios in parentheses show that a man with a bachelor's degree earns 2.7 times in annual income as much as a man with eight or fewer years of schooling. Across the board, women earn less than men, although like men, added years of schooling boosts their income. Keep in mind that for

both men and women, some of the greater earnings have to do with social background, because the people with the most schooling are likely to come from well-off families to begin with.

Greater Opportunity: Expanding Higher Education

With some 19.1 million people enrolled in colleges and universities, the United States is a world leader in providing a college education to its people. This country also enrolls more students from abroad than any other.

One reason for this achievement is that there are more than 4,400 colleges and universities in the United States. This number includes 2,719 four-year institutions (which award bachelor's degrees) and 1,690 two-year colleges (which award associate's degrees). Some two-year colleges are private, but most are publicly funded community colleges that serve a local area (usually a city or a county) and charge a low tuition (National Center for Education Statistics, 2010).

Because higher education is a path to better jobs and higher income, the government makes money available to help certain categories of people pay the costs of college. After World War II, the GI Bill provided college funds to veterans, enabling tens of thousands of men and women to attend college. Some branches of the military continue to offer college money to enlistees; in addition, veterans continue to benefit from government grants and scholarships.

Community Colleges

Since the 1960s, the expansion of state-funded community colleges has greatly increased access to higher education. According to the National Center for Education Statistics (2010), the 1,690 two-year colleges across the United States now enroll 41 percent of all college undergraduates.

Community colleges provide a number of specific benefits. First, their low cost places college courses and degrees within reach of millions of families who could not otherwise afford them. Many

Table 14–2 Median Income by Sex and Educational Attainment, 2008

Education	Men	Women
Professional degree	$100,000 (4.1)	$71,297 (3.8)
Doctorate	100,000 (4.1)	74,025 (4.0)
Master's degree	80,962 (3.3)	57,512 (3.1)
Bachelor's degree	65,800 (2.7)	47,026 (2.5)
1–3 years of college	45,821 (1.9)	32,626 (1.8)
4 years of high school	39,009 (1.6)	28,382 (1.5)
9–11 years of school	29,678 (1.2)	20,405 (1.1)
0–8 years of school	24,255 (1.0)	18,634 (1.0)

Notes: Figures are for persons aged twenty-five years and over working full time. The earnings ratio, in parentheses, indicates what multiple of the lowest income level a person with the indicated amount of additional schooling earns.

Source: U.S. Census Bureau (2009).

○ Making the Grade

Review the Applying Theory table to be sure you understand the three theoretical approaches to education.

○ Making the Grade

The social-conflict approach claims that schooling transforms family privilege into personal merit. This means that, although we understand that earning a college degree is a personal achievement, family privilege plays a major part in getting people to college in the first place.

● APPLYING THEORY ●

Education

	Structural-Functional Approach	Symbolic-Interaction Approach	Social-Conflict Approach
What is the level of analysis?	Macro-level	Micro-level	Macro-level
What is the importance of education for society?	Schooling performs many vital tasks for the operation of society, including socializing the young and encouraging discovery and invention to improve our lives. Schooling helps unite a diverse society by teaching shared norms and values.	How teachers define their students—as well as how students think of themselves—can become real to everyone and affect students' educational performance.	Schooling maintains social inequality through unequal schooling for rich and poor. Within individual schools, tracking provides privileged children with a better education than poor children.

students at community colleges today are the first in their families to pursue a college degree. The low cost of community colleges is especially important during periods of economic recession. When the economy slumps and people lose their jobs, college enrollments soar, especially at community colleges. ● Go to **mysoclab.com**

Second, community colleges have special importance to minorities. Currently, almost half of all African American and Hispanic undergraduates in the United States attend community colleges.

Third, although community colleges serve local populations, some attract students from around the world. Many community colleges recruit students from abroad, and about 20 percent of all foreign students enrolled on a U.S. campus are studying at community colleges (National Center for Education Statistics, 2010).

Fourth, the top priority of faculty who work at large universities is typically research, but the most important job for community college faculty is teaching. So even though teaching loads are heavy (typically four or five classes each semester), community colleges appeal to faculty who find their greatest pleasure in the classroom. Community college students often get more attention from faculty than students at large universities (Jacobson, 2003). During the recent economic recession, community college enrollments have increased dramatically. Seeing Sociology in the News on pages 416–17 provides details.

Privilege and Personal Merit

If attending college is a rite of passage for rich men and women, as social-conflict analysis suggests, then *schooling transforms social privilege into personal merit.* But given our cultural emphasis on individualism, we tend to see credentials as badges of ability rather than as symbols of family affluence (Sennett & Cobb, 1973).

When we congratulate the new graduate, we rarely recognize the resources—in terms of both money and cultural capital—that made this achievement possible. Yet young people from families with incomes exceeding $200,000 a year average more than 375 points higher on the SAT exam than those whose families earn less than $20,000 a year (College Board, 2010). The richer students are thus more likely to get into college; once there, they are also more likely to complete their studies and get a degree. In a *credential society* such as ours, which evaluates people on the basis of their schooling, companies hire those with the best education. This process ends up helping people who are already advantaged and hurting those who are already disadvantaged (Collins, 1979).

○ **CRITICAL REVIEW** Social-conflict analysis links formal education to social inequality to show how schooling transforms privilege into personal worthiness and disadvantage into personal deficiency. However, the social-conflict approach overlooks the extent to which schooling provides upward mobility for talented women and men from all backgrounds. In addition, despite claims that schooling supports the status quo, today's college curricula challenge social inequality on many fronts.

The *Applying Theory table* sums up what the theoretical approaches show us about education.

○ **CHECK YOUR LEARNING** Explain several ways in which education is linked to social inequality.

The New York Times

New Meaning for Night Class at Two-Year Colleges

BY ABBY GOODNOUGH
October 29, 2009

BOSTON—Winston Chin hustles on Tuesdays from his eight-hour shift as a lab technician to his writing class at Bunker Hill Community College, a requirement for the associate's degree he is seeking in hopes of a better job.

He is a typical part-time student, with one exception. His class runs from 11:45 p.m. to 2:30 a.m., the consequence of an unprecedented enrollment spike that has Bunker Hill scrambling to accommodate hundreds of newcomers. In the dead of night, he and his classmates dissect Walt Whitman poems and learn the finer points of essay writing, fueled by unlimited coffee, cookies and an instructor who does push-ups beforehand to stay lively.

Similar booms have forced many of the nation's community colleges to add makeshift parking lots, rent extra space and keep thousands of students on waiting lists this fall. While Bunker Hill offers two midnight classes—the other is Psychology 101—and Clackamas Community College in Oregon holds welding classes until 2 a.m.,

others have added classes as early as 6 a.m. to make room for the jobless and others whom the recession has nudged back to school.

The deluge also includes an unusually large number of recent high school graduates, diverted from more expensive four-year colleges by the economic downturn.

"I liken myself to the old woman who lives in a shoe," said Mary L. Fifield, the president of Bunker Hill, where enrollment is up 16 percent over last fall. "The seams are tearing, and people are just popping out all over."

Virtually every state is dealing with enrollment booms at community colleges, the American Association of Community Colleges says, with some in California reporting increases of 35 percent. The demand comes amid deep cuts to higher education budgets, but also at a hopeful time for community colleges: President Obama recently announced a $12 billion plan to increase the number of community college graduates by five million by 2020.

"It shines a spotlight on a sector of higher education that by and large has been viewed as

the lowest rung on the ladder," Dr. Fifield said. "Now we have the president of the United States talking about community colleges as an engine that will drive and sustain economic success in this country."

Most of the students in Mr. Chin's writing class, who range in age from 18 to 59, are employed but hoping a degree will lead to more stable, higher paying jobs. Some start work as early as 4 a.m. or finish as late as 11 p.m., making the class time more appealing. They include a taxi dispatcher who dreams of going to medical school, a Dunkin' Donuts cashier who wants to be a homicide detective and a landscaper who wants to be a state trooper. . . .

Mr. Chin, who took the midnight class because other writing classes were full, wants to become a surgical nurse. At 57, he has three small children and has not been a student since graduating from high school.

"I probably would have taken something early in the morning if I'd had my pick of classes," he said. "But this is working out. I never really need more than about four hours of sleep anyway."

Problems in the Schools

Intense debate revolves around schooling in the United States. Because we expect schools to do so much—equalize opportunity, instill discipline, and fire the imagination—people are divided on whether public schools are doing their job. Although half of adults give their local schools a grade of A or B, just as many give a grade of C or below (Bushaw & McNee, 2009).

Discipline and Violence

When many of today's older teachers think back to their own student days, school "problems" consisted of talking out of turn, chewing gum, breaking the dress code, or cutting class. Today, schools are grappling with serious issues such as drug and alcohol abuse, teenage pregnancy, and outright violence. Although almost everyone agrees that schools should teach personal discipline, many people think the job is no longer being done.

Schools do not create violence; in most cases, violence spills into schools from the surrounding society. In the wake of a number of school shootings in recent years, many school districts have adopted zero-tolerance policies that require suspension or expulsion for serious misbehavior or bringing weapons on campus.

Deadly school shootings—including the deaths of thirty-three students at Virginia Tech University in 2007 and of eight students at

Northern Illinois University in 2008—have shocked the nation. Such tragic incidents also raise serious questions about balancing students' right to privacy (typically, the law prohibits colleges from informing parents of a student's grades or mental health issues) and the need to ensure the safety of the campus population. In the Virginia Tech case, for example, had the university been able to bring the disturbed young man's mental health problems to the attention of the police or his family, the tragedy might have been prevented (Gibbs, 2007; Shedden, 2008).

Student Passivity

If some schools are plagued by violence, many more are filled with students who are bored. Some of the blame for their passivity can be placed on the fact that electronic devices, from television to iPods, now claim far more of young people's time than school, parents, and community activities. But schools must share the blame because the educational system itself encourages student passivity (Coleman, Hoffer, & Kilgore, 1981).

Bureaucracy

The small, personal schools that served local communities a century ago have evolved into huge education factories. In a study of high schools across the United States, Theodore Sizer (1984:207–9) identified five ways in which large, bureaucratic schools undermine education:

Mr. Chin and his classmates get plenty of parking—a rarity at community colleges these days. Holyoke Community College, in Holyoke, Massachusetts, where enrollment is up 13 percent over last fall, turned its tennis courts into parking lots; it also sent postcards to all 7,500 students urging them to take public transportation to class. . . .

But with state allocations down sharply this year because of the economy, many community colleges have not been able to keep up with the demand. At Miami Dade College, whose 170,000 students make it the nation's largest community college, about 30,000 could not get every class they wanted this fall; about 5,000 others were shut out completely.

At De Anza College in Cupertino, California, about 8,000 students found themselves on wait lists last month, as did 7,500 students at Central Oregon Community College. . . .

Colleen Roach, Bunker Hill's spokeswoman, said higher student fees and an influx of federal stimulus money helped the college offer dozens more classes this fall. It is planning to add a third midnight course, Sociology 101, next spring, along with five business and science courses that will run to 11:45 p.m.

Dr. Fifield said putting dynamic instructors in charge of the late-night classes was crucial.

"Not everyone is going to be able to keep people awake until 2:45 in the morning," she said.

Wick Sloane, who teaches the midnight writing class at Bunker Hill, tried to transport Mr. Chin and the other students from the windowless, concrete-walled classroom one recent night with an essay by Edward Abbey, the nature writer, about encountering a mountain lion in the New Mexican desert. When one student answered a question with a giant yawn around 2:15, Mr. Sloane asked, "Can everyone make it about fifteen more minutes?"

For homework, he assigned an essay analyzing Calpurnia's rhetoric in Shakespeare's "Julius Caesar," leading one student to ask whether Shakespeare used an alias. The room started buzzing with opinions.

"Do you want to stay and debate who Shakespeare was?" Mr. Sloane asked.

They did not, but not for lack of enthusiasm. "He's got me engaged," Mr. Chin said, "which is not easy at this time of night."

WHAT DO YOU THINK?

1. According to the article, what are some of the reasons for the recent increase in community college enrollments?

2. What are the personal goals that are driving students at community colleges to obtain an additional degree? If you are a community college student, what are your goals?

3. What categories of people might decide to take a Sociology 101 class at midnight? What categories of people would have difficulty doing this?

1. **Rigid uniformity.** Bureaucratic schools run by outside specialists (such as state education officials) generally ignore the cultural character of local communities and the personal needs of their children.

2. **Numerical ratings.** School officials define success in terms of numerical attendance rates and dropout rates, and teachers "teach to the tests," hoping to raise test scores. Overlooked in the process are dimensions of schooling that are difficult to quantify, such as creativity and enthusiasm.

3. **Rigid expectations.** Officials expect fifteen-year-olds to be in the tenth grade and eleventh graders to score at a certain level on a standardized verbal achievement test. Rarely are exceptionally bright and motivated students permitted to graduate early. Likewise, poor performers are pushed from grade to grade, doomed to fail year after year.

4. **Specialization.** High school students learn Spanish from one teacher, receive guidance from another, and are coached in sports by still others. Students shuffle between fifty-minute periods throughout the school day. As a result, no school official comes to know the child well.

5. **Little individual responsibility.** Highly bureaucratic schools do not empower students to learn on their own. Similarly, teachers have little say in how they teach their classes; any change in the pace of learning or other deviation from the set curriculum risks disrupting the system.

Of course, with 62 million schoolchildren in the United States, schools have to be bureaucratic to get the job done. But Sizer recommends that we "humanize" schools by eliminating rigid scheduling, reducing class size, and training teachers more broadly to make them more involved in the lives of their students. Overall, as James Coleman (1993) has suggested, schools should be less "administratively driven" and more "output-driven." Perhaps this transformation could begin by ensuring that graduation from high school depends on what students have learned rather than on how many years they have spent in the building.

College: The Silent Classroom

Passivity is also common among college and university students (Gimenez, 1989). Sociologists rarely study the college classroom—a curious fact considering how much time they spend there. One exception was a study of a coeducational university where David Karp and William Yoels (1976) found that even in small classes, only a few students speak up. Thus passivity is a classroom norm, and students even become irritated if one of their number is especially talkative.

According to Karp and Yoels, most students think classroom passivity is their own fault. But as anyone who watches young people

● Seeing Sociology
  in Everyday Life

How many of your classes encourage active student
discussion? Is participation more common in some disciplines
than in others? Why?

functional illiteracy a lack of the reading and writing skills needed for
everyday living.

outside of class knows, they are usually active and vocal. It is clearly
the schools that teach students to be passive and to view instructors
as experts who serve up "knowledge" and "truth." Students see their
proper role as quietly listening and taking notes. As a result, the
researchers estimate, just 10 percent of college class time is used for
discussion.

Faculty can bring students to life in their classrooms by making
use of four teaching strategies: (1) calling on students by name when
they volunteer, (2) positively reinforcing student participation, (3)
asking analytical rather than factual questions and giving students
time to answer, and (4) asking for student opinions even when no one
volunteers a response (Auster & MacRone, 1994).

Dropping Out

If many students are passive in class, others are not there at all. The problem of *dropping out*—quitting before earning a high school diploma—
leaves young people (many of whom are disadvantaged to begin with)
unprepared for the world of work and at high risk of poverty.

The dropout rate has declined slightly in recent decades; currently, 8 percent of people between the ages of sixteen and twenty-
four are high school dropouts, a total of 3 million young women and
men. Dropping out is least common among non-Hispanic whites
(4.8 percent), more likely among non-Hispanic African Americans (9.9 percent), and most common among Hispanics (18.3
percent) (National Center for Education Statistics, 2009).

Some students drop out because of problems with the
English language, others because of pregnancy, and some
because they must work to support their family. For
children growing up in families with income in
the bottom 25 percent, the dropout rate is
more than seven times higher than for
children living in high-income families
(National Center for Education Statistics, 2009). These data suggest that
many dropouts are young people
whose parents also have little schooling, revealing a multigenerational cycle
of disadvantage.

Dropping out is actually the norm
in many large urban school systems.

For all categories of people in the United
States, dropping out of school greatly
reduces the chances of getting a good job
and earning a secure income. Why is the
dropout rate particularly high among
Hispanic Americans?

Fewer than half of all children end up graduating from high school
in many of this country's largest school districts—including Minneapolis (graduation rate of just 45 percent), Atlanta (44 percent),
Los Angeles (44 percent), Baltimore (42 percent), Milwaukee (41
percent), and Detroit (38 percent) (Swanson, 2009).

Academic Standards

Perhaps the most serious educational issue confronting our society is
the quality of our nation's schooling. *A Nation at Risk,* a comprehensive study of the quality of U.S. schools conducted by the National
Commission on Excellence in Education, begins with this alarming
statement:

> If an unfriendly foreign power had attempted to impose on America
> the mediocre educational performance that exists today, we might
> well have viewed it as an act of war. As it stands, we have allowed this
> to happen to ourselves. (1983:5)

Supporting this claim, the report notes that "nearly 40 percent of
seventeen-year-olds cannot draw inferences from written material; only
one-fifth can write a persuasive essay; and only one-third can solve
mathematical problems requiring several steps" (1983:9). Furthermore,
scores on the Scholastic Assessment Test (SAT) show little improvement over time. In 1967, median scores were 516 on the mathematics test and 543 on the verbal test; by 2009, the average in
mathematics had dropped 1 point to 515, and the verbal average had slipped to just 501. Nationwide, one-third of
high school students—and more than half of those
in urban schools—fail to master even the basics
in reading, math, and science on the
National Assessment of Educational
Progress examination (Marklein, 2000;
Barnes, 2002a; National Assessment of
Educational Progress, 2007; College
Board, 2009).

For many people in this country, even
basic literacy is at issue. **Functional illiteracy,** *a lack of the reading and writing skills
needed for everyday living,* is a problem for
one in three U.S. children. For older people, about 30 million U.S. adults (about
14 percent of the total) lack basic skills
in reading and writing.

A Nation at Risk recommended
drastic reform. First, it called for
schools to require *all* students to
complete several years of English,
mathematics, social studies, general
science, and computer science. Second,

Seeing Sociology in Everyday Life

Recall that U.S. students spend only about 13 percent of their waking hours in school. Do you think they should spend more time in school? Explain your answer.

Making the Grade

School choice is favored by those who see a market system as providing competition among service providers and choice to service consumers. Critics claim market models generate inequality; they favor government systems that attempt to provide the same service to everyone.

it warned schools not to promote students until they meet achievement standards. Third, it stated that teacher training must improve and teachers' salaries be raised to draw talent into the profession. The report concluded that schools must meet public expectations and that citizens must be prepared to pay for a job well done.

What has happened in the years since *A Nation at Risk* was issued? In some respects, schools have improved. A report by the National Center for Education Statistics (2008) noted some decline in the dropout rate, a trend toward schools' offering more challenging courses, and a larger share of high school graduates going to college. At the same time, the evidence suggests that a majority of elementary school students are falling below standards in reading; in many cases, they can't read at all. In short, although some improvement is evident, much remains to be done.

The United States spends more on schooling its children than almost any other nation—half again more than Japan and double the average in Europe. Even so, a recent report comparing the academic performance of fifteen-year-olds in fifty-seven countries found that the United States placed twenty-ninth in science and thirty-fifth in mathematics. Such statistics fuel fears that our country is losing its leadership in science to other nations, including China, India, and South Korea (OECD, 2007).

Cultural values play a part in how hard students work at their schooling. For example, U.S. students are generally less motivated and do less homework than students in Japan. Japanese young people also spend forty-three more days in school each year than U.S. students. Perhaps one approach to improving school performance is simply to have students spend more time in school.

Grade Inflation

Academic standards depend on the use of grades that have clear meaning and are awarded for work of appropriate quality. Yet recent decades have seen substantial *grade inflation,* the awarding of ever-higher grades for average work. Though not necessarily found in every school, grade inflation is evident in both high schools and colleges.

One study of high school grades revealed a dramatic change in the distribution of grades between 1968 and 2007. In 1968, the high school records of students who had just entered college included more grades of C+ and below than grades of A–, A, and A+. By 2007, however, these A grades outnumbered grades of C+ and below by more than ten to one (Pryor et al., 2009).

A few colleges and universities have enacted policies that limit the share of A grades (generally to one-third of all grades). But there is little evidence that grade inflation will be reversed anytime soon. As a result, the C grade (which used to mean "middle of the pack") may all but disappear, making just about every student "above average."

What accounts for grade inflation? In part, today's teachers are concerned about the morale and self-esteem of their students and

perhaps their own popularity. In any case, teachers clearly are not as "tough" as they used to be. At the same time, the ever more competitive process of getting into college and graduate school puts pressure on high schools and colleges to award high grades (Astin et al., 2002).

Current Issues in U.S. Education

Our society's schools continuously confront new challenges. This section explores several recent and important educational issues.

School Choice

Some analysts claim that our schools teach poorly because they have no competition. Giving parents options for schooling their children might force all schools to do a better job. This is the essence of a policy called *school choice.*

The goal of school choice is to create a market for education so that parents and students can shop for the best value. According to one proposal, the government would give vouchers to families with school-age children and allow them to spend the money at public, private, or parochial schools. In recent years, major cities, including Indianapolis, Minneapolis, Milwaukee, Cleveland, Chicago, and Washington, D.C., as well as the states of Florida and Illinois, have experimented with choice plans designed to make public schools perform better to win the confidence of families.

Supporters claim that giving parents a choice about where to enroll their children is the only sure way to improve all schools. But critics (including teachers' unions) charge that school choice amounts to giving up on our nation's commitment to public education and that it will do little to improve schools in the central cities, where the need is greatest (A. Cohen, 1999; Morse, 2002).

In 2002, President George W. Bush signed a new education bill that downplayed vouchers in favor of another approach to greater choice. Starting in the 2005–06 school year, all public schools began testing every child in reading, mathematics, and science in grades three through eight. Although the federal government may provide more aid to schools with students who do not perform well, if those schools do not show improvements in test scores over time, low-income students will have the choice of special tutoring or transportation to another school. This program, called "No Child Left Behind," has helped identify which schools are not doing a good job educating children and has raised some measures of school performance. At the same time, however, little change has occurred in many of the worst-performing schools (Lindlaw, 2002; Wallis & Steptoe, 2007).

By 2010, fully one-third of this nation's public schools had been labeled as failing, and a large majority of U.S. adults claimed that the No Child Left Behind Act had not improved public education. The

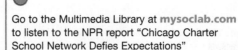

● Seeing Sociology
in Everyday Life

Have you ever attended a magnet school, charter school, or
for-profit school? If so, was it a good experience?

Go to the Multimedia Library at **mysoclab.com**
to listen to the NPR report "Chicago Charter
School Network Defies Expectations"

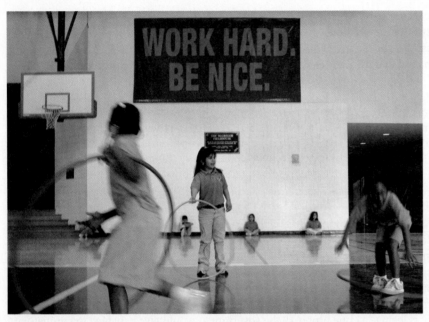

Charter schools, one part of the school choice movement, encourage personal
discipline and academic excellence. Do you support school choice? Why or why not?

public schools, enrolling hundreds of thousands of students, are now run by private businesses for profit.

Research confirms that many public school systems suffer from bureaucratic bloat, spending far too much and teaching far too little. And U.S. society has long looked to competition to improve quality. Evidence suggests that for-profit schools have greatly reduced administrative costs, but the educational results appear mixed. Although some companies claim to improve student learning, some cities have cut back on business-run schools. In recent years, school boards in Baltimore, Miami, Hartford, and Boston have canceled the contracts of for-profit schooling corporations. But other cities have been willing to give for-profit schooling a try. For example, after Philadelphia's public school system failed to graduate one-third of its students, the state of Pennsylvania took charge of that city's schools and turned most of them over to for-profit companies. Although there was some evidence of improvement in student performance, by 2010 school officials were still dissatisfied and so they turned over most of these schools to independent companies that operate as nonprofit organizations. Overall, we do not yet have clear evidence as to which type of schooling works best. As a result, the debate over public and private operation of our schools continues, with each side claiming to speak for the well-being of the schoolchildren caught in the middle (Winters, 2002; Sizer, 2003; Richburg, 2008).

Home Schooling

Home schooling is gaining popularity across the United States. About 1.5 million children (almost 3 percent of all school-age children) have their formal schooling at home.

Why do parents undertake the enormous challenge of schooling their own children? A couple of decades ago, many of the parents who pioneered home schooling (which is now legal in every state) did not believe in public education because they wanted to give their children a strongly religious upbringing. Today, however, the majority are mothers and fathers who simply do not believe that public schools are doing a good job and who think they can do better. To benefit their children, many parents are willing to change work schedules and to relearn algebra or other necessary subjects. Many belong to groups in which parents combine their efforts, specializing in what each knows best.

Advocates of home schooling point out that given the poor performance of many public schools, no one should be surprised that a growing number of parents are stepping up to teach their own children. Even more impressive is that this system works—on average, students who learn at home outperform those who learn in school. Critics argue that home schooling reduces the amount of federal funding going

Obama administration has asked Congress to focus attention on the 5,000 schools with the lowest student performance and to shift the goal from raising test scores to raising graduation rates and preparing students for careers (Gallup, 2009; Dillon, 2010).

A more modest form of school choice involves *magnet schools,* more than 2,700 of which now exist across the country. Magnet schools offer special facilities and programs to promote educational excellence in a particular field, such as computer science, foreign languages, science and mathematics, or the arts. In school districts with magnet schools, parents can choose the one best suited to their child's particular talents and interests.

Another school choice strategy involves *charter schools,* public schools that are given more freedom to try new policies and programs. There are more than 4,000 such schools in forty-one states, Washington, D.C., and Puerto Rico; they enroll 1.3 million students, 60 percent of whom are minorities. In many of these schools, students have demonstrated high academic achievement—a requirement for renewal of the charter (National Center for Education Statistics, 2010). ● Go to **mysoclab.com**

A final development in the school choice movement is *schooling for profit.* Supporters of this plan say school systems can be operated more efficiently by private profit-making companies than by local governments. Private schooling is nothing new, of course; more than 28,000 schools in the United States are currently run by private organizations and religious groups. What is new is that hundreds of

Go to the Multimedia Library at **mysoclab.com**
to view the *Core Concepts in Sociology* video
"Attracting and Retaining Good Teachers"

● Seeing Sociology
in Everyday Life

Have you considered a career in teaching? If so, why? If not,
what changes might make the field more appealing to you?

to local public schools, which ends up hurting the majority of students. In addition, as one critic points out, home schooling "takes some of the most affluent and articulate parents out of the system. These are the parents who know how to get things done with administrators" (Chris Lubienski, quoted in Cloud & Morse, 2001:48).

Schooling People with Disabilities

Many of the 6.6 million children with disabilities in the United States have difficulty getting to and from school; once there, many with crutches or wheelchairs cannot negotiate stairs and other obstacles in school buildings. Children with developmental disabilities such as mental retardation need extensive personal attention from specially trained teachers. As a result, many children with mental and physical disabilities have won the right to a public education only after persistent efforts by parents and other concerned citizens (Horn & Tynan, 2001).

Not quite half of all children with disabilities are schooled in special facilities; a slight majority attend public schools, most joining regular classes. Including students with disabilities in the overall educational program is called *mainstreaming*. This form of *inclusive education* works best for physically impaired students who have no difficulty keeping up academically with the rest of the class. Another benefit is that mainstreaming allows all students to learn to interact with people who are different from themselves.

Adult Education

In recent years, almost 100 million U.S. adults have been enrolled in some type of schooling. These older students range in age from the mid-twenties to the seventies and beyond and make up 39 percent of students in degree-granting programs. Adults in school are more likely to be women than men, and most have above-average incomes.

Why do adults return to the classroom? The most common reasons given are to advance a career or train for a new job, but many are in class simply for personal enrichment (National Center for Education Statistics, 2006). During economic downturns, as we have experienced in recent years, the number of adults returning to the classroom (including many who are out of work) typically goes up.

The Teacher Shortage

A final challenge for U.S. schools is hiring enough teachers to fill the classrooms. A number of factors—including low salaries, frustration over extensive bureaucracy, and retirement of aging teachers, as well as rising enrollment and increases in class size—have combined to create more than 300,000 teaching vacancies in the United States each year.

How will these slots be filled? About the same number of people graduate with education degrees annually. Most of them do not

have a degree in a specific field, such as mathematics, biology, or English, and many have trouble passing state certification tests in the subject they want to teach. As a result, many schools, especially in low-income neighborhoods, are taught by teachers who may be just one chapter ahead of their students (Quaid, 2008).

This means that the teacher shortage is really a shortage of *good* teachers. For our nation's public schools to improve, two things must happen: First, teachers who do not teach well must receive additional training or lose their jobs, and second, well-qualified people need to be attracted into the classroom (Ripley, 2008). ● Go to **mysoclab.com**

Getting rid of bad teachers (and perhaps bad principals too) means changing rules that make it difficult or impossible to fire someone after a few years on the job. Gaining well-qualified teachers depends on adopting various recruitment strategies. Some schools offer incentives such as higher salaries (the average salary for a thirty-year-old teacher in public schools is only about $37,000 a year) to draw into teaching people who have already had successful careers. Some schools provide signing bonuses (especially for hard-to-fill positions in disciplines such as chemistry) or give housing allowances (in cities such as New York, where housing is often out of reach to teachers). President Obama (2007) has stated that he believes that school districts should pay highly qualified and effective teachers as much as $100,000 a year—but, he adds, they also should be able to dismiss unqualified and ineffective teachers.

Other policy ideas include having community colleges play a larger role in teacher education and having government and school boards make it easier for good teachers to get the certification they need to enter the classroom. Finally, many school districts are going global, actively recruiting in countries such as Spain, India, and the Philippines to bring talented women and men from around the world to U.S. classrooms (Evelyn, 2002; Ripley, 2008; Wallis, 2008).

Debate about education in the United States extends beyond the issues noted here. The Seeing Sociology in Everyday Life box on page 422 highlights the declining share of college students who are men.

Schooling: Looking Ahead

Although the United States still leads the world in sending people to college, the public school system continues to struggle with serious problems. In terms of quality of schooling, this country is falling behind many other nations, a fact that calls into question the future strength of the United States on the world stage.

Many of the problems of schooling discussed in this chapter have their roots in the larger society. We cannot expect schools *by themselves* to provide high-quality education. Schools will improve only to the extent that students, teachers, parents, and local communities commit themselves to educational excellence. In short, educational problems are *social* problems for which there is no quick fix.

● Seeing Sociology
in Everyday Life

Are you personally concerned about the gender balance on your
campus? Why or why not?

Go to the Multimedia Library at **mysoclab.com**
to hear author John Macionis respond to the
question "How Is Health a Social Issue?"

SEEING SOCIOLOGY IN EVERYDAY LIFE

The Twenty-First-Century Campus: Where Are the Men?

MEG: I mean, where are the men on this campus? Seems like they're hard to find.

TRICIA: Does it matter? I'd rather focus on my work anyway.

MARK: But, hey, it's really cool for us guys!

A century ago, the campuses of colleges and universities across the United States might as well have hung out a sign that read "Men Only." Almost all of the students and faculty were male. There were a small number of women's colleges, but many more schools—including some of the most prestigious U.S. universities, including Yale, Harvard, and Princeton—barred women outright.

Since then, women have won greater social equality. By 1980, the number of women enrolled at U.S. colleges finally matched the number of men.

In a surprising trend, however, the share of women on campus has continued to increase. As a result, in 2008, men accounted for only 43 percent of all U.S. undergraduates. Meg DeLong noticed the gender imbalance right away when she moved into her dorm at the University of Georgia at Athens; she soon learned that just 39 percent of her first-year classmates were men. In some classes there were few men, and women usually dominated discussions. Out of class, DeLong and many other women soon complained that having so few men on campus hurt their social life. Not surprisingly, most of the men felt otherwise (Fonda, 2000).

What accounts for the shifting gender balance on U.S. campuses? One theory is that young men are drawn away from college by the lure of jobs, especially in high technology. This pattern is sometimes termed the "Bill Gates syndrome," after the Microsoft founder, who dropped out of college and soon became the world's richest person. In addition, analysts point to an anti-intellectual male culture. Young women are drawn to learning and seek to do well in school, but young men attach less importance to studying. Rightly or wrongly, more men seem to think they can get a good job without investing years of their lives and a considerable amount of money in getting a college degree.

The gender gap is evident in all racial and ethnic categories and at all class levels. Among African Americans on campus, only 36 percent are men. The lower the income level, the greater the gender gap in college attendance.

Many college officials are concerned about a lack of men on campus. In an effort to attract more balanced enrollments, some colleges are adopting what amounts to affirmative action programs for males. But courts in several states have ruled such policies illegal. Many colleges are therefore turning to more active recruitment; admissions officers are paying special attention to male applicants and stressing a college's strength in mathematics and science—areas traditionally popular with men. In the same way that colleges across the country are striving to increase their share of minority students, the hope is that they can also succeed in attracting a larger share of men.

WHAT DO YOU THINK?

1. Among high school students, are men less concerned than women about academic achievement? Why or why not?

2. Is there a gender imbalance on your campus? Does it create problems? If so, what problems? For whom?

3. What programs or policies do you think might increase the number of men going to college?

For much of the twentieth century, there were just two models for education in the United States: public schools run by the government and private schools operated by nongovernmental organizations. In recent decades, however, many new ideas about schooling have emerged, including schooling for profit and a wide range of "school choice" programs. In the decades ahead, we will probably see some significant changes in mass education, guided in part by the results of social science research into the outcomes of different strategies.

Another factor that will continue to shape schools is information technology. Today, all but the poorest primary and sec-

ondary schools use computers for instruction. Computers prompt students to be more active and allow them to progress at their own pace. Even so, computers will never bring to the educational process the personal insights or imagination of a motivated human teacher.

Nor will technology ever solve all the problems that plague our schools, including violence and rigid bureaucracy. What we need is a broad plan for social change that refires this country's ambition to provide universal schooling of the highest quality—a goal that we have yet to achieve.

○ Making the Grade

In high-income societies today, few deaths result from infectious diseases; most deaths result from chronic illnesses.

Health and Medicine

Another institution that expands greatly in modern societies is **medicine,** *the social institution that focuses on fighting disease and improving health.* In ideal terms, according to the World Health Organization (1946:3), **health** is *a state of complete physical, mental, and social well-being.* This definition underscores the important fact that health is as much a social as a biological issue. ● Go to **mysoclab.com**

Health and Society

Society affects people's health in four major ways:

1. **Cultural patterns define health.** Standards of health vary from culture to culture. A century ago, yaws, a contagious skin disease, was so common in sub-Saharan Africa that people there considered it normal (Dubos, 1980). In the United States, a rich diet is so common that most adults consider overeating to be normal and are now overweight. "Health," therefore, is sometimes a matter of having the same conditions or diseases as one's neighbors (Pinhey, Rubinstein, & Colfax, 1997).

   What people see as healthful also reflects what they think is morally good. Members of our society (especially men) think a competitive way of life is "healthy" because it fits our cultural mores, but stress contributes to heart disease and many other illnesses. People who object to homosexuality on moral grounds often call it "sick," even though it is natural from a biological point of view. Thus ideas about health act as a form of social control, encouraging conformity to cultural norms.

2. **Cultural standards of health change over time.** Early in the twentieth century, some doctors warned women not to go to college because higher education strained the female brain. Others claimed that masturbation was a threat to health. We now know that both of these ideas are false. Fifty years ago, on the other hand, few doctors understood the dangers of cigarette smoking or too much sun exposure, practices that we now recognize as serious health risks. Even patterns of basic hygiene change over time. Today, most people in the United States bathe or shower every day; this is three times as often as fifty years ago (Gillespie, 2000).

3. **A society's technology affects people's health.** In poor nations, infectious diseases are widespread because of malnutrition and poor sanitation. As industrialization raises living standards, people become healthier. But industrial technology also creates new threats to health. As Chapter 15 ("Population, Urbanization, and Environment") explains, rich societies endanger health by overtaxing the world's resources and creating pollution.

4. **Social inequality affects people's health.** All societies distribute resources unequally. Overall, the rich have far better physical, mental, and emotional health than the poor.

Health: A Global Survey

Because health is closely linked to social life, human well-being has improved over the long course of history as societies developed more advanced technology. Differences in societal development are also the cause of striking differences in health around the world today.

Health in Low-Income Countries

With only simple technology, our ancestors could do little to improve health. Hunters and gatherers faced frequent food shortages, which sometimes forced mothers to abandon their children. Those lucky enough to survive infancy were still vulnerable to injury and illness, so half died by age twenty and few lived to forty (Scupin, 2000; Nolan & Lenski, 2004).

As societies developed agriculture, food became more plentiful. Yet social inequality also increased, so that elites enjoyed better health than peasants and slaves, who lived in crowded, unsanitary shelters and often went hungry. In the growing cities of medieval Europe, human waste and refuse piled up in the streets, spreading infectious diseases, and plagues periodically wiped out entire towns (Mumford, 1961).

In much of the world, poverty cuts decades off the life expectancy found in rich countries. In low-income nations of sub-Saharan Africa, for example, people have a life expectancy of barely fifty, and in the poorest countries, most people die before reaching their teens.

The World Health Organization reports that 1 billion people around the world—one person in six—suffer from serious illness due to poverty. Poor sanitation and malnutrition kill people of all ages. In a classic vicious circle, poverty breeds disease, which reduces people's ability to work, increasing poverty. When medical technology is used to control infectious disease, the populations of poor nations soar. But without enough resources to provide for the current population, poor societies can ill afford population increases. Therefore, programs that lower death rates in poor countries will succeed only if they are coupled with programs that reduce birth rates.

Health in High-Income Countries

By 1800, as the Industrial Revolution took hold, factory jobs in cities attracted people from the countryside. Cities quickly became overcrowded, causing serious sanitation problems. Factories fouled the air with smoke, and workplace accidents were common.

Table 14–3 Leading Causes of Death in the United States, 1900 and 2007

1900	2007
1. Influenza and pneumonia	1. Heart disease
2. Tuberculosis	2. Cancer
3. Stomach and intestinal disease	3. Stroke
4. Heart disease	4. Lung disease (noncancerous)
5. Cerebral hemorrhage	5. Accidents
6. Kidney disease	6. Alzheimer's disease
7. Accidents	7. Diabetes
8. Cancer	8. Influenza and pneumonia
9. Disease in early infancy	9. Kidney disease
10. Diphtheria	10. Blood disease

Sources: Information for 1900 is from William C. Cockerham, *Medical Sociology,* 2nd ed. (Englewood Cliffs, N.J.: Prentice Hall, 1986), p. 24; information for 2007 is from Jiaquan Xu, Kenneth D. Kochanek, & Betzaida Tejada-Vera, "Deaths: Final Data for 2007," *National Vital Statistics Reports,* vol. 58, no. 19 (Hyattsville, Md: National Center for Health Statistics, 2010).

Gradually, industrialization raised living standards, providing better nutrition and safer housing for most people, so that after about 1850, health began to improve. Also around this time, medical advances began to control infectious diseases. In 1854, a researcher named John Snow mapped the street addresses of London's cholera victims and found that they had all drunk water from the same well. Not long afterward, scientists linked cholera to a specific bacterium and developed a vaccine against the deadly disease. Armed with scientific knowledge, early environmentalists campaigned against common practices such as discharging raw sewage into rivers used for drinking water. By the early twentieth century, death rates from infectious diseases had fallen sharply.

Table 14–3 shows that the leading killers in 1900—influenza and pneumonia—account for few deaths in the United States today. It is now chronic illnesses, such as heart disease, cancer, and stroke, that cause most deaths, usually in old age.

Health in the United States

Because the United States is a rich nation, health is generally good by world standards. Still, some categories of people have much better health than others.

Who Is Healthy? Age, Gender, Class, and Race

Social epidemiology is *the study of how health and disease are distributed throughout a society's population.* Social epidemiologists examine the origin and spread of epidemic diseases and try to understand how people's health is tied to their physical and social environments.

In the United States, a twenty-year gap in average life expectancy separates the richest and poorest communities. This difference can be examined through the lens of age, gender, social class, and race.

Age and Gender

Death is now rare among young people. Still, young people do fall victim to accidents and, in recent decades, to acquired immune deficiency syndrome (AIDS).

Throughout the life course, women have better health than men. First, girls are less likely than boys to die before or immediately after birth. As socialization begins, males become more aggressive and individualistic, resulting in higher rates of accidents, violence, and suicide. As the Thinking About Diversity box explains, the combination of chronic impatience, uncontrolled ambition, and outbursts of hostility that doctors call "coronary-prone behavior" is a fairly close match with our culture's definition of masculinity.

Social Class and Race

Government researchers tell us that 79 percent of people in families with incomes over $75,000 think their health is excellent or very good, but only 51 percent of people in families earning less than $35,000 say the same. Conversely, only about 4 percent of higher-income people describe their health as fair or poor, compared with 19 percent of low-income people (Adams, Heyman, & Vickerie, 2009).

Research suggests that African Americans are no different from whites in terms of their desire for good health and willingness to seek medical help. But poverty among African Americans—three times the rate for whites—helps explain why black people are more likely to die in infancy and, as adults, to suffer the effects of violence, drug abuse, and poor health (Hayward et al., 2000; Schnittker, Pescosolido, & Croghan, 2005). Figure 14–2 on page 426 shows that the life expectancy of white children born in 2007 is almost five years greater than for African American children (78.4 years versus 73.6). Gender is an even stronger predictor of health than race, since African American women outlive men of either race. From another angle, 81 percent of white men but just 67 percent of African American men will live to age sixty-five. The comparable figures for women are 88 percent for whites and 79 percent for African Americans.

Infant mortality—the death rate among children under one year of age—is twice as high for disadvantaged children in the United States as for children born into privileged families. Although the health of the richest children in our country is the best in the world, our poorest children are as vulnerable to disease as those in low-income nations such as Nigeria and Vietnam.

Cigarette Smoking

Cigarette smoking tops the list of preventable health hazards in the United States. Only after World War I did smoking become popular

Seeing Sociology in Everyday Life

Have you ever thought about gender as a health issue? Explain.

Seeing Sociology in Everyday Life

Sixteen states have enacted laws banning smoking in all public buildings. Would you support making this ban a national policy? Why or why not?

THINKING ABOUT DIVERSITY: RACE, CLASS, & GENDER

Masculinity: A Threat to Health?

JEFF: Cindy! If you don't get out of there in ten seconds, I'm gonna break the door down!

CINDY: Chill out, bro! I have as much right to be in the bathroom as you do. I'm not finished.

JEFF: Are you going to take *all day?*

CINDY: Why are you guys always in such a hurry?

Doctors call it "coronary-prone behavior." Psychologists call it "Type A personality." Sociologists recognize it as our culture's idea of masculinity. This combination of attitudes and behavior, common among men in our society, includes chronic impatience ("Get outta my way!"), uncontrolled ambition ("I've gotta have it. I *need* that!"), and free-floating hostility ("Why are people *such idiots?*").

This pattern, although normal from a cultural point of view, is one major reason that men who are driven to succeed are at high risk of heart disease. By acting out the Type A personality, we may get the job done, but we set in motion complex biochemical processes that are very hard on the human heart.

Here are a few questions to help you determine your own degree of risk (or that of someone important to you):

1. **Do you believe that you have to be aggressive to succeed?** Do nice guys finish last? For your heart's sake, try to remove hostility from your life. Here's a place to start: Eliminate profanity from your speech. Try to replace aggression with compassion, which can be surprisingly effective in dealing with other people. Medically speaking, substituting compassion and humor for irritation and aggravation will improve your health.

2. **How well do you handle uncertainty and opposition?** Do you lose patience with other people ("Why won't the waiter take my order?" "This jerk just doesn't get it!")? We all like to know what's going on, and we want others to go along with us. But the world often doesn't work that way. Accepting uncertainty and opposition

makes us more mature and certainly healthier.

3. **Are you uncomfortable showing positive emotions?** Many men think that giving and accepting love—from women, from children, and from other men—is a sign of weakness. But the medical truth is that love supports health and anger damages it.

As human beings, we have a great deal of choice about how we live. Think about the choices you make, and reflect on how our society's idea of masculinity often makes us hard on others (including those we love) and, just as important, hard on ourselves.

WHAT DO YOU THINK?

1. What aspects of masculinity are harmful to health?

2. Why are so many people unaware of how masculinity can be harmful to health?

3. How can sociology play a part in changing men's health for the better?

Sources: Friedman & Rosenman (1974) and M. P. Levine (1990).

---

in this country. Despite growing evidence of its dangers, smoking remained fashionable until around a generation ago. Today, however, an increasing number of people consider smoking a mild form of social deviance, and an increasing number of states have banned smoking in public buildings (Niesse, 2007).

The adult popularity of cigarettes peaked in 1960, when 45 percent of adults in the United States smoked. By 2008, only 21 percent were lighting up, according to the Centers for Disease Control and Prevention (CDC, 2009). Another sign of the times is that thirty-eight states have banned smoking in most or all public places, such as restaurants and bars.

All the same, quitting is difficult because cigarette smoke contains nicotine, a physically addictive drug. Many people smoke to cope with stress: Divorced and separated people are likely to smoke, as are the unemployed and people serving in the armed forces. Smoking is much more common among working-class people than among those with more income and education. A larger share of men (23 percent) than women (18 percent) smoke. But cigarettes, the only form of tobacco use popular among women, have taken a toll on women's health. By 1987, lung cancer had surpassed breast cancer as a cause of death among U.S. women, who now account for 39 percent of all smoking-related deaths (CDC, 2008; Pampel, 2006).

Whites live longer than African Americans, just as females typically outlive males.

Diversity Snapshot

FIGURE 14–2   **Life Expectancy of U.S. Children Born in 2007**

Both gender and race have a powerful effect on life expectancy.

Source: Xu et al. (2010).

Some 443,000 men and women die prematurely each year as a direct result of cigarette smoking, a figure that exceeds the death toll from alcohol, cocaine, heroin, homicide, suicide, automobile accidents, and AIDS combined (CDC, 2008). Smokers also suffer more often from minor illnesses such as the flu, and pregnant women who smoke increase the likelihood of spontaneous abortion, prenatal death, and low-birthweight babies. Even nonsmokers exposed to cigarette smoke have a high risk of smoking-related diseases.

Tobacco is an $89 billion industry in the United States. In 1997, the tobacco industry admitted that cigarette smoking is harmful to health and agreed to stop marketing cigarettes to young people. Despite the antismoking trend in the United States, the percentage of college students who smoke has now passed 30 percent and continues to rise (College Tobacco Prevention Resource, 2006; U.S. Department of Health and Human Services, 2010). In addition, the use of chewing tobacco, also a threat to health, is increasing among the young.

The tobacco industry has increased marketing abroad, where there is less regulation of tobacco products. In many countries, especially in Asia, a large majority of men smoke. Worldwide, more than 1 billion adults (about 25 percent of the total) smoke, consuming some 6 trillion cigarettes annually, and smoking is on the rise. One result of the rise in global smoking is that cancer is likely to overtake heart disease as the world's number one killer in the next year or two (Stobbe, 2008; World Health Organization, 2009). The harm

that comes from cigarette smoking is real. But the good news is that about ten years after quitting, an ex-smoker's health is about as good as that of someone who never smoked at all.

Eating Disorders

An **eating disorder** is *an intense form of dieting or other unhealthy method of weight control driven by the desire to be very thin.* One eating disorder, *anorexia nervosa,* is characterized by dieting to the point of starvation; another is *bulimia,* which involves binge eating followed by induced vomiting to avoid weight gain.

Eating disorders involve gender, race, and class: 95 percent of people who suffer from anorexia nervosa or bulimia are women, mostly from white, affluent families. For women, U.S. culture equates slimness with being successful and attractive to men. Conversely, we tend to stereotype overweight women (and to a lesser extent men) as lazy, sloppy, and even stupid (M. P. Levine, 1987; A. E. Becker, 1999).

Research shows that most college-age women believe that "guys like thin girls," that being thin is crucial to physical attractiveness, and that they are not as thin as men would like. In fact, most college women actually want to be thinner than most college men want them to be. Men typically express more satisfaction with their own body shapes (Fallon & Rozin, 1985).

Because few women are able to meet our culture's unrealistic standards of beauty, many women develop a low self-image. Our idealized image of beauty leads many young women to diet to the point of risking their health and even their lives.

Obesity

Eating disorders such as anorexia nervosa and bulimia are serious, but they are not the biggest eating-related problem in the United States. Obesity in the population as a whole is rapidly reaching crisis proportions. The government reports that 63 percent of U.S. adults are overweight, which is defined in terms of a *body mass index* (BMI) of 25.0 to 29.9, or roughly 10 to 30 pounds over a healthy weight for one's height. Forty-two percent of all overweight people in the United States are clinically obese, with a BMI over 30.0, which means that they are at least 30 pounds over their healthy weight. National Map 14–2 shows the increasing trend toward obesity in the United States.

Being overweight can limit physical activity and raises the risk of a number of serious diseases, including heart disease, stroke, and diabetes. According to the U.S. government, the cost of treating diseases caused by obesity plus the cost of lost days at work due to such illnesses equals almost $150 billion every year. Most seriously, some 112,000 people die each year in the United States from diseases related to being overweight (Ferraro & Kelley-Moore, 2003; R. Stein, 2005; CDC, 2007).

Calculate your *body mass index* (BMI): Divide your weight in pounds by the square of your height in inches, and multiply the result by 703 (or go to http://www.nhlbisupport.com/bmi). A BMI of 18.5 to 24.9 is normal, 25.0 to 29.9 is considered overweight, and 30.0 and above is obese. What is your BMI? Are you surprised by the results?

▭▮ **Read** "Let Them Eat Fat: The Heavy Truths about American Obesity" by Greg Crister on **mysoclab.com**

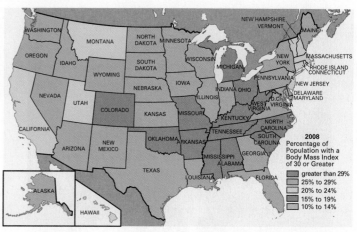

Seeing Ourselves

NATIONAL MAP 14–2

Obesity across the United States, 1996 and 2008

The map on the left shows the percentage of each state's population that was medically obese in 1996; the one on the right shows the figures for 2008. What factors do you think are responsible for the trend toward more and more obesity in our country?

Source: Centers for Disease Control and Prevention (2010).

A cause for national concern is the fact that about one in six young people in this country is already overweight, and the proportion is increasing (CDC, 2010). This trend suggests that the members of this new generation will experience more medical problems as they reach middle age and may ultimately reverse the historical trend toward greater life expectancy.

What are the social causes of obesity? One factor is that we live in a society in which more and more people have jobs that keep them sitting in front of computer screens rather than engaging in the type of physical labor that was common a century ago. Even when we are not on the job, most of the work around the house is done by machines (or other people). Children spend more of their time sitting as well, watching television or playing video games.

Then, of course, there is diet. The typical person in the United States is eating more salty, sugary, and fatty foods than ever before (Wells & Buzby, 2008). And meals are getting larger: The Department of Agriculture reported that in 2000, the typical U.S. adult consumed 140 more pounds of food each year than was true a decade earlier. Comparing old and new editions of cookbooks, recipes that used to say they would feed six now say they will feed four. The odds of being overweight go up among people with lower incomes partly because they may lack the education to make healthy choices and partly because stores in low-income communities offer a greater selection of low-cost, high-fat snack foods and fewer healthful fruits and vegetables (Hellmich, 2002). ▭▮ **Read** on **mysoclab.com**

Sexually Transmitted Diseases

Sexual activity, though both pleasurable and vital to the continuation of our species, can transmit more than fifty types of *sexually transmitted diseases* (STDs). Because our culture associates sex with sin, some people regard sexually transmitted diseases (STDs) not only as illnesses but also as marks of immorality.

STDs grabbed national attention during the "sexual revolution" of the 1960s, when infection rates rose dramatically as people became sexually active at younger ages and had a greater number of partners. This means that STDs are an exception to the general decline in infectious diseases over the course of the past century. By the late 1980s, the rising danger of STDs, especially AIDS, generated a sexual counterrevolution as people moved away from casual sex (Kain, 1987; Laumann et al., 1994). The following sections briefly describe several common STDs.

Gonorrhea and Syphilis

Gonorrhea and syphilis, among the oldest known diseases, are caused by microscopic organisms that are almost always transmitted by sexual contact. Untreated, gonorrhea causes sterility, and syphilis can damage major organs and result in blindness, mental disorders, and death.

In 2008, some 333,000 cases of gonorrhea and 13,500 cases of syphilis were recorded in the United States, although the actual numbers may be several times higher. Most cases are contracted by non-Hispanic

Making the Grade

The increase in sexually transmitted diseases is one exception
to the downward trend in infectious diseases.

Go to the Multimedia Library at **mysoclab.com**
to view the ABC *Primetime* video "AIDS in
Black America"

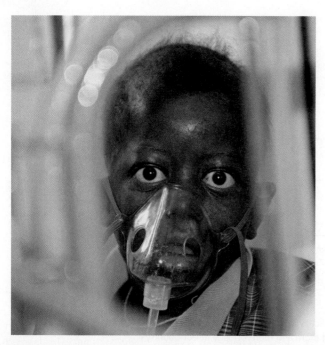

In the African nation of Kenya, about 300 people die from AIDS every day.
In parts of sub-Saharan Africa, the epidemic is so great that half of all
children will eventually become infected with HIV. This young Nairobi child,
who already has AIDS, is fighting for his life.

African Americans (70 percent), with lower numbers among non-
Hispanic whites (19 percent), Latinos (9 percent), and Asian and
Native Americans (under 2 percent) (CDC, 2010).

Both gonorrhea and syphilis can be cured easily with antibiotics
such as penicillin. Thus neither is a major health problem in the
United States.

Genital Herpes

Genital herpes is a virus that is fairly common, infecting at least 24
million adolescents and adults in the United States (one in six).
Though far less serious than gonorrhea and syphilis, herpes is incurable. People with genital herpes may not have any symptoms, or they
may experience periodic, painful blisters on the genitals accompanied by fever and headache. Although it is not fatal to adults, women
with active genital herpes can transmit the disease during a vaginal
delivery, and it can be deadly to newborns. Therefore, infected women
often give birth by cesarean section (Sobel, 2001; CDC, 2010).

AIDS

The most serious of all sexually transmitted diseases is acquired
immune deficiency syndrome (AIDS). Identified in 1981, it is
incurable and almost always fatal. AIDS is caused by the human
immunodeficiency virus (HIV), which attacks white blood cells, weakening the immune system. AIDS thus makes a person vulnerable to
a wide range of other diseases that eventually cause death.

AIDS deaths in the United States numbered 14,110 in 2007. But
officials recorded some 35,962 new cases in the United States that
year, raising the total number of cases on record to 1,018,428. Of
these, 562,793 have died (CDC, 2009).

Globally, HIV infects some 33 million people—half of them
under age twenty-five—and the number continues to rise. The global
death toll now exceeds 25 million, with less than 1 percent of all deaths
occurring in the United States in 2008. Global Map 14–2 shows that
sub-Saharan Africa has the highest HIV infection rate and accounts
for 68 percent of all world cases. A United Nations study found that
across much of sub-Saharan Africa, fifteen-year-olds face a fifty-fifty
chance of becoming infected with HIV. The risk is especially high for
girls, not only because HIV is transmitted more easily from men to
women but also because many African cultures encourage women to
be submissive to men. According to some analysts, the AIDS crisis
now threatens the political and economic security of Africa, which
affects the entire world (Ashford, 2002; UNAIDS, 2008).

Upon infection, people with HIV display no symptoms at all, so
most are unaware of their condition. Symptoms of AIDS may not
appear for a year or longer, during which time an infected person may
infect others. Within five years, one-third of infected people who have
gone untreated develop full-blown AIDS; half develop AIDS within
ten years; and almost all become sick within twenty years. In low-
income countries, the progression of the illness is much more rapid,
with many people dying within a few years of becoming infected.

HIV is infectious but not contagious. That means that HIV is
transmitted from person to person through blood, semen, or breast
milk but not through casual contact such as shaking hands, hugging,
sharing towels or dishes, swimming together, or even coughing and
sneezing. The risk of transmitting AIDS through saliva (as in kissing)
is extremely low. The risk of transmitting HIV through sexual activity is greatly reduced by the use of latex condoms. However, abstinence or an exclusive relationship with an uninfected person is the
only sure way to avoid infection.

Specific behaviors place people at high risk for HIV infection.
Anal sex can cause rectal bleeding, allowing easy transmission of HIV
from one person to another. The fact that many homosexual and
bisexual men engage in anal sex helps explain why these categories
of people account for 47 percent of AIDS cases in the United States.

Sharing needles used to inject drugs is a second high-risk behavior. At present, intravenous drug users account for 28 percent of people with AIDS, so sex with an intravenous drug user is also very risky.
Because intravenous drug use is more common among poor people
in the United States, AIDS is becoming a disease of the socially disadvantaged. Minorities make up a majority of all people with AIDS:

Parker Marsden goes to a small college in Minnesota; although aware of AIDS, he does not know anyone infected with HIV.

Mukoya Saarelma-Maunumaa lives in Namibia, where as many as half the people in some rural regions are infected with HIV; he has lost his father and two cousins to AIDS.

Percentage of Population Aged 15 to 49 with HIV/AIDS

20.0% and greater
10.0% to 19.9%
5.0% to 9.9%
1.0% to 4.9%
0.1% to 0.9%
Less than 0.1%
No data

World average = 0.9%

Window on the World

GLOBAL MAP 14–2

HIV/AIDS Infection of Adults in Global Perspective

Sixty-eight percent of all global HIV infections are in sub-Saharan Africa. In Swaziland, one-fourth of people between the ages of fifteen and forty-nine are infected with HIV/AIDS. This very high infection rate reflects the prevalence of other sexually transmitted diseases and infrequent use of condoms, two factors that promote transmission of HIV. South and Southeast Asia account for about 13 percent of global HIV infections. In Thailand, 1.4 percent of people aged fifteen to forty-nine are now infected. All of North and South America taken together account for 9 percent of global HIV infections. In the United States, 0.6 percent of people aged fifteen to forty-nine are infected. The incidence of infection in Muslim nations is extremely low by world standards.

Source: Population Reference Bureau (2009).

Non-Hispanic African Americans (12.8 percent of the population) account for 49 percent of people with AIDS, and Latinos (15.4 percent of the population) represent 19 percent of all AIDS cases. Eighty percent of all women and children with the disease are African American or Latino. By contrast, Asian Americans and Native Americans together account for only about 2 percent of people with AIDS (CDC, 2009). 🔘 Go to **mysoclab.com**

Use of any drug, including alcohol, also increases the risk of being infected with HIV to the extent that it impairs judgment. In other words, even people who understand the risks may make bad choices

● Seeing Sociology
in Everyday Life

Have you considered writing your own will? Why or why not?

euthanasia assisting in the death of a person suffering from an incurable disease

regarding sexual activity or intravenous drug use when under the influence of alcohol, marijuana, or some other drug.

In the United States, 47 percent of people with AIDS became infected through homosexual contact, but heterosexual activity can transmit HIV, and the danger rises with the number of sexual partners one has, especially if they fall into high-risk categories. Worldwide, heterosexual relations are the primary means of HIV transmission, accounting for two-thirds of all infections.

Treating just one person with AIDS costs hundreds of thousands of dollars, and the figure tends to rise as new therapies appear. At present, government health programs, private insurance, and personal savings rarely cover more than a fraction of the cost of treatment. In addition, there is the mounting cost of caring for U.S. children orphaned by AIDS—about 1,000 per year in New York City, about 75,000 annually nationwide, and worldwide around 15 million per year (Norwood, 2010). Overall, there is little doubt that AIDS is both a medical and a social problem of monumental proportions.

In the early 1980s, the U.S. government responded slowly to the AIDS crisis, largely because gays and intravenous drug users were widely viewed as deviant. But funding to combat AIDS has increased (the 2011 federal budget provides $27 billion), and researchers have already identified some drugs, including protease inhibitors, that suppress the symptoms of the disease. But educational programs remain the most effective weapon against AIDS because prevention is the only way to stop a disease that so far has no cure.

Ethical Issues surrounding Death

Now that technological advances are giving human beings the power to draw the line separating life and death, we must decide how and when to do so. In other words, questions about the use of medical technology have added an ethical dimension to health and illness.

When Does Death Occur?

Common sense suggests that life ends when breathing and heartbeat stop. But the ability to revive or replace a heart and artificially sustain respiration makes this definition of death obsolete. So medical and legal experts in the United States now define death as an *irreversible* state involving no response to stimulation, no movement or breathing, no reflexes, and no indication of brain activity (Ladd, 1979; Wall, 1980; D. G. Jones, 1998).

Do People Have a Right to Die?

Today, medical personnel, family members, and patients themselves face the burden of deciding when the life of a terminally ill person should end. Among the most difficult cases are the roughly 10,000 people in the United States in a permanent vegetative state who cannot express their own desires about life and death.

Generally speaking, the first duty of doctors and hospitals is to protect a patient's life. Even so, a mentally competent person in the process of dying can refuse medical treatment or even nutrition either at the time or, in advance, through a document called a *living will* that states the extent of medical care a person would want or not want in the event of an illness or injury that leaves the person unable to make decisions.

Mercy killing is the common term for **euthanasia,** *assisting in the death of a person suffering from an incurable disease.* Euthanasia (from the Greek, meaning "a good death") poses an ethical dilemma, being at once an act of kindness and a form of killing.

Whether there is a "right to die" is one of today's most difficult issues. All people with incurable diseases have a right to refuse treatment that might prolong their lives. But whether a doctor should be allowed to help bring about death is at the heart of today's debate. In 1994, three states—Washington, California, and Oregon—asked voters whether doctors should be able to help people who wanted to die. Only Oregon's proposition passed, and the law was quickly challenged and remained tied up in court until 1997, when voters again endorsed it. Since then, Oregon doctors have legally assisted in the death of more than 450 terminally ill patients. In 1997, however, the U.S. Supreme Court decided that under the U.S. Constitution, there is no "right to die," a decision that has slowed the spread of such laws. Only in 2008 did Washington become the second state to allow physician-assisted suicide.

Supporters of *active* euthanasia—allowing a dying person to enlist the services of a doctor to bring on a quick death—argue that there are circumstances (such as when a dying person is suffering great pain) that make death preferable to life. Critics counter that permitting active euthanasia invites abuse. They fear that patients will feel pressure to end their lives to spare family members the burden of caring for them and the high costs of hospitalization. Research in the Netherlands, where physician-assisted suicide is legal, indicates that about one-fifth of all such deaths have occurred without a patient's explicitly requesting to die (Gillon, 1999).

In the United States, a majority of adults express support for giving dying people the right to choose to die with a doctor's help (NORC, 2009). Therefore, the right-to-die debate is sure to continue.

The Medical Establishment

Throughout most of human history, health care was the responsibility of individuals and their families. Medicine emerges as a social institution only as societies become more productive and people take on specialized work.

Members of agrarian societies today still turn to traditional health practitioners, including acupuncturists and herbalists. In industrial societies, medical care falls to specially trained and licensed professionals, from anesthesiologists to X-ray technicians. The medical establishment of modern, industrial societies took form over the past 200 years.

● Seeing Sociology
in Everyday Life

Do you believe people have a "right to die"? Under what
circumstances?

holistic medicine an approach to health care that emphasizes the
prevention of illness and takes into account a person's entire physical and
social environment

The Rise of Scientific Medicine

In colonial times, herbalists, druggists, barbers, midwives, and ministers practiced the healing arts. But not all were effective. Unsanitary
instruments, lack of anesthesia, and simple ignorance made surgery a terrible ordeal, and doctors probably killed as many people as they saved.

Doctors made medicine into a science by following scientific
procedures to study the human body and how it works and emphasizing surgery and the use of drugs to fight disease. Pointing to their
specialized knowledge, doctors gradually established themselves as
self-regulating professionals with medical degrees. The American
Medical Association (AMA), founded in 1847, symbolized the growing acceptance of a scientific model of medicine.

Still, traditional practitioners of health care had their supporters. The AMA opposed them by seeking control of the certification
process. In the early 1900s, state licensing boards agreed to certify
only doctors trained in the scientific programs approved by the AMA.
As a result, schools teaching other healing skills began to close, which
soon limited the practice of medicine to individuals holding an M.D.
degree. Accordingly, the prestige and income of doctors rose dramatically; today, men and women with M.D. degrees earn, on average, $250,000 annually.

Practitioners who did things differently, such as osteopathic physicians, concluded that they had no choice but to fall in line and follow
AMA standards. Thus osteopaths (with D.O. degrees), originally concerned with treating illness by manipulating the skeleton and muscles,
today treat illness with drugs in much the same way as medical doctors
(with M.D. degrees). Chiropractors, herbal healers, and midwives still
practice with their own special approaches but have lower standing
within the medical profession. Debates between people supporting scientific medicine and those favoring traditional healing practices continue today, both in the United States and in many other countries.

Scientific medicine, taught in expensive, urban medical schools,
also changed the social profile of doctors so that most physicians
came from privileged backgrounds and practiced in cities. Women,
who had played a large part in many fields of healing, were pushed
aside by the AMA. Some early medical schools did train women and
African Americans, but with few financial resources, most of these
schools ran out of money and closed. Only in recent decades has the
social diversity of the medical profession increased, with women and
African Americans representing 32 percent and 6 percent of physicians, respectively (U.S. Bureau of Labor Statistics, 2010).

Holistic Medicine

The scientific model of medicine has been tempered by the introduction of **holistic medicine,** *an approach to health care that emphasizes
the prevention of illness and takes into account a person's entire physical and social environment.* Holistic practitioners agree on the need for

The rise of scientific medicine during the nineteenth century resulted in
new skills and technology for treating many common ailments that had
afflicted humanity for centuries. At the same time, however, scientific
medicine pushed forms of health care involving women to the margins and
placed medicine under the control of men living in cities. We see this
pattern in the A. F. Seligmann painting *General Hospital,* showing an
all-male medical school class in Vienna, Austria, in 1880.

drugs, surgery, artificial organs, and high technology, but they emphasize treating the whole person rather than just symptoms and focus
on health rather than disease. There are three foundations of holistic
health care (Gordon, 1980; Patterson, 1998):

1. **Treat patients as people.** Holistic practitioners are concerned
   not only with symptoms but also with how people's environment
   and lifestyle affect health. Holistic practitioners extend the bounds
   of conventional medicine, taking an active role in fighting poverty,
   environmental pollution, and other dangers to public health.

2. **Encourage responsibility, not dependency.** A scientific
   approach to medicine puts doctors in charge of health, and
   patients are to follow doctors' orders. Holistic medicine tries to
   shift some responsibility for health from doctor to patient by

Seeing Sociology
in Everyday Life

Point to specific ways in which people should take personal responsibility for their own health. In what ways should society change to promote public health?

Go to the Multimedia Library at **mysoclab.com** to view the *Core Concepts in Sociology* video "Health Care Outside the United States"

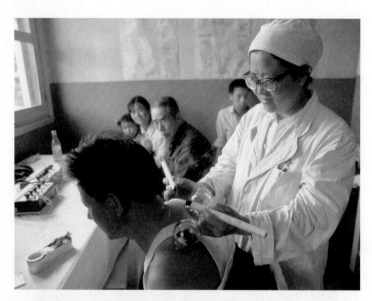

Traditional healers work to improve people's health throughout the world. This patient is receiving a traditional needle therapy in Suining, a city in China's Sichuan province. Do you think people in the United States are accepting of traditional healing practices? Why or why not?

emphasizing health-promoting behavior. Holistic medicine favors an *active approach to health* rather than a *reactive approach to illness.*

3. **Provide personal treatment.** Scientific medicine treats patients in impersonal offices and hospitals, both disease-centered settings. Holistic practitioners favor, as much as possible, a personal and relaxed environment such as the home.

In sum, holistic care does not oppose scientific medicine but shifts the emphasis from treating disease to achieving the greatest well-being for everyone. Considering that the AMA certifies more than fifty medical specialties, there is a need for practitioners concerned with the whole patient.

Paying for Medical Care: A Global Survey

As medicine has come to rely on advanced technology, the costs of medical care in industrial societies have skyrocketed. Countries throughout the world have adopted different strategies to meet these costs. ● Go to **mysoclab.com**

People's Republic of China

This economically growing but still mostly agrarian nation faces the immense task of providing for the health of more than 1.3 billion people. China has experimented with private medicine, but the government controls most health care.

China's "barefoot doctors," roughly comparable to U.S. paramedics, bring some modern methods of medical care to peasants in rural villages. Traditional healing arts, involving acupuncture and medicinal herbs, are still widely practiced. The Chinese approach to health is based on a holistic concern for the interplay of mind and body (Kaptchuk, 1985).

Russian Federation

The Russian Federation has transformed what was a state-dominated economy into more of a market system. For this reason, medical care is in transition. But the state remains in charge of medical care, and the government claims that everyone has a right to basic medical care.

As in China, people in the Russian Federation do not choose a doctor but report to a local government health facility. Physicians have much lower incomes than medical doctors in the United States, earning about the same salary as skilled industrial workers (by contrast, U.S. doctors earn roughly five times as much as industrial workers in the United States). Also, about 70 percent of Russia's doctors are women, compared to 32 percent in the United States. As in our society, occupations dominated by women in the Russian Federation offer lower pay.

In recent years, the Russian Federation has suffered setbacks in health, due in part to a falling standard of living. Rising demand for medical care has strained a bureaucratic system that at best provides highly standardized and impersonal care. The optimistic view is that as living standards rise, the quality of medical service will improve. In Russia's uncertain times, what does seem clear is that inequalities in medical care will increase (Specter, 1995; Landsberg, 1998; Mason, 2004; Zuckerman, 2006).

Sweden

In 1891, Sweden began a mandatory, comprehensive system of government medical care. Citizens pay for this program with their taxes, which are among the highest in the world. Typically, doctors are government employees, and most hospitals are government-managed. Sweden's system is called **socialized medicine,** *a medical care system in which the government owns and operates most medical facilities and employs most physicians.*

Great Britain

In 1948, Great Britain also established socialized medicine by creating a dual system of medical services. All British citizens are entitled to medical care provided by the National Health Service, but those who can afford it can also go to doctors and hospitals that operate privately.

Seeing Sociology in Everyday Life

The head of the Ford Motor Company said recently that in building a car, the cost of medical care for workers is now greater than the cost of steel. How do you think the rising cost of medical care affects an average family's budget?

Canada

Since 1972, Canada has had a "single-payer" model of medical care that provides care to all Canadians. Like a giant insurance company, the Canadian government pays doctors and hospitals according to a set schedule of fees. Like Great Britain, Canada also has some physicians working outside the government-funded system and setting their own fees, although costs are regulated by the government.

Canada boasts of providing care for everyone at a lower cost than the (nonuniversal) medical system in the United States. However, the Canadian system uses less state-of-the-art technology and responds more slowly, meaning that people may wait months for major surgery. The Canadian system provides care for all its citizens, regardless of income, unlike the United States, in which lower-income people are often denied medical care (Rosenthal, 1991; Macionis & Gerber, 2008).

> July 31, Montreal, Canada. I am visiting the home of an oral surgeon who appears (judging by the large home) to be doing pretty well. Yet he complains that the provincial governments in Canada, in an effort to hold down medical costs, cap doctors' salaries at several hundred thousand dollars (exact caps vary from province to province). Therefore, he explains, many specialists have left for the United States, where they can earn much more; other doctors and dentists simply limit their practices.

Japan

Physicians in Japan operate privately, but a combination of government programs and private insurance pays medical costs. As shown in Figure 14–3, the Japanese approach medical care much like the Europeans, with most medical expenses paid through the government.

Paying for Medical Care: The United States

Even after the historic passage of the new health care bill in 2010, the United States stands alone among high-income nations in having no universal, government-operated program of medical care. Ours is a **direct-fee system,** *a medical care system in which patients pay directly for the services of physicians and hospitals.* Europeans look to government to fund 70 to nearly 90 percent of medical costs (paid for through taxation), but the U.S. government pays just 42 percent of this country's medical costs (U.S. Department of Health and Human Services, 2010).

In the United States, rich people can buy the best medical care in the world, but poor people are worse off than their counterparts in Europe. This difference translates into relatively high death rates

Global Snapshot

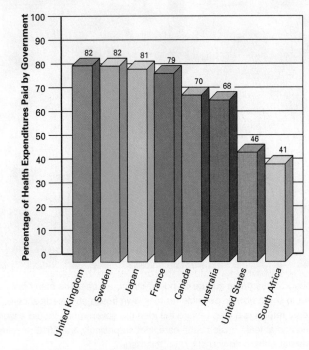

FIGURE 14–3   Extent of Socialized Medicine in Selected Countries

The governments of most high-income countries pay a greater share of their people's medical costs than the U.S. government does.

Source: World Bank (2010).

among both infants and adults in the United States compared with many European countries (Population Reference Bureau, 2010).

Several states, including Maine, Vermont, and Massachusetts, have enacted programs that provide health care to everyone. Why does the United States have no national program that provides universal care? First, because our culture stresses self-reliance, our society has limited the scope of government programs. Second, at least until recently, political support for a national medical program has not been strong, even among labor unions, which have concentrated on winning medical care benefits from employers. Third, the AMA and the insurance industry have strongly and consistently opposed national medical care.

Medical expenditures in the United States have increased dramatically, from $12 billion in 1950 to more than $2 trillion in 2008 (U.S. Department of Health and Human Services, 2010). This amounts to more than $7,600 per person, more than any other nation spends for medical care. Who pays the medical bills?

Seeing Sociology in Everyday Life

Do you support the 2010 health care reforms enacted by Congress? Do they go far enough? Too far? Explain your position.

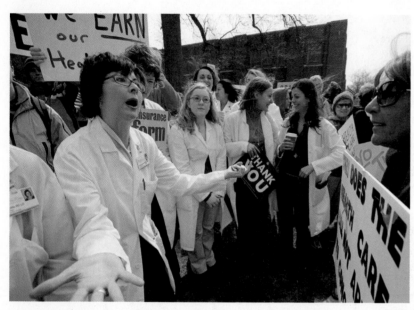

The United States has a culture of individualism, which leads many people to think that people should be responsible for their own health and medical care. The 2010 health care reform is a step toward the idea the government should ensure that everyone has at least basic health care. Not surprisingly, the 2010 reforms were controversial. Where do you stand on this issue?

Private Insurance Programs

In 2008, about 176 million people in the United States (58.5 percent) received medical care benefits from a family member's employer or labor union. Another 27 million people (9 percent) purchased some private coverage on their own. Combining these figures, 67 percent of the U.S. population has private insurance, although few such programs pay all medical costs (U.S. Census Bureau, 2009).

Public Insurance Programs

In 1965, Congress created Medicare and Medicaid. Medicare pays some of the medical costs for people over age sixty-five; in 2008, it covered 43 million men and women, 14 percent of the population. In the same year, Medicaid, a medical insurance program for the poor, provided benefits to another 43 million people, about 14 percent of the population. An additional 11.6 million military veterans (4 percent) can obtain free care in government-operated hospitals. In all, 29 percent of this country's people get medical benefits from the government, but most also have private insurance.

Health Maintenance Organizations

About 65 million people (22 percent) in the United States belong to a **health maintenance organization (HMO),** *an organization that provides comprehensive medical care to subscribers for a fixed fee.* HMOs

vary in cost and benefits, and none provides full coverage. Fixed fees make these organizations profitable if subscribers stay healthy; therefore, many take a preventive approach to health. However, HMOs have been criticized for refusing to pay for medical procedures that they consider unnecessary. Congress is currently debating the extent to which patients can sue HMOs to obtain better care.

In all, 85 percent of the U.S. population has some medical care coverage, either private or public. Yet most plans do not provide full coverage, so serious illness threatens even middle-class people with financial hardship. Most programs also exclude many medical services, such as dental care and treatment for mental health and substance abuse problems. Worse, 46 million people (about 15 percent of the population) have no medical insurance at all, even though 73 percent of these people are working. Almost as many lose their coverage temporarily each year because of layoffs or job changes. Caught in the medical care bind are mostly low- to moderate-income people who cannot afford the cost of the preventive medical care they need to stay healthy (Brink, 2002; U.S. Census Bureau, 2009).

The 2010 Health Care Reform

In 2010, Congress passed a law, known as the Patient Protection and Affordable Care Act, that made significant changes to the way this country pays for health care. The act has a huge cost—estimated at almost $1 trillion over the next ten years—and change will take effect in stages.

Here are some of the most important features of the new law:

1. **The insurance tax.** Starting right away, all families will pay an insurance tax. Lower-income families, however, will receive subsidies to help pay the cost of the insurance; high-income families will pay higher taxes on their income to help fund the program.

2. **Insurance reform.** Within six months of passage, insurance companies will no longer be permitted to drop customers because they get sick, nor can companies legally refuse coverage to children because of preexisting conditions. In addition, insurance companies cannot set caps on the amount of money they will pay to any individual for medical expenses over a lifetime. By 2014, insurance companies will no longer be able to refuse coverage to anyone of any age due to a preexisting health condition.

3. **Coverage for children.** Parents can include in their own health care plans coverage for their children up to the age of twenty-six.

Seeing Sociology
in Everyday Life

Most nursing programs require at least a basic course in sociology.
Can you see why?

sick role patterns of behavior defined as appropriate for people who are ill

4. **Government-mandated insurance.** By 2014, all families will be required to purchase insurance coverage. Government will regulate both the benefits available and the costs.

5. **Penalties for failure to comply.** The law provides penalties for people who do not buy insurance; these penalties will increase over time.

In all, the Patient Protection and Affordable Care Act will provide health insurance to some 32 million of the 46 million people in the United States who currently do not have this protection. The Obama administration claims that this law, although providing something short of universal health care coverage, is nonetheless a major step toward that goal.

The Nursing Shortage

Another issue in medical care is the shortage of nurses across the United States. In 2008, there were more than 3 million registered nurses (people with the degree of R.N.), but about 116,000 positions in hospitals and another 100,000 jobs in nursing homes were unfilled.

The field of nursing continues to attract young people. Almost 500,000 people have entered the field of nursing since 2004. Even so, in a society where the share of older people is rising rapidly, the number of new nurses continues to fall short of the rapidly expanding need. One reason for the shortage is that nursing schools do not have enough teachers, which limits the number of graduates. A broader reason is that today's young women have a wide range of job choices, and fewer are drawn to the traditionally female occupation of nursing. This fact is evident in the rising median age of working nurses, which is now forty-seven. Another is that many of today's nurses are unhappy with their working conditions, citing heavy patient loads, too much required overtime, a stressful working environment, and a lack of recognition and respect from supervisors, physicians, and hospital managers. In fact, one recent survey found that a majority of working nurses say they would not recommend the field to others, and many R.N.'s are leaving the field for other jobs.

The nursing shortage is harming heath care. One study estimates that more than 6,000 hospital patients die each year for lack of immediate treatment due to the shortage of nurses. Such facts are bringing change to this profession. Salaries, which range from about $50,000 for general-duty nurses in residential care and child care facilities to $100,000 for certified nurse-anesthetists, are on the rise. Some hospitals and doctors are also offering signing bonuses in efforts to attract new nurses. In addition, nursing programs are trying harder to recruit a more diverse population, seeking more minorities (which are currently underrepresented) and, especially, more men (who now make up only 8 percent of R.N.'s) (Marquez, 2006; American Association of Colleges of Nursing, 2010; U.S. Bureau of Labor Statistics, 2010; U.S. Department of Health and Human Services, 2010).

Throughout the United States, there is a serious shortage of nurses. One strategy for filling this need is to recruit more men into this profession; currently, men account for only 8 percent of nurses with R.N. degrees.

Theoretical Analysis of Health and Medicine

Each of the theoretical approaches in sociology helps us organize and understand facts and issues concerning human health.

Structural-Functional Analysis: Role Theory

Talcott Parsons (1951) viewed medicine as society's strategy to keep its members healthy. Parsons considered illness dysfunctional because it reduces people's abilities to perform their roles.

The Sick Role

Society responds to illness not only by providing medical care but also by allowing people a **sick role,** *patterns of behavior defined as appropriate for people who are ill.* According to Parsons, the sick role releases people from everyday obligations such as going to work or attending classes. However, people cannot simply claim to be ill; they must "look the part" and, in serious cases, get the help of a medical expert. After assuming the sick role, the patient must want to get better and must do whatever is needed to regain good health, including cooperating with health professionals.

○ Making the Grade

Be sure you can explain how health and illness are
socially constructed.

● Seeing Sociology
in Everyday Life

Have you ever had, or even considered, cosmetic surgery?
Explain your reasons.

The Physician's Role

Physicians evaluate people's claims of sickness and help restore the sick
to normal routines. To do this, physicians use their specialized knowledge and expect patients to follow "doctor's orders" in order to complete treatment.

○ **CRITICAL REVIEW**   Parsons's analysis links illness and
medicine to the broader organization of society. Others have
extended the concept of the sick role to some nonillness situations such as pregnancy (Myers & Grasmick, 1989).

One limitation of the sick-role concept is that it applies to
acute conditions (such as the flu or a broken leg) better than to
chronic illnesses (such as heart disease), which may not be
reversible. In addition, a sick person's ability to assume the sick
role (to take time off from work to regain health) depends on the
person's resources. Finally, illness is not completely dysfunctional; it can have some positive consequences. Many people
who experience a serious illness consider it an opportunity to
reevaluate their lives and gain a better sense of what is truly
important to them (D. G. Myers, 2000; Ehrenreich, 2001).

○ **CHECK YOUR LEARNING**   Define the sick role. How
does turning illness into a role in this way help society operate?

Symbolic-Interaction Analysis:
The Meaning of Health

Using the symbolic-interaction approach, society is less a grand system than a complex and changing reality. In this view, health and medical care are socially constructed by people in everyday interaction.

The Social Construction of Illness

If both health and illness are socially constructed, people in a poor
society may view malnutrition as normal. Similarly, many members
of our own society give little thought to the harmful effects of a rich
diet.

Our response to illness is based also on social definitions that
may or may not square with medical facts. People with AIDS may
be forced to deal with prejudice that has no medical basis. Likewise,
students may pay no attention to symptoms of illness on the eve of
vacation but head for the infirmary hours before a midterm examination with a case of the sniffles. In short, health is less an objective
fact than a negotiated outcome.

How people define a medical situation may actually affect how
they feel. Medical experts marvel at *psychosomatic* disorders (a fusion
of the Greek words for "mind" and "body"), when state of mind
guides physical sensations (Hamrick, Anspaugh, & Ezell, 1986).
Applying the Thomas theorem (presented in Chapter 4, "Social

Interaction in Everyday Life"), we can say that once health or illness
is defined as real, it can become real in its consequences.

The Social Construction of Treatment

Also in Chapter 4, we used Erving Goffman's dramaturgical approach
to explain how doctors tailor their physical surroundings (their office)
and their behavior (the "presentation of self") so that others see them
as competent and in charge.

The sociologist Joan Emerson (1970) further illustrates this
process of reality construction in her analysis of the gynecological
examination carried out by a male doctor. The situation could be seriously misinterpreted because a man touching a woman's genitals is
conventionally viewed as a sexual act and possibly an assault.

To ensure that the situation is defined as impersonal and professional, medical personnel wear uniforms, and the examination room
is furnished with nothing but medical equipment. The doctor's manner is designed to make the patient feel that to him, examining the
genital area is no different from treating any other part of the body.
A female nurse is usually present during the examination, not only
to assist the physician but also to avoid any impression that a man
and woman are "alone together."

Managing situational definitions is rarely taught in medical
schools. This oversight is unfortunate, because as Emerson's analysis shows, understanding how medical personnel construct reality
in the examination room is as important as mastering the medical
skills needed for treatment. One recent study found that physicians
who were weak in social skills, even if they were well-trained medically, were much more likely to be the targets of complaints and lawsuits filed by patients (Tamblyn, 2008).

The Social Construction of Personal Identity

A final insight provided by the symbolic-interaction approach is how
surgery can affect people's social identity. The reason that medical
procedures can have a major effect on how we think of ourselves is
that our culture places great symbolic importance on some organs
and other parts of our bodies. People who lose a limb (say, in military
combat) typically experience serious doubts about being "as much of
a person" as before. The effects of surgery can be important even when
there is no obvious change in physical appearance. For example, Jean
Elson (2004) points out that one out of three women in the United
States eventually has her uterus surgically removed in a procedure
known as a *hysterectomy*. In interviews with women who had undergone the procedure, Elson found that the typical woman faced serious self-doubt about gender identity—asking, in other words, "Am
I still a woman?" Only 10 percent of hysterectomies are for cancer;
most are for pain, bleeding, or cysts—serious conditions but not so
dangerous that other types of treatment might be considered. Perhaps, Elson points out, doctors might be more willing to consider

○ Seeing Sociology
in Everyday Life

How do you think soldiers who lose a hand, an arm, or a leg
feel about themselves afterward? In terms of personal and
social identity, what healing and rebuilding are needed?

○ Making the Grade

In general, the social-conflict approach claims that any
institution (in this case, medicine) would operate more in
the interest of the population as a whole if it were under
government rather than market control.

alternative treatment if they were aware of how symbolically important the loss of the uterus is to many women.

Many women who undergo breast surgery have much the same reaction, doubting their own feminine identity and worrying that men will no longer find them attractive. For men to understand the significance of such medical procedures, it is only necessary to imagine how a male might react to the surgical loss of any or all of his genitals.

○ **CRITICAL REVIEW** The symbolic-interaction approach reveals that what people view as healthful or harmful depends on a host of factors that are not, strictly speaking, medical. This approach also shows that in any medical procedure, both patient and medical staff engage in a subtle process of reality construction. Finally, this approach has helped us understand the symbolic importance of limbs and other bodily organs; the loss of any part of the body—through accident or elective surgery—can have important consequences for personal identity.

By directing attention to the meanings people attach to health or illness, the symbolic-interaction approach draws criticism for implying that there are no objective standards of well-being. Certain physical conditions do indeed cause specific changes in people, regardless of how we may view those conditions. For example, people who lack sufficient nutrition and safe water suffer from their unhealthy environment, whether they define their surroundings as normal or not.

A recent study shows that the share of beginning college students in the United States who describe their physical health as "above average" is lower today than it was in 1985. Do you think this trend reflects changing perceptions or a real decline in health (due, say, to eating more unhealthy food)? The study also found that more women than men see their health as below average—can you offer any possible reasons?

○ **CHECK YOUR LEARNING** Explain what it means to say that both health and the treatment of illness are socially constructed.

Social-Conflict and Feminist Analysis

Social-conflict analysis points out the connection between health and social inequality. Some analysts, taking a cue from Karl Marx, tie medicine to the operation of capitalism. In addition, feminists link medicine to sexism and gender stratification. Most attention has gone to three main issues: access to medical care, the effects of the profit motive, and the politics of medicine.

Access to Care

Health is important to everyone. But by requiring individuals to pay directly for medical care, capitalist societies allow the richest people

Definitions of health are based on cultural standards, including ideas about beauty. Every year, millions of people undergo cosmetic surgery to bring their appearance into line with societal definitions of how people ought to look.

to have the best health. The access problem is more serious in the United States than in most other high-income nations because we do not have a universal medical care system.

Conflict theorists argue that capitalism provides excellent health care for the rich but at the expense of the rest of the population. Most of the 46 million people in the United States who lack any medical care coverage at present have moderate to low incomes.

The Profit Motive

Some social-conflict analysts go further, arguing that the real problem is not access to medical care but capitalist medicine itself. The profit motive turns doctors, hospitals, and the pharmaceutical industry into multibillion-dollar corporations. The drive for higher profits encourages unnecessary tests and surgery and a reliance on expensive drugs rather than focusing on improving people's lifestyles and living conditions.

Of more than 25 million surgical operations performed in the United States each year, three-fourths are elective, meaning that they are intended to promote long-term health and are not prompted by a medical emergency. Of course, any medical procedure or use of drugs is risky and harms between 5 and 10 percent of patients. Therefore, social-conflict theorists argue that surgery reflects not just the medical needs of patients but also the financial interests of surgeons and hospitals (Cowley, 1995; Nuland, 1999).

Finally, say conflict theorists, our society is too tolerant of doctors' having a direct financial interest in the tests and procedures they

○ Making the Grade

The Apply Theory table below is a learning tool to help you understand theoretical approaches to health.

○ Seeing Sociology in Everyday Life

Looking ahead, what patterns regarding health and illness would you predict for our society fifty years from now?

● APPLYING THEORY ●

Health

	Structural-Functional Approach	Symbolic-Interaction Approach	Social-Conflict Approach
What is the level of analysis?	Macro-level	Micro-level	Macro-level
How is health related to society?	Illness is dysfunctional for society because it prevents people from carrying out their daily roles. The sick role releases people who are ill from responsibilities while they try to get well.	Societies define "health" and "illness" differently according to their living standards. How people define their own health affects how they actually feel (psychosomatic conditions).	Health is linked to social inequality, with rich people having more access to care than poor people. Capitalist medical care places the drive for profits over the needs of people, treating symptoms rather than addressing poverty and sexism as causes of illness.

order for their patients (Pear & Eckholm, 1991). Medical care should be motivated by a concern for people, not profits.

Medicine as Politics

Although science claims to be politically neutral, feminists feel that scientific medicine often takes sides on significant social issues. For example, the medical establishment has always strongly opposed government medical care programs and only recently allowed a significant number of women to join the ranks of physicians. The history of medicine shows that not only has racial and sexual discrimination kept women and people of color out of medicine but also that discrimination has been supported by "scientific" opinions about, say, the inferiority of women and other minorities (Leavitt, 1984). Consider the diagnosis of "hysteria," a term that has its origins in the Greek word *hyster*, meaning "uterus." In choosing this word to describe a wild, emotional state, the medical profession suggested that being a woman is somehow the same as being irrational.

According to conflict theory, scientific medicine explains illness in terms of bacteria and viruses, ignoring the damaging effects of poverty, racism, and sexism. In effect, scientific medicine hides the bias in our medical system by transforming this social issue into simple biology.

○ **CRITICAL REVIEW**   Social-conflict analysis provides still another view of the relationships among health, medicine, and society. According to this approach, social inequality is the reason some people have better health than others.

The most common objection to the conflict approach is that it minimizes the advances in U.S. health brought about by scientific medicine and higher living standards. Though there is plenty of room for improvement, health indicators for our population as a whole rose steadily over the course of the twentieth century, and they compare well with those in other high-income nations.

○ **CHECK YOUR LEARNING**   How are health and medical care linked to social classes, capitalism, and gender stratification?

Sociology's three major theoretical approaches, summed up in the Applying Theory table, explain why health and medicine are social issues.

But advancing technology will not solve every health problem. On the contrary, as the Controversy & Debate box explains, today's advancing technology is raising new questions and concerns.

The famous French scientist Louis Pasteur (1822–1895), who spent much of his life studying how bacteria cause disease, said just before he died that health depends less on bacteria than on the social environment in which the bacteria are found (Gordon, 1980:7). Explaining Pasteur's insight is sociology's contribution to human health.

Health and Medicine: Looking Ahead

In the early 1900s, deaths from infectious diseases such as diphtheria and measles were widespread. Because scientists had yet to develop penicillin and other antibiotics, even a simple infection from a minor

Making the Grade

The box below presents a case of cultural lag: Our scientific ability has progressed beyond our certainty about when or even if we should act on what we know.

Go to the Multimedia Library at **mysoclab.com** to listen to the NPR report "Tailoring Treatment to Patients' Genetics"

CONTROVERSY & DEBATE

The Genetic Crystal Ball: Do We Really Want to Look?

FELISHA: Before I get married, I want my partner to have a genetic screening. It's like buying a house or a car—you should check it out before you sign on the line.

EVA: Do you expect to get a warranty, too?

The discovery of deoxyribonucleic acid, or DNA, was one of the greatest medical breakthroughs of all time. The spiraling DNA molecule is found in every cell of the human body and contains the blueprint for making each one of us human as well as different from every other person.

Your body is composed of roughly 100 trillion cells, most of which contain a nucleus of twenty-three pairs of chromosomes (one of each pair comes from each parent). Each chromosome is packed with DNA in segments called genes. Genes guide the production of proteins, the building blocks of the human body.

If genetics sounds complicated (and it is), the social implications of genetic knowledge are even more complex. Scientists discovered the structure of the DNA molecule in 1952, but it wasn't until 2000 that scientists had mapped most of the human genome. Charting our genetic landscape will help us understand how each bit of DNA shapes our being. Go to **mysoclab.com**

But do we really want to turn the key to understanding life itself? And what do we do with this knowledge once we have it? Research has already identified genetic abnormalities that cause many diseases, including sickle-cell anemia, muscular dystrophy, Huntington's disease, cystic fibrosis, and some forms of cancer. Gazing into a person's genetic "crystal ball," doctors may be able to manipulate segments of DNA to prevent diseases before they appear.

But many people urge caution in such research, warning that genetic information can easily be abused. At its worst, genetic mapping opens the door to Nazi-like efforts to breed a "super race." In 1994, the People's Republic of China began to use genetic information to regulate marriage and childbirth with the purpose of avoiding "new births of inferior quality."

All over the world, many parents will want to use genetic testing to predict the health (or even the eye color) of their future children. What if they want to abort a fetus because it falls short of their standards? When genetic manipulations become possible, should parents be able to create "designer children"?

Then there is the issue of "genetic privacy." Can a woman request a genetic evaluation of her fiancé before agreeing to marry? Can life insurance companies demand genetic testing before issuing policies? Should employers be allowed to screen job applicants to weed out those whose future illnesses might drain their company's health care funds? Clearly, what is scientifically possible is not always morally desirable. Society is already struggling with questions about the proper use of our expanding knowledge of human genetics. Such ethical dilemmas will multiply as genetic research moves forward in the years to come.

WHAT DO YOU THINK?

1. Traditional wedding vows join couples "in sickness and in health." Do people have a right to know the future health prospects of a partner before marriage? Why or why not?

2. Should parents be permitted to genetically "design" their children? Why or why not?

3. Should genetic research companies be allowed to patent their discoveries so that they can profit from the results, or should this information be made available to everyone? Explain your answer.

Sources: D. Thompson (1999) and Golden & Lemonick (2000).

---

wound was sometimes life-threatening. Today, a century later, most members of our society take good health and long life for granted.

More people in the United States are taking personal responsibility for their health. Even so, there are some grounds for concern. The increasing obesity epidemic is one major problem. If this trend continues, the younger generation may become the first in some time with a lower rather than higher average life span. Every one of us can live better and longer if we eat sensibly and in moderation, exercise regularly, and avoid tobacco.

Another health problem that our society faces, discussed throughout this chapter, is the double standard that offers good health to the rich but causes higher rates of disease for the poor. International comparisons reveal that the United States lags in some measures of human health because of the large share of our population

who live with low income at the margins of our society. An important question, even after the recent reforms, is what our rich society should do about the millions of people who still live with low income and without the security of medical care.

Finally, we find that health problems are far greater in low-income nations than in the United States. The good news is that life expectancy for the world as a whole has been rising—from forty-eight years in 1950 to sixty-nine years today—and the biggest gains have been in poor countries (Population Reference Bureau, 2010). But in much of Latin America, Asia, and especially Africa, hundreds of millions of adults and children lack not only medical attention but adequate food and safe water as well. Improving the health of the world's poorest people is a critical challenge in the years to come.

Seeing Sociology in Everyday Life

How does society affect patterns of health?

Certain occupations put people at higher-than-average risk of accident or death. One example is coal mining, which has long been one of the deadliest jobs. Although the death toll from mining accidents in the United States has gone down over time, even miners who manage to avoid mine collapses or explosions typically suffer harm from years of breathing coal dust. Look at the photos below: How do they link health to a way of life?

> **HINT** Among the most dangerous jobs in the United States are farming (dangers come from using power equipment), mining, timber cutting, truck driving, and constructing tall buildings. Many members of the military also face danger on a daily basis. In general, people in the working class are at greater risk than middle-class people, who typically work in offices; men also predominate in the most dangerous jobs. Overall, about 5,000 U.S. (nonmilitary) workers lose their lives every year in workplace accidents.

Crews on fishing boats such as this one spend months at a time battling high seas and often frigid temperatures. As documented on the television show *The Deadliest Catch*, it is a rare and fortunate fishing season that brings no death or serious injury. What other jobs threaten the health and well-being of U.S. workers?

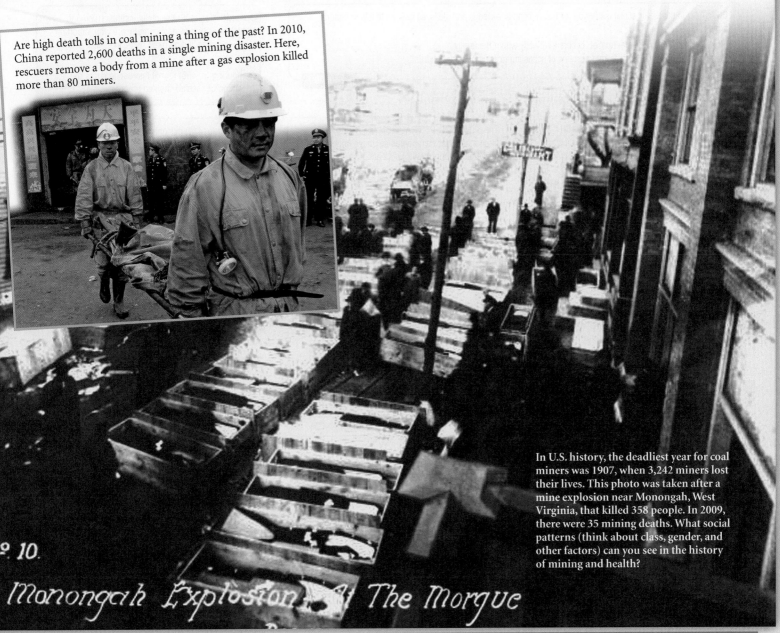

Are high death tolls in coal mining a thing of the past? In 2010, China reported 2,600 deaths in a single mining disaster. Here, rescuers remove a body from a mine after a gas explosion killed more than 80 miners.

In U.S. history, the deadliest year for coal miners was 1907, when 3,242 miners lost their lives. This photo was taken after a mine explosion near Monongah, West Virginia, that killed 358 people. In 2009, there were 35 mining deaths. What social patterns (think about class, gender, and other factors) can you see in the history of mining and health?

º 10.

Monongah Explosion At The Morgue

Applying SOCIOLOGY in Everyday Life

1. Think about the effects of schooling on health. In what ways does getting a college degree (and perhaps a graduate or professional degree) improve a person's likelihood of leading a healthy life?

2. Visit a secondary school near your college or home. Does it have a tracking policy? If so, find out how it works. How much importance does a student's family background have in making a tracking assignment?

3. Given the importance of sexuality in our thinking about women in the United States (and how they think about themselves), how do you think medical procedures such as mastectomy (surgical removal of part or all of a breast) affect women's personal and social identity? (To learn more about these experiences, see Elson, 2004.)

Making the Grade

VISUAL SUMMARY

Education: A Global Survey

EDUCATION is the major social institution for transmitting knowledge and skills, as well as teaching cultural norms and values.

- In preindustrial societies, education occurs informally within the family.
- Industrial societies develop formal systems of schooling to educate their children.

pp. 406–09

Theoretical Analysis of Schooling

The **STRUCTURAL-FUNCTIONAL APPROACH** highlights major functions of schooling, including socialization, cultural innovation, social integration, and the placement of people in the social hierarchy.

- Latent functions of schooling include providing child care and building social networks.

p. 409

The **SYMBOLIC-INTERACTION APPROACH** helps us understand that stereotypes can have important consequences for how people act. If students think they are academically superior, they are likely to perform better; students who think they are inferior are likely to perform less well.

pp. 409–10

The **SOCIAL-CONFLICT APPROACH** links schooling to the hierarchy involving class, race, and gender.

- Formal education serves as a means of generating conformity to produce obedient adult workers.
- Standardized achievement tests have been criticized as culturally biased tools that may lead to labeling less privileged students as personally deficient.
- Tracking has been challenged by critics as a program that gives privileged youngsters a richer education.
- The great majority of young people in the United States attend state-funded public schools. A small proportion of students—usually the most well-to-do—attend elite private college preparatory schools.
- Largely due to the high cost of college, only 69% of U.S. students enroll in college directly after high school graduation.

pp. 410–16

See the Applying Theory table on page 415.

Problems in the Schools

- *Violence* permeates many schools, especially in poor neighborhoods.
- The bureaucratic character of schools fosters *high dropout rates* and *student passivity*.
- *Declining academic standards* are reflected in today's lower average scores on achievement tests, the functional illiteracy of a significant proportion of high school graduates, and grade inflation.

pp. 416–19

Current Issues in U.S. Education

The **SCHOOL CHOICE MOVEMENT** seeks to make schools more accountable to the public. Innovative options include

- magnet schools
- schooling for profit
- charter schools

pp. 419–20

HOME SCHOOLING

- The original pioneers of home schooling did not believe in public education because they wanted to give their children a strongly religious upbringing.
- Home schooling advocates today point to the poor performance of public schools.

pp. 420–21

ADULT EDUCATION

- Adults represent a growing proportion of students in the United States.
- Most older learners are women who are engaged in job-related study.

p. 421

THE TEACHER SHORTAGE

- More than 300,000 teaching vacancies exist in the United States each year due to low salaries, frustration, retirements, and rising enrollment and class size.
- To address this shortage, many school districts are recruiting teachers from abroad.

p. 421

SCHOOLING PEOPLE WITH DISABILITITES

- Children with mental or physical disabilities have historically been schooled in special classes.
- *Mainstreaming* affords them broader opportunities and exposes all children to a more diverse student population.

p. 421

education (p. 406) the social institution through which society provides its members with important knowledge, including basic facts, job skills, and cultural norms and values

schooling (p. 406) formal instruction under the direction of specially trained teachers

tracking (p. 411) assigning students to different types of educational programs

functional illiteracy (p. 418) a lack of the reading and writing skills needed for everyday living

⊕ Explore on mysoclab.com

Health and Medicine

HEALTH is a social issue because personal well-being depends on a society's level of technology and its distribution of resources. A society's culture shapes definitions of health.

`p. 423`

medicine (p. 423) the social institution that focuses on fighting disease and improving health

health (p. 423) a state of complete physical, mental, and social well-being

Health: A Global Survey

HEALTH VARIES OVER TIME:
- With industrialization, health improved dramatically in Western Europe and North America in the nineteenth century.
- A century ago, infectious diseases were leading killers; today, most people in the United States die in old age of chronic illnesses such as heart disease, cancer, or stroke.

`p. 423`

HEALTH VARIES AROUND THE WORLD:
- Poor nations suffer from inadequate sanitation, hunger, and other problems linked to poverty.
- Life expectancy in low-income nations is about twenty-five years less than in the United States; in the poorest nations, half the children do not survive to adulthood.

`pp. 423–24`

Health in the United States

HEALTH FACTS
- More than three-fourths of U.S. children born today will live to at least age sixty-five.
- Throughout the life course, women have better health than men, and people of high social position enjoy better health than the poor.

`pp. 424–25`

CURRENT ISSUES in U.S. health care include
- cigarette smoking, which is the greatest preventable cause of death
- eating disorders and obesity
- the increase in sexually transmitted diseases
- ethical dilemmas associated with advancing medical technology and the right to die

`pp. 425–30`

social epidemiology (p. 424) the study of how health and disease are distributed throughout a society's population

eating disorder (p. 426) an intense form of dieting or other unhealthy method of weight control driven by the desire to be very thin

euthanasia (p. 430) assisting in the death of a person suffering from an incurable disease; also known as *mercy killing*

The Medical Establishment

🕮 Read on mysoclab.com

THE RISE OF SCIENTIFIC MEDICINE
- Health care was historically a family concern but with industrialization became the responsibility of trained specialists.
- The model of scientific medicine is the foundation of the U.S. medical establishment.

`p. 430–32`

PAYING FOR MEDICAL CARE: A GLOBAL SURVEY
- Socialist societies define medical care as a right; governments offer basic care equally to everyone.
- Capitalist societies view medical care as a commodity to be purchased, although most capitalist governments help pay for medical care through socialized medicine or national health insurance.

`pp. 432–33`

PAYING FOR MEDICAL CARE: THE UNITED STATES
- Most people have private or government health insurance, but about 46 million people in the United States do not have health insurance.
- The 2010 health care reforms moved the United States much closer to the goal of having everyone covered by health insurance.

`pp. 433–35`

holistic medicine (p. 431) an approach to health care that emphasizes the prevention of illness and takes into account a person's entire physical and social environment

socialized medicine (p. 432) a medical care system in which the government owns and operates most medical facilities and employs most physicians

direct-fee system (p. 433) a medical care system in which patients pay directly for the services of physicians and hospitals

health maintenance organization (HMO) (p. 434) an organization that provides comprehensive medical care to subscribers for a fixed fee

Theoretical Analysis of Health and Medicine

The **STRUCTURAL-FUNCTIONAL APPROACH** considers illness dysfunctional because it reduces people's abilities to perform their roles (Talcott Parsons). Society responds to illness by defining roles:
- The *sick role* excuses the ill person from routine social responsibilities.
- The *physician's role* is to use specialized knowledge to take charge of the patient's recovery.

`pp. 435–36`

The **SYMBOLIC-INTERACTION APPROACH** investigates how health and medical care are socially constructed by people in everyday interaction:
- Our response to illness is not always based on medical facts.
- How people define a medical situation may affect how they feel.

`pp. 436–37`

The **SOCIAL-CONFLICT** and **FEMINIST APPROACHES** focus on the unequal distribution of health and medical care. They criticize the U.S. medical establishment for
- its overreliance on drugs and surgery.
- the dominance of the profit motive.
- overemphasis on the biological rather than the social causes of illness.

`pp. 437–38`

sick role (p. 435) patterns of behavior defined as appropriate for people who are ill

📖 *See the Applying Theory table on page 438.*

15 Population, Urbanization, and Environment

- Why should we worry about the rapid rate of global population increase?

- What makes city and rural living different?

- How is the state of the natural environment a social issue?

Watch the *Core Concepts in Sociology* video "Population Growth and Decline" on **mysoclab.com**

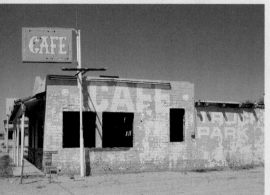

Looking for a new place to live after you finish college? Crosby, North Dakota, would really like you to call it home. The town's officials will do more than welcome you—they will give you a free piece of land on which to build a house. As a bonus, they will throw in a free membership in the local country club.

The old cattle town of Ellsworth, Kansas, also wants you. The town leaders will match Crosby's offer of free land and go one better, giving you $1,000 cash toward your down payment on a new home.

Perhaps the best deal of all is found in Plainville, another small Kansas town. In addition to free land, you can forget about property taxes for the next ten years!

Why are these towns so eager to attract new residents? The answer is that they are all in the Great Plains, the region of the United States extending from North Dakota all the way down to Texas that has lost much of its population in recent decades. The governments of Crosby (current population 1,100), Ellsworth (2,500), and Plainville (2,000) are offering these incentives because they are worried that unless there is a turnaround, their towns may disappear like hundreds of other nearby communities already have (Greene, 2005).

All across the Great Plains, towns are hanging on by a thread. This chapter investigates population patterns, explaining why people move from place to place, why some cities get so large, and why small towns sometimes die. It will also look at the effects on the physical environment of population change and our way of life.

Demography: The Study of Population

When humans first began to cultivate plants some 12,000 years ago, Earth's entire *Homo sapiens* population was about 5 million, or about the number of people living in Colorado today. Very slow growth pushed the total in 1 C.E. to perhaps 300 million, or about the population of the United States today.

Starting around 1750, world population began to spike upward. We are currently adding nearly 83 million people to the planet each year; the world now holds 6.8 billion people.

The causes and consequences of this drama are the focus of **demography,** *the study of human population.* Demography (from the Greek, meaning "description of people") is a cousin of sociology that analyzes the size and composition of a population and studies how and why people move from place to place. Demographers not only collect statistics but also raise important questions about the effects of population growth and suggest how it might be controlled. The following sections present basic demographic concepts.

Fertility

The study of human population begins with how many people are born. **Fertility** is *the incidence of childbearing in a country's population.* During a woman's childbearing years, from the onset of menstruation (typically in the early teens) to menopause (usually in the late forties), she is capable of bearing more than twenty children. But *fecundity,* or maximum possible childbearing, is sharply reduced by cultural norms, finances, and personal choice.

Demographers describe fertility using the **crude birth rate,** *the number of live births in a given year for every 1,000 people in a population.* To calculate a crude birth rate, divide the number of live births in a year by the total population and multiply the result by 1,000. In the United States in 2008, there were 4.25 million live births in a population of 304 million, yielding a crude birth rate of 14.0 (Hamilton, Martin, & Ventura, 2010).

January 18, Coshocton County, Ohio. Having just finished off the mountains of meat and potatoes that make up a typical Amish meal, our group of college students has gathered in the living room of Jacob and Anna Raber, members of this rural Amish community. Anna, a mother of four, is telling us about Amish life. "Most of the women I know have five or six children," she says with a smile, "but certainly not everybody—some have eleven or twelve!"

Global Snapshot

(a)	(b)	(c)

FIGURE 15–1 **(a) Crude Birth Rates and Crude Death Rates, (b) Infant Mortality Rates, and (c) Life Expectancy around the World, 2009**

By world standards, North America has a low birth rate, an average death rate, a very low infant mortality rate, and high life expectancy.

[1] United States and Canada.

[2] Australia, New Zealand, and South Pacific Islands.

Source: Population Reference Bureau (2009).

A country's birth rate is described as "crude" because it is based on the entire population, not just women in their childbearing years. In addition, this measure ignores differences among various categories of the population: Fertility among the Amish, for example, is quite high, and fertility among Asian Americans is low. But the measure is easy to calculate and allows rough comparisons of the fertility of one country or region to others. Part (a) of Figure 15–1 shows that compared to the rest of the world, the crude birth rate of North Americans is low.

Mortality

Population size also reflects **mortality,** *the incidence of death in a country's population.* To measure mortality, demographers use the **crude death rate,** *the number of deaths in a given year for every 1,000 people in a population.* This time, we take the number of deaths in a year, divide by the total population, and multiply the result by 1,000. In 2008, there were 2.45 million deaths in the U.S. population of 304 million, yielding a crude death rate of 8.1 (Tejada-Vera & Sutton, 2009). Part (a) of Figure 15–1 shows that in global context, this rate is about average.

A third useful demographic measure is the **infant mortality rate,** *the number of deaths among infants under one year of age for each 1,000 live births in a given year.* To compute infant mortality, divide the number of deaths of children under one year of age by the number of live births during the same year and multiply the result by 1,000. In 2008, there were 27,600 infant deaths and 4.25 million live births in the United States. Dividing the first number by the second and multiplying the result by 1,000 yields an infant mortality rate of 6.49. Part (b) of Figure 15–1 indicates that by world standards, North American infant mortality is very low.

But remember the differences among various categories of people. For example, African Americans, with three times the burden of poverty compared to whites, have an infant mortality rate of 12.9, more than twice the rate for non-Hispanic whites of 5.7.

Low infant mortality greatly raises **life expectancy,** *the average life span of a country's population.* U.S. males born in 2007 can expect to live 75.4 years, and females can look forward to 80.4 years. As part (c) of Figure 15–1 shows, life expectancy for North Americans is twenty-three years greater than that typical of low-income countries of Africa.

Migration

Population size is also affected by **migration,** *the movement of people into and out of a specified territory.* Movement into a territory, or *immigration,* is measured as an *in-migration rate,* calculated as the number of people entering an area for every 1,000 people in the

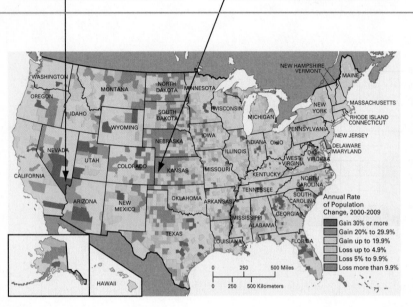

Cheryl Richardson, age 36, has just moved to Las Vegas to work in the expanding tourism industry, which has boosted the region's population.

Tom and Ellen Posten, in their sixties, live in Wichita County, Kansas; like many other families in the area, their children have all moved out of the county in search of better jobs.

Explore population density in your local community and in counties across the United States on mysoclab.com

Seeing Ourselves

NATIONAL MAP 15–1
Population Change across the United States

This map shows that since 2000, population has been moving from the heartland of the United States toward the coasts. What do you think is causing this internal migration? What categories of people do you think remain in counties that are losing population?

Explore on mysoclab.com

Source: U.S. Census Bureau (2009).

Annual Rate of Population Change, 2000-2009

- Gain 30% or more
- Gain 20% to 29.9%
- Gain up to 19.9%
- Loss up to 4.9%
- Loss 5% to 9.9%
- Loss more than 9.9%

population. Movement out of a territory, or *emigration,* is measured in terms of an *out-migration rate,* the number leaving for every 1,000 people. Both types of migration usually happen at the same time; the difference is the *net migration rate.*

All nations experience some degree of internal migration, that is, movement within their borders from one region to another. National Map 15–1 shows where the U.S. population is moving and the places being left behind (as suggested by the chapter opening, notice the heavy losses in the Plains States in the middle of the country).

Migration is sometimes voluntary, as when people leave a small town to move to a larger city. In such cases, "push-pull" factors are usually at work: A lack of jobs "pushes" people to move, and more opportunity elsewhere "pulls" people to someplace new. Migration can also be involuntary, such as the forced transport of 10 million Africans to the Western Hemisphere as slaves or when Hurricane Katrina caused tens of thousands of people to flee New Orleans.

Population Growth

Fertility, mortality, and migration all affect the size of a society's population. In general, rich nations (such as the United States) grow almost as much from immigration as from natural increase; poorer nations (such as Pakistan) grow almost entirely from natural increase.

To calculate a population's *natural growth rate,* demographers subtract the crude death rate from the crude birth rate. The natural growth rate of the U.S. population in 2008 was 5.9 per 1,000 (the crude birth rate of 14.0 minus the crude death rate of 8.1), or about 0.6 percent annual growth.

Global Map 15–1 shows that population growth in the United States and other high-income nations is well below the world average

of 1.2 percent. Earth's low-growth continents are Europe (currently posting no growth) and North America (increasing by 0.6 percent). Near the global average are Oceania (1.1 percent), Asia (1.2 percent), and Latin America (1.4 percent). The highest-growth region of the world is Africa (2.4 percent).

A handy rule for estimating population growth is to divide a society's population growth into the number 70; this yields the *doubling time* in years. Thus an annual growth rate of 2 percent (found in parts of Latin America) doubles a population in thirty-five years, and a 3 percent growth rate (found in some countries in Africa) drops the doubling time to just twenty-three years. The rapid population growth of the poorest countries is deeply troubling because these countries can barely support the populations they have now.

Population Composition

Demographers also study the makeup of a society's population at a given point in time. One variable is the **sex ratio,** *the number of males for every 100 females in a nation's population.* In 2008, the sex ratio in the United States was 97, or 97 males for every 100 females. Sex ratios are ordinarily below 100 because, on average, women outlive men. Because Plainville, Kansas, has an aging population, its sex ratio is 89, or 89 males for every 100 females. In India, however, the sex ratio is 108 because parents value sons more than daughters and may either abort a female fetus or, after birth, give more care to a male infant, raising the odds that a female child will die.

A more complex measure is the **age-sex pyramid,** *a graphic representation of the age and sex of a population.* Figure 15–2 on page 450 presents the age-sex pyramids for the United States and Mexico. Higher death rates as people age give these figures a rough pyramid shape. In the

Amélie Bouchard, age 34, lives in Canada, a nation with a low birth rate and slowly increasing population.

Amat Al-Sharafi, age 35, has four children and lives in Yemen, a country where the birth rate is high and population is rapidly increasing.

Annual Population Growth
- 3.0% and higher
- 2.0% to 2.9%
- 1.0% to 1.9%
- Below 1.0%

Window on the World

GLOBAL MAP 15–1   Population Growth in Global Perspective

The richest countries of the world—including the United States, Canada, and the nations of Europe—have growth rates below 1 percent. The nations of Latin America and Asia typically have growth rates around 1.5 percent, a rate that doubles a population in forty-seven years. Africa has an overall growth rate of 2.4 percent (despite only small increases in countries with a high rate of AIDS), which cuts the doubling time to twenty-nine years. In global perspective, we see that a society's standard of living is closely related to its rate of population growth: Population is rising fastest in the world regions that can least afford to support more people.

Source: Population Reference Bureau (2009).

U.S. pyramid, the bulge near the middle reflects the high birth rates during the "baby boom" from the mid-1940s to the mid-1960s. The contraction for people in their twenties and thirties reflects the subsequent "baby bust." The birth rate of 14.0 in 2008 is still well below its high of 25.3 in 1957.

Comparing the U.S. and Mexican age-sex pyramids shows different demographic trends. The pyramid for Mexico, like that of other lower-income nations, is wide at the bottom (reflecting higher birth rates) and narrows quickly by what we would call middle age (due to higher mortality). In short, Mexico is a much younger society,

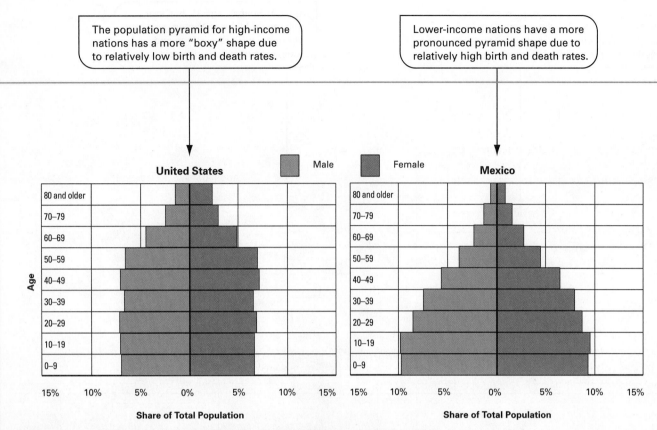

The population pyramid for high-income nations has a more "boxy" shape due to relatively low birth and death rates.

Lower-income nations have a more pronounced pyramid shape due to relatively high birth and death rates.

United States

Male   Female

Mexico

| Age |
| 80 and older |
| 70–79 |
| 60–69 |
| 50–59 |
| 40–49 |
| 30–39 |
| 20–29 |
| 10–19 |
| 0–9 |

15% 10% 5% 0% 5% 10% 15%

Share of Total Population

15% 10% 5% 0% 5% 10% 15%

Share of Total Population

FIGURE 15–2   Age-Sex Population Pyramids for the United States and Mexico, 2010

By looking at the shape of a country's population pyramid, you can tell its level of economic development and predict future levels of population increase.

Source: U.S. Census Bureau (2010).

with a median age of twenty-six, compared to thirty-seven in the United States. With a larger share of women still in their child-bearing years, therefore, Mexico's crude birth rate (19) is half again the size of our own (14.0), and its annual rate of population growth (1.1 percent) is almost twice the U.S. rate (0.6 percent).

History and Theory of Population Growth

In the past, people wanted large families because human labor was the key to productivity. In addition, until rubber condoms were invented in the mid-1800s, preventing pregnancy was uncertain at best. But high death rates from infectious diseases put a constant brake on population growth.

A major demographic shift began about 1750 as the world's population turned upward, reaching the 1 billion mark by 1800. This milestone (which took all of human history to reach) was matched barely a century later in 1930, when a second billion people were added to the planet. In other words, not only was population increasing, but the *rate* of growth was accelerating. Global population reached 3 billion by 1962 (just thirty-two years later) and 4 billion by

1974 (only twelve years later). The rate of world population increase has slowed recently, but the planet passed the 5 billion mark in 1987 and the 6 billion mark in 1999 and now stands at 6.8 billion. In no previous century did the world's population even double. In the twentieth century, it *quadrupled.*

Currently, the world is gaining almost 83 million people each year; 98 percent of this increase is in poor countries. Experts predict that Earth's population will be more than 9 billion in 2050 (United Nations Population Division, 2010). Given the world's troubles feeding its present population, such an increase is a matter of urgent concern.

Malthusian Theory

The sudden population growth 250 years ago sparked the development of demography. Thomas Robert Malthus (1766–1834), an English economist and clergyman, warned that rapid population increase would lead to social chaos. Malthus (1926, orig. 1798) calculated that population would increase in what mathematicians call a *geometric progression,* illustrated by the series of numbers 2, 4, 8, 16, 32, and so on. At such a rate, Malthus concluded, world population would soon soar out of control.

Seeing Sociology in Everyday Life

Using the age-sex pyramid for the United States shown in Figure 15–2, why do you think many people are concerned that there will not be enough workers to pay for the retirement of the baby boom generation? How does the pyramid shape change as more and more baby boomers enter retirement?

demographic transition theory a thesis that links population patterns to a society's level of technological development

Food production would also increase, Malthus explained, but only in an *arithmetic progression* (as in the series 2, 3, 4, 5, 6, and so on) because even with new agricultural technology, farmland is limited. Thus Malthus presented a troubling vision of the future: people reproducing beyond what the planet could feed, leading ultimately to widespread starvation and war over what resources were left.

Malthus recognized that artificial birth control or abstaining from sex might change his prediction. But he considered one morally wrong and the other impractical. Famine and war therefore stalked humanity in Malthus's mind, and he was justly known as "the dismal parson."

CRITICAL REVIEW Fortunately, Malthus's prediction was flawed. First, by 1850, the European birth rate began to drop, partly because with industrialization, children were becoming an economic liability rather than an asset and partly because people began using artificial birth control. Second, Malthus underestimated human ingenuity: Modern irrigation techniques, fertilizers, and pesticides have increased farm production far more than he could have imagined.

Some people criticized Malthus for ignoring the role of social inequality in world abundance and famine. For example, Karl Marx (1967, orig. 1867) objected to his view of suffering as a "law of nature" rather than the curse of capitalism. More recently, "critical demographers" have claimed that saying poverty is caused by a high birth rate in low-income countries amounts to blaming the victims. On the contrary, they see global inequality as the real issue (Horton, 1999; Kuumba, 1999).

Still, Malthus offers an important lesson. Habitable land, clean water, and fresh air are limited resources, and increased economic productivity has taken a heavy toll on the natural environment. In addition, medical advances have lowered death rates, pushing up world population. In principle, of course, no level of population growth can go on forever. People everywhere must become aware of the dangers of population increase.

CHECK YOUR LEARNING What did Malthus predict about human population increase? About food production? What was his overall conclusion?

Demographic Transition Theory

A more complex analysis of population change is **demographic transition theory,** *a thesis that links population patterns to a society's level of technological development.* Figure 15–3 on page 452 shows the demographic consequences at four levels of technological development. Preindustrial, agrarian societies (Stage 1) have high birth rates because of the economic value of children and the absence of birth control. Death rates are also high due to low living standards and

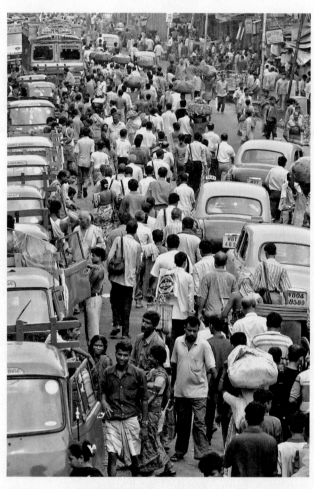

This street scene in Kolkata (Calcutta), India, conveys the vision of the future found in the work of Thomas Robert Malthus, who feared that population increase would overwhelm the world's resources. Can you explain why Malthus had such a serious concern about population? How is demographic transition theory a more hopeful analysis?

limited medical technology. Outbreaks of disease cancel out births, so population rises and falls with only a modest overall increase. This was the case for thousands of years in Europe before the Industrial Revolution.

Stage 2, the onset of industrialization, brings a demographic transition as death rates fall due to greater food supplies and scientific medicine. But birth rates remain high, resulting in rapid population growth. It was during Europe's Stage 2 that Malthus formulated his ideas, which accounts for his pessimistic view of the future. The world's poorest countries today are in this high-growth stage.

In Stage 3, a mature industrial economy, the birth rate drops, curbing population growth once again. Fertility falls because most

The United States is in this historical stage, with both a low birth rate and a low death rate.

	Stage 1	Stage 2	Stage 3	Stage 4
Birth Rate **Death Rate**		Natural Increase		
Level of Technology	Preindustrial	Early Industrial	Mature Industrial	Postindustrial
Population Growth	Very Slow	Rapid	Slowing	Very Slow

FIGURE 15–3 Demographic Transition Theory

Demographic transition theory links population change to a society's level of technological development.

children survive to adulthood, so fewer are needed, and because high living standards make raising children expensive. In short, affluence transforms children from economic assets into economic liabilities. Smaller families, made possible by effective birth control, are also favored by women working outside the home. As birth rates follow death rates downward, population growth slows further.

Stage 4 corresponds to a postindustrial economy in which the demographic transition is complete. The birth rate keeps falling, partly because dual-income couples gradually become the norm and partly because the cost of raising and schooling children continues to increase. This trend, coupled with steady death rates, means that population grows only very slowly or even decreases. This is the case today in Japan, Europe, and the United States.

CRITICAL REVIEW   Demographic transition theory suggests that the key to population control lies in technology. Instead of the runaway population increase feared by Malthus, this theory sees technology slowing growth and spreading material plenty.

Demographic transition theory is linked to modernization theory, one approach to global development discussed in Chapter 9 ("Global Stratification"). Modernization theorists are optimistic that poor countries will solve their population problems as they industrialize. But critics, notably dependency theorists, strongly disagree. Unless there is a redistribution of global resources, they maintain, our planet will become increasingly divided into affluent "haves," enjoying low population growth, and poor "have-nots," struggling in vain to feed more and more people.

CHECK YOUR LEARNING   Explain the four stages of demographic transition theory.

Global Population Today: A Brief Survey

What can we say about population in today's world? Drawing on the discussion so far, we can identify important patterns and reach several conclusions.

The Low-Growth North

When the Industrial Revolution began in the Northern Hemisphere, population growth in Western Europe and North America was a high 3 percent annually. But in the centuries since, the growth rate has steadily declined, and in 1970, it fell below 1 percent. As our postindustrial society settles into Stage 4, the U.S. birth rate is at about the replacement level of 2.1 children per woman, a point demographers call **zero population growth,** *the rate of reproduction that maintains population at a steady level.* More than seventy nations, almost all of them rich, are at or below the point of zero population growth.

Among the factors that serve to hold down population in these postindustrial societies are the high proportion of men and women in the labor force, the rising costs of raising children, trends toward later marriage and singlehood, and the widespread use of contraceptives and abortion.

In high-income nations, then, population increase is not the pressing problem that it is in poor countries. On the contrary, many governments in high-income countries are concerned about a future problem of *underpopulation* because declining population size may be difficult to reverse and also because the swelling ranks of the elderly will have fewer and fewer young people to look to for support (Kent & Mather, 2002; United Nations Population Division, 2009).

The High-Growth South

Population is a critical problem in poor nations of the Southern Hemisphere. No nation in the world lacks industrial technology entirely; demographic transition theory's Stage 1 applies only to remote rural areas of low-income nations. But much of Latin America, Africa, and Asia is at Stage 2, with mixed agrarian and industrial economies. Advanced medical technology, supplied by rich societies, has sharply reduced death rates, but birth rates remain high. This is why poor societies now account for two-thirds of Earth's people and 98 percent of global population increase. Read on mysoclab.com

In poor countries around the world, birth rates have fallen from an average of about six children per woman in 1950 to three or four today. But fertility this high will only intensify global poverty. That is why leaders in the battle against global poverty point to the importance of reducing fertility rates in low-income nations. Notice, too, that

Seeing Sociology in Everyday Life

Typically, immigrants are younger than most people in their new country. What is the likely effect of high immigration on a country's ability to support more and more older people?

zero population growth the rate of reproduction that maintains population at a steady level

a key element in controlling world population growth is improving the status of women. Why? Because of this simple truth: Give women more life choices, and they will have fewer children. History has shown that women who are free to decide when and where to marry, bear children as a matter of choice, and have access to education and to good jobs will limit their own fertility (Axinn & Barber, 2001; Roudi-Fahimi & Kent, 2007).

The Demographic Divide

High- and low-income nations display very different population dynamics, a gap that is sometimes called the *demographic divide.* In Italy, a high-income, very low growth nation, women average just over one child in their lifetimes. Such a low birth rate means that the number of annual births is actually less than the number of deaths. This means that at the moment, Italy is actually *losing* population. Looking ahead to 2050 and even assuming some gains from immigration, Italy's population is projected to be about the same as it is today. The share of elderly people in Italy—now 20 percent—will only increase as time goes on.

Look at how different the patterns are in a low-income nation such as the Democratic Republic of the Congo in Central Africa. There women still have an average of six to seven children, so even with a high mortality rate, this nation's population will triple by 2050. The share of elderly people is extremely low—about 3 percent—and half the country's people are below the age of fifteen. With such a high growth rate, it is no surprise that the problem of poverty is bad and getting worse: About three-fourths of the people are undernourished (Population Reference Bureau, 2009).

In sum, a demographic divide now separates rich countries with low birth rates and aging populations from poor countries with high birth rates and very young populations. Just as humanity has devised ways to reduce deaths around the world, so it must now bring down population growth, especially in poor countries where projections suggest a future as bleak as that imagined by Thomas Malthus centuries ago.

China stands out as a nation that that has taken a strong stand on reducing the rate of population increase. That country's one-child policy, enacted back in the 1970s, has reduced China's potential population by about 250 million. Yet as the Thinking About Diversity box on page 454 explains, this policy has been controversial.

In much of the world today, mortality is falling. To limit population increase, the world—especially poor nations—must control births as successfully as it is fending off deaths.

Fertility in the United States has fallen during the past century and is now quite low. But some categories of the U.S. population have much higher fertility rates. One example is the Amish, a religious society living in rural areas of Ohio, Pennsylvania, and other states. It is common for Amish couples to have five, six, or more children. Why do you think the Amish favor large families?

Urbanization: The Growth of Cities

October 8, Hong Kong. The cable train grinds to the top of Victoria Peak, where we behold one of the world's most spectacular vistas: the city of Hong Kong at night. A million bright, colorful lights ring the harbor as ships, ferries, and traditional Chinese junks churn by. Few cities match Hong Kong for sheer energy: This small city is as economically productive as the state of Wisconsin or the nation of Finland. We could sit here for hours entranced by the spectacle of Hong Kong.

Throughout most of human history, the sights and sounds of great cities such as Hong Kong, New York, and Paris were simply unimaginable. Our distant ancestors lived in small, nomadic groups, moving from place to place as they depleted vegetation or hunted migratory game. The small settlements that marked the emergence of civilization in the Middle East some 12,000 years ago held only a small fraction of Earth's people. Today, the largest three or four cities of the world hold as many people as the entire planet did back then.

● Seeing Sociology
  in Everyday Life

With global population increasing, would you support expanding
the one-child policy to other countries? Why or why not?

●○ Making the Grade

As China's economy continues to grow, what would
demographic transition theory predict about that nation's
birth rate?

THINKING ABOUT DIVERSITY: RACE, CLASS, & GENDER

What's Happened to the Girls? China's One-Child Policy

The parents had argued for hours. But the man was determined and the woman was exhausted. The father wrestled the sleeping baby girl from the mother's arms. The decision was now made; the girl had to go. The father put several extra layers of clothing on his daughter and lay the newborn girl in a cardboard box lined with blankets. Next to her, he placed a small bottle of milk. He walked off into the dark night toward the distant village, leaving behind the sobbing of his beloved wife—the baby's mother—who cried out, "Please, I beg you, bring back my baby!"

Yet in her heart, she too knew that this must be done. Half an hour later, the father arrived in the village and found his way to the local school. For the last time, he kissed his daughter goodbye. He set her makeshift crib on the steps of the school's front entrance, knowing that when dawn broke in an hour or so, she would be found and cared for. With tears in his eyes, he said a quick prayer to his ancestors to keep the baby safe from harm. Then he turned and again disappeared into the night, knowing that he would never see or hear from her again.

This story may be heartbreaking, but it is one that has occurred tens of thousands of times in China. What would prompt parents to give up a child? Why would a father abandon his daughter in a public place? The answer lies in China's population control policy and the nation's cultural traditions.

Back in the 1970s, the high Chinese birth rate was fueling an extremely rapid population increase. Government leaders could see that the country's economic development depended on controlling population growth. As a result, they passed a law stating that a family can have only one child. Families who follow the one-child policy can expect rewards such as a better job, a higher salary, and maybe even a larger apartment. On the other hand, parents who violate the law by having a second child face a stiff fine, and their second child may not be eligible for educational and health care benefits.

The government actively promotes the one-child message in the mass media, in popular songs, and in the schools. But education is not the government's only tactic—enforcement officials can be found in most neighborhoods and workplaces. Most Chinese willingly comply with the policy, praising it as good for the country. Those who do not must face the consequences.

Modern China is determined to control population increase. But China is also a country steeped in a tradition of male dominance. If government rules permit only one child, most families would prefer a boy. Why? Parents see boys as a better investment because sons will carry on the family name and must care for their aging parents. On the other hand, girls will end up caring for their husbands' parents, leading most Chinese to see raising daughters as a waste of precious resources. The Chinese government has expanded women's rights and opportunities, but patriarchal traditions are deeply rooted in the country's history, and as is true everywhere, attitudes change slowly.

Around the world, the one-child policy has attracted both praise and condemnation. On the positive side, analysts agree that it has succeeded in its goal of reducing the rate of population increase. This trend, in turn, has helped raise living standards and lifted China to the ranks of

middle-income nations. Many one-child families are happy with the added income from women who now work outside the home, and parents now have more to spend on a child's schooling.

But the one-child policy also has a dark side, shown in the story that began this box. Since the law was passed, as many as 1 million girls have "disappeared." In some cases, parents who learn that the woman is carrying a female fetus may choose abortion so they can "try again." In other cases, family members decide to kill a female infant soon after birth. In still other cases, girls survive but are never recorded in the birth statistics so that they grow up as "noncitizens" who can never go to school or receive treatment at a local health clinic. Finally, some parents, like those described earlier, give up or abandon their daughter in the hope that the child may find a home elsewhere.

China's one-child policy has certainly held population increase in check. But it has had a dramatic toll on the female population of China. In one recent year, the nation's birth records showed almost 1 million fewer girls than boys. The Chinese population is now about 250 million lower than it would have been without the one-child policy, but it is also steadily becoming more and more male.

WHAT DO YOU THINK?

1. Point to the reasons China's one-child policy has attracted praise and also blame. On balance, do you think this is a good policy? Can you think of a better way to control population? Explain.

2. What about cases where parents think they can afford additional children? Should family size be a couple's decision? Or does government have a responsibility to look out for the entire country's well-being?

3. Do you now understand why almost all of the babies U.S. parents adopt from China are girls?

China's one-child policy is advertised on billboards throughout the country.

Sources: Hesketh & Lu (2005), Baochang et al. (2007), and Yardley (2008).

● Seeing Sociology
in Everyday Life

As the sections describing preindustrial and industrial cities
explain, the size and shape of a city provides clues to a society's technology and culture.

urbanization the concentration of population into cities

Urbanization is *the concentration of population into cities.* Urbanization both redistributes population within a society and transforms many patterns of social life. We will trace these changes in terms of three urban revolutions: the emergence of cities beginning 10,000 years ago, the development of industrial cities after 1750, and the explosive growth of cities in poor countries today.

The Evolution of Cities

Cities are a relatively new development in human history. Only about 12,000 years ago did our ancestors begin founding permanent settlements, which paved the way for the *first urban revolution.*

The First Cities

Hunting and gathering forced people to move all the time; however, once our ancestors discovered how to domesticate animals and cultivate crops, they were able to stay in one place. Raising their own food also created a material surplus, which freed some people from food production and allowed them to build shelters, make tools, weave cloth, and take part in religious rituals. The emergence of cities led to both specialization and higher living standards.

The first city that we know of was Jericho, which lies to the north of the Dead Sea in what is now the West Bank. When first settled 10,000 years ago, it was home to only 600 people. But as the centuries passed, cities grew to tens of thousands of people and became the centers of vast empires. By 3000 B.C.E., Egyptian cities flourished, as did cities in China about 2000 B.C.E. and in Central and South America about 1500 B.C.E. In North America, however, only a few Native American societies formed settlements; widespread urbanization did not take place until the arrival of European settlers in the seventeenth century.

Preindustrial European Cities

European cities date back some 5,000 years to the Greeks and, later, the Romans, both of whom formed great empires and founded cities across Europe, including Vienna, Paris, and London. With the fall of the Roman Empire, the so-called Dark Ages began as people withdrew within defensive walled settlements and warlords battled for territory. Only in the eleventh century did Europe become more peaceful; trade flourished once again, allowing cities to grow.

Medieval cities were quite different from those familiar to us today. Beneath towering cathedrals, the narrow, winding streets of London, Brussels, and Florence teemed with merchants, artisans, priests, peddlers, jugglers, nobles, and servants. Occupational groups such as bakers, carpenters, and metalworkers clustered in distinct sections or "quarters." Ethnicity also defined communities as people sought to keep out those who differed from themselves. The term "ghetto" (from the Italian word *borghetto*, meaning "outside the city walls") was first used to describe the neighborhood into which the Jews of Venice were segregated.

Industrial European Cities

As the Middle Ages came to a close, steadily increasing commerce enriched a new urban middle class called the *bourgeoisie* (French, meaning "townspeople"). Earning more and more money, the bourgeoisie soon rivaled the hereditary nobility.

By about 1750, the Industrial Revolution triggered a *second urban revolution,* first in Europe and then in North America. The tremendous productive power of factories caused cities to grow bigger than ever before. London, the largest European city, reached 550,000 people by 1700 and exploded to 6.5 million by 1900 (A. F. Weber, 1963, orig. 1899; Chandler & Fox, 1974).

Cities not only grew but changed shape as well. Older winding streets gave way to broad, straight boulevards to handle the increasing flow of commercial traffic. Steam and electric trolleys soon crisscrossed the expanding cities. Because land was now a commodity to be bought and sold, developers divided cities into regular-sized lots (Mumford, 1961). The center of the city was no longer the cathedral but a bustling central business district filled with banks, retail stores, and tall office buildings.

With a new focus on business, cities became ever more crowded and impersonal. Crime rates rose. Especially at the outset, a few industrialists lived in grand style, but most men, women, and children barely survived by working in factories.

Organized efforts by workers eventually brought improvements to the workplace, better housing, and the right to vote. Public services such as water, sewer systems, and electricity further improved urban living. Today, some urbanites still live in poverty, but a rising standard of living has partly fulfilled the city's historical promise of a better life.

The Growth of U.S. Cities

As noted, most of the Native Americans who inhabited North America for thousands of years before the arrival of Europeans were migratory people who formed few permanent settlements. The spread of villages and towns came after European colonization.

Colonial Settlement, 1565–1800

In 1565, the Spanish built a settlement at Saint Augustine, Florida, and in 1607, the English founded Jamestown, Virginia. However, the first lasting settlement came in 1624 when the Dutch established New Amsterdam, later renamed New York.

New York and Boston (founded by the English in 1630) started out as tiny villages in a vast wilderness. They resembled medieval towns in Europe, with narrow, winding streets that still curve through

● Seeing Sociology
in Everyday Life

Looking at the table below, imagine how the lives of
people who lived a century ago differed from what we
experience today. What are some differences?

metropolis a large city that socially and economically dominates an urban area

suburbs urban areas beyond the political boundaries of a city

megalopolis a vast urban region containing a number of cities and their surrounding suburbs

Table 15–1 Urban Population of the United States, 1790–2040

Year	Population (in millions)	Urban Portion
1790	3.9	5.1%
1800	5.3	6.1
1820	9.6	7.3
1840	17.1	10.5
1860	31.4	19.7
1880	50.2	28.1
1900	76.0	39.7
1920	105.7	51.3
1940	131.7	56.5
1960	179.3	69.9
1980	226.5	73.7
2000	281.4	79.0
2020*	290.7	84.9
2040*	342.6	88.8

*Projection.

Sources: U.S. Census Bureau (2009) and United Nations Population Division (2009).

lower Manhattan and downtown Boston. When the first census was completed in 1790, as Table 15–1 shows, just 5 percent of the nation's people lived in cities.

Urban Expansion, 1800–1860

Early in the nineteenth century, towns sprang up along the transportation routes that opened the American West. By 1860, Buffalo, Cleveland, Detroit, and Chicago were all changing the face of the Midwest, and about one-fifth of the U.S. population lived in cities.

Urban expansion was greatest in the northern states; New York City, for example, had ten times the population of Charleston, South Carolina. The evolution of the United States into the industrial-urban North and the agrarian-rural South was one major cause of the Civil War (Schlesinger, 1969).

The Metropolitan Era, 1860–1950

The Civil War (1861–1865) gave an enormous boost to urbanization as factories strained to produce weapons. Especially in the North, waves of people deserted the countryside for cities in hopes of finding better jobs. Joining them were tens of millions of immigrants, most from Europe, forming a culturally diverse urban mix.

In 1900, New York's population soared past the 4 million mark, and Chicago, a city that had scarcely 100,000 people in 1860, was closing in on 2 million. Such growth marked the beginning of the **metropolis** (Greek for "mother city"), *a large city that dominates an urban area socially and economically.* Metropolises became the economic centers of the United States. By 1920, urban areas were home to a majority of the U.S. population.

Industrial technology pushed city populations higher and higher. In the 1880s, the tallest buildings, supported by steel girders and equipped with mechanical elevators, were ten stories high. In 1930, New York's Empire State Building was hailed as an urban wonder, soaring 102 stories into the clouds.

Urban Decentralization, 1950–Present

The industrial metropolis reached its peak about 1950. Since then, something of a turnaround, called *urban decentralization,* has occurred as people have left downtown areas for outlying **suburbs,** *urban areas beyond the political boundaries of a city.* The old industrial cities of the Northeast and Midwest stopped growing, and some lost considerable population in the decades after 1950. The urban landscape of densely packed central cities evolved into sprawling suburban regions.

Suburbs and Urban Decline

Imitating European nobility, some of the rich in the United States split their time between town houses in the city and country homes beyond the city limits. But not until after World War II did ordinary people find a suburban home within their reach. Thanks to more and more cars in circulation, new four-lane highways, government-backed mortgages, and inexpensive tract homes, suburbs grew rapidly. By 1999, most of the U.S. population lived in suburbs, where they frequented nearby shopping malls rather than the older downtown shopping districts (Pederson, Smith, & Adler, 1999; Macionis & Parrillo, 2010).

As many older cities of the Snowbelt—the Northeast and Midwest—lost higher-income taxpayers to the suburbs, they struggled to pay for expensive social programs for the poor who remained. Many cities fell into financial crisis, and inner-city decay became severe. Especially to white suburbanites, the inner cities became synonymous with slum housing, crime, drugs, unemployment, the poor, and minorities (Stahura, 1986; Galster, 1991).

The decline of central cities has also led to a decline in the importance of public space (Goldberger, 2002). Historically, city life was played out on the streets. The French word for a sophisticated person is *boulevardier,* which literally means "street person." However, this term has a negative meaning in the United States today. The activity that once took place on public streets and in public squares now takes place in shopping malls, the lobbies of cineplex theaters, and gated residential communities—all privately owned spaces. Further reducing the vitality of today's urban places is the spread of television, the Internet, and other media that people use without leaving home.

Sunbelt Cities and Urban Sprawl

As the older Snowbelt cities fell into decline, Sunbelt cities in the South and West grew rapidly. The soaring populations of cities such

<table>
<tr><td>

● Seeing Sociology
in Everyday Life

Is there a class difference in people's use of the streets as a place to meet and greet others? For example, do you think working-class people are more likely to use the streets in this way than middle-class suburbanites?

</td><td>

● Making the Grade

The megalopolis, edge cities, and the "rural rebound" are all aspects of population decentralization as cities spread outward after 1950.

</td></tr>
</table>

as Los Angeles and Houston reflected a population shift to the Sunbelt, where 60 percent of people in the United States now live. In addition, most of today's immigrants enter the country in the Sunbelt region. In 1950, nine of the ten largest U.S. cities were in the Snowbelt; in 2008, seven of the top ten were in the Sunbelt (U.S. Census Bureau, 2010).

Unlike their colder counterparts, these cities came of age after urban decentralization began. So while Snowbelt cities have long been enclosed by a ring of politically independent suburbs, Sunbelt cities have pushed their boundaries outward to include suburban communities. Chicago covers 227 square miles; Houston is more than twice that size, and the greater Houston metropolitan region covers almost 9,000 square miles—an area the size of the state of New Hampshire.

The great sprawl of Sunbelt cities has its drawbacks. Many people in cities such as Atlanta, Dallas, Phoenix, and Los Angeles claim that unplanned growth results in traffic-clogged roads leading to unattractive developments and schools that cannot keep up with the inflow of children. Not surprisingly, voters in many communities across the United States have passed ballot initiatives seeking to limit urban sprawl (Lacayo, 1999; Romero & Liserio, 2002; W. Sullivan, 2007).

In recent decades, many U.S. cities in the Sunbelt have spread outward in a process called urban sprawl. Los Angeles, for example, now covers about 500 square miles, and even with a vast system of freeways, people moving around the city often find themselves stuck in slow-moving traffic. What are other disadvantages of urban sprawl?

Megalopolis: The Regional City

Another result of urban decentralization is urban regions, or regional cities. The U.S. Census Bureau (2010) recognizes 374 *metropolitan statistical areas* (MSAs). Each includes at least one city with 50,000 or more people. The bureau also recognizes 581 *micropolitan statistical areas,* urban areas with at least one city of 10,000 to 50,000 people. *Core-based statistical areas* (CBSAs) include both metropolitan and micropolitan statistical areas.

The biggest CBSAs contain millions of people and extend into several states. In 2008, the biggest CBSA was New York and its adjacent urban areas in Long Island, western Connecticut, northern New Jersey, and eastern Pennsylvania, with a total population of more than 22 million. Next in size is the CBSA in southern California that includes Los Angeles, Riverside, and Long Beach, with a population of almost 18 million.

As regional cities grow, they begin to overlap. In the early 1960s, the French geographer Jean Gottmann (1961) coined the term **megalopolis** to designate *a vast urban region containing a number of cities and their surrounding suburbs.* Along the East Coast, a 400-mile megalopolis stretches all the way from New England to Virginia. Other supercities cover the eastern coast of Florida and stretch from Cleveland west to Chicago.

Edge Cities

Urban decentralization has also created *edge cities,* business centers some distance from the old downtowns. Edge cities—a mix of corporate office buildings, shopping malls, hotels, and entertainment complexes—differ from suburbs, which contain mostly homes. The population of suburbs peaks at night, but the population of edge cities peaks during the workday.

As part of expanding urban regions, most edge cities have no clear physical boundaries. Some do have names, including Las Colinas (near the Dallas–Fort Worth airport), Tyson's Corner (in Virginia, near Washington, D.C.), and King of Prussia (northwest of Philadelphia). Other edge cities are known only by the major highways that flow through them, including Route 1, which runs through Princeton, New Jersey, and Route 128 near Boston (Garreau, 1991; Macionis & Parrillo, 2010).

The Rural Rebound

Over the course of U.S. history, as shown by the data in Table 15–1, the urban population of the nation has increased steadily. Immigration has played a part in this increase because most newcomers settle in cities. There has also been considerable migration from rural areas to urban places, typically by people seeking greater social, educational, and economic opportunity.

Gemeinschaft a type of social organization in which people are closely tied by kinship and tradition

Gesellschaft a type of social organization in which people come together only on the basis of individual self-interest

Seeing Sociology
in Everyday Life

How might Tönnies explain social patterns such as our high rate of divorce, widespread fear of crime, and incidents of "road rage" on the highways?

The rural rebound has been most pronounced in towns that offer spectacular natural beauty. There are times when people living in the scenic town of Park City, Utah, cannot even find a parking space.

However, in the 1990s, three-fourths of the rural counties across the United States gained population, a trend analysts have called the "rural rebound." Most of this gain resulted from migration of people from urban areas. This trend has not affected all rural places: As the opening to this chapter explains, many small towns in rural areas (especially in the Plains States) are struggling to stay alive. But even in these areas, the losses have slowed in recent years (K. M. Johnson, 1999; D. Johnson, 2001).

The greatest gains have come to rural communities that offer scenic and recreational attractions, such as lakes, mountains, and ski areas. People are drawn not only to the natural beauty of rural communities but also to their slower pace: less traffic, a lower crime rate,

and cleaner air. A number of companies have relocated to rural counties as well, which has increased economic opportunity for the rural population (K. M. Johnson, 1999; Johnson & Fuguitt, 2000).

Urbanism as a Way of Life

Early sociologists in Europe and the United States focused their attention on the rise of cities. We briefly examine their accounts of urbanism as a way of life.

Ferdinand Tönnies:
Gemeinschaft and *Gesellschaft*

In the nineteenth century, the German sociologist Ferdinand Tönnies (1855–1937) studied how life in the new industrial metropolis differed from life in rural villages. From this contrast, he developed two concepts that have become a lasting part of sociology's terminology.

Tönnies (1963, orig. 1887) used the German word **Gemeinschaft** ("community") to refer to *a type of social organization in which people are closely tied by kinship and tradition.* The *Gemeinschaft* of the rural village, Tönnies explained, joins people in what amounts to a single primary group.

By and large, argued Tönnies, *Gemeinschaft* is absent in the modern city. On the contrary, urbanization creates **Gesellschaft** ("association"), *a type of social organization in which people come together only on the basis of individual self-interest.* In the *Gesellschaft* way of life, individuals are motivated by their own needs rather than by a desire to help improve the well-being of everyone. By and large, city dwellers have little sense of community or common identity and look to other people mainly when they need something. Tönnies saw in urbanization the weakening of close, long-lasting social relations in favor of the brief and impersonal ties or secondary relationships typical of business.

Emile Durkheim: Mechanical and Organic Solidarity

The French sociologist Emile Durkheim agreed with much of Tönnies's thinking about cities. However, Durkheim countered that urbanites do not lack social bonds; they simply organize social life differently than rural people do.

Durkheim described traditional, rural life as *mechanical solidarity,* social bonds based on common sentiments and shared moral values. With its emphasis on tradition, Durkheim's concept of mechanical solidarity bears a strong similarity to Tönnies's *Gemeinschaft.* Urbanization erodes mechanical solidarity, Durkheim explained, but it also generates a new type of bonding, which he called *organic solidarity,* social bonds based on specialization and interdependence. This concept, which parallels Tönnies's *Gesellschaft,* reveals an important

● Seeing Sociology
 in Everyday Life

How would Simmel explain cases of people turning away
from others in need on the grounds that they simply "don't
want to get involved"?

● Making the Grade

Tönnies's concept of *Gemeinschaft* corresponds to Durkheim's
mechanical solidarity; *Gesellschaft* corresponds to organic
solidarity.

Peasant Dance (left, c. 1565), by Pieter Breughel the Elder, conveys the essential unity of rural life forged by generations
of kinship and neighborhood. By contrast, Lily Furedi's *Subway (right)* communicates the impersonality common to
urban areas. Taken together, these paintings capture Tönnies's distinction between *Gemeinschaft* and *Gesellschaft.*

Pieter Breughel the Elder (c. 1525/30–1569), *Peasant Dance*, c. 1565, Kunsthistorisches Museum, Vienna/Superstock. Lily Furedi, American. *Subway*.
Oil on canvas, 99 x 123 cm. National Collection of Fine Arts, Washington, D.C./Smithsonian Institute.

difference between the two thinkers. Both felt that the growth of
industrial cities weakened tradition, but Durkheim optimistically
pointed to a new kind of solidarity. Where societies had been built
on *likeness*, Durkheim now saw social life based on *difference.*

For Durkheim, urban society offers more individual choice,
moral tolerance, and personal privacy than people find in rural villages. In sum, Durkheim thought that something is lost in the process
of urbanization, but much is gained.

Georg Simmel: The Blasé Urbanite

The German sociologist Georg Simmel (1858–1918) offered a micro-
level analysis of cities, studying how urban life shapes individual experience. According to Simmel, individuals see the city as a crush of
people, objects, and events. To prevent being overwhelmed by all this
stimulation, urbanites develop a *blasé attitude,* tuning out much of
what goes on around them. Such detachment does not mean that city
dwellers lack compassion for others; they simply keep their distance
as a survival strategy so that they can focus their time and energy on
the people and things that really matter to them.

The Chicago School:
Robert Park and Louis Wirth

Sociologists in the United States soon joined the study of rapidly
growing cities. Robert Park (1864–1944), a leader of the first U.S.

sociology program at the University of Chicago, sought to add a street-
level perspective by getting out and studying real cities. As he said of
himself, "I suspect that I have actually covered more ground, tramp-
ing about in cities in different parts of the world, than any other living man" (1950:viii). Walking the streets, Park found the city to be
an organized mosaic of distinctive ethnic communities, commercial
centers, and industrial districts. Over time, he observed, these "natural areas" develop and change in relation to one another. To Park, the
city was a living organism—a human kaleidoscope.

Another major figure in the Chicago School of urban sociology
was Louis Wirth (1897–1952). Wirth (1938) is best known for blending the ideas of Tönnies, Durkheim, Simmel, and Park into a comprehensive theory of urban life.

Wirth began by defining the city as a setting with a large, dense, and
socially diverse population. These traits result in an impersonal, superficial, and transitory way of life for city dwellers. Living among millions of others, urbanites come into contact with many more people
than residents of rural areas. Thus when city people take notice of others at all, they usually know them not in terms of *who they are* but *what
they do*—as, for instance, the bus driver, the pharmacist, or the grocery
store clerk. These specialized urban relationships are sometimes pleasant for all concerned, but we should remember that self-interest rather
than friendship is the main reason behind the interaction.

The impersonal nature of urban relationships, together with the
great social diversity found in cities today, makes city dwellers more

urban ecology the study of the link between the physical and social dimensions of cities

○ Making the Grade

Urban ecology was a significant part of urban sociology until about 1970; after that, it declined in importance as urban political economy gained the attention of sociologists.

THINKING ABOUT DIVERSITY: RACE, CLASS, & GENDER

Minorities Now a Majority in the Largest U.S. Cities

According to the 2000 census, minorities—Hispanics, African Americans, and Asians—were now a majority of the population in 48 of the 100 largest U.S. cities, up from 30 in 1990, and the number has surely increased since then.

What accounts for the change? One reason is that large cities have been losing their non-Hispanic white populations. For example, by 2000, Santa Ana, California, had lost 38 percent of the white population it had in 1990; the drop was 40 percent in Birmingham, Alabama, and a whopping 53 percent in Detroit, Michigan. The white share of the population of all 100 of the largest cities fell from 52.1 percent in 1990 to 43.8 percent in 2000, as the figure shows.

But perhaps the biggest reason for the minority-majority trend is the increase in immigration. Immigration, coupled with higher birth rates among new immigrants, resulted in a 43 percent gain in the Hispanic population (almost 4 million people) of the largest 100 cities between 1990 and 2000. The Asian population also surged by

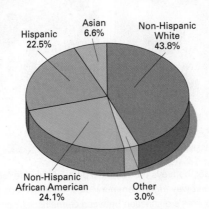

Population Profile for the 100 Largest U.S. Cities, 2000

Racial and ethnic minorities make up a majority of the population of this country's 100 largest cities.

Source: U.S. Census Bureau (2001).

40 percent (more than 1.1 million people). The African American population was steady over the course of the 1990s.

Political officials and other policymakers examine these figures closely. Clearly, the future vitality of the largest U.S. cities depends on meeting the needs and taking advantage of the contributions of their swelling minority populations.

WHAT DO YOU THINK?

1. Why are the minority populations of large U.S. cities increasing?

2. What positive changes and challenges does a minority-majority bring to a city?

3. Before Hurricane Katrina, African Americans represented 60 percent of the population of New Orleans; afterward, the share was about 40 percent. What difference might this change make in the city's immediate future?

Sources: Schmitt (2001) and U.S. Census Bureau (2009).

---

tolerant than rural villagers. Rural communities often jealously enforce their narrow traditions, but the heterogeneous population of a city rarely shares any single code of moral conduct (T. C. Wilson, 1985, 1995).

○ **CRITICAL REVIEW** In both Europe and the United States, early sociologists presented a mixed view of urban living. Rapid urbanization troubled Tönnies and Wirth, who saw personal ties and traditional morality lost in the anonymous rush of the city. Durkheim and Park emphasized urbanism's positive face, pointing to more personal freedom and greater personal choice.

One problem with all of these views is that they paint urbanism in broad strokes that overlook the effects of class, race, and gender. There are many kinds of urbanites—rich and poor, black and white, Anglo and Latino, women and men—all leading distinctive lives (Gans, 1968). As the Thinking About Diversity box explains, the share of racial and ethnic minorities in the largest U.S. cities increased sharply during the 1990s. We see social diversity most clearly in cities, where various categories of

people are large enough to form visible communities (Macionis & Parrillo, 2007).

○ **CHECK YOUR LEARNING** Of these urban sociologists—Tönnies, Durkheim, Park, and Wirth—which were more positive about urban life? Which were more negative? In each case, explain why.

Urban Ecology

Sociologists (especially members of the Chicago School) developed **urban ecology**, *the study of the link between the physical and social dimensions of cities.* For example, why are cities located where they are? The first cities emerged in fertile regions where the ecology favored raising crops. Preindustrial people, concerned with defense, built their cities on mountains (ancient Athens was perched on an outcropping of rock) or surrounded by water (Paris and Mexico City were built on islands). With the Industrial Revolution, economic considerations placed all major U.S. cities near rivers and natural harbors that facilitated trade.

Go to the Multimedia Library at **mysoclab.com** to view the *Core Concepts in Sociology* video "Challenges Facing Cities"

Seeing Sociology in Everyday Life

The decline of industrial production is evident in the decline of industrial cities, such as Detroit.

Urban ecologists also study the physical design of cities. In 1925, Ernest W. Burgess, a student and colleague of Robert Park's, described land use in Chicago in terms of *concentric zones*. City centers, Burgess observed, are business districts bordered by a ring of factories, followed by residential rings with housing that becomes more expensive the farther it is from the noise and pollution of the city's center.

Homer Hoyt (1939) refined Burgess's observations, noting that distinctive districts sometimes form *wedge-shaped sectors*. For example, one fashionable area may develop next to another, or an industrial district may extend outward from a city's center along a train or trolley line.

Chauncy Harris and Edward Ullman (1945) added yet another insight: As cities decentralize, they lose their single-center form in favor of a *multicentered model*. As cities grow, residential areas, industrial parks, and shopping districts typically push away from one another. Few people want to live close to industrial areas, for example, so the city becomes a mosaic of distinct districts.

Social area analysis investigates what people in particular neighborhoods have in common. Three factors seem to explain most of the variation in neighborhood types: family patterns, social class, and race and ethnicity (Shevky & Bell, 1955; R. J. Johnston, 1976). Families with children look for areas with large apartments or single-family homes and good schools. The rich seek high-prestige neighborhoods, often in the central city near cultural attractions. People with a common race or ethnic heritage cluster in distinctive communities.

Brian Berry and Philip Rees (1969) tied together many of these insights. They explained that distinct family types tend to settle in the concentric zones described by Burgess. Specifically, households with few children tend to cluster toward the city's center, and those with more children live farther away. Social class differences are primarily responsible for the sector-shaped districts described by Hoyt; the rich occupy one "side of the tracks" and the poor the other. And racial and ethnic neighborhoods are found at various places throughout the city, consistent with Harris and Ullman's multicentered model.

Urban Political Economy

In the late 1960s, many large U.S. cities were rocked by major riots. As public awareness of racial and economic inequality increased, some analysts turned away from the ecological approach to a social-conflict understanding of city life. The *urban political-economy model* applies Karl Marx's analysis of conflict in the workplace to conflict in the city (Lindstrom, 1995). 🔵 Go to **mysoclab.com**

Political economists reject the ecological approach's view of the city as a natural organism with particular districts and neighborhoods

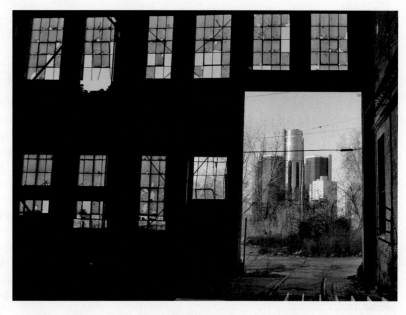

The industrial revolution created great cities across the United States. In recent decades, however, the movement of industry abroad has brought decline to Detroit and other older cities in the "rustbelt." From this abandoned warehouse, we see the headquarters of General Motors, which, in 2009, declared bankruptcy. What do you see as the future of such cities?

developing according to an internal logic. Instead, they see city life as defined by people with power: corporate leaders and political officials. Capitalism, which transforms the city into real estate traded for profit and concentrates wealth in the hands of the few, is the key to understanding city life. From this point of view, the decline in industrial Snowbelt cities after 1950 was the result of deliberate decisions by the corporate elite to move their production facilities to the Sunbelt (where labor is cheaper and less likely to be unionized) or move them out of the country entirely to low-income nations (Molotch, 1976; Castells, 1977, 1983; Lefebvre, 1991; Jones & Wilson, 1999).

CRITICAL REVIEW The fact that many U.S. cities are in crisis, with widespread poverty, high crime, and barely functioning schools, seems to favor the political-economy view over the urban ecology approach. But one criticism applies to both: They focus on U.S. cities during a limited period of history. Much of what we know about industrial cities does not apply to preindustrial towns in our own past or the rapidly growing cities in many poor nations today. It is unlikely that any single model of cities can account for the full range of urban diversity.

CHECK YOUR LEARNING In your own words, explain what the urban ecology theories and the urban political-economy theory teach us about cities.

ecology the study of the interaction of living organisms and the natural environment

natural environment Earth's surface and atmosphere, including living organisms, air, water, soil, and other resources necessary to sustain life

ecosystem a system composed of the interaction of all living organisms and their natural environment

environmental deficit profound long-term harm to the natural environment caused by humanity's focus on short-term material affluence

○ Making the Grade

Be sure you understand when and where the three urban revolutions occurred.

Urbanization in Poor Nations

> **November 16, Cairo, Egypt.** People call the vast Muslim cemetery in Old Cairo the "City of the Dead." In truth, it is very much alive: Tens of thousands of squatters have moved into the mausoleums, making this place an eerie mix of life and death. Children run across the stone floors, clotheslines stretch between the monuments, and an occasional television antenna protrudes from a tomb roof. With Cairo gaining 1,000 people a day, families live where they can.

Twice in its history, the world has experienced a revolutionary expansion of cities. The first urban revolution began about 8000 B.C.E. with the first urban settlements and continued until permanent settlements were in place on several continents. About 1750, the second urban revolution took off; it lasted for two centuries as the Industrial Revolution spurred rapid growth of cities in Europe and North America.

A third urban revolution is now under way. Today, 75 percent of people in high-income countries are already city dwellers. But extraordinary urban growth is occurring in low-income nations. In 1950, about 25 percent of the people in poor countries lived in cities. In 2008, the world became mostly urban for the first time in history, with more than half of humanity living in cities (Population Reference Bureau, 2009).

Not only are more people urban, but cities are also getting bigger. In 1950, only seven cities in the world had populations over 5 million, and only two of these were in low-income countries. By 2007, forty-nine cities had passed this mark, and two-thirds of them were in less developed nations (Brockerhoff, 2000; United Nations, 2008).

This third urban revolution is the result of many poor nations entering the high-growth Stage 2 of demographic transition theory. Falling death rates have fueled population increases in Latin America, Asia, and especially Africa. For urban areas, the rate of increase is *twice as high* because in addition to natural increase, millions of people leave the countryside each year in search of jobs, health care, education, and conveniences such as running water and electricity. As cities grow, so do suburbs.

Cities do offer more opportunities than rural areas, but they provide no quick fix for the problems of escalating population and grinding poverty. Many cities in less developed nations—including Mexico City, Egypt's Cairo, India's Kolkata (formerly Calcutta), and Manila in the Philippines—are simply unable to meet the basic needs of much of their population. All these cities are surrounded by wretched shantytowns, settlements of makeshift homes built from discarded materials. As noted in Chapter 9 ("Global Stratification"), even city dumps are home to thousands of poor people, who pick through the waste hoping to find enough to eat or sell to make it through another day.

Environment and Society

The human species has prospered, rapidly expanding over the entire planet. An increasing share of the global population now lives in large, complex settlements that offer the promise of a better life than that found in rural villages.

But these advances have come at a high price. Never before in history have human beings placed such demands on the planet. This disturbing development brings us to focus on the interplay of the natural environment and society. Like demography, **ecology** is another cousin of sociology, formally defined as *the study of the interaction of living organisms and the natural environment.* Ecology rests on the research of natural scientists as well as social scientists. We shall focus on the aspects of ecology that involve familiar sociological concepts and issues.

The **natural environment** is *Earth's surface and atmosphere, including living organisms, air, water, soil, and other resources necessary to sustain life.* Like every other species, humans depend on the natural environment to survive. Yet with our capacity for culture, humans stand apart from other species; we alone take deliberate action to remake the world according to our own interests and desires, for better and for worse.

Why is the environment of interest to sociologists? Environmental problems, from pollution to global warming, do not arise from the natural world operating on its own. Such problems result from the choices and actions of human beings, making them *social* problems.

The Global Dimension

The study of the natural environment requires a global perspective. The reason is simple: Regardless of political divisions between nations, the planet is a single **ecosystem,** which encompasses *the interaction of all living organisms and their natural environment.*

The Greek meaning of *eco* is "house," reminding us that this planet is our home and that all living things and their natural environment are interrelated. A change in any part of the natural environment sends ripples through the entire global ecosystem.

Consider, from an ecological point of view, our national love of eating hamburgers. People in North America (and, increasingly, around the world) have created a huge demand for beef, which has greatly expanded ranching in Brazil, Costa Rica, and other Latin American nations. To produce the lean meat sought by fast-food corporations, cattle in Latin America feed on grass, which uses a great deal of land. Latin American ranchers clear the land for grazing by cutting down thousands of square miles of forests each year. These

○ Making the Grade

I = PAT is an important environmental idea; be sure you understand its meaning.

○ Seeing Sociology in Everyday Life

Can you identify ways in which the mass media and our popular culture (music, films, and television) encourage people to support the logic of growth?

tropical forests are vital to maintaining Earth's atmosphere. Deforestation ends up threatening everyone, including the people back in the United States enjoying their hamburgers (N. Myers, 1984a).

Technology and the Environmental Deficit

Sociologists point to a simple formula: $I = PAT$, where environmental impact (I) reflects a society's population (P), its level of affluence (A), and its level of technology (T). Members of simpler societies—the hunters and gatherers described in Chapter 2 ("Culture")—hardly affect the environment because they are few in number, are poor, and have only simple technology. Nature affects all aspects of their lives as they follow the migration of game, watch the rhythm of the seasons, and suffer from natural catastrophes, such as fires, floods, droughts, and storms.

Societies at intermediate stages of sociocultural evolution have a somewhat greater capacity to affect the environment. But the environmental impact of horticulture (small-scale farming), pastoralism (the herding of animals), and even agriculture (the use of animal-drawn plows) is limited because people still rely on muscle power for producing food and other goods.

Human control of the natural environment increased dramatically with the changes brought about by the Industrial Revolution. Muscle power gave way to engines that burn fossil fuels: coal at first and then oil. The use of such machinery affects the environment in two ways: It consumes more natural resources and releases more pollutants into the atmosphere. Even more important, humans armed with industrial technology are able to bend nature to their will, tunneling through mountains, damming rivers, irrigating deserts, and drilling for oil in the arctic wilderness and on the ocean floor. This explains why people in rich nations, who represent just 23 percent of humanity, account for half of the world's energy use (World Bank, 2009).

Not only do industrial societies use more energy, but they produce 100 times more goods than agrarian societies do. Higher living standards are good in some ways, but they increase the problems of solid waste (because people ultimately throw away most of what they produce) and pollution (industrial production generates smoke and other toxic substances).

From the start, people recognized the material benefits of industrial technology. But only a century later did they begin to see its long-term effects on the natural environment. Today, we realize that the technological power to make our lives better can also put the lives of future generations at risk, and there is a national debate about how to address this issue. Seeing Sociology in the News on pages 464–65 describes one high school's efforts to address environmental issues.

Evidence is mounting that we are running up an **environmental deficit,** *profound long-term harm to the natural environment caused by*

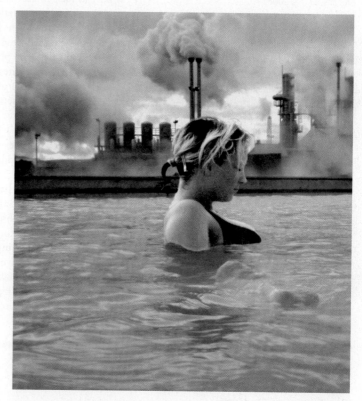

The most important insight sociology offers about our physical world is that environmental problems do not simply "happen." Rather, the state of the natural environment reflects the ways in which social life is organized—how people live and what they think is important. The greater the technological power of a society, the greater that society's ability to threaten the natural environment.

humanity's focus on short-term material affluence (Bormann, 1990). The concept of environmental deficit is important for three reasons. First, it reminds us that environmental concerns are *sociological*, reflecting societies' priorities about how people should live. Second, it suggests that much environmental damage—to the air, land, and water—is *unintended*. By focusing on the short-term benefits of, say, cutting down forests, strip mining, or using throwaway packaging, we fail to see the long-term environmental effects. Third, in some respects, the environmental deficit is *reversible*. Inasmuch as societies have created environmental problems, societies can undo many of them.

Culture: Growth and Limits

Whether we recognize environmental dangers and decide to do something about them is a cultural matter. Thus along with technology, culture has powerful environmental consequences.

Rolling Stone

Boyz Under the Hood

BY DAVID KUSHNER
December 18, 2008

Even among the roughest schools in the country, West Philadelphia High School stands out. Situated among boarded-up abandoned buildings and graffiti-covered crack houses, the school has had dozens of arson fires. A Spanish teacher was beaten bloody with a fire extinguisher. A music instructor got a broken jaw after being slugged by a pupil for trying to take away a cell phone. One 15-year-old girl was left for dead after having her face slashed while waiting for her school bus. She survived, but needed 114 stitches.

But in the automotive shop class in a garage next door, a group of African American students and their scrappy white teacher are making their school famous for something else: building the world's greenest car. Kids in baggy jeans and sideways hats mill around a sleek purple car they built that runs on biodiesel. Sparks fly from a chainsaw as one boy cuts through an aluminum plate, his long afro held back by the strap of his scuffed goggles.

Behind a windowed wall, half a dozen girls are busy at their iMacs. Samantha Wright . . . boots up a solar charging station she designed using an image of a rundown Philadelphia parking lot from Google Earth, and augmented it with green roofs and cars. "The photoactive panels convert the sunlight into direct energy," she explains, pointing to a carport onscreen. "We're changing the world, man. I never expected to be doing that."

Like the other kids in the shop, Wright, the daughter of a phone sex worker and absentee dad, overcame incredible odds to find a haven here at the Electric Vehicle X Club, an after-school program that has been turning these cars and kids around, and that's not all. While Washington and Detroit hit the skids on delivering alternative fuel cars for the masses, these inner-city teens are churning out some of the most badass and competitive eco-wheels on the planet for as little as $15,000. As the blog Treehugger puts it, they're "sending a message to the major U.S. auto manufacturers: if we can do it, why can't you?"

In addition to clocking their suburban opponents at state science fairs, the EVX Club has crushed colleges and high-financed corporate start-ups with back-to-back titles in the coveted Northeast Sustainable Energy Association's Tour De Sol, a prestigious eco-car challenge. They modified a Saturn to run on soybean fuel, and transformed a Slovakian kit car into a wildly sporty hybrid called the Hybrid X. "Hybrids don't have to be slow and ugly like a Prius," says 18-year-old EV member, Lawrence Jones-Mahoney. "They can be efficient and cool."

Now the team is racing to prove their cars—and themselves—to the world. They're the dark horse entrants in the Progressive Automotive X-Prize: a worldwide contest to build a car, suitable for mass production, that gets 100 miles per gallon. The contest runs through summer 2010, and the winner gets $10 million. . . .

Simon Hauger, the 38-year-old neighborhood hero who runs the West Philly High auto school, is working overtime with his students to win. But the checkered flag is theirs. "The fact that

The Logic of Growth

When you turn on the television news, you might hear a story like this: "The government reported bad economic news today, with the economy growing by only half a percent during the first quarter of the year." If you stop to think about it, our culture defines an economy that isn't growing as "stagnant" (which is bad) and an economy that is getting smaller as a recession or a "depression" (which is *very* bad). What is "good" is *growth*—the economy getting bigger and bigger. More cars, bigger homes, more income, more spending—the idea of *more* is at the heart of our cultural definition of living well (McKibben, 2007).

One of the reasons we define growth in positive terms is that we value *material comfort,* believing that money and the things it buys improve our lives. We also believe in the idea of *progress,* thinking that the future will be better than the present. In addition, we look to *science* to make our lives easier and more rewarding. In simpler terms, "having things is good," "life gets better," and "people are clever." Taken together, such cultural values form the *logic of growth.*

An optimistic view of the world, the logic of growth holds that more powerful technology has improved our lives and that new discoveries will continue to do so in the future. Throughout the history of the United States and other high-income nations, the logic of growth has been the driving force behind settling the wilderness, building towns and roads, and pursuing material affluence.

However, "progress" can lead to unexpected problems, including strain on the environment. The logic of growth responds by arguing that people (especially scientists and other technology experts) will find a way out of any problem placed in our path. If, for example, the world runs short of oil, scientists will come up with hydrogen, solar, or nuclear engines or some as yet unknown technology to meet the world's energy needs.

Environmentalists counter that the logic of growth is flawed because it assumes that natural resources such as clean air, fresh water, and fertile soil will always be plentiful. We can and will exhaust these *finite* resources if we continue to pursue growth at any cost. Echoing Malthus, environmentalists warn that if we call on the planet to support increasing numbers of people, we will surely destroy the environment—and ourselves—in the process.

The Limits to Growth

If we cannot invent our way out of the problems created by the logic of growth, perhaps we need another way of thinking about the world. Environmentalists therefore counter that growth must have limits. Stated simply, the *limits-to-growth thesis* is that humanity must put in place policies to control the growth of population, production, and the use of resources in order to avoid environmental collapse.

we've come this far," Hauger says, looking around the room, "we've already won." . . .

When a go-kart was donated to the school, Hauger decided to start an after-school science group that would work on building an electric motor for the kart. He called it the Electric Vehicle Club. One by one, kids trickled in after school—gang members, drug dealers. One kid had a 150 IQ, but a mom on crack and a dad dying of AIDS. The kid was bouncing between foster homes and stealing credit cards on the side. But when Hauger slapped a wrench in the kid's hand, he was transformed. "When he would work on a project, he would block out all the crap in his life," Hauger recalls, "and he became a mad scientist. Working on this made all the math and science hands on." . . .

As word of Hauger's club spread, kids got turned on not only by getting under the hood, but by making cars that can better the planet—and busting labels along the way. "There's a stereotype that urban kids are just violent and don't care about anything," says Wright, "but we know the environment is important, and we can do something about it."

For the EV club's next project, they modified a silver Jeep Wrangler to go electric. Clueless how to proceed, they hit the Net—downloading instructions from an obscure eco-geek magazine called *Mother Earth*. With Hauger guiding them and improvising plenty, they ripped out the gas engine and stored 217 lead acid batteries in a custom aluminum casing. When they drove their electric hot rod Jeep into the city's science fair of microscopes and Bunsen burners, jaws dropped. "The judges didn't know what to do with it," Hauger recalls. Then they gave West Philly High the top prize. . . .

As the current 15 kids on the EVX team mill around the garage, talk turns to the plans for the Auto X prize. "As crazy as it sounds, I think we have a shot at winning," Hauger says. While the competition is focusing on high-priced cars that look like the Jetsons, the EVX team is taking a decidedly more accessible—and they hope—winning approach. . . .

. . . The EVX team's legacy is already spreading among those in the eco-car pursuit. "It's inspiring that a contest can inspire a group like that to

compete," says Darryl Siry, spokesperson for Tesla, "it says something about who they are. I recommend they not listen to people who tell them this is how it's done. Innovation comes from figuring out solutions and answers to problems in new ways."

WHAT DO YOU THINK?

1. Do you think that many people think of environmental issues as the concerns mainly of more well-off people? Explain.

2. Would you make environmental study part of the curriculum of every school in the country? Why or why not?

3. What specific strategies or policies would you suggest to encourage greater environmental understanding on the part of this country's young people?

Adapted from the original article, "Boyz Under the Hood" by David Kushner, from RolllingStone.com, December 18, 2008, copyright ©2008 Rolling Stone LLC. All rights reserved. Reprinted by permission.

In *The Limits to Growth,* a controversial book that played a large part in launching the environmental movement, Donella Meadows and her colleagues (1972) used a computer model to calculate the planet's available resources, rates of population growth, amount of land available for cultivation, levels of industrial and food production, and amount of pollutants released into the atmosphere. The model reflects changes that have occurred since 1900 and projects forward to the end of the twenty-first century. The authors concede that such long-range predictions are speculative, and some critics think they are plain wrong (Simon, 1981).

But right or wrong, the conclusions of the study call for serious consideration. The authors claim that we are quickly consuming Earth's finite resources. Supplies of oil, natural gas, and other energy sources are declining and will continue to drop, a little faster or more slowly depending on the conservation policies of rich nations and the speed with which other nations such as India and China continue to industrialize. Within the next 100 years, resources will run out, crippling industrial output and causing a decline in food production.

This limits-to-growth theory shares Malthus's pessimism about the future. People who accept it doubt that current patterns of life are sustainable for even another century. Perhaps we can all learn to live with less. This may not be as hard as you might think: Research shows, for example, that as material consumption has gone up in

recent decades, there has been no increase in levels of personal happiness (D. G. Myers, 2000). In the end, environmentalists warn, either make fundamental changes in how we live, placing less strain on the natural environment, or widespread hunger and conflict will force change on us.

Solid Waste: The Disposable Society

Across the United States, people generate a massive amount of solid waste—about 1.4 billion pounds *each and every day.* Figure 15–4 on page 466 shows the composition of a typical community's trash.

As a rich nation of people who value convenience, the United States has become a *disposable society.* We consume more products than virtually any other nation, and many of these products have throwaway packaging. For example, fast food is served in cardboard, plastic, and Styrofoam containers that we throw away within minutes. But countless other products, from film to fishhooks, are elaborately packaged to make them more attractive to the customer and to discourage tampering and theft.

Manufacturers market soft drinks, beer, and fruit juices in aluminum cans, glass jars, and plastic containers, which not only use up finite resources but also create mountains of solid waste. Countless items are intentionally designed to be disposable: pens, razors, flashlights, batteries, even cameras. Other goods, from lightbulbs to

● Seeing Sociology
in Everyday Life

Do you think that having more, in a materialistic sense, is the
path to personal happiness? Why or why not?

● Seeing Sociology
in Everyday Life

Think about how specific ways we live put more or less strain
on the natural environment.

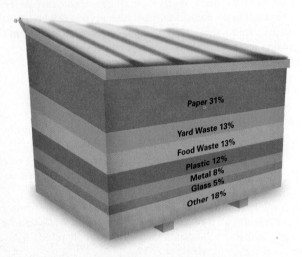

FIGURE 15–4   Composition of Community Trash

We throw away a wide range of material, with paper the single largest
part of our trash.

Source: U.S. Environmental Protection Agency (2009).

automobiles, are designed to have a limited useful life, after which
they become unwanted junk. As Paul Connett (1991) points out,
even the words we use to describe what we throw away—*waste, trash,
refuse, garbage, rubbish*—show how little we value what we cannot
immediately use. But this was not always the case, as the Seeing Sociology in Everyday Life box explains.

Living in a rich society, the average person in the United States
consumes hundreds of times more energy, plastics, lumber, and other
resources than someone living in a low-income nation such as
Bangladesh or Tanzania (and nearly twice as much as someone living in many other high-income countries such as Japan or Sweden).
This high level of consumption means that we in the United States
not only use a disproportionate share of the planet's natural resources
but also that we generate most of the world's refuse.

We like to say that we throw things "away." But more than half
of our solid waste never goes away. It ends up in landfills, which are,
literally, filling up. Material in landfills can also pollute groundwater
stored under Earth's surface. Although in most places laws now regulate what can be discarded in a landfill, the Environmental Protection Agency has identified 1,269 dump sites across the United States
containing hazardous materials that are polluting water both above
and below the ground. In addition, what goes into landfills all too
often stays there, sometimes for centuries. Tens of millions of tires,
disposable diapers, and other items that we bury in landfills each
year do not decompose and will be an unwelcome legacy for future
generations.

Environmentalists argue that we should address the problem of
solid waste by doing what many of our grandparents did: turn
"waste" into a resource. One way to do this is through *recycling*,
reusing resources we would otherwise throw away. Recycling is an
accepted practice in Japan and many other nations, and it is becoming more common in the United States, where we now reuse about
33 percent of waste materials. The share is increasing as more munic-
ipalities pass laws requiring reuse of certain materials such as glass
bottles and aluminum cans and as the business of recycling becomes
more profitable.

Water and Air

Oceans, lakes, and streams are the lifeblood of the global ecosystem.
Humans depend on water for drinking, bathing, cooling, cooking,
recreation, and a host of other activities.

According to what scientists call the *hydrologic cycle*, the planet
naturally recycles water and refreshes the land. The process begins as
heat from the sun causes Earth's water, 97 percent of which is in the
oceans, to evaporate and form clouds. Because water evaporates at
lower temperatures than most pollutants, the water vapor that rises
from the seas is relatively pure, leaving various contaminants behind.
Water then falls to the Earth as rain, which drains into streams and
rivers and finally returns to the sea. Two major concerns about water,
then, are supply and pollution.

Water Supply

Less than one-tenth of 1 percent of Earth's water is suitable for drinking. It is not surprising, then, that for thousands of years, water rights
have figured prominently in laws around the world. Today, some
regions of the world, especially the tropics, enjoy plentiful fresh water,
using only a small share of the available supply. High demand, coupled with modest reserves, makes water supply a matter of concern in
much of North America and Asia, where people look to rivers rather
than rainfall for their water. In China, deep aquifers are dropping rapidly. In the Middle East, water supply is reaching a critical level. Iran
is rationing water in its capital city. In Egypt, people can consume
just one-sixth as much water from the Nile River today as in 1900.
Across northern Africa and the Middle East, as many as 1 billion people may lack the water they need for irrigation and drinking by 2025
("China Faces Water Shortage," 2001; International Development
Research Center, 2006).

Rising population and the development of more complex technology have greatly increased the world's appetite for water. The
global consumption of water (now estimated at almost 4,000 cubic
kilometers, or 140 trillion cubic feet, per year) has doubled since
1950 and is rising steadily. As a result, even in parts of the world that
receive plenty of rainfall, people are using groundwater faster than

SEEING SOCIOLOGY IN EVERYDAY LIFE

Why Grandma Macionis Had No Trash

Grandma Macionis, we always used to say, never threw away anything. She was born and raised in Lithuania—the "old country"—where growing up in a poor village shaped her in ways that never changed, even after she came to the United States as a young woman and settled in Philadelphia.

In her later years, when I knew her, I remember the family traveling together to her house to celebrate her birthday. We never knew what to get Grandma because although she didn't have all that much, she never seemed to need anything. She lived a simple life and had simple clothes and showed little interest in "fancy things." She used everything until it wore out. Her kitchen knives, for example, were worn narrow from decades of sharpening. And she hardly ever threw anything away—she recycled all her garbage as compost for her vegetable garden.

After opening a birthday present, she would carefully save the box, wrapping paper, and ribbon, which meant as much to her as whatever gift they surrounded. We all expected her to save every bit of whatever she was given, smiling to each other as we watched

her put everything away, knowing she would find a way to use it all again and again.

As strange as Grandma sometimes seemed to her grandchildren, she was a product of her culture. A century ago, there was little "trash." If a pair of socks wore thin, people mended them, probably more than once. When they were beyond repair, they were used as rags for clean-

Grandma Macionis, in the 1970s, with the author.

ing or sewn, along with other old clothing, into a quilt. For her, everything had value, if not in one way, then in another.

During the twentieth century, as women joined men working outside of the home, income went up and families began buying more and more "time-saving" products. Before long, few people cared about the home recycling that Grandma practiced. Soon cities sent crews from block to block to pick up truckloads of discarded material. The era of "trash" had begun.

WHAT DO YOU THINK?

1. Just as Grandma Macionis was a product of her culture, so are we. What cultural values make people today demand time-saving products and "convenience" packaging?

2. Do you recycle drink containers, paper, or other materials? Why or why not?

3. In what ways does this box demonstrate that the state of the natural environment is a social issue?

it can be replenished naturally. In the Tamil Nadu region of southern India, for example, people are drawing so much groundwater that the local water table has fallen 100 feet over the past several decades. Mexico City—which has sprawled to some 1,400 square miles—has pumped so much water from its underground aquifer that the city has sunk 30 feet in the past century and continues to drop about 2 inches per year. Farther north in the United States, the Ogallala aquifer, which lies below seven states from South Dakota to Texas, is now being pumped so rapidly that some experts fear it could run dry in just a few decades.

In light of such developments, we must face the reality that water is a valuable and finite resource. Greater conservation of water by individuals (the average person in the United States consumes 3 million gallons in a lifetime) is part of the answer. However, households around the world account for just 10 percent of water use. We need to reduce water consumption by industry, which uses 20 percent of the global total, and farming, which consumes 70 percent of the total for irrigation.

Perhaps new irrigation technology will reduce demand for water in the future. But here again, we see how population increase, as well as economic growth, strains our ecosystem (Postel, 1993; Population Action International, 2000; United Nations World Water Assessment Programme, 2009; U.S. Geological Survey, 2009).

Water Pollution

In large cities from Mexico City to Cairo to Shanghai, many people have no choice but to drink contaminated water. Infectious diseases such as typhoid, cholera, and dysentery, all caused by waterborne microorganisms, spread rapidly through these populations. In addition to ensuring ample *supplies* of water, we must protect the *quality* of water.

Water quality in the United States is generally good by global standards. However, even here the problem of water pollution is steadily growing. Across the United States, rivers and streams absorb hundreds of millions of pounds of toxic waste each year. This pollution

● Seeing Sociology
in Everyday Life

Have you experienced changes in your own world resulting
from global warming or other issues discussed here?

rain forests regions of dense forestation, most of which circle the globe close to the equator

global warming a rise in Earth's average temperature due to an increasing concentration of carbon dioxide in the atmosphere

environmental racism patterns of development that expose poor people, especially minorities, to environmental hazards

results not just from intentional dumping but also from the runoff of agricultural fertilizers and lawn chemicals.

A special problem is *acid rain*—rain made acidic by air pollution—which destroys plant and animal life. Acid rain (or snow) begins with power plants burning fossil fuels (oil and coal) to generate electricity; this burning process releases sulfuric and nitrous oxides into the air. As the wind sweeps these gases into the atmosphere, they react with the air to form sulfuric and nitric acids, which turns atmospheric moisture acidic.

This is a clear case of one type of pollution causing another: Air pollution (from smokestacks) ends up contaminating water (in lakes and streams that collect acid rain). Acid rain is truly a global phenomenon because the regions that suffer the harmful effects may be thousands of miles from the source of the pollution. For instance, British power plants have caused acid rain that has devastated forests and fish in Norway and Sweden, 1,000 miles to the northeast. In the United States, we see a similar pattern as midwestern smokestacks have harmed the natural environment of upstate New York and New England.

Air Pollution

Because we are surrounded by air, most people in the United States are more aware of air pollution than contaminated water. One of the unexpected consequences of industrial technology—especially the factory and the motor vehicle—has been a decline in air quality. In London, fifty years ago, factory smokestacks, automobiles, and coal fires used to heat households all added up to what was probably the worst urban air quality in the world. The fog that some residents jokingly called "pea soup" was in reality a deadly mix of pollutants: In 1952, an especially thick haze that hung over London for five days killed 4,000 people.

Air quality improved in the final decades of the twentieth century. Rich nations passed laws that banned high-pollution heating, including the coal fires that choked London. In addition, scientists devised ways to make factories and motor vehicles operate much more cleanly. The cleanest of today's automobiles emit only a small percentage of the pollutants released by the typical car in 1960.

If people in high-income countries can breathe a bit more easily than they once did, those living in poor societies face problems of air pollution that are becoming more serious. One reason is that people in low-income countries still rely on wood, coal, peat, or other "dirty" fuels to cook their food and heat their homes. In addition, nations eager to encourage short-term industrial development may pay little attention to the longer-term dangers of air pollution. As a result, many cities in Latin America, Eastern Europe, and Asia are plagued by air pollution as bad as London's pea soup back in the 1950s.

The Rain Forests

Rain forests are *regions of dense forestation, most of which circle the globe close to the equator.* The largest tropical rain forests are in South America (notably Brazil), west-central Africa, and Southeast Asia. In all, the world's rain forests cover some 1.5 billion acres, or 4.5 percent of Earth's total land surface (United Nations Environment Programme, 2009).

Like other global resources, rain forests are falling victim to the needs and appetites of the surging world population. As noted earlier, to meet the demand for beef, ranchers in Latin America clear forested areas to increase their supply of grazing land. We are also losing rain forests to the hardwood trade. People in rich nations pay high prices for mahogany and other woods because, as the environmentalist Norman Myers (1984b:88) puts it, they have "a penchant for parquet floors, fine furniture, fancy paneling, weekend yachts, and high-grade coffins." Under such economic pressure, the world's rain forests are now less than half their original size, and they continue to shrink by at least 1 percent (58,000 square miles) annually, which amounts to about one acre every second. Unless we stop this loss, the rain forests will vanish before the end of this century, and with them will go protection for Earth's biodiversity and climate.

Global Warming

Why are rain forests so important to our natural environment? One reason is that they cleanse the atmosphere of carbon dioxide (CO_2). Since the beginning of the Industrial Revolution, the amount of carbon dioxide produced by humans (mostly from factories and automobiles) has risen sharply. Much of this CO_2 is absorbed by the oceans. But plants also take in carbon dioxide and in the process expel oxygen. This is why the rain forests—our largest concentration of plant life—are vital to maintaining the chemical balance of the atmosphere.

The problem is that production of carbon dioxide is rising while the amount of plant life on Earth is shrinking. To make matters worse, rain forests are being destroyed mostly by burning, which releases even more CO_2 into the atmosphere. Experts estimate that the atmospheric concentration of carbon dioxide is now 40 percent higher than it was 150 years ago (Gore, 2006; United Nations Environment Programme, 2009; National Oceanic and Atmospheric Administration, 2010).

High above Earth, carbon dioxide acts like the glass roof of a greenhouse, letting heat from the sun pass through to the surface while preventing much of it from radiating away from the planet. The result of this *greenhouse effect,* say ecologists, is **global warming,** *a rise in Earth's average temperature due to an increasing concentration of carbon dioxide in the atmosphere.* Over the past century, the global temperature has risen about 1.3° Fahrenheit (to

Go to the Multimedia Library at **mysoclab.com** to listen to the NPR report "Sources of Global Warming"

Seeing Sociology in Everyday Life

Do you worry much about global warming? Why or why not?
Do you think global warming could affect you personally? How?

an average of 58° F.). Scientists warn that it could rise by 5° to 10° F. during this century. Already, the polar ice caps are melting, and scientists predict that increasing temperatures could melt so much ice that the sea level would rise to cover low-lying land all around the world. Were this to happen, water would cover all of Bangladesh, for example, and much of the coastal United States, including Washington, D.C., right up to the steps of the White House. On the other hand, the U.S. Midwest, currently one of the most productive agricultural regions in the world, probably would become arid.

Some scientists point out that we cannot be sure of the consequences of global warming. Others point to the fact that global temperature changes have been taking place throughout history, perhaps having little or nothing to do with rain forests. A few are optimistic, suggesting that higher concentrations of carbon dioxide in the atmosphere might speed up plant growth (because plants thrive on this gas), and this increase might correct the imbalance and nudge Earth's temperature downward once again. But the consensus of scientists is clear: Global warming is a serious problem that threatens the future for all of us (Kerr, 2005; Gore, 2006; International Panel on Climate Change, 2007; National Oceanic and Atmospheric Administration, 2010). ● Go to **mysoclab.com**

Water is vital to life, and it is also in short supply. The state of Gujarat, in western India, has experienced a long drought. In the village of Natwarghad, people crowd together, lowering pots into the local well, taking what little water is left.

Declining Biodiversity

Our planet is home to as many as 30 million species of animals, plants, and microorganisms. As rain forests are cleared and humans extend their control over nature, several dozen unique species of plants and animals cease to exist each day.

But given the vast number of living species, why should we be concerned about the loss of a few? Environmentalists give four reasons. First, our planet's biodiversity provides a varied source of human food. Using agricultural high technology, scientists can cross familiar crops with more exotic plant life, making food more bountiful and more resistant to insects and disease. Thus biodiversity helps feed our planet's rapidly increasing population.

Second, Earth's biodiversity is a vital genetic resource used by medical and pharmaceutical researchers to provide hundreds of new compounds each year that cure disease and improve our lives. For example, children in the United States now have a good chance of surviving leukemia, a disease that was almost a sure killer two generations ago, because of a compound derived from a tropical flower called the rosy periwinkle. The oral birth control pill, used by tens of millions of women in this country, is another product of plant research, this one involving the Mexican forest yam.

Third, with the loss of any species of life—whether it is the magnificent California condor, the famed Chinese panda, the spotted owl, or even a single species of ant—the beauty and complexity of our natural environment are diminished. And there are clear warning signs: Three-fourths of the world's 10,000 species of birds are declining in number.

Finally, unlike pollution, the extinction of any species is irreversible and final. An important ethical question, then, is whether people living today have the right to impoverish the world for those who will live tomorrow (N. Myers, 1991; E. O. Wilson, 1991; Brown et al., 1993).

Environmental Racism

Environmental problems threaten us all. But most environmental issues harm some people more than others. Conflict theory has given birth to the concept of **environmental racism,** *patterns of development that expose poor people, especially minorities, to environmental hazards.* Historically, factories that spew pollution have stood near neighborhoods housing the poor and people of color. Why? In part, the poor themselves were drawn to factories in search of work, and their low incomes often meant they could afford housing only in undesirable neighborhoods. Sometimes the only housing that fit their budgets stood in the very shadow of the plants and mills where they worked.

○ Making the Grade

With its focus on inequality, environmental racism is linked to the social-conflict approach.

ecologically sustainable culture a way of life that meets the needs of the present generation without threatening the environmental legacy of future generations

Nobody wants a factory or dump nearby, but the poor have little power to resist. Through the years, the most serious environmental hazards have been located near Newark, New Jersey (not in upscale Bergen County), in southside Chicago (not in wealthy Lake Forest), or on Native American reservations in the West (not in affluent suburbs of Denver or Phoenix) (Commission for Racial Justice, 1994; Bohon & Humphrey, 2000).

Looking Ahead: Toward a Sustainable Society and World

The demographic analysis presented in this chapter points to some disturbing trends. We see, first, that our planet's population has reached record levels because birth rates remain high in poor nations and death rates have fallen just about everywhere. Reducing fertility will remain a pressing issue throughout this century. Even with some recent decline in the rate of population increase, the nightmare of Thomas Malthus is still a real possibility, as the Controversy & Debate box explains.

Further, population growth remains greatest in the poorest countries of the world, which cannot support their present populations, much less their future ones. Supporting 83 million additional people on our planet each year, 81 million of whom are in poor societies, will take a global commitment to provide not only food but also housing, schools, and employment. The well-being of the entire world may ultimately depend on resolving the economic and social problems of poor, overpopulated countries and bridging the widening gulf between "have" and "have-not" nations.

Urbanization is continuing, especially in poor countries. People have always sought out cities in the hope of finding a better life. But the sheer numbers of people who live in the emerging global supercities, including Mexico City, São Paulo (Brazil), Kinshasa (Democratic Republic of the Congo), Mumbai (India), and Manila (Philippines), have created urban problems on a massive scale.

Throughout the world, humanity is facing a serious environmental challenge. Part of this problem is population increase, which is greatest in poor societies. But part of the problem is the high levels of consumption in rich nations such as our own. By increasing the planet's environmental deficit, our present way of life is borrowing against the well-being of our children and their children. Globally, members of rich societies, who currently consume so much of Earth's resources, are mortgaging the future security of the poor countries of the world.

The answer, in principle, is to create an **ecologically sustainable culture,** *a way of life that meets the needs of the present generation without threatening the environmental legacy of future generations.* Sustainable living depends on three strategies.

First, we need to *bring population growth under control.* The current population of 6.8 billion is already straining the natural environment. Clearly, the higher world population climbs, the more difficult environmental problems will become. Even if the recent slowing of population growth continues, the world will have 9 billion people by 2050. Few analysts think that Earth can support this many people; most argue that we must hold the line at about 7 billion, and some argue that we must *decrease* population in the coming decades (Smail, 2010).

A second strategy is to *conserve finite resources.* This means meeting our needs with a responsible eye toward the future by using resources efficiently, seeking alternative sources of energy, and in some cases, learning to live with less.

A third strategy is to *reduce waste.* Whenever possible, simply using less is the best solution. Learning to live with less will not come easily, but keep in mind that as our society has consumed more and more in recent decades, people have not become any happier (D. G. Myers, 2000). Recycling programs, too, are part of the answer, and recycling can make everyone part of the solution to our environmental problems.

If human ingenuity created the threats to our environment we now face, can humans also solve these problems? In recent years, a number of designs for small, environmentally friendly cars show the promise of new technology. But do such innovations go far enough? Will we have to make more basic changes to our way of life to ensure human survival in the centuries to come?

CONTROVERSY & DEBATE

Apocalypse: Will People Overwhelm the Planet?

NUSHAWN: I'm telling you, there are too many people already! Where is everyone going to live?

TABITHA: Have you ever been to Kansas? Or Wyoming? There's plenty of empty space out there.

MARCO: Maybe now. But I'm not so sure there'll be all that room for our children—or their children. . . .

Are you worried about the world's rapidly increasing population? Think about this: By the time you finish reading this box, more than 1,000 people will have been added to our planet. By this time tomorrow, global population will have risen by more than 200,000. Currently, as the table shows, there are four births for every two deaths on the planet, pushing the world's population upward by almost 83 million people annually. Put another way, global population growth amounts to adding another Germany to the world each year.

It is no wonder that many demographers and environmentalists are deeply concerned about the future. Earth has an unprecedented population: The 2.8 billion people we have added since 1974 alone exceed the planet's total in 1900. Might Thomas Malthus—who predicted that overpopulation would push the world into war and suffering—be right after all? Lester Brown and other *neo-Malthusians* predict a coming apocalypse if we do not change our ways. Brown (1995) admits that Malthus failed to imagine how much technology (especially fertilizers and plant genetics) could boost the planet's agricultural output. But he maintains that Earth's rising population is rapidly outstripping its finite resources. Families in many poor countries can find little firewood, members of rich countries are depleting the oil reserves, and everyone is draining our supply of clean water and poisoning the planet with waste. Some ana-

lysts argue that we have already passed Earth's "carrying capacity" for population and that we need to hold the line or even reduce global population to ensure our long-term survival.

But other analysts, the *anti-Malthusians,* sharply disagree. Julian Simon (1995) points out that two centuries after Malthus predicted catastrophe, Earth supports almost six times as many people who, on average, live longer, healthier lives than ever before. With more advanced technology, people have devised ways to increase productivity and limit population increase. As Simon sees it, this is cause for celebration. Human ingenuity has consistently proved the doomsayers wrong, and Simon is betting that it will continue to do so.

WHAT DO YOU THINK?

1. Where do you place your bet? Do you think Earth can support 8 or 10 billion people? Explain your reasoning.

2. Almost all current population growth is in poor countries. What does this mean for the future of rich nations? For the future of poor ones?

3. What should people in rich countries do to ensure the future of children everywhere?

Sources: Brown (1995), Simon (1995), Scanlon (2001), and Smail (2007).

Global Population Increase, 2009

	Births	Deaths	Net Increase
Per year	138,949,000	56,083,000	82,866,000
Per month	11,579,083	4,673,583	6,905,500
Per day	380,682	155,652	227,030
Per hour	15,862	6,402	9,460
Per minute	264	107	158
Per second	4.4	1.8	2.6

In the end, making all three of these strategies work depends on a more basic change in the way we think about ourselves and our world. Our *egocentric* outlook sets our own interests as standards for how to live; a sustainable environment demands an *ecocentric* outlook that helps us see that the present is tied to the future and that everyone must work together. Most nations in the southern half of the world are *underdeveloped,* unable to meet the basic needs of their people. At the same time, most countries in the northern half of the world are *overdeveloped,* using more resources than Earth can sustain over time. The changes needed to create a sustainable ecosystem will not come easily, and they will be costly. But the price of *not*

responding to the growing environmental deficit will certainly be greater (Brown et al., 1993; Population Action International, 2000; Gore, 2006).

Finally, consider that the great dinosaurs dominated this planet for some 160 million years and then perished forever. Humanity is far younger, having existed for a mere 250,000 years. Compared to the rather dimwitted dinosaurs, our species has the gift of great intelligence. But how will we use this ability? What are the chances that humans will continue to flourish 160 million years—or even 160 years—from now? The answer depends on the choices made by just one of the 30 million species living on Earth: human beings.

Why is the environment a social issue?

As this chapter explains, the state of the natural environment depends on how society is organized, especially the importance a culture attaches to consumption and economic growth.

> **HINT** If expansion is "good times," then contraction is a "recession" or perhaps even a "depression." Such a worldview means that it is normal—or even desirable—to live in a way that increases stress on the natural environment. Sustainability, an idea that is especially important as world population increases, depends on learning to live with what we have or maybe even learning to live with less. Although many people seem to think so, it really doesn't require a 6,000-pound SUV to move around urban areas. Actually, it might not require a car at all. This new way of thinking requires that we do not define social standing and personal success in terms of what we own and what we consume. Can you imagine a society like that? What would it be like?

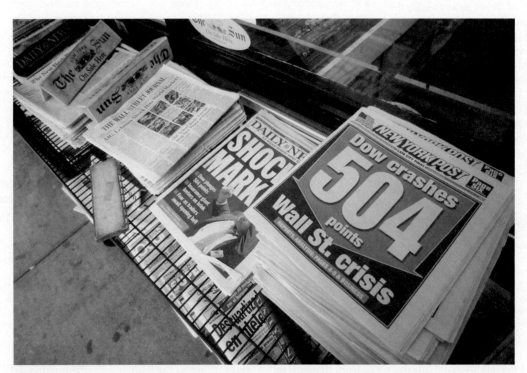

We learn to see economic expansion as natural and good. When the economy stays the same for a number of months, we say we are experiencing "stagnation." How do we define a period when the economy gets smaller, as happened during the fall of 2008?

What would it take to convince members of our society that smaller (rather than bigger) might be better? Why do we seem to prefer not just bigger cars but bigger homes and more and more material possessions?

Applying SOCIOLOGY in Everyday Life

1. Here is an illustration of the problem of runaway growth (Milbrath, 1989:10): "A pond has a single water lily growing on it. The lily doubles in size each day. In thirty days, it covers the entire pond. On which day does it cover half the pond?" When you realize the answer, discuss the implications of this example for population increase.

2. Draw a mental map of a city familiar to you with as much detail of specific places, districts, roads, and transportation facilities as you can. Compare your map to a real one or,

better yet, a map drawn by someone else. Try to account for the differences.

3. As an interesting exercise, carry a trash bag around for a single day, and collect everything you throw away. Most people are surprised to find that the average person in the United States discards close to 5 pounds of paper, metal, plastic, and other materials daily (over a lifetime, that's about 50 tons).

Making the Grade

Population, Urbanization, and Environment

Demography: The Study of Population

👁 Watch on **mysoclab.com**

✓ *Demography analyzes the size and composition of a population and how and why people move from place to place. Demographers collect data and study several factors that affect population (p. 446).*

FERTILITY
- Fertility is the incidence of childbearing in a country's population.
- Demographers describe fertility using the **crude birth rate**.

pp. 446–47

MORTALITY
- Mortality is the incidence of death in a country's population.
- Demographers measure mortality using both the **crude death rate** and the **infant mortality rate.**

p. 447

MIGRATION
- The **net migration rate** is the difference between the in-migration rate and the out-migration rate.

pp. 447–48

🧭 Explore on **mysoclab.com**

POPULATION GROWTH
In general, rich nations grow as much from immigration as from natural increase; poorer nations grow almost entirely from natural increase.

p. 448

POPULATION COMPOSITION
Demographers use **age-sex pyramids** to show graphically the composition of a population and to project population trends.

pp. 448–50

demography (p. 446) the study of human population

fertility (p. 446) the incidence of childbearing in a country's population

crude birth rate (p. 446) the number of live births in a given year for every 1,000 people in a population

mortality (p. 447) the incidence of death in a country's population

crude death rate (p. 447) the number of deaths in a given year for every 1,000 people in a population

infant mortality rate (p. 447) the number of deaths among infants under one year of age for each 1,000 live births in a given year

life expectancy (p. 447) the average life span of a country's population

migration (p. 447) the movement of people into and out of a specified territory

sex ratio (p. 448) the number of males for every 100 females in a nation's population

age-sex pyramid (p. 448) a graphic representation of the age and sex of a population

History and Theory of Population Growth

- Historically, world population grew slowly because high birth rates were offset by high death rates.
- About 1750, a demographic transition began as world population rose sharply, mostly due to falling death rates.
- In the late 1700s, Thomas Robert Malthus warned that population growth would outpace food production, resulting in social calamity.
- **Demographic transition theory** contends that technological advances gradually slow population increase.
- World population is expected to exceed 9 billion by 2050.

pp. 450–53

demographic transition theory (p. 451) a thesis that links population patterns to a society's level of technological development

zero population growth (p. 452) the rate of reproduction that maintains population at a steady level

✓ *Currently, the world is gaining 83 million people each year, with 98% of this increase taking place in poor countries (p. 450).*

📖 Read on **mysoclab.com**

Urbanization: The Growth of Cities

The **FIRST URBAN REVOLUTION** began with the appearance of cities about 10,000 years ago.
- By about 2,000 years ago, cities had emerged in most regions of the world except North America and Antarctica.
- Preindustrial cities have low buildings; narrow, winding streets; and personal social ties.

pp. 453–55

A **SECOND URBAN REVOLUTION** began about 1750 as the Industrial Revolution propelled rapid urban growth in Europe.
- The physical form of cities changed as planners created wide, regular streets to allow for more trade.
- The emphasis on commerce, as well as the increasing size of cities, made urban life more impersonal.

p. 455

urbanization (p. 455) the concentration of population into cities

metropolis (p. 456) a large city that socially and economically dominates an urban area

suburbs (p. 456) urban areas beyond the political boundaries of a city

megalopolis (p. 457) a vast urban region containing a number of cities and their surrounding suburbs

IN THE UNITED STATES, urbanization has been going on for more than 400 years and continues today.
- Urbanization came to North America with European colonists.
- By 1850, hundreds of new cities had been founded from coast to coast.
- By 1920, a majority of the U.S. population lived in urban areas.
- Since 1950, the decentralization of cities has resulted in the growth of suburbs and edge cities and a rebound in rural population.
- Nationally, Sunbelt cities—but not the older Snowbelt cities—are increasing in size and population.

pp. 455–58

Urbanism as a Way of Life

✓ *Rapid urbanization during the nineteenth century led early sociologists to study the differences between rural and urban life. These early sociologists included, in Europe, Tönnies, Durkheim, and Simmel, and in the United States, Park and Wirth.*

FERDINAND TÖNNIES built his analysis on the concepts of *Gemeinschaft* and *Gesellschaft.*

- *Gemeinschaft*, typical of the rural village, joins people in what amounts to a single primary group.
- *Gesellschaft*, typical of the modern city, describes individuals motivated by their own needs rather than the well-being of the community.

p. 458

EMILE DURKHEIM agreed with much of Tönnies's thinking but claimed that urbanites do not lack social bonds; the basis of social soldarity simply differs in the two settings.

- **Mechanical solidarity** involves social bonds based on common sentiments and shared moral values. This type of social solidarity is typical of traditional, rural life.
- **Organic solidarity** arises from social bonds based on specialization and interdependence. This type of social solidarity is typical of modern, urban life.

pp. 458–59

Gemeinschaft (p. 458) a type of social organization in which people are closely tied by kinship and tradition

Gesellschaft (p. 458) a type of social organization in which people come together only on the basis of individual self-interest

urban ecology (p. 460) the study of the link between the physical and social dimensions of cities

GEORG SIMMEL claimed that the overstimulation of city life produced a blasé attitude in urbanites.

p. 459

ROBERT PARK, at the University of Chicago, claimed that cities permit greater social freedom.

pp. 459–60

LOUIS WIRTH saw large, dense, heterogeneous populations creating an impersonal and self-interested, though tolerant, way of life.

pp. 459–60

Urbanization in Poor Nations

- The world's first urban revolution took place about 8000 B.C.E. with the first urban settlements.
- The second urban revolution took place after 1750 in Europe and North America with the Industrial Revolution.
- A third urban revolution is now occurring in poor countries. Today, most of the world's largest cities are found in less developed nations.

p. 462

Environment and Society

The state of the **ENVIRONMENT** is a social issue because it reflects how human beings organize social life.

- Societies increase the **environmental deficit** by focusing on short-term benefits and ignoring the long-term consequences brought on by their way of life.
- The more complex a society's technology, the greater its capacity to alter the natural environment.

pp. 462–63

- The *logic-of-growth thesis* supports economic development, claiming that people can solve environmental problems as they arise.
- The *limits-to-growth thesis* states that societies must curb development to prevent eventual environmental collapse.

pp. 464–65

ecology (p. 462) the study of the interaction of living organisms and the natural environment

natural environment (p. 462) Earth's surface and atmosphere, including living organisms, air, water, soil, and other resources necessary to sustain life

ecosystem (p. 462) the interaction of all living organisms and their natural environment

environmental deficit (p. 463) profound long-term harm to the natural environment caused by humanity's focus on short-term material affluence

rain forests (p. 468) regions of dense forestation, most of which circle the globe close to the equator

global warming (p. 468) a rise in Earth's average temperature due to an increasing concentration of carbon dioxide in the atmosphere

environmental racism (p. 469) patterns of development that expose poor people, especially minorities, to environmental hazards

ecologically sustainable culture (p. 470) a way of life that meets the needs of the present generation without threatening the environmental legacy of future generations

ENVIRONMENTAL ISSUES include

- *Disposing of solid waste:* More than half of what we throw away ends up in landfills, which are filling up and which can pollute groundwater under Earth's surface.
- *Protecting the quality of water and air:* The supply of clean water is already low in some parts of the world. Industrial technology has caused a decline in air quality.
- *Protecting the rain forests:* Rain forests help remove carbon dioxide from the atmosphere and are home to a large share of this planet's living species. Under pressure from development, the world's rain forests are now half their original size and are shrinking by about 1% annually.
- *Global warming:* Increasing levels of carbon dioxide in the atmosphere are causing the average temperature of the planet to rise, melting the ice caps and bringing other dramatic changes to the natural environment.
- *Environmental racism:* Conflict theory has drawn attention to the fact that the poor, especially minorities, suffer most from environmental hazards.

pp. 465–70

16 Social Change: Modern and Postmodern Societies

- Why do societies change?

- How do social movements both encourage and resist social change?

- What do sociologists say is good and bad about today's society?

The five-story red brick apartment building at 253 East Tenth Street in New York has been standing for more than a century. In 1900, one of the twenty small apartments in the building was occupied by thirty-nine-year-old Julius Streicher; Christine Streicher, age thirty-three; and their four young children. The Streichers were immigrants, both having come in 1885 from their native Germany to New York, where they met and married.

The Streichers probably considered themselves successful. Julius operated a small clothing shop a few blocks from his apartment; Christine stayed at home, raised the children, and did housework. Like most people in the country at that time, neither Julius nor Christine had graduated from high school, and they worked for ten to twelve hours a day, six days a week. Their income—average for that time—was about $35 a month, or about $425 per year. (In today's dollars, that would be slightly more than $11,000, which would put the family well below the poverty line.) They spent almost half of their income for food; most of the rest went for rent.

Today, Dorothy Sabo resides at 253 East Tenth Street, living alone in the same apartment where the Streichers spent much of their lives. Now eighty-seven, she is retired from a career teaching art at a nearby museum. In many respects, Sabo's life has been far easier than the life the Streichers knew. For one thing, when the Streichers lived there, the building had no electricity (people used kerosene lamps and candles) and no running water (Christine Streicher spent most of every Monday doing laundry using water she carried from a public fountain at the end of the block). There were no telephones, no television, and of course no computers. Today, Dorothy Sabo takes such conveniences for granted. Although she is hardly rich, her pension and Social Security amount to several times as much (in constant dollars) as the Streichers earned.

Sabo has her own worries. She is concerned about the environment and often speaks out about global warming. But a century ago, if the Streichers and their neighbors were concerned about "the environment," they probably would have meant the smell coming up from the street. At a time when motor vehicles were just beginning to appear in New York City, carriages, trucks, and trolleys were all pulled by horses—thousands of them. These animals dumped 60,000 gallons of urine and 2.5 million pounds of manure on the streets each and every day—an offensive mixture churned and splashed by countless wheels onto everything and everyone within a stone's throw of the streets (Simon & Cannon, 2001).

It is difficult for most people today to imagine how different life was a century ago. Not only was life much harder back then, but it was also much shorter. Statistical records show that life expectancy was just forty-six years for men and forty-eight years for women, compared to about seventy-five and eighty years today, respectively (Xu et al., 2010).

Over the course of the past century, much has changed for the better. Yet as this chapter explains, social change is not all positive. Change has negative consequences too, causing unexpected new problems. Early sociologists had a mixed assessment of *modernity,* changes brought about by the Industrial Revolution. Likewise, today's sociol-

ogists point to both good and bad aspects of *postmodernity,* the transformations caused by the Information Revolution and the postindustrial economy. One thing is clear: For better or worse, the rate of change has never been faster than it is now.

What Is Social Change?

In earlier chapters, we examined relatively fixed or *static* social patterns, including status and role, social stratification, and social institutions. We also looked at the *dynamic* forces that have shaped our way

● Seeing Sociology
in Everyday Life

What would you say have been the two or three most important changes to our society that have occurred during your lifetime? Explain your answer.

social change the transformation of culture and social institutions over time

of life, ranging from innovations in technology to the growth of bureaucracy and the expansion of cities. These are all dimensions of **social change,** *the transformation of culture and social institutions over time.* This complex process has four major characteristics:

1. **Social change happens all the time.** People used to say that the only sure things in life were "death and taxes." Yet our thoughts about death have changed dramatically as life expectancy in the United States has nearly doubled in the past century. And back in the Streichers' day, people in the United States paid little or no taxes on their earnings; taxation increased dramatically over the course of the twentieth century, along with the size and scope of government. In short, just about everything in life, even the "sure things," is subject to the twists and turns of change.

   Still, some societies change faster than others. As Chapter 2 ("Culture") explained, hunting and gathering societies change quite slowly; members of technologically complex societies, by contrast, can witness significant change within a single lifetime.

   It is also true that in any society, some cultural elements change faster than others. William Ogburn's theory of *cultural lag* (see Chapter 2) asserts that material culture (that is, things) changes faster than nonmaterial culture (ideas and attitudes). For example, genetic technology that allows scientists to alter and perhaps even create life has developed more rapidly than our ethical standards for deciding when and how to use the technology.

2. **Social change is sometimes intentional but often unplanned.** Industrial societies actively promote many kinds of change. Scientists seek more efficient forms of energy, and advertisers try to convince us that we cannot live without the latest electronic gadget. Yet rarely can anyone envision all the consequences of changes as they are set in motion.

   Back in 1900, when the country still relied on horses for transportation, people looked ahead to motor vehicles that would take a single day to carry them distances that used to take weeks or months. But no one could see how much the mobility provided by automobiles would alter life in the United States, scattering family members, threatening the environment, and reshaping cities and suburbs. Nor could automotive pioneers have predicted the more than 37,000 deaths that occur in car accidents each year in the United States alone (National Highway Traffic Safety Administration, 2009).

These young men are performing in a hip-hop dance marathon in Hong Kong. Hip-hop music, dress style, and dancing have become popular in Asia, a clear case of cultural diffusion. Social change occurs as cultural patterns move from place to place, but people in different societies don't always attach the same meanings to these patterns. How might Chinese youth understand hip-hop differently from the young African Americans in the United States who originated it?

3. **Social change is controversial.** The history of the automobile shows that social change brings both good and bad consequences. Cars brought an end to the muck of urine and manure on city streets, but they spewed carbon monoxide into the air. In the same contradictory way, capitalists benefited from greater production and profits made possible by the Industrial Revolution at the same time that workers pushed back against the machines that they feared would make their skills obsolete.

   Today, as in the past, people disagree about how we ought to live and what we should welcome as "progress." We see this disagreement every day in the changing patterns of social interaction between black people and white people, women and men, and homosexuals and heterosexuals that are celebrated by some people and opposed by others.

4. **Some changes matter more than others.** Some changes (such as clothing fads) have only passing significance; others (like the invention of computers) may change the world. Will the Information Revolution turn out to be as important as the Industrial Revolution? Like the automobile and television, computers have both positive and negative effects, providing new kinds of jobs while eliminating old ones, isolating people in offices while linking people in global electronic networks, offering vast amounts of information while threatening personal privacy.

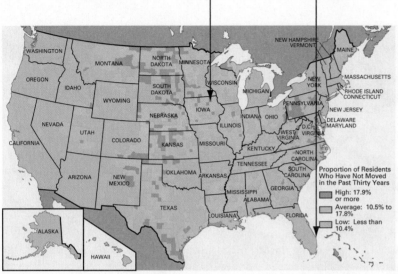

Martina Serfass, age 54, is a nurse who lives near Decorah, Iowa; most of the people in her community have lived there all their lives.

Serge Smith-Heiser, age 27, lives in an apartment complex in Fort Lauderdale, Florida, and thinks of his city as a place where people come and go. He arrived two years ago in search of a new job.

Explore residential stability in your local community and in counties across the United States on mysoclab.com

Seeing Ourselves

NATIONAL MAP 16–1
Who Stays Put? Residential Stability across the United States

Overall, only about 15 percent of U.S. residents have not moved during the past thirty years. Counties with a higher proportion of "long-termers" typically have experienced less change over recent decades: Many neighborhoods have been in place since before World War II, and many of the same families live in them. As you look at the map, what can you say about these stable areas? What accounts for the fact that most of these counties are rural and at some distance from the coasts?

Explore on mysoclab.com

Source: U.S. Census Bureau (2000).

Causes of Social Change

Social change has many causes. In a world linked by sophisticated communication and transportation technology, change in one place often sets off change elsewhere.

Culture and Change

Chapter 2 ("Culture") identified three important sources of cultural change. First, *invention* produces new objects, ideas, and social patterns. Rocket propulsion research, which began in the 1940s, has produced sophisticated spacecraft that can reach toward the stars. Today we take such technology for granted; during the present century, a significant number of people may well have an opportunity to travel in space.

Second, *discovery* occurs when people take notice of existing elements of the world. For example, medical advances offer a growing understanding of the human body. Beyond their direct effects on human health, medical discoveries have extended life expectancy, setting in motion the "graying" of U.S. society (see Chapter 3, "Socialization: From Infancy to Old Age").

Third, *diffusion* creates change as products, people, and information spread from one society to another. Ralph Linton (1937a) recognized that many familiar aspects of our culture came from other lands. For example, the cloth used to make our clothing was developed in Asia, the clocks we see all around us were invented in Europe, and the coins we carry in our pockets were devised in what is now Turkey.

In general, material things change more quickly than cultural ideas. For example, breakthroughs such as the science of cloning occur faster than our understanding of when—and even whether—they are morally desirable.

Conflict and Change

Inequality and conflict within a society also produce change. Karl Marx saw class conflict as the engine that drives societies from one historical era to another. In industrial-capitalist societies, he maintained, the struggle between capitalists and workers pushes society toward a socialist system of production.

In the more than 125 years since Marx's death, this model has proved simplistic. Yet Marx correctly foresaw that social conflict arising from inequality (involving not just class but also race and gender) would force changes in every society, including our own, to improve the lives of working people.

Ideas and Change

Max Weber also contributed to our understanding of social change. Although Weber acknowledged that conflict could bring about change, he traced the roots of most social changes to ideas. For example, people with charisma (Martin Luther King Jr. is an example) can carry a message that changes the world.

Weber highlighted the importance of ideas by revealing how the religious beliefs of early Protestants set the stage for the spread of industrial capitalism (see Chapter 13, "Family and Religion"). The fact that industrial capitalism developed primarily in areas of Western Europe where the Protestant work ethic was strong proved to Weber (1958, orig. 1904–05) the power of ideas to bring about change.

Demographic Change

Population patterns also play a part in social change. The typical U.S. household was almost twice as large in 1900 (4.8 people) as it is today

●— Seeing Sociology
in Everyday Life

Look at the various changes in the United States over the past
century. In each case, think about how the change affected
everyday social life.

social movement an organized activity that encourages
or discourages social change

(2.6 people). Women are having fewer children, and more people are
living alone. Change is also taking place as our population grows
older. As Chapter 3 ("Socialization: From Infancy to Old Age")
explained, 13 percent of the U.S. population was over age sixty-five in
2008, three times the proportion back in 1900. By the year 2030, seniors will account for 20 percent of the total (U.S. Census Bureau,
2009). Medical research and health care services already focus extensively on the elderly, and life will change in countless other ways as
homes and household products are redesigned to meet the needs of
growing numbers of older consumers.

Migration within and between societies is another demographic
factor that promotes change. Between 1870 and 1930, tens of millions of immigrants entered the industrial cities in the United States.
Millions more from rural areas joined the rush. As a result, farm
communities declined, cities expanded, and by 1920 the United
States had for the first time become a mostly urban nation. Similar
changes are taking place today as people moving from the Snowbelt to the Sunbelt mix with new immigrants from Latin America
and Asia.

Where in the United States have demographic changes been greatest, and where have they been less pronounced? National Map 16–1
provides one answer, showing counties where the largest share of people have lived in their present homes for thirty years or more.

Social Movements and Change

A final cause of social change lies in the efforts of people like us. People commonly band together to form a **social movement,** *an organized activity that encourages or discourages social change.* Our nation's
history includes all kinds of social movements, from the colonial drive
for independence to today's organizations supporting or opposing
abortion, gay rights, and the death penalty.

Social movements are about connecting people who share some
political goal. Computer technology, including smartphones and
social networking Internet sites, has made it possible for people to
connect as never before. Seeing Sociology in the News on page 482
takes a closer look at the power of networking sites such as Facebook
to support effective social movements.

Types of Social Movements

Researchers classify social movements according to the type of
change they seek (Aberle, 1966; Cameron, 1966; Blumer, 1969). One
variable asks, Who is changed? Some movements target selected
people, and others try to change everyone. A second variable asks,
How much change? Some movements seek only limited change in
our lives; others pursue a radical transformation of society. Combining these variables results in four types of social movements, shown
in Figure 16–1.

Alterative social movements are the least threatening to the status quo because they seek limited change in only part of the population. Their aim is to help certain people *alter* their lives. Promise
Keepers is one example of an alterative social movement; it encourages men to live more spiritual lives and be more supportive of their
families.

Redemptive social movements also target specific individuals,
but they seek more radical change. Their aim is to help certain people *redeem* their lives. For example, Alcoholics Anonymous is an
organization that helps people with an alcohol addiction achieve a
sober life.

Reformative social movements aim for only limited change but
target everyone. The environmental movement seeks to interest
everyone in protecting the natural environment.

Revolutionary social movements are the most extreme of all,
working for major transformation of an entire society. Sometimes
pursuing specific goals, sometimes spinning utopian dreams, these
social movements, including both the left-wing Communist party
(pushing for government control of the entire economy) and right-
wing militia groups (seeking the destruction of "big government")
seek to radically change our way of life.

Claims Making

In 1981, the Centers for Disease Control and Prevention began to
track a strange disease that was killing people, most of them homosexual men. The disease came to be known as AIDS (acquired
immune deficiency syndrome). Although AIDS was clearly a
deadly disease, it was given little public or media attention. Only

FIGURE 16–1   Four Types of Social Movements

There are four types of social movements, reflecting who is changed
and how great the change is.

Source: Based on Aberle (1966).

USA Today

Facebook Helps Spark Movements

BY DAVID UNZE
March 25, 2010

Austin Lee spent three years advocating for a skate park in St. Cloud, Minnesota, before he turned to Facebook.

The seventeen-year-old used to work the phones to keep his friends and supporters updated about his efforts. But when he took his campaign to the social networking site, he says his message really started to take off. The site's value as a grassroots organizing tool was never more clear to Lee than when sixty of his 1,085 followers confirmed within a day of getting an update from him that they would be able to attend a key City Council meeting on the project.

"Facebook, I think, made a huge impact," he said.

The effort paid off. The council approved a $500,000 skate plaza last month and council members agreed the Facebook community played a role. John Libert, vice president of the St. Cloud City Council, said he's never gotten more e-mails and other communications about a single issue than the skate plaza in his four years on the council.

"It was definitely effective. It did influence me, to the extent that the number of people who were out there supporting it" was so large, he said. Facebook is becoming a core component for social movements, from constituent outreach for political campaigns to building support for causes, says Andrew Noyes, manager of public policy communications for Facebook.

A growing number of people are discovering that Facebook, with its 350 million members, "is about way more than simply connecting with friends," Noyes said.

The use of Facebook to rally political support got a huge boost when President Obama relied on it during his candidacy to get his message out, Noyes said. Newly elected Senator Scott Brown, R-Mass., embraced Facebook during his campaign, Noyes said, an illustration of how the GOP is waking up to the power of social media. . . .

Levi Russell, communications director for Tea Party Express, the planned national bus tour that will host rallies across the nation to promote fiscal conservatism and protest Obama administration policies between March 27 and April 15, says the group started its first Facebook page a little less than a year ago, and has been growing by the thousands.

"Facebook allows us to promote and organize events in a whole new way," he said. "While it is not our primary communication tool, it is one of the most targeted and flexible tools we use. Our supporters are able to really take ownership of events in their area by sharing, discussing, and inviting their friends in a very visual and tangible format."

College students looking to get support for issues have also turned to Facebook.

Casey Allen Sears, a student at The College of William and Mary in Williamsburg, Virginia, helped start a Facebook group this month in opposition to Virginia Attorney General Ken Cuc-

cinelli's letter about discrimination policies at state public universities. Cuccinelli wrote that Virginia's public universities could not adopt policies that prohibit discrimination based on sexual orientation "absent specific authorization from the General Assembly."

The Facebook group promoted a protest against Cuccinelli's assertion that public universities should back away from policies against discrimination on the basis of sexual orientation.

"In the forty-eight hours from the creation of the event, we had more than 700 people saying they were attending," Sears said. "It's really easy to organize a mass movement." . . .

WHAT DO YOU THINK?

1. According to the article, why are Facebook and other computer-based networking systems becoming a "core component for social movements"?

2. Do you think the use of Facebook for political purposes will make this country more democratic? Why or why not?

3. Have you ever used Facebook or a similar networking site as part of an effort to organize a political demonstration or other social movement activity? Explain.

Adapted from "Facebook Helps Spark Movements" by David Unze. Source: *USA Today*, a division of Gannett Co., Inc. March 25, 2010. Reprinted with permission.

---

about five years later did the public begin to take notice of the rising number of deaths and start to think of AIDS as a serious social threat.

The change in public thinking was the result of **claims making,** *the process of trying to convince the public and public officials of the importance of joining a social movement to address a particular issue.* In other words, for a social movement to form, some issue has to be defined as a problem that demands public attention. Usually, claims making begins with a small number of people. In the case of AIDS, the gay community in large cities (notably San Francisco and New York) mobilized to convince people of the dangers posed by this deadly disease. Over time, if the mass media give the issue attention and public officials speak out on behalf of the problem, it is likely that the social movement will gain strength.

Considerable public attention has now been given to AIDS, and there is ongoing research aimed at finding a cure. The process of claims making goes on all the time for dozens of issues. Today, for

example, a movement to ban the use of cell phones in automobiles has pointed to the thousands of automobile accidents each year related to the use of phones while driving; six states have now passed laws banning the use of handheld phones, and debate continues in others (McVeigh, Welch, & Bjarnason, 2003; Governors Highway Safety Association, 2010; Macionis, 2010).

Explaining Social Movements

Sociologists have developed several explanations of social movements. *Deprivation theory* holds that social movements arise among people who feel deprived of something, such as income, safe working conditions, or political rights. Whether you feel deprived or not, of course, depends on what you expect in life. Thus people band together in response to **relative deprivation,** *a perceived disadvantage arising from some specific comparison.* This concept helps explain why movements for change surface in both good and bad times: It is not people's absolute standing that counts but how they perceive claims making the process of trying to convince the public and public officials of the importance of joining a social movement to address a particular issue

relative deprivation a perceived disadvantage arising from some specific comparison

○ Making the Grade

Review the discussion in Chapter 5 ("Groups and Organizations") on page 122 to see how we use reference groups to decide whether we are being deprived or not.

their situation in relation to the situations of others (J. C. Davies, 1962; Merton, 1968).

Mass-society theory, a second explanation, argues that social movements attract socially isolated people who join a movement in order to gain a sense of identity and purpose. From this point of view, social movements have a personal as well as a political agenda (Melucci, 1989).

Resource mobilization theory, a third theoretical scheme, links the success of any social movement to the resources that are available to it, including money, human labor, and the mass media. Because most social movements begin small, they must look beyond themselves to mobilize the resources required for success (Valocchi, 1996; Zhao, 1998; Passy & Giugni, 2001; Packer, 2003).

Fourth, *culture theory* points out that social movements depend not only on money and other material resources but also on cultural symbols. People must have a shared understanding of injustice in the world before they will mobilize to bring about change. In addition, specific symbols (such as photographs of the World Trade Center towers engulfed in flames after the September 11, 2001, terrorist attacks) helped mobilize people to support the U.S. military campaigns in Afghanistan and Iraq (McAdam, McCarthy, & Zald, 1996; J. E. Williams, 2002).

Fifth, *new social movements theory* points out the distinctive character of recent social movements in postindustrial societies. Rather than being local matters, these movements are typically national or international in scope, and most focus on quality-of-life issues, such as the natural environment, world peace, or animal rights, rather than more traditional economic issues. This broader scope of contemporary social movements results from closer ties between governments and between ordinary people around the world, who are now linked by the mass media and new information technology (Kriesi, 1989; Pakulski, 1993; Jenkins & Wallace, 1996).

Sixth and finally, *political economy theory* is a Marxist approach that claims that social movements arise in opposition to the capitalist economic system, which fails to meet the needs of the majority of people. Despite great economic productivity, U.S. society is in crisis, with millions of people unable to find good jobs, living below the poverty line, and surviving without health insurance. Social movements arise as workers organize to demand higher wages, citizens rally for a health policy that protects everyone, and people march in opposition to spending billions to fund wars while ignoring basic needs at home (Buechler, 2000).

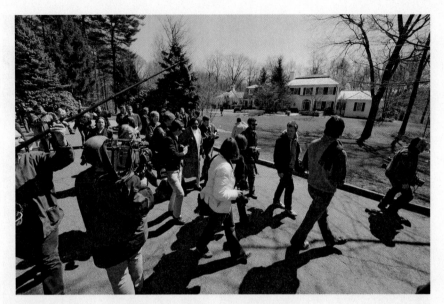

Political debate is a matter of claims making by various organizations. After the insurance giant AIG was saved from collapse by a massive government bailout, executives took millions of dollars in bonuses for themselves, claiming this served the interest of the company. The action prompted one organization to visit the executives' homes, denouncing the bonuses as little more than greed and demanding that the money be returned.

Stages in Social Movements

Social movements typically unfold in four stages: emergence, coalescence, bureaucratization, and decline. The *emergence* of social movements occurs as people begin to think that all is not well. Some, such as the civil rights and women's movements, are born of widespread dissatisfaction. Others emerge as a small group tries to mobilize the population, as when gay activists raised public concern about AIDS.

Coalescence takes place when a social movement defines itself and develops a strategy for attracting new members and "going public." Leaders determine policies and decide on tactics, which may include demonstrations or rallies to attract media attention.

As it gains members and resources, a social movement may undergo *bureaucratization.* As a movement becomes established, it depends less on the charisma and talents of a few leaders and more on a professional staff, which increases the chances for the movement's long-term survival.

Finally, social movements *decline* as resources dry up, the group faces overwhelming opposition, or members achieve their goals and lose interest. Some well-established organizations outlive their original causes and move on to new crusades; others lose touch with the idea of changing society and choose instead to become part of the "system" (Piven & Cloward, 1977; F. D. Miller, 1983).

disaster an event, generally unexpected, that causes extensive harm to people and damage to property

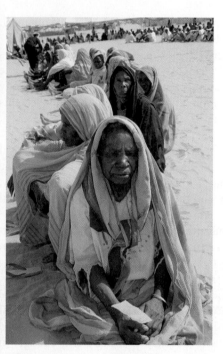

Sociologists classify disasters into three types. The 2010 earthquake in Haiti, which claimed several hundred thousand lives, is an example of a natural disaster. The 2010 oil spill in the Gulf of Mexico is an example of a technological disaster. The slaughter of hundreds of thousands of people and the displacement of millions more from their homes in the Darfur region of Sudan since 2003 is an example of an intentional disaster.

Disasters: Unexpected Change

Sometimes change results from events that are both unexpected and unwelcome. A **disaster** is *an event, generally unexpected, that causes extensive harm to people and damage to property*. Disasters are of three types. Floods, earthquakes, forest fires, and hurricanes (such as Hurricane Katrina, which devastated the Gulf Coast in 2005) are examples of *natural disasters* (Erikson, 2005a). A second type is the *technological disaster*, which is widely regarded as an *accident* but is more accurately the result of our inability to control technology (Erikson, 2005a). The nuclear accident at the Chernobyl power plant in Ukraine in 1986 and the spilling of millions of gallons of oil in the Gulf of Mexico in 2010 were technological disasters. A third type is the *intentional disaster*, in which one or more organized groups deliberately harm others. War, terrorist attacks, and the genocide that took place in Yugoslavia (1992–95), Rwanda (2000), and the Darfur region of Sudan (2003–10) are examples of intentional disasters.

The full scope of the harm caused by disasters may become evident only many years after the event. The Thinking Globally box describes a technological disaster that is still affecting people and their descendants more than half a century after it took place.

Kai Erikson (1976, 1994, 2005a) has investigated disasters of all types and has reached three major conclusions about the social consequences of disasters. First, we all know that disasters harm people and destroy property, but what most people don't realize is that disasters also cause social damage by disrupting human community. When a dam burst and sent a mountain of water down West Virginia's Buffalo Creek in 1972, it killed 125 people, destroyed 1,000 homes, and left 4,000 people homeless. After the waters had gone and help was streaming into the area, the people were paralyzed not only by the loss of family members and friends but also by the loss of their way of life. Even four decades later, they have been unable to rebuild the community life that they once knew. We can know when disasters start, Erikson points out, but we cannot know when they will end.

Second, Erikson explains that the social damage is more serious when an event involves some toxic substance, as is common with technological disasters. As the case of radiation falling on Utrik Island shows us, people feel "poisoned" when they have been exposed to a dangerous substance that they fear and over which they have no

● Seeing Sociology
in Everyday Life

What social damage do you think was caused by the 1986
explosion and massive radiation leak at the Chernobyl nuclear
plant in Ukraine?

modernity social patterns resulting from industrialization

modernization the process of social change begun by industrialization

THINKING GLOBALLY

A Never-Ending Atomic Disaster

It was just after dawn on March 1, 1954, and the air was already warm on Utrik Island, a small bit of coral and volcanic rock in the South Pacific that is one of the Marshall Islands. The island was home to 159 people, who lived by fishing much as their ancestors had done for centuries. The population knew only a little about the outside world—a missionary from the United States taught the local children, and two dozen military personnel lived at a small U.S. weather station with an airstrip where a single plane touched down each week.

At 6:45 A.M., the western sky suddenly lit up brighter than anyone had ever seen, and seconds later, a rumble like a massive earthquake rolled across the island. Some of the Utrik people thought the world was coming to an end. Their world, at least as they had known it, had changed forever.

About 160 miles to the west, on Bikini Island, the United States military had just detonated an atomic bomb, a huge device with 1,000 times the power of the bomb used at the end of World War II to destroy the Japanese city of Hiroshima. The enormous blast vaporized the island and sent a massive cloud of dust and radiation into the atmosphere. The military expected the winds to take the cloud north into an open area of the ocean, but the cloud blew east instead. By noon, the radiation cloud had engulfed a Japanese fishing boat ironically called the *Lucky Dragon,* exposing the twenty-three people on board to a dose of radiation that would eventually sicken or

kill them all. By the end of the afternoon, the deadly cloud spilled across Utrik Island.

The cloud was made up of coral and rock dust, all that was left of Bikini Island. The dust fell softly on Utrik Island, and the children, who remembered pictures of snow shown to them by their missionary teacher, ran out to play in the white powder that was piling up everywhere. No one realized that it was contaminated with deadly radiation.

Three-and-one-half days later, the U.S. military landed planes on Utrik Island and informed all the people that they would have to leave

immediately, taking nothing with them. For three months, the island people were held at another military base, and then they were returned home.

Many of the people who were on the island that fateful morning died young, typically from cancer or other diseases associated with radiation exposure. But even today, those who survived consider themselves and their island poisoned by the radiation, and they believe that the poison will never go away. The radiation may or may not still be in their bodies, but it has worked its way deep into their culture. More than half a century after the bomb exploded, people still talked about the morning that "everything changed." The damage from this disaster turns out to be much more than medical—it was a social transformation that left the people with a deep belief that they are all sick, that life will never be the same, and that the people who live on the other side of the world could have prevented the disaster but did not.

WHAT DO YOU THINK?

1. In what sense is a disaster like this one never really over?

2. In what ways did the atomic bomb test change the culture of the Utrik people?

3. What does this account lead us to expect about the long-term consequences of other disasters such as Hurricane Katrina, which damaged much of the Gulf Coast in 2005?

Source: Based on Erikson (2005a).

control. People in Ukraine felt much the same way after the 1986 explosion and radiation leak at the Chernobyl nuclear plant.

Third, the social damage is most serious when the disaster is caused by the actions of other people. This can happen through negligence or carelessness (as in technological disasters) or through willful action (intentional disasters). Our belief that "other people will do us no harm" is a foundation of social life, Erikson claims. But when others act carelessly (as in the case of an oil spill) or intentionally in ways that harm us (as in the case of genocide in Darfur), survivors typically lose their trust in others to a degree that may never go away.

Modernity

A central concept in the study of social change is **modernity,** *social patterns resulting from industrialization.* In everyday terms, *modernity* (its Latin root means "lately") refers to the present in relation to the past. Sociologists use this catchall concept to describe the many social patterns set in motion by the Industrial Revolution, which began in Western Europe in the 1750s. **Modernization,** then, is *the process of social change begun by industrialization.* The timeline inside the back cover of this book highlights important events that mark the emergence

Seeing Sociology in Everyday Life

Look at the various changes in the United States over the past century as summarized in the table below. In each case, think about how the change affected everyday social life.

Making the Grade

Be sure you understand the four traits of modernization identified by Peter Berger.

Table 16–1 The United States: A Century of Change

	1900	2000
National population	76 million	281 million
Share living in cities	40%	80%
Life expectancy	46 years (men), 48 years (women)	74 years (men), 79 years (women)
Median age	22.9 years	35.3 years
Average household income	$8,000 (in 2000 dollars)	$40,000 (in 2000 dollars)
Share of income spent on food	43%	15%
Share of homes with flush toilets	10%	98%
Average number of cars	1 car for every 2,000 households	1.3 cars for every household
Divorce rate	about 1 in 20 marriages	about 8 in 20 marriages
Average gallons of petroleum products consumed	34 per person per year	1,100 per person per year

of modernity. Table 16–1 provides a summary of change in the United States over the course of the twentieth century.

Peter Berger (1977) identified four major characteristics of modernization:

1. **The decline of small, traditional communities.** Modernity involves "the progressive weakening, if not destruction, of the ... relatively cohesive communities in which human beings have found solidarity and meaning throughout most of history" (1977:72). For thousands of years, in the camps of hunters and gatherers and in the rural villages of Europe and North America, people lived in small communities where life revolved around family and neighborhood. Such traditional worlds gave each person a well-defined place that, although limiting range of choice, offered a strong sense of identity, belonging, and purpose.

   Small, isolated communities still exist in the United States, of course, but they are home to only a tiny percentage of our nation's people. These days, their isolation is only geographic: Except among those who are extremely poor, cars, telephones, television, and computers give rural families the pulse of the larger society and connect them to the entire world.

2. **The expansion of personal choice.** People in traditional, preindustrial societies view their lives as shaped by forces beyond human control—gods, spirits, fate. As the power of tradition weakens, people come to see their lives as an unending series of options, a process Berger calls *individualization*. For instance, many people in the United States choose a particular "lifestyle" (sometimes adopting one after another), showing an openness to change. Indeed, it is a common belief that people *should* take control of their lives.

3. **Increasing social diversity.** In preindustrial societies, strong family ties and powerful religious beliefs enforce conformity and discourage diversity and change. Modernization promotes a more rational, scientific worldview as tradition loses its hold and people gain more individual choice. The growth of cities, the expansion of

impersonal bureaucracy, and the social mix of people from various backgrounds combine to encourage diverse beliefs and behavior.

4. **Orientation toward the future and a growing awareness of time.** Premodern people focus on the past; people in modern societies think more about the future. Modern people are not only forward-looking but also optimistic that new inventions and discoveries will improve their lives.

   Modern people organize daily routines down to the very minute. With the introduction of clocks in the late Middle Ages, Europeans began to think not in terms of sunlight and seasons but in terms of hours and minutes. Focused on personal gain, modern people demand precise measurement of time and are likely to agree that "time is money." Berger points out that one good indicator of a society's degree of modernization is the share of people who keep track of time by continually glancing at their wristwatches (or nowadays, their cell phones).

Finally, recall that modernization touched off the development of sociology itself. As Chapter 1 ("Sociology: Perspective, Theory, and Method") explained, the discipline originated in the wake of the Industrial Revolution in Western Europe at a point when social change was proceeding rapidly. Early European and U.S. sociologists tried to analyze the rise of modern society and its consequences, both good and bad, for human beings.

Ferdinand Tönnies: The Loss of Community

The German sociologist Ferdinand Tönnies produced a lasting account of modernization in his theory of *Gemeinschaft* and *Gesellschaft* (see Chapter 15, "Population, Urbanization, and Environment"). Like Peter Berger, whose work he influenced, Tönnies (1963, orig. 1887) viewed modernization as the progressive loss of *Gemeinschaft*, or human community. As Tönnies saw it, the Industrial Revolution weakened the

○ Making the Grade

Durkheim's concepts match up with those of Tönnies, but be sure to get it right: Mechanical solidarity corresponds to *Gemeinschaft,* and organic solidarity is the same as *Gesellschaft.*

[▭●] Read "Bowling Alone: America's Declining Social Capital" by Robert D. Putnam on **mysoclab.com**

social fabric of family and tradition by introducing a businesslike emphasis on facts, efficiency, and money. European and North American societies gradually became rootless and impersonal as people came to associate with one another mostly on the basis of self-interest—the state Tönnies termed *Gesellschaft.*

Early in the twentieth century, at least some parts of the United States could be described using Tönnies's concept of *Gemeinschaft.* Families that had lived for many generations in small villages and towns were bound together into a hardworking and slowly changing way of life. Telephones (invented in 1876) were rare; not until 1915 could one place a coast-to-coast call (see the timeline inside the back cover of this book). Living without television (introduced commercially in 1933 and not widespread until after 1950), families entertained themselves, often gathering with friends in the evening to share stories, sorrows, or song. Lacking rapid transportation (Henry Ford's assembly line began in 1908, but cars became common only after World War II), many people knew little of the world beyond their hometown.

Inevitable tensions and conflicts divided these communities of the past. But according to Tönnies, the traditional spirit of *Gemeinschaft* meant that people were "essentially united in spite of all separating factors" (1963:65, orig. 1887).

Modernity turns society inside out so that, as Tönnies put it, people are "essentially separated in spite of uniting factors" (1963:65, orig. 1887). This is the world of *Gesellschaft,* where, especially in large cities, most people live among strangers and ignore the people they pass on the street. Trust is hard to come by in a mobile and anonymous society in which people put their personal needs ahead of group loyalty and a majority of adults believe "you can't be too careful" in dealing with people (NORC, 2009:1811). No wonder researchers conclude that even as we have become more affluent, the social health of modern societies has declined (D. G. Myers, 2000). [▭●] Read on **mysoclab.com**

○ **CRITICAL REVIEW** Tönnies's theory of *Gemeinschaft* and *Gesellschaft* is the most widely cited model of modernization. The theory's strength lies in its synthesis of various dimensions of change: growing population, the rise of cities, and increasingly impersonal interaction. But modern life, though often impersonal, still has some degree of *Gemeinschaft.* Even in a world of strangers, modern friendships can be strong and lasting. In addition, some analysts think that Tönnies favored—perhaps even romanticized—traditional societies while overlooking bonds of family and friendship that continue to flourish in modern societies.

○ **CHECK YOUR LEARNING** As types of social organization, how do *Gemeinschaft* and *Gesellschaft* differ?

George Tooker's 1950 painting *The Subway* depicts a common problem of modern life: Weakening social ties and eroding traditions create a generic humanity in which everyone is alike yet each person is an anxious stranger in the midst of others.

Source: George Tooker, *The Subway,* 1950, egg tempera on gesso panel, 18 1/8 × 36 1/8 inches, Whitney Museum of American Art, New York. Purchased with funds from the Juliana Force Purchase Award, 50.23. Photograph © Whitney Museum of American Art

Emile Durkheim: The Division of Labor

The French sociologist Emile Durkheim shared Tönnies's interest in the important social changes that resulted from the Industrial Revolution. For Durkheim (1964a, orig. 1893), modernization was marked by an increasing **division of labor,** or *specialized economic activity.* Every member of a traditional society performs more or less the same activities; modern societies function by having people perform highly specific jobs.

Durkheim explained that preindustrial societies are held together by *mechanical solidarity,* or shared moral sentiments (see Chapter 15). Members of such societies view everyone as basically alike, doing the same work and belonging together. Durkheim's concept of mechanical solidarity is virtually the same as Tönnies's *Gemeinschaft.*

With modernization, the division of labor (job specialization) becomes more and more pronounced. To Durkheim, this change means less mechanical solidarity but more of another kind of tie: *organic solidarity,* mutual dependency between people engaged in specialized work. Put simply, modern societies are held together not by likeness but by difference: All of us must depend on others to meet most of our needs. Organic solidarity corresponds to Tönnies's concept of *Gesellschaft.*

Despite obvious similarities in their thinking, Durkheim and Tönnies viewed modernity somewhat differently. To Tönnies, modern *Gesellschaft* amounted to the loss of social solidarity because people lose the "natural" and "organic" bonds of the rural village, leaving only the "artificial" and "mechanical" ties of the big city. Durkheim

division of labor (p. 487) specialized economic activity

anomie a condition in which society provides little moral guidance to individuals

Go to the Multimedia Library at **mysoclab.com** to hear author John Macionis discuss "What Is Distinctive about the Modern World?"

In traditional societies, such as Amish communities in the United States, everyone does much the same work. These societies are held together by strong moral beliefs. Modern societies, illustrated by urban areas in this country, are held together by a system of production in which people perform specialized work and rely on one another.

had a different view of modernity, even reversing Tönnies's language to bring home the point. Durkheim labeled modern society "organic," arguing that modern society is no less natural than any other, and he described traditional societies as "mechanical" because they are so regimented. Durkheim viewed modernization not so much as a loss of community as a change from community based on bonds of likeness (kinship and neighborhood) to community based on economic interdependence (the division of labor). Durkheim's view of modernity is thus both more complex and more positive than Tönnies's view.

CRITICAL REVIEW Durkheim's work, which resembles that of Tönnies, is a highly influential analysis of modernity. Of the two, Durkheim was more optimistic; still, he feared that modern societies might become so diverse that they would collapse into **anomie,** *a condition in which society provides little moral guidance to individuals.* Living with weak moral norms, modern people can become egocentric, placing their own needs above those of others and finding little purpose in life.

The suicide rate, which Durkheim considered a good index of anomie, did in fact increase in the United States over the course of the twentieth century, and the vast majority of adults report that they see moral questions not in clear terms of right and wrong but as confusing "shades of gray" (NORC, 2009:478). Yet shared norms and values seem strong enough to give most people a sense of meaning and purpose. Whatever the hazards of anomie, most people value the personal freedom modern society gives us.

CHECK YOUR LEARNING Define mechanical solidarity and organic solidarity. In his view of the modern world, what makes Durkheim more optimistic than Tönnies?

Max Weber: Rationalization

For Max Weber, modernity meant replacing a traditional worldview with a rational way of thinking. In preindustrial societies, tradition acts as a constant brake on social change. To traditional people, "truth" is roughly the same as "what has always been" (1978:36, orig. 1921). To modern people, however, "truth" is the result of rational calculation. Because they value efficiency and have little reverence for the past, modern people adopt social patterns that allow them to achieve their goals.

Echoing Tönnies's and Durkheim's claim that industrialization weakens tradition, Weber characterized modern society as "disenchanted." The unquestioned truths of an earlier time had been challenged by rational thinking. In short, said Weber, modern society turns away from the gods just as it turns away from the past. Throughout his life, Weber studied various modern "types"—the scientist, the capitalist, the bureaucrat—all of whom share the forward-looking, rational, and detached worldview that he believed was coming to dominate humanity. ● Go to **mysoclab.com**

CRITICAL REVIEW Compared with Tönnies and especially Durkheim, Weber was very critical of modern society. He knew that science could produce technological and organizational wonders, yet he worried that science was carrying us away

○ Making the Grade

Be sure you see what, from Weber's point of view, the scientist, the capitalist, and the bureaucrat (all pictured below) have in common.

○ Making the Grade

Marx claimed capitalism was the foundation of modern society; Weber claimed that capitalism (along with science and bureaucracy) rests on a more basic foundation—rationality.

from more basic questions about the meaning and purpose of human existence. Weber feared that rationalization, especially in bureaucracies, would erode the human spirit with endless rules and regulations.

○ **CHECK YOUR LEARNING** What did Weber mean by describing the modern world as "disenchanted"? In what ways are scientists, capitalists, and bureaucrats all "disenchanted"?

Some of Weber's critics think that the alienation Weber attributed to bureaucracy actually stemmed from social inequality. This issue leads us to the ideas of Karl Marx.

Karl Marx: Capitalism

For Karl Marx, modern society was synonymous with capitalism; he saw the Industrial Revolution primarily as a *capitalist* revolution. Marx traced the emergence of the bourgeoisie in medieval Europe to the expansion of commerce. The bourgeoisie gradually displaced the feudal aristocracy as the Industrial Revolution gave it control of a powerful new productive system.

Marx agreed that modernity weakened small communities (as described by Tönnies), increased the division of labor (as noted by Durkheim), and encouraged a rational worldview (as Weber claimed). But he saw these simply as conditions necessary for capitalism to flourish. According to Marx, capitalism draws population away from farms and small towns into an ever-expanding market system centered in the cities; specialization is needed for efficient

factories; and rationality is illustrated by the capitalists' endless pursuit of profit.

Earlier chapters have painted Marx as a spirited critic of capitalist society, but his vision of modernity also includes a good bit of optimism. Unlike Weber, who viewed modern society as an "iron cage" of bureaucracy from which there was no escape, Marx believed that social conflict in capitalist societies would sow the seeds of revolutionary change, leading to an egalitarian socialism. Such a society, as he saw it, would harness the wonders of industrial technology to enrich people's lives and rid the world of social classes, the source of conflict and so much suffering. Although Marx's evaluation of modern capitalist society was highly negative, he imagined a future of human freedom, creativity, and community.

○ **CRITICAL REVIEW** Marx's theory of modernization is a complex theory of capitalism. But he underestimated the dominance of bureaucracy in shaping modern societies. In socialist societies, in particular, the stifling effects of bureaucracy have turned out to be as bad as, or even worse than, the dehumanizing aspects of capitalism. The upheavals in Eastern Europe and the former Soviet Union in the 1990s revealed the depth of popular opposition to oppressive state bureaucracies.

○ **CHECK YOUR LEARNING** Of the four theorists just discussed—Tönnies, Durkheim, Weber, and Marx—who comes across as the most optimistic about modern society? Who was the most pessimistic? Explain your choices.

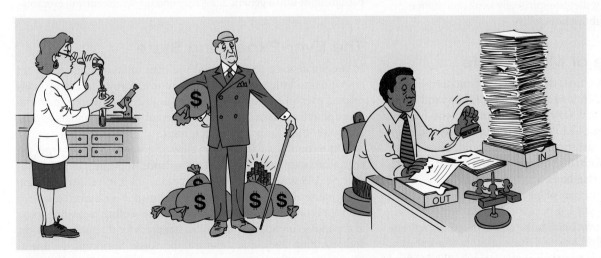

Max Weber maintained that the distinctive character of modern society was its rational worldview. Virtually all of Weber's work on modernity centered on types of people he considered typical of their age: the scientist, the capitalist, and the bureaucrat. Each is rational to the core: The scientist is committed to the orderly discovery of truth, the capitalist to the orderly pursuit of profit, and the bureaucrat to orderly conformity to a system of rules.

● Seeing Sociology in Everyday Life

Identify five examples of "mass culture" that are the same throughout the United States. Name five more that differ from region to region.

Structural-Functional Analysis: Modernity as Mass Society

> November 11, on Interstate 275. From the car window, we see BP and Sunoco gas stations, a Kmart and a Walmart, an AmeriSuites hotel, a Bob Evans, a Chi-Chi's Mexican restaurant, and a McDonald's. This road happens to circle Cincinnati, Ohio. But it could be in Boston, Saint Louis, Denver, San Diego, or almost anywhere else in the United States.

The rise of modernity is a complex process involving many dimensions of change, described in earlier chapters and reviewed here in the Summing Up table. How can we make sense of so many changes going on at once? Sociologists have two broad explanations of modern society, one guided by the structural-functional approach and the other based on social-conflict theory.

The first explanation, guided by the structural-functional approach and drawing on the ideas of Tönnies, Durkheim, and Weber, understands modernity as the emergence of a *mass society* (Kornhauser, 1959; Nisbet, 1969; Berger, Berger, & Kellner, 1974; Pearson, 1993). A **mass society** is *a society in which prosperity and bureaucracy have weakened traditional social ties*. A mass society is productive; on average, people have more income than ever. At the same time, it is marked by weak kinship and impersonal neighborhoods, leaving individuals to feel socially isolated. Although many people have material plenty, they are spiritually weak and often experience moral uncertainty about how to live.

The Mass Scale of Modern Life

Mass-society theory argues, first, that the scale of modern life has greatly increased. Before the Industrial Revolution, Europe and North America formed a mosaic of rural villages and small towns. In these local communities, which inspired Tönnies's concept of *Gemeinschaft*, people lived out their lives surrounded by kin and guided by a shared heritage. Gossip was an informal yet highly effective way of ensuring conformity to community standards. Such small communities tolerated little social diversity—the state of mechanical solidarity described by Durkheim.

For example, before 1690, English law demanded that everyone participate regularly in the Christian ritual of Holy Communion (Laslett, 1984). On the North American continent, only Rhode Island among the New England colonies tolerated any religious dissent. Because social differences were repressed in favor of conformity to established norms, subcultures and countercultures were few, and change proceeded slowly.

Increasing population, the growth of cities, and specialized economic activity driven by the Industrial Revolution gradually altered this pattern. People came to know one another by their jobs (for example, as "the doctor" or "the bank clerk") rather than by their kinship group or hometown. People looked on most others simply as strangers. The face-to-face communication of the village was eventually replaced by the impersonal mass media: newspapers, radio, television, and computer networks. Large organizations steadily assumed more and more responsibility for the daily needs that had once been fulfilled by family, friends, and neighbors; public education drew more and more people to schools; police, lawyers, and courts supervised a formal criminal justice system. Even charity became the work of faceless bureaucrats working for various social welfare agencies.

Geographic mobility, mass communication, and exposure to diverse ways of life all weaken traditional values. People become more tolerant of social diversity, defending individual rights and freedom of choice. Treating people differently because of their race, sex, or religion comes to be defined as backward and unjust. In the process, minorities at the margins of society gain greater power and broader participation in public life. The election of Barack Obama—an African American—to the highest office in the United States is surely one indicator that ours is now a modern society (West, 2008).

The mass media give rise to a national culture that washes over the traditional differences that used to set off one region from another. As one analyst put it, "Even in Baton Rouge, La., the local kids don't say 'y'all' anymore; they say 'you guys' just like on TV" (Gibbs, 2000:42). Mass-society theorists fear that the transformation of people of various backgrounds into a generic mass may end up dehumanizing everyone.

The Ever-Expanding State

In the small-scale preindustrial societies of Europe, government amounted to little more than a local noble. A royal family formally reigned over an entire nation, but in the absence of swift transportation and efficient communication, even absolute monarchs had far less power than today's political leaders.

As technological innovation allowed government to expand, the centralized state grew in size and importance. At the time of independence, the U.S. government was a tiny organization, its primary function being national defense. Since then, government has assumed responsibility for more and more areas of social life: schooling, regulating wages and working conditions, establishing standards for products of all sorts, and providing financial assistance to the elderly, the ill, and the unemployed. To pay for such programs, taxes have soared: Today's average worker in the United States labors more than four months each year just to pay for the broad array of services the government provides.

In a mass society, power resides in large bureaucracies, leaving people in local communities with little control over their lives. For

○ Making the Grade

This table is a good summary of trends that define our modern society. It also reviews much of what you have studied in earlier chapters.

○ Making the Grade

As you read about mass society theory, keep in mind the theories of Tönnies, Durkheim, and Weber on which it is based.

SUMMING UP

Traditional and Modern Societies: The Big Picture

Elements of Society	Traditional Societies	Modern Societies
Cultural Patterns		
Values	Homogeneous; sacred character; few subcultures and countercultures	Heterogeneous; secular character; many subcultures and countercultures
Norms	Great moral significance; little tolerance of diversity	Variable moral significance; high tolerance of diversity
Time orientation	Present linked to past	Present linked to future
Technology	Preindustrial; human and animal energy	Industrial; advanced energy sources
Social Structure		
Status and role	Few statuses, most ascribed; few specialized roles	Many statuses, some ascribed and some achieved; many specialized roles
Relationships	Typically primary; little anonymity or privacy	Typically secondary; much anonymity and privacy
Communication	Face to face	Face-to-face communication supplemented by mass media
Social control	Informal gossip	Formal police and legal system
Social stratification	Rigid patterns of social inequality; little mobility	Fluid patterns of social inequality; high mobility
Gender patterns	Pronounced patriarchy; women's lives centered on the home	Declining patriarchy; increasing share of women work in the paid labor force
Settlement patterns	Small-scale; population typically small and widely dispersed in rural villages and small towns	Large-scale; population typically large and concentrated in cities
Social Institutions		
Economy	Based on agriculture; much manufacturing in the home; little white-collar work	Based on industrial mass production; factories become centers of production; increasing white-collar work
State	Small-scale government; little state intervention in society	Large-scale government; much state intervention in society
Family	Extended family as the primary means of socialization and economic production	Nuclear family still has some socialization functions but is more a unit of consumption than of production
Religion	Religion guides worldview; little religious pluralism	Religion weakens with the rise of science; extensive religious pluralism
Education	Formal schooling limited to elites	Basic schooling becomes universal, with growing share of people receiving advanced education
Health	High birth and death rates; short life expectancy because of low standard of living and simple medical technology	Low birth and death rates; longer life expectancy because of higher standard of living and sophisticated medical technology
Social Change	Slow; change evident over many generations	Rapid; change evident within a single generation

example, state officials mandate that local schools must meet educational standards, local products must be government-certified, and every citizen must maintain extensive tax records. Although such regulations may protect people and enhance social equality, they also force us to deal more and more with nameless officials in distant and often unresponsive bureaucracies, and they undermine the autonomy of families and local communities.

○ **CRITICAL REVIEW** The growing scale of modern life certainly has positive aspects, but only at the cost of our cultural heritage. Modern societies increase individual rights, have greater tolerance of social differences, and raise living standards (Inglehart & Baker, 2000). But they are prone to what Weber feared most—excessive bureaucracy—as well as to Tönnies's self-centeredness and Durkheim's anomie. The size, complexity, and

Making the Grade

Mass-society theory is critical of the expansion of the modern state, claiming that large bureaucracies encourage dehumanization. Class-society theory takes a more positive view of the expanding state, claiming that it helps reduce social inequality.

Making the Grade

Mass society theory claims the problem with modern society is that it has become too big and impersonal; class society theory claims the problem with modern society is that it is too unequal.

tolerance of diversity of modern societies all but doom traditional values and families, leaving individuals isolated, powerless, and materialistic. As Chapter 12 ("Economics and Politics") noted, voter apathy is a serious problem in the United States. But should we be surprised that individuals in vast, impersonal societies such as ours end up thinking that no one person can make much of a difference?

Critics sometimes say that mass-society theory romanticizes the past. They remind us that many people in the small towns of our past were eager to set out for a better standard of living in cities. This approach also ignores problems of social inequality. Critics say mass-society theory attracts social and economic conservatives who defend conventional morality and are indifferent to the historical inequality of women and other minorities.

CHECK YOUR LEARNING In your own words, state the mass-society analysis of modernity.

Social-Conflict Analysis: Modernity as Class Society

The second explanation of modernity derives mostly from the ideas of Karl Marx. From a social-conflict perspective, modernity takes the form of a **class society,** *a capitalist society with pronounced social stratification.* While agreeing that modern societies have expanded to a

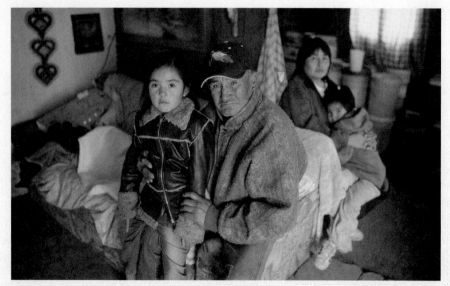

Social-conflict theory sees modernity not as an impersonal mass society but as an unequal class society in which some categories of people are second-class citizens. This Arizona family, like many Native Americans, lives on a reservation, where poverty is widespread and many trailer homes do not have electricity or running water.

mass scale, this approach views the heart of modernization as an expanding capitalist economy, marked by inequality (Habermas, 1970; Harrington, 1984; Buechler, 2000).

Capitalism

Class-society theory follows Marx in claiming that the increasing scale of social life in modern times has resulted from the growth and greed unleashed by capitalism. Because a capitalist economy pursues ever-greater profits, both production and consumption steadily increase.

According to Marx, capitalism rests on "naked self-interest" (Marx & Engels, 1972:337, orig. 1848). This self-centeredness weakens the social ties that once united small communities. Capitalism also treats people as commodities: a source of labor and a market for capitalist products.

Capitalism supports science not just as the key to greater productivity but also as an ideology that justifies the status quo. Modern societies encourage people to view human well-being as a technical puzzle that can be solved by engineers and other scientific experts rather than through the pursuit of social justice. For example, a capitalist culture seeks to improve health through advances in scientific medicine rather than by eliminating poverty, despite the fact that poverty is a core cause of poor health.

Businesses also raise the banner of scientific logic, trying to increase profits through greater efficiency. As Chapter 12 ("Economics and Politics") explained, capitalist corporations have reached enormous size and control unimaginable wealth as a result of global expansion. From the class-society point of view, the expanding scale of life is less a function of *Gesellschaft* than the inevitable and destructive consequence of capitalism.

Persistent Inequality

Modernity has gradually worn away some of the rigid categories that divided preindustrial societies. But class-society theory maintains that elites persist in the form of capitalist millionaires instead of nobles born to wealth and power. In the United States, we may have no hereditary monarchy, but the richest 5 percent of the population controls about 60 percent of all privately held property (Keister, 2005; Wolff, 2009).

What of the state? Mass-society theorists argue that the state works to increase equality and fight social problems. Marx disagreed; he doubted that the state could accomplish more than minor reforms because, as he saw it, real power lies in the hands of the capitalists who control the economy. Other class-society

Making the Grade

Both mass- and class-society theories are critical of modernity: the first because of what is lost (traditional social ties), the second because of what remains (persistent social inequality).

Seeing Sociology in Everyday Life

Have you ever felt difficulty deciding "who you are"? Do you try to be a different person in different settings? If you answer "yes" to such questions, how might you link such experiences to modernity?

SUMMING UP

Two Interpretations of Modernity

	Mass Society	Class Society
Process of modernization	Industrialization; growth of bureaucracy	Rise of capitalism
Effects of modernization	Increasing scale of life; rise of the state and other formal organizations	Expansion of the capitalist economy; persistence of social inequality

theorists add that to the extent that working people and minorities do enjoy greater political rights and a higher standard of living today, these changes were the result of political struggle, not government goodwill. Despite our pretensions of democracy, they conclude, most people are powerless in the face of wealthy elites.

CRITICAL REVIEW Class-society theory dismisses Durkheim's argument that people in modern societies suffer from anomie, claiming instead that most people deal with alienation and powerlessness. Not surprisingly, the class-society interpretation of modernity enjoys widespread support among liberals and radicals who favor greater equality and seek extensive regulation (or abolition) of the capitalist marketplace.

A basic criticism of class-society theory is that it overlooks the increasing prosperity of modern societies and the fact that discrimination based on race, ethnicity, religion, and gender is now illegal and is widely regarded as a social problem. In addition, most people in the United States do not want an egalitarian society; they prefer a system of unequal rewards that reflects personal differences in talent and effort.

Based on socialism's failure to generate a high overall standard of living, few observers think that a centralized economy would cure the ills of modernity. Many other problems in the United States—including unemployment, industrial pollution, and unresponsive government—are also found in socialist nations.

CHECK YOUR LEARNING In your own words, state the class-society analysis of modernity. What are several criticisms of it?

The Summing Up table compares views of modern society offered by mass-society theory and class-society theory. Mass-society theory focuses on the increasing impersonality of social life and the growth of government; class-society theory stresses the expansion of capitalism and the persistence of inequality.

Modernity and the Individual

Both mass- and class-society theories look at the broad patterns of change since the Industrial Revolution. From these macro-level approaches, we can also draw micro-level insights into how modernity shapes individual lives.

Mass Society: Problems of Identity

Modernity freed individuals from the small, tightly knit communities of the past. Most members of modern societies have the privacy and freedom to express their individuality. However, mass-society theory suggests that so much social diversity, widespread isolation, and rapid social change make it difficult for many people to establish any coherent identity at all (Wheelis, 1958; Berger, Berger, & Kellner, 1974).

Chapter 3 ("Socialization: From Infancy to Old Age") explained that people's personalities are mostly a product of their social experiences. The small, homogeneous, and slowly changing societies of the past provided a firm, if narrow, foundation for building a personal identity. Even today, Amish and Mennonite communities that flourish in the United States teach young men and women "correct" ways to think and behave. Not everyone born into an Amish community can tolerate such rigid demands for conformity, but most members establish a well-integrated and satisfying personal identity (Kraybill & Olshan, 1994; Kraybill & Hurd, 2006).

Mass societies are quite another story. Socially diverse and rapidly changing, they offer only shifting sands on which to build a personal identity. Left to make many life decisions on their own, people—especially those with greater wealth—face a confusing range of options. The freedom to choose has little value without standards to guide the selection process; in a tolerant mass society, people may find little reason to choose one path over another. As a result, many people shuttle from one identity to another, changing their lifestyles, relationships, and even religions in search of an elusive "true self." Given the widespread relativism of modern societies, people without

○ Making the Grade

Riesman's tradition-directedness corresponds to Tönnies's *Gemeinschaft* and Durkheim's mechanical solidarity. Other-directedness is linked to *Gesellschaft* and organic solidarity.

a moral compass lack the security and certainty once provided by tradition.

To David Riesman (1970, orig. 1950), modernization brings changes in **social character**, *personality patterns common to members of a particular society*. Preindustrial societies promote what Riesman calls **tradition-directedness**, *rigid conformity to time-honored ways of living*. Members of such societies model their lives on those of their ancestors, so that "living the good life" amounts to "doing what people have always done."

Tradition-directedness corresponds to Tönnies's *Gemeinschaft* and Durkheim's mechanical solidarity. Culturally conservative, tradition-directed people think and act alike. Unlike the conformity often found in modern societies, the uniformity of tradition-directedness is not an effort to imitate a popular celebrity or follow the latest trend. Instead, people are alike because they all draw on the same solid cultural foundation. Amish women and men exemplify tradition-directedness; in the Amish culture, tradition ties everyone to ancestors and descendants in an unbroken chain of righteous living.

Members of diverse and rapidly changing societies define a tradition-directed personality as deviant because it seems so rigid. Modern people prize personal flexibility, the capacity to adapt, and sensitivity to others. Riesman calls this type of social character **other-directedness**, *openness to the latest trends and fashions, often expressed by imitating others*. Because their socialization occurs in societies that are continuously in flux, other-directed people develop fluid identities marked by superficiality, inconsistency, and change. They try on different "selves" almost like new clothing, seek out role models, and engage in varied performances as they move from setting to setting (Goffman, 1959). In a traditional society, such "shiftiness" marks a person as untrustworthy, but in a changing, modern society, the chameleonlike ability to fit in almost virtually anywhere is very useful.

In societies that value the up-to-date rather than the traditional, people look to others for approval, using members of their own generation rather than elders as role models. Peer pressure can be irresistible to people without strong standards to guide them. Our society urges people to be true to themselves, but when social surroundings change so rapidly, how can people develop the self to which they should be true? This problem lies at the root of the identity crisis so widespread in industrial societies today. "Who am I?" is a nagging question that many of us struggle to answer. In truth, this problem is not so much us as the inherently unstable mass society in which we live.

Class Society: Problems of Powerlessness

Class-society theory paints a different picture of modernity's effects on individuals. This approach maintains that persistent inequality under-

mines modern society's promise of individual freedom. For some people, modernity serves up great privilege, but for many others, everyday life means coping with economic uncertainty and a gnawing sense of powerlessness (K. S. Newman, 1993; Ehrenreich, 2001).

For racial and ethnic minorities, the problem of relative disadvantage looms even larger. Similarly, although women participate more broadly in modern societies, they continue to run up against traditional barriers of sexism. This approach rejects mass-society theory's claim that people suffer from too much freedom; according to class-society theory, our society still denies a majority of people full participation in social life.

As Chapter 9 ("Global Stratification") explained, the expanding scope of world capitalism has placed more of Earth's population under the influence of multinational corporations. As a result, 80 percent of the world's income is concentrated in high-income nations, where just 23 percent of its people live. Is it any wonder, class-society theorists ask, that people in poor nations seek greater power to shape their own lives?

The problem of widespread powerlessness led Herbert Marcuse (1964) to challenge Max Weber's claim that modern society is rational. Marcuse condemned modern society as irrational for failing to meet the needs of so many people. Although modern capitalist societies produce unparalleled wealth, poverty remains the daily plight of more than 1 billion people. Marcuse added that technological advances further reduce people's control over their own lives. The advent of high technology has generally conferred a great deal of power on a core of specialists—not the majority of people—who now dominate discussion of when to go to war, what our energy policy should be, and how people should pay for health care. Countering the popular view that technology *solves* the world's problems, Marcuse believed that science *causes* them. In sum, class-society theory asserts that people suffer because modern societies have concentrated both wealth and power in the hands of a privileged few.

Modernity and Progress

In modern societies, most people expect and applaud social change. We link modernity to the idea of *progress* (from the Latin, meaning "moving forward"), a state of continual improvement. We equate stability with stagnation.

Given our bias in favor of change, members of our society tend to regard traditional cultures as backward. But change, particularly toward material affluence, is a mixed blessing. As the Thinking Globally box on page 496 shows, social change is too complex simply to equate with progress.

Even getting rich has both advantages and disadvantages, as the cases of the Kaiapo and Gullah show. Historically, among people in

○ Making the Grade

In a sense, mass-society theory claims that modern people have too much freedom and choice; class-society theory claims that we have too little.

○ Seeing Sociology
in Everyday Life

In 1970, Alvin Toffler coined the phrase "future shock" to describe the effect of social change that comes so rapidly that it overwhelms us. Do you think the pace of change has become overwhelming? Does our world need more change, or do we have too much already? Explain your answers.

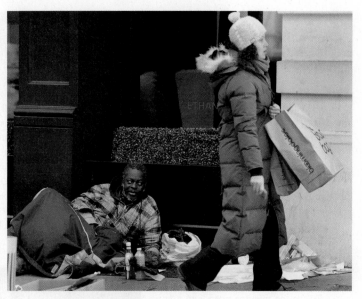

Mass-society theory relates feelings of anxiety and lack of meaning in the modern world to rapid social change that washes away tradition. This notion of modern emptiness is captured in the photo at the left. Class-society theory, by contrast, ties such feelings to social inequality, by which some categories of people are made into second-class citizens (or not made citizens at all), an idea expressed in the photo at the right.

the United States, a rising standard of living has made lives longer and more comfortable. At the same time, many people wonder whether today's routines are too stressful, with families often having little time to relax or to spend time together. Perhaps this is why, in the United States, measures of happiness have declined (D. G. Myers, 2000; Inglehart, Welzel, & Foa, 2009).

Science, too, has its pluses and minuses. People in the United States are more confident than people living in most other industrial societies that science improves our everyday lives (Inglehart & Welzel, 2010). But surveys also show that many adults in the United States feel that science "makes our way of life change too fast" (NORC, 2009:1329).

New technology has always sparked controversy. Just over a century ago, the introduction of automobiles and telephones allowed more rapid transportation and more efficient communication, improving people's lives. At the same time, such technology also weakened traditional attachments to hometowns and even to families. Today, people might wonder whether computer technology will do the same thing: giving us access to people around the world but shielding us from the community right outside our doors; providing more information than ever before but in the process threatening personal privacy. In short, we all realize that social change comes faster all the time, but we may disagree about whether a particular change is good or bad for society.

Modernity: Global Variation

October 1, Kobe, Japan. Riding the computer-controlled monorail high above the streets of Kobe or the 200-mile-per-hour bullet train to Tokyo, we see Japan as the society of the future, in love with high technology. Yet the Japanese remain strikingly traditional in other respects: Few corporate executives and almost no politicians are women, young people still show seniors great respect, and public orderliness contrasts with the relative chaos of many U.S. cities.

Japan is a nation both traditional and modern. This contradiction reminds us that although it is useful to contrast traditional and modern social patterns, the old and the new often coexist in unexpected ways. In the People's Republic of China, ancient Confucian principles are mixed with contemporary socialist thinking. In Saudi Arabia and Qatar, a love of the latest modern technology is mixed with respect for the ancient principles of Islam. Likewise, in Mexico and much of Latin America, people observe centuries-old Christian rituals even as they struggle to move ahead economically. In short, although we may think of tradition and modernity as opposites, combinations of traditional and modern are far from unusual, and they are found throughout the world.

○ Making the Grade

The importance of a global perspective is seeing that "tradition" and "modernity" are not simply opposites but are often found in unexpected combinations in societies around the world.

postmodernity social patterns characteristic of postindustrial societies

---

THINKING GLOBALLY

Does "Modernity" Mean "Progress"? The Kaiapo of the Amazon and the Gullah of Georgia

The firelight flickers in the gathering darkness. Chief Kanhonk sits, as he has done at the end of the day for many years, ready to begin an evening of animated talk and storytelling (Simons, 2007). This is the hour when the Kaiapo, a small society in Brazil's lush Amazon region, celebrate their heritage. Because the Kaiapo are a traditional people with no written language, the elders rely on evenings by the fire to pass along their culture to their children and grandchildren. In the past, evenings like this have been filled with tales of brave Kaiapo warriors fighting off Portuguese traders in pursuit of slaves and gold.

But as the minutes pass, just a few older villagers assemble for the evening ritual. "It is the Big Ghost," one man grumbles, explaining the poor turnout. The "Big Ghost" has indeed descended on them; its bluish glow spills from windows throughout the village. The Kaiapo children—and many adults as well—are watching sitcoms on television. Buying a television and a satellite dish several years ago has had consequences far greater than anyone imagined. In the

end, what their enemies failed to do with guns, the Kaiapo may well do to themselves with prime-time programming.

The Kaiapo are among the 230,000 native peoples who inhabit Brazil. They stand out because of their striking body paint and ornate ceremonial dress. During the 1980s, they became rich from gold mining and harvesting mahogany trees. Now they must decide if their newfound fortune is a blessing or a curse.

To some, affluence means the opportunity to learn about the outside world through travel and television. Others, like Chief Kanhonk, are not so sure. Sitting by the fire, he thinks aloud, "I have been saying that people must buy useful things like knives and fishing hooks. Television does not fill the stomach. It only shows our children and grandchildren white people's things." Bebtopup, the oldest priest, nods in agreement: "The night is the time the old people teach the young people. Television has stolen the night" (Simons, 2007:522).

Far to the north, half an hour by ferry from the coast of Georgia, lies the swampy island community of Hog Hammock. The seventy African American residents of the island today trace their ancestry back to the first slaves who settled here in 1802.

Walking past the brightly painted houses that stand among yellow pine trees draped with Spanish moss, a visitor can easily feel transported back in time. The local people, known as Gullahs (or in some places, Geechees), speak a

Postmodernity

If modernity was the product of the Industrial Revolution, could the Information Revolution be creating a postmodern era? A number of scholars think so, and they use the term **postmodernity** to refer to *social patterns characteristic of postindustrial societies.*

Precisely what postmodernism is remains a matter of debate. The term has been used for decades in literary, philosophical, and even architectural circles. It has moved into sociology on a wave of social criticism that has been building since the spread of left-leaning politics in the 1960s. Although there are many variations of postmodern thinking, all share the following five themes (Hall & Neitz, 1993; Inglehart, 1997; Rudel & Gerson, 1999):

1. **In important respects, modernity has failed.** The promise of modernity was a life free from want. As postmodernist critics see it, however, the twentieth century was unsuccessful in solving

social problems such as poverty because many people still lack financial security.

2. **The bright light of "progress" is fading.** Modern people look to the future expecting their lives to improve in significant ways. Members (and even leaders) of a postmodern society are less confident about what the future holds. The strong optimism that carried society into the modern era more than a century ago has given way to widespread pessimism, especially in recent years due to the weak economy.

3. **Science no longer holds the answers.** The defining trait of the modern era was a scientific outlook and a confident belief that technology would make life better. But postmodern critics argue that science has failed to solve many old problems (such as poor health) and has even created new problems (such as air and water pollution and declining natural resources).

Postmodernist thinkers discredit science, claiming that it implies a singular truth. On the contrary, they maintain, there

○ Making the Grade

Just as the Industrial Revolution marks the onset of modernity, the new postindustrial economy (or Information Revolution) marks the onset of postmodernity.

○ Making the Grade

An important sociological insight is that social change always has both positive and negative consequences, so it is simplistic to equate change with "progress."

creole, a mixture of English and West African languages. They fish, living much the same as they have for hundreds of years.

But the future of this way of life is now in doubt. Few young people who are raised in Hog Hammock can find work; beyond fishing and making traditional crafts, there are simply no jobs to do. "We have been here nine generations and we are still here," says one local. Then, referring to the nineteen children who now live on the island, she adds, "It's not that they don't want to be here; it's that there's nothing here for them—they need to have jobs" (Curry, 2001:41).

Just as important, with people on the mainland looking for waterside homes for vacations or year-round living, the island is now becoming prime real estate. Not long ago, one larger house went up for sale and the community was shocked to learn of an asking price over $1 million. The locals know only too well that higher property values will mean high taxes that few can afford to pay. In short, Hog Hammock is likely to become another Hilton Head, once a Gullah community on the South Carolina coast that is now home to well-to-do people from the mainland.

The odds are that before long, the people of Hog Hammock will be selling their homes and moving inland. But few people are happy at the thought of selling out, even for a good price. On the contrary, moving away will mean the end of their cultural heritage.

The stories of the Kaiapo and the people of Hog Hammock show us that change is not a simple path toward "progress." These people may be moving toward modernity, but this process will have both positive and negative consequences. In the end, both groups of people may enjoy a higher standard of living with better shelter, more clothing, and new technology. But their newfound affluence will come at the price of their traditions. The drama of these people is now being played out around the world as more and more traditional cultures are being lured away from their heritage by the affluence and materialism of rich societies.

WHAT DO YOU THINK?

1. Why is social change both a winning and a losing proposition for traditional people?

2. Do the changes described here improve the lives of the Kaiapo? What about the Gullah community?

3. Do traditional people have any choice about becoming modern? Explain your view.

is no one truth. This means that objective reality does not exist; rather, many realities result from social construction.

4. **Cultural debates are intensifying.** Many people have all the material things they really need, which allows ideas to take on more importance. In this sense, postmodernity is also a postmaterialist era in which issues such as social justice, the environment, and animal rights command more and more public attention.

5. **Social institutions are changing.** Just as industrialization brought sweeping transformation to social institutions, the rise of postindustrial society is remaking society all over again. For example, the Industrial Revolution placed *material things* at the center of productive life; the Information Revolution emphasizes *ideas.* Similarly, the postmodern family no longer conforms to any one pattern; on the contrary, individuals are choosing among many family forms.

○ **CRITICAL REVIEW** Analysts who claim that the United States and other high-income nations are entering a postmodern era criticize modernity for failing to meet human needs. In defense of modernity, there have been marked increases in longevity and living standards over the past century. Even if we were to accept postmodernist views that science is bankrupt and progress is a sham, what are the alternatives?

○ **CHECK YOUR LEARNING** In your own words, state the defining characteristics of a postmodern society.

Looking Ahead: Modernization and Our Global Future

Imagine the entire world's population reduced to a single village of 1,000 people. About 230 residents of this "global village" are from high-income countries. Another 196 people are so poor that their lives are at risk.

○ Seeing Sociology
in Everyday Life

Do you think there is too much of a "me first" attitude in
today's world? Explain your view.

○ Seeing Sociology
in Everyday Life

Does the balance between individual freedom and personal
responsibility differ for men and women? If so, how, and why?

SEEING SOCIOLOGY IN EVERYDAY LIFE Personal Freedom and Social Responsibility: Can We Have It Both Ways?

SAMUEL: I feel that being free is the most important thing. Let me do what I want!

SANJI: But if everyone felt that way, what would the world be like?

DOREEN: Isn't there a way to be true to ourselves and also take account of other people?

One issue we all have to work out is making personal decisions that take proper account of other people. But what, exactly, do we owe others? To see the problem, consider an event that took place in New York in 1964.

Shortly after midnight on a crisp March evening, Kitty Genovese drove into the parking lot of her apartment complex. She turned off the engine, locked the car doors, and headed across the blacktop toward the entrance to her building. Out of nowhere, a man holding a knife lunged at her, and as she screamed in terror and pain, he stabbed her repeatedly. Windows opened above as curious neighbors looked down to see what was going

on. The attack continued for more than thirty minutes until Genovese lay dead in her doorway. The police never identified her killer, and the follow-up investigation revealed a stunning fact:

In today's world, people can find new ways to express age-old virtues such as extending a helping hand to their neighbors in need. In the wake of Hurricane Katrina, thousands of college students from across the country converged on New Orleans to help repair the damage to the stricken city. Are there opportunities for you to get involved in your own community?

Not one of the dozens of neighbors who witnessed the attack on Kitty Genovese went to her aid or even called the police.

Decades after this tragic event, we still confront the question of what we owe others. As members of a modern society, we prize our individual rights and personal privacy, but we sometimes withdraw from public responsibility and turn a cold shoulder to people in need. When a cry for help is met by indifference, have we pushed our modern idea of personal freedom too far? In a society of expanding individual rights, can we keep a sense of human community?

These questions highlight the tension between traditional and modern social systems, which is evident in the writings of all the sociologists discussed in this chapter. Tönnies, Durkheim, and others concluded that in some respects, traditional community and modern individualism don't mix. That is, society can unite its members as a

---

The tragic plight of the world's poor shows that some desperately needed change has not yet occurred. Chapter 9 ("Global Stratification") presented two competing views of why 1 billion people around the world are so poor. *Modernization theory* claims that in the past, the entire world was poor and that technological change, especially the Industrial Revolution, enhanced human productivity and raised living standards in many nations. From this point of view, the solution to global poverty is to promote technological development and market economies around the world.

For reasons suggested earlier, however, global modernization may be difficult. Recall that David Riesman portrayed preindustrial people as *tradition-directed* and likely to resist change. So modernization theorists claim that rich nations should help poor countries grow economically. Industrial nations can speed development by exporting technology to poor regions, welcoming students from these countries, and providing foreign aid to stimulate economic growth.

The review of modernization theory in Chapter 9 points to some success for these policies in Latin America and more dramatic results in the small Asian countries of Taiwan, South Korea, and Singapore and in Hong Kong (part of the People's Republic of China). But jump-starting development in the poorest countries of the world poses greater challenges. Even where dramatic change has occurred, modernization involves a trade-off. Traditional people, such as Brazil's Kaiapo, may gain wealth through economic development, but only at the cost of losing their traditional identity and values as they are drawn into a global "McCulture," which is based on Western materialism, pop music, trendy clothes, and fast food. One Brazilian anthropologist expressed optimism about the future of the Kaiapo: "At least they quickly understood the consequences of watching television. . . . Now [they] can make a choice" (Simons, 2007:523).

But not everyone thinks that modernization is really an option. According to a second approach to global stratification, *dependency*

● Seeing Sociology
in Everyday Life

Think of people you admire. Do you admire them for their
personal achievement, social responsibility, or a combination of
the two?

● Seeing Sociology
in Everyday Life

After reading the box below, think of ways your campus
encourages a sense of community and social responsibility.

moral community only by limiting their range of personal choices about how to live. In short, although we value both community and freedom, we can't have it both ways.

The famed sociologist Amitai Etzioni (1993, 1996, 2003) has tried to strike a middle ground. The *communitarian movement* rests on the simple idea that with rights must come responsibilities. Put another way, our pursuit of self-interest must be balanced by a commitment to the larger community.

Etzioni claims that modern people have become too concerned about individual rights. We expect the system to work for us, but we are reluctant to support the system. For example, we believe that people accused of a crime deserve their day in court, but fewer and fewer of us are willing to perform jury duty; similarly, we are quick to accept government services but reluctant to support these services with our taxes.

The communitarians advance four proposals toward balancing individual rights with public responsibilities. First, our society should stop the expanding "culture of rights" by which we put our own interests ahead of social responsibility. The Constitution, which is quoted so often when discussing individual rights, does not guarantee us the right to do whatever we want. Second, we must remember that we cannot take from society without giving something back. Third, the well-being of everyone may require limiting our individual rights; for example, pilots and bus drivers who are responsible for public safety may be asked to take drug tests. Fourth, no one can ignore key responsibilities such as obeying the law and responding to a cry for help from someone like Kitty Genovese.

The communitarian movement appeals to many people who believe in both personal freedom and social responsibility. But Etzioni's proposals have drawn criticism from both sides of the political spectrum. To those on the left, problems ranging from voter apathy to street crime cannot be solved by some vague idea of "social responsibility." As they see it, what is needed is expanded government programs to protect people and lessen inequality.

Conservatives, on the political right, see different problems in Etzioni's proposals (Pearson, 1995). As they see it, the communitarian movement favors liberal goals, such as confronting prejudice and protecting the environment, but says little about conservative goals, such as strengthening religious beliefs and supporting traditional families.

Etzioni responds that the criticism coming from both sides suggests he has found a moderate, sensible answer to a serious problem. But the debate may also indicate that in a society as diverse as the United States, people who are so quick to assert their rights are not so ready to agree on their responsibilities.

WHAT DO YOU THINK?

1. Have you ever failed to come to the aid of someone in need or danger? Why did you not take action?

2. Half a century ago, President John F. Kennedy stated, "Ask not what your country can do for you; ask what you can do for your country." Do you think people today support this idea? Why or why not?

3. Are you willing to serve on a jury? Do you mind paying your fair share of taxes? Would you be willing to perform a year of national service after you graduate from college? Explain your answers.

---

theory, today's poor societies have little ability to modernize, even if they want to. From this point of view, the major barrier to economic development is not traditionalism but global domination by rich capitalist societies.

Dependency theory asserts that rich nations achieved their modernization at the expense of poor ones, by taking their valuable natural resources and exploiting their human labor. Even today, the world's poorest countries remain locked in a disadvantageous economic relationship with rich nations, dependent on wealthy countries to buy their raw materials and in return provide them with whatever manufactured products they can afford. According to this view, continuing ties with rich societies will only perpetuate current patterns of global inequality.

Whichever approach you find more convincing, keep in mind that change in the United States is no longer separate from change in the rest of the world. At the beginning of the twentieth century, most people in today's high-income countries lived in relatively small settlements with limited awareness of the larger world. Today, the world has become one huge village because the lives of all people are increasingly interconnected.

The twentieth century witnessed unprecedented human achievement. Yet solutions to many problems of human existence—including finding meaning in life, resolving conflicts between societies, and eliminating poverty—have eluded us. The Seeing Sociology in Everyday Life box examines one dilemma: balancing individual freedom and personal responsibility. To this list of pressing matters new concerns have been added, such as controlling population growth and establishing an environmentally sustainable society. In the coming years, we must be prepared to tackle such problems with imagination, compassion, and determination. Our growing understanding of human society gives us reason to be hopeful that we can get the job done.

Seeing Sociology in Everyday Life

Is tradition the opposite of modernity?

Conceptually, this may be true. But as this chapter explains, traditional and modern social patterns combine in all sorts of interesting ways in our everyday lives. Look at the photographs below, and identify elements of tradition and modernity. Do they seem to go together, or are they in conflict? Why?

> **HINT** Although sociologists analyze tradition and modernity as conceptual opposites, every society combines these elements in various ways. People may debate the virtues of traditional and modern life, but the two patterns are found almost everywhere. Technological change always has social consequences—for example, the use of cell phones changes people's social networks and economic opportunities; similarly, the spread of McDonald's changes not only what people eat but where and with whom they share meals.

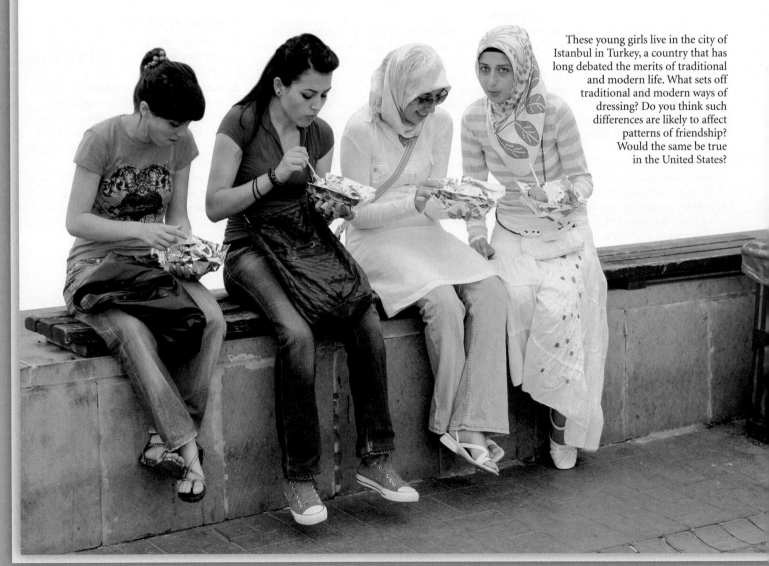

These young girls live in the city of Istanbul in Turkey, a country that has long debated the merits of traditional and modern life. What sets off traditional and modern ways of dressing? Do you think such differences are likely to affect patterns of friendship? Would the same be true in the United States?

When the first McDonald's restaurant opened in the city of Kiev in Ukraine, many people stopped by to taste a hamburger and see what "fast food" was all about. As large corporations expand their operations around the world, do they tip the balance away from tradition in favor of modernity? How?

In Riyadh, Saudi Arabia, these young men are shopping for the latest in cell phones. Does such modern technology threaten a society's traditions?

Applying SOCIOLOGY in Everyday Life

1. How do tradition and modernity combine in your life? Point to several ways in which you are traditional and several ways in which you are thoroughly modern.

2. Ask people in your class or friendship group to make five predictions about U.S. society in the year 2050, when today's twenty-year-olds will be senior citizens. Compare notes. On what issues is there agreement?

3. Do you think the rate of social change has been increasing? Do some research about modes of travel—including walking, riding animals, bicycles, trains, cars, airplanes, and rockets. At what point in history did each of these ways of moving come into being? What pattern do you see?

Making the Grade

Social Change: Modern and Postmodern Societies

What Is Social Change?

⊙-|Watch on mysoclab.com

SOCIAL CHANGE is the transformation of culture and social institutions over time. Every society changes all the time, sometimes faster, sometimes more slowly. Social change often generates controversy.

pp. 478–79

social change (p. 479) the transformation of culture and social institutions over time

Causes of Social Change

CULTURE
- *Invention* produces new objects, ideas, and social patterns.
- *Discovery* occurs when people take notice of existing elements of the world.
- *Diffusion* creates change as products, people, and information spread from one society to another.

p. 480

SOCIAL CONFLICT
- Karl Marx claimed that class conflict between capitalists and workers pushes society toward a socialist system of production.
- Social conflict arising from class, race, and gender inequality has resulted in social changes that have improved the lives of working people.

p. 480

IDEAS
Max Weber traced the roots of most social changes to ideas:
- The fact that industrial capitalism developed first in areas of Western Europe where the Protestant work ethic was strong demonstrates the power of ideas to bring about change.

p. 480

DEMOGRAPHIC FACTORS
Population patterns play a part in social change:
- The aging of U.S. society has resulted in changes to family life and the development of consumer products to meet the needs of the elderly.
- Migration within and between societies promotes change.

pp. 480–81

social movement (p. 481) an organized activity that encourages or discourages social change

claims making (p. 482) the process of trying to convince the public and public officials of the importance of joining a social movement to address a particular issue

relative deprivation (p. 482) a perceived disadvantage arising from some specific comparison

disaster (p. 484) an event, generally unexpected, that causes extensive harm to people and damage to property.

Disasters

Disasters cause unexpected social change:
- *natural disasters* (example: Hurricane Katrina)
- *technological disasters* (example: nuclear accident at the Chernobyl power plant)
- *intentional disasters* (example: Darfur genocide)

pp. 484–85

⊕-|Explore on mysoclab.com

Social Movements

TYPES OF SOCIAL MOVEMENTS
- *Alterative social movements* seek limited change in specific individuals (example: Promise Keepers).
- *Redemptive social movements* seek radical change in specific individuals (example: Alcoholics Anonymous).
- *Reformative social movements* seek limited change in the whole society (example: the environmental movement).
- *Revolutionary social movements* seek radical change in the whole society (example: the Communist party).

p. 481

EXPLANATIONS OF SOCIAL MOVEMENTS
- *Deprivation theory:* Social movements arise among people who feel deprived of something, such as income, safe working conditions, or political rights.
- *Mass-society theory:* Social movements attract socially isolated people who join a movement in order to gain a sense of identity and purpose.
- *Resource mobilization theory:* Success of a social movement is linked to available resources, including money, labor, and the mass media.
- *Culture theory:* Social movements depend not only on money and resources but also on cultural symbols that motivate people.
- *New social movements theory:* Social movements in postindustrial societies are typically international in scope and focus on quality-of-life issues.

pp. 482–83

What Is Modernity?

MODERNITY refers to the social consequences of industrialization, which include the decline of traditional communities, the expansion of personal choice, increasing social diversity, and a focus on the future.
- **Ferdinand Tönnies** described modernization as the transition from *Gemeinschaft* to *Gesellschaft*, characterized by the loss of traditional community and the rise of individualism.
- **Emile Durkheim** saw modernization as a society's expanding division of labor. *Mechanical solidarity*, based on shared activities and beliefs, is gradually replaced by *organic solidarity*, in which specialization makes people interdependent.
- **Max Weber** saw modernity as the decline of a traditional worldview and the rise of rationality. Weber feared the dehumanizing effects of rational organization.
- **Karl Marx** saw modernity as the triumph of capitalism over feudalism. Capitalism creates social conflict, which Marx claimed would bring about revolutionary change leading to an egalitarian socialist society.

pp. 485–89

modernity (p. 485) social patterns resulting from industrialization

modernization (p. 485) the process of social change begun by industrialization

division of labor (p. 487) specialized economic activity

anomie (p. 488) Durkheim's term for a condition in which society provides little moral guidance to individuals

▭-|Read on mysoclab.com

VISUAL SUMMARY

Theoretical Analysis of Modernity

STRUCTURAL-FUNCTIONAL THEORY: MODERNITY AS MASS SOCIETY

- According to **mass-society theory,** modernity increases the scale of life, enlarging the role of government and other formal organizations in carrying out tasks previously performed by families in local communities.
- Cultural diversity and rapid social change make it difficult for people in modern societies to develop stable identities and to find meaning in their lives.

pp. 490–92

SOCIAL-CONFLICT THEORY: MODERNITY AS CLASS SOCIETY

- According to **class-society theory,** modernity involves the rise of capitalism into a global economic system resulting in persistent social inequality.
- By concentrating wealth in the hands of a few, modern capitalist societies generate widespread feelings of alienation and powerlessness.

pp. 492–93

mass society (p. 490) a society in which prosperity and bureaucracy have weakened traditional social ties

class society (p. 492) a capitalist society with pronounced social stratification

See the Summing Up tables on pages 491 and 493.

Modernity and the Individual

Both mass-society theory and class-society theory are macro-level approaches; from them, however, we can also draw micro-level insights into how modernity shapes individual lives.

p. 493

social character (p. 494) personality patterns common to members of a particular society

tradition-directedness (p. 494) rigid conformity to time-honored ways of living

other-directedness (p. 494) openness to the latest trends and fashions, often expressed by imitating others

MASS SOCIETY: PROBLEMS OF IDENTITY

- Mass-society theory suggests that the great social diversity, widespread isolation, and rapid social change of modern societies make it difficult for individuals to establish a stable social identity.

David Riesman described the changes in social character that modernity causes:

- Preindustrial societies exhibit **tradition-directedness:** Everyone in society draws on the same solid cultural foundation, and people model their lives on those of their ancestors.
- Modern societies exhibit **other-directedness:** Because their socialization occurs in societies that are continuously in flux, other-directed people develop fluid identities marked by superficiality, inconsistency, and change.

pp. 493–94

CLASS SOCIETY: PROBLEMS OF POWERLESSNESS

- Class-society theory claims that the problem facing most people today is economic uncertainty and powerlessness.
- Herbert Marcuse claimed that modern society is irrational because it fails to meet the needs of so many people.
- Marcuse also believed that technological advances further reduce people's control over their own lives.
- People suffer because modern societies have concentrated both wealth and power in the hands of a privileged few.

p. 494

Modernity and Progress

Social change is too complex and controversial simply to be equated with progress:

- A rising standard of living has made lives longer and materially more comfortable; at the same time, many people are stressed and have little time to relax with their families; measures of happiness have declined in recent decades.
- Science and technology have brought many conveniences to our everyday lives, yet many people are concerned that life is changing too fast; the introduction of automobiles and advanced communication technology have weakened traditional attachments to hometowns and even to families.

pp. 494–95

Modernity: Global Variation

Although we often think of tradition and modernity as opposites, traditional and modern elements coexist in most societies.

p. 495

Postmodernity

POSTMODERNITY refers to the cultural traits of postindustrial societies. Postmodern criticism of society centers on the failure of modernity, and specifically science, to fulfill its promise of prosperity and well-being.

pp. 496–97

postmodernity (p. 496) social patterns characteristic of postindustrial societies

These questions are similar to those found in the test bank that accompanies this textbook.

Chapter 1 Sociology: Perspective, Theory, and Method

Multiple-Choice Questions

1. **What does the sociological perspective show us about whom any individual chooses to marry?**
   a. There is no explaining personal feelings like love.
   b. People's actions reflect human free will.
   c. The operation of society guides many of our personal choices.
   d. In the case of love, opposites attract.

2. **The personal value of studying sociology includes**
   a. seeing the opportunities and constraints in our lives.
   b. the fact that it is good preparation for a number of careers.
   c. becoming more active participants in society.
   d. All of the above are correct.

3. **The discipline of sociology first developed in**
   a. countries experiencing rapid social change.
   b. countries with strong traditions.
   c. countries with a history of warfare.
   d. the world's poorest countries.

4. **Which early sociologist coined the term *sociology* in 1838?**
   a. Karl Marx
   b. Auguste Comte
   c. Adam Smith
   d. Herbert Spencer

5. **Sociology's social-conflict approach draws attention to**
   a. how structure contributes to the overall operation of society.
   b. how people construct meaning through interaction.
   c. patterns of social inequality.
   d. the stable aspects of society.

6. ***Empirical evidence* refers to**
   a. quantitative rather than qualitative data.
   b. what people consider "common sense."
   c. information we can verify with our senses.
   d. patterns found in every known society.

7. **When trying to measure people's "social class," you would have to keep in mind that**
   a. no measurement can ever be both reliable and valid.
   b. there are several ways to operationalize this variable.
   c. there is no way to measure "social class."
   d. in the United States, everyone agrees on what "social class" means.

8. **Interpretive sociology is a research orientation that**
   a. focuses on people's actions.
   b. sees an objective reality "out there."
   c. seeks to increase social justice.
   d. focuses on the meanings people attach to behavior.

9. **In research using participant observation, the problem of "breaking in" to a setting is often solved with the help of a**
   a. key informant.
   b. research assistant.
   c. bigger budget.
   d. sample.

10. **The critical sociology research orientation is linked most closely to which theoretical approach?**
   a. structural-functional approach
   b. social-conflict approach
   c. symbolic-interaction approach
   d. None of the above is correct.

Essay Questions

1. Explain why using the sociological perspective can make us seem less in control of our lives. In what ways does it actually give us greater power over our lives?

2. Guided by the discipline's three major theoretical approaches, come up with sociological questions about (a) television, (b) war, and (c) colleges and universities.

3. Discuss positivist sociology, interpretive sociology, and critical sociology so that you present each orientation clearly. Why might a sociologist prefer one orientation to another? Why is it important for a student of sociology to understand all three?

Chapter 2 Culture

Multiple-Choice Questions

1. **Of all the world's countries, the United States is the most**
   a. multicultural.
   b. culturally uniform.
   c. slowly changing.
   d. resistant to cultural diversity.

2. **Ideas created by members of a society are part of**
   a. high culture.
   b. material culture.
   c. norms.
   d. nonmaterial culture.

3. **Sociologists define a symbol as**
   a. any gesture that creates conflict within a population.
   b. any element of material culture.

c. anything that has meaning to people who share a culture.

d. any pattern that causes culture shock.

4. **U.S. culture holds a strong belief in**

a. the traditions of the past.

b. individuality.

c. equality of condition for all.

d. "being" rather than "doing."

5. **Cheating on a final examination is an example of violating campus**

a. folkways.

b. symbols.

c. mores.

d. high culture.

6. **Which of the following phrases describes the concept of ethnocentrism?**

a. taking pride in your ethnicity

b. judging an unfamiliar culture using the standards of your own culture

c. seeing another culture as better than your own

d. judging another culture by its own standards

7. *Subculture* **refers to**

a. a part of the population lacking culture.

b. elements of popular culture.

c. people who embrace high culture.

d. cultural patterns that set apart a segment of a society's population.

8. **Which region of the United States has the largest share of people who speak a language other than English at home?**

a. the Southwest

b. the Northeast

c. the Northwest

d. the South

9. **In human history, the "dawn of civilization" took place with the development of**

a. hunting and gathering.

b. pastoralism.

c. industry.

d. agriculture.

10. **Which theoretical approach focuses on the link between culture and social inequality?**

a. the structural-functional approach

b. the social-conflict approach

c. the symbolic-interaction approach

d. the sociobiology approach

ANSWERS: 1(a); 2(d); 3(c); 4(b); 5(c); 6(b); 7(d); 8(a); 9(d); 10(b).

Essay Questions

1. In the United States, hot dogs, hamburgers, French fries, and ice cream have long been considered national favorites. What cultural patterns help explain this country's love of these foods?

2. From what you have learned in this chapter, do you think that a global culture is emerging? Do you think the idea of global culture is positive or negative? Explain your answer.

Chapter 3   Socialization: From Infancy To Old Age

Multiple-Choice Questions

1. **Kingsley Davis's study of Anna, the girl isolated for five years, shows that**

a. humans have the same instincts found in other animal species.

b. without social experience, a child never develops personality.

c. personality is present in all humans at birth.

d. many human instincts disappear in the first few years of life.

2. **Most sociologists take the position that**

a. most human behavior is directed by instincts.

b. biological instincts develop in humans at puberty.

c. it is human nature for us to nurture.

d. All of the above are correct.

3. **Lawrence Kohlberg explored socialization by studying**

a. cognition.

b. the importance of gender in socialization.

c. the development of biological instincts.

d. moral reasoning.

4. **Carol Gilligan added to Kohlberg's findings by showing that**

a. girls and boys typically use different standards in deciding what is right and wrong.

b. girls are more interested in right and wrong than boys are.

c. boys are more interested in right and wrong than girls are.

d. today's children are far less interested in right and wrong than their parents are.

5. **The "self," said George Herbert Mead, is**

a. the part of the human personality made up of self-awareness and self-image.

b. the presence of culture within the individual.

c. basic drives that are self-centered.

d. present in infants from birth.

6. **Why is the family so important to the socialization process?**

a. Family members provide necessary care for infants and children.

b. Families give children social identity in terms of class, ethnicity, and religion.

c. Parents greatly affect a child's self-concept.

d. All of the above are correct.

7. **Compared to higher-income parents, lower-income parents are more likely to emphasize which of the following as a desirable trait in children?**

a. independence

b. creativity

c. obedience

d. imagination

8. In global perspective, which statement about childhood is correct?
   a. In every society, the first ten years of life are a time of play and learning.
   b. Rich societies extend childhood much longer than poor societies do.
   c. Poor societies extend childhood much longer than rich societies do.
   d. Childhood is defined by being biologically immature.

9. Members of high-income societies typically define people in old age as
   a. the wisest of all.
   b. the most up-to-date on current fashion and trends.
   c. less socially important than younger adults.
   d. All of the above are correct.

10. According to Erving Goffman, the purpose of a total institution is
    a. to reward someone for achievement in the outside world.
    b. to give a person more choices about how to live.
    c. to encourage lifelong learning in a supervised setting.
    d. to radically change a person's personality or behavior.

ANSWERS: 1(b); 2(c); 3(d); 4(a); 5(a); 6(d); 7(c); 8(c); 9(c); 10(d).

Essay Questions

1. State the two sides of the "nature-nurture" debate. In what important way are human nature and nurture *not* opposed to each other?

2. Point to several common themes in the ideas of Freud, Piaget, Kohlberg, Gilligan, Mead, and Erikson. In what ways do their theories differ?

Chapter 4   Social Interaction in Everyday Life

Multiple-Choice Questions

1. Which of the following concepts defines who we are in relation to others?
   a. role
   b. status
   c. role set
   d. role strain

2. In U.S. society, which of the following is typically a master status?
   a. occupation
   b. age
   c. sex
   d. physical or mental disability

3. *Role set* refers to
   a. all the roles found in any one society.
   b. a number of roles attached to a single status.
   c. a number of roles that are more or less the same.
   d. the leadership roles within any one organization.

4. Frank excels at football at his college, but with the time sports demands, he doesn't have enough time to study. He is experiencing the problem of
   a. role set.
   b. role strain.
   c. role conflict.
   d. role exit.

5. The Thomas theorem states that
   a. our statuses and roles are the key to our personality.
   b. most people rise to their level of incompetence.
   c. people know the world only through their language.
   d. situations defined as real are real in their consequences.

6. Which of the following is the correct meaning of "presentation of self"?
   a. efforts to create impressions in the minds of others
   b. acting out a master status
   c. thinking back over the process of role exit
   d. trying to draw attention away from others

7. Research supports the conclusion that people around the world
   a. rarely display any emotion when "on the job."
   b. are prompted by the same "triggers" to display emotions.
   c. experience the same six basic emotions.
   d. follow the same rules about when and where to display emotions.

8. In terms of dramaturgical analysis, tact is understood as
   a. helping someone take on a new role.
   b. helping someone "save face."
   c. making it difficult for someone to perform a role.
   d. negotiating a situation to get your own way.

9. In her study of human emotion, Arlie Hochschild explains that many companies
   a. try to regulate the emotions of workers.
   b. want workers to lack all emotion.
   c. encourage workers to express their true emotions.
   d. profit from making customers more emotional.

10. People are likely to "get" a joke when they
    a. know something about more than one culture.
    b. have a different social background than the joke teller.
    c. understand the two different realities being presented.
    d. know why someone wants to tell the joke.

ANSWERS: 1(b); 2(d); 3(b); 4(c); 5(d); 6(a); 7(c); 8(b); 9(a); 10(c).

Essay Questions

1. Explain Erving Goffman's claim that we engage in a "presentation of self." What are the elements of this presentation? Apply this approach to an analysis of a college professor teaching a class.

2. In what ways are human emotions rooted in our biology? In what ways are emotions guided by culture?

Chapter 5   Groups and Organizations

Multiple-Choice Questions

1. What name did Charles Horton Cooley give to a small social group whose members share personal and lasting relationships?
   a. expressive group
   b. in-group

c. primary group

d. secondary group

2. **Which type of group leadership is concerned with getting the job done?**
   a. laissez-faire leadership
   b. secondary group leadership
   c. expressive leadership
   d. instrumental leadership

3. **The research done by Solomon Asch, in which subjects were asked to pick lines of the same length, showed that**
   a. groups encourage their members to conform.
   b. most people are stubborn and refuse to change their minds.
   c. groups often generate conflict.
   d. group members rarely agree on everything.

4. **Which of the following concepts refers to a social group that someone uses as a point of reference in making an evaluation or decision?**
   a. out-group
   b. reference group
   c. in-group
   d. primary group

5. **A network is correctly thought of as**
   a. the most close-knit social group.
   b. a category of people with something in common.
   c. a social group in which most people know one another.
   d. a web of weak social ties.

6. **From the point of view of a nurse, a hospital is a**
   a. normative organization.
   b. coercive organization.
   c. utilitarian organization.
   d. All of the above are correct.

7. **Bureaucracy is a type of social organization characterized by**
   a. specialized jobs.
   b. offices arranged in a hierarchy.
   c. lots of rules and regulations.
   d. All of the above are correct.

8. **According to Robert Michels, bureaucracy always means**
   a. inefficiency.
   b. oligarchy.
   c. alienation.
   d. specialization.

9. **Rosabeth Moss Kanter claims that large business organizations**
   a. need to "open up" opportunity to encourage all workers to perform well.
   b. must have clear and stable rules to survive in a changing world.
   c. do well or badly depending on how talented the leader is.
   d. suffer if they do not adopt the latest technology.

10. **The "McDonaldization of society" means that**
    a. organizations can provide food for people more efficiently than families can.
    b. impersonal organizations concerned with efficiency, predictability, uniformity, and control are more and more common.

c. it is possible for organizations to both achieve their goals and meet human needs.

d. society today is one vast social network.

ANSWERS: 1(c); 2(d); 3(a); 4(b); 5(d); 6(c); 7(d); 8(b); 9(a); 10(b).

Essay Questions

1. How do primary groups differ from secondary groups? Give examples of each type of group in your own life.

2. According to Max Weber, what are the six traits that define bureaucracy? What is the advantage of this organizational form? What are several problems that often go along with it?

Chapter 6   Sexuality and Society

Multiple-Choice Questions

1. **What is the term for humans who have some combination of female and male genitalia?**
   a. asexual people
   b. bisexual people
   c. transsexual people
   d. intersexual people

2. **A global perspective on human sexuality shows us that**
   a. although sex involves our biology, it is also a cultural trait that varies from place to place.
   b. people everywhere in the world have the same sexual practices.
   c. people in all societies are uncomfortable talking about sex.
   d. All of the above are correct.

3. **Why is the incest taboo found in every society?**
   a. It limits sexual competition between members of families.
   b. It helps define people's rights and obligations toward one another.
   c. It helps connect members of a family to others in the larger society.
   d. All of the above are correct.

4. **The sexual revolution came of age during the**
   a. 1890s.
   b. 1920s.
   c. 1960s.
   d. 1980s.

5. **Survey data show that the largest share of U.S. adults reject which of the following sexual practices?**
   a. extramarital sex
   b. homosexuality
   c. premarital sex
   d. sex simply for pleasure

6. **According to the Laumann study of sexuality in the United States,**
   a. only one-third of the adult population is sexually active.
   b. there is great diversity in levels of sexual activity, so no one stereotype is correct.

c. single people have more sex than married people.

d. most married men admit to cheating on their wives at some point in their marriage.

7. **Which concept refers to sexual attraction to people of both sexes?**
    a. heterosexuality
    b. homosexuality
    c. bisexuality
    d. asexuality

8. **Compared to 1950, the U.S. rate of teenage pregnancy today is**
    a. higher.
    b. the same, but more teens become pregnant by choice.
    c. the same, but more pregnant teens are married.
    d. lower.

9. **By what point in their lives do half of young people in the United States today experience sexual intercourse?**
    a. when they marry
    b. by the middle of college
    c. by the end of high school
    d. by age thirteen

10. **If we look back in history, we see that once a society develops birth control technology,**
    a. social control of sexuality becomes more strict.
    b. the birth rate actually goes up.
    c. attitudes about sexuality become more permissive.
    d. people no longer express concern about incest.

ANSWERS: 1(d); 2(a); 3(d); 4(c); 5(a); 6(b); 7(c); 8(d); 9(c); 10(c).

Essay Questions

1. What was the "sexual revolution"? What changed? Can you point to reasons for the change?

2. Identify four sexual orientations. Based on what researchers have discovered, how do people take on a sexual orientation?

Chapter 7   Deviance

Multiple-Choice Questions

1. **Crime is a special type of deviance that**
    a. refers to violations of formally enacted criminal law.
    b. always involves punishment.
    c. refers to the violation of any societal norms.
    d. causes the greatest harm to society.

2. **Emile Durkheim explains that deviance is**
    a. defined by the rich and used against the poor.
    b. harmful not just to victims but to society as a whole.
    c. often at odds with public morality.
    d. found in every society because it has useful consequences.

3. **Using Robert Merton's strain theory, a person selling illegal drugs for a living would fall into which of the following categories?**
    a. conformist
    b. innovator
    c. retreatist
    d. ritualist

4. **Labeling theory states that deviance**
    a. is a normal part of social life.
    b. always changes an offender's social identity.
    c. arises not from what people do as much as from how others respond to the action.
    d. All of the above are correct.

5. **When Jake's friends began calling him a "dope-head," he left the group and spent more time smoking marijuana. He also began hanging out with others who used drugs, and by the end of the term, he had dropped out of college. Edwin Lemert would say this situation illustrates**
    a. a case of primary deviance.
    b. the onset of secondary deviance.
    c. the formation of a deviant subculture.
    d. the beginning of retreatism.

6. **A social-conflict analysis links deviance to**
    a. who does and does not have power in the society.
    b. a society's moral values.
    c. how often the behavior occurs.
    d. how harmful the behavior is.

7. **Stealing a laptop computer from the study lounge in your college dorm is an example of which of the following criminal offenses?**
    a. a burglary
    b. motor vehicle theft
    c. robbery
    d. larceny-theft

8. **The FBI's criminal statistics used in this chapter reflect**
    a. all crimes that occur.
    b. offenses known to the police.
    c. offenses that result in an arrest.
    d. offenses that result in a criminal conviction.

9. **Most people arrested for violent crime in the United States are**
    a. white.
    b. African American.
    c. Hispanic.
    d. Asian.

10. **Which of the following is the oldest justification for punishing an offender?**
    a. deterrence
    b. societal protection
    c. retribution
    d. rehabilitation

ANSWERS: 1(a); 2(d); 3(b); 4(c); 5(b); 6(a); 7(d); 8(b); 9(a); 10(c).

Essay Questions

1. How does a sociological view of deviance differ from the common-sense notion that bad people do bad things?

2. How is social power linked to the creation of crime or other types of deviance? In your response, consider social class and race. Does gender also fit this pattern? Explain.

Chapter 8   Social Stratification

Multiple-Choice Questions

1. *Social stratification* refers to
   a. job specialization in modern societies.
   b. ranking categories of people in a hierarchy.
   c. the fact that some people work harder than others.
   d. inequality of personal talent and individual effort.

2. A caste system is social stratification
   a. based on individual achievement.
   b. based on merit.
   c. based on birth.
   d. in which just two categories of people are unequal.

3. Sonja has two advanced degrees, an average salary, and is working at a low-prestige job. Which concept best describes her situation?
   a. low status consistency
   b. horizontal social mobility
   c. upward social mobility
   d. high status consistency

4. According to the Davis-Moore thesis,
   a. equality is functional or useful for society.
   b. the more inequality a society has, the more productive it is.
   c. more important jobs must offer enough rewards to draw talent from less important work.
   d. societies with more meritocracy are less productive than those with caste systems.

5. Karl Marx claimed that society "reproduces the class structure." By this he meant that
   a. society benefits from inequality.
   b. class differences are passed on from one generation to the next.
   c. class differences are the same everywhere in the world.
   d. a classless society is impossible.

6. Max Weber claimed that social stratification is based on
   a. economic class.
   b. social status or prestige.
   c. power.
   d. All of the above are correct.

7. The wealthiest 20 percent of people in the United States own about how much of the country's privately owned wealth?
   a. 35 percent
   b. 55 percent
   c. 85 percent
   d. 95 percent

8. Which of the following jobs is an example of high-prestige work?
   a. telephone operator
   b. college professor
   c. child care worker
   d. cashier

9. Which of the following is another term for the working class?
   a. upper-middle class
   b. average-middle class
   c. lower class
   d. lower-middle class

10. Which quintile (20 percent) of the U.S. population has seen the greatest change in income over the last generation?
    a. the top quintile
    b. the middle quintile
    c. the lowest quintile
    d. All quintiles have seen the same change.

11. Change in social position during a person's own lifetime is called
    a. intergenerational social mobility.
    b. intragenerational social mobility.
    c. structural social mobility.
    d. horizontal social mobility.

12. Which age category of the U.S. population has the highest poverty rate?
    a. young people under the age of eighteen
    b. adults in their thirties
    c. middle-aged people in their forties
    d. seniors over age sixty-five

ANSWERS: 1(b); 2(c); 3(a); 4(c); 5(b); 6(d); 7(c); 8(b); 9(d); 10(a); 11(b); 12(a).

Essay Questions

1. Explain why social stratification is a creation of society and not just a reflection of individual differences.

2. How do caste and class systems differ? How are they the same? Why does industrialization introduce a measure of meritocracy into social stratification?

3. What is the extent of poverty in the United States? Who are the poor in terms of age, race and ethnicity, and gender?

Chapter 9   Global Stratification

Multiple-Choice Questions

1. In global perspective, the richest 20 percent of all people earn about what share of the entire world's income?
   a. 17 percent
   b. 370 percent
   c. 57 percent
   d. 77 percent

2. The United States, Canada, and Japan are all
   a. high-income countries.
   b. middle-income countries.
   c. low-income countries.
   d. in different income categories.

3. Low-income nations
   a. are evenly spread in all world regions.
   b. are found mostly in Africa and Asia.
   c. are all in Latin America.
   d. contain a majority of the world's people.

4. China and India are now
   a. the world's two poorest nations.
   b. two of the world's low-income nations.
   c. two of the world's middle-income nations.
   d. two of the world's high-income nations.

5. Which of the following is the range of annual personal income for people living in middle-income nations?
   a. $250 to $1,000
   b. $1,000 to $2,499
   c. $2,500 to $12,000
   d. $12,001 to $25,000

6. How does poverty in poor nations compare to poverty in the United States?
   a. In poor nations, poverty is more likely to involve men.
   b. In most poor nations, the problem of poverty is close to being solved.
   c. Poor nations contain a smaller number of poor people than the United States.
   d. In poor nations, there is far more absolute poverty.

7. *Neocolonialism* refers to the process by which
   a. rich countries gain new colonies to replace older ones.
   b. multinational corporations dominate the economy of a poor country.
   c. rich countries grant independence to their former colonies.
   d. large corporations do business in many countries at once.

8. Which of the following statements is the basis of modernization theory?
   a. The main cause of poverty in the world is low productivity due to simple technology and traditional culture.
   b. Poor nations can never become rich if they remain part of the global capitalist economy.
   c. The main cause of poverty in the world is the operation of multi-national corporations.
   d. Most poor nations were richer in the past than they are today.

9. According to Walt Rostow, which is the final stage of economic development?
   a. drive to technological maturity
   b. traditional
   c. high mass consumption
   d. take-off

10. Dependency theory differs from modernization theory by saying that
    a. poor nations are responsible for their own poverty.
    b. capitalism is the best way to produce economic development.

c. economic development is not a good idea for poor countries.
d. global stratification results from the exploitation of poor countries by rich countries.

ANSWERS: 1(d); 2(a); 3(b); 4(c); 5(c); 6(d); 7(b); 8(a); 9(c); 10(d).

Essay Questions

1. What are the differences between relative and absolute poverty? Describe global social stratification using both concepts.

2. Why do many analysts claim that economic development in low-income countries depends on raising the social standing of women?

Chapter 10   Gender Stratification

Multiple-Choice Questions

1. Gender is not just a matter of personal traits but also a matter of differences in
   a. power.
   b. wealth.
   c. prestige.
   d. All of the above are correct.

2. The anthropologist Margaret Mead studied gender in three societies in New Guinea and found that
   a. all societies define femininity in much the same way.
   b. all societies define masculinity in much the same way.
   c. what is feminine in one society may be masculine in another.
   d. the meaning of gender is changing everywhere toward greater equality.

3. For all of us raised in U.S. society, gender shapes our
   a. feelings.
   b. thoughts.
   c. actions.
   d. All of the above are correct.

4. There is a "beauty myth" in U.S. society that encourages
   a. women to believe that their personal importance depends on their looks.
   b. beautiful women to think they do not need men.
   c. men to improve their physical appearance in order to attract women.
   d. women to disregard beauty in favor of personal achievement.

5. In the United States, what share of women work for income?
   a. 80 percent
   b. 60 percent
   c. 40 percent
   d. 20 percent

6. In the U.S. labor force,
   a. men and women have the same types of jobs.
   b. men and women earn the same pay.
   c. women are still concentrated in several types of jobs.
   d. a majority of working women hold "pink-collar" jobs.

7. For which of the following categories of people in the United States is it true that women do more housework than men?
   a. people who work for income
   b. people who are married
   c. people who have children
   d. All of the above are correct.

8. In the United States, women in the labor force working full time earn how much for every dollar earned by men working full time?
   a. 77 cents
   b. 87 cents
   c. 91 cents
   d. 97 cents

9. Before the 2010 elections, women held about what percentage of seats in Congress?
   a. 7 percent
   b. 17 percent
   c. 37 percent
   d. 57 percent

10. The Equal Rights Amendment, which would expand the rights and opportunities of women, reflects which of the following types of feminism?
   a. socialist feminism
   b. liberal feminism
   c. radical feminism
   d. All of the above are correct.

Essay Questions

1. How do the concepts "sex" and "gender" differ? Why is the chapter called "Gender Stratification" rather than "Sex Stratification?"

2. Why is gender correctly considered a dimension of social stratification? How does gender intersect other dimensions of inequality, such as class, race, and ethnicity?

Chapter 11   Race and Ethnicity

Multiple-Choice Questions

1. *Race* refers to _____ considered important in a society, and *ethnicity* refers to _____.
   a. biological traits; cultural traits
   b. cultural traits; biological traits
   c. our differences; what we all have in common
   d. what we all have in common; our differences

2. People of Hispanic descent make up what share of the U.S. population?
   a. 45.4 percent
   b. 35.4 percent
   c. 25.4 percent
   d. 15.4 percent

3. A minority is defined as a category of people who
   a. at one time were disadvantaged.
   b. are less than half of a society's population.
   c. are defined as different and are disadvantaged.
   d. are below average in terms of income.

4. In the United States, four states have a "minority majority." Which of the following states is *not* one of them?
   a. California
   b. Florida
   c. Texas
   d. New Mexico

5. Research using the Bogardus social distance scale shows that U.S. college students
   a. are less prejudiced than students fifty years ago.
   b. believe that Arabs and Muslims should be kept out of the country.
   c. have the strongest prejudice against African Americans.
   d. All of the above are correct.

6. *Prejudice* is a matter of _____, and *discrimination* is a matter of _____.
   a. biology; culture
   b. attitudes; behavior
   c. choice; social structure
   d. social structure; culture

7. The United States is not truly pluralistic today because
   a. part of our population lives in "ethnic enclaves."
   b. this country has a history of slavery.
   c. different racial and ethnic categories are unequal in social standing.
   d. All of the above are correct.

8. Which concept is illustrated by immigrants from Ecuador coming to the United States and learning to speak the English language?
   a. genocide
   b. segregation
   c. assimilation
   d. pluralism

9. When the first Europeans came to the Americas in the late 1400s, Native Americans
   a. followed shortly thereafter.
   b. had just migrated from Asia.
   c. came on ships with them from Europe.
   d. had inhabited this land for 30,000 years.

10. Which is the largest category of Asian Americans in the United States?
   a. Chinese Americans
   b. Japanese Americans
   c. Korean Americans
   d. Vietnamese Americans

Essay Questions

1. What is the difference between race and ethnicity? What does it mean to say that race and ethnicity are socially constructed?

2. What is a minority? Pointing to specific facts in this chapter, support the claim that African Americans and Arab Americans are both minorities in the United States.

Chapter 12   Economics and Politics

Multiple-Choice Questions

1. The economy is the social institution that guides
   a. the production of goods and services.
   b. the distribution of goods and services.
   c. the consumption of goods and services.
   d. All of the above are correct.

2. Building houses and making cars are examples of production in which economic sector?
   a. the primary sector
   b. the secondary sector
   c. the tertiary sector
   d. the service sector

3. Which of the following factors is a result of the globalization of the economy?
   a. Certain areas of the world specialize in one sector of economic activity.
   b. Industrial jobs in the United States are being lost to other countries.
   c. More and more products pass through several nations before reaching the consumer.
   d. All of the above are correct.

4. Socialist economies differ from capitalist economies by
   a. being more productive.
   b. creating less economic equality.
   c. creating more economic equality.
   d. making greater use of commercial advertising.

5. The largest 2,568 corporations, each with assets exceeding $2.5 billion, represent about what share of all corporate assets in the United States?
   a. 80 percent
   b. 60 percent
   c. 30 percent
   d. 10 percent

6. Modern societies, including the United States, rely mostly on which type of authority?
   a. charismatic authority
   b. traditional authority
   c. rational-legal authority
   d. no authority at all

7. In which type of political system does power reside in the hands of the people as a whole?
   a. democracy
   b. aristocracy
   c. totalitarianism
   d. monarchy

8. In the 2008 U.S. presidential election, about what share of registered voters actually cast a vote?
   a. 93 percent
   b. 83 percent
   c. 63 percent
   d. 23 percent

9. The Marxist political-economy model suggests that
   a. power is concentrated in the hands of a small "power elite."
   b. an antidemocratic bias is built into the capitalist system.
   c. power is widely spread throughout society.
   d. many people do not vote because they are basically satisfied with their lives.

10. Which of the following wars resulted in the highest loss of life to people in the United States?
    a. Civil War
    b. World War II
    c. Korean War
    d. Vietnam War

ANSWERS: 1(d); 2(b); 3(d); 4(c); 5(a); 6(c); 7(a); 8(c); 9(b); 10(a).

Essay Questions

1. In what specific ways did the Industrial Revolution change the U.S. economy? How is the Information Revolution changing the economy once again?

2. Discuss the pluralist, power-elite, and Marxist political-economy models of political power, explaining how each differs from the others. Which of these models do you think makes the most sense? Why?

Chapter 13   Family and Religion

Multiple-Choice Questions

1. The family is a social institution that is found in
   a. every society.
   b. low-income nations but typically not in high-income nations.
   c. high-income nations but typically not in low-income nations.
   d. most but not all societies.

2. What is the term sociologists use for a group containing parents, children, and other kin?
   a. extended family
   b. nuclear family
   c. family of affinity
   d. conjugal family

3. Sociologists claim that marriage in the United States follows the principle of homogamy, which means that partners are
   a. people of the same sex.
   b. people who are socially alike in terms of class, age, and race.
   c. people who marry due to social pressure.
   d. selected based on love rather than by parents.

4. Which theoretical approach helps us see that people select partners who have about the same to offer as they do?
   a. the structural-functional approach
   b. the social-conflict approach
   c. the social-exchange approach
   d. the feminist approach

5. In the United States, many Latino families are characterized by
   a. strong extended kinship.
   b. parents exerting a great deal of control over their children's courtship.
   c. traditional gender roles.
   d. All of the above are correct.

6. What term did Emile Durkheim use to describe the everyday aspects of our lives?
   a. religion
   b. sacred
   c. profane
   d. ritual

7. Max Weber's famous thesis states that particular religious ideas set in motion a wave of change that resulted in
   a. increasing social conflict.
   b. a return to the traditions of the Middle Ages.
   c. the Protestant Reformation.
   d. the Industrial Revolution and the rise of capitalism.

8. Which type of religious organization is most integrated into the larger society?
   a. cult
   b. church
   c. sect
   d. counterculture

9. About what share of the U.S. population claims to identify with a religious tradition?
   a. 84 percent
   b. 64 percent
   c. 44 percent
   d. 24 percent

10. The term "secularization" refers to which of the following?
   a. religion becoming more important in people's lives
   b. the increasing popularity of religious fundamentalism
   c. a decline in the importance of religion and the sacred
   d. churches trying to resist social change

ANSWERS: 1(a); 2(a); 3(b); 4(c); 5(d); 6(c); 7(d); 8(b); 9(a); 10(c).

Essay Questions

1. Sociologists point to ways in which family life reflects not just individual choices but the structure of society as well. Provide three examples of how society shapes family life.

2. Explain Karl Marx's claim that religion tends to support the status quo. Develop a counterclaim, based on Max Weber's analysis of Calvinism and the rise of capitalism.

Chapter 14   Education, Health, and Medicine

Multiple-Choice Questions

1. In the United States and in other countries, laws requiring all children to attend school were enacted following
   a. national independence.
   b. the Industrial Revolution.
   c. World War II.
   d. the invention of computers.

2. Japan differs from the United States in that attending college there depends more on
   a. athletic ability.
   b. race and ethnicity.
   c. scores on achievement tests.
   d. family wealth.

3. According to the structural-functional approach, schooling carries out the task of
   a. linking together a diverse population with common norms and values.
   b. creating new elements of culture.
   c. socializing young people.
   d. All of the above are correct.

4. Social-conflict analysis highlights how education
   a. reflects and reinforces social inequality.
   b. helps prepare students for their future careers.
   c. has both latent and manifest functions.
   d. All of the above are correct.

5. The importance of community colleges to U.S. higher education is reflected in the fact that they
   a. greatly expand the opportunity to attend college.
   b. enroll more than 40 percent of all U.S. college students.
   c. enroll almost half of all African American and Hispanic college students.
   d. All of the above are correct.

6. Health is a social issue because
   a. cultural patterns define what people view as healthy.
   b. social inequality affects people's health.
   c. a society's technology affects people's health.
   d. All of the above are correct.

7. In the very poorest nations of the world today, a majority of people die before reaching
   a. their teens.
   b. the age of fifty.
   c. the age of sixty-five.
   d. the age of seventy-five.

8. Which is the greatest cause of death among young people in the United States?
   a. cancer
   b. AIDS

c. accidents

d. influenza

9. **In the United States, the greatest preventable cause of death is**

   a. sexually transmitted diseases.

   b. automobile accidents.

   c. cigarette smoking.

   d. AIDS.

10. **About what share of U.S. adults are overweight?**

   a. two-thirds

   b. one-half

   c. one-third

   d. one-fifth

ANSWERS: 1(b); 2(c); 3(d); 4(a); 5(d); 6(d); 7(a); 8(c); 9(c); 10(a).

Essay Questions

1. Why does industrialization lead societies to expand their systems of schooling? In what ways has schooling in the United States been shaped by our economic, political, and cultural systems?

2. Using the structural-functional approach, why is schooling important to the operation of society? From a social-conflict point of view, how does schooling reproduce social inequality in each generation?

3. Why is health a social issue as much as a biological issue? What are several ways in which health and medicine are linked to social inequality?

Chapter 15 Population, Urbanization, and Environment

Multiple-Choice Questions

1. *Demography* is defined as the study of

   a. democratic political systems.

   b. human culture.

   c. human population.

   d. the natural environment.

2. **Which region of the world has both the lowest birth rate and the lowest infant mortality rate?**

   a. Latin America

   b. Europe

   c. Africa

   d. Asia

3. **Typically, high-income nations grow mostly from _____, while low-income nations grow from _____.**

   a. immigration; natural increase

   b. emigration; natural increase

   c. natural increase; immigration

   d. internal migration; natural increase

4. **In general, the higher the average income of a country,**

   a. the faster the population increases.

   b. the slower the population increases.

   c. the lower the level of immigration.

   d. the lower the level of urbanization.

5. **In the United States, urban decentralization has caused**

   a. the expansion of suburbs.

   b. the development of vast urban regions.

   c. the growth of edge cities.

   d. All of the above are correct.

6. **Which of the following concepts did Ferdinand Tönnies use to refer to people coming together on the basis of individual self-interest?**

   a. mechanical solidarity

   b. organic solidarity

   c. *Gesellschaft*

   d. *Gemeinschaft*

7. **The world's third urban revolution is now taking place in**

   a. the United States.

   b. Europe and Japan.

   c. middle-income nations.

   d. low-income nations.

8. **The *environmental deficit* refers to**

   a. long-term harm to the environment caused by a shortsighted focus on material affluence.

   b. the public's lack of interest in the natural environment.

   c. the fact that natural scientists ignore the social dimensions of environmental problems.

   d. the lack of funding for important environmental programs.

9. **Which of the following statements reflects the limits-to-growth thesis?**

   a. People are rapidly consuming Earth's finite resources.

   b. Whatever problems technology creates, technology can solve.

   c. Quality of life on Earth is getting better.

   d. Higher living standards today will benefit future generations.

10. **Environmental racism is the idea that**

   a. few minorities are represented within the environmental movement.

   b. prejudice is the major cause of pollution and other environmental problems.

   c. environmental dangers are greatest for the poor and minorities.

   d. All of the above are correct.

ANSWERS: 1(c); 2(b); 3(a); 4(b); 5(d); 6(c); 7(d); 8(a); 9(a); 10(c).

Essay Questions

1. According to demographic transition theory, how does economic development affect population patterns?

2. According to Ferdinand Tönnies, Emile Durkheim, Georg Simmel, and Louis Wirth, what characterizes urbanism as a way of life? Note several differences in the ideas of these thinkers.

Chapter 16   Social Change: Modern and Postmodern Societies

Multiple-Choice Questions

1. Sociologists use the term "modernity" to refer to social patterns that emerged
   a. with the first human civilizations.
   b. with the founding of cities.
   c. after the Industrial Revolution.
   d. along with the Information Revolution.

2. Which of the following are common causes of social change?
   a. the invention of things, ideas, and social patterns
   b. diffusion from one cultural system to another
   c. the discovery of existing things
   d. All of the above are correct.

3. Karl Marx highlighted the importance of which of the following factors in the process of social change?
   a. immigration and demographic factors
   b. ideas
   c. social conflict
   d. cultural diffusion

4. Max Weber's analysis of the rise of rational, modern society highlighted the importance of which of the following factors in the process of social change?
   a. invention
   b. ideas
   c. social conflict
   d. cultural diffusion

5. Which term did Ferdinand Tönnies use to describe a modern society?
   a. *Gesellschaft*
   b. *Gemeinschaft*
   c. mechanical solidarity
   d. organic solidarity

6. According to Emile Durkheim, modern societies have
   a. respect for established tradition.
   b. widespread alienation.
   c. common values and beliefs.
   d. an increasing division of labor.

7. The 2010 Gulf of Mexico oil spill is one recent case of
   a. a natural disaster.
   b. a technological disaster.
   c. an intentional disaster.
   d. an everyday disaster.

8. Which of the following statements about modernity as a mass society is *not* correct?
   a. There is more poverty now than in past centuries.
   b. Kinship ties have become weaker.
   c. Bureaucracy, including government, has expanded in size.
   d. People experience greater moral uncertainty about how to live.

9. Sociologists who describe modernity in terms of class-society theory focus on which of the following?
   a. rationality as a way of thinking about the world
   b. mutual interdependency
   c. the rise of capitalism
   d. the high risk of anomie

10. David Riesman described the other-directed social character typical of modern people as
    a. rigid conformity to tradition.
    b. eagerness to follow the latest fashions and fads.
    c. highly individualistic.
    d. All of the above are correct.

ANSWERS: 1(c); 2(d); 3(c); 4(b); 5(a); 6(d); 7(b); 8(a); 9(c); 10(b).

Essay Questions

1. Discuss how Tönnies, Durkheim, Weber, and Marx described modern society. Point out the similarities and differences in their understandings of modernity.

2. What traits lead some people to call the United States a "mass society"? Why do other analysts describe the United States as a "class society"?

Glossary

abortion   the deliberate termination of a pregnancy

absolute poverty   a lack of resources that is life-threatening

achieved status   a social position a person takes on voluntarily that reflects personal ability and effort

Afrocentrism   emphasizing and promoting African cultural patterns

ageism   prejudice and discrimination against older people

age-sex pyramid   a graphic representation of the age and sex of a population

agriculture   large-scale cultivation using plows harnessed to animals or more powerful energy sources

alienation   the experience of isolation and misery resulting from powerlessness

animism   the belief that elements of the natural world are conscious life forms that affect humanity

anomie   Durkheim's term for a condition in which society provides little moral guidance to individuals

anticipatory socialization   learning that helps a person achieve a desired position

ascribed status   a social position a person receives at birth or takes on involuntarily later in life

asexuality   a lack of sexual attraction to people of either sex

assimilation   the process by which minorities gradually adopt patterns of the dominant culture

authoritarianism   a political system that denies the people participation in government

authority   power that people perceive as legitimate rather than coercive

beliefs   specific ideas that people hold to be true

bisexuality   sexual attraction to people of both sexes

blue-collar occupations   lower-prestige jobs that involve mostly manual labor

bureaucracy   an organizational model rationally designed to perform tasks efficiently

bureaucratic inertia   the tendency of bureaucratic organizations to perpetuate themselves

bureaucratic ritualism   a focus on rules and regulations to the point of undermining an organization's goals

capitalism   an economic system in which natural resources and the means of producing goods and services are privately owned

capitalists   people who own and operate factories and other businesses in pursuit of profits

caste system   social stratification based on ascription, or birth

cause and effect   a relationship in which change in one variable (the independent variable) causes change in another (the dependent variable)

charisma   extraordinary personal qualities that can infuse people with emotion and turn them into followers

church   a religious organization that is well integrated into the larger society

civil religion   a quasi-religious loyalty binding individuals in a basically secular society

claims making   the process of trying to convince the public and public officials of the importance of joining a social movement to address a particular issue

class society   a capitalist society with pronounced social stratification

class system   social stratification based on both birth and individual achievement

cohabitation   the sharing of a household by an unmarried couple

cohort   a category of people with something in common, usually their age

colonialism   the process by which some nations enrich themselves through political and economic control of other nations

community-based corrections   correctional programs operating within society at large rather than behind prison walls

concept   a mental construct that represents some aspect of the world in a simplified form

concrete operational stage   Piaget's term for the level of human development at which individuals first see causal connections in their surroundings

conspicuous consumption   buying and using products because of the "statement" they make about social position

corporate crime   the illegal actions of a corporation or people acting on its behalf

corporation   an organization with a legal existence, including rights and liabilities, separate from that of its members

correlation   a relationship in which two (or more) variables change together

counterculture   cultural patterns that strongly oppose those widely accepted within a society

crime   the violation of a society's formally enacted criminal law

crimes against the person   crimes that direct violence or the threat of violence against others; also known as *violent crimes*

crimes against property   crimes that involve theft of money or property belonging to others; also known as *property crimes*

criminal justice system   the organizations—police, courts, and prison officials—that respond to alleged violations of the law

criminal recidivism   later offenses by people previously convicted of crimes

critical sociology   the study of society that focuses on the need for social change

crude birth rate   the number of live births in a given year for every 1,000 people in a population

crude death rate   the number of deaths in a given year for every 1,000 people in a population

cult   a religious organization that is largely outside a society's cultural traditions

cultural integration   the close relationships among various elements of a cultural system

cultural lag   the fact that some cultural elements change more quickly than others, disrupting a cultural system

cultural relativism   the practice of judging a culture by its own standards

cultural transmission   the process by which one generation passes culture to the next

cultural universals   traits that are part of every known culture

culture   the ways of thinking, the ways of acting, and the material objects that together form a people's way of life

culture shock   personal disorientation when experiencing an unfamiliar way of life

Davis-Moore thesis   the functional analysis claiming that social stratification has beneficial consequences for the operation of society

democracy   a political system that gives power to the people as a whole

demographic transition theory   a thesis that links population patterns to a society's level of technological development

demography   the study of human population

denomination   a church, independent of the state, that recognizes religious pluralism

dependency theory   a model of economic and social development that explains global inequality in terms of the historical exploitation of poor nations by rich ones

descent   the system by which members of a society trace kinship over generations

deterrence the attempt to discourage criminality through the use of punishment

deviance the recognized violation of cultural norms

direct-fee system a medical care system in which patients pay directly for the services of physicians and hospitals

disaster an event, generally unexpected, that causes extensive harm to people and damage to property

discrimination unequal treatment of various categories of people

division of labor specialized economic activity

dramaturgical analysis Erving Goffman's term for the study of social interaction in terms of theatrical performance

dyad a social group with two members

eating disorder an intense form of dieting or other unhealthy method of weight control driven by the desire to be very thin

ecologically sustainable culture a way of life that meets the needs of the present generation without threatening the environmental legacy of future generations

ecology the study of the interaction of living organisms and the natural environment

economy the social institution that organizes a society's production, distribution, and consumption of goods and services

ecosystem the interaction of all living organisms and their natural environment

education the social institution through which society provides its members with important knowledge, including basic facts, job skills, and cultural norms and values

ego Freud's term for a person's conscious efforts to balance innate pleasure-seeking drives with the demands of society

empirical evidence information we can verify with our senses

endogamy marriage between people of the same social category

environmental deficit profound long-term harm to the natural environment caused by humanity's focus on short-term material affluence

environmental racism patterns of development that expose poor people, especially minorities, to environmental hazards

ethnicity a shared cultural heritage

ethnocentrism the practice of judging another culture by the standards of one's own culture

ethnomethodology Harold Garfinkel's term for the study of the way people make sense of their everyday surroundings

Eurocentrism the dominance of European (especially English) cultural patterns

euthanasia assisting in the death of a person suffering from an incurable disease; also known as *mercy killing*

exogamy marriage between people of different social categories

experiment a research method for investigating cause and effect under highly controlled conditions

expressive leadership group leadership that focuses on the group's well-being

extended family a family composed of parents and children as well as other kin; also known as a *consanguine family*

faith belief based on conviction rather than on scientific evidence

family a social institution found in all societies that unites people in cooperative groups to care for one another, including any children

family violence emotional, physical, or sexual abuse of one family member by another

feminism support of social equality for women and men

feminization of poverty the trend of women making up an increasing proportion of the poor

fertility the incidence of childbearing in a country's population

folkways norms for routine or casual interaction

formal operational stage Piaget's term for the level of human development at which individuals think abstractly and critically

formal organization a large secondary group organized to achieve its goals efficiently

functional illiteracy a lack of the reading and writing skills needed for everyday living

fundamentalism a conservative religious doctrine that opposes intellectualism and worldly accommodation in favor of restoring traditional, otherworldly religion

Gemeinschaft a type of social organization in which people are closely tied by kinship and tradition

gender the personal traits and social positions that members of a society attach to being female or male

gender-conflict approach a point of view that focuses on inequality and conflict between women and men

gender roles (sex roles) attitudes and activities that a society links to each sex

gender stratification the unequal distribution of wealth, power, and privilege between men and women

generalized other Mead's term for widespread cultural norms and values we use as a reference in evaluating ourselves

genocide the systematic killing of one category of people by another

gerontocracy a form of social organization in which the elderly have the most wealth, power, and prestige

gerontology the study of aging and the elderly

Gesellschaft a type of social organization in which people come together only on the basis of individual self-interest

global economy economic activity that crosses national borders

global perspective the study of the larger world and our society's place in it

global stratification patterns of social inequality in the world as a whole

global warming a rise in Earth's average temperature due to an increasing concentration of carbon dioxide in the atmosphere

government a formal organization that directs the political life of a society

groupthink the tendency of group members to conform, resulting in a narrow view of some issue

hate crime a criminal act against a person or a person's property by an offender motivated by racial or other bias

health a state of complete physical, mental, and social well-being

health maintenance organization (HMO) an organization that provides comprehensive medical care to subscribers for a fixed fee

heterosexism a view that labels anyone who is not heterosexual as "queer"

heterosexuality sexual attraction to someone of the other sex

high culture cultural patterns that distinguish a society's elite

high-income countries the nations with the highest overall standards of living

holistic medicine an approach to health care that emphasizes the prevention of illness and takes into account a person's entire physical and social environment

homogamy marriage between people with the same social characteristics

homophobia discomfort over close personal interaction with people thought to be gay, lesbian, or bisexual

homosexuality sexual attraction to someone of the same sex

horticulture the use of hand tools to raise crops

hunting and gathering the use of simple tools to hunt animals and gather vegetation for food

id Freud's term for the human being's basic drives

ideology cultural beliefs that justify particular social arrangements, including patterns of inequality

incest taboo a norm forbidding sexual relations or marriage between certain relatives

income earnings from work or investments

industry the production of goods using advanced sources of energy to drive large machinery

infant mortality rate the number of deaths among infants under one year of age for each 1,000 live births in a given year

in-group a social group toward which a member feels respect and loyalty

institutional prejudice and discrimination bias built into the operation of society's institutions

instrumental leadership group leadership that focuses on the completion of tasks

intergenerational social mobility upward or downward social mobility of children in relation to their parents

interpretive sociology the study of society that focuses on discovering the meanings people attach to their social world

intersection theory analysis of the interplay of race, class, and gender, often resulting in multiple dimensions of disadvantage

intersexual people people whose bodies (including genitals) have both female and male characteristics

intragenerational social mobility a change in social position occurring during a person's lifetime

kinship   a social bond based on common ancestry, marriage, or adoption

labeling theory   the idea that deviance and conformity result not so much from what people do as from how others respond to those actions

language   a system of symbols that allows people to communicate with one another

latent functions   the unrecognized and unintended consequences of any social pattern

liberation theology   the combining of Christian principles with political activism, often Marxist in character

life expectancy   the average life span of a country's population

looking-glass self   Charles Horton Cooley's term for a self-image based on how we think others see us

low-income countries   nations with a low standard of living in which most people are poor

macro-level orientation   a broad focus on social structures that shape society as a whole

manifest functions   the recognized and intended consequences of any social pattern

marriage   a legal relationship, usually involving economic cooperation, sexual activity, and childbearing

Marxist political-economy model   an analysis that explains politics in terms of the operation of a society's economic system

mass media   the means for delivering impersonal communications to a vast audience

mass society   a society in which prosperity and bureaucracy have weakened traditional social ties

master status   a status that has special importance for social identity, often shaping a person's entire life

matriarchy   a form of social organization in which females dominate males

measurement   a procedure for determining the value of a variable in a specific case

medicalization of deviance   the transformation of moral and legal deviance into a medical condition

medicine   the social institution that focuses on fighting disease and improving health

megalopolis   a vast urban region containing a number of cities and their surrounding suburbs

meritocracy   social stratification based on personal merit

metropolis   a large city that dominates an urban area socially and economically

micro-level orientation   a close-up focus on social interaction in specific situations

middle-income countries   nations with a standard of living about average for the world as a whole

migration   the movement of people into and out of a specified territory

military-industrial complex   the close association of the federal government, the military, and defense industries

minority   any category of people distinguished by physical or cultural difference that a society sets apart and subordinates

miscegenation   biological reproduction by partners of different racial categories

modernity   social patterns resulting from industrialization

modernization   the process of social change begun by industrialization

modernization theory   a model of economic and social development that explains global inequality in terms of technological and cultural differences between nations

monarchy   a political system in which a single family rules from generation to generation

monogamy   marriage that unites two partners

monopoly   the domination of a market by a single producer

mores   norms that are widely observed and have great moral significance

mortality   the incidence of death in a country's population

multiculturalism   a perspective recognizing the cultural diversity of the United States and promoting equal standing for all cultural traditions

multinational corporation   a large business that operates in many countries

natural environment   Earth's surface and atmosphere, including living organisms, air, water, soil, and other resources necessary to sustain life

neocolonialism   a new form of global power relationships that involves not direct political control but economic exploitation by multinational corporations

network   a web of weak social ties

nonverbal communication   communication using body movements, gestures, and facial expressions rather than speech

norms   rules and expectations by which a society guides the behavior of its members

nuclear family   a family composed of one or two parents and their children; also known as a *conjugal family*

oligarchy   the rule of the many by the few

oligopoly   the domination of a market by a few producers

organizational environment   factors outside an organization that affect its operation

organized crime   a business supplying illegal goods or services

other-directedness   openness to the latest trends and fashions, often expressed by imitating others

out-group   a social group toward which a person feels a sense of competition or opposition

participant observation   a research method in which investigators systematically observe people while joining them in their routine activities

pastoralism   the domestication of animals

patriarchy   a form of social organization in which males dominate females

peer group   a social group whose members have interests, social position, and age in common

personality   a person's fairly consistent patterns of acting, thinking, and feeling

personal space   the surrounding area over which a person makes some claim to privacy

plea bargaining   a legal negotiation in which a prosecutor reduces a charge in exchange for a defendant's guilty plea

pluralism   a state in which people of all races and ethnicities are distinct but have equal social standing

pluralist model   an analysis of politics that sees power as spread among many competing interest groups

political revolution   the overthrow of one political system in order to establish another

politics   the social institution that distributes power, sets a society's goals, and makes decisions

polygamy   marriage that unites a person with two or more spouses

popular culture   cultural patterns that are widespread among a society's population

pornography   sexually explicit material intended to cause sexual arousal

positivism   a scientific approach to knowledge based on "positive" facts as opposed to mere speculation

positivist sociology   the study of society based on systematic observation of social behavior

postindustrial economy   a productive system based on service work and computer technology

postindustrialism   the production of information using computer technology

postmodernity   social patterns characteristic of postindustrial societies

power   the ability to achieve desired ends despite resistance from others

power-elite model   an analysis of politics that sees power as concentrated among the rich

prejudice   a rigid and unfair generalization about an entire category of people

preoperational stage   Piaget's term for the level of human development at which individuals first use language and other symbols

presentation of self   Erving Goffman's term for a person's efforts to create specific impressions in the minds of others

primary group   a small social group whose members share personal and lasting relationships

primary sector   the part of the economy that draws raw materials from the natural environment

primary sex characteristics   the genitals, organs used for reproduction

profane   occurring as an ordinary part of everyday life

profession   a prestigious white-collar occupation that requires extensive formal education

proletarians   people who sell their labor for wages

prostitution   the selling of sexual services

queer theory   a body of research findings that challenges the heterosexual bias in U.S. society

race a socially constructed category of people who share biologically transmitted traits that members of a society consider important

race-conflict approach a point of view that focuses on inequality and conflict between people of different racial and ethnic categories

racism the belief that one racial category is innately superior or inferior to another

rain forests regions of dense forestation, most of which circle the globe close to the equator

rationality a way of thinking that emphasizes deliberate, matter-of-fact calculation of the most efficient way to accomplish a particular task

rationalization of society Weber's term for the historical change from tradition to rationality as the main type of human thought

reference group a social group that serves as a point of reference in making evaluations and decisions

rehabilitation a program for reforming the offender to prevent later offenses

relative deprivation a perceived disadvantage arising from some specific comparison

relative poverty the lack of resources of some people in relation to those who have more

reliability consistency in measurement

religion a social institution involving beliefs and practices based on recognizing the sacred

religiosity the importance of religion in a person's life

research method a systematic plan for doing research

resocialization radically changing an inmate's personality by carefully controlling the environment

retribution an act of moral vengeance by which society makes the offender suffer as much as the suffering caused by the crime

role behavior expected of someone who holds a particular status

role conflict conflict among the roles connected to two or more statuses

role set a number of roles attached to a single status

role strain tension among the roles connected to a single status

routinization of charisma the transformation of charismatic authority into some combination of traditional and bureaucratic authority

sacred set apart as extraordinary, inspiring awe and reverence

Sapir-Whorf thesis the idea that people see and understand the world through the cultural lens of language

scapegoat a person or category of people, typically with little power, whom other people unfairly blame for their own troubles

schooling formal instruction under the direction of specially trained teachers

science a logical system that develops knowledge from direct, systematic observation

scientific management Frederick Taylor's term for the application of scientific principles to the operation of a business or other large organization

secondary group a large and impersonal social group whose members pursue a specific goal or activity

secondary sector the part of the economy that transforms raw materials into manufactured goods

secondary sex characteristics bodily development, apart from the genitals, that distinguishes biologically mature females and males

sect a religious organization that stands apart from the larger society

secularization the historical decline in the importance of the supernatural and the sacred

segregation the physical and social separation of categories of people

self George Herbert Mead's term for the part of an individual's personality composed of self-awareness and self-image

sensorimotor stage Piaget's term for the level of human development at which individuals experience the world only through their senses

sex the biological distinction between females and males

sexism the belief that one sex is innately superior to the other

sex ratio the number of males for every 100 females in a nation's population

sexual harassment comments, gestures, or physical contacts of a sexual nature that are deliberate, repeated, and unwelcome

sexual orientation a person's romantic and emotional attraction to another person

sick role patterns of behavior defined as appropriate for people who are ill

significant others people, such as parents, who have special importance for socialization

social change the transformation of culture and social institutions over time

social character personality patterns common to members of a particular society

social-conflict approach a framework for building theory that sees society as an arena of inequality that generates conflict and change

social construction of reality the process by which people creatively shape reality through social interaction

social control attempts by society to regulate people's thoughts and behavior

social dysfunction any social pattern that may disrupt the operation of society

social epidemiology the study of how health and disease are distributed throughout a society's population

social functions the consequences of a social pattern for the operation of society as a whole

social group two or more people who identify with and interact with one another

social institution a major sphere of social life, or societal subsystem, organized to meet human needs

social interaction the process by which people act and react in relation to others

socialism an economic system in which natural resources and the means of producing goods and services are collectively owned

socialization the lifelong social experience by which people develop their human potential and learn culture

socialized medicine a medical care system in which the government owns and operates most medical facilities and employs most physicians

social mobility a change in position within the social hierarchy

social movement an organized activity that encourages or discourages social change

social stratification a system by which a society ranks categories of people in a hierarchy

social structure any relatively stable pattern of social behavior

societal protection rendering an offender incapable of further offenses temporarily through imprisonment or permanently by execution

society people who interact in a defined territory and share a culture

sociobiology a theoretical approach that explores ways in which human biology affects how we create culture

socioeconomic status (SES) a composite ranking based on various dimensions of social inequality

sociological perspective the special point of view of sociology that sees general patterns of society in the lives of particular people

sociology the systematic study of human society

state capitalism an economic and political system in which companies are privately owned but cooperate closely with the government

state church a church formally linked to the state

status a social position that a person holds

status consistency the degree of uniformity in a person's social standing across various dimensions of social inequality

status set all the statuses a person holds at a given time

stereotype a simplified description applied to every person in some category

stigma a powerfully negative label that greatly changes a person's self-concept and social identity

structural-functional approach a framework for building theory that sees society as a complex system whose parts work together to promote solidarity and stability

structural social mobility a shift in the social position of large numbers of people due more to changes in society itself than to individual efforts

subculture cultural patterns that set apart some segment of a society's population

suburbs urban areas beyond the political boundaries of a city

superego Freud's term for the cultural values and norms internalized by an individual

survey a research method in which subjects respond to a series of statements or questions on a questionnaire or in an interview

symbol anything that carries a particular meaning recognized by people who share a culture

symbolic-interaction approach a framework for building theory that sees society as the product of the everyday interactions of individuals

technology   knowledge that people use to make a way of life in their surroundings

terrorism   acts of violence or the threat of violence used as a political strategy by an individual or a group

tertiary sector   the part of the economy that involves services rather than goods

theoretical approach   a basic image of society that guides thinking and research

theory   a statement of how and why specific facts are related

Thomas theorem   W. I. Thomas's claim that situations defined as real are real in their consequences

total institution   a setting in which people are isolated from the rest of society and controlled by an administrative staff

totalitarianism   a highly centralized political system that extensively regulates people's lives

totem   an object in the natural world collectively defined as sacred

tracking   assigning students to different types of educational programs

tradition   values and beliefs passed from generation to generation

tradition-directedness   rigid conformity to time-honored ways of living

transsexuals   people who feel they are one sex even though biologically they are the other

triad   a social group with three members

urban ecology   the study of the link between the physical and social dimensions of cities

urbanization   the concentration of population into cities

validity   actually measuring exactly what you intend to measure

values   culturally defined standards that people use to decide what is desirable, good, and beautiful and that serve as broad guidelines for social living

variable   a concept whose value changes from case to case

victimless crimes   violations of law in which there are no obvious victims

war   organized, armed conflict among the people of two or more nations, directed by their governments

wealth   the total value of money and other assets, minus outstanding debts

welfare capitalism   an economic and political system that combines a mostly market-based economy with extensive social welfare programs

welfare state   a system of government agencies and programs that provides benefits to the population

white-collar crime   crime committed by people of high social position in the course of their occupations

white-collar occupations   higher-prestige jobs that involve mostly mental activity

zero population growth   the rate of reproduction that maintains population at a steady level

References

* Blue type denotes reference citations new to this eleventh edition.

AARP FOUNDATION. "GrandFacts." October 2007. http://www.grandfactsheets.org/doc/National%20Resources%20Fact%20Sheet.pdf

ABERLE, DAVID F. *The Peyote Religion among the Navaho.* Chicago: Aldine, 1966.

"Abramoff Effect: Leaping Out of Bed with the Lobbyists." *New York Times* (January 16, 2006). http://www.researchnavigator.com

ADAMS, PATRICIA F., KATHLEEN M. HEYMAN, and JACQUELINE L. VICKERIE. "Summary Health Statistics for the U.S. Population: National Health Interview Survey, 2008." National Center for Health Statistics. *Vital and Health Statistics.* Ser. 10, No. 243 (2009). http://www.cdc.gov/nchs/data/series/sr_10/sr10_243.pdf

ADLER, JERRY. "When Harry Called Sally . . ." *Newsweek* (October 1, 1990):74.

ADORNO, THEODORE W., ELSE FRENKEL-BRUNSWIK, DANIEL J. LEVINSON, and R. NEVITT SANFORD. *The Authoritarian Personality.* New York: Harper, 1950.

AKERS, RONALD L., MARVIN D. KROHN, LONN LANZA-KADUCE, and MARCIA RADOSEVICH. "Social Learning and Deviant Behavior." *American Sociological Review.* Vol. 44, No. 4 (August 1979):636–55.

ALAN GUTTMACHER INSTITUTE. "Teen Pregnancy: Trends and Lessons Learned." *Issues in Brief.* 2002 Series, No. 1. 2002. http://www.guttmacher.org/pubs/tgr/05/1/gr050107.html

———. "U.S. Teenage Pregnancy Statistics: National and State Trends and Trends by Race and Ethnicity." Rev. September 2006. http://www.guttmacher.org/pubs/2006/09/12/USTPstats.pdf

ALBON, JOAN. "Retention of Cultural Values and Differential Urban Adaptation: Samoans and American Indians in a West Coast City." *Social Forces.* Vol. 49, No. 3 (March 1971):385–93.

ALI, LORRAINE, and VANESSA JUAREZ. "We Love This Country." *Newsweek* (April 7, 2003). http://www.newsweek.com/2003/04/06/we-love-this-country.html

ALI, LORRAINE, TAMARA LIPPER, and MOHAMMED MACK. "Voters: A Demographic Shift." *Newsweek* (October 25, 2004). http://www.newsweek.com/2004/10/24/voters-a-demographic-shift.html

ALLAN, EMILIE ANDERSEN, and DARRELL J. STEFFENSMEIER. "Youth, Underemployment, and Property Crime: Differential Effects of Job Availability and Job Quality on Juvenile and Young Adult Arrest Rates." *American Sociological Review.* Vol. 54, No. 1 (February 1989):107–23.

ALLEN, MIKE. "Card Check Battle Starts Tomorrow." *Politico* (March 9, 2009). http://www.politico.com/news/stories/0309/19786.html

ALLEN, THOMAS B., and CHARLES O. HYMAN. *We Americans: Celebrating a Nation, Its People, and Its Past.* Washington, D.C.: National Geographic Society, 1999.

ALLEN, WALTER R. "African American Family Life in Social Context: Crisis and Hope." *Sociological Forum.* Vol. 10, No. 4 (December 1995):569–92.

ALTONJI, JOSEPH G., ULRICH DORASZELSKI, and LEWIS SEGAL. "Black/White Differences in Wealth." *Economic Perspectives.* Vol. 24, No. 1 (First Quarter 2000):38–50.

AMATO, PAUL R. "What Children Learn from Divorce." *Population Today.* Vol. 29, No. 1 (January 2001):1, 4.

AMERICAN ASSOCIATION OF COLLEGES OF NURSING (AACN). "Table 10: Race/Ethnicity of Students Enrolled in Generic (Entry-Level) Baccalaureate, Master's, and Doctoral (Research-Focused) Programs in Nursing, 2000–2009." 2010. http://www.aacn.nche.edu/IDS/pdf/EthnicityTbl.pdf

AMERICAN BAR ASSOCIATION. "First-Year and Total J.D. Enrollment by Gender, 1947–2008." 2010. http://www.abanet.org/legaled/statistics/charts/stats%20-%206.pdf

AMERICAN GAMING ASSOCIATION. "States with Gaming." May 2009. http://www.americangaming.com/Industry/factsheets/general_info_detail.cfv?id=15

AMERICAN PSYCHOLOGICAL ASSOCIATION. *Violence and Youth: Psychology's Response.* Washington, D.C.: American Psychological Association, 1993.

AMERICAN SOCIOLOGICAL ASSOCIATION. *Code of Ethics.* Washington, D.C.: American Sociological Association, 1997.

———. *The Importance of Collecting Data and Doing Social Scientific Research on Race.* Washington, D.C.: American Sociological Association, 2003.

———. "Careers in Sociology." Rev. July 19, 2007. http://www.asanet.org/cs/root/leftnav/careers_and_jobs/careers_in_sociology

AMNESTY INTERNATIONAL. "Abolitionist and Retentionist Countries." 2008a. http://www.amnesty.org/en/death-penalty/abolitionist-and-retentionist-countries

———. "Secrecy Surrounds Death Penalty." 2008b. http://www.amnesty.org/en/news-and-updates/report/secrecy-surrounds-death-penalty-20080415

———. "The Death Penalty in 2008." 2010. http://www.amnesty.org/en/death-penalty/death-sentences-and-executions-in-2008

ANDERSON, ELIJAH. "The Code of the Streets." *Atlantic Monthly.* Vol. 273 (May 1994):81–94.

———. "The Ideologically Driven Critique." *American Journal of Sociology.* Vol. 197, No. 6 (May 2002):1533–50.

ANDERSON, JOHN WARD. "Early to Wed: The Child Brides of India." *Washington Post* (May 24, 1995):A27, A30.

ANNAN, KOFI. "Astonishing Facts." *New York Times* (September 27, 1998):16.

ANTI-SLAVERY INTERNATIONAL. 2008. "Slavery Remains Despite Years of Successes." http://www.antislavery.org/archive/press/latestpressrelease.htm

———. "Today's Fight for Tomorrow's Freedom." 2010. http://www.antislavery.org/english/default.aspx

APPLEBOME, PETER. "70 Years after Scopes Trial, Creation Debate Lives." *New York Times* (March 10, 1996):1, 10.

ARIÈS, PHILIPPE. *Centuries of Childhood: A Social History of Family Life.* New York: Vintage Books, 1965.

ARMSTRONG, ELISABETH. *The Retreat from Organization: U.S. Feminism Reconceptualized.* Albany: State University of New York Press, 2002.

"Army Apologizes" (January 7, 2009). http://www.reuters.com/article/idUSTRE50674G20090107

ASANTE, MOLEFI KETE. *Afrocentricity.* Trenton, N.J.: Africa World Press, 1988.

ASCH, SOLOMON. *Social Psychology.* Englewood Cliffs, N.J.: Prentice Hall, 1952.

ASHFORD, LORI S. "Young Women in Sub-Saharan Africa Face a High Risk of HIV Infection." *Population Today.* Vol. 30, No. 2 (February/March 2002):3, 6.

ASTIN, ALEXANDER W., LETICIA OSEGUERA, LINDA J. SAX, and WILLIAM S. KORN. *The American Freshman: Thirty-Five-Year Trends.* Los Angeles: UCLA Higher Education Research Institute, 2002.

ATLAS, TERRY. "The Human Cost of China's Boom Times." *U.S. News and World Report* (March 12, 2007):21.

"Atomic Education Urged by Einstein." *New York Times* (May 25 1946):13.

AUSTER, CAROL J., and MINDY MACRONE. "The Classroom as a Negotiated Social Setting: An Empirical Study of the Effects of Faculty Members' Behavior on Students' Participation." *Teaching Sociology.* Vol. 22, No. 4 (October 1994):289–300.

AXINN, WILLIAM G., and JENNIFER S. BARBER. "Mass Education and Fertility Transition." *American Sociological Review.* Vol. 66, No. 4 (August 2001):481–505.

BAINBRIDGE, JAY, MARCIA K. MEYERS, and JANE WALDFOGEL. "Childcare Reform and the Employment of Single Mothers." *Social Science Quarterly.* Vol. 84, No. 4 (December 2003):771–91.

BAKALAR, NICHOLAS. "Reactions: Go On, Laugh Your Heart Out." *New York Times* (March 8, 2005). http://www.nytimes.com/2005/03/08/health/08reac.html

BAKER, PATRICIA S., WILLIAM C. YOELS, JEFFREY M. CLAIR, and RICHARD M. ALLMAN. "Laughter in the Triadic Geriatric Encounters: A Transcript-Based Analysis." In REBECCA J. ERIKSON and BEVERLY CUTHBERTSON-JOHNSON, eds., *Social Perspectives on Emotion.* Vol. 4. Greenwich, Conn.: JAI Press, 1997:179–207.

BALTZELL, E. DIGBY. *The Protestant Establishment: Aristocracy and Caste in America.* New York: Vintage Books, 1964.

———. "Introduction to the 1967 Edition." In W.E.B. DU BOIS, *The Philadelphia Negro: A Social Study.* New York: Schocken Books, 1967.

———. *Puritan Boston and Quaker Philadelphia.* New York: Free Press, 1979.

———. *Sporting Gentlemen: From the Age of Honor to the Cult of the Superstar.* New York: Free Press, 1995.

BARASH, DAVID P. *The Whisperings Within.* New York: Penguin Books, 1981.

BARNES, JULIAN E. "Wanted: Readers." *U.S. News & World Report* (September 9, 2002a):44–45.

———. "War Profiteering." *U.S. News & World Report* (May 13, 2002b):20–24.

BARON, JAMES N., MICHAEL T. HANNAN, and M. DIANE BURTON. "Building the Iron Cage: Determinants of Managerial Intensity in the Early Years of Organizations." *American Sociological Review.* Vol. 64, No. 4 (August 1999):527–47.

BARONE, MICHAEL. "Cultures Aren't Equal." *U.S. News & World Report* (August 22, 2005):26.

BAROVICK, HARRIET. "Tongues That Go Out of Style." *Time* (June 10, 2002):22.

BARR, ROBERT. "Archbishop of Canterbury Is Enthroned." *Yahoo! News* (February 27, 2003). http://news.yahoo.com

BARTLETT, DONALD L., and JAMES B. STEELE. "How the Little Guy Gets Crunched." *Time* (February 7, 2000):38–41.

———. "Wheel of Misfortune." *Time* (December 16, 2002):44–58.

BAUER, P. T. *Equality, the Third World, and Economic Delusion.* Cambridge, Mass.: Harvard University Press, 1981.

BAYDAR, NAZLI, and JEANNE BROOKS-GUNN. "Effect of Maternal Employment and Child-Care Arrangements on Preschoolers' Cognitive and Behavioral Outcomes: Evidence from Children from the National Longitudinal Survey of Youth." *Developmental Psychology.* Vol. 27, No. 6 (November 1991):932–35.

BEARAK, BARRY. "Lives Held Cheap in Bangladesh Sweatshops." *New York Times* (April 15, 2001):A1, A12.

BEARMAN, PETER S., JAMES MOODY, and KATHERINE STOVEL. "Chains of Affection." *American Journal of Sociology.* Vol. 110, No. 1 (July 2004):44–91.

BECKER, ANNE E. "The Association of Television Exposure with Disordered Eating among Ethnic Fijian Adolescent Girls." Paper presented at the annual meeting of the American Psychiatric Association, Washington, D.C., May 19, 1999.

BECKER, HOWARD S. *Outside: Studies in the Sociology of Deviance.* New York: Free Press, 1966.

BEDARD, PAUL. "Washington Whispers." *U.S. News & World Report* (March 25, 2002):2.

BEEGHLEY, LEONARD. *The Structure of Social Stratification in the United States.* Needham Heights, Mass.: Allyn & Bacon, 1989.

BEGLEY, SHARON. "Gray Matters." *Newsweek* (March 7, 1995):48–54.

BELLAH, ROBERT N. *The Broken Covenant.* New York: Seabury Press, 1975.

BELLER, EMILY, and MICHAEL HOUT. "Intergenerational Social Mobility: The United States in Comparative Perspective." *The Future of Children.* Vol. 16, No. 2 (Fall 2006). http://www.futureofchildren.org/information2826/information_show.htm?doc_id=389282

BEM, SANDRA LIPSITZ. *The Lenses of Gender: Transforming the Debate on Sexual Inequality.* New Haven, Conn.: Yale University Press, 1993.

BENEDICT, RUTH. "Continuities and Discontinuities in Cultural Conditioning." *Psychiatry.* Vol. 1, No. 2 (May 1938):161–67.

BENJAMIN, LOIS. *The Black Elite: Facing the Color Line in the Twilight of the Twentieth Century.* Chicago: Nelson-Hall, 1991.

BENOKRAITIS, NIJOLE, and JOE R. FEAGIN. *Modern Sexism: Blatant, Subtle, and Overt Discrimination.* 2nd ed. Englewood Cliffs, N.J.: Prentice Hall, 1995.

BERGAMO, MONICA, and GERSON CAMAROTTI. "Brazil's Landless Millions." *World Press Review.* Vol. 43, No. 7 (July 1996):46–47.

BERGER, PETER L. *Invitation to Sociology.* New York: Anchor Books, 1963.

———. *The Sacred Canopy: Elements of a Sociological Theory of Religion.* Garden City, N.Y.: Doubleday, 1967.

———. *Facing Up to Modernity: Excursions in Society, Politics, and Religion.* New York: Basic Books, 1977.

———. *The Capitalist Revolution: Fifty Propositions about Prosperity, Equality, and Liberty.* New York: Basic Books, 1986.

BERGER, PETER L., BRIGITTE BERGER, and HANSFRIED KELLNER. *The Homeless Mind: Modernization and Consciousness.* New York: Vintage Books, 1974.

BERGESEN, ALBERT, ed. *Crises in the World-System.* Beverly Hills, Calif.: Sage, 1983.

BERNARD, JESSIE. *The Female World.* New York: Free Press, 1981.

———. *The Future of Marriage.* 2nd ed. New Haven, Conn.: Yale University Press, 1982.

BERRY, BRIAN L., and PHILIP H. REES. "The Factorial Ecology of Calcutta." *American Journal of Sociology.* Vol. 74, No. 5 (March 1969):445–91.

BERTEAU, CELESTE. "Disconnected Intimacy: AOL Instant Messenger Use among Kenyon College Students." Senior thesis. Kenyon College, 2005.

BESECKE, KELLY. "Speaking of Meaning in Modernity: Reflexive Spirituality as a Cultural Resource." *Sociology of Religion.* Vol. 62, No. 3 (2003):365–81.

———. "Seeing Invisible Religion: Religion as a Societal Conversation about Transcendent Meaning." *Sociological Theory.* Vol. 23, Vol. 2 (June 2005):179–96.

BESHAROV, DOUGLAS J., and LISA A. LAUMANN. "Child Abuse Reporting." *Society.* Vol. 34, No. 4 (May/June 1996):40–46.

BEST, RAPHAELA. *We've All Got Scars: What Boys and Girls Learn in Elementary School.* Bloomington: Indiana University Press, 1983.

BIAN, YANJIE. "Chinese Social Stratification and Social Mobility." *Annual Review of Sociology.* Vol. 28 (2002):91–116.

BIANCHI, SUZANNE M., and DAPHNE SPAIN. "Women, Work, and Family in America." *Population Bulletin.* Vol. 51, No. 3 (December 1996).

BLACKWOOD, EVELYN, and SASKIA WIERINGA, eds. *Female Desires: Same-Sex Relations and Transgender Practices across Cultures.* New York: Columbia University Press, 1999.

BLANKENHORN, DAVID. *Fatherless America: Confronting Our Most Urgent Social Problem.* New York: HarperCollins, 1995.

BLANTON, KIMBERLY. "Borrowers Sue Subprime Lender, Allege Race Bias." *Boston Globe.* July 13, 2007. http://www.boston.com/business/personalfinance/articles/2007/07/13/borrowers_sue_subprime_lender_allege_race_bias/

BLAU, JUDITH R., and PETER M. BLAU. "The Cost of Inequality: Metropolitan Structure and Violent Crime." *American Sociological Review.* Vol. 47, No. 1 (February 1982):114–29.

BLAU, PETER M. *Exchange and Power in Social Life.* New York: Wiley, 1964.

———. *Inequality and Heterogeneity: A Primitive Theory of Social Structure.* New York: Free Press, 1977.

BLAU, PETER M., TERRY C. BLUM, and JOSEPH E. SCHWARTZ. "Heterogeneity and Intermarriage." *American Sociological Review.* Vol. 47, No. 1 (February 1982):45–62.

BLAUSTEIN, ALBERT P., and ROBERT L. ZANGRANDO. *Civil Rights and the Black American.* New York: Washington Square Press, 1968.

BLUMER, HERBERT G. "Collective Behavior." In ALFRED McCLUNG LEE, ed., *Principles of Sociology.* 3rd ed. New York: Barnes & Noble Books, 1969:65–121.

BOBO, LAWRENCE, and VINCENT L. HUTCHINGS. "Perceptions of Racial Group Competition: Extending Blumer's Theory of Group Position to a Multiracial Social Context." *American Sociological Review.* Vol. 61, No. 6 (December 1996):951–72.

BOGARDUS, EMORY S. "Social Distance and Its Origins." *Sociology and Social Research.* Vol. 9 (July/August 1925):216–25.

———. *A Forty-Year Racial Distance Study.* Los Angeles: University of Southern California Press, 1967.

BOHANNAN, CECIL. "The Economic Correlates of Homelessness in Sixty Cities." *Social Science Quarterly.* Vol. 72, No. 4 (December 1991):817–25.

BOHLEN, CELESTINE. "Facing Oblivion, Rust-Belt Giants Top Russian List of Vexing Crises." *New York Times* (November 8, 1998):1, 6.

BOHON, STEPHANIE A., and CRAIG R. HUMPHREY. "Courting LULUs: Characteristic of Suitor and Objector Communities." *Rural Sociology.* Vol. 65, No. 3 (September 2000):376–95.

BONANNO, ALESSANDRO, DOUGLAS H. CONSTANCE, and HEATHER LORENZ. "Powers and Limits of Transnational Corporations: The Case of ADM." *Rural Sociology.* Vol. 65, No. 3 (September 2000):440–60.

BONNER, JANE. Research presented in the Public Broadcast System telecast *The Brain #6: The Two Brains.* Videocassette VHS 339. Newark, N.J.: WNET-13 Films, 1984.

BONO, AGOSTINO. "John Jay Study Reveals the Extent of Abuse Problem." http://www.americancatholic.org/news/clergysexabuse/johnjaycns.asp

BOOTH, ALAN, and ANN C. CROUTER, eds. *Just Living Together: Implications of Cohabitation on Families, Children, and Policy.* Mahwah, N.J.: Erlbaum, 2002.

BOOTH, WILLIAM. "By the Sweat of Their Brows: A New Economy." *Washington Post* (July 13, 1998):A1, A10–A11.

BORMANN, F. HERBERT. "The Global Environmental Deficit." *BioScience.* Vol. 40, No. 2 (1990):74.

BOSWELL, TERRY E. "A Split Labor Market Analysis of Discrimination against Chinese Immigrants, 1850–1882." *American Sociological Review.* Vol. 51, No. 3 (June 1986):352–71.

BOSWELL, TERRY E., and WILLIAM J. DIXON. "Marx's Theory of Rebellion: A Cross-National Analysis of Class Exploitation, Economic Development, and Violent Revolt." *American Sociological Review.* Vol. 58, No. 5 (October 1993):681–702.

BOTT, ELIZABETH. *Family and Social Network.* New York: Free Press, 1971; orig. 1957.

BOWEN, WILLIAM G., and DEREK K. BOK. *The Shape of the River: Long-Term Consequences of Considering Race in College and University Admissions.* Princeton, N.J.: Princeton University Press, 1999.

BOWLES, SAMUEL, and HERBERT GINTIS. *Schooling in Capitalist America: Educational Reform and the Contradictions of Economic Life.* New York: Basic Books, 1976.

BOYER, DEBRA. "Male Prostitution and Homosexual Identity." *Journal of Homosexuality.* Vol. 17, Nos. 1–2 (1989):151–84.

BOYLE, ELIZABETH HEGER, FORTUNATA SONGORA, and GAIL FOSS. "International Discourse and Local Politics: Anti-Female-Genital-Cutting Laws in Egypt, Tanzania, and the United States." *Social Problems.* Vol. 48, No. 4 (November 2001):524–44.

BRADY CAMPAIGN. "Firearm Facts." April 2008. http://www.bradycampaign.org/issues/gvstats/firearmoverview/

BRIANS, CRAIG LEONARD, and BERNARD GROFMAN. "Election Day Registration's Effect on U.S. Voter Turnout." *Social Science Quarterly.* Vol. 82, No. 1 (March 2001):170–83.

BRINES, JULIE, and KARA JOYNER. "The Ties That Bind: Principles of Cohesion in Cohabitation and Marriage." *American Sociological Review.* Vol. 64, No. 3 (June 1999):333–55.

BRINK, SUSAN. "Living on the Edge." *U.S. News & World Report* (October 14, 2002):58–64.

BROCKERHOFF, MARTIN P. "An Urbanizing World." *Population Bulletin.* Vol. 55, No. 3 (September 2000):1–44.

BRODKIN, KAREN B. "How Did Jews Become White Folks?" In JOHN J. MACIONIS and NIJOLE V. BENOKRAITIS, eds. *Seeing Ourselves: Classic, Contemporary, and Cross-Cultural Readings in Sociology.* 7th ed. Upper Saddle River, N.J.: Prentice Hall, 2007.

BROOKS, DAVID. *Bobos in Paradise: The New Upper Class and How They Got There.* New York: Simon & Schuster, 2000.

BROWN, LESTER R. "Reassessing the Earth's Population." *Society.* Vol. 32, No. 4 (May/June 1995):7–10.

BROWN, LESTER R., ET AL., eds. *State of the World 1993: A Worldwatch Institute Report on Progress toward a Sustainable Society.* New York: Norton, 1993.

BRUXELLES, SIMON DE. "Crimespotting: The New Way to Make Money on the Internet." *London Times* (October 6, 2009). http://www.timesonline.co.uk/tol/news/uk/crime/article6862398.ece

BUCKS, BRIAN K., ARTHUR B. KENNICKELL, TRACI L. MACH, and KEVIN B. MOORE. "Changes in U.S. Family Finances from 2004 to 2007: Evidence from the Survey of Consumer Finances." February 2009. http://www.federalreserve.gov/pubs/bulletin/2009/pdf/scf09.pdf

BUECHLER, STEVEN M. *Social Movements in Advanced Capitalism: The Political Economy and Cultural Construction of Social Activism.* New York: Oxford University Press, 2000.

BURKETT, ELINOR. "God Created Me to Be a Slave." *New York Times Magazine* (October 12, 1997):56–60.

BUSHAW, WILLIAM J., and JOHN A. McNEE. "Americans Speak Out." *Phi Delta Kappan.* Vol. 91, No. 1 (September 2009):9–23.

BUSSOLO, MAURIZIO, RAFAEL DE HOYOS, DENIS MEDVEDEV, and VICTOR SULLA. "Demographic Change, Economic Growth, and Income Distribution: An Empirical Analysis Using Ex-Ante Microsimulations." Paper prepared for Global Economic Prospects, 2007.

CALIFORNIA NEWSREEL. "Race: The Power of an Illusion: Genetic Diversity Quiz." 2003. http://www.pbs.org/race/000_About/002_04_a-godeeper.htm

CAMARA, EVANDRO. Personal communication, 2000.

CAMERON, WILLIAM BRUCE. *Modern Social Movements: A Sociological Outline.* New York: Random House, 1966.

CAP Index (2009), www.capindex.com

CARLSON, NORMAN A. "Corrections in the United States Today: A Balance Has Been Struck." *American Criminal Law Review.* Vol. 13, No. 4 (Spring 1976):615–47.

CARMICHAEL, STOKELY, and CHARLES V. HAMILTON. *Black Power: The Politics of Liberation in America.* New York: Vintage Books, 1967.

CASTELLS, MANUEL. *The Urban Question.* Cambridge, Mass.: MIT Press, 1977.

———. *The City and the Grass Roots.* Berkeley: University of California Press, 1983.

CASTILLA, EMILIO J. "Gender, Race, and Meritocracy in Organizational Careers." *American Journal of Sociology.* Vol. 113, No. 6 (May 2008):1479–1526.

CATALYST. "Research and Knowledge." 2010. http://www.catalyst.org/page/64/browse-research-knowledge

CENTER FOR AMERICAN WOMEN AND POLITICS. "Women in Elective Office, 2010." 2010. http://www.cawp.rutgers.edu/fast_facts/levels_of_office/documents/elective.pdf

CENTER FOR RESPONSIVE POLITICS. "110th Congress Casualty List." 2009. http://www.opensecrets.org/index.php

CENTER FOR THE STUDY OF THE AMERICAN ELECTORATE. "2008 Turnout Report: African-Americans, Anger, Fear and Youth Propel Turnout to Highest Level Since 1960." December 17, 2008. http://www1.american.edu/ia/cdem/csae/electionstudies

CENTER FOR WOMEN'S BUSINESS RESEARCH. "Key Facts about Women-Owned Businesses." 2009. http://www.nfwbo.org/facts/index.php

CENTERS FOR DISEASE CONTROL AND PREVENTION (CDC). "Annual Smoking-Attributable Mortality." *Morbidity and Mortality Weekly Report*. Vol. 54, No. 25 (July 1, 2005):625–28.

———. *Sexually Transmitted Disease Surveillance, 2005*. Atlanta: U.S. Department of Health and Human Services, 2006.

———. "Tobacco Use among Adults—United States, 2005." *Morbidity and Mortality Weekly Report*. Vol. 55, No. 42 (October 27, 2006):1145–48.

———. "Youth Risk Behavior Surveillance—United States, 2005." *Morbidity and Mortality Weekly Report*. Vol. 55, No. 5 (June 9, 2006).

———. "Smoking and Tobacco Use Fact Sheet: Cigarette Smoking-Related Mortality." September 2006. http://www.cdc.gov/tobacco/data_statistics/Factsheets/cig_smoking_mort.htm

———. *HIV/AIDS Surveillance Report, 2005*. Vol. 17, rev. ed. Atlanta: U.S. Department of Health and Human Services, 2007.

———. "Cigarette Smoking among Adults—United States, 2006." *Morbidity and Mortality Weekly Report*. Vol. 56, No. 44 (November 9, 2007):1157–61.

———. "Overweight and Obesity: Economic Consequences." May 2007. http://www.cdc.gov/nccdphp/dnpa/obesity/economic_consequences.htm

———. *Sexually Transmitted Disease Surveillance, 2006*. Atlanta: U.S. Department of Health and Human Services, 2007.

———. "Targeting Tobacco Use: The Nation's Leading Cause of Preventable Death." March 2008. http://www.cdc.gov/NCCDPHP/publications/aag/osh.htm

———. "Trends in the Prevalence of Sexual Behaviors: National Youth Risk Behavior Survey, 1991–2007." 2008. http://www.cdc.gov/HealthyYouth/sexualbehaviors/index.htm

———. *HIV/AIDS Surveillance Report, 2007*. Vol. 19. Atlanta: U.S. Department of Health and Human Services. 2009. http://www.cdc.gov/hiv/topics/surveillance/

———. *Morbidity and Mortality Weekly Reports*. 2009. http://www.cdc.gov/mmwr/preview/mmwrhtml/mm5745a2.htm

———. "Behavioral Risk Factor Surveillance System: Mapping." 2010, http://www.cdc.gov/brfss/index.htm

———. *Sexually Transmitted Diseases*. Atlanta: U.S. Department of Health and Human Services. 2010. http://www.cdc.gov/std/stats/default.htm

CENTRAL INTELLIGENCE AGENCY. *The World Factbook*. 2010 (updated biweekly). https://www.cia.gov/library/publications/the-world-factbook/index.html

CHAGNON, NAPOLEON A. *Yanomamö: The Fierce People*. 4th ed. Austin, Tex.: Holt, Rinehart and Winston, 1992.

CHANDLER, TERTIUS, and GERALD FOX. *3000 Years of Urban History*. New York: Academic Press, 1974.

CHANG, LESLIE T. *Factory Girls: From Village to City in a Changing China*. New York: Spiegel & Grau, 2008.

CHEN, SHAHUA, and MARTIN RAVALLION. "The Developing World Is Poorer than We Thought, but No Less Successful in the Fight against Poverty." 2008. http://go.worldbank.org/C9GR27WRJ0

CHERLIN, ANDREW J., LINDA M. BURTON, TERA R. HART, and DIANE M. PURVIN. "The Influence of Physical and Sexual Abuse on Marriage and Cohabitation." *American Sociological Review*. Vol. 69, No. 6 (December 2004):768–89.

"China Faces Water Shortage." *Popline*. Vol. 23 (December 2001):1–4.

CHIRICOS, TED, RANEE MCENTIRE, and MARC GERTZ. "Perceived Racial and Ethnic Composition of Neighborhood and Perceived Risk of Crime." *Social Problems*. Vol. 48, No. 3 (August 2001):322–40.

CHODOROW, NANCY. *Femininities, Masculinities, Sexualities: Freud and Beyond*. Lexington: University of Kentucky Press, 1994.

CHOPRA, ANUJ. "Iranian Rap Music Bedevils the Authorities." *U.S. News & World Report* (March 24, 2008):33.

CHRONICLE OF HIGHER EDUCATION. *Almanac 2007–08*. 2007. http://chronicle.com/free/almanac/2007/nation/nation_index.htm#faculty

———. "A Profile of College Presidents, 1986 and 2006." February 26, 2007. http://chronicle.com/stats/acesurvey/data.htm share

CHUA-EOAN, HOWARD. "Profiles in Outrage." *Time* (September 25, 2000):38–39.

CIMINO, RICHARD, and DON LATTIN. "Choosing My Religion." *American Demographics*. Vol. 21, No. 4 (April 1999):60–65.

CLARK, ANDREW. "Wal-Mart, the U.S. Retailer, Taking Over the World by Stealth." *Guardian*, January 12, 2010. http://www.guardian.co.uk/business/2010/jan/12/walmart-companies-to-shape-the-decade

CLARK, KIM. "Bankrupt Lives." *U.S. News & World Report* (September 16, 2002):52–54.

CLARK, MARGARET S., ed. *Prosocial Behavior*. Newbury Park, Calif.: Sage, 1991.

CLAWSON, DAN, and MARY ANN CLAWSON. "What Has Happened to the U.S. Labor Movement? Union Decline and Renewal." *Annual Review of Sociology*. Vol. 25 (1999):95–119.

CLOUD, JOHN, and JODIE MORSE. "Home Sweet School." *Time* (August 27, 2001):46–54.

CLOWARD, RICHARD A., and LLOYD E. OHLIN. *Delinquency and Opportunity: A Theory of Delinquent Gangs*. New York: Free Press, 1966.

COHEN, ADAM. "A First Report Card on Vouchers." *Time* (April 26, 1999):36–38.

COHEN, ALBERT K. *Delinquent Boys: The Culture of the Gang*. New York: Free Press, 1971; orig. 1955.

COHEN, PHILIP N., and MATT L. HUFFMAN. "Individuals, Jobs, and Labor Markets: The Devaluation of Women's Work." *American Sociological Review*. Vol. 68, No. 3 (June 2003):443–63.

COHN, D'VERA. "Do Parents Spend Enough Time with Their Children?" Population Reference Bureau. January 2007. http://www.prb.org/Articles/2007/DoParentsSpendEnoughTimeWithTheirChildren.aspx

COLE, GEORGE F., and CHRISTOPHER E. SMITH. *Criminal Justice in America*. 3rd ed. Belmont, Calif.: Wadsworth, 2002.

COLEMAN, JAMES S. "The Design of Organizations and the Right to Act." *Sociological Forum*. Vol. 8, No. 4 (December 1993):527–46.

COLEMAN, JAMES S., and THOMAS HOFFER. *Public and Private High Schools: The Impact of Communities*. New York: Basic Books, 1987.

COLEMAN, JAMES S., THOMAS HOFFER, and SALLY KILGORE. *Public and Private Schools: An Analysis of Public Schools and Beyond*. Washington, D.C.: National Center for Education Statistics, 1981.

COLEMAN, JAMES S., ET AL. *Equality of Educational Opportunity*. Washington, D.C.: U.S. Government Printing Office, 1966.

COLEMAN, RICHARD P., and LEE RAINWATER. *Social Standing in America*. New York: Basic Books, 1978.

COLLEGE BOARD. "Tables & Related Items, 2008." 2008. http://professionals.collegeboard.com/data-reports-research/sat/cb-seniors-2008/tables

———. "2009 College-Bound Seniors: Total Group Profile Report." 2009. http://professionals.collegeboard.com/profdownload/cbs-2009-national-TOTAL-GROUP.pdf

———. "Public Four-Year Tuition Continues to Rise at Faster Rate than Private Four-Year Tuition." October 20, 2009. http://www.collegeboard.com/press/releases/208962.html

COLLEGE TOBACCO PREVENTION RESOURCE. "College Tobacco Resources, 1990–2005." 2006. http://www.ttac.org/college/pdfs/TTACFINALLitReview.pdf

COLLINS, RANDALL. *The Credential Society: A Historical Sociology of Education and Stratification*. New York: Academic Press, 1979.

COLLYMORE, YVETTE. "Migrant Street Children on the Rise in Central America." *Population Today*. Vol. 30, No. 2 (February/March 2002):1, 4.

COLTON, HELEN. *The Gift of Touch: How Physical Contact Improves Communication, Pleasure, and Health*. New York: Seaview/Putnam, 1983.

COMMISSION FOR RACIAL JUSTICE. *CRJ Reporter*. New York: United Church of Christ, 1994.

COMTE, AUGUSTE. *Auguste Comte and Positivism: The Essential Writings*. GERTRUD LENZER, ed. New York: Harper Torchbooks, 1975, orig. 1851–54.

CONGRESSIONAL BUDGET OFFICE. "Growing Disparities in Life Expectancy." April 17, 2008. http://www.cbo.gov/ftpdocs/91xx/doc9104/04-17-LifeExpectancy_Brief.pdf

CONNETT, PAUL H. "The Disposable Society." In F. HERBERT BORMANN and STEPHEN R. KELLERT, eds., *Ecology, Economics, and Ethics: The Broken Circle*. New Haven, Conn.: Yale University Press, 1991:99–122.

COOLEY, CHARLES HORTON. *Human Nature and the Social Order*. New York: Schocken Books, 1964; orig. 1902.

CORPORATE LIBRARY. "Executive Compensation." 2010. http://www.thecorporatelibrary.com/info.php?id=60ec

CORRELL, SHELLEY J. "Gender and the Career Choice Process: The Role of Biased Self-Assessment." *American Journal of Sociology*. Vol. 106, No. 6 (May 2001):1691–1730.

CORTESE, ANTHONY J. *Provocateur: Images of Women and Minorities in Advertising*. Lanham, Md.: Rowman & Littlefield, 1999.

COURTWRIGHT, DAVID T. *Violent Land: Single Men and Social Disorder from the Frontier to the Inner City*. Cambridge, Mass.: Harvard University Press, 1996.

COWLEY, GEOFFREY. "The Prescription That Kills." *Newsweek* (July 17, 1995):54.

COX, HARVEY. *The Secular City*. Rev. ed. New York: Macmillan, 1971.

CQ PRESS ELECTRONIC LIBRARY. *Political Handbook of the World Online Edition*. May 15, 2010. http://www.cqpress.com/product/PH-World-2008-OE.html

CROSSETTE, BARBARA. "Female Genital Mutilation by Immigrants Is Becoming Cause for Concern in the U.S." *New York Times International* (December 10, 1995):11.

CROUSE, JAMES, and DALE TRUSHEIM. *The Case against the SAT*. Chicago: University of Chicago Press, 1988.

CTIA. "Quick Facts." June 2009. http://www.ctia.org/media/industry_info/index.cfm/AID/10323

CUMMINGS, SCOTT, and THOMAS LAMBERT. "Anti-Hispanic and Anti-Asian Sentiments among African Americans." *Social Science Quarterly*. Vol. 78, No. 2 (June 1997):338–53.

CURRIE, ELLIOTT. *Confronting Crime: An American Challenge*. New York: Pantheon Books, 1985.

CURRY, ANDREW. "The Gullahs' Last Stand?" *U.S. News & World Report* (June 18, 2001):40–41.

CURTIS, JAMES E., DOUGLAS E. BAER, and EDWARD G. GRABB. "Nations of Joiners: Explaining Voluntary Association Membership in Democratic Societies." *American Sociological Review*. Vol. 66, No. 6 (December 2001):783–805.

CURTISS, SUSAN. *Genie: A Psycholinguistic Study of a Modern-Day "Wild Child."* New York: Academic Press, 1977.

DAHL, ROBERT A. *Who Governs?* New Haven, Conn.: Yale University Press, 1961.

———. *Dilemmas of Pluralist Democracy: Autonomy vs. Control*. New Haven, Conn.: Yale University Press, 1982.

DAHRENDORF, RALF. *Class and Class Conflict in Industrial Society*. Stanford, Calif.: Stanford University Press, 1959.

DALMIA, SHIKRA. "Obama and Big Labor." *Forbes* (October 29, 2008). http://www.forbes.com/2008/10/28/obama-card-check-oped-cx_sd_1029dalmia.html

DANG, ALAIN, and CABRINI VIANNEY. *Living in the Margins: A National Survey of Lesbian, Gay, Bisexual, and Transgender Asian and Pacific Islander Americans*. New York: National Gay and Lesbian Task Force Policy Institute, 2007.

DARROCH, JACQUELINE E., ET AL. "Teenage Sexual and Reproductive Behavior in Developed Countries: Can More Progress Be Made?" 2001. [Online] Available May 30, 2005, at http://www.guttmacher.org/pubs/eurosynth_rpt.pdf

DARWIN, CHARLES. *On the Origin of Species by Means of Natural Selection, or the Preservation of Favoured Races in the Struggle for Life.* London: Murray, 1859

DAVIDSON, JULIA O'CONNELL. *Prostitution, Power, and Freedom.* Ann Arbor: University of Michigan Press, 1998.

DAVIES, CHRISTIE. *Ethnic Humor around the World: A Comparative Analysis.* Bloomington: Indiana University Press, 1990.

DAVIES, JAMES B., SUSANNA SANDSTRÖM, ANTHONY SHORROCKS, and EDWARD N. WOLFF. *The World Distribution of Household Wealth.* Discussion Paper No. 2008/03. Helsinki: United Nations University–World Institute for Development Economics Research. February 2008. http://www.wider.unu.edu/publications/working-papers/discussion-papers/2008/en_GB/dp2008-03/

DAVIES, JAMES C. "Toward a Theory of Revolution." *American Sociological Review.* Vol. 27, No. 1 (February 1962):5–19.

DAVIES, MARK, and DENISE B. KANDEL. "Parental and Peer Influences on Adolescents' Educational Plans: Some Further Evidence." *American Journal of Sociology.* Vol. 87, No. 2 (September 1981):363–87.

DAVIS, DONALD M., cited in "TV Is a Blonde, Blonde World." *American Demographics,* special issue: *Women Change Places.* 1993.

DAVIS, KINGSLEY. "Final Note on a Case of Extreme Isolation." *American Journal of Sociology.* Vol. 52, No. 5 (March 1947):432–37.

———. "Sexual Behavior." In ROBERT K. MERTON and ROBERT NISBET, eds., *Contemporary Social Problems.* 3rd ed. New York: Harcourt Brace Jovanovich, 1971:313–60.

DAVIS, KINGSLEY, and WILBERT MOORE. "Some Principles of Stratification." *American Sociological Review.* Vol. 10, No. 2 (April 1945):242–49.

DEATH PENALTY INFORMATION CENTER. "Innocence and the Death Penalty." 2010. http://www.deathpenaltyinfo.org/innocence-and-death-penalty

DECARLO, SCOTT, ed. "The Global 2000." Forbes.com. April 8, 2009. http://www.forbes.com/lists/2009/18/global-09_The-Global-2000_Rank.html

DEDRICK, DENNIS K., and RICHARD E. YINGER. "MAD, SDI, and the Nuclear Arms Race." Unpublished manuscript. Georgetown, Ky.: Georgetown College, 1990.

DEFENSE FINANCE AND ACCOUNTING SERVICE. "Military Pay Tables, 2010." 2010. http://www.dfas.mil/militarypay/militarypaytables.html

DEFINA, ROBERT H., and THOMAS M. ARVANITES. "The Weak Effect of Imprisonment on Crime, 1971–1998." *Social Science Quarterly.* Vol. 83, No. 3 (September 2002):635–53.

DELACROIX, JACQUES, and CHARLES C. RAGIN. "Structural Blockage: A Cross-National Study of Economic Dependency, State Efficacy, and Underdevelopment." *American Journal of Sociology.* Vol. 86, No. 6 (May 1981):1311–47.

DEMERATH, N. J., III. "Who Now Debates Functionalism? From *System, Change, and Conflict* to 'Culture, Choice, and Praxis.'" *Sociological Forum.* Vol. 11, No. 2 (June 1996):333–45.

DEMUTH, STEPHEN, and DARRELL STEFFENSMEIER. "The Impact of Gender and Race-Ethnicity in the Pretrial Release Process." *Social Problems.* Vol. 51, No. 2 (May 2004):222–42.

DERBER, CHARLES. *The Wilding of America: Money, Mayhem, and the New American Dream.* 3rd ed. New York: Worth, 2004.

DEUTSCHER, IRWIN. *Making a Difference: The Practice of Sociology.* New Brunswick, N.J.: Transaction, 1999.

DICKLER, JESSICA. "Best-Paid Executives: The Gender Gap Exaggerated." *Fortune: 50 Most Powerful Women in Business.* October 3, 2007. http://money.cnn.com/2007/10/02/news/newsmakers/mpwpay/index.htm

DILLON, SAM. "Administration Seeks Converts to Education Plan." *New York Times.* March 16, 2010. http://www.nytimes.com/2010/03/17/education/17educ.html

DIXON, WILLIAM J., and TERRY BOSWELL. "Dependency, Disarticulation, and Denominator Effects: Another Look at Foreign Capital Penetration." *American Journal of Sociology.* Vol. 102, No. 2 (September 1996):543–62.

DOBYNS, HENRY F. "An Appraisal of Techniques with a New Hemispheric Estimate." *Current Anthropology.* Vol. 7, No. 4 (October 1966):395–446.

DOLLARD, JOHN, ET AL. *Frustration and Aggression.* New Haven, Conn.: Yale University Press, 1939.

DOMHOFF, G. WILLIAM. *Who Rules America Now? A View of the '80s.* Englewood Cliffs, N.J.: Prentice Hall, 1983.

DONAHUE, JOHN J., III, and STEVEN D. LEAVITT. Research cited in "New Study Claims Abortion Is behind Decrease in Crime." *Population Today.* Vol. 28, No. 1 (January 2000):1, 4.

DONOVAN, VIRGINIA K., and RONNIE LITTENBERG. "Psychology of Women: Feminist Therapy." In BARBARA HABER, ed., *The Women's Annual, 1981: The Year in Review.* Boston: Hall, 1982:211–35.

DOWNEY, DOUGLAS B., PAUL T. VON HIPPEL, and BECKETT A. BROH. "Are Schools the Great Equalizer? Cognitive Inequality during the Summer Months and School Year." *American Sociological Review.* Vol. 59, No. 5 (October 2004):613–35.

DOYLE, JAMES A. *The Male Experience.* Dubuque, Iowa: Brown, 1983.

DU BOIS, W. E. B. *The Philadelphia Negro: A Social Study.* New York: Schoken Books, 1967 (orig. 1899).

DUBOS, RENÉ. *Man Adapting.* Enlarged ed. New Haven, Conn.: Yale University Press, 1980.

DUDLEY, KATHRYN MARIE. *Debt and Dispossession: Farm Loss in America's Heartland.* Chicago: University of Chicago Press, 2000.

DUNCAN, CYNTHIA M. *Worlds Apart: Why Poverty Persists in Rural America.* New Haven, Conn.: Yale University Press, 1999.

DUNCAN, GREG J., W. JEAN YEUNG, JEANNE BROOKS-GUNN, and JUDITH R. SMITH. "How Much Does Childhood Poverty Affect the Life Chances of Children?" *American Sociological Review.* Vol. 63, No. 3 (June 1998):406–23.

DURKHEIM, EMILE. *The Division of Labor in Society.* New York: Free Press, 1964a; orig. 1893.

———. *The Rules of Sociological Method.* New York: Free Press, 1964b; orig. 1895.

———. *The Elementary Forms of Religious Life.* New York: Free Press, 1965; orig. 1915.

———. *Suicide.* New York: Free Press, 1966; orig. 1897.

DWORKIN, ANDREA. *Intercourse.* New York: Free Press, 1987.

EBAUGH, HELEN ROSE FUCHS. *Becoming an Ex: The Process of Role Exit.* Chicago: University of Chicago Press, 1988.

EBOH, CAMILLUS. "Nigerian Woman Loses Appeal against Stoning Death." *Yahoo! News* (August 19, 2002). http://news.yahoo.com

ECK, DIANA L. *A New Religious America: How a "Christian Country" Has Become the World's Most Religiously Diverse Nation.* San Francisco: HarperSanFrancisco, 2001.

ECONOMIST. "The Big Mac Index: Sandwiched." July 24, 2008. http://www.economist.com/finance/displaystory.cfm?story_id=11793125

EDWARDS, TAMALA M. "Revolt of the Gentry." *Time* (June 15, 1998):34–35.

———. "Flying Solo." *Time* (August 28, 2000):47–55.

EHRENREICH, BARBARA. *The Hearts of Men: American Dreams and the Flight from Commitment.* Garden City, N.Y.: Anchor Books, 1983.

———. "The Real Truth about the Female Body." *Time* (March 15, 1999):56–65.

———. *Nickel and Dimed: On (Not) Getting By in America.* New York: Henry Holt, 2001.

EICHLER, MARGRIT. *Nonsexist Research Methods: A Practical Guide.* Winchester, Mass.: Unwin Hyman, 1988.

EKMAN, PAUL. "Biological and Cultural Contributions to Body and Facial Movements in the Expression of Emotions." In A. RORTY, ed., *Explaining Emotions.* Berkeley: University of California Press, 1980a:73–101.

———. *Face of Man: Universal Expression in a New Guinea Village.* New York: Garland Press, 1980b.

ELIAS, ROBERT. *The Politics of Victimization: Victims, Victimology, and Human Rights.* New York: Oxford University Press, 1986.

ELLIOT, DELBERT S., and SUZANNE S. AGETON. "Reconciling Race and Class Differences in Self-Reported and Official Estimates of Delinquency." *American Sociological Review.* Vol. 45, No. 1 (February 1980):95–110.

ELLISON, CHRISTOPHER G., JOHN P. BARTKOWSKI, and MICHELLE L. SEGAL. "Do Conservative Protestant Parents Spank More Often? Further Evidence from the National Survey of Families and Households." *Social Science Quarterly.* Vol. 77, No. 3 (September 1996):663–73.

ELSON, JEAN. *Am I Still a Woman? Hysterectomy and Gender Identity.* Philadelphia: Temple University Press, 2004.

EMERSON, JOAN P. "Behavior in Private Places: Sustaining Definitions of Reality in Gynecological Examinations." In H. P. DREITZEL, ed., *Recent Sociology.* Vol. 2. New York: Collier, 1970:74–97.

EMERSON, MICHAEL O., GEORGE YANCEY, and KAREN J. CHAI. "Does Race Matter in Residential Segregation? Exploring the Preferences of White Americans." *American Sociological Review.* Vol. 66, No. 6 (December 2001):922–35.

ENGELS, FRIEDRICH. *The Origin of the Family.* Chicago: Kerr, 1902; orig. 1884.

ENGLAND, PAULA. "Three Reviews on Marriage." *Contemporary Sociology.* Vol. 30, No. 6 (November 2001):564–65.

ENGLAND, PAULA, JOAN M. HERMSEN, and DAVID A. COTTER. "The Devaluation of Women's Work: A Comment on Tam." *American Journal of Sociology.* Vol. 105, No. 6 (May 2000):1741–60.

ERIKSON, ERIK H. *Childhood and Society.* New York: Norton, 1963; orig. 1950.

ERIKSON, KAI T. *Everything in Its Path: Destruction of Community in the Buffalo Creek Flood.* New York: Simon & Schuster, 1976.

———. *A New Species of Trouble: Explorations in Disaster, Trauma, and Community.* New York: Norton, 1994.

———. Lecture at Kenyon College, February 7, 2005a.

———. *Wayward Puritans: A Study in the Sociology of Deviance.* New York: Wiley, 2005b; orig. 1966.

ESTES, RICHARD J. "The Commercial Sexual Exploitation of Children in the U.S., Canada, and Mexico." Reported in "Study Explores Sexual Exploitation." *Yahoo! News* (September 10, 2001). http://news.yahoo.com

ETZIONI, AMITAI. *A Comparative Analysis of Complex Organization: On Power, Involvement, and Their Correlates.* Rev. and enlarged ed. New York: Free Press, 1975.

———. "How to Make Marriage Matter." *Time* (September 6, 1993):76.

———. "The Responsive Community: A Communitarian Perspective." *American Sociological Review.* Vol. 61, No. 1 (February 1996):1–11.

———. *My Brother's Keeper: A Memoir and a Message.* Lanham, Md.: Rowman & Littlefield, 2003.

EUROPEAN UNION. EUROPEAN COMMUNITIES STATISTICAL OFFICE. "Eurostat." 2010. http://epp.eurostat.ec.europa.eu/portal/

EVELYN, JAMILAH. "Community Colleges Play Too Small a Role in Teacher Education, Report Concludes." *Chronicle of Higher Education Online.* October 24, 2002. http://chronicle.com/daily/2002/10/2002102403n.htm

EWERS, JUSTIN. "Saving Symbols of Shame." *U.S. News & World Report* (March 10, 2008):31.

EXECUTIVE LEADERSHIP COUNCIL. "Women and Minorities on *Fortune* 100 Boards." January 28, 2008. http://www.elcinfo.com/reports.php

FALLON, A. E., and P. ROZIN. "Sex Differences in Perception of Desirable Body Shape." *Journal of Abnormal Psychology.* Vol. 94, No. 1 (1985):100–105.

FATTAH, HASSAN. "A More Diverse Community." *American Demographics.* Vol. 24, No. 7 (July/August 2002):39–43.

FEAGIN, JOE R., and VERA HERNÁN. *Liberation Sociology.* Boulder, Colo.: Westview Press, 2001.

FEDERAL BUREAU OF INVESTIGATION. CRIMINAL JUSTICE INFORMATION SERVICES DIVISION. *Crime in the United States, 2007.* 2008. http://www.fbi.gov/ucr/cius2007/index.html

———. *Crime in the United States, 2008*. 2009. http://www.fbi.gov/ucr/cius2008/index.html

FEDERAL COMMUNICATIONS COMMISSION. "Trends in Telephone Service: Industry Analysis and Technology Division Wireline Competition Bureau." August 2008. http://hraunfoss.fcc.gov/edocs_public/attachmatch/DOC-284932A1.pdf

FEDERAL ELECTION COMMISSION. "FEC Records Slight Increase in the Number of PACs." Press release, January 17, 2008. http://www.fec.gov/press/press2008/20080117paccount.shtml

———. "2007–2008 Financial Activity of Senate and House General Election Campaigns, (January 1, 2007 – December 31, 2008)." http://www.fec.gov/press/press2009/2009Dec29Cong/2009Dec29Cong.shtml

FELLMAN, BRUCE. "Taking the Measure of Children's TV." *Yale Alumni Magazine* (April 1995):46–51.

"Female Opinion and Defense since September 11th." *Society*. Vol. 39, No. 3 (March/April 2002):2.

FENG HOU and JOHN MYLES. "The Changing Role of Education in the Marriage Market: Assortive Marriage in Canada and the united States Since the 1970s." *Canadian Journal of Sociology*. Vol. 33, No. 2 (2008):335-64.

FERNANDEZ, ROBERTO M., and NANCY WEINBERG. "Sifting and Sorting: Personal Contacts and Hiring in a Retail Bank." *American Sociological Review*. Vol. 62, No. 6 (December 1997):883–902.

FERRARO, KENNETH F., and JESSICA A. KELLEY-MOORE. "Cumulative Disadvantage and Health: Long-Term Consequences of Obesity?" *American Sociological Review*. Vol. 68, No. 5 (October 2003):707–29.

FERREE, MYRA MARX, and BETH B. HESS. *Controversy and Coalition: The New Feminist Movement across Four Decades of Change*. 3rd ed. New York: Routledge, 1995.

FETTO, JOHN. "Me Gusta TV." *American Demographics*. Vol. 24, No. 11 (January 2003):14–15.

FINE, GARY ALAN. "Nature and the Taming of the Wild: The Problem of 'Overpick' in the Culture of Mushroomers." *Social Problems*. Vol. 44, No. 1 (February 1997):68–88.

FIREBAUGH, GLENN. "Growth Effects of Foreign and Domestic Investment." *American Journal of Sociology*. Vol. 98, No. 1 (July 1992):105–30.

———. "Does Foreign Capital Harm Poor Nations? New Estimates Based on Dixon and Boswell's Measures of Capital Penetration." *American Journal of Sociology*. Vol. 102, No. 2 (September 1996):563–75.

FIREBAUGH, GLENN, and FRANK D. BECK. "Does Economic Growth Benefit the Masses? Growth, Dependence, and Welfare in the Third World." *American Sociological Review*. Vol. 59, No. 5 (October 1994):631–53.

FIREBAUGH, GLENN, and KENNETH E. DAVIS. "Trends in Antiblack Prejudice, 1972–1984: Region and Cohort Effects." *American Journal of Sociology*. Vol. 94, No. 2 (September 1988):251–72.

FIREBAUGH, GLENN, and DUMITRU SANDU. "Who Supports Marketization and Democratization in Post-Communist Romania?" *Sociological Forum*. Vol. 13, No. 3 (September 1998):521–41.

FISHER, ELIZABETH. *Woman's Creation: Sexual Evolution and the Shaping of Society*. Garden City, N.Y.: Anchor/Doubleday, 1979.

FISHER, ROGER, and WILLIAM URY. "Getting to Yes." In WILLIAM M. EVAN and STEPHEN HILGARTNER, eds., *The Arms Race and Nuclear War*. Englewood Cliffs, N.J.: Prentice Hall, 1988:261–68.

FLAHERTY, MICHAEL G. "A Formal Approach to the Study of Amusement in Social Interaction." *Studies in Symbolic Interaction*. Vol. 5. New York: JAI Press, 1984:71–82.

———. "Two Conceptions of the Social Situation: Some Implications of Humor." *Sociological Quarterly*. Vol. 31, No. 1 (Spring 1990):93–106.

FONDA, DAREN. "The Male Minority." *Time* (December 11, 2000):58–60.

FORD, CLELLAN S., and FRANK A. BEACH. *Patterns of Sexual Behavior*. New York: Harper Bros., 1951.

FORTUNE. "Rankings: 2010 Fortune 500." 2010. http://money.cnn.com/magazines/fortune/rankings/

FOUCAULT, MICHEL. *The History of Sexuality: An Introduction*. Vol. 1. ROBERT HURLEY, trans. New York: Vintage, 1990; orig. 1978.

FOWLER, BREE. "GM 3Q Global Sales Drop 11 Percent, Trail Toyota." *USA Today*, October 29, 2008. http://www.usatoday.com/money/economy/2008-10-29-1630144436_x.htm

FOX, JUSTIN. "Why Denmark Loves Globalization." *Time* (November 15, 2007). http://www.time.com/time/magazine/article/0,9171,1684528,00.html

FRANK, ANDRÉ GUNDER. *On Capitalist Underdevelopment*. Bombay: Oxford University Press, 1975.

———. *Crisis in the World Economy*. New York: Holmes & Meier, 1980.

———. *Reflections on the World Economic Crisis*. New York: Monthly Review Press, 1981.

FRANKLIN, JOHN HOPE. *From Slavery to Freedom: A History of Negro Americans*. 3rd ed. New York: Vintage Books, 1967.

FRAZIER, E. FRANKLIN. *Black Bourgeoisie: The Rise of a New Middle Class*. New York: Free Press, 1965.

FREEDMAN, ESTELLE B. *No Turning Back: The History of Feminism and the Future of Women*. New York: Ballantine Books, 2002.

FREEDOM HOUSE. "Freedom in the World Comparative and Historical Data." 2010. http://www.freedomhouse.org/template.cfm?page=439

FRENCH, MARILYN. *Beyond Power: On Women, Men, and Morals*. New York: Summit Books, 1985.

FRIAS, SONIA M., and RONALD J. ANGEL. "Stability and Change in the Experience of Partner Violence among Low-Income Women." *Social Science Quarterly*. Vol. 88, No. 5 (May 2007):1281–1306.

FRIEDMAN, MEYER, and RAY H. ROSENMAN. *Type A Behavior and Your Heart*. New York: Fawcett Crest, 1974.

FULLER, REX, and RICHARD SCHOENBERGER. "The Gender Salary Gap: Do Academic Achievement, Intern Experience, and College Major Make a Difference?" *Social Science Quarterly*. Vol. 72, No. 4 (December 1991):715–26.

FURSTENBERG, FRANK F., JR., and ANDREW J. CHERLIN. *Divided Families: What Happens to Children When Parents Part*. Cambridge, Mass.: Harvard University Press, 1991.

———. "Children's Adjustment to Divorce." In BONNIE J. FOX, ed. *Family Patterns, Gender Relations*. 2nd ed. New York: Oxford University Press, 2001.

GAGE, ELENI N. "Oaxaca's Alternative Lifestyle Scene." *Travel and Leisure* (November 2005). http://travelandleisure.com/articles/stepping-out/1

GAGNÉ, PATRICIA, RICHARD TEWKSBURY, and DEANNA McGAUGHEY. "Coming Out and Crossing Over: Identity Formation and Proclamation in a Transgender Community." *Gender and Society*. Vol. 11, No. 4 (August 1997):478–508.

GALANO, ANA MARIA. "Land Hungry in Brazil." *Courier* (July/August 1998). http://www.unesco.org/courier/1998_08/uk/somm/intro.htm

GALLAGHER, CHARLES A. "Miscounting Race: Explaining Whites' Misperceptions of Racial Group Size." *Sociological Perspectives*. Vol. 46, No. 3 (2003):381–96.

GALLUP. "U.S. Schools: Whole Lotta Cheatin' Going On." May 11, 2004. http://www.gallup.com/Home.aspx

——— . http://www.gallup.com/poll/1612/Education.aspx

GALSTER, GEORGE. "Black Suburbanization: Has It Changed the Relative Location of Races?" *Urban Affairs Quarterly*. Vol. 26, No. 4 (June 1991):621–28.

GAMORAN, ADAM. "The Variable Effects of High-School Tracking." *American Sociological Review*. Vol. 57, No. 6 (December 1992):812–28.

GANS, HERBERT J. *People and Plans: Essays on Urban Problems and Solutions*. New York: Basic Books, 1968.

GARDYN, REBECCA. "The Mating Game." *American Demographics*. Vol. 24, No. 7 (July/August 2002):33–37.

GARFINKEL, HAROLD. "Conditions of Successful Degradation Ceremonies." *American Journal of Sociology*. Vol. 61, No. 2 (March 1956):420–24.

———. *Studies in Ethnomethodology*. Cambridge, Mass.: Polity Press, 1967.

GARREAU, JOEL. *Edge City*. New York: Doubleday, 1991.

GEERTZ, CLIFFORD. "Common Sense as a Cultural System." *Antioch Review*. Vol. 33, No. 1 (Spring 1975):5–26.

GERBER, THEODORE P., and MICHAEL HOUT. "More Shock than Therapy: Market Transition, Employment, and Income in Russia, 1991–1995." *American Journal of Sociology*. Vol. 104, No. 1 (July 1998):1–50.

GERLACH, MICHAEL L. *The Social Organization of Japanese Business*. Berkeley: University of California Press, 1992.

GESCHWENDER, JAMES A. *Racial Stratification in America*. Dubuque, Iowa: Brown, 1978.

GEWERTZ, DEBORAH. "A Historical Reconsideration of Female Dominance among the Chambri of Papua New Guinea." *American Ethnologist*. Vol. 8, No. 1 (1981):94–106.

GIBBS, NANCY. "The Pulse of America along the River." *Time* (July 10, 2000):42–46.

———. "What Kids (Really) Need." *Time* (April 30, 2001):48–49.

———. "Darkness Falls." *Time* (April 30, 2007):36–52.

GIDDENS, ANTHONY. *The Transformation of Intimacy*. Cambridge: Polity Press, 1992.

GILBERT, NEIL. "Family Life: Sold on Work." *Society*. Vol. 42, No. 3 (2005):12–17.

GILBERTSON, GRETA A., and DOUGLAS T. GURAK. "Broadening the Enclave Debate: The Dual Labor Market Experiences of Dominican and Colombian Men in New York City." *Sociological Forum*. Vol. 8, No. 2 (June 1993):205–20.

GILLESPIE, MARK. "Trends Show Bathing and Exercise Up, TV Watching Down." Gallup.com. January 2000. http://www.gallup.com/poll/3352/Trends-Show-Bathing-Exercise-Up-Watching-Down.aspx

GILLIGAN, CAROL. *In a Different Voice: Psychological Theory and Women's Development*. Cambridge, Mass.: Harvard University Press, 1982.

GILLON, RAANAN. "Euthanasia in the Netherlands: Down the Slippery Slope?" *Journal of Medical Ethics*. Vol. 25, No. 1 (February 1999):3–4.

GIMENEZ, MARTHA E. "Silence in the Classroom: Some Thoughts about Teaching in the 1980s." *Teaching Sociology*. Vol. 17, No. 2 (April 1989):184–91.

GIOVANNINI, MAUREEN. "Female Anthropologist and Male Informant: Gender Conflict in a Sicilian Town." In JOHN J. MACIONIS and NIJOLE V. BENOKRAITIS, eds., *Seeing Ourselves: Classic, Contemporary, and Cross-Cultural Readings in Sociology*. 2nd ed. Englewood Cliffs, N.J.: Prentice Hall, 1992:27–32.

GLEICK, ELIZABETH. "The Marker We've Been Waiting For." *Time* (April 7, 1997):28–42.

GLENMARY RESEARCH CENTER. *Religious Congregations and Membership in the United States, 2000*. Nashville, Tenn.: Glenmary Research Center, 2002.

GLOBAL MARCH AGAINST CHILD LABOUR. *Worst Forms of Child Labour Report, 2005*. 2008. http://www.globalmarch.org/worstformsreport/world/index.html

GLUECK, SHELDON, and ELEANOR GLUECK. *Unraveling Juvenile Delinquency*. New York: Commonwealth Fund, 1950.

GOESLING, BRIAN. "Changing Income Inequalities within and between Nations: New Evidence." *American Sociological Review*. Vol. 66, No. 5 (October 2001):745–61.

GOFFMAN, ERVING. *The Presentation of Self in Everyday Life*. Garden City, N.Y.: Anchor Books, 1959.

———. *Asylums: Essays on the Social Situation of Mental Patients and Other Inmates*. Garden City, N.Y.: Anchor Books, 1961.

———. *Stigma: Notes on the Management of Spoiled Identity*. Englewood Cliffs, N.J.: Prentice Hall, 1963.

———. *Interactional Ritual: Essays on Face to Face Behavior*. Garden City, N.Y.: Anchor Books, 1967.

———. *Gender Advertisements*. New York: Harper Colophon, 1979.

GOLDBERG, BERNARD. *Bias: A CBS Insider Exposes How the Media Distort the News*. Washington, D.C.: Regnery, 2002.

GOLDBERG, STEVEN. *The Inevitability of Patriarchy*. New York: Morrow, 1974.

GOLDBERGER, PAUL. Lecture delivered at Kenyon College, September 22, 2002.

GOLDEN, FREDERIC, and MICHAEL D. LEMONICK. "The Race Is Over." *Time* (July 3, 2000):18–23.

GOLDSMITH, H. H. "Genetic Influences on Personality from Infancy." *Child Development*. Vol. 54, No. 2 (April 1983):331–35.

GOLDSTEIN, JOSHUA R., and CATHERINE T. KENNEY. "Marriage Delayed or Marriage Forgone? New Cohort Forecasts of First Marriage for U.S. Women." *American Sociological Review*. Vol. 66, No. 4 (August 2001):506–19.

GOODE, WILLIAM J. "The Theoretical Importance of Love." *American Sociological Review*. Vol. 24, No. 1 (February 1959):38–47.

———. "Encroachment, Charlatanism, and the Emerging Profession: Psychology, Sociology, and Medicine." *American Sociological Review*. Vol. 25, No. 6 (December 1960):902–14.

GORDON, JAMES S. "The Paradigm of Holistic Medicine." In ARTHUR C. HASTINGS ET AL., eds., *Health for the Whole Person: The Complete Guide to Holistic Medicine*. Boulder, Colo.: Westview Press, 1980:3–27.

GORE, AL. *An Inconvenient Truth: The Crisis of Global Warming*. Emmaus, Pa.: Rodale Books, 2006.

GORMAN, CHRISTINE. "Stressed-Out Kids." *Time* (December 25, 2000):168.

GORSKI, PHILIP S. "Historicizing the Secularization Debate: Church, State, and Society in Late Medieval and Early Modern Europe, ca. 1300 to 1700." *American Sociological Review*. Vol. 65, No. 1 (February 2000):138–67.

GOTHAM, KEVIN FOX. "Race, Mortgage Lending, and Loan Rejections in a U.S. City." *Sociological Focus*. Vol. 31, No. 4 (October 1998):391–405.

GOTTFREDSON, MICHAEL R., and TRAVIS HIRSCHI. "National Crime Control Policies." *Society*. Vol. 32, No. 2 (January/February 1995):30–36.

GOTTMANN, JEAN. *Megalopolis*. New York: Twentieth Century Fund, 1961.

GOULD, STEPHEN J. "Evolution as Fact and Theory." *Discover* (May 1981):35–37.

GOVERNORS HIGHWAY SAFETY ASSOCIATION. "Cell Phone and Texting Laws." July 2010. http://www.ghsa.org/html/stateinfo/laws/cellphone_laws.html

GRAYBOW, MARTHA. "Women Directors Help Boost the Bottom Line." *Yahoo! News* (October 1, 2007). http://news.yahoo.com

GREEN, GARY PAUL, LEANN M. TIGGES, and DANIEL DIAZ. "Racial and Ethnic Differences in Job-Search Strategies in Atlanta, Boston, and Los Angeles." *Social Science Quarterly*. Vol. 80, No. 2 (June 1999):263–90.

GREENBERG, DAVID F. *The Construction of Homosexuality*. Chicago: University of Chicago Press, 1988.

GREENE, BOB. "Empty House on the Prairie." *New York Times* (March 2, 2005). http://www.nytimes.com/2005/03/02/opinion/02greene.html

GREENHOUSE, STEVEN. "Many Entry-Level Workers Find Pinch of Rough Market." *New York Times* (September 4, 2006). http://www.nytimes.com/2006/09/04/us/04labor.html

GREENSPAN, STANLEY I. *The Four-Thirds Solution: Solving the Child-Care Crisis in America*. Cambridge, Mass.: Perseus, 2001.

GRIER, PETER. "How to Slow the Spread of the Bomb." *Christian Science Monitor* (June 5, 2006). http://news.yahoo.com/s/csm/20060605

GROSS, MATT. "It's My (Virtual) World." *New York Times* (November 3, 2006). http://www.nytimes.com/2006/11/03/travel/escapes/03second.html

Gu, BAOCHANG, ZHENZHEN ZHENG, FENG WANG, and YONG CAI. "Globalization, Policy intervention, and Reproduction: Below Replacement Fertility in China." (2007). Annual Meeting of the Population Association of America.

GURNETT, KATE. "On the Forefront of Feminism." *Albany Times Union* (July 5, 1998):G-1, G-6.

GUTIERREZ, CARL. "Bear Stearns Announces More Job Cuts." *Forbes* (October 3, 2007). http://www.forbes.com/markets/2007/10/03/bear-stearns-layoffs-markets-equity-cx_cg_1003markets23.html

GWYNNE, S. C., and JOHN F. DICKERSON. "Lost in the E-Mail." *Time* (April 21, 1997):88–90.

HABERMAS, JÜRGEN. *Toward a Rational Society: Student Protest, Science, and Politics*. JEREMY J. SHAPIRO, trans. Boston: Beacon Press, 1970.

HADDEN, JEFFREY K., and CHARLES E. SWAIN. *Prime-Time Preachers: The Rising Power of Televangelism*. Reading, Mass.: Addison-Wesley, 1981.

HAGAN, JACQUELINE MARIA. "Social Networks, Gender, and Immigrant Incorporation: Resources and Restraints." *American Sociological Review*. Vol. 63, No. 1 (February 1998):55–67.

HAGOPIAN, ELAINE C. *Civil Rights in Peril: The Targeting of Arabs and Muslims*. London: Photo Press, 2004.

HALBERSTAM, DAVID. *The Reckoning*. New York: Avon Books, 1986.

HALBFINGER, DAVID M., and STEVEN A. HOLMES. "Military Mirrors Working-Class America." *New York Times* (March 30, 2003). http://www.nytimes.com/2003/03/30/international/worldspecial/30DEMO.html

HALL, JOHN R., and MARY JO NEITZ. *Culture: Sociological Perspectives*. Englewood Cliffs, N.J.: Prentice Hall, 1993.

HAMER, DEAN, and PETER COPELAND. *The Science of Desire: The Search for the Gay Gene and the Biology of Behavior*. New York: Simon & Schuster, 1994.

HAMILTON, ANITA. "Speeders, Say Cheese." *Time* (September 17, 2001):32.

HAMILTON, BRADY E., JOYCE A. MARTIN, and STEPHANIE J. VENTURA. "Births: Preliminary Data for 2007." *National Vital Statistics Reports*. Vol. 57, No. 12 (March 18, 2009). http://www.cdc.gov/nchs/data/nvsr/nvsr57/nvsr57_12.pdf

———. "Births: Preliminary Data for 2008." *National Vital Statistics Reports*. Vol. 58, No. 16 (April 6, 2010). http://www.cdc.gov/nchs/data/nvsr/nvsr58/nvsr58_16.pdf

HAMRICK, MICHAEL H., DAVID J. ANSPAUGH, and GENE EZELL. *Health*. Columbus, Ohio: Merrill, 1986.

HANDLIN, OSCAR. *Boston's Immigrants, 1790–1865: A Study in Acculturation*. Cambridge, Mass.: Harvard University Press, 1941.

HANEY, CRAIG, W. CURTIS BANKS, and PHILIP G. ZIMBARDO. "Interpersonal Dynamics in a Simulated Prison." *International Journal of Criminology and Penology*. Vol. 1 (1973):69–97.

HANEY, LYNNE. "After the Fall: East European Women since the Collapse of State Socialism." *Contexts*. Vol. 1, No. 3 (Fall 2002):27–36.

HARFORD, TIM. "The American Dream: Getting to the Starting Line." Forbes.com. October 9, 2007. http://www.forbes.com/entrepreneurs/2007/10/09/income-mobility-opportunity-ent-dream1007-cx_th_1009harford.html

———. "The Beauty of Everyday Economics." *U.S. News & World Report* (January 28, 2008):14.

HARLOW, HARRY F., and MARGARET KUENNE HARLOW. "Social Deprivation in Monkeys." *Scientific American* (November 1962):137–46.

HARPSTER, PAULA, and ELIZABETH MONK-TURNER. "Why Men Do Housework: A Test of Gender Production and the Relative Resources Model." *Sociological Focus*. Vol. 31, No. 1 (February 1998):45–59.

HARRIES, KEITH D. *Serious Violence: Patterns of Homicide and Assault in America*. Springfield, Ill.: Thomas, 1990.

HARRINGTON, MICHAEL. *The New American Poverty*. New York: Penguin Books, 1984.

HARRIS, CHAUNCY D., and EDWARD L. ULLMAN. "The Nature of Cities." *Annals of the American Academy of Political and Social Sciences*. Vol. 242, No. 1 (November 1945):7–17.

HARRIS, DAVID R., and JEREMIAH JOSEPH SIM. "Who Is Multiracial? Assessing the Complexity of Lived Race." *American Sociological Review*. Vol. 67, No. 4 (August 2002):614–27.

HARRIS, MARVIN. *Cultural Anthropology*. 2nd ed. New York: Harper & Row, 1987.

HARRISON, C. KEITH. "Black Athletes at the Millennium." *Society*. Vol. 37, No. 3 (March/April 2000):35–39.

HARTOCOLLIS, ANEMONA. "Man Is Convicted of Attempted Murder as Hate Crime in Village Rampage." *New York Times* (March 2, 2007):B6.

HAYDEN, THOMAS. "Losing Our Voices." *U.S. News & World Report* (May 26, 2003):42.

HAYWARD, MARK D., EILEEN M. CRIMMINS, TONI P. MILES, and YU YANG. "The Significance of Socioeconomic Status in Explaining the Racial Gap in Chronic Health Conditions." *American Sociological Review*. Vol. 65, No. 6 (December 2000):910–30.

HEATH, BRAD. "Fraud Cases Fell as Crisis Loomed." *USA Today* (December 16, 2009):1A.

HEATH, JULIA A., and W. DAVID BOURNE. "Husbands and Housework: Parity or Parody?" *Social Science Quarterly*. Vol. 76, No. 1 (March 1995):195–202.

HELGESEN, SALLY. *The Female Advantage: Women's Ways of Leadership*. New York: Doubleday, 1990.

HELIN, DAVID W. "When Slogans Go Wrong." *American Demographics*. Vol. 14, No. 2 (February 1992):14.

HELLMICH, NANCI. "Environment, Economics Partly to Blame." *USA Today* (October 9, 2002):9D.

HENLEY, NANCY, MYKOL HAMILTON, and BARRIE THORNE. "Womanspeak and Manspeak: Sex Differences in Communication, Verbal and Nonverbal." In JOHN J. MACIONIS and NIJOLE V. BENOKRAITIS, eds., *Seeing Ourselves: Classic, Contemporary, and Cross-Cultural Readings in Sociology*. 2nd ed. Englewood Cliffs, N.J.: Prentice Hall, 1992.

HERMAN, DIANNE. "The Rape Culture." In JOHN J. MACIONIS and NIJOLE V. BENOKRAITIS, eds., *Seeing Ourselves: Classic, Contemporary, and Cross-Cultural Readings in Sociology*. 5th ed. Upper Saddle River, N.J.: Prentice Hall, 2001.

HERON, MELONIE, ET AL. "Deaths: Final Data for 2006." *National Vital Statistics Reports*. Vol. 57, No. 14 (April 17, 2009). http://www.cdc.gov/nchs/data/nvsr/nvsr57/nvsr57_14.pdf

HERPERTZ, SABINE C., and HENNING SASS. "Emotional Deficiency and Psychopathy." *Behavioral Sciences and the Law*. Vol. 18, No. 5 (September/October 2000):567–80.

HERRNSTEIN, RICHARD J., and CHARLES MURRAY. *The Bell Curve: Intelligence and Class Structure in American Life*. New York: Free Press, 1994.

HESKETH, T., and LU, L. "The Effect of China's One-Child Policy After 25 Years." *New England Journal of Medicine*. Vol. 353, No. 1 (September 2005):1171–76.

HESS, BETH B. "Breaking and Entering the Establishment: Committing Social Change and Confronting the Backlash." *Social Problems*. Vol. 46, No. 1 (February 1999):1–12.

HEWLETT, SYLVIA ANN, and CAROLYN BUCK LUCE. "Off-Ramps and On-Ramps: Keeping Talented Women on the Road to Success." *Harvard Business Review*. Vol. 83, No. 3 (March 2005):43–54.

HEYMANN, PHILIP B. "Civil Liberties and Human Rights in the Aftermath of September 11." *Harvard Journal of Law and Public Policy*. Vol. 25, No. 2 (Spring 2002):441–57.

HIGHTOWER, JIM. *Eat Your Heart Out: Food Profiteering in America*. New York: Crown, 1975.

HILL, MARK E. "Race of the Interviewer and Perception of Skin Color: Evidence from the Multi-City Study of Urban Inequality." *American Sociological Review*. Vol. 67, No. 1 (February 2002):99–108.

HIRSCHI, TRAVIS. *Causes of Delinquency*. Berkeley: University of California Press, 1969.

HOCHSCHILD, ARLIE RUSSELL. "Emotion Work, Feeling Rules, and Social Structure." *American Journal of Sociology*. Vol. 85, No. 3 (November 1979):551–75.

———. *The Managed Heart*. Berkeley: University of California Press, 1983.

HOPE, TRINA L., HAROLD G. GRASMICK, and LAURA J. POINTON. "The Family in Gottfredson and Hrischi's General Theory of Crime: Structure, Parenting, and Self-Control." *Sociological Focus*. Vol. 36, No. 4 (November 2003):291–311.

HORN, WADE F., and DOUGLAS TYNAN. "Revamping Special Education." *Public Interest*. No. 144 (Summer 2001):36–53.

HORTON, HAYWARD DERRICK. "Critical Demography: The Paradigm of the Future?" *Sociological Forum*. Vol. 14, No. 3 (September 1999):363–67.

HOUT, MICHAEL. "More Universalism, Less Structural Mobility: The American Occupational Structure in the 1980s." *American Journal of Sociology*. Vol. 95, No. 6 (May 1998):1358–1400.

HOUT, MICHAEL, CLEM BROOKS, and JEFF MANZA. "The Persistence of Classes in Post-Industrial Societies." *International Sociology*. Vol. 8, No. 3 (September 1993):259–77.

HOUT, MICHAEL, and CLAUDE S. FISHER. "Why More Americans Have No Religious Preference: Politics and Generations." *American Sociological Review*. Vol. 67, No. 2 (April 2002):165–90.

HOUT, MICHAEL, ANDREW M. GREELEY, and MELISSA J. WILDE. "The Demographic Imperative in Religious Change in the United States." *American Journal of Sociology*. Vol. 107, No. 2 (September 2001):468–500.

HOWDEN, DANIEL. "Latin America's New Socialist Revolution." *New Zealand Herald* (December 20, 2005). http://www.nzherald.co.nz

HOYT, HOMER. *The Structure and Growth of Residential Neighborhoods in American Cities*. Washington, D.C.: Federal Housing Administration, 1939.

HSU, FRANCIS L. K. *The Challenge of the American Dream: The Chinese in the United States*. Belmont, Calif.: Wadsworth, 1971.

HUCHINGSON, JAMES E. "Science and Religion." *Miami* (Fla.) *Herald* (December 25, 1994):1M, 6M.

HUFFMAN, KAREN. *Psychology in Action*. New York: Wiley, 2000.

HUNTER, JAMES DAVISON. *American Evangelicalism: Conservative Religion and the Quandary of Modernity*. New Brunswick, N.J.: Rutgers University Press, 1983.

———. "Conservative Protestantism." In PHILIP E. HAMMOND, ed., *The Sacred in a Secular Age*. Berkeley: University of California Press, 1985:50–66.

———. *Evangelicalism: The Coming Generation*. Chicago: University of Chicago Press, 1987.

HYMOWITZ, KAY S. "Kids Today Are Growing Up Way Too Fast." *Wall Street Journal* (October 28, 1998):A22.

IANNACCONE, LAURENCE R. "Why Strict Churches Are Strong." *American Journal of Sociology*. Vol. 99, No. 5 (March 1994):1180–1211.

IDE, THOMAS R., and ARTHUR J. CORDELL. "Automating Work." *Society*. Vol. 31, No. 6 (September/October 1994):65–71.

IGNATIUS, ADI. "Why Putin Will Still Run Russia." *Time*. (March 2, 2008). http://www.time.com/time/world/article/0,8599,1718775,00.html

INCIARDI, JAMES A. *Elements of Criminal Justice*. 2nd ed. New York: Oxford University Press, 2000.

INCIARDI, JAMES A., HILARY L. SURRATT, and PAULO R. TELLES. *Sex, Drugs, and HIV/AIDS in Brazil*. Boulder, Colo.: Westview Press, 2000.

INGLEHART, RONALD. *Modernization and Postmodernization: Cultural, Economic, and Political Change in 43 Societies*. Princeton, N.J.: Princeton University Press, 1997.

INGLEHART, RONALD, and WAYNE E. BAKER. "Modernization, Cultural Change, and the Persistence of Traditional Values." *American Sociological Review*. Vol. 65, No. 1 (February 2000):19–51.

INGLEHART, RONALD and CHRISTIAN WELZEL. *Modernization, Culture Change, and Democracy*. New York: Cambridge University Press, 2005.

———. "World Values Survey: Inglehart-Welzel Cultural Map of the World." 2010. //www.worldvaluessurvey.com/

INGLEHART, RONALD, CHRISTIAN WELZEL, and ROBERTO FOA. "Happiness Trends in 24 Countries, 1946–2006." 2010. http://www.worldvaluessurvey.org/wvs/articles/folder_published/article_base_106

INGLEHART, RONALD, ET AL. *World Values Surveys and European Values Surveys, 1981–1984, 1990–1993, and 1995–1997*. Computer file. Ann Arbor, Mich.: Interuniversity Consortium for Political and Social Research, 2000.

INTERNAL REVENUE SERVICE. "SOI Tax Stats: Returns of Active Corporations, Table 2." 2008. http://www.irs.gov/taxstats/article/0,,id=170544,00.html

———. "SOI Tax Stats: Individual Statistical Tables by Tax Rate and Income Percentile." 2009. http://www.irs.gov/taxstats/indtaxstats/article/0,,id=133521,00.html

INTERNATIONAL DEVELOPMENT RESEARCH CENTER. *Growing Better Cities: Urban Agriculture for Sustainable Development*. Ottawa, Canada. 2006.

INTERNATIONAL LABOUR ORGANIZATION. INTERNATIONAL PROGRAMME ON THE ELIMINATION OF CHILD LABOUR (ILO-IPEC). "Global Child Labour Trends, 2000–2004." June 2006. http://www.ilo.org/ipec/Informationresources/lang–en/index.htm

INTERNATIONAL MONETARY FUND. *World Economic Outlook*. October 2007. http://www.imf.org/external/pubs/ft/weo/2007/02

INTERNATIONAL PANEL ON CLIMATE CHANGE. *Climate Change, 2007*. New York: United Nations, 2007.

INTERNATIONAL TELECOMMUNICATION UNION. *World Telecommunication Development Report*. Data cited in WORLD BANK, *2008 World Development Indicators*. Washington, D.C.: World Bank, 2008.

INTERNATIONAL TELECOMMUNICATION UNION. *World Telecommunication Development Report*. Data cited in WORLD BANK, *2009 World Development Indicators*. Washington, D.C.: World Bank, 2009.

INTER-PARLIAMENTARY UNION. "Women in National Parliaments." 2008. http://www.ipu.org/wmn-e/classif.htm; http://www.ipu.org/wmn-e/world.htm

———. "Women in National Parliaments." October 31, 2009. http://www.ipu.org/english/home.htm

ISRAEL, GLENN D., LIONEL J. BEAULIEU, and GLEN HARTLESS. "The Influence of Family and Community Social Capital on Educational Achievement." *Rural Sociology*. Vol. 66, No. 1 (March 2001):43–68.

ITZKOFF, DAVE. "Television: A Brave New World for TV? Virtually." *New York Times* (June 24, 2007). http://www.nytimes.com/2007/06/24/arts/television/24itzk.html

JACOBS, DAVID, and RONALD E. HELMS. "Toward a Political Model of Incarceration: A Time-Series Examination of Multiple Explanations for Prison Admission Rates." *American Journal of Sociology*. Vol. 102, No. 2 (September 1996):323–57.

JACOBSON, JENNIFER. "Professors Are Finding Better Pay and More Freedom at Community Colleges." *Chronicle of Higher Education* (March 7, 2003). http://chronicle.com/article/Professors-Are-Finding-Better/18498/

JACQUET, CONSTANT H., and ALICE M. JONES. *Yearbook of American and Canadian Churches, 1991*. Nashville, Tenn.: Abingdon Press, 1991.

JANIS, IRVING L. *Victims of Groupthink*. Boston: Houghton Mifflin, 1972.

———. *Crucial Decisions: Leadership in Policymaking and Crisis Management*. New York: Free Press, 1989.

JENKINS, J. CRAIG. *Images of Terror: What We Can and Can't Know about Terrorism*. Hawthorne, N.Y.: Aldine de Gruyter, 2003.

JENKINS, J. CRAIG, and MICHAEL WALLACE. "The Generalized Action Potential of Protest Movements: The New Class, Social Trends, and Political Exclusion Explanations." *Sociological Forum*. Vol. 11, No. 2 (June 1996):183–207.

JOHNSON, BARRY W., and BRIAN G. RAUB. "Personal Wealth, 2001." *Statistics of Income Bulletin* (Winter 2005–06). 2006. http://www.irs.gov/pub/irs-soi/01pwart.pdf

JOHNSON, CATHRYN. "Gender, Legitimate Authority, and Leader-Subordinate Conversations." *American Sociological Review*. Vol. 59, No. 1 (February 1994):122–35.

JOHNSON, DIRK. "Death of a Small Town." *Newsweek* (September 10, 2001):30–31.

JOHNSON, KENNETH M. "The Rural Rebound." *Population Reference Bureau Reports on America*. Vol. 1, No. 3 (September 1999). http://www.prb.org/Content/NavigationMenu/PRB/AboutPRB/Reports_on_America/ReportonAmericaRuralRebound.pdf

JOHNSON, KENNETH M., and GLENN V. FUGUITT. "Continuity and Change in Rural Migration Patterns, 1950–1995." *Rural Sociology*. Vol. 65, No. 1 (March 2000):27–49.

JOHNSON, PAUL. "The Seven Deadly Sins of Terrorism." In BENJAMIN NETANYAHU, ed., *International Terrorism*. New Brunswick, N.J.: Transaction Books, 1981:12–22.

JOHNSTON, R. J. "Residential Area Characteristics." In D. T. HERBERT and R. J. JOHNSTON, eds., *Social Areas in Cities. Vol. 1: Spatial Processes and Form*. New York: Wiley, 1976:193–235.

JONES, ANDREW E. G., and DAVID WILSON. *The Urban Growth Machine: Critical Perspectives*. Albany: State University of New York Press, 1999.

JONES, CHARISSE. "Upon Release from Prison, Some Can Feel Lost." *USA Today* (December 14, 2007):5A.

JONES, D. GARETH. "Brain Death." *Journal of Medical Ethics*. Vol. 24, No. 4 (August 1998):237–43.

JONES, KATHARINE W. *Accent on Privilege: English Identities and Anglophilia in the U.S.* Philadelphia: Temple University Press, 2001.

JORDAN, ELLEN, and ANGELA COWAN. "Warrior Narratives in the Kindergarten Classroom: Renegotiating the Social Contract?" *Gender and Society*. Vol. 9, No. 6 (December 1995):727–43.

JOSEPHY, ALVIN M., JR. *Now That the Buffalo's Gone: A Study of Today's American Indians*. New York: Knopf. 1982.

KAIN, EDWARD L. "A Note on the Integration of AIDS into the Sociology of Human Sexuality." *Teaching Sociology*. Vol. 15, No. 4 (July 1987):320–23.

KALLEBERG, ARNE L., BARBARA F. RESKIN, and KEN HUDSON. "Bad Jobs in America: Standard and Nonstandard Employment Relations and Job Quality in the United States." *American Sociological Review*. Vol. 65, No 2 (April 2000):256–78.

KAMINER, WENDY. "Volunteers: Who Knows What's in It for Them?" *Ms.* (December 1984):93–96, 126–28.

———. "Demasculinizing the Army." *New York Times Review of Books* (June 15, 1997):7.

KANE, EMILY W. "Racial and Ethnic Variations in Gender-Related Attitudes." *Annual Review of Sociology*. Vol. 26 (2000):419–39.

KANTER, ROSABETH MOSS. *Men and Women of the Corporation*. New York: Basic Books, 1977.

KANTER, ROSABETH MOSS, and BARRY A. STEIN. "The Gender Pioneers: Women in an Industrial Sales Force." In ROSABETH MOSS KANTER and BARRY A. STEIN, eds., *Life in Organizations*. New York: Basic Books, 1979:134–60.

KANTROWITZ, BARBARA, and PAT WINGERT. "Unmarried with Children." *Newsweek* (May 28, 2001):46–52.

———. "What's at Stake." *Newsweek* (January 27, 2003):30–37.

KAO, GRACE. "Group Images and Possible Selves among Adolescents: Linking Stereotypes to Expectations by Race and Ethnicity." *Sociological Forum*. Vol. 15, No. 3 (September 2000):407–30.

KAPLAN, DAVID E., and MICHAEL SCHAFFER. "Losing the Psywar." *U.S. News & World Report* (October 8, 2001):46.

KAPTCHUK, TED. "The Holistic Logic of Chinese Medicine." In BERKELEY HOLISTIC HEALTH CENTER, *The New Holistic Health Handbook: Living Well in a New Age*. SHEPARD BLISS ET AL., eds. Lexington, Mass.: Steven Greene Press, 1985:41.

KARATNYCKY, ADRIAN. "The 2001–2002 Freedom House Survey of Freedom: The Democracy Gap." In *Freedom in the World: The Annual Survey of Political Rights and Civil Liberties, 2001–2002*. New York: Freedom House, 2002:7-18.

KARJANE, HEATHER M., BONNIE S. FISHER, and FRANCIS T. CULLEN. "Sexual Assault on Campus: What Colleges and Universities Are Doing about It." December 2005. http://www.ncjrs.gov/pdffiles1/nij/205521.pdf

KARP, DAVID A., and WILLIAM C. YOELS. "The College Classroom: Some Observations on the Meaning of Student Participation." *Sociology and Social Research*. Vol. 60, No. 4 (July 1976):421–39.

KARRFALT, WAYNE. "A Multicultural Mecca." *American Demographics*. Vol. 25, No. 4 (May 2003):54–55.

KAUFMAN, LESLIE. "Surge in Homeless Families Sets Off Debate on Cause." *New York Times* (July 29, 2004). http://www.nytimes.com/2004/06/29/us/surge-in-homeless-families-sets-off-debate-on-cause.html

KAUFMAN, ROBERT L. "Assessing Alternative Perspectives on Race and Sex Employment Segregation." *American Sociological Review*. Vol. 67, No. 4 (August 2002):547–72.

KAUFMAN, WALTER. *Religions in Four Dimensions: Existential, Aesthetic, Historical, and Comparative*. Pleasantville, N.Y.: Reader's Digest Press, 1976.

KAY, PAUL, and WILLETT KEMPTON. "What Is the Sapir-Whorf Hypothesis?" *American Anthropologist*. Vol. 86, No. 1 (March 1984):65–79.

KEISTER, LISA A. *Wealth in America: Trends in Wealth Inequality.* New York: Cambridge University Press, 2000.

———. "Religion and Wealth: The Role of Religious Affiliation and Participation in Early Adult Asset Accumulation." *Social Forces.* Vol. 82, No. 1 (September 2003):175–207.

KEISTER, LISA A., and STEPHANIE MOLLER. "Wealth Inequality in the United States." *Annual Review of Sociology.* Vol. 26 (2000):63–81.

KENT, MARY M., and MARK MATHER. "What Drives U.S. Population Growth?" *Population Bulletin.* Vol. 57, No. 4 (December 2002):3–40.

KENTOR, JEFFREY. "The Long-Term Effects of Foreign Investment Dependence on Economic Growth, 1940–1990." *American Journal of Sociology.* Vol. 103, No. 4 (January 1998):1024–46.

———. "The Long-Term Effects of Globalization on Income Inequality, Population Growth, and Economic Development." *Social Problems.* Vol. 48, No. 4 (November 2001):435–55.

KERR, RICHARD A. "Climate Models Heat Up." *Science Now* (January 26, 2005):1–3.

KewalRamani, Angelina, Lauren Gilbertson, Mary Ann Fox, and Stephen Provasnik. *Status and Trends in the Education of Racial and Ethnic Minorities, 2005.* National Center for Education Statistics. September 2007. http://nces.ed.gov/pubs2007/minoritytrends/

KEYS, JENNIFER. "Feeling Rules That Script the Abortion Experience." Paper presented at the annual meeting of the American Sociological Association, Chicago, August 2002.

KILBOURNE, BROCK K. "The Conway and Siegelman Claims against Religious Cults: An Assessment of Their Data." *Journal for the Scientific Study of Religion.* Vol. 22, No. 4 (December 1983):380–85.

KILGORE, SALLY B. "The Organizational Context of Tracking in Schools." *American Sociological Review.* Vol. 56, No. 2 (April 1991):189–203.

KING, KATHLEEN PIKER, and DENNIS E. CLAYSON. "The Differential Perceptions of Male and Female Deviants." *Sociological Focus.* Vol. 21, No. 2 (April 1988):153–64.

KINKEAD, GWEN. *Chinatown: A Portrait of a Closed Society.* New York: HarperCollins, 1992.

KINSEY, ALFRED, WARDELL BAXTER POMEROY, and CLYDE E. MARTIN. *Sexual Behavior in the Human Male.* Philadelphia: Saunders, 1948.

KINSEY, ALFRED, WARDELL BAXTER POMEROY, CLYDE E. MARTIN, and PAUL H. GEBHARD. *Sexual Behavior in the Human Female.* Philadelphia: Saunders, 1953.

KITTRIE, NICHOLAS N. *The Right to Be Different: Deviance and Enforced Therapy.* Baltimore: Johns Hopkins University Press, 1971.

KIVANT, BARBARA. "Reassessing Risk." *Time* (November 17, 2008): Global 1–4.

KLUCKHOHN, CLYDE. "As an Anthropologist Views It." In ALBERT DEUTSCH, ed., *Sex Habits of American Men.* New York: Prentice Hall, 1948.

KOHLBERG, LAWRENCE. *The Psychology of Moral Development: The Nature and Validity of Moral Stages.* New York: Harper & Row, 1981.

KOHLBERG, LAWRENCE, and CAROL GILLIGAN. "The Adolescent as Philosopher: The Discovery of Self in a Postconventional World." *Daedalus.* No. 100 (Fall 1971):1051–86.

KOHN, MELVIN L. *Class and Conformity: A Study in Values.* 2nd ed. Homewood, Ill.: Dorsey Press, 1977.

KOHUT, ANDREW. "Post-Election Perpsectives." Pew Research Center. November 13, 2008. http://pewresearch.org/pubs/1039/post-election-perspectives

KONO, CLIFFORD, DONALD PALMER, ROGER FRIEDLAND, and MATTHEW ZAFONTE. "Lost in Space: The Geography of Corporate Interlocking Directorates." *American Journal of Sociology.* Vol. 103, No. 4 (January 1998):863–911.

KORNHAUSER, WILLIAM. *The Politics of Mass Society.* New York: Free Press, 1959.

KOZOL, JONATHAN. *Rachel and Her Children: Homeless Families in America.* New York: Crown, 1988.

———. *Savage Inequalities: Children in America's Schools.* New York: Harper Perennial, 1992.

KRAL, BRIGITTA. "The Eyes of Jane Elliott." *Horizon Magazine.* 2000. http://www.horizon-mag.com/4/jane-elliott.asp

KRAYBILL, DONALD B. *The Riddle of Amish Culture.* Baltimore: Johns Hopkins University Press, 1989.

———. "The Amish Encounter with Modernity." In DONALD B. KRAYBILL and MARC A. OLSHAN, eds., *The Amish Struggle with Modernity.* Hanover, N.H.: University Press of New England, 1994:21–33.

KRAYBILL, DONALD B., and JAMES P. HURD. *Horse-and-Buggy Mennonites: Hoofbeats of Humility in a Postmodern World.* University Park: Pennsylvania State University Press, 2006.

KRAYBILL, DONALD B., and MARC A. OLSHAN, eds. *The Amish Struggle with Modernity.* Hanover, N.H.: University Press of New England, 1994.

KROLL, LUISA, MATTHEW MILLER, and TATIANA SERAFIN. "Forbes Special Report: The World's Billionaires." Forbes.com. March 11, 2009. http://www.forbes.com/2009/03/11/worlds-richest-people-billionaires-2009-billionaires_land.html

KRUGMAN, PAUL. "For Richer: How the Permissive Capitalism of the Boom Destroyed American Equality." *New York Times Magazine* (September 20, 2002):62–67, 76–77, 141–42.

KRUKS, GABRIEL N. "Gay and Lesbian Homeless/Street Youth: Special Issues and Concerns." *Journal of Adolescent Health.* Special Issue. No. 12 (1991):515–18.

KRYSAN, MARIA. "Community Undesirability in Black and White: Examining Racial Residential Preferences through Community Perceptions." *Social Problems.* Vol. 49, No. 4 (November 2002):521–43.

KÜBLER-ROSS, ELISABETH. *On Death and Dying.* New York: Macmillan, 1969.

KUBRIN, CHARLES E. "Gangstas, Thugs, and Hustlas: Identity and the Code of the Street in Rap Music." *Social Problems.* Vol. 52, No. 3 (2005):360–78.

KUNKEL, DALE, ET AL. *Sex on TV, 2005.* Menlo Park, Calif.: Henry J. Kaiser Family Foundation, 2005. http://www.kff.org/entmedia/entmedia110905pkg.cfm

KUUMBA, M. BAHATI. "A Cross-Cultural Race/Class/Gender Critique of Contemporary Population Policy: The Impact of Globalization." *Sociological Forum.* Vol. 14, No. 3 (March 1999):447–63.

KUZNETS, SIMON. "Economic Growth and Income Inequality." *American Economic Review.* Vol. 14, No. 1 (March 1955):1–28.

———. *Modern Economic Growth: Rate, Structure, and Spread.* New Haven, Conn.: Yale University Press, 1966.

LACAYO, RICHARD. "The Brawl over Sprawl." *Time* (March 22, 1999):44–48.

LACEY, MARC. "A Distinct Lifestyle: The Muxe of Mexico." *New York Times* (December 7, 2008):4.

LADD, JOHN. "The Definition of Death and the Right to Die." In JOHN LADD, ed., *Ethical Issues Relating to Life and Death.* New York: Oxford University Press, 1979:118–45.

LAGORIO, CHRISTINE. "Pepperdine in a Treehouse." *New York Times* (January 7, 2007). http://query.nytimes.com/gst/fullpage.html?res=9E02E4DE1730F934A35752C0A9619C8B63

LAI, H. M. "Chinese." In *Harvard Encyclopedia of American Ethnic Groups.* Cambridge, Mass.: Harvard University Press, 1980:217–33.

LANDSBERG, MITCHELL. "Health Disaster Brings Early Death in Russia." *Washington Times* (March 15, 1998):A8.

LANGAN, PATRICK A., and DAVID J. LEVIN. "Recidivism of Prisoners Released in 1994." Bureau of Justice Statistics Special Report. June 2002. http://bjs.ojp.usdoj.gov/index.cfm?ty=pbdetail&iid=1134

LANGBEIN, LAURA I., and ROSEANA BESS. "Sports in School: Source of Amity or Antipathy?" *Social Science Quarterly.* Vol. 83, No. 2 (June 2002):436–54.

LAPCHICK, RICHARD with ALEJANDRA DIAZ-CAMERON and DEREK McMECHAN. "The 2009 Racial and Gender Report Card: Major League Baseball." Orlando: Institute for Diversity and Ethics in Sports. University of Central Florida. http://web.bus.ucf.edu/sportbusiness/?page=1445

LAPPÉ, FRANCES MOORE, and JOSEPH COLLINS. *World Hunger: Twelve Myths.* New York: Grove Press/Food First Books, 1986.

LAREAU, ANNETTE. "Invisible Inequality: Social Class and Childrearing in Black Families and White Familes." *American Sociological Review.* Vol. 67, No. 5 (October 2002):747–76.

LaROSSA, RALPH, and DONALD C. REITZES. "Two? Two and One-Half? Thirty Months? Chronometrical Childhood in Early Twentieth-Century America." *Sociological Forum.* Vol. 166, No. 3 (September 2001):385–407.

LASLETT, PETER. *The World We Have Lost: England before the Industrial Age.* 3rd ed. New York: Scribner, 1984.

LAUMANN, EDWARD O., JOHN H. GAGNON, ROBERT T. MICHAEL, and STUART MICHAELS. *The Social Organization of Sexuality: Sexual Practices in the United States.* Chicago: University of Chicago Press, 1994.

LEACH, COLIN WAYNE. "Democracy's Dilemma: Explaining Racial Inequality in Egalitarian Societies." *Sociological Forum.* Vol. 17, No. 4 (December 2002):681–96.

LEACOCK, ELEANOR. "Women's Status in Egalitarian Societies: Implications for Social Evolution." *Current Anthropology.* Vol. 19, No. 2 (June 1978):247–75.

LEAVITT, JUDITH WALZER. "Women and Health in America: An Overview." In JUDITH WALZER LEAVITT, ed., *Women and Health in America.* Madison: University of Wisconsin Press, 1984:3–7.

LEE, BARRET A., and MATTHEW MARLEY. "The Right Side of the Tracks: Affluent Neighborhoods in the Metropolitan United States." *Social Science Quarterly.* Vol. 88, No. 3 (2007):766–89.

LEE, SHARON M., and BARRY EDMONSTON. "New Marriages, New Families: U.S. Racial and Hispanic Intermarriage." *Population Bulletin.* Vol. 60, No. 2 (June 2005):3–36. http://www.prb.org/pdf05/60.2NewMarriages.pdf

LEFEBVRE, HENRI. *The Production of Space.* Oxford: Blackwell, 1991.

LEFF, LISA. "California Gay Marriage Vote Still Undecided." *Yahoo! News* (November 5, 2008). http://news.yahoo.com

LEMERT, EDWIN M. *Social Pathology: A Systematic Approach to the Theory of Sociopathic Behavior.* New York: McGraw-Hill, 1951.

———. *Human Deviance, Social Problems, and Social Control.* 2nd ed. Englewood Cliffs, N.J.: Prentice Hall, 1972.

LEMONICK, MICHAEL D. "The Search for a Murder Gene." *Time* (January 20, 2003):100.

LENGERMANN, PATRICIA MADOO, and JILL NIEBRUGGE-BRANTLEY. *The Women Founders: Sociology and Social Theory, 1830–1930.* New York: McGraw-Hill, 1998.

LENGERMANN, PATRICIA MADOO, and RUTH A. WALLACE. *Gender in America: Social Control and Social Change.* Englewood Cliffs, N.J.: Prentice Hall, 1985.

LENSKI, GERHARD E. *Power and Privilege: A Theory of Social Stratification.* New York: McGraw-Hill, 1966.

LEONARD, EILEEN B. *Women, Crime, and Society: A Critique of Theoretical Criminology.* White Plains, N.Y.: Longman, 1982.

LEOPOLD, EVELYN. "Sudan's Young Endure 'Unspeakable' Abuse: Report." *Yahoo! News* (April 19, 2007). http://news.yahoo.com

LeVay, SIMON. *The Sexual Brain.* Cambridge, Mass.: MIT Press, 1993.

LEVER, JANET. "Sex Differences in the Complexity of Children's Play and Games." *American Sociological Review.* Vol. 43, No. 4 (August 1978):471–83.

LEVINE, MICHAEL P. "Reducing Hostility Can Prevent Heart Disease." *Mount Vernon* (Ohio) *News* (August 7, 1990):4A.

LEVINE, SAMANTHA. "The Price of Child Abuse." *U.S. News & World Report* (April 9, 2001):58.

———. "Playing God in Illinois." *U.S. News & World Report* (January 13, 2003):13.

LEVINSON, F. JAMES, and LUCY BASSETT. "Malnutrition Is Still a Major Contributor to Child Deaths." Population Reference Bureau. 2007. http://www.prb.org/pdf07/Nutrition2007.pdf

LEWIN, TAMAR. "Girls' Gains Have Not Cost Boys, Report Says." *New York Times* (May 20, 2008). http://www.nytimes.com/2008/05/20/education/20girls.html?partner=permalink&exprod=permalink

LEWIS, M. PAUL, ed. *Ethnologue: Languages of the World.* 16th ed. Dallas, Tex.: SIL International, 2009.

LEWIS, OSCAR. *The Children of Sanchez.* New York: Random House, 1961.

LIAZOS, ALEXANDER. "The Poverty of the Sociology of Deviance: Nuts, Sluts, and Perverts." *Social Problems.* Vol. 20, No. 1 (Summer 1972):103–20.

———. *People First: An Introduction to Social Problems.* Needham Heights, Mass.: Allyn & Bacon, 1982.

LICHTER, DANIEL T., and MARTHA L. CROWLEY. "Poverty in America: Beyond Welfare Reform." *Population Bulletin.* Vol. 57, No. 2 (June 2002):3–34.

LICHTER, DANIEL T., and RUKMALIE JAYAKODY. "Welfare Reform: How Do We Measure Success?" *Annual Review of Sociology.* Vol. 28 (2002):117–41.

LICHTER, S. ROBERT, and DANIEL R. AMUNDSON. "Distorted Reality: Hispanic Characters in TV Entertainment." In CLARA E. RODRIGUEZ, ed., *Latin Looks: Images of Latinas and Latinos in the U.S. Media.* Boulder, Colo.: Westview Press, 1997:57–79.

LIN, NAN, KAREN COOK, and RONALD S. BURT, eds. *Social Capital: Theory and Research.* Hawthorne, N.Y.: Aldine de Gruyter, 2001.

LIN, NAN, and WEN XIE. "Occupational Prestige in Urban China." *American Journal of Sociology.* Vol. 93, No. 4 (January 1988):793–832.

LINDAUER, DAVID L., and AKILA WEERAPANA. "Relief for Poor Nations." *Society.* Vol. 39, No. 3 (March/April 2002):54–58.

LINDLAW, SCOTT. "President Signs Education Bill." *Yahoo! News* (January 8, 2002). http://news.yahoo.com

LINDSTROM, BONNIE. "Chicago's Post-Industrial Suburbs." *Sociological Focus.* Vol. 28, No. 4 (October 1995):399–412.

LING, PYAU. "Causes of Chinese Emigration." In AMY TACHIKI ET AL., eds., *Roots: An Asian American Reader.* Los Angeles: UCLA Asian American Studies Center, 1971:134–38.

LINO, MARK, and ANDREA CARLSON. "Expenditures on Children by Families, 2008." Miscellaneous Publication No. 1528-2008. U.S. Department of Agriculture Center for Nutrition Policy and Promotion. July 2009. http://www.cnpp.usda.gov/Publications/CRC/crc2008.pdf

———. "Expenditures on Children by Families, 2009." U.S. Department of Agriculture, Center for Nutrition Policy and Promotion. Washington, D.C.: U.S. Government Printing Office, 2010.

LINTON, RALPH. "One Hundred Percent American." *American Mercury.* Vol. 40, No. 160 (April 1937a):427–29.

———. *The Study of Man.* New York: Appleton-Century, 1937b.

LIPSET, SEYMOUR MARTIN. "Canada and the United States." CHARLES F. DONAN and JOHN H. SIGLER, eds. Englewood Cliffs, N.J.: Prentice Hall, 1985.

LIPTAK, ADAM. "More than 1 in 100 Adults Are Now in Prison in U.S." *New York Times* (February 29, 2008):A14.

———. "Justices, 5–4, Reject Corporate Spending Limit in Political Campaigns." *New York Times* (January 22, 2010). http://www.nytimes.com/2010/01/22/us/politics/22scotus.html

LISKA, ALLEN E., and BARBARA D. WARNER. "Functions of Crime: A Paradoxical Process." *American Journal of Sociology.* Vol. 96, No. 6 (May 1991):1441–63.

LITTLE, CRAIG, and ANDREA RANKIN. "Why Do They Start It? Explaining Reported Early-Teen Sexual Activity." *Sociological Forum.* Vol. 16, No. 4 (December 2001):703–29.

LIU, MELINDA, and DUNCAN HEWITT. "The Rise of the Sea Turtles." *Newsweek* (August 18, 2008):29–31.

LOBO, SUSAN. "Census-Taking and the Invisibility of Urban American Indians." *Population Today.* Vol. 30, No. 4 (May/June 2002):3–4.

LOGAN, JOHN R., RICHARD D. ALBA, and WENQUAN ZHANG. "Immigrant Enclaves and Ethnic Communities in New York and Los Angeles." *American Sociological Review.* Vol. 67, No. 2 (April 2002):299–322.

LOGAN, JOHN R., DEIDRE OAKLEY, and JACOB STOWELL. "School Segregation in Metropolitan Regions, 1970–2000: The Impacts of Policy Change on Public Education." *American Journal of Sociology.* Vol. 113, No. 6 (May 2008):1611–44.

LONG, JASON, and JOSEPH FERRIE. "The Path to Convergence: Intergenerational Occupational Mobility in Britain and the U.S. in Three Eras." *Economic Journal.* Vol. 117, No. 3 (March 2007):C61–C71. http://search.ebscohost.com/login.aspx?direct=true&db=buh&AN=24719931&loginpage=Login.asp&site=ehost-live

LOOMIS, CAROL. "Getting Women to the Highest Levels." *Fortune: 50 Most Powerful Women in Business.* October 4, 2007. [Online] Available May 12, 2008, at http://money.cnn.com/2007/10/04/magazines/fortune/loomis_boards.fortune/index.htm

LORD, MARY. "Good Teachers the Newest Imports." *U.S. News & World Report* (April 9, 2001):54.

LORD, WALTER. *A Night to Remember.* Rev. ed. New York: Holt, Rinehart and Winston, 1976.

LOVEMAN, MARA. "Is 'Race' Essential?" *American Sociological Review.* Vol. 64, No. 6 (December 1999):890–98.

LOWREY, YING. "Women in Business, 2006: A Demographic Review of Women's Business Ownership." Office of Economic Research, Office of Advocacy, U.S. Small Business Administration. 2006. http://www.sba.gov/advo/research/rs280tot.pdf

LUND, DALE A. "Caregiving." *Encyclopedia of Adult Development.* Phoenix, Ariz.: Oryx Press, 1993:57–63.

LYND, ROBERT S., and HELEN MERRELL LYND. *Middletown in Transition.* New York: Harcourt, Brace & World, 1937.

MABRY, MARCUS, and TOM MASLAND. "The Man after Mandela." *Newsweek* (June 7, 1999):54–55.

MACE, DAVID, and VERA MACE. *Marriage East and West.* Garden City, N.Y.: Doubleday/Dolphin, 1960.

MACIONIS, JOHN J. "Intimacy: Structure and Process in Interpersonal Relationships." *Alternative Lifestyles.* Vol. 1, No. 1 (February 1978):113–30.

———. "A Sociological Analysis of Humor." Presentation to the Texas Junior College Teachers Association, Houston, 1987.

———. *Social Problems.* 4th ed. Upper Saddle River, N.J.: Prentice Hall, 2010.

MACIONIS, JOHN J., and LINDA GERBER. *Sociology* (6th Canadian ed.). Scarborough, Ontario: Prentice Hall Allyn & Bacon Canada, 2008.

MACIONIS, JOHN J., and VINCENT R. PARRILLO. *Cities and Urban Life.* 4th ed. Upper Saddle River, N.J.: Prentice Hall, 2007.

———. *Cities and Urban Life.* 5th ed. Upper Saddle River, N.J.: Prentice Hall, 2010.

MACKAY, JUDITH. *The Penguin Atlas of Human Sexual Behavior.* New York: Penguin, 2000.

MADDOX, SETMA. "Organizational Culture and Leadership Style: Factors Affecting Self-Managed Work Team Performance." Paper presented at the annual meeting of the Southwest Social Science Association, Dallas, February 1994.

MALTHUS, THOMAS ROBERT. *First Essay on Population 1798.* London: Macmillan, 1926; orig. 1798.

MANZA, JEFF, and CLEM BROOKS. "The Religious Factor in U.S. Presidential Elections, 1960–1992." *American Journal of Sociology.* Vol. 103, No. 1 (July 1997):38–81.

Marathonguide.com (2010). http://www.marathonguide.com/index.cfm?SRED=18

MARCUSE, HERBERT. *One-Dimensional Man.* Boston: Beacon Press, 1964.

MARÍN, GERARDO, and BARBARA VAN OSS MARÍN. *Research with Hispanic Populations.* Newbury Park, Calif.: Sage, 1991.

MARKLEIN, MARY BETH. "Optimism Rises as SAT Math Scores Hit 30-Year High." *USA Today* (August 30, 2000):1A.

MARKOFF, JOHN. "Remember Big Brother? Now He's a Company Man." *New York Times* (March 31, 1991):7.

MARQUAND, ROBERT. "Worship Shift: Americans Seek Feeling of 'Awe.'" *Christian Science Monitor* (May 28, 1997):1, 8.

MARQUAND, ROBERT, and DANIEL B. WOOD. "Rise in Cults as Millennium Approaches." *Christian Science Monitor* (March 28, 1997):1, 18.

MARQUARDT, ELIZABETH, and NORVAL GLENN. *Hooking Up, Hanging Out, and Hoping for Mr. Right.* New York: Institute for American Values, 2001.

MARQUEZ, LAURA. "Nursing Shortage: How It May Affect You." *ABC News.* January 21, 2006. http://abcnews.go.com/WNT/Health/story?id=1529546

MARSHALL, SUSAN E. "Ladies against Women: Mobilization Dilemmas of Antifeminist Movements." *Social Problems.* Vol. 32, No. 4 (April 1985):348–62.

MARTIN, CAROL LYNN, and RICHARD A. FABES. "The Stability and Consequences of Young Children's Same-Sex Peer Interactions." *Developmental Psychology.* Vol. 37, No. 3 (May 2001):431–46.

MARTIN, JOYCE A., ET AL. "Births: Final Data for 2006." *National Vital Statistics Reports.* Vol. 57, No. 7 (January 7, 2009). http://www.cdc.gov/nchs/data/nvsr/nvsr57/nvsr57_07.pdf

MARTINEZ, RAMIRO, JR. "Latinos and Lethal Violence: The Impact of Poverty and Inequality." *Social Problems.* Vol. 43, No. 2 (May 1996):131–46.

MARULLO, SAM. "The Functions and Dysfunctions of Preparations for Fighting Nuclear War." *Sociological Focus.* Vol. 20, No. 2 (April 1987):135–53.

MARX, KARL. *Karl Marx: Early Writings.* T. B. BOTTOMORE, ed. New York: McGraw-Hill, 1964; orig. 1848.

———. *Capital.* FRIEDRICH ENGELS, ed. New York: International Publishers, 1967; orig. 1867.

MARX, KARL, and FRIEDRICH ENGELS. "Manifesto of the Communist Party." In ROBERT C. TUCKER, ed., *The Marx-Engels Reader.* New York: Norton, 1972:331–62; orig. 1848.

MASON, DAVID S. "Fairness Matters: Equity and the Transition to Democracy." *World Policy Journal.* Vol. 20, No. 4 (Winter 2003–04). 2004. http://www.worldpolicy.org/journal/articles/wpj03-4/mason.htm

MASSEY, DOUGLAS S., and NANCY A. DENTON. "Hypersegregation in U.S. Metropolitan Areas: Black and Hispanic Segregation along Five Dimensions." *Demography.* Vol. 26, No. 3 (August 1989):373–91.

MATHER, MARK, and KELVIN POLLARD. "U.S. Population Projected to Hit 400 Million in 2039." Population Reference Bureau. August 2008. http://www.prb.org/Articles/2008/us400million.aspx

MATTHIESSEN, PETER. *Indian Country.* New York: Viking Press, 1984.

MAUER, MARC. *The Crisis of the Young African American Male and the Criminal Justice System.* Report prepared for U.S. Commission on Civil Rights, Washington, D.C., April 15–16, 1999. http://www.sentencingproject.org/Admin/Documents/publications/rd_crisis oftheyoung.pdf

MAYO, KATHERINE. *Mother India.* New York: Harcourt, Brace, 1927.

MCADAM, DOUG, JOHN D. MCCARTHY, and MAYER N. ZALD. "Introduction: Opportunities, Mobilizing Structures, and Framing Processes—Toward a Synthetic, Comparative Perspective on Social Movements." In DOUG MCADAM, JOHN D. MCCARTHY, and MAYER N. ZALD, eds., *Comparative Perspectives on Social Movements: Political Opportunities, Mobilizing Structures, and Cultural Framings.* New York: Cambridge University Press, 1996:1–19.

MCDONALD'S CORPORATION. "2008 Annual Report." April 2009. http://www.aboutmcdonalds.com/mcd/investors/publications.html

MCGEEHAN, PATRICK, and MATHEW R. WARREN. "Adding to Recession's Pain, Thousands to Lose Job Benefits." *New York Times* (January 11, 2009). http://www.nytimes.com/2009/01/12/nyregion/12benefits.html

MCGIRK, TIM. "Crossing the Lines." *Time* (February 27, 2006):36–43.

MCKEE, VICTORIA. "Blue Blood and the Color of Money." *New York Times* (June 9, 1996):49–50.

MCKIBBEN, BILL. *Deep Economy: The Wealth of Communities and the Durable Future.* New York: Times Books, 2007.

MCLANAHAN, SARA. "Life without Father: What Happens to the Children?" *Contexts.* Vol. 1, No. 1 (Spring 2002):35–44.

MCLEOD, JANE D., and MICHAEL J. SHANAHAN. "Poverty, Parenting, and Children's Mental Health." *American Sociological Review.* Vol. 58, No. 3 (June 1993):351–66.

McLeod, Jay. *Ain't No Makin' It: Aspirations and Attainment in a Low-Income Neighborhood.* Boulder, Colo.: Westview Press, 1995.

McVeigh, Rory, Michael Welch, and Thoroddur Bjarnason. "Hate Crime Reporting as a Successful Social Movement Outcome." *American Sociological Review.* Vol. 68, No. 6 (December 2003):843–67.

Mead, George Herbert. *Mind, Self, and Society.* Charles W. Morris, ed. Chicago: University of Chicago Press, 1962; orig. 1934.

Mead, Margaret. *Sex and Temperament in Three Primitive Societies.* New York: Morrow, 1963; orig. 1935.

Meadows, Donella H., Dennis L. Meadows, Jorgan Randers, and William W. Behrens III. *The Limits to Growth: A Report on the Club of Rome's Project on the Predicament of Mankind.* New York: Universe, 1972.

Meltzer, Bernard N. "Mead's Social Psychology." In Jerome G. Manis and Bernard N. Meltzer, eds., *Symbolic Interaction: A Reader in Social Psychology.* 3rd ed. Needham Heights, Mass.: Allyn & Bacon, 1978.

Melucci, Alberto. *Nomads of the Present: Social Movements and Individual Needs in Contemporary Society.* Philadelphia: Temple University Press, 1989.

Merton, Robert K. "Social Structure and Anomie." *American Sociological Review.* Vol. 3, No. 6 (October 1938):672–82.

———. *Social Theory and Social Structure.* New York: Free Press, 1968.

Metz, Michael E., and Michael H. Miner. "Psychosexual and Psychosocial Aspects of Male Aging and Sexual Health." *Canadian Journal of Human Sexuality.* Vol. 7, No. 3 (Summer 1998):245–60.

Metzger, Kurt. "Cities and Race." *Society.* Vol. 39, No. 1 (December 2001):2.

Michels, Robert. *Political Parties.* Glencoe, Ill.: Free Press, 1949; orig. 1911.

Milanovic, Branko. "Global Inequality Recalculated: The Effect of New 2005 PPP Estimates on Global Inequality." World Bank. August 2008. http://siteresources.worldbank.org/INTDECINEQ/Resources/Global_Inequality_Recalculated.pdf

Milbrath, Lester W. *Envisioning a Sustainable Society: Learning Our Way Out.* Albany: State University of New York Press, 1989.

Milgram, Stanley. "Behavioral Study of Obedience." *Journal of Abnormal and Social Psychology.* Vol. 67, No. 4 (November 1963):371–78.

———. "Group Pressure and Action against a Person." *Journal of Abnormal and Social Psychology.* Vol. 69, No. 2 (August 1964):137–43.

———. "Some Conditions of Obedience and Disobedience to Authority." *Human Relations.* Vol. 18, No. 1 (February 1965):57–76.

———. "The Small World Problem." *Psychology Today* (May 1967):60–67.

Miller, Alan S., and Rodney Stark. "Gender and Religiousness: Can Socialization Explanations Be Saved?" *American Journal of Sociology.* Vol. 107, No. 6 (May 2002):1399–1423.

Miller, Arthur G. *The Obedience Experiments: A Case of Controversy in Social Science.* New York: Praeger, 1986.

Miller, Frederick D. "The End of SDS and the Emergence of Weatherman: Demise through Success." In Jo Freeman, ed., *Social Movements of the Sixties and Seventies.* White Plains, N.Y.: Longman, 1983:279–97.

Miller, Matthew, and Duncan Greenberg. "The Forbes 400." September 30, 2009. http://www.forbes.com/2009/09/30/forbes-400-gates-buffett-wealth-rich-list-09_land.html

Miller, Matthew, and Peter Newcomb, eds. "The Forbes 400." *Forbes* (Special issue, October 10, 2005).

Miller, Terry, Kim Holmes, and Anthony B. Kim. "2010 Index of Economic Freedom." January 20, 2010. http://www.heritage.org/index/Default.aspx

Miller, Walter B. "Lower-Class Culture as a Generating Milieu of Gang Delinquency." In Marvin E. Wolfgang, Leonard Savitz, and Norman Johnston, eds., *The Sociology of Crime and Delinquency.* 2nd ed. New York: Wiley, 1970:351–63; orig. 1958.

Miller, William J., and Rick A. Matthews. "Youth Employment, Differential Association, and Juvenile Delinquency." *Sociological Focus.* Vol. 34, No. 3 (August 2001):251–68.

Mills, C. Wright. *The Power Elite.* New York: Oxford University Press, 1956.

———. *The Sociological Imagination.* New York: Oxford University Press, 1959.

Miracle, Tina S., Andrew W. Miracle, and Roy F. Baumeister. *Human Sexuality: Meeting Your Basic Needs.* Upper Saddle River, N.J.: Prentice Hall, 2003.

Miringoff, Marc, and Marque-Luisa Miringoff. "The Social Health of the Nation." *Economist.* Vol. 352, No. 8128 (July 17, 1999):suppl. 6–7.

Mirowsky, John. "The Psycho-Economics of Feeling Underpaid: Distributive Justice and the Earnings of Husbands and Wives." *American Journal of Sociology.* Vol. 92, No. 6 (May 1987):1404–34.

Mitchell, Chris. "The Killing of Murder." *New York Magazine* (January 8, 2008). http://nymag.com/news/features/crime/2008/42603/

Moghadam, Valentine M. "The 'Feminization of Poverty' and Women's Human Rights." UNESCO Gender Equality and Development Section. July 2005. http://portal.unesco.org/shs/en/files/8282/11313736811Feminization_of_Poverty.pdf/Feminization%2Bof%2BPoverty.pdf

Molotch, Harvey. "The City as a Growth Machine." *American Journal of Sociology.* Vol. 82, No. 2 (September 1976):309–33.

Montaigne, Fen. "Russia Rising." *National Geographic.* Vol. 200, No. 5 (September 2001):2–31.

Moore, Gwen, et al. "Elite Interlocks in Three U.S. Sectors: Nonprofit, Corporate, and Government." *Social Science Quarterly.* Vol. 83, No. 3 (September 2002):726–44.

Moore, Wilbert E. "Modernization as Rationalization: Processes and Restraints." In Manning Nash, ed., *Essays on Economic Development and Cultural Change in Honor of Bert F. Hoselitz.* Chicago: University of Chicago Press, 1977:29–42.

———. *World Modernization: The Limits of Convergence.* New York: Elsevier, 1979.

Morell, Virginia. "Minds of Their Own: Animals Are Smarter than You Think." *National Geographic.* Vol. 213, No. 3 (March 2008):36–61.

Morin, Richard. "Getting a Grad Degree in Cheating." September 27, 2006. Pew Research Center. http://pewresearch.org/pubs/68/getting-a-grad-degree-in-cheating

Morse, Jodie. "A Victory for Vouchers." *Time* (July 8, 2002):32–34.

Mosher, William D., Anjani Chandra, and Jo Jones. *Sexual Behavior and Selected Health Measures: Men and Women 15–44 Years of Age, United States, 2002.* 2005. http://www.cdc.gov/nchs/products/pubs/pubd/ad/361-370/ad362.htm

Mouw, Ted. "Job Relocation and the Racial Gap in Unemployment in Detroit and Chicago, 1980 to 1990." *American Sociological Review.* Vol. 65, No. 5 (October 2000):730–53.

MSNBC. "Cop-Killer Suspect Shot Dead by Officer." December 1, 2009. http://www.msnbc.msn.com/id/34194122/

"Much Ado about Evolution." *Time* (November 21, 2005):23.

Muller, Chandra, and Christopher G. Ellison. "Religious Involvement, Social Capital, and Adolescents' Academic Progress: Evidence from the National Education Longitudinal Study of 1988." *Sociological Focus.* Vol. 34, No. 2 (May 2001):155–83.

Mumford, Lewis. *The City in History: Its Origins, Its Transformations, and Its Prospects.* New York: Harcourt, Brace & World, 1961.

Munroe, Susan. "Abolition of Capital Punishment in Canada." About.com: Canada Online. July 2007. http://canadaonline.about.com/od/crime/a/abolitioncappun.htm

Murdock, George Peter. "Comparative Data on the Division of Labor by Sex." *Social Forces.* Vol. 15, No. 4 (May 1937):551–53.

———. "The Common Denominator of Cultures." In Ralph Linton, ed., *The Science of Man in World Crisis.* New York: Columbia University Press, 1945:123–42.

———. *Social Structure.* New York: Free Press, 1965; orig. 1949.

Myers, David G. *The American Paradox: Spiritual Hunger in an Age of Plenty.* New Haven, Conn.: Yale University Press, 2000.

Myers, Norman. "Humanity's Growth." In Edmund Hillary, ed., *Ecology 2000: The Changing Face of the Earth.* New York: Beaufort Books, 1984a:16–35.

———. "The Mega-Extinction of Animals and Plants." In Sir Edmund Hillary, ed., *Ecology 2000: The Changing Face of the Earth.* New York: Beaufort Books, 1984b:82–107.

———. "Biological Diversity and Global Security." In F. Herbert Bormann and Stephen R. Kellert, eds., *Ecology, Economics, and Ethics: The Broken Circle.* New Haven, Conn.: Yale University Press, 1991:11–25.

Myers, Sheila, and Harold G. Grasmick. "The Social Rights and Responsibilities of Pregnant Women: An Application of Parsons' Sick Role Model." Paper presented to the Southwestern Sociological Association, Little Rock, Ark., March 1989.

Myrdal, Gunnar. *An American Dilemma: The Negro Problem and Modern Democracy.* New York: Harper Bros., 1944.

National Center for Counterterrorism. "2008 Report on Terrorism." April 30, 2009. http://wits.nctc.gov/Reports.do

National Center for Education Statistics. *Adult Education Participation in 2004–05.* May 2006a. http://nces.ed.gov/pubs2006/adulted

———. *Digest of Education Statistics.* "2005 Tables." 2006b. http://nces.ed.gov/programs/digest

———. *Dropout Rates in the United States, 2005.* Washington, D.C.: U.S. Government Printing Office. 2007.

———. *Digest of Education Statistics.* "2007 Tables." March 2008. http://nces.ed.gov/programs/digest/d07/tables_1.asp

———. "Trends in International Mathematics and Science Study (TIMSS)." March 3, 2009. http://nces.ed.gov/timss/index.asp

———. *Digest of Education Statistics, 2009.* "2009 Tables." March 2010. http://nces.ed.gov/programs/digest/d09/tables_1.asp

National Center for Health Statistics. "Health Data Interactive." 2009. http://www.cdc.gov/nchs/hdi.htm

———. "Health, United States, 2009." 2010. http://www.cdc.gov/nchs/hus.htm

National Coalition of Anti-Violence Programs. "Anti-Lesbian, Gay, Bisexual and Transgender Violence in 2007." 2008. http://www.ncavp.org/

National Conference of State Legislatures. "Marriages." 2009. http://www.ncsl.org/programs/cyf/cousins.htm

———. "State Traffic Safety Legislation." 2010. http://www.ncsl.org/programs/transportation/trafsafdb.cfm

National Highway Traffic Safety Administration. "2007 Traffic Safety Annual Assessment: Alcohol-Impaired Driving Fatalities." August 2008. http://www-nrd.nhtsa.dot.gov/Pubs/811016.PDF

———. "2008 Traffic Safety Annual Assessment: Highlights." June 2009. http://www-nrd.nhtsa.dot.gov/Pubs/811172.PDF

National Oceanic and Atmospheric Association. "State of the Climate Global Analysis: Annual 2009." February 12, 2010. http://www.ncdc.noaa.gov/sotc/?report=global&year=2009&month=13gtemp

Navarro, Mireya. "Puerto Rican Presence Wanes in New York." *New York Times* (February 28, 2000):A1, A20.

———. "For Younger Latinas, a Shift to Smaller Families." *New York Times* (December 5, 2004). http://www.nytimes.com/2004/12/05/national/05latina.html

Nelson, Amy L. "The Effect of Economic Restructuring on Family Poverty in the Industrial Heartland, 1970–1990." *Sociological Focus.* Vol. 31, No. 2 (May 1998):201–16.

Neuhouser, Kevin. "The Radicalization of the Brazilian Catholic Church in Comparative Perspective." *American Sociological Review.* Vol. 54, No. 2 (April 1989):233–44.

Newman, Katherine S. *Declining Fortunes: The Withering of the American Dream.* New York: Basic Books, 1993.

Newman, William M. *American Pluralism: A Study of Minority Groups and Social Theory.* New York: Harper & Row, 1973.

Newport, Frank. "Americans Turn More Negative toward Same-Sex Marriage." Gallup News Service. April 2005. http://www.gallup.com/poll/15889/Americans-Turn-More-Negative-Toward-SameSex-Marriage.aspx

NEW YORK COMMUNITY MEDIA ALLIANCE. *Many Voices, One City: The NYCMA Guide to the Ethnic Press of New York.*. 4th ed. New York: New York Community Media Alliance, 2008. http://www.indypressny.org/

NIELSEN MEDIA RESEARCH. (Nielsen Media Research, 2008). http://en-us.nielsen.com

———. "Nielsen Three Screen Report." 2009. http://en-us.nielsen.com/main/insights/nielsen_a2m2_three

NIESSE, MARK. "Some Bars Pan Hawaii's Tough Smoking Ban." *Yahoo! News* (February 19, 2007). http://news.yahoo.com

NISBET, ROBERT A. *The Quest for Community.* New York: Oxford University Press, 1969.

NOCK, STEVEN L., JAMES D. WRIGHT, and LAURA SANCHEZ. "America's Divorce Problem." *Society.* Vol. 36, No. 4 (May/June 1999):43–52.

NOLAN, PATRICK, and GERHARD E. LENSKI. *Human Societies: An Introduction to Macrosociology.* 10th ed. Boulder, Colo.: Paradigm, 2007.

NORC. *General Social Surveys, 1972–2006: Cumulative Codebook.* Chicago: National Opinion Research Center, 2007.

———. *General Social Surveys, 1972–2008: Cumulative Codebook.* Chicago: National Opinion Research Center, 2009. http://www.norc.org/GSS+Website/

NORWOOD, CHRIS. "Yes, America Has AIDS Orphans—Lots." *Huffington Post.* April 21, 2010. http://www.huffingtonpost.com/chris-norwood/yes-america-has-aids-orph_b_184239.html?view=print

NOVAK, VIVECA. "The Cost of Poor Advice." *Time* (July 5, 1999):38.

NULAND, SHERWIN B. "The Hazards of Hospitalization." *Wall Street Journal* (December 2, 1999):A22.

OAKES, JEANNIE. "Classroom Social Relationships: Exploring the Bowles and Gintis Hypothesis." *Sociology of Education.* Vol. 55, No. 4 (October 1982):197–212.

———. *Keeping Track: How High Schools Structure Inequality.* New Haven, Conn.: Yale University Press, 1985.

OBAMA, BARACK. *The Audacity of Hope: Thoughts on Reclaiming the American Dream.* New York: Random House, 2007.

OECD (ORGANISATION FOR ECONOMIC CO-OPERATION AND DEVELOPMENT). *Society at a Glance: OECD Social Indicators.* Paris: OECD, 2007.

———. "Education at a Glance, 2009: OECD Indicators." 2009. http://www.oecd.org/edu/eag2009

———. "OECD Factbook, 2009: Economic, Environmental, and Social Statistics." 2009. http://oberon.sourceoecd.org/vl=473271/cl=32/nw=1/rpsv/factbook2009/index.htm

———. "Tax Burdens Falling in OECD Economies as Crisis Takes Its Toll." November 24, 2009. http://www.oecd.org/document/47/0,3343,en_2649_34487_44115887_1_1_1_1,00.html

———. "Stat Extracts." 2010. http://stats.oecd.org/WBOS/index.aspx

OGBURN, WILLIAM F. *On Culture and Social Change.* Chicago: University of Chicago Press, 1964.

O'HARROW, ROBERT, JR. "ID Theft Scam Hits D.C. Area Residents." *Yahoo! News* (February 21, 2005). http://news.yahoo.com

OHLEMACHER, STEPHEN. "Obama's Victory May Show the Way to Win in Future." *USA Today* (November 9, 2008). http://www.usatoday.com/news/politics/2008-11-08-1164297038_x.htm

OLSEN, GREGG M. "Remodeling Sweden: The Rise and Demise of the Compromise in a Global Economy." *Social Problems.* Vol. 43, No. 1 (February 1996):1–20.

OLYSLAGER, FEMKE, and LYNN CONWAY. "On the Calculation of the Prevalence of Transsexualism." 2007. http://ai.eecs.umich.edu/people/conway/TS/Prevalence/Reports/Prevalence%20of%20Transsexualism.pdf

OLZAK, SUSAN. "Labor Unrest, Immigration, and Ethnic Conflict in Urban America, 1880–1914." *American Journal of Sociology.* Vol. 94, No. 6 (May 1989):1303–33.

"Online Privacy: It's Time for Rules in Wonderland." *Business Week* (March 20, 2000):82–96.

ORLANSKY, MICHAEL D., and WILLIAM L. HEWARD. *Voices: Interviews with Handicapped People.* Columbus, Ohio: Merrill, 1981.

ORHANT, MELANIE. "Human Trafficking Exposed." *Population Today.* Vol. 30, No. 1 (January 2002):1, 4.

OSTRANDER, SUSAN A. "Upper-Class Women: The Feminine Side of Privilege." *Qualitative Sociology.* Vol. 3, No. 1 (Spring 1980):23–44.

———. *Women of the Upper Class.* Philadelphia: Temple University Press, 1984.

OUCHI, WILLIAM. *Theory Z: How American Business Can Meet the Japanese Challenge.* Reading, Mass.: Addison-Wesley, 1981.

"Our Cheating Hearts." Editorial. *U.S. News & World Report* (May 6, 2002):4.

OVADIA, SETH. "Race, Class, and Gender Differences in High School Seniors' Values: Applying Intersection Theory in Empirical Analysis." *Social Science Quarterly.* Vol. 82, No. 2 (June 2001):341–56.

OWEN, CAROLYN A., HOWARD C. ELSNER, and THOMAS R. MCFAUL. "A Half-Century of Social Distance Research: National Replication of the Bogardus Studies." *Sociology and Social Research.* Vol. 66, No. 1 (1977):80–98.

PACKARD, MARK. Personal communication (2002).

PACKER, GEORGE. "Smart-Mobbing the War." *New York Times Magazine* (March 9, 2003):46–49.

PAKULSKI, JAN. "Mass Social Movements and Social Class." *International Sociology.* Vol. 8, No. 2 (June 1993):131–58.

PAMPEL, FRED C. "Socioeconomic Distinction, Cultural Tastes, and Cigarette Smoking." *Social Science Quarterly.* Vol. 87, No. 1 (March 2006):19–35.

PARIS, PETER J. "The Religious World of African Americans." In JACOB NEUSNER, ed. *World Religions in America: An Introduction.* Rev. and expanded ed. Louisville, Ky.: Westminster/John Knox Press, 2000:48–65.

PARK, ROBERT E. *Race and Culture.* Glencoe, Ill.: Free Press, 1950.

PARKER-POPE, TARA. "Love, Sex, and the Changing Landscape of Infidelity." *New York Times.* (October 27, 2008). http://www.nytimes.com/2008/10/28/health/28.well.html?_r=1

PARRILLO, VINCENT N. "Diversity in America: A Sociohistorical Analysis." *Sociological Forum.* Vol. 9, No. 4 (December 1994):42–45.

PARRILLO, VINCENT, and CHRISTOPHER DONOGHUE. "Updating the Bogardus Social Distance Studies: A New National Survey." *Social Science Journal.* Vol. 42, No. 2 (April 2005):257–71.

PARSONS, TALCOTT. "Age and Sex in the Social Structure of the United States." *American Sociological Review.* Vol. 7, No. 4 (August 1942):604–16.

———. *The Social System.* New York: Free Press, 1951.

———. *Essays in Sociological Theory.* New York: Free Press, 1954.

———. *Societies: Evolutionary and Comparative Perspectives.* Englewood Cliffs, N.J.: Prentice Hall, 1966.

PASSY, FLORENCE, and MARCO GIUGNI. "Social Networks and Individual Perceptions: Explaining Differential Participation in Social Movements." *Sociological Forum.* Vol. 16, No. 1 (March 2001):123–53.

PATTERSON, ELISSA F. "The Philosophy and Physics of Holistic Health Care: Spiritual Healing as a Workable Interpretation." *Journal of Advanced Nursing.* Vol. 27, No. 2 (February 1998):287–93.

PATTILLO-MCCOY, MARY. "Church Culture as a Strategy of Action in the Black Community." *American Sociological Review.* Vol. 63, No. 6 (December 1998):767–84.

PAUL, PAMELA. "News, Noticias, Nouvelles." *American Demographics.* Vol. 23, No. 11 (November 2001):26–31.

PAXTON, PAMELA, MELANIE M. HUGHES, and JENNIFER L. GREEN. "The International Women's Movement and Women's Political Participation, 1893–2003." *American Sociological Review.* Vol. 71, No. 6 (December 2006):898–920.

PEAR, ROBERT, and ERIK ECKHOLM. "When Healers Are Entrepreneurs: A Debate over Costs and Ethics." *New York Times* (June 2, 1991):1, 17.

PEARSON, DAVID E. "Post-Mass Culture." *Society.* Vol. 30, No. 5 (July/August 1993):17–22.

———. "Community and Sociology." *Society.* Vol. 32, No. 5 (July/August 1995):44–50.

PEASE, JOHN, and LEE MARTIN. "Want Ads and Jobs for the Poor: A Glaring Mismatch." *Sociological Forum.* Vol. 12, No. 4 (December 1997):545–64.

PEDERSON, DANIEL, VERN E. SMITH, and JERRY ADLER. "Sprawling, Sprawling . . ." *Newsweek* (July 19, 1999):23–27.

PERLMUTTER, PHILIP. "Minority Group Prejudice." *Society.* Vol. 39, No. 3 (March/April 2002):59–65.

PERRUCCI, ROBERT. "Inventing Social Justice: SSSP and the Twenty-First Century." *Social Problems.* Vol. 48, No. 2 (May 2001):159–67.

PERRY, ALEX. "South Africa Looks for a Leader." *Time.* (April 27, 2009):38–41.

PETERS, ARNO. *Peters Atlas of the World.* New York: Harper & Row, 1990.

PETERSEN, TROND, ISHAK SAPORTA, and MARC-DAVID L. SEIDEL. "Offering a Job: Meritocracy and Social Networks." *American Journal of Sociology.* Vol. 106, No. 3 (November 2000):763–816.

PETERSILIA, JOAN. "Probation in the United States: Practices and Challenges." *National Institute of Justice Journal.* No. 233 (September 1997):4.

PETERSON, PAUL E., and ELENA LLAUDET. "On the Public-Private School Achievement Debate." Paper prepared for the annual meetings of the American Political Science Association, Philadelphia, August 2006. http://www.hks.harvard.edu/pepg/PDF/Papers/PEPG06-02-PetersonLlaudet.pdf

PEW CENTER ON THE STATES. "One in 100: Behind Bars in America 2008." 2008. http://www.pewcenteronthestates.org/uploadedFiles/One%20in%20100.pdf

PEW FORUM ON RELIGION & PUBLIC LIFE. "A Slight but Steady Majority Favors Keeping Abortion Legal—but Most Also Favor Restrictions." September 16, 2008a. http://pewforum.org/docs/?DocID=350

———. "U.S. Religious Landscape Survey." February 2008b. http://religions.pewforum.org/reports

———. "A Religious Portrait of African-Americans." January 30, 2009a. http://pewforum.org/docs/?DocID=389#a

———. "Same-Sex Marriage: Redefining Marriage around the World." January 22, 2009b. http://pewforum.org/docs/?DocID=235

———. "Scientists and Belief." Nov. 5, 2009c. http://pewforum.org/docs/?DocID=474

PEW RESEARCH CENTER. "As Marriage and Parenthood Drift Apart, Public Is Concerned about Social Impact." July 1, 2007a. http://pewsocialtrends.org/pubs/526/marriage-parenthood

———. "Muslim Americans: Middle Class and Mostly Mainstream." May 22, 2007b. http://pewresearch.org/assets/pdf/muslim-americans.pdf

———. "Social and Demographic Trends: Reports." 2008. http://pewsocialtrends.org/pubs

PHILADELPHIA, DESA. "Tastier, Plusher—and Fast." *Time* (September 30, 2002):57.

PHILLIPS, MELANIE. "What about the Overclass?" *Public Interest.* No. 145 (Fall 2001):38–43.

PINCHOT, GIFFORD, and ELIZABETH PINCHOT. *The End of Bureaucracy and the Rise of the Intelligent Organization.* San Francisco: Berrett-Koehler, 1993.

PINHEY, THOMAS K., DONALD H. RUBINSTEIN, and RICHARD S. COLFAX. "Overweight and Happiness: The Reflected Self-Appraisal Hypothesis Reconsidered." *Social Science Quarterly.* Vol. 78, No. 3 (September 1997):747–55.

PINKER, STEVEN. *The Language Instinct.* New York: Morrow, 1994.

———. "Are Your Genes to Blame?" *Time* (January 20, 2003):98–100.

PIVEN, FRANCES FOX, and RICHARD A. CLOWARD. *Poor People's Movements: Why They Succeed, How They Fail.* New York: Pantheon Books, 1977.

"Places Where the System Broke Down." *Time* (September 19, 2005):34–41.

PLEIS, JOHN, and JACQUELINE W. LUCAS. "Summary Health Statistics for U.S. Adults: National Health Interview Survey, 2007." Series 10. Data From the National Health Survey. (2009). No. 240.

PLEIS, J. R., J. W. LUCAS, and B. W. WARD. "Summary Health Statistics for U.S. Adults: National Health Interview Survey, 2008." Series 10. Data From the National Health Survey. (2009). No. 242.

PODOLNY, JOEL M., and JAMES N. BARON. "Resources and Relationships: Social Networks and Mobility in the Workplace." *American Sociological Review*. Vol. 62, No. 5 (October 1997):673–93.

POLSBY, NELSON W. "Three Problems in the Analysis of Community Power." *American Sociological Review*. Vol. 24, No. 6 (December 1959):796–803.

POMER, MARSHALL I. "Labor Market Structure, Intragenerational Mobility, and Discrimination: Black Male Advancement out of Low-Paying Occupations, 1962–1973." *American Sociological Review*. Vol. 51, No. 5 (October 1986):650–59.

POPENOE, DAVID. "American Family Decline, 1960–1990: A Review and Appraisal." *Journal of Marriage and the Family*. Vol. 55, No. 3 (August 1993a):527–55.

———. "Parental Androgyny." *Society*. Vol. 30, No. 6 (September/October 1993b):5–11.

———. "Can the Nuclear Family Be Revived?" *Society*. Vol. 36, No. 5 (July/August 1999):28–30.

POPENOE, DAVID, and BARBARA DAFOE WHITEHEAD. *Should We Live Together? What Young Adults Need to Know about Cohabitation before Marriage*. New Brunswick, N.J.: National Marriage Project, 1999.

POPULATION ACTION INTERNATIONAL. *People in the Balance: Population and Resources at the Turn of the Millennium*. Washington, D.C.: Population Action International, 2000.

POPULATION REFERENCE BUREAU. "2009 World Population Data Sheet." August 2009. http://www.prb.org/pdf09/09WPDS_Eng.pdf

———. "Datafinder." 2010. http://www.prb.org/DataFinder.aspx

PORTES, ALEJANDRO, and LEIF JENSEN. "The Enclave and the Entrants: Patterns of Ethnic Enterprise in Miami before and after Mariel." *American Sociological Review*. Vol. 54, No. 6 (December 1989):929–49.

POSTEL, SANDRA. "Facing Water Scarcity." In LESTER R. BROWN ET AL., eds., *State of the World, 1993: A Worldwatch Institute Report on Progress toward a Sustainable Society*. New York: Norton, 1993:22–41.

POTTER, DENA. "Fear of Dem Crackdown Leads to Boom in Gun Sales." (November 8, 2008). http://www.dailyamerican.com/articles/2009/04/20/business/business091.txt

POWELL, BILL. "Postcard: Dongguan." *Time* (December 15, 2008):4.

PRIMEGGIA, SALVATORE, and JOSEPH A. VARACALLI. "Southern Italian Comedy: Old to New World." In JOSEPH V. SCELSA, SALVATORE J. LA GUMINA, and LYDIO TOMASI, eds., *Italian Americans in Transition*. New York: American Italian Historical Association, 1990:241–52.

PRYOR, JOHN H., ET AL. *The American Freshman: National Norms for Fall 2007*. Los Angeles: UCLA Higher Education Research Institute, 2007.

———. *The American Freshman: National Norms for Fall 2009*. Los Angeles: UCLA Higher Education Research Institute, 2010.

PUTKA, GARY. "SAT to Become a Better Gauge." *Wall Street Journal* (November 1, 1990):B1.

PYLE, RALPH E. "Trends in Religious Stratification: Have Religious Group Socioeconomic Distinctions Declined in Recent Decades?" *Sociology of Religion*. Vol. 67, No. 1 (Spring 2006):61–79.

PYLE, RALPH E., and JEROME R. KOCH. "The Religious Affiliation of American Elites, 1930s to 1990s: A Note on the Pace of Disestablishment." *Sociological Focus*. Vol. 34, No. 2 (May 2001):125–37.

QUAID, LIBBY. "Study: Math Teachers One Chapter ahead of Students." *Yahoo! News* (November 25, 2008). http://news.yahoo.com

QUILLIAN, LINCOLN, and DEVAH PAGER. "Black Neighbors, Higher Crime? The Role of Racial Stereotypes in Evaluations of Neighborhood Crime." *American Journal of Sociology*. Vol. 107, No. 3 (November 2001):717–67.

QUINNEY, RICHARD. *Class, State and Crime: On the Theory and Practice of Criminal Justice*. New York: McKay, 1977.

RALEY, R. KELLY, T. ELIZABETH DURDEN, and ELIZABETH WILDSMITH. "Understanding Mexican-American Marriage Patterns using a Life Course Approach." *Social Science Quarterly*. Vol. 85, No. 4 (December 2004):872–90.

RAND, MICHAEL R. "Criminal Victimization, 2008." National Crime Victimization Survey. (September 2009). http://bjs.ojp.usdoj.gov/content/pub/pdf/cv08.pdf

RANK, MARK R., and THOMAS A. HIRSCHL. "Rags or Riches? Estimating the Probabilities of Poverty and Affluence across the Adult American Life Span." *Social Science Quarterly*. Vol. 82, No. 4 (December 2001):651–69.

RAPHAEL, RAY. *The Men from the Boys: Rites of Passage in Male America*. Lincoln: University of Nebraska Press, 1988.

RECKLESS, WALTER C., and SIMON DINITZ. "Pioneering with Self-Concept as a Vulnerability Factor in Delinquency." *Journal of Criminal Law, Criminology, and Police Science*. Vol. 58, No. 4 (December 1967):515–23.

RESKIN, BARBARA F., and DEBRA BRANCH MCBRIER. "Why Not Ascription? Organizations' Employment of Male and Female Managers." *American Sociological Review*. Vol. 65, No. 2 (April 2000):210–33.

RICHBURG, KEITH B. "School Privatization Plan Sputters." *Boston Globe* (June 29, 2008). http://www.boston.com/news/nation/articles/2008/06/29/school_privatization_plan_sputters

RIDEOUT, VICTORIA. "Parents, Children, and Media: A Kaiser Family Foundation Survey." June 2007. http://www.kff.org/entmedia/upload/7638.pdf

RIDGEWAY, CECILIA L. *The Dynamics of Small Groups*. New York: St. Martin's Press, 1983.

RIDGEWAY, CECILIA L., and LYNN SMITH-LOVIN. "The Gender System and Interaction." *Annual Review of Sociology*. Vol. 25 (August 1999):191–216.

RIESMAN, DAVID. *The Lonely Crowd: A Study of the Changing American Character*. New Haven, Conn.: Yale University Press, 1970; orig. 1950.

RIPLEY, AMANDA. "Can She Save Our Schools?" *Time* (December 8, 2008):36–44.

RITZER, GEORGE. *The McDonaldization of Society: An Investigation into the Changing Character of Contemporary Social Life*. Thousand Oaks, Calif.: Pine Forge Press, 1993.

———. *The McDonaldization Thesis: Explorations and Extensions*. Thousand Oaks, Calif.: Sage, 1998.

———. "The Globalization of McDonaldization." *Spark* (February 2000):8–9.

RITZER, GEORGE, and DAVID WALCZAK. *Working: Conflict and Change*. 4th ed. Englewood Cliffs, N.J.: Prentice Hall, 1990.

ROBERTS, DONALD F., ULLA G. FOEHR, and VICTORIA RIDEOUT. *Generation M: Media in the Lives of 8–18-Year-Olds*. Kaiser Family Foundation, March 2005. http://www.kff.org/entmedia/7251.cfm

ROBERTS, J. DEOTIS. *Roots of a Black Future: Family and Church*. Philadelphia: Westminster Press, 1980.

ROBINSON, THOMAS N., ET AL. "Effects of Reducing Children's Television and Video Game Use on Aggressive Behavior." *Archives of Pediatrics and Adolescent Medicine*. Vol. 155, No. 1 (January 2001):17–23.

ROESCH, ROBERTA. "Violent Families." *Parents*. Vol. 59, No. 9 (September 1984):74–76, 150–52.

ROGERS, RICHARD G., REBECCA ROSENBLATT, ROBERT A. HUMMER, and PATRICK M. KRUEGER. "Black-White Differentials in Adult Homicide Mortality in the United States." *Social Science Quarterly*. Vol. 82, No. 3 (September 2001):435–52.

ROMERO, FRANCINE SANDERS, and ADRIAN LISERIO. "Saving Open Spaces: Determinants of 1998 and 1999 'Antisprawl' Ballot Measures." *Social Science Quarterly*. Vol. 83, No. 1 (March 2002):341–52.

ROOF, WADE CLARK, and WILLIAM MCKINNEY. *American Mainline Religion: Its Changing Shape and Future*. New Brunswick, N.J.: Rutgers University Press, 1987.

ROSEN, JEFFREY. *The Unwanted Gaze*. New York: Random House, 2000.

ROSENBERG, MICA. "Mexican Transvestite Fiesta Rocks Indigenous Town." Reuters (November 23, 2008). http://www.reuters.com/article/lifestyleMolt/idUSTRE4AM1PB20081123

ROSENDAHL, MONA. *Inside the Revolution: Everyday Life in Socialist Cuba*. Ithaca, N.Y.: Cornell University Press, 1997.

ROSENFELD, RICHARD. "Crime Decline in Context." *Contexts*. Vol. 1, No. 1 (Spring 2002):20–34.

ROSENFELD, MICHAEL J., and BYONG-SOO KIM. "The Independence of Young Adults and the Rise of Interracial and Same-Sex Unions." *American Sociological Review*. Vol. 70, No. 4 (August 2005):541–62.

ROSENTHAL, ELIZABETH. "Canada's National Health Plan Gives Care to All, with Limits." *New York Times* (April 30, 1991):A1, A16.

ROSSI, ALICE S. "Gender and Parenthood." In ALICE S. ROSSI, ed., *Gender and the Life Course*. New York: Aldine, 1985:161–91.

ROSTOW, WALT W. *The Stages of Economic Growth: A Non-Communist Manifesto*. Cambridge: Cambridge University Press, 1960.

———. *The World Economy: History and Prospect*. Austin: University of Texas Press, 1978.

ROTHENBERG, PAULA. *White Privilege*. 3rd ed. New York: Worth, 2008.

ROTHMAN, STANLEY, and AMY E. BLACK. "Who Rules Now? American Elites in the 1990s." *Society*. Vol. 35, No. 6 (September/October 1998):17–20.

ROTHMAN, STANLEY, STEPHEN POWERS, and DAVID ROTHMAN. "Feminism in Films." *Society*. Vol. 30, No. 3 (March/April 1993):66–72.

ROUDI-FAHIMI, FARZANEH, and MARY MEDERIOS KENT. "Challenges and Opportunities: The Population of the Middle East and North Africa." *Population Bulletin*. Vol. 65, No. 2 (June 2007). Washington, D.C.: Population Reference Bureau, 2007.

ROUSSEAU, CARYN. "Unions Rally at Wal-Mart Stores." *Yahoo! News* (November 22, 2002). http://dailynews.yahoo.com

ROZELL, MARK J., CLYDE WILCOX, and JOHN C. GREEN. "Religious Constituencies and Support for the Christian Right in the 1990s." *Social Science Quarterly*. Vol. 79, No. 4 (December 1998):815–27.

RUBIN, JOEL. "E-Mail Too Formal? Try a Text Message." Columbia News Service, March 7, 2003. http://www.jrn.columbia.edu/studentwork/cns/2003-03-07/85.asp

RUBIN, LILLIAN BRESLOW. *Worlds of Pain: Life in the Working-Class Family*. New York: Basic Books, 1976.

RUDEL, THOMAS K., and JUDITH M. GERSON. "Postmodernism, Institutional Change, and Academic Workers: A Sociology of Knowledge." *Social Science Quarterly*. Vol. 80, No. 2 (June 1999):213–28.

RULE, JAMES, and PETER BRANTLEY. "Computerized Surveillance in the Workplace: Forms and Delusions." *Sociological Forum*. Vol. 7, No. 3 (September 1992):405–23.

RUSSELL, CHERYL. "Are We in the Dumps?" *American Demographics*. Vol. 17, No. 1 (January 1995):6.

RYAN, WILLIAM. *Blaming the Victim*. Rev. ed. New York: Vintage Books, 1976.

RYMER, RUSS. *Genie*. New York: HarperPerennial, 1994.

SACHS, JEFFREY D. "The Case for Bigger Government." *Time* (January 19, 2009):34–36.

SAINT JAMES, MARGO, and PRISCILLA ALEXANDER. "What Is COYOTE?" 2004. http://www.coyotela.org/what-is.html

SAINT JEAN, YANICK, and JOE R. FEAGIN. *Double Burden: Black Women and Everyday Racism*. Armonk, N.Y.: Sharpe, 1998.

SALA-I-MARTIN, XAVIER. *The World Distribution of Income*. Working Paper No. 8933. Cambridge, Mass.: National Bureau of Economic Research, 2002.

SALE, KIRKPATRICK. *The Conquest of Paradise: Christopher Columbus and the Columbian Legacy*. New York: Knopf, 1990.

SAMUELSON, ROBERT J. "The Rich and Everyone Else." *Newsweek* (January 27, 2003):57.

SANSOM, WILLIAM. *A Contest of Ladies*. London: Hogarth, 1956.

SAPIR, EDWARD. "The Status of Linguistics as a Science." *Language*. Vol. 5, No. 4 (1929):207–14.

———. *Selected Writings of Edward Sapir in Language, Culture, and Personality*. DAVID G. MANDELBAUM, ed. Berkeley: University of California Press, 1949.

SAPORITO, BILL. "Can Wal-Mart Get Any Bigger?" *Time* (January 13, 2003):38–43.

———. "Spotlight: Toyota's Recall." *Time* (February 15, 2010):17.

SAX, LINDA J., ET AL. *The American Freshman: National Norms for Fall 2003.* Los Angeles: UCLA Higher Education Research Institute, 2003.

SCANLON, STEPHAN J. "Food Availability and Access in Less Industrialized Societies: A Test and Interpretation of Neo-Malthusian and Technoecological Theories." *Sociological Forum.* Vol. 16, No. 2 (June 2001):231–62.

SCHAFFER, MICHAEL. "American Dreamers." *U.S. News & World Report* (August 26, 2002):12–16.

SCHEFF, THOMAS J. *Being Mentally Ill: A Sociological Theory.* 2nd ed. New York: Aldine, 1984.

SCHLESINGER, ARTHUR M., JR. "The City in American Civilization." In A. B. CALLOW JR., ed., *American Urban History.* New York: Oxford University Press, 1969:25–41.

SCHLOSSER, ERIC. *Fast-Food Nation: The Dark Side of the All-American Meal.* New York: Perennial, 2002.

SCHMITT, ERIC. "Whites in Minority in Largest Cities, the Census Shows." *New York Times* (April 30, 2001):A1, A12.

SCHNEIDER, MARK, MELISSA MARSCHALL, PAUL TESKE, and CHRISTINE ROCH. "School Choice and Culture Wars in the Classroom: What Different Parents Seek from Education." *Social Science Quarterly.* Vol. 79, No. 3 (September 1998):489–501.

SCHNITTKER, JASON, BERNICE A. PESCOSOLIDO, and THOMAS W. CROGHAN. "Are African Americans Really Less Willing to Use Health Care?" *Social Problems.* Vol. 52, No. 2 (May 2005):255–71.

SCHOEN, ROBERT, and YEN-HSIN ALICE CHENG. "Partner Choice and the Differential Retreat from Marriage." *Journal of Marriage and the Family.* Vol. 68 (2006):1–10.

SCHOFER, EVAN, and MARION FOURCADE-GOURINCHAS. "The Structural Contexts of Civil Engagement: Voluntary Association Membership in Comparative Perspective." *American Sociological Review.* Vol. 66, No. 6 (December 2001):806–28.

SCHUR, LISA A., and DOUGLAS L. KRUSE. "What Determines Voter Turnout? Lessons from Citizens with Disabilities." *Social Science Quarterly.* Vol. 81, No. 2 (June 2000): 571–87.

SCHWARTZ, CHRISTINE R., and ROBERT D. MARE. "Trends in Educational Assortative Marriage from 1940 to 2003." July 2005. http://www.ccpr.ucla.edu/ccprwpseries/ccpr_017_05.pdf

SCOMMEGNA, PAOLA. "Increased Cohabitation Changing Children's Family Settings." *Population Today.* Vol. 30, No. 7 (July 2002):3, 6.

SEAGER, JONI. *The Penguin Atlas of Women in the World.* 3rd ed. New York: Penguin Putnam, 2003.

SEGAL, MADY WECHSLER, and AMANDA FAITH HANSEN. "Value Rationales in Policy Debates on Women in the Military: A Content Analysis of Congressional Testimony, 1941–1985." *Social Science Quarterly.* Vol. 73, No. 2 (June 1992):296–309.

SENNETT, RICHARD. *The Corrosion of Character: The Personal Consequences of Work in the New Capitalism.* New York: Norton, 1998.

SENNETT, RICHARD, and JONATHAN COBB. *The Hidden Injuries of Class.* New York: Vintage Books, 1973.

SENTENCING PROJECT. "Felony Disenfranchisement Laws in the United States." September 2008a. http://www.sentencingproject.org/Admin%5CDocuments%5Cpublications%5Cfd_bs_fdlawsinus.pdf

———. "Incarceration." 2008b. http://www.sentencingproject.org/IssueAreaHome.aspx?IssueID=2

SHEA, RACHEL HARTIGAN. "The New Insecurity." *U.S. News & World Report* (March 25, 2002):40.

SHEDDEN, DAVID. "School Shootings (1997–2008)." Poynter Institute. April 16, 2008. http://www.poynter.org/column.asp?id=49&aid=1025

SHELDON, WILLIAM H., EMIL M. HARTL, and EUGENE MCDERMOTT. *Varieties of Delinquent Youth.* New York: Harper Bros., 1949.

SHERKAT, DARREN E., and CHRISTOPHER G. ELLISON. "Recent Developments and Current Controversies in the Sociology of Religion." *Annual Review of Sociology.* Vol. 25 (1999):363–94.

SHERMAN, LAWRENCE W., and DOUGLAS A. SMITH. "Crime, Punishment, and Stake in Conformity: Legal and Informal Control of Domestic Violence." *American Sociological Review.* Vol. 57, No. 5 (October 1992):680–90.

SHEVKY, ESHREF, and WENDELL BELL. *Social Area Analysis.* Palo Alto, Calif.: Stanford University Press, 1955.

SHIPLEY, JOSEPH T. *Dictionary of Word Origins.* Totowa, N.J.: Rowman & Allanheld, 1985.

SHIVELY, JOELLEN. "Cowboys and Indians: Perceptions of Western Films among American Indians and Anglos." *American Sociological Review.* Vol. 57, No. 6 (December 1992):725–34.

SHOVER, NEAL, and ANDREW HOCHSTETLER. *Choosing White-Collar Crime.* New York: Cambridge University Press, 2006.

SHUPE, ANSON. *In the Name of All That's Holy: A Theory of Clergy Malfeasance.* Westport, Conn.: Praeger, 1995.

SHUPE, ANSON, WILLIAM A. STACEY, and LONNIE R. HAZLEWOOD. *Violent Men, Violent Couples: The Dynamics of Domestic Violence.* Lexington, Mass.: Lexington Books, 1987.

SIMMEL, GEORG. *The Sociology of Georg Simmel.* KURT WOLFF, ed. New York: Free Press, 1950; orig. 1902.

SIMON, JULIAN. *The Ultimate Resource.* Princeton, N.J.: Princeton University Press, 1981.

———. "More People, Greater Wealth, More Resources, Healthier Environment." In THEODORE D. GOLDFARB, ed., *Taking Sides: Clashing Views on Controversial Environmental Issues.* 6th ed. Guilford, Conn.: Dushkin, 1995.

SIMON, ROGER, and ANGIE CANNON. "An Amazing Journey." *U.S. News & World Report* (August 6, 2001):10–19.

SIMONS, MARLISE. "The Price of Modernization: The Case of Brazil's Kaiapo Indians." In JOHN J. MACIONIS and NIJOLE V. BENOKRAITIS, eds., *Seeing Ourselves: Classic, Contemporary, and Cross-Cultural Readings in Sociology.* 7th ed. Upper Saddle River, N.J.: Prentice Hall, 2007.

SIVARD, RUTH LEGER. *World Military and Social Expenditures, 1987–88.* 12th ed. Washington, D.C.: World Priorities, 1988.

SIZER, THEODORE R. *Horace's Compromise: The Dilemma of the American High School.* Boston: Houghton Mifflin, 1984.

———. "Private Profit, Public Good?" *Frontline* interview. July 3, 2003. http://www.pbs.org/wgbh/pages/frontline/shows/edison/etc/private.html

SKOCPOL, THEDA. *States and Social Revolutions: A Comparative Analysis of France, Russia, and China.* Cambridge: Cambridge University Press, 1979.

SMAIL, J. KENNETH. "Let's *Reduce* Global Population!" In JOHN J. MACIONIS and NIJOLE V. BENOKRAITIS, eds., *Seeing Ourselves: Classic, Contemporary, and Cross-Cultural Readings in Sociology.* 8th ed. Upper Saddle River, N.J.: Prentice Hall, 2010:413–17.

SMITH, ADAM. *An Inquiry into the Nature and Causes of the Wealth of Nations.* New York: Modern Library, 1937; orig. 1776.

SMITH, DOUGLAS A. "Police Response to Interpersonal Violence: Defining the Parameters of Legal Control." *Social Forces.* Vol. 65, No. 3 (March 1987):767–82.

SMITH, DOUGLAS A., and PATRICK R. GARTIN. "Specifying Specific Deterrence: The Influence of Arrest on Future Criminal Activity." *American Sociological Review.* Vol. 54, No. 1 (February 1989):94–105.

SMITH, DOUGLAS A., and CHRISTY A. VISHER. "Street-Level Justice: Situational Determinants of Police Arrest Decisions." *Social Problems.* Vol. 29, No. 2 (December 1981):167–77.

SMITH, RYAN A. "Race, Gender, and Authority in the Workplace: Theory and Research." *Annual Review of Sociology.* Vol. 28 (2002):509–42.

SMITH, TOM W. "Anti-Semitism Decreases but Persists." *Society.* Vol. 33, No. 3 (March/April 1996):2.

———. "Are We Grown Up Yet? U.S. Study Says Not 'til 26." *Yahoo! News* (May 23, 2003). http://news.yahoo.com

——— *American Sexual Behavior: Trends, Sociodemographic Differences, and Risk Behavior.* Chicago: National Opinion Research Center, March 2006. http://www.norc.org/NR/rdonlyres/2663F09F-2E74-436E-AC81-6FFBF288E183/0/AmericanSexualBehavior2006.pdf

SMITH-LOVIN, LYNN, and CHARLES BRODY. "Interruptions in Group Discussions: The Effects of Gender and Group Composition." *American Journal of Sociology.* Vol. 54, No. 3 (June 1989):424–35.

SMOLOWE, JILL. "When Violence Hits Home." *Time* (July 4, 1994):18–25.

SNELL, MARILYN BERLIN. "The Purge of Nurture." *New Perspectives Quarterly.* Vol. 7, No. 1 (Winter 1990):1–2.

SNYDER, HOWARD N. "Sexual Assault of Young Children as Reported to Law Enforcement: Victim, Incident, and Offender Characteristics." U.S. Department of Justice. 2000. http://bjs.ojp.usdoj.gov/index.cfm?ty=pbdetail&iid=1147

SOBEL, RACHEL K. "Herpes Tests Give Answers You Might Need to Know." *U.S. News & World Report* (June 18, 2001):53.

SOUTH, SCOTT J., and STEVEN F. MESSNER. "Structural Determinants of Intergroup Association: Interracial Marriage and Crime." *American Journal of Sociology.* Vol. 91, No. 6 (May 1986):1409–30.

SOWELL, THOMAS. *Ethnic America.* New York: Basic Books, 1981.

———. *Race and Culture.* New York: Basic Books, 1994.

———. "Ethnicity and IQ." In STEVEN FRASER, ed., *The Bell Curve Wars: Race, Intelligence, and the Future of America.* New York: Basic Books, 1995:70–79.

SPECTER, MICHAEL. "Plunging Life Expectancy Puzzles Russia." *New York Times* (August 2, 1995):A1, A2.

SPEIER, HANS. "Wit and Politics: An Essay on Laughter and Power." ROBERT JACKALL, ed. and trans. *American Journal of Sociology.* Vol. 103, No. 5 (March 1998):1352–1401.

SPENCER STUART. "Leading CEOs: A Statistical Snapshot of S&P 500 Leaders." December 2008. http://www.spencerstuart.com/research/articles/975

SPITZER, STEVEN. "Toward a Marxian Theory of Deviance." In DELOS H. KELLY, ed., *Criminal Behavior: Readings in Criminology.* New York: St. Martin's Press, 1980:175–91.

STACEY, JUDITH. *Patriarchy and Socialist Revolution in China.* Berkeley: University of California Press, 1983.

———. *Brave New Families: Stories of Domestic Upheaval in Late-Twentieth-Century America.* New York: Basic Books, 1990.

———. "Good Riddance to 'The Family': A Response to David Popenoe." *Journal of Marriage and the Family.* Vol. 55, No. 3 (August 1993):545–47.

STACK, STEVEN, IRA WASSERMAN, and ROGER KERN. "Adult Social Bonds and the Use of Internet Pornography." *Social Science Quarterly.* Vol. 85, No. 1 (March 2004):75–88.

STAHURA, JOHN M. "Suburban Development, Black Suburbanization, and the Black Civil Rights Movement since World War II." *American Sociological Review.* Vol. 51, No. 1 (February 1986):131–44.

STAPINSKI, HELENE. "Let's Talk Dirty." *American Demographics.* Vol. 20, No. 11 (November 1998):50–56.

STARK, RODNEY. *Sociology.* Belmont, Calif.: Wadsworth, 1985.

STARK, RODNEY, and WILLIAM SIMS BAINBRIDGE. "Of Churches, Sects, and Cults: Preliminary Concepts for a Theory of Religious Movements." *Journal for the Scientific Study of Religion.* Vol. 18, No. 2 (June 1979):117–31.

STARK, RODNEY, and ROGER FINKE. *Acts of Faith: Explaining the Human Side of Religion.* Berkeley: University of California Press, 2000.

STATISTICS CANADA. "Ethnic Diversity and Immigration." January 13, 2009. http://www41.statcan.ca/2008/30000/ceb30000_000-eng.htm

STEELE, RANDY. "Awful but Lawful." *Boating* (June 2000):36.

STEELE, SHELBY. *The Content of Our Character: A New Vision of Race in America.* New York: St. Martin's Press, 1990.

STEIN, ROB. "Fewer U.S. Deaths Linked to Obesity." *Washington Post* (April 20, 2005):A10.

STEPHENS, JOHN D. *The Transition from Capitalism to Socialism.* Urbana: University of Illinois Press, 1986.

STEYN, MARK. "Is Canada's Economy a Model for America?" *Imprimis.* Vol. 37, No. 1 (January 2008):1–7.

STIER, HAYA. "Continuity and Change in Women's Occupations following First Childbirth." *Social Science Quarterly.* Vol. 77, No. 1 (March 1996):60–75.

STOBBE, MIKE. "Cancer to Be World's Top Killer by 2010, WHO Says." *Guardian* (December 12, 2008). http://www.guardian.co.uk/uslatest/story/0,,-8147108,00.html

STOCKHOLM INTERNATIONAL PEACE RESEARCH INSTITUTE. *SIPRI Yearbook, 2009: Armaments, Disarmament and International Security.* Stockholm: SIPRI. June 2009. http://www.sipri.org/yearbook/2009

STORMS, MICHAEL D. "Theories of Sexual Orientation." *Journal of Personality and Social Psychology.* Vol. 38, No. 5 (May 1980):783–92.

STORY, LOUISE. "Top Hedge Fund Managers Do Well in a Down Year." *New York Times* (March 25, 2009). http://www.nytimes.com/2009/03/25/business/25hedge.html

STOUFFER, SAMUEL A., ET AL. *The American Soldier: Adjustment during Army Life.* Princeton, N.J.: Princeton University Press, 1949.

STOUT, DAVID. "Supreme Court Splits on Diversity Efforts at University of Michigan." *Yahoo! News* (June 23, 2003). http://news.yahoo.com

STRATTON, LESLIE S. "Why Does More Housework Lower Women's Wages? Testing Hypotheses involving Job Effort and Hours Flexibility." *Social Sciences Quarterly.* Vol. 82, No. 1 (March 2001):67–76.

STUESSY, JOE, and SCOTT LIPSCOMB. *Rock and Roll: Its History and Stylistic Development.* 6th ed. Upper Saddle River, N.J.: Prentice Hall, 2008.

SULLIVAN, ANDREW. Lecture delivered at Kenyon College, April 4, 2002.

SULLIVAN, BARBARA. "McDonald's Sees India as Golden Opportunity." *Chicago Tribune* (April 5, 1995):B1.

SULLIVAN, WILL. "Road Warriors." *U.S. News & World Report* (May 7, 2007):42–49.

SUMNER, WILLIAM GRAHAM. *Folkways.* New York: Dover, 1959; orig. 1906.

SUN, LENA H. "WWII's Forgotten Internees Await Apology." *Washington Post* (March 9, 1998):A1, A5, A6.

SUTHERLAND, EDWIN H. "White Collar Criminality." *American Sociological Review.* Vol. 5, No. 1 (February 1940):1–12.

SWARTZ, STEVE. "Why Michael Milken Stands to Qualify for Guinness Book." *Wall Street Journal* (March 31, 1989):1, 4.

SZASZ, THOMAS S. *The Myth of Mental Illness: Foundations of a Theory of Personal Conduct.* New York: Dell, 1961.

———. *The Manufacturer of Madness: A Comparative Study of the Inquisition and the Mental Health Movement.* New York: Harper & Row, 1970.

———. "Cleansing the Modern Heart." *Society.* Vol. 40, No. 4 (May/June 2003):52–59.

———. "Protecting Patients against Psychiatric Intervention." *Society.* Vol. 41, No. 3 (March/April 2004):7–10.

TAJFEL, HENRI. "Social Psychology of Intergroup Relations." *Annual Review of Psychology.* Palo Alto, Calif.: Annual Reviews, 1982:1–39.

TAKAKI, RONALD. *Strangers from a Different Shore.* Boston: Back Bay Books, 1998.

TALLICHET, SUZANNE E. "Barriers to Women's Advancement in Underground Coal Mining." *Rural Sociology.* Vol. 65, No. 2 (June 2000):234–52.

TAMBLYN, ROBYN; cited in SHELDON LEWIS, "Which Doctors Will Annoy Their Patients?" *Spirituality and Health.* Vol. 11, No. 2 (March/April 2008):28.

TANNEN, DEBORAH. *You Just Don't Understand: Women and Men in Conversation.* New York: Morrow, 1990.

———. *Talking from 9 to 5: How Women's and Men's Conversational Styles Affect Who Gets Heard, Who Gets Credit, and What Gets Done at Work.* New York: Morrow, 1994.

TAVRIS, CAROL, and CAROL WADE. *Psychology in Perspective.* 3rd ed. Upper Saddle River, N.J.: Prentice Hall, 2001.

TAX FOUNDATION. "America Celebrates Tax Freedom Day." 2010. http://www.taxfoundation.org/taxfreedomday/

TEENAGE RESEARCH UNLIMITED. Loveisrespect.org, National Teen Dating Abuse Helpline: Resource Center. 2008. http://www.loveisrespect.org/resource-center/

TEJADA-VERA, BETZAIDA, and PAUL D. SUTTON. "Births, Marriages, Divorces, and Deaths: Provisional Data for 2008." *National Vital Statistics Reports.* Vol. 57, No. 19 (July 29, 2009). http://www.cdc.gov/nchs/data/nvsr/nvsr57/nvsr57_19.pdf

TERRY, DON. "In Crackdown on Bias, a New Tool." *New York Times* (June 12, 1993):8.

THOMAS, EVAN, and MARTHA BRANT. "Injection of Reflection." *Newsweek* (November 19, 2007):40–41.

THOMAS, PIRI. *Down These Mean Streets.* New York: Signet, 1967.

THOMAS, W. I. "The Relation of Research to the Social Process." In MORRIS JANOWITZ, ed., *W. I. Thomas on Social Organization and Social Personality.* Chicago: University of Chicago Press, 1966:289–305; orig. 1931.

THOMAS, W. I., and DOROTHY SWAINE THOMAS. *The Child in America: Behavior Problems and Programs.* New York: Knopf, 1928.

THOMMA, STEVEN. "Christian Coalition Demands Action from GOP." *Philadelphia Inquirer* (September 14, 1997):A2.

THOMPSON, DICK. "Gene Maverick." *Time* (January 11, 1999):54–55.

THOMPSON, MARK, and DOUGLAS WALLER. "Shield of Dreams." *Time* (May 8, 2001):45–47.

THORNBERRY, TERRANCE, and MARGARET FARNSWORTH. "Social Correlates of Criminal Involvement: Further Evidence on the Relationship between Social Status and Criminal Behavior." *American Sociological Review.* Vol. 47, No. 4 (August 1982):505–18.

THORNE, BARRIE, CHERIS KRAMARAE, and NANCY HENLEY, eds. *Language, Gender, and Society.* Rowley, Mass.: Newbury House, 1983.

TILLY, CHARLES. "Does Modernization Breed Revolution?" In JACK A. GOLDSTONE, ed., *Revolutions: Theoretical, Comparative, and Historical Studies.* New York: Harcourt Brace Jovanovich, 1986:47–57.

TITTLE, CHARLES R., WAYNE J. VILLEMEZ, and DOUGLAS A. SMITH. "The Myth of Social Class and Criminality: An Empirical Assessment of the Empirical Evidence." *American Sociological Review.* Vol. 43, No. 5 (October 1978):643–56.

TOCQUEVILLE, ALEXIS DE. *The Old Regime and the French Revolution.* STUART GILBERT, trans. Garden City, N.Y.: Anchor/Doubleday, 1955; orig. 1856.

TOLSON, JAY. "The Trouble with Elites." *Wilson Quarterly.* Vol. 19, No. 1 (Winter 1995):6–8.

TÖNNIES, FERDINAND. *Community and Society (Gemeinschaft und Gesellschaft).* New York: Harper & Row, 1963; orig. 1887.

TOOSSI, MITRA. "Labor Force Projections to 2016: More Workers in Their Golden Years." *Monthly Labor Review* (November 2007):33–52. http://www.bls.gov/opub/mlr/2007/11/art3full.pdf

TOPPO, GREG. "Big City Schools Struggle with Graduation Rates." *USA Today* (June 20, 2006). http://www.usatoday.com/news/education/2006-06-20-dropout-rates_x.htm

TOPPO, GREG, and ANTHONY DEBARROS. "Reality Weighs Down Dreams of College." *USA Today* (February 2, 2005):A1.

TORRES, LISA, and MATT L. HUFFMAN. "Social Networks and Job Search Outcomes among Male and Female Professional, Technical, and Managerial Workers." *Sociological Focus.* Vol. 35, No. 1 (February 2002):25–42.

TREAS, JUDITH. "Older Americans in the 1990s and Beyond." *Population Bulletin.* Vol. 50, No. 2 (May 1995).

TROELTSCH, ERNST. *The Social Teaching of the Christian Churches.* New York: Macmillan, 1931.

TUCKER, JAMES. "New Age Religion and the Cult of the Self." *Society.* Vol. 39, No. 2 (February 2002):46–51.

TUMIN, MELVIN M. "Some Principles of Stratification: A Critical Analysis." *American Sociological Review.* Vol. 18, No. 4 (August 1953):387–94.

TUMULTY, KAREN. "Should They Stay or Should They Go?" *Time.* Vol. 167, No. 15 (April 10, 2006):30–41.

TURNER, JONATHAN. *On the Origins of Human Emotions: A Sociological Inquiry into the Evolution of Human Emotions.* Stanford, Calif.: Stanford University Press, 2000.

TYLER, S. LYMAN. *A History of Indian Policy.* Washington, D.C.: U.S. Department of the Interior, Bureau of Indian Affairs, 1973.

UDRY, J. RICHARD. "Biological Limitations of Gender Construction." *American Sociological Review.* Vol. 65, No. 3 (June 2000):443–57.

UGGEN, CHRISTOPHER. "Ex-Offenders and the Conformist Alternative: A Job-Quality Model of Work and Crime." *Social Problems.* Vol. 46, No. 1 (February 1999):127–51.

UGGEN, CHRISTOPHER, and JEFF MANZA. "Democratic Contraction? Political Consequences of Felon Disenfranchisement in the United States." *American Sociological Review.* Vol. 67, No. 6 (December 2002):777–803.

UNAIDS. "Fast Facts about HIV Prevention." 2008a. http://www.unaids.org/en/KnowledgeCentre/Resources/FastFacts/

———. "2008 Report on the Global AIDS Epidemic." August 2008b. http://www.unaids.org/en/KnowledgeCentre/HIVData/GlobalReport/2008/2008_Global_report.asp

UNESCO. Data reported in "Tower of Babel Is Tumbling Down—Slowly." *U.S. News & World Report* (July 2, 2001):9.

UNESCO INSTITUTE OF STATISTICS. "Data Centre." 2008. http://stats.uis.unesco.org/unesco/tableviewer/document.aspx?ReportId=143

———. "Data Centre." 2009. http://stats.uis.unesco.org/unesco/TableViewer/document.aspx?ReportId=143

———. Data Centre. Custom Table, VAR: Adult literacy rate (%). 2010

UNICEF. "ChildInfo Statistics by Area: Child Survival and Health, 2004." 2004. http://www.childinfo.org/survival_health.html

———. "Gender Equality: The Big Picture." August 25, 2004. http://www.unicef.org/gender/index_bigpicture.html

———. "Female Genital Mutilation/Cutting." April 2008. http://www.childinfo.org/areas/fgmc/tables.php

———. "The State of the World's Children, 2008." 2008. http://www.unicef.org/sowc08/index.php

———. "Understanding Children's Work." 2008. http://www.ucw-project.org/

———. "ChildInfo Statistics by Area: Child Protection/Female Genital Mutilation/Cutting." November 2009. http://www.childinfo.org/protection.html

United Nations. *Human Development Report 2004.* New York: Oxford University Press, 2004.

———. "2006 Report on the Global AIDS Epidemic." 2006a. http://www.unaids.org/en/HIV_data/2006GlobalReport/default.asp

———. UNAIDS. "WHO AIDS Epidemic Update, December 2006." December 2006b. http://www.unaids.org/en/HIV_data/epi2006/default.asp

———. "2007 AIDS Epidemic Update. Joint United Nations Programme on HIV/AIDS (UNAIDS) and World Health Organization (WHO)." 2007. http://data.unaids.org/pub/EPISlides/2007/2007_epiupdate_en.pdf

———. "Executive Summary." *World Urbanization Prospects: The 2007 Revision.* February 2008a. http://www.un.org/esa/population/publications/wup2007/2007WUP_ExecSum_web.pdf

———. "Millenium Development Goals." 2008b. http://www.un.org/millenniumgoals/

———. "2007 UNAIDS Annual Report: Knowing Your Epidemic." Joint United Nations Programme on HIV/AIDS (UNAIDS). 2008c. http://data.unaids.org/pub/Report/2008/jc1535_annual_report07_en.pdf

———. "World Contraceptive Use, 2008." 2008. http://www.un.org/esa/population/publications/contraceptive2008/WCU2008.htm

UNITED NATIONS DEVELOPMENT PROGRAMME. *Human Development Report 1990.* New York: Oxford University Press, 1990.

———. *Human Development Report 2007–2008.* New York: Palgrave Macmillan, 2007. http://hdr.undp.org/en/

———. "Human Development Indices: A Statistical Update." December 18, 2008. http://hdr.undp.org/en/statistics/data/

———. *Human Development Report 2009.* New York: Palgrave Macmillan, 2009. http://hdr.undp.org/en/reports/global/hdr2009/

UNITED NATIONS ENVIRONMENTAL PROGRAMME. "Vital Forest Graphics: Stopping the Downswing?" June 8, 2009. http://www.fao.org/forestry/home/en/

UNITED NATIONS FOOD AND AGRICULTURE ORGANIZATION. *The State of Food Insecurity in the World, 2008.* Rome: Food and Agriculture Organization of the United Nations, 2008. http://www.fao.org/docrep/011/i0291e/i0291e00.htm

———. "Prevalence of Undernourishment in Total Population: Food Security Statistics." 2010. http://www.fao.org/faostat/foodsecurity/index_en.htm

UNITED NATIONS POPULATION DIVISION. "World Population Prospects: The 2006 Revision" and "World Urbanization Prospects: The 2007 Revision." 2008. http://esa.un.org/unup

———. "World Population Prospects: The 2008 Revision." March 2009. http://www.un.org/esa/population/unpop.htm

———. "World Population Prospects: The 2009 Revision." March 2010. http://www.un.org/esa/population/unpop.htm

UNITED NATIONS STATISTICS DIVISION. "Undata." http://data.un.org/Browse.aspx?d=CDB

UNITED NATIONS WORLD FOOD PROGRAMME. "Undernutrition: Women and Children Paying the Price." October 9, 2008. http://www.wfp.org/english/?n=37

UNITED NATIONS WORLD WATER ASSESSMENT PROGRAMME. "World Water Development Report 3: Water in a Changing World." March 2009. http://www.unesco.org/water/wwap/wwdr/

U.S. BUREAU OF INTERNATIONAL LABOR AFFAIRS. "Office of Child Labor, Forced Labor and Human Trafficking (OCFT)." 2008. http://www.dol.gov/ilab/programs/ocft/

U.S. BUREAU OF JUSTICE STATISTICS. "Criminal Victimization in the United States: Statistical Tables." September 2, 2009. http://bjs.ojp.usdoj.gov/index.cfm?ty=pbdetail&iid=1975

———. "Federal Justice Statistics Resource Center." 2010. http://fjsrc.urban.org/index.cfm

U.S. BUREAU OF LABOR STATISTICS. "American Time Use Survey, 2008: Results." June 2009. http://www.bls.gov/tus/

———. "Consumer Expenditure Survey, 2008." 2009. http://www.bls.gov/cex/tables.htm

———. "Employment Projections: Labor Force (Demographic) Data." December 10, 2009. http://www.bls.gov/emp/emplab1.htm

———. "Employment Situation." December 9, 2009. http://www.bls.gov/news.release/empsit.toc.htm

———. "Highlights of Women's Earnings in 2008." July 2009. http://www.bls.gov/cps/cpswom2008.pdf

———. "Census of Fatal Occupational Injuries (CFOI)." 2010. http://www.bls.gov/iif/oshcfoi1.htm

———. "Current Employment Statistics: CES (National)." 2010. http://www.bls.gov/ces/home.htm

———. "International Labor Comparisons." January 29, 2010. http://www.bls.gov/fls/tables

———. "Labor Force Statistics from the Current Population Survey." 2010. http://www.bls.gov/cps/home.htm

U.S. CENSUS BUREAU. *The Two or More Races Population, 2000.* Census 2000 Brief No. C2KBR/01-6. Washington, D.C.: U.S. Government Printing Office, 2001.

———. *Language Use and English-Speaking Ability, 2000.* Census 2000 Brief No. C2KBR-29. Washington, D.C.: U.S. Government Printing Office, 2003.

———. *County and City Data Book, 2007* (14th ed.). Washington, D.C.: U.S. Government Printing Office, November 2007. http://www.census.gov/prod/www/abs/ccdb07.html

———. "National Population Projections: Tables and Charts." August 14, 2008. http://www.census.gov/population/www/projections/

———. "Who's Minding the Kids? Child Care Arrangements, Spring 2005." Rev. February 28, 2008. http://www.census.gov/population/www/socdemo/child/ppl-2005.html

———. "American Community Survey, 2009." 2009. http://factfinder.census.gov/

———. "Current Population Survey." September 10, 2009. http://www.census.gov/cps/

———. "Foreign Trade Statistics." 2009. http://www.census.gov/foreign-trade/statistics/index.html

———. "Housing Vacancies and Homeownership (CPS/HVS): Annual Statistics, 2008." 2009. http://www.census.gov/hhes/www/housing/hvs/annual08/ann08ind.html

———. "International Data Base." December 2009. http://www.census.gov/ipc/www/idb/tables.html

———. "Newsroom: Facts for Features and Special Editions." January 28, 2009. http://www.census.gov/Press-Release/www/releases/archives/facts_for_features_special_editions/index.html

———. "Population Estimates." June 2009. http://www.census.gov/popest/estimates.html

———. "State and Metropolitan Area Data Book: Metropolitan and Micropolitan Area Data Tables." February 4, 2009. http://www.census.gov/compendia/smadb/SMADB-metro.html

———. *Statistical Abstract of the United States, 2009* (128th ed.). Washington, D.C.: U.S. Government Printing Office, 2008). http://www.census.gov/compendia/statab/

———. "Families and Living Arrangements." 2010. http://www.census.gov/population/www/socdemo/hh-fam.html

———. "Federal, State, and Local Governments: State Government Tax Collections." January 28, 2010. http://www.census.gov/govs/statetax/

———. "State and County QuickFacts." 2010. http://www.fedstats.gov/qf/

———. *Statistical Abstract of the United States, 2010* (129th ed.). Washington, D.C.: U.S. Government Printing Office, 2009. http://www.census.gov/compendia/statab/

U.S. CONFERENCE OF MAYORS. *Hunger and Homelessness Survey: A Status Report on Hunger and Homelessness in America's Cities: A 23-City Survey.* Washington, D.C.: U.S. Conference of Mayors, 2007. http://usmayors.org/HHSurvey2007/hhsurvey07.pdf

U.S. DEPARTMENT OF HEALTH AND HUMAN SERVICES. ADMINISTRATION FOR CHILDREN AND FAMILIES. *Temporary Assistance for Needy Families (TANF) Program: Third Annual Report to Congress.* Washington, D.C.: U.S. Government Printing Office, August 2000.

———. *Child Maltreatment, 2007.* Washington, D.C.: U.S. Government Printing Office, 2009. http://www.acf.hhs.gov/programs/cb/pubs/cm07/index.htm

U.S. DEPARTMENT OF HEALTH AND HUMAN SERVICES; HEALTH RESOURCES AND SERVICES ADMINISTRATION. "The Registered Nurse Population: 2008 Survey." 2010. http://bhpr.hrsa.gov/healthworkforce/rnsurvey/initialfindings2008.pdf

U.S. DEPARTMENT OF HEALTH AND HUMAN SERVICES. SUBSTANCE ABUSE AND MENTAL HEALTH SERVICES ADMINISTRATION (SAMHSA). *Results from the 2008 National Survey on Drug Use and Health: National Findings.* DHHS Publication No. SMA 08-4343. Rockville, Md., 2010. http://oas.samhsa.gov/NSDUHlatest.htm

U.S. DEPARTMENT OF HOMELAND SECURITY. *2008 Yearbook of Immigration Statistics.* Washington, D.C.: U.S. Government Printing Office, 2009. http://wwww.dhs.gov/ximgtn/statistics/publications/yearbook.shtm

U.S. DEPARTMENT OF HOUSING AND URBAN DEVELOPMENT. "Annual Homeless Assessment Report to Congress." July 2009. http://www.hudhre.info/documents/4thHomelessAssessmentReport.pdf

U.S. DEPARTMENT OF LABOR. "Employment and Earnings." 2008. http://www.bls.gov/cps/#annual

———. BUREAU OF LABOR STATISTICS. "Labor Force Statistics from the Current Population Survey." 2008. http://www.bls.gov/cps/home.htm

———. "Quick Facts on Registered Nurses (RNs)." 2008. http://www.dol.gov/wb/factsheets/Qfnursing-07.htm

———. "Employment Situation." December 9, 2009. http://www.bls.gov/news.release/empsit.toc.htm

———. "Highlights of Women's Earnings in 2008." July 2009. http://www.bls.gov/cps/cpswom2008.pdf

———. "List of Goods Produced by Child Labor or Forced Labor." September 2009. http://www.dol.gov/ilab/programs/ocft/PDF/2009TVPRA.pdf

———. "Women in the Labor Force: A Databook." 2009. http://www.bls.gov/cps/wlf-databook2009.htm

U.S. DEPARTMENT OF STATE. "Independent States in the World." August 19, 2008. http://www.state.gov/s/inr/rls/4250.htm

———. "2008 Report on Terrorism." April 30, 2009. http://wits.nctc.gov/Reports.do

———. "2009 Report on International Religious Freedom." 2010. http://www.state.gov/g/drl/rls/irf/2009/index.htm

U.S. DEPARTMENT OF THE ARMY. "Physical Fitness Training, Appendix A: Physiological Differences between the Sexes." 1992. http://www.usma.edu/dpe/testing/FM21-20/Appa.pdf

U.S. ENVIRONMENTAL PROTECTION AGENCY. "Municipal Solid Waste Generation, Recycling, and Disposal in the United States: Facts and Figures for 2008." November 2009. http://www.epa.gov/osw/nonhaz/municipal/

———. "National Priorities List (NPL): Superfund Sites." 2010. http://www.epa.gov/superfund/sites/query/queryhtm/nplfin1.htm

U.S. EQUAL EMPLOYMENT OPPORTUNITY COMMISSION. "Job Patterns for Minorities and Women in Private Industry, 2007." March 23, 2009. http://www.eeoc.gov/eeoc/statistics/employment/jobpat-eeo1/2007/index.html

U.S. GEOLOGICAL SURVEY. "Estimated Use of Water in the United States in 2005." 2009. http://water.usgs.gov/watuse/

U.S. HOUSE OF REPRESENTATIVES. *1991 Green Book.* Washington, D.C.: U.S. Government Printing Office, 1991.

———. Legislative Resources. (2010). http://www.house.gov

U.S. OFFICE OF MANAGEMENT AND BUDGET. "The Budget for Fiscal Year 2010." 2010. http://www.gpoaccess.gov/usbudget/fy10/pdf/summary.pdf

U.S. OFFICE OF PERSONNEL MANAGEMENT. "Employment and Trends." 2010. http://www.opm.gov/feddata/html/empt.asp

U.S. SENATE. "Women in the Senate." 2010. http://www.senate.gov/reference/reference_index_subjects/Women_in_Congress_vrd.htm

U.S. SMALL BUSINESS ADMINISTRATION. *Women's Business Ownership.* August 2006. [Online] Available May 28, 2008, at http://www.sba.gov/advo/research/rs280tot.pdf

U.S. SOCIAL SECURITY ADMINISTRATION. "2009 Annual Report of the Board of Trustees of the Federal Old-Age and Survivors Insurance and Federal Disability Insurance Trust Funds." 2009. http://www.ssa.gov/OACT/TR/2009

UPTHEGROVE, TAYNA R., VINCENT J. ROSCIGNO, and CAMILLE ZUBRINSKY CHARLES. "Big Money Collegiate Sports: Racial Concentration, Contradictory Pressures, and Academic Performance." *Social Science Quarterly.* Vol. 80, No. 4 (December 1999):718–37.

VALDEZ, A. "In the Hood: Street Gangs Discover White-Collar Crime." *Police.* Vol. 21, No. 5 (May 1997):49–50, 56.

VALLAS, STEPHEN P., and JOHN P. BECK. "The Transformation of Work Revisited: The Limits of Flexibility in American Manufacturing." *Social Problems.* Vol. 43, No. 3 (August 1996):339–61.

VALOCCHI, STEVE. "The Emergence of the Integrationist Ideology in the Civil Rights Movement." *Social Problems.* Vol. 43, No. 1 (February 1996):116–30.

VAN BIEMA, DAVID. "America's Unfaithful Faithful." *Time* (February 25, 2008). http://www.time.com/time/nation/article/0,8599,1716987,00.html?xid=feed-yahoo-full-nation

VENTURA, STEPHANIE J., JOYCE C. ABMA, WILLIAM D. MOSHER, and STANLEY K. HENSHAW. "Estimated Pregnancy Rates for the United States, 1990–2005: An Update." *National Vital Statistics Reports.* Vol. 58, No. 4 (October 14, 2009). http://www.cdc.gov/nchs/data/nvsr/nvsr58/nvsr58_04.pdf

VINOVSKIS, MARIS A. "Have Social Historians Lost the Civil War? Some Preliminary Demographic Speculations." *Journal of American History.* Vol. 76, No. 1 (June 1989):34–58.

VISSER, JELLE. "Union Membership Statistics in 24 Countries." *Monthly Labor Review* (January 2006):38–49. http://www.bls.gov/opub/mlr/2006/01/art3full.pdf

VOGEL, EZRA F. *The Four Little Dragons: The Spread of Industrialization in East Asia.* Cambridge, Mass.: Harvard University Press, 1991.

VOGEL, LISE. *Marxism and the Oppression of Women: Toward a Unitary Theory.* New Brunswick, N.J.: Rutgers University Press, 1983.

VOLD, GEORGE B., and THOMAS J. BERNARD. *Theoretical Criminology.* 3rd ed. New York: Oxford University Press, 1986.

WALDFOGEL, JANE. "The Effect of Children on Women's Wages." *American Sociological Review.* Vol. 62, No. 2 (April 1997):209–17.

WALKER, KAREN. "'Always There for Me': Friendship Patterns and Expectations among Middle- and Working-Class Men and Women." *Sociological Forum.* Vol. 10, No. 2 (June 1995):273–96.

WALL, THOMAS F. *Medical Ethics: Basic Moral Issues.* Washington, D.C.: University Press of America, 1980.

WALLERSTEIN, IMMANUEL. *The Modern World-System: Capitalist Agriculture and the Origins of the European World-Economy in the Sixteenth Century.* New York: Academic Press, 1974.

———. *The Capitalist World-Economy.* New York: Cambridge University Press, 1979.

———. "Crises: The World Economy, the Movements, and the Ideologies." In ALBERT BERGESEN, ed., *Crises in the World-System.* Beverly Hills, Calif.: Sage, 1983:21–36.

———. *The Politics of the World Economy: The States, the Movements, and the Civilizations.* Cambridge: Cambridge University Press, 1984.

WALLIS, CLAUDIA. "How to Make Great Teachers." *Time.* February 14, 2008. http://www.time.com/time/nation/article/0,8599,1713174,00.html

WALLIS, CLAUDIA, and SONJA STEPTOE. "How to Fix No Child Left Behind." *Time.* Vol. 169, No. 23 (June 4, 2007):34–41.

WAL-MART. "Corporate Facts: Wal-Mart by the Numbers"; "Wal-Mart International Operational Data Sheet, April 2008"; and "2009 Annual Report to Shareholders." 2009. http://walmartstores.com/FactsNews/FactSheets/

WALSH, BRYAN. "How Business Saw the Light." *Time* (January 15, 2007):56–57.

WARNER, R. STEPHEN. "Work in Progress toward a New Paradigm for the Sociological Study of Religion in the United States." *American Journal of Sociology.* Vol. 98, No. 5 (March 1993):1044–93.

WARNER, W. LLOYD, and PAUL S. LUNT. *The Social Life of a Modern Community.* New Haven, Conn.: Yale University Press, 1941.

WARR, MARK, and CHRISTOPHER G. ELLISON. "Rethinking Social Reactions to Crime: Personal and Altruistic Fear in Family Households." *American Journal of Sociology.* Vol. 106, No. 3 (November 2000):551–78.

WATERS, MELISSA S., WILL CARRINGTON HEATH, and JOHN KEITH WATSON. "A Positive Model of the Determination of Religious Affiliation." *Social Science Quarterly.* Vol. 76, No. 1 (March 1995):105–23.

WATTS, DUNCAN J. "Networks, Dynamics, and the Small-World Phenomenon." *American Journal of Sociology.* Vol. 105, No. 2 (September 1999):493–527.

WEBER, ADNA FERRIN. *The Growth of Cities.* New York: Columbia University Press, 1963; orig. 1899.

WEBER, MAX. *The Protestant Ethic and the Spirit of Capitalism.* New York: Scribner, 1958; orig. 1904–05.

———. *Economy and Society: An Outline of Interpretive Sociology.* GUENTHER ROTH and CLAUS WITTICH, eds. Berkeley: University of California Press, 1978; orig. 1921.

WEIDENBAUM, MURRAY. "The Evolving Corporate Board." *Society.* Vol. 32, No. 3 (March/April 1995):9–20.

WEINBERG, GEORGE. *Society and the Healthy Homosexual.* Garden City, N.Y.: Anchor Books, 1973.

WEISBERG, D. KELLY. *Children of the Night: A Study of Adolescent Prostitution.* Lexington, Mass.: Heath, 1985.

WEITZMAN, LENORE J. *The Divorce Revolution: The Unexpected Social and Economic Consequences for Women and Children in America.* New York: Free Press, 1985.

———. "The Economic Consequences of Divorce Are Still Unequal: Comment on Peterson." *American Sociological Review.* Vol. 61, No. 3 (June 1996):537–38.

WELLS, HODAN FARAH, and JEAN C. BUZBY. *Dietary Assessment of Major Trends in U.S. Food Consumption, 1970–2005.* Economic Information Bulletin No. (EIB 33). Washington, D.C.: U.S. Department of Agriculture, March 2008.

WENDLE, JOHN. "Russia's Millionaires Keep Their Heads Up." *Time.* (January 12, 2009):4.

WESSELMAN, HANK. *Visionseeker: Shared Wisdom from the Place of Refuge.* Carlsbad, Calif.: Hay House, 2001.

WEST, CORNEL. "The Obama Moment." *U.S. News & World Report* (November 17, 2008): 29.

WHEELIS, ALLEN. *The Quest for Identity.* New York: Norton, 1958.

WHITAKER, MARK. "Ten Ways to Fight Terrorism." *Newsweek* (July 1, 1985):26–29.

WHITE, JACK E. "I'm Just Who I Am." *Time* (May 5, 1997):32–36.

WHITE, RALPH, and RONALD LIPPITT. "Leader Behavior and Member Reaction in Three 'Social Climates.'" In DORWIN CARTWRIGHT and ALVIN ZANDER, eds., *Group Dynamics.* Evanston, Ill.: Row & Peterson, 1953:586–611.

WHORF, BENJAMIN LEE. "The Relation of Habitual Thought and Behavior to Language." In *Language, Thought, and Reality.* Cambridge, Mass.: Technology Press of MIT; New York: Wiley, 1956:134–59; orig. 1941.

WHYTE, WILLIAM FOOTE. *Street Corner Society.* 3rd ed. Chicago: University of Chicago Press, 1981; orig. 1943.

WILCOX, CLYDE. "Race, Gender, and Support for Women in the Military." *Social Science Quarterly.* Vol. 73, No. 2 (June 1992):310–23.

WILDAVSKY, BEN. "Small World, Isn't It?" *U.S. News & World Report* (April 1, 2002):68.

WILES, P. J. D. *Economic Institutions Compared.* New York: Halsted Press, 1977.

WILKES, RIMA, and JOHN ICELAND. "Hypersegregation in the Twenty-First Century." *Demography.* Vol. 41, No. 1 (February 9, 2004):23–36.

WILLIAMS, JOHNNY E. "Linking Beliefs to Collective Action: Politicized Religious Beliefs and the Civil Rights Movement." *Sociological Forum.* Vol. 17, No. 2 (June 2002):203–22.

WILLIAMS, PETER W. "America's Religions: From Their Origins to the Twenty-First Century.* Urbana: University of Illinois Press, 2002.

WILLIAMS, RHYS H., and N. J. DEMERATH III. "Religion and Political Process in an American City." *American Sociological Review.* Vol. 56, No. 4 (August 1991):417–31.

WILLIAMS, ROBIN M., JR. *American Society: A Sociological Interpretation.* 3rd ed. New York: Knopf, 1970.

WILLIAMSON, JEFFREY G., and PETER H. LINDERT. *American Inequality: A Macroeconomic History.* New York: Academic Press, 1980.

WILLIAMSON, SAMUEL H. "Seven Ways to Compute the Relative Value of a U.S. Dollar Amount, 1774 to Present." Measuring Worth. April 2010. http://www.measuringworth.com/uscompare

WILSON, EDWARD O. "Biodiversity, Prosperity, and Value." In F. HERBERT BORMANN and STEPHEN R. KELLERT, eds., *Ecology, Economics, and Ethics: The Broken Circle.* New Haven, Conn.: Yale University Press, 1991:3–10.

WILSON, JAMES Q. "Crime, Race, and Values." *Society.* Vol. 30, No. 1 (November/December 1992):90–93.

WILSON, THOMAS C. "Urbanism and Tolerance: A Test of Some Hypotheses Drawn from Wirth and Stouffer." *American Sociological Review.* Vol. 50, No. 1 (February 1985):117–23.

———. "Urbanism and Unconventionality: The Case of Sexual Behavior." *Social Science Quarterly.* Vol. 76, No. 2 (June 1995):346–63.

WILSON, WILLIAM JULIUS. *When Work Disappears: The World of the New Urban Poor.* New York: Knopf, 1996a.

———. "Work." *New York Times Magazine* (August 18, 1996b):26 ff.

WINSHIP, CHRISTOPHER, and JENNY BERRIEN. "Boston Cops and Black Churches." *Public Interest* (Summer 1999):52–68.

WINTER, GREG. "Wider Gap Found between Wealthy and Poor Schools." *New York Times* (October 6, 2004). http://www.nytimes.com/2004/10/06/education/06gap.html

WINTERS, REBECCA. "Trouble for School Inc." *Time* (May 27, 2002):53.

WIRTH, LOUIS. "Urbanism as a Way of Life." *American Journal of Sociology.* Vol. 44, No. 1 (July 1938):1–24.

WITKIN, GORDON. "The Crime Bust." *U.S. News & World Report* (May 25, 1998):28–40.

WITTENAUER, CHERYL. "Saggy Pants May Not Be Lawful." (2007). http://www.yahoonews.com

WOLF, NAOMI. *The Beauty Myth: How Images of Beauty Are Used against Women.* New York: Morrow, 1990.

WOLFF, EDWARD N. "Recent Trends in Household Wealth in the United States: Rising Debt and the Middle-Class Squeeze." Levy Economics Institute of Bard College. June 2007. http://www.levy.org/pubs/wp_502.pdf

WOLFGANG, MARVIN E., ROBERT M. FIGLIO, and THORSTEN SELLIN. *Delinquency in a Birth Cohort.* Chicago: University of Chicago Press, 1972.

WOLFGANG, MARVIN E., TERRENCE P. THORNBERRY, and ROBERT M. FIGLIO. *From Boy to Man, from Delinquency to Crime.* Chicago: University of Chicago Press, 1987.

WONDERS, NANCY A., and RAYMOND MICHALOWSKI. "Bodies, Borders, and Sex Tourism in a Globalized World: A Tale of Two Cities—Amsterdam and Havana." *Social Problems.* Vol. 48, No. 4 (November 2001):545–71.

WONG, BUCK. "Need for Awareness: An Essay on Chinatown, San Francisco." In AMY TACHIKI ET AL., eds., *Roots: An Asian American Reader.* Los Angeles: UCLA Asian American Studies Center, 1971:265–73.

WOODWARD, KENNETH L. "Feminism and the Churches." *Newsweek* (February 13, 1989):58–61.

WORLD BANK. *2007 World Development Indicators.* Washington, D.C.: World Bank, 2007.

———. *2008 World Development Indicators.* Washington, D.C.: World Bank, 2008.

———. "Education Statistics." 2009, 2010 (updated regularly). http://go.worldbank.org/ITABCOGIV1

———. *World Development Indicators, 2009.* Washington, D.C.: World Bank, 2009.

WORLD HEALTH ORGANIZATION. *Constitution of the World Health Organization.* New York: World Health Organization Interim Commission, 1946.

———. "Female Genital Mutilation: New Knowledge Spurs Optimism." *Progress in Sexual and Reproductive Health Research.* No. 72. 2006. http://www.who.int/reproductive-health/hrp/progress/72.pdf

———. "Eliminating Female Genital Mutilation." 2008a. http://www.who.int/reproductivehealth/publications/fgm/9789241596442/en/index.html

———. "The Global Burden of Disease: 2004 Update, Summary Tables." October 2008b. http://www.who.int/healthinfo/global_burden_disease/estimates_regional/en/index.html

———. "Major Causes of Death: A Primer." Fact sheet No. 310. November 2008c. http://www.who.int/mediacentre/factsheets/fs310/en/index2.html

———. "WHO Report on the Global Tobacco Epidemic, 2009." 2009. http://www.who.int/tobacco/mpower/2009/en/index.html

WORLD VALUES SURVEY. "Inglehart-Welzel Cultural Map of the World." 2008. http://www.worldvaluessurvey.com/

WORSLEY, PETER. "Models of the World System." In MIKE FEATHERSTONE, ed., *Global Culture: Nationalism, Globalization, and Modernity.* Newbury Park, Calif.: Sage, 1990:83–95.

WRIGHT, EARL, II. "The Atlanta Sociological Laboratory, 1896–1924: A Historical Account of the First American School of Sociology." *Western Journal of Black Studies.* Vol. 26, No. 3 (2002a):165–74.

———. "Why Black People Tend to Shout! An Earnest Attempt to Explain the Sociological Negation of the Atlanta Sociological Laboratory Despite Its Possible Unpleasantness." *Sociological Spectrum.* Vol. 22, No. 3 (2002b):325–61.

WRIGHT, JAMES D. "Ten Essential Observations on Guns in America." *Society*. Vol. 32, No. 3 (March/April 1995):63–68.

WRIGHT, QUINCY. "Causes of War in the Atomic Age." In WILLIAM M. EVAN and STEPHEN HILGARTNER, eds., *The Arms Race and Nuclear War*. Englewood Cliffs, N.J.: Prentice Hall, 1987:7–10.

WRIGHT, RICHARD A. *In Defense of Prisons*. Westport, Conn.: Greenwood Press, 1994.

WRIGHT, ROBERT. "Sin in the Global Village." *Time* (October 19, 1998):130.

WU, XIAOGANG, and DONALD G. TREIMAN. "Inequality and Equality under Chinese Socialism: The Hukou System and Intergenerational Occupational Mobility." *American Journal of Sociology*. Vol. 113, No. 2 (September 2007): 415–45.

XU, JIAQUAN, KENNETH D. KOCHANEK, and BETZAIDA TEJADA-VERA. "Deaths: Preliminary Data for 2007." *National Vital Statistics Reports*. Vol. 58, No. 1 (August 19, 2009). http://www.cdc.gov/nchs/data/nvsr/nvsr58/nvsr58_01.pdf

YABROFF, JENNIE. "The Myths of Teen Sex." *Newsweek* (June 9, 2008):55.

YANG, FENGGANG, and HELEN ROSE FUCHS EBAUGH. "Transformations in New Immigrant Religions and Their Global Implications." *American Sociological Review*. Vol. 66, No. 2 (April 2001):269–88.

YARDLEY, JIM. "China Sticking with One-Child Policy." *New York Times* (March 11, 2008). http://www.nytimes.com/2008/03/11/world/asia/11china.html?_r=1

YEATTS, DALE E. "Creating the High Performance Self-Managed Work Team: A Review of Theoretical Perspectives." Paper presented at the annual meeting of the Southwest Social Science Association, Dallas, February 1994.

YOELS, WILLIAM C., and JEFFREY MICHAEL CLAIR. "Laughter in the Clinic: Humor in Social Organization." *Symbolic Interaction*. Vol. 18, No. 1 (1995):39–58.

ZAGORSKY, JAY. "Divorce Drops a Person's Wealth by 77 Percent." Press release, January 18, 2006. http://www.eurekalert.org/pub_releases/2006-01/osu-dda011806.php

ZHAO, DINGXIN. "Ecologies of Social Movements: Student Mobilization during the 1989 Prodemocracy Movement in Beijing." *American Journal of Sociology*. Vol. 103, No. 6 (May 1998):1493–1529.

ZIMBARDO, PHILIP G. "Pathology of Imprisonment." *Society*. Vol. 9, No. 1 (April 1972):4–8.

ZUCKERMAN, MORTIMER B. "The Russian Conundrum." *U.S. News & World Report* (March 13, 2006):64.

Photo Credits

CHAPTER 1: (c) Erik Isakson / CORBIS All Rights Reserved. 1; Jupiterimages\Thinkstock, 2; Gary He\AP Wide World Photos, 5; Caroline Penn\CORBIS- NY, 7 (top left); Minh-Thu Pham, 7 (top center); Paul Liebhardt\Paul W. Liebhardt, 7 (top right); Paul Liebhardt\Paul W. Liebhardt, 7 (bottom left); UpperCut Images\SuperStock, Inc., 7 (bottom center); Paul Liebhardt\Paul W. Liebhardt, 7 (bottom right); Steve Liss\Getty Images/Time Life Pictures, 8; Frank Zullo\Photo Researchers, Inc., 9; Courtesy of the Library of Congress, 13; Art Resource/Schomburg Center for Research in Black Culture, 14; PCN Photography\Alamy Images, 16; Vic Bider\PhotoEdit Inc., 19; (c) Bob Sacha / CORBIS All Rights Reserved, 22; Ter Foxx\Alamy Images, 23; Jupiter Images/Polka Dot\Alamy Images Royalty Free, 25; Reuben Burrell/ Hampton University/Lois Benjamin, 26; Michael Doolittle\The Image Works, 28; Photodisc/Getty Images, 31; Victor Malafronte\Getty Images Inc. - Hulton Archive Photos, 32; (c) Mark Savage / Corbis Entertainment / CORBIS All Rights Reserved, 33; Paul Skipper\AP Wide World Photos, 33.

CHAPTER 2: Vinicius Tupinamba\Shutterstock, 36; Reprinted by permission of Charles Schwab Corporation, 38; Paul W. Liebhardt, 39 (top left); Boaz Rottem\Alamy Images, 39 (top center); Marvin Dembinsky Photo Associates\Alamy Images, 39 (top right); Paul W. Liebhardt, 39 (middle left); Jon Arnold Images Ltd.\Alamy.com, 39 (middle center); Hubertus Kanus\Photo Researchers, Inc., 39 (middle right); Photononstop\SuperStock, Inc., 39 (bottom right); Suzy Bennett\Alamy Images, 39 (bottom center); Getty Images, Inc - Stockbyte Royalty Free, 39 (bottom right); Hazel Thompson/The New York Times, 40; Herve Collart\CORBIS- NY, 41; Margo Silver/Stone/Getty Images, 42; Fancy/Veer\Corbis RF, 43; Twentieth Century-Fox Film CorpThe Kobal Collection.The Pictur\Picture Desk, Inc./Kobal Collection, 46; Monty Brinton/CBS\Getty Images Inc., 48; (c) Andy Rain / epa / CORBIS All Rights Reserved, 50; Michael Buckner/Discovery Channel\Getty Images Inc., 51; Michael Ochs Archive\Getty Images, Inc. - Getty News, 54 (left); Carlos Rene Perez\AP Wide World Photos, 54 (center); (c) Bettmann/CORBIS, 54 (right); Aurora Photos\Alamy Images, 56; GoGo Images Corporation\Alamy Images, 60; (c) Bettmann/CORBIS, 61 (left); Canadian Government Travel Bureau, 61 (right); Barson Collection\Getty Images Inc. - Hulton Archive Photos, 62; 20th Century Fox Television\Picture Desk, Inc./Kobal Collection, 62; Marvel/Sony Pictures\Picture Desk, Inc./Kobal Collection, 63.

CHAPTER 3: Nick White / Digital Vision, 66; Blend Images\SuperStock, Inc., 68; Drawings from Dr. Annie Sparrow/Human Rights Watch, 70; Superstock Royalty Free, 72; Henry Ossawa Tanner, *The Banjo Lesson*, 1893. Oil on canvas. 49" x 35 1/2". Hampton University Museum, Hampton, Virginia, 75; Nigel Treblin/AFP/Getty Images, 79; SHNS photo by Bob D'Amico\Newscom, 80; Christopher Futcher\PhotoEdit Inc., 83; Ryan Remiorz, CP\AP Wide World Photos, 85 (left); James Devaney\WireImage\Getty Images Inc., 85 (second from left); Henny Ray Abrams\AP Wide World Photos, 85 (second from right); Evan Agostini\AP Wide World Photos, 85 (right); Warner Bros.\Everett Collection, 86; James Porto\Getty Images, Inc. – Taxi, 87; (c) Remi Benali / CORBIS All Rights Reserved, 88; (c) Anders Ryman / CORBIS All Rights Reserved; 89; Chung Sung-Jun\Getty Images Inc., 89.

CHAPTER 4: Jupiterimages/Commstock/Getty Images, 92; Ingram Publishing\SuperStock, Inc., 94; zumasportsworld\Newscom, 95; Michael Hanson\Getty Images, Inc. - Aurora, 96; Goodshoot\Thinkstock, 99; Staton R. Winter/The New York Times, 100; (C)2006 David Sipress from cartoonbank.com. All Rights Reserved, 102; apaphotos\Newscom, 103; Paul W. Liebhardt, 104 (left, center, and right); Barbara Penoya\Getty Images, Inc.- Photodisc./Royalty Free, 105 (left); David Young-Wolff\PhotoEdit Inc., 105 (second from left); Andy Crawford (c) Dorling Kindersley, 105 (third from left); Lucian Coman\Shutterstock, 105 (third from right); Jupiter Images - Thinkstock Images Royalty Free, 105 (second from right); Thinkstock Royalty Free, 105 (right); (c) Furgolle/Image Point FR / CORBIS All Rights Reserved, 106; Kevpix\Alamy Images, 108; Photodisc/Getty Images, 109; Dana Edelson\AP Wide World Photos, 110; zumawirewestphotos\Newscom, 111, George Doyle\Getty Images – Stockbyte, 113.

CHAPTER 5: Digital Vision\Thinkstock, 116; Historic Site of the Original McDonalds, 118; Michael Newman\PhotoEdit Inc., 119; Jonathan Green. *Friends*, 1992. Oil on Masonite, 14 in. x 11 in. © Jonathan Green. http://www.jonathangreenstudios.com, 124; Chris Haston\NBCU Photo Bank, 126; George Tooker *Government Bureau*, 1956, egg tempera on gesso panel, 19 5/8 x 29 5/8 inches. The Metropolitan Museum of Art,

George A. Hearn Fund, 1956 (56.78). Photograph courtesy of The Metropolitan Museum of Art/Art Resource, NY., 129; nyul\Fotolia, LLC - Royalty Free, 133; (c) Catherine Karnow / CORBIS All Rights Reserved, 135 (left); David Levenson\Alamy Images, 135 (right); Lillian Graeble, 136; Don Smetzer Photographer, 138; © David Young-Wolff/PhotoEdit, 139; Robert Harbison, 139.

CHAPTER 6: Getty Images, Inc./Peter Wafzig/Contributor, 142; Blend Images\Alamy Images, 144; Photobank\Alamy Images, 145 (top left); John Cancalosi\Alamy Images, 145 (top center); Peter Adams\Alamy Images, 145 (top right); William Waterfall / PacificStock.com, 145 (bottom left); Pete Turner Studio, 145 (bottom center); George Holton\Photo Researchers, Inc., 145 (bottom right); Newscom/David Tonnessen/Pacific Coast News, 146; Brand X Pictures\Alamy Images Royalty Free, 148 (left); Thomas Schweizer\CORBIS- NY, 148 (right); Getty Images, Inc./Shaul Schwarz, 153; Getty Images, Inc./ABC/Randy Holmes, 154; (c) Helen King / Corbis Edge / CORBIS All Rights Reserved, 160; AKG-Images, 162; Richard Lord\The Image Works, 163; Getty Images, Inc./Shaul Schwarz, 166; Newscom/Wenn Photo, 167.

CHAPTER 7: iStockphoto/Thinkstock, 171; (C)Santa Fabio, 172; Melissa Moore\The Image Works, 173; Jose Azel\Aurora Photos, Inc., 174; Jim Cole\AP Wide World Photos, 175; Hector Mata\Getty Images, Inc. - Agence France Presse, 177; Yellow Dog Productions/Getty Images, Inc., 180; Bob Gathany/The Hunstville Times/Landov, 181; [Photographer]/Stone/Getty Images, 182; Christine Cornell/Agence France Presse/Getty Images, 183; Zuma Press\Newscom, 186; (C)The New Yorker Collection 2000 David Sipress from cartoonbank.com. All Rights Reserved, 189; Kayte M. Deioma/PhotoEdit Inc., 192; Newscom, 193; US Information Agency, 195; A. Ramey/PhotoEdit Inc., 197; Charlie Campbell/The Star-Democrat/AP Wide World Photos, 198; Miguel Angel Morenatti/AP Wide World Photos, 199; Bill Greenblatt/UPI/Landov Media, 199.

CHAPTER 8: www.jupiterimages.com, 202; Interfoto/Alamy, 204; William Albert Allard/National Geographic Image Collection, 205; Tomasz Tomaszewski/National Geographic Image Collection, 207; Getty Images/De Agostini Editore Picture Library, 208; (c) Matthieu Paley / CORBIS All Rights Reserved, 210; Kevin Winter\Getty Images Inc., 213; Rich Pedroncelli/AP Wide World Photos, 214; Getty Images, Inc., 216; Hill Street Studios/Getty Images, Inc. - Blend Images, 220; Thinkstock, 223 (left); H. Mark Weidman/Alamy Images, 223 (right); PhotoEdit, Inc./ Jeff Greenberg, 224; Russell Lee\CORBIS- NY, 225; Penny Tweedie/Stone/Getty Images, 226; Indianapolis Star, Charlie Nye\AP Wide World Photos, 230; Henry Ossawa Tanner (1859-1937) *The Thankful Poor*. Private Collection. Art Resource, NY., 235; David Urbina/PhotoEdit Inc., 236; David De Lossy/Photodisc/Getty Images, 238; Ronnie Kaufman/CORBIS- NY, 239.

CHAPTER 9: Jay Directo/ Agence France Presse/ Getty Images, 242; Getty Images, Inc. AFP, 244; WARWICK KENT\Photolibrary.com, 246 (top left); Alamy.com, 246 (top right); PAUL NEVIN\Photolibrary.com, 246 (bottom); (c) Alison Wright / CORBIS All Rights Reserved, 248; UPI/Pedro Cerda/Newscom, 249 (left); Chesnot/SIPA/AP, 249 (right); Sucheta Das\CORBIS- NY, 253; Malcolm Linton\Getty Images, Inc. - Getty News, 257; Maciej Dakowicz\Alamy Images, 258; Joe McDonald\CORBIS- NY, 259 (left); Robert van der Hilst\CORBIS- NY, 259 (center); Wolfgang Kaehler\CORBIS- NY, 259 (right); Andrea Comas\CORBIS- NY, 261; Jenny Matthews\Alamy Images, 262; Fabio Liverani\Nature Picture Library, 263; RABIH MOGHRABI/AFP/Getty Images/Newscom, 266; Dubai Travel/Matt Shonfeld\Redux Pictures, 267; Kamran Jebreili\AP Wide World Photos, 267.

CHAPTER 10: Hemera/Thinkstock, 270; CORBIS- NY, 272; Suzanne Porter\Alamy Images, 274; Jean Louis Batt]/Stone/Getty Images, 276; Newscom, 277; AP Wide World Photos, 278; Michael Newman\PhotoEdit Inc., 284; Kuenzig/laif\Aurora Photos, Inc., 286; Sven Hagolani\Zefa\Corbis RF, 287; FPG\Getty Images Inc. - Hulton Archive Photos, 289; John Bazemore\AP Wide World Photos, 290; Image courtesy of The Advertising Archives, 294; Image courtesy of The Advertising Archives, 295.

CHAPTER 11: Nick White/Digital Vision/Thinkstock, 298; Bryant Mason, 300; David Young-Wolff\PhotoEdit Inc., 301 (top left); David Young-Wolff\PhotoEdit Inc., 301 (top center); Owen Franken\CORBIS- NY, 301 (top right); Charles O'Rear\CORBIS- NY, 301 (bottom left); Paul W. Liebhardt, 301 (bottom center); Buddy Mays\Alamy Images, 301 (bottom right); Joe Raedle\Getty Images Inc., 304; David Young-Wolff\PhotoEdit Inc.,

305; (c) Cheryl Diaz Meyer / Dallas Morning News / CORBIS All Rights Reserved, 311; Western History Collections, University of Oklahoma Libraries. Phillips Collection 357, 312; CORBIS- NY, 314 (left); Courtesy of the Library of Congress, 314 (second from left); Photographs and Prints Division, Schomburg Center for Research in Black Culture/The New York Public Library/Astor, Lenox and Tilden Foundations, 314 (second from right); UPI\CORBIS- NY, 314 (right); (c) Phil Schermeister / CORBIS All Rights Reserved, 317; Jim West\Alamy Images, 319; Peter Yates\CORBIS- NY, 321; Carl D. Walsh\Aurora Photos, Inc., 322; Image courtesy of The Advertising Archives, 324; Image courtesy of The Advertising Archives, 325.

CHAPTER 12: Getty Images, Inc., 328: Spencer Tirey\AP Wide World Photos, 330; Chris Thomaidis\Getty Images Inc. - Stone Allstock, 331; Ho Phillip\Shutterstock, 335 (left); T. Lehne/Lotuseaters\Alamy Images, 335 (right); National Geophysical Data Center, 336; (c) Stephanie Maze / CORBIS All Rights Reserved, 337; Newscom/Zuma Wire World Photos, 340; Alamy Images, 343; Rob Colvin\Getty Images, Inc - Artville LLC, 344; Chor Sokunthea/Reuters\CORBIS- NY, 346; Vincent Thian\AP Wide World Photos, 347; Lee Celano/The New York Times\Redux Pictures, 351 (left); David Hancock\Alamy Images, 351 (right); Newscom, 354; Newscom, 356; Joe McNally, Life Magazine (C)TimePix, 360; Dr. Billy Ingram/WireImage\Getty Images Inc., 362; William Thomas Cain\Getty Images Inc., 363; Paul Warner\AP Wide World Photos, 363.

CHAPTER 13: Tim Pannell/Corbis Yellow/Corbis RF, 366; Michael Newman\PhotoEdit Inc., 368; Getty Images, Inc., 369; Newscom, 371; PNC/Brand X\Jupiter Images PictureArts Corporation/Brand X Royalty Free, 372; AP Wide World Photos, 374; (C)The New Yorker Collection 1983 Robert Weber from cartoonbank.com. All Rights Reserved., 375; Zefa/ CORBIS-NY, 379; Mark J. Barrett\Creative Eye/MIRA.com, 381; The Des Moines Register, Christopher Gannon\AP Wide World Photos, 383; (c) Ronnie Kaufman / Blend Images / CORBIS RF. All Rights Reserved., 385; Michael Newman\PhotoEdit Inc., 386; Charlie Saceda\CORBIS- NY, 387; (c) Doranne Jacobson International Images, 390; (c) Galen Rowell / CORBIS All Rights Reserved, 391; Tony Freeman\PhotoEdit Inc., 394; Phil Date\Shutterstock, 396; Anna Belle Lee Washington/SuperStock, Inc., 397; (c) Gary Braasch/Bettmann/CORBIS All Rights Reserved, 398; Larry Williams\CORBIS- NY, 400; Denver Post/Glen Martin\AP Wide World Photos, 401; Denver Post/Glen Martin\AP Wide World Photos, 401.

CHAPTER 14: Getty Images, Inc./Joe Raedle/Staff/Getty Images News, 404; (C)Michael Newman/PhotoEdit. All rights reserved., 406; Antony Njuguna/Reuters\Landov Media, 409; PICTURE DESK KOBAL COLLECTION ART ARCHIVE ADV ARCHIVE TRAVELSITE/Baer Karin/Fox-TV, 410; Cleve Bryant\PhotoEdit Inc., 411 (left); Jim Cummins\CORBIS- NY, 411 (right); PhotoEdit, Inc., 413; Spencer Grant\PhotoEdit Inc., 418; Pat Sullivan\AP Wide World Photos, 420; SuperStock, Inc., 422; Steve Prezant\CORBIS- NY, 425; George Mulala\Photolibrary/Peter Arnold, Inc., 428; Adalbert Franz Seligmann *Allgemeines Krankenhaus* (General Hospital) 19th Century Painting, canvas. "Professor Theodor Billroth lectures at the General Hospital, Vienna. 1880." Erich Lessing/Art Resource, NY, 431; (c) Tom Nebbia / CORBIS All Rights Reserved,

432; (c) Phil Schermeister / CORBIS All Rights Reserved, 434; Rodney White\AP Wide World Photos, 435; (c) Lauren Greenfield/Institute for Artist Management, 437; Dan Rafla\Aurora Photos, Inc., 440; Xinhua/Wang Song\AP Wide World Photos, 441; Mine Safety and Health Administration (MSHA)\U.S. Department of Labor, 441.

CHAPTER 15: NB Photos\Alamy Images, 444; Nina Raingold\Getty Images Inc., 446; AP Wide World Photos,451; (c) David and Peter Turnley/Bettmann/CORBIS All Rights Reserved, 453; (c) Bohemian Nomad Picturemakers / CORBIS All Rights Reserved, 454; Ric Francis\AP Wide World Photos, 457; Michael Smtih\Getty Images Inc., 458; Pieter Breughel the Elder (c. 1525/30-1569), *Peasant Dance*, c. 1565, Kunsthistorisches Museum, Vienna/Superstock, Inc., 459 (left); Lily Furedi (1896-1969) American, *Subway* ca. 1934. Oil on canvas, 39 in. x 48 1/4 in. (99.1 x 122.6 cm). Transfer from the U.S. Department of the Interior, National Park Service. Smithsonian American Art Museum, Washington, DC, USA, Art Resource, NY, 459 (right); Paul Sancya\AP Wide World Photos, 461; Wilfried Krecichwost/Zefa\CORBIS- NY, 463; Dave Amit/Reuters\Landov Media, 469; Valery Hache/Agence France Presse/Getty Images, 470; Richard B. Levine\Newscom, 472; David Cooper/Toronto Star\ZUMA Press, 473.

CHAPTER 16: FREDERIC J. BROWN/Staff\Getty Images, Inc. AFP, 476; Laimute Druskis\Pearson Education/PH College, 478; Mike Clarke/AFP\Getty Images, Inc. AFP, 479; Stan Honda/Agence France Presse\Getty Images, 483; AFP Photo/Eitan Abramovich/Newscom, 484 (left); Barry Lewis\Alamy Images, 484 (center); Salah Omar/AFP\Getty Images, Inc. - Agence France Presse, 484 (right); CORBIS- NY, 485; George Tooker (b. 1920), *The Subway*, 1950, egg tempera on gesso panel, 18 1/8 x 36 1/8", Whitney Museum of American Art, New York, purchased with funds from the Juliana Force Purchase Award, 50.23. Photograph courtesy of The Whitney Museum of American Art, 487; Peter Finger\CORBIS- NY, 488 (left); Photos.com, 488 (right); Pearson Education/PH College, 489; (c) Alison Wright / CORBIS All Rights Reserved, 492; Wally Santana\AP Wide World Photos, 495 (left); Timothy A Clary\Getty Images, Inc. AFP, 495 (right); Mauri Rautkari, 496; Kelly-Mooney Photography\CORBIS- NY, 497; Jim West\Alamy Images, 498; Paul Prescott\Alamy Images, 500; Shawn Baldwin/The New York Times\Redux Pictures, 501; Efrem Lukatsky\AP Wide World Photos, 501.

TIMELINE: *1807:* MPI/ Getty Images, Inc. – Hulton Archive Photos; *1829:* Association of American Railroads; *1848:* North Carolina Museum of History; *1876:* AT&T Archives; *1886:* Irene Springer/ Pearson Education/PH College; *1893:* Library of Congress; *1902:* Library of Congress; *1910:* Tim Ridley/Dorling Kindersley Media Library; *1912:* Chris Alan Wilton/ Getty Images, Inc. – Image Bank; *1913:* Library of Congress; *1921:* Getty Images, Inc. – Hulton Archive Photos; *1927:* Corbis/Bettmann; *1931:* Texas State Library and Archives; *1945:* U.S. Air Force; *1946:* Unisys Corporation; *1947:* Corbis/Bettmann; *1953:* Corbis/Bettmann; *1964:* CBS Photo/ Getty Images, Inc. – Hulton Archive Photos; *1969:* Robert F. Bukaty/AP Wide World Photos; *1969:* NASA/ Johnson Space Center; *1980:* Laima Druskis/ Pearson Education/PH College; *1981:* Jan Butchofsky-Houser/ Corbis/Bettmann; *1987:* John Serafin; *1990s:* Gerald Lopez/ Dorling Kindersley Media Library; *2000:* Brady/Pearson Education/ PH College.

Name Index

Subject Index

Davis-Moore thesis, 211–12
Death and dying
  (*see also* Mortality rates)
  defining, 430
  ethical issues, 430
  euthanasia, 430
  instinct, 70
  leading causes of, in U.S., 424
  median age, map of global, 252
  penalty, 191, 195–96
  right-to-die debate, 430
  as a stage of life, 85–86
  of a spouse, 376
  stages of, 86
Death rates
  Civil War and, 357
  crude, 447
  war and, 357
Debt bondage, 254
Deception, spotting, 102–3
Declaration of Independence, 9, 314–15
Decline, social movements and, 483
De facto segregation, 311
Degradation ceremony, 178
De jure segregation, 311
Demeanor, social interaction and, 103
Democracy
  bureaucracy and, 347
  defined, 347
  economic inequality and, 347
  freedom and, 347, 361
  gap, 361
  political freedom, map of, 348
  U.S. value, 44
Democratic leadership, 120
Democratic party, 350, 351, 353
Democratic Republic of the Congo, as a
    middle-income country, 249
Demographics of African Americans, Asian
    Americans, Arab Americans, and Hispanic
    Americans, 320
Demographic divide, 453
Demographic transition theory, 451–52
Demography
  (*see also* Population/population growth)
  defined, 446
  fertility, 446–47
  migration, 447–48
  mortality, 447
  social change and, 480–81
Denial of death, 86
Denmark
  freedom and equality, 337
  homosexual marriages, 383
  welfare capitalism, 335
Denominations, 39
Dependency theory
  capitalist world economy, 261–62
  colonialism and, 261
  compared to modernization theory, 264
  defined, 260
  evaluation of, 263
  high-income countries and, 262
  historical, 260–61
  modernity and, 498–99
Dependent variables, 18, 23
Deprivation theory, 482–83
Descent patterns, 369–70
Descriptive statistics, 18
Deterrence
  of criminals, 193–94
  of war, 359–60
Development, human (*see* Human develop-
    ment)
Deviance
  (*see also* Crime)
  biological context, 172–73
  capitalism and, 183
  control theory, 181
  cultural differences, 174
  defined, 172–75
  differential association theory, 181
  Durkheim's work, 175
  functions of, 175
  gender differences and, 185–86
  heroes versus villains, 198–99
  Hirschi's control theory, 181

labeling theory, 178–82
  medicalization of, 179–80
  Merton's strain theory, 176
  personality factors, 173–74
  power and, 182
  primary, 178
  Puritans, example of, 175–76
  secondary, 178
  social-conflict analysis, 182–83, 185
  social control, 172
  social foundations of, 174–75
  stigma, 178
  subcultures, 176–77, 180
  strain theory, 176
  structural-functional analysis, 175–77, 185
  Sutherland's differential association
      theory, 181
  symbolic-interaction analysis, 177–82, 185
Deviant career, 178
Dharma, 258
Differential association theory, 181
Diffusion
  culture, 53
  social change and, 480
Diplomacy, peace and, 360
Direct-fee system, 433
Disabled
  education for, 421
  master status, 96
Disarmament, peace and, 360
Disasters
  defined, 484
  impact of, 484–85
  intentional, 484
  natural, 484
  technological, 484
Discipline problems, school, 416
Discoveries
  cultural change and, 53
  social change and, 480
Discrimination
  (*see also* Racial discrimination)
  defined, 309
  institutional, 309–10
  prejudice and, 308–10
  women and, 280
  workplace, 131
Disposable society, 465–66
Diversity
  (*see also* Cultural diversity; Social diversity)
  biodiversity, declining, 469
  language, in the U.S., 52
  racial, in the U.S., 76
  religious, across U.S., 393
  workplace, 340–41, 342
Divine right, 346
Division of labor, 487–88
Divorce
  causes of, 380
  children and, 380–81
  child support, 380–81
  rates for U.S., 379–80
DNA, as criminal evidence, 195
Doe v. *Bolton*, 164
Domestication of animals, 48
Domestic violence, 381–82
Double standards, 21, 279
  sexual behavior and, 59–60, 149
Down These Mean Streets (Thomas), 99
Downward social mobility, 227
Dramaturgical analysis
  defined, 101
  elements of, 15
  embarrassment and tact, 104–5
  gender performances, 103–4
  idealization, 104
  nonverbal communication, 102–3
  performances, 101–2
  presentation of self, 101–5
Dred Scott case, 314–15
Dropout, school, 418–19
Drug abuse
  AIDS/HIV and, 429–30
  deviance and medicalization of, 180
Drug trade
  crime and, 190–91
  decline in, 197

Dubai, 266–67
Due process, 192
Durkheim, work of
  on deviance, 175
  division of labor, 487–88
  on mechanical and organic solidarity,
      458–59
  on religion, 386, 387
  suicide and, 4, 11, 488
Dyad, 122–23
Earnings (*see* Economy; Global economy;
    Income)
Eastern Europe (*see* Europe, eastern)
Eating disorders, 426
Ecocentric, 471
Ecologically sustainable culture, 470
Ecology
  defined, 462
  urban, 460–61
Economic elites, 337
Economic equality, capitalism versus socialism
    and, 336
Economic inequality
  (*see also* Income inequality)
  in China, 210
  democracy and, 347
  increasing world, 265
  in selected countries, 211
  socialism and, 337
  in the Soviet Union, 208–9
Economic productivity, capitalism versus
    socialism and, 336
Economic systems
  capitalism, 334
  socialism, 334–35
  state capitalism, 335
  welfare capitalism, 335
Economy
  (*see also* Global economy; Income)
  agricultural revolution, 330
  capitalism, 334
  capitalism, state, 335
  capitalism, welfare, 335
  in China, 211
  corporations, 342–45
  crime rates and, 177
  defined, 330, 331
  education and role of, 406–7
  future issues, 345
  historical overview, 330–31
  Industrial Revolution, 330–31
  information revolution, 331, 341–42
  laissez-faire, 334
  map, agricultural employment, 333
  map, service sector work, 333
  perestroika, in Soviet Union, 209
  political-economy model/theory, 353–54,
      355, 483
  politics and, 350
  postindustrial, 331
  postindustrial society and, 331, 338–41
  sectors of, 332
  socialism, 334–35
  urban political, 461
  Wallerstein's capitalist world, 261–62
Ecosystem, 462
Ecuador
  economic inequality, 211
  gross domestic product, 251
  as a middle-income country, 251
  quality of life index, 251
  socialism and, 337
Edge cities, 457
Education
  (*see also* Colleges; Schools)
  academic standards, 418–19
  adult, 421
  affirmative action, 322–23
  of African Americans, 309–10, 315, 412
  of Asian Americans, 316, 317
  Brown v. *Board of Education of Topeka*, 309–10
  busing, 412
  defined, 406, 407
  disabled students, 421
  discipline, 416
  dropouts, 418–19
  economic development and, 406–7

functions of, 409
  future for, 421–22
  gender differences, 220, 222, 273, 277, 281
  GI Bill, 414
  global view, 406–9
  grade inflation, 419
  hidden curriculum, 76
  of Hispanic Americans, 318
  home schooling, 420–21
  illiteracy map, 407
  in India, 407–8
  in Japan, 408
  of Japanese Americans, 316
  mainstreaming/inclusive, 421
  mandatory, 408
  of Native Americans, 312
  problems in, 416–19
  progressive, 409
  public versus private, 411–12
  school choice, 419–20
  segregation, 309, 311
  social class and, 222–25
  social-conflict analysis, 415
  social inequality and, 220, 222, 410–15
  social interaction and, 409–11
  structural-functional analysis, 415
  student passivity, 416–17
  symbolic-interaction analysis, 415
  teacher shortage, 421
  terrorism and effects on, 409
  in the U.S., 408–21
  violence and, 416
Efficiency
  McDonaldization concept, 134
  U.S. value, 44
Ego, 70
Egypt
  female genital mutilation, 286
  population growth and control, 462
  sibling marriages in ancient, 147
  water supply problems, 466
Elderly
  (*see also* Aging)
  biological changes, 83–84
  children caring for, 376
  culture and, 84–85
  death and dying, 85–86
  death of spouse/partner, 376
  defined, 82–83
  income and, 85
  poverty and, 232
  sex and, 151–52
  socialization and, 82–85
  statistics, 83, 84
Elections (*see* Voting)
Electronic church/religion, 399
Electronic mail (*see* E-mail)
El Salvador, as a middle-income country, 249
E-mail
  organizational structure and effects of, 128
  privacy issues, 136–37
  symbols used in, 43
Embarrassment, social interaction and, 104
Emergence, social movements and, 483
Emigration, 448
Emotions
  biological side of, 105
  cultural side of, 105–6
  on the job, 106
  managing, 106–7
  social interaction and, 105–6
Empirical evidence, 16
Employment (*see* Labor; Work/workplace)
Empty nest syndrome, 376
Enclosure movement, 9
Endogamy, 369
Energy, industrialization and, 331
England (*see* Britain)
English language, 45, 51, 52, 57
Entrepreneurs, women as, 279
Environment
  acid rain, 468
  air pollution, 468
  biodiversity, declining, 469
  deficit, 463
  future for, 470–71
  global, 462–63

Rebellion, 176
Recidivism, criminal, 195
Recycling, 466, 467
Redemptive social movements, 481
Red tape, bureaucratic, 129
Reference groups, 122
Reformative social movements, 481
Reformatories, 194
Rehabilitation, of criminals, 194
Relative deprivation, 482
Relative opportunity, 176
Relative poverty, 232, 251
Relativism, cultural, 53–57
Reliability, 18
Religion
  (*see also* name of)
  affiliation, changing, 394–95
  in agrarian societies, 49, 392
  basic concepts, 386
  capitalism and, 389
  civil, 396
  in colonial America, 313
  defined, 386
  diversity across U.S., map, 393
  electronic, 399
  ethnicity and, 393–94
  functions of, 387
  fundamentalism, 397–99
  future for, 399
  in history, 391–92
  in horticultural societies, 49, 392
  in hunting and gathering societies, 48, 391–92
  in industrial societies, 392
  membership across U.S., map, 393
  New Age, 396–99
  in pastoral societies, 392
  postdenominational society, 396
  in preindustrial societies, 392
  race and, 394
  revival, 397–98
  science and, 398–99
  secularization, 395
  social change and, 389
  social class and, 393
  social-conflict analysis, 388–89
  sociology and, 386
  structural-functional analysis, 387, 389
  symbolic-interaction analysis, 387–88, 389
  in the U.S., 392–93
Religiosity
  defined, 392, 400–401
  globally, 392
  importance of, 392–93
Religious affiliation
  college students and, 395
  diversity across U.S., map, 393
  membership across U.S., map, 393
  racial/ethnic, 393–94
  social class and, 393
Religious organization, types of
  churches, 390
  cults, 391
  denominations, 390
  sects, 390–91
  state church, 390
Remarriage, 381
Renaissance, 10–11
Repression, 71
Reproduction
  family and new technology, 384
  in vitro fertilization, 384
  sex determination, 146
  test tube babies, 384
Republican party, 350, 353
Research (*see* Sociological investigation)
Research methods
  data, using existing, 28–29, 30
  defined, 22
  experiments, 22–23, 30
  participant observation, 26–28, 30
  summary of, 30
  surveys, 24–25, 30
Research orientations, 21
Reservations
  Japanese Americans on, 317
  Native Americans on, 312, 378
Residential patterns

industrial societies and, 369
  preindustrial societies and, 369
Resocialization, 86–87
Resource-mobilization theory, 483
Retreatism, 176
Retreatist subculture, 176
Retribution, 193
Retrospective labeling, 179
Revivalism, 397–98
Revolution, capitalist, 489
Revolution, political
  common traits, 355
  defined, 354–55
Revolutionary social movements, 481
Revolutionary War, 552
Rhesus monkeys, social isolation experiment, 69
Right(s)
  due process, 192
  individual, 9
  informed consent, 22
  -to-die debate, 430
Ritual, defined, 386
Ritualism
  bureaucratic, 128–29
  deviance, 176
Roe v. *Wade*, 164, 165
Roles
  (*see also* Gender roles)
  conflict, 97
  defined, 95–96
  exit, 97
  leadership, 120
  set, 96, 97
  strain, 97
Roman Catholic Church
  (*see also* Catholicism)
  liberation theology, 389
  parochial schools, 411
Roman Empire, early cities in, 455
Romania
  market reforms, 337
  socialism, decline of, 336
Romantic love, 373–74
Routinization of charisma, 346
Rural areas
  political party identification and, 351
  population growth in, 457–58
  poverty, 233, 234
  presidential election of 2008 and, 353
Rural life (*Gemeinschaft*), 458, 486–87
Russia
  (*see also* Soviet Union)
  economic inequality, 211
  as a high-income country, 247, 248, 251
  market reforms, 337
  medicine in, 432
  social inequality in, 217
  social stratification in, 209
Russian Revolution, 208–9, 355
Rwanda
  genocide, 311, 484
  quality of life, 260
Sacred, defined, 386
Sambia, homosexuality and, 152
Same-sex marriage, 33, 155–57, 383
Samoa, modesty, 147
Sampling, 24
  snowball, 25
Sanctions, 46
Sandwich generation, 376
Sapir-Whorf thesis, 43–44
SAT (Scholastic Assessment Test) scores, 273, 418
Saudi Arabia
  ban on red flowers, 174
  constraints put on women, 185
  as a high-income country, 5, 247, 248, 251
  modernity, 495
  monarchy in, 346
Scapegoat theory, 307–8
Scholastic Assessment Test (SAT) scores, 273, 418
Schooling
  (*see also* Education)
  defined, 406
  functions of, 409
  for profit, 420
School problems (*see* Education)

Schools
  (*see also* Education)
  charter, 420
  choice of, 419–20
  Christian academies, 411
  funding issues, 412, 413
  home, 420–21
  inequality in, 410–15
  magnet, 420
  parochial, 411
  private boarding, 411
  public, 409–13
  public versus private, in the U.S., 411–13
  socialization and, 76, 409
  tracking, 411
Charles Schwab & Co., 38
Science
  defined, 16
  medicine and, 431
  pros and cons of, 495
  religion and, 398–99
  sociology and, 9–11
  U.S. value, 44
Scientific management, 130–31
Scientific medicine, 431
Scientific stage, 10
SDI (*see* Strategic defense initiative)
Secondary deviance, 178
Secondary economic sector, 332
Secondary groups, 118–19, 120
Secondary sex characteristics, 146
Second world countries (*see* Middle-income
  countries)
Sects, 390–91
Secularization, 395
Segregation
  (*see also* Racial segregation)
  Brown v. *Board of Education of Topeka*,
    309–10
  defined, 311
Self
  defined, 73
  development in adolescents, 83
  looking-glass, 73
  Mead's social self theory, 73–74
  play and the development of, 73–74
  presentation of, 101–5
Self-aware, 73
Self-employment, 339–40
Self-fulfilling prophecy, 409–10
Semai, 40, 48, 256, 356–57
Seneca Falls convention, 272
Senegal, female genital mutilation, 286
Sensorimotor stage, 71
Separate but equal, 309
September 11, 2001, attacks
  bureaucratic ritualism and, 129
  impact of, 355–56
  social distance, 305
  USA Patriot Act, 137
Serbs, 311
Servile forms of marriage, 254
Services, defined, 330
Service-sector employment
  changes in, 338
  map of global, 333
Settlement houses, Hull House, 13
Seventh-Day Adventists, 398
Sex and sexuality
  adolescents and, 156, 158
  age and changes in, 151–52
  anal, HIV/AIDS transmission and, 428
  attitudes in the U.S., 148–52
  between adults, 151
  characteristics, 146
  contraception use globally, map of, 150
  counterrevolution, 149–50
  cultural differences, 152–53, 162–63
  cultural variations, 146–47
  defined, 145–46
  determination of, 146
  difference between gender and, 146
  double standards and, 59–60, 149
  extramarital, 19, 151
  family and new reproductive technology, 384
  frequency of, 151
  incest taboo, 147–48, 371

Kinsey studies, 147, 149, 151, 154
  marriage and satisfaction, 374–75
  media, influence of, 166–67
  orientation, 152–55
  premarital, 150–51
  queer theory, 164
  revolution, 148–49
  social-conflict analysis of, 161, 163–65
  social construction of, 162
  structural-functional analysis of, 161–62
  symbolic-interaction analysis of, 161, 162
Sexism
  costs of, 274–76
  defined, 274
  institutional, 274
  patriarchy and, 274–76
Sex ratio, defined, 448
Sex roles (*see* Gender roles)
Sexual counterrevolution, 149–50
Sexual harassment, 186, 285–87
Sexual issues
  abortion, 164–65
  adolescent pregnancy, 156, 158
  homosexuality, attitudes toward, 152,
    153–55, 383
  pornography, 156–57
  prostitution, 157–58, 159, 162
  rape, 158–61
  sexual harassment, 186, 285–87
Sexually transmitted diseases (STDs)
  AIDS/HIV, 428–30
  genital herpes, 428
  gonorrhea, 427–28
  syphilis, 427–28
Sexual orientation
  asexuality, 152
  biology and, 153–54
  bisexuality, 152, 155
  defined, 152
  heterosexuality, 152, 164
  homosexuality, 152, 154–55
  intersexual, 146
  society and, 152–53
  transsexuals, 146
Sexual revolution, 148–49
Sexual violence
  date rape, 158–61
  female genital mutilation, 163, 284, 285, 286
  pornography and, 156–57, 287
  as a power issue, 158, 284
  rape, 158, 284, 381
Sex workers, 157
Shaman, 48
Shame, norms and, 47
Shantytowns, 462
Shock probation, 196
Siberia, homosexuality in, 152
Sibling marriages, 147–48, 371
Sick role, 435
Sierra Leone
  female genital mutilation, 286
  social status of women, 274
Significant others, 73–74
Singapore
  as a high-income country, 248
  modernization theory, 259, 260
  state capitalism, in, 335
Single-parent families, 382, 383
Slavery
  African Americans, 314–15
  agrarian societies and, 49
  chattel, 254, 257
  child, 254
  colonialism and, 254
  debt bondage, 254
  forced migration and, 448
  global, 254–55
  human trafficking, 254
  poverty and, 254
  servile forms of marriage, 254
  Thirteenth Amendment, 315
Slovakia, market reforms, 336, 337
Smiling, social interaction and, 103
Smoking
  gender differences, 425
  globally, 426
  health effects, 424–26

Snowball sampling, 25
Snowbelt cities, 456
Social area analysis, 461
Social behaviorism (Mead), 73–74
Social change
 (*see also* Modernity)
 causes of, 480–83
 characteristics of, 479
 critical sociology and, 20–21
 culture and, 480
 defined, 478–79
 demographic, 480–81
 deviance and, 175
 ideas and, 480
 Marx and, 480
 religion and, 389
 social conflict and, 480
 social movements and, ideas and, 481–83
 sociology and, 9
Social character, 494
Social classes
 (*see also* Social stratification)
 average-middles, 224
 in Britain, 206–8
 in China, 209–10
 class system, 206
 crime and, 189
 deviance and, 183
 family life and, 226–27, 377
 gender roles and, 226–27
 global economy and effects on U.S., 231
 group dynamics and, 123
 health and, 225, 424
 homelessness, 235–36
 language and, 208
 lower, 225
 lower-uppers, 223
 meritocracy, 206
 middle, 223–24
 military, 357
 mobility, 227–31
 political party identification and, 350–51
 politics and, 226
 religious affiliation and, 393
 in Russia, 209
 socialization and, 75–76
 status consistency, 206
 in the U.S., 222–25
 upper, 222–23
 upper-middles, 223–24
 upper-uppers, 223
 values/attitudes and, 225–26
 working, 225
Social cohesion, religion and, 387
Social-conflict approach
 culture and, 58–59
 description of, 12, 15
 deviance and, 182–83, 185
 education and, 415
 family and, 372, 373
 gender stratification and, 288, 289–90
 health/medicine and, 437–38
 Marx and, 492
 modernity and, 492–93
 religion and, 388–89
 sexuality and, 161, 163–65
 social stratification and, 215
 sports and, 16–17
Social construction
 of gender, 107–8
 of humor, 108–11
 of illness, 436
 of personal identity, 436–37
 of reality, 97–101, 112–13
 of sexuality, 162–63
 of treatment, 436
Social control
 conformity and, 181
 defined, 172, 173
 deviance and, 172
 education and, 410–11
 religion and, 393
 sexual behavior and, 161–62
 theory, Hirschi's, 181
Social crisis, 4–5
Social distance
 defined, 305

scale, 305, 306
Social diversity
 group dynamics and, 123
 modernity and, 486
Social dysfunction, defined, 12
Social epidemiology, 424
Social-exchange analysis, 15
 family and, 372, 373
Social functions, defined, 11, 12
Social groups
 conformity, 120–22
 defined, 118, 119
 diversity of, 123
 formal organizations compared to, 123, 127
 in- and out-, 122
 leadership, 119–20
 networks, 123–24
 peers, 76–77
 primary and secondary, 118–19, 120
 reference, 122
 size of, 122–23
 special-interest, 351
 superiority and, 46
Social inequality
 (*see also* Social classes; Social stratification)
 agrarian societies and, 49
 ancestry and, 222
 culture and, 58
 deviance and, 182–83, 185
 education and, 220, 410–15
 ethnicity and, 222
 gender and, 222
 health and, 423
 income, 218, 219
 industrial societies and, 49
 Kuznets curve, 217–19
 modernity and, 494
 power, 219–20
 race and, 222
 religion and, 388–89
 sexuality and, 163
 sports and, 16–17
 in the U.S., 219–36
 wealth, 219–20
 work, 220, 221
Social institutions, defined, 345
Social integration
 education and, 409
 suicide rates and, 4
Social interaction
 defined, 94, 95
 dramaturgical analysis, 101–5
 education and, 409–10
 embarrassment, 104–5
 emotions, 105–6
 gender performances, 103–4
 humor, 108–11
 idealization, 104
 language, 107–8, 109
 nonverbal communication, 102–3
 performances, 101–2
 roles and, 95–97
 social construction of reality, 97–101,
  112–13
 status and, 95
Socialism
 collapse of, in the Soviet Union, 209
 compared to capitalism, 335–36
 countries that follow, 335
 decline of, 335
 defined, 334
 features of, 334–35
Social isolation
 human development and, 69
 Rhesus monkey experiment, 69
Social issues, politics and, 345
Socialist feminism, 291, 292
Socialization
 anticipatory, 77, 122
 defined, 68, 69
 education and, 409–10
 Erikson's developmental stages, 74–75
 family and, 75–76, 371
 Freud's personality theory, 70–71
 gender and, 76, 276–77
 Gilligan's gender and moral development
  theory, 72–73

human development, 68–69
 Kohlberg's moral development theory, 72
 life course, 79–86
 Mead's social self theory, 73–74
 media and, 77–79
 nature versus nurture, 68–69
 peers and, 76–77
 Piaget's cognitive theory, 71
 resocialization, 86–87
 schools and, 76
 social behaviorism, 73–74
 social isolation, 69
 total institutions, 86
 totalitarianism and, 349
Socialized medicine, 432, 433
Social marginality, 4–5
Social mobility
 defined, 209
 downward, 227
 gender differences and, 229–30
 horizontal, 228
 income levels and, 228–29
 intergenerational, 228
 intragenerational, 228
 marriage and, 230–31
 meritocracy and, 209
 myth versus reality, 228–29, 238–39
 problems with, 231–32
 race and, 229
 in the Soviet Union, 209
 structural, 209, 228
 in the U.S., 227–32
 upward, 227
Social movements
 claims making, 481–82
 defined, 481
 explanations for, 482–83
 stages in, 483
 types of, 481
Social responsibility, personal freedom versus,
  498–99
Social self (*see* Self)
Social stratification
 (*see also* Global stratification)
 in Britain, 206–8
 caste system, 205–6
 in China, 209–10
 class system, 206
 conflict and, 213–16
 Davis-Moore thesis, 211–12
 defined, 204–5
 estate system, 206
 functions of, 211–13
 gender and, 277–81
 global perspective, 217–19
 ideology of, 210–11
 income inequality map, 218
 interaction and, 216–17
 Kuznets curve, 217–19
 meritocracy, 206
 poverty and, 232–34, 255
 in Russia, 209
 social-conflict approach, 215
 in the Soviet Union, former, 208–9
 status consistency, 206
 structural-functional approach, 215
 symbolic-interaction approach, 215
 technology and, 217–19
 Weber's views, 214–15
Social structure
 defined, 11–12
 roles, 95–97
 status, 96
Societal protection, 194
Societies
 agrarian, 49
 credential, 415
 defined, 40
 deviance and influence of, 174
 disposable, 465–66
 health and, 423, 440–41
 homosexuality and influence of, 152–53
 horticulture, 48–49
 hunting and gathering, 48
 industrial, 49
 mass, 490–91, 493
 McDonaldization concept, 133–36, 138–39

pastoralism, 48
 postindustrial, 49
 rationalization of, 126
 sexual orientation and influence of, 152–53
 technology and, 47–49
 traditional versus modern, 491, 500–501
Sociobiology, culture and, 59–60
Sociocultural evolution
 agrarian societies, 49
 cities, development of, 9, 453, 455–58
 defined, 48
 horticulture societies, 48–49
 hunting and gathering societies, 48
 industrial societies, 49
 pastoralism, 48
 postindustrial societies, 49
 religion, 49
Socioeconomic status (SES)
 (*see also* Social inequality; Social classes)
 African Americans and, 315
 Arab Americans and, 321
 Asian Americans and, 316
 defined, 215
 Hispanic Americans and, 318
 Native Americans and, 313
Sociological imagination, 5, 6
Sociological investigation
 critical sociology, 20–21
 data, using existing, 28–29, 30
 ethics and, 22
 experiments, 22–23, 30
 funding, 22
 gender and, 21–22
 global, 22
 historical, 29
 interpretive sociology, 20, 21
 methods, 22–29
 participant observation, 26–28, 30
 positivist sociology, 10–11, 16–20, 21
 relationship between theory and methods, 21
 research methods, 22–39
 statistics, use of, 18
 surveys, 24–25, 30
 tables, use of, 26
 ten steps in, 29–31
Sociological perspective
 applications of, 7–9
 crisis, 4–5
 defined, 2, 4
 importance of, 5–7
 marginality, 4–5
 role of, 2–5
Sociological research (*see* Sociological
  investigation)
Sociological theory
 defined, 11
 feminism and gender-conflict approach,
  12–13
 race-conflict approach, 13–14
 research orientations and, 21
 social-conflict approach, 12, 15
 sociological, 11–15
 structural-functional approach,
  11–12, 15
 symbolic-interaction approach, 14–15
Sociology
 careers in, 8–9
 critical, 20–21
 defined, 2, 4
 first use of term, 10
 interpretive, 20, 21
 origins of, 9–11
 personal growth and, 7–8
 positivist, 10–11, 16–20, 21
 public policy and, 7
 religion and, 386
 science and, 9–11
 social change and, 9
 theory, 11–15
Solidarity
 mechanical, 458–59, 487
 organic, 458–59, 487
Solid waste, 465–66
Somalia
 child labor, 82
 female genital mutilation, 285, 286
 modernization theory, 257

SOCIETY IN HISTORY: TIMELINES

A timeline is a visual device that helps us understand historical change. The timeline at the right represents 5 billion years of the history of the planet Earth. This timeline is divided into three sections, each of which is drawn to a different scale of time. The first section, The Earth's Origins, begins with the planet's origins 5 billion years before the present (B.P.) and indicates that another full billion years passed before the earliest forms of life appeared. The second section, Our Human Origins, shows that plants and animals continued to evolve for billions more years until, approximately 12 million years ago, our earliest human ancestors came onto the scene. In the third section of this timeline, Earliest Civilization, we see that what we call civilization is relatively recent indeed, with the first permanent settlements occurring in the Middle East a scant 12,000 years ago. But the written record

of our species' existence extends back only half this long, to the time humans invented writing and first farmed with animal-driven plows some 5,000 years B.P.

Sociology came into being in the wake of the many changes to society wrought by the Industrial Revolution over the last few centuries—just the blink of an eye in evolutionary perspective. The lower timeline provides a close-up look at the events and trends that have defined The Modern Era, most of which are discussed in this text. Innovations in technology are charted in the panel below the line and provide a useful backdrop for viewing the milestones of social progress highlighted in the panel above the line. Major contributions to the development of sociological thought are traced along the very bottom of this timeline.

SOCIAL MILESTONES

Slave trade underway (began 1619)

Colonization of Latin America/India underway

U.S. is small, agrarian society

Death rates fall in Europe and United States

Opening of U.S. Western frontier

Chinese immigration to U.S. begins

European colonization of Africa

Japanese immigration to U.S. begins

"Great European Immigration"

1890 Rise of blues

1849 Elizabeth Blackwell is first woman to earn M.D. degree

1883 U.S. adopts Standard time zones

1861 First department store (Marshall Field's, Chicago)

1790 First U.S. census

1892 Pledge of Allegiance written

1789 George Washington sworn in as first U.S. president

1821 First women's college (Troy Female Seminary)

1857 Dred Scott decision

1870 First African American elected to U.S. House of Representatives

1886 Statue of Liberty

1776 U.S. Independence from Great Britain

WOMEN bring all VOTERS into the world Let Women Vote

1848 Women's suffrage movement begins

1859 Charles Darwin's Origin of Species

1872 First woman runs for U.S. president

1890 Massacre at Wounded Knee

1787 Court defines a slave as 3/5 a citizen

Negroes for Sale.

1851 The New York Times founded

1865 U.S. bans slavery

1884 NYC outlaws wifebeating

1892 First sociology department (University of Chicago)

Rev. War 1775–1783

1807 U.S. bans slave trade

U.S. Civil War 1861–1865

TECHNOLOGY

| 1775 | 1800 | 1825 | 1850 | 1875 | 1900 |

1879 Light bulb invented

1793 Eli Whitney invents the cotton gin

1839 Photography invented

1895 Radio invented

1869 Transcontinental railroad completed

1825 Erie Canal opens

1844 Telegraph invented

1850 Rubber condom invented

1885 First 10-story skyscraper (Chicago)

1825 First U.S. textile mills (in New England)

1876 Telephone invented

1847 Founding of American Medical Association signals rise of scientific medicine

1893 First car (the Duryea)

1860 Isaac Singer invents sewing machine and forms first multinational corporation

1880 Home refrigerator invented

1877 Phonograph invented

1829 Steam locomotive invented

1860 Louis Pasteur kills germs in milk by heating (pasteurization)

1886 Coca-Cola invented

Industrial Revolution begins to transform Europe

Industrialization underway in U.S.

1889 Jukebox invented

| WORLD POPULATION | 1 billion | | |
| U.S. POPULATION | 5.3 million | 23.2 million | 76.0 million |

THEORY

1776 Adam Smith applauds capitalism

1798 Malthus warns of perilous population increase

1838 Comte coins term "sociology"

1848 Marx challenges capitalist class conflict

1896 Freud formulates psychoanalysis

1897 Durkheim studies suicide